The Tools & Techniques *of* Financial Planning

Stephan R. Leimberg, Martin J. Satinsky,
Robert T. LeClair, Robert J. Doyle, Jr.

The
NATIONAL
UNDERWRITER
Company

Professional Publishing Group
P.O. Box 14367 • Cincinnati, OH 45250-0367
1-800-543-0874 • www.nationalunderwriter.com

ISBN 0-87218-195-2

published by

NULAW SERVICES

a department of

THE NATIONAL UNDERWRITER COMPANY

Copyright © 1986, 1987, 1988, 1993, 1998
The National Underwriter Company
P.O. Box 14367
Cincinnati, Ohio 45250-0367

Fifth Edition

3rd Printing

Printed in the United States of America

DEDICATION

Stephan R. Leimberg

*To my daughters, Charlee and Lara,
my son-in-law, Rob, and my grandson, Max —
I love you so very much!*

Martin J. Satinsky

To Marcia

Robert T. LeClair

To Bion B. Howard, friend and teacher

Robert J. Doyle, Jr.

*To Kathy, my loving and understanding wife,
and to my three principal inspirations,
Erin, Stevie, and Bob*

ABOUT THE AUTHORS

Stephan R. Leimburg

Stephan R. Leimberg is CEO of Leimberg and LeClair, Inc., an estate and financial planning software company and President of Leimberg Associates, Inc., a publishing and software company in Bryn Mawr, Pennsylvania. He is an Adjunct Professor in the Masters of Taxation Program of Temple University School of Law, holds a B.A. from Temple University, and a J.D. from Temple University School of Law.

Leimberg is the author of numerous books on estate, financial, and employee benefit and retirement planning and a nationally known speaker. Leimberg is the creator and principal author of the entire four book *Tools and Techniques* series including *The Tools and Techniques of Estate Planning, The Tools and Techniques of Financial Planning, The Tools and Techniques of Employee Benefit and Retirement Planning,* and *The Tools and Techniques of Life Insurance Planning.* Leimberg recently co-authored, with noted attorney Howard Zaritsky, *Tax Planning with Life Insurance, The New Book of Trusts - Post '97 Tax Law* with attorneys Charles K. Plotnick and Daniel Evans, and *How to Settle an Estate* with Charles K. Plotnick.

Leimberg is co-creator of many software packages for the financial services professional including *NumberCruncher '98* (estate planning), *Business QuickView* (business valuation, projection, and analysis), *Toolkit* (financial planning), *IRS Factors Calculator* (actuarial computations), and *Financial Calculator II*. His most recent software packages are *Estate Planning Quickview* (Estate Planning Flow Charts), *Planning Ahead for a Secure Retirement* (PowerPoint Client Seminar) and *Toward a Zero Estate Tax* (PowerPoint Client Seminar).

A nationally known speaker, Professor Leimberg has addressed the Miami Tax Institute, the NYU Tax Institute, the Notre Dame Law School and Duke University Law School's Estate Planning Conference, the National Association of Estate Planners and Councils, and the AICPA's National Estate Planning Forum. Leimberg has also spoken to the Federal Bureau of Investigation, and the National Aeronautics and Space Administration.

Leimberg was awarded the Excellence in Writing Award of the American Bar Association's Probate and Property Section. He has been honored as Estate Planner of the Year by the Montgomery County Estate Planning Council and as Distinguished Estate Planner by the Philadelphia Estate Planning Council. He is also a recipient of the President's Cup of the Philadelphia Life Underwriters, a two time Boris Todorovitch Lecturer, and the First Ben Feldman Lecturer.

Leimberg was named 1998 Edward N. Polisher Lecturer of the Dickinson School of Law.

Dr. Robert T. LeClair

Robert T. LeClair, Ph.D., is Associate Professor of Finance at Villanova University, Villanova, Pennsylvania. He is a graduate of the Wharton School of the University of Pennsylvania and received his MBA and Ph.D. degrees from Northwestern University's Kellogg Graduate School of Management. Prior to joining the faculty at Villanova, Dr. LeClair served on the faculties of The American College, Bryn Mawr, Pennsylvania, and the University of Illinois at Champaign-Urbana, Illinois.

Dr. LeClair is also a faculty member in finance of the National School of Banking, a professional education program for the thrift industry. The School, conducted at Fairfield University, Fairfield, Connecticut, is sponsored by America's Community Bankers (ACB) which is headquartered in Washington, D.C.

Dr. LeClair is active as a lecturer for John Cabot University in Rome, Italy. In Rome, he has been a speaker for various United Nations organizations including the World Food Program and the Food and Agriculture Organization. He has also presented courses developed by the American Management Association for Italian business executives.

Dr. LeClair is a frequent speaker for business groups and professional organizations in the areas of finance, investment, retirement planning, taxation, and personal financial planning. He has also been active as a consultant for numerous banks, thrift institutions, insurance companies, and professional associations. These include: Commerce Clearing House, Shenandoah Life Insurance Co., Jewel Companies, Inc., CNA Financial Corp., Continental Bank, America's Community Bankers, the Pennsylvania Credit Union League, the National Board of Medical Examiners, National Liberty Corporation, Eagle Software Publishing, Fidelcor, Inc., and the Archdiocese of Philadelphia.

In addition to magazine and journal articles, his other publications include: *Money and Retirement; A Consumer's Guide to Personal Investing* and *Financial Planning Software Tool Kit*. He has also co-authored and published three computer software packages: *The Financial and Estate Planner's NumberCruncher* and *Financial Planning Toolkit*.

Martin J. Satinsky

Marty Satinsky has been providing tax and financial planning services to individuals and businesses for over twenty years. He has worked with regional and international accounting firms, including seven years as a tax partner with Coopers & Lybrand.

In his current practice, Martin J. Satinsky & Associates, P.C., Mr. Satinsky specializes in Tax Consulting and Litigation Support Services. He is also President of Independent Financial Advisory Services, Inc., a fee based personal financial planning service.

An accomplished author on personal financial matters, he has co-authored many books on income and estate taxes and personal financial planning, including the *Accountant's Guide to Employee Benefit Plans*.

A frequent lecturer, Mr. Satinsky has also been an instructor at the American College, Temple University Law School, Georgetown University Law School, Syracuse University Law School and the University of Pennsylvania. He is currently a professor at the Philadelphia College of Textiles and Science Master Tax Program.

Mr. Satinsky is a graduate of the Pennsylvania State University and the Law School of the University of Pennsylvania. He received his Master of Law degree in Taxation from Temple University Law School.

Mr. Satinsky is a Certified Public Accountant in Pennsylvania and has been admitted to the Pennsylvania Bar. He is a member of the American Institute of Certified Public Accountants, and the Pennsylvania Institute of Certified Public Accountants, as well as the American Bar Association, and the Philadelphia Bar Association. He has served as an officer of the Philadelphia Estate Planning Council and also as a member of the AICPA Personal Financial Planning Member Services Committee and the PICPA Personal Financial Planning Committee.

Mr. Satinsky has conducted seminars on life insurance issues for the Philadelphia Bar Education Center, the AICPA and PICPA, and is a principal in Second Opinion Financial Systems, Inc., a company dedicated to improved understanding of how life insurance works.

Mr. Satinsky is president of the Jewish Community Centers of Greater Philadelphia and treasurer of the Philadelphia Bar Education Center. He has been active with the Federation of Jewish Agencies in Philadelphia and Washington, D.C. and was elected vice president of the Syracuse Jewish Federation.

Robert J. Doyle, Jr.

Robert J. Doyle, Jr. is an associate of Surgent & Associates, the country's leading purveyor of continuing professional education seminars and self-study materials for CPAs in the areas of taxation and financial planning. He has served as the subject matter expert and speaker for courses on "Everything You Need to Know About IRAs, Roth IRAs, SIMPLEs, and SEPs," "MBA in a Day," "Comprehensive Tools and Techniques of Investment Planning," "What Every CPA Should Know About Retirement Plan Distributions," "Advanced Strategies and Tactics of Wealth Accumulation and Retirement Planning," "A Technical Guide to Using the Wall Street Journal," and "What Every CPA Should Know About Insurance Products and Planning."

About the Authors

Before joining Surgent & Associates, Robert J. Doyle, Jr. was Senior Vice President of Mandeville Financial Services, Inc. (MFS), a diversified insurance, employee benefits, and executive compensation consulting firm and life insurance agency. MFS was part of the Mandeville Group, which included operations in property and liability insurance, real estate sales, management, maintenance, and appraisals, and personal and commercial motor vehicle sales and leasing.

Mr. Doyle has served as Adjunct Professor of Taxation in the graduate tax program of Widener University Graduate School of Management where he has taught courses in taxation of investments and taxation for financial planning. Mr. Doyle also spent 15 years as Associate Professor of Finance and Insurance at The American College where he was responsible for designing and writing courses in retirement and wealth accumulation planning for the College's CLU and ChFC professional designation programs. He did his graduate study as a Huebner Fellow at the Wharton School of the University of Pennsylvania. He holds the MA and MBA degrees from the Wharton School, a BA from Macalester College, is a CLU and a Chartered Financial Consultant (ChFC).

Mr. Doyle is the author of a dozen books and monographs including *Can You Afford to Retire?*® (Probus Publishing Company) and *The Tools and Techniques of Life Insurance Planning* (The National Underwriter). He has published numerous articles in the academic, professional, trade, and lay press on insurance, investments, taxation, business valuation, executive compensation, qualified and nonqualified plans, wealth accumulation, and retirement planning, and is a frequent speaker to business organizations, professional associations, and civic groups. He has been a main platform speaker at both the National Forum of the American Society of CLU & ChFC and the Fifth Annual National Conference on Financial Planning sponsored by Commerce Clearing House and The American College. He has appeared as a financial planning expert on radio and television talk shows around the country and videotaped a series of financial planning segments sponsored by The American Society of CLU & ChFC that have aired on various financial news broadcasts.

Mr. Doyle is also the author of several financial and tax planning software programs including Brentmark's *IRS Factors Calculator*, a tool to compute the value of annuities, life estates, remainders, and terms of years for gift and estate tax purposes. He has served as a design consultant and financial planning expert in the development of several commercial software packages including Financial Data's *NumberCruncher*® and *ToolKit*®, *Money*® *Magazine's WealthBuilder*®, and The Vanguard Group's *Retireß*. He is also the author of an IRA analysis software package that evaluates the regular IRA to Roth IRA rollover decision and an aftertax financial calculator that permits planners to do time-value computations that include realistic ordinary and capital gain tax effects.

Mr. Doyle is an avid competitive amateur golfer and a member of Rotary International.

PREFACE TO THE FIFTH EDITION

Much has changed since the Fourth Edition was published (1993) — and yet much has remained the same.

The tax law has changed — and we have expanded and updated TOOLS AND TECHNIQUES OF FINANCIAL PLANNING for all those tax law changes affecting it.

The tools and techniques of financial planning have changed. Asset allocation is a major professional buzzword. There are now Roth IRAs and SIMPLE IRAs, as well as traditional IRAs. Education funding includes education IRAs, qualified state tuition programs, and interest on qualified education loans. Segmented planning, a concentration on immediate and intermediate goals such as education funding, retirement funding, disability funding, and post death liquidity funding, is now the term of preference in the profession.

Our authors have remained the same. We have an attorney, a CPA, a PhD, and an MBA, all with extensive practical as well as theoretical insight into the problems of both clients and planners.

We were fortunate enough to obtain the assistance of Edward Graves, an MBA acknowledged as one of the country's leading experts on life insurance to review and update the chapter on that subject, Dr. Michael J. Roszkowski of the American College and Dr. Glenn E. Snelbecker of Temple University to provide a very useful guideline to assessing the risk taking propensities and expectations of clients through easy-to-apply psychometric tests.

The book was carefully edited by these tax attorneys on the staff of The National Underwriter Company: William J. Wagner, J.D., LL.M., CLU; Deborah A. Miner, J.D., CLU, ChFC; Darlene K. Chandler, J.D., CLU, ChFC; April K. Caudill, J.D., CLU, ChFC; Joseph F. Stenken, J.D.; Mary E. Bell, J.D.; and Sonya E. King, J.D., LL.M.

Our sister books have changed. At one time, there was only THE TOOLS AND TECHNIQUES OF ESTATE PLANNING. Now there two other sibling texts, THE TOOLS AND TECHNIQUES OF EMPLOYEE BENEFIT AND RETIREMENT PLANNING and THE TOOLS AND TECHNIQUES OF LIFE INSURANCE PLANNING . Financial planners seeking easily accessed information in those areas will find a familiar chapter format and writing style with all the essential information on a topic in one place.

Economics have changed. Economic upturns, lower interest rates, and the mergers and acquisitions of many financial institutions since the last edition have alerted clients as well as planners of the importance of diversification and constant asset appropriateness checks. This edition contains an entire chapter on the very latest tools available to assure clients safety of principal coupled with consistent growth and steady income.

Computers and computer graphics have become more useful as communications and persuasions tools; a simple pie or bar chart conveys in a millisecond what columns of numbers take minutes, hours, or never succeed in transmitting. This edition contains dozens of such graphs to make the point to planners who in turn can learn by experiencing that "seeing is believing".

So many things have changed. Therefore the need for this fifth edition of TOOLS AND TECHNIQUES OF FINANCIAL PLANNING.

Yet so many things have remained the same.

The need for a planner to continue to study and learn remains.

The need for a planner to understand the person — as well as the statement of financial condition, as Dr. Jerald W. Mason, education director for the International Association for Financial Planning, called it — is more important than ever.

The need for honesty and objectivity and ethics and competence is greater than ever.

The need to seek out and solve problems remains.

Our goals in writing this book have not changed. We want to help people help people obtain and retain financial dignity and achieve their economic dreams.

My co-authors and I invite you to share in our knowledge and experience — and to give us more feedback so that we can make the sixth edition more useful to you.

STEPHAN R. LEIMBERG

ABOUT THE TOOLS AND TECHNIQUES OF FINANCIAL PLANNING

Financial planning is fascinating and challenging (not only to the novice—but also to the seasoned professional) because it involves the interplay between clients, those they love, their personal and financial goals, the barriers to reaching those goals, and the tools and techniques and other resources available to meet those objectives.

No two people, or problems, are ever the same. There are no perfect answers either. Clients must understand that there are no "cost free" solutions. Every transaction has costs or downsides, and each suggestion the planner makes must be measured against that cost.

In other words, financial planning is much more than merely accumulating as much property or income as possible; it is far more complex because people and their relationship to each other, to their property, and to their objectives are involved.

There is no "quick fix" route to learning financial planning. The field is constantly changing, vast, and affected directly and indirectly (and sometimes in uncertain ways) by a multiplicity of factors.

WHO IS THE FINANCIAL PLANNER?

Every individual's finances are planned, some by inaction, lack of concern, or failure to appreciate the multitude of problems standing between them and their goals. They allow fate to do their planning. The results are often disappointing and sometimes disastrous. Others take a careful, calculated, and systematic approach to financial security. Their peace of mind is justified by the existence of a judicious mix of assets producing both adequate income and sufficient capital to safely meet their goals.

In this most general sense anyone who earns, spends, saves, invests, owns, manages, marries, shares ownership, buys, sells, gives, protects what is theirs, inherits, or retires can be said to be a financial planner. This book, however, is designed for use by the planner who earns the right, by the acquisition of knowledge and dedication to the financial security of others (rather than merely by charging a fee or commission) to call himself or herself a *professional*.

It is foolhardy, even negligent in some cases, to expect that any adviser, no matter how bright or knowledgeable will know everything necessary to properly execute a comprehensive financial plan. For this reason, a financial planning team should include several other advisors: a CPA (for tax matters), an attorney (for legal matters and drafting), a ChFC or CFP (for specific financial advice), a CLU (for life insurance), and a CPCU (for property and casualty insurance advice). The term "team" implies more than the sum of its parts and requires constant interaction and cooperation among the members to the extent necessary to achieve the client's goals.

Who should lead the financial planning process? In practice, financial planning typically will be initiated by one member of the team. Others will contribute in varying degrees. The extent to which each will participate will be determined by the circumstances of the particular case, the experience, skills, and personalities of the parties, and their relationship with the client.

Since the client is the ultimate planner, he or she should always be considered the single most important member of the financial planning team. The professional must:

(1) Uncover and describe the nature and extent of the client's problems and professionally impress the client with the urgency and significance of action.

(2) Discuss the viable alternatives.

(3) Explain what should be done and why.

(4) Match the plan to what the client really needs and wants (and can understand and is likely to accomplish).

(5) Match the plan to the client's risk taking propensity, investment philosophy, and order of priorities.

(6) Explain why present arrangements fail to accomplish the client's objectives or maximize the utility of his resources.

Absent any one or more of these, it is likely that the client's present "plan" will continue.

THE OBJECTIVES OF
TOOLS AND TECHNIQUES

The objectives of this book are to provide the reader with accurate, up to date, highly practical, lucid, comprehensive, and detailed information on a wide range of financial planning tools and techniques.

Through our unique format (one concept at a time—with all aspects of that subject explained in one place), we have striven to accomplish these objectives in a succinct yet creative manner useful to the layman or novice. We also feel that *The Tools and Techniques of Financial Planning* will become a "briefcase essential" for even the most sophisticated and seasoned planner who wishes to review and update knowledge of basic investment products and concepts and the impact of tax law on these. It can also be an invaluable aid to any planner who needs a well-organized approach for explaining financial planning tools and techniques to individual clients (or to potential clients in seminars) and who is concerned with client-suitability of the products and services he offers.

ABOUT THE FORMAT

The Tools and Techniques of Financial Planning, like its companion texts, the classic *The Tools and Techniques of Estate Planning*, *The Tools and Techniques of Employee Benefit and Retirement Planning*, and *The Tools and Techniques of Life Insurance Planning* is a unique way to learn, review, and share information.

The Tools and Techniques of Financial Planning is divided into three main divisions:

(1) the techniques of financial planning,

(2) the tools of financial planning, and

(3) helpful tables, checklists, and charts in the appendices.

The "Ten Minute Financial Planner," the first chapter in the "techniques" section, will serve as an excellent overview for those new to the field, and a perspective refreshing review for the practiced professional, and can be used as a basis for seminar presentations to clients of almost all financial planners. This chapter is followed by a chapter devoted entirely to the financial planning process and sixteen more chapters invaluable to anyone who wants an in-depth pragmatic understanding of the essential elements of a thorough financial plan.

The "tools" of financial planning are the various investments that are available to meet the needs of clients for income and wealth or to protect and assure the continuation of income and the preservation of wealth they already have. There are 33 easy-to-read chapters covering every major device currently available to clients.

The third major section of the book, the appendices, will provide the planner with the numbers to quantify both a client's needs and resources in terms of either present or future dollars. The investment matrix, designed especially for this book, is a due diligence device to help the planner make an objective and realistic analysis of what investment is most proper for a given client.

Each chapter is presented in a straightforward manner that allows the reader to readily ascertain the similarities and distinctions in each of the various tools and techniques available. This format provides for easy comparison through uniformity.

Common subtitles in these chapters include:

(1) "WHAT IS IT?" (A description of the tool or technique.)

(2) "WHEN IS THE USE OF THIS TOOL INDICATED?" (A checklist of situations or circumstances in which the utilization of the tool or technique would be appropriate.)

(3) "ADVANTAGES" (A list and explanation of why or how the particular tool might benefit a client.)

(4) "DISADVANTAGES" (A list and explanation of why or how the particular tool might not be appropriate in a specific situation.)

(5) "TAX IMPLICATIONS" (A succinct description of how the income tax law—and in many cases the gift or estate tax law—affects or is affected by the subject of the chapter.)

(6) "ALTERNATIVES" (A list of other tools or techniques that are in one or more ways comparable to the one under consideration and which should also be checked for suitability.)

(7) "WHERE AND HOW DO I GET IT?" (A practical step-by-step guideline for the financial planner and/or client which explains how to purchase a given financial planning tool. This section not only explains "where" but also "how" to buy a bond, stock, or other investment.)

(8) "WHAT FEES OR OTHER ACQUISITION COSTS ARE INVOLVED?" (A description of typical commissions, storage, and other acquisition costs associated with a particular investment vehicle which makes it easier to compare one with another.)

(9) "HOW DO I SELECT THE BEST OF ITS TYPE?" (This section highlights the decisions that must be made after the investor and adviser have determined the specific type of investment to make.)

(10) "WHERE CAN I FIND OUT MORE ABOUT IT?" (A list of easy to find or key references for more detailed and specific information on any given topic.)

(11) "QUESTIONS AND ANSWERS" (This section answers commonly asked questions about the subject matter.)

Because of their special nature (for example, the chapter on income taxation) certain chapters of *The Tools and Techniques of Financial Planning* contain their own special format.

Specially designed matrix and evaluation tools (easily convertible to computer spreadsheets) can be found in Appendix H. These should be consulted both before and after reading any chapter to give the planner a basis for comparing and contrasting various tools and techniques and ascertaining client suitability.

The Tools and Techniques of Financial Planning also includes a Glossary and several additional appendices containing numerous tables and other helpful guidance for the financial planner.

The Financial Planning TOOLKIT and NumberCruncher Estate Planning software (610-527-5216) were used to produce many of the illustrations in this book.

WHO WILL FIND THE BOOK USEFUL

Every present and aspiring member of the financial planning team will find *The Tools and Techniques of Financial Planning* useful, including bankers, stockbrokers, accountants, attorneys, instructors of financial planning courses at colleges and universities, instructors of adult education and personal finance courses, law schools, CPA firms, insurance agents, para-professionals, and even clients themselves.

CONTENTS

		Page
Dedications		iii
About the Authors		v
Preface		ix
About the TOOLS AND TECHNIQUES OF FINANCIAL PLANNING		xi

PART I TECHNIQUES

Chapter 1	The Ten Minute Financial Planner	1
Chapter 2	The Financial Planning Process	21
Chapter 3	Budgeting	27
Chapter 4	Education Funding	37
Chapter 5	Estate Planning	77
Chapter 6	How to Evaluate Life Insurance Products	101
Chapter 7	How to Review a Will	119
Chapter 8	Income Tax Concepts	129
Chapter 9	Investment Advisers: Regulation and Registration	151
Chapter 10	Financial Leveraging	159
Chapter 11	Personal Financial Statements	163
Chapter 12	Rate of Return Computations: Part I	173
Chapter 13	Rate of Return Computations: Part II	181
Chapter 14	Retirement Plan Distribution Planning	191
Chapter 15	Risk and Reward	199
Chapter 16	Risk Tolerance and Risk Aversion	215
Chapter 17	Asset Allocation and Personal Portfolio Management	229

PART II TOOLS

Chapter 18	Annuities	247
Chapter 19	Certificates of Deposit	261
Chapter 20	Collectibles	265
Chapter 21	Commodities	269
Chapter 22	Common Stocks	273
Chapter 23	Convertible Securities	281
Chapter 24	Corporate Bonds	287
Chapter 25	Financial Futures	295
Chapter 26	Gold and Other Precious Metals	301
Chapter 27	Individual Retirement Accounts: Roth	307
Chapter 28	Individual Retirement Accounts: Traditional	319
Chapter 29	Keogh (HR-10) Plans	337
Chapter 30	Life Insurance	343
Chapter 31	Money Market Funds	355
Chapter 32	Mortgage-Backed Securities	359
Chapter 33	Municipal Bonds	369

Chapter 34 Mutual Funds 375
Chapter 35 Oil and Gas 391
Chapter 36 Preferred Stock 397
Chapter 37 Publicly Traded (Master) Limited Partnerships 401
Chapter 38 Put and Call Stock Options 411
Chapter 39 Qualified Pension and Profit-Sharing Plans 417
Chapter 40 Real Estate as an Investment 423
Chapter 41 REITs (Real Estate Investment Trusts) 435
Chapter 42 REMICs (Real Estate Mortgage Investment Conduits) 445
Chapter 43 Retirement Plan Rollovers 459
Chapter 44 SEPs (Simplified Employee Pensions) 465
Chapter 45 SIMPLE Plans 469
Chapter 46 Stripped Bonds 475
Chapter 47 Tax Shelters: General Concepts 477
Chapter 48 U.S. Government Securities 481
Chapter 49 World Wide Investing 485
Chapter 50 Zero-Coupon Bonds 491

APPENDICES

Appendix A Compound Interest Table 493
Appendix B Present Value Table 499
Appendix C Compound Annual Annuity in Advance 503
Appendix D Compound Annual Annuity in Arrears 509
Appendix E Compound Discount Table 515
Appendix F Present Value of Annuity Due 519
Appendix G Tax Exempt Equivalents 523
Appendix H Investment Matrix 527
Appendix I Income Tax Rate Tables 537
Appendix J Million Dollar Goal Guide 539
Appendix K Sample Letter of Instructions 541

GLOSSARY 543

INDEX 549

Chapter 1

THE TEN MINUTE FINANCIAL PLANNER

It takes a multiplicity of courses and years of experience to become a skilled financial planner. Even then, you have to continue reading, listening, and learning. So you won't learn from this chapter or even this whole book (or any other book) everything you need to know to be a financial planner. But in ten minutes, this chapter can give you an overview (or review) that will set the stage for you to be (or will get you back on track to being) an effective financial services professional.

In the paragraphs below we will (a) define financial planning, (b) discuss the "co-op" approach, (c) consider the process of planning, (d) list and explain the golden principles of financial planning, (e) outline for you what a full blown financial planning report to a client should cover, (f) list ten steps to success, and (g) tell you where you can learn much more.

FINANCIAL PLANNING DEFINED

Financial planning is

(1) creating order out of chaos,

(2) a deliberate and continuing process by which a sufficient amount of capital is accumulated and conserved and adequate levels of income are attained to accomplish the financial and personal objectives of the client,

(3) the development and implementation of coordinated plans for the achievement of a client's overall financial objectives, and/or

(4) income tax planning, retirement planning, estate planning, investment and asset allocation planning, and risk management planning.

Select one of the above, or select all. There seems to be no one universally accepted definition of what financial planning is. That's understandable since the planner's role must be as different as the needs of clients and their ability or willingness to pay for advice. No two people or problems will ever be exactly the same.

For many clients, the creation of a simple and workable system that will help them control their cash and pay their bills on time will be successful financial planning. For others successful financial planning will involve the full time efforts of a planner, staff, and sophisticated computer support. Most planners will be working with clients whose needs fall somewhere between these two extremes.

The financial problems our clients face in their lives can be categorized by the letters L-I-V-E-S.

L. LACK OF LIQUIDITY (The inability to quickly turn invested capital into spendable cash without incurring unreasonable cost. This problem can result in a forced sale of assets at pennies on the dollar. For instance, if a client must sell stocks or mutual fund shares in a "down market," or if an executor must sell a valuable real estate portfolio to pay death tax and administrative expenses, the buyer will offer to pay the lowest possible price for the most precious asset. A forced sale often becomes a "fire sale.")

I. INADEQUATE RESOURCES (Insufficient capital or income in the event of death, disability, at retirement, or for special needs.)

I. INFLATION (Not enough has been done to "inflation proof" the client's portfolio. Figure 1.1 emphasizes the crippling impact of inflation on each dollar's ability to buy goods and services.)

I. IMPROPER DISPOSITION OF ASSETS (The client is leaving the wrong asset to the wrong person at the wrong time and in the wrong manner. Picture, for instance, a client leaving a sports car to a 10-year old child or $100,000 cash to a 21 year old college student.)

V. VALUE (Not enough has been done to stabilize and maximize the financial security value of the client's business and other assets.)

E. EXCESSIVE TAXES (Excessive taxes add to the cost of an investment and retard progress toward a client's objectives.)

S. SPECIAL NEEDS (Clients have desires that go beyond mere quantifiable goals. Psychological assurance and comfort should be part of the financial planning process. For example, a client may want to provide financial care for a spouse or children who are disabled or emotionally troubled.)

But rather than further proliferate the definitional morass, it may be more productive to examine what it is you must do and what it is you are expected to know as a "financial planner."

The College For Financial Planning has completed an extensive study of the professional responsibilities and knowledge requirements of financial planners. The survey, conducted by Dr. Larry Skurnik, a Measurement Research Specialist, covered a large number of CFPs and ChFCs as well as others in the field. The broad categories of inquiry are instructive as to what you must do and know as a practicing financial services professional.

What you must do is

(1) evaluate client needs,

(2) explain financial planning concepts,

(3) clarify client goals,

(4) analyze information,

(5) prepare comprehensive financial plans,

(6) implement comprehensive financial plans,

(7) monitor comprehensive financial plans, and

(8) establish and maintain accurate records and perform other professional functions.

What you must know are

(1) communications skills,

(2) risk management,

(3) investment planning,

(4) tax planning,

(5) retirement planning, and

(6) estate planning.

The College For Financial Planning Study indicates that aside from a necessary "must know" common core of skills and information, what you, as a planner, must be able to do or know depends on

(1) your background,

(2) personal characteristics,

(3) whether you are a sole practitioner, a member of a firm of planners, or an employee with a narrower range of responsibilities,

(4) the major tasks and duties of your job, and

(5) the market in which you work.

In short, the planner must have competence in many areas and compassion and concern for the financial well being of others.

THE "CO-OP" APPROACH TO FINANCIAL PLANNING

No single financial planner can possibly know all that needs to be known or do all that needs to be done for every client. Nevertheless, no transaction should ever be recommended to a client until the planner acquires a working knowledge of how that recommendation will affect and be affected by

(1) taxes (income, gift, estate) at both the federal and state level,

(2) retirement planning (including a practical understanding of Social Security, inflation, and the psychological dynamics of retirement planning),

(3) estate planning (which encompasses property law, domestic relations law, and other state laws as well as tax law),

(4) wealth and asset management (which requires, aside from knowledge of various products and their alternatives, an understanding of cash flow implications and present and future value and rate of return computations), and

(5) risk-reward principles (both economic and psychological).

Since no one person can know all these things in great depth, a truly professional financial planner must view himself or herself as part of a financial planning "cooperative" with the client and with other professionals, with each professional adding to the efficiency and effectiveness of the plan.

The first step in working as a member of this cooperative is to become aware of

(1) the client's long, intermediate, and short range goals,

(2) the problems faced by and opportunities available to the client in the quest to achieve those goals,

(3) what each of the other professional advisers has already done for the client, and

(4) what each of the other professional advisers may be able to contribute to the improvement of the client's plan to achieve his goals.

It is extremely important that, no matter who is the coordinator of this cooperative effort, each member of the cooperative be offered the opportunity to participate in the process.

Most importantly, the client, the principal member of the cooperative, must never be forgotten. Clients who are not given an opportunity to express their desires or thoughts or who do not understand a suggestion or the rationale for it will not implement or continue the plan and will resent paying what the planner feels is a reasonable price for the service rendered.

THE FINANCIAL PLANNING PROCESS—BY THE NUMBERS

Where do I start? Most new financial planners, and many who have been in the field for a long time, face this question. The high expense of doing business exacts a cruel price from those who do not develop a cost effective and systematic approach to every stage in the financial planning process (including the business of being in business, which is beyond the scope of this book but which is certainly a key factor in determining a planner's success or failure).

The planner who does not develop (or discover in books such as this or in computer programs such as those described in this book) procedures, forms, strategies, checklists, and worksheets is doomed to endlessly reinvent the wheel.

There is no "right" answer as to where you begin because the process is circular (as you'll note in Chapter 2, "The Financial Planning Process"). But most planners follow a course that looks something like this:

1. Meet with the client and gather and then analyze the data. (This step involves not only gathering data but also obtaining documents relative to the services promised. This may include wills, trusts, marital agreements, tax returns, employee benefit plans, and buy-sell agreements. Information must be comprehensive, accurate, and in some cases intimate.)

2. Uncover the client's personal objectives, quantify them, and then prioritize them. (The difference between a dream and a realistic and achievable goal is the reduction of "What I'd like when..." to specific dollar needs at a given date and the conversion of that "then" figure into what needs to be done now to "get there when." For example, "I'd like a secure and comfortable retirement" is a dream. "I need $800,000 producing income at 5% or greater when I am age sixty, twenty years from now" is the reduction of the dream to a dollar goal. But that itself must be converted into, "I need to invest an additional $2,000 a month and earn at least X% interest for each of the next twenty years, together with the assets already at work, to achieve my goal.") Dollar quantification of each of a client's goals is one of the most important tasks of a financial planner.

Once the planner has measured the client's needs, the planner must establish an order of priorities and then give first preference to those things the client feels are most important.

3. Analyze and discover weaknesses in the client's present plan. ("Where is the client financially? Where does the client want to be at given times or events? Is there too little discretionary cash flow? Are invested funds earning too low a rate? What stands in the client's way? Are the client's income tax payments needlessly high? What is the impact of inflation on the client's real rate of return? What changes in circumstances such as divorce, inheritance, illness, death, or changes in job or residence have occurred in the past or may affect the plan in the future?")

Consider how assets are (a) positioned (b) taxed and (c) risk managed. ("Are assets protected against damage, loss, theft, or legal liability? How is income (a) directed (b) taxed (c) protected? What is the client's attitude toward planning and is the client organized and disciplined enough to carry out a new plan?")

4. Formulate and test a new plan. ("What tools and techniques can most efficiently accomplish the client's objectives within comfortable risk-reward parameters? Considering the available resources, which alternatives are most appropriate? Does the new plan position assets in line with stated objectives and direct discretionary cash flow toward weak areas? Will the plan work on paper, and what are the downside risks if it doesn't? Does the action being considered create reward without undue risk or remove risk without excessive cost? Does the new plan

Figure 1.1

| EROSION OF PURCHASING POWER | | | | | |

Amount $100,000
Annual Rate of Inflation 0.030

After Years	0.010	0.020	0.030	0.040	0.050
1	99,010	98,039	97,087	96,154	95,238
2	98,030	96,117	94,260	92,456	90,703
3	97,059	94,232	91,514	88,900	86,384
4	96,098	92,385	88,849	85,480	82,270
5	95,147	90,573	86,261	82,193	78,353
6	94,205	88,797	83,748	79,031	74,622
7	93,272	87,056	81,309	75,992	71,068
8	92,348	85,349	78,941	73,069	67,684
9	91,434	83,676	76,642	70,259	64,461
10	90,529	82,035	74,409	67,556	61,391

Reprinted courtesy *Financial Planning* TOOLKIT, Leimberg and LeClair, Inc.

mesh with the client's lifestyle and attitudes? Can the client and the client's family understand the plan and accept it as their own?")

5. Execute the new or revised plan. ("What products and services need to be acquired and what is the best way to do that? Which members of the financial planning cooperative should be responsible for carrying out the various parts of the plan? Who will be responsible for the overall implementation of the plan and for communication to the client and to other members of the financial planning co-operative?")

6. Periodically review the revised plan. ("How often should the plan be reviewed? What events should trigger a review other than the passage of time? Procedurally, how will the review process be implemented?")

GOLDEN PRINCIPLES OF FINANCIAL PLANNING

There is nothing new (including this maxim) under the sun. Yet, there is a very good reason why certain sayings, rules of thumb, or guidelines have been around so long: they work! The rate of change in the tax law affecting financial planning has been surpassed only by the rapid change in the investment and insurance products and services designed to meet clients' needs.

Despite these continuing changes, certain principles remain golden. Consider that regardless of how sophisticated

you or your operation becomes, or how long you are planning the financial affairs of others, these principles will shine:

1. Cover your assets before taking greater risk. Never suggest that a client proceed to the next level of risk before the gains already made have been protected. This is the basic principle behind risk management as well as the proper assessment of life and disability income needs.

2. Seek first a return *of* principal before a return *on* principal. Put safety of principal and certainty of income before gain on capital or growth of income. This "safety first" caveat is really another way of saying, "Don't be greedy or you may lose it all." An adviser must always remind a client of the balance between risk and reward, but protection of principal must always come first.

3. No risk, no reward. Strong profits are not gained by faint hearts. Money is made and taxes are saved by taking prudent (defined on a client-by-client basis) risk. It is important for clients to recognize that there are three types of risk: financial risk, purchasing power risk, and lost opportunity risk.

    Doing nothing is the greatest risk of all. At only 3% inflation, $100,000 loses more than 25% of its purchasing power in just ten years, as the Financial Planning TOOLKIT printout shown in Figure 1.1 illustrates. And the average rate of inflation during the past 15 years (even considering the very low rates of the last few years) has

The Tools and Techniques of Financial Planning

been almost double that 3% rate! Client's ignore inflation—even low rates of inflation at great peril.

4. Without both liquidity and marketability, there is no flexibility. Liquidity is a measure of the investor's ability to turn all or most of an investment back into cash, with little or no loss. Marketability is a measure of the speed and ease at which a buyer (through sale, trade, or otherwise) can dispose of his investment.

   If a client does not have enough cash or assets that can quickly, inexpensively, and easily be turned into cash, how will he or she meet an emergency or take advantage of an opportunity? Inadequate cash often translates into either a forced sale or a lost opportunity. This problem becomes especially acute when an investor dies and large and often unexpected cash drains (payable according to the IRS's timetable) occur and too often a fire sale results.

5. A successful investor has to be right three times. To profit from any investment, it is not good enough to merely select the right investment; it is also necessary that the asset be purchased and sold at the right time and also in the right manner. Selection, timing, and titling (i.e., the right decision concerning who should hold legal title to property) are all keys to success (as is keeping the spread or commission and loading charges paid on an investment as low as possible).

6. An investor should never put all his eggs into one basket. But if they are put in one basket, the basket must be watched carefully. Diversification is one of the most important principles of financial planning. It is the driving force behind the success of the mutual fund. Although it is conceivable that a person could diversify into mediocrity, this result is not likely if diversification is combined with the other golden principles.

   Diversification should be not only "horizontal" and "vertical" but, if feasible, "multidimensional." That means an investor should, if economically possible, diversify in terms of investment vehicles (for instance, divide capital between stocks, real estate, and money markets), within a class or type of investment, by geographic location, and through timing (different maturities within the same type of investment and dollar cost averaging as explained in number 20 below).

   The letters H-P-M will help in the remembrance of the goals and advantages of diversification.

   H—Diversify to achieve the *highest after-tax return* consistent with asset growth and income needs.

P—Diversify to acquire the *proper balance of liquidity and marketability.*

M—Diversify to *match a client's risk-taking propensity and temperament.*

   It is the authors' opinion that few people should invest in individual stocks until they have first built up sizeable mutual fund portfolios.

7. Put yourself on your own payroll—at the top of the payroll.

   If a client doesn't know where to start, he probably won't start. The place to start is on top. The point is that most people pay their bills and end with little, if anything, for themselves. Reverse that chaos with order, the right order, and help the client to use the budgetary process to take care of himself first. Clients should budget for savings and investment, just as they budget for the payment of monthly debt.

8. Capitalize on the miracle of the "forgotten" automatic investment.

   By far, the greatest financial security most individuals have results from having put aside money on a regular automatic basis before they see it or consider it "spendable." This includes salary savings plans, employer sponsored pension and profit sharing and thrift plans, as well as what must be the most common example of all, the month after month reminder that life insurance premiums are due. That "forgotten" money compounds year after year (putting into play the power of compound interest) so that when you need it the most, it's there in the amount needed.

9. It is as important to increase the rate of investing as it is to increase the rate of return.

   It is far easier and safer to find or create small incremental increases of discretionary cash to invest each month over a long period of time than to uncover or create large lumps of assets at one time or dramatically increase investment return. In fact, a small increase in input of regular investment is equal to a dramatic increase in the rate of return on current investment.

   We suggest that clients increase the amount they invest each week or month until they reach the "ouch" point. The ouch point is reached when the level of investment begins to have an adverse impact on their standard of living. By constantly raising the "ouch point," more and more is being invested on a regular basis, putting less pressure on the assets already saved to meet objectives. This is another way of saying that by increasing investment input, the return (spelled R-I-S-K) that must be obtained by current investments to meet a given goal is reduced.

Increasing the level of investments also provides an additional hedge against inflation as well as a "luxury level" in excess of merely meeting the "bare bones" financial objective.

Master planner Harold Gourgues, in his *Financial Planning Handbook* (New York Institute of Finance/ Prentice Hall) describes the use of a "rate of return matrix" to properly align assets. The principles behind this system are these two questions:

How "fast" do assets have to "move" to get to their goal on time? (In other words,"What internal rate of return must be realized on the current income producing assets and current stream of investable income to meet the quantified financial goals of the client?")

What risks must be taken to move assets faster toward their goal of reaching the desired amount?

In the event the current mix of assets and the current level of investment result in a projected shortage of college or retirement funds, solutions include

(a) trying a new mix of assets (increasing risk) to increase average rate of return,

(b) increasing capital,

(c) increasing annual contributions,

(d) taking down capital at retirement,

(e) retiring at a later date to buy more time, or

(d) using a combination of these solutions

Discretionary cash flow (investable cash) can be increased by

(a) reducing income or other taxes imposed during the client's lifetime, and by

(b) programming and controlling moderate to major expenses (two techniques, simple budgeting and controlling of inflows and outflows of cash and the use of

financial management accounts, will help to create or improve discretionary cash flow).

10. Let purpose help define the level of risk taken.

If the client's need to satisfy a given objective is great (for example, he has two children and anticipates a minimum need of $60,000 for college education funds in six years), he may not be willing to risk significant capital to obtain 2 or 3 percent higher return. On the other hand, if a client has allocated a given amount of money as a crapshoot and has no special purpose for the money, he or she will probably be willing to take much higher risks more often.

Be sure the client understands not only the level of risk the client is taking but also all the risks the client is taking. For instance, it may appear that a 4% return in a savings account with a major bank is a riskless investment. Likewise, a fully secured loan of $100,000 to a major financial institution seems risk free. Yet in both cases the purchasing power of the investor's capital is invisibly eroded by inflation. This is just one of the hidden risks that must be understood by clients. (Another risk is that the institution will become insolvent.) Still another risk is "alternative risk." Had the money been placed in an alternative investment, to what level would it have grown?

11. Assets and income maintain their utility only to the extent they maintain or increase their purchasing power.

As Figure 1.2 illustrates, it will be difficult for an investor to maintain a $100,000 a year purchasing power even if he has $1,000,000 of income producing assets earning 6% if inflation erodes that buying power at only a 3% rate.

By the tenth year, it will take $130,477 to buy what $100,000 would have purchased in the first year. Invasion of the fund producing the income is necessary from the beginning, since even in the first year there is a $40,000 gap between what is produced and what is needed. By the thirteenth year, the fund will be sufficiently depleted that the income will no longer be maintainable. (Consider as you ponder this harsh reality that a sixty-five year old female has a life expectancy of about seventeen years.)

12. Increase expenditures (especially nondeductible ones) at a lower rate than you increase your income.

Controlling inefficient spending and debt acquisition is the lowest risk way to increase dollars available for

Figure 1.2

INFLATION-ADJUSTED INCOME & ASSET ANALYSIS

Desired Income From Investments $100,000

Income Producing Assets $1,000,000

Assumed Return on Investments 0.060

Assumed Inflation Rate 0.030

Year	Inflation Adjusted Income	Value of Assets	Income From Assets	Use of Capital	Assets at End of Year
1	$100,000	$1,000,000	$60,000	$40,000	$960,000
2	$103,000	$960,000	$57,600	$45,400	$914,600
3	$106,090	$914,600	$54,876	$51,214	$863,386
4	$109,273	$863,386	$51,803	$57,470	$805,916
5	$112,551	$805,916	$48,355	$64,196	$741,720
6	$115,927	$741,720	$44,503	$71,424	$670,296
7	$119,405	$670,296	$40,218	$79,187	$591,109
8	$122,987	$591,109	$35,467	$87,520	$503,589
9	$126,677	$503,589	$30,215	$96,462	$407,127
10	$130,477	$407,127	$24,428	$106,049	$301,078
11	$134,392	$301,078	$18,065	$116,327	$184,751
12	$138,423	$184,751	$11,085	$127,338	$57,413
13	$142,576	$57,413	$3,445	$139,131	$0
14	$146,853	$0	$0	$146,853	$0
15	$151,259	$0	$0	$151,259	$0
16	$155,797	$0	$0	$155,797	$0
17	$160,471	$0	$0	$160,471	$0
18	$165,285	$0	$0	$165,285	$0
19	$170,243	$0	$0	$170,243	$0
20	$175,351	$0	$0	$175,351	$0

Reprinted courtesy *Financial Planning* TOOLKIT, Leimberg and LeClair, Inc.

investment. Although budgeting is often considered the least sophisticated aspect of financial planning, in a surprising number of cases monetary waste and uncontrolled cash flow are not only major impediments to financial success but also to financial stability or survival.

13. Think of financial security only in terms of the bottom line.

It's not what you earn that counts; it's what you get to keep.

Too many clients judge the health of their wealth at the top line. But getting ahead in terms of absolute wealth or absolute income is a false security. Many planners use the analogy of a funnel; wealth and income are diverted from a straight path down the funnel to the client and his or her family because of (1) taxes, and (2) slippage.

Consider that state and federal taxes, expenses of producing income, inflation, and transfer costs will significantly diminish the purchasing power of what's left on the bottom line. Remember that it's only what makes it to the bottom line that generates purchasing power. For instance, Figure 1.3 shows that after taxes, the true return on a taxable investment is far less than it otherwise appears.

The Tools and Techniques of Financial Planning

Figure 1.3

TRUE RETURN TABLE THE TRUE RETURN ON MONEY IS:						
TAXABLE RATE OF RETURN	COMBINED FEDERAL & STATE TAX BRACKET					
	0.15	0.30	0.35	0.40	0.45	0.50
0.02	0.017	0.014	0.013	0.012	0.011	0.010
0.03	0.026	0.021	0.020	0.018	0.017	0.015
0.04	0.034	0.028	0.026	0.024	0.022	0.020
0.05	0.043	0.035	0.033	0.030	0.028	0.025
0.06	0.051	0.042	0.039	0.036	0.033	0.030
0.07	0.060	0.049	0.046	0.042	0.039	0.035
0.08	0.068	0.056	0.052	0.048	0.044	0.040
0.09	0.077	0.063	0.058	0.054	0.049	0.045
0.10	0.085	0.070	0.065	0.060	0.055	0.050
0.11	0.093	0.077	0.072	0.066	0.060	0.055
0.12	0.102	0.084	0.078	0.072	0.066	0.060
0.13	0.110	0.091	0.084	0.078	0.071	0.065
0.14	0.119	0.098	0.091	0.084	0.077	0.070
0.15	0.128	0.105	0.098	0.090	0.082	0.075
0.16	0.136	0.112	0.104	0.096	0.088	0.080
0.17	0.145	0.119	0.111	0.102	0.094	0.085
0.18	0.153	0.126	0.117	0.108	0.099	0.090
0.19	0.162	0.133	0.124	0.114	0.105	0.095
0.20	0.170	0.140	0.130	0.120	0.110	0.100
0.21	0.179	0.147	0.137	0.126	0.116	0.105
0.22	0.187	0.154	0.143	0.132	0.121	0.110
0.23	0.196	0.161	0.150	0.138	0.127	0.115
0.24	0.204	0.168	0.156	0.144	0.132	0.120
0.25	0.213	0.175	0.163	0.150	0.138	0.125

This bottom line philosophy must be extended to all phases of financial and estate planning. For example, if a sixty year old executive dies and leaves $9,000,000 in his pension plan to his granddaughter, the transfer is subject to a federal estate tax, a generation-skipping transfer tax (assuming he had already utilized his exclusion), an income tax, probably a state inheritance or estate tax, and in many states, a state income tax. If the pension plan is fully subject to tax at the maximum federal tax rates, the grandchild will receive about 12 cents on the dollar.

Retirement Plan	$ 1.00
Estate Tax (55%)	(.55)
Net	.45
Generation-Skipping Tax (55%)	(.25)
Net	.20
Income Tax (39.6%)	(.08)
Net	.12

14. He is wise who can turn top tax dollars into assets or spendable income without undue risk.

Marginal income tax rates are what eat into the last dollar of income, if permitted. High tax brackets indicate planning opportunities. A good planner will search for opportunities to accomplish the following key objectives of financial and estate planning (for more information on the estate planning process, see our companion text, *The Tools and Techniques of Estate Planning*):

(a) *Create* estate tax free wealth. For instance, it is possible to transfer wealth from one generation to another through a death benefit only plan or an irrevocable life insurance trust.

(b) *Divide* and conquer the tax systems. The progressive nature of the income, estate, and gift tax systems can be used against each other by creating more taxpayers, each

The Tools and Techniques of Financial Planning

Figure 1.4

AFTER-TAX RETURN/COST CALCULATOR	
Federal Tax Bracket	0.280
State Tax Bracket	0.070
Combined Marginal Tax Bracket	0.330
Before-Tax Return on Investment	0.080
After-Tax Return on Investment	0.054
Before-Deduction Borrowing Rate	0.120
Net Cost of Borrowing	0.080

Reprinted courtesy *Financial Planning* TOOLKIT, Leimberg and LeClair, Inc.

at lower brackets. Using the annual gift tax exclusion to shift income to lower tax brackets, thereby lowering the resulting income tax, is an example.

(c) *Deduct.* It is obvious that deductions reduce tax liability. The benefit of a deduction is directly related to the marginal tax bracket you are in; the higher the bracket, the greater the benefit from the deduction. The formula for computing the tax saving from a deduction is

(Amount of deduction) x (investor's marginal tax rate).

So the tax saving to an investor in a 28% bracket with a $1,000 deduction appears to be $280. We say, "appears to be" since a planner must take into consideration state as well as federal taxes and the interplay between them.

The Financial Planning TOOLKIT illustration in Figure 1.4 shows that an individual's combined income tax bracket is much higher than the federal bracket alone, even though a deduction from the federal bracket may be allowed for the state tax paid. The illustration also points out that the return on the individual's investments is substantially lowered, but the net cost of borrowing is also significantly lowered by the leverage of the tax deduction.

(d) *Defer.* Deferring income from one tax year to another or over many years has multiple advantages. First, deferral of receipt translates into a deferral of taxation. Money that otherwise would have taken a one way trip to Washington, D.C., on April 15th can be used year after year to earn income for the client. Deferral of tax is, temporarily at least, like a no or low cost loan from the IRS.

Second, in some cases it may be possible to defer long enough so that the tax on the deferred income need never be paid. For instance, the internal build up within a life

insurance contract is never taxed if the policy is held by the owner until the death of the insured. Money inside a Roth IRA not only can accumulate tax free for many years, but also can be received income tax free.

Third, income that may be taxed in a high bracket year can be deferred to a lower bracket year. For example, a 40% combined federal and state bracket reduces the after-tax return of a 10% investment yield to 6%. (See True Return Table, Figure 1.3.) The same investment yields 7% if the investor is in a 30% bracket when the income becomes taxable.

Of course, it is important to consider nontax factors such as the possibility that the creditor who is able to pay in the year of deferral may not be able to pay in the later year.

Deferral is accomplished through a variety of mechanisms, such as

(i) deferring interest income by, for example, purchasing T-bills maturing in a later tax year or by purchasing U.S. Savings bonds,

(ii) contracting with an employer for a nonqualified deferred compensation plan,

(iii) sending out bills late in December with the expectation that they will not be paid until January (i.e., the following tax year for cash basis taxpayers), and

(iv) postponing the due date of interest a debtor is liable to pay you from this year to a future tax year.

(e) *Discount.* Pay real estate and other local taxes early where the taxing entity provides an advantageous discount. This technique will increase cash flow but requires cash flow control (budgeting) to work.

Figure 1.5

				Tax Free Proceeds		Cash Value as
End Yr.	Amount Payable	Cumulative Premiums	Cost Per $	Above Premiums	Cash Value	% of Premium
1	$1,000,000	$27,430	$0.03	$972,570	$410	1.5%
5	$1,034,000	$137,150	$0.13	$896,850	$11,094	8.1%
10	$1,132,400	$246,870	$0.22	$885,530	$294,567	119.3%
20	$1,214,900	$246,870	$0.20	$968,030	$601,135	243.5%

DISCOUNTING THE FEDERAL ESTATE TAX

Reprinted courtesy *Financial Planning* TOOLKIT, Leimberg and LeClair, Inc.

Another "discount" device that should not be overlooked by planners is the ability to pay federal estate tax at a "discount" through properly arranged (out of the estate but available for the estate) life insurance. The Financial Planning TOOLKIT illustration in Figure 1.5 shows how a substantial estate tax payment can be made for literally pennies on the dollar.

(f) *Eliminate* the tax on wealth. Through devices such as a private annuity, it is possible to transfer wealth through one or more generations free of federal estate tax.

(g) *Freeze* the growth on wealth and shift it to another generation. Private annuities, installment sales, and certain recapitalizations are all techniques that can stop or slow down the buildup of assets and assist in the "intentional defunding" of a client's estate and the shift of assets (and therefore income) from the client to younger generations.

(h) *Gelt* (Yiddish for "money") trip through time. Among the most valuable of the financial planner's tools is the ability to use time value of money concepts (see Chapters 12 and 13, "Rate of Return Computations") by literally "turning the actuarial tables" against the IRS. Techniques such as GRITs (grantor retained income trusts), GRATs (grantor retained annuity trusts), and GRUTs (grantor retained unitrusts) can result in hundreds of thousands and even millions of dollars of estate transfer cost savings as well as significant income tax advantages. (These estate planning devices are covered in detail in our sister book, *The Tools and Techniques of Estate Planning*.)

15. The essence of risk management is protecting the ground that's already been gained without losing more in the process.

Consider the effect on discretionary cash flow of dollars misdirected toward unnecessary insurance premiums or the potential damage to a client's financial security caused by underinsurance. Insure only what is of measurable value or need and cannot be easily or economically replaced without insurance.

There are three key categories of risk management that must be considered by the financial planner:

(a) property (fire, storm, loss, theft, shipwreck),

(b) income (death, accident, sickness), and

(c) liability.

16. It's not enough just to make money; an investor has to create automatic mechanisms to make money with the money he's made.

To reach any financial goal first requires (a) better positioning of what the client already has and then (b) automatic and cost-effective channeling of the return on investments. For example, most mutual funds and many stocks provide automatic (and low or no commission) dividend reinvestment plans.

17. Always use the lowest risk solution that satisfies the need.

The planner must

(a) measure the client's needs,

(b) establish an order of needs, and

(c) give first preference to what the client most wants to accomplish.

If each level of need is satisfied before moving to the next higher level, needs and risk should typically match. For instance, one of the most primary and "first level" needs is for an emergency fund. (The term "first level" refers to the analogy that financial planning builds security from a firm foundation at the ground level and then moves up floor by floor to the roof, or from the base to the apex of a pyramid, with each new level representing a higher risk.) When many of the foundation and first floor level needs have been satisfied, the client can afford to take greater risk and therefore attempt to achieve a greater return.

Stated in different terms, risk, like income taxes, should increase progressively but only after lower bracket financial needs have been satisfied. This can be called the "hierarchy of financial needs and risks" equation.

18. At a certain point, action must replace cogitation and articulation.

The finest plan is worthless until executed. It is extremely important to establish a timetable that lists not only the action to be taken but also the party who is responsible for each phase of the plan. This should be broken down into segments small enough to be accomplished but large enough so that everyone in the financial planning cooperative retains perspective and can see and appreciate the role played by others.

The creation of a full blown financial planning timetable is an extremely valuable exercise because it will force you to consider not only what must be done, but also the capacity of those involved to accomplish the plan according to a schedule which will be distributed to all concerned parties. This changes concepts into commitments.

19. No tool or technique is without cost.

Perhaps the most insidious trap a planner can fall into is giving too much attention to one problem area without giving enough attention to the others that may be affected by a suggested move. Do not create more problems for the future than you solve in the present by ignoring or failing to consider other problems you may be creating. Saving estate taxes on a small amount of estate taxable at a 37% bracket sounds good, but not if the saving is at the expense of a much higher income tax on a large taxable base not far down the road.

Before you suggest any transaction, use this checklist to consider each of the following and their implications for all parties concerned:

(a) the federal income tax,

(b) the federal gift tax,

(c) the federal estate tax,

(d) the federal generation-skipping transfer tax,

(e) state taxes of all 4 of the above varieties,

(f) the alternative minimum tax (AMT),

(g) cash flow at both the business and personal level,

(h) property law, domestic law, and other state laws,

(i) psychological and emotional implications including issues of control, flexibility, and certainty,

(j) legal, ethical, and moral implications,

(k) implementation problems, aggravation, and cost, and

(l) the relation of all these to each other and to the client's personal goals.

20. Patience and discipline are the parents of financial success.

Clients who lack either the patience or the discipline to follow through on a long range plan will end up, if with anything other than broken dreams, with a number of uncoordinated products or hastily conceived packages.

Financial success depends upon

(a) the ability and willingness to suppress greed,

(b) efficiency (low tax, low load),

(c) willingness to take risk,

(d) discipline (and patience),

(e) education, and

(f) wisdom—knowing when to start and when enough is enough.

Discipline is the principle behind "dollar cost averaging," a long-recognized and respected strategy for successful investing.

Combining dollar cost averaging with diversification can be accomplished through regular monthly mutual fund purchases. The investor buys the same dollar amount of the fund (the same concept will work with any type of investment) each month, regardless of the current share price of the fund. That means the investor buys more shares when the market price is low and fewer shares when the market price is high. Mathematically, dollar cost averaging will result in an average cost lower than the average price over the acquisition period.

Risk is reduced by diversification over time. Of course, so is the potential for gain.

Three points should be made about this "patience and discipline" technique. First, it works only if the investor does in fact stay with the system for an extended period of time. This is particularly important as the market price per share is dropping. Second, the benefit of dollar cost averaging will be leveraged if the client increases the dollar amount of his or her investment during the time of declining prices and decreases the dollar amount invested as prices go up. Third, this system does not maximize profit potential. In fact, it guarantees that potential return is not maximized. If an investor is sure that the market has bottomed out and will be rising, a much greater profit may be obtained by investing all available funds at that point.

21. Whether it is better to "own" or "loan" depends on one's own situation.

An investor "loans" when he or she provides capital and in exchange receives a fixed or guaranteed rate of return. At a specified time or event, the investor recovers the original capital placed into the investment. Loan-type investments include bonds, money markets, savings accounts, and C.D.s.

Own-type investments are made when an investor buys an asset or an interest in property with the hope and expectation that the asset will increase in value over time but with no fixed or guaranteed assurance of the rate or amount. This category of investment includes common stocks, mutual funds, real estate, precious metals, and collectibles.

Loaning or owning are the only two choices an investor has when deciding what category of investment to make. Both have advantages and disadvantages.

Loan-type investment advantages:

(a) The interest is predictable.

(b) The amount of capital to be received is predictable.

(c) The time capital will be recovered is predictable.

(d) The investment is always liquid.

Loan-type investment disadvantages:

(a) In an inflationary economy, the investor's principal will lose purchasing power if the investor does not accumulate and reinvest his earnings since what is recovered is exactly what was in existence at the beginning of the investment in absolute dollars but greatly diminished in terms of purchasing power. For instance, at only a 4% inflation rate, $100,000 loaned out today will have the purchasing power of only $67,566 ten years from now. (Note that the average rate of inflation over the last 20 years was almost 6%!)

(b) Interest payments will typically remain level and not increase.

(c) After taxes, it will be difficult, or even impossible for interest rates to keep up with inflation rates over an extended period of time.

Own-type investment advantages:

(a) There is an opportunity for growth of capital.

(b) There is an opportunity for growth of income.

Own-type investment disadvantages:

(a) It is impossible to predict the value at any given time in the future.

(b) Both income and capital may drop or even be lost.

(c) Often, this type of property is illiquid. An emergency creating the necessity for a forced sale will result in much less received than the original investment. A lack of liquidity may also result in the loss of opportunity to achieve even higher return.

Financial risk tends to increase as an investor adds more own-type investments to his "rate of return matrix" (portfolio), but purchasing power risk tends to decrease (assuming the potential return is in fact realized). On the other hand, financial risk tends to decrease as an investor adds more loan-type investments to his "rate of return matrix," but purchasing power risk tends to increase.

Diversification to reduce both financial and purchasing power risk is the obvious answer; the investor must

Figure 1.6

COMPUTING THE AFTER TAX COST OF AN INVESTMENT AFTER TAX RETURN	
AMOUNT OF INVESTMENT	$10,000
RATE OF RETURN	0.120
INCOME	$1,200
COMBINED FEDERAL AND STATE TAX RATE	0.40
AFTER-TAX RETURN	$720
AFTER TAX COST OF INVESTMENT	
AMOUNT BORROWED	$10,000
INTEREST RATE	0.090
INTEREST EXPENSE	$900
AFTER-TAX COST (IF DEDUCTIBLE)	$540
AFTER-TAX RETURN	$720
AFTER-TAX COST	$540
ADVANTAGE	$180

mix the investments in his portfolio to defend against these two risks, or risk the consequences in return for the potential rewards.

22. Debt, like spending, should be at the discretion of and fully controlled by the investor.

When a client has no choice about debt and must borrow, two rules should always be followed. First, find the lowest true rate of interest available under favorable terms. Second, never borrow more than can be paid back under the schedule agreed upon.

Better yet, position your client's budget so that borrowing, as investing, is discretionary. This means the planner's goal should be to make the decision to borrow a matter of the client's choice. Aside from the emotional and psychological constraints and the very important principle that no investment decision can be made in a vacuum, the decision can be made on an analytical formula basis:

Borrow only when it is probable that the return on the investment will exceed (after taxes are considered) the cost of the borrowed funds.

For instance, assume a client could invest $10,000 at 12%. His after-tax return, as shown by the example in Figure 1.6, would be $720 if his combined tax bracket was 40%. If the investment was financed by a loan which required a 9% payment, the after-tax cost of the loan would be $540, assuming the interest was fully deductible. The $180 spread ($720-$540) would be the true net advantage of the investment.

This is an example of the important financial concept known as "leveraging" (see Chapter 10, "Leveraging"). Whenever part or all of the investment is made with borrowed money, leveraging is at work, for the client if things go well, against the client if things don't go well. In this example, even though the return to the client seems small in terms of absolute dollars, if the investment is considered in terms of the percentage return on the investor's own equity, the return is infinite since none of his money was involved.

Few investments use the 100% leverage found in the example above. In most cases of leveraging, a portion of the investment is borrowed and a portion of the investment is made with the investor's own assets. There is therefore both leverage (debt) and equity (ownership) in most leveraged investments.

Where there will be both debt and equity and the goal is to maximize the return on the investor's capital, use this rule of thumb:

Maximize leverage where the reasonably predictable after-tax return will exceed the reasonably predictable after-tax cost of the debt.

A financial planner should assist a client with the question of the debt to equity mix by doing a debt to equity analysis.

Where the rate of return on an investment is higher than the cost to borrow money, an investor increases the after-tax return on his equity by increasing the leveraging, that is, by increasing the ratio of debt to equity in the investment. In other words, it is better to borrow than to own.

Where the rate of return is lower than the cost to borrow, an investor increases after-tax return by increasing the ratio of equity to debt. In other words, it is better to own than to borrow.

Keep in mind that these maxims must be themselves tempered by the concept of "opportunity costs." Opportunity costs are the costs of missing an alternative (and better) use of the investor's money (whether the money is owned or borrowed) and the after-tax income the investor's money could have earned in the alternative investment. An investor must always ask whether he is making the best use of his money (whether that money is owned or borrowed).

Opportunity costs are not a relevant consideration if any after-tax alternative return (after considering any borrowing costs) is the same as the after-tax return (after considering any borrowing costs) on the chosen investment.

But if the after-tax return (after considering any costs of borrowing) on any alternative investment is greater than the after-tax return (after considering any costs of borrowing) on the chosen investment (if you could have made more on any equity and received a greater differential on any borrowed money in another investment), then your overall return on equity effectively decreases as you increase equity in the chosen investment.

Financial leverage can be further enhanced by "tax leverage" (see item 23, below), the favorable condition that occurs when a deduction is allowed against taxable income or a tax credit is allowed against a tax because a client has purchased a "Code blessed" investment. The tax benefit either lowers investment cost or increases investment return.

"Double leverage," where both financial leverage and tax leverage are present in the same investment, accelerates the result. If the result is positive and the investor makes a profit, that profit will be dramatically higher than

it would have been without leverage. Conversely, the double leverage significantly increases the investor's risk.

Borrowing to finance all or a part of the purchase price of an asset will meet or beat inflation if (a) the asset's value appreciates in price at or above the inflation rate, and (b) the after-tax cost of the interest payable is equal to or less than the difference between appreciation and inflation.

Keep in mind the limitation on the deduction of investment interest. (See Chapter 8, "Income Tax Concepts.")

23. Tax leverage is a concept similar to financial leverage and can provide similar advantages. Tax leverage occurs when an investment provides tax benefits that allow an investor to defer taxes that would otherwise have been paid currently if the investment had not been made or had been made in some other form. Tax leverage allows an investor to use money that would otherwise be paid to Uncle Sam in taxes to earn additional returns on investment. What's even better, the "loan" from the government is interest free. There is, of course, a risk in using tax leverage: there is the chance that tax law changes will eliminate the tax benefits of the investment—and an investment that is a winner with tax advantages might not be a winner without those advantages.

Tax leverage is created in essentially two ways. What have been called tax shelters or tax-advantaged investments typically use special provisions in the Internal Revenue Code that provide up-front deductions or credits to encourage certain types of investments. As a result, although an investor must put up, say, $10,000, the actual cost to him is $10,000 less the taxes saved because of the deductions or credits. There is no free lunch, though, and taxes that are saved up front typically must be paid at some later date. But in the meantime the investor has enjoyed the use of the tax money at zero interest.

Tax leverage is also created when taxes on investment earnings are deferred. For example, the earnings in life insurance policies and annuities and series EE savings bonds typically accumulate on a tax-deferred basis. However, the most common example of this type of tax leverage is the tax deferral on capital appreciation. The tax on gains on stocks, real estate, and other capital assets is generally deferred until the asset is sold. Each year that investors enjoy tax-deferral on their earnings, they receive additional interest-free "loans" from the government that leverage future earnings just as if they had borrowed money at zero interest.

The Tools and Techniques of Financial Planning

Many investments provide both types of tax leverage. For example, contributions to qualified retirement plans and IRAs are often tax deductible and taxes on the earnings within the plans are deferred until the funds are distributed.

One feature that makes tax leverage different from financial leverage is that the amount of the "loan" that must be repaid (the deferred taxes) depends on the tax rate at the time proceeds from the investment are received in a taxable transaction. If an investor is in a lower tax bracket when the taxes must ultimately be paid, part of the loan is in essence "forgiven." In contrast, if the investor is in a higher tax bracket when the deferred taxes must be paid, the amount of the "loan" is increased. However, in many cases even if an investor is in a higher tax bracket when the deferred taxes must be paid, the benefit of the tax deferral will outweigh the cost of the additional taxes.

24. The after-tax return on the repayment of debt is essentially risk free.

Sooner or later, an investor must repay debt incurred to finance an investment. In essence, this repayment is an important alternative to other investments. Repayment offers almost certain savings of the after-tax interest cost that would have been paid had the debt not been paid off. These savings can be thought of as "earnings" on the money used to pay the debt. With the lower tax brackets, the cost of interest (and the savings that can be realized by paying off debt) has increased. In many cases the after-tax return from the elimination of debt will be as good if not better than many investment alternatives.

25. When planning for retirement, the wise planner and client will assume a lower than hoped for rate of return on investments, a higher than anticipated level of inflation and cost of living, and put less reliance on what social security or a pension will provide.

In some cases it is best to show a "worst case," "best case," and "probable case" scenario rather than just one set of figures. Clients often put undue reliance on figures that are mathematically accurate but are built on dubious long range assumptions. In the authors' opinion, few clients can realize, net after taxes, a long term steady and loss free growth in excess of 6 or 7 percent. Likewise, the authors suggest inflation planning be based on at least a 3 to 5 percent assumption.

26. When doing estate planning, the wise planner will assume the highest reasonable liquidity demands and the lowest reasonable cash to meet those needs.

Few executors or widows have complained of having too much cash.

The above comments regarding the wisdom of presenting a range of possibilities to clients, and the false reliance that clients tend to place on overly optimistic numbers in a report (especially those done by computer) apply here, too.

27. The best investment, bar none, is education.

Clients should not rely solely on any planner. Good planners will encourage clients to read the business and financial reports in the newspapers and keep up with the impact of politics and world economic and social events on their financial security. The difference between financial dignity and financial despair may be an awareness of what's coming.

28. Before making any suggestion to a client regarding any investment or any Tool or Technique, the planner should ask and answer these questions:

(a) What are the advantages—and disadvantages—of the viable alternatives?

(b) Which of the viable alternatives provides the highest return at the least cost with the greatest certainty?

(c) What happens if the client takes no action?

WHAT A FINANCIAL PLANNING REPORT SHOULD COVER

The "product" of the financial planning professional's analysis should be a carefully prepared document that summarizes for the client, the client's family, and the client's advisers:

(1) Analysis—WHERE YOU ARE NOW

(2) Objectives—WHERE YOU WANT TO BE

(3) Strategy—HOW TO GET TO WHERE YOU WANT TO BE

The actual presentation can (and in many cases should) be brief. Or it can be long. The length of the report must be determined by the task set by the client—does the client want you to do a full analysis or just solve one or two problems?, by time and cost considerations, and by your style as a professional and your feelings as to how much the client needs to know to have confidence in and take action on your suggestions.

A good rule of thumb is, "Overstate and bore, understate and score." Most clients prefer to have their problems and potential solutions stated as succinctly (and as graphically) as possible. We suggest liberal use of graphs and checklists.

Here's a checklist for a table of contents for a full blown analysis:

WHERE YOU ARE NOW

(1) balance sheet

(2) cash flow analysis

    (a) normal situation—current

    (b) normal situation—projected

    (c) death of "breadwinner"

    (d) disability of "breadwinner"

    (e) retirement

(3) asset liquidity analysis

WHERE YOU WANT TO BE

Quantification of goals

(1) increasing investable income

(2) improving liquidity

(3) reducing risk

(4) increasing income at death, disability, or retirement

(5) increasing financial security for heirs and satisfying charitable objectives

HOW TO GET TO WHERE YOU WANT TO BE

(1) tax strategy

(2) investment strategy

(3) risk management strategy

(4) wealth transfer strategy

SUMMARY AND ASSIGNMENT OF RESPONSIBILITIES

(1) summary

(2) who must take action

(3) what must be done

(4) timetable (see above)

(5) date of next review

TEN STEPS TO SUCCESS

While there is no "magic formula" for assuring success, and certainly none that will provide "instant success," here are those steps we feel are essential to your success as a financial planner:

(1) Increase the scope and depth of your technical knowledge of financial planning subjects. The more you know about a wide range of financial planning subjects the better you can serve your clients. But it is not enough that you know the field better; your clients and prospective clients must perceive that you have an ever increasing expertise. Consider what you are doing and what you must continue to do to impress clients with your technical competence.

(2) Develop a "value added" strategy. "No one cares how much you know until they know how much you care." A great deal of your success in financial planning will be due to how much your clients perceive you care about them for reasons that go beyond your fees or commissions. Show clients how to stabilize and maximize the value of the assets they already have and they will be more willing to listen to your advice and more likely to purchase the services or products that you are there to offer them. Relate in a very personal way to their needs, desires, and individual circumstances. Consider where a client would rate your skills, knowledge, and delivery if asked to place these on a continuum that has at one extreme "high touch" high care competence and at the other end hit-and-run "high tech boilerplate."

(3) Increase your "product" range. Whether or not you sell what you consider products—and whether or not you even think you sell anything—you do. The attorney or accountant or "fee for services" financial planner "sells" the client on his competence and capability

and willingness to uncover and solve problems in the most efficient manner consistent with the client's objectives. The "product" that "nonsales" planners sell is every bit as real as a stock, bond, annuity, or life insurance contract. The improvement of net worth, increase of net income or reduction of risk are all examples of the "products" of the financial planner who does not accept commissions. You increase your potential for success and enhance your ability to fully implement plans, directly or indirectly, by being able to provide—or help obtain for your client—a broad spectrum of services, tools and techniques. (One way to enhance your skills portfolio is to associate with one or more other planners whose skills are complementary to yours.)

(4) Increase your client contact. Quality must be leveraged by quantity. The more often you see your clients (or interact with them by phone, mail, or seminar), the more likely you will continue to service or sell them. Find new and creative ways of keeping in touch more often. For example, send your clients financial planning literature on a regular basis.

(5) Provide continuity of service. Does the client know he will always be able to reach you? Will someone different answer his or her call and serve that account after the initial interview? People like to know that they won't get a "runaround" when the time comes for service after the sale.

(6) Enhance your consumer reputation. Consider what you can do to add prestige to your name. What are you planning to do to enhance the overall value judgment by your clients as to the professional level of your services? In a nutshell, how can you get them to really appreciate (and tell their friends) how good you are? Putting on no-sell or soft-sell public interest seminars, writing newspaper columns and sending copies to clients and other financial services professionals, appearing on radio or TV talk shows about taxes, investing, cash control (we once called this budgeting), or living wills, and of course doing a darn good job for currently existing clients are all ways of enhancing your reputation.

(7) Keep "creative records." This does not mean cooking or juggling the books. It does mean that you must improve your ability to provide clients with current financial status reports on a regular basis. But it's not enough to send raw data out often. Ask yourself—from the client's perspective—if you would feel the report you get (a) is up to date, (b) is accurate, (c) is easy to comprehend, and (d) lends itself to making decisions regarding taking further action in the future

(Should I buy, sell, or hold? How much have I gained? Lost?). Are the record systems and data bases you have created for your clients also designed to help you cross market new products and services to these same people or help you with your public relations?

(8) Automate and develop your operation to the proper scale. Do you have the computer capacity to service your targeted market efficiently enough to provide clients with excellent service yet provide yourself with a suitable profit? Is your staff large enough to handle the multifaceted problems of financial planning yet small (spell that F-L-E-X-I-B-L-E) enough to adapt to new market conditions quickly? How long did it take you to gear up after the last tax law change? What capacities do you need and what should you do to take the maximum advantage of the next tax law change? Is your office library extensive—and up-to-date?

(9) Plan to make mistakes—in a safe environment. Find out what you don't know, what misconceptions you have or what interpersonal relationship errors you are making in an environment that doesn't "waste" clients or prospective clients. Take CLU/ChFC/CFP review classes just to see if the things that go without saying are still going. Role play with colleagues in interactive mock cases that test how you would respond to given problems. Examine not only what you say but how you would say it. Change places to see how you would feel if you were on the receiving end of the questions that you asked or the answers that you gave.

(10) Focus more on the bottom line. Emphasize more often that the only financial security your clients have is what is left—on the bottom line. Remind them that they can spend and their families can live on only what is left after taxes, inflation, and transfer costs. Spend more time improving your business and your bottom line by increasing the efficiency and productivity of your operation.

The bottom line (in financial planning that's all that counts) is that people want three things from financial planners: (1) adequate solutions to their problems, (2) someone they can trust, and (3) a "value added" to the products and services they purchase.

PROFESSIONAL FINANCIAL PLANNING EDUCATION

The professional adviser who does not continue his or her education is both a fool and a thief. So here's a list of some of the sources for gaining knowledge.

The major organizations that are involved in the education of financial services professionals are THE AMERICAN COLLEGE, THE AMERICAN SOCIETY OF CLU & ChFC, THE COLLEGE FOR FINANCIAL PLANNING, THE IBCFP (INTERNATIONAL BOARD OF STANDARDS AND PRACTICES FOR CERTIFIED FINANCIAL PLANNERS, INC.), THE ICFP (INSTITUTE OF CERTIFIED FINANCIAL PLANNERS), and THE IAFP (INTERNATIONAL ASSOCIATION FOR FINANCIAL PLANNING). These are separate organizations in separate locations with separate governing bodies. We suggest that you write to both the American College and the College for Financial Planning for information about their courses.

The American College

The American College was founded in 1927 and is fully accredited by the Middle States Association of Colleges and Schools. The American College is located in Bryn Mawr, Pennsylvania (phone 610-526-1000). American College courses are developed by a resident faculty in Bryn Mawr and studied independently or in local classes. Testing is administered at local examination centers.

The American College offers the ten course CLU (Chartered Life Underwriter) designation for persons principally interested in the life insurance services (more than 85,000 have graduated from this course) and the ten course ChFC (Chartered Financial Consultant) for those principally interested in providing financial planning services (more than 30,000 have graduated from this course).

The American College offers graduate level courses for continuing education requirements or as a preliminary to enrollment in the Graduate School of Financial Sciences. The Graduate School of Financial Sciences at the American College offers the course leading to the Master of Science in Financial Services (over 2,000 MSFS degrees have been awarded).

The American Society of CLU and ChFC

The American Society, headquartered in Bryn Mawr, Pennsylvania (phone 610-526-2500), was established over sixty years ago. It now has 226 chapters, and about 35,000 members. Its function is to provide continuing education and other professional services to members and to publicize the profession to the public.

The College For Financial Planning

The College for Financial Planning is an academic institution based in Denver, Colorado (phone 303-220-1200). Among its programs, the College for Financial Planning offers the Certified Financial Planner program, a two year, six part program that provides the educational requirements for obtaining the CFP (Certified Financial Planner) license from the International Board of Standards and Practices for Certified Financial Planners, Inc. (IBCFP), see below. Almost 50,000 students have graduated from the Certified Financial Planner program, and almost 17,000 students are currently pursuing the program. Organized classes and examinations are available throughout the country.

The College for Financial Planning also offers graduate level courses in its Master of Science degree program. The master's degree is awarded to those who successfully complete 12 courses, with a concentration in one of four specialty areas: wealth management, tax planning, retirement planning, and estate planning. Over 400 students have graduated from the Master of Science program, and almost 1,000 students are now working toward the master's degree.

The College for Financial Planning also offers a basic Foundations in Financial Planning course for those interested in gaining an understanding of the fundamentals of financial planning and for those interested in pursuing the College's paraprofessional program leading to the Financial Paraplanner certificate. Over 5,000 students have completed the Foundations course, with about 2,500 of those going on to earn the paraplanner certificate.

The College for Financial Planning also offers a number of professional development programs open to people working in the financial planning field.

IBCFP

The International Board of Standards and Practices for Certified Financial Planners, Inc. (IBCFP) (phone 303-830-7500), administers the comprehensive exam that leads to the Certified Financial Planner (CFP) license.

The IBCFP requirements for certification as a CFP include subscribing to a Code of Ethics and Professional Responsibility. The IBCFP is empowered to discipline CFPs who violate that Code. This gives the Board an ability to regulate the practices of CFPs.

ICFP

The Institute of Certified Financial Planners based in Denver, Colorado (phone 303-759-4900), is a professional membership organization closely associated with the College for Financial Planning and has two types of members: (1) those who have earned the CFP designation and (2) those who are studying for it. There are over 31,000 in the first category and almost 3,000 in the second. There are 75 societies (chapters) throughout the country with over 12,000 members.

The ICFP produces continuing education opportunities for its members including a practice oriented Residency program.

IAFP

The International Association for Financial Planning is based in Atlanta, Georgia (phone 800-945-IAFP). The IAFP was established in 1969 to recognize the common interests of financial planners and to explain their profession to financial services professionals. The IAFP now has 113 chapters and over 17,000 members.

SUMMARY

Time is up. Or, we should say, the time to learn more about The TOOLS AND TECHNIQUES OF FINANCIAL PLANNING is just beginning. Enjoy.

Chapter 2

THE FINANCIAL PLANNING PROCESS

"People don't plan to fail; they fail because they don't plan."

It is important to understand the concept of financial planning as a process, not a product or a service. It is a series of interrelated activities that you engage in on a continuing basis. It is not something that you complete, even successfully, and then put away or forget. Financial planning must be done regularly in order to take into account changes in your personal circumstances, the availability of new products, and varying conditions in the financial markets.

Many new devices have drastically altered the way people and businesses handle money, as well as the rates of return earned on liquid funds. Good examples of these are brokerage multi-service accounts, money market bank accounts, and universal life insurance.

Choosing a professional to guide you through the financial planning process can be as crucial as the plan itself. Finding someone with the appropriate professional credentials is important. However, a planner with whom you feel comfortable as well as one who has been recommended by satisfied clients is just as important. Personal financial planners, including certified financial planners (CFP), chartered financial consultants (ChFC), chartered life underwriters (CLU), and stockbrokers, are each trained in different areas of financial planning and consulting, so it is in your best interest to research the background of the planner you choose to make sure the planner's training is best suited to your needs. The best financial plan will take all relevant information into consideration and offer advice and implementation techniques that are reasonable to meet your goals and objectives.

As new products appear and market conditions change, even the best prepared financial plan will tend to become obsolete and out of date. Changes in your personal situation may also require adjustments in the overall plan. Births, deaths, marriage, divorce, or a new business can have a great impact on your personal planning.

The following activities in the process of financial planning should be carried out regularly and, where necessary, may involve qualified professional advisers:

Gathering background information

Establishing financial objectives

Developing financial plans

Executing and controlling plans

Measuring performance

The flowchart shown in Figure 2.1 provides a summary of the individual activities involved in the process and shows the relationships between them.

GATHERING BACKGROUND INFORMATION

Effective planning requires comprehensive information on all aspects of your financial program. Such information includes a record of income and expenditures as well as your individual or family financial position.

Prior to setting your objectives, you will need information regarding the sex, health, age, lifestyle, tastes, and preferences of individual family members. Much of this information is subjective, and attitudes may shift considerably over the years. Such changes make it important that you update your plan regularly. Keeping your records on a personal computer will enable you to revise your data and add new information whenever necessary.

Another important area of background analysis has to do with your attitudes toward the degree of risk you are willing to accept in your financial plan. Feelings about investment risk, personal financial security, and independence are just as important as your income statement or net worth. An awareness of these feelings enables you to establish realistic, acceptable objectives. By ignoring these feelings you may develop a "good plan" that is simply out of touch with your personality. Such plans are not likely to be implemented, and a great deal of time and effort will have been wasted.

Unfortunately, attitudes toward risk are very difficult to measure for a number of reasons. First, defining the nature of risk is highly subjective and will vary considerably from one person to another. Second, attitudes about risk are likely to change dramatically over an individual or family's life cycle. What seemed perfectly reasonable to the 25-year-old bachelor

Figure 2.1

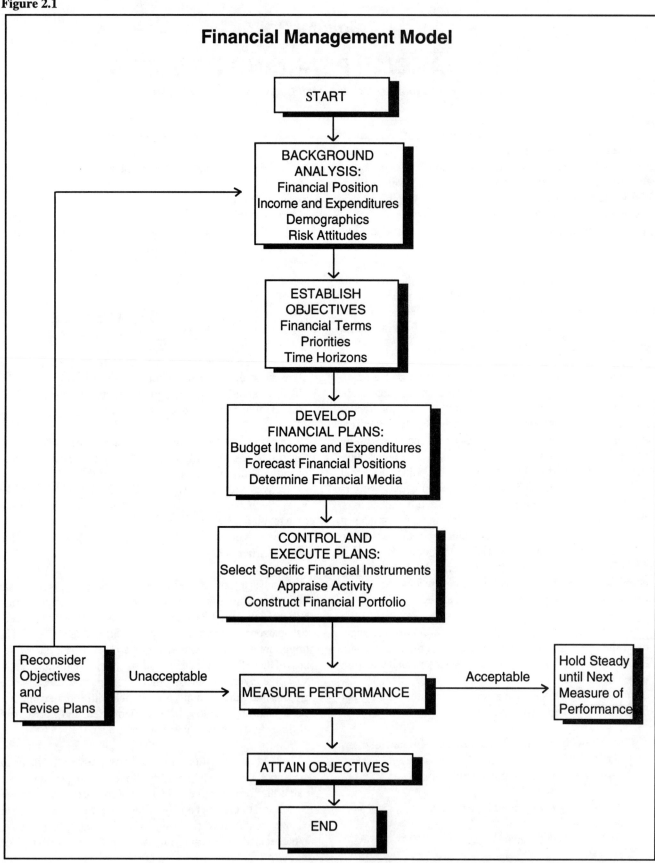

Financial Management Model

START

BACKGROUND
ANALYSIS:
Financial Position
Income and Expenditures
Demographics
Risk Attitudes

ESTABLISH
OBJECTIVES
Financial Terms
Priorities
Time Horizons

DEVELOP
FINANCIAL PLANS:
Budget Income and Expenditures
Forecast Financial Positions
Determine Financial Media

CONTROL AND
EXECUTE PLANS:
Select Specific Financial Instruments
Appraise Activity
Construct Financial Portfolio

Reconsider
Objectives
and
Revise Plans

Unacceptable → MEASURE PERFORMANCE

Acceptable →

Hold Steady
until Next
Measure of
Performance

ATTAIN OBJECTIVES

END

may be totally unacceptable to the 40-year-old father of four children. Finally, risk attitudes are a function of many personal psychological factors that may be difficult to deal with. Yet you should try, through discussions with family members and other advisers, to determine your feelings about risk and be alert to significant changes that may occur over time.

ESTABLISHING FINANCIAL OBJECTIVES

Stating your financial objectives in a concrete way is a difficult but essential part of the planning process. One reason many plans fail is that financial goals are not described in operational terms. Objectives often are presented in vague language that is difficult to translate into action.

Each of your objective statements should have the following characteristics. First, it should be well-defined and clearly understood by everyone involved. Unless you really know and understand what you are trying to accomplish, you probably will not succeed.

Writing down your objectives is one way of working toward a set of clear and useful statements. Comments such as "I want a safe and secure retirement income" do not provide much guidance for financial planning. They merely express a wish that may be very real to you but is hard to put into effective terms and plans.

Second, good financial objectives are generally stated in quantitative terms. Only by attaching numbers to your plans can you know when the objective has been accomplished. This is a particularly important factor in regard to long-term objectives, such as those concerning education funds or retirement. It is desirable to measure progress toward your goals at various points along the way.

For example, the goal of having a particular sum for retirement in 20 years can be reviewed each year to see if the necessary progress has been made. If earnings have been lower than anticipated, you may have to make larger contributions in future years. If a higher rate of return has actually been realized, your contributions can be reduced. Such fine tuning is impossible unless numbers are associated with plan objectives. Adding numbers to objectives will also help to make them easier to understand by all members of the family.

Finally, each of your goals or objectives should have a time dimension attached to it. When will a particular goal be accomplished? How much progress have you made since the last review? How much time remains until the goal is to be accomplished? These questions and similar ones can be an-

swered only if you have established a schedule with objectives listed at particular points in time.

Some parts of your plan, such as retirement objectives, will have very long time lines. Others, such as a change in savings, may be accomplished in a few months or a year. Whether long term or short term, the timing aspect of objectives is very important. Even long-term goals can be broken down into shorter time periods, which can be included in an annual review of your plan.

After your objectives have been written out, they should be put in order of priority. This ranking process is necessary since many objectives normally will compete for limited resources. It's not likely that you will be able to satisfy all of your wishes at the same time. Some goals will be more important, more urgent, than others. Critical short-term needs may have to be satisfied ahead of long-range plans.

Once certain goals have been reached, funds may be channeled to other areas. An example would be the funding of children's education. After this goal has been met, you may allocate money previously spent on education costs to building a retirement fund or some other long-range objective. Unless you have assigned specific priorities to these and other goals, it will be difficult for you to organize and carry out an effective plan. Conversely, a set of well-integrated financial objectives can make the actual planning process a relatively easy task.

Individuals and families should have workable objectives in each of the following areas:

STANDARD OF LIVING — Maintaining a particular lifestyle generally takes most of a person's resources. Setting an objective in this area calls for you to analyze required spending (such as food and housing costs) as well as optional spending (travel, vacations, and entertainment). If almost all of your income is being spent in this area, it will be very difficult to accomplish your other objectives.

One widely used rule of thumb states that no more than 80% of gross income should be spent on maintaining a given standard of living. The remaining 20% of income should be allocated to the other financial objectives. Obviously, this guideline will vary from one person or family to another. But unless a significant portion of your income can be directed toward the remaining objectives, you are not likely to reach your goals.

SAVINGS — Everyone recognizes the need for money that can be used to meet an emergency or other special need. However, determining the ideal level of savings can be a complicated problem. It will depend on the nature of your income, personal risk attitudes, stability of employment, and other factors such as the type of health and dental insurance coverage you have.

It is recommended that you maintain savings equal to at least three months' disposable income. These funds should be kept in a safe and highly liquid form where the rate of return is a secondary consideration. Today a money market mutual fund or a bank money market account offers an excellent vehicle for savings. These investments offer a high degree of safety, ready access to your money, and a very good rate of return.

PROTECTION — This objective covers life, health, disability, property, and liability insurance coverage. It should be designed to provide protection against insurable risks and related losses. Objectives in this area should take into account any coverage that is provided through public programs such as Social Security as well as group insurance offered as an employee benefit.

Analysis of this area should be done in cooperation with experienced professional advisers. Consult a Chartered Life Underwriter (CLU) in determining the amount of life insurance you need and what type of insurance best suits your individual situation. Discuss your property and liability insurance requirements with an agent who holds the Chartered Property and Casualty Underwriter (CPCU) designation.

ACCUMULATION (INVESTMENT) — This is the most complex objective in a number of ways. It relates to the future buildup of capital for significant financial needs. These needs can be as diverse as a child's college education, a wedding, or a vacation home. The sheer number and variety of such goals makes it difficult to define this objective and to set priorities.

Adding to the difficult nature of this planning area is the generally long time involved, which may extend for twenty years or more. Finally, the wide variety of possible investments that you can use adds to the overall complexity. Regardless of the reason for building capital, the critical ingredients in this objective are the ability to quantify needed amounts and to state target dates for accumulation. An annual review in this area is essential.

FINANCIAL INDEPENDENCE (RETIREMENT) — This objective may be thought of as a particularly important example of the accumulation objective. It concerns the building of assets over a long time. Financial independence may be desired at a particular age and may or may not actually correspond with retirement from work. Instead, you may wish to have security and financial independence while continuing to work at an enjoyable occupation or profession.

More than most others, this area will be affected by changes in government programs such as Social Security and benefits paid by employers. Also, since the planning period is such a long one, this objective should be broken down into subgoals that can be evaluated, analyzed, and reworked over the years.

ESTATE PLANNING — Objectives in this area are typically concerned with the preservation and distribution of wealth after the estate owner's death. However, accomplishing such goals may call for you to take a number of actions well before that time. Having a will prepared is the most fundamental act in estate planning, and yet thousands of persons die each year without having done so. These people die intestate, leaving the distribution of their assets to state laws and the courts.

For larger estates, avoidance or minimization of estate taxes is an important consideration. These objectives can be accomplished, but they call for careful planning and implementation prior to the owner's death. The use of various trust instruments, distribution of assets through gifts, and proper titling of property can all result in a smaller taxable estate. However, carrying out such a program will take time and should be considered as various assets are being acquired. This is also an area in which professional guidance is generally necessary. You should consult an attorney to draft a will or prepare a trust document.

DEVELOPING FINANCIAL PLANS

Once realistic, well-defined objectives have been established, you can begin to develop actual plans. This planning stage includes the budgeting of income and expenditures for the near term along with a forecast of future activity. You should also make a projection of your financial position for the next several years. This will give you an idea of future growth and the returns necessary to reach your overall net worth objective.

Your plans should identify the financial instruments that will be included in programs to meet specific objectives. For example, you should identify specific savings media if you need more emergency funds. You may consider regular savings accounts, money market certificates, or shares in a money market fund. If an investment program is called for, you should determine the appropriate types of investments such as securities, real estate, or mutual funds.

CONTROLLING AND EXECUTING PLANS

The next stage of the financial planning model calls for you to set the plan in motion. This may involve the purchase or sale of various assets, changes in your life insurance protection, additional liability coverage, and other changes. All of these activities should be closely monitored and appraised to see that they are effective in accomplishing your objectives. The outcome of some actions will be apparent quickly, while others may take a long time to produce results.

MEASURING PERFORMANCE

Measuring performance is an important step; it helps you determine the progress you are making toward the attainment of your objectives. If performance to date is acceptable, you may not need to take any particular corrective action until the next scheduled review. However, if you determine that progress to date is not satisfactory, action will be necessary. This may include a review of your plans to see if they are still valid and an analysis of the financial environment to take note of unexpected changes.

If your original objectives are no longer realistic and desirable, you will want to review and alter them. In that case your entire plan may have to be recycled through each of the stages described above. This model of financial planning is a dynamic one that is continually repeated as personal, financial, and environmental factors change.

Chapter 3

BUDGETING

WHAT IS IT?

Budgeting can be defined as the ability to estimate the amount of money to be received and spent for various purposes within a given time frame. For purposes of this text, however, budgeting should be thought of as a deliberate plan for spending and investing the resources available to the investor. It ultimately serves as a yardstick against which to measure actual investment results.

HOW DOES IT WORK?

In simplest terms, the budgeting process works as a result of the establishment of a working budget model by an investor, followed by the comparative analysis of actual investment results with the expected results used to create the planning budget. It is the comparison of budget results with expectations that yields the benefits of the process to the user.

WHEN IS THE USE OF THIS TECHNIQUE INDICATED?

1. When there is a need to measure periodic progress towards the achievement of specific goals (a) within a defined time frame and (b) within the confines of limited resources.

2. When the elements of economic activity are of sufficient complexity to warrant continuous monitoring of the details.

3. When there is a need to provide guidelines for evaluating the economic performance of various elements or individuals.

4. When there is a need to communicate a planning strategy to those affected by the budget.

5. When there is a need to provide incentives (goals) for the performance of individuals involved.

6. Budgeting may be indicated for the following specific purposes:

    (a) Controlling household expenses

    (b) Accomplishing desired wealth accumulation/savings goals, such as

        (1) saving for retirement

        (2) funding the children's education

        (3) saving for vacation

    (c) Monitoring the performance of a specific investment, such as

        (1) a securities portfolio

        (2) rental property

        (3) a closely-held business

ADVANTAGES

1. Budgeting helps coordinate activity of the investor and financial counseling team in developing objectives.

2. Budgeting reveals inefficient, ineffective, or unusual utilization of resources.

3. Budgeting makes family members aware of the need to conserve resources and helps to allocate roles in achieving overall financial objectives to various individuals.

4. Budgeting provides a means of financial self-evaluation and a guideline to measure actual performance.

5. Budgeting allows the recognition and forces the anticipation of problems before they occur, and thus permits corrective action or preparation to be taken.

6. Budgeting highlights the possibility of, and the need for, alternative courses of action.

7. Budgeting provides a motivation for performance.

DISADVANTAGES

1. To the extent the data utilized are inaccurate, the conclusions drawn from the budget may be misleading.

2. Many individuals have a psychological aversion to the record keeping required and may not maintain sufficient information for the budget to be of use.

3. A rote dependence on budgeted numbers inhibits creativity, tends to stifle "risk taking," and encourages mechanical thinking. Such an investor may forfeit opportunities or fail to minimize losses.

HOW IS IT IMPLEMENTED?

The principal purpose of an investor's budget is to control and evaluate performance. Therefore, the basic sources of information in developing a budget are personal financial statements, prior years' tax returns, canceled checks, and projections of income and expenditures for the target period. Once initial estimates have been made, they must be adjusted in light of special circumstances or considerations.

Here are some guidelines to use when establishing a budget:

(a) Make the budget flexible enough so that it will work even if there are emergencies, unexpected opportunities, or other unforeseen circumstances.

(b) Keep the budget period short enough so that the estimates you make will involve the minimum amount of guesswork.

(c) Establish a budget period long enough to utilize an investment strategy and a workable series of investment procedures. A typical family budget will cover twelve months and coincide with a calendar year.

(d) Make the budget simple, short, and understandable.

(e) Follow the form and content of the budget consistently.

(f) Eliminate any extraneous information.

(g) Do not attempt to obtain absolute accuracy, especially with insignificant items.

(h) Tailor the budget to specific goals and objectives.

(i) Remember that a budget is also a guideline against which actual results are to be measured. Unexpected results, highlighted by comparison with the budget, should be analyzed. It may be that the unexpected variance is in fact the norm, and should therefore be incorporated in a revised budget.

(j) Determine, in advance, all the variables that may influence the amounts of specific items of income and expenditures. Income items include expected annual raises and increases or decreases in interest or dividend rates. Expenditures include increased costs, changing tastes or preferences, or changes in family circumstances.

Here is how to construct an income-expenditure budget:

STEP 1. Estimate the family's annual income. Identify fixed amounts of income expected from

(a) salary

(b) bonus

(c) self-employment (business)

(d) real estate

(e) dividends—close corporations

(f) dividends—publicly traded corporations

(g) interest—savings accounts

(h) interest—taxable bonds

(i) interest—tax free bonds

(j) trust income

(k) other fixed payment income

(l) variable sources of income

If a family experiences an irregular income flow, or because of extreme variations of income finds it difficult to predict, two income estimates should be developed. One estimate should be based on the lowest amount of income that might be received, while the other should show a higher, but still reasonable figure.

STEP 2. Develop expenditure estimates broken down between fixed and discretionary expenses. Canceled checks and charge account receipts serve as a good basis for developing the following expenditure estimates:

FIXED

(a) housing (mortgage or rental payments)

(b) utilities

(c) food, groceries, etc.

(d) clothing & cleaning

(e) income taxes

(f) social security

(g) property taxes

(h) transportation

(i) medical & dental

(j) debt repayment

(k) household supplies & maintenance

(l) life & disability insurance

(m) property & liability insurance

(n) current school expenses

DISCRETIONARY

(a) vacations, travel, etc.

(b) recreation & entertainment

(c) gifts & contributions

(d) household furnishings

(e) education fund

(f) savings

(g) investments

(h) other

STEP 3. Determine the excess or shortfall of income within the budget period.

STEP 4. Consider available methods of increasing income or decreasing expenses.

STEP 5. Calculate both income and expenses as a percentage of the total and determine if there is a better or preferable allocation of resources.

Figure 3.3 (at the end of this chapter) is an illustration of the Sample family's 1998 personal budget using *Financial Plan-*

ning TOOLKIT computer software. This example reflects a $5,800 excess of budgeted income over expenditures for the year. With this estimate of the year's expected financial results available early in the year, the Sample family can plan their investment or spending of the projected excess.

However, as the illustration in Figure 3.4 (at the end of this chapter) indicates, if Mr. Sample does not receive his expected bonus of $15,000, the family will have a budgeted shortfall of $4,500. This is so even after a projected reduction in income taxes of $4,500 (from $28,000 to $23,500) and in Social Security taxes of $200 (from $7,700 to $7,500) as a result of not receiving the bonus. On this basis, the Sample family must modify their spending and investing plans for the year. This example illustrates the importance of preparing budgets reflecting conservative as well as optimistic results.

Figure 3.5 (at the end of this chapter) is a printout of a blank budget form from *Financial Planning* TOOLKIT that you may find helpful in preparing your personal budget.

WHERE CAN I FIND OUT MORE ABOUT IT?

1. Lawrence Gitman, *Personal Financial Planning* (Dryden Press, 1996).

2. *Financial Planning TOOLKIT* (Leimberg & LeClair, Inc.).

3. David Scott, *The Guide to Personal Budgeting* (Globe Pecquet Press, 1995).

4. *Basic Budgeting* (Credit Union Nat'l Assoc., 1990).

5. *Armed Forces Guide to Personal Financial Planning: Strategies for Managing Your Budget, Savings, Insurance, Taxes, and Investments* (Stackpole Books, 1998).

QUESTIONS AND ANSWERS

Question — How long a period should the typical family budget cover?

Answer — A family budget should project income and expenditure activity for any planning period an investor feels is convenient or appropriate for a specific purpose. Most planners budget for twelve months at a time. This typically coincides with a calendar year, but may also be a fiscal period, such as a school year. Generally, the budget is calculated on a month-by-month basis.

It is often appropriate to budget for longer periods of time, such as the four-year costs of funding a college education. However, for any long-range budgeting, it is important to keep in mind that the accuracy of the budget will decrease as the length of the period covered increases.

Question — Are there special techniques that should be used by clients with highly irregular income flows or expenditures?

Answer — Families that experience difficulty in predicting income or who may have highly variable cash outflows should consider two budgets—one based on the lowest income and highest expenditures expected ("worst case" budget), and the second based on the client's reasonable expectations of income and expenses ("most probable" budget).

In some cases it may also make sense to prepare a budget based on the highest possible income and lowest possible expenditures ("best case" budget). This third alternative budget is often used where a client wants to see whether the cost of a "hoped for" expenditure, such as an expensive new car, is within reach if everything falls into place.

Question — What variables should be considered in establishing a budget?

Answer — It is important to identify all major variables that can influence both income and expenses. The client's income can be affected by salary increases, bonuses, dividend or interest rate changes, proceeds from the sale of stocks or other assets, inheritances, etc. A client's expenditures can vary as a result of increased costs of living, unexpected business expenses, financial catastrophes, such as uninsured theft or fire losses, changes in tastes or preferences, and large-scale expenses, such as college or retirement.

Question — Why is it often helpful to divide a budget between fixed and variable components?

Answer — Many planners divide an income statement into income that is (a) fixed and certain and (b) variable or uncertain. Expenditures should be divided between those that are (a) fixed and (b) discretionary.

A budget based on only fixed and certain income would be considered conservative. Limiting expenditures to this conservative estimate of income will assure the client that fixed and expected costs can be covered. Any "excess" income can then be used for investments or discretionary spending.

Alternatively, excess income can be placed in a "contingency" fund, which every family should have for emergencies or opportunities. Some families, rather than building contingency funds, have emergency lines of credit through various banks or credit cards. This enables them to invest any excess income, or use it to increase their standard of living. There are two drawbacks to using this technique. First, the interest charged on such credit card borrowing is usually quite high. Second, the client must have sufficient income to repay the loan.

Annual expenditures can be classified as fixed or discretionary. But the term "fixed" applies only in the short run and can often be changed without imposing a radical shift in the client's lifestyle. Even the most "fixed" of all expenditures, housing, can be changed if necessary to meet financial requirements or objectives.

Discretionary expenditures, by definition, can be foregone or timed through proper budgeting so that they are incurred when sufficient income is available.

Question — How much should be allocated in a family's budget for "emergencies" and where should that money be kept?

Answer — Budgeting should allocate cash reserves for (a) emergencies, (b) scheduled forthcoming purchases, (c) investment opportunities, and (d) liquidity needs.

These cash reserves should be invested according to the speed at which they must be available if needed. In other words, funds should be placed in investments suitable for the needs to be satisfied.

Very short term reserves to meet day to day needs should be placed in an interest bearing checking account. It is often suggested that no more than $5,000 (or 5 percent of total cash reserves if lower) be kept in such accounts.

It has also been suggested that intermediate reserves to meet month to month needs for at least three months should be held in a money market account. This fund would typically comprise no more than 30 percent of total cash reserves.

Long term cash reserves can be held in single premium deferred annuities or in cash value life insurance. This pool of dollars should be enough to carry the family for at least six months at its present standard of living.

Question — If I can increase my investment contributions each year, what impact will this have on my ability to accumulate a stated amount of future capital?

Answer — The ability to increase future contributions to an investment program means that you could start with smaller amounts for the first several years than would otherwise be required. For example, suppose that you wanted to accumulate a retirement fund of $100,000 over the next twenty years. If you make uniform annual contributions, you will have to pay $2,718 a year for twenty years, assuming a six percent after-tax return on invested funds. However, if you could increase your contributions by five percent each year, the amount of your annual payment would be lower than this figure for the first nine years. The first year payment would be only

$1,806. Payments would be higher during the final eleven years, but your income is likely to be greater as well. See Figure 3.1 for a listing of the entire payment schedule for this accumulation program.

Question — If I want to withdraw an increasing amount from my retirement fund to keep up with inflation, how will this affect the required capital?

Answer — Increasing the amount of your withdrawals from a fund on a regular basis will add to the amount of necessary capital, or shorten the time that the fund will provide income. For example, a fund of $529,701 will allow you to make withdrawals of $50,000 each year for twenty years assuming an after-tax interest rate of seven percent. If you wanted to be able to increase the amount

Figure 3.1

CONTRIBUTIONS REQUIRED TO REACH A GOAL IF CONTRIBUTIONS INCREASE ANNUALLY			
Desired Future Value (Financial Goal) $100,000			
Accumulation Period (Years) 20			
After-Tax Return on Invested Capital 0.060			
Annual Percentage Increase in Contributions 0.050			
Year-End	**Required Contribution**	**Cumulative Contributions**	**Total Accumulation**
1	$1,806	$1,806	$1,806
2	1,896	3,701	3,810
3	1,991	5,692	6,029
4	2,090	7,782	8,481
5	2,195	9,977	11,185
6	2,304	12,281	14,160
7	2,420	14,701	17,429
8	2,541	17,242	21,016
9	2,668	19,909	24,944
10	2,801	22,710	29,242
11	2,941	25,652	33,938
12	3,088	28,740	39,062
13	3,243	31,982	44,648
14	3,405	35,387	50,732
15	3,575	38,962	57,351
16	3,754	42,716	64,545
17	3,941	46,657	72,360
18	4,138	50,795	80,840
19	4,345	55,141	90,035
20	4,563	59,703	100,000

Reprinted with permission from *Financial Planning* TOOLKIT, Leimberg & LeClair, Inc.

of the withdrawals by five percent each year, ($52,500 in year two, $55,125 in year three, etc.) then you would need to have $785,844 as a beginning capital balance (see Figure 3.2).

Figure 3.2

LUMP SUM NEEDED TO PROVIDE INCREASING ANNUAL PAYMENTS	
Amount of Initial Annual Payment Desired	$50,000
Desired % Increase in Annual Payments	0.050
Number of Years Payments Should Last	20
After-Tax Return (%) on Invested Capital	0.070
Principal Needed to Fund Annuity	$785,844
Reprinted with permission from *Financial Planning* TOOLKIT, Leimberg & LeClair, Inc.	

Figure 3.3 — Sample family budget

INCOME AND EXPENSES REPORT		
Annual Income and Expenses For 1998		

Annual Income

	Amount	% of Total Income
Salary/Bonus 1:	$125,000	74.4%
Salary/Bonus 2:	$30,000	17.9%
Self-Employment (Business):	0	0.0%
Dividends — Close Corporation Stock:	0	0.0%
Dividends — Investments:	$3,000	1.8%
Interest on Savings Accounts:	$2,000	1.2%
Interest on Bonds, Taxable:	$5,000	3.0%
Interest on Bonds, Exempt:	$3,000	1.8%
Trust Income:	0	0.0%
Rental Income:	0	0.0%
Other Sources:	0	0.0%
Total Annual Income:	$168,000	

Annual Expenditures - Fixed Expenses

Housing (Mortgage/Rent):	$15,500	9.2%
Utilities & Telephone:	$7,000	4.2%
Food, Groceries, Etc.:	$10,500	6.3%
Clothing and Cleaning:	$7,000	4.2%
Income Taxes:	$28,000	16.7%
Social Security:	$7,700	4.6%
Real Estate Taxes:	$5,000	3.0%
Transportation:	$8,000	4.8%
Medical/Dental Expenses:	$8,000	4.8%
Debt Repayment:	$5,000	3.0%
Housing Supplies/Maint.:	$6,000	3.6%
Life Insurance:	$8,000	4.8%
Prop. & Liability Ins.:	$5,000	3.0%
Current School Exp.:	$4,500	2.7%
Total Fixed Expenses:	$125,200	74.9%

Variable Expenses

Vacations, Travel, Etc.:	$4,000	2.4%
Recreation/Entertainment:	$5,000	3.0%
Contributions, Gifts:	$7,500	4.5%
Household Furnishings:	$5,000	3.0%
Education Fund:	$5,000	3.0%
Savings:	$3,000	1.8%
Investments:	$2,500	1.5%
Other Expenses:	$5,000	3.0%
Total Variable Expenses:	$37,000	22.2%
Total Expenses:	$162,200	97.1%
Net Saving:	$5,800	3.0%

Reprinted with permission from *Financial Planning* TOOLKIT, Leimberg & LeClair, Inc.

Figure 3.4 — Alternate Sample family budget

INCOME AND EXPENSES REPORT		

Annual Income and Expenses For 1998

Annual Income

	Amount	% of Total Income
Salary/Bonus 1:	$110,000	71.9%
Salary/Bonus 2:	$30,000	19.6%
Self-Employment (Business):	$0	0.0%
Dividends — Close Corporation Stock:	$0	0.0%
Dividends — Investments:	$3,000	2.0%
Interest on Savings Accounts:	$2,000	1.3%
Interest on Bonds, Taxable:	$5,000	3.3%
Interest on Bonds, Exempt:	$3,000	2.0%
Trust Income:	$0	0.0%
Rental Income:	$0	0.0%
Other Sources:	$0	0.0%
Total Annual Income:	$153,000	

Annual Expenditures - Fixed Expenses

	Amount	% of Total Income
Housing (Mortgage/Rent):	$15,500	10.1%
Utilities & Telephone:	$7,000	4.6%
Food, Groceries, Etc.:	$10,500	6.9%
Clothing and Cleaning:	$7,000	4.6%
Income Taxes:	$23,500	15.4%
Social Security:	$7,500	4.9%
Real Estate Taxes:	$5,000	3.3%
Transportation:	$8,000	5.2%
Medical/Dental Expenses:	$8,000	5.2%
Debt Repayment:	$5,000	3.3%
Housing Supplies/Maint.:	$6,000	3.9%
Life Insurance:	$8,000	5.2%
Prop. & Liability Ins.:	$5,000	3.3%
Current School Exp.:	$4,500	2.9%
Total Fixed Expenses:	$120,500	78.8%

Variable Expenses

	Amount	% of Total Income
Vacations, Travel, Etc.:	$4,000	2.6%
Recreation/Entertainment:	$5,000	3.3%
Contributions, Gifts:	$7,500	4.9%
Household Furnishings:	$5,000	3.3%
Education Fund:	$5,000	3.3%
Savings:	$3,000	2.0%
Investments:	$2,500	1.6%
Other Expenses:	$5,000	3.3%
Total Variable Expenses:	$37,000	24.3%
Total Expenses:	$157,500	103.1%
Net Saving:	$-4,500	-3.0%

Reprinted with permission from *Financial Planning* TOOLKIT, Leimberg & LeClair, Inc.

Figure 3.5 — Blank budget form

Budget — Annual Income and Expenses for:	1998	
Annual Income	Amount	(%)
Salary/Bonus 1	0	0.0
Salary/Bonus 2	0	0.0
Self-Employment (Business)	0	0.0
Rental Income	0	0.0
Dividends — Close Corporation Stock	0	0.0
Dividends — Investments	0	0.0
Interest — Savings Accounts	0	0.0
Interest — Bonds, Taxable	0	0.0
Interest — Bonds, Exempt	0	0.0
Trust Income	0	0.0
Other Sources	0	0.0
Total Annual Income	$0	0.0
Annual Expenditures		
Fixed Expenses		
Housing (Mortgage/Rent)	0	0.0
Utilities & Telephone	0	0.0
Food, Groceries, Etc.	0	0.0
Clothing and Cleaning	0	0.0
Income Taxes	0	0.0
Social Security	0	0.0
Real Estate Taxes	0	0.0
Transportation	0	0.0
Medical/Dental Expenses	0	0.0
Debt Repayment	0	0.0
Housing Supplies/Maint.	0	0.0
Life Insurance	0	0.0
Prop. & Liability Ins.	0	0.0
Current School Expense	0	0.0
Total Fixed Expenses	$0	0.0
Variable Expenses		
Vacations, Travel, Etc.	0	0.0
Recreation/Entertainment	0	0.0
Contributions, Gifts	0	0.0
Household Furnishings	0	0.0
Education Fund	0	0.0
Savings	0	0.0
Investments	0	0.0
Other Expenses	0	0.0
Total Variable Expenses	$0	0.0
Total Income	$0	0.0
Total Expenses	$0	0.0
Net Saving (Borrowing)	$0	0.0

Reprinted with permission from *Financial Planning* TOOLKIT, Leimberg & LeClair, Inc.

Chapter 4

EDUCATION FUNDING

OVERVIEW

The expense of educating children has become one of the greatest financial burdens facing parents because of both the large and constantly increasing annual costs and because of the increasing number of years of college and graduate or professional school education required. Except for the purchase of a home and the accumulation of a retirement fund, paying for school is one of the highest priorities — and one of the most expensive decisions — that parents will ever make.

Although this discussion will focus on college education expenses, financial planners should also consider that many clients will provide secondary and even primary school education for their children at private institutions with costs approaching and in some cases even exceeding college tuition. Ironically, attendance at a fine private high school may increase the probability of admission to one of the better (spelled expensive) colleges.

How much financing is actually needed will depend upon many factors including the family's educational goals and the time remaining until the goals have to be met. Families often have some combination of the following goals:

(1) to provide private school education at the elementary and secondary level,

(2) to provide funding of all or a portion of the college costs of one or more children at a private institution,

(3) to provide all or a portion of the college costs of one or more children at public institutions,

(4) to provide funding for all or a portion of the other educational programs such as graduate or professional school education for one or more children, and

(5) to provide an education fund for grandchildren or others.

As with other financial goals, parents must determine education funding goals for their children and set priorities. Many parents will not be able to achieve all their goals and must weigh potential tradeoffs among them. For instance, parents who send their children to private elementary and secondary schools are using resources they could be applying to a college education fund. However, if the private elementary and secondary schooling provides a child with a sufficiently advanced education, the child may qualify for the more elite and well-endowed private college institutions that typically have more financial resources for aid and scholarships. Consequently, resources spent on elementary and secondary school education may be an investment that pays off in lower absolute dollar expenditures for college education at what are considered the more prestigious and elite colleges or universities.

The balance of this chapter is divided into two major sections. Part I is a procedure and worksheet section to show you how to compute how much funding is necessary. Part II deals with the tools and techniques available for funding educational expenses.

PART I: COMPUTING THE REQUIRED EDUCATION FUNDING NEED

Estimating college education costs and funding requirements involves essentially 4 steps:

(1) estimating education costs in current dollars;

(2) projecting future education costs in inflated dollars;

(3) determining the required current lump-sum investment; and

(4) determining the required periodic investment.

Each of these steps is discussed in turn below followed by a simplified college cost worksheet.

Estimating Expenses

For more and more of our children, college is becoming a normal stop in the road to a career and adulthood. About half of the nation's high school graduates enrolled in college ten years ago, but by 1996 two-thirds were college bound. As a result of these trends, financing college has become one of the largest costs that many families face.

College costs also continue to increase. If recent annual increases were to continue at the same pace, the cost of one year in a four-year public college for a resident student would balloon from an average of around $10,000 today to $16,000 in a decade and almost $26,000 in 20 years.

Despite these trends, paying for a child's college education is more within reach than many people think. For one thing, The Taxpayer Relief Act of 1997 (TRA '97) includes provisions intended to make college more affordable. Still the costs of higher education can be expected to put a strain on the finances of most families, especially when more than one child is in college. Scholarships and financial aid may be insufficient or unavailable for many students. Also, the use of loans can stretch college financing for parents well beyond graduation day and saddle graduates with a heavy load of debt.

Understanding College Costs

What are parents paying for when their child attends college? There are several components to college costs, but for simplicity we'll divide them into three categories:

• Tuition;

• Room and Board;

• Everything else.

Tuition costs vary widely, as Figure 4.1 shows. For the 1997-1998 academic year, some 73% of students paid tuition and fees of less than $8,000, according to The College Board. Official tuition and fees were $20,000 or more for only about 6% of students.

Private four-year colleges and universities, which teach about one-quarter of the nation's 14 million students, charge the highest tuition. Their average tuition of $13,700 for the 1997-98 school year is more than four times the $3,100 average tuition charged by four-year public colleges and universities.

The wide disparity between tuition levels arises because, unlike their public counterparts, private institutions can't rely on tax revenues for support. (Note that many students may not be charged full tuition, especially the higher amounts listed by private schools, because colleges sometimes "discount" their published tuition as part of a financial aid offer.)

Room and board expenses typically constitute the next-highest costs after tuition and fees. As you would expect, these costs take up a greater portion of total college costs — about twice as much — for resident students than for commuters.

Everything else — books and supplies, transportation, laundry money, football tickets, pizza, activity fees, and so forth — make up the rest of the costs.

Figure 4.1

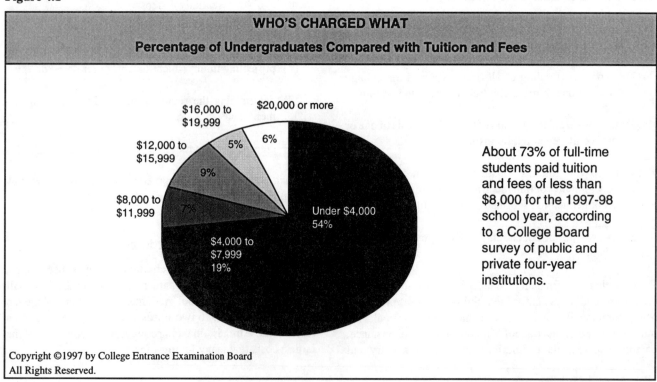

Copyright ©1997 by College Entrance Examination Board
All Rights Reserved.

Figure 4.2

SAMPLE UNDERGRADUATE BUDGETS AT FOUR-YEAR COLLEGES				
1996-97 School Year				
	Public College		**Private College**	
	Commuter	**Resident**	**Commuter**	**Resident**
Tuition and fees	$3,111	$3,111	$13,664	$13,664
Room and board	1,963	4,631	1,913	5,549
Transportation	960	573	854	537
Books and supplies	643	634	628	628
Other expenses	1,465	1,390	1,201	1,043
Total costs (rounded)	$8,130	$10,070	$18,260	$21,420

Private colleges are considerably more expensive than public schools, and resident students pay much more in room and board than commuters. Tack on between $4,300 and $6,400 if your child is an out-of-state resident at a public school.

Copyright ©1997 by College Entrance Examination Board
All Rights Reserved.

When all of the costs of attending college are added up (see Figure 4.2), one year of school in 1997-98 might cost an average of anywhere from about $8,100 to more than $21,000, or even up to $30,000 for the most prestigious and expensive private colleges and universities!

Is a College Education Worth the Cost?

One important question arises: Is the time, money and effort of attending college worthwhile? Yes, when looked at strictly from an earnings point of view (see Figure 4.3). U.S. Census data show that college graduates earn an average of 62% more than high school graduates — an income advantage that has increased significantly over the years.

The President's Council of Economic Advisors also offers a rough estimate of the worth of a college degree. They have estimated that the return on an "investment" in a college education is between 11% and 13% a year for life.

Figure 4.3

HOW EDUCATION PAYS OFF	
Level of education	**Mean Income**
Less than ninth grade	$12,470
High school dropout	15,993
High school graduate	22,080
Some college	27,656
Associate degree	29,108
Bachelor's	39,136
Master's	59,867
Doctorate	72,340
Professional degree	92,256

More years of school lead to higher incomes, according to U.S. Census Bureau data.

Figure 4.4

STATE UNIVERSITIES 1997-98 COSTS			
University	Tuition for state residents	Room & board	Tuition for nonresidents
U. of Alabama	$2,594	$4,550	$6,582
U. of Alaska/Fairbanks	2,960	3,790	6,480
U. of Arizona	2,060	4,930	8,640
U. of Arkansas	2,280	2,740	5,090
U. of California/L.A.	4,007	6,181	12,401
U. of Colorado/Boulder	3,309	4,370	15,022
U. of Connecticut	5,242	5,462	13,760
U. of Delaware	4,430	4,590	11,690
U. of the Dist. of Col.	1,612	N/A	4,444
U. of Florida	1,930	4,610	7,850
U. of Georgia	2,838	4,323	8,790
U. of Hawaii/Hilo	1,322	4,810	6,938
U. of Idaho	1,944	3,600	8,284
U. of Illinois/Urbana-Champaign	4,338	5,078	9,924
Indiana U./Bloomington*	3,783	4,284	11,331
U. of Iowa	2,642	3,780	9,240
U. of Kansas	2,385	3,950	8,690
U. of Kentucky	2,736	4,700	7,536
Louisiana State U./Baton Rouge*	2,687	3,570	3,650
U. of Maine/Orono*	4,730	4,820	11,270
U. of Md./College Pk.	4,460	5,667	10,589
U. of Mass./Amherst	5,329	4,520	12,324
U. of Michigan/Ann Arbor*	5,710	5,140	17,738
U. of Minn./Twin Cities*	4,319	4,056	11,004
U. of Mississippi	2,631	2,510	5,451
U. of Missouri/Columbia	4,016	4,290	10,962
U. of Montana	2,766	4,237	7,193
U. of Nebraska/Lincoln*	2,638	3,525	6,120
U. of Nevada/Las Vegas	2,110	6,100	7,545
U. of New Hampshire*	5,261	4,354	14,231
Rutgers U. of N.J./New Brunswick*	5,105	5,134	8,200
U. of New Mexico	2,165	4,618	8,174
State U. of N.Y./Albany	4,145	5,241	9,045
U. of N.C./Chapel Hill*	2,161	4,500	10,693
U. of N. Dakota	2,969	3,117	6,470
Ohio State U./Columbus*	3,468	4,907	10,335
U. of Oklahoma*	2,186	3,909	5,582
U. of Oregon	3,646	4,646	12,014
Pennsylvania State U.*	5,624	4,460	11,964
U. of Rhode Island	4,574	5,824	11,008
U. of S. Carolina/Columbia	3,480	3,830	8,910
U. of S. Dakota	2,754	2,968	5,153
U. of Tennessee/Knoxville*	2,220	3,620	6,474
U. of Texas/Austin	2,867	3,901	9,287
U. of Utah	2,190	6,633	6,299
U. of Vermont	7,559	5,252	18,107
U. of Virginia*	4,648	4,003	14,434
U. of Washington	3,375	5,418	10,674
West Virginia U.	2,336	4,832	7,356
U. of Wisconsin/Madison	3,180	4,860	10,750
U. of Wyoming	2,326	4,244	7,414

DATA SOURCE: U.S. News & World Report: America's Best Colleges 1998 Exclusive Rankings.

* 1996-97 Costs

Figure 4.5

THE TOP PRIVATE SCHOOLS (1997-98)		
	Tuition	Room and Board
Amherst College (MA)	$23,064	$6,000
Barnard College (NY)*	20,324	8,374
Bennington (VT)*	23,700	4,100
Boston University (MA)	22,278	7,570
Brandeis (MA)	22,851	6,970
Brown University (RI)	23,124	6,776
Carnegie-Mellon U. (PA)	20,375	6,225
Columbia (NY)	22,650	7,332
Dartmouth (NH)	23,011	6,495
Duke University (NC)	22,179	6,830
Georgetown U. (DC)	21,405	8,091
Harvard (MA)	22,802	7,278
John Hopkins U. (MD)	21,700	7,355
M.I.T. (Mass. Institute of Tech.)	23,100	6,550
Northwestern U. (IL)	19,152	6,520
Princeton (NJ)	22,920	6,515
Sarah Lawrence (NY)	22,936	7,219
Skidmore College (NY)	21,975	6,354
Smith College (MA)	21,512	7,250
Stanford (CA)	21,300	7,560
Swarthmore College (PA)	22,000	7,500
Tufts University (MA)	22,811	6,838
University of Chicago (IL)	22,671	7,604
University of Pennsylvania	22,250	7,280
Vanderbilt University (TN)	21,467	7,430
Wellesley College (MA)	21,660	6,670
Wheaton College (MA)	20,820	6,470
Yale (CT)	23,100	6,850

DATA SOURCE: U.S. News & World Report: America's Best Colleges 1998 Exclusive Rankings.

* 1996-97 Costs

Adjusting for Inflation

Until recently, college costs have been climbing steadily at an annual rate from 7% to 12%.

Year	Tuition Inflation Rate**	Overall Inflation Rate*
Last 5 years (1992 — 1996)	7.34%	2.84%
Last 10 years (1987 — 1996)	7.42%	3.68%
Last 15 years (1982 — 1996)	7.35%	3.55%
Last 20 years (1977 — 1996)	7.40%	5.14%

* SBBI 1997 Yearbook Ibbotson Associates
** U.S. Department of Education, Tuition Only

In 1997 and 1998, the annual rate of increase for college education costs has slowed to about 5%. However, college costs have consistently grown faster than both the typical family's income and the overall rate of inflation.

If costs continue to grow at the 7% annual rate that many financial advisers suggest using as the reasonably conservative (high-end) inflation rate for planning purposes, future college costs will quickly grow to incredible numbers. As Figure 4.6 shows, the parents of a child born in 1998 who can expect their child to start college in about the year 2016 should anticipate average total 5-year college education costs to range from about $133,000 (as a commuter to a public four-year college) to almost $350,000 (as a resident at a private four-year college). Moreover, surveys indicate that most

Figure 4.6

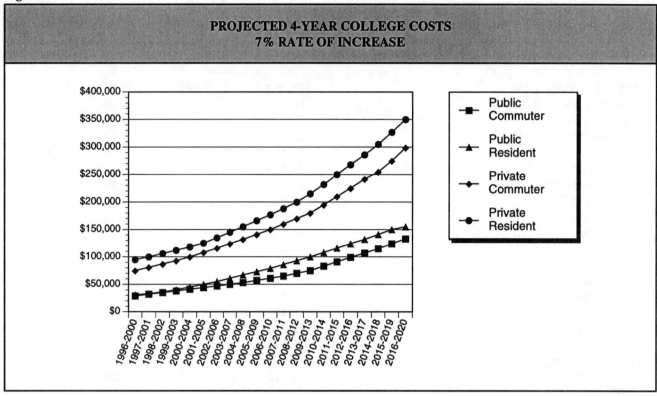

PROJECTED 4-YEAR COLLEGE COSTS
7% RATE OF INCREASE

people are not saving enough for college and that they also tend to underestimate how much college will cost.

Figures 4.4 and 4.5 give specific college data for various state and private colleges and can serve as starting points for estimating college tuition and room and board costs in current dollars. If your clients can identify some particular college or university that they favor and to which they plan to send their children, more up-to-date and accurate information about current and projected costs can be obtained by calling the placement director or financial aid officer of that school. Keep in mind that in addition to tuition and room and board, students will need funds for books, fees, clothes and miscellaneous entertainment expenses and, if they are away from home, travel. Costs for books and lab fees in the sciences, for example, can run as high as $1,000 per semester.

Planners can estimate future college costs by using the formula for computing the future value of a lump-sum value:

FORMULA 1

$$FV = PV \times (1 + I)^N$$

Where FV is the Future Value (future costs) of one year's college education,

PV is the Present Value (current cost) of one year's college education,

I is the assumed inflation rate, and

N is the number of years until the payment must be made.

Most planners, however, will prefer to use financial tables, financial calculators, or computer programs such as *The Financial and Estate Planner's NumberCruncher* to perform this computation. The Compound Interest Table in Appendix A has the necessary factors to compute future education costs using the following formula:

FORMULA 2

$$FV = PV \times FVfactor$$

Where FV and PV are defined as above and

FVfactor is the factor from the Compound Interest Table of Appendix A for the selected values of I (the assumed inflation rate) and N (the number of years until the child begins college).

For example, assume that

(1) the current annual costs (PV) for your client's choice of college is $21,420 per year (the current average private school resident level),

(2) your client's child is now 4 years old (which means N = 14 years assuming the child will be age 18 when beginning college), and

(3) the assumed inflation rate (I) is 7 percent.

The future value factor from the Table in Appendix A for I = 7 percent and N = 14 years is 2.5785. Applying Formula 2, the estimated first-year cost after adjustment for inflation is $55,231:

$$FV = \$21,420 \times 2.5785 = \$55,231.$$

For each successive year of college the cost could be estimated in a similar manner using the FV factors from the table for N = 15, 16, 17, etc., until the end of the projected college term. In most cases, a suitable estimate of the total cost can be determined by multiplying the first-year cost by the number of years of college, generally 4. In this case the total estimated cost is $220,924 ($55,231 x 4) for 4 years of college.

Determining the Required Current Lump-sum Investment

According to a government survey, 70 percent of families with annual incomes of $30,000 or more are managing to set aside money for future college bills. But the median amount being set aside is an obviously inadequate $904 a year. As described above, assuming annual costs rise 7 percent per year from a current average private school resident level of $21,420, parents with a four year-old child in 1998 will confront college bills that can total over $220,000. To be ready to handle bills of that magnitude, the parents would have to set aside in 1998 a lump-sum investment of about $97,715 in an account earning 6 percent net after tax, or about $825 a month net after tax every year until the child is age 18. Even if the parents could earn 10 percent net after tax on their money, they would still need a lump-sum investment of about $58,200 in 1998, or would have to save almost $600 a month until their child is age 18. (Examples of how to compute these amounts follow.) Few investments can provide such returns over such a long period of time—especially after taxes are considered. Those few investments that might provide such returns do so with significant risk that capital as well as income may be lost. Clearly, many parents may find themselves grossly underfunded when it comes time to pay college bills for their children.

To estimate the current lump-sum investment required to fund future education expenses the following time value formula may be applied:

FORMULA 3

$$PV = FV \times \frac{1}{(1+r)^N}$$

Where FV is the total estimated future education cost as determined above,

PV is the present value (required investment) of the future costs,

r is the assumed after-tax rate of return, and

N is the number of years until the child begins college.

The critical assumption when determining the required current investment is r, the assumed after-tax rate of return. The after-tax rate of return depends both on the type of assets in which the funds will be invested and on the tax that will apply to the earnings on those assets. You may wish to review Chapter 15 on Risk and Reward for a historical perspective on before-tax rates of return from various asset categories. Later in this chapter the tax aspects of various accumulation strategies are discussed. We recommend planners use about a 6 percent after-tax rate of return as a reasonable conservative estimate of the long-term after-tax rate of return. If more aggressive investments and/or tax-deferring strategies are contemplated, an effective after-tax rate as high as 8 percent may be reasonable.

The Present Value Table in Appendix B may be used with the following formula to derive the same result as Formula 3:

FORMULA 4

$$PV = FV \times PVfactor$$

Where PV and FV are defined as above, and

PVfactor is the factor from the Present Value Table of Appendix B for the selected values of r (the assumed rate of return) and N (the number of years until the child begins college).

For example, assume that

(1) the total future costs are calculated (from above) to be $220,924,

(2) the child will begin college in 14 years, and

(3) the assumed after-tax rate of return is 6 percent.

In this case the PVfactor from the Present Value Table of Appendix B is 0.4423. Applying Formula 4, the estimated current lump-sum investment required to fund the child's education is $97,715:

$$PV = \$220,924 \times 0.4423 = \$97,715$$

If the parents have already earmarked assets for the child's education, the current value of these assets should be subtracted from the present value amount derived using Formula 4, to determine their current deficit. For example, if in the case described above the parents have already earmarked $22,500 for their child's education, their current deficit would be $75,215 ($97,715 - $22,500).

Determining the Required Periodic Investment

Most clients will not have sufficient assets to fully fund their children's education without some additional periodic investing. The amount they must save each year (or each month) depends principally on how long they have to accumulate the necessary funds; the earlier they start their funding, the less they will have to save each period. The level of required periodic investment necessary to fund their current deficit is determined using the following time-value formula:

FORMULA 5

$$Pmt = Current\ Deficit \div \frac{1 - (1 + r)^{-Nf}}{r \div (1 + r)}$$

To compute the *annual* payments that are necessary to fund the deficit, use r, the assumed after-tax rate of return you used when determining the current funding deficit (as described above), and Nf, which equals the number of years over which the funding will take place.

To compute the *monthly* payments that would be required, divide the annual rate of return, r, by 12 to determine the monthly rate of return and multiply Nf by 12 and use these values in Formula 5 for r and Nf, respectively.

Note: The rate of return (r) assumed when using Formula 5 must be equal to the rate of return used in Formula 3. However, the number of years for funding (Nf) *does not* have to equal the number of years until the child begins college (N). For example, a client may wish to determine the amount required each year to fund the deficit in 5 years, even though the child will not begin college for 10 years. More commonly, clients will want to know how much they will have to invest each year until the child's last year of school, which is typically 3 years longer than the number of years until the child begins college; however, this could result in underfunding because as principal is removed each year, the rate of return is received on a lesser and lesser amount. For purposes of the calculations below, the number of years for funding will equal the number of years until the child begins college.

The Present Value of an Annuity Due Table in Appendix F can be used with the following formula to compute the same result as in Formula 5:

FORMULA 6

$$Pmt = Current\ Deficit \div PVADfactor$$

where Pmt is defined as above and

PVADfactor is the Present Value of an Annuity Due factor from Table F for the selected values of r and N.

For example, assume that

(1) the current deficit is $75,215 (as determined above),

(2) the number of years of annual funding, Nf, is 14 years (until the child who is currently age 4 begins her first year of college at age 18), and

(3) the assumed after-tax annual rate of return, r, is 6 percent.

The PVADfactor from Appendix F when r equals 6 percent and Nf equals 14 years is 9.8527. Therefore, the required annual funding is

$$Pmt = \$75,215 \div 9.8527 = \$7,634$$

The required monthly funding can be approximated by dividing the required annual funding by 12. In the case presented, your client would need to invest about $636 per month at a 6 percent after-tax rate of return for the next 14 years to fully fund the current deficit in the estimated amount required for the child's education.

Assuming that the rate of return on the assets already earmarked for the child's education equals that assumed in Formula 6, the combined amounts will equal the FV amount in Formula 4.

Simplified College Cost Worksheet

For many clients the Simplified College Cost Worksheet (Figure 4.7) will provide adequate estimates to get them started

Figure 4.7

SIMPLIFIED COLLEGE COST WORKSHEET	
1. Enter child's AGE	_____
2. YEARS to College (18 - child's AGE)	_____
3. Annual College COSTS (current dollars)	_____
4. Assumed College INFLATION Rate (%)	_____%
5. College INFLATION FACTOR (Factor from Compound Interest Table, Appendix A, for Years In Step 2 and INFLATION Rate in Step 4.	_____
6. Estimated FUTURE ANNUAL COSTS (Step 3 x Step 5)	_____
7. Estimated TOTAL Future Costs (Step 6 x number of years of college)	_____
FUNDING REQUIREMENTS	
8. Assumed After-tax RATE OF RETURN (%)	_____%
9. Present Value of Future LUMP-SUM Factor (Factor from Present Value Table, Appendix B, for YEARS in Step 2 and RATE OF RETURN in Step 8.)	_____
10. Total LUMP-SUM INVESTMENT Currently Required (Step 7 - Step 9)	_____
11. AMOUNT ALREADY EARMARKED for Education	_____
12. Additional LUMP-SUM Funding Required (Step 10 - Step 11)	_____
13. YEARS OF FUNDING	_____
14. Present Value of an Annuity Due Factor (Factor from Present Value of an Annuity Due Table, Appendix F, for YEARS in Step 13 and RATE OF RETURN in Step 8.)	_____
15. ANNUAL TARGET AMOUNT to Invest (Step 12 ÷ Step 14)	_____
16. Approximate MONTHLY TARGET AMOUNT to Invest (Step 15 ÷ Step 12)	_____

Figure 4.8

COMPLETED COLLEGE COST WORKSHEET	
1. Enter child's AGE	<u>4 years</u>
2. YEARS to College (18 - child's AGE)	<u>14 yrs.</u>
3. Annual College COSTS (current dollars)	<u>21,420</u>
4. Assumed College INFLATION Rate (%)	<u>7%</u>
5. College INFLATION FACTOR (Factor from Compound Interest Table, Appendix A, for Years in Step 2 and INFLATION Rate in Step 4.)	<u>2.5785</u>
6. Estimated TOTAL Future Cost (Step 3 x Step 5)	<u>55,231</u>
7. Estimated TOTAL Future Cost (Step 6 x number of years of college)	<u>x4</u> $ <u>220,924</u>

FUNDING REQUIREMENTS	
8. Assumed After-tax RATE OF RETURN (%)	<u>6%</u>
9. Present Value of Future LUMP-SUM Factor (Factor from Present Value Table, Appendix B, for YEARS in Step 2 and RATE OF RETURN in Step 8.)	<u>0.4423</u>
10. Total LUMP-SUM INVESTMENT Currently Required (Step 7 x Step 9)	<u>97.715</u>
11. AMOUNT ALREADY EARMARKED for Education	<u>$22,500</u>
12. Additional LUMP-SUM Funding Required (Step 10 - Step 11)	<u>75,215</u>
13. YEARS OF FUNDING	<u>14</u>
14. Present Value of an Annuity Due Factor (Factor from Present Value of an Annuity Due Table, Appendix F, for YEARS in Step 13 and RATE OF RETURN in Step 8.)	<u>9.8527</u>
15. ANNUAL TARGET AMOUNT to Invest (Step ÷ Step 14)	$ <u>7,634</u>
16. Approximate MONTHLY TARGET AMOUNT to Invest (Step 15 ÷ Step 12)	$ <u>636</u>

on a savings program to meet their college funding requirements. The Simplified College Cost Worksheet incorporates the four steps discussed above in one simple planning tool. In Figure 4.8 the numbers from the example above are illustrated.

In cases where your clients must fund the education of several children, planning to "smooth out" the required funding schedule so that the required payments are not too burdensome in any given year involves additional complexity. However, a "unified" funding schedule can be devised in the following manner:

(A) Using steps 1 through 10 of the Simplified College Cost Worksheet, determine the current required lump-sum investment for each child.

(B) Add together the amounts derived in step (A) for all children to find the aggregate current required lump-sum investment. Place this value in step 10 of the Simplified College Cost Worksheet.

(C) Use the remaining steps in the Simplified College Cost Worksheet to derive a level funding schedule over the desired funding period.

For example, assume that your clients

(1) have an annual before-tax family income of $100,000;

(2) have three children, ages 4, 6, and 10;

(3) plan to fund 75 percent of the cost of their children's education at a private institution whose current tuition, fees, room and board is about $21,420 per year (your clients believe the children should assume responsibility for 25 percent of the cost of their schooling);

(4) believe they can invest at about a 6 percent after-tax rate of return;

(5) have $30,000 currently earmarked to pay for their children's education;

(6) estimate college costs will rise at 7 percent per year; and

(7) want to fund their current deficit over the period until their youngest child begins his senior year in college.

Figure 4.9 shows the analysis for this case. Based on these assumptions, your clients would have to invest about $18,725 per year, or about $1,560 a month, for the next 14 years to pay 75 percent of their children's estimated college expenses. The annual payment represents more than 18 percent of the family's current before-tax income. As this example demonstrates, funding college education can be a substantial burden for most families, even for those with considerable incomes.

Clearly, if a family can raise its effective after-tax rate of return through the use of income-shifting, tax-reducing, and tax-deferring techniques, they can substantially reduce their required funding. For example, Figure 4.10 shows the analysis for the client described above assuming that the effective after-tax rate of return is raised to 8 percent. In this case, the required annual funding is $16,122 (monthly, $1,343), or about 14 percent less than that required when the after-tax rate of return is assumed to be 6 percent. The following sections of this chapter discuss various income-shifting, tax-reducing, and tax-deferring strategies and techniques that can help your clients increase their effective after-tax rate of return on their education funds.

PART II: TOOLS AND TECHNIQUES FOR FUNDING EDUCATION EXPENSES

There are seven methods of financing a child's education:

(A) on a pay-as-you go basis out of current assets and income,

(B) through government tax incentives,

(C) from scholarships and loans,

(D) children may work their way through school,

(E) the parents may engage in a systematic plan of early savings and investment,

(F) the parents may give gifts to children set aside sufficiently early to compound over a long period of time, or

(G) through a combination of these techniques.

Most parents will use some combination of these techniques.

Pay-As-You-Go

From a planning perspective, using current assets and income on a pay-as-you-go system or depending on scholarships and loans are the least favorable methods for financing education expenses. Financing an education out of current income or assets is the most expensive alternative because it takes the least advantage of the time value

Figure 4.9

COLLEGE COST ANALYSIS			
	4-yr. Old	**6-yr. Old**	**10-yr. Old**
1. Enter child's AGE	4	6	10
2. YEARS to College (18 - child's AGE)	14	12	8
3. Annual College COSTS (current dollars)	16,065*	16,065*	16,065*
4. Assumed College INFLATION Rate (%)	7%	7%	7%
5. College INFLATION FACTOR (Factor from Compound Interest Table, Appendix A, for Years in Step 2 and INFLATION Rate in Step 4.)	2.5785	2.2522	1.7182
6. Estimated FUTURE ANNUAL COSTS (Step 3 x Step 5)	$41,424	$36,182	$27,603
7. Estimated TOTAL Future cost (Step 6 x number of years of college)	$165,696	$144,728	$110,412

FUNDING REQUIREMENTS			
8. Assumed After-tax RATE OF RETURN (%)	6%	6%	6%
9. Present Value of Future LUMP-SUM Factor (Factor from present Value Table, Appendix B, for YEARS in Step 2 and RATE OF RETURN in Step 8.)	0.4423	0.4970	0.6274
10. Total LUMP-SUM INVESTMENT Currently Required	$73,287	$71,930	$69,272
10a. SUM of Line 10, all columns		$214,489	
11. AMOUNT ALREADY EARMARKED for Education		$30,000	
12. Additional LUMP-SUM Funding Required (Step 10a - Step 11)		$184,489	
13. YEARS OF FUNDING		14**	
14. Present Value of an Annuity Due Factor (Factor from Present Value of an Annuity Due Table, Appendix F, for YEARS in Step 13 and the RATE OF RETURN in Step 8.)		9.8527	
15. ANNUAL TARGET AMOUNT to Invest (Step 12 ÷ Step 14)		$18,725	
16. Approximate MONTHLY TARGET AMOUNT to Invest (Step 15 ÷ Step 12)		$1,560	

* 21,420 total current cost x 75 percent that parent plans to fund for

** Years until youngest child starts first year of college

Figure 4.10

COLLEGE COST ANALYSIS ASSUMING 8 PERCENT RETURN			
	4-yr. Old	6-yr. Old	10-yr. Old
1. Enter child's age	4	6	10
2. YEARS to College (18 - child's AGE)	14	12	8
3. Annual College COSTS (current dollar)	$16,065*	$16,065*	$16,065*
4. Assumed College INFLATION Rate (%)	7%	7%	7%
5. College INFLATION FACTOR (Factor from Compound Interest Table, Appendix A, for Years in Step 2 and INFLATION Rate in Step 4.)	2.5785	2.2522	1.7182
6. Estimated FUTURE ANNUAL COSTS (Step 3 x Step 5)	$41,424	$36,182	$27,603
7. Estimated TOTAL Future Cost (Step 6 x number of years of college)	$165,696	$144,728	$110,412
FUNDING REQUIREMENTS			
8. Assumed After-tax RATE OF RETURN (%)	8%	8%	8%
9. Present Value of Future LUMP-SUM Factor (Factor from Present Value Table, Appendix B, for YEARS in Step 2 and RATE OF RETURN in Step 8.)	0.3405	0.3971	0.5403
10. Total LUMP-SUM INVESTMENT Currently Required (Step 7 x Step 9)	$56,419	$57,471	$59,656
10a. SUM of Line 10, all columns		$173,546	
11. AMOUNT ALREADY EARMARKED for Education		$ 30,000	
12. Additional LUMP-SUM Funding Required (Step 10a - Step 11)		$143,546	
13. YEARS OF FUNDING		14**	
14. Present Value of an Annuity Due Factor (Factor from Present Value of an Annuity Due Table, Appendix F, for YEARS in Step 13 and RATE OF RETURN in Step 8.)		8.9038	
15. ANNUAL TARGET AMOUNT to Invest (Step 12 ÷ Step 14)		$ 16,122	
16. Approximate MONTHLY TARGET AMOUNT to Invest (Step 15 ÷ Step 12)		$1,343	

* $21,420 total current cost x 75 percent parents plan to fund
** Years until youngest child starts first year of college

of money and the favorable tax treatment available for funds which might have been set aside for this purpose. In addition, this method places the greatest strain on current disposable income.

Government Provided Tax Credits and Other College Financing Tax Incentives

Hope Scholarship Credit and Lifetime Learning Credit For Higher Education Expenses

A taxpayer may take advantage of new tax features with respect to an eligible student: the "hope scholarship" credit and the "lifetime learning" credit.

Hope Scholarship Credit

Individual taxpayers are allowed to claim a nonrefundable hope scholarship credit against federal income taxes *per student per year* in an amount equal to the sum of: (1) 100 percent on the first $1,000 of qualified tuition and related expenses; and (2) 50 percent on the next $1,000 of qualified tuition and related expenses. Thus, for 1998, the maximum credit available is $1,500 ($1,000 + (50% x $1,000)). The credit may be claimed only with respect to expenses of a student for two taxable years and only with respect to expenses for a student who has not completed the first two years of post-secondary education before the beginning of the taxable year in which the credit is claimed.

This credit can only be used if the student is an *eligible student* for at least one academic period which begins during the taxable year. An eligible student is one who: (1) is enrolled in a degree, certificate, or other program (including a program of study abroad approved for credit by the institution at which such student is enrolled) leading to a recognized educational credential at an eligible educational institution; (2) carries at least one-half the normal full-time work load for the course of study the student is pursuing; and (3) has not been convicted of a felony (under state or federal law) relating to the possession or distribution of a controlled substance by the end of the taxable year with or within which the academic period ends.

PLANNING POINT — If qualified tuition and related expenses are paid during the taxable year for an academic period that begins during the first three months of the following year, the academic period is treated as beginning during the current year. This permits, for example, the payment in December of 1998 for the college term beginning on February 1, 1999 to qualify for the tax credit in 1998. It has other implications as well. Most post-secondary education is administered on a fall through spring term. For moderate-level expenses, the operation of the above rules may require not electing a credit for the fall semester freshman year but electing the spring freshman-fall sophomore year and spring sophomore-fall junior year as the time to elect the Hope credit. Alternatively, prepayment of the spring semester during the fall semester may allow the taxpayer to take full advantage of the credit. For example, suppose the annual qualified tuition and related expenses are $3,000. Payment of the freshman fall term expenses in 1998 results in a credit of $1,250 (100 percent x $1,000 + 50 percent x $500). In 1999, payment of $3,000 for the freshman spring and sophomore terms results in a credit of $1,500 (100 percent x $1,000 + 50 percent x $1,000). Because the credit had now been claimed in two taxable years, no further expenses would qualify for the credit. If instead taxpayer had prepaid the $1,500 spring freshman (1999) semester fees in 1998 and again in 1999 prepaid the $1,500 for the sophomore (2000) spring semester, the taxpayer would be entitled to a $1,500 credit in both years.

Beginning in 2002, the maximum hope scholarship credit amount of $1,500 will be indexed for inflation, by adjusting the $1,000 amounts used to calculate the maximum credit, rounded to the next lowest multiple of $100. Thus, in the year in which the inflation adjustment reaches $1,100, the maximum credit will be $1,650 ((100 percent x $1,100) + (50 percent x $1,100)).

Lifetime Learning Credit

The taxpayer may also claim a nonrefundable lifetime learning credit against federal income taxes in an amount equal to 20 percent of qualified tuition and fees incurred during the taxable year which do not exceed $5,000 ($10,000 for taxable years beginning in 2003 and thereafter). In contrast with the hope scholarship credit, the lifetime learning credit is applied on a per taxpayer basis rather than on a per student basis for the taxable year.

The qualified tuition and related expenses to which the lifetime learning credit applies do not include those expenses with respect to an individual for whom a hope scholarship credit is allowed for the taxable year. Expenses related to educational programs leading to a degree or certificate programs and in certain cases those which do not lead to a degree or certificate, may qualify for the lifetime learning credit. Expenses incurred at either the undergraduate or graduate-level (or professional degree program) may qualify for the credit. In addition to allowing a credit for the tuition and fees of a student who attends classes on at least a half-time basis as part of a degree or certificate program, the lifetime learning credit is also available with respect to expenses related to any course of instruction at an eligible education institution (whether enrolled in by the student on a full-time, half-time, or less than half-time basis) to acquire or improve the student's job skills. In contrast to the hope scholarship credit, the maximum amount of the lifetime learning credit that may be claimed on a taxpayer's return will not vary based on the number of students in the taxpayer's family.

Qualified tuition and fees paid with the proceeds of a loan generally are eligible for the lifetime learning credit (rather than the loan itself).

The hope scholarship credit and the lifetime learning credit share certain common features:

Qualified tuition and related expenses are those (1) for the enrollment or attendance of (2) the taxpayer, the taxpayer's spouse, or any dependent for whom the taxpayer is allowed a personal exemption at an eligible education institution for courses of instruction of such individual at the institution.

PLANNING POINT — In the case of divorcing or divorced parents, consideration of projected levels of adjusted gross income is a factor to be considered in determining who is entitled to the dependency exemption, since only a spouse who can claim the exemption and meets the AGI limits can take full advantage of the credits. This can in appropriate circumstances suggest that the divorce or separation agreement be structured so that the credits are available to one of the spouses.

• The expenses of education involving sports, games, or hobbies are not qualified tuition expenses unless this education is part of the student's degree program. Charges and fees associated with meals, lodging, student activities, athletics, insurance, transportation, and similar personal, living or family expenses are also not included. Neither credit is available for expenses incurred to purchase books. Qualified tuition and fees do not include expenses covered by educational assistance that is not required to be included in the gross income of either the student or the taxpayer claiming the credit. Thus, total qualified tuition and fees are reduced by any scholarship or fellowship grants excludable from gross income under Code section 117 and any other tax free educational benefits received by the student during the taxable year (such as employer-provided educational assistance excludable under Code section 127). In addition, such tuition and fees are reduced by any payment (other than a gift, bequest, devise, or inheritance within the meaning of Code section 102(a)) which is excludable under any United States law. Moreover, a lifetime learning credit is not allowed with respect to any education expense for which a deduction is claimed under Section 162 or any other section of the Code.

• If a student is claimed as a dependent by the parent or other taxpayer, the student is not entitled to claim either credit for that taxable year on the student's own tax return. If a parent (or other taxpayer) claims a student as a dependent, any qualified tuition and related expenses paid by the student are treated as paid by the parent (or other taxpayer) for purposes of the credits. On the other hand, if a child is not claimed as a dependent by the parent (or by any other taxpayer) for the taxable year, then the child has the option of electing either the hope scholarship or lifetime learning credit for qualified higher education expenses paid during that year.

PLANNING POINT — Because a parent (or other taxpayer) who claims a student as a dependent may treat qualified tuition and related expenses paid by the student as paid by the parent (or other taxpayer) for purposes of the credit, income-shifting to the eligible student becomes attractive because the source of the funds for payment is taxed at presumably no more than a 15 percent rate, yet it applies as an offset against the perhaps 28 percent tax rate of the taxpayer.

• Eligible educational institutions are defined by reference to §481 of the Higher Education Act of 1965. Such institutions generally are accredited post-secondary educational institutions offering credit toward a bachelor's degree, an associate's degree, or another recognized post-secondary credential. Certain proprietary institutions and post-secondary vocational institutions also are eligible educational institutions. The institution must be eligible to participate in Department of Education student aid programs.

• Neither credit is allowed unless the taxpayer includes the name and taxpayer identification number on the taxpayer's tax return.

CAUTION — Neither credit is available to married taxpayers who file separate returns. This is particularly a problem in the context of a divorcing couple. In determining whether a couple is married their legal relationship is generally examined as of the end of the taxable year. If they are legally separated under a divorce decree or separate maintenance, they are not considered married. In a typical scenario, there will be at least one taxable year in which the couple is separated or estranged to the point that (assuming good advice) one of them will not subject themselves to the joint and several liability of the tax return. Should this occur at the time the couple's children are going to college (or one of the estranged couple is taking graduate work or other courses), the credits are threatened. It is another issue that must be negotiated in the divorce process.

• The hope scholarship and lifetime learning credit amount that a taxpayer may otherwise claim is phased out ratably for taxpayers with modified AGI between $40,000 and $50,000 ($80,000 and $100,000 for joint returns). *Modified AGI* includes amounts otherwise excluded with respect to income earned abroad (or income from Puerto Rico or U.S. possessions).

PLANNING POINT — The phase-out suggests tax strategies to reduce the taxpayer's adjusted gross income, which might include increasing the amount of §401(k) elective deferrals by employees, increasing the level of contribution to a self-employed's Keogh plan, and shifting investment income to another family member, including the student. Each of these strategies can be justified independent of the credit but under certain circumstances, for taxpayers on or near the cusp, the available credit together with other new features makes each of these more attractive.

Example: A sole proprietor otherwise having adjusted gross income of $90,000 has a child about to enter college which will entail $10,000 of annual qualified tuition expenses. How should he do this?

STRATEGY ONE: Pay expenses out of current income. Assuming the sole proprietor doesn't have a huge amount of itemized deduction and personal exemptions, this will be paid out of 28 percent income. Grossing up, the proprietor is with respect to the tuition out-of-pocket $13,889 ($10,000/.72). If the hope scholarship credit is used there is a $1,500 credit phased down to $750. That is the $1,500 credit is reduced by $750 ($1,500 - [$1,500 x {$90,000 - $80,000}/$20,000]). Net cost thus is, on an after-tax basis, $13,139 ($13,889 after-tax cost of tuition - $750 tax savings by credit).

STRATEGY TWO: Reduce AGI to $80,000 by setting up a Keogh profit-sharing plan and contributing the $10,000 in strategy one to it. This may well require borrowing the $10,000 to pay the tuition — but more on that later. This frees up from phase out the $750 credit reduction in strategy one. Now, the net after-tax cost of college is $12,389.

NOTE — The application of the hope scholarship or lifetime learning credit is elective. Nevertheless, no election may be made for a taxable year in which any portion of a distribution from an Education IRA (discussed below) is excluded from income.

PLANNING POINT — Qualified tuition and related fees cannot be allocated to the different credits. For example, the payment of $7,000 tuition for one individual cannot be broken down into a $2,000 hope scholarship segment and a $5,000 lifetime learning segment. On the other hand, tuition and related expenses can be allocated to different credits on a student basis. Thus, a taxpayer may claim the lifetime learning credit for a taxable year with respect to one or more students, even though the taxpayer also claims a hope scholarship credit (or claims an exclusion from gross income for certain distributions from qualified state tuition programs or Education IRAs) for that same taxable year with respect to *other students*. If, for a taxable year, a taxpayer claims a hope scholarship credit with respect to a student (or claims an exclusion for certain distributions from an Education IRA with respect to a student), then the lifetime learning credit will not be available with respect to that same student for that year (although the lifetime learning credit may be available with respect to that same student for other taxable years).

Withdrawals from IRAs for Educational Purposes

An individual generally is not subject to income tax on amounts held in an IRA, including earnings on contributions, until the amounts are withdrawn from the IRA. Amounts withdrawn from an IRA are includable in gross income (except to the extent of nondeductible contributions). In addition, a 10-percent additional tax generally applies to distributions from IRAs made before age 59½, unless the distribution is made: (1) on account of death or disability; (2) in the form of annuity payments; (3) for medical expenses of the individual and his spouse and dependents that exceed 7.5 percent of AGI; or (4) for medical insurance of the individuals and his spouse and dependents (without regard to the 7.5 percent AGI floor) if the individual has received unemployment compensation for at least 12 weeks, and the withdrawal is made in the year such unemployment compensation is received or the following year.

TRA '97 added an additional exception to the 10-percent additional tax for distributions from an IRA to the extent such distributions (other than those already excluded from the penalty) do not exceed the qualified higher education expenses of the taxpayer for the taxable year. For these purposes, qualified higher education expenses are those furnished to (i) the taxpayer, (ii) the taxpayer's spouse, or (iii) any child or grandchild of the taxpayer or the taxpayer's spouse, at an eligible educational institution. A child includes a son, daughter, stepson, or stepdaughter, and under Code section 152, an adopted child and, in certain circumstances, a foster child. Qualified higher education expenses are reduced by any amount excludable from gross income relating to the redemption of a qualified U.S. savings bond and certain scholarships and veterans benefits.

NOTE — The amount of qualified higher deduction expenses for any taxable year is reduced by: (1) the amount of scholarships or fellowship grants excludable from gross income under Code section 117; (2) any other tax free educational benefits received by the student during the taxable year (such as employer-provided educational assistance excludable under Section 127); and (3) any payment (other than a gift bequest, devise or inheritance within the meaning of Code section 102(a)) which is excludable under any United States law.

Education IRAs

TRA '97 added a new tax-qualified vehicle to help finance education called an "educational individual retirement account" which, while generally exempt from income tax, is subject to tax on its unrelated business taxable income. An Education IRA is a trust or custodial account created or organized in the United States exclusively for the purpose of paying the qualified higher education expenses of the designated beneficiary of the trust (and designated as an individual retirement account at the time created or organized), but only if the written governing instrument creating the trust meets certain requirements, one of which limits its utility. Contributions may only be made in cash and no contributions may be made to the account after the date on which such beneficiary attains age 18. The maximum aggregate contributions (other than rollovers) for a taxable year cannot exceed $500. Such contributions are nondeductible.

NOTE — Education IRA is a misnomer, because the account is not an individual retirement account under Code section 408, and practitioners and clients are likely to be confused by thinking of this vehicle as an IRA. Certain provisions mirror similar provisions applicable to an IRA, but the Education IRA is subject to those requirements separately and not because it is an IRA. For example, an IRA that invests in collectibles is generally treated as making a distribution. No such treatment appears applicable to an Education IRA. The Service's position is that the $500 limitation is applied to the beneficiary. Thus, the parents and grandparents may not each make separate $500 contributions on behalf of a single child.

As with traditional IRAs, the trustee must be a bank or other person who demonstrates that the manner in which that person will administer the trust will be consistent with the require-

ments of an Education IRA. The assets of the trust cannot be commingled with other property except in a common trust fund or common investment fund. However, no part of the trust assets may be invested in life insurance contracts. Upon the death of the designated beneficiary, any balance to the credit of the beneficiary must be distributed within 30 days after the date of death to the estate of such beneficiary.

For these purposes, the term "qualified education expenses" has the meaning given by qualified state tuition programs. It also includes amounts paid or incurred to purchase tuition credits or certificates, or to make contributions to an account, under a qualified state tuition program for the benefit of the beneficiary of the account. Note that any higher education expenses taken into account for an exclusion for a distribution from an Education IRA may not be taken into account for purposes of any other deductions or credits (e.g., hope scholarship or lifetime learning credits). An eligible educational institution has the meaning given by qualified state tuition programs.

The maximum amount which can be contributed to an Education IRA is reduced by an amount which bears the same ratio to that maximum amount as the excess of the contributor's modified adjusted gross income (MAGI) from such taxable year, over $95,000 ($150,000 in the case of a joint return), bears to $15,000 ($10,000 in the case of a joint return). MAGI is the adjusted gross income of the taxpayer for the taxable year increased by any amount excluded from gross income for foreign earned income and housing, amounts earned in Puerto Rico and certain U.S. possessions.

Example: T, a joint return filer, has MAGI of $154,000. The maximum amount T may contribute to an Education IRA is $300. That is, the maximum contribution is: $500 - {[($154,000 - $150,000)/ $10,000] x $500} = $300.

Distributions from an Education IRA are not included in the gross income of the distributee to the extent of the beneficiary's qualified higher education expenses during the taxable year. In the simple case where the distributions are not offset by any qualified higher education expenses during the taxable year, the distribution is included in the distributee's gross income according to the annuity rules of Code section 72.

If the distributions exceed the qualified higher education expenses during the taxable year, the distributee includes in gross income the amount which would have been included under Code section 72 in the preceding sentence but subtracting from it such amount multiplied by a fraction, the numerator of which is the qualified higher education expenses during the taxable year and the denominator of which is the aggregate distribution during the taxable year.

Example: J has contributed a total of $3,000 on behalf of T. A distribution is made during the taxable year in the amount of $4,000. The value of the account at the end of the year in which the distribution is made is $1,000. The exclusion ratio is $\frac{3}{5}$ [$3,000/($4,000 + $1,000)]. If T has no qualified higher education expenses during the taxable year, the amount included in income is $1,600 ($\frac{2}{5}$ x $4,000). If T has $4,000 of qualified higher education expenses, $2,400 is excluded as a return of capital, and $1,600 is excluded under the special exclusion for expenses attributable to qualified higher education expenses during the taxable year.

If T has $3,000 of qualified higher education expenses, the amount included in income equals $400 [$1,600 - ($1,600 x ($3,000 ÷ $4,000))].

PLANNING POINT — A taxpayer may elect to waive the application of this paragraph for any taxable year.

For purposes of the gift and generation-skipping transfer tax, any contribution to an Education IRA on behalf of any designated beneficiary is treated as a completed gift to such beneficiary that is not a future interest in property, and not a qualified transfer under Code section 2503(e) (i.e., it qualifies for exclusion under the annual exclusion limitation). Generally, no distribution from an Education IRA will be treated as a taxable gift. The lone exception is with respect to a transfer by reason of a change in the designated beneficiary (or a rollover to the account of a new beneficiary) if the new beneficiary is a generation below the generation of the old beneficiary.

For estate tax purposes, the value in an Education IRA is generally not included in the gross estate of the donor or beneficiary.

- However, amounts distributed on account of the death of the beneficiary are included in the gross estate of the designated beneficiary.

- If the donor has made the election to treat certain excess contributions as made ratably over a five-year period and dies before the close of such five-year period, the gross estate of the donor includes the portion of such contributions properly allocable to periods after the date of death of the donor.

In addition, to the extent a payment or distribution from an Education IRA is includable in gross income, the recipient is subject to an additional penalty tax of 10-percent of the amount which is so includable. The penalty is avoided in the following circumstances:

- The payment or distribution is made to a beneficiary (or to the estate of the designated beneficiary) on or after the death of the designated beneficiary;

- The payment or distribution is attributable to the designated beneficiary's being disabled; or

- The payment or distribution is made on account of a scholarship, allowance, or payment described in Code section 25A(g)(2) received by the account holder to the extent the amount of her payment or distribution does not exceed the amount of the scholarship, allowance, or payment;

- The distribution of any excess contribution made during a taxable year on behalf of a designated beneficiary which is received on or before the day prescribed by law (including extensions of time) for filing the contributor's return for that taxable year and is accompanied by the amount of net income attributable to the excess contribution. For these purposes, the net income attributable to the excess contribution is included in gross income for the taxable year in which such excess contribution was made.

A distribution otherwise taxable from an Education IRA is tax exempt to the extent that the amount received is paid not later than the 60th day after the date of such payment or distribution into another Education IRA for the benefit of the same beneficiary or a member of the family of such beneficiary who has not attained age 30 as of such date. However, the rollover does not avoid tax with respect to any payment or distribution if the rollover was applied to any prior payment or distribution during the 12-month period ending on the date of the payment or distribution.

Any change in the beneficiary of an Education IRA will not be treated as a distribution if the new beneficiary is a member of the family of the old beneficiary and has not yet attained age 30 as of the date of such change.

In the case of divorce, the transfer of an individual's interest in an Education IRA to an individual's spouse or former spouse under a divorce or separation instrument will not be considered a taxable transfer made by such individual notwithstanding any other provision of the income tax, and such interest will, after such transfer, be treated as an Education IRA with respect to which such spouse is the account holder.

On the death of the holder of the Education IRA:

- If the account holder's surviving spouse or family member acquires such holder's interest in an Education IRA by reason of being the designated beneficiary of such account at the death of the account holder, such Education IRA will be treated as if the spouse or family member were the account holder, provided the surviving spouse or family member has not yet attained age 30.

- If anyone other than the account holder's surviving spouse or family member acquires such holder's interest in an Education IRA by reason of being the designated beneficiary of such account at the death of the account holder, it ceases being an Education IRA as of the date of death, and an amount equal to the fair market value of the assets in such account on the date will be includable in income: (1) if such person is not the estate of such holder, in such holder's gross income for the taxable year which includes such date; or (2) if such person is the estate of such holder, in such holder's gross income for the last taxable year of such holder. An appropriate deduction will be allowed under Code section 691(c) to any person (other than the decedent or the decedent's spouse) with respect to amounts included in gross income by such person.

- Any balance remaining in the Education IRA at the end of the 30-day period following the designated beneficiary's death will be deemed distributed.

An Education IRA is also subject to two restrictions applicable to IRAs. It loses its tax-exemption in the event of a prohibited transaction, and any pledge of the account is treated as a distribution to the extent of the amount pledged. For these purposes, an individual for whose benefit an Education IRA is established and any contributor to such account are not considered engaged in a prohibited transaction with respect to any transaction concerning such account (which would otherwise be taxable) if §503(d) applies with respect to such transaction.

The Education IRA is also subject to the six-percent tax on excess contributions to certain plans. For these purposes, an excess contribution is: (1) the amount by which the amount contributed for the taxable year to such accounts exceeds $500 or lesser MAGI phased out amount; or (2) and generally, any amount contributed to an Education IRA for any taxable year in which any amount is contributed during such year to a qualified state tuition program for the benefit of such beneficiary. For these purposes, the excess contribution tax does not apply if the contribution is returned before the due date of the contributor's income tax return for the taxable year, including extensions; however, any earnings on these amounts are includable in the gross income for the contributor for the taxable year in which the contributions were made. Excess contributions from previous taxable years, to the extent not

corrected, will continue to be taxed as excess contributions in subsequent years.

Any balance remaining in an Education IRA at the time a beneficiary becomes 30 years old must be distributed within 30 days, and the earnings portion of such a distribution may be includable in gross income of the beneficiary and subject to an additional 10-percent penalty tax because the distribution was not for educational purposes. However, prior to the beneficiary reaching age 30, tax-free (and penalty-free) transfers and rollovers of account balances may be allowed from one Education IRA benefitting one beneficiary to another Education IRA benefiting a different beneficiary (as well as redesignations of the named beneficiary), provided that the new beneficiary is a member of the family of old beneficiary, and has not yet attained age 30. In any event, an Education IRA can continue to be rolled over by changing the designation of the beneficiary before reaching age 30. Any balance remaining in the Education IRA at the end of the 30-day period following the designated beneficiary attaining age 30 shall be deemed distributed.

Figure 4.11 summarizes the key elements of the various types of IRAs as financing vehicles for college education.

Exclusion for Employer Provided Educational Assistance

An employee's gross income and wages do not include amounts paid or incurred by the employer for educational assistance provided to the employee if such amounts are paid or incurred pursuant to an educational assistance program that meets certain requirements. This exclusion is limited to $5,250 of educational assistance with respect to an individual during a calendar year. The exclusion does not apply to graduate-level courses. In the absence of the exclusion, educational assistance is excludable from income only if it is related to the employee's current job. The exclusion for employer-provided educational assistance expires for courses beginning after May 31, 2000.

Scholarships and Loans

Reliance on scholarships or special student loans is quite questionable, especially given the present financial aid trend away from outright grants and favorable loans. Even if favorable student loans are available, a client may not wish to saddle a child with large loans that must be paid off at a time when the child begins a career. Loans to parents generally are made at market interest rates and repayment commences shortly after the loans are taken out.

Most college aid packages include a combination of grants, loans, and work-study programs. Two federal grants

Figure 4.11

Comparing IRAs: Focus On College Savings			
	Education IRA	**Roth IRA**	**Traditional IRA (Deductible)**	**Traditional IRA (Nondeductible)**
Who may use this type of IRA?	Beneficiaries under age 18. Contributions may come from parents, grandparents, or other interested parties. There is no earned income requirement (but contributions may be limited by AGI, as shown below)	Anyone with earned income, subject to limits below.	1. Individual not in an employer-sponsored plan. 2. Participant in an employer pension plan, subject to AGI limits below. 3. Individual whose spouse is covered by an employer pension plan, subject to AGI limits below	Anyone with earned income as well as nonworking spouses.
Tax Treatment of Contributions?	Nondeductible	Nondeductible	Deductible	Nondeductible
Annual maximum contribution?	$500 per child under age 18, regardless of the contributions permitted under other types of IRAs. No contribution is allowed, however, for any year in which anyone contributes to a qualified state tuition program for the same beneficiary.	$2,000 per person, in total to all Roth and traditional IRAs or, if lower, 100% of earned income.	$2,000 per person, in total to all Roth and traditional IRAs or, if lower, 100% of earned income.	$2,000 per person, in total to all Roth and traditional IRAs or, if lower, 100% or earned income.
Tax on withdrawals if used for qualified education expenses?	No (Balances must be withdrawn by the time the beneficiary reaches age 30 but can be rolled over to the Education IRA of another child in the same family.)	Yes (Earnings are taxed, unless the withdrawal occurs after age 59 1/2 and the account has been open for at least five years).	Yes	Yes (Earnings are taxed.)
Penalty on withdrawals if used for qualified education expenses?	No	No	No	No
AGI limitations in 1998?*	Individual returns: $95,000 to $110,000. Joint returns: $150,000 to $160,000.	Individual returns: $95,000 $110,000. Joint returns: $150,000 to $160,000.	1. None 2. Individual returns: $30,000 to $40,000. Joint returns: $50,000 to $60,000. 3. Joint AGI of $150,000 to $160,000	None

* The allowable contribution, or deduction, depends on adjusted gross income (AGI). A maximum amount is allowed if AGI is no more than the bottom income number in the ranges shown. None is permitted if AGI exceeds the top number in the ranges. A partial amount is allowed for incomes in between.

are available, Pell Grants and Supplemental Educational Opportunity Grants. Pell Grants are limited. The maximum award for the 1997-1998 award year was $2,700. Due to federal funding limits the actual maximum grants may be less than this amount. Supplemental Educational Opportunity Grants are limited to a maximum of $4,000 per year. Both of these federal grants are awarded only to academically promising students who also qualify under the financial needs formulas.

Most states have programs similar to the Supplemental Educational Opportunity Grants program for students who are residents of and attend school within the state. These grants generally provide amounts less than $4,000 per year and are available only to students who demonstrate need.

Most colleges and universities also offer their own grants or scholarships. These funds are predominantly given to students who demonstrate financial need and superior academic potential. Many schools offer some scholarships to the most gifted students, regardless of need, but competition for these grants is especially intense.

Low-interest federal loans are still available and some high-income families may qualify. *Perkins Loans* (formerly called National Direct Student Loans) are awarded by colleges on a first-come, first-served basis. The college decides whether the applicant needs the loan. Students from families with income under $30,000 are typically given preference, but gifted students with solid academic credentials may also qualify under this program. Depending on when a student applies, the level of need, and the funding level of the school, a student can borrow up to: (1) $3,000 for each year of undergraduate study up to a total of $15,000; and (2) $5,000 for each year of graduate or professional study up to a total of $30,000, including any Federal Perkins Loans borrowed as an undergraduate. Interest is only 5% and payments on these loans don't begin until after graduation. The loans are repaid over 10 years.

Stafford Student Loans are generally available to students who have financial need remaining after their Expected Family Contribution (EFC), Federal Pell Grant eligibility, and aid from other sources are subtracted from the cost of their attendance. The government will pay the interest on the loan while the student is in school, for the first six months after the student leaves school, and when the student qualifies to have payments deferred. This type of loan is called a subsidized loan.

Students who do not have financial need remaining may still borrow a Stafford Loan for the amount of their EFC or the annual Stafford Loan borrowing limit for their grade level, whichever is less. Because an unsubsidized loan is not awarded on the basis of need, the Student's EFC is not taken into account. In this case the loan is unsubsidized; interest is charged from the time the loan is disbursed until it is paid in full. However, the borrower may elect either to pay the interest as it accrues or to allow it to accumulate and be added to the principal amount of the loan. Students may receive a subsidized Stafford Loan and an unsubsidized Stafford Loan for the same enrollment period.

Dependent undergraduate students can borrow up to the following amounts (in 1998):

• $2,625 if they are first-year students enrolled in a program of study that is at least a full academic year;

• $3,500 if they have completed their first year of study and the remainder of their program is at least a full academic year;

• $5,500 a year if they have completed two years of study and the remainder of their program is at least a full academic year.

Independent undergraduate students or dependent students whose parents are unable to get a PLUS Loan (a parent loan) can borrow up to:

• $6,625 if they are first-year students enrolled in a program of study that is at least a full academic year. (At least $4,000 of this amount must be in unsubsidized loans.)

• $7,500 if they have completed their first year of study and the remainder of their program is at least a full academic year. (At least $4,000 of this amount must be in unsubsidized loans.)

• $10,500 a year if they have completed two years of study and the remainder of their program is at least a full academic year. (At least $5,000 of this amount must be in unsubsidized loans.)

The amounts described here are the maximum yearly amounts a student can borrow in both subsidized and unsubsidized Stafford Loans, individually or in combination, based on guidelines for 1998. Because students cannot borrow more than the cost of attendance minus both the amount of any Pell Grant they are eligible for and any other financial aid they will get, they may receive less than the annual maximum amounts.

The interest rate on Stafford Loans is variable (adjusted annually) but will never exceed 8.25%. From July 1, 1997 through June 30, 1998, the rate was 8.25% during repayment and 7.66% while a borrower was in school, a grace period, or a deferment. Students who have loans outstanding will be notified any time there is a rate change.

After students graduate, leave school, or drop below half-time enrollment, they have a six-month "grace period" before they must begin repayment. During this period, borrowers will receive information about repayment and will be notified of the date repayment begins. However, borrowers are responsible for beginning repayment on time, even if they do not receive this information. Payments are usually due monthly.

Most states also have subsidized loan programs similar to the federal loan programs. To qualify, students typically must (1) demonstrate need, (2) be a resident of the state, and (3) attend a state college or university.

Parent Loans for Undergraduate Students (PLUS) to meet students' education costs are available through both the FEEL and Direct Loan programs. Parents who do not have a bad credit history can borrow a PLUS Loan to pay the education expenses of a child who is a dependent student enrolled at least half time in an eligible program at an eligible school. These loans are available from most banks.

To be eligible to receive a PLUS Loan, parents generally will be required to pass a credit check. A parent cannot be turned down for having no credit history — only for having an adverse one. If parents do not pass the credit check, they might still be able to receive a loan if someone, such as a relative or friend who is able to pass the credit check, agrees to endorse the loan. An endorser promises to repay the loan if a student's parents fail to do so. Parents might also qualify for a loan even if they do not pass the credit check as long as they can demonstrate that extenuating circumstances exist. The student and the parents must also meet other general eligibility requirements for federal student financial aid.

The yearly limit on a PLUS Loan is equal to the student's cost of attendance minus any other financial aid the student gets. If the cost of attendance is $10,000, for example, and a student receives $6,000 in other financial aid, the parents can borrow up to $4,000.

The student's school will receive the money in at least two installments. No one payment may exceed half of the loan amount. The school might require the parents to endorse a disbursement check and send it back to the school. The school will then apply the money to the student's tuition and fees, room and board, and other school charges. If any loan money remains, the parents will receive the amount as a check or in cash, unless they authorize that it be released to the student. Any remaining loan money must be used for education expenses.

The interest rate is variable, but it will never exceed 9%. From July 1, 1997 through June 30, 1998, the interest rate was 8.98%. The interest rate is adjusted each year of repayment.

Parents will be notified of interest rate changes throughout the life of the loan. Interest is charged on the loan from the date the first disbursement is made until the loan is paid off. Generally, the first payment is due within 50 days after the final loan disbursement for the year. There is no grace period on these loans. Interest begins to accumulate at the time the first disbursement is made, and parents will begin repaying both principal and interest while their child is in school.

A Stafford Loan or PLUS Loan *may* be canceled under any of the following conditions:

- The borrower dies (or the student on whose behalf a parent borrowed dies).

- The borrower becomes totally or permanently disabled.

- The loan is discharged in bankruptcy.

- The school closes before the student completes the program of study.

- The school falsely certifies the loan.

Even if a student does not complete the program of study at the school, does not like the school or the program of study, or does not obtain employment after completing the program of study, these loans must nonetheless be repaid. Neither type of loan (Stafford or PLUS) can be canceled for these reasons.

Repayment assistance (not a cancellation, but another way to repay) may be available if a student serves in the military. For more information, contact your recruiting officer.

Most colleges and universities have their own loan funds as well. The qualifying criteria are generally similar to those used for loans, although most schools use the funds to help attract top students as well, regardless of the family's financial need. For example, the Consortium on Financing Higher Education, which encompasses the Ivy League and other schools, provides annual loans of up to $15,000 for 15 years at a variable rate that floats 200 basis points (2 percent) above the prime rate.

Students who qualify as "independents" are rated for college aid without considering parents' income or assets and, therefore, are much more likely to qualify for subsidized loans. However, qualifying for independent status is not an easy affair. (See "Independent Student Status" below.)

If parents incur unexpected expenses or if their accumulated savings are less than anticipated, both student loans and loans to parents may be good planning supplements. However at the centerpiece of any plan for financing education, reliance upon the future availability of loan programs is risky. Careful consideration of alternative (or at least supplementary) planning vehicles will help insure a client's ability to finance a child's education.

Deduction of Student Loan Interest and Educational Expenses

The Tax Reform Act of 1986 repealed the deduction for personal interest. After enactment, student loan interest generally was treated as personal interest and thus was not allowable as an itemized deduction from income. In addition, taxpayers generally have not been permitted to deduct education and training expenses.

However, a deduction for education expenses generally has been allowed under Code section 162 if the education or training (1) maintains or improves a skill required in a trade or business currently engaged in by the taxpayer, or (2) meets the express requirement of the taxpayer's employer, or requirements of applicable law or regulations, imposed as a condition of continued employment. More generally, education expenses are not deductible if they relate to certain minimum educational requirements or to education or training that enables a taxpayer to begin working in a new trade or business. In the case of an employee, education expenses (if not reimbursed by the employer) may be claimed as an itemized deduction only if such expenses relate to the employee's current job and only to the extent that the expenses, along with other miscellaneous deductions, exceed two percent of the taxpayer's adjusted gross income (AGI).

TRA '97 added provisions which permit the deduction of student loan interest in certain circumstances. An individual who has paid interest on a *qualified education loan* may claim a deduction for such interest expenses under Code section 221. A qualified education loan is any indebtedness incurred by the taxpayer solely to pay *qualified higher education expenses* that are incurred on behalf of the taxpayer, the taxpayer's spouse or a dependent (as of the time the debt was incurred), which are paid or incurred within a reasonable period of time before or after the debt was incurred, and which are attributable to education furnished during a period during which the recipient was an *eligible student*. However, a debt owed to a related person cannot be a qualified education loan. In contrast, a refinancing of a qualified education loan is treated as a qualified education loan.

Qualified higher education expenses are the cost of attendance at an *eligible education institution*, reduced by the amount excluded under an educational assistance plan, qualified education bonds, or qualified tuition program distributions and the amount of any scholarship, allowance, or payment excluded with respect to the hope scholarship and lifetime learning credits. An eligible education institution is the same as for the hope scholarship and lifetime learning credits, but also includes an institution conducting an internship or residency program leading to a degree or certificate awarded by an institution of higher education, a hospital, or a health care facility which offers postgraduate training.

An eligible student is defined the same as for the hope scholarship and lifetime learning credits (described later). In addition, the following requirements apply:

- The deduction is taken "above the line" in computing adjusted gross income.

- The deduction is allowed only with respect to interest paid on a qualified education loan during *the first 60 months* (whether or not consecutive) in which interest payments are required. Months during which the qualified education loan is in deferral or forbearance do not count against the 60-month period. For purposes of counting the 60 months, any qualified education loan and all refinancing (that is treated as a qualified education loan) of such loan are treated as a single loan.

- No deduction is allowed to an individual if that individual is claimed as a dependent on another taxpayer's return for the taxable year.

The amount of the deduction is limited in two ways:

- First, the amount allowable cannot exceed $1,000 in 1998, $1,500 in 1999, $2,000 in 2000, and $2,500 in 2001 and thereafter.

- Second, the maximum amount otherwise allowable as a deduction is reduced by the maximum amount deductible (according to the limits above) multiplied by the ratio that the excess of the taxpayer's *modified adjusted gross income* over $40,000 ($60,000 for married taxpayers filing jointly) bears to $15,000. For these purposes, modified adjusted gross income is computed after applying the Social Security inclusion, moving expenses and passive loss rules, but without regard to either the student loan interest deduction, the exclusion for amounts received in redemption of qualified education savings bonds, the foreign earned income exclusion and foreign housing exclusion, and amounts excluded from certain United States possessions or Puerto Rico.

- The maximum deduction amount is *not* indexed for inflation, however the threshold amounts listed above are indexed for inflation occurring after the year 2002, rounded down to the next closest multiple of $5,000. As a result of this reduction based on MAGI, for single taxpayers no deduction may be taken if MAGI exceeds $55,000 and the amount that may be deducted is reduced proportionately if MAGI is between $40,000 and $55,000. For married taxpayers filing a joint return, no deduction may be taken if MAGI exceeds $75,000, and the amount that may be deducted is reduced proportionately if MAGI is between $60,000 and $75,000. Married taxpayers filing separately may not take the deduction.

Certain eligible education institutions, or any person in a trade or business, or any governmental agency, that receives $600 or more in qualified education loan interest from an individual during a calendar year must provide an information report on such interest to the IRS and to the payor.

Given the limitations on deductibility, many parents may not qualify to deduct interest on educational loans or may not be able to deduct all of the interest they pay on such loans. One possible alternative is to use home equity loans to help finance college education expenses. Interest on home equity loans of up to $100,000 may be deductible regardless of how the proceeds are used. In many cases this may be a more tax-effective and less costly means to finance college education expenses than various educational loan programs.

Cancellation of Certain Student Loans

Prior to TRA '97, in the case of an individual, gross income subject to federal income tax did not include any amount from the forgiveness (in whole or in part) of certain student loans, provided that the forgiveness was contingent on the student's working for a certain period of time in certain professions for a broad class of employers.

Student loans eligible for this special rule must have been made to an individual to assist the individual in attending an educational institution that normally maintains a regular faculty and curriculum and normally has a regularly enrolled body of students in attendance at the place where its education and activities are regularly carried on. Loan proceeds may have been used not only for tuition and required fees, but also to cover room and board expenses (in contrast to tax free scholarships under Code section 117, which are limited to tuition and required fees). In addition, the loan must have been made by (1) the United States (or an instrumentality or agency thereof), (2) a state (or any political subdivision thereof), (3) certain tax-exempt public benefit corporations

that control a state, county, or municipal hospital and whose employees have been deemed to be public employees under state law, or (4) an educational organization that originally received the funds from which the loan was made from the United States, a state, or a tax-exempt public benefit corporation. Thus, loans made with private, non-governmental funds are not qualifying student loans for purposes of the Code section 108(f) exclusion.

TRA '97 expanded this exclusion. An individual's gross income does not include forgiveness of loans made by tax-exempt charitable organizations (e.g., educational organizations or private foundations) if the proceeds of such loans are used to pay costs of attendance at an educational institution or to refinance outstanding student loans and the student is not employed by the lender organization. As under present law, the Section 108(f) exclusion applies only if the forgiveness is contingent on the student's working for a certain period of time in certain professions for any of a broad class of employers. In addition, in the case of loans made by tax-exempt charitable organizations, the student's work must fulfill a public service requirement. The student must work in an occupation or area with unmet needs and such work must be performed for or under the direction of a tax-exempt charitable organization or a governmental entity.

Children Working

Parents are widely divided on whether children should help to pay for their college education by working during the school year. Some parents believe that their children will appreciate their college education more and apply themselves more diligently to their college studies if they have to work to pay for part of their education. Other parents are concerned that work during the school year may distract children from their studies and adversely affect their performance. Should the parents favor children working during the college months? Some studies indicate that students who work up to twenty hours per week during the school year perform no worse, and in some cases perform better, than their colleagues who do not work during the school year.

Students who decide that their financial situation requires them to work during the school year to make ends meet may qualify for the Federal work-study (FWS) program. The FWS Program provides part-time jobs for undergraduate and graduate students with financial need, allowing them to earn money to help pay education expenses. The program encourages community service work and work related to the recipient's course of study. FWS can help students get a foot in the door by allowing them to gain valuable experience in their chosen field before they leave school.

Students in the FWS program are paid by the hour. No FWS student may be paid by commission or fee. The school must pay students directly at least once a month. Wages for the FWS program must equal at least the current federal minimum wage but may be higher, depending on the type of work the student does and the skills required. The total FWS award depends on when the student applies, financial need, and the funding level at the student's school. The amount FWS students can earn cannot exceed their total FWS award. When assigning work hours, the employer or financial aid administrator will consider the award amount, the student's class schedule, and the student's academic progress.

The jobs available under the FWS program are usually provided by the student's school or by private nonprofit organization or public agencies, and the work performed must be in the public interest. In some cases a FWS student's school may also have agreements with private for-profit employers for FWS jobs. This type of job must be relevant to the student's course of study.

Parents are more likely to favor their children working during the summer months. The planner should advise the parents that the college aid formula used when awarding aid to students presumes that students will work during their summer vacations and will contribute that money to the payment of their college expenses.

Systematic Saving and Gifts

For most parents, careful and early planning is essential to financing their children's education. Tax benefits can be used to increase the efficiency of long-term savings. In addition to the value of long-term compounding over time, the client will find that shifting the ownership of dollars saved to the child (or to an entity taxed at the child's tax bracket) may increase the after-tax yield on the fund. The earlier the client implements a long-term savings plan and the younger the child is at the time the savings program is undertaken, the longer the interest and dividends produced by the fund will be compounding. These factors in turn enhance the efficiency of the savings effort. Although tax law changes have reduced the opportunities for income shifting to lower tax bracket children, some opportunities still remain.

The College Aid Formula

Unfortunately, shifting assets from a client to a child may have adverse consequences with respect to the child's eligibility for financial aid. As will be discussed in more detail below, a standard formula is used for all applicants for financial aid to determine what is called the "expected family contribu-

tion." The federal formula approved by Congress to calculate the expected family contribution (EFC) is called the Federal Methodology (FM). The federal methodology is used to determine eligibility for federal funds. If a college or university relies on a different formula for awarding its own funds, that formula is called the Institutional Methodology (IM). Different colleges and universities may use different institutional methodologies.

The EFC is the sum of the student contribution and the parent contribution:

EFC = Student Contribution + Parent Contribution

The calculation of the expected student contribution changes from school to school, but is generally 35% of the student's assets and 50% of the student's summer earnings. (The federal calculation is 50% of the summer earnings above $1,750 and 35% of the student's reported assets.)

The parental contribution depends on the number of parents with earned income, their income and assets, the age of the older parent, the family size, and the number of family members enrolled in post-secondary education. Income is not just the adjusted gross income from the tax return, but also includes nontaxable income such as social security benefits and child support. The Higher Education Amendments of 1992 eliminated home equity from the EFC, but many private schools and universities still use a parent's home equity as a way of rationing their school's own grant and scholarship funds. Money set aside for retirement in a pension plan such as a 401K, IRA Keogh, or 403(b) is usually not counted as an asset. However, the funds contributed to a tax-deferred retirement program during the previous year must be included on the official financial aid form (FAFSA) as "other untaxed income." In addition, an asset protection allowance shelters a portion of the assets from the calculation of the parent contribution. The asset protection allowance increases with the age of the parents to allow for emergencies and retirement needs.

The need analysis system assumes that the parents contribute 6% to 12% of their assets above a threshold, and 25% of the gross income above a threshold (the minimum living allowance, which depends on the number of family members living at home), less an allowance for family members in college. The following formulas is meant to be illustrative — the federal formula is a bit more complicated — but gives a fairly good estimate of the parent contribution (PC) for each student in college.

For the following formulas, let n be the number of family members in college.

Estimated Parental Contribution (EPC)

EPC = 12% (assets - $30,000) + 25% (income - $18,000) - (n - 1) x $900

Parental Contribution (PC)

$$PC = \frac{EPC + (n - 1) \times \$500}{n}$$

For example, assume the value of the parent's qualifying assets are $75,000, their income is $50,000, and they have two students in college.

EPC = (12% x $45,000) + (25% x $32,000) - 900 = $12,500

$$PC = \frac{12,500 + 500}{2} = \$6,500 \text{ per student}$$

Low-income families are most likely to qualify for aid but even families with incomes in excess of $70,000 may qualify. Do not arbitrarily assume children will not qualify for aid if your client's income is substantial—a family's income is only one factor in determining who receives aid. The parent's home equity, real estate assets, investments, and savings are all counted when determining the parent's contribution.

The family financial burdens, such as medical bills, the size of the family, the number of children in private schools or colleges, and the years until the parents expect to retire all reduce the required parental contribution amount according to the aid formula. In addition, the larger the student's income and savings the smaller, all else equal, the aid award.

Planning Tips for Reducing the Expected Family Contribution

There are several consequences of the structure of the needs analysis formula that are worth noting.

If a child is unlikely to qualify for aid, income-shifting techniques can be employed to help accumulate funds for education. If a child would otherwise qualify for aid in the absence of income shifting and asset shifting to the child, employing these shifting techniques may be counter-productive and parents would often do better accumulating funds themselves.

The obvious disincentives of such formulas for computing the expected family contribution put parents in a "Catch-22" position. Lower-income parents who are conscientious and thrifty may be less likely to receive aid then higher income but more profligate parents. In addition, the assets and income of parents are "taxed" by the federal methodology need analysis formula at a much lower rate than those of the student. This means that it may not be to the advantage of the parties to shift income and assets to their children, despite potential income tax savings.

For example, parents who have managed to save $50,000 would be expected to contribute about $2,400 of it to help pay for a child's college expenses when the college works out the aid package for the child. If these assets had been transferred to the child, about $17,400 (35%), or $15,000 more than if the parents owned the assets, would be used when computing the child's aid award. Although a family financial status is equal in either case, the aid award from the college will be considerably smaller when the assets are owned by the child.

Generally, after application of the aid formulas, the practical effect is that no more than about 6% of a parent's assets (excluding their home equity and retirement programs) are expected to be used for the child's educational costs. For virtually all parents, the first $40,000 to $50,000 of their assets (depending on their age and family size) will be ignored completely in the federal methodology need analysis formula.

Since the student's assets are "taxed" at a much higher rate than the parents' assets, the family should spend down the student's assets before using any of the parents' assets to pay for the student's education. Otherwise the student's assets will again be subject to the high "tax" rate during the next year's needs analysis. Just because the formula assumes that students contribute 35% of their assets and parents only about 6%, doesn't mean you have to treat those percentages as targets.

The parent contribution is divided by the number of family members in college. Changes in the number of family members in college can significantly affect the amount of aid received. For example, even families that are well off may become eligible for financial aid when two or more family members are enrolled in college at the same time. So parents should not assume that they are ineligible for aid just because they make too much money or own a house.

[Thus the single greatest thing a parent can do to effect his children's eligibility is to go back to school themselves. Many private schools, however, exclude parents in college from their needs analysis calculations.]

Note that the family members must be enrolled at least half-time and working toward a degree at a qualifying institution to be counted as being in college.

The financial aid award or "package" is based on the assets and earnings for the year before the student matriculates in college. So parents should be careful about financial activity the year before their children enter college. For example, parents who avoid creating or recognizing capital gains during the child's senior year in high school will be at an advantage in the federal methodology need analysis system.

If the parents' income varies substantially from year to year, try to rearrange income fluctuations in their favor. For example try to defer income from the base year for determining aid to the next year. Also try to defer deductions from the year prior to the base year or accelerate deductions from the year after the base year to the base year.

Business property is not treated in the same manner as the primary residence or any other real estate holdings in the needs analysis. If part of the primary residence is used for business purposes, be sure to indicate it on the financial statement.

Consumer debt (car payments, credit card payments, payments on personal notes, and so on) is not given credit in the needs analysis formula. However, home equity loans do reduce the home equity reported in the needs analysis. Therefore, using home equity loans to replace other consumer debt will lower the family assets in the needs analysis formula and increase the potential aid award.

Parents should consider making any large, planned purchases in cash to reduce liquid assets right before filling out the financial aid form. For example, if your client has been planning on buying a new car or making home improvements, he should be advised to pay for it prior to filling out the form. The reduced savings will reduce the family asset value.

Company-sponsored savings plans such as 401(k) plans or tax-deferred annuity plans for employees of non-profit institutions should be used by the client. These assets do not count as "available income" or assets on the needs analysis form.

Additionally, tax-deferred investments such as single-pay life, whole life, variable life, and universal life insurance and annuities do not count as assets in the needs analysis formula. This makes these instruments especially attractive for maximizing the potential financial aid award.

Independent Student Status

As noted earlier, students who qualify as independents are rated for college aid without including their parent's income or assets. This status may benefit some students who would otherwise not qualify to receive aid. Further relief may now be available in the wake of more liberalized rules for determining this "independent" student status.

Students are considered independent if they meet any of the following criteria:

1. They will be 24 years old by December 31 of the award year, even if they are still living at home;

2. They are orphans or wards of the state;

3. They are armed forces veterans;

4. They have legal dependents other than a spouse;

5. They are graduate students or students at professional schools and will not be claimed as an exemption by their parents for the first calendar year of the award year;

6. They are married and will not be claimed as a tax exemption by their parents for the first calendar year of the award year.

The school may ask students that claim to be independent to submit proof before they can receive any federal student aid. Students who think they have unusual circumstances (other than one of those conditions listed above) that would make them independent may talk to their school's aid administrator. The aid administrator can change a student's status if he thinks the student's circumstances warrant it based on the documentation provided. But remember, the aid administrator will not automatically do this. The decision is based on his judgment, and it's final — a student cannot appeal the aid administrator's decision to the U.S. Department of Education.

Income-Shifting Techniques

Education funding can be optimized if the funds are accumulated in a tax-advantaged way. Although the so-called "kiddie tax" taxes a child's unearned income above certain limits at the parent's marginal rate, shifting income to children in a lower tax bracket still has some value as a way of achieving this objective. The rules and their education planning implications are summarized below.

Taxation of Children

For children under age 14 who have at least one parent living at the close of the tax year, unearned income (investment income) in excess of $1,400 is generally taxed at the parent's marginal tax rate. There is no tax on the first $700 of unearned income and the next $700 is taxed to the child at the child's 15 percent bracket resulting in a $105 tax. (Note: these numbers apply to 1998 and are adjusted annually for inflation.)

The kiddie tax rules will apply without regard to the source of the unearned income or the income-producing property (parents, grandparents, or even savings created by the child's own labor).

A dependent child with gross income in excess of the standard deduction, or with unearned income of more than $700, generally must file a tax return. However, a parent may report a child's income on the parent's return and forego filing a return for the child if the child's gross income for the taxable year (1) is more than $700 and less than $7,000 and (2) includes interest and dividend income only. The parent will pay no tax on the first $700 of the child's income and a 15% tax rate on the second $700.

Earned income is taxed to the child at the child's tax bracket regardless of the child's age. All income of a child age 14 or over is taxed to the child at the child's tax bracket.

Gifts to children may make tax sense. Up to $20,000 of joint gifts of a present interest per year will not cause a gift tax liability, and for children age 14 or over, income from property given will be taxed at the child's tax rate. For children under age 14, unearned income (over $1,400) will be subject to the kiddie tax unless it is in a tax-free or tax-deferred form. Use of Minor's trusts and/or Crummey trusts allow additional splitting and shifting of income to low-bracket children.

Taxation of Trusts

The income shifting benefits of certain pre-TRA '86 trust vehicles (such as Clifford trusts and spousal remainder trusts) are effectively unavailable as income-shifting devices, because in most cases they are treated as "grantor trusts." The income and deductions of such trusts are taxable to the grantor, not the income beneficiary. However, Clifford and spousal remainder trusts in existence before March 1, 1986 were grandfathered, and thus are not treated as grantor trusts. The trust income from a grandfathered trust is taxable to the beneficiary and not to the grantor; however, the income taxable to beneficiaries under age 14 is taxed at the parent's marginal tax rate under the kiddie tax rules until a child is age 14 or older. From that point, income paid out from those types of trusts will be taxed to the child at the child's bracket. The objective of shifting the tax burden on income to the lower tax bracket child is therefore thwarted, unless tax-exempt or tax-deferred income can be generated.

Trusts are required to use a calendar year for tax purposes; however, tax-exempt and charitable trusts are exceptions to this rule.

For tax years beginning in 1998, the indexed tax rate brackets for trusts are: fifteen (15) percent on the first $1,700 of taxable income; twenty-eight (28) percent on taxable income between $1,700 and $4,000; thirty-one (31) percent on taxable income between $4,000 and $6,100; thirty-six (36) percent on taxable income between $6,100 and $8,350; and 39.6 percent on taxable income over $8,350.

The 2 percent floor on miscellaneous itemized deductions applies to trusts and estates, as well as to individuals.

Quarterly payments of estimated tax are required of trusts in the same manner as they are of individual taxpayers.

The combination of the compressed trust tax rate schedule for undistributed trust income, the kiddie tax rules for distributions of trust income to children under the age of 14, and the college aid formulas that apply a "tax" (contribution) rate on assets held by children at 35% as compared to an effective average parental asset "tax" (contribution) rate of about 6% has essentially eliminated the opportunity for the effective use of trusts for income and asset shifting to children for college funding purposes. Trusts may still be effectively used for other financial planning purposes or special cases, such as in the case of divorce, special needs for children, and the like, that may include funding for a child's education among their other support objectives, but these are uses beyond the scope of this discussion of college education funding.

Taxation of Fellowships and Scholarships

Scholarships and fellowship grants of degree candidates are excludable from gross income only to the extent spent on tuition and course-related expenses. Any portion of the money that pays for room and board and other noneducation costs is taxable. Also, IRS rulings require scholarships that are awarded to students who have teaching, research, or other responsibilities associated with the grant to be allocated between the "service" portion and the scholarship portion. The portion of a grant or scholarship allocated to service is considered taxable income to the student.

Non-degree candidates receive no exclusion.

Income-Shifting and Parents' Support Obligations

The use of income shifting techniques to help fund a child's education should not be recommended without some consideration of the tax impact they may have as a result of a parent's support obligations. As a general rule, if resources are used to satisfy the parent's legal obligation to support a child, the parent, not the child, is subject to tax on the income. While the basic concept is easily understood, this issue has long been a subject with unknown boundaries. The principal question is whether or not a parent's legal obligation to support a child includes the obligation to pay for a child's college education.

The implication of the applicable case law is generally that in states where a college education is considered a normal support obligation of the parents, funds that have been transferred to a child are the child's money. Therefore, those assets may not be used to pay college expenses even though the parents gave the child the money with express purpose of using it to fund the child's college education! In other words, using the funds to pay the normal support obligations of the parents, including paying college education expenses in states that extend the support obligation to college education, is a breach of fiduciary duty. Such breaches could result in fines and penalties and would normally require that the parents make complete restitution. In addition, custodial funds used to pay college expenses would be taxable to the parents in a state where the parents have an obligation of support that extends to college education.

In general the courts have considered a number of factors such as the parents' means, ability to pay, and station in life in determining whether a college education is a normal support obligation. If, after assessing your client's financial status, college financing needs, and their parental support obligation in their state, it appears that income shifting may serve their purposes, the tools and techniques described in this chapter should be considered.

Prepaid College Tuition Plans

A prepaid tuition plan is a college savings plan that is guaranteed to rise in value at the same rate as college tuition. For example, if a family purchases shares that are worth half a year's tuition at a state college, they will always be worth half a year's tuition, even ten years later when tuition rates will have probably doubled. (Other types of college savings plans, such as the Education IRA established by TRA '97, do not include a tuition lock.)

Prepaid tuition plans are often exempt from local and state taxes, and the federal tax obligation is levied on the beneficiary when the plan is used. Most plans are guaranteed by the full faith and credit of the state that offers them, but the nature of the guarantee differs from state to state.

Most plans offer monthly and annual investment options, in addition to lump sum investments. In a typical plan, the family purchases shares that represent a percentage of a year's tuition. The price of these shares, of course, increases every year. Most plans include features that make it easy to set aside

money regularly, such as payroll deduction and automatic transfers from a checking or savings account.

There are two main types of plans. Some states provide one type and some the other:

- Prepaid Unit. The prepaid unit plan sells units that represent a fixed percentage of tuition. Everybody pays the same price for the units, and the price of a unit increases every year in pace with the increase in the cost of college education.

- Contracts. The contract plan sells contracts, where the parent agrees to purchase a specified number of years of tuition. The purchase price depends on whether the payment is on a lump sum or installment basis and on the age of the child. Most contract plans offer lower prices for younger children, since the state has more time to invest the money.

Many prepaid tuition plans are aimed at middle-income families, although several states have been adding provisions to make them more affordable to lower income families. According to the U.S. General Accounting Office (GAO), investors in prepaid tuition plans tend to be middle- and upper-income families. A study by the American Association of State Colleges and Universities concurs with these findings.

Prepaid tuition plans do not guarantee admission into college.

The main benefit of a prepaid tuition plan is that it allows the student's parents or legal guardian (and in some cases, grandparents or friends of the family) to lock in tuition at current rates, offering peace of mind. The simplicity of the plans is also attractive, and most plans offer a better rate of return on an investment than bank certificates of deposit and savings accounts.

Unfortunately, most plans may be used only at public colleges and universities, with only a few states extending the plan to selected in-state private schools. If the child ultimately decides not to attend a participating school, the value of the plan is significantly reduced. If the child decides to attend an out-of-state school, many plans let the family redeem their shares, but at a lower rate of return, and do not allow the proceeds to be used at trade schools or other for-profit institutions of higher education. For example, Massachusetts will return to a family their initial investment adjusted for inflation (CPI), and Florida gives the family the initial investment adjusted for the increase in in-state tuition or a five percent annual return, whichever is less. If the child decides not to go to college, in general the family will only get back what they originally contributed with no interest added, and there may be a cancellation penalty. However, most plans allow a sibling to use the plan in such circumstances. If the family moves out of state but the child attends a participating school, the family can still use the plan but may be held responsible for the difference between out-of-state and in-state tuition.

Thus, it is important that a family carefully evaluate their options before investing in a prepaid tuition plan. There are many benefits to a prepaid tuition plan, but such plans are not for everyone.

Prepaid Tuition Plan Checklist

- What are the fees? Is there an enrollment fee or a load?

- What is the minimum and maximum investment?

- Is the plan exempt from state and local taxes? Are contributions to the plan tax deductible?

- Who is eligible to participate in the plan? Must the student (or a parent) be a state resident?

- Which schools participate in the plan?

- What happens if the child goes to an out-of-state school or if the child decides not to go to college? What happens if the child receives a scholarship from the school?

- What happens if the child dies or becomes disabled?

- What happens if the family moves out of state but the child still attends a participating school?

- Does the participant have to name a specific school when buying the contract? If the plan is school-specific, what happens if a child chooses a different school or isn't admitted by the school?

- Are there any age restrictions?

- Are shares in the plan guaranteed by the state?

- How are shares indexed to tuition? Are they guaranteed to equal actual tuition increases, the state average increase, or a projected increase?

- What expenses are included in the plan? Does the plan cover just tuition and fees, or does it also include room and board?

- What payment options, such as lump-sum and monthly installment, are available?

- Can payments be made through electronic funds transfer (EFT) , allowing them to be deducted automatically from payroll checks and bank accounts?

- Who can purchase shares on behalf of the student? Must they be a resident of the state? Can grandparents and friends of the family purchase shares, or just the parents?

- Can the investment in the plan be canceled? If so, how is the amount of the refund calculated?

- How are shares redeemed when the child matriculates in college?

Tax Status of Prepaid Tuition Plans

Investments in prepaid tuition plans are usually exempt from local and state income tax, but are still subject to federal income tax. The federal income tax obligation is deferred until the shares in the plan are redeemed (when the child attends college), and is then levied on the student who benefits from the plan, not the parents. This offers additional tax savings since the student's tax bracket is likely to be more favorable than the parent's tax bracket. Federal income tax will be due on the difference between the current value of the shares in tuition dollars and their original cost. The annual increase in value is not subject to annual capital gains tax, and contributions to a child's plan are not subject to gift taxes. Prepaid tuition plan funds can be used only at non-profit public and private institutions of higher education. For details on the federal tax status of prepaid tuition plans, see Section 529 of the Internal Revenue Code.

Impact of Prepaid Tuition Plans on Contributions to Education IRAs

Generally, no contribution is permitted to an Education IRA for a beneficiary in the same tax year in which a contribution is made to a state prepaid tuition program for the same beneficiary. Also, families may not take advantage of the hope scholarship or lifetime learning tax credits in the same year as they take a distribution from an Education IRA for the student. Accordingly, parents should plan on using the hope scholarship credit during the first two years of college, and on liquidating the Education IRA the last two years of college.

Impact of Prepaid Tuition Plans on Aid Eligibility

A major problem with prepaid tuition plans is the negative impact on eligibility for federal student aid. The federal need analysis methodology currently treats the value of the benefits received by the student from the plan each academic year as a resource, which means that it reduces financial need (or cost of attendance, which yields the same effect) by 100%. Thus every dollar saved in a prepaid tuition plan reduces eligibility for student financial aid by a dollar. This is in contrast with assets saved in the parents' names, which reduce aid eligibility by about six percent, and assets saved in the student's name, which reduce aid eligibility by about 35%. Moreover, even though amounts saved in prepaid tuition plans reduce aid eligibility by 100%, they do not reduce the parent contribution. The states recognize these problems and are lobbying to have them changed.

The impact on eligibility for state aid is often much more favorable. Several states have provisions that shelter the savings from the state need analysis process. For example, Pennsylvania's TAP accounts do not have any impact on eligibility for state grants and loans. Virginia's program treats amounts in prepaid tuition plans as student assets.

Prepaid Tuition Plans should not be reported as a family asset on the Free Application for Federal Student Aid (FAFSA), but should instead be reported as a resource. Since the rules may change, students should contact the financial aid administrator at the schools to which they are applying to find out about the impact of the plan on applications for financial aid.

Pros and Cons of Prepaid Tuition Plans

There are many considerations to be weighed before deciding to invest in a prepaid tuition plan. Aside from the restrictions on choice of college, the key consideration is a trade off between risk and return. A family with financial savvy might be better off investing the funds on their own.

Prepaid tuition plans encourage parents to save for their children's education and offer then peace of mind. They are not necessarily the best way to save for college, but provide a safe, affordable, and convenient option for families who may not be very knowledgeable about investing.

The low risk of prepaid tuition plans is an important consideration. Most parents do not start saving until very late in the game. Even the financial advisors who tell parents that they could do better on their own will acknowledge that as college approaches the family should move the college savings into lower-risk investments. If college is less than five years away, the family should put the college fund in low risk investments like certificates of deposit, zero-coupon bonds, and prepaid tuition plans.

Before investing in a prepaid tuition plan, parents should carefully evaluate the plan and their other investment options.

From an investment perspective, a prepaid tuition plan is a low-risk, tax-advantaged investment vehicle, with earnings indexed to the average increase in tuition. Since tuition rates seem to increase at about twice the inflation rate, the earning potential is probably greater than the interest earned from bank savings accounts and certificates of deposit (CDs). On the other hand, the negative impact on eligibility for federal student aid should be taken into account.

If parents are willing to accept a greater amount of risk, they might be able to do better investing on their own. Some planners advise families to invest in a diversified portfolio of mutual funds. For example, the Standard & Poor's 500 index (S&P 500) has historically gone up by about 10% to 11% a year, offering a slightly better rate of return than most prepaid tuition plans after taking taxes into account. On the other hand, the S&P 500 is not guaranteed to always increase at the same rate, and in some years it might have a worse return than a prepaid tuition plan. The opportunity for greater returns comes with a correspondingly greater risk.

The best advice is to carefully evaluate the options before considering any investment. Some of the key point to consider when evaluating a prepaid tuition plan are:

- *Safety.* Prepaid tuition plans are low risk, because they are guaranteed to increase at the "tuition inflation rate," typically between six percent and eight percent. Investments in prepaid tuition plans are not subject to the unpredictability and volatility of the stock market. They are also often guaranteed by the full faith and credit of the state that runs the plan. On the other hand, this also means that the earning potential is more limited than that of riskier investments.

- *Tax Exempt.* Prepaid tuition plans are usually exempt from state and city taxes and the federal tax obligation is at the child's rate and is deferred until matriculation.

- *Negative Impact on Aid Eligibility.* Prepaid tuition plans reduce eligibility for federal student financial aid by 100%, in contrast with other investment vehicles.

- *Limitations on School Choice.* All plans are designed for students who intend to matriculate at a state college or university. Some restrict the plans to public schools, while others include selected private institutions. If the student decides to go to school out of state or attend a school that doesn't participate, the main benefit of the plan is eliminated. Most plans offer a lower rate of return if the shares are not used to pay for tuition at an in-state school. (A few of the more recently established state plans allow the proceeds to be used at any

Figure 4.12

COMPOUND TAX SAVINGS FROM SHIFTING $1,200 OF UNEARNED INCOME PRE YEAR TO CHILD AT 6% AFTER TAX			

Years Prior to Need	Parent's Tax Bracket		
	36 Percent	31 Percent	28 Percent
18	12,331	10,167	8,870
17	11,257	9,282	8,097
16	10,243	8,446	7,368
15	9,287	7,658	6,680
14	8,385	6,914	6,031
13	7,534	6,212	5,419
12	6,731	5,550	4,842
11	5,974	4,926	4,297
10	5,259	4,336	3,783
09	4,585	3,781	3,298
08	3,949	3,256	2,841
07	3,349	2,762	2,409
06	2,783	2,295	2,002
05	2,249	1,855	1,618
04	1,745	1,439	1,255
03	1,270	1,047	914
02	822	678	591
01	399	329	287

accredited nonprofit U.S. college or university, basing the amount of the benefit on the average in-state public tuition cost.) On the other hand, many plans allow shares to be transferred to other members of the family.

- *Return on Investment.* The effective rate of return may depend on the school, since the plan's earnings are indexed to the average rate of tuition increase, and an individual school's tuition may grow at a faster or slower rate. Depending on the nature of the plan, the package may not include all of the college expenses. For example, many plans are limited to tuition and fees, and do not cover room and board. So the family may need to plan for these additional costs as well.

- *Affordability.* The minimum investment amount is typically much lower than that required by most mutual funds, making prepaid tuition plans more accessible to lower income families.

- *Simplicity.* Prepaid tuition plans appeal to parents who may not have the time or knowledge to manage their own investments. Most plans sell shares that represent a fixed percentage of a year's tuition, a concept that is easily understood by most parents.

- *Discipline.* Prepaid tuition plans typically require parents to begin contributing on a regular schedule, years before their children matriculate in college. By requiring consistent and systematic payments at regular intervals, prepaid tuition plans get parents to start saving and investing for college sooner.

Prepaid tuition plans may also be useful in other circumstances, such as divorce settlements and probate of a will.

As of 1998, twenty-three states — Alabama, Alaska, Arizona, Colorado, Florida, Illinois, Indiana, Louisiana, Massachusetts, Michigan, Mississippi, Missouri, New Hampshire, New Jersey, New York, Ohio, Pennsylvania, South Carolina, Tennessee, Texas, Virginia, Wisconsin, and Wyoming — offer prepaid tuition plans. Seven states — Arkansas, California, Illinois, Missouri, Nevada, New Hampshire, and Oregon — offer savings bond programs. Four states — Indiana, Kentucky, Louisiana, and Utah — offer savings funds or savings plan trusts. Georgia offers the Georgia HOPE Scholarship Program using the proceeds from the state lottery.

Gifts to Minors

The most direct method of funding education for children is by using a plan of giving under the Uniform Gifts to Minors Act (UGMA), or under the Uniform Transfers to Minors Act (UTMA). For children 14 years of age or older, income-shifting benefits are possible, since they are not subject to the kiddie tax. However, gifts to children who are at least 14 do not leave much time for accumulating a large college fund out of tax savings.

For younger children, at least $1,400 (in 1998) per year of unearned income can be sheltered from the parent's tax rate. Therefore, assuming the parents are in a 36 percent, 31 percent, or 28 percent bracket, the tax savings can be $504, $434, or $392 per year less the $105 of tax paid by the child on the second $700 of income received by the child (based on inflation-adjusted amounts for 1998). This can amount to a significant savings if the gift program is started early.

A gift to a UGMA or UTMA account, generally called a custodial account, generally qualifies for the annual gift tax exclusion. The gift is completed by opening an account and transferring property to a custodian for the benefit of the minor child. Specially drafted legal documents usually are not required; however, the minor must have a social security number.

The types of assets which can be transferred to a custodial account are defined by state law. In some states, the asset categories are limited to money, securities, and insurance policies. Other states have expanded the list to include real estate, partnership interests, and other investment properties. The trend has been to a broader definition of eligible investments for custodial accounts. Your banker or broker can tell you which types of investments qualify for custodial accounts in your state.

The custodian of the custodial account has general investment powers over the account and has discretion to apply the principal and income in the account for the benefit of the minor. The property placed in a custodial account vests immediately and irrevocably in the minor at the time of transfer. Also, the entire principal and income of the custodial account must be delivered to the minor when the custodianship ends (typically at age 18 or 21). If the minor dies during the custodianship, the balance in the account must be delivered to the minor's estate.

The income from a custodial account is taxed to the minor unless and to the extent that the income is used to discharge a legal obligation of another person, in which case the income is taxed to that person. If, for example, the funds are used to meet the parent's legal obligation to support the minor, the income will be taxed to the parent.

The major advantages of the custodial account are its

(1) simplicity,

(2) low cost, and

(3) ease of administration.

The possible disadvantages include

(1) loss of parental control over assets,

(2) inflexible distribution requirements at termination of custodianship,

(3) questions about education as a "support" item,

(4) the kiddie tax rules, which reduce or eliminate tax savings, and

(5) the prospect of the child receiving more money than he is capable of managing (or willing to apply toward the intended purposes).

The types of assets that are placed in a custodial account can have a significant effect on the tax benefits. If a child is under age 14, the custodial account could be partially funded with tax-free, tax-deferred, or low-income/high-appreciation investments in order to postpone realization of excess taxable income until the child attains age 14. Such investments include:

EE bonds;

Zero coupon municipal bonds;

Tax-deferred annuities;

Single-premium life insurance;

Growth stocks;

Stocks in a closely held business;

Land; or

Other growth-oriented assets that do not produce significant current income.

Gifts of Appreciated Assets to Minors

Gifts of appreciated assets can provide significant tax savings. Such gifts are especially suitable when planning opportunities are limited because of the children being near the age when the funds are needed. If the child is age 14 or older, the tax on the gain can be shifted to the child's bracket by giving the appreciated asset and having the sale made in the name of the child. For example, assume parents own stock worth $20,000 that they acquired for $5,000 five years ago. If the parents are in the 31 percent tax bracket and the child is in the 15 percent tax bracket, the family can save up to $1,570 in taxes by giving the stock to the child, who immediately sells it to pay college expenses. This tax savings is computed as follows:

Taxable Gain Transferred from Parent to Child:

Market Value	$20,000	
Less Cost	(5,000)	
Gain	$15,000	
Parents' tax rate	x .20	
Parents tax		$ 3,000
Child's tax cost		
Taxable gain	$15,000	
Less excludible portion	(700)	
Taxable income	$14,300	
Child's tax rate	x .10	
Child's tax		$ 1,430
Family Tax Savings		$ 1,570

The gift of appreciated property qualifies for the annual $10,000 ($20,000 joint) gift tax exclusion and the parent's holding period carries over to the child.

Interest-Free Loans and Below-Market Interest Loans

Under the rules for below-market loans, interest-free or low-interest "demand loans" (loans which may be called at any time by the lender) are treated as follows: the lender (parent) is deemed to have made a loan to the borrower (child) at the "applicable federal rate," a rate which is established and published monthly by the IRS. At the end of the calendar year, the child is deemed to have paid the parent interest at a rate equal to the applicable federal rate; therefore, the parent has interest income as if the imputed interest had been paid. The parent is then deemed to have made a gift to the child in the amount of that interest. The interest deemed to have been paid by the child will be subject to the general limitations on deduction of interest.

The imputed interest rules were devised to prevent income-splitting, but there are certain limited exceptions.

The first exception to the general rule applies if the total amount of outstanding loans to a child does not exceed $10,000. However, if the loan is directly attributable to the purchase or carrying of income-producing assets, the rules do apply. What this means is that if the loan proceeds are invested in income-producing assets or placed in a savings account, the $10,000 exception will not apply.

The second exception allows a loan of up to $100,000 to escape the rules, as long as the child's net investment income (from all sources) for the year does not exceed $1,000. If the child's net investment income does exceed $1,000, the amount of interest treated as being transferred is limited to the amount of the child's net investment income.

The application of the $10,000 exception depends on how the specific funds are spent; in contrast, the application of the $100,000 exception depends on how much investment income the child has. The following examples illustrate these rules:

Example 1. Assume a father makes a loan of $10,000 to his son who has net investment income of $2,000. The son uses the loan to pay tuition. Assuming the principal purpose of the loan is not tax avoidance, the imputed interest rules do not apply because the loan qualifies under the $10,000 de minimis exception. However, if the son had placed the $10,000 in a savings account, the interest would have to be imputed.

Example 2. Mother makes a $100,000 loan to her son who has no investment income. Son uses the money to buy a house. The imputed interest rules do not apply and the loan qualifies under the $100,000 exception. But, if son had $5,000 of investment income that year, the imputed interest rules would apply. However, the imputed interest would be limited to the amount of net investment income, $5,000.

The Family Partnership

A gift to children of an interest in a family partnership can also be an income-splitting device. The tax savings are limited, however, by the kiddie tax rules for children under age 14. If the child is age 14 or older, the income will be taxed at the child's tax rate.

There are several potential pitfalls in the use of family partnerships for family income shifting:

(1) In most cases, children will not be recognized as partners unless it can be shown that the children are competent to manage their own affairs. Consequently, partnership interests owned by minors should generally be held in trust or in an UGMA account with an independent custodian.

(2) Many states recognize a trust as a legal partner but there are some that do not.

(3) If the partnership interest is given to the trust by the parent, an independent trustee relationship should be established.

(4) Control by the parent in any form can jeopardize recognition of the partnership interest.

(5) If the trust for the children receives its partnership interest by gift and does not contribute any services, capital must be a significant factor in producing the income of the partnership for the Internal Revenue Service to recognize the children's partnership interest.

(6) A child's interest in a personal service partnership (one in which most of the income is generated by commissions and fees) is generally not recognized by the Internal Revenue Service. This is because the partnership would be unable to satisfy the IRS requirement that capital be a significant income-producing factor.

S Corporations

A family-owned S corporation can be used to shift income to children in much the same way that a family partnership can. In contrast with the family partnership, S corporation stock can be owned even if capital is not a significant income-producing factor. However, this is not true in the case of a professional corporation electing S corporation treatment; shares cannot be transferred to a family member who is not licensed if the shareholders must be professionally licensed under state law to hold shares. For example, a doctor's stock in her medical S corporation cannot be transferred to her minor daughter or to a trust for her benefit—even if it were a trust that could otherwise hold S corporation stock.

Income-shifting and splitting may be accomplished by transferring S corporation shares to children because the tax treatment of S corporations resembles that of a partnership. Income, losses, deductions, and credits are passed through to the shareholders and are reported on the shareholder's individual returns. The kiddie tax rules apply to S corporation income. Therefore, the benefits of income splitting will be limited unless the child has attained age 14. (But planners should keep in mind estate tax and other advantages).

In most cases, children will not be providing significant services to the corporation. However, children may be employed by the corporation to perform services commensurate with their age and abilities. Consequently, an S corporation can be used to shift income in two ways: through payment for services to the corporation and through distributions of profits to children who are shareholders.

In some cases it may be wise to use a custodial account or trust to hold the minor's stock. The use of a custodial account may be less complicated and less expensive, but does not provide for as much flexibility as a trust. In most states, the custodial arrangement ends at age 18, at which time the children take possession of the stock. At that point, the children may use the funds for any purpose they desire (which may or may not include paying for their college education).

If a trust is used to hold minor children's stock, the trust must be a "QSST" (Qualified Subchapeter S Trust). What constitutes a qualified subchapter S trust is beyond this discussion; there are complex restrictions on areas such as how the trust is to be structured, who is eligible to be a beneficiary, and how income is to be distributed.

A QSST is indicated when

(1) a parent does not want to give stock to a child outright, or

(2) does not want the child to have ownership of the stock until he or she reaches a certain age, or

(3) if parents wish to distribute income on the stock to one beneficiary and later distribute the income and stock outright to another beneficiary when the trust terminates. (For example, the trust instrument could state that the income from the trust would go to the parent's child throughout his or her lifetime, and the remainder of the trust would go to a grandchild upon the child's death.)

Using the S corporation form for a family business, and transferring shares to children is especially suitable when the family may desire to transfer ownership of the business outright to the children at some later date as well as providing income for a college education.

Employing Children

One of the best methods for shifting income to children is to employ them in a family-owned business. Employing children has a double tax benefit. First, income is shifted to the lower-tax-bracket children and, second, the parent-employer receives a deduction for the amount paid in wages. The salary paid must be reasonable in relation to the services rendered, but the work performed need not be either significant or regular. For example, a child may be employed to clean the office, cut the grass, clear sidewalks of snow, perform maintenance or janitorial services, open the mail, make deliveries, or other similar tasks.

If the business is not incorporated, the services performed by a child under the age of eighteen are excluded from Social Security coverage. The business may deduct the salary or wage payment, but avoid the added expense of Social Security taxes that would be required if the compensation were paid to unrelated employees.

A parent/business owner employing a child in the business may generally claim a dependency exemption for the child if (a) the parent/business owner furnishes more than one-half the child's support and (b) the child is under 19 years of age or is a full-time student under age 24. If the child is 24 years of age or older and a full-time student, the parent is not entitled to the dependency exemption unless the child earns less than the exemption amount ($2,700 for tax years beginning in 1998).

A child who is a dependent may not claim any personal exemption but is allowed a standard deduction equal to the greater of (a) $700 or (b) the sum of $250 and the dependent's earned income (up to the appropriate standard deduction limit, e.g., $4,250 for single taxpayers for 1998; thereafter, indexed for inflation). In other words, in 1998, a child with earned income pays zero tax on the first $4,250 of earned income. Therefore, by employing a child, the business owner in the 31 percent bracket will save $1,318 in taxes for the first $4,250 in wages paid to each child. On any compensation in excess of $4,250 paid, the business owner will save the difference in taxes between the child's low-bracket amount and the parent's 31 percent bracket amount.

Children over 17 years of age can work any job, whether hazardous or not, for an unlimited number of hours. Under the Federal Fair Labor Standards Act, children aged 16 and 17 are restricted to nonhazardous jobs. They may work any type of nonhazardous job for an unlimited number of hours. If children are age 14 or 15, they may work no more than 3 hours on a school day and 18 hours in a school week, and are restricted to nonhazardous jobs. Fourteen is the minimum age for most nonfarm work unless the child works for the parent in a nonhazardous job, in a nonmanufacturing business owned by the parent. In that situation there is no minimum age. Planners must also check state and city laws regarding employment of minors.

The Gift-Leaseback Technique

The Tax Court has approved the gift-leaseback technique as a legitimate means of reducing tax liability and income-shifting. In the typical situation the taxpayer, such as a professional or perhaps a shareholder in a closely held corporation, establishes a trust for the children. Business property such as office buildings, furniture, equipment, autos, trucks, or machinery, is transferred to the trust, which agrees to lease it back to the taxpayer. The lease payments are then deductible by the high-bracket taxpayer and reported as income to the low-bracket trust beneficiaries (or to the trust if the income is accumulated).

If the children (the trust beneficiaries) have no other income, the first $700 of the shifted income to each child is exempt from tax (because of the dependent's exemption). The next $700, regardless of age, is taxed at the child's tax rates. If the child is under age 14, distributed income in excess of $1,400 is taxed at the parent's rates. This can be avoided by having the trust retain the income. If the child is 14 or over, the distributed income is taxed at the child's rates. When the property is ultimately transferred to the income beneficiary, or the residual beneficiary, if different, gains on sales of assets are taxable to the beneficiary, not the grantor. The parent taxpayer will also continue to be entitled to a personal exemption for each dependent child who is at least 50 percent supported, so long as the dependency tests are met.

Investment Vehicles

The selection of an appropriate investment vehicle for college education funds depends on many factors, including the time until the funds are needed, whether the parent or child will be the owner of the asset, the client's attitudes towards risk and return, tax rates, and the like. In other chapters of this book we have detailed descriptions of various investment vehicles. These chapters can assist you in selecting those which are most appropriate for your client's education fund. However, many clients are especially interested in investments that are particularly suitable for their children who are under age 14 (and thus subject to the kiddie tax rules), that provide tax advantages, or that provide certainty of value when college costs must be paid. The following sections briefly describe some of the investments that can meet these objectives.

Investments for Children Under Age 14; Investments for Tax Deferral

If funds are being transferred to a child under age 14, investments that minimize taxable income while providing relatively certain growth potential would be most suitable, since they will minimize the effect of the kiddie tax. Among those that the financial planner should consider are:

(1) Variable and Universal Life Insurance. Inside buildup is tax deferred or tax free; child may borrow cash value without paying tax on gains to pay college costs; secure.

(2) Deep-discount bonds. Market discounts on bonds issued before July 19, 1984 with low coupons (such as those issued in the 1950's and early 1960's) accrue on a tax-deferred basis. By leveraging the purchase of the bonds appropriately, you can create a combination investment where the interest expense just offsets the interest income that the bond pays and eliminates all taxable income during the holding period. In effect, such leveraging converts the taxable interest into tax-deferred discount that is recovered and taxed when the bonds mature. In other words, they become the equivalent of tax-deferred zero-coupon bonds. In addition, on maturity or sale of the bonds, the discount on these pre-July 19, 1984 bonds is treated as capital gain, not ordinary income. As a result, the discount will be subject to a maximum rate of 20%. These bonds also provide high certainty of value at maturity if they are high quality.

(3) Municipal bonds. Interest is free of federal income tax and, in many cases, state income tax. (See chapter 33.)

(4) High-growth, low-dividend stocks. Tax on gain is deferred until recognized upon disposition. If leveraged, interest expense offsets dividend income and increases growth potential. In this way, leveraged growth stocks are similar to deep-discount bonds, except that there is much less certainty of value when the funds are needed for college. However, if there is at least 10 years until college begins, the risk/return potential is favorable as compared with bonds. (See Chapter 15, "Risk and Reward" for further discussion of the risk and return relationships of various assets for various holding periods.)

(5) High-growth, low-dividend stock mutual funds. Similar to high-growth, low-dividend stocks except that leveraging possibilities are more limited and some capital gains must be recognized and are subject to tax when the fund declares capital gains dividends each year.

(6) Series EE savings bonds. Tax on accruing interest is deferred; high certainty of value.

Special Income Exclusion for Series EE Bonds

For Series EE bonds purchased after 1989, a parent who redeems these bonds — and pays certain education expenses of his child in the same year — may be entitled to exclude the accrued interest on the bonds. This exclusion is subject to the following limitations:

BOND OWNERSHIP REQUIREMENT. In order to qualify for the exclusion, the owner must have purchased the bonds after having attained the age of 24, and must be the sole owner of the bonds or own the bonds jointly with a spouse. The exclusion is not available to an individual who is the owner of a Series EE bond which was purchased by another individual, other than a spouse. For example, the exclusion is not available if a parent purchases a Series EE bond and puts the bond in the name of a child or another dependent. Also, the exclusion is not available for married taxpayers who do not file jointly. Furthermore, the exclusion is not available for any bonds which might be obtained as part of a tax-free rollover of matured Series E savings bonds into Series EE savings bonds.

QUALIFIED EDUCATIONAL EXPENSES. Qualifying educational expenses include tuition and required fees for a taxpayer, or the taxpayer's spouse or dependents, net of scholarships, fellowships, employer-provided educational assistance, and other tuition reduction amounts at an eligible educational institution. Such expenses do not include expenses with respect to any course or other education involving sports, games, hobbies, other than as part of a degree or certificate granting program.

LIMITATION WHERE REDEMPTION AMOUNT EXCEEDS QUALIFIED EXPENSES. If the aggregate redemption amount, that is, principal plus interest, of all Series EE bonds redeemed by the taxpayer during the taxable year does not exceed the amount of the student's qualified educational expenses, all interest for the year on the bonds is potentially excludable. For example, if the redemption amount is $10,000 ($5,000 each of principal and interest), and qualified educational expenses are $12,000, the entire $5,000 of interest may be excluded from income (subject to the phaseout described below). However, where the redemption amount exceeds the qualified educational expenses, the amount of excludable interest is reduced on a pro-rata basis. For example, if the redemption amount is $10,000 ($5,000 each of principal and interest), and qualified educational expenses are $8,000, then the ratio of expenses to redemption amount is 80 percent ($8,000/$10,000) and $4,000 (5,000 x .80) of the interest may thus be excluded from income.

PHASEOUT OF EXCLUSION WHERE INCOME EXCEEDS CERTAIN AMOUNTS. The exclusion is phased out for taxpayers with what is called "modified adjusted gross income" (MAGI) of $52,250 (as indexed for 1998, $78,350 for joint filers) or more for the taxable year. No amount is excludable for taxpayers whose MAGI exceeds $67,250 (in 1998; $108,350 for joint filers).

Modified adjusted gross income (MAGI) is defined as the taxpayer's adjusted gross income for the taxable year including what would otherwise be excluded foreign earned income (or certain income of residents of Puerto Rico, Guam, American Samoa, or the Northern Mariana Islands), the partial inclusion of Social Security and Tier 1 Railroad Retirement benefits, the adjustments for contributions of retirement savings, and the adjustments with respect to limitations of passive activity losses and credits.

The amount that may be excluded when a taxpayer's MAGI falls within the phaseout range may be determined using the following formulas.

For singles and heads of households whose MAGI exceeds $52,250:

(1) Adjusted Exclusion = Unadjusted Exclusion x [1 - (MAGI - $52,250) / $15,000].

For married taxpayers whose MAGI exceeds $78,350:

(2) Adjusted Exclusion = Unadjusted Exclusion x [1 - (MAGI - $78,350) / $30,000].

Example 1. Assume a married taxpayer filing jointly who has a MAGI of $83,350 redeems bonds worth $10,000 ($5,000 principal and $5,000 interest) and pays qualified educational expenses of $13,000. The unadjusted exclusion is $5,000 since the qualified expenses exceed the redemption amount. Therefore, the adjusted exclusion using the formula shown in (2) above is $4,167 [$5,000 x (1 - ($83,350- $78,350)/ $30,000)].

Example 2. Assume a single taxpayer who has a MAGI of $62,250 redeems bonds worth $12,000 ($6,000 each of principal and interest) and pays qualified educational expenses of $9,000. The unadjusted exclusion is 75 percent of $6,000, or $4,500. (Remember, if the redemption amount exceeds the qualified expenses, the amount

of interest that is excludable is determined by multiplying the interest by the ratio of the total expenses to the total redemption amount.) Therefore, the adjusted exclusion using the formula shown in (1) above is $1,500 [$4,500 x (1 - ($62,250 - $52,250)/ $15,000)].

The phaseout levels are indexed annually for inflation; consequently, the phaseout will begin at higher nominal (but essentially the same real) level of income in future years.

Investments with Certainty in Reinvestment Rate or Return

One problem facing any accumulation program is the uncertainty regarding the rate that can be earned on reinvested income and, consequently, the uncertainty regarding the amount that will ultimately be accumulated by the target date. If your client wants certainty of value when the funds are needed to pay college expenses, the following investments should be considered:

(1) Zero-coupon bonds. Zeros sell at a discount from face value and pay no cash interest. At maturity zeros pay their face value. Consequently, investors who hold the bonds to maturity are guaranteed that they will receive a rate of return equal to the original yield to maturity regardless of what happens to reinvestment rates over the term until the bond matures. However, most zero-coupon bonds are callable. Therefore, investors bear some risk, if the bonds are called before maturity, that they will not be able to reinvest the proceeds at a rate comparable to their original yield on the bonds.

(2) Stripped bonds. Stripped bonds are artificially created zero-coupon bonds. These bonds are created by investment bankers who "strip" the coupons from the bond and sell the principal portion at a discount from face value. Strips are sometimes issued with "call protection," a guarantee against early redemption of the bonds that would force investors to reinvest the proceeds at potentially lower yields. The call protection feature is especially attractive on municipal bond strips since municipal bonds are generally much more likely to be called than taxable bonds.

(3) Bunny bonds. These are bonds issued with rights to purchase additional bonds with the same coupon and terms as the original bond. Bunny bondholders may direct their coupon payments on the bonds to be used to purchase additional bonds, thus guaranteeing their reinvestment rate of return.

(4) College Sure CDs. College Savings Bank of Princeton, New Jersey offers CDs whose interest payments are tied to an index of the tuition costs of major colleges and universities. Investors are guaranteed that the CDs will mature with a value that has kept pace with increases in the cost of college tuition.

(5) Deep-discount bonds. These are similar to zero-coupon bonds. Investors are guaranteed that the portion of the return attributable to the discount will accrue at the original yield to maturity if the bonds are held to maturity.

WHERE CAN I FIND OUT MORE?

(1) *Applying for Financial Aid* (American College Testing Program, Iowa City, IA, yearly publication).

(2) *Profiles of American Colleges* (Barron's Educational Series, Inc., Woodbury, NY, yearly).

(3) *Getting Through the College Aid Maze* (College Planning Service, Hauppage, NY, 1986).

(4) *Don't Miss Out: the Ambitious Student's Guide to Financial Aid* (Octameron Associates, Alexandria, VA, yearly).

(5) *The A's and B's: Your Guide to Academic Scholarships* (Octameron Associates, Alexandria, VA, yearly).

(6) *College Loans from Uncle Sam* (Octameron Associates, Alexandria, VA, yearly).

(7) John Lyons, *How to Pay Your Way Through College (the Smart Way): How to Make More than $5,000 a Year in College—by the Students who Actually Did It!* (Banbury Books, Inc. Wayne, PA, 1984.)

(8) *The Student Guide*: The Student Guide is published by the U.S. Department of Education and provides definitive information about federal aid programs, including Pell Grants, Federal Direct Loans, Federal Family Education Loans (FEEL), Federal Supplemental Educational Opportunity Grants (FSEOG), Federal Work-Study (FWS), and Federal Perkins Loans (Federal Student Aid Information Center, Washington D.C., yearly).

(9) *Cash for College and Timely Information for Parents and Students (TIPS)*: The NAFSA Public Page includes the complete text of two publications for students and their families from the National Association of Student Financial Aid Administrators (NASFAA). The Cash for College pamphlet summarizes basic information about getting financial aid for college. The Timely Information for Parents and Students (TIPS) book provides an in-depth overview of student financial aid (Washington D.C., NASFAA - serial).

(10) *Preparing Your Child for College: A Resource Book for Parents (1996-1997)*: This is an online version of the 57 page publication by the U.S. Department of Education. It talks about the benefits of a college education and how to prepare your children for college educationally and financially. The topics include choosing a college, how much college will cost, how you will be able to afford it, the most common sources of financial aid, some ways to keep college costs down, setting up a long-range plan, and sources of further information. This booklet is also available as a ZIP file for anonymous FTP. This publication is also available from the Consumer Information Center on their gopher. A paper copy may be ordered by calling 1-800-USA-LEARN (Washington D.C., U.S. Dept. of Education, serial).

(11) *A Guide to Student Aid Programs and Procedures*: Published by the National Association of Student Financial Aid Administrators, 1920 L Street, N.W., Suite 200, Washington D.C., 20036.

(12) *Websites* - A helpful list of websites that can assist in college planning can be found on The Vanguard Group website at www.vanguard.com.

Chapter 5

ESTATE PLANNING

Many financial planners view the accumulation of wealth as the primary objective of most clients and, indeed, for most clients, building wealth is a primary goal. But wealth may fail to accomplish many of the client's most important goals and needs if, at the client's death or disability, it is lost or poorly used. Thus, planning for these events is an important part of the financial planner's art.

The purpose of this chapter is to provide an overview of estate planning and to alert planners to common problems and classic opportunities of estate planning. Because it is an overview, it does not cover all the tools or techniques of estate planning nor does it treat any in depth. (We wrote THE TOOLS AND TECHNIQUES OF ESTATE PLANNING for those who want a solid foundation in estate planning and recommend the latest edition to all financial planners.)

The following topics will be covered:

(1) The definition and objectives of estate planning

(2) Why client control is so important

(3) People planning

(4) Why estate planning is not only for the wealthy

(5) Problems clients face

(6) Steps in the planning process

(7) Events triggering a need for a review

(8) The will as the cornerstone of the process

(9) Intestacy

(10) Letter of instructions

(11) Administration of an estate

(12) Joint ownership

(13) Trusts

(14) Gift giving

(15) Computing the federal estate tax

(16) The generation-skipping transfer tax

ESTATE PLANNING DEFINED

In the broadest sense estate planning is the accumulation, conservation, and distribution of wealth in the manner that most efficiently and effectively accomplishes the client's objectives. An alternative definition emphasizing the "planning" aspect is that estate planning is a goal-oriented activity that uses tax minimization tools and techniques to provide the greatest possible financial security for an individual and his beneficiaries. Regardless of which definition is used, it is obvious that estate planning is a key element of overall financial planning.

THE IMPORTANCE OF CONTROL

Every estate is planned. Some estates are planned by default: by inaction some people allow their estate plan to be dictated by the federal and state governments. The person who dies without a valid will (that is, dies "intestate") allows the state in which he lived to draw one for him and determine who his heirs will be and how and when they will receive their inheritance. Those heirs must live with what is left by the system of income and death taxation structured by the federal and state governments even though those costs could have been significantly reduced by thoughtful planning. Few clients would agree to purchase a "one size fits all" wardrobe, yet that is exactly what happens when, by default, they allow the state government to decide who will receive their property, when and in what manner their property will be received, and even who will be the guardians of their children's assets or persons.

The best estate planning is controlled by the estate owner and the financial services professionals he enlists. Such people use a variety of methods for reducing taxes and the other causes of estate erosion and they employ numerous tax and nontax tools and techniques to accomplish the client's objectives.

PEOPLE PLANNING

There are only two reasons for a client to engage in estate planning. The most obvious incentive is to build, conserve, and distribute assets. The less obvious, but more important, reason is the need for "people planning." In fact, from the financial planner's perspective, people planning should be the first and foremost consideration. People planning is the anticipation of the financial and psychological needs of those people and organizations the client loves or feels a duty towards. It involves providing adequate financial security in terms of absolute dollars and providing emotional assurance that loved ones will be able to continue their way of life. A great deal of what estate planning is designed to do is give people peace of mind.

Consider the extent of needs of the client who has minor children. "Would you leave young children at home without a babysitter?" "Would you allow a stranger to choose that person for your children?" Few clients would answer affirmatively to either question, yet it is incredible how many clients haven't named a guardian for their children in their wills. Think about the client with the exceptionally artistic or intellectually gifted child. Will the child have the financial means to fully develop that talent if the client doesn't prepare now? If the client dies or becomes disabled, who will care for a retarded, emotionally disturbed, or physically handicapped child or other dependent who is not self sufficient? What provision has been made for the spouse or child who is not intellectually or emotionally equipped or lacks experience (or just does not want) to manage large sums of money, a portfolio of securities, or an active business? Who will take care of aging parents and other relatives who depend on the client if the client does not or cannot care for them? Who cares for the client if the client cannot? (If the client does not prepare future care for himself in the event of a disability or prepare for his retirement, who will?)

IS ESTATE PLANNING ONLY FOR THE RICH?

At this point, it should be obvious that wealth should not be the planner's sole focus, although money is an essential part of the estate planning equation. It is a common misconception among most clients that estate planning is only for the wealthy. Although it is essential for those who have accumulated substantial wealth, estate planning may be even more important for those of modest or moderate wealth. Every dollar lost unnecessarily to taxes or administrative costs hurts survivors more when the estate is small. (The rich man's family can afford his mistakes better than the family of the man of modest or moderate wealth). Money saved and income provided by a well thought out tax savings device, even if it's only putting the right title on a bank savings account, will have the greatest significance where the potential tax threatens to wipe out a proportionately larger part of the client's assets.

PROBLEMS CLIENTS FACE

An estate often breaks up when the estate owner dies (or becomes disabled) — not because that person has done anything wrong — but because that person hasn't done anything. It is impossible to solve problems until you know what they are. What are the problems that clients need to address?

There are six major estate planning problems that the financial planner should consider in addressing the needs of clients:

(1) Lack of liquidity. This means insufficient cash. Test to see if there are enough assets in the client's estate that can quickly and inexpensively be turned into cash to meet tax demands and other estate settlement costs. Identify the specific source(s) from which the estate will pay last illness and funeral expenses, current and long term bills and debts, unpaid income taxes, attorney's, accountant's, and appraiser's fees, federal and state death taxes, and the additional costs of estate administration. A lack of liquidity is extremely serious because it often results in a forced sale at pennies on the dollar of the most valuable or important assets the client has (such as the family business or a precious heirloom). Sacrifice sales of assets with substantial income producing power, or the family business or farm not only results in a disproportionately large loss of income but sometimes results in a devastating psychological trauma that emotionally cripples survivors.

(2) Improper disposition of assets. Check various dispositive instruments such as life insurance policies, wills, trusts, joint bank accounts, pension plans and other employee benefit plans to see if assets are going to the wrong person at the wrong time or in the wrong manner. For instance, it would be inappropriate to put a high powered sports car in the hands of a child. Yet hundreds of thousands of dollars worth of assets are often left outright to beneficiaries who are unwilling or who are legally and/or intellectually or emotionally unable to manage them properly. An incompetent and his money are soon parted.

(3) Inadequate income or capital. It is essential that the financial planner quantify and verify that the client has adequate income sources or sufficient capital to provide for:

(a) retirement,

(b) the "special needs" discussed below,

(c) the family at the client's death, and

(d) the client if he becomes disabled. A long term disability is a "living death." The loss of income due to the disability is often coupled with a massive financial drain caused by the illness itself. Both problems are compounded by the inadequate management of currently owned assets. Together, these forces tend to diminish the client's net worth with frightening speed.

(4) Asset values destabilized and not maximized. Compare the value and marketability of assets "before and after" the various types of changes that occur over the life cycle of a client. For instance, will a client's business be worth the same (in terms of income producing ability or financial net worth) after his death, disability, or divorce as it was worth before such an event? The lack of a backup management team, the failure of heirs to note a change in consumer preferences, or product or equipment obsolescence may result in a rapid decline in the value of a decedent's business. Does the client have a buy-sell agreement? Is it in writing? Does the price in that agreement reflect the current worth of that business? Is the agreement funded adequately so that his family's fortune is not dependent on the business? Is a life insurance policy worth as much to a client's family if it is paid to his estate rather than to a named beneficiary (perhaps because the primary beneficiary died and there was no secondary beneficiary named)? Are assets needlessly exposed to the claims of creditors? Check to see what must be done to stabilize and maximize the value of the client's business and other assets.

(5) Excessive taxes and transfer costs. Is the client paying unreasonably high income taxes? Is there an opportunity to reduce or defer income tax? Run a hypothetical probate. (See "Computing the Federal Estate Tax" below.) See if the client will be paying more in death taxes and other estate settlement costs than necessary. Often, through various commonly used estate planning tools or techniques many thousands of dollars of income and transfer taxes can be saved within a family unit.

(6) Special needs. Uncover and address what may be the most important and difficult of all the estate planning problems the typical client has — his "special" problems. Special problems include a spouse who can not or will not handle money, property, or a family business. Such problems may also include the care of a dependent who is physically, emotionally, intellectually handicapped or mentally disturbed. Consider the importance of providing the proper financial support for exceptionally gifted children. Special needs also include the desire to provide meaningful financial support to schools, churches, synagogues, or other institutions and charities.

STEPS IN THE ESTATE PLANNING PROCESS

There are seven major steps in the estate planning process designed (a) to measure the client's needs, (b) to establish an order of priority in addressing these needs, and (c) to give first preference to those needs or problems which the client feels are most important. These seven steps are:

(1) Gather comprehensive and accurate data on all aspects of the client and the client's family including goals and desires.

(2) Categorize the data into general problem areas such as the six major areas described above.

(3) Estimate estate transfer costs and other liquidity needs. This amount is generally the sum of cash bequests in the client's will plus

(a) funeral and administrative expenses,

(b) debts and taxes,

(c) the state death tax payable, and

(d) the net federal estate tax payable.

(4) Set priorities for problems and prepare alternative solutions to each.

(5) With the client and other advisers, formulate the overall plan (decide what can and should be done and the order in which things should be done) and determine the implementation procedure (decide which parties are responsible for each task and establish a timetable for action).

(6) Test and implement the plan.

(7) Review the plan.

REVIEWING THE ESTATE PLAN

As is the case with financial planning, an estate plan is good for only as long as it fits the needs, desires, and circumstances of the parties involved. As these factors change, so must the plan. Among the events that should trigger a review are:

(1) Marriage or remarriage, separation or divorce.

(2) Birth or death.

(3) Change of job.

(4) Move to a new state.

(5) Significant change in income, wealth, or living standard.

(6) Change in health.

(7) Major change in tax law.

Automatic in-depth estate analysis reviews should be scheduled at least every three years in addition to normal annual financial security checkups. (We call these "Financial Fire Drills.")

THE WILL: CORNERSTONE OF THE ESTATE PLANNING PROCESS

Defined

A will is the legal expression or testament of a "testator's" wishes as to the disposition of his "probate" estate at the time of his death. A will does not and cannot direct the disposition of assets which pass outside of probate. Among these "nonprobate" assets are assets which pass at death by contract or by operation of law such as:

(1) life insurance payable to a named beneficiary other than the estate or its executor (as executor),

(2) qualified retirement plan proceeds,

(3) IRA death benefits,

(4) jointly owned property (real or personal) with right of survivorship,

(5) nonqualified deferred compensation death benefits, and

(6) assets in a revocable or irrevocable living trust.

A will can be changed or revoked at any time prior to the testator's death. It becomes operative only upon the testator's

death and applies only to the probate assets and situation that exist at that time.

Anyone can draft his own will. But only an attorney should. The knowledge of tax, corporate, domestic relations, property, trust, real estate, and securities laws that must be considered and integrated into the will-writing process makes the "do it yourself" will dangerous and expensive. The costs, unfortunately, of an error of omission or commission must be paid by those least able to afford the expense, the testator's survivors. The more affordable and recommended method — employing a competent attorney — will usually run about $100 for a simple will and approximately $1,500 to $5,000, depending on their complexity, for a will and trust. Wills, like any other tool or technique in estate planning, must be part of the entire process and must consider assets passing outside the probate estate.

A well drafted will should provide a plan for distributing probate assets according to the testator's desires and the beneficiaries' needs giving due consideration to federal and state tax and other laws. It should consider the potential for change in all these factors after the will is drawn. A will should be complete and unambiguous with respect to the testator's desires.

There is no standard format that every will must follow and every state has its own laws regarding the requirements for a valid will. Most wills should contain at least the following features (for an in-depth discussion, see Chapter 7, "How to Review a Will"):

(1) introduction,

(2) direction to pay debts and expenses,

(3) tax apportionment clause,

(4) disposition of personal property,

(5) disposition of real property,

(6) residuary clause,

(7) powers clause,

(8) appointment of fiduciary,

(9) common disaster or simultaneous death clause,

(10) execution clause,

(11) witness clause.

Each of these provisions must be carefully tailored to the client's individual needs and circumstances by an attorney familiar with state law as well as tax law.

Grounds For Contesting A Will

Every state imposes its own requirements that must be met if a will is to be considered valid. Generally, the requirements of a valid will are

(1) The testator must have "capacity"— both legal and mental. This means the testator must have been the statutory age (18 or 21 in most states) or older, and must have

(a) a full knowledge of the act in which he is involved,

(b) an understanding of the property he owns,

(c) a knowledge of the disposition he wants to make, and

(d) an appreciation of the parties who are the natural objects of his bounty.

(Typically, if there is legal capacity, the courts will presume there is mental capacity. A contestant to the validity of a will on the ground of "incapacity" has the burden of proving a lack of capacity with clear and convincing evidence.)

(2) The testator must have freedom of choice. A will is considered invalid if by clear and convincing evidence, it can be shown that the testator was subject to the undue influence of some other person at the time the will was drawn and executed. The types of undue influence that can prove a lack of freedom of choice include threats, misrepresentations, inordinate flattery, or a physical or mental or emotional coercion.

(3) The will must be properly executed. Every state has a specific statute that spells out the form a will must take (usually in writing), where it must be signed (typically at its logical conclusion), how it must be signed (usually in ink), and the requirements for the signature of witnesses (three witnesses is the maximum any state requires). Some states allow a will to be "self proving." This means if a testator's signing of the will is witnessed by at least three individuals who sign in the presence of each other and of a notary, those witnesses do not have to appear at the probate of the will. This can save time, money, and aggravation. It is suggested that professionals consider that clients of-

ten move to a new state after signing a will. Therefore, the document should routinely comply with the most stringent requirements of any state rather than meet the least demanding state's rules.

Codicils

A will can be changed through a "codicil." Because the will does not become effective until the testator's death, it can be changed at any time until then. The codicil is a simple and convenient way to make minor changes in a will. Usually it is a very short document which states the change desired but reaffirms all the existing provisions in the will except for that change.

The codicil must be executed in accordance with the same formalities as a will. It should be typed, signed, and witnessed in the same manner as the will.

There are situations in which a new will, rather than a codicil, is indicated. The old will should be destroyed and a new will rather than a codicil should be used when:

(1) Significant changes are to be made.

(2) The size of the gift in the will is to be reduced or where a beneficiary is to be deleted. (It may offend the beneficiary or even encourage a will contest if the change is made by codicil because if a codicil is used the original will must nonetheless be probated.)

Conversely, the old will should be retained and a codicil or a new will should be used when:

(1) The testator is older or in poor health and there is a strong potential that the will may be contested. (If for any reason the new will fails, the prior will may qualify and protect most of the testator's intended gift.)

(2) A charitable gift was made in the first will and now a larger charitable gift is contemplated but there is a high probability that the new will may be contested. (The original will can be used to show that the larger gift to charity is not merely an afterthought or the result of a mind unduly influenced by the charity).

Revocation and Modification

Wills, of course, can be revoked. Actually, both the testator and the law can revoke or modify a will. A testator can revoke a will by:

(1) making a later will which revokes a prior will,

(2) making a codicil expressly revoking a will,

(3) making a later will inconsistent with a former will,

(4) physically mutilating, burning, tearing, or defacing the will with the intention of revoking it.

State law can revoke or modify a will automatically under circumstances which vary from state to state but often include:

(1) Divorce of the testator. (In some states, if the testator divorces after making a will, all the provisions in the will relating to the former spouse are invalid.)

(2) Marriage of the testator. (If the testator marries after making a will, the spouse receives the portion of the probate estate he would have received had the testator died without a valid will — unless the will provides for a larger share.)

(3) Birth or adoption. (If the testator did not provide for a child born or adopted after the will was made and did not clearly state in the will that the omission was intentional, the child receives that share of the estate that the child would have received after a surviving spouse's share is taken out, had there been no will. (See the discussion of intestacy below.)

(4) Murder. (Many states have "slayers bounty" statutes that prohibit a person who participated in a willful and unlawful murder from acquiring property as a result of the deed.)

Aside from providing for contesting the validity of a will and for its revocation, many states provide another way by which the dispositive result can be changed: this is known as a "right of election." A right of election, typically given only to a surviving spouse, is a right to choose to "take against the will," that is, to take a specified portion of the probate estate regardless of what the will provides. One state, for instance, allows a surviving spouse to take that share the spouse would have been allowed had the deceased died without a valid will. This right is generally forfeited by a spouse who deserted the testator or who participated in the testator's willful and unlawful murder.

Safeguarding the Will

Safeguarding the will is extremely important. Usually, a will should be kept together with all a client's important

documents in a safe deposit box. (Check first on your state's rules that take effect when a safe deposit box owner dies. Although some states "freeze" the contents of the box and require that it remain sealed until state tax authorities can inventory the contents of the box, in most states a surviving spouse can quickly gain access to the will). Although some authorities recommend leaving the original of a will with the attorney who wrote it, this may make it awkward for the executor to exercise his right to choose the estate's attorney, a right provided by many states' laws regardless of who drew the will. Some states provide for the "lodging" of a will; a mechanism for filing and safekeeping it in the office of the probate court (sometimes called orphans' or surrogate's court).

INTESTACY

The absence of a valid will at death is called "intestacy." State intestacy laws provide a will for the person who did not draw his own. State law, therefore, determines (a) who is entitled to receive an intestate decedent's probate property, (b) how such individuals will receive their shares (typically outright in a lump sum), and (c) when those shares will be paid out (usually, at the conclusion of the probate process or, if later, when the beneficiary reaches legal majority).

Generally, intestacy statutes enumerate certain preferred classes of survivors:

Decedent's spouse,

Decedent's children and other descendants,

Decedent's parents,

Decedent's brothers and sisters.

The distribution of a typical intestate estate is shown in Figure 5.1.

LETTER OF INSTRUCTIONS

A "letter of instructions" is an informal nonlegal way to convey highly personal thoughts and directions that cannot or should not be included in a will. A letter of instructions (see the sample form in Appendix K) might provide the following information:

(1) Location of the will and other key documents.

(2) Funeral and burial instructions (remember that a will is often not opened until long after the funeral).

Figure 5.1

DISTRIBUTION OF A TYPICAL INTESTATE ESTATE		
Decedent Dies Leaving	**Distribution**	
Spouse and children or their descendants	Spouse receives one third	Children receive two thirds divided equally
Spouse and one child or child's descendants	Spouse receives one half	Child receives one half
Spouse but no children or their descendants, and decedent's mother or father survives	Spouse receives $10,000 plus one half of balance	Father and mother or surviving parent (if one is already deceased) receive one half of balance
Spouse but no children or their descendants, and no parent survives	Spouse receives $10,000 plus one half of balance	Brothers and sisters receive other half of balance divided equally
Spouse but no children or their descendants, and no parent, brother, sister, niece, nephew, grandparent, uncle, or aunt survives	Spouse receives all	
Child or children but no spouse		Child or children receive all divided equally
No spouse and no children or their descendants, and decedent's mother or father survives		Mother and father receive all
No spouse and no children or their descendants, and no parent of the decedent survives		Brothers and sisters receive all divided equally

(3) Suggestions or recommendations as to the continuation, sale, or liquidation of a business (it is easier to speak frankly and freely in the letter than in the will).

(4) Personal matters the client might prefer not to be made public (such as statements that might seem unkind, harsh, or inconsiderate but that would prove of value to the executor; for instance, a letter of instructions could provide guidance as to who could or could not be trusted or how to handle a spendthrift spouse or child addicted to drugs).

(5) Legal and accounting services (remember that because of the high personal liability that "comes with the job," executors typically have the legal right to

their own choice of counsel — regardless of who may be named in the will).

(6) An explanation of why certain actions were taken in the will (which may help avoid litigation). For instance, "I left only $1,000 for my son, Bouillabaisse, because..."

HOW AN ESTATE IS ADMINISTERED

The administration of an estate can be a short and relatively simple process or it can be a drawn out and complex nightmare involving thousands of hours of work and dozens or even hundreds of difficult choices. Essentially, however, there are three main stages common to all administrations:

(1) safeguarding and collecting the decedent's assets,

(2) paying of debts and taxes,

(3) distribution of any remainder to the heirs specified in the will or under state intestacy law.

In other words, when a person dies a process similar to a business liquidation occurs. Money owed to the decedent is collected, creditors (including all taxing authorities) must be satisfied, and what is left is distributed to the appropriate individuals and organizations.

This process—also called probate—is generally supervised through a local court called a probate court (although sometimes called an orphans' or surrogate's court). The person who represents the decedent and in many ways "stands in the shoes of the decedent" with respect to legal matters is generally called the "personal representative." Male personal representatives, serving in situations where the decedent died "testate," i.e., with a valid will, are called executors. More than one executor can serve at a time and can be one or more individuals, corporate fiduciaries, or a combination of one or more persons and one or more corporations. The female counterpart of an executor is an "executrix."

When there is no valid will, the court will appoint an administrator (or administratrix). This person has much the same responsibility and same powers as an executor (although an executor's power can be expanded by the will beyond those permitted under state law).

Why is the administrative process important? There are three major reasons. The first is that bank accounts could not be collected and contracts could not be enforced if there were no one legally charged with that responsibility and given that authority. The second reason is that without the probate process, title to property would be forever clouded with uncertainty. Real estate could not be made marketable because there would be no "chain of title" and no mechanism for proving that claims against the real estate had been satisfied. The third reason the administration process is important is the assurance to both the testator and heirs that the court will see that the decedent's wishes are carried out and that the appropriate heirs receive the property to which they are entitled. The probate process is therefore a device to safeguard the interests of the estate's beneficiaries (as well as to assure state taxes are paid, which they would in most states whether or not an asset "avoids probate").

JOINT OWNERSHIP DEFINED

Aside from community property in which each spouse is, generally speaking, deemed to own half of a married couple's assets, the major ways that people hold title to property are (1) sole name, (2) tenancy in common, (3) joint tenancy with right of survivorship, and (4) tenancy by the entirety.

At death property owned in the sole name of the client will pass under the client's will if there is a valid will or by state intestacy laws if no valid will exists.

Tenancy in common means that each tenant (co-owner) holds an interest that can be left to whomever he chooses. The property interest of a tenant in common will pass just as sole name property passes — either by will or intestacy. For instance, assume Ted and Steve own BlackandBlue Acre as tenants in common: at Ted's death his one half interest in the property will pass to the person or persons named in his will (or under state intestacy laws if he had no valid will). During Ted's lifetime, he has the right to give away or sell his interest in the property. He does not need the consent of his co-tenant, Steve, to take either action.

A joint tenancy with right of survivorship is a form of property ownership which can involve any number of persons who may or may not be related by blood or marriage. At any time, any co-tenant can sever (sell or give away) his interest without the consent of the other co-tenant. At the death of one co-tenant, his interest passes to the other owner(s) by operation of law regardless of his will and regardless of state intestacy law. That interest passes free from the claims of the decedent's creditors, heirs, or personal representatives. For instance, if Ted and Steve were joint tenants with right of survivorship, at Ted's death, his interest would pass automatically and immediately to the surviving co-tenant, Steve.

A tenancy by the entirety is similar to a joint tenancy. The decedent's interest will pass immediately and automatically outside the probate estate to the surviving joint tenant. But there are some major differences:

(1) A tenancy by the entirety can exist only between a husband and wife.

(2) A tenancy by the entirety cannot be severed unilaterally; such property can be sold or given away only by (a) mutual agreement, (b) by divorce or (c) conveyance by both spouses to a third party.

(3) A joint tenancy with right of survivorship can exist with any type of property. In some states a tenancy by the entirety can exist only with respect to real property while some other states do not recognize such tenancies at all.

Advantages and Disadvantages Of Joint Ownership

The major advantage of joint tenancy with right of survivorship is that it offers a sense of family security, quick and easy transfer of property at death, exemption of the property from the claims of the deceased co-tenant's creditors, and avoidance of the delays and costs of probate. This type of property arrangement is well suited to smaller less complex estates of married couples where gift and death taxes are not major factors.

But there are disadvantages that must be considered. First, jointly owned property cannot be controlled by will. Therefore, the first owner to die has lost control of the ultimate disposition of the property. This loss is particularly destructive where the parties are (a) unmarried co-habiting couples, (b) three or more relatives, (c) friends, or (d) partners. For instance, assume a widowed mother adds a son's name to the title of her home as a joint tenant with right of survivorship. Consider:

(1) "senior citizens benefits" lost or reduced,

(2) the implication if the new co-tenant sells or gives away or loses his interest to creditors or to tax liens,

(3) if the new co-tenant dies first, the parent may have to pay inheritance tax to get her own property back,

(4) the mother may remarry and wish to give or will her share to her new spouse or future children,

(5) upon the divorce of the son, the mother may be a co-tenant with her ex-daughter in law (and the ex-daughter in law's new husband or boyfriend).

There are other disadvantages besides the loss of control and the loss of ability to direct how the property will be managed or invested. Higher potential tax costs may be incurred upon both the creation and the severance of jointly held property. For instance, a mother who purchases and pays for property and then places it in her name and her son's name is making a gift to the son. Upon the termination of the tenancy, if the son receives the entire proceeds (say on the sale of a jointly owned home), the mother is making a second gift to the son. At both times the mother is transferring an interest to the son that he did not have before.

TRUSTS DEFINED

A trust is a legal arrangement which facilitates the transfer, management, investment, and disposition of property and/or its income. Formally, a trust is the relationship created when one party, the "grantor" (also known as the settlor or creator) transfers cash or other property (the principal or "res" — pronounced "race") to a second party, the "trustee" (the person responsible for carrying out the terms of the trust) for the benefit of third parties, the beneficiaries (who may or may not include the grantor).

The trustee holds legal title to the property placed in the trust. But that property, and any income it produces, must be used solely for the benefit of trust beneficiaries. The trust should be evidenced by a written document which details both substantive provisions (such as the limitations on the beneficiary's receipt of income or principal) and administrative provisions (such as how trust funds are or are not to be invested).

In general the trust document should spell out each of the following points:

(1) how the assets in the trust are to be managed and invested,

(2) who is to receive the income and eventually the principal,

(3) how income and principal are to be paid and upon what events or ages beneficiaries will receive their shares,

(4) who are the trustees and what are their powers and responsibilities.

A "living" trust (also called an "intervivos" trust) is one established during the lifetime of the grantor. A "testamentary" trust is one created under a will and doesn't actually take effect until the probate of the will. Living trusts may be "revocable" (the grantor reserves the right to change the terms of the trust or recover trust property at any time) or "irrevocable" (the terms of the trust cannot be altered or amended by the grantor and assets in the trust cannot be recovered during the existence of the trust).

Purposes of Trusts

There are literally dozens of reasons why property is placed into trust. Most trusts are used either (a) to achieve a client's "people oriented" management, conservation, and dispositive objectives, (b) to save income, estate, or generation-skipping transfer taxes and transfer costs, or (c) to protect assets from the claims of creditors.

Some of the nontax situations that should trigger consideration of trusts in the mind of the financial planner include:

(1) When the client believes the beneficiary is unwilling or unable to invest, manage, or handle the responsibility of an outright gift. This is particularly important where the beneficiary lacks legal, emotional or intellectual maturity, physical capacity, or technical training to handle large sums of money or assets which require competent and constant management.

(2) When the client wants to postpone full ownership for some given period of time (such as until a child reaches age 30) or prevent ownership outside a narrow class of beneficiaries. For example, many parents want to provide financial security for their children but don't want assets to end up in the hands of former sons in law or daughters in law.

(3) When the client fears the possible results of an outright "no strings attached" transfer which lessens the donees' dependence on him.

(4) When the proposed gift property does not lend itself to fragmentation but the donor desires to spread beneficial ownership among a number of people. For instance, real estate or a large life insurance policy (and the ultimate proceeds generated at death) are often better held by a single trust than jointly by several individuals.

(5) When the gift consists of more than one property and there are two or more beneficiaries and the client is worried that the value of one property may appreciate and the other may fall. If the properties are left in trust, all beneficiaries can share appreciation (and risk) equally.

(6) When creditor protection is important. Arranged properly, trusts can provide protection from both the donor's and beneficiary's creditors.

(7) When privacy is important. Assets which pass through probate, either through the will or by intestacy, become public knowledge. But neither the terms of a living trust (revocable or irrevocable) nor the value of the property placed in it during the donor's lifetime is subject to public scrutiny.

(8) When the client is concerned that an outright gift to a minor child will return to the client or go to the wrong relative or in-law at the child's death.

Aside from the nontax advantages, there are many tax reasons for setting up a trust. With an irrevocable trust the burden of income taxes can be shifted from the client's tax bracket to the trust (if the income is retained by the trust and accumulated) or to the trust's beneficiary (if the income is paid out to it or split between the trust and its beneficiary). In spite of the "kiddie tax" rules — which provide in general that the unearned income of a child under age 14 will be taxed to the child, but at the parents' tax rate — significant income tax savings are still possible.

A well drafted irrevocable trust can save thousands of dollars of income taxes because

(1) income accumulated in the trust is taxed to the trust at its tax bracket regardless of the age of the child or grandchild who will eventually receive that money.

(2) income can be split between the trust and a child age 14 and over. The advantage is that income is held in the lower tax brackets longer.

Estate tax savings and state death tax savings can also be realized with an irrevocable trust. Both the property in the trust and the income it produces will be out of the client's estate if the trust has been drawn properly.

On the other hand, a revocable trust will not save any income, estate, or generation-skipping tax at either the state or federal level.

Selection of a Trustee

Guiding a client toward the selection of the proper trustee is an important task. The financial planner should be sure the client understands that more than one trustee can be named (such as two or more individuals or one or more persons and a professional trustee such as a bank). Such fiduciaries are jointly liable for mistakes. There is no perfect trustee; instead, there are advantages and disadvantages to any trustee. Figure 5.2 offers a checklist helpful in making the proper selection:

The best solution to the selection process is often a combination of corporate fiduciary and one or more family members (who should be prohibited from voting on issues which directly affect them).

Types of Trusts

There is almost no limit to the types of trusts that can be created or what they can do. Trusts have been classified in many different ways — aside from revocable and irrevocable and intervivos and testamentary. The following answers to five questions provide a good guide to identifying types of trusts.

Figure 5.2

ATTRIBUTE	BANK	SPOUSE/ CHILD	INDEPENDENT THIRD PARTY	EXPLANATION
perpetual existence	yes	no	no	Although banks go on holiday, they never die, become disabled, or retire. Banks may, however, "lose interest" if the amount of trust funds in question falls below a given sum.
experience	yes	no	no	Few individuals have the investment expertise, bookkeeping, tax and state law knowledge banks have. Even most accountants are not equipped to do proper trust accounting.
objectivity	yes	no	yes	Impartiality is extremely important to minimize conflicts of interest in decision making and allocating assets and income among beneficiaries. A family member chosen as trustee may be unduly influenced or pressured by other family members to make decisions in their interest. The potential to use a trustee's powers to control, punish, or reward family members is high (some would say this is an advantage rather than a disadvantage).
physical safety	yes	no	no	Banks and trust companies are audited both internally and externally and have substantial physical safeguards for financial assets.
investment policy	conservative	?	?	Some clients think a conservative investment policy is an advantage while others believe such a philosophy results in less favorable investment returns than might otherwise be obtained. Will individuals follow the investment policy laid out in the trust? Banks are not inclined to handle assets such as family businesses and tend to sell or liquidate them.
turnover	yes	no	no	Over the course of a period of time, the personnel in a bank is likely to change considerably. This may or may not occur if individuals are named as trustees.

The Tools and Techniques of Financial Planning

Figure 5.2 continued

ATTRIBUTE	BANK	SPOUSE/ CHILD	INDEPENDENT THIRD PARTY	EXPLANATION
flexibility	?	?	?	Out of concern for potential surcharge by beneficiaries and because of state government oversight, corporate trustees tend to be less flexible than individual trustees with respect to "bending the provisions" in the trust. Individuals sometimes have greater compassion (some say they can be "swayed" more easily).
fees	yes	?	?	Banks will typically charge an annual fee based on a percentage of both the principal and income of the trust. Some banks also charge a distribution fee based on a percentage of the principal paid from the trust. Individuals may or may not charge fees - although in some cases because of the time, risk, and difficulty of the task, individuals should charge fees.
knows beneficiaries	no	yes	?	A trustee's knowledge of the circumstances and needs of the beneficiaries is most helpful. Typically, a spouse or adult sibling or a third party individual will have such knowledge while few banks do.
time and inclination	yes	?	?	Few individuals have the time or inclination to give proper attention to the investment and management of assets.
favorable taxation	yes	?	?	Where family members are given broad powers as trustee, unexpected and adverse income, estate, or generation-skipping taxes may result.

(1) who gets the income?

(2) who is taxable on trust income?

(3) who gets the trust's assets?

(4) are trust assets excludable (or deductible) from the gross estate?

(5) can the client recover trust assets?

The chart in Figure 5.3 classifies a few of the better known kinds of trusts by the answers to these questions.

GIFT GIVING

Why does good financial planning often include gift giving? Clients are often encouraged to make gifts for many reasons. Some of these are:

(1) Giving gifts, especially gifts of income producing assets, is a way to reduce probate costs and substantially reduce or eliminate income taxes and the death tax on wealth.

(2) A gift creates certainty and avoids the unknown. For instance, a client who wants to be sure a gift goes to a

The Tools and Techniques of Financial Planning

Figure 5.3

				Are Trust Assets Excludable from or Deductible by Your Estate?	Can You Get Trust Assets Back?
TRUSTS — A SUMMARY*					
<u>Type of Trust</u>	**Who Gets <u>the Income?</u>**	**Who Is Taxable <u>on Trust Income?</u>**	**Who Gets <u>the Assets</u>**	**Are Trust Assets Excludable from or Deductible <u>by Your Estate?</u>**	**Can You Get Trust <u>Assets Back?</u>**
Revocable	You do	You	You choose	No	Yes
Irrevocable	Terms of trust determine	Trust if income retained, beneficiary if paid out. Taxed at beneficiary's bracket if 14 or over, otherwise taxed to beneficiary at parent's bracket	Terms of trust determine	Yes	No
2503(c) minor's	Held in trust or paid to minor	Trust if held, minor if paid out. Taxed to minor at parent's bracket if minor under 14, otherwise to minor at minor's bracket	Minor at age 21	Yes	No
Charitable remainder	You do	You	Charity	Yes	No
Marital (power of appointment)	Surviving spouse	Surviving spouse	Surviving spouse or person he/she appoints	Yes	N/A
Marital Q.T.I.P.	Surviving spouse	Surviving spouse	Parties you select	Yes	N/A
Credit equivalent bypass (C.E.B.T.)	Surviving spouse for life, then children	Surviving spouse for life, then children	Children	Yes	N/A
Grantor retained income (G.R.I.T.)	You do	You	Parties you select	Yes, if you survive specified term	No

*As is the case with any chart, the consequences shown above are only overviews. There are many exceptions.

Adapted from *Keeping Your Money: How to Avoid Taxes and Probate Through Estate Planning*, by Plotnick and Leimberg, © 1987 Charles Plotnick and Stephan Leimberg. Reproduced by permission of John Wiley & Sons, Inc.

child (rather than a former spouse or a creditor) will not wait to leave it by will. Wills can be broken or elected against and creditors' claims are an ever present danger, but a gift is a sure thing.

(3) Giving affords the client the pleasure of seeing the recipient enjoy the gift and the opportunity to see how that gift and the income it produces are handled. Lifetime gifts help the client decide whether, when, and how to make additional gifts during lifetime or at death.

(4) A lifetime gift is private. Only the donee (and perhaps tax authorities) have the right to any of the details. This makes it less likely that beneficiaries will fall prey to the advice of those people who always seem to know how to invest other people's money.

Reducing or Eliminating the Tax on Gifts

Federal tax law imposes a tax on gifts regardless of whether the gift is made during lifetime or at death. There are four ways the gift tax can be reduced or in most cases eliminated even in the case of substantial gifts. These four are:

(1) the gift tax annual exclusion,

(2) split gifts,

(3) the gift tax marital deduction, and

(4) the unified credit.

The gift tax annual exclusion allows anyone, married or single, to give up to $10,000 (indexed for inflation after 1998) in cash or other property to each of any number of donees (whether or not they are related to the donor) entirely gift tax free each year. These gifts can be made to individuals or to other parties such as an organization or charity.

Gifts made by a husband or wife to a third party such as a child can be "split," that is, treated as if half was made by each of the spouses. The gift will be treated as if each spouse gave half even if one contributed the entire amount. Gift splitting doubles the annual exclusion amount to $20,000 per donee. A further advantage of gift splitting is that, because gift tax rates are "progressive" (the tax grows disproportionately higher the more a person gives), making two smaller gifts creates a lower total tax than one larger gift. For example, a taxable gift (the amount over and above any allowable annual exclusion) of $100,000 results in a tax of $23,800. If the same gift were split so that each spouse was considered to have given a taxable gift

of $50,000, the tax on each gift would be only $10,600, a total of $21,200 (a saving of $2,600).

The gift tax marital deduction eliminates the tax entirely on gifts between spouses. Federal gift tax law allows one spouse to give another an unlimited amount free of gift tax (over and above the amount allowed as an annual exclusion). There is no upper limit on how much a client can give gift tax free to his or her spouse during lifetime. Gifts to a spouse who is not a U.S. citizen generally qualify for a $100,000 annual exclusion rather than the marital deduction.

There may be no tax payable even on that portion of a gift which, after any allowable annual exclusion, is still taxable. This is because a large dollar for dollar reduction in the gift tax payable is allowed to every taxpayer. This is called the "unified credit" because it can be allocated in any manner desired against gifts made during lifetime or at death to offset the taxes generated by the federal unified gift and estate transfer tax system. The unified credit in 1998 is $202,050. This offsets the tax on taxable property worth up to $625,000. So any client, married or not, could give during lifetime or leave at death up to $625,000 to anyone, whether or not related, and pay no federal estate tax. The credit which is not used during lifetime is available at death to offset estate taxes. The credit is scheduled to increase as follows:

Year	Exclusion Equivalent	Unified Credit
1987-1997	$600,000	$192,800
1998	$625,000	$202,050
1999	$650,000	$211,300
2000-2001	$675,000	$220,550
2002-2003	$700,000	$229,800
2004	$850,000	$287,300
2005	$950,000	$326,300
2006-	$1,000,000	$345,800

Helping the Client Select the Right Property

Planners should give a great deal of consideration to what property a client should—or should not—give, as well as the timing of that gift. These are some guidelines:

(1) Give income producing property if the client is in a high income tax bracket and the donee is in a lower bracket.

(2) Give assets likely to appreciate substantially in value. Make the gift when the gift tax value (and therefore the gift tax cost) is lowest. Life insurance, given away while the insured is alive, is a good example. Another example of good property to give away is the stock of

a business; give it to a family member before a lucrative contract is signed.

(3) Give away property owned in a state other than the one in which you live. This prevents "ancillary administration," a costly process involving probate in the state where the property is located as well as probate in the state of the decedent's domicile. For instance, clients who live in Florida and who own a home in Maryland but no longer use it might give away the home to avoid the additional probate.

The wise planner knows not only "what to give" but just as important, "when" to make that gift. A gift should never be made if for financial security or psychological reasons the client is depending on it or the income it produces or may have such a need at any time in the future. Tax savings should never be achieved at the cost of even one night's lost sleep. But if the client can — in every respect — afford to make the gift, then the time to do it is now. Get it out of the client's estate as quickly as possible to save income taxes and compound the potential estate tax savings.

If an asset fluctuates in value, it should be given away when its market value is low. If sale of the property by the client would result in a loss, it should be sold by the client rather than given away. The loss, if allowable, could be taken by the client (but could not be taken by the donee). The net proceeds could then be given away.

Discourage an older or ill client from giving away highly appreciated property. Although the gift may save some probate costs and inheritance taxes, the beneficiaries will end up paying more income taxes when the property is later sold. Why? because appreciated property generally gets a "step-up in basis" (cost for purposes of calculating taxable gain) if it is held until death but will not get that step-up if it is given away even a moment before death. Instead, its basis in the hands of the beneficiaries is the client's basis regardless of how low that was. For instance, if stock was purchased 40 years ago for $10 a share and it's now worth $1,000, the $990 built in gain is never subjected to income tax, either to the client or to his heirs, if it is held to the client's death. If the property is given away, the donee must carry over the donor's $10 a share basis.

HOW TO COMPUTE
THE FEDERAL ESTATE TAX

The federal estate tax system was designed to "redistribute" wealth and is often, by intent and in result, "confiscatory." Financial planners who want to help clients keep more of their wealth within the family unit must understand how the federal estate tax system works and how the tax is computed. Study the form below, Figure 5.4, as you read the following explanations of how the tax is computed. A more comprehensive explanation can be found in the appendix of our companion text, THE TOOLS AND TECHNIQUES OF ESTATE PLANNING.

An Overview

The first step is the computation of the gross estate. This is the total of all property the client owns in his own name at death. It also includes some property which is not technically owned by the client but which the tax law requires the executor to include.

After the gross estate is computed, certain adjustments are allowed. These adjustments include deductions for funeral and administrative expenses as well as for certain debts and taxes. The result is appropriately called the "adjusted gross estate."

One or more deductions can be taken from the adjusted gross estate. These deductions are for (a) property passing in a qualifying manner to a surviving spouse (the "marital deduction"), (b) property passing to a charity (the "charitable deduction"), and (c) qualified family-owned business interests. The result of subtracting the allowable deductions is the taxable estate.

The term, "taxable estate" is a somewhat misleading term since the tax is not based on this amount but upon the "tentative tax base." The tentative tax base is the sum of the taxable estate and "adjusted taxable gifts," the taxable portion of lifetime gifts that weren't already included in the gross estate. For instance, if a divorced client had given his daughter $100,000 in cash, the taxable gift would be $90,000 ($100,000 less the $10,000 annual exclusion). That $90,000 would be added to the client's taxable estate. The federal estate tax rates are applied to the total of the taxable estate and the adjusted taxable gifts.

Once the tax is computed, it may be reduced by one or more credits. These credits, which provide a dollar for dollar reduction of the tax, are:

(1) the unified credit,

(2) the credit for state death taxes,

(3) the credit for foreign death taxes,

(4) the credit for tax on prior transfers.

Figure 5.4 — Computing the Federal Estate Tax

	STAGE 1	(1)	Gross Estate			$_____
minus						
		(2)	Funeral and administration expenses (estimated as ____% of ____)		$_____	
		(3)	Debts and taxes			$_____
		(4)	Losses		$_____	
			Total deductions		$_____	
equals						
	STAGE 2	(5)	Adjusted gross estate			$_____
minus						
		(6)	Marital deduction			$_____
		(7)	Charitable deduction		$_____	
			Total deductions		$_____	$_____
equals						
	STAGE 3	(8)	Taxable estate			$_____
plus						
		(9)	Adjusted taxable gifts (post-1976 lifetime taxable transfers not included in gross estate)		$_____	
equals						
		(10)	Tentative tax base (total of taxable estate and adjusted taxable gift)			$_____
compute						
		(11)	Tentative Tax			$_____
minus						
		(12)	Gift taxes which would have been payable on post-1976 gifts			$_____
equals						
	STAGE 4	(13)	Estate tax payable before credits			$_____
minus						
		(14)	Tax credits			
			(a) Unified credit	$_____		
			(b) State death tax credit	$_____		
			(c) Credit for foreign death taxes	$_____		
			(d) Credit for tax on prior transfers	$_____		
			Total reduction	$_____		$_____
equals						
	STAGE 5	(15)	TOTAL ESTATE TAX			$_____

© 1998 Stephan R. Leimberg

Figure 5.5

DETERMINATION OF CASH REQUIREMENTS FOR 1998		
Value of Gross Estate:		$4,200,000
Funeral & Administration Expenses:	$76,000	
Debts & Taxes:	$125,000	
Other Losses:	$0	
Total Deductions:		$201,000
Adjusted Gross Estate:		$3,999,000
Marital Deduction	$0	
Charitable Deduction	$0	
Total Deductions:		$0
Taxable Estate:		$3,999,000
Adjusted Taxable Gifts:		$0
Tentative Tax Base:		$3,999,000
Tentative Tax:		$1,840,250
Gift Taxes Paid or Payable on Post-1976 Gifts:		$0
Federal Estate Tax Payable Before Credits:		$1,840,250
Tax Credits		
Unified Credit:	$202,050	
State Death Tax Credit:	$280,296	
Credit for Foreign Death Taxes:	$0	
Credit for Tax on Prior Transfers:	$0	
Total Reduction:		$482,346
Net Federal Estate Tax Payable:		$1,357,904
Summary of Cash Needs		
Funeral & Administration Expenses:	$76,000	
Debts & Taxes:		$125,000
Losses:		$0
Federal Estate Tax Payable	$1,357,904	
State Death Tax Payable:	$280,296	
Total Cash Bequests:	$0	
Total Cash Requirements:	$1,839,200	
Liquidity Situation		
Liquidity Presumed Available	$700,000	
Total Cash Requirements:	$1,839,200	
Liquidity Surplus:	-$1,139,200	

It is important for the financial planner to note that total liquidity costs (demands on the executor for cash) include the following:

(1) funeral and administration costs,

(2) debts and unpaid income, gift, and real estate taxes,

(3) state death tax,

(4) the net federal estate tax(es),

(5) total cash bequests.

Figure 5.5 shows an example of an actual computation.

A Detailed Examination

Run what estate planners call a "hypothetical probate," a financial guesstimate of how much, in taxes and other expenses, would be incurred by the estate if the client died today. This exercise will give the client a good idea of how much liquidity is needed to avoid a forced sale of assets to raise needed cash. It also provides a "base line" for measuring the progress and tax saving realized through planning.

STEP 1: COMPUTE THE GROSS ESTATE. Make a list of the property owned by the client in each of the following eight categories and state the estimated value:

Category 1—Property in client's name only.

Include all property the client owned in his own name at death such as

(1) cash, stocks, bonds, notes, real estate, or mortgages payable to the client

(2) tangible (touchable) personal (movable) property such as watches, rings, and other personal effects

(3) bank accounts (checking and savings) in the client's own name

(4) the right to future income such as the right to partnership profits, dividends, interest payments, or bonuses earned but not actually received at death.

Category 2—Gifts in which income or control over the property or the income was retained.

This category encompasses property ostensibly given away before death, but in which the donor retained certain rights such as the right to income produced by the property or the right to use, possess, or enjoy the property itself. Giving away property but keeping the right to enjoy or control it or determine who will receive the property or its income is an incomplete disposition. The donee's full and complete possession and enjoyment doesn't start (and therefore the decedent's ownership doesn't end) until the decedent dies. That retained right will cause the entire value of the property—measured as of the date of the client's death—to be includable in his estate.

Category 3—Gifts made conditional on surviving the decedent.

Where a client gives away property during lifetime but conditions the recipient's right to it upon surviving the client and there is a meaningful probability that the property will return to the client's estate (or be subject to disposition under the client's will or by intestacy), the value of the transferred property will be included in the client's estate.

For instance, suppose a client gave real estate worth $100,000 in trust to his son. Assume the trust provides, "the real estate is to go to my son but if he does not survive me, it is to go to the person I name in my will." The client's right to recover the property if the condition (survivorship) is not met is called a "reversionary interest." This reversionary interest is created by an incomplete disposition. Because the transfer of the reversionary interest will take effect at death, the value of the interest may be included in the client's estate.

Category 4—Gifts with respect to which the client retained the right to alter, amend, revoke, or terminate the gift.

If a client makes a gift but retains the right to change the gift, i.e., to alter the size or amend the conditions of the gift or revoke or terminate the gift at whim, the value of the property subject to that power (measured at the time of death rather than at the time of the gift) will be in his estate. This provision is broadly construed by the IRS. The mere power to control the date a beneficiary will receive an interest is enough to cause inclusion. In fact, even if the client retains any of the forbidden powers as trustee the IRS will include the property in his estate.

Category 5—Annuities or similar arrangements purchased by the client or on his behalf that are payable to the client for life and then to the client's designated heir.

If the client purchased an annuity (a systematic liquidation of principal and interest) which he is receiving or has the right to receive at the time of his death, and payments are to last for the client's life and will continue for the lifetime of his chosen survivor, the present value of the survivor's interest will be in the client's estate at his death. For instance, suppose a client (or the client's employer on behalf of the client as an employee benefit) purchased an annuity that would provide payments of $30,000 per year for the client's life and would then continue payments to the client's daughter. The present value (according to actuarial tables published in Treasury regulations) of the income stream the daughter is expected to receive will be includable in the client's estate.

There are limitations. First, if the annuity payments end at the client's death, there is nothing that can be transferred and nothing is includable in the estate. Second, to the extent the survivor can prove contribution of a portion of the cost of the annuity, that percentage of the value of the survivor annuity will not be includable in the client's estate. For instance, if the client's daughter paid for 25 percent of the annuity, only 75 percent of the discounted value of payments to be made to the daughter will be includable in the client's estate. (Payments made by an employer are treated as if made by the employee for this purpose).

Category 6—Jointly held property where a person automatically receives the client's property merely by surviving.

Where property is owned as "joint tenants with right of survivorship" or as "tenants by the entireties," upon the death of either joint tenant, the survivor automatically becomes owner. There are two rules that apply to such jointly held property: (1) the "50-50" rule and (2) the "percentage of contribution" rule.

The 50-50 rule applies only to property held solely between spouses (furthermore, the interest must have been created after 1976); it cannot be used where anyone other than the husband and wife is a joint tenant. The rule provides that only half of property held jointly with right of survivorship will be in the estate of the first to die, regardless of which spouse paid (or how much either spouse contributed toward) the purchase price. For instance, assume a $200,000 home was purchased entirely from the wife's income. Assume the house appreciated to $800,000 by the date of the husband's death. Under the 50-50 rule, $400,000 would be includable in the husband's estate even though he actually made no contribution. Since this portion will pass to the husband's surviving spouse, it will qualify for the estate tax marital deduction and therefore will not generate any federal estate tax.

All property held jointly with right of survivorship that does not fall under the 50-50 rule is subject to the "percentage of contribution" rule (also known as the "consideration furnished" rule). This rule provides that such property is taxed in the estate of the first joint tenant to die except to the extent the survivor can prove contribution to the original purchase price from funds other than any acquired as a gift from the decedent. For instance, two brothers purchased property worth $300,000 and the younger contributed $100,000. At the death of the older brother, when the property was worth $900,000, only $600,000 would be includable in the older brother's estate. Because the survivor must be able to prove the amount of his contribution to the property, regardless of

how long a period passes between purchase and the death of the first joint tenant, it is essential that the financial planner point out the importance of meticulous long term record keeping.

Category 7—General powers of appointment (the unlimited right to specify who receives someone else's property).

A client may be given by someone else, such as a parent, the right to say who will receive that relative's assets (which may be currently held in trust). This power to appoint (choose the ultimate recipient of the property) will cause the assets subject to the power to be included in the estate of the person who holds that power, if it is so broad that it is considered a "general" power. A power will be considered "general" if the holder can name himself (or his estate or his creditors) recipient of the assets. Thus, if a father creates a trust with $1,000,000 of assets and gives his son the right to specify who will receive those assets and the son has the right to have the trustee pay them to the son, the value of the assets in the trust will be included in the son's estate at the son's death.

Category 8—Life insurance owned by the client or over which the client has certain rights, or which is payable to the client's estate.

Life insurance proceeds are included in a client's estate (1) if the client owns the policy at death or has any "incidents of ownership" (significant property rights) in the policy, or (2) if the proceeds are payable to the client's estate (regardless of who owned the policy or who held the incidents of ownership).

If a client, at the time of death, owns life insurance on his life or had given it away within three years of his death, it will be included in his estate regardless of who was named as beneficiary. Any right to benefit from the policy in a meaningful way or to determine who can benefit from the policy in an economic sense will cause inclusion. Some of these incidents of ownership that cause estate tax inclusion are the right to:

(1) cash the policy in, or surrender it,

(2) change the beneficiaries,

(3) veto an owner's change of beneficiaries,

(4) borrow policy cash values,

(5) use the policy as collateral for loans.

Life insurance owned by a corporation that the client controlled (that is, he owned more than 50 percent of the voting stock of the corporation) is also includable in a client's estate to the extent it is payable to a party other than the corporation or its creditors. The entire proceeds (to the extent so payable), not merely the client's ownership percentage, is includable. Planners should remember that these proceeds may also be considered a dividend for income tax purposes. This means that the potential taxes on the proceeds could be as high as 94.6 percent (55 percent estate tax maximum plus 39.6 percent income tax).

The second rule that applies to life insurance proceeds is that the payment will be in the client's estate no matter who owned the policy or held incidents of ownership in it if it is payable to the client's estate or for the estate's benefit. For example, even if the policy was purchased and owned by the client's son, it would still be includable in the client's estate if the estate's executor (as executor) was named as beneficiary or if a creditor of the client received the proceeds.

These are the eight main categories of interests that cause inclusion of assets in the gross estate of a client. When doing a hypothetical estate probate, total the values of all the assets that fall under these categories. Don't worry that the figures are not exact. In the planning stage the goal should be a "guesstimation" of the estate's greatest potential need for cash. Err on the conservative side. A planner will never be sued by a surviving spouse who received "too much" cash.

STEP 2: ADJUST THE GROSS ESTATE.

The next step is to adjust the gross estate. An executor can deduct from the gross estate funeral expenses including interment, burial lot or vault, grave marker, and perpetual care costs. Administrative costs are also deductible. These include:

(1) expenses incurred in the collection and preservation of assets passing under the will,

(2) costs incurred in paying off debts,

(3) expenses incurred in distributing what's left to the appropriate beneficiaries.

Administrative expenses include court costs, accounting fees, appraiser's fees, brokerage costs, executor's commissions, and attorney's fees. These costs will vary widely and be affected by (a) location, (b) size of the estate, (c) complexity of the administrative problems. For

instance, bank accounts, money market certificates, and life insurance are all good examples of "low probate cost," highly liquid assets. Where the estate has little cash and many assets or properties which must be appraised, the estate settlement expenses will be higher. Many planners, as a rule of thumb, estimate 5 to 7 percent of the probate estate for administrative expenses in a small to moderate sized estate (under $1,200,000) and 3 to 5 percent in a larger estate.

Debts and taxes are also deductible. The executor can deduct all the client's bona fide debts including mortgages owed at death. Deductible taxes include income, gift, and property taxes owed but not paid at death. Casualty losses incurred during the administration of the estate are deductible but most financial planners ignore this area unless assisting in an actual estate probate.

The sum of these deductions is taken from the gross estate. The result is appropriately called the "adjusted gross estate."

STEP 3: COMPUTE THE TAXABLE ESTATE.

Deductions may be taken to reduce the adjusted gross estate still further: (1) the marital deduction for certain transfers to a surviving spouse, (2) the charitable deduction for certain transfers to a qualified charity, and (3) the deduction for qualified family-owned business interests.

The marital deduction is the most important deduction in most estates of married couples. This is because it is the largest deduction most estates receive. It's allowed for property passing outright, or in a manner that's tantamount to outright, to a surviving spouse. This deduction is virtually unlimited. A client can leave his entire estate to his surviving spouse and regardless of its size the deduction could wipe out the federal estate tax entirely. Use of a qualified domestic trust is generally required if the surviving spouse is not a U.S. citizen.

The charitable deduction, like the marital deduction, is virtually unlimited. Conceivably, a client could leave his entire estate to charity and no matter how large the bequest it would all be deductible.

The estate of a business owner may be able to deduct up to $675,000 of business interests from the estate under Code section 2057 as qualified family-owned business interests.

The result of subtracting these deductions is the "taxable estate."

Figure 5.6 — Estate Tax Rate Schedule

ESTATE TAX	
If the amount with respect to which the tentative tax to be computed is:	**The tentative tax is:**
Not over $10,000	18 percent of such amount.
Over $10,000 but not over $20,000	$1,800, plus 20 percent of the excess of such amount over $10,000.
Over $20,000 but not over $40,000	$3,800, plus 22 percent of the excess of such amount over $20,000.
Over $40,000 but not over $60,000	$8,200, plus 24 percent of the excess of such amount over $40,000.
Over $60,000 but not over $80,000	$13,000, plus 26 percent of the excess of such amount over $60,000.
Over $80,000 but not over $100,000	$18,200, plus 28 percent of the excess of such amount over $80,000.
Over $100,000 but not over $150,000	$23,800, plus 30 percent of the excess of such amount over $100,000.
Over $150,000 but not over $250,000	$38,800, plus 32 percent of the excess of such amount over $150,000.
Over $250,000 but not over $500,000	$70,800, plus 34 percent of the excess of such amount over $250,000.
Over $500,000 but not over $750,000	$155,800, plus 37 percent of the excess of such amount over $500,000.
Over $750,000 but not over $1,000,000	$248,300, plus 39 percent of the excess of such amount over $750,000.
Over $1,000,000 but not over $1,250,000	$345,800, plus 41 percent of the excess of such amount over $1,000,000.
Over $1,250,000 but not over $1,500,000	$448,300, plus 43 percent of the excess of such amount over $1,250,000.
Over $1,500,000 but not over $2,000,000	$555,800, plus 45 percent of the excess of such amount over $1,500,000.
Over $2,000,000 but not over $2,500,000	$780,800, plus 49 percent of the excess of such amount over $2,000,000.
Over $2,500,000 but not over $3,000,000	$1,025,800, plus 53% of the excess of such amount over $2,500,000.
Over $3,000,000	$1,290,800, plus 55% of the excess of such amount over $3,000,000.

Phase-out of graduated rates and unified credit.—

The tentative tax shall be increased by an amount equal to 5 percent of so much of the amount (with respect to which the tentative tax is to be computed) as exceeds $10,000,000 but does not exceed the amount at which the average tax under this section is 55 percent [$17,184,000].

Figure 5.7

CREDIT FOR STATE DEATH TAXES

If the adjusted taxable estate is:	The maximum tax credit shall be:
Not over $90,000	*8/10*ths of 1% of the amount by which the adjusted taxable estate exceeds $40,000.
Over $90,000 but not over $140,000	$400 plus 1.6% of the excess over $90,000.
Over $140,000 but not over $240,000	$1,200 plus 2.4% of the excess over $140,000.
Over $240,000 but not over $440,000	$3,600 plus 3.2% of the excess over $240,000.
Over $440,000 but not over $640,000	$10,000 plus 4% of the excess over $440,000.
Over $640,000 but not over $840,000	$18,000 plus 4.8% of the excess over $640,000.
Over $840,000 but not over $1,040,000	$27,600 plus 5.6% of the excess over $840,000.
Over $1,040,000 but not over $1,540,000	$38,800 plus 6.4% of the excess over $1,040,000.
Over $1,540,000 but not over $2,040,000	$70,800 plus 7.2% of the excess over $1,540,000.
Over $2,040,000 but not over $2,540,000	$106,800 plus 8% of the excess over $2,040,000.
Over $2,540,000 but not over $3,040,000	$146,800 plus 8.8% of the excess over $2,540,000.
Over $3,040,000 but not over $3,540,000	$190,800 plus 9.6% of the excess over $3,040,000.
Over $3,540,000 but not over $4,040,000	$238,800 plus 10.4% of the excess over $3,540,000.
Over $4,040,000 but not over $5,040,000	$290,800 plus 11.2% of the excess over $4,040,000.
Over $5,040,000 but not over $6,040,000	$402,800 plus 12% of the excess over $5,040,000.
Over $6,040,000 but not over $7,040,000	$522,800 plus 12.8% of the excess over $6,040,000.
Over $7,040,000 but not over $8,040,000	$650,800 plus 13.6% of the excess over $7,040,000.
Over $8,040,000 but not over $9,040,000	$786,800 plus 14.4% of the excess over $8,040,000.
Over $9,040,000 but not over $10,040,000	$930,800 plus 15.2% of the excess over $9,040,000.
Over $10,040,000	$1,082,800 plus 16% of the excess over $10,040,000.

The term "adjusted taxable estate" means the taxable estate reduced by $60,000.

STEP 4: COMPUTE THE TENTATIVE TAX BASE.

The term "taxable estate" is a misnomer because the tax is not calculated on the taxable estate. "Adjusted taxable gifts," that is, the taxable portion of certain lifetime gifts (post 1976 taxable gifts that were not already includable in the gross estate), are added back at this point in the computation.

When adjusted taxable gifts are added to the taxable estate, the sum is called the "tentative tax base." This is the base upon which the tax rates (see Figure 5.6) are applied. A glance at the rate schedule shows that once the tentative tax base reaches $3,000,000 the rate on every additional dollar is at least 55 percent. The words, "tentative tax" are used because the tax computed by applying the rates to the base is not yet the final amount: it is next lowered by one or more credits.

STEP 5: COMPUTE THE NET ESTATE TAX PAYABLE.

Any gift taxes paid during the client's lifetime can be subtracted from the otherwise payable tentative tax. Then certain credits may be allowed. The two most important of these credits are the unified credit and the credit for

state death taxes. The unified credit is a dollar for dollar reduction against the federal estate tax otherwise payable. An amount equal to the unified credit in the year of death will be eliminated assuming no part of the credit was used during the client's lifetime. The estate tax rate is boosted from 55 percent to 60 percent on amounts between $10,000,000 and $17,184,000 (see Figure 5.6). If technical corrections phase out the benefit of the unified credit, the 60 percent bracket will extend even higher.

The second major credit is the one allowed for state death taxes. The table in Figure 5.7 illustrates the amount of this credit. The credit is limited to the lower of (a) the state death tax actually paid or (b) the amount of credit from the government's table.

The third credit is for death taxes paid to a foreign country. This credit is designed to eliminate double taxation on property taxable both by the United States and by a foreign government.

The fourth credit is called the credit for tax on prior transfers. The purpose of this credit is to minimize the impact of estate taxation where the same property is includable in the estates of two or more persons who die within a short time (ten years or less) of each other. The closer the two deaths occur, the greater the credit allowed in the estate of the second decedent.

COMPUTING THE TAX ON GENERATION-SKIPPING TRANSFERS

There is yet another level of potential federal tax — the tax on transfers which skip a generation. This generation-skipping transfer tax (GSTT) is imposed at a flat 55 percent, on transfers to grandchildren or others of that generation or younger. Although it is of concern to only wealthy clients, inflation coupled with long term growth of assets puts a surprising number of people into situations where planning for the tax can result in significant savings.

Three examples of how the GSTT works follow and illustrate how harsh the tax can be. The examples assume none of the GSTT exceptions described below is applicable:

(1) The "taxable distribution": The client sets up a trust that provides income or principal distributions to her daughter or granddaughter at the trustee's discretion. At the time the trustee distributes either income or principal to the granddaughter, the result is a taxable distribution. If the trustee distributed $100,000 of trust income, the result would be a 55 percent tax, $55,000. The granddaughter would net only $45,000.

(2) The "taxable termination": The client sets up a trust which provides income to her son for life. At the son's death, assets in the trust pass to the son's son, the client's grandchild. At the son's death, the amount passing to the grandson becomes taxable. If $1,000,000 was placed into the trust, there would be a tax of $550,000 (55 percent of $1,000,000). The grandson would receive only $450,000.

(3) The "direct skip": The client makes a lifetime gift of cash or other property to her grandson. If the gift was worth $1,000,000, the grandparent would be liable for a 55 percent tax on the $1,000,000 transfer. Here, the tax is paid by the grandparent and is not paid from the gift itself. So the grandson nets the full $1,000,000.

Planners should recognize that it is possible that the cost of making a generation-skipping transfer can be greater than the value of the entire gift. For example, assume a client who is already in the 55 percent gift tax bracket writes a check to his granddaughter for $2,000,000. The generation-skipping transfer tax will be 55 percent of the $2,000,000, or $1,100,000. In addition, since the transfer was a gift, the client must pay a gift

tax at the rate of 55 percent on the gift, another $1,100,000. To add insult to tax injury, the client is deemed to be making a second gift, a gift of the generation-skipping transfer tax ($1,100,000) upon which must be paid an additional 55 percent gift tax. The total tax is therefore $2,805,000. That's 140 percent of the value of the gift!

An important exception to the GSTT is that each donor can transfer up to $1,000,000 (indexed for inflation after 1998) before becoming subject to the tax. This exemption can be increased to $2,000,000 by "splitting" the exemption with a spouse (i.e., treating each spouse as if he or she made half the transfer). Also, gifts of up to $10,000 (indexed for inflation after 1998) a year ($20,000 if the gift is split) can be made to an unlimited number of donees without being subjected to the GSTT (although a gift in trust requires a separate share for each exclusion).

STATE DEATH TAXES

Some clients will be subject to state death taxes. Clients of modest or moderate wealth may lose far more to state death taxation than to the federal estate tax system. About one-half of the states impose a tax equal to the maximum amount for which a state death tax credit is available (see Figure 5.7). All other states impose a tax equal to the greater of the regular state death tax or the maximum amount for which a state death tax credit is available. Planning can lower state death taxes considerably.

CONCLUSION

Estate planning is an essential part of the overall financial planning process. It is possible for most clients to efficiently and effectively conserve and distribute an estate in a manner that both minimizes taxes and accomplishes personal objectives. These results can be achieved only if the client can be helped to become aware of the scope and urgency of the problems and overcome a natural unwillingness to address difficult and sometimes distasteful issues (such as his own mortality). Above all, the planner must:

(1) show compassion and care for reasons beyond possible compensation,

(2) become competent in estate planning and/or work with other advisers who are,

(3) learn the goals, circumstances, and needs of all the people involved,

(4) bring the client and the client's family into the planning process as much as possible.

Chapter 6

HOW TO EVALUATE LIFE INSURANCE PRODUCTS

Attorneys, accountants, and other financial services professionals are constantly required to provide a second opinion as to the efficacy of a life insurance policy for the particular client and to assist in selecting between competing policies. This chapter will focus on the factors that must be considered by professionals in evaluating life insurance products. Rule-of-thumb guidelines will be stated that should speed up the decision-making process and help the professional determine if the criteria he is considering follow generally accepted life insurance planning principles.

This chapter is divided into five Parts:

Part I — selection of the type of insurance product (or product mix) that is appropriate for the client

Part II — determination of the proper amount of coverage

Part III — deciphering life insurance policy illustrations

Part IV — policy comparison measurements

Part V — company comparison measurements

PART I: HOW TO SELECT THE TYPE OF INSURANCE PRODUCT OR PRODUCT MIX APPROPRIATE FOR THE CLIENT

The selection of the particular type of life insurance coverage appropriate for a given client should be a function of four factors:

(1) the client's personal preferences, prejudices, and priorities;

(2) the amount of insurance needed;

(3) the client's ability and willingness to pay a given level of premiums (cash flow considerations); and

(4) holding period probabilities (duration of need considerations).

Preferences, Prejudices, and Priorities

The selection of a particular type of life insurance policy or policy mix is to a great extent a very personal decision. Just as some individuals prefer by psychological nature to lease an automobile or rent an apartment, others prefer to purchase a car or own a home. Some clients prefer to make their purchases with a minimum down payment and stretch out the length of payments as long as possible while others prefer to make a relatively large down payment and to pay off the loan or mortgage as quickly as possible. To many clients there is emotional comfort in "owning" while others feel that owning ties them down and restricts their freedom of choice and flexibility. Similar comparisons can be made with respect to life insurance policies.

Some clients do not want to "pay, pay, pay... and have nothing to show for it at the end of the term" while others have been told all their lives to "buy term and invest the difference." In the real world both positions are correct — and not correct. Even the advice of knowledgeable planners has been tainted by their own prejudices. For most clients the right course of action usually lies where they are most comfortable — since peace of mind is really the impetus for the purchase of life insurance in the first place.

Another useful analogy is the purchase of technology tools by professionals. Some tend to purchase the highest quality, most expensive tools that they can afford so that the tool will serve them well over a lifetime (or at least the reasonably expected lifetime of the tool). They do not tend to purchase lower priced, lower quality tools that will have to be replaced because they wear out, were inadequate to begin with, or would just plain break.

But others cannot afford to (or will choose not to) purchase top quality tools. They may have other priorities. They may prefer to have the money to invest or to spend on current consumption. They may end up spending more over the length of their careers on tools and be inconvenienced in the process of continually having to replace the original tool. Although this "preference/priority" decision is not necessarily the most logical, it is a strong and important process that requires the planner to take into consideration the client's psychological makeup.

The rule-of-thumb here is:

Buy term if the client has a high risk-taking propensity.

Buy term if the client has a "lease rather than own" preference.

Buy some type of whole life insurance if the client has an "own rather than loan" type personality.

Buy some type of whole life insurance if the client wants something to show for his money at any given point. The more important it is for the client to have cash values and dividends at any given point the more whole life type coverage is indicated.

Buy a mix of term and whole life if the client is — like most clients — not solidly on one end of the spectrum or the other.

Amount of Insurance Needed

When the amount of insurance needed is so great (as it often is for families with young children or for couples with high living standards relative to their incomes) that only term insurance or a term/whole life type combination is feasible, the need for death protection should be given first priority.

This results in a simple rule of thumb:

Buy term insurance when there is no way to satisfy the death need without it. The term insurance can be converted to another form of protection at a later date if and when appropriate.

Buy a combination of term and permanent insurance when the client can cover the entire death need and can and is willing to allocate additional dollars to appropriate permanent coverage.

Cash Flow Considerations

There are a large number of premium payment configurations that provide considerable flexibility for policyowners.

Some clients will prefer to prepay for their coverage and take advantage of the tax-deferred internal buildup of investment return. This limits the total amount of premium that will be paid even if the insured lives well beyond life expectancy.

Other clients will be more comfortable with the payment of premiums at regular intervals for a fixed period or for the life of the insured (or for the working life of the insured). This "installment" purchase of life insurance benefits the policyowner who dies shortly after the policy is purchased since a much lower total premium would be paid before death.

Note that conceptually, the insurance company itself is indifferent as to which premium payment method is selected since all of these patterns of payment, if applied to the same level of death benefit and continued for the same duration of time, will have the same actuarial value. So client abilities to pay and preferences are the major factors in the decision.

The rule of thumb is:

Prepay coverage (buy limited payment whole life permanent type insurance) if the client expects to live longer than average.

Pay on the installment basis (purchase term or low outlay whole life type coverage) if the client believes he or she faces a greater than average mortality risk.

Purchase YRT (Yearly Renewable Term) if the client wants or needs to pay absolutely minimal initial premiums but is willing to pay increasingly larger premiums each consecutive year to keep the same level of coverage in force.

Duration of Need Considerations

In many cases the planner's decision must be dictated at least in part by how long the need is expected to last.

Some rules of thumb here are:

Buy term insurance if the need will probably last for 10 years or less.

Buy term and/or whole life if the need will probably last for 10 to 15 years.

Buy some type of whole life coverage if the need will probably last for 15 years or longer.

Buy some type of whole life coverage if the policy will probably be continued up to or beyond the insured's age 55.

Buy some type of whole life coverage if the policy is purchased to solve a buy-sell need.

Buy some type of whole life coverage if the policy is designed to pay death taxes or transfer capital efficiently from one generation to another.

PART II: HOW TO DETERMINE THE AMOUNT OF COVERAGE

There is no perfect or even universally agreed upon answer to the question, "How do you determine how much life insurance a client needs?" From the client's perspective, the ultimate answer is, "I don't need any life insurance — but those I love do."

There are two basic approaches to insurance needs analysis: (1) "human-life value" and (2) "capital needs."

The human-life value approach attempts to evaluate the economic worth of a person to those dependent on his ability to generate income. Essentially it assumes that death occurs today and measures the economic loss — the loss of income that would have been generated — had the client lived to the end of his working lifetime. The human-life value concept then reduces the economic worth of an individual to its present value at a given discount rate.

The capital needs approach (some call this the programming approach) attempts to determine the various expenses that must be met if the income provider dies. These needs will vary considerably from client to client and should consider:

(1) the composition and circumstances of the surviving family;

(2) their current living standard;

(3) the standard of living to which they are assumed to adjust;

(4) capital required to pay lump-sum outlays such as last illness (final) expenses, burial costs, death taxes, estate settlement costs, taxes and debts payable at death, and educational expenses; and

(5) capital required to satisfy special needs such as providing for permanently dependent children, parents, or other relatives or for charitable or other bequests.

The planner must work with the client first to quantify needs based on current living expenses and then to separate absolute needs, desires, and wishes. In other words the planner should develop not one, but two, or, better yet, three, insurance needs analyses showing (1) "survival level financial security needs," (2) "comfort level needs," and (3) "flourish level needs." We suggest the planner print out and share with the client a projection of insurance needs based on each of these three levels and let the client choose the one that the client is most comfortable with (and can afford).

The amount of life insurance the client should purchase would be the difference between the level of needs the client chooses (i.e., the cost of satisfying the client's selected level of objectives) and the amount of capital assets already available to meet that chosen level of needs.

The computer printout in Figure 6.1, from *Financial Planning TOOLKIT*, is a simple and quick means of calculating a client's surplus or deficit.

Note: the assumptions and weaknesses inherent in both the human-life value and the capital needs approach can result in considerably different dollar needs amounts.

Here are some guidelines to safeguard the security of survivors:

Assume the client may die today but review your analysis every year. Needs, circumstances, and reasonable assumptions can all change considerably within a short period of time.

Assume income-producing assets earn — after tax — no more than four to six percent over a five or more year period.

Assume no liquidation or invasion of principal. Although some planners feel that this is an unduly conservative or even unrealistic assumption, the use of an "income only" assumption is at least balanced by the inflationary pressures on living costs. In other words inflation will use up any excess capital just as certainly as a systematic liquidation of accumulated assets. Alternatively, if needs are computed based on an invasion of principal, assume a conservative after-tax earnings rate on the unpaid balance. Note also that an invasion of principal results in no legacy available for heirs.

Consider both the current impact of state and federal death taxes and the impact of normal growth of assets and inflation upon the death tax that will be levied.

Consider the purchase of more insurance than is currently indicated if the need for coverage is expected to increase in the future. This will eliminate the insurability problem often faced by executives, business owners, and professionals who are under constant stress and whose standards of living are constantly rising. (Note that constantly increasing financial needs may be indicative of an unrealistic escalation of goals and objectives relative to the client's increases in income. Such a situation may warrant a reevaluation of the client's objectives, a need for cash-control management, and a reconsideration of the client's priorities.)

Figure 6.1

INSURANCE NEEDS ANALYSIS	
INPUT: Name: Sam Sample	
Current Cash Needs:	
INPUT: Final Expenses	$20,000
INPUT: Emergency Fund	$25,000
INPUT: Mortgage Fund	$100,000
INPUT: Notes & Loans Payable	$10,000
INPUT: Taxes Payable	$4,000
INPUT: Education Expenses (NPV)	$75,000
INPUT: Other	$10,000
Total Cash Needs:	$244,000
Capital Needs:	
INPUT: Capital Required for Lifetime Income of $3,500 per Month at .070% interest	$600,000
INPUT: Capital Required for $1,000 Monthly Income for Adjustment Period of 2 Year(s)	$24,000
Total Capital Needs	$624,000
Total Needs	$868,000
Less Capital Assets:	
INPUT: Life Insurance	$200,000
INPUT: Cash, Savings, Etc.	$25,000
INPUT: Investment Assets	$200,000
INPUT: Social Security (NPV)	$100,000
INPUT: Pension Benefits	$50,000
INPUT: Other	$25,000
Total Capital Assets	$575,000
Surplus or (Deficit)	($293,000)

PART III: HOW TO DECIPHER POLICY ILLUSTRATIONS

The first step in understanding a policy illustration is to identify the columns that state:

(1) yearly premium payments;

(2) year-end policy cash values;

(3) projected policy dividends;

(4) cumulative cash value at given policy durations;

(5) the death benefit from the basic policy; and

(6) the death benefit provided by any dividends.

In other words the planner should ask: "What does the client pay year by year compared to what he gets if he lives and what his family receives if he dies?" and "What portion of those amounts are guaranteed and what portion of those amounts are projections?" Also ask, "What interest or other assumptions are built into these figures?"

Financial services professionals should examine a policy illustration with particular emphasis on:

(1) Surrender charges;

(2) Cash value projections;

(3) Policy loans; and

(4) Dividends.

Surrender charges. Determine what the company charges if the client surrenders the policy in a given year by looking at the cash value columns. Where there are two columns for cash values — one which reflects the net surrender value of the contract and the other the year-end cash value for the policy — the difference between these two amounts is the surrender charge for the given year.

Cash value projections. Ascertain the "premium level safety" by looking at the cash value projections on universal life and interest-sensitive life products. It is common under these two types of policies to show future cash values based on (a) the guaranteed interest rate and also (b) one or more higher interest rates related to either (i) current portfolio earnings or (ii) whatever earnings level the agent has selected for the illustration.

Question the long term reasonableness of the assumptions. Are they unrealistic? Does the cash value associated with the guaranteed interest rate drop to zero after some years of duration? This indicates that the premium being charged for the contract will at that point become inadequate to support the coverage in force if the insurer is only able to credit cash values with the guaranteed interest rate. The client will be forced to pay higher premiums unless the contract earns interest higher than the guaranteed rate. If the illustration shows positive cash values at all policy durations, the premium will be adequate to carry the policy indefinitely   if the insurance company credits interest on the cash value at the higher illustrated rates.

Policy loans. Check the illustration to see if loans are part of a systematic plan of borrowing to pay premiums. This is called a "minimum deposit" plan. This is evidenced by a regular pattern of increasing outstanding loan balances where the increases are tied closely to the interest rate applicable to the previous outstanding balance and the premium payment due under the contract.

Dividends. Remember that dividends are not guaranteed and that many insurance companies have significantly reduced dividends below their original projections. Check the interest rate that the insurer will pay on any dividend left with

it to earn interest (the interest is currently taxable even though the dividend itself will not be taxable to the client). If the client is in poor health or desires additional insurance to build up at net (no commission or overhead) cost, dividends should be used to purchase "paid-up additional insurance" (agents call these "paid-up ads"). Alternatively, the dividends could be used to purchase one-year term insurance (also a very cost-effective purchase) and the balance of any dividend remaining should be reflected in the dividend column.

Here are some questions to ask:

Is the illustration from the home office or printed on the agent's (or some other source's) computer? Demand a ledger printout from the insurance company's home office to compare one policy with another.

Is the interest rate used reasonable over a long period of time?

Are dividends "puffed"? (Does the past history of the company suggest that it was "overly optimistic" when the projected dividends of the past are compared with the actual dividends paid in the past — or when compared with the records of other companies' products you are examining? This can have a significant impact upon when or if premiums will "vanish" or when they will unexpectedly reappear.

Are cash flow amounts in one illustration comparable with those in another? Cash flow amounts will be similar only if death benefit amounts and premium payments as well as any projected policy loans or withdrawals are for similar amounts for each policy duration. The more the values of these variables differ from one illustration to another, the less meaningful are differences in cash values, death benefits, or dividend levels.

In comparing universal life products, demand to know what variables are incorporated in the illustration and then insist that all competitive illustrations use the same (reasonable) assumptions.

PART IV: HOW TO COMPARE POLICIES

At best, life insurance is a very complicated product that is extremely difficult to evaluate and compare. Fortunately, there are at least seven commonly used measures for policy comparison that can be of help in comparing purchase alternatives. Keep in mind that none of these methods does or could take into account all of the factors that should be considered when making the purchase decision. But if several measures are used and the planner keeps in mind the strengths

Figure 6.2

TRADITIONAL NET COST METHOD
$25,000 POLICY FOR A MALE AGE 35
(per $1,000 of coverage)

Year	Premium	Dividends	Cash Value	Terminal Dividends	Surrender Charges
1	$22.24	$0.00	$0.00	$0.00	$2.00
2	22.24	3.40	16.00	0.00	1.75
3	22.24	4.00	33.00	0.00	1.50
4	22.24	4.70	51.00	0.00	1.00
5	22.24	5.50	69.00	0.00	0.50
6	22.24	6.00	84.00	1.05	0.00
7	22.24	6.75	104.00	2.35	0.00
8	22.24	7.50	122.00	3.25	0.00
9	22.24	8.25	141.00	4.25	0.00
10	22.24	9.00	160.00	5.25	0.00
TOTALS	$222.40	$55.10	$160.00	$5.25	$0.00

(1)	Total premiums	$222.40
(2)	Total dividends	55.10
(3)	Total Net premiums	$167.30
(4)	Cash Value in Year	$160.00
	+ Terminal Dividend	5.25
	- Surrender Charge	0.00
	Net Cash Value	165.25
(5)	Total Net Cost	$2.05
(6)	Divided by Number of Years	10
	Traditional Net Cost per $1,000 per year	0.205

and weaknesses of each during the comparison process, they will be quite helpful in at least eliminating policies that should not be considered.

The seven commonly used policy comparison techniques are:

(1) the "net cost" method;

(2) the "interest-adjusted net cost" method;

(3) the "equal outlay" method;

(4) the "cash accumulation" method;

(5) the "Linton yield" method;

(6) the "Belth yearly rate of return" method; and

(7) the "Belth yearly price of protection" method.

Traditional Net Cost Method

The traditional "net cost" method works like this:

(1) Add the premiums on the ledger sheet over a stated period of time such as 10, 15, or 20 years.

Figure 6.3

	INTEREST-ADJUSTED COST METHOD $25,000 POLICY FOR A MALE AGE 35 (per $1,000 of coverage)					

	Premiums		Dividends			
Year	Per Year	Accum. at 5.00%	Per Year	Accum. at 5.00%	Cash Value	Terminal Dividends
1	$22.24	$23.35	$0.00	$0.00	$0.00	$0.00
2	22.24	47.87	3.40	3.57	16.00	0.00
3	22.24	73.62	4.00	7.95	33.00	0.00
4	22.24	100.65	4.70	13.28	51.00	0.00
5	22.24	129.03	5.50	19.72	69.00	0.00
6	22.24	158.84	6.00	27.01	84.00	1.05
7	22.24	190.13	6.75	35.44	104.00	2.35
8	22.24	222.99	7.50	45.09	122.00	3.25
9	22.24	257.49	8.25	56.01	141.00	4.25
10	22.24	293.72	9.00	68.26	160.00	5.25
TOTALS	$222.40	$293.72	$55.10	$68.26	$160.00	$5.25

(1)	Premiums Compounded at	5.00%	$293.72	
(2)	Dividends Compounded at	5.00%	68.26	

(3)	Future Value of Net Premiums		$225.46
(4)	Cash Value	$160.00	
	+ Terminal Dividends	5.25	
	- Surrender Charge	0.00	
	Net Cash Value		165.25

(5)	Future Value of Net Cost	$60.21
(6)	Annuity Factor	13.207
	Interest-adjusted Cost per $1,000	$4.56

(2) Add the dividends projected on the ledger sheet over the same period of time.

(3) Subtract the total dividends from the total premiums to find the total net premiums paid over the period you are measuring.

(4) Add the cash value and any "terminal dividends" shown on the ledger statement.

(5) Subtract the total cash value and terminal dividends from the total net premiums to arrive at the total net cost of the policy over the selected period.

(6) Divide your result by the face amount of the policy (in thousands) and again by the number of years in the selected period to arrive at the net cost of insurance per thousand dollars of coverage per year. This method is illustrated in Figure 6.2.

This is the easiest method to understand and use but its simplicity is its weakness. This measure ignores the time value of money. This makes it possible to manipulate policy illustrations by shifting cash flows. Even without intentional manipulation the traditional net cost method grossly under-states the cost of insurance coverage and in many cases implies that the average annual cost of coverage is zero or negative. The result could be misleadingly low measures of policy costs. Few states sanction this method for comparing policy costs although it can be used by the planner, together with the other methods described below, to make a quick and rough first-level relative comparison of policies.

Interest-Adjusted Net Cost Index

The interest-adjusted net cost method works like this:

(1) Accumulate each year's premium at some specified rate of interest (most policy illustrations use a five percent rate). Do the calculation over a selected period of time such as 10, 15, or 20 years.

(2) Accumulate each year's dividends projected on the ledger sheet at the same assumed rate of interest over the same period of time.

(3) Subtract the total dividends (plus interest) from the total premiums (plus interest) to find the future value of the total net premiums paid over the period you are measuring.

(4) Add the cash value and any "terminal dividends" shown on the ledger statement.

(5) Subtract the total cash value and terminal dividends from the future value of the net premiums to arrive at the total net cost of the policy over the selected period.

(6) Divide your result by the future value of annuity factor for the rate assumed and the period selected. The result is the level annual cost for the policy.

(7) Divide the level annual cost for the policy by the number of thousands in the face amount of coverage. The result is the interest-adjusted net cost per thousand dollars of coverage.

The policy with the lowest number (the low-value index) would be the most favorable policy under this method. This method is illustrated in Figure 6.3.

Planners usually will not have to do this computation since most ledger sheets will contain this number at the bottom of the front page of the policy illustration.

Most states require that prospective policyowners be provided with a policy's interest-adjusted net cost index. Planners should therefore understand how this measure works, understand its limitations, and be able to explain it to sophisticated clients.

Among the weaknesses of the interest-adjusted net cost method are these:

(1) If the policies being compared are not quite similar, the index results will be misleading. For instance, if the outlays differ significantly, a hypothetical side fund should be established to accumulate the differences in the annual outlays at the assumed rate of interest to properly adjust for the differences. This will be the case where an existing policy is compared with a potential replacement. There will almost always be a material difference in the projected cash flows. This makes the interest-adjusted net cost method unsuitable (unless adjusted) for "replacement" comparisons.

(2) This method is subject to manipulation (although to a lesser extent than the traditional net cost method) and in the commonly used measuring periods such as 10 or 20 years can be made to provide more favorable estimates of cost than for other selected periods.

(3) The interest-adjusted method is valid only to the extent that the projections of cash flows materialize as assumed. Therefore, the calculation cannot consider the impact of an overly optimistic dividend scale.

The Equal Outlay Method

The equal outlay method works like this: The client is assumed to pay out (his outlay) the same premium for each of the policies that are to be compared with each other. Likewise, the client is assumed to purchase, in each policy under comparison, essentially equal amounts of death benefits year by year.

The equal outlay method is easiest to employ when comparing flexible premium type policies such as universal life because it is easy for the illustration to be generated with equal annual contributions.

Planners should demand that

(1) cash values should be projected using the guaranteed rates for the policy,

(2) separate illustrations should be run showing a selected intermediate interest rate assumption, and

(3) separate illustrations should be run showing the current interest rate the company credits to policies.

An inspection of the projected cash values in future years should make it possible to identify the policy with the highest cash values and, therefore, to determine which is the best purchase.

Figure 6.4

					EQUAL OUTLAY METHOD		

Ordinary Life (O.L.) versus Yearly renewable term (YRT)*
$100,000 face value for age 35 male nonsmoker

Year	O.L. Prem.	YRT Prem.	Diff. in Prem.	Diff. Accum. at 6%	O.L. Surrend. Values	YRT Plus Side fund	O.L. with Paid-up Additions
1	$1,445	$145	$1,300	$1,378	$0	$101,378	$100,010
2	1,445	148	1,297	2,836	175	102,836	100,111
3	1,445	154	1,291	4,374	1,670	104,374	100,309
4	1,445	162	1,283	5,997	3,324	105,997	100,848
5	1,445	172	1,273	7,706	5,167	107,706	101,817
6	1,445	185	1,260	9,504	7,189	109,504	103,231
7	1,445	200	1,245	11,394	9,435	111,394	105,105
8	1,445	219	1,226	13,377	11,986	113,377	107,458
9	1,445	242	1,203	15,455	14,768	115,455	110,316
10	1,445	268	1,177	17,629	17,898	117,629	113,678
11	1,445	299	1,146	19,902	21,243	119,902	117,611
12	1,445	333	1,112	22,275	25,007	122,275	122,056
13	1,445	373	1,072	24,748	29,147	124,748	127,057
14	1,445	417	1,028	27,322	33,634	127,322	132,669
15	1,445	466	979	29,999	38,579	129,999	138,903
16	1,445	521	924	32,779	44,126	132,779	145,821
17	1,445	581	864	35,661	50,167	135,661	153,454
18	1,445	646	799	38,648	56,913	138,648	161,813
19	1,445	716	729	41,739	64,238	141,739	171,062
20	1,445	791	654	44,937	72,295	144,937	181,159

* Assumes dividends are used to purchase paid-up additions.

In this case the yearly renewable term option is superior until years 10 to 12. After the tenth year, the surrender cash value of the whole life policy exceeds the side fund accumulated with the yearly renewable term options. However, the whole life policy's death benefit, assuming dividends are used to buy paid-up additions, does not exceed the total death benefit (term insurance plus side fund) of the yearly renewable term option until after year 12. This example demonstrates, as is typical, that term policies will often be a better choice when insurance needs are shorter term. But term policies are generally increasingly less attractive the longer the duration of the insurance need.

The procedure will be more complicated where the equal outlay method is used to compare a fixed premium contract with one or more flexible premium policies. Here, the net premium level (adjusted for any dividends) and the death benefit of the flexible premium policies must be made to match the corresponding values for the fixed premium contract for all years over the period of comparison. This makes it possible to compare future cash values in the same manner as when comparing two flexible premium policies.

The equal outlay method can also be used to compare two or more fixed-premium policies or to compare a term policy to a whole life policy in the following manner: Hypothetically, "invest" the differences in net annual outlay in a side fund at some reasonable after-tax rate of return which essentially keeps the two alternatives equal in annual outlay. Compare (a) cash values including side fund amounts and (b) total death benefits including side fund amounts.

Note, quite often the result of this computation will show that term insurance (or a lower-outlay whole life policy) with a side fund will out-perform a permanent type whole life plan during a period of perhaps the first seven to 10 years but then lose that edge when the projection is carried to a longer duration. See Figure 6.4.

There are a number of disadvantages of the equal outlay method:

(1) When comparing a fixed to a flexible premium contract, the underlying assumptions of the contracts are not the same and, therefore, the analysis cannot fairly compare them. For instance, most universal life cash value projections are based on "new money assumptions" while ordinary life policy dividends are usually based on the "current portfolio rate" of the insurer (a rate which often varies significantly from the new money rate).

In recent periods the new money rate has typically been greater than the portfolio rate. If this trend continues, cash values in universal life contracts are more likely to materialize as projected. But if these economic conditions hold true, then it is likely that the portfolio rate will also rise. This means dividends paid would increase relative to those projected based on the current portfolio rate. The equal outlay method does not take into consideration either the fluctuations in rates or the differences in how they are computed.

(2) The required adjustments in most comparisons can quickly become burdensome. In many cases it is quite difficult to equate death benefits under the comparison policies while maintaining equal outlays.

(3) When comparing an existing policy with a potential replacement policy, the analysis must consider any cash value in the existing policy at the time of the comparison. Generally, it is easiest to assume that the cash value will be paid into the new policy. Otherwise, the analysis should probably account for the time value of that cash value and should, as closely as possible, equate total death benefits including any side fund.

(4) The results even after many adjustments have been made will be ambiguous. Quite often the results can be interpreted as favoring one policy for certain durations and favoring the other for other holding periods.

Cash Accumulation Method

The cash accumulation method works like this:

(1) Equate outlays (much in the same manner as the equal outlay method) for the policies being compared.

(2) Change the face amount of the lower premium policy so that the sum of the side fund plus the face amount equals the face amount of the higher premium policy. Note that this would yield the same result as where it is possible to set both death benefits and premium

payments exactly equal — in flexible premium policies.

(3) Accumulate any differences in premiums at an assumed rate of interest.

(4) Compare the cash value/side fund differences over given periods of time to see which policy is preferable to the other. This method is illustrated in Figure 6.5.

The cash accumulation method is ideal for comparing term with permanent insurance. But the analysis must be done with caution; the use of the appropriate interest rate is critical since, as is the case with any time-value measurement, a higher assumed interest rate will generally favor a lower premium policy/side fund combination relative to a higher premium policy.

We suggest a two part approach: If the comparison is performed without regard to a specific client and merely to determine the relative ranking of the policies, the planner should assume a relatively conservative risk-free after-tax rate comparable to the rate that the client expects to earn on the cash values of the higher premium policy. This would more closely equate the combination of the lower premium/side fund with the risk-return characteristics of the higher premium policy.

Alternatively, if the comparison is being conducted for a specific client, the planner should use that individual's long-run after-tax opportunity cost rate of return which may be considerably higher than the rate of return anticipated on the cash value of the higher premium policy.

A full and fair comparison is made more difficult because of the impact of death taxes, probate costs, and creditor laws. This is because the cash accumulation method uses a hypothetical side fund to make the comparison. But money in the side fund — if it in fact were created — would not be eligible for the exemptions or special rate reductions afforded to the death proceeds of life insurance. Therefore each dollar from that side fund would be subjected to a level of taxation that life insurance dollars would not. Likewise, the side fund would be subjected to the normal probate fees and attorney's costs to which cash or other property is subject. Furthermore, this method does not consider the value of state law creditor protection afforded to the death benefits in a life insurance policy but not to amounts held in most other types of investments. The bottom line is that the side fund money may appear to have more value than it actually would in the hands of those for whom it was intended.

It is therefore apparent that the cash accumulation method has strengths that overcome many of the weaknesses of other

Figure 6.5

	**CASH ACCUMULATION METHOD**

Ordinary Life (O.L.) versus Yearly Renewable Term (YRT)*
$100,000 face value for age 35 male nonsmoker

Year	O.L. Prem.	YRT Prem.	Diff. in Prem.	Side fund at 6.000%	O.L. Surrend. Value	YRT Face Amount	Plus Side fund	O.L. with Paid-up Additions
1	$1,445	143	$1,302	$1,380	$0	$98,630	$100,010	$100,010
2	1,445	144	1,301	2,842	175	97,269	100,111	100,111
3	1,445	148	1,297	4,388	1,670	95,921	100,309	100,309
4	1,445	154	1,291	6,020	3,324	94,828	100,848	100,848
5	1,445	162	1,283	7,741	5,167	94,076	101,817	101,817
6	1,445	173	1,272	9,554	7,189	93,677	103,231	103,231
7	1,445	187	1,258	11,460	9,435	93,645	105,105	105,105
8	1,445	206	1,239	13,461	11,986	93,997	107,458	107,458
9	1,445	229	1,216	15,557	14,768	94,759	110,316	110,316
10	1,445	257	1,188	17,750	17,898	95,928	113,678	113,678
11	1,445	292	1,153	20,037	21,243	97,574	117,611	117,611
12	1,445	332	1,113	22,420	25,007	99,636	122,056	122,056
13	1,445	381	1,064	24,893	29,147	102,164	127,057	127,057
14	1,445	439	1,006	27,453	33,634	105,216	132,669	132,669
15	1,445	507	938	30,094	38,579	108,809	138,903	138,903
16	1,445	589	856	31,807	44,126	113,014	145,821	145,821
17	1,445	685	760	35,582	50,167	117,872	153,454	162,454
18	1,445	797	648	38,403	56,913	123,410	161,813	161,813
19	1,445	929	516	41,254	64,238	129,808	171,062	171,062
20	1,445	1,084	361	44,112	72,295	137,047	181,159	181,159

* Assumes dividends are used to purchase paid-up additions.

The whole life policy and the term rates used in this example are the same as those used in the equal outlay example (Figure 6.5). The cash accumulation example differs from the equal outlay example chiefly in that it keeps the total death benefits equal each year under each option by adjusting the face amount of the term coverage. This method unambiguously identifies the whole life policy as the superior strategy for years 10 and beyond.

comparison methods but also contains weaknesses that prevent it from being the single best answer to the financial planner's policy comparison problem.

Linton Yield Method

The Linton yield method works like this: The planner computes the rate of return that the policyowner must earn on a hypothetical (or real) side fund assuming death benefits and outlays are held equal for every year over the period being studied. The policy that should be selected according to this method is the one which has the highest Linton yield, that is,

the policy which — given an assumed schedule of costs (term rates) — has the highest rate of return.

In essence this method is just the reverse of the interest-adjusted method which holds the assumed interest rate level and solves for cost; the Linton method holds cost level and solves for interest. It should therefore be an excellent way to check the interest-adjusted method results since the two methods should rank policies virtually identically.

Planners can compare dissimilar policies through the Linton yield method. Note, however, that the same term rates must be used for each policy that is being evaluated or the results will

Figure 6.6

	20-YEAR LINTON YIELD							
	Ordinary Life (O.L.) versus Yearly Renewable Term (YRT)*							
	$100,000 face value for age 35 male nonsmoker							
Year	**O.L. Prem.**	**YRT Prem.**	**Diff. in Prem.**	**Side fund at 9.696%**	**O.L. Surrend. Value**	**YRT Face Amount**	**YRT Plus Side fund**	**O.L. with Paid-up Additions**
1	$1,445	$143	$1,302	$1,428	$3	$98,582	$100,010	$100,010
2	1,445	144	1,301	2,994	175	97,117	100,111	100,111
3	1,445	147	1,298	4,708	1,670	95,601	100,309	100,309
4	1,445	153	1,292	6,582	3,324	94,266	100,848	100,848
5	1,445	160	1,285	8,630	5,167	93,187	101,817	101,817
6	1,445	171	1,274	10,864	7,189	92,367	103,231	103,231
7	1,445	184	1,261	13,301	9,435	91,804	105,105	105,105
8	1,445	200	1,245	15,956	11,986	91,502	107,458	107,458
9	1,445	221	1,224	18,846	14,768	91,470	110,316	110,316
10	1,445	246	1,199	21,988	17,898	91,690	113,678	113,678
11	1,445	276	1,169	25,403	21,243	92,208	117,611	117,611
12	1,445	310	1,135	29,112	25,007	92,944	122,056	122,056
13	1,445	350	1,095	33,135	29,147	93,922	127,057	127,057
14	1,445	397	1,048	37,498	33,634	95,171	132,669	132,669
15	1,445	451	994	42,225	38,579	96,678	138,903	138,903
16	1,445	513	932	47,341	44,126	98,480	145,821	145,821
17	1,445	584	861	52,875	50,167	100,579	153,454	153,454
18	1,445	665	780	58,857	56,913	102,956	161,813	161,813
19	1,445	757	688	65,319	54,238	105,743	171,062	171,062
20	1,445	861	584	72,293	72,295	108,866	181,159	181,159

* Assumes dividends are used to purchase paid-up additions.

The difference between Ordinary Life premiums and Yearly Renewable Life premiums is invested at 9.696% in the side fund. Side fund equals cash value in year 20.

be misleading. The higher the term rate that is used, the higher the Linton yield that will be produced — and of course the reverse is also true. This emphasizes the importance of using this method only for a relative comparison of policies and not to measure the "true rate of return" actually credited to the cash value of a given policy.

Computationally, the Linton yield method is a variation on the cash accumulation method. Using the cash accumulation method described above, the Linton yield is the rate of return that equates the side fund with the cash surrender value for a specified period of years. For example, in the cash accumulation method example above, the side fund was just about equal to the cash surrender value in year 10 when the side fund was invested at six percent. Therefore, the Linton yield for the whole life policy (assuming the YRT rates are competitive) is

about six percent for 10 years. Figure 6.6 shows that the 20-year Linton yield for this policy is 9.696 percent.

Belth Yearly Rate of Return Method

The Belth yearly rate of return method works like this:

(1) Compute the "benefits" from the policy for the year (benefits are the sum of (a) end of each year's cash value, (b) dividends paid during the year, and (c) the net death benefit for the policy year).

(2) Compute the "investment" in the policy for the year (investment is defined as the sum of (a) the premium paid for the year plus (b) the cash value at the beginning of the year).

(3) Divide the benefits for the year by the investment for the year and subtract one from the result. Stated as a formula, the computation is:

$$\text{Yearly rate of return} = \frac{\text{Benefit}}{\text{Investments}} - 1$$

(4) Repeat the calculations for each year over the desired duration or planning period. See Figure 6.7.

This yearly rate of return method is especially useful to compare policies over many different durations. The policy with the highest yearly rates in the greatest number of years is generally the best choice.

As is the case with the comparison methods described above, this system has its weaknesses and potential flaws.

(1) The calculated yearly rates of return may be misleading where cash values are small.

(2) The results can be manipulated or unintentionally affected by the term rate assumed. The planner must specify an assumed yearly cost for insurance in order to calculate the benefits for the policy year. In other words one year term rates must be used. But if the term rates used are neither competitive nor realistic, the results will not accurately portray how well a "buy term, invest the difference" plan performs in comparison to a "buy whole life and build the cash values" plan.

(3) Typically, no one policy will be better than another year after year. This means the "best policy" may not be easy to select. One policy may provide the higher yearly rates of return in early years but not in later years.

Belth Yearly Price of Protection Method

The Belth yearly price of protection method works like this:

(1) Accumulate the client's "investment" in the policy for one year at an assumed rate of interest. (Investment is the sum of (a) the previous year end cash value plus (b) the current premium).

(2) Compute the sum of (a) the end of the year cash value plus (b) any dividend.

(3) Subtract the result of (2) from the result of (1).

(4) Divide the result of (3) by the net amount at risk in thousands to derive the cost of protection for the year. See Figure 6.7.

The result is an estimate of the cost in any given year of the net death benefit (death benefit minus cash value). The policy with the lowest yearly price of protection in the most years is generally the contract that should be selected under this method.

The flaws and potential weaknesses of this method are:

(1) The yearly prices of protection may have no relation to the actual mortality costs charged against the policy in any given year. To compare the calculated yearly "prices" (which have been critically affected by the rate of return assumed by the planner) with term insurance rates may be misleading. But, if the same assumed rate of interest is used when computing the yearly prices for all policies under consideration, the yearly rates for each policy should provide a good indication of where various policies stand in relation to others. Planners should use an assumed rate as close as possible to the rate actually used by the insurance company in its cash value and dividend illustrations. This will enable a fair comparison of the yearly prices of protection from the policy to yearly renewable term insurance.

(2) Where the net amount at risk for the year is relatively small, the yearly prices of protection will tend to fluctuate widely and have little meaning.

(3) As is the case with the previous method, in some years one policy may look better while in other years another policy will appear more favorable. This method may not always lead to an clear choice.

Summary of Methods

The Summary of Key Points of Common Cost Comparison Methods in Figure 6.8 should prove helpful in reviewing these methods and in deciding which should be used or how to properly overcome their flaws.

Other considerations in using these techniques are:

(1) Remember that policy comparisons based on policy illustrations created by a source other than an insurance company's home office may not be officially sanctioned, accurate, or complete. Demand computer printouts from the insurer's home office for comparative purchasing purposes.

(2) Policy dividend projections are not guarantees — a point the consumer often does not hear or understand (or sometimes does not want to hear or understand).

Figure 6.7

BELTH YEARLY RATE OF RETURN (YROR) AND YEARLY PRICE OF PROTECTION METHODS (YPOP)*							
Year	O.L. Prem.	Dividends	O.L. Cash Values	YRT Per $1000	Yearly Benefits	Yearly Investments	YROR	YPOP at 9.000%
1	$1,445	$3	$0	$1.45	$148	$1,445	-89.779%	$15.72
2	1,445	26	122	1.48	296	1,445	-79.494%	14.28
3	1,445	53	1,352	1.54	1,557	1,567	-0.640%	3.07
4	1,445	149	2,618	1.62	2,925	2,797	4.569%	2.89
5	1,445	278	3,919	1.72	4,363	4,063	7.377%	2.41
6	1,445	418	5,252	1.85	5,845	5,364	8.961%	1.87
7	1,445	572	6,619	2.00	7,378	6,697	10.168%	1.16
8	1,445	742	8,020	2.19	8,963	8,064	11.146%	0.31
9	1,445	928	9,455	2.42	10,602	9,465	12.011%	(0.73)
10	1,445	1,133	10,923	2.68	12,294	10,900	12.797%	(1.97)
11	1,445	1,355	12,423	2.99	14,039	12,368	13.516%	(3.39)
12	1,445	1,584	13,960	3.33	15,830	13,868	14.150%	(4.97)
13	1,445	1,837	15,527	3.73	17,679	15,405	14.764%	(6.78)
14	1,445	2,116	17,127	4.17	19,588	16,972	15.415%	(8.97)
15	1,445	2,424	18,757	4.66	21,559	18,572	16.087%	(11.54)
16	1,445	2,766	20,418	5.21	23,598	20,202	16.811%	(14.62)
17	1,445	3,140	22,105	5.81	25,698	21,863	17.541%	(18.16)
18	1,445	3,552	23,823	6.46	27,867	23,550	18.332%	(22.39)
19	1,445	4,011	25,570	7.16	30,114	25,268	19.178%	(27.39)
20	1,445	4,514	27,345	7.91	32,434	27,015	20.059%	(33.21)

* Dividends are not used to buy paid-up additions.

Yearly benefit = cash value + dividend + death protection benefit
Death protection benefit = YRT rate x ($100,000 - cash value) x .001
Yearly investment = premium + prior year's cash value
YROR = (yearly benefit ÷ yearly investment) - 1
YPOP = ((premium + cash value prior year) x (1 + interest rate) - cash value - dividend)
      ÷ ($100,000 - cash value) x .001

The financial adviser should not only emphasize this in comparing policies but also in making presentations to clients.

(3) The longer the period into the future that values are projected or illustrated the less likely they are to be either precise or accurate.

(4) The method used to decide rates credited to cash values and to allocate the amount of dividends to policyowners and then apportion them among policyowners will significantly affect policy comparisons. Check to see if the company is using the "port-folio" method or the "investment year" method (sometimes called the "new money" method).

Most companies now use the investment year method. Under the investment year method the assets acquired with the premiums paid during a particular year are treated as a separate cell of the insurance company's general asset account. The investment returns earned by the assets in each calendar-year cell are credited to the cell. Each year as the composition of the cell changes because of maturities, repayments, sales, and other transactions, the changing investment performance of the cell is allocated to the policies that

Figure 6.8

SUMMARY OF KEY POINTS OF COMMON COST COMPARISON METHODS

	Traditional Net Cost	Interest Adjusted Net Cost	Equal Outlay	Cash Accumulation	Linton Yield	Belth Yield	Belth Price
Technique	Sum premiums less CV and dividends; ignores interest	Sum premiums at interest less sum dividends at interest and CV	Accumulate premium differences at interest	Accumulate premium differences at interest while holding death benefits constant	Accumulate premium differences at interest rate that causes equal future values and equal death benefits	Ratio of "benefits" to "investment"	Policy "investment" less benefits
Solves for:	"Net cost"	Average net cost	Surrender value and death benefit differences	Surrender value differences	Average rate of return that causes equality	Yearly rate of return	Yearly price of protection
Assumptions needed	Money has no time value	Rate of return	(1) Rate of return (2) Equal outlay (3) Equal death benefits	(1) Rate of return (2) Equal outlay	(1) YRT rates (2) Equal outlay (3) Equal death benefits	YRT rates	Rate of return
Compares similar policies	No	Yes	Yes, but often ambiguous results	Yes	Yes, if common YRT rates used	Yes, if common YRT rates used	Yes
Compares dissimilar policies?	No	No	Yes, but results often ambiguous	Yes	Yes	Yes	Yes
Requires computer?	No	No, but time consuming	No, but time consuming	Yes	Yes	No	No
Good for replacement evaluation?	No	No	Yes, with modification	Yes, with modification	Yes, with modification	Yes, but results often ambiguous	Yes, but results often ambiguous

paid the premiums to acquire the assets in the cell. This method promotes equity since policyholders receive the investment results that are directly attributable to their premium contributions.

If the portfolio method is used, all policies are credited with the rate earned on the company's overall portfolio, despite the fact that earnings on premium dollars received in some years may actually be earning higher or lower returns than the portfolio rate. For instance, in periods of declining interest rates, the premium dollars received on new policies will probably be invested by the company at rates that are lower than the company earns on its existing portfolio. If the portfolio method is used, these new policyholders will benefit at the expense of the prior policyholders because they will be credited with higher returns than their premium dollars are actually earning. Conversely, if interest rates are increasing, use of the portfolio method will be disadvantageous for new policyholders, but beneficial to existing policyholders. Make sure all the illustrations are based on the same method if possible.

(5) Supplementary benefits and riders affect policy comparisons. For example, the total premium for a policy with waiver of premium should be adjusted to take into account the extra charge.

(6) In comparing whole life insurance to "buy term and invest the difference" be sure to consider the value of

    (a) protection from creditors,

    (b) probate savings,

    (c) federal gift/estate tax savings implications,

    (d) state gift/death tax savings implications,

    (e) dividend options (such as one year term),

    (f) loan/collateral uses,

    (g) settlement (annuity) options.

Where To Find Policy Rating Information

The most authoritative independent sources of information on premiums, cash values, dividends, interest adjusted indexes, dividend histories, settlement option values, and other essential data for policy comparison are:

(1) *Best's Flitcraft Compend* available from the A.M. Best Company, Oldwick, New Jersey.

(2) *Best's Review*, a monthly magazine, runs policy comparisons and each year compares dividend histories of different companies. This magazine is also a valuable source of information about new products.

(3) *Consumer's Reports* does some evaluations for non-professionals but is unfortunately limited in the number of companies and policies reviewed.

(4) The *Life Insurance Consumer's Handbook* written by Professor Joseph Belth and published by the University of Indiana is another source of useful information on individual policy statistics.

PART V: HOW TO COMPARE LIFE INSURANCE COMPANIES

Financial planners doing a policy comparison invite malpractice suits by not investigating an insurance company as surely as they invite a law suit when they have not done "due diligence" in investigating a security. Advisers must consider:

(1) quantitative investment performance and financial soundness;

(2) corporate management philosophy and ethics; and

(3) qualitative aspects of company performance.

Performance and Soundness

Sources to quantify the strength of a company's investment performance and financial soundness are available from the *Best's Reports* of the A. M. Best Co. and the insurer ratings from Standard & Poor's. It is essential that the financial planner test each company under consideration for these factors because

(1) Competitive changes in the life insurance industry have reduced the safety margins with respect to (i) surplus accounts, (ii) mortality assumptions, (iii) expenses, (iv) investment assumptions. Levels below those traditionally maintained by insurance companies are not uncommon. This translates into an impaired ability to deal with unforeseen increases in expenses, decreases in investment performance, or increases in mortality.

(2) Some insurance companies have invested heavily in high risk assets such as "junk bonds."

(3) At the same time that safety margins are shrinking, underwriting profits are being threatened by perhaps the greatest threat ever faced by insurance companies, AIDS. It is impossible to predict the impact of AIDS on the financial health of the insurance industry.

(4) The stock market has dramatically illustrated how quickly it can rise and fall.

Note that the portfolio return in any given year is a relatively meaningless figure; an evaluation of investment performance must take into account at least two and preferably five or more years. Insurers who have been investing in higher risk/higher return portfolios invite considerable volatility in return for the opportunity.

The financial planner must also go beyond easily obtained statistics and consider many other interconnected and interrelated factors such as the company's efficiency in carrying out administrative and claims handling functions. A company which is highly efficient in these areas may offset lower investment returns and provide more value per premium dollar to the client than a company having a higher portfolio yield but less efficient operations.

Corporate Management Philosophy

Qualitative aspects of a company should not be ignored in the comparative process. Planners should ask:

(1) Will (and can) the company do what it says it will do?

(2) How realistic are its projections?

(3) What is the company's past "promised vs. delivered" track record? Some companies take a conservative stance on projected dividends and actively try to deliver a significantly better performance while others "puff" their projections. Comparing projected with actually paid dividends over a 20 year period will show the amount by which actual dividends exceeded projected dividends (or vice versa) and gives some indication of how well the company has done sharing its earnings relative to what it led those same policyowners to hope for when the policy was sold.

(4) Has the company had its ratings reduced at any time in the recent past? (Check ratings for a duration of at least

five years rather than rely on a single year's rating). A reduction in rating is unusual and could be an indication of potentially serious problems. A company with a B rating downgraded from an A+ may be more of a risk than a C+ rating company recently upgraded from a C rating.

Qualitative Aspects of Company Performance

Be sure also to consider:

(1) speed of service;

(2) quality and accuracy of service;

(3) courtesy; and

(4) geographic availability.

These factors can vary widely within a single company because of differences in staff and management at various agency locations and change over time as a result of retirements, disabilities, and deaths of personnel. Yet top management of most companies sets the standards and there is often some consistency within a given company. Ask other professionals and policyholders about the reputation of the companies and agents under consideration.

Seek out staff who hold professional designations such as CLU (Chartered Life Underwriter), CFP (Certified Financial Planner), ChFC (Chartered Financial Consultant), or who have advanced degrees such as a Masters of Law in Taxation or a state authorized specialization. These designations or degrees indicate preparation and dedication above minimal requirements for the profession.

CONCLUSION

Due diligence in advising clients on the selection of the appropriate life insurance product requires that the financial planner first determine the proper type of policy or appropriate product mix. This step is often preceded by or occurs simultaneously with the determination of the amount of insurance the client's family or business needs. Planners must then thoroughly understand a policy illustration and its underlying assumptions. The two final stages are to measure one policy against another using an objective and quantifiable method with a minimum of weaknesses and to likewise measure the soundness of the companies that stand behind the policies being compared.

Chapter 7

HOW TO REVIEW A WILL: A CHECKLIST FOR THE ESTATE AND FINANCIAL PLANNER

Note: A version of this article under the title "How To Review a Will" has appeared in the magazine *Financial Planning* in two parts, April and May, 1988.

INTRODUCTION

A will is the legal document that specifies how a person wants to dispose of the real and personal property he owns in his own name at the time of his death. Most mentally competent adults have the legal capacity to draw a will. But few persons are knowledgeable enough to do so properly. Only an attorney should draft a will and even most attorneys should not attempt to draw their own.

Despite this, every member of the estate planning team, including the financial planner, should know how to review a will.

First, it is necessary to coordinate the will properly with other dispositive documents such as employee benefit plans. For example, if the will is not synchronized with an executive's pension, group insurance, and 401(k) plan, there is no way to minimize overall death taxes and provide for a smooth and efficient estate administration.

Second, it is impossible to know if there will be appropriate liquidity unless the will and its various dispositive schemes are examined.

Third, wills become outdated and tax laws change (for instance, a marital deduction provision in a will drafted before September 13, 1981, may not qualify for the unlimited marital deduction and TRA '97 increased the unified credit in a series of steps and introduced a family-owned business exclusion). The circumstances, needs, and desires of the parties are always in flux. The attorney who drafted the will may have died and it may have been many years since the will was revised or reviewed by either the client or attorney.

Every professional in the estate planning team must therefore be able to examine a will and spot — in general terms at least — what's wrong.

"What's wrong" with a given will is more often a question of what has been omitted or what has changed or what are the present objectives of the client than what has been improperly drafted. "What's wrong" is even more often the failure of the draftsman to match the facts of the case or the circumstances or desires of the parties with the documents. "What's wrong" may be something the accountant, for instance, knows that no other professional knows. "What's wrong" may be that the will has not been updated for years and no longer addresses the current circumstances or client goals or latest tax law. "What's wrong" may be that a will alone—without a trust or the use of other tools or techniques—is inadequate or does not maximize the possibility to accomplish the client's objectives with greater certainty and lesser cost.

The following is a (by no means complete) checklist designed to give each member of the estate planning team the tools needed to examine a will:

INTRODUCTORY CLAUSE

Start with the introductory ("exordium") clause which should be the first paragraph in the will. The purpose of this preamble is to

(1) identify the testator, the person disposing of property at death;

(2) establish domicile, the county that will have legal jurisdiction for purposes of determining the validity of the will and interpreting will provisions, for purposes of state inheritance taxation (technically, what is said in a will about the testator's domicile is not dispositive but is evidence which will usually be considered even if subordinated to proof of facts to the contrary);

(3) declare that the document in question is intended to dispose of the testator's property at death and no matter how many wills have been written in the past, this is meant to be the last will; and

(4) revoke all prior wills. This is designed to nullify old and forgotten wills — and "codicils" (legally effective modifications of existing wills).

An example of this introductory clause is:

I, Edward Grieg, a resident of and domiciled in the city of Bryn Mawr in Montgomery County, Pennsylvania, declare this to be my last will. I revoke all wills and codicils made prior to this will.

Planners should check:

(1) Is the spelling of the client's name correct? Has the client's full name been used?

(2) Is the client "A/K/A" ("also known as"), i.e., is there some other name by which the client is known and should that name be listed?

(3) Is the domicile correct? For tax or other planning purposes, would it make sense to begin to document a different domicile? Will the will meet all the statutory requirements of the stated domicile? If the client spends a great deal of time in more than one residence, could the address mentioned in the will trigger a "double domicile" problem (e.g., where more than one state claims the decedent was a domiciliary of the state and therefore has the right to impose an inheritance tax)?

(4) Is there a reason prior wills and codicils should not be revoked? Instead of a new will, should the present document be a codicil making a small change but otherwise ratifying an existing will? For instance, if there is a potential for an attack on this will on the grounds of mental incompetency, fraud, or undue influence, a prior will providing a similar disposition will help prove the mental capacity of the testator and may discourage would-be contestants from attacking the current will. Conversely, if a beneficiary has been deleted, a new will should be drawn rather than a codicil to avoid the mention of the eliminated beneficiary.

After the introductory clause, the will can take either of two directions. It can (1) describe the steps that take place in administering the testator's estate (such as payment of debts and taxes and then payment of legacies) or it can (2) dispose of legacies first and describe obligations later. We will take the former approach in formulating this checklist.

DEBTS CLAUSE

The next clause usually pertains to the payment of debts, expenses, and costs. The purposes of this clause are:

(1) To state the source from which each debt will be paid. (This is an extremely important point because of the death

tax implications. For instance, if a surviving spouse rather than some other beneficiary must pay debts, to that extent the marital deduction will be decreased and taxes may be increased. Furthermore, if the burden falls on the wrong person(s), the testator's goals may not be met.)

(2) To establish as debts items which might not otherwise be considered the testator's obligations.

An example of the payment of debts clause is:

I direct all of my debts (including any expenses of my last illness) and my funeral expenses be paid.

Planners should check:

(1) Does the testator have any rights to property held in the trust of another person (a so-called "power of appointment") and, if so, what effect does the debts clause have on that property? Does it expose that property to the claims of creditors?

(2) Will the beneficiaries receive more or less than the client intended when the will was drawn because of the operation of this provision? Has the size of the debt changed since the will was drawn? What will be the federal and state death tax impact of the clause?

(3) What is the effect of the Equal Rights Amendment in the state of domicile? In some states the will of a married woman should contain a direction to pay debts and taxes. Otherwise, the burden of her funeral and medical expenses will be placed on her surviving husband — thus barring a deduction for payment of those expenses by her estate.

(4) Did the will provide detailed funeral arrangements? Most authorities feel this is inadvisable since the will may not be found or may not be accessible in sufficient time after the testator's death. Should such provisions be placed in a "Letter of Instructions," an informal and nonlegal list of requests, suggestions, and recommendations that should not be placed in the will?

(5) Does the client intend that "payment of debts" include the mortgage on property left to a specific individual? In some states, absent an express direction to the contrary, when specific property is left to an individual (a "specific bequest"), any debt on that property will not be paid off. In other states, such a clause will require the executor to satisfy the mortgage. Does the named beneficiary of a life insurance policy that has been pledged as the collateral for a loan have the right to have the loan paid off because of the "pay my [just] debts" clause? The planner must

check state law. In at least one state the answer depends on who the lender is. The result, absent specific direction to the contrary, is one way if the lender is the insurance company (the beneficiary takes only the net proceeds) and another (the beneficiary is entitled to have the estate pay off the debt out of other estate assets) if the creditor is an independent lending institution.

TAX CLAUSE

The clause pertaining to the payment of death taxes can either be stated next or appear after the provisions disposing of property.

The purpose of the tax clause is to establish the source for the payment of the federal estate tax, the state inheritance and estate tax, and any federal or state generation-skipping transfer tax.

This is an example of a tax clause:

I direct that all inheritance, estate, transfer, succession, legacy and other death taxes upon property required to be included in my taxable estate whether or not passing under this Will [except (1) transfer taxes levied pursuant to the provisions of Chapter 13 of the Internal Revenue Code of 1986, relating to "generation-skipping transfers," or any similar state law, and (2) taxes on property held in trust under the Will (or any revocable trust) of my spouse], and any interest and penalties thereon, shall be charged against and paid from my residuary estate passing under Article *FOURTH* of Part I of this my Will.

Planners should check:

(1) State "apportionment" statutes. If there is no tax clause in the will or if it does not adequately address the payment of a particular death tax, state law will allocate the burden of taxes among the beneficiaries. Many states require beneficiaries to pay a share of estate taxes unless the will provides otherwise. The result is often an inappropriate or unintended reduction of the shares of certain beneficiaries or adverse tax consequences. (For example, there may be a spiraling reduction of the estate tax marital deduction. The deduction is allowed only for the net amount passing to the surviving spouse. If that amount is reduced by an estate tax burden, the tax increases — further reducing the amount passing to the spouse, etc.) An "anti-apportionment" tax clause may be the solution. For instance, suppose you wanted a child to receive $100,000 of your client's $2,000,000 estate

free and clear. Without special provision, that child would be forced to pay his share of taxes, or 1/20 of the total federal and state death taxes. With a special tax clause, the child will receive the entire $100,000.

(2) Does the client expect or want property passing outside the probate estate to pay its share of tax if it in fact generates tax? For instance, assume $1,000,000 of pension proceeds (or life insurance) is payable to the client's two oldest children and $1,000,000 of cash is payable to the client's two youngest children. Who is to pay the tax on the $2,000,000? What if the $1,000,000 of pension proceeds (or life insurance) is state inheritance tax exempt but the cash is not? Unless the will provides to the contrary, estate taxes must be paid by recipients of property passing outside the will. The will should specify who pays taxes on both probate and nonprobate property.

(3) Assume a sizable amount of property will pass through a revocable living trust. Is the tax clause in that instrument coordinated with the tax clause in the will or are they incompatible? What if assets under the will are to "pour over" into a previously funded trust which itself will generate significant estate taxes. Is there (should there be) a will provision calling upon the trust to help the estate pay taxes? Does the trust have a provision recognizing and empowering a "call" on its assets to pay the probate estate's taxes?

(4) Who is to pay the tax on a generation-skipping transfer? Absent a contrary direction, the taxes will probably be payable from the assets of the fund subject to the tax. Some draftsmen specifically provide that such taxes are not to be imposed on the "skip person's" estate.

(5) Assume the facts indicate that very large taxable gifts have been made by the client. The taxable portion of these gifts — to the extent not included in the client's gross estate — will be considered "adjusted taxable gifts." They will increase the rate of federal estate tax payable on the taxable estate remaining. Will an unexpectedly high burden be placed on the assets remaining because of these prior gifts and should the tax clause take such gifts into account in apportioning the tax burden?

(6) Should certain beneficiaries be insulated from tax for either tax reasons or to accomplish the dispositive goals of the client or better meet the needs of the beneficiaries? For example, should a child to whom property has been given be exempted by the will from paying the estate tax on that property?

TANGIBLE PERSONAL PROPERTY CLAUSE

A clause pertaining to the disposition of tangible personal property is often next. The purposes of this clause are:

(1) to provide for who will receive personal property and the terms under which they will receive it; and

(2) to make special dispositions among the persons and the organizations of the testator's choice.

An example of the tangible personal property dispositive clause is:

I give to my daughter, Eva Grieg, all of my clothing, household furnishings, jewelry, automobiles, books, pictures, and all other articles of tangible personal property owned by me at the date of my death. If my daughter, Eva Grieg, does not survive me, I give the property mentioned above in equal shares to my grandchildren, Gretta and Gail Grieg or the survivor who is alive at the date of my death.

or

I give the Philadelphia Museum of Art my painting of "Helga" by Andrew Wyeth.

Planners should check:

(1) Does (or should) the client make specific bequests of all "intimate" items such as a watch or ring? Absent such provisions, if personal property has been left to several individuals, the result is often needless expense in determining who gets what or reducing the estate to cash (not to mention the potential for bitter intrafamily fights). If specific bequests have been made, has each item been described in enough detail so that there will be no confusion as to which diamond ring the testator meant? (Use the same description as is found in the insurance policy covering the loss or theft of the item).

(2) Has provision been made in case the item specifically left to a beneficiary is not owned by the decedent at death? For instance, what if one ring is sold and the proceeds are used to purchase a second. Does the named beneficiary receive the second ring?

(3) If the item specifically bequeathed has been lost, stolen, etc. and the loss has been covered by insurance, would the client want the named beneficiary to receive the insurance? In many states the bequest of an item of personal property does not — absent specific direction to the contrary — also pass the insurance covering the item.

(4) Does the client intend to pass — under the category of personal property — cash in a safe deposit box, travelers' checks, and cash found in his home or on his person? Does the client know that cash on deposit is typically not considered tangible personal property?

(5) If the client has property in many different places, consider allowing the executor — at the expense of the estate — to take possession of the property "as and where is" (a provision which will permit the beneficiary to receive the property free of delivery costs and protect the fiduciary and beneficiaries during administration from the risk that specific assets will be lost).

(6) The phrase "personal effects" may not encompass items of household use or even a car. Consider specific mention of items of tangible personal property.

(7) Is there a "catchall" phrase that passes the residue of tangible personalty? The phrase, "all other tangible personal property" should dispose of any residual property.

(8) Should the will confirm that certain property such as household furnishings, silverware, etc. belongs to someone else?

(9) Does this clause dispose of property by referring to an instrument outside the will? This "incorporation by reference" is not recommended since it often leads to litigation.

(10) The use of the term "contents" should be avoided. Personal property should not be described by its location.

General checkup of legacies:

(1) Has property been left outright to a minor who is legally incapable of handling it or to a person under a physical, mental, or emotional handicap who does not have the physical or intellectual capacity?

(2) Are all beneficiaries named alive? Are there "backup" beneficiaries (at least two) for each beneficiary? Are they the beneficiaries the client currently desires?

(3) Are any of the gifts conditioned on events or circumstances which are impossible, "against public policy," or in violation of the Constitution? For example, a bequest would be invalidated by the courts if it were made on the condition that the recipient first divorce her spouse.

(4) Are there gifts to "my issue" (which would unintentionally disinherit an adopted person)?

(5) Do gifts to charities meet state law requirements? Has the charity's full legal (corporate) name and address been stated? (The popular name is often different from the full legal name). Have you checked the IRS's "Cumulative List of Organizations" or obtained assurances from the charity itself to make sure the gift to the charity will qualify for a tax deduction? Has the client named a backup charity? Check to be sure the will specifies that taxes are to be paid from the portion of the residue not passing to charity. Otherwise, what should be a tax-free bequest must bear its portion of the total taxes. That reduces the charity's share and therefore increases taxes. This in turn creates a new cycle of problems.

(6) If someone is intentionally omitted, have you checked state law to see if such an omission is permissible? Are there defamatory statements in the will concerning an heir? (At the probate of the will, such statements may become libelous and expose the client's estate to an action for damages.)

(7) Does the will make so many specific bequests of cash that the residuary estate doesn't have enough left to pay estate taxes? Keep in mind that the IRS can attach the assets of any beneficiary for the unpaid estate tax. Check to be sure the executor will have a sufficient reserve of funds for paying estate tax and all the bequests to residuary beneficiaries.

(8) Note that a tangible personal property clause should nearly always be used where the residue of the estate will be paid to a trust. Few clients want trusts involved in handling personal effects such as jewelry, or household furniture, antiques, or cars.

DEVISES OF REAL ESTATE CLAUSE

The next clause pertains to "devises," testamentary grants of real property. The purposes of the devises clause are:

(1) to specify which real estate is to be disposed of under the will and to dispose of that real estate, and

(2) to handle the problems where the property has been sold or destroyed prior to the testator's death.

An example of a devise is:

I leave my residence located at 207 Rawles Run Lane, Bryn Mawr, Pa. to my daughter, Larrissa Grieg. If, at the time of my death, I am no longer using the property at 207 Rawles Run Lane as my residence, then this devise is to be void and of no effect; however, if I own any other real estate which I am using as my residence at that time, then, in such an event, I devise such other real estate to my daughter, Larrissa Grieg. If my daughter, Larrissa Grieg, does not survive me, this devise shall lapse and such real estate shall become part of my residuary estate.

SPECIFIC BEQUESTS OF INTANGIBLES AND CASH

After disposing of tangible personal property and real estate, the will may then cover specific gifts of intangibles (property where the item itself is evidence of value) such as gifts of cash or accounts receivable. An example of a gift of an intangible asset is:

I give 100 shares of Rohm and Haas stock to my niece, Danielle Green.

or

I give the sum of Five Thousand ($5,000) dollars to my sister, Sara Black, if she survives me.

Planners should check:

(1) Has provision been made in the event the primary beneficiary does not survive the decedent?

(2) Does the will spell out what gift, if any, is made if the decedent does not possess, at the time of death, the stock mentioned in the will? What if the stock had been sold but new stock was purchased with the proceeds?

RESIDUARY CLAUSE

The next clause is called the "residuary clause." The purposes of the residuary clause are to:

(1) transfer all assets not disposed of up to this point,

(2) (in some cases) provide a mechanism for "pouring over" assets from the will to a previously established (inter vivos) trust (if a pourover is made, it is important to review the trust as carefully as the will itself), and

(3) provide for an alternative disposition in case the primary beneficiary has died or the trust to which probate assets (assets passing under a valid will or by intestacy) were to be poured over was for some reason invalid, previously revoked, or never came into existence.

An example of a residuary clause is:

All the rest, residue, and remainder of the property which I own at the date of my death, real and personal, tangible or intangible, regardless of where it is situated, I leave to my daughter, Larrissa Grieg. But if Larrissa Grieg does not survive me, then I leave the said property in equal shares to my grandchildren, Ronald Reimus and Reginald Reimus or to the survivor of them.

Planners should check:

(1) Has a spouse been disinherited? If so, is the client aware of the "elective rights" (rights to a portion of the probate estate and perhaps certain other property owned by the decedent at death regardless of what the will provides) the surviving spouse has even if the will is valid? (It may be possible to control the surviving spouse to some degree by inserting a provision at least as attractive as the spouse's intestate share or by a provision reducing or eliminating the share of a person in whom the spouse is interested if he exercises his right of election. An alternative is a pre- or post-nuptial agreement).

(2) Has the client, inadvertently, exercised a "power of appointment" (a right to direct the disposition of property in a trust established by someone else)? In some states, a residuary clause automatically exercises a general power of appointment unless the trust requires that it must be specifically referred to in order to make a valid exercise or unless the will itself states that no exercise is intended.

(3) Is there a disposition to a young adult, minor, or a person legally, mentally, or emotionally incompetent that should be made in trust? Is there provision for the executor to retain the property during the minority of such a person or to use income or principal for that person's benefit? Has the right person been named as the custodian of a child's property and are there backups in case that person is unwilling or unable to serve?

(4) Is there a default provision in case a trust into which the residue was to have poured is for any reason revoked or never came into existence?

(5) If a child dies, will that child's share pass to the parties desired by the client?

(6) Does the will address the possibility of the birth of a child to the client (it's never too late)?

(7) Has the client, in lieu of leaving his residuary estate outright to his spouse, created a marital deduction formula disposition through a so-called formula clause?

Marital deduction formula clauses are very important to review and analyze. They are often found in the wills of clients who own assets of at least the unified credit equivalent ($625,000, scheduled to increase to $1,000,000 by 2006). Such clauses typically divide the client's estate into two parts, one "marital" and the other "nonmarital." The marital portion passes property to the client's surviving spouse as part of the marital deduction and may contain an outright or trust disposition. The nonmarital portion is designed to set aside property exempted from federal estate tax by reason of the client's available unified credit and passes property to persons other than the surviving spouse (or to a credit equivalent "bypass trust" for the benefit of the surviving spouse that will not be included in the spouse's estate on his death).

The language used in the formula typically takes the form of a fixed sum (a "pecuniary marital deduction") or a fraction of the client's residuary estate (a "fractional share marital deduction"). The formula clause (especially if it is a pecuniary one) will also have to contain a provision for funding the marital deduction when assets are distributed to it.

If the marital deduction clause directs that the property is to be held in trust, the surviving spouse must be entitled to all of the trust's net income in each year and no other person may be interested in the income or principal during the survivor's lifetime.

Any planner who regularly reviews client wills should familiarize himself with marital deduction requirements, or, at least, direct inquiries to persons who have expertise in this area.

If the client owns an interest in a business, it is important to consider the Code section 2033A family-owned business interest exclusion.

POWERS CLAUSE

The next clause is often one pertaining to the powers of the executor (and trustee if the will establishes a "testamentary trust," a trust created at the testator's death under the will). The purposes of the powers clause are to:

(1) give the executor (and trustee) specific power and authority over and above those provided by state law to enable the executor to conserve and manage the property, and

(2) limit, where desired and appropriate, the executor's power and authority (for instance, the client may not want the executor to make certain investments), and

(3) provide authority to continue a business (or handle other property with special management or investment prob-

lems) and the special flexibility necessary to accomplish that objective, and

(4) protect the executor against suit by other beneficiaries by specifying the powers necessary to accomplish the executor's role.

An (abbreviated) example of a powers clause is:

I authorize my executor (as well as any substitute executor) in his, her, or its discretion, with respect to all property, real and personal, in addition to the powers conferred by law, to:

1. retain assets

2. purchase investments

3. hold cash

4. vote and grant proxies

5. sell, exchange, or dispose of

6. distribute in cash or in kind

7. delegate to agents

8. assign or compromise claims

9. borrow funds

10. lease, manage, develop real estate

11. abandon property

12. make certain tax elections

13. receive and use employee benefits

Planners should check:

(1) Are there any assets or problems in this case which require special powers to fulfill the desires of the client or provide the executor with sufficient flexibility? (Beware of "boilerplate" clauses). Are there powers that should be added? Are there "standard" powers that should be removed or modified.

(2) Will any power adversely affect the estate tax marital deduction? For instance, a marital deduction trust, under Code section 2056(b)(5) or (b)(7), must provide that the surviving spouse receive all income at least annually. Consider the impact of a power allowing the trustee under a testamentary trust to retain nonincome producing property. Unless the will/trust also contains a provision allowing the surviving spouse to demand that the trust assets be sold or made income producing, the marital deduction may be lost. Will such a power thwart other objectives of the testator? For instance, what if the unproductive property was stock in a family corporation? A sale of such stock would raise income but could cause the loss of family control of the corporation.

The draftsman might consider including a "savings clause" that would nullify any power, duty, or discretionary authority that might jeopardize the marital deduction.

(3) Will any of the powers granted cause a conflict of interest? For instance, if the executor is a bank, discretionary authority to invest in its own securities or common trust funds will cause a conflict that must be specifically "forgiven" by the will (assuming the client wants to do so). Is the executor a business partner or co-shareholder of the insured? What problems might they create?

(4) Is there specific authority for the executor to make distribution "in kind" (as opposed to selling estate assets and making the distribution in cash?) In some states absent specified power to do so, the executor may have no choice: the distribution must be made in cash.

APPOINTMENT OF FIDUCIARIES CLAUSE

The appointment of the executor, trustee of any testamentary trust, and guardian of any minor child, often comes toward the end of the will.

The purposes of the fiduciary appointment clause are:

(1) to name the individual(s) or corporate fiduciary or combinations of individual(s) and fiduciaries who will administer the testator's estate and any trust which the will creates;

(2) to give the executor the appropriate power to act on behalf of the estate and carry out the terms of the will;

(3) to specify if and how the executor is to be compensated;

(4) state whether or not the executor is to post bond;

(5) to specify the authority of and decision making process for co-executors; and

(6) to name guardian(s) and successor guardian(s) of any minor child of the testator.

An example of the appointment clause is:

I appoint my nephew, Farnsworth Dowlrimple III, as the executor under this will. If for any reason he fails to qualify or ceases to act, I appoint the Left Bank and Trust of Overflow, Pa. as my executor. I confer upon my executor all the powers enumerated in clause _____ above. No executor shall be required to furnish any bond or other security in any jurisdiction. I direct that my nephew, Farnsworth, shall receive no compensation for his services as Executor and that the Left Bank and Trust of Overflow, Pa. be entitled to be compensated for its services as executor in accordance with its regularly adopted schedule of compensation in effect and applicable at the time of the performance of such services.

Planners should check:

(1) Does the client trust the individual who is currently named as executor and backup executor? Is that individual or corporate fiduciary legally qualified to act as executor? (Has the attorney who drew the will been named as executor? Typically, absent special circumstances, this raises a number of ethical questions and raises the spectre of a conflict of interest.)

(2) Should the executor's bond be waived?

(3) Is the executor named willing to serve? (How recently has the client checked?)

(4) Is the guardian for minors willing to act? Is he able to act? Is that person suitable?

(5) Is a prolonged estate (or trust) administration anticipated? If so, consider giving executors (trustees) the power to appoint successors by filing an instrument with the probate or other appropriate court.

TESTATOR'S SIGNING CLAUSE

The next to the last clause in a will is typically the testator's signing or "testimonium" provision. The purposes of the testimonium clause are

(1) to establish that the document is intended to be the testator's last will,

(2) to meet statutory requirements that require the testator's signature at the logical conclusion of the will, and

(3) to state the date on which the will was signed.

An example of a testimonium clause is:

In witness of the above, I subscribe my name, this 11th day of September, 1998 at Bryn Mawr, Pennsylvania to this, my last will, which consists of 13 pages (each of which I have initialed at the bottom).

Planners should check:

(1) Is the will signed by the testator at its logical end? Is each page numbered? Is the page count correct?

(2) Are there duplicate or triplicate signed wills in existence? If the testator was given a signed duplicate which is not found at his death, it is possible that a presumption will arise that the testator destroyed it with the intention of revoking it. The potential for litigation is therefore increased significantly. The better practice is for only one original to be executed.

ATTESTATION CLAUSE

The final clause in a will is the "attestation" provision. The purposes of the attestation (often called the witness) clause are to:

(1) witness the testator's signing,

(2) comply with statutory requirements,

(3) underline the testamentary character of the document, and

(4) comply with state law requirements in cases where the testator signed by a mark (such as an "X") or where, at the testator's direction and on his behalf, the will was signed by someone else (as would be the case where the testator was physically incapable of signing but mentally competent).

An example of an attestation clause is:

This will was signed by Edward Grieg, the testator, and declared to be his last will in our presence. We, at his request and in his presence and in the presence of each other, state that we witnessed his signing and declaration and at his request we have signed our names as witnesses this 11th day of September, 1998.

Planners should check:

(1) Are there three witnesses to the testator's signing? Although most states require less, three witness will comply with the most stringent probate requirements of any state and as a practical matter provide stronger evidence of the competence and testamentary intent of the testator.

(2) Were any of the witnesses beneficiaries under the will? This is inadvisable for at least two reasons: First, the witnesses may become incompetent to testify as to the execution or validity of the will. Second, witnesses who are also beneficiaries may be prevented from receiving bequests under the will.

(3) Are the addresses of the witnesses stated? Although addresses may not be legally required, they make it easier to locate and identify witnesses when needed.

(4) Is the will "self proving"? I.e., in some states a notarized affidavit attached to the will signed by the witnesses (and in some states, the testator, also) which describes the circumstances of the execution of the will may permit the will to be admitted to probate without the requirement that the witnesses be found or appear before the court in the probate proceeding.

OTHER CLAUSES

There are, of course, many other clauses which should be considered in reviewing a will. Some additional points for the planner to check are:

(1) Is the federal estate tax marital deduction important? If so, consider that the Uniform Simultaneous Death Act, which applies in most states, presumes that the testator survives in the event of a simultaneous death involving the testator and a beneficiary. This would cause a loss of the estate tax marital deduction unless the will superseded state law by providing a "common disaster" clause. This provision makes the presumption that the testator's spouse is deemed to have survived.

(2) Does the will consider the possibility that one or more beneficiaries will disclaim? The will should state who

will receive property if the named beneficiary renounces his interest. The transfer is then treated as if the decedent had left property directly to the ultimate recipient.

(3) Have the provisions in the will been coordinated with other dispositive instruments? For instance, is the will coordinated with all trusts, with employee benefit plans, buy-sell agreements, and life insurance beneficiary designations?

(4) Are the problems of minors, incompetents, and other beneficiaries with special needs or circumstances properly addressed in the will? In other words, is the right asset going to the right person at the right time and in the right manner?

Has the client considered the financial burden that may be placed on the guardians of minor children, and have appropriate financial provisions been made so that they can afford to raise both the client's children and their own? (Some may want to set up a special life insurance funded trust that, if necessary, can provide to the guardians needed dollars, but, if not, will go to the client's children later in life.)

(5) Is the client's spouse's will coordinated with the client's will?

(6) Is there a "spendthrift clause" to provide protection against the claims of creditors?

SUMMARY

Although only an attorney should draft a will, every member of the estate planning team should make it a practice to review a client's will on a regular basis. The nonattorney's role in the will review process should be thought of not as a replacement for or as a means of "second guessing" the attorney, but rather as a source of additional strength in the planning process. The estate planner can provide in that regard a valuable resource to ascertain how the client's total dispositive plan can most effectively and efficiently meet the current needs, circumstances, and goals of both the client and the client's beneficiaries.

Chapter 8

INCOME TAX CONCEPTS

WHY TAXES ARE IMPORTANT TO THE INVESTOR

An investor must consider taxes (federal, state, and local) as part of the cost of any investment. The objective of financial planning is to maximize the utility of invested capital in order to accomplish the client's financial and personal goals. Consequently, the planner must attempt to minimize the tax element of the investment cost in a manner that is consistent with those goals. An understanding of the basic concepts of the income tax law is therefore essential.

The complexity of the federal income tax law (not to mention the various state and local income tax laws) is almost overwhelming. Specific tax advice should be given only by qualified tax specialists. But planners and clients must both have a working knowledge of (1) the issues involved in the acquisition and disposition of an investment asset, (2) the issues relating to income and expenses during the period the investment is held, and (3) the federal income tax rate structure. This chapter will focus on these three broad areas and subdivide them as follows:

(1) Acquisition and Disposition Issues

    (a) Basis (including the "at risk" rules)

    (b) Business Energy and Rehabilitation Tax Credits

    (c) Timing of reporting gain or loss upon disposition

    (d) Character of gain or loss upon disposition

(2) Issues relating to income and expenses while the investment is held

    (a) Income defined

    (b) Character of income or loss

    (c) Deductible expenses

    (d) Timing of recognition of income and expenses

    (e) Impact of "tax preference items" (Alternative Minimum Tax)

(3) The Federal income tax rate structure

    (a) Income tax rates

    (b) The "kiddie" tax

TAX ISSUES AFFECTING THE ACQUISITION AND DISPOSITION OF AN INVESTMENT

Basis

GENERAL RULES—Basis is a key concept to the investor because it is the starting point for determining the amount of gain or loss. It is also the measure of the maximum amount of depreciation or amortization allowable for certain types of assets.

An investor's original basis in a purchased asset is its cost. The cost of property is the amount the investor paid for it in cash or other property. For example, if Bob buys a rental property for $100,000 cash, his original basis in the acquired property is $100,000.

When property other than—or in addition to—cash is used to acquire an investment (and the transaction does not qualify as a tax free exchange), the cost (basis) of the property acquired is the sum of any cash paid and the fair market value of any property given. For instance, if Bob purchased the rental property for $10,000 cash plus stock of IBM worth $90,000, Bob's original basis in the rental property would be $100,000 (the sum of the $10,000 cash paid plus the $90,000 fair market value of the stock).

Typically, when an investor exchanges one property for another, the market value of the property given up and the market value of the property received will be approximately equal. The fair market value of both properties will, as a practical matter, usually be ascertained by reference to the property whose value is most easily determined. In the example in the previous paragraph, it is easy to determine Bob's basis in the rental property since Bob paid for the property with cash ($10,000) and publicly traded IBM stock ($90,000) the value of which can be easily found.

When property is acquired subject to a mortgage or other debt, the basis of the property is not merely the amount of the investor's equity in the property; the basis is the total of the cash and value of other property paid plus the amount of the debt. For example, if Rich buys a $1,000,000 apartment house, paying $250,000 in cash and borrowing the remaining $750,000, his basis in the property is the full $1,000,000.

"AT RISK" RULES—An investor's ability to create basis through the use of debt is limited by the at risk rules. These rules provide that losses are deductible only to the extent the investor is personally at risk.

The at risk rules limit deductions for borrowing that attempt to be characterized as at risk for tax purposes when there is no economic risk to the investor. For instance, assume Georgia wants to purchase a $100,000 interest in an oil drilling venture. She intends to invest $20,000 of her own funds while borrowing the $80,000 balance. The bank providing the loan to Georgia has agreed to make a nonrecourse loan to her. In other words, the bank will rely solely on the value of the property as its collateral for the debt. In the event Georgia cannot repay the loan, the bank cannot look to Georgia's other assets to cover the unpaid balance. Since the most Georgia can lose on the investment is her $20,000 of cash, her deductions will be limited to that $20,000 (plus the amount of income generated from the investment).

The at risk rules cover essentially all investment activities except for real estate acquired before 1987. With respect to real estate subject to the at risk rules, "qualified nonrecourse financing" is treated as an additional amount at risk. "Qualified" financing is generally defined as borrowings (except convertible debt) from persons or entities actively engaged in the business of lending money (such as banks), and not the former owner of the property. Loans from or guaranteed by a federal, state, or local government agency will also qualify.

Aside from real estate investments, the at risk rules apply to the following examples of activities when engaged in by an individual for the production of income:

(1) Holding, producing, or distributing motion picture films or video tapes.

(2) Farming.

(3) Exploring for or exploiting oil and gas reserves or geothermal deposits.

(4) Leasing of depreciable personal property.

An investor is considered at risk to the extent of

(1) Cash invested, plus

(2) The basis of property invested, plus

(3) Amounts borrowed for use in the investment which are secured by the investor's assets (other than the property used in the investment activity), plus

(4) Amounts borrowed to the extent the investor is personally liable for its repayment, plus

(5) When the investment is made in partnership form,

(a) The investor-partner's undistributed share of partnership income, plus

(b) The investor-partner's proportionate share of partnership debt, to the extent he is personally liable for its repayment.

An investor is not considered at risk with respect to nonrecourse debt (other than qualified nonrecourse financing, see above) used to finance the activity or to finance the acquisition of property used in the activity or with respect to any other arrangement for the compensation or reimbursement of any economic loss. For example, if Georgia is able to obtain commercial insurance against the risk that the oil drilling fund will not return her original $20,000 cash investment, she would not even be considered at risk on that amount.

Losses limited by the at risk provisions are not lost; these amounts may be carried over and deducted in subsequent years (but only if the investor's at risk amount is sufficiently increased).

The benefit of previously deducted losses must be recaptured when the investor's at risk amount is reduced below zero. For example, assume Tania's loss deductions from her interest in an oil drilling venture total $5,000 through the end of last year. Her basis in the venture at the end of last year (after the deductions) was $1,000. In the current year Tania received $3,000 in cash distributions. That distribution reduces Tania's basis by $3,000 to -$2,000.

Since an investor cannot have a negative basis in an investment for tax purposes, Tania must recapture the $2,000 of prior year deductible losses in order to bring her basis up to zero. In addition, Tania will not be able to deduct any losses from the venture in the current year because she has a zero basis.

PROPERTY ACQUIRED FROM A DECEDENT—When an investor dies, the beneficiary of his property does not carry over the decedent's basis. Instead, the basis of property acquired from or passing from a decedent is the fair market value of the property as of the date of (a) the investor's death, or (b) the federal estate tax alternate valuation date if that date (typically six months after the date of death) is elected by the estate's executor. Therefore, if the value of an investment held until death increases from the date of its acquisition, the potential gain (or loss in the case of a decrease in value) is never recognized for income tax purposes. An increase in the property's basis to its federal estate tax value is called a "step-up" in basis.

Note that this stepped-up basis is obtained even though no one pays income tax on the intervening appreciation. For example, if an individual had purchased stock which cost him $10,000 and which had a fair market value of $50,000 at the time of his death, his beneficiary would receive a $50,000 basis for the stock. The $40,000 appreciation in the value of the stock would never be taxed. If the beneficiary then sold the property for $65,000, his taxable gain would be only $15,000.

The alternate valuation method may be elected by an executor or administrator only if the election will decrease (a) the value of the gross estate and (b) the amount of the federal estate tax imposed. Generally, an election to use the alternate valuation date means that property will be included in the gross estate at its fair market value as of six months after the decedent's death. However, if any property is distributed, sold, exchanged, or otherwise disposed of within six months after the decedent's death, the value of the property at that disposition date becomes the "alternate value."

For instance, assume property was purchased for $10,000 and is worth $50,000 on the date of a widower's death. Assume that his executor sells the asset for $45,000 three months after his death. If the alternate valuation date is elected, the valuation date for this property would be the date of its sale. Its basis becomes $45,000. The estate realizes no tax gain or loss because the $45,000 amount realized on the sale is equal to the property's $45,000 basis.

PROPERTY ACQUIRED BY GIFT—When property is acquired by lifetime gift and there is a gain on the sale by the donee, the general rule is that the property in the hands of the donee has the same basis (subject to an adjustment discussed below) it had in the hands of the donor. This is called a "substituted" or "transferred" or "carryover" basis; the donee of the gift—the new owner, computes his basis by reference to the basis in the hands of the donor. In other words, the donor's basis is transferred and carried over to the donee so that gain will not escape tax but merely be deferred. The gain remains deferred only until the donee disposes of the property in a taxable transaction.

For example, assume that Alex purchases stock for $3,000. After it appreciates in value to $9,000, he gives it to Sara. The basis of the stock in Sara's hands for determining gain on a later sale by Sara is still $3,000. Therefore, if she sells it for $10,000, she has a $7,000 gain.

When the donor's basis is used, it is subject to an adjustment for any gift taxes paid on the net appreciation in the value of the gift (but not above the amount of the gift tax paid). For instance, in the example in the paragraph above, if the gift tax were $1,500, the donee's basis would be the $3,000 carryover basis plus $1,000 adjustment, a total of $4,000. The addition to basis is computed according to the following formula:

$$\frac{\text{Net Appreciation in Value of Gift}}{\text{Value of Gift at Transfer}} \quad \text{x} \quad \text{Gift Tax Paid}$$

In our example, the computation would be

$$\frac{9,000 - \$3,000}{\$9,000} \quad \text{x} \quad \$1,500 \quad = \quad \begin{array}{l}\text{Adjustment to}\\ \$3,000\\ \text{Carryover Basis}\end{array}$$

The basis rule for determining loss on the sale of property acquired by gift is different from the rule for determining the amount of the gain on the sale. For purposes of determining the amount of a loss, the basis of the property in the hands of the donee is the lesser of (a) the donor's basis or (b) the fair market value of the property at the time of the gift. The purpose of this special provision is to prevent investors from gaining a tax benefit by transferring property with a built-in loss to persons who could take advantage of tax losses.

Assume, for instance, that in the example above the value of the stock at the time of the gift was only $1,000. If Alex sold the stock, he would have a capital loss of $2,000 ($3,000 basis - $1,000 amount realized): If Alex had other capital losses of at least $3,000 but no capital gains, the $2,000 loss would be of no immediate tax benefit to him. Were it not for the special provision, Alex might give the stock to his father who had capital gains. If his father were allowed to use Alex's $3,000 basis, his father could sell the stock, take a $2,000 loss, and obtain the tax benefit from the loss which Alex himself could not have used. For this reason, the father, in determining his loss on the sale, must use as his basis the $1,000 fair market value of the property at the time of the gift since that is lower than Alex's $3,000 basis. If Alex's father sold the property for $900, he would only recognize a $100 loss on the sale ($900 proceeds less $1,000 basis). If Alex's father sold the property at a time when it was worth only $1,200 (or any other amount between the $1,000 fair market value at the date of the gift or the $3,000 carryover basis), no gain or loss would be recognized.

General Business Tax Credits

A credit is a dollar-for-dollar reduction in the investor's tax. The energy, rehabilitation, and low-income tax credits are incentives to encourage investment in certain types of property used in a trade or business, including rental property (and therefore stimulate economic growth).

The energy credit is a percentage of the taxpayer's qualified investment in energy property and is generally limited to 10%. This category includes solar energy and geothermal property. The rehabilitation credit is available for expenditures incurred to rehabilitate buildings that are certified historic structures or were initially placed in service before 1936. The credit is limited to 10 percent of qualified rehabilitation expenditures for buildings which are not certified historic structures. Rehabilitation expenditures for buildings which qualify as certified historic structures are eligible for a credit of 20 percent. Both the rehabilitation credits apply to residential as well as nonresidential properties. A credit is available for investment in certain low-income housing (see Chapter 40, Real Estate as an Investment).

The energy, rehabilitation, and low-income housing credits are aggregated with certain other credits to form the general business credit. The amount of the general business credit which may offset income taxes in any one year is limited.

The energy and rehabilitation tax credits are not without cost. The investor must reduce his basis for both purposes of computing future depreciation deductions and computing gain or loss upon the sale or other taxable disposition of the asset. The property's basis must be reduced by

(1) 50 percent of the business energy tax credit, and

(2) 100 percent of the rehabilitation credits.

Upon early disposition of property for which an energy or rehabilitation credit was claimed and which reduced the investor's tax liability, some or all of the investment credit must be "recaptured," (i.e., reported as an additional tax). Property which is held at least five full years from the date it was placed in service is not subject to recapture. Likewise, early dispositions triggered by the investor's death or by a tax free transfer to a corporation in exchange for its stock will not result in recapture.

If recapture is required, the investor must add to his tax a portion of the credit as indicated in the following table:

If Disposition Occurs Before the End of	Percentage of Investment Credit to be Recaptured
1 Year	100%
2 Years	80%
3 Years	60%
4 Years	40%
5 Years	20%

This recapture has the effect of increasing the investor's basis in the property (which was previously reduced when the credit was claimed). This adjustment to basis is treated as if it were made immediately before the disposition.

However, the low-income housing credit is subject to a 15 year recapture period rather than the 5-year schedule above. For additional information on the rehabilitation credit and the low-income housing credit, see Chapter 40, Real Estate as an Investment.

Timing of Reporting Gain or Loss Upon Disposition

The timing of reporting gain or loss is critical to the success of the investor. Deferring income until a later year, particularly a year in which the investor is in a lower tax bracket, or accelerating a deduction into a year in which the taxpayer has a great deal of income, can significantly enhance the after tax return from an investment.

The problems of the correct year to report income or take deductions flow from the requirement that income is to be reported on the basis of annual periods. Although there are a few exceptions, as a general rule investors must report income and claim deductions according to annual accounting periods.

Most individuals are cash basis taxpayers. A "cash basis" investor (one who reports income as it is received and who takes deductions as expenses are paid) generally will recognize a gain or loss from the disposition of an asset at the time the transaction is "closed." The mere signing of an agreement to sell does not trigger the recognition of gain or loss. A transaction is not closed until the seller transfers title to the property in exchange for cash or other proceeds.

INSTALLMENT SALES—An investor can defer the recognition of gain until the actual receipt of cash or other property in exchange for the asset sold. The key ingredient in an installment sale is that at least one payment will be received by the seller in a year after the year of sale.

The installment sale provisions are particularly important to investors who have sold an asset for a substantial profit and have received a cash down payment and notes of the purchaser for the balance due. Usually these notes are not readily transferable. Without the installment sale rules, the investor would incur a large tax in one year, even if he does not have sufficient cash to pay the tax. Installment sales are also indicated when an investor wants to sell property to another party who does not have enough liquid assets to pay for the property in a lump sum at closing.

The basic rules for installment sale reporting include the following:

(1) A seller of property can defer as much or as little as desired and payments can be set to fit the seller's financial needs. Even if payments are received in the year of sale, the installment method may still be used for the unpaid balance. For instance, a sale for $1,000,000 will qualify even if $300,000 is received in the year of sale and the remaining $700,000 (plus interest on the unpaid balance) is paid over the next five years.

(2) No payment has to be made in the year of sale. For example, the parties could agree that the entire purchase price for payment of a $1,000,000 parcel of land will be paid five years after the sale (with interest being earned on the $1,000,000 during the five year period). The only requirement is that at least one payment must be made in a taxable year after the year of sale. This means that an investor should contract to have payments made to him at the time when it is most advantageous or least disadvantageous.

(3) Installment sale treatment is automatic unless the investor affirmatively elects not to have installment treatment apply.

(4) The installment note receivable may be independently secured (such as with a letter of credit obtained from a bank) without triggering the recognition of income when the note is secured.

The computation of the gain recognized with each receipt of cash from an installment sale can be illustrated as follows:

Assume an investor purchased land which cost her $10,000. Five years later she sells the land for $50,000. Upon closing she receives $20,000 cash plus a note for the remaining $30,000. The note provides for three annual payments of $10,000 plus interest of 10% on the unpaid balance. The investor's cash received each year is as follows:

	SALE PROCEEDS	INTEREST	TOTAL
Year of Sale	$20,000	—	$20,000
First Installment	10,000	$3,000	13,000
Second Installment	10,000	2,000	12,000
Third Installment	10,000	1,000	11,000
Total	$50,000	$6,000	$56,000

Computation Of Gain. The rule used to compute gain in an installment sale is:

Income is realized in the same proportion which the gross profit (selling price less seller's adjusted basis) bears to the total contract price (amount to be received by the seller). The installment method of reporting is not available for losses. Losses are recognized in full in the year of sale and may be deductible, subject to certain limitations. In addition, upon the sale of certain depreciable property, gain must be recognized in the year of sale to the extent of the "depreciation recapture" amount, even if no cash is received in that year.

This rule results in the following treatment of the components of the proceeds:

A. Recovery of basis   Tax free
B. Gain   Capital gain or ordinary income
C. Interest   Ordinary income

The amount of each component in any given payment is computed as follows:

$$\frac{\text{Recovery of Basis}}{} = \frac{\text{Adjusted basis of property sold}}{\text{Total sale proceeds}} \times \frac{\text{Amount received}}{\text{(excluding interest)}}$$

In the example above the numbers would be as follows:

Year of Sale	$\frac{\$10,000}{\$50,000}$	X	$20,000	=	$4,000
First Installment	$\frac{\$10,000}{\$50,000}$	X	$10,000	=	$2,000
Second Installment	$\frac{\$10,000}{\$50,000}$	X	$10,000	=	$2,000
Third Installment	$\frac{\$10,000}{\$50,000}$	X	$10,000	=	$2,000

$$\text{Gain} = \frac{\text{Total sale proceeds less Adjusted basis of property sold}}{\text{Total sale of proceeds}} \times \frac{\text{Amount received}}{\text{(excluding interest)}}$$

In the example above the numbers would be as follows:

Year of Sale	$\dfrac{\$40,000}{\$50,000}$	x	$20,000	=	$16,000
First Installment	$\dfrac{\$40,000}{\$50,000}$	x	$10,000	=	$8,000
Second Installment	$\dfrac{\$40,000}{\$50,000}$	x	$10,000	=	$8,000
Third Installment	$\dfrac{\$40,000}{\$50,000}$	x	$10,000	=	$8,000

Interest. In this example the interest payable each year was specified in the contract and was therefore easily determinable. The amount of the interest income each year is stated in the facts above.

In the event that interest is not specified in the agreement, or the interest rate stated is less than a "test" amount, an interest amount will be "imputed." This means the law will treat the parties as if they had agreed to a minimum rate of interest on the unpaid balance. Since the total cash received will remain unchanged, the effect of imputing an interest element is to reduce the total sales price. For example, if the parties in the transaction above had agreed that the seller would be paid $10,000 in the year of the sale, with four subsequent annual installments of $10,000, it is obvious that the seller is not receiving interest on the unpaid balance—assuming that the sales price is $50,000. The tax law treats the parties as if they had in fact agreed upon a sales price of less than $50,000 together with annual interest on the unpaid balance.

The interest rate that must be used by parties in seller financed transactions is governed by rules relating to the "applicable federal rate" (AFR). The AFRs (which vary, depending on the term of the loan and frequency of payments) are published monthly by the Internal Revenue Service. AFRs are used to set imputed rates of interest on interest free and below market interest loans as well as other interest sensitive transactions.

Seller financing of more than $3,823,100 in 1998 (as indexed annually) is subject to an imputed interest rate of 100% of the AFR unless the stated rate is in excess of the AFR. If the seller financing is for less than the indexed amount (where no interest rate is specified or if the specified rate is less than 9% compounded semiannually or a lower AFR), the effective interest rate will be the lesser of 9% compounded semiannually or the AFR.

Several limitations are imposed on the use of the installment sale method of accounting for gain on the sale of property, the most important of which are discussed here. One

such limitation is that the installment sale method may not be used for the sale of stock or securities that are traded on an established securities market. A second limitation is that dealers are prohibited from using the installment sale method.

Two special rules apply to certain installment sales of property with a sales price exceeding $150,000:

(1) If the aggregate outstanding balance of such sales exceeds $5,000,000 in face value, an interest surcharge is imposed in the year of sale, as well as any subsequent year that the installment obligations are outstanding.

(2) If the holder of such an installment obligation pledges the installment receivable as security for a loan, the net proceeds of the secured loan will be treated as a payment received on the installment receivable, thus accelerating the recognition of the income otherwise deferred.

These rules generally apply to *any* non-dealer sales whether of real or personal property, with exceptions for: (1) certain farm property, (2) timeshares and residential lots, and (3) personal use property.

As a final note on installment sales, strict rules govern the use of the installment method for sales between related parties.

Character of Gain or Loss

The effect of having the gain from the sale of property treated as a capital gain rather than ordinary income can be substantial; *net capital gains* are discussed in further detail below. The distinction between capital gains and ordinary income is important. Capital losses can be used only to offset capital gains and a limited amount of ordinary income (no more than $3,000 per year—although unused capital losses may be carried forward and utilized in future years).

The amount of capital gain or loss upon a taxable sale or exchange is determined by computing the difference between the sales price or proceeds received and the investor's tax basis (usually his cost) in the "capital asset." A formula often used for this computation is

Amount Realized - Adjusted Basis = Gain

Alternatively,

Adjusted Basis - Amount Realized = Loss

Income Tax Concepts

In certain situations it may be necessary to treat part of the gain as ordinary income as a result of provisions in the tax law, such as those dealing with original issue discount and depreciation recapture discussed below.

With certain limited exceptions, all securities held by investors are considered capital assets. Most other assets held for investment purposes are also considered capital assets. In general, the following rules apply to the treatment of capital gains and losses:

(1) *Net capital gain* (i.e., the excess of long-term capital gains over short-term capital losses) is determined by first separating the long-term capital gains and losses into three tax rate groups. These groups are: (a) the 28% group, which generally includes collectibles gain and Section 1202 gain, (b) the 25% group (i.e., Section 1250 gain) and (c) the 20% group consisting of long-term capital gains and losses not falling under (a) or (b). Any net short-term capital losses are then applied to reduce any net gain from the 28% group, 25% group and 20% group in that order.

(2) *Adjusted net capital gain* (i.e., net capital gain reduced, but not below zero, by the sum of unrecaptured Section 1250 gain and the 28% rate gain). The reduced capital gains tax rate applies only to adjusted net capital gain.

(3) An investor's capital losses must be used first to offset any capital gains. Investors are allowed to offset net capital losses against ordinary income on a dollar for dollar basis — but only to the extent of $3,000 per year ($1,500 in the case of married taxpayers filing separately).

(4) Any excess capital losses (from (3), above) may be carried forward indefinitely and used to offset future years' capital gains and up to $3,000 per year of ordinary income.

HOLDING PERIOD — A capital asset falls into its category of short-term or long-term based upon the time it is held. The calculation of the holding period begins on the day after the property is acquired. The same date in each successive month is considered the first day of a new month. The holding period includes the date on which the property is sold or exchanged. If property is acquired on the 1st day of a month, the holding period begins on the first day of the following month. The specific holding periods are as follows:

Short-term — held for less than one year.

Long-term — held for more than one year. For assets sold on or after December 31, 1997, assets in this category are taxed at a maximum rate of 20% (10% to the extent of income in the 15% bracket). Special lower rates for assets held more than five years are effective for years after 2000.

Special rules apply in the case of gains or losses of:

(1) Regulated futures contracts.

(2) Nonequity option contracts.

(3) Foreign currency contracts.

(4) Short sales.

(5) Wash sales.

(6) Tax straddles.

(7) Constructive sales.

"Tacking" of a holding period is allowed in the case of gifts, tax free exchanges, and certain other nontaxable exchanges. Tacking means an investor may add the holding period of the prior owner(s) to his own. For instance, if Sara gives Lara stock Sara bought 3 years ago, Lara's holding period would include the 3 years Sara held the stock, as well as the period Lara actually held the stock.

When an asset is acquired through bequest or inheritance, it automatically is treated as though it was held by the recipient for the long-term holding period. This rule applies even if the decedent held the asset for less than one year. For example, assume Sam purchased shares in a mutual fund one month before his death. Sam's heir, Sandi, could sell the shares 4 months after Sam's death and still obtain long-term treatment on any gain.

Many investors buying stocks, bonds, mutual funds, or other investments have multiple holdings of the same types of assets. It therefore becomes necessary to be able to identify each separate share or unit of a multiple investment so that each share's own basis and holding period can be determined.

If an investor is unable to adequately identify the lot from which securities are sold or transferred, a "FIFO" (first-in, first-out) method must be used. This means that the investor will be deemed to have sold the securities in the order in which they were acquired. In some cases involving mutual fund shares, the investor may be allowed to use an "average basis" method for ascertaining both tax basis and holding period.

TAX ISSUES RELATING TO INCOME AND EXPENSES WHILE THE INVESTMENT IS HELD

Income Defined

Tax law defines "income" in very broad terms. Income includes "all income from whatever source derived" that is not specifically excluded by a section of the Internal Revenue Code. The implication is that if an item is considered something other than a return of an investor's capital, it will be taxable unless otherwise excluded. The Supreme Court has defined income as "gains received from capital, from labor, or from both combined, provided it be understood to include profit gained through a sale or conversion of capital assets."

Common items realized by an investor that are specifically enumerated by the Internal Revenue Code as income include:

(1) Gains derived from dealings in property.

(2) Interest.

(3) Rents.

(4) Royalties.

(5) Dividends.

(6) Annuities.

(7) Income from an interest in an estate or trust.

Note that the tax is levied only on income. The distinction in answering the question of whether an item is income lies between the terms "income" and "capital." An investor may recover, income tax free, his capital investment in an asset. This tax free recovery of capital concept is inherent in the formula described above for computing gain:

Amount Realized - Adjusted Basis = Gain

Among the very few items common to an investor specifically excluded from income by the Internal Revenue Code are:

(1) Interest on certain governmental obligations (e.g., many "municipal bonds").

(2) Certain improvements by the lessee on the lessor's property.

(3) Generally, death proceeds received under a life insurance contract.

"Whose income is it?" is an important issue that must be resolved by financial planners. An individual can be taxed on income which he never receives but which is received by someone else.

Income is taxed to the person who

(1) Earns it.

(2) Creates the right to receive it.

(3) Owns or controls property which is the source of the income.

(4) Controls the right to control who will enjoy the benefit of it.

The tax rule governing income shifting is known as the "assignment of income doctrine." According to this doctrine, although the income itself may be shifted from one individual to another (which may create gift tax problems), the burden of income taxation will not change. The person who earns the income—or owns or controls the source of the income—is deemed to have received it and then passed it on to its actual recipient. For example, if an attorney directs a client to pay his fee to the attorney's mother, or a wealthy investor who owns an office building directs that all tenants pay rent directly to his widowed sister, although the income will be shifted, the tax liability will not.

Although merely assigning income will not shift the burden of taxation, an assignment of an income producing asset will cause the income derived from that asset to be taxed to the assignee. For example, if an individual makes a gift of securities or any other income producing property to his son, income produced by that property after the transfer will be taxed to the son.

To accomplish income shifting tax objectives, the transfer of the property must be made before the income is actually earned and must be (1) complete, (2) bona fide, and (3) the transferor must retain no control over either the property or the income it produces.

Character of Income or Loss

Under current tax law it is necessary to distinguish among:

(1) earned income or losses (such as salary, or active business income or losses),

(2) "investment" income (such as interest, dividends, royalties, and annuities), and

(3) "passive activity" income or losses.

These separate categories of income are important, since an investor may not use passive activity losses (and credits) to offset earned income or investment income. (Losses from active business endeavors may be offset against income from other active businesses, investment income, or passive activity income.) The passive activity loss limitations apply to estates and trusts, personal service corporations, and pass-through entities such as partnerships and S corporations, in generally the manner they apply to individuals. Passive activity losses of closely-held C corporations (where 5 or fewer shareholders own more than 50% of the stock value) can offset trade or business (earned) income, but not investment income of the corporation.

Disallowed passive activity losses and credits may be carried forward and treated as deductions and credits from passive activities in the next taxable year. Suspended losses from a passive activity are allowed in full when the taxpayer disposes of his entire interest in the passive activity in a fully taxable transaction. Suspended credits may not be claimed in full in the year the taxpayer disposes of the interest in the passive activity. Such credits are carried forward until used to offset tax liability from passive activity income. However, upon a fully taxable disposition of a passive activity, a taxpayer may elect to increase the basis of property immediately before the transaction by an amount equal to the portion of any suspended credit that reduced the basis of the property for the taxable year in which the credit arose.

PASSIVE ACTIVITY DEFINED—In general, the term passive activity means any activity that involves the conduct of any trade or business in which the taxpayer has an interest but does not "materially participate."

The definition of passive activity generally includes any rental activity of either real or tangible personal property regardless of whether the individual materially participates. With respect to equipment leasing, short-term rental to certain users (where the lessor provides substantial services) is an active business rather than a passive activity.

In general, "working interests" in oil and gas property held directly or indirectly via a pass-through entity where the investor's liability is not limited (e.g., general partnership) will be treated as an active trade or business, not a passive activity.

MATERIAL PARTICIPATION DEFINED—In general, a taxpayer will be treated as materially participating in an activity only if the taxpayer is involved in the operations of the activity on a regular, continuous, and substantial basis. Substantial and bona fide management decision-making by an

individual may constitute material participation. For example, if the managerial services are performed on a full-time basis and the success of the business is dependent upon the exercise of business judgment by an individual, such services would constitute material participation. This test applies regardless of whether an individual owns an interest in the activity directly or through a pass-through entity such as a general partnership or an S corporation.

Limited partnership interests are generally treated as not materially participating.

NET INVESTMENT INCOME DEFINED—Net investment income is not treated as passive activity income and therefore cannot be offset by passive activity losses. Net investment income means gross income from interest, dividends, annuities, or royalties not derived in the ordinary course of a trade or business,

LESS

Expenses (other than interest) that are clearly and directly allocable to such gross income,

LESS

Interest expense properly allocable to such gross income,

PLUS

Gains from the disposition of property generating the interest, dividend, royalty, etc. income,

LESS

Losses from the disposition of property generating the interest, dividend, royalty, etc. income.

Investment income earned within a pass-through entity, such as a partnership or S corporation, retains its character when reported to each investor in the entity, and cannot be used to reduce the passive activity losses that pass through to each investor.

TREATMENT OF FORMER PASSIVE ACTIVITY—If an activity is a former passive activity for any taxable year and has suspended losses or credits from prior years when the activity was passive, the suspended losses may be offset against the current year's income from the activity, and the suspended credits may offset any current year's regular tax liability allocable to that activity. Any remaining suspended losses or credits continue to be treated as derived from a passive activity. Such losses and credits can be used to offset income or tax from that activity in years after it changed from passive to active, as well as income or tax from other passive activities.

DISPOSITIONS OF AN ENTIRE INTEREST IN A PASSIVE ACTIVITY—Upon the taxable disposition (including abandonment) of an entire interest in a passive activity (or former passive activity), any suspended losses from the activity are no longer treated as passive activity losses and are allowable as a deduction against the taxpayer's income in the following order:

(1) Income or gain from the passive activity for the taxable year (including any gain recognized on the disposition).

(2) Net income or gain for the taxable year from all passive activities.

(3) Any other income or gain.

When an interest in a passive activity is transferred upon the death of the taxpayer, suspended losses may be deducted against income, but only to the extent such losses exceed the amount by which the basis of the interest in the activity is "stepped-up" at the taxpayer's death. For example, assume that Fred has a zero basis in a limited partnership interest just before his death. Fred had a suspended loss in the partnership of $50,000. The value of the interest reflected on his estate tax return is $20,000. Fred's heir to the partnership interest, his son, therefore receives a step up in basis in the property of $20,000. Only $30,000 of the $50,000 suspended losses can be used on Fred's final income tax return.

If an entire interest in a passive activity is disposed of in an installment sale, suspended losses may be deducted each year based on the ratio of the gain recognized each year to the total gain on the sale.

If an interest in a passive activity is disposed of by gift, the basis of the interest to the transferee is increased by the amount of the suspended losses generated from the interest. Such suspended losses added to the transferee's basis are not allowed as a deduction in any taxable year. The increase in basis will, of course, reduce the gain (or possibly increase the loss) from the ultimate taxable sale by the transferee.

SPECIAL RULES FOR RENTAL REAL ESTATE— Where an individual owns an interest in rental real estate in which he actively participates, the individual may deduct up to $25,000 ($12,500 in the case of married taxpayers filing separately) of such losses (which, as previously noted, are passive activity losses) or claim an equivalent amount of credits from the rental activity each year, regardless of the general limitations imposed on passive activities. This $25,000 annual allowance is reduced by 50% of the taxpayer's adjusted gross income (determined without regard to passive activity losses, taxable social security benefits, or IRA deductions) that exceeds $100,000 ($50,000 for married taxpayers filing separately). Consequently, the special $25,000 allowance is fully phased-out for taxpayers with adjusted gross income greater than $150,000 ($75,000 for married taxpayers filing separately).

Any losses in excess of the $25,000, or reduced allowable amount, from rental real estate where there is active participation are carried over as suspended passive activity losses. Such losses may be used in computing the $25,000 allowable amount in subsequent years in which the investor actively participates in the rental real estate activity.

The requirement for "active participation" is less stringent than the test for "material participation" used in distinguishing a passive activity from an active interest in a trade or business. Generally less personal involvement will be required. However, an individual can never be considered to actively participate in a rental property during a period where neither the individual nor the individual's spouse have at least a 10% interest in the property. Except as provided in regulations, a limited partnership interest in real estate does not qualify as active participation.

In the case of the rehabilitation and low-income housing credits (but not losses), the $25,000 allowance applies on a credit-equivalent basis, regardless of whether the individual actively participates in the rental real estate activity. Even if the interest is in a limited partnership, the credits may be claimed (up to the $25,000 credit equivalent). The phaseout of the credit equivalent for rehabilitation credits, regardless of when the property was placed in service, starts at adjusted gross income of $200,000, rather than $100,000. Similarly, with respect to property placed in service prior to 1990, phaseout of the $25,000 credit equivalent for the low-income housing tax credit starts at adjusted gross income of $200,000, rather than $100,000. With respect to property placed in service after 1989, there is no phaseout of the $25,000 credit equivalent for the low-income housing tax credit. The credit equivalent of the $25,000 allowance is $7,000 for an individual in the 28% tax bracket.

Deductible Expenses

A deduction is permitted for many of the investment expenses incurred by an investor. These expenses fall into two major categories: (1) interest paid on amounts borrowed in order to acquire or hold taxable investments, and (2) other expenses paid in connection with the production of income.

Income Tax Concepts

DEDUCTIBILITY OF INTEREST—Subject to some complex rules and limitations, interest paid or accrued within the taxable year on indebtedness may be deductible. Before discussing these limitations, the following general concepts regarding interest should be reviewed:

(1) The meaning and significance of the term "indebtedness."

(2) Whether an item is "interest."

(3) The effect of one person paying the interest of another's indebtedness.

What is meant by the term "indebtedness"? Indebtedness implies a debtor-creditor relationship. The investor must be unconditionally obligated to pay what he owes while his counterpart, the creditor, must be legally able to demand payment.

The requisites described above are lacking in the case of a gift. If Abe gives a promissory note to his minor daughter, Bea, and, according to the terms of the note, Abe pays Bea interest on the note, the payments will not be deductible. This is because there is no consideration given by the daughter to her father in return for the note. The daughter has no right to enforce payment. In actuality, she has the mere promise of her father to make gifts to her (disguised as interest) in the future.

Perhaps the most common interest deduction denial situation affecting investors is in the case of stock disguised as debt. The importance of the distinction between corporate debt and corporate equity is obvious; interest paid by a corporation on its bonds is deductible, but a dividend paid on its stock is not. Factors weighed by the IRS and the courts in distinguishing between debt and equity include:

(1) Whether there is a fixed maturity date.

(2) Whether the amount is payable in any event or is contingent upon corporate profits.

(3) Whether there is subordination or preference over any other indebtedness.

(4) What the ratio of debt to equity is.

(5) Whether the debt is convertible to stock.

(6) Whether stock and debt are proportionately held by the same individuals.

In essence, these factors are used to answer the question, "Is the investor (the owner of the security) primarily a bona fide creditor, looking for a fixed and reasonably stable and secure rate of return together with a preferential position on his debtor's assets, or is he an entrepreneur accepting the risks of the business in return for the benefits of ownership?"

What is meant by the word "interest"? Interest can be defined as the compensation allowed by law or fixed by the parties for the use of money. No interest deduction is allowed, regardless of the label given to a particular payment, unless the investor has incurred (1) a valid obligation, (2) to pay a fixed or determinable sum of money, (3) in return for the use of money.

The tax law does not stipulate how interest must be computed or paid. Generally, it will be figured as a percentage of the principal sum (e.g., 10% of the amount of the note). Sometimes interest is represented by a "discount." Series EE U.S. Savings Bonds are a good illustration. An individual might purchase a bond for $500 which will pay $1,000 at maturity. The investor receives no annual interest payments. The difference between what the investor pays for the bond and what he receives when it matures is interest.

It should be noted that many corporate bonds are also issued at a discount. However, although the tax law permits the purchaser of a Series EE bond to defer recognizing income until the bonds mature, the purchaser of corporate bonds issued at a discount must report the interest as income when earned, even though it is not yet received. This annual recognition of income on discount corporate and similar bonds is governed by the Original Issue Discount (OID) rules. Essentially, the OID rules require an investor to determine the amount of the annual discount income he must report, using a constant interest rate (a compound interest method). This results in less income reportable in the early years and greater income in later years.

Interest implies a payment for the use of money. Sometimes mortgages contain penalty clauses if the mortgagor prepays the loan. These penalty payments are for the use of money and are therefore—as payments for the privilege of prepaying mortgage indebtedness—deductible as interest.

"Points" may also be considered interest. Points are premiums in addition to the stated interest rate paid by borrowers to obtain a loan. This additional charge is typically calculated as a percentage of the loan amount (typically 1% to 3%) and is assessed and paid at the inception of the loan. If the fee was paid by the investor as compensation for the use of money, it is interest and therefore deductible. Typically points are deductible ratably over the term of the loan; yet, if certain requirements are met, points can be deductible in the year paid. On the other hand, if all or a part of the charge was for services provided by the lending institution, such as appraisal fees, that portion will not be considered interest.

If one person pays the interest on another person's debt, the deduction will be disallowed; the indebtedness must be that of the individual claiming the interest deduction. If there is a joint and several liability (such as when a husband and wife are joint obligors or comakers of a note), since the obligation to pay the interest extends to each, the entire amount of interest is deductible by whichever co-debtor makes the payment.

RULES LIMITING THE DEDUCTIBILITY OF INTEREST—Under current law, essentially all the interest expenses of an individual investor (other than interest incurred in the ordinary course of a trade or business in which the individual materially participates) are subject to some limitations. These limitations can be most easily described by the categories to which the debt is properly allocable. These categories include:

(1) Passive activity interest,

(2) Investment interest, and

(3) Personal interest.

Generally, the allocation of interest is based on the use of the proceeds of the underlying debt. Any interest expense properly allocable to a passive activity is added to other passive activity expenses in determining the annual limitation on the deductibility of passive activity losses (discussed above).

"Investment interest" generally includes interest expense paid on indebtedness properly allocable to property held for investment (other than passive activity investments). Investment interest is deductible only to the extent of "net investment income." (Interest expense incurred with respect to rental real estate eligible for the $25,000 passive activity loss exception, discussed above, is not investment interest.) Investment interest generally includes interest expense:

— allocable to the production of "portfolio" income (dividends, interest, royalties, etc.).

— allocable to a trade or business in which the investor does not materially participate, (unless the activity is treated as a passive activity, in which case the interest expense is subject to the passive activity loss limitations).

— allocable to the portfolio income of a passive activity.

"Net investment income" means the excess of investment income over investment expenses. Investment income includes portfolio income (dividends, interest, royalties, etc.), rents (except from passive activity investments), net short-term and long-term capital gains, and ordinary income gains from the sale of investment property (other than passive activity investment property). Investment expenses include expenses (except interest) related to these sources of investment income.

Annual interest deductions that are disallowed solely due to the investment interest expense limitation rule may be carried over indefinitely and deducted in future years.

Individuals, estates and trusts are not allowed to deduct personal interest paid or accrued during the taxable year. Personal interest is defined to include all interest except:

(1) Interest expense incurred or continued in connection with the conduct of a trade or business.

(2) Investment interest.

(3) Interest taken into account in computing a taxpayer's income or losses from passive activities.

(4) "Qualified residence interest."

(5) Interest on qualified educational loans (as discussed below).

(6) Interest payable resulting from allowable extensions of payments of estate tax (on the value of reversionary or remainder interests in property).

With respect to mortgage debt incurred after October 13, 1987, interest is deductible on mortgage acquisition indebtedness up to a total of $1 million ($500,000 in the case of married taxpayers filing separately), covering up to two homes. "Acquisition indebtedness" is debt incurred to finance the purchase or improvement of either of the two qualified residences. The amount of acquisition indebtedness upon which the interest deduction is computed must be reduced as principal payments are made and cannot be increased by refinancing unless the additional debt received from the refinancing is used for additional improvements.

In addition to interest on acquisition indebtedness, interest may be deducted on home equity indebtedness of up to $100,000 ($50,000 for married taxpayers filing separately). "Home equity indebtedness" must be secured by the same two qualified residences as the acquisition indebtedness. However, there is no limitation on the use of the home equity indebtedness funds.

Interest on qualified residence debt incurred prior to October 14, 1987 is treated as acquisition indebtedness that is not subject to the $1,000,000 limitation, and is deductible in full. In other words, such amounts are grandfathered under the post-October 14, 1987 rules. However, the amount of pre-

October 14, 1987 debt reduces (but not below zero) the amount of the $1,000,000 limitation on acquisition indebtedness incurred after October 13, 1987 (but does not reduce the amount of home equity debt which can be incurred after that date). Any refinancing of pre-October 14, 1987 acquisition indebtedness that extends the term of the debt beyond the original term or exceeds the principal amount of the original debt will no longer qualify under the grandfather provision. However, the interest on a debt with a "balloon" type principal payment requirement is deductible for the term of the first refinancing of such acquisition indebtedness, not to exceed 30 years.

Interest payments due and paid after December 31, 1997 on loans for qualified educational expenses are deductible for taxpayers with modified adjusted gross income (MAGI) up to certain limits. Qualified educational expenses include tuition, fees, room and board, and related expenses. The maximum deduction is $1,000 in 1998, $1,500 in 1999, $2,000 in 2000 and $2,500 in 2001 and thereafter. No deduction is allowed for an individual who is claimed as a dependent on another taxpayer's return. The deduction is allowed only during the first 60 months in which interest payments are due.

If MAGI exceeds certain limits, the deduction for interest on education loans is reduced. For single taxpayers, no deduction may be taken if MAGI is in excess of $55,000 and the amount of the deduction is reduced proportionally if MAGI is between $40,000 and $55,000. For married taxpayers filing jointly, no deduction may be taken if MAGI is in excess of $75,000 and the amount of the deduction is reduced proportionately if MAGI is between $60,000 and $75,000. No such deduction may be taken by married taxpayers filing separately.

Other limitations on the deductibility of interest expense have been in the law for some time. More specifically, interest that would otherwise be deductible cannot be deducted if it is allocable to a class of income wholly exempt from tax. The rationale is that if the income items are entirely excluded from gross income, it is not necessary or appropriate to permit any interest deduction.

Interest on indebtedness incurred to purchase or carry tax-exempt obligations (such as municipal bonds) is not deductible. This rule makes it difficult for an investor borrowing money for investment purposes to deduct interest on those loans if he also holds tax-exempt bonds for investment.

The problem is that the IRS may be able to make a connection between the interest paid on the new loans and the currently existing tax-exempt securities. Likewise, an investor who has financed the purchase of taxable income securities may have difficulty deducting the interest if he later purchases significant amounts of tax free bonds. It will be presumed that interest was incurred to purchase or carry tax free indebtedness whenever the investor has outstanding indebtedness which is not directly connected with personal expenditures and is not incurred or continued in connection with the active conduct of a trade or business. This harsh inference may be made by the IRS even though the indebtedness is ostensibly incurred or continued to purchase or carry taxable income investments.

The tax law provides a number of other limitations on the deduction of interest, which are of importance to investors. One such restriction is imposed on interest incurred to purchase or carry "market discount bonds" (bonds purchased after original issue at a price below both its redemption price and its original issue price because of an increase in the interest rates available on newly issued alternative investments). Such interest is not currently deductible to the extent the investor has deferred the recognition of current income. The interest deduction may be claimed at the time the investor reports the "market discount income," essentially the unreported interest which has accrued on the bond from the date of purchase until the date of disposition.

A similar restriction is imposed on interest expenses incurred in financing noninterest-bearing short-term obligations such as Treasury Bills. If the investor acquired the short-term obligation through a loan, the net interest expense is not deductible to the extent of the ratable portion of the bond discount attributable to the current year (the disallowed interest is deductible upon the disposition of the bond). Interest is currently deductible if the investor elects to include the discount as income in the taxable year it is earned.

DEDUCTIBILITY OF INVESTMENT EXPENSES OTHER THAN INTEREST—Many expenses incurred by an investor will be deductible (subject to the 2% floor on miscellaneous itemized deductions) if certain requirements are met. These requirements are that the expenses must be incurred:

(1) For the production or collection of income, or

(2) For the management, conservation, or maintenance of property held for the production of income, or

(3) In connection with the determination, collection, or refund of any tax.

Additionally, an investor's expenses must be: (1) ordinary and necessary; (2) paid or incurred in the taxable year; and (3) expenses rather than capital expenditures. An expense is considered ordinary if it normally occurs or is likely to occur in connection with an investment similar to the one for which an expense deduction is claimed.

Common deductible investment related expenses include:

1. Rental expenses of a safe deposit box used to store taxable securities.

2. Subscriptions to investment advisory services.

3. Investment counsel fees (whether or not the advice is followed).

4. Custodian's fees.

5. Service charges in connection with a dividend reinvestment plan.

6. Service, custodial, and guaranty fees charged by the issuer of mortgage backed pass-through certificates.

7. Bookkeeping services.

8. Office expenses such as rent, water, telephone, stamps, and stationary incurred in connection with investment activities.

9. Secretarial services relating to the management of rental property and investment record keeping.

10. Premiums paid for indemnity bond required for issuance of a new stock certificate to replace lost, stolen, destroyed, or mislaid certificates.

11. Fees incurred for tax advice (including (a) preparation of income tax returns, (b) cost of tax books used in preparing tax returns, (c) tax advice from attorneys and accountants, (d) legal fees for obtaining a Letter Ruling from the IRS, and (e) legal or accounting fees contesting a tax deficiency or claiming a refund—whether or not successfully).

However, deductible investment related expenses of individuals are subject to a limitation. Such expenses are only deductible to the extent they exceed 2% of the taxpayer's "adjusted gross income" (AGI). Thus, for example, if Jon's deductible investment related expenses equal $4,500 in a year in which his AGI is $200,000, his allowable deduction for such expenses is limited to $500 ($4,500 less $4,000 [2% of $200,000]).

Common investment related expenses that are not deductible (because they are personal in nature or because they are not ordinary and necessary) include travel to attend shareholders' meetings. An investment related expense need not be essential in order for it to be considered necessary. However, it must be one which the investor reasonably believes is

appropriate and helpful. Generally the courts will not question the investor's determination. The standard of what is or is not both ordinary and necessary depends on the situation in the community where the issue arises. If most investors in the same situation would have incurred the same expenditure, the ordinary and necessary tests would be met.

It is essential that an expense be "paid or incurred in the taxable year." This issue is further discussed below in the consideration of "timing of recognition of income and expenses."

To be deductible, an expense must meet one additional major test; it must not be a capital expenditure. If an outlay is an expense, it can be deducted immediately. If an outlay is considered the cost or part of the cost of an asset, it must be "capitalized." This means that the outlay must be added to the investor's basis in the asset. If the asset is depreciable or amortizable, this increased basis will result in additional deductions over the life of the asset. The increased basis may otherwise be used to lower the gain or increase the loss upon a sale or other taxable disposition of the investment.

Common expenditures which are considered capital in nature and are therefore not currently deductible include:

(1) Brokers' commissions and fees in connection with acquiring investments (these are added to the basis of the property).

(2) Selling expenses (these are offset against selling price in determining capital gains and losses).

(3) Expenses to defend, acquire, or perfect title to property (these are added to the basis of the property).

Timing of Recognition of Income and Expenses

Income is reportable in the year that it is received by a cash basis taxpayer. An expense will generally be deductible when it is paid by a cash basis taxpayer. The cash basis method is therefore essentially an "in and out of pocket" method of reporting. Items do not have to be received or paid in cash; receipts and payments in property are income and deduction items to the extent of the fair market value of the property.

Income of an accrual basis taxpayer is reportable when it is earned, even if the income is not received until a subsequent year. An expense will generally be deductible by an accrual basis taxpayer when the liability for payment has become fixed and determinable. Most individuals are cash basis taxpayers. The following discussion will focus on the application of the general rules applicable to cash basis investors and four of the major exceptions.

A cash basis investor generally will include interest, royalty, dividend, and other investment income, as well as gains from the sale of investments, in gross income in the year in which cash or other property is received. The following examples illustrate the application of this general rule:

(1) Dividend income is included when the check is received by the shareholder (even if the check is received in a year subsequent to when the dividend was declared or the year when the actual check was issued).

(2) Gain on the sale of property generally, under the installment sale rules, is taxed in the year sales proceeds are received.

A cash basis investor generally will deduct interest and other expenses incurred in connection with his investments, as well as losses from the sale of investments, from gross income in the year in which cash or other property is paid. Thus, interest expense, investment advisory fees, and other deductible expenses are deductible in the year paid. However, losses on the sale of securities generally are deductible on the trade date (even if delivery and receipt of the proceeds occur in the following year).

The four major exceptions to the general rules governing cash basis investors are:

(1) The doctrine of "constructive receipt."

(2) The "economic benefit" ("cash equivalent") theory.

(3) "Restricted property" rules.

(4) "Prepaid deduction" limitations.

CONSTRUCTIVE RECEIPT—Under the doctrine of constructive receipt, an item must be included in an investor's gross income even though it is not actually reduced to his possession if it is (a) credited to his account, or (b) set apart for him, or (c) otherwise available so that he can obtain it at his own volition without any substantial conditions or restrictions.

The purpose of the doctrine is to prevent an investor from determining at will the year in which he will report income. Without the doctrine of constructive receipt, an investor could postpone the taxability of income until the year in which he chose to reduce the item to his actual possession. For example, a cash basis taxpayer must report interest credited to his bank savings account regardless of whether he withdraws the interest or leaves it on deposit.

Constructive receipt will not apply if the taxpayer's control of the income is restricted in some meaningful manner. For instance, an investor will not be considered to have constructively received money or other property if:

(1) it is only conditionally credited, or

(2) it is indefinite in amount, or

(3) the payor has no funds, or

(4) the money is available only through the surrender of a valuable right, or

(5) receipt is subject to any other substantial limitation or restriction.

The doctrine of constructive receipt is particularly important to individuals whose employers have enhanced their financial security through nonqualified deferred compensation arrangements. For instance, an athlete or a high salaried executive may prefer not to crowd compensation into a high bracket year and may want to spread it into later years, particularly if he will be in a lower tax bracket in such later years.

Through an agreement with his employer (entered into before services are performed), an employee can defer a portion of his compensation and therefore the tax on that compensation. Typically the employer will purchase life insurance and/or make certain investments to finance his obligations under the deferred compensation plan. But the employee will be successful in his attempt to defer the tax on the income only if he avoids the doctrine of constructive receipt. If the employee is able to withdraw funds at will or if funds are irrevocably set aside beyond the claims of the corporation's creditors for the benefit of the employee, his goal of deferring taxation will be thwarted.

ECONOMIC BENEFIT—When an employee receives from his employer a benefit that is the equivalent of cash, the value of that benefit is currently taxable. The most common example is where an executive receives group term life insurance coverage in excess of the amount excludable from federal income tax. The employee is required to include in income an amount (computed from government tables) which represents the economic benefit he receives when premium payments are paid by his employer.

There is an important difference between the doctrine of constructive receipt and the economic benefit theory. The constructive receipt doctrine requires the inclusion of income when a taxpayer has an unrestricted choice—to take or not to take—income set apart for him or credited to his account. It is concerned with the issue of "When is income realized by the taxpayer?"

Conversely, the economic benefit theory requires income to be included even if the taxpayer cannot "take" the income. Under the economic benefit theory, all that is necessary to trigger taxation is that an employee receive from his employer a benefit that is the equivalent of cash, something with a (1) current, (2) real, and (3) measurable value. The economic benefit theory is concerned with the issue "Has the taxpayer enjoyed a present benefit from his employer capable of measurement and subject to tax?" It relates to the problem of "What is income?"

RESTRICTED PROPERTY—Property is often transferred by an employer to an employee in connection with the performance of services. A business may give or sell stock or other property to a key employee but withhold, by separate agreement, significant rights. For example, an employer may transfer stock to an employee but restrict the employee's right to vote the stock or sell it. The idea is that the property rights will be withheld (restricted) by the employer until the employee has performed certain specified services. If the employee fails to achieve his goal or meet the specified requirements, the stock or other property may be forfeited.

Suppose an employer pays a bonus to an executive in the form of company stock. Assume the ownership of this stock is subject to certain restrictions including a provision that if the employee leaves the company within a five year period, he will forfeit the stock and will receive no compensation. Such property is appropriately called "restricted stock" or "restricted property."

If an employee is given property with no restrictions, the entire value of the property would constitute current compensation income. For instance, an employee who receives a bonus of 100 shares of his employer's stock currently selling for $200 a share realizes $20,000 of income. But, if certain tests are met, an employer can compensate an employee in a manner that delays the tax until the employee is given full rights in the property.

The general rules governing restricted property (the so-called "Section 83" rules) provide that transfers of restricted property will be reportable as income in the first tax year in which the employee's rights are (1) not subject to any substantial risk of forfeiture or (2) transferable free of this risk. In other words, an employee will not be subject to tax on restricted property as long as his rights to that property are forfeitable (subject to a substantial risk of forfeiture) and not transferable by him free of such risk. (This means that if the employee should sell or give the property away, the recipient of the property must also be under a substantial risk that he (the new owner) would forfeit the property if the employee failed to satisfy the conditions necessary to obtain full ownership.)

"Substantial risk of forfeiture" means that rights in transferred property are conditioned, directly or indirectly, upon the future performance (or refraining from performance) of substantial services by any person or upon the occurrence of a condition related to the purpose of the transfer. In addition, there must be a realistic and substantial possibility of forfeiture if the specified condition is not satisfied. The following examples illustrate common situations which probably would not be considered substantial restrictions:

(1) A consulting contract with a retiring executive which called for only occasional services at the executive's discretion.

(2) A requirement that an employee must return the property if he commits a felony.

(3) A "noncompetition provision" (since this is largely within the employee's control).

What happens when the restrictions expire? At the lapse of the restrictions, the employee must include in income the value of the property at that time. Sometimes an employer will remove restrictions in stages so that an employee may "earn out" of the restrictions.

There are two important exceptions to the general rule that the employee becomes taxable on the fair market value of the property (less any amount the employee may have paid for the property) at the time the restrictions lapse. The first of these exceptions is known as the "employee's election." The second exception is the "fair market value rule."

Under the employee's election, the employee has a "gambler's choice;" he can elect to have the value of the restricted property taxed to him immediately in the year it is received (even though it remains nontransferable or subject to a substantial risk of forfeiture). If an employee makes this election within 30 days of receipt of the property, the general restricted property rules do not apply. Any appreciation in the value of the property is treated as capital gain rather than as compensation. The employee pays no tax at the time the risk of forfeiture expires (and will pay no tax until the property is sold or otherwise disposed of in a taxable exchange). But if the property is later forfeited, no deduction is allowed for the loss.

An employee who makes this election must be willing to pay ordinary income tax on the fair market value of the property in the year he receives the stock or other property. He is gambling that the value of the property will increase considerably before the restrictions lapse (in which case he may be eligible to pay tax on any realized gain as capital gain). He is also gambling that he will not forfeit the stock before he is able to sell or dispose of it without restriction.

The second exception to the strict rule of includability of the fair market value of the property (upon the lapse of restrictions) concerns restrictions that affect value. This exception pertains to value-affecting restrictions which—by their terms—will never lapse. For instance, if the restricted property can be sold only at book value and that restriction, by its terms, will never lapse, that amount will be treated as the property's fair market value.

An employer's compensation deduction will be allowed at the time the employee recognizes income from restricted property. The amount of the deduction will be the same as the amount of income recognized by the employee.

PREPAID DEDUCTIONS—In certain situations, a cash basis investor can control the year in which he will take deductions. He can, for instance, prepay certain taxes and take the deduction in the year of payment even though the expenses relate to future years. This ability to "time" deductions is limited. Multiple years' prepaid rent and insurance premiums, for example, cannot be deducted in the year of payment. Deductions generally must be spread over the period covered by the prepayment where the deduction of the prepayment would "materially" distort income.

Special rules apply to the deductibility of interest expense for all taxpayers, whether they use the cash or accrual method of accounting. A cash basis investor must deduct prepaid interest over the period of the loan, to the extent the interest represents the cost of using the borrowed funds during each taxable year in the period. Points paid on an investment loan must be deducted ratably over the term of the loan. An investor on the accrual method of accounting accrues interest ratably over the loan period. This means it must be deducted ratably even if the interest is prepaid.

Impact of "Tax Preference Items" (Alternative Minimum Tax)

The tax law imposes an "alternative minimum tax" so that individuals with substantial economic income will not be able to avoid a tax liability by using exclusions, deductions, and credits. The "AMT" attempts to broaden the "taxable income base" to insure that at least some tax liability will be incurred by most investors.

The computation of the alternative minimum tax is extremely complex. The following discussion is designed to cover only the essential elements of the AMT.

The alternative minimum tax is 26% of an investor's "alternative minimum taxable income" (AMTI) not exceeding $175,000 ($87,500 for married taxpayers filing separately) and 28% of AMTI exceeding that amount. Preferential tax rates for long-term capital gains are also used in determining an individual's AMT. Alternative minimum taxable income is computed as follows:

(1) Taxable income

PLUS or LESS

(2) Adjustments to taxable income (listed below)

PLUS

(3) The amount of an investor's "preference items" (specified items, described below, on which the investor is receiving preferential tax treatment)

LESS

(4) An exemption up to (a) $45,000 for a married couple filing jointly, (b) $33,750 for a single taxpayer, or (c) $22,500 for a married couple filing separately (and an estate or trust).

(The exemption amount is reduced by 25% of the amount by which AMTI exceeds $150,000 for married taxpayers filing jointly, $112,500 for single taxpayers, and $75,000 for married taxpayers filing separately.)

If the tax computed under this formula does not exceed the investor's regular tax, the AMT does not apply. If the computed AMT exceeds the investor's regular tax, the excess of the AMT over the regular tax is added to his tax liability.

The following is a simplified example of the computation of the AMT:

Assume Dr. and Mrs. Ginsburg file a joint return for 1998. They have two dependent children. Their regular tax was computed to be $36,784.

(1)	Their taxable income is	$135,000
(2)	Their AMT adjustments to taxable income are	30,000
(3)	Their tax preference items total	57,000
		$222,000
(4)	Their exemption amount is ($45,000 less $18,000) (25% of $222,000 less $150,000)	(27,000)
(5)	Their alternative minimum taxable income is	$195,000
(6)	Their "potential" AMT is	$ 51,100

The excess of the Ginsburgs' potential AMT ($51,100) over their regular tax ($36,784) is $14,316. This amount becomes their alternative minimum tax liability and is added to their regular tax. They would therefore pay a total tax of $51,100.

The adjustments to taxable income include the following:

(1) For property placed in service after 1986, depreciation deductions are adjusted to conform to special rules for the AMT.

(2) Mining exploration and development costs, circulation expenditures, and research and development expense deductions must be adjusted to conform with special AMT amortization rules.

(3) Gains or losses on the sale of property are adjusted to reflect the special depreciation rules used for AMT purposes.

(4) Long-term contracts entered into after February 28, 1986 must be accounted for using the percentage-of-completion method for purposes of the AMT.

(5) Net operating loss (NOL) deductions are calculated under special AMT rules and cannot offset more than 90% of AMT income.

(6) Certain itemized deductions allowable in computing regular taxable income must be added back in computing AMTI. These itemized deductions include state and local taxes, certain interest and miscellaneous deductions (including reimbursed employee business expenses), to the extent allowable in computing regular taxable income. In addition, the medical expense deduction is subject to a 10% floor under the AMT as compared to a 7.5% of AGI floor used in computing regular taxable income. For purposes of this adjustment item, the phaseout of itemized deductions for certain upper income taxpayers is not taken into account.

(7) Incentive Stock Options (ISOs). Upon the exercise of an ISO, the excess of the fair market value of the option stock over the option exercise price (the "bargain element") is added in computing AMTI in the year of exercise. When the option stock is subsequently sold, the previously computed bargain element amount is subtracted in computing AMTI in the year of sale.

(8) Passive activity losses are not allowed in determining AMTI, except to the extent the taxpayer is insolvent.

Items considered "tax preferences" which must be added to AMTI include:

(1) The excess of accelerated depreciation or ACRS deductions over straight-line depreciation on real property placed in service before 1987 (to the extent not taken into account in computing the adjustment to taxable income discussed above).

(2) Percentage depletion in excess of cost basis.

(3) Accelerated depreciation on depreciable personal property placed in service before 1987 that is leased (to the extent not taken into account in computing the adjustment to taxable income discussed above).

(4) Amortization of certified pollution control facilities.

(5) Certain excess intangible drilling costs.

(6) Tax-exempt interest on certain "private activity" (e.g., Industrial Development) bonds issued after August 7, 1986 (with certain limited exceptions).

(7) Use of the installment method by dealers in personal property.

(8) 42% of the amount excuded under Section 1202 (gains on sales of certain small business stock). For stock with holding periods beginning after 2000, the percentage is changed to 28%.

ALTERNATIVE MINIMUM TAX CREDIT—Individuals are allowed a credit against their regular tax liability in years in which their regular tax exceeds the computed alternative minimum tax. The amount of the credit is based on the amount of alternative minimum tax paid in excess of the regular tax computed. The credit is not available to the extent the prior years' AMT was attributed to excess percentage depletion, tax-exempt interest, or non-AMT itemized deductions.

The credit is limited to the amount necessary to reduce the regular tax to the amount of AMT computed for the year in which the credit is claimed. For example, assume Stanley's computed regular tax for 1998 is $45,000, while his AMT for 1998 is $36,000. Stanley may use up to $9,000 of AMT credits carried over from prior years to reduce the tax he must pay in 1998 from $45,000 to $36,000.

TAX PLANNING FOR THE AMT—The existence of the alternative minimum tax places a premium on planning techniques. With the availability of the AMT credit, it is less critical to undertake some of the more drastic planning concepts when the taxpayer will be able to use the AMT credit within a year or two after the AMT tax would be due. Here are some planning ideas and considerations:

In order to avoid or minimize the effect of the AMT,

(1) Determine the maximum amount of deductions or losses that an investor can claim before becoming subject to the AMT. Once an investor reaches the point where the AMT applies, any additional deductions will yield at most a 26% (or 28% as determined by AMTI) tax benefit.

(2) An investor can reduce or eliminate tax preference items by

(a) Electing to capitalize excess intangible drilling costs, mining exploration expenses, and research and experimentation expenses, and amortize them over the permissible AMT periods.

(b) Electing the AMT or straight line methods of computing depreciation.

(c) Considering an early disposition (in the year of exercise) of stock acquired through the exercise of an Incentive Stock Option.

When it has been determined that the investor will be subject to the AMT,

(1) The investor should consider deferring current year deductions (which will be of minimal value because of the AMT) and save them for a future year when they will be more valuable, by

(a) Postponing charitable contributions.

(b) Postponing elective medical treatments.

(c) Delaying making estimated state tax payments.

(2) The investor should accelerate ordinary income, since it will be taxed at no greater than the AMT rate. This can be accomplished, for example, by exercising options under an Incentive Stock Option Plan (ISO) and selling the stock within the same year. (This has the double advantage of qualifying the ordinary income from the accelerated sale of the ISO for the maximum AMT tax rate and eliminating the ISO as a tax preference item.)

THE FEDERAL TAX RATE STRUCTURE

Financial planning is so closely tied with minimizing income taxes that it has become necessary for financial planners to have a complete understanding of the federal income tax rate structure. This section of the income tax concepts chapter will briefly explain the current status of the federal income tax rate structure and the workings of what is known as the "kiddie tax."

Income Tax Rates

The income tax rates are applied to a taxpayer's taxable income, which can be defined as the amount of income that remains after a taxpayer subtracts all deductions and exemptions from gross income. Currently, the income tax rates are 15%, 28%, 31%, 36%, and 39.6%. The different schedules of rates will apply depending on whether the taxpayer is single, a surviving spouse, married filing separately, married filing jointly, or a head of household. The effect of a taxpayer's tax rate, bracket, and filing status on his income tax liability can be seen below.

For tax years beginning in 1998, income *over* the following amounts is taxed at the marginal tax rate above each column:

	28%	31%	36%	39.6%
Married Filing Jointly (and Surviving Spouses)	$42,350	$102,300	$155,950	$278,450
Heads of Households	$33,950	$87,700	$142,000	$278,450
Single	$25,350	$61,400	$128,100	$278,450
Married Filing Separately	$21,175	$51,150	$77,975	$139,225
Trusts and Estates	$1,700	$4,000	$6,100	$8,350

For tax years beginning in 1998, the personal and dependency exemption amount is $2,700; however, certain upper income taxpayers are subject to a phaseout of their personal and dependency exemptions. Specifically, the dollar amounts for personal and dependency exemptions of taxpayers with adjusted gross income above certain levels will be reduced by an "applicable percentage." The applicable percentage is 2 points for every $2,500 (or fraction thereof; $1,250 for married individuals filing separately) by which the taxpayer's adjusted gross income (for 1998) exceeds the following threshold amounts: Married filing jointly (and surviving spouses) — $186,800; Heads of households — $155,650; Single — $124,500; Married filing separately — $93,400. These dollar amounts are indexed for inflation.

In other words, the personal exemption amount for a single taxpayer whose adjusted gross income is $137,000 would be reduced by 10%. If his adjusted gross income were $248,000, the amount of the personal exemption would be zero, since it is reduced by 100% at that income level for a single person. The reduction of the exemption amount applies to all personal and dependency exemptions claimed by a taxpayer.

An additional limitation phases out some of the itemized deductions of certain taxpayers. The provision reduces the aggregate of most itemized ("below-the-line") deductions dollar-for-dollar by the lesser of (1) 3% of the amount of a taxpayer's adjusted gross income that exceeds (for 1998) $124,500 ($62,250 in the case of a married taxpayer filing separately), or (2) 80% of the amount of itemized deductions otherwise allowable for the year. The income amounts at which the limit is imposed are indexed for inflation. The limitation is not applicable to the medical expense deduction, the investment interest deduction, or certain casualty loss deductions, and does not apply to estates and trusts.

The Kiddie Tax—Unearned Income of Certain Minor Children

The "net unearned income" of a child who has not reached age 14 by year end and who has at least one parent alive at year end is subject to a special tax computation. The tax payable by the child on the net unearned income is essentially the additional amount of tax that the parent would have had to pay if the net unearned income of the child were included in the parent's taxable income.

If the parents have two or more minor children with unearned income to be taxed at the parents' marginal tax rate, all of the children's applicable unearned income will be added together and the tax calculated. The tax is then allocated to each child based on the child's pro rata share of the unearned income.

There are three levels of a minor's unearned income involved in the calculation of the tax on such income:

(1) Generally, the first $700 of a minor child's unearned income is exempt from tax because of the child's standard deduction. (The standard deduction of a child claimed as a dependent is limited to the greater of (a) $700 or (b) the sum of $250 and the amount of his earned income, not to exceed the regular standard deduction amount. After the first $700 is used to offset the child's unearned income, any excess is available to offset earned income of the child).

(2) The next $700 of unearned income is taxable at the child's bracket.

(3) Unearned income in excess of the first $1,400 will be taxed to the child at the appropriate parent's rate.

COMPUTATION OF THE TAX

(A) The amount of tax at the applicable parent's bracket reflected on a child's tax return is computed as follows:

(1) Compute the tax the child would have to pay on earned and unearned income at the child's rates. $_____
(2) Compute the sume of
  (a) the tax payable if the child had no "net unearned income," plus $_____
  (b) the child's share of the "allocable parental tax." $_____
    Total $_____

The tax on the unearned income of children under age 14 is the greater of (1) or (2).

The term "unearned income" means income from sources other than wages, salaries, professional fees, and other amounts received as compensation for personal services actually rendered.

(B) The net unearned income of a minor child can be computed as follows:

(1) State the total unearned income (or the child's taxable income if lower). $_____
(2) Calculate the amount not taxable at the parent's bracket — the sum of
  (a) up to $700 (standard deduction amount), plus
  (b) an additional amount which is the greater of (i) $700 or (ii) the allowable deductions directly related to the production of the child's unearned income, assuming the child claims itemized deductions. [This is the amount of unearned income taxable at the child's tax bracket.] $_____
    Total $_____
(3) Net unearned income is (1) minus (2). $_____

The $700 amounts used in this computation are adjusted annually for inflation.

(C) The amount of the tax on net unearned income of all the minor children of an applicable parent is computed as follows:

(1) State the tax that would have been imposed on the parent's taxable income if all the net unearned income of all the parent's children under age 14 were added to the parent's taxable income. $_____
(2) State the tax that would have been imposed on the parent's taxable income if none of the net unearned income of the parent's children under age 14 were includible. $_____
(3) The allocable tax computed at parent's marginal rate is (1) minus (2). $_____

(D) The tax computed at the parent's marginal tax rate is allocated to a particular child as follows:

(1) State the total allocable tax computed at $_____
the parent's marginal rate.

(2) State the child's net unearned income. $_____

(3) State the aggregate net unearned income $_____
of all children of the parent under age 14.

(4) Divide (2) by (3). $_____

(5) The child's share of allocable tax $_____
computed at the parent's marginal bracket
is (4) X (1).

In the case of unmarried parents, the parent whose taxable income is used in computing the tax on the unearned income of the minor child is the custodial parent. In the case of parents who are married but filing separately the marginal rate of the parent with the greater taxable income will be used in the calculation.

The so-called kiddie tax rules apply regardless of the source of the child's assets producing the unearned income. It doesn't matter whether the child earned the assets producing the income, or received the assets (or funds) as an inheritance or a gift from grandparents or parents.

If a child can be claimed as a dependent on a parent's return, the child may not claim a personal exemption and the child's standard deduction is limited to the greater of (1) $700 or (2) the sum $250 and the child's earned income (up to the maximum of that year's standard deduction—e.g., $4,250 in 1998).

Many parents will be able to elect to include their children's unearned income over $1,400 on their own return, thus avoiding the necessity of filing a return for each child. The election is available if the child has income of more than $700 but less than $7,000, all of which is from interest and dividends. Additionally, there is a tax of $105 or 15% of the income over $700 (whichever is less) for each child to whom the election applies.

Chapter 9

INVESTMENT ADVISERS— REGULATION AND REGISTRATION

INTRODUCTION

The Securities and Exchange Commission (SEC) regulates investment advisers and their activities under the Investment Advisers Act of 1940. One of the central elements of the regulatory program is the requirement that, unless you are exempt under specific provisions of the Act, you must register with the Commission as an investment adviser. Part I of this chapter describes the regulatory process and Part II provides detailed information on how to register as an investment adviser.

Investment advisers that have less than $25 million of assets under management and are subject to state securities regulation are generally prohibited from registering with the SEC. Assets under management are defined as securities portfolios with respect to which an investment adviser provides continuous and regular supervisory or management services. Investment advisers with $25 million of assets under management or in those states that do not regulate investment advisers must register with the SEC as described below. In addition, many states have investment adviser laws that are patterned after the federal investment adviser law, described below.

PART I—REGULATION

Definition of an Investment Adviser

The Investment Advisers Act of 1940 provides a three-part definition for determining who is an investment adviser. An investment adviser is a person who (1) provides advice, or issues reports or analyses, regarding securities; (2) is in the business of providing such services; and (3) provides such services for compensation.[1] All three prongs of this test must be met for the definition to apply.

It is important to note that the SEC defines compensation as "the receipt of any economic benefit," which includes commissions on the sale of products.

Exclusions From the Definition

The Investment Advisers Act excludes certain organizations and individuals from the definition of an investment adviser. These include:

(1) banks and bank holding companies;

(2) lawyers, accountants, engineers, or teachers, if their performance of advisory services is solely incidental to their professions;

(3) brokers or dealers if their performance of advisory services is solely incidental to the conduct of their business as brokers or dealers, and they do not receive any special compensation for their advisory services;

(4) publishers of bona fide newspapers, news magazines, or business or financial publications of general and regular circulation;

(5) those persons whose advice is related only to securities which are direct obligations of or guaranteed by the United States.

Caution must be exercised by practitioners relying on the exclusions provided under (2) and (3), above. The SEC has taken the position that the "incidental practice" exception provided by these sections is not available to individuals who hold themselves out to the public as providing financial planning, pension consulting, or other financial advisory services. It is the view of the SEC that if persons are promoting or advertising themselves as providing such services, it is unlikely that these services are merely incidental to their businesses.

In addition to these exclusions, the 1940 Act allows some advisers to be exempt from registration if they meet certain limited criteria discussed in the next section.

Exemptions From Registration

The Act provides limited exemptions from registration. Particularly important is the exemption for investment advisers who, during the course of the preceding twelve (12) months, had fewer than fifteen (15) clients and who do not hold themselves out generally to the public as investment advisers.[2]

This is a very limited exemption and applies only if both conditions are met. Even if an investment adviser has fewer than fifteen clients, he is not exempt if he holds himself out to the public as an investment adviser in any manner. Examples of this public notice include:

(1) maintaining a listing as an investment adviser in a telephone, business, building, or other directory;

(2) expressing willingness to existing clients or others to accept new clients;

(3) using a letterhead indicating any investment adviser activity.

This exemption also is not available to an investment adviser who advises an investment company (mutual fund) registered under the Investment Company Act of 1940, or a business development company that has elected to be treated as such under that Act.

Another exemption provides that any investment adviser, all of whose clients are residents of the same state as the principal office and place of business, is exempt if he does not furnish advice or analysis concerning any security listed or traded on any national securities exchange.[3]

Are Financial Planners Investment Advisers?

Financial planning as such or the provision of investment advice in connection with non-financial planning services triggers the issue of whether there is an investment adviser for purposes of the Act. As described above, the Act defines an investment adviser as "any person who, for compensation, engages in the business of advising others, either directly or through publications or writings, as to the value of securities or as to the advisability of investing in, purchasing, or selling securities, or who, for compensation and as part of a regular business, issues or promulgates analyses or reports concerning securities."[4]

(1) A person includes a natural person as well as a company, irrespective of the form of its organization.[5]

(2) A security includes any note, stock, bond, debenture, evidence of indebtedness, certificate of interest or participation in any profit-sharing agreement, collateral-trust agreement, pre-organization certificate or

subscription, transferable share, or investment contract (including variable annuities).[6]

However, financial planning may encompass a wide variety of services, principally advisory in nature, which may, or may not, trigger the registration requirement. These services may be broadly segmented in three service categories:

(1) Generally, financial planning services involve preparing a financial program for a client based on the client's financial circumstances and objectives. This information normally would cover present and anticipated assets and liabilities, including insurance, savings, investments, and anticipated retirement or other employee benefits. The program developed for the client usually includes general recommendations for a course of activity, or specific actions to be taken by the client. Recommendations may be made, for example, that the client obtain insurance or revise existing coverage, establish an individual retirement account, increase or decrease funds held in savings accounts, or invest funds in securities. A financial planner may develop tax or estate plans for clients or refer clients to an accountant or attorney for these services. The provider of such services in most cases assists the client in implementing the recommended program by, among other things, making specific recommendations to carry out the general recommendations of the program, or by selling the client insurance products, securities, or other investments. The financial planner may also review the client's program periodically and recommend revisions. Persons providing such financial planning services use various compensation arrangements. Some financial planners charge clients an overall fee for developing an individual client program while others charge clients an hourly fee. In some instances financial planners are compensated, in whole or in part, by commissions on the sale to the client of insurance products, interests in real estate, securities (such as common stocks, bonds, limited partnership interests, and mutual funds), or other investments.

(2) A second common form of service relating to financial matters is provided by pension consultants who typically offer, in addition to administrative services, a variety of advisory services to employee benefit plans and their fiduciaries based upon an analysis of the needs of the plan. These advisory services may include advice as to the types of funding media available to provide plan benefits, general recommendations as to what portion of plan assets should be invested in various investment media, including securities, and in some cases, recommendations regarding investment

152

in specific securities or other investments. Pension consultants may also assist plan fiduciaries in determining plan investment objectives and policies and in designing funding media for the plan. They may also provide general or specific advice to plan fiduciaries as to the selection or retention of persons to manage the assets of the plan. Persons providing these services to plans are customarily compensated for their services through fees paid by the plan, its sponsor, or other persons; by means of sales commissions on the sale of insurance products or investments to the plan; or through a combination of fees and commissions.

(3) A rarer form of financial advisory service is that provided by persons offering a variety of financially related services to entertainers or athletes based upon the needs of the individual client. Such persons, who often use the designation "sports representative" or "entertainment representative," offer a number of services to clients, including the negotiation of employment contracts and development of promotional opportunities for the client, as well as advisory services related to investments, tax planning, or budget and money management. Such persons providing these services to clients may assume discretion over all or a portion of a client's funds by collecting income, paying bills, and making investments for the client. Such representatives are customarily compensated for their services primarily through fees charged for negotiation of employment contracts but may also receive compensation in the form of fixed charges or hourly fees for other services provided, including investment advisory services.

The SEC has issued guidance concerning the application of the Act in Investment Advisers Act Release No. 1092 (IA 1092). According to IA 1092, all of the facts and circumstances must be examined in determining whether a person providing integrated advisory services meets the definition of an investment adviser.

(1) A person who provides advice, or issues or promulgates reports or analyses, which concern securities, generally is an investment adviser.

• This includes analysis of rate of return on current portfolio and opinions concerning the efficacy of the asset allocation to achieve the financial goals.

• This also includes giving advice as to the selection or retention of an investment manager if the advice is based on the client's investment objectives.

• Providing a list of investment mangers without recommendation in conjunction with a financial planning business is considered investment advice, while the providing of a list of money managers is not considered investment advice.

(2) A person who advises clients concerning the relative advantages and disadvantages of investing in securities in general as compared to other investments is an investment adviser.

In general, therefore, any person engaging in any of the types of financial planning services described above is considered an investment adviser unless otherwise qualifying under one of the exclusions or exemptions described above.

The clearest instance of an investment adviser being in the business of giving such advice is where the person clearly holds himself to others as such adviser or as one who gives such advice.

In a case where the person's principal business is the giving of financial services other than investment advice the person is still considered to be in the business if there are discussions concerning investments that go beyond a discussion of the advisability of investing in securities in general terms[7] or if the giving of investment advice is regularly a part of the business activities.[8] The giving of advice need not be the principal business activity for the person to be in the business of giving investment advice.

> **Example**: A CPA is reviewing the tax return with a client. In response to the client's question about reducing taxes, the CPA indicates that municipal bonds would reduce such taxes. If such statements are regularly made in the course of reviewing clients' tax returns or assets, the CPA is in the business of giving investment advice.

According to the SEC, a person is considered to be in the business of giving advice with respect to securities if that person:

(1) Holds himself out as an investment adviser or as a provider of investment advice;

(2) Receives separate or additional compensation that is a clearly definable charge for the provision of advice about securities, regardless of whether the compensation is separate or included in overall compensation;

(3) Provides specific investment advice other than in rare, isolated, or non-periodic instances.[9]

The SEC will also consider other financial services activities offered to clients. For example, if a financial planner structures his planning so as to give only generic, non-specific investment advice as a financial planner, but then gives specific securities advice in his capacity as a registered representative of a dealer or as an agent of an insurance company, the person would not be able to assert that he was not "in the business" of giving investment advice.

Compensation Element

The compensation element of being an investment adviser is satisfied by the receipt of any economic benefit, whether in the form of an advisory fee or some other fee relating to the total services rendered, commissions, or some combination of the foregoing. It is not necessary that the person who provides investment advisory and other services to a client charge a separate fee for the investment advisory portion of the total services. The compensation element is satisfied if a single fee is charged for a number of different services, including investment advice or the issuing of reports or analyses concerning securities. But the fact that no separate fee is charged for the investment advisory portion of the service could be relevant to whether the person is "in the business" of giving investment advice.

It is not necessary that an adviser's compensation be paid directly by the person receiving investment advisory services, only that the investment adviser receive compensation from some source for his services. A person providing a variety of services to a client, including investment advisory services, for which the person receives any economic benefit, for example, by receipt of a single fee or commissions upon the sale to the client of insurance products or investments, is providing advisory services for compensation.

Subsidiaries and Affiliates

The controlling entity of a registered investment adviser may likewise have to register unless the controlled entity has a separate, independent existence evidenced by:

(1) Being adequately capitalized;

(2) Having a buffer between the subsidiary's personnel and the parent's;

(3) Having employees, officers, and directors who are not otherwise engaged in an investment advisory business of the parent;

(4) Determining the investment advice given to clients and not limiting sources of investment information to its parent; and

(5) Keeping its investment advice confidential until communicated to its clients.[10]

The Exception For Accountants

Even if an accountant is considered to be an investment adviser in the business of providing investment advice, an accountant may be specifically excluded from the definition of an investment adviser for purposes of the Act. The issue is whether the investment advice is given solely incidental to the practice of accounting.[11] There are no specific regulatory or judicial announcements to guide accountants on the meaning of the incidental rule; however, the SEC has issued a "No-Action" letter in which it enumerated three factors to be considered:[12]

(1) Whether the accountant (or firm) holds himself out to the public as an investment adviser;

(2) Whether the services rendered are in connection with and reasonably related to accounting services; and

(3) Whether the fee charged for advisory services is based on the same factors as those used to determine the accounting fee.

The No-Action letter provides that the exception is not available to an accountant who holds himself out, or a firm that holds itself out, to the public as providing financial planning, pension consulting, or other financial advisory services. In such case, the performance of investment advisory services by such a person is deemed to be incidental to the practice of financial planning or pension consulting profession and not incidental to the practice of accounting. In this respect, financial planning appears to be considered as something outside the practice of accounting for purposes of this exception.

Even if an accountant is an investment adviser and cannot rely on the accountants exemption, there are exemptions from registration which may be available. However, such persons remain liable under the Act's anti-fraud provisions.

Brochure Rule

Investment advisers are generally required to deliver a written disclosure statement (brochure) on their background and business practices upon entering into an advisory contract with a client.[13] The brochure rule is designed to assure that clients are provided with pertinent information useful in the selection or retention of an investment adviser.

The rule also requires investment advisers, on an annual basis, to deliver (or to offer in writing to deliver) to clients a free brochure. Advisory contracts with investment companies and contracts for impersonal advisory services of less than $200 per year are exempt from the brochure rule. An adviser entering into a contract for impersonal advisory services of more than $200 per year need only offer to deliver a brochure.

The information required by the brochure rule is included in Part II of Form ADV, the registration form for investment advisers. To comply with the brochure rule, an investment adviser may deliver either: (1) Part II of Form ADV, or (2) another document containing at least that information.

Books and Records—Inspections

The 1940 Adviser's Act and the SEC's rules require that advisers maintain and preserve specified books and records and make them available to Commission examiners for inspection. This rule allows computer and microfilm record-keeping under certain conditions.[14]

Prohibited Contractual and Fee Provisions

The Act requires advisory contracts to provide that the contract may not be assigned without the client's consent. If the investment adviser is a partnership, the contract must provide that the adviser will notify the client of a change in its membership.

The Act also prohibits any type of fee arrangement contingent on capital gains or appreciation in the client's account. There is a statutory exception from the performance fee prohibition for contracts with a registered investment company or certain clients with more than $1 million in managed assets if specific conditions are met.[15] In addition, performance fee contracts are permitted with clients with $500,000 under the adviser's management or a net worth in excess of $1 million under certain conditions.[16]

Restrictions on Use of the Term "Investment Counsel"

A registered investment adviser may not use the term "investment counsel" unless its principal business is acting as an investment adviser and a substantial portion of its business is providing "investment supervisory services." Investment

supervisory services are the giving of continuous advice on the investment of funds on the basis of the individual needs of each client.[17]

Anti-Fraud Provisions

Fraudulent activities by investment advisers are prohibited. This applies to all investment advisers, registered or not.[18] SEC regulations establish restrictions on advertising by investment advisers, custody or possession of a client's funds or securities, and when advisers may pay cash referral fees.[19]

Misstatements or misleading omissions of material facts and fraudulent acts and practices in connection with the purchase or sale of securities or the conduct of an investment advisory business are prohibited.[20] As a fiduciary, an investment adviser owes his clients undivided loyalty and may not engage in activity in conflict with a client's interest. U. S. Supreme Court rulings have also held that advisers have an affirmative obligation "of utmost good faith and full and fair disclosure of all material facts" to their clients, as well as a duty to avoid misleading them.

Three rules are particularly important:

(1) All investment advisers are prohibited from using any advertisement that contains any untrue statement of material fact or which is otherwise misleading. Specific prohibitions apply to the use of testimonials, past specific recommendations, and charts, graphs, formulas, and similar devices.[21]

(2) Regulations detail how client funds and securities in the custody of the adviser must be held and require the adviser to provide specified information to clients. Under these rules, advisers with custody must have an annual, unannounced examination of the funds and securities by an independent public accountant and file that report with the SEC.[22]

(3) An investment adviser is prohibited from paying cash fees for soliciting clients, on a direct or indirect basis, except under specific conditions.[23]

Responsibility for Compliance— SEC Assistance

This chapter merely highlights selected provisions of the 1940 Investment Advisers Act and its rules. It does not state all applicable regulatory provisions. You should consult the Act (15 U.S.C. 80b-1 et. seq.) and its rules and regulations, which are found in Title 17, Part 275 of the Code of Federal Regulations.

We recommend that advisers obtain the rules and regulations (Title 17, CFR, Part 240 through the end). They are available from:

Superintendent of Documents
Government Printing Office
Washington, DC 20402-9325
(202) 512-1800

The rules and regulations can also be accessed through the Government Printing Office's website, www.gpo.gov.

The staff of the SEC, Division of Investment Management is available to answer specific questions on regulation and registration of advisers. You may also contact the nearest Regional or Branch Office of the SEC.

The SEC's website also has an explanation of the investment adviser registration requirements. The address is www.sec.gov/rules/othern/advfaq.htm.

State Requirements

Most states have securities laws requiring registration of investment advisers. In the majority of the states with these laws, the laws are patterned on the 1940 Act and the same three-pronged definition determines who is and who is not an investment adviser. Some states have amended their securities laws in recent years to bring financial planners within the definition of investment adviser.

Most of the states require completion of the ADV form or their own version of the ADV form; most also have an exam requirement and a filing fee. In some states a bond must be posted. The amounts vary from state to state. Requests for information about the requirements of any particular state should be addressed to that state's officials. The name and address of those officials can be obtained by contacting:

North American Securities Administrators Assoc.
10 G Street NE, Suite 710
Washington, DC 20002
(202) 737-0900
www.nasaa.org

PART II—REGISTRATION

Introduction

A person subject to SEC registration as an investment adviser must file Form ADV, keep it current by filing periodic amendments, and file a brief report annually. These requirements are discussed below.

A person subject to registration also must comply with the "brochure rule," (described above) which requires most advisers to provide clients and prospective clients with information about the adviser's business practices and educational and business background. For more information about the brochure rule, consult the document "General Information on the Regulation of Investment Advisers" (contact the nearest regional office of the Securities and Exchange Commission for a copy) or Rule 204-3.[24]

General Filing Requirements

FORMS—Copies of Forms ADV and ADV-W can be obtained from the SEC's Office of Consumer Affairs and Information Services in Washington, DC, or from a local Commission office.

COPIES—All adviser filings must be submitted in triplicate and typewritten. Copies can be filed, but each must be signed manually. If an applicant fails to submit three copies, the filing will be returned and may be declared delinquent when it is resubmitted. An applicant should keep a fourth copy of all filings for his own records.

NAME and SIGNATURES—Full names are required. Initials may not be used, unless an individual legally has only an initial. Each copy of an execution page must contain an original manual signature. If the registration application is filed by a sole proprietor, it should be signed by the proprietor; if filed by a partnership, it should be signed in the name of the partnership by a general partner; if filed by a corporation, it should be signed in the corporation's name by an authorized principal officer.

Form ADV

Form ADV is the application for registration with the SEC as an investment adviser. Its Part I asks for information that is used to review the application and in the SEC's investment advisory program. Part II requires information on the background and business practices of the investment adviser, and can be given to clients to comply with the "brochure rule." Both parts must be filed with the SEC.

Within 45 days after a registration application is filed, the SEC must grant registration or begin proceedings to deny it. The only grounds for denial are if the Commission finds that the adviser has committed prohibited acts and the public interest requires denial.

Make sure that all items of the form and accompanying schedules are properly completed in full. If the registration application filed is incomplete, it will be returned and the 45 day period will not begin again until a complete application is submitted.

Amending Form ADV

Form ADV must be amended to be updated. Rule 204-1 governs which information must be corrected promptly and which must be corrected within 90 days of the end of the fiscal year.

Amending the form requires completing the execution page (page one) and the entire page containing the updated items. Circle the items being amended. Rule 204-1(a) and (b) and the instructions to Form ADV give more complete information on amendments.

Balance Sheets

All registrants must maintain "true, accurate, and current books and records" as specified in Rule 204-2.[25] However, not all registrants are required to submit financial statements to the Commission. Registrants who must file a balance sheet are those with custody or possession of client funds or securities, or those requiring prepayment of advisory fees six months or more in advance and in excess of $500 per client.

If an adviser is required to submit a balance sheet, it must be audited by an independent public accountant. It is filed annually on Schedule G as an amendment to Form ADV.

Withdrawal From Registration—Form ADV-W

If an adviser is no longer engaged in business as an investment adviser, he may apply to withdraw his registration by filing Form ADV-W (Notice of Withdrawal from Registration as an Investment Adviser) in accordance with the instructions on the form. He must file Form ADV-W to withdraw his registration voluntarily.

Additional Information

Form ADV and ADV-W contain instructions for completing and filing these forms. For questions concerning registration, contact:

Office of Applications and Reports Services
Branch of Registrations and Examinations
U. S. Securities and Exchange Commission
6432 General Green Way
Alexandria, VA 22312
(202) 942-7820

WHERE CAN I FIND OUT MORE ABOUT IT?

1. The American Society of CLU & ChFC's bimonthly publication, *Society Page* includes a recurring column on regulatory issues affecting the insurance and financial services professions.

2. *ICFP Government Affairs Handbook* provides a guide to the state and federal laws and regulations of the financial planning profession.

FOOTNOTE REFERENCES

Investment Advisers — Regulation and Registration

1. 15 USC §80b-2(a)(11).
2. 15 USC §80b-3(b)(3).
3. 15 USC §80b-3(b)(1).
4. 15 USC §80b-2(a)(11).
5. 15 USC §80b-2(a)(16).
6. 15 USC §80b-2(a)(18).
7. IA 770.
8. IA 1092.
9. IA 1092 indicates that asset allocation advice concerning the percentages of various assets that should be held is considered equivalent to giving advice with respect to specific securities.
10. Richard E. Ellis/R.E. Holdings Limited, SEC No-Action Letter (Sept. 17, 1981).
11. 15 USC §80b-2(a)(11)(B).
12. Hauk, Soule, & Fasani, P.C., SEC No-Action Letter (May 2, 1986).
13. 17 CFR 275.204-3.
14. 15 USC §80b-4; 17 C.F.R. 275.204-2.
15. 15 USC §80b-5(b).
16. 17 CFR 275.205-3.
17. 15 USC §§80b-2(a)(13), 80b-8(c).
18. 15 USC §80b-6.
19. 17 CFR 275.206(4)-1, 275.206(4)-2, 275.206(4)-3.
20. 15 USC §§77q, 78j(b), 80b-6; 17 C.F.R. 240.10b-5.
21. 17 CFR 275.206(4)-1.
22. 17 CFR 275.206(4)-2.
23. 17 CFR 275.206(4)-3.
24. 17 CFR 275.204-3.
25. 17 CFR 275.204-2.

Chapter 10

FINANCIAL LEVERAGING

WHAT IS IT?

Financial leveraging is the use of borrowed funds at a fixed or controllable interest rate in order to obtain an investment which will provide a current return or appreciation at a rate greater than the cost of the borrowed funds. In other words, financial leveraging is borrowing money at one rate and investing it at a higher rate.

In this chapter, the term "leveraging" refers to financial leveraging, in other words, the advantage of using borrowed money to enhance the return on a client's investment. In other chapters, the term leverage may be given a different meaning.

HOW DOES IT WORK?

The operations of a commercial bank provide a good illustration of the day-to-day use of leveraging. The owners of the bank use their own funds to provide approximately ten percent of the bank's assets. For simplicity, assume that the bank obtains the balance of its cash needs through the following sources:

	COST
Checking accounts	0%-3%
Savings accounts	4%-6%
Certificates of Deposit	5%-7%

If these funds (90% of which are someone else's money) are lent or invested at a 14% average return, it is easy to see how the bank makes money.

Leveraging also enables an investor to purchase a larger asset than his own available funds will permit. For example, if an individual wishes to purchase a $100,000 real estate investment which he expects to appreciate by 20% over the next year, but he has only $20,000 available to invest, the individual would leverage the investment by borrowing the other $80,000 he needs for the investment.

The application of leveraging to personal financial planning can best be explained by way of an example. Assume an investor wishes to purchase undeveloped land at a price of $50,000. The investor believes he can have the zoning for the property changed within a year, allowing him to sell the land for $75,000. The investor has arranged with his bank to borrow $40,000 of the purchase price for the needed one year at a fixed rate of 10%, with all interest payable with the principal at the end of the one-year term. The investor will therefore be required to invest only $10,000 of his own funds. In deciding whether to invest $50,000 of his own funds or to invest only $10,000 and borrow the balance under the terms provided by the bank, the investor would make the following analysis:

Purchase Price: $50,000
Expected Sale Price: $75,000
Holding Period: one year
Investor's Tax Bracket: 31%

		Leverage	Financing
(1)	Initial Equity	$50,000	$10,000
(2)	Loan Principal	—	40,000
(3)	Sales Price	75,000	75,000
(4)	Gain on Sale [(3) - (1) - (2)]	25,000	25,000
(5)	Interest Cost [.10 x (2)]	—	4,000
(6)	Tax on Sale [.31 x (4)]	7,750	7,750
(7)	Tax benefit of interest [.31 x (5)]	—	1,240
(8)	Net Return [(4) - (5) - (6) + (7)]	17,250	14,490
	Return on Investor's Equity [(8)/(1)]	$17,250 / $50,000 = 34.5%	$14,490 / $10,000 = 144.90%

In evaluating whether leveraging is appropriate for this investment, the investor must review not only the potential rewards of leveraging, but also the associated risks. What if he is not able to obtain the expected zoning change and can sell the property in one year for only $35,000? The investor must still repay the bank the $40,000 borrowed plus the interest of $6,000. The results of this investment would look like this:

Purchase Price: $50,000
Sale Price: $35,000
Holding Period: one year

Investor's Tax Bracket: 31% (Loss on sale will be a capital loss, offsetting other gains of investor.)

		No Leverage	80% Financing
(1)	Initial Equity	$50,000	$10,000
(2)	Loan Principal	—	40,000
(3)	Sales Price	35,000	35,000
(4)	Gain on Sale [(3) - (1) - (2)]	(15,000)	(15,000)
(5)	Interest Cost [.10 x (2)]	—	4,000
(6)	Tax Benefit of loss [.31 x (4)]	4,650	4,650
(7)	Tax benefit of interest [.31 x (5)]	—	1,240
(8)	Net Loss [(4) - (5) + (6) + (7)]	(10,350)	(13,110)

Return on Investor's Equity [(8)/(1)]	($10,350)/$50,000 = -20.7%	($13,110)/$10,000 = -131.1%

This example illustrates the concept of "negative leverage," the risk that the investment will not generate enough cash income to pay off the debt. The result could be the loss of the entire investment, including not only the capital put into the investment, but also the cash needed to repay the borrowed money.

Even if the investor can afford to lose only $10,000, if he believes the risk of loss is small, then leveraging may still make sense. However, a loss in such a case, could be devastating to the investor if he can sell the land for only $35,000. Where will he get the $15,120 to cover his net loss?

WHEN IS THE USE OF THIS TECHNIQUE INDICATED?

1. When the investor does not have the available cash to finance the purchase of a particular asset.

2. When the investor can borrow money at a rate lower than the expected return on an investment. Leveraged debt should be incurred only when the investment will earn more than the cost of borrowing.

3. When the investment itself can generate sufficient "cash flow" to cover "debt service" (the annual cost of interest and any principal payable on the debt).

4. Where the goal of the investment is long term appreciation rather than a current return, and the investor has other available resources to cover the annual cost of debt service.

5. During periods of high inflation. At such times, borrowing money enables an investor to purchase an asset immediately. The appreciation in that asset offsets the effects of inflation. The investor can pay off the debt in the future with dollars which have been "cheapened" by the effects of inflation.

ADVANTAGES

1. Leveraging makes it possible to purchase an asset the investor might not otherwise be able to afford.

2. Leveraging may significantly increase the return on the investor's equity.

3. When used to obtain depreciable property, leveraging increases the tax benefits to the investor. This is because depreciation and investment tax credit may be based on the full purchase price of the asset, and not just the amount of the investor's equity. For example, if David Kurt purchased an office building costing $100,000 (exclusive of land), his depreciation will be computed on the full $100,000, even though he may have used only $20,000 of his own funds.

4. Leveraging permits the investor to spread a limited amount of available funds throughout a number of investments. This enhanced diversification adds to the safety of principal.

5. The creditor will have an interest in the financial soundness of the investment. In order to protect that interest, before a loan is made, most lenders will make an independent investigation of the underlying value of the property and the borrower's ability to pay both interest and principal. This provides the investor with an objective evaluation of the appropriateness of the venture.

DISADVANTAGES

1. "Reverse leverage" is the most serious disadvantage of borrowing money to purchase an investment. Reverse leverage means that the cost of servicing the debt (both interest and principal) exceeds the total return (both cash flow and appreciation). For example, if the annual debt service for a $100,000 loan is $15,000 and the annual cash flow from the investment is only $8,000, the investor must fund the $7,000 shortfall from other income or assets.

2. If the primary purpose of the investment is to obtain appreciation, and there is little or no current income generated, the annual debt service payment requirements may place significant cash flow pressures on the investor.

3. Leveraging automatically increases the risks of an investment since the debt must be repaid, regardless of the return the investor receives.

4. The creditor, as a "partner" in the venture, may impose certain restrictions on the investor. For example, a bank may limit the amount of salary that can be paid to the sole shareholder of a corporation borrowing funds to finance the purchase of a new manufacturing facility. Similarly, a brokerage firm lending money to a customer to help him purchase securities may require him to provide other securities as collateral. Therefore, the cost of this "margin account" is not only the interest on the borrowed funds, but also the limitations on the free use of the securities used as additional collateral.

5. Borrowing to finance the purchase of an investment asset may restrict an individual's ability to borrow for other purposes. Other potential creditors may determine that the individual cannot safely handle any further indebtedness.

HOW IS IT IMPLEMENTED?

Once you have determined that an investment may be appropriate for leveraging:

(1) Determine your borrowing capacity. No matter how much you may want to borrow, prospective lenders will impose limitations on the amount they are willing to lend.

(2) Determine the appropriate amount of leverage. The factors you should examine include:

(a) The availability of future funds to meet debt service requirements. An investor's borrowing should be limited to his ability to meet debt payments as they come due. The future funds needed may be derived from the cash flow of the investment itself ("self-funding") or from outside sources such as other investments, the investor's personal income, or other borrowed funds.

(b) The spread between the expected return on the investment and the cost to borrow. The higher the expected rate of return, the greater the advantage of leverage (and therefore the greater the risk the investor should be willing to take). For example, if you expect to earn 20% on your money and it cost you only 14% to borrow, you would tend to borrow more than if the money cost you 18%. The 2% spread between the 18% cost to borrow and the 20% expected return may still

make leveraging worthwhile, but the spread is *only* 2%. In other words, there is little margin for error. With the 6% spread between 14% and 20%, even if the return on the investment drops 3% below the projected 20%, the investor still has positive leverage.

(c) The greater the tax advantages of borrowing (all other things being equal), the more the investor should borrow. Subject to limitations imposed by the tax law on deductions and other tax benefits relating to investment property (see Chapter 8), the investor receives the same type and level of tax benefits from borrowed funds as he does from the use of his own capital. Therefore, financial leveraging is also tax leveraging. For example, an investor who purchases an office building for $100,000 of his own funds receives depreciation deductions based on that amount. He obtains neither financial nor tax leverage. But if the same individual had purchased a $500,000 building using his $100,000 and $400,000 of borrowed money, his depreciation deductions would be five times higher.

(3) Determine the alternative sources for leverage borrowing. Such alternatives might include (a) bank financing (either secured by the investment property, other personal assets, or possibly unsecured), (b) margin borrowing from a brokerage house (secured by your portfolio of securities), (c) the cash value of insurance policies, (d) seller financing (often called "purchase-money" financing), and (e) borrowing from friends and family.

WHERE CAN I FIND OUT MORE?

1. *Tax Facts on Investments (Tax Facts 2)* (The National Underwriter Company).

2. Lilian Chew, *Managing Derivative Risks: The Use and Abuse of Leverage* (John Wiley & Sons, 1996).

3. David Sarota, *Essentials of Real Estate Investment* (Real Estate Education Co., 1997)

4. Friedman and Harris, *Keys to Investing in Real Estate* (Barrons, 1993)

5. *What is Margin?* (Merrill Lynch, Pierce, Fenner & Smith, Inc.).

6. Lawrence Gitman, *Personal Financial Planning* (Dryden Press, 1996).

QUESTIONS AND ANSWERS

Question — What is a margin account?

Answer — A margin account enables an investor to use unencumbered securities to borrow cash which in turn is used to purchase additional securities. Essentially, a margin account with a broker is one which provides loans secured by stocks and other securities held by the brokerage firm.

Question — What are the advantages of a margin account?

Answer — A margin account enables an investor to borrow cash readily, with a minimum of paperwork and without the need to sell or transfer stocks to finance the loan. The investor pays a competitive rate of interest to the broker on this "secured loan."

Borrowing funds to purchase stocks may increase the size of the profit the investor may realize beyond what would be possible if only personal funds were used. This is a classic example of the enhancement of purchasing power available through leveraging; by buying more stocks with the additional money borrowed from the brokerage firm, the investor increases his potential gain as well as possible dividends.

For example, assume an investor buys 750 shares of the Martin-Stephans Corporation at $50 a share. He uses his own money and pays $37,500. Assume the stock appreciates $10 a share. It is then worth a total of $45,000, for a gain of $7,500. If the investor had used leverage through a margin account, the gain could have been increased significantly. For instance, he could have bought one-third more shares at a 75% margin. Although he would still have invested $37,500 of his own money for 750 shares, he can borrow $12,500 to purchase an additional 250 shares. If the 1000 share total appreciates $10 a share, his profit is $10,000. As a result of leveraging, his profit has increased by $2,500 (before the after-tax interest cost of borrowing the $12,500).

Question — What is a "leveraged lease"?

Answer — A leveraged lease is one in which the lessor finances a portion of the purchase price of the leased property with debt. Sometimes this debt is "nonrecourse." This means that the borrower has no personal liability. A nonrecourse loan is secured by specific assets of the borrower. For example, in many real estate financing transactions, the lender may look only to the property itself as security for the loan.

Chapter 11

PERSONAL FINANCIAL STATEMENTS

WHAT IS IT?

Personal financial statements provide a summary of an individual's financial position. The financial statements most commonly thought of in a business context are the "Balance Sheet" and the "Income Statement." In personal financial planning, the financial statements which are most commonly used are the "Balance Sheet" (the American Institute of Certified Public Accountants [AICPA] refers to this as a "Statement of Financial Condition") and the "Cash Flow Statement."

As with business financial statements, a personal "balance sheet" reflects a person's assets, liabilities, and net worth as of a given date. A personal "cash flow statement" shows an individual's cash receipts (e.g., income) and cash disbursements (e.g., expenses) for a given period of time. The cash flow statement is often presented in conjunction with a statement of an individual's taxable income.

HOW DOES IT WORK?

The preparation of personal financial statements requires the compilation of the individual's "personal financial data" into the formal statements used in the financial planning process. Some individuals have developed the habit of maintaining financial statements on a regular basis. Other clients will not begin the financial statement process until a specific need arises, and often will need professional help. These statements are essential before a financial planner can effectively begin the planning process.

Figure 11.1 is an example of a personal balance sheet, using the format illustrated in the AICPA's Personal Financial Statements Guide. Such statements of financial condition are generally accompanied by notes which are an integral part of these statements. Note 1 is a general statement that the assets are stated at their estimated current values, and the liabilities at their estimated current amounts. The other notes are referenced at the end of the description of the specific assets and liabilities to which they apply. They generally describe the methods used to determine the estimated current values of assets and the estimated current amounts of liabilities and any other information warranting disclosure to the users of the statements.

Contingent liabilities are listed on the balance sheet without specific amounts reflected. This is because it is not possible to determine whether or how much the individual may be required to pay. An example of a contingent liability is a personal guaranty of a debt of a closely held corporation controlled by the individual. Such contingent liabilities generally receive substantial explanation in the notes to the financial statements.

Figure 11.2 is an example of a combined personal statement of cash flow and taxable income which can be extremely useful in the financial planning process. (A blank form for this statement which is suitable for photocopying appears in Figure 11.3 at the end of this chapter.)

WHEN IS THE USE OF THIS TECHNIQUE INDICATED?

1. It is the essential starting point in the determination of personal financial goals. The financial statements are critical in order to determine (a) "what you have" and (b) "what you need to get where you want to be."

2. When an individual would like to borrow money for an investment and must prove to the lender an ability to make debt service payments and assure the creditor that there is adequate security for the loan.

3. When a "tax shelter" or other investment is contemplated and the investor must prove to the promoters that all the financial criteria established in the prospectus can be met. These criteria typically include:

   (a) minimal income and marginal tax bracket

   (b) minimal net worth of prospective investor

   (The net worth required will vary significantly, depending on such factors as the risk involved in the investment and the amount of future funding the investor may be called upon to provide.)

4. As the starting point for the budgeting process.

5. As the starting point for the income or cash flow projection process. For example, "Do I have enough to retire?"

6. When a "capital needs analysis" is required to determine life or disability income insurance shortfalls.

ADVANTAGES

1. Provides a means for summarizing an individual's financial position in a format commonly used in financial analysis.

2. Provides an individual with an orderly reference point to evaluate his current financial position relative to financial goals.

3. May force an individual to focus realistically on what needs to be done to achieve projected goals and provide motivation for the appropriate action.

DISADVANTAGES

1. May be difficult and time consuming to compile, especially if financial statements are not maintained on a regular basis.

2. A "fair market value" balance sheet may require expensive appraisals and asset valuations. (Balance sheets prepared under "generally accepted accounting principles" are usually based on the original or depreciated cost of assets, rather than their current fair market value. Such statements tend to understate net worth.)

HOW IS IT IMPLEMENTED?

The financial records of most individuals are both informal and incomplete. In many cases a client will have organized and recorded only a small portion of his assets and liabilities. This means that the financial planner must be prepared to assist the client in gathering the necessary information from numerous sources, such as:

(1) income tax returns,

(2) real estate and personal property tax returns,

(3) client's accountant,

(4) bank records, including checking and savings account statements, loan balance statements, etc.,

(5) client's attorney,

(6) stock broker's statements,

(7) property and life insurance records,

(8) listing of safe deposit box contents,

(9) the client.

The following basic guidelines (suggested by the Personal Financial Statements Guide of the AICPA) should be considered in creating personal financial statements:

(1) Reflect assets and liabilities on an accrual rather than cash basis. For example, if Lara Leimberg, the famous author, had earned $30,000 of royalties which she had not yet received, that amount should be shown as an account receivable on her personal balance sheet. This would be the case even if she reported income for tax purposes on a cash basis.

(2) Assets and liabilities should be presented by order of liquidity and maturity. The most liquid assets, such as cash, should be at the top. This helps to highlight the ability to meet immediate cash needs, the amount of liquid assets available for immediate consumption, or to take advantage of investment opportunities. From an estate planning perspective, listing assets in order of liquidity also emphasizes the importance of adequate cash (or equivalents) to meet estate settlement needs.

(3) Statements should include only the proportionate interest of a joint or community property owner. The extent of that interest and its value must be determined under the property laws of the appropriate state. An attorney's advice might be necessary to ascertain whether an interest should be included, and if so, to what extent.

(4) If a business interest comprises a significant portion of a client's total assets, it should be segregated and shown separately from other investments.

(5) If real estate or a business interest is encumbered with a large debt, that debt should be presented separately from the asset. This is particularly true if the liability may be satisfied from sources unrelated to the investment. For example, if Charlee Leimberg, the real estate investor, purchased a $600,000 building and obtained a $400,000 mortgage on which she was personally liable, the real estate and the related mortgage should be presented separately.

(6) Assets should be presented at estimated current values. Likewise, liabilities should be shown at their estimated current amounts. The current value of an asset is the amount at which an exchange would occur between a hypothetical "informed and willing" buyer and seller, neither of whom is under compulsion to consummate the transaction.

Personal Financial Statements

Figure 11.1

Robert and Rebecca Stone Statements of Financial Condition December 31, 1997 and 1996		

| | December 31, | |
	1997	1996
ASSETS		
Cash	$ 7,400	$ 31,200
Bonus Receivable	40,000	20,000
Investments		
Marketable Securities (Note 2)	321,000	281,400
Stock Options (Note 3)	56,000	48,000
RobReb Limited Partnership (Note 4)	96,000	84,000
Stone & Stone, Inc. (Note 5)	1,100,000	950,000
Vested Interest in deferred profit sharing plan	222,800	197,800
Remainder interest in testamentary trust (Note 6)	343,800	257,600
Cash value of life insurance ($87,200 and $85,800),		
less loans payable to insurance companies		
($76,200 and $75,400) (Note 7)	11,000	10,400
Residences (Note 8)	380,000	360,000
Personal effects (excluding art and jewelry) (Note 9)	110,000	100,000
Art and Jewelry (Note 9)	80,000	73,000
	$2,768,000	$2,413,400

| December 31, | | |
	1997	1996
LIABILITIES		
Income taxes - current year balance	$ 17,600	$ 800
Demand 12.0% note payable to bank	50,000	52,000
Mortgage payable (Note 10)	196,400	198,000
Contingent liabilities (Note 11)		
	264,000	250,800
Estimated income taxes on the differences between the		
estimated current values of assets and the estimated		
current amounts of liabilities and their tax bases		
(Note 12)	478,000	320,000
Net worth	2,026,000	1,842,600
	$2,768,000	$2,413,400

Figure 11.2

	CASH FLOW		TAXABLE INCOME
Robert and Rebecca Stone **Statement of Cash Flow and Taxable Income** **Calendar Year 1997**			
CASH RECEIPTS & INCOME:			
Salary — Husband	$70,000		$ 70,000
Wife	90,000		90,000
Bonus — Husband	25,000		25,000
Wife	5,000		5,000
Interest	3,500		3,500
Maturity [Cash-in] of			
Notes Receivable, etc.			
Dividend	2,500		2,500
Cash Distributed/Taxable Income from Business:			
Assets Sales:			
Sales Proceeds	25,000	$25,000	
Less: Basis		(5,000)	
Equals: Gain (Loss)			20,000
Rental Property:			
Rental Income	14,000		14,000
Less: Depreciation			(3,000)
Less: Debt Service	(6,500)	(6,500)	
Add Back:			
Principal Payments		1,200	
Equals: Interest Expense			(5,300)
Less: Other Expenses	(4,500)		(4,500)
Partnership Cash Distributed/Taxable			
Income (Loss)	(4,500)		(1,500)
Cash Distributed/Taxable Income (Loss)			
from Other Investments			
Other Cash Receipts/Taxable Income			
[Trusts, Gifts, Loans, etc.]	5,000		5,000
Total Cash Receipts & Income	$232,000		$220,700

Figure 11.2 (continued)

CASH DISBURSEMENTS & EXPENSES:	CASH FLOW	TAXABLE INCOME
Employee Business Expenses	$ 2,500	$ 2,500
IRA-Keogh Contributions*,	4,000	4,000
Alimony Paid,		
Medical Expenses	2,500	2,500
Less: Nondeductible Amount		(2,500)
State & Local Taxes —		
Income	6,000	6,000
Real Estate	2,500	2,500
Personal Property	1,200	1,200
Federal Income Taxes Paid or W/H	55,000	
Other Deductible Taxes		
Nondeductible Taxes		
(e.g., FICA)	10,800	
Debt Service Payments —		
Mortgage— Interest	9,500	9,500
— Principal	1,200	
Other — Interest	4,500	
— Principal	8,000	
Charitable Contributions	15,000	15,000
Political Contributions		
Casualty Losses		
(Net of Insurance Proceeds)		
Other Deductible Amounts	3,000	3,000
Nondeductible Personal Expenses		
(Food, Clothing, Vacations, Education,		
Furnishings, Gifts, etc.)	62,000	
Investments	30,000	
Standard Deduction		
Personal and Dependency Exemptionsÿ		10,600
Total Cash Disbursements & Expenses	$217,700	$ 54,300
Net Cash Inflow (Outflow)		
& Taxable Income	$ 14,300	$166,400

*Neither spouse participated in an employer-sponsored retirement plan.

‡The couple has two dependent children and the exemption amount for 1997 was $2,650.

Any material transaction costs (such as commissions) should be considered when estimating current values. Taxes on unrecognized gain that would be incurred upon the conversion of the asset to cash are often shown separately as a liability. For instance, assume an investor purchased land for $300,000 which is now worth $700,000. Obviously, upon the sale of the land the investor would recognize a $400,000 gain. The estimated tax liability should be shown in order to realistically reflect the true net worth of the asset. Similarly, if an individual has a vested pension worth $500,000, the tax to be paid when the money is taken should be included on the balance sheet as a liability.

Value can generally be determined through:

(a) recent sales of similar assets,

(b) capitalization of past or prospective earnings,

(c) liquidation values,

(d) adjustment of historical cost based on changes in a specific price index,

(e) the use of appraisals (specialists may have to be consulted in estimating the value of works of art, jewelry, real estate, restricted securities, and closely held businesses),

(f) the use of the discounted amounts of projected cash receipts and disbursements.

(7) Receivables should be discounted using appropriate interest rates as of the date the financial statement is compiled.

(8) Marketable securities (which include both debt and equity investments) should be shown at their quoted market prices. If the security is traded on an exchange, the determinative value will be the closing price of the security nearest to the date of the financial statements. If the security is traded over the counter, the mean of the bid prices or of the bid and asked prices will generally provide a fair estimation of current value. These quotations are available from a number of financial reporting services.

(9) Adjustments should be made to recognize the importance of a majority, minority, or large block interest in equity securities. A controlling interest may have proportionately more value than a recently sold minority interest, but a large block of stock might not sell at as high a per share price as a small number of shares recently sold.

(10) Restrictions on the transfer of a security may indicate the desirability of an adjustment to recent market price.

(11) In the absence of a published price for an option, the value of an option should be determined by reference to the value of the assets subject to the option. The planner should also consider both the exercise price and the length of the option period.

(12) Life insurance should be valued at its "interpolated terminal reserve" value plus any unearned premium as of the balance sheet date. The amount of any loans against the policy can be netted against the policy value.

WHERE CAN I FIND OUT MORE ABOUT IT?

1. *Personal Financial Statements Guide* (American Inst. of CPAs).

2. Elizabeth Lewin, *Your Personal Financial Fitness Program* (Facts on File Pubs., 1983).

3. *The Professional Plan* (Blankenship & Co.).

4. *The Professional Financial Planning System* (Micro Planning Systems).

5. Ochi & Hughes, *Accounting With Lotus 1-2-3* (Wadsworth Elec. Pub. Co., 1983).

6. *Financial and Estate Planners' NumberCruncher I* (Leimberg & LeClair, Inc.).

QUESTIONS AND ANSWERS

Question — How do you estimate the value of a business or other asset through "capitalization of income"?

Answer — The projected flow of income from a business or other asset can be converted into an estimate of its present value. This is called "capitalizing the income." Capitalization of income is a simple, reasonably accurate and commonly accepted means to estimate fair market value.

If a business generates $100,000 of annual earnings, its value would approximate $500,000 if the "capitalization rate" assumed is 20% ($100,000 annual earnings divided by 20% equals the capitalized value of $500,000).

Another way of computing the value of a business or other asset using capitalized earnings is to multiply the annual income amount ($100,000) by the number of years earnings are reasonably estimated to continue (5 years). Thus, an earnings multiplier of "5 times earnings"

The Tools and Techniques of Financial Planning

produces the same value as applying a capitalization rate of 20%.

Two questions must be answered before the financial planner can use a value arrived at through this method: (1) What adjustments must be made to earnings to realistically reflect the "true" earnings of the business or other asset? *and* (2) What capitalization rate is appropriate?

The earnings of a business must be adjusted to take into consideration (1) excessive (or unrealistically low) salaries and other forms of compensation paid to shareholder-employees, (2) excessive (or unrealistically low) rents paid to shareholders, (3) nonrecurring or unusual income or expense items, such as fire losses or insurance recoveries, (4) excessive depreciation, (5) major changes in accounting procedures, (6) widely fluctuating or cyclical profits, (7) strong upward or downward earnings trends, and (8) other factors that may distort the reflection of normal earnings.

In determining the appropriate capitalization rate (earnings multiplier) to be applied to a particular valuation, consider the following:

(a) A higher capitalization rate results in a lower value. For instance, a business producing after-tax income of $50,000, capitalized at 6%, would be valued at $833,333. The same income, capitalized at 15%, would result in a valuation of $333,333. (A 6% capitalization rate is the same as using an earnings multiplier of approximately 16.67. A 15% capitalization rate is the same as multiplying the earnings by about 6.67.)

(b) A lower capitalization rate (and therefore a higher valuation) is appropriate when you are dealing with a stable business, one with a large capital asset base, and one with established goodwill.

(c) A higher capitalization rate (and therefore a lower valuation) is appropriate when you are dealing with a small business, one with little capital, a relatively short financial history, or shallow management resources. A business involved in a speculative venture or one which depends on the presence of only one or two key people will generally warrant a higher capitalization rate.

There are situations where the capitalization of earnings approach is inappropriate or will lead to an unrealistic valuation. For example, raw land, producing no current income, but expected to result in substantial appreciation for the investor, cannot be valued using this method.

Question — When should book value be used in determining the value of a closely held business?

Answer — Book value (book value of assets minus book value of liabilities) is an appropriate method of valuation when the business is:

(a) An investment company with essentially no intrinsic value other than the underlying value of its assets.

(b) A real estate development business and land and/or buildings are the major profit making factor.

(c) Dependent on one or two key individuals for its success. Such business are typically worth only "liquidation value" upon the death, disability, or termination of employment of such key people.

(d) In the process of liquidation. The financial planner should consider the impact of a sacrifice sale as well as the resulting tax liability in determining the net realizable value to the owner.

(e) Highly competitive but only marginally profitable. In such cases profits of the past are an unreliable tool to measure potential future earnings.

(f) Relatively new.

(g) Experiencing large deficits.

Book value should not be used when invested capital is a minor element in the generation of profits or the client does not have enough voting power to force the liquidation of the business.

Book value should rarely be used as the sole determinant of valuation; it should be used in conjunction with or as a means of testing the relevancy of the capitalization of earnings and other methods.

Question — What adjustments must be made to book value in order for it to result in a realistic valuation?

Answer — Most financial planners begin with an accountant's balance sheet, prepared in accordance with generally accepted accounting principles. Such balance sheets are generally based upon historic data and do not reflect the current market value of the underlying assets.

Consider making adjustments under the following circumstances:

(a) When assets are valued at original cost, thus not reflecting any subsequent appreciation or depreciation.

(b) When assets have been depreciated more rapidly than their economic value has actually declined.

(c) When one or more assets with significant economic value have been "written off."

(d) When the business possesses material "off balance sheet assets," such as a long-term lease at an unusually favorable rent.

(e) When the business carries franchises, goodwill, results of successful research and development, or other intangible assets on its books at nominal (if any) cost.

(f) When the business has poor experience in the collection of accounts receivable.

(g) When the firm possesses inventory that is either obsolete or for some other reason is not readily marketable.

(h) When the firm's working capital or liquidity position is unfavorable.

(i) When the assets of the business are encumbered with significant long term debt.

(j) Where the retained earnings are high only because they have been accumulated over a long period of time. Such a business may have poor current earnings and its potential for future profits may be minimal.

Question — What are "goodwill" and "going concern value"?

Answer — In the broadest sense, goodwill is synonymous with the entire intangible value inherent in the operation of a business. But, in the narrower and more technically accurate sense, the intangible value attributable to identifiable intangible assets, such as franchises, patents, secret formulas, trademarks, exclusive licenses, favorable leases, and customer lists, should be separately identified.

What is left, therefore, is a much more restrictive definition of goodwill; goodwill is the expectation of repeat sales due to such factors as (a) advantageous location, (b) superior management expertise, and/or (c) relationships built between consumers and employees.

Goodwill, in its most restrictive sense, is therefore the ability of location, management expertise, and customer relationships to generate earnings that are in excess of the fair market value and that can reasonably be anticipated on the net tangible and identifiable intangible assets of the business.

Going concern value is that element of value possessed by a firm which is an existing establishment, doing business, with earnings sufficient to realize a fair rate of return on the net tangible assets required for continued business operations.

A planner should examine the following factors to determine if an enterprise has a going concern value: (1) experienced management, (2) trained and functioning sales and production personnel, (3) in-place operating facilities, (4) established sources of supply, (5) an established and operative system for distributing the products and services offered by the business, (6) consumer demand for the firm's products, and (7) the ability to continue—uninterrupted—the business and production functions described above in the event of a change of ownership for any reason. The absence of any of these factors may substantially impair the going concern value of the enterprise.

Figure 11.3

	CASH FLOW	TAXABLE INCOME
Statement of Cash Flow and Taxable Income **Calendar Year**		

CASH RECEIPTS & INCOME:
Salary — Husband
   Wife
Bonus — Husband
   Wife
Interest
Maturity [Cash-in] of
 Notes Receivable, etc.
Dividend
Cash Distributed/Taxable Income from Business:
Assets Sales:
 Sales Proceeds
 Less: Basis   ————
Equals: Gain (Loss)
Rental Property:
Rental Income
 Less: Depreciation
 Less: Debt Service
 Add Back:
     Principal Payments
 Equals: Interest Expense   ————
Less: Other Expenses
Partnership Cash Distributed/Taxable
 Income (Loss)
Cash Distributed/Taxable Income (Loss)
 from Other Investments
Other Cash Receipts/Taxable Income
 [Trusts, Gifts, Loans, etc.]
Total Cash Receipts & Income

Figure 11.3 (continued)

	CASH FLOW	TAXABLE INCOME
CASH DISBURSEMENTS & EXPENSES:		
Employee Business Expenses		
IRA-Keogh Contributions		
Alimony Paid		
Medical Expenses		
Less: Nondeductible Amount		
State & Local Taxes —		
Income		
Real Estate		
Personal Property		
Federal Income Taxes Paid or W/H		
Other Deductible Taxes		
Nondeductible Taxes		
(e.g., FICA)		
Debt Service Payments —		
Mortgage — Interest		
— Principal		
Other — Interest		
— Principal		
Charitable Contributions		
Political Contributions		
Casualty Losses		
(Net of Insurance Proceeds)		
Other Deductible Amounts		
Nondeductible Personal Expenses		
(Food, Clothing, Vacations, Education,		
Furnishings, Gifts, etc.)		
Investments		
Standard Deduction		
Personal and Dependency Exemptions		
Total Cash Disbursements & Expenses	————	————
Net Cash Inflow (Outflow)	════	════
& Taxable Income		

Chapter 12

RATE OF RETURN COMPUTATIONS
PART I — DETERMINING PRESENT AND FUTURE VALUES

(Ascertaining The Time Value Of Money)

WHAT IS IT?

Rate of return computations pertain to the fundamentals of the time value of money and the relationship of this important concept to sound financial decisions. Present and future value computations provide quantitative techniques for determining the value of time in tax and financial decision making and are essential in understanding:

(1) the effect of time on the profitability of an investment,

(2) how the projected value of an investment's future economic returns affects the price that should be paid for it,

(3) how to compute the value of an investment's future economic return.

Sound financial decisions depend on an understanding of the basic mathematics of compound interest. This concept is essential in analyzing the financial consequences of almost any investment.

The concept of investment, by definition, implies a delay in consumption or enjoyment. For an individual to forego current consumption or enjoyment in favor of future consumption, there must be some reward. That reward is called "profit," which must be large enough to justify (at least in the mind of the investor) the expected delay. The measure of the profit is typically called the "rate of return," or the "rate of interest."

This chapter (Rate of Return Computations, Part I) will provide a guide to basic present and future value computations. Chapter 13 (Rate of Return Computations, Part II) will deal with other analytical techniques and computations for analyzing the rate of an investment's return, using the material of this chapter as a building block.

HOW DOES IT WORK?

The particular type of investment which a given individual will make depends both on his financial resources and risk preferences. But regardless of preferences, there are three basic underlying rate of return principles that should govern every investment: (1) "timing," (2) "quality," and (3) "quantity."

(1) TIMING — An early return of principal and income is preferable to a later return. For example, given two potential investments, one providing $1,000 now and the other providing $1,000 a year from now, the former investment should be the one selected.

This "sooner is better than later" concept will be referred to as "timing." Tax law provides a good example of the advantages of timing. An important technique in income tax planning, and an integral part of a tax shelter investment, is the use of accelerated depreciation to recover the investor's capital more quickly. The timing benefit of accelerated depreciation as compared to straight line depreciation is the result of keeping tax dollars in the hands of the taxpayer for a longer period of time. This provides a quicker recovery of cost than would be possible through a slower form of depreciation.

(2) QUALITY — An investment with less risk is preferable to one with greater risk. Therefore, if two alternative investments offer the same rate of return, but it is more likely that the principal of the second investment could be lost, the former investment should be the one selected. This "likelihood of pay back" concept is referred to as "quality."

(3) QUANTITY — Assuming investment risks are equal and the timing of the return is identical, the investment with the highest rate of return is preferable. Therefore, if two investments have equal timing and are equally risky, but one has a higher rate of return, it should be the one selected. This "more is better than less" concept will be referred to as "quantity."

This chapter focuses on the principles inherent in the first and third of these three concepts (timing and quantity) and their interrelationship. It is only through a "time adjusted analysis" that an investment with a higher yield but a longer investment life can be effectively compared with an investment with a lower yield but a shorter life span.

In summary, the proper measure of the financial consequences of investment alternatives will focus not only on risk and the sum of the cash flows, but also reflect the differences in the expected timing of their receipt. An example of the attempt to bring all these factors into balance in making a comparison can be found in the "interest adjusted" method of comparing life insurance policies. Emphasis is placed, not only on how much is returned in excess of the policy owner's cost, but also on how quickly cash values build and how rapidly dividends are paid.

WHEN IS THE USE OF THIS TECHNIQUE INDICATED?

1. When an investor wishes to analyze an investment or compare alternative investments where any of the following factors is involved:

    a) "Timing" (When and/or how often must cash be put in and/or taken out of the investment?)

    b) "Quantity" (At what interest rate is the investment earning or growing?)

ADVANTAGES

1. Makes it possible to determine whether an investor can afford to commit funds to a particular investment for the length of time required.

2. Permits a quantitative comparison of alternative investments with different rates of return and different investment life spans.

DISADVANTAGES

1. Heavy reliance on quantitative techniques for evaluating alternatives may overshadow the need to review subjectively the appropriateness of an investment. There are times when an investor should rely on his "gut feelings" and "play a hunch."

2. There are such a large number of measurement devices that the choice of the wrong one in a given situation may easily occur. For example, what would be the appropriate measuring tool to use in estimating the value of an investment 10 years from now? It would not be helpful to measure the future value of a *series* of payments during that period. It would, however, be appropriate to compute the future value (in 10 years) of a single, lump sum invested today.

3. The results of any quantitative analysis are only as good as the initial information provided. Financial analysis is subject to the same danger often raised by computer users: "Garbage in, garbage out." For example, in evaluating the present value of a retirement fund needed 10 years from now, it would be a mistake to use an interest rate of 18% if you know that an investment can never earn at a rate greater than 14% per year. The use of an 18% interest assumption would provide an overly optimistic and misleading answer. In turn, this would lead to the possible underfunding of retirement needs.

HOW IS IT IMPLEMENTED?

The right measurement device in a particular situation depends upon the nature of the problem to be solved. In this section we will review each of the basic time value of money concepts used in financial planning.

I. Computing the Future Value of a Lump Sum

PROBLEM: If I have a lump sum of $_____ today, how do I calculate the value of that lump sum years in the future assuming I earn ___% on my investment?

SOLUTION: Go to Appendix A, Compound Interest Table (future value of a lump sum). This table reflects the amount $1 will be worth in a given number of years at various interest rates. For example, to find how much $10,000 invested today will be worth in 5 years, if it grows at the rate of 10% per year, you would multiply $10,000 by the factor found in the "5-year" row under the 10% column. That factor is 1.6105. Therefore, $10,000 invested today will be worth $16,105 in 5 years.

This compound interest table provides a quick way to determine the future value of an investment or other asset such as a family home. However, this table contains only a limited number of years and interest rate assumptions. To compute the future value of an asset where the number of years or interest rate is not covered by the table, it is necessary to utilize the following formula:

$$F_n = P(1 + i)^n$$

In this formula,

n = The Number of Years (Periods) in the Future

F = Future Value Amount

P = Present Value Amount

The Tools and Techniques of Financial Planning

i = Interest Rate for Each Year (Period)

Applying the formula to our example,

$$F_n = P (1 + i)^n$$

$$F_5 = \$10,000 (1 + .10)^5$$

$$F_5 = \$16,105$$

The formula is a shortcut way of expressing the annual 10% compounding, in our example, of the initial $10,000 investment for the 5-year investment period. The actual, manual computation for the entire investment period can be charted as follows:

	Beginning Balance		Interest @ 10%		Ending Balance
Year 1	$10,000	+	$1,000	=	$11,000
Year 2	$11,000	+	$1,100	=	$12,100
Year 3	$12,100	+	$1,210	=	$13,310
Year 4	$13,310	+	$1,331	=	$14,641
Year 5	$14,641	+	$1,464	=	$16,105

The Compound Interest Table in Appendix A carries compounding factors to four decimal places; other compound interest tables may show more or fewer decimal places and therefore cause the final result to be different. For example, if the table in Appendix A showed a value of only 1.610 (i.e., due to rounding), the final result would have been $16,100, $5 less than the amount computed using either the formula or the longhand chart. This discrepancy highlights one of the shortcomings of tables. In addition, differences resulting from using such tables become more pronounced as the compounding period becomes longer or the present value amount becomes larger.

A further shortcoming of tables is evident when, for example, the interest rate or the compounding period is more complex (such as an interest rate of 10.375%, or a compounding period of 20 years, 7 months). In such cases most tables could not be used. Although the formula is cumbersome, it would be the only way to compute the desired future value.

Fortunately, the formula does not have to be applied manually. A pocket calculator can handle the multiple computations necessary. Many calculators are sophisticated enough (using preprogramed "microchips") to perform the calculation by merely entering the **P** (principal), **n** (number of periods), and **i** (interest rate) numbers. Many such calculators are surprisingly inexpensive (as low as $25). In addition, personal computers easily can be programed to perform the formula computations, as well as provide a printout of the future value at any interim period.

II. Computing the Present Value of a Future Lump Sum

PROBLEM: If I will have a lump sum of $_____ in ___ years, how do I calculate the present value of my investment, assuming it will earn interest at the rate of ___? In other words, what is the equivalent today of $_____ payable as a lump sum ___ years in the future?

SOLUTION: Go to Appendix B, Present Value Table (present value of a future lump sum). This table reflects the present value of $1 received at the end of a given number of years in the future at various interest rates. For example, to find out the present value of $100,000 to be received in 20 years, assuming a growth rate of 10% per year, you would multiply $100,000 by the factor found in the "20-year" row under the 10% column. That factor is 0.1486. Therefore the $100,000 to be received in 20 years has a present value of $14,860.

This present value table was compiled using the following mathematical formula which can be used in cases which are not included in the table:

$$P = \frac{F_n}{(1+ i)^n}$$

Again, in this formula,

P = Present Value Amount

F = Future Value Amount

n = The Number of Years (Periods) Until the Future Payment

i = Interest Rate for Each Year (Period)

Applying the formula to our example,

$$P = \frac{F_n}{(1 + i)^n}$$

$$P = \frac{\$100,000}{(1 + .1)^{20}}$$

$$P = \$14,900$$

[We have deliberately used a 20-year term in this example to point out how difficult it would be to try a manual computation, similar to the one reflected in the chart above (used to illustrate the manual computation of the future value of a lump sum). It continues to become obvious that, without the appropriate table, a calculator or computer is really needed for these kinds of computations.]

A careful look at these first two formulas will reveal that they are really the same formula, but used to solve for different unknown elements.

The first formula is used to determine the future value of a lump sum when the present value, number of years, and interest rate are known.

The second formula is used to determine the present value when the future value, number of years, and interest rate are known.

Either formula can be used to compute any one of the four factors in the equation, so long as the other three are known. For example, either formula could be used if you wanted to know how many years it would take for a present value of $14,860 to grow to $100,000, if the annual interest rate earned on the amount was 10%. You could also use either the table in Appendix A or Appendix B, provided the three known elements can be located in the table. For example, using the table in Appendix B, the Present Value Table, looking under the 10% column we can see that it will take 20 years for a present value of 0.1486 to grow to $1. Multiplying these amounts by 100,000, we see that it will take 20 years for a present value of $14,860 to grow to $100,000.

If the present value in the above example were $15,000, rather than $14,860, the present value table could be used only to estimate the actual period needed to compound the $15,000 to $100,000 at a 10% interest rate. In this case the formula would be needed to arrive at the actual compounding period required. It would then make sense to use a financial calculator or a computer to solve the problem.

Plugging this information into the second formula, the solution would look like this:

$$P = \frac{F_n}{(1+i)^n}$$

$$\$14,900 = \frac{\$100,000}{(1+.10)^n}$$

$$n = 20 \text{ years}$$

As a further example, let's calculate the interest rate at which $14,860 would have to grow in order to compound to $100,000 in 20 years. Using the second formula:

$$P = \frac{F_n}{(1+i)^n}$$

$$\$14,900 = \frac{\$100,000}{(1+i)^{20}}$$

$$i = .10 \text{ or } 10\%$$

III. Calculating the Future Value of a Regular Series of Payments

PROBLEMS:

A. If, beginning today, I invest $_____ a year for ___ years, how do I calculate what the value of that series of investments would be ___ years from now assuming I earn a compounded interest rate of ___% on my investments?

This type of problem requires the calculation of the future value of a regular series of payments. Where each payment is made at the beginning of a compounding period (for example, at the beginning of each year), the process is known as an "annuity due" or an "annuity in advance."

B. What if the first payment in my series of investments is not made until one year from now? In this case the process is known as an "ordinary annuity" or an "annuity in arrears."

SOLUTIONS:

A. Go to Appendix C, Compounded Annual Annuity (In Advance) Table (future value of an annuity due). This table reflects the amount to which $1 deposited at the beginning of each year will accumulate at compound interest for a given number of years at various interest rates. For example, to find out how much $1,000 a year, invested at the *beginning* of each year, will be worth at the end of 20 years, if the invested annual payments grow at the rate of 10% per year, you would multiply $1,000 by the factor found in the "20-year" row under the 10% column. That factor is 63.0025. Therefore, the investments of $1,000 per year, as of the beginning of each year, would be worth $63,002.50 at the end of 20 years.

This annuity table was compiled using the following formula which can be used in cases not included in the table:

$$F_n = A(1+i)\left[\frac{(1+i)^n - 1}{i}\right]$$

In this formula,

F = Future Value Amount

A = The Amount of the Annual (Annuity) Investment (Payment)

n = The Number of Years (Periods) of Annual Investments (Payments)

i = Interest Rate for each Year (Period)

Applying the formula to our example,

$$F_n = A(1 + i) \left[\frac{(1 + i)^n - 1}{i} \right]$$

$$F_{20} = \$1,000 (1 + .10) \left[\frac{(1 + .10)^{20} - 1}{.10} \right]$$

$$F_{20} = \$63,002$$

In an investment context, a common example of an "annuity due" is the amount an investor would deposit at the beginning of each year in order to provide funds for retirement at a specified retirement age.

B. Go to Appendix D, Compounded Annual Annuity (In Arrears) Table (future value of an ordinary annuity). This table reflects the amount to which $1 deposited at the end of each year will accumulate at compound interest for a given number of years at various interest rates. For example, to find out how much $1,000 a year, invested at the end of each year, will be worth at the end of 20 years, if the invested annual payments grow at the rate of 10% per year, you would multiply $1,000 by the factor found in the "20-year" row under the 10% column. That factor is 57.2750. Therefore, the investments of $1,000 per year, as of the end of each year, would be worth $57,275 at the end of 20 years.

This annuity table was compiled using the following mathematical formula which can be used in cases not included in the table:

$$F_n = A \left[\frac{(1 + i)^n - 1}{i} \right]$$

In this formula,

F = Future Value Amount

n = The Number of Years (Periods) of Annual Investments (Payments)

A = The Amount of the Annual (Annuity) Investment (Payment)

i = Interest Rate for each Year (Period)

Applying the formula to our example,

$$F_n = A \left[\frac{(1 + i)^n - 1}{i} \right]$$

$$F_{20} = \$1,000 \left[\frac{(1 + .10)^{20} - 1}{.10} \right]$$

$$F_{20} = \$57,275$$

In an investment context, an example of an "ordinary annuity" is the deposits an investor would make at the end of each year in order to provide funds for retirement at a specified retirement age.

It is important to compare the future value of the series of payments made at the beginning of each year ($63,002) with the future value of the series of payments made at the end of each year ($57,275). This $5,727 difference is due partially to the extra $1,000 payment made, but mainly results from the additional compounding on all of the payments.

IV. Computing the Present Value of a Regular Series of Receipts

PROBLEM: If, beginning today, I receive $_____ a year for ___ years, how do I calculate the present value of that series of payments, assuming a ___% discount rate?

SOLUTION: Go to Appendix E, Compound Discount Table (present value of an ordinary annuity). This table reflects the present value of $1 received annually at the end of each year for a given number of years at various discount rates.

For example, to compute the present value of $1,000 received at the end of each year for a 20-year period, discounted at the rate of 10% per year, you would multiply $1,000 by the factor found in the "20-year" row under the 10% column. That factor is 8.5136. Therefore, the receipt of $1,000 at the end of each year for the next 20 years has a present value of $8,513.60.

This annuity table was compiled using the following formula which can be used in cases not included in the table:

$$P = A(1/i) \left[1 - \frac{1}{(1 + i)^n} \right]$$

In this formula,

P = Present Value Amount

A = The Amount of the Annual (Annuity) Receipts

i = Interest Rate for each Year (Period)

n = The Number of Years (Periods) of Annual Receipts

Applying the formula to our example,

$$P = A(1/i)\left[1 - \frac{1}{(1 + i)^n}\right]$$

$$P = \$1{,}000\,(1/.10)\left[1 - \frac{1}{(1 + .10)^{20}}\right]$$

$$P = \$8{,}513$$

V. Practical Examples

1. PROBLEM: Rich Stevens, age 53, has just inherited $100,000 which he would like to use as part of his retirement nest egg. Rich would like to know just how much the $100,000 will be worth in 12 years, when he will reach age 65, assuming the funds can be invested for the entire period at a 12% annual rate. He would also like to know what the future value of the $100,000 will be in only 7 years, when he reaches age 60, in case he decides to retire early.

SOLUTION: Using the table in Appendix A, the future value of the $100,000 at the end of 12 years and 7 years can be computed as follows:

	Present Value		12% Interest Factor		Future Value
12 Years	$100,000	X	3.8960	=	$389,600
7 Years	$100,000	X	2.2107	=	$221,170

2. PROBLEM: Now that Rich knows how much the $100,000 inheritance will be worth in both cases, he would like to know how much he could withdraw from the fund in equal installments at the end of each year from the year he reaches age 65 until he reaches age 70½, the year he must start withdrawing funds from his Individual Retirement Account (IRA). Rich assumes the funds will continue to earn at a 12% annual rate. In other words, Rich would like to know the annual year-end payment from (1) a 6-year annuity (from age 65 to the year he will be 70½), earning 12% annually on a principal sum of $389,600, and (2) an 11-year annuity (from age 60 to the year he will be 70½), earning 12% annually on a principal sum of $221,070.

SOLUTION: Using the table in Appendix E, the year-end annual annuity payment amounts can be computed as follows:

	Principal Sum		12% Annuity Factor		Annual Annuity Amount
6-Year Annuity	$389,600	÷	4.1114	=	$94,761
11-Year Annuity	$221,070	÷	5.9377	=	$37,232

3. PROBLEM: Rich has determined that he will need $60,000 per year from the inheritance fund to handle his living needs until he reaches age 70½. Assuming the fund will continue to earn 12% annually, at what age can Rich afford to retire? (Rich has already decided not to touch his IRA funds until the latest possible date, believing he can cover his living costs with the inheritance until that time. He is even willing to adjust his retirement date by a year or so if need be.)

SOLUTION: This problem is more difficult, but a reasonably accurate answer can be computed using "trial and error" and the tables in Appendix A and Appendix E.

We have already determined that if Rich waits until age 65 to retire, the inheritance will grow, at a 12% annual interest rate, to $389,600 when he retires. The $389,600 will provide him with a 6-year annual annuity of $94,761, until he reaches age 70½. This annual annuity is $34,761 per year more than the $60,000 Rich believes he needs. Therefore, Rich should be able to retire before reaching age 65.

On the other hand, we have also computed that Rich's inheritance will grow, at a 12% rate, to only $221,070 by the time he reaches age 60. In this case the resulting annual annuity would be only $37,232 until he reaches age 70½, 11 years after retiring. This annual annuity is $22,768 ($60,000 - $37,232) per year short of Rich's $60,000 estimated annual need until reaching age 70½. Consequently, it does not appear that Rich can retire as early as age 60.

On a trial and error basis, let's compute what would happen if Rich retires at age 62. The $100,000 would grow for 9 years at 12% to $277,310, computed as follows, using the table in Appendix A.

	Present Value		12% Interest Factor		Future Value
9 Years	$100,000	X	2.7731	=	$277,310

The $277,310 would provide Rich a 12% annuity for 9 years, until he reaches age 70½, of $52,046, computed as follows, using the table in Appendix E:

	Principal Sum		12% Annuity Factor		Annual Annuity Amount
9-Year Annuity	$277,310	^	5.3282	=	$52,046

On this basis, Rich falls $7,954 short of reaching his goal of a $60,000 annual annuity if he retires at age 62. Let's see what happens if he retires at age 63. The $100,000 would grow for 10 years at a 12% to $310,580, computed as follows, using the table in Appendix A.

	Present Value		12% Interest Factor		Future Value
10 Years	$100,000	X	3.1058	=	$310,580

The $310,580 would provide Rich a 12% annuity for 8 years, until he reaches age 70½, of $62,521, computed as follows, using the table in Appendix E:

	Principal Sum		12% Annuity Factor		Annual Annuity Amount
8-Year Annuity	$310,580	÷	4.9676	=	$62,521

On this basis, Rich will exceed his goal of a $60,000 annual annuity by $2,521, if he retires at age 63. Therefore, although the tables in Appendix A and Appendix E cannot provide an exact retirement date, they can be used to provide a reasonable approximation. In this case, Rich Stevens can attain his retirement goal of a $60,000 annual annuity, to last until he reaches age 70 ½, using his $100,000 inheritance, if he retires sometime just before attaining age 63.

4. PROBLEM: Rich has decided that he wants to retire at age 60. He would like to know how much of his other funds need be set aside with his $100,000 inheritance in order to reach his goal of a $60,000 annuity from age 60 until the year he reaches age 70 ½. Rich assumes the funds can continue to earn at a 12% annual rate.

SOLUTION: The first step in determining the amount which must be added to the $100,000 inheritance is to determine the lump sum needed as of the anticipated retirement date in 7 years (age 60). At age 60, Rich will need $356,262 in order to provide an annual annuity of $60,000 for the 11 years from age 60 until the year he reaches age 70½. This lump sum can be computed as follows, using the table in Appendix E (present value of an annuity):

	Annual Annuity Amount		12% Annuity Factor		Principal Sum
11-Year Annuity	$60,000	X	5.9377	=	$356,262

In order for Rich to accumulate $356,262 by the time he retires at age 60, he must currently invest, at a 12% annual rate, a lump sum amount of $161,137, which can be computed in the following manner, using the table in Appendix B:

	Future Value		12% Interest Factor		Present Value
7 Years	$356,262	X	0.4523	=	$161,137

Since Rich has $100,000 from his inheritance, he must add $61,137 in order to accumulate the $356,262 needed to fund an 11-year, $60,000 annuity, to begin in 7 years, when Rich reaches age 60.

5. PROBLEM: Suppose Rich Stevens does not have $61,137 of other funds? How much must he set aside at the beginning of each year over the next seven years, together with the $100,000 lump sum from his inheritance, to reach his $356,262 objective at age 60?

SOLUTION: The $100,000 will grow to $221,070 in the 7 years until Rich reaches age 60, assuming a 12% annual interest rate (see the solution to Problem 1 for this computation). The shortfall at age 60 would be $135,192, the difference between the $356,262 needed and the $221,070 compounded from the original $100,000 inheritance. The $135,192 shortfall can be funded with annual investments of $11,964 computed as follows, using the table in Appendix C:

	Future Value		12% Interest Factor		Annual Investment
7 Years	$135,192	÷	11.2997	=	$11,964

WHERE CAN I FIND OUT MORE?

1. Frank Fabozzi, *Fixed Income Mathematics: Analytical and Statistical Techniques* (Irwin Professional Publishers, 1996).

2. David Spaulding, *Measuring Investment Performance: Calculating and Evaluating Investment Risk and Return* (McGraw-Hill, 1997).

3. Robert Rachlin, *Return on Investment Manual: Tools and Applications for Managing Financial Results* (Sharpe, 1997).

4. Arefaine Yohannes, *The Irwin Guide to Risk and Reward* (Irwin Professional Publishers, 1996).

5. Birrer & Carrica, *Present Value Applications for Accountants and Financial Planners* (Quorum Books, 1990).

6. Charles Akerson, *The Internal Rate of Return in Real Estate Investments* (American Inst. of Real Estate Appraisers, 1988).

7. David Leahigh, *A Pocket Guide to Finance* (Dryden Press, 1996).

8. *Calculator Analysis for Business and Finance* (Texas Instrument, Inc.).

9. *HP-12C Owner's Handbook and Problem-Solving Guide* (Hewlett-Packard Co.).

QUESTIONS AND ANSWERS

Question — Assume you are offered a 10% rate of return on one investment, compounded annually. You are examining alternative investments but they are all compounded on a semiannual or monthly basis. How can you determine which investment will yield the greatest return?

Answer — The question can be restated by asking, "What is the 'effective' yield on an investment that has a 'stated' or 'nominal' annual interest rate, but compounds more frequently (most commonly semiannually, quarterly, monthly, or daily)?"

Where the number of compounding periods differs from the number of payment periods, to compare alternative investments it is sometimes necessary to convert the stated interest rates to equivalent effective interest rates.

For example, if a $1,000 investment compounds semi-annually at an annual stated rate of 10%, the interest earned in the first six months will be added to the original amount of the investment and will thus earn interest for the remainder of the year. Therefore, at the end of 6 months, $50 (10% x $1,000 x ½ year) will be added to the original $1,000 principal. For the balance of the year, $1,050 will be earning interest at the annual rate of 10%. A sum of $52.50 will be earned in the second half of the year (10% x $1,050 x ½ year). The total interest earned for the year on the initial $1,000 is $102.50, resulting in a 10.25% effective rate for the year, compounded on a semiannual basis.

The more frequently an investment is compounded the higher the effective annual interest rate. For example, a monthly compounding of an investment with a 10% stated annual interest rate has an effective annual rate of 10.471%.

Use the following formula to determine the effective annual interest rate where the nominal annual interest rate is compounded more frequently than annually:

$$\text{Effective Rate} = (1 + (i \div n))^n - 1$$

In this formula,

n = The Number of Compounding Periods in a Year

i = Nominal Annual Interest Rate

Applying the formula to a nominal annual interest rate of 10% which is compounded quarterly:

$$\text{Effective Rate} = (1 + (i \div n))^n - 1$$

$$\text{Effective Rate} = (1 + (.10 \div 4))^4 - 1$$

$$\text{Effective Rate} = 10.381\%$$

Thus, a quarterly compounding of an investment with a 10% stated annual interest rate has an effective annual rate of 10.381%.

Chapter 13

RATE OF RETURN COMPUTATIONS
PART II — OTHER ANALYTICAL METHODS OF COMPARISON

WHAT IS IT?

An analytical method of comparison is an objective way to assess the relative risks and potential rewards from alternative investments. Although the ultimate decision as to which (if any) investment should be made may be subjective, the assessment should initially be based on both factual and measurable information.

The techniques discussed in this chapter are all based on the "time value of money" concept. The general principles of "present value" and "compounded future value," discussed in Part I (Chapter 12) may be sufficient in themselves to evaluate the return on a particular investment. But, in many cases, the more sophisticated approaches described below may be appropriate or necessary.

HOW DOES IT WORK?

This chapter will examine five comparative techniques commonly used to evaluate alternative investment opportunities. These are (1) "Net Present Value" (NPV), (2) "Internal Rate of Return" (IRR), (3) "Adjusted Rate of Return" (ARR), (4) "Pay Back Period," and (5) "Cash-on-Cash."

All of these devices have the same goal; they are all designed to measure the return on an investor's principal. This is the concept of "Return on Investment (ROI)."

(1) *Net Present Value* is the difference between the present value of all future benefits of an investment and the present value of all capital contributions. This method measures the tradeoff between the cash invested and the benefits projected.

(2) *Internal Rate of Return* is that rate at which the present value of all the future benefits an investor will receive from an investment exactly equals the present value of all the capital contributions the investor will be required to make. IRR is generally used to compare the *effective* interest rates of two or more investments.

(3) *Adjusted Rate of Return*, often called "effective rate of return," is calculated by assuming that all of the investment's benefits (not only cash inflows but also tax savings) are

invested at the "alternative reinvestment rate." The alternative reinvestment rate is the after-tax rate at which money can be safely invested.

(4) *Pay Back Period* measures the relative periods of time needed to recover the investor's capital (income received after the pay back period will be considered gain).

(5) *Cash on Cash*, as its name implies, analyzes an investment by dividing the annual cash flow by the amount of the cash investment in order to determine the cash return on the cash invested.

ADVANTAGES

1. These methods of comparison offer a way to measure the potential return on alternative investments in a logical and consistent manner.

2. The use of mathematics (assuming the accuracy of the input) balances an investor's natural inclination to "play a hunch" by introducing objectivity into the decision-making process.

3. The use of more than one comparative method will help the investor more effectively recognize and evaluate risk/reward parameters.

DISADVANTAGES

1. There are a number of unknowns in the measurement process. For instance, an investor can only estimate or project how much money will be received from a given investment and when that cash inflow and outflow will occur. There is no way to completely guaranty either the amount or timing of cash flows.

These uncertainties, though drawbacks, should not preclude the use of analytical techniques. There is no single technique which can be applied to every case. The method that most closely reflects the investor's perception of how return should be measured is the one which should be used. It is important that the chosen method be used *consistently*. In many cases more than one analytical technique should be used in order to corroborate the results of the other approaches.

2. Undue reliance on mathematical quantitative evaluation techniques, as noted in the previous chapter, may create a false sense of security. Such excessive reliance can both hinder the investor's ability to utilize appropriate subjective analytical skills and inhibit the consideration of external factors which may affect the viability of the investment.

3. It is often difficult to know which measuring device to select. The use of an inappropriate technique will often result in drawing an inappropriate conclusion.

4. In practice it is often difficult to obtain accurate and comprehensive data.

WHEN IS THE USE OF THIS TECHNIQUE INDICATED?

The five techniques discussed in this chapter are all useful when an investor wants to compare alternative investments that are seemingly similar with respect to risk and it is desirable to distinguish the investments by measuring their relative rewards in terms of: (1) "timing" — when and/or how often cash must be invested in and/or may be taken out of the investment, and (2) "quantity" — the rate of interest the investment will earn or the rate at which it will grow.

A second reason for the use of these "return on investment" techniques is to evaluate one particular investment in comparison with a so-called "safe" alternative, such as a U.S. Treasury Note. Used in this manner, the "safe" alternative serves as a benchmark to determine whether the potential reward from the investment under consideration is sufficient relative to the associated risks.

HOW IS IT IMPLEMENTED?

I. Net Present Value

Net present value is an extension of the present value concepts discussed in the previous chapter. Present value is the amount that must be invested now to produce a given future value. For instance, if I assume I can invest money at 10%, I must have $1,000 now in order to have it grow to $1,100 one year from now. $1,000 is the present value of $1,100 to be received in one year. Obviously, the present value is affected by (1) the interest (investment analysts call this the

"discount") rate, as well as (2) the length of the investment period.

Present value is a simple means of comparing two investments. For example, I am considering an investment of $1,000 which will pay me $1,200 three years from now. I can also invest the $1,000 in an alternative investment of equal risk and earn 10% on my money. Which investment should I make?

An easy way to compare the investments is to compute the present value of the $1,200 payable three years from now at a 10% discount rate. The present value of the first investment is only $902, while obviously, the present value of $1,000 in hand today is $1,000. Therefore, from a pure present value standpoint, the proposed investment is inferior to the alternative of simply investing the $1,000 at 10%.

"Net" present value is the difference between (a) the present value of all future benefits to be realized from an investment and (b) the present value of all capital contributions into the investment. A negative net present value should result in an almost automatic rejection of the investment. A positive net present value indicates that the investment is worth further consideration since the present value of the stream of dollars you will recover exceeds the present value of the stream of dollars you will have to pay out.

The problem is, what discount rate should be used in computing the present values of the cash inflows and cash outflows? Usually this discount rate will be the minimal acceptable rate of return. This is usually found by determining the cost of capital or, as in the example above, determining the rate an alternative investment of similar quality can earn. In the example above, the rate was 10%. Once this so-called "reinvestment rate" is determined, it can be used as the discount factor to compute the present value of the money invested and the present value of the expected return.

These present value amounts are then netted against each other. If the result is positive, the investment will exceed the reinvestment rate and should be considered. If the net present value is a negative number and falls short of the reinvestment rate, the investment under consideration should be rejected.

To the extent that a proposed investment yields a positive net present value, the investment provides a potential "cushion" for safety. It may also allow the investor to incur certain additional costs (such as attorney's, accountant's, or financial planner's fees in connection with the analysis of the investment) and still achieve the desired reinvestment rate.

An example of the use of net present value analysis may be helpful:

Assume that at the beginning of the year an individual has been shown an investment opportunity requiring a lump sum outlay of $10,000. Currently the funds he would use for this investment are in a money market fund earning 6% annually, net after taxes. The investment proposal projects the following after-tax cash flows at the end of each year:

Year	Amount Received
1	$ 2,000
2	1,500
3	750
4	500
5	10,000
Total Receipts	$14,750

Based solely on net present value analysis, should he make the investment?

The first step in the analysis would be to determine the appropriate reinvestment rate. In this example, the investor currently is earning a net after tax return of 6% in what he believes is a "safe" investment. To warrant any further consideration, this proposed investment must have a net present value of at least the benchmark reinvestment rate of 6%.

Does the proposed investment meet that benchmark? Look at the NumberCruncher™ illustration that follows:

NET PRESENT VALUE OF A STREAM OF INCOME

INPUT: EFFECTIVE INTEREST RATE 0.06

YEAR	AMOUNT RECEIVED
INPUT: 0 (CURRENT YEAR)	$ 2,000
1	$ 1,500
2	$ 750
3	$ 500
4	$ 10,000
5	$ 0
6	$ 0
7	$ 0
8	$ 0
9	$ 0
TOTAL	$ 14,750

PRESENT VALUE (PMTS. AT END OF PERIOD) .... $ 11,720

PRESENT VALUE (PMTS. AT START OF PERIOD) .... $ 12,423

The illustration above indicates that the stream of dollars projected to be received from the proposed investment has a present value of $11,720 assuming a 6% discount rate. The net present value is a positive $1,720 (the difference between the present value of the future stream of cash inflows, $11,720, and the $10,000 present value of the lump sum outflow of $10,000). Therefore, the proposal does deserve further consideration.

But what if the investor demands a rate of return from the proposed investment higher than his benchmark rate of 6% in order to compensate for the additional risk? If he sets a 15% rate as his minimum, the present value of the stream of dollars from the proposed investment is only $8,624, as illustrated below:

NET PRESENT VALUE OF A STREAM OF INCOME

INPUT: EFFECTIVE INTEREST RATE 0.15

YEAR	AMOUNT RECEIVED
INPUT: 0 (CURRENT YEAR)	$ 2,000
1	$ 1,500
2	$ 750
3	$ 500
4	$ 10,000
5	$ 0
6	$ 0
7	$ 0
8	$ 0
9	$ 0
TOTAL	$ 14,750

PRESENT VALUE (PMTS. AT END OF PERIOD .... $ 8,624

PRESENT VALUE (PMTS. AT START OF PERIOD .... $ 9,818

The illustration above indicates that the stream of dollars projected to be received from the proposed investment has a present value of only $8,624 assuming a 15% discount rate. The net present value is a negative $1,376 (the difference between the present value of the future stream of cash inflows, $8,624, and the $10,000 present value of the lump sum outflow of $10,000). Therefore, the proposal does not deserve further consideration.

What discount rate when applied to the expected stream of cash inflows from the proposed investment has a present value exactly equal to the $10,000 lump sum investment? As the following example shows, that discount rate is 10.5%:

NET PRESENT VALUE OF A STREAM OF INCOME

INPUT: EFFECTIVE INTEREST RATE 0.105

YEAR	AMOUNT RECEIVED
INPUT: 0 (CURRENT YEAR)	$ 2,000
1	$ 1,500
2	$ 750
3	$ 500
4	$ 10,000
5	$ 0
6	$ 0
7	$ 0
8	$ 0
9	$ 0
TOTAL	$ 14,750

PRESENT VALUE (PMTS. AT END OF PERIOD ....$ 10,000

PRESENT VALUE (PMTS. AT START OF PERIOD ....$ 11,050

This computation illustrates the concept of Internal Rate of Return, discussed more fully below.

How To Compute Net Present Value

A. Lump Sum Investment, Single Future Receipt

Assume an individual makes a lump sum investment at the beginning of year one of $10,000. The expected return on this investment is $15,000 (after tax) to be received as a single amount at the end of year five. The investor's discount rate (for an alternative "safe" investment) is 6% after tax. What is the net present value of the investment under consideration?

To compute the net present value of the investment, the following basic steps are necessary:

(1) Compute the present value of the $10,000 investment. Since only one payment is required (immediately at the beginning of the cash flow period), the present value of that payment would be $10,000.

(2) Compute the present value of the $15,000 future amount to be received (at the end of year five) using the 6% discount rate. Refer to the Present Value Table in Appendix B. The applicable factor for the present value of $1 at the end of 5 years, using a 6% discount rate, is 0.7473. This factor is multiplied by the $15,000 amount to be received in the future. The present value is therefore $11,210 ($15,000 x 0.7473).

(3) Subtract the present value of the $10,000 lump sum investment ($10,000) from the present value of the $15,000 single payment to be received ($11,210). The net amount is +$1,210; a "positive" net present value. [Note that if the $15,000 were not received until the end of seven years, the present value of the receipt would be only $9,977 ($15,000 x 0.6651 discount factor), resulting in a "negative" net present value of $23.]

B. Lump Sum Investment, Multiple Future Receipts

Assume an individual makes a lump sum investment at the beginning of year one of $10,000, the present value of which is $10,000 [Step (1)].

The expected return on this investment (received at each year end) and the present value of each receipt, discounted at 6% are as follows [Step 2]:

Year	Amount Received	PV @ 6%
1	$ 2,000	$ 1,887
2	1,500	1,335
3	750	630
4	500	396
5	$14,750	$11,721
Total Receipts	$14,750	$11,721

[The present value amounts in this table were computed using the Present Value Table in Appendix B. Since these factors are taken to only four decimal places, they will not be as accurate as the computation of the present value of total receipts computed above using NumberCruncher™ ($11,720).]

The net present value is therefore $1,721 ($11,721 present value of the future flow of receipts, less $10,000 present value of the lump sum investment) [Step 3].

C. Multiple Investments, Multiple Future Receipts

Continuing the above example, assume that instead of one $10,000 investment at the beginning of year one, there will be two $5,000 payments, one at the beginning of year one, and the other at the beginning of year two. The present value of the investment, using the same 6% discount rate would be computed as follows [Step 1]:

	Year	PV Payment	@ 6%
[Beginning]	1	$ 5,000	$ 5,000
[Beginning]	2	5,000	4,717
Total Payments		$10,000	$ 9,717

When multiple investment payments are required over a period of time, the present value of these payments must be determined. In this example, the present value of the first $5,000 investment is $5,000. The present value of the second $5,000 is $4,717, $5,000 multiplied by the present value factor of 0.9434 (since the payment is made at the beginning of the second year, the present value factor for the end of the first year is appropriate). If we assume the present value of the receipts are the same as above, $11,721 [Step 2], then the net present value of this investment is $2,004 ($11,721 - $9,717) [Step 3].

II. Internal Rate of Return

When we discussed the concept of net present value (NPV), we defined it as the difference between the present value of all future benefits to be realized from an investment and the present value of all capital contributions into the investment. The discount (interest) rate at which these two present values will be equal is the Internal Rate of Return (IRR) of the investment.

Stated in other terms, in computing IRR the interest rate we are trying to find is that rate at which inflows and outflows of cash, discounted to present value, will equal the original principal. It is a method of determining what percentage rate of return cash inflows will provide based on a known investment (cash outflow) and estimated cash inflows.

Internal rate of return is really the same as a present value computation except that the discount rate is either not known or not given. The financial advisor is therefore attempting to find that rate which will discount the future cash inflows so that they will precisely equal the investor's initial investment.

Confused? Let's try an example.

Assume your client is considering the purchase of a $100,000 unit of a limited partnership. The full $100,000 is due at the beginning of the year. You have estimated that, after taxes, she should be receiving the following cash inflows at the end of each year:

End of Year	In-Flow
1	$ 10,000
2	10,000
3	120,000

If we were to do a NPV analysis of this investment, looking at several alternative rates of return, it would look as presented in Figure 13.1.

At an 8% rate, this investment has a positive net present value of $13,092. That is, if you had invested $100,000 at 8% (for example, in a certificate of deposit) the present value of the future cash inflow should be $100,000. But, in the investment above, you will see that the present value of the expected cash inflows is actually $113,092, $13,092 higher than it should be at 8%. Therefore, it is obvious that the investment is generating a significantly higher rate of return than 8%.

At a 10% rate, this investment has a positive net present value of $7,513. That is, if you had invested $100,000 at 10% the present value of the future cash inflow should be $100,000. But, in the investment above, you will see that the present value of the expected cash inflows is actually $107,513, $7,513 higher than it should be at 10%. Therefore, it appears that the investment is generating a higher rate of return than 10%.

At a 20% rate, this investment has a negative net present value of $15,279. That is, if you had invested $100,000 at 20% the present value of the future cash inflow should be $100,000. But, in the investment above, you will see that the present value of the expected cash inflows is actually $84,721, $15,279 lower than it should be at 20%. Therefore, it is obvious that the investment is generating a lower rate of return than 20%.

What is the actual rate of return on this investment? Obviously somewhere between 10% and 20%. Internal rate of return is a method of computing that exact rate. The chart in Figure 13.1 illustrates that the internal rate of return of the investment is approximately 12.9%. That is, the present value of the cash outflows($100,000) is roughly equal to the present value of the cash inflows ($100,089) when discounted at a 12.9% rate.

The NumberCruncher™ illustration below indicates the exact computation:

INTERNAL RATE OF RETURN ON AN INVESTMENT	INPUT:	0	($100,000)
		1	$10,000
		2	$10,000
		3	$120,000
		4	$0
INPUT: ESTIMATED IRR 0.129		5	$0
		6	$0
		7	$0
		8	$0
		9	$0
CUMULATIVE CASH FLOW $40,000		10	$0
(TOTAL INCOME MINUS OUTLAYS)		11	$0
		12	$0
		13	$0
		14	$0
		15	$0
CALCULATED INTERNAL			
	====	16	$0
RATE OF RETURN (%) 0.129	====	17	$0
		18	$0
		19	$0

Figure 13.1

Outflows	Amount Paid	Present Value of Amount Paid @			
		8%	10%	12.9%	20%
Year 1 (Beginning of year)	-$100,000	-$100,000	-$100,000	-$100,000	-$100,000

Inflows	Amount Received	Present Value of Amount Received @			
		8%	10%	12.9%	20%
Year 1	$ 10,000	$ 9,259	$ 9,091	$ 8,857	$ 8,333 (End of year)
2	10,000	8,573	8,264	7,845	6,944
3	120,000	95,260	90,158	83,387	69,446
Total of Present Value of Inflows		$113,092	$107,513	$100,089	$ 84,721
Net Present Value (NPV)		$ 13,092	$ 7,513	$ 89	-$ 15,279

What are the shortcomings of IRR? There are several: Many investments cannot be purchased unless the investor is able to borrow to make the investment. Loans, of course, require repayment. Will the cash inflows from the investment meet the cash demands from the loan? Cash inflows and cash outflows do not always match. For instance, an investor might borrow $100,000 for 15 years at the rate of 14%. The loan requires monthly payments of $1,331.74 for a full payback of the loan principal and interest at the end of the 15 years. IRR analysis can tell us if the investment will yield greater than 14%, but it will not tell us whether the investment will provide sufficient monthly cash inflows to service the debt.

A second flaw in IRR analysis is that it inherently assumes that the cash inflows will be reinvested at the computed internal rate of return of the investment itself. It is often impossible to invest the cash generated from an investment at the rate at which the investment is earning (which is why you invested your money there in the first place). The essential question is whether or not the internal rate of return is earned on the entire investment amount during the life of the investment.

Most investments with periodic cash inflows do not return a rate equal to the computed internal rate of return. This is because the IRR, as its name implies, refers only to the rate earned within the investment (i.e., internally). Once cash is distributed from the investment, it is often difficult to reinvest the distributed amounts at the same or better rate than that provided by the investment itself.

What the financial advisor should examine is which investment will produce the largest aggregate increase (after taxes) in the investor's net worth.

Perhaps an example will help. Assume your client has a choice between two real estate investments, both requiring an immediate outlay of $100,000. The cash inflows are as follows:

| | CASH INFLOWS FROM | |
YEAR	Wildwood Property	Avalon Property
1	$10,000	$60,000
2	15,000	48,000
3	20,000	14,000
4	92,960	4,060
IRR	10%	15%

Which of the two is a more appropriate investment? Looking purely to the IRR of the two alternatives, the Avalon property appears to be a better deal. It also returns a greater amount of the investor's capital more quickly than the Wildwood property. However, this may be a disadvantage. For instance, assume the cash generated from the Avalon property

can be reinvested at only 5%. At the end of four years the investor will have received a total of $141,140, an increase in net worth of $41,140. The investment in the Wildwood property, which keeps more of the invested capital at work at 10%, results in the investor receiving $142,070, an increase in net worth of $42,070. The Wildwood property, therefore, yields a net worth advantage of $930. The higher the rate at which the cash inflows can be reinvested, the better the Avalon alternative becomes.

A third flaw in the IRR concept is that if the investor must borrow money (or withdraw funds from an alternative investment) at a given rate of interest in order to meet a cash demand of the investment, that rate will typically not be identical to the internal rate of return of the investment. In other words, a subsequent investment (a negative cash flow) must be provided from someplace outside of the investment under analysis. It is inappropriate to assume that the external rate (the rate at which funds outside the investment can be borrowed or are otherwise earning) is the same as the computed internal rate of return. The following example may be helpful in understanding the effect of the flaw:

Assume an investment involves the following cash flows:

YEAR	OUT FLOW	IN FLOW
1	-10,000	
2		$6,000
3		5,000
4		4,000
5		2,000
6	- 3,000	

The internal rate of return of this investment is 24%. But this assumes that the investor will have to borrow the $3,000 in year 6 at 24% or has funds otherwise invested also earning 24%. This may be totally unrealistic. Because this inherent flaw will often lead to improper conclusions, it is often necessary to make adjustments in using the internal rate of return concept. We discuss such an adjustment below under the heading of "Adjusted Rate of Return."

How To Compute Internal Rate of Return

In an earlier example we assumed a client was considering the purchase of a $100,000 unit of a limited partnership, and that, after taxes, she should be receiving the following cash inflows:

End of Year	In-Flow
1	$ 10,000
2	10,000
3	120,000

Figure 13.2

Outflows	Amount Paid	Present Value of Amount Paid @			
		8%	10%	12.9%	20%
Year 1 (Beginning of year)	-$100,000	-$ 100,000	-$100,000	-$100,000	-$100,000

Inflows	Amount Received	Present Value of Amount Received @			
		8%	10%	20%	12.9%
Year 1	$ 10,000	$ 9,259	$ 9,091	$ 8,333	$ 8,857 (End of year)
2	10,000	8,573	8,264	6,944	7,845
3	120,000	95,260	90,158	69,446	83,387
Total of Present Value of Inflows		$113,092	$107,513	$ 84,721	$100,089
Net Present Value (NPV)		$ 13,092	$ 7,513	-$ 15,279	$ 89

In manually computing the IRR of this investment the first step is to compute the NPV using a preliminary estimate of the IRR. If the first computation results in a positive NPV, a second calculation, using a higher discount rate, will be necessary. If a negative NPV is computed, the recalculation will require a lower discount rate. The process would have to continue until you arrive at a NPV of $0 (i.e., the rate at which the present value of the cash outflows equals the present value of the cash inflows.

The chart in Figure 13.2 provides an example of the series of iterative computations which might be necessary:

If we use 8% as our initial (test) discount rate, we find a positive net present value, and therefore must try a higher discount rate. On our second attempt, using 10%, we still have a positive NPV. Our third computation, using 20%, yields a negative NPV. Therefore, the IRR must be between 10% and 20%.

After several attempts, we finally try a rate of 12.9% which results in a positive NPV of only $89. We're getting close. For most planning purposes, this would be close enough. To do the job more accurately and efficiently, we could use a business calculator or a computer.

III. Adjusted Rate of Return

The Adjusted Rate of Return (ARR) method (also referred to as the Effective Rate of Return method) is generally a more meaningful and realistic approach to measuring investment return than IRR. ARR goes a step further than IRR since it recognizes that the cash flow from an investment may be "reinvested" at a rate which is different from the rate produced internally by the investment.

ARR is computed by assuming that all the benefits derived (i.e., cash distributions and taxes saved) from an investment are earning an "alternative investment rate." This alternative investment rate is the after-tax rate at which an individual feels that money can be safely invested (for example, in bank CDs or other federally insured investments).

Effectively, the ARR is the combined rate at which the investment is earning both internally and externally (on the distributions and tax benefits). If the external, alternative investment rate is less than the internal rate of return, the adjusted rate of return will be somewhere in between (essentially a weighted average of the two).

Conceptually, ARR is computed as follows:

(1) Compute the amount of future benefits at the end of the investment period by totalling:

(a) the amount of cash distributed to the investor during the investment period,

(b) any tax savings derived from the investment during that time,

(c) income earned on the distributed cash and/or tax savings, and

(d) any cash proceeds at the end of the investment period (such as from the sale of the investment property).

(2) Determine the discount rate at which the original investment would have had to grow to equal the first amount. That rate is the adjusted rate of return.

Confused again? Let's try another example.

For simplicity, we'll ignore tax implications.

Ronnie Smith invests $10,000 in the stock of Z-Rocks Corp. at the beginning of year one. At the end of each year she is paid dividends of $1,000. At the end of the third year, she sells the stock for $15,000. The annual dividends are placed in a money market fund which yields an average return of 8% per year.

The internal rate of return on this investment would be 23.3%, determined as shown is Figure 13.3.

The 23.3% rate can be computed using the formula for determining the present value of a future lump sum, discussed in the Chapter 12. This can easily be computed using a business calculator, such as the Hewlett-Packard HP-12C™, by inputting (1) the present value ($10,000), (2) the future value ($18,246), and (3) the term (three years), and solving for the rate.

There are several conclusions the planner can draw from this analysis. First, since the internal rate of return is higher than the rate of return available for the distributed dividends, the IRR computation does not accurately reflect the actual yield on this investment. The rate differential between the IRR and the ARR of approximately 1.1% is the result of the lower reinvestment rate.

Second, if available, the investor might consider a dividend reinvestment program for the Z-Rocks Corp. stock since we know that the internal rate is higher than the external rate available.

IV. Pay Back Period

Pay back period analysis is a "time value of money" concept. This method compares alternative investments by measuring the length of time required to recover the original investment. From this perspective, the investment that returns the original capital in the shortest period of time is the "best" investment.

The major flaw in this analytical technique is obvious: taken to its extreme, an indiscriminate investor would choose a deal requiring a $10,000 investment which paid back $15,000 in one year rather than an alternative which required the same capital outlay but returned $25,000 in two years.

V. Cash on Cash

Cash-on-Cash analysis, as its name implies, focuses on the *amount* of cash generated by the investment. It ignores both taxes and the potential gain from any sale.

To compute cash on cash return, divide the annual cash flow by the cash investment. For example, when we examined the adjusted rate of return method, we used the illustration of a woman who plans to invest $10,000 in the stock of Z-Rocks Corp. Each year she would receive a dividend of $1,000, and expects to receive $15,000 upon the sale of the stock in three years.

She is considering an alternative investment for the $10,000, Eye-B-Em Stock, which yields a cash distribution of only

Figure 13.3

INTERNAL RATE OF RETURN INPUT:		0	($10,000)
ON AN INVESTMENT		1	$1,000
		2	$1,000
		3	$16,000
		4	$0
INPUT: ESTIMATED IRR	0.200	5	$0
		6	$0
		7	$0
		8	$0
		9	$0
CUMULATIVE CASH FLOW $8,000		10	$0
(TOTAL INCOME MINUS OUTLAYS)		11	$0
		12	$0
		13	$0
		14	$0
		15	$0
CALCULATED INTERNAL		16	$0
	= ===		
RATE OF RETURN (%)	0.233	17	$0
	= ===		
		18	$0
		19	$0

The adjusted rate of return is computed as follows:

(1)   (a) Amount of cash distributed during the investment period (Dividends for 3 years). $3,000
    (b) Tax savings (ignored for simplicity).
    (c) Income earned on the dividends.
       1st year dividend (paid at year end) invested at 8% for 2 years   166
       2nd year dividend (paid at year end) invested at 8% for 1 year.   80
    (d) Cash proceeds of sale. $15,000

                          $18,246

The $18,246 represents the future amount of all the benefits of this investment. This is often called the "Gross Terminal Value."

(2)   Discount rate at which $10,000 investment growth to $18,246 in three years: 22.2%

$600 per year, but which she believes will be worth $25,000 at the end of the three year investment period. Under the cash-on-cash method her return on the first investment is 10% per year ($1,000 dividend divided by the $10,000 investment), while the return on the alternative is only 6% per year ($600 divided by the $10,000 investment).

Using only the cash-on-cash method to evaluate the investments, she would choose the Z-Rocks stock, because of the higher annual dividend. However, if she had compared the investments by looking at their relative internal rates of return or adjusted rates of return, she would probably have chosen the alternative.

WHERE CAN I FIND OUT MORE?

1. Frank Fabozzi, *Fixed Income Mathematics: Analytical and Statistical Techniques* (Irwin Professional Publishers, 1996).

2. David Spaulding, *Measuring Investment Performance: Calculating and Evaluating Investment Risk and Return* (McGraw-Hill, 1997).

3. Robert Rachlin, *Return on Investment Manual: Tools and Applications for Managing Financial Results* (Sharpe, 1997).

4. Arefaine Yohannes, *The Irwin Guide to Risk and Reward* (Irwin Professional Publishers, 1996).

5. Birrer & Carrica, *Present Value Applications for Accountants and Financial Planners* (Quorum Books, 1990).

6. Charles Akerson, *The Internal Rate of Return in Real Estate Investments* (American Inst. of Real Estate Appraisers, 1988).

7. David Leahigh, *A Pocket Guide to Finance* (Dryden Press, 1996).

8. *Calculator Analysis for Business and Finance* (Texas Instrument, Inc.).

9. *HP-12C Owner's Handbook and Problem-Solving Guide* (Hewlett-Packard Co.).

QUESTIONS AND ANSWERS

Question — What is meant by "sensitivity analysis?"

Answer — In any quantitative analysis it is necessary to make a number of assumptions and predictions (and at times, just some "guesstimates"). These inputs include (a) yields, (b) rates of inflation, (c) growth rates, (d) effective tax rates, and (e) timing of inflows and outflows.

Obviously, these variables, by definition, cannot be predicted with certainty. Therefore, it is important to determine the sensitivity of the results of your analysis to fluctuations (upward or downward) in any of the variables relevant to decision-making. Sensitivity analysis can be defined as a procedure by which relevant variables are changed one at a time to determine the effect on the overall results.

Sensitivity analysis utilizes the mathematical methods of comparison discussed above. It enables the planner to ascertain which assumptions or predictions must be emphasized or modified in order to obtain a more realistic or accurate conclusion.

Sensitivity analysis can be used to establish parameters of potential results such as "worst down side risk," "highest upside potential" and "most probable result." Once the "worst case-best case" and most probable scenarios have been developed, the investor can then make subjective judgments as to whether or not the investment is appropriate.

Question — In analyzing the viability of a real estate investment, how do you determine what rental revenues, expenses, and final selling price to use in your analytical computations?

Answer — Forecasting revenues, expenses, and final selling price in a real estate investment involves a multiplicity of factors, such as (a) market demand for the specific location, (b) price and availability of comparable properties, (c) technological and other factors which may result in a greater or lesser property value, (d) government restrictions on alternative uses, and (e) neighborhood influences. The determination of what values to use will be based primarily on available historical data which will require modifications based on expected future trends.

Question — How can a planner help an investor determine how long to hold an investment?

Answer — The internal rate of return and adjusted rate of return concepts can be used to mechanically determine the most desirable holding period. For instance, IRR analysis could be used to ascertain the rate if the investment were held for 5 years, 6 years, 7 years, etc. Mathematically, the number of years which produces the highest IRR would be the one selected.

Some investment analysts ask, "What would the incremental effect be if the investment were held one additional year?" This "one-year-more" concept is often called the "marginal method." It compares the benefit of waiting one more year to the benefit of investing the cumulative benefits received in an alternative investment.

Basing the decision solely on the mathematical results of this marginal analysis, it will make sense to remain in the original investment for at least one more year as long as the marginal IRR is greater than what the investor can receive from an alternative investment.

Chapter 14

RETIREMENT PLAN DISTRIBUTION PLANNING

Employer retirement plans, such as qualified pension or profit-sharing plans or Section 403(b) tax-deferred annuity plans of tax-exempt employers can allow employees to accumulate substantial retirement benefits. Even a middle-level employee may have an account balance of hundreds of thousands of dollars available at retirement or termination of employment. Careful planning is important in order to make the right choices about this plan distribution, not only to get the right result in financial planning for retirement, but also to avoid adverse tax results.

General objectives should be identified first. If an employee does not immediately need the plan distribution for retirement income, a major objective will be to spread the distribution over the longest possible period in order to provide deferral of taxation and to allow the plan account to build up income on a tax-deferred basis. On the other hand, if an employee depends on the plan as a primary source of retirement income, choosing the right options to meet retirement planning needs may be more important than tax-oriented planning, although it is still important to avoid excessive taxation.

WHAT OPTIONS DOES THE PLAN PROVIDE?

The first step is to examine plan documents to see what plan distribution options are available. Usually the plan's Summary Plan Description (SPD) explains these in adequate detail. But the underlying plan document may have to be examined to resolve questions. Furthermore, in the event the SPD and plan document provisions differ, the terms of the plan document will govern. By federal law participants in qualified (and certain other) retirement plans must be provided with an SPD and must be allowed to examine the plan document and copy it for a reasonable copying fee.

Not all plans provide the maximum flexibility allowed in distributions under federal law. If the plan provisions are not flexible, the distribution must be designed as well as possible within these limitations. However, plans can be amended to change distribution provisions. If your client is a controlling shareholder or key employee of the employer, it may be possible to change the plan prior to the distribution to provide more favorable results.

Defined Benefit Plan Distribution Provisions

Defined benefit plans must provide a married participant with a *joint and survivor annuity* as the automatic form of benefit. The joint and survivor annuity benefit provides a stated benefit to the participant and spouse while both are living, with a survivor annuity to the nonparticipant spouse. If the nonparticipant spouse dies before the participant spouse, there is generally no further death benefit under this option. The annuity amount for the surviving nonparticipant spouse can be anywhere from 50 percent up to 100 percent of the amount payable during the joint lives. Some plans allow a participant to choose an amount of survivor annuity within these limits.

For an unmarried participant, the plan's automatic form of benefit is usually a life annuity—typically monthly payments to the participant for life, with no further payments after the participant's death.

Many plans allow participants to elect to receive some other form of benefit from a list of options in the plan. However, to elect any option that eliminates the benefit for a married participant's spouse, the spouse must consent on a notarized written form. This is not just a legal formality. In consenting to another form of benefit, the spouse gives up property rights in the participant's qualified plan that are guaranteed under federal law. Thus, the spouse should receive something in return for consenting to give up spousal rights. An ill-advised consent, especially where the spouse is not represented by his or her own legal or financial adviser, could be deemed to be an "uninformed consent" at some later time— typically after the participant's death. This could mean the original consent would be nullified by the courts.

Typically plans offer, as an option to the joint and single life annuity, a *period certain* annuity. A period certain annuity provides payments for a specified period of time—usually 10 to 20 years—even if the participant, or the participant and spouse, die before the end of that period. Thus, the period certain annuity provides benefits for the participant's heirs even if the participant (or participant and spouse) die early. Because of this guarantee feature, the annual or monthly payments under a period certain option are less than they would be under an option where payments end at death. A period certain option therefore should be chosen if the participant wants to make sure that his heirs are provided for in case both he and his spouse die shortly after retirement. For example, the participant and spouse might choose this option if they were both in poor health, or if they wanted to make sure that their children (or other heirs) with large financial needs were provided for in the event of their deaths.

Defined benefit plans may allow participants to choose joint annuities with a beneficiary other than a spouse—for example, an annuity for the life of a participant and a son or daughter. Federal tax rules limit the amount of annuity payable to a much younger beneficiary in order to ensure that the participant personally receives at least a minimum portion of the total value of the plan benefit and that plan payments are not unduly deferred beyond the participant's death. (See the minimum distribution rules discussed below, under "Penalty for Distributions Too Late or Not Enough.") Thus, a much younger beneficiary (except for a spouse) generally would not be allowed to receive a 100 percent survivor annuity benefit.

Defined Contribution Plan Distribution Provisions

Defined contribution plans include such plans as profit sharing, 401(k), and money purchase plans. Section 403(b) tax-deferred annuity plans also have distribution provisions similar to defined contribution plans. Defined contribution plans sometimes provide annuity benefits like those in defined benefit plans. In fact, certain kinds of defined contribution plans (e.g., money purchase pension plans) must provide to a married participant a joint and survivor annuity as the automatic form of benefit. Others do not have to meet the joint and survivor requirements as long as the plan provides for the spouse to receive any unpaid nonforfeitable benefit remaining at the death of the participant.

Annuity benefits are computed by converting the participant's account balance in the defined contribution plan into an equivalent annuity. The TIAA/CREF plan for college teachers, for example, is a defined contribution plan that primarily offers annuity options. In some plans the participant can elect to have his account balance used to purchase an annuity from an insurance company. The same considerations in choosing annuity options then apply as have already been discussed.

Defined contribution plans often provide a lump-sum distribution option, and sometimes only a lump-sum option. Defined contribution plans often also allow the option of taking out periodic distributions over the retirement years, which are not necessarily in the form of an annuity. That is, the participant simply takes out money as it is needed, subject to the minimum distribution requirements discussed later. Lump-sum or periodic distribution provisions provide much flexibility in planning.

TAX IMPLICATIONS

For some plan participants, retirement income adequacy is more important than minimizing taxes to the last dollar. Nevertheless, taxes on both the federal and state levels must never be ignored. The planner must consider

(a) the direct income tax on the lump-sum or periodic distribution,

(b) penalty taxes,

(c) estate taxes, and

(d) generation skipping transfer taxes.

A qualified plan distribution may be subject to federal, state, and local taxes, in whole or in part. This section will focus only on the federal tax treatment. The federal tax treatment is generally the most significant because federal tax rates are usually higher than state and local rates. Also, many state and local income tax laws provide a full or partial exemption or specially favorable tax treatment for distributions from qualified retirement plans.

Nontaxable and Taxable Amounts

Qualified plans often contain after-tax employee money—that is, contributions that have already been taxed. These amounts generally can be distributed to the employee tax free, although the order in which they are recovered for tax purposes depends on the kind of distribution.

Generally, distributions—whether annuity payments or amounts distributed or withdrawn before any annuity payments begin—are deemed to include both taxable and nontaxable amounts in each payment. In the case of distributions and withdrawals before annuitization, the nontaxable amount will be proportionate to the ratio of total after-tax contributions to the plan account balance. The treatment of annuity payments is explained below.

There is an exception in the case of distributions and withdrawals before annuitization with respect to employee after-tax contributions made before 1987 to certain previously-existing plans. Such amounts will be treated as being paid entirely with non-taxable employee after-tax money until the pre-1987 employee after-tax money has been completely distributed.

Taxable distributions may also be subject to an early withdrawal penalty (see below).

The first step in determining the tax on any distribution is to determine the participant's cost basis in the plan benefit.

The participant's cost basis can include:

(a) the total after-tax contributions made by the employee to a contributory plan.

(b) the total cost of life insurance reported as taxable income by the participant (the P.S. 58 costs) if the plan distribution is received under the same contract that provided the life insurance protection. (If the plan trustee cashes in the contract before distribution, this cost basis amount is not available. For a person who is now or was self-employed, P.S. 58 costs are also not available.)

(c) any employer contributions previously taxed to the employee—for example, where a nonqualified plan later becomes qualified.

(d) certain employer contributions attributable to foreign services performed before 1963.

(e) amounts paid by the employee in repayment of loans that were treated as distributions.

Taxation of Annuity Payments

The annuity rules of Code section 72 apply to periodic plan distributions made over more than one taxable year of the employee in a systematic liquidation of the participant's benefit. Amounts distributed are taxable in the year received, except for a proportionate recovery of the cost basis. The method used for recovery of the cost basis depends on the participant's annuity starting date.

If the annuity starting date is after December 31, 1997 and the annuity is payable over two or more lives, the excludable portion of each monthly payment is determined by dividing the employee's cost basis by the number of payments shown in the table below:

If the combined ages of the annuitants are:	Number of Payments
Not more than 110	410
More than 110 but not more than 120	360
More than 120 but not more than 130	310
More than 130 but not more than 140	260
More than 140	210

If (A) the annuity starting date is after November 18, 1996 and before January 1, 1998 and is payable over two or more

lives, or (B) the annuity starting date is after November 18, 1996 and the annuity is payable over one life, the excludable portion of each monthly payment is determined by dividing the employee's cost basis by the number of payments shown in the table below:

Age	Number of Payments
Not more than 55	360
More than 55 but not more than 60	310
More than 60 but not more than 65	260
More than 65 but not more than 70	210
More than 70	160

In the case of participants with an annuity starting date after July 1, 1986 and before November 19, 1996, the cost basis is recovered through the calculation of an exclusion ratio that is applied to each payment to determine the nontaxable amount.

The exclusion ratio is:

$$\frac{\text{Investment in the contract}}{\text{Expected return}}$$

Basically, the "investment in the contract" is the participant's cost basis. In the case of a life annuity, the "expected return" is determined by multiplying the total annual payment by the participant's life expectancy. Life expectancies are determined under tables found in Treasury Regulations for Section 72 (Reg. §1.72-9).

Example: Fred Retiree retired in 1995 at age 65 with a pension of $500 per month for his life. Fred's cost basis in the plan was $20,000. Using a life expectancy of 20 years, Fred's exclusion ratio was calculated as follows:

$$\frac{\$20,000}{\$120,000} = \frac{1}{6}$$

The numerator is Fred's cost basis; the denominator is Fred's annual pension of $6,000 multiplied by his life expectancy. Therefore, 1/6 of each payment Fred receives will be nontaxable. The remainder of each payment is taxable as ordinary income.

Once the exclusion ratio is determined it continues to apply until the cost basis is fully recovered. Payments made subsequently are taxable in full. If the participant dies before the cost basis is fully recovered, an income tax deduction for the unrecovered basis is allowed on the participant's final return. Special tables are used for joint life expectancies and separate computations may be necessary to determine expected return in some situations, such as where there is a period certain guarantee.

A simplified "safe harbor" method (for annuity starting dates after July 1, 1986 and before November 19, 1996) was provided by the IRS in Notice 88-118 (1988-2 CB 450). This alternative to the use of the exclusion ratio applied only to payments from a qualified plan or Section 403(b) tax-deferred annuity plan which were to be paid for the life of the employee or the joint lives of the employee and beneficiary. Under this method, the employee's investment in the contract was divided by the number of expected monthly payments set out in the IRS table below. The number of payments was based on the employee's age at the annuity starting date and the same table was used for both single life and joint and survivor annuity payments. The resulting dollar amount was excluded from each payment until the cost basis was fully recovered.

Age	Number of Payments
55 and under	300
55-60	260
61-65	240
66-70	170
71 and over	120

Lump-Sum Distributions

A lump-sum distribution may be desirable for retirement planning purposes, but the distribution may be large enough to push most of it into the highest tax bracket. In determining the tax on a lump-sum distribution, the first step is to calculate the taxable amount of the distribution. The taxable amount consists of (a) the total value of the distribution less (b) after-tax contributions and other items constituting the employee's cost basis. If employer securities are included in the distribution, the net unrealized appreciation of the stock is generally subtracted from the value of a lump-sum distribution.

For qualified plans only (total distributions from IRAs or Section 403(b) annuities are not technically "lump-sum distributions") there is a limited relief from this result in tax years beginning before January 1, 2000: a special one-time 5-year averaging tax computation that a participant may elect if the lump-sum distribution (a) is received after age 59½ and (b) meets the following 5 requirements:

(a) it is made in one taxable year of the recipient,

(b) it represents the entire amount of the employee's benefit in the plan,

(c) it is payable on account of the participant's death, attainment of age 59½, separation from service (non-self-employed person) or disability (self-employed person only),

(d) the employee participated in the plan for at least 5 taxable years prior to the tax year of distribution (a death benefit is exempted from this requirement), and

(e) the distribution is made on or before December 31, 1999.

In determining whether the distribution is a total distribution, all pension plans maintained by the employer are treated as a single plan, all profit-sharing plans are treated as a single plan, and all stock bonus plans are treated as one plan.

If the distribution meets all of these qualifications, the taxable amount is eligible for 5-year averaging. The recipient of the distribution must elect this treatment. Only one election is permitted and the election is available only if the distribution is received on or after the participant attained age 59½.

Five-year averaging is not available to a recipient of a death benefit unless the deceased plan participant had attained age 59½. (If the recipient is a spouse, the distribution can be rolled over to an IRA—see Chapter 28. For other beneficiaries, a lump sum distribution is fully taxable.)

Five-year averaging is available to a spouse or former spouse of a participant who receives a total distribution of a plan interest under a qualified domestic relations order (QDRO) pursuant to a divorce or separation agreement only if a total distribution would be eligible for five-year averaging if paid to the participant.

For participants who had attained age 50 before January 1, 1986, some of the more liberal rules of prior law were preserved: any otherwise available averaging can be elected on death, disability or separation from service even if the participant was not age 59½ or over at the time of distribution.

Certain amounts accumulated prior to 1974 are eligible for capital gain treatment at the participant's election. If the participant was in the plan before 1974, the distribution is separated into pre-1974 and post-1973 portions on the basis of months of plan participation before and after January 1, 1974. Participants who attained age 50 before January 1, 1986, may elect to have the pre-1974 capital gain portion taxed at a 20% rate (the pre-1987 long-term capital gain maximum).

Any portion of the distribution not eligible for capital gain treatment is eligible for 5-year averaging, provided the distribution was received before January 1, 2000. Capital gain treatment is not mandatory; a pre-1974 plan participant can elect simply to treat the entire distribution under the 5-year averaging provision, assuming such treatment is otherwise available.

Five year averaging works as follows. First, a "minimum distribution allowance" is subtracted from the taxable amount. The minimum distribution allowance is the *lesser of* $10,000 or one-half of the total taxable amount, *reduced by* 20 percent of the total taxable amount in excess of $20,000. In other words, if the taxable amount is $70,000 or more the minimum distribution allowance disappears. The remaining taxable amount after the minimum distribution allowance is divided by 5 and a separate tax is determined on this portion. The tax is based on the single taxpayer rate without any deductions or exclusions. The tax determined in this manner is multiplied by 5.

1. Total taxable amount $40,000
2. Minimum distribution allowance
    $10,000 - [20% x ($40,000 - $20,000)]   -6,000
3. Balance $34,000
4. 1/5 of balance   6,800
5. Tax on line 4 amount (at 1998 rates)   1,020
6. Total tax (5 x line 5) $ 5,100

For individuals who attained age 50 before January 1, 1986, lump-sum distributions may be treated under a 10-year averaging provision (using 1986 rates and taking into account the prior law zero bracket amount), even in years beginning after 1999, when 5-year averaging is not available. Like the election to use capital-gain treatment for pre-1974 amounts, this grandfathering provision will ordinarily be elected if it provides lower taxes than using 5-year averaging. Generally, the higher the distribution amount, the less likely the taxpayer is to benefit from this special treatment.

Taxation of Death Benefits

In general, the same income tax treatment applies to death benefits paid to beneficiaries as to lifetime benefits payable to participants. Either the annuity rules or the lump-sum special tax provisions are used by the beneficiary receiving a death benefit. However, an additional income tax benefit is available, in that if the death benefit is payable under a life insurance contract held by the qualified plan, the pure insurance amount of the death benefit is excludable from income taxation. The pure insurance amount is the difference between the policy's face amount and its cash value at the date of death. (For decedents dying before August 21, 1996, an additional amount of up to $5,000 could be excluded as an employee death benefit.)

Example: Alan Participant, age 62, dies in 1998 before retirement. His beneficiary receives a lump-sum death benefit from the plan of $100,000. The $100,000 is the proceeds of a cash value life insurance contract; the contract's cash value at Alan's death was $60,000. Alan reported a total of $10,000 of P.S. 58 insurance costs on his income tax returns during his lifetime. The taxable amount of the $100,000 distribution to the beneficiary is $100,000 less the following items:

(a) the pure insurance amount of $40,000 ($100,000 less the cash value of $60,000),

(b) Alan's cost basis of $10,000 of P.S. 58 costs.

The taxable amount of this benefit is therefore $50,000. The beneficiary may be eligible for 5-year (or 10-year) averaging on this taxable amount (within the limitations described above) or capital-gain treatment for at least a portion of any pre-1974 amounts.

Federal Estate Tax on Distributions

The value of a qualified plan death benefit is subject to inclusion in the decedent's gross estate for federal estate tax purposes. However, only high-income plan participants will actually be subject to estate tax. First, there is a high minimum tax credit applicable to the estate tax which essentially eliminates estate taxes for gross estates less than $625,000 in 1998, increasing to $1,000,000 by 2006. In addition, the unlimited marital deduction for federal estate tax purposes eliminates federal estate tax upon the death of the first spouse on property transferred to the surviving spouse in a qualifying manner.

In some cases, however, avoiding federal estate tax can be significant. For example, the estate may be relatively large and the participant may be single or unwilling to pay the death benefit to the spouse. Therefore, the marital deduction is not always available. Also, even when the death benefit is payable to a spouse, federal estate tax is not really avoided; a spouse is often about the same age as the decedent, and thus much of the property transferred to the spouse is potentially subject to federal estate tax within a few years at the surviving spouse's death.

Some authorities believe it is possible to design a qualified plan so that death benefits can be excluded from the participant's estate. Here is the rationale: The federal estate tax law provides that all of a decedent's property is includable in the estate unless there is a specific exclusionary provision. Qualified plan death benefits are not subject to any specific exclusion, so they are generally includable. There is, however, a specific provision in the Internal Revenue Code that applies to life insurance: Section 2042 provides that life insurance proceeds are includable in a decedent's estate only if the decedent had incidents of ownership in the insurance policies (or if proceeds are payable to the decedent's estate). An incident of ownership includes the right to designate the beneficiary as well as similar rights under the policy. Some planners have attempted to design qualified plan death benefits using life insurance policies in which the decedent has no incidents of ownership. Some methods for doing this include the use of separate trusts or subtrusts under the plan for holding insurance policies, together with irrevocable beneficiary designations. At this point the law is not entirely clear on whether these provisions will in fact avoid incidents of ownership. A conservative view is that they will not.

LUMP-SUM VS. DEFERRED PAYMENTS: THE TRADEOFFS

Often plan participants have a choice between a single lump-sum plan distribution and a series of deferred payments. This requires a choice between competing advantages.

Advantages of a lump-sum distribution include:

(a) 5-year averaging tax treatment, if the distribution is received before January 1, 2000, and is otherwise eligible, and

(b) freedom to invest plan proceeds at the participant's—not the plan administrator's—discretion.

The contrasting advantages of a deferred payout are:

(a) deferral of taxes until money is actually distributed,

(b) continued sheltering of income on the plan account from taxes while money remains in the plan, and

(c) security of retirement income.

There is not one single favored alternative but rather competing advantages. In a given situation, a lump-sum distribution may save more taxes, and in others the deferred payment may be a better tax choice. The conclusion depends on many variables—the participant's tax bracket, tax rates, rates of investment return, and the number of years of deferral. A full analysis of these for an individual may be complex. It should certainly be done where very large sums are involved. In other cases, it may be adequate to make a good estimate of the result.

PENALTY TAXES

In addition to these complicated regular tax rules, distributions must be planned so that recipients avoid—or at least are not surprised by—two types of tax penalties. These are summarized as follows.

Penalty for Distributions Too Soon

Early distributions from qualified plans, 403(b) tax-deferred annuity plans, IRAs and SEPs are subject to a penalty of 10 percent of the taxable amount of the distribution, except for distributions:

(1) made on or after attainment of age 59½;

(2) made to the plan participant's beneficiary or estate on or after the participant's death;

(3) attributable to the participant's disability;

(4) that are part of a series of substantially equal periodic payments made at least annually over the life or life expectancy of the participant, or of the participant and beneficiary (separation from the employer's service is required, except for IRAs);

(5) made following separation from service after attainment of age 55 (not applicable to IRAs);

(6) certain tax credit ESOP dividend payments; or

(7) distributions to the extent of medical expenses deductible for the year under Code Section 213, whether or not actually deducted.

In addition certain distributions made from IRAs for the payment of health insurance premiums by unemployed individuals, and certain distributions used for higher education expenses or first-time home purchases may be exempt from the penalty. (See IRC Secs. 72(t)(2)(D)-(F).)

Penalty for Distributions Too Late or Not Enough

(1) Distributions from qualified plans, 403(b) tax-deferred annuity plans, IRAs, SEPs, and 457 governmental deferred compensation plans generally must begin by April 1 of the calendar year after the participant attains age 70½. However, for years beginning after 1996, distributions from qualified plans are not subject to this rule if the participant has not retired and is not a more than 5% owner (as defined for top heavy purposes). Instead, distributions may be deferred until April 1 of the year following retirement. Distributions from traditional IRAs may not be deferred until retirement under this rule. (Special rules apply for individuals who turned 70½ before 1989.)

(2) There is an annual *minimum* distribution required; if distribution is less than the minimum there is a penalty

of 50 percent of the amount that should have been distributed but was not.

(3) The minimum initial annual distribution is determined by dividing the participant's account balance (as of the last plan valuation date prior to the year in which distributions must begin) by the participant's life expectancy (or participant and beneficiary's joint life expectancy) from IRS regulations. Payments can be stretched out by recalculating life expectancy annually. (Other minimum limits may also apply.)

(4) If the beneficiary is not a spouse, the minimum distribution may be further increased (using a factor in proposed IRS regulations) to insure that the participant's share of the benefit is at least a minimum amount of the expected total. This factor will come into effect where the beneficiary is more than 10 years younger than the participant.

Chapter 15

RISK AND REWARD

Everyone wants to invest for high returns with low risk. However, as every student of investments is taught, if you want high returns you must bear correspondingly high risks. But is this always so? And how is risk related to returns?

For financial planners who are helping their clients achieve their investment and accumulation goals these are fundamental questions. As the following discussion will demonstrate, risk, as measured by potential deviations or fluctuations from the expected or average return for a given class of investment assets, depends critically on the investor's investment planning horizon. As an investor's planning horizon increases, the risk of substantial deviations from the expected or average return for any given type of investment declines. More importantly, as the planning horizon increases, risk (as measured by the range of worst possible outcomes) decreases. For longer investment planning horizons the so-called "riskier" investments, such as common stocks, have historically had higher or better "worst" performances than "less risky" investments, such as T-bills and bonds. Armed with a solid understanding of the relationship between risk and investment planning horizon returns financial planners can help their clients achieve their accumulation objectives for various planning horizons by selecting investments that maximize potential returns within acceptable risk levels.

HISTORICAL PERSPECTIVE - NOMINAL AND REAL RETURNS

Historically, investments with greater risk have provided higher returns. Figure 15.1 shows total annual compound and simple nominal returns (with reinvestment of cash flows), standard deviations (a measure of risk that is essentially the average amount by which any given period's return varies from the average return for all periods) for common stocks (based upon the S&P composite index), small capitalization stocks (the bottom 20 percent of the stocks listed on the New York Stock Exchange ranked by capitalization), long-term AAA-rated corporate bonds, long-term government bonds, U.S. Treasury bills, and the consumer price index for the period 1926 through 1997. Figure 15.2 shows real (inflation-adjusted) returns for the same period.[1]

Small stocks, which have experienced the greatest yearly fluctuation of returns as indicated by the standard deviation of 33.89 percent, have provided the highest annual compound return over this period. U.S. Treasury bills, which have had the lowest yearly fluctuation in returns, have also had the lowest annual compound return. Each of the other investments rank as expected with respect to their return given their risk, as measured by the fluctuation (standard deviation) in their annual returns. These results confirm that in the long run returns are positively related to the risk associated with the

Figure 15.1

Nominal Returns (Unadjusted for Inflation) Since 1926			
Series	Compound Return	Simple Return	Standard Deviation
Small stocks	12.712%	17.729%	33.89%
Common stocks	10.996	12.958	20.32
Long-term corporate bonds	5.733	6.059	8.76
Long-term government bonds	5.189	5.562	9.24
Intermediate government bonds	5.258	5.406	5.74
U.S. Treasury bills	3.759	3.808	3.24
Inflation	3.098	3.196	4.51

Figure 15.2

Real Returns (Inflation Adjusted) Since 1926			
Series	Compound Return	Simple Return	Standard Deviation
Small stocks	9.325%	14.203%	33.26%
Common stocks	7.660	9.659	20.46
Long-term corporate bonds	2.556	3.019	9.96
Long-term government bonds	2.028	2.538	10.53
Intermediate government bonds	2.095	2.329	7.03
U.S. Treasury bills	0.641	0.727	4.17
Inflation	0.000	0.000	0.00

investment. In other words, the more risk there is, the greater the potential reward.

Over any short-term holding period, however, an investor cannot expect returns on the higher-risk investments to necessarily exceed the returns on the lower-risk investments. Of course, that is exactly why the high-risk investments are considered risky. Since the high-risk investments have widely fluctuating returns year by year, an investor with a five-year investment horizon who invests in small stocks, for instance, may experience low or negative returns over that relatively short time period. The investor may lose money relative to an equivalent investment in Treasury bills. Similarly, returns on small stocks over that relatively short time period may be exceptionally high and exceed the long-term average return for small stocks many times over.

In general, investors can expect that as their investment horizon lengthens, the returns they realize will tend to deviate less from the long-term average for the type of investment they have selected. The practical implication of this result is that investors with longer-term investment objectives should be willing to invest in what are considered higher-risk, higher-return instruments than they would tolerate for shorter-term

objectives. Investors who can tolerate the high-risk investments for shorter-term objectives must understand that they may realize extraordinary results - either high returns or high losses.

HISTORICAL PERSPECTIVE - RISK PREMIUMS

Figure 15.3 presents risk premiums for the six basic asset classes introduced in Figure 15.1 for the period of 1926 through 1997. A *risk premium* is the average additional return an investor receives for bearing the additional risk of a given investment relative to a given safer alternative.

The *real riskless interest rate* serves as the basis for all the other risk premiums. The real riskless interest rate is based on the difference in returns between consumer goods (inflation as measured by the CPI) and U.S. Treasury bills, which are a very short-term, almost risk-free asset (using risk of capital and income as the criterion).

The *bond maturity premium* measures the additional return investors receive for bearing the interest-rate risk of longer-

Figure 15.3

Risk Premiums			
Series	Compound Return	Simple Return	Standard Deviation
Equity risk premiums (stocks-bills)	6.97%	8.87%	21.14%
Small stock premiums (small stocks-stocks)	1.55	4.22	22.18
Default premiums (LT corps-LT govts)	0.52	0.48	2.94
Maturity premiums (LT govts-bills)	1.38	1.69	8.76
Real interest rates (bills-inflation)	0.64	0.59	4.77

term but essentially default-free government bonds relative to Treasury bills. Since long-term bond prices fluctuate more than prices of short-term bonds for a given change in interest rates, long-term bondholders face the risk of capital loss if they must sell before the bonds mature.

The *bond default premium* measures the additional return investors receive for bearing the risk of default on corporate bonds relative to government bonds of equal maturity. The total risk premium for corporate bonds relative to Treasury bills may be approximated by adding the bond maturity premium to the default premium.

The *equity risk premium* is a measure of the additional return an investor receives from an investment in common stocks relative to an investment in Treasury bills.

The *small stock premium* is a measure of the additional return from an investment in small capitalization stocks relative to an investment in S&P 500 stocks. The total risk premium for an investment in small stocks relative to Treasury bills may be approximated by adding the equity risk premium for S&P stocks to the small stock premium.

One of the most startling observations from Figure 15.3 is that the real riskless compound rate of return has been less than 2/3 of one percent (0.64 percent). These historical data suggest that investors who invest exclusively in Treasury bills can expect little more than a break-even return after inflation. In contrast, based on experience from 1926 through 1997, investors in common stocks can expect a long-term compound real rate of return that is about 7 percent higher than the return on Treasury bills and 7.7 percent higher than inflation. Investors in small stocks can expect a compound long-term real (inflation-adjusted) rate of return of about 9.33 percent.

COMMON STOCK (S&P COMPOSITE) RETURNS

Over the period 1926 through 1997, nominal stock returns were positive in almost 70 percent of the years. Real (inflation adjusted) returns were positive about two-thirds of the time. The longest period over which an investor would have had a negative nominal total return (unadjusted for inflation) on an S&P composite common stock investment was the 14-year period of 1929-1942. However, during the 18-year period from June 1964 through September 1982, a common stock investor would have had a negative real rate of return (adjusted for inflation). Although real returns were negative over this period, in nominal terms the value of investment would have more than tripled.

Five-Year Returns

Looking at all possible five-year periods from 1926 through 1997 the nominal average annualized compound return was 10.54 percent. Nominal annualized compound rates of return were positive in almost 90 percent of the five-year periods. They ranged from a high of 23.92 percent from 1950 to 1954 to a low of -12.47 percent from 1928 to 1932 - a minimum/maximum range of 36.39 percent. There is about a 99 percent probability that any given five-year nominal annualized compound return will fall between -10.63 and 31.71 percent.

The real average annualized compound return was over 7 percent. Real compound annualized five-year returns were positive about 80 percent of the time. They ranged from a high of 23.51 percent from 1932 to 1936 to a low of -9.34 percent from 1937 to 1941 — a minimum/maximum range of 32.85 percent. Based on the historical distribution of returns, the real annual five-year return should fall within the range of -12.93 to 26.99 percent 99 percent of the time.

Ten-Year Returns

The average nominal annualized compound return was 10.89 percent for all 10-year periods over the period 1926 through 1997. Nominal annualized compound returns were positive in almost 97 percent of the 10-year holding periods. They ranged from a high of 20.1 percent from 1948 to 1958 to a low of -0.89 percent from 1928 to 1938 - a minimum/maximum range of about 21 percent. This range is about half the size of the five-year holding-period minimum/maximum range. Based on the historical distribution of returns, the 10-year nominal annualized return should fall within the range of -3.2 to 24.9 percent 99 percent of the time.

The average real annual compound return was 7.08 percent. Real annual compound returns were positive for 89 percent of the 10-year periods. They ranged from a high of 17.9 percent from 1948 to 1958 to a low of -3.8 percent from 1964 to 1974 — a minimum/maximum range of 21.7 percent, or about two-thirds the size of the five-year minimum/maximum range. The 10-year real annualized return should fall between -7.12 and 21.28 percent 99 percent of the time.

Twenty-Year Returns

Looking at 20-year periods, the average nominal annualized compound return was 10.93 percent. Nominal annualized returns were positive for all of the 20-year holding periods. They ranged from a high of 16.86 percent from 1942 to 1961 to a low of 3.11 percent from 1928 to 1948 — a minimum/maximum range of 13.75 percent range, which is about one-

Figure 15.4

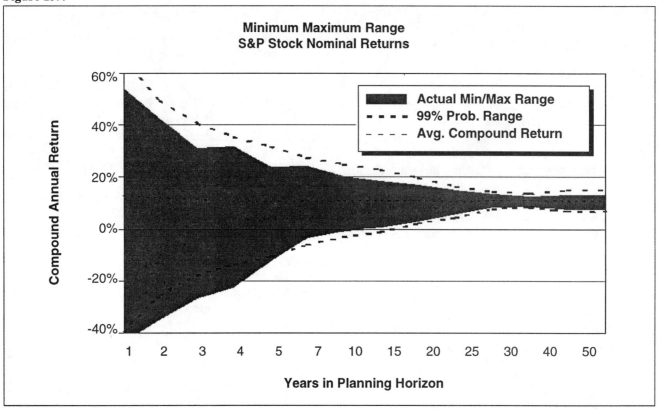

third the size of the five-year holding-period minimum/maximum range. Approximately 99 percent of the time, 20-year nominal annualized returns should fall between 2.16 and 19.70 percent.

The average real annualized compound return was 6.78 percent. Real annualized returns were positive in all 20-year holding periods. They ranged from a high of 13.04 percent from 1942 to 1961 to a low of 0.84 percent from 1965 to 1984 — a minimum/maximum range of 12.2 percent, or about one third the five-year range. Based on the historic distribution of returns, the real 20-year annualized compound return has a 99 percent chance of falling within the range of -2.64 to 16.20 percent.

Planning Horizon And Minimum/Maximum Range

These results demonstrate that investors can generally expect both the real and nominal returns they realize on a portfolio of common stocks to deviate less from the long-term average return for common stocks when their planning horizon is longer. In other words, common stocks become less risky (with no reduction in expected return) when an investor's planning horizon for stock investments

is longer. Perhaps more importantly, the downside risk, as measured by the probability of negative average annual compound returns that are less than zero, declines as the holding period increases. Specifically, the probability of earning a negative real return for a one-year investment in S&P stocks is about 32 percent (or 1 in 3). For a 20-year holding period, the probability that the average real annual compound return will be negative is just over 3 percent (or 1 in 32). Consequently common stocks may be suitable investments for long-term accumulation objectives for many investors who would be unwilling to bear the risk of common stocks for short-term accumulation objectives. Figures 15.4 and 15.5 graphically demonstrates this point for nominal and real rates of return.

Figure 15.6 shows total nominal and real compound annualized rates of return for S&P 500 stocks for planning horizons ranging from one year to 50 years. It also shows the maximum and minimum values for each planning horizon, the minimum/maximum range (computed as the difference between the minimum and maximum values), and the standard deviation of the planning-horizon returns. Smaller standard deviations mean less volatility and imply less risk. Finally, based on the historical distribution of returns, it shows the range into which you can expect annualized returns to fall 99 percent of the time.

Figure 15.5

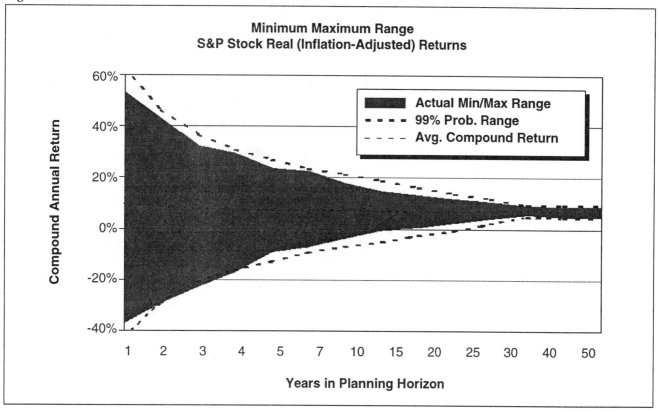

SMALL CAPITALIZATION STOCK RETURNS

Returns on small stocks, similar to returns on S&P common stocks, were positive in over 70 percent of the years 1926 through 1997. The simple one-year nominal average return was 17.73 percent. The one-year nominal average compound return was 12.71 percent. The 15-year period from 1928 to 1942 was the longest period over which an investor would have earned a negative return in either real or nominal terms. During the 18-year period (1964-1982) when the real returns on S&P common stocks were negative, small stocks grew at an 8.2 percent annual compound rate of return — enough to increase investor wealth in real terms four-fold. The simple real (inflation-adjusted) one-year average return was 14.20 percent The one-year real average compound return was 9.32 percent.

Five-Year Returns

Looking at five-year periods, the average nominal annualized return was 13.74 percent. Nominal annualized compound returns were positive in about 87 percent of the periods. They ranged from a high of 45.90 percent from 1941 to 1945 to a low of -27.54 percent from 1928 to 1932 - a minimum/maximum range of 73.44 percent. Based on this history, an investor

could expect nominal five-year annualized rates of return to fall between -21.60 and 61.95 percent 99 percent of the time.

The average real annualized return was 9.98 percent. Real annualized compound returns were positive in over 82 percent of the five-year periods. They ranged from a high of 47.06 percent from 1932 to 1936 to a low of -23.38 percent from 1928 to 1932 - a minimum/maximum range of 70.44 percent. The real five-year annualized compound rate of return should fall between about -21.27 and 51.28 percent 99 percent of the time.

Ten-Year Returns

Looking at 10-year periods, the average nominal annualized return was 14.13 percent. Nominal annualized returns for 10-year periods were positive almost 97 percent of the time. They ranged from a high of 30.38 percent from 1975 to 1984 to a low of -5.70 percent from 1929 to 1938 - a minimum/maximum range of 36.08 percent, or half the five-year range. Ten-year nominal annualized compound returns can be expected to fall between -3.84 and 34.89 percent in all but one year in 100.

The average real annualized return was 10.13 percent. Real 10-year period annual returns were positive over 90 percent of

Figure 15.6

S&P 500 STOCK RISK-RETURN ANALYSIS (1926-1997)										
Nominal Returns (10.996% Compound, 12.958% Simple Over Entire Period)										
	Annualized Returns					99% Probability Range				
Yrs in Planning Horizon	Average Compound ROR (%)	Actual Min ROR (%)	Actual Max ROR (%)	Actual Min-Max Range (%)	Pct Periods ROR>0 (%)	Stnd Dev (%)	Prob ROR<0 (%)	Min ROR (%)	Max ROR (%)	Min-Max Range (%)
1	12.958	-43.34	53.99	97.33	72.22	20.32	26.18	-39.38	65.30	104.68
2	11.880	-34.77	41.70	76.47	83.10	14.60	20.80	-25.74	49.50	75.24
3	11.256	-26.95	31.15	58.10	87.14	11.36	16.08	-18.00	40.51	58.51
4	10.757	-22.66	31.62	54.28	89.86	9.52	12.92	-13.76	35.28	49.04
5	10.543	-12.47	23.92	36.38	89.71	8.22	9.98	-10.63	31.71	42.34
7	10.650	-3.49	24.23	27.72	93.94	6.55	5.19	-6.21	27.51	33.73
10	10.887	-0.89	20.06	20.95	96.83	5.46	2.30	-3.17	24.94	28.11
15	10.870	0.64	18.24	17.60	100.00	4.64	0.96	-1.08	22.82	23.91
20	10.927	3.11	16.86	13.75	100.00	3.40	0.07	2.16	19.70	17.54
25	10.381	5.94	15.02	9.08	100.00	2.32	0.00	4.40	16.36	11.96
30	10.956	8.47	13.49	5.02	100.00	1.33	0.00	7.52	14.39	6.87
40	10.955	8.85	12.49	3.63	100.00	1.04	0.00	8.29	13.62	5.34
50	10.878	7.69	13.12	5.42	100.00	1.57	0.00	6.84	14.92	8.07
Real Returns (7.660% Compound, 9.659% Simple Over Entire Period)										
1	9.659	-37.37	53.39	90.76	68.06	20.46	31.85	-43.05	62.37	105.42
2	8.492	-29.25	42.69	71.94	74.65	14.64	28.10	-29.22	46.20	75.43
3	7.812	-22.94	32.14	55.08	80.00	11.17	24.22	-20.97	36.59	57.56
4	7.274	-17.28	29.45	46.73	76.81	9.13	21.28	-16.24	30.79	47.03
5	7.034	-9.34	23.51	32.85	79.41	7.75	18.20	-12.93	26.99	39.92
7	7.044	-7.27	22.31	29.58	86.36	6.37	13.43	-9.36	23.45	32.81
10	7.079	-3.76	17.87	21.63	88.89	5.51	9.95	-7.12	21.28	28.40
15	6.838	-0.58	14.64	15.22	93.10	4.68	7.21	-5.22	18.90	24.12
20	6.782	0.84	13.04	12.20	100.00	3.66	3.18	-2.64	16.20	18.84
25	6.495	2.60	11.75	9.14	100.00	2.79	0.99	-0.69	13.68	14.37
30	6.995	4.35	10.58	6.23	100.00	1.88	0.01	2.16	11.83	9.68
40	7.031	5.70	9.15	3.44	100.00	0.89	0.00	4.73	9.33	4.59
50	6.750	4.77	8.84	4.07	100.00	0.98	0.00	4.22	9.28	5.06

the time. They ranged from a high of 21.47 percent from 1975 to 1984 to a low of -3.80 percent from 1929 to 1938 - a minimum/maximum range of 25.27 percent, or about one-third the five-year range. Real 10-year annualized compound returns should fall within -4.68 and 26.86 percent 99 percent of the time.

Twenty-Year Returns

Looking at 20-year periods, nominal annual returns averaged 14.81 percent and were positive in all 20-year periods. Nominal returns range from a high of 21.13 percent from 1942 to 1961 to a low of 5.74 percent from 1929 to 1948 - a minimum/maximum range of 15.39 percent, or almost one-fifth of the five-year range. Similarly, the range in which the 20-year annual compound return can be expected to fall 99 percent of the time is 6.07 to 24.16 percent, again about one-fifth the size of the five-year range.

The average real annualized return was 10.51 percent. Real annual compound returns for 20-year periods were positive in all 20-year periods. They ranged from a high of 17.18 percent from 1942 to 1961 to a low of 3.96 percent from 1929 to 1948 - a minimum/maximum range of 13.22 percent, or less than one-fifth the five-year range. There is a 99 percent chance that the real 20-year annual return will fall between 2.38 and 19.18 percent.

Planning Horizon And Minimum/ Maximum Range

Similar to the results for S&P stocks, generally the real rate of return on a portfolio of small capitalization stocks has deviated less from the long-term average expected return when the investor's planning horizon was longer.

Figure 15.7

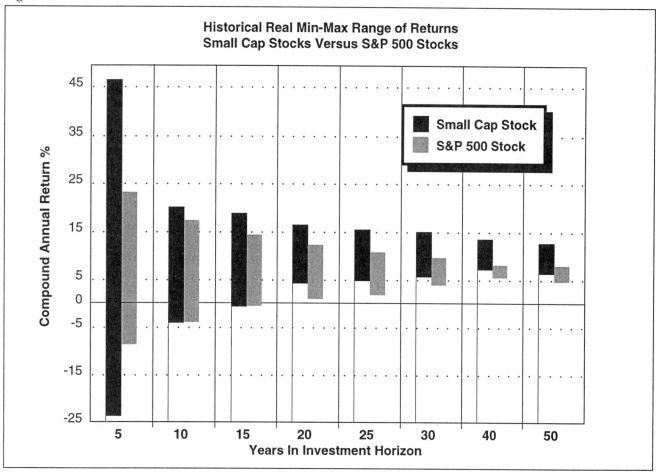

Historical Real Min-Max Range of Returns
Small Cap Stocks Versus S&P 500 Stocks

The minimum/maximum range of returns for any given planning horizon is greater for small capitalization stocks than for S&P stocks. Therefore, although small capitalization stocks become less risky the longer the investor's planning horizon (in the sense that the investor's actual return is less likely to deviate substantially from the long-term expected averages), the returns on small capitalization stocks still fluctuate more on average for any given period than returns on S&P common stocks. However, the risk of small stocks decreases more than the risk of S&P stocks as the planning horizon increases. Specifically, the historical five-year minimum/maximum range of returns for small stocks was more than twice as large as the range for S&P stocks (73.44 percent nominal and 70.44 percent real for small stocks versus 36.39 percent nominal and 32.85 percent real for S&P stocks).

In contrast, the historical 20-year minimum/maximum ranges for small stocks and S&P stocks are almost identical (15.39 percent nominal and 13.22 percent real for small stocks versus 13.75 percent nominal and 12.20 percent real for S&P stocks). And for all periods of 20 years or longer, small capitalization stocks have absolutely dominated S&P stocks

in terms of nominal returns. The maximum and minimum annualized nominal compound returns for small stocks for any period of 20 years or more were always greater than the corresponding maximum and minimum values for S&P stocks.

Conclusions

Looking at real inflation-adjusted returns, small capitalization stocks similarly dominated S&P stocks for all holding periods of 10 years or more. Consequently, for long-term accumulation objectives, investors can capture a substantial expected annual return premium (1.55 percent real compound small stock premium) with virtually no increase in risk by shifting from a portfolio of S&P stocks to a portfolio of small capitalization stocks. Figure 15.7 compares real (inflation-adjusted) minimum/maximum ranges for both S&P stocks and small capitalization stocks for planning horizons ranging from one year to 50 years. When risk is viewed as downside or loss possibilities, small stocks look even better relative to S&P stocks for longer planning horizons. For planning horizons up to five years, small stocks have a higher probability

Figure 15.8

SMALL CAP STOCK RISK-RETURN ANALYSIS (1926-1997)										
Nominal Returns (12.712% Compound, 17.729% Simple Over Entire Period)										
		Annualized Returns				99% Probability Range				
Yrs in Planning Horizon	Average Compound ROR (%)	Actual Min ROR (%)	Actual Max ROR (%)	Actual Min-Max Range (%)	Pct Periods ROR>0 (%)	Stnd Dev (%)	Prob ROR<0 (%)	Min ROR (%)	Max ROR (%)	Min-Max Range (%)
1	17.729	-58.01	142.87	200.87	70.83	33.89	34.86	-48.95	148.85	197.79
2	15.602	-45.15	73.69	118.84	74.65	25.04	30.28	-38.02	105.05	143.06
3	14.613	-46.73	71.31	118.04	80.00	20.45	26.63	-31.15	84.42	115.58
4	13.941	-38.50	64.17	102.68	81.16	17.86	23.73	-26.38	71.89	98.28
5	13.745	-27.54	45.90	73.44	86.76	15.22	19.83	-21.60	61.95	83.54
7	13.879	-18.22	35.78	54.00	90.91	10.91	10.34	-12.22	46.34	58.56
10	14.130	-5.70	30.38	36.08	96.83	7.37	2.39	-3.84	34.89	38.73
15	14.536	-1.30	23.33	24.63	94.83	5.39	0.28	0.97	29.63	28.67
20	14.814	5.74	21.13	15.39	100.00	3.48	0.00	6.07	24.16	18.10
25	13.799	7.16	19.62	12.46	100.00	2.83	0.00	6.67	21.33	14.65
30	14.461	8.84	18.83	10.00	100.00	2.49	0.00	8.16	21.07	12.90
40	14.515	11.10	17.90	6.80	100.00	1.80	0.00	9.95	19.24	9.29
50	14.545	9.80	17.46	7.66	100.00	2.15	0.00	9.06	20.27	11.21
Real Returns (9.325% Compound, 14.203% Simple Over Entire Period)										
1	14.203	-59.27	141.63	200.90	70.83	33.26	38.54	-50.31	140.52	190.82
2	11.973	-43.47	71.52	114.99	73.24	24.19	34.66	-38.85	95.38	134.23
3	10.916	-43.80	67.12	110.92	75.71	19.23	31.32	-31.47	74.03	105.50
4	10.192	-34.22	59.80	94.02	76.81	16.30	28.49	-26.20	60.94	87.14
5	9.977	-23.38	47.06	70.44	82.35	13.48	24.53	-21.27	51.28	72.56
7	10.052	-14.46	25.30	39.76	83.33	9.28	14.55	-12.42	37.28	49.70
10	10.132	-3.80	21.47	25.27	90.48	6.02	4.34	-4.68	26.86	31.54
15	10.333	-0.42	19.31	19.74	96.55	4.62	1.05	-1.12	22.90	24.02
20	10.508	3.96	17.18	13.22	100.00	3.26	0.04	2.38	19.18	16.79
25	9.782	5.00	16.21	11.21	100.00	2.82	0.01	2.75	17.22	14.46
30	10.366	6.08	15.40	9.33	100.00	2.42	0.00	4.31	16.71	12.40
40	10.46	8.24	13.64	5.40	100.00	1.37	0.00	6.98	14.04	7.05
50	10.277	7.35	12.83	5.49	100.00	1.47	0.00	6.53	14.14	7.61

than S&P stocks of earning an average real compound annual return that is negative. However, for longer planning horizons the probability of negative returns is less for small stocks than for S&P stocks. For instance, for 20-year periods the probability of negative returns for small stocks is 0.04 percent, or less than 1 in 2,500. In contrast, for S&P stocks, the probability is 3.18 percent, or about 80 times greater than for small stocks.

LONG-TERM CORPORATE BONDS

The average one-year nominal simple rate of return and the average one-year inflation-adjusted real simple rate of return on long-term corporate bonds was 6.059 percent and 3.019 percent, respectively, over the period 1926 through 1997. In about 78 percent of the years long-term corporate bonds had positive nominal compound returns. Returns ranged from

42.56 percent to -8.09 percent. Based on history, an investor should expect nominal annual returns to fall within -13.48 and 29.21 percent 99 percent of the time. Long-term corporate bonds had positive inflation-adjusted real annual compound returns in 64 percent of the years. Real returns ranged from a high of 37.25 percent to a low of -15.45 percent.

Five-year, 10-year, and 20-year nominal annualized compound returns for long-term corporate bonds ranged from 22.51 percent, 16.32 percent, and 10.57 percent, respectively, on the high side, to -2.22 percent, 0.98 percent, and 1.34 percent respectively, on the low side. Therefore the respective minimum/maximum ranges were 24.73 percent, 15.34 percent, and 9.23 percent.

Real annualized compound returns ranged from 18.60 percent, 11.94 percent, and 5.44 percent on the high side

Figure 15.9

CORPORATE BOND RISK-RETURN ANALYSIS (1926-1997)
Nominal Returns (5.733% Compound, 6.059% Simple Over Entire Period)

Yrs in Planning Horizon	Annualized Returns					99% Probability Range				
	Average Compound ROR (%)	Actual Min ROR (%)	Actual Max ROR (%)	Actual Min-Max Range (%)	Pct Periods ROR>0 (%)	Stnd Dev (%)	Prob ROR<0 (%)	Min ROR (%)	Max ROR (%)	Min-Max Range (%)
1	6.059	-8.09	42.56	50.65	77.78	8.67	23.69	-13.48	29.21	42.68
2	5.850	-3.48	24.86	28.35	83.10	6.29	17.05	-8.98	22.68	31.66
3	5.801	-3.59	22.14	25.73	88.57	5.49	13.99	-7.34	20.49	27.83
4	5.711	-2.66	23.19	25.85	89.86	4.97	11.84	-6.21	18.90	25.11
5	5.701	-2.22	22.51	24.73	95.59	4.69	10.44	-5.56	18.08	23.64
7	5.652	-0.63	17.25	17.88	98.48	4.22	8.34	-4.57	16.79	21.37
10	5.487	0.98	16.32	15.33	100.00	3.84	7.04	-3.88	15.62	19.49
15	5.124	1.02	13.66	12.64	100.00	3.41	6.09	-3.24	14.09	17.33
20	4.723	1.34	10.57	9.23	100.00	2.79	4.08	-2.17	12.02	14.19
25	4.251	1.34	9.59	8.25	100.00	2.28	2.78	-1.42	10.20	11.62
30	4.334	1.79	8.86	7.07	100.00	2.00	1.31	-0.67	9.55	10.21
40	4.286	2.62	7.09	4.47	100.00	1.40	0.08	0.76	7.92	7.16
50	4.563	3.47	6.07	2.60	100.00	0.80	0.00	2.52	6.64	4.12
Real Returns (2.556% Compound, 3.019% Simple Over Entire Period)										
1	3.019	-15.45	37.25	52.70	63.89	9.96	39.55	-19.76	31.07	50.82
2	2.736	-14.47	21.89	36.36	67.61	7.65	37.31	-15.52	24.25	39.77
3	2.625	-12.80	18.64	31.44	64.29	6.73	35.89	-13.56	21.32	34.87
4	2.482	-11.70	18.62	30.33	59.42	6.06	34.93	-12.10	19.07	31.16
5	2.429	-10.35	18.60	28.95	58.82	5.71	34.16	-11.26	17.87	29.13
7	2.255	-5.58	13.16	18.74	59.09	5.12	33.53	-10.11	16.04	26.15
10	1.878	-5.22	11.94	17.16	53.97	4.37	33.76	-8.72	13.50	22.22
15	1.294	-3.89	9.76	13.65	58.62	3.32	35.13	-6.84	10.03	16.87
20	0.786	-2.69	5.44	8.13	52.83	2.12	35.78	-4.51	6.33	10.84
25	0.557	-1.97	3.82	5.78	52.08	1.54	36.11	-3.34	4.58	7.92
30	0.593	-1.52	3.35	4.87	55.81	1.39	33.71	-2.94	4.23	7.17
40	0.597	-1.90	2.54	4.45	63.64	1.30	32.51	-2.71	4.00	6.72
50	0.675	-0.30	2.05	2.36	82.61	0.68	16.14	-1.07	2.45	3.52

to -10.35 percent, -5.22 percent, and -2.69 percent on the low side, respectively, for 5, 10, and 20-year periods. Therefore the respective real minimum/maximum ranges were 28.95 percent, 17.16 percent, and 8.13 percent. These results are perfectly consistent with expectations regarding risk level and holding periods relative to the other asset categories. Perhaps one of the most notable items is the consistently high probability of negative real returns for all holding periods. The chance for negative real returns stays at around 33 percent (or 1 in 3) for planning horizons as long as 40 years.

Stocks And Corporate Bonds Compared

Although the long-term corporate bond minimum/maximum ranges for various periods were smaller than the corresponding ranges for either S&P stocks or small capitalization stocks, both S&P stocks and small capitalization stocks absolutely dominated long-term corporate bonds for longer planning horizons.

Figure 15.10 compares real return minimum/maximum ranges for both S&P stocks and long-term corporate bonds for periods ranging from one year to 50 years. For all periods, the maximum real annualized compound returns for S&P stocks have always been considerably higher than the corresponding values for long-term bonds. For periods of about 8 years or longer, the S&P stock's minimum real annualized compound returns have been equal to or greater than the corresponding values for long-term bonds. In fact, for planning horizons of about 25 years or longer, the minimum values for S&P stocks have always been greater than the maximum values for long-term bonds. For shorter planning horizons (five or less years), although the upside potential of S&P stocks as indicated by the maximum return values is considerably greater than for

Figure 15.10

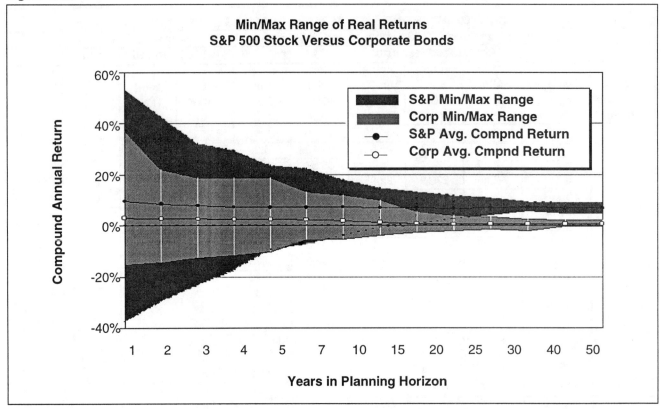

Min/Max Range of Real Returns
S&P 500 Stock Versus Corporate Bonds

bonds, the downside risk as indicated by minimum return values for S&P stocks is significantly lower than for corporate bonds.

LONG-TERM U.S. GOVERNMENT BONDS

Over the entire period from 1926 through 1997, compound annual real (inflation-adjusted) long-term government bond returns were only 2.028 percent. Nominal long-term government bond returns were positive in 72 percent of the years. Nominal annual returns ranged from 40.35 percent in 1982 to -9.19 percent in 1967. Real long-term government bond returns were positive in slightly less than 60 percent of the years. Real annual returns ranged from 35.12 percent in 1982 to -15.46 percent in 1946.

Over this entire period the highest nominal annualized compound returns were 21.62 percent for five-year periods, 15.56 percent for 10-year periods, and 10.45 percent for 20-year periods. The lowest nominal annualized returns were -2.14 percent, -0.07 percent, and 0.68 percent for 5, 10, and 20-year periods, respectively. The nominal minimum/maximum ranges for 5, 10, and 20-year periods were 23.76 percent, 15.63 percent, and 9.77 percent, respectively.

The highest real annualized compound return was 17.73

percent for five-year periods, 11.21 percent for 10-year periods, and 5.25 percent for 20-year periods. The lowest real annualized compound returns were -10.10 percent, -5.36 percent, and -3.06 percent for 5, 10, and 20-year periods, respectively. The real minimum/maximum ranges for 5, 10, and 20-year periods were 27.83 percent, 16.57 percent, and 8.31 percent, respectively. Notable is the consistently high probability of negative real returns over any given planning horizon. The probability of negative real returns ranges from about 40 percent for shorter planning horizons to almost 50 percent for longer planning horizons.

Stocks And Long-Term Government Bonds Compared

Once again, the minimum/maximum annualized compound return range declines as the planning horizon increases. And, consistent with their risk rating, the minimum/maximum annual compound return range for long-term U.S. government bonds for any given planning horizon is smaller than for either S&P common stocks or small capitalization stocks. However, similar to corporate bonds, for longer planning horizons (about 10 years or longer) long-term government bonds have been absolutely dominated by both S&P stocks and small capitalization stocks. For periods of 10 years or longer, both the maximum and minimum annual compound

Figure 15.11

LONG-TERM GOVT BOND RISK-RETURN ANALYSIS (1926-1997)										
Nominal Returns (5.189% Compound, 5.562% Simple Over Entire Period)										
Annualized Returns						99% Probability Range				
Yrs in Planning Horizon	Average Compound ROR (%)	Actual Min ROR (%)	Actual Max ROR (%)	Actual Min-Max Range (%)	Pct Periods ROR>0 (%)	Stnd Dev (%)	Prob ROR<0 (%)	Min ROR (%)	Max ROR (%)	Min-Max Range (%)
1	5.562	-9.19	40.35	49.53	72.22	9.24	27.20	-15.14	30.39	45.53
2	5.278	-4.83	27.71	32.54	81.69	6.30	19.64	-9.53	22.10	31.63
3	5.216	-4.91	23.49	28.41	85.71	5.46	16.45	-7.80	19.76	27.57
4	5.113	-2.84	20.90	23.74	88.41	4.89	14.23	-6.64	18.10	24.74
5	5.108	-2.14	21.62	23.76	91.18	4.71	13.19	-6.18	17.52	23.70
7	5.060	-0.88	16.07	16.95	98.48	4.27	11.15	-5.26	16.32	21.59
10	4.907	-0.07	15.56	15.63	98.41	3.89	9.67	-4.53	15.12	19.65
15	4.593	0.40	13.53	13.14	100.00	3.47	8.65	-3.87	13.69	17.56
20	4.210	0.68	10.45	9.76	100.00	2.84	6.39	-2.79	11.63	14.42
25	3.742	0.82	9.23	8.41	100.00	2.31	4.87	-2.00	9.77	11.77
30	3.796	1.53	8.63	7.10	100.00	2.02	2.75	-1.26	9.07	10.33
40	3.745	2.26	6.71	4.45	100.00	1.42	0.35	0.16	7.44	7.28
50	4.042	2.80	5.70	2.89	100.00	0.93	0.00	1.68	6.45	4.77
Real Returns (2.028% Compound, 2.538% Simple Over Entire Period)										
1	2.538	-15.46	35.12	50.58	59.72	10.53	42.02	-21.08	31.91	52.99
2	2.170	-13.69	24.66	38.36	63.38	7.51	39.89	-15.66	23.11	38.77
3	2.042	-12.27	19.96	32.24	64.29	6.46	38.65	-13.48	19.87	33.34
4	1.884	-10.98	16.42	27.39	59.42	5.68	37.88	-11.84	17.38	29.22
5	1.837	-10.10	17.73	27.83	54.41	5.38	37.36	-11.11	16.36	27.47
7	1.667	-5.68	12.02	17.70	56.06	4.83	37.13	-10.03	14.63	24.66
10	1.307	-5.36	11.21	16.57	47.62	4.11	38.03	-8.68	12.21	20.90
15	0.778	-4.46	9.44	13.90	41.38	3.22	40.90	-7.13	9.25	16.38
20	0.291	-3.06	5.25	8.31	35.85	2.10	44.86	-4.97	5.79	10.76
25	0.065	-2.46	3.47	5.93	37.50	1.53	48.60	-3.80	4.06	7.86
30	0.073	-2.00	3.13	5.13	48.84	1.37	48.14	-3.40	3.65	7.06
40	0.074	-2.27	2.18	4.45	57.58	1.24	47.86	-3.09	3.32	6.41
50	0.172	-0.81	1.70	2.51	47.83	0.69	40.24	-1.58	1.95	3.54

returns for these assets have been greater than the corresponding values for long-term government bonds. For periods exceeding about 20 years, for Small Cap Stocks, and 25 years, for S&P 500 Stocks, the minimum real returns on the stocks have exceeded the maximum real returns on long-term government bonds.

MID-TERM GOVERNMENT BONDS

Over the entire period 1926 through 1997, compound annual real (inflation-adjusted) mid-term government bond returns were about 2.1 percent. Nominal mid-term government bond returns were positive in over 90 percent of the years. Nominal annual returns ranged from 29.10 percent in 1982 to -5.14 percent in 1994. Real mid-term government bond returns were positive in slightly less than 60 percent of the years. Real annual returns ranged from 24.29 percent in 1982 to -14.53 percent in 1946.

Over this entire period the highest nominal annualized compound returns were 16.98 percent for five-year periods, 13.13 percent for 10-year periods, and 9.85 percent for 20-year periods. The lowest nominal annualized returns were 0.96 percent, 1.25 percent, and 1.58 percent for 5, 10, and 20-year periods, respectively. The nominal minimum/maximum ranges for 5, 10, and 20-year periods were 16.02 percent, 11.88 percent, and 8.27 percent, respectively.

The highest real annualized compound returns were 13.24 percent for five-year periods, 8.87 percent for 10-year periods, and 4.40 percent for 20-year periods. The lowest real

Figure 15.12

MID-TERM GOVT BOND RISK-RETURN ANALYSIS (1926-1997)										
Nominal Returns (5.258% Compound, 5.562% Simple Over Entire Period)										
Annualized Returns						99% Probability Range				
Yrs in Planning Horizon	Average Compound ROR (%)	Actual Min ROR (%)	Actual Max ROR (%)	Actual Min-Max Range (%)	Pct Periods ROR>0 (%)	Stnd Dev (%)	Prob ROR<0 (%)	Min ROR (%)	Max ROR (%)	Min-Max Range (%)
1	5.406	-5.14	29.10	34.24	90.28	5.74	16.52	-8.09	20.55	28.64
2	5.320	-0.84	18.87	19.71	97.18	4.39	10.43	-5.21	16.82	22.03
3	5.315	0.53	16.50	15.97	100.00	3.98	8.38	-4.33	15.77	20.10
4	5.288	1.19	17.44	16.25	100.00	3.74	7.21	-3.82	15.11	18.93
5	5.303	0.96	16.98	16.02	100.00	3.64	6.63	-3.57	14.87	18.44
7	5.300	1.07	13.93	12.86	100.00	3.47	5.80	-3.21	14.44	17.66
10	5.228	1.25	13.13	11.87	100.00	3.31	5.25	-2.93	13.96	16.89
15	5.057	1.44	11.27	9.83	100.00	3.12	4.84	-2.66	13.29	15.95
20	4.808	1.58	9.85	8.26	100.00	2.78	3.79	-2.08	12.10	14.18
25	4.408	1.87	9.26	7.38	100.00	2.39	2.95	-1.55	10.67	12.22
30	4.558	2.21	8.52	6.31	100.00	2.17	1.58	-0.87	10.24	11.12
40	4.516	2.80	7.10	4.30	100.00	1.52	0.12	0.67	8.49	7.82
50	4.688	3.54	6.04	2.50	100.00	0.87	0.00	2.47	6.95	4.49
Real Returns (2.095% Compound, 2.329% Simple Over Entire Period)										
1	2.329	-14.53	24.29	38.81	59.72	7.03	37.99	-14.27	21.59	35.86
2	2.175	-11.05	14.90	25.95	67.61	5.53	35.53	-11.25	17.29	28.53
3	2.115	-7.77	14.15	21.91	64.29	4.94	34.08	-9.91	15.49	25.40
4	2.039	-6.46	13.09	19.55	65.22	4.49	33.02	-8.93	14.11	23.04
5	2.014	-5.11	13.24	18.36	67.65	4.27	32.29	-8.41	13.43	21.84
7	1.889	-5.53	9.31	14.84	68.18	3.90	31.85	-7.71	12.33	20.04
10	1.608	-4.06	8.87	12.93	66.67	3.35	31.92	-6.68	10.51	17.19
15	1.217	-2.72	7.08	9.80	67.24	2.58	32.13	-5.22	8.02	13.24
20	0.860	-2.13	4.40	6.53	69.81	1.71	30.94	-3.46	5.34	8.80
25	0.703	-1.15	3.50	4.65	66.67	1.28	29.25	-2.54	4.04	6.58
30	0.802	-1.12	3.03	4.14	62.79	1.18	24.92	-2.20	3.88	6.08
40	0.816	-1.17	2.55	3.72	69.70	1.11	23.22	-2.01	3.71	5.73
50	0.794	0.01	2.03	2.02	100.00	0.56	7.78	-0.64	2.24	2.88

annualized compound returns were -5.11 percent, -4.06 percent, and -2.13 percent for 5, 10, and 20-year periods, respectively. The real minimum/maximum ranges for 5, 10, and 20-year periods were 18.35 percent, 12.93 percent, and 6.53 percent, respectively. The probability of negative real returns ranges from just over 14 percent for shorter planning horizons to about 2.5 percent for longer planning horizons.

Stocks And Mid-Term Government Bonds Compared

Similar to long-term corporate bonds and long-term government bonds, mid-term government bonds have experienced negative real returns over some periods for all planning horizons up to 50 years. Small cap stocks and S&P 500 stocks, in contrast, have not experienced negative real returns for most periods exceeding 15 years and have never had negative

real returns over any period of 20 years or longer.

U.S. TREASURY BILLS AND INFLATION

The real inflation-adjusted U.S. Treasury bill return over the entire period from 1926 through 1997 was only 0.641 percent compounded annually. The nominal compound rate was 3.759 percent. The real riskless interest rate is often reported as being between 3 to 4 percent, which does not seem to be supported if we define the real riskless interest rate as the premium on T-bills over the rate of inflation.

The studies that have measured the real riskless interest rate at 3 to 4 percent have typically used high-grade long-term corporate bond yields to measure the riskless rates. Since long-term corporate bond yields incorporate both promised

Figure 15.13

	T-BILL RISK-RETURN ANALYSIS (1926-1997)									
	Nominal Returns (3.759% Compound, 3.808% Simple Over Entire Period)									
	Annualized Returns					99% Probability Range				
Yrs in Planning Horizon	Average Compound ROR (%)	Actual Min ROR (%)	Actual Max ROR (%)	Actual Min-Max Range (%)	Pct Periods ROR>0 (%)	Stnd Dev (%)	Prob ROR<0 (%)	Min ROR (%)	Max ROR (%)	Min-Max Range (%)
1	3.808	-0.02	14.71	14.73	98.61	3.24	11.53	-4.15	12.32	16.47
2	3.800	0.00	12.96	12.96	100.00	3.19	11.26	-4.06	12.20	16.25
3	3.792	0.00	12.15	12.14	100.00	3.15	11.03	-3.97	12.09	16.06
4	3.782	0.02	11.70	11.69	100.00	3.12	10.87	-3.91	12.00	15.91
5	3.772	0.07	11.12	11.05	100.00	3.09	10.78	-3.88	11.93	15.81
7	3.776	0.10	10.44	10.34	100.00	3.07	10.62	-3.83	11.89	15.72
10	3.788	0.15	9.17	9.03	100.00	3.04	10.33	-3.75	11.82	15.57
15	3.808	0.22	8.32	8.10	100.00	2.95	9.54	-3.52	11.60	15.13
20	3.767	0.42	7.72	7.30	100.00	2.75	8.28	-3.09	11.04	14.13
25	3.505	0.57	7.07	6.50	100.00	2.42	7.11	-2.55	9.88	12.43
30	3.677	0.94	6.77	5.83	100.00	2.21	4.60	-1.88	9.50	11.38
40	3.651	1.52	5.85	4.33	100.00	1.58	0.96	-0.36	7.80	8.16
50	3.704	2.33	4.99	2.66	100.00	0.91	0.00	1.37	6.08	4.71
	Real Returns (0.641% Compound, 0.727% Simple Over Entire Period)									
1	0.727	-15.07	12.55	27.62	65.28	4.17	43.95	-9.66	12.12	21.78
2	0.664	-11.51	12.13	23.64	63.38	3.82	43.87	-8.84	11.00	19.84
3	0.609	-8.41	11.07	19.48	62.86	3.54	43.85	-8.19	10.11	18.30
4	0.555	-6.81	9.40	16.21	60.87	3.31	43.96	-7.66	9.39	17.05
5	0.508	-6.08	8.42	14.50	61.76	3.16	44.20	-7.36	8.93	16.29
7	0.394	-6.72	7.45	14.17	59.09	2.91	45.19	-6.89	8.15	15.04
10	0.201	-5.08	4.65	9.73	57.14	2.49	47.29	-6.08	6.84	12.92
15	0.006	-3.71	3.07	6.78	65.52	2.02	50.29	-5.12	5.37	10.49
20	-0.144	-3.04	2.29	5.33	62.26	1.54	54.01	-4.06	3.91	7.97
25	-0.170	-2.31	1.36	3.68	56.25	1.21	55.79	-3.26	3.00	6.26
30	-0.050	-1.75	1.36	3.12	46.51	1.07	52.07	-2.76	2.73	5.49
40	-0.022	-1.21	1.36	2.57	42.42	0.92	51.15	-2.37	2.38	4.75
50	-0.154	-0.87	1.02	1.89	34.78	0.49	62.51	-1.40	1.11	2.51

future maturity premiums and default premiums, as well as promised future real interest rates, measures of the real riskless rate that use high-grade long-term corporate bond yields probably overstate the real rate of return.

Throughout the entire period from 1926 through 1997, U.S. Treasury bill returns often tracked inflation rates very closely. However, in certain sub-periods, such as the deflationary period between 1926 and 1932 where the annual rate of inflation was -0.4 percent while bills returned 2.7 percent annually, this close relationship has broken down.

Five, 10, and 20-year annual nominal compound returns from rolling over one-month bills ranged from highs of 11.12 percent in 1979 through 1983, 9.17 percent in 1977 through 1986, and 7.72 percent in 1967 through 1986, respectively, to lows of 0.07 percent in 1937 through 1941, 0.15 percent in

1933 through 1942, and 0.42 percent in 1931 through 1950, respectively. The corresponding nominal minimum/maximum ranges were 11.05 percent, 9.02 percent, and 7.30 percent.

The 5, 10, and 20-year annualized real compound returns ranged from 8.42 percent, 4.65 percent, and 2.29 percent on the high side to -6.08 percent, -5.08 percent, and -3.04 percent on the low side, respectively. The real minimum/maximum ranges for these periods were 14.50 percent, 9.73 percent, and 5.33 percent, respectively. The probability of experiencing negative real rates of return starts at an incredibly high 44 percent for one-year holding periods and increases consistently for longer holding periods to almost 62 percent for 50-year holding periods.

Figure 15.14

	INFLATION ANALYSIS (1926-1997)									
	Average Inflation Rate 3.098% Compound, 3.196% Simple Over Entire Period)									
	Annualized Inflation Rate					99% Probability Range				
Yrs in Planning Horizon	Average Compound Inflation Rate (%)	Actual Min IR (%)	Actual Max IR (%)	Actual Min-Max Range (%)	Pct Periods IR>0 (%)	Stnd Dev (%)	Prob IR<0 (%)	Min IR (%)	Max IR (%)	Min-Max Range (%)
1	3.196	-10.30	18.17	28.46	86.11	4.51	23.94	-8.43	14.82	23.25
2	3.222	-9.91	13.49	23.40	87.32	4.10	21.59	-7.34	13.78	21.12
3	3.249	-8.64	11.56	20.20	87.14	3.76	19.38	-6.44	12.94	19.37
4	3.278	-6.50	10.90	17.40	89.86	3.50	17.44	-5.73	12.29	18.02
5	3.307	-5.42	10.06	15.48	89.71	3.36	16.22	-5.34	11.95	17.28
7	3.415	-4.40	9.32	13.71	89.39	3.13	13.79	-4.66	11.49	16.14
10	3.603	-2.57	8.67	11.24	90.48	2.71	9.16	-3.37	10.58	13.95
15	3.805	-1.59	7.30	8.90	94.83	2.17	4.00	-1.79	9.40	11.20
20	3.907	0.07	6.36	6.29	100.00	1.69	1.04	-0.44	8.26	8.70
25	3.670	1.34	5.77	4.43	100.00	1.38	0.40	0.11	7.23	7.12
30	3.718	1.35	5.38	4.03	100.00	1.21	0.11	0.60	6.83	6.23
40	3.671	1.45	4.63	3.19	100.00	1.02	0.02	1.04	6.30	5.26
50	3.864	2.29	4.61	2.32	100.00	0.72	0.00	2.00	5.73	3.73

In 1973 through 1980 the real riskless rate of return averaged -0.7 percent per year. In the more recent period of 1981 through 1990 Treasury bill returns stayed historically high, with an average nominal compound annual rate of 5 percent (3.89% real compound rate). Since 1990, the real compound rate of return has averaged 1.81 percent. Since the depression era, real interest rates reached a monthly high of 13.9 percent (annualized) in March 1982.

Five, 10, and 20-year annualized inflation rates ranged from a high of 10.06 percent in 1977 through 1981, 8.67 percent in 1973 through 1982, and 6.36 percent in 1965 through 1984, respectively, to a low of -5.42 percent in 1928 through 1932, -2.57 percent in 1926 through 1935, and 0.07 percent in 1926 through 1945, respectively.

Although Treasury bill rates and inflation rates have been closely correlated over the period from 1926 to 1997, in some periods real rates of return have been substantially negative or substantially positive. Since nominal interest rates are never negative, real rates of return will always be significantly high in periods of deflation. The exceptionally high real rates of return experienced in the period from 1981 to 1990 may be attributable to exceptionally high premiums for the uncertainty of inflation after the unprecedented rise in inflation in the late 1970s.

CONCLUSIONS AND IMPLICATIONS

Figure 15.15 graphically shows real minimum/maximum ranges for periods ranging from five to 50 years.

Looking at real inflation adjusted returns, S&P stocks have historically performed better than what are called less risky long-term corporate and government bonds for planning horizons as short as five years. Although the minimum/maximum range for S&P stocks is larger than the minimum/maximum ranges for these "safer" investments, the worst five-year performance for S&P stocks (-9.34 percent real annual compound rate of return) over the period was still slightly better than the worst performance for long-term corporate and government bonds (-10.35 percent and -10.10 percent, respectively). At the same time, the average performance and the best performance for S&P stocks were vastly better than for either long-term corporate or government bonds. In fact, in terms of downside risk (worst five-year period) T-bills did only slightly better than S&P stocks (-6.08 percent for T-bills versus -9.34 percent for S&P stocks).

For 10-year periods or longer, S&P stocks have dominated corporate and government bonds and T-bills in real inflation-adjusted terms. In fact, in real inflation-adjusted terms small capitalization stocks have dominated S&P stocks and all other investment categories for 10-year investment horizons or longer.

The fact that the worst performance for a given horizon over the entire period for S&P stocks or small stocks was better than the worst performance for the other investment categories does not mean that S&P stocks or small stocks

Figure 15.15

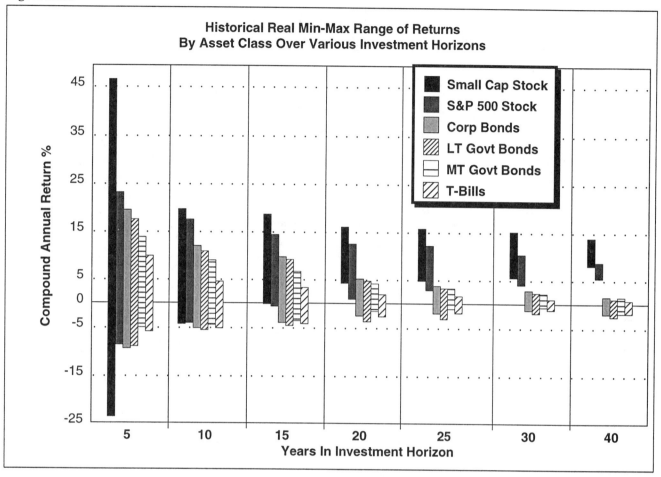

outperformed the other categories in each period. For example, in the 10-year period between 1969 and 1978 the real compound annual return on small stocks was -2.05 percent as compared with only -1.47 percent for long-term government bonds.

Although stocks are considerably riskier than bonds and T-bills (as measured by the 99 percent confidence range) for a one-year investment horizon, the relative risk increasingly diminishes for longer investment horizons. This concept is demonstrated in another way in Figure 15.16. Figure 15.16 shows relative performance probabilities among the various asset categories for one-year and 15-year investment periods. Reading across the table, the values are the probabilities (based on historical returns since 1926) that the asset type named in the left column will outperform (have higher average annual real inflation-adjusted compound returns than) the asset type named in the top row. For example, S&P 500 stocks have a 59.3 percent probability of outperforming long-term corporate bonds in any one-year period and an 85.4 percent probability over any 15-year horizon.

Figure 15.16 also includes the probability that the average

annual real compound return for each asset type will exceed 0 percent for any one-year or 15-year investment period. Stocks have a slightly higher probability of positive returns for any one-year period than bonds and T-bills (but, also a much greater downside potential if returns are negative). The probability of positive real returns on small cap stocks and S&P 500 stocks increases dramatically to almost 100 percent and to over 93 percent, respectively, for 15-year investment horizons. In contrast, the probability of positive returns for bonds remains virtually level at around 60 percent, regardless of the investment horizon. For T-bills the probability of real positive returns declines to less than 50 percent as the investment period increases to 15 years. For investment horizons exceeding 15-years these trends continue.

For any given investment period, bonds and T-bills may outperform stocks. But for longer investment planning horizons, the probability of this happening diminishes drastically. The basic conclusion is this: Stocks provide much higher expected returns and are actually less risky than bonds and T-bills when your investment horizon exceeds 10 to 15 years.

The fact that equities can be expected to be superior long

Figure 15.16

RELATIVE PERFORMANCE PROBABILITIES (%): AVERAGE ANNUAL REAL COMPOUND RETURNS FOR 1-YEAR AND 15-YEAR HORIZONS														
	Small Cap Stocks		S&P 500 Stocks		Long-Term Corp Bonds		Long-Term Govt Bonds		Mid-term Gov't Bonds		Treasury Bills		ZERO*	
Horizon:	1 Yr.	15 Yr.	1 Yr.	15 Yr.	1 Yr.	15 Yr.	1 Yr.	15 Yr.	1 Yr.	15 Yr.	1 Yr.	15 Yr.	1 Yr.	15 Yr.
Small Cap Stocks	NA	NA	56.7	81.0	57.5	92.9	58.1	94.7	58.0	94.1	60.0	97.1	61.5	99.0
S&P 500 Stocks	43.3	19.0	NA	NA	59.3	85.4	60.0	88.5	60.2	85.9	62.9	91.3	64.6	93.1
Long-Term Corp Bonds	42.5	7.1	40.7	14.6	NA	NA	55.5	88.7	56.0	52.2	59.7	69.4	60.4	64.9
Long-Term Govt Bonds	41.9	5.3	40.0	11.5	44.5	11.3	NA	NA	50.9	36.5	56.8	61.7	58.0	59.1
Mid-Term Govt Bonds	42.0	5.9	39.8	14.1	44.0	47.8	49.1	63.5	NA	NA	62.3	82.1	62.0	67.9
Treasury Bills	40.0	2.9	37.1	8.7	40.3	30.6	43.2	38.3	37.7	17.9	NA	NA	56.1	49.7
ZERO	38.5	1.0	35.4	6.9	39.6	35.1	42.0	40.9	38.0	32.1	43.9	50.3	NA	NA

*ZERO is 0% real inflation-adjusted return. The values in the ZERO row are the probabilities that the average annual real compound returns on the assets in the top row will be less than 0% for the given horizon. Similarly, the values in the ZERO columns are the probabilities that the average annual real compound returns on the assets in the left column will be greater than 0%.

KEY: ACROSS: Probabilities that average annual real compound returns on assets in left column will exceed the average annual real compound returns on assets in top row.
DOWN: Probabilities that average annual real compound returns on assets in top row will be less than the average annual real compound returns on assets in left column.

DATA: Probabilities are determined based on 1926-1997 historical series from Ibbotson Associates, Chicago, Illinois.

term investment instruments does not mean investors should invest exclusively in stocks if their investment horizon is long term. Sound investment management principles dictate that investors should virtually never invest in just one asset class at the exclusion of all others. What it does mean, all else being equal, is that the proportion of wealth invested in stocks relative to bonds, money market instruments, and other "lower risk" fixed income types of investments can be greater for longer investment horizons or without increasing the total risk of the portfolio over longer planning horizons.

The conclusion to be drawn from these analyses is that the actual risk - in the most important sense of downside performance - associated with what are considered the riskier investments (S&P stocks or small stocks) may be less than that associated with the "safer" investments (corporate and government bonds and T-bills) when the investment planning horizon is longer term. Investors looking to fund their Keoghs or IRAs or to otherwise invest for retirement or long-term accumulation objectives and who have at least a 10-year investment horizon will almost certainly be better off investing in stocks than in bonds or money market investments. These analyses further suggest that variable life insurance or variable deferred annuities invested in equity portfolios should be considered by many healthy people with longer-term accumulation and protection objectives. Although yearly returns will vary much more widely for stocks than for bonds or money-market instruments, the up years should more than offset the down years. The investor should expect superior overall returns with very little risk that the stock investment will under perform a longer-term bond investment.

Investing for shorter-term objectives, such as education funding for a child who will attend college in the next five years, bonds or money market instruments present much less risk than stocks that the funding will fail to meet desired goals. Also all long-term investment goals ultimately become short-term goals as the target date approaches. Investors who invested in stocks for their long-term goals but who are unwilling to bear the additional risk of stock investments for short-term goals should typically begin to shift assets from stocks to bonds and money market instruments within five years of their target. By carefully choosing when they shift the investments they can essentially "lock in" the almost certainly higher returns earned on stocks over the major part of the accumulation period and reduce the risk of major losses in the years the funds are needed.

FOOTNOTE REFERENCES

1.   Data is derived from *Stocks, Bonds, Bills, and Inflation*, an annual yearbook published by Ibbotson Associates, 225 North Michigan Avenue, Suite 700, Chicago, Illinois 60601-7676.

Chapter 16

RISK TOLERANCE AND RISK AVERSION*

Risk can mean quite different things to different people. A 1984 survey conducted by Louis Harris and Associates for The Insurance Information Institute found that of the people surveyed, "risk" means:

"danger" .... to 84%
"possible loss" .... to 77%
"uncertainty" .... to 58%
"challenge" .... to 50%
"opportunity" .... to 41%
"thrill" .... to 23%

These findings show that people vary in how favorably or unfavorably they view risk. Some approach risk in positive terms (a challenge or an opportunity) while others look at risk in negative terms (danger or possible loss). The most neutral connotation carried by the word "risk" is uncertainty.

To economists, "risk" typically involves probabilities that actual future returns will be below expected returns. It is generally accepted (and typically expected in the long run) that the greater the risk, the greater the return one can expect from an investment. This relationship is frequently illustrated in the form of a "risk-return trade-off" graph similar to the one shown in Figure 16.1. This graph shows that as risk goes up, so does expected reward. Different classes of investment products can be identified in terms of their risk-return potentials and can be plotted on this type of graph at given risk-return junctures.

Propensity for accepting risk regarding investments can be considered on a continuum. Clients who are highly tolerant of risk would place on one end ("risk-tolerant" or "risk-taking") and those who avoid risks at almost all costs would fall on the other ("risk-aversive" or "risk-avoider"). Those in the middle are sometimes called "risk-indifferent" or "risk-neutral."

Risk Tolerant   Risk Indifferent   Risk Adversive

WHY/WHEN IS THIS INFORMATION NEEDED?

The financial planner has an obligation to assist his clients in identifying investments that are consistent with their risk-return expectations.

Figure 16.1

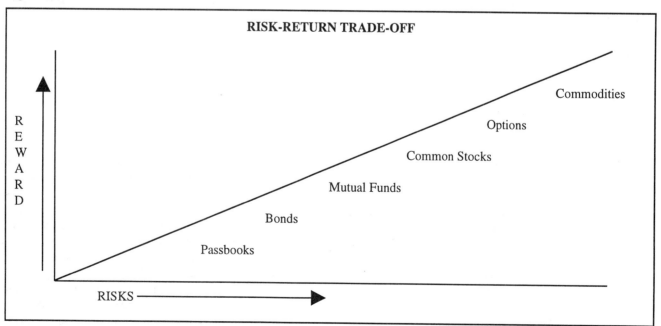

RISK-RETURN TRADE-OFF

Commodities

Options

Common Stocks

Mutual Funds

Bonds

Passbooks

REWARD

RISKS ———————→

* This chapter was written especially for this publication by psychologists Dr. Glen Shelbecker and Dr. Michael Roszkowski.

To a significant extent, client satisfaction (or, if greatly dissatisfied, client propensity for malpractice litigation) depends on the financial planner's ability to guide the client toward "satisfactory returns" (i.e., a rate of investment return/growth sufficiently high to satisfy expectations while keeping perceived risk within the client's risk-taking tolerance). Fortunately for planners, clients who know their own inclinations toward taking risks are likely to help a planner match their investment choices with their risk tolerance. Unfortunately for planners, few clients understand their own mental machinery and many have irrational fears and idiosyncrasies that keep them from making sound choices in many investment situations.

Clients' risk-return expectations are not fixed. A financial planner needs to recognize that both changing "personal" and "outside" factors (as well as objective information) about a given investment tend to influence a client's risk tolerance position at any given time. This means that an accurate assessment of a clients' risk-return expectations is needed not only when the financial plan is being prepared but also with (a) major changes in the economy, (b) as a result of increases or reductions in family obligations, or (c) whenever circumstances cause changes in their risk-return expectations.

WHAT DO WE KNOW ABOUT JUDGING RISK-TAKING PROPENSITY AND WHAT NEW INFORMATION IS NEEDED?

There are many resources available to aid financial planners in their work. But most of these resources tend to focus more on investment products than on the client. The financial planner typically must depend on clients' oral or written statements concerning their views about risk and return expectations, with minimal provisions for comparing a given client's views with those of other investors or even for detecting how stable the client's views have been over time. It is often not known whether a client's views about the risks and returns of investment products are consistent with views commonly held by financial planners.

Risk-taking is a subject that has been of interest to psychologists and economists for quite some time. The psychological literature and the business research literature contain many different measures of risk as well as theories concerning the conditions under which people are more or less risk-tolerant.

Unfortunately, only a small portion of this information is directly related to how a planner can better match product to risk-taking propensity, better meet the needs of clients, and avoid litigation. Most other information is, at best, of only marginal value. When using information about risk tolerance,

financial planners need to consider the extent to which the various published risk measures and findings are relevant to risk-taking with regard to investments.

PROBLEMS IN MEASURING CLIENTS' RISK TOLERANCE

Assessing a client's risk propensity is not an easy task for a number of reasons, including these five:

(1) There are few, if any, "standardized" instruments designed for application in a financial planning context. Most existing devices appear to have been created by various financial planning concerns for their local "in-house" use or are adaptations of techniques that were meant for use in scientific studies of risk-taking. No one measure has yet emerged as the standard by which the others can be evaluated.

(2) Although some psychologists view risk-taking as a general personal attribute, most psychologists consider risk propensity to be a complex set of attitudes that are situation-specific. Therefore, one cannot safely label a client as a "risk-taker" or a "risk-averter" by simply observing his behavior in a single situation or context.

(3) The degree of risk-taking or risk-aversion ascribed to an individual is very dependent on the type of measure used. For example, one recent study found that, in the same group of managers, the percentage of individuals who could be labeled "risk-takers" ranged from 0% to 94% depending on the technique employed.

(4) Similarly, a client's risk tolerance is not fixed. It may change from time to time depending, for example, on family responsibilities, job security, and other pertinent conditions.

(5) A measure of "risk tolerance," like all measurement procedures and devices, needs to meet acceptable standards of reliability and validity, particularly when the information is being used to draw inferences for individuals rather than large groups of people. Simply put, a properly constructed risk tolerance test must measure a characteristic consistently (reliability). Furthermore, evidence must be obtained to document that the measuring device does, in fact, measure what it purports to measure (validity). Few, if any, of the popular methods that financial planners use to evaluate their clients' "risk tolerance" have been subjected to the rigorous procedures necessary to demonstrate reliability and validity according to guidelines pre-

sented in the *Standards for Educational and Psychological Testing*. Thus, techniques being used by financial planners may not be providing dependable and accurate information.

CURRENT APPROACHES TO THE MEASUREMENT OF RISK TOLERANCE

A wide range of approaches has ·been devised for the measurement of risk tolerance—most of them for scientific research purposes. Many of these experimental procedures are not directly applicable to a financial planning setting without substantial modifications, but they illustrate the basis through which much of the risk tolerance findings have been obtained. Various characteristics can be used to classify currently available approaches to the measurement of risk tolerance including (a) the context of the risk-taking, and (b) the format used to gauge the client's risk-taking propensity.

Some psychologists believe that there are four major contexts or categories of situations in which decisions are made involving risk. These are:

(1) Monetary Risk: Examples include situations involving gambling, investments, and job security.

(2) Physical Risk: Situations involving risk of bodily harm are examples of this type of risk.

(3) Social Risk: Potential loss of esteem in the eyes of another typifies this risk category.

(4) Ethical Risk: The compromise of one's standards or religious beliefs or a conflict of interest are common examples of this type of risk.

Four broad classifications of the methods used to assess how a person reacts to risk are discussed below. Examples of some more specific techniques are provided under each classification.

I. SELF-REPORTED PREFERENCES FOR SELECTED INVESTMENT PRODUCTS—This is the most common approach that financial planners use to measure risk tolerance. Questionnaires found in most fact-finders typically address preferences for selected investment products. They generally ask the respondent either to rank the products in terms of their preferences or to indicate how they prefer to distribute their total funds among the various options of investment presented. In both measurement approaches, the products all have associated "risk-return" probabilities, which are either assumed to be known by the client or (preferably) are specified as part of the measurement procedures.

An example of one such test is shown in Figure 16.2. A variation of the same test, as shown in Figure 16.3, groups the investments into broader classes such as high risk, moderate risk, and low risk.

Information regarding risk tolerance is sometimes inferred from an examination of the client's objectives. For example, the individual may be asked to:

Rank the following six financial objectives in terms of their importance to you. A rank of 1 means that this

Figure 16.2

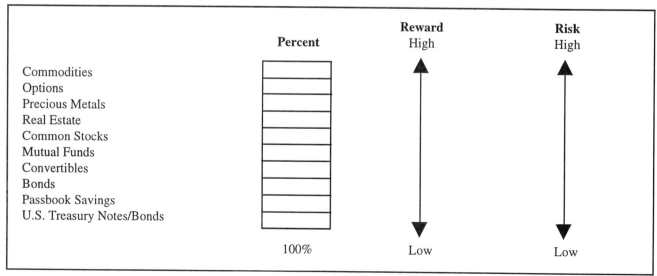

Figure 16.3

High Risk Vehicles (Commodities, Options, Real Estate, Precious Metals, Collectibles)	_____%
Moderate Risk Vehicles (Mutual Funds, Variable Annuities, Blue-chip Stocks, Municipal Bonds)	_____%
Low Risk Vehicles (Money Market Funds, Tax Deferred Fixed Annuities, Certificates of Deposit, U.S. Government Bonds, Life Insurance)	_____%

Total: 100%

objective is the *most* important one, and a rank of 6 means that it is the *least* important one.

____ Liquidity

____ Safety of Principal

____ Appreciation

____ Protection from Inflation

____ Current Income

____ Tax Reduction

A primary concern with safety of principal is considered characteristic of the risk-averse individual. A concern for inflation protection and the desire to thwart the destruction of future purchasing power by inflation is generally viewed as more typical of a risk-tolerant investor.

There are both advantages and disadvantages to this first type of methodology. The advantages are that these kinds of measurement tools are relatively easy to construct, they are simple, and the method is directly related to the subjects the financial planner must consider. But these tools have often been created by persons who do not appreciate or who are unaware of the problems and nuances inherent in measuring attitudes. Most only have what is called "face validity." In other words the test seems to measure what it claims to measure but often, because of many of the factors that will be

discussed below, does not in fact represent an accurate gauge of the client's risk-taking propensity.

II. PREFERENCES FOR PROBABILITIES/PAYOFFS IN VARIOUS SIMULATIONS—The "Choice Dilemmas" procedure is an example of the "probabilities/payoffs testing approach." This procedure typically involves the presentation of several different situations or cases to the client. Each situation allows for two alternative courses of action, one "risky" and the other "safe." The risky course of action has larger potential payoffs. Odds are given for the chance of success for the risky course of action, e.g., 1 in 10, 3 in 10, 5 in 10, 7 in 10, etc. The client's task is to pick the odds that would make the more risky course of action sufficiently attractive to be chosen over the safe course of action.

For example, a respondent might be given this hypothetical situation and asked which choice he would pick:

A single parent with two children (one in high school, one in college) has recently inherited $10,000 that can be invested. The nature of other family investments indicates that some degree of risk seems reasonable. The person is debating between investing in a blue-chip stock or in a newly founded corporation (Company C) that is more risky. If Company C's new high-tech product is successful, it could double in value. What is the lowest probability for the stock doubling over a three-year period that would justify investing these funds in Company C's stock?

_____ 1 in 10

_____ 3 in 10

_____ 5 in 10

_____ 7 in 10

_____ 9 in 10

_____ none

A number of dilemmas of this sort are presented. After the respondent has selected probabilities for each task, a total score is computed to indicate the person's overall tolerance for risk across the hypothetical situations. The situations usually involve a broad range of dilemmas so that the respondents' scores will reveal how they say they would handle different risky situations.

The advantages of this type of testing tool are that it provides standardized situations and that most people feel it is "fun" to take. But the concept has a major disadvantage. All of the situations are hypothetical. They do not produce the personal interest and the "emotional arousal" that takes place in real life risk decisions.

III. CHOICES MADE INVOLVING RISK IN NATU-RALLY-OCCURRING LIFE SITUATIONS—Scales of this type measure risk tolerance by asking the person to indicate how he has handled actual "real life" activities generally considered to involve risk-taking. Items in these inventories address activities in various sports, work, interpersonal situations, and financial matters that involve varying degrees of risk. For example, jobs such as air traffic controller or a race car driver would be rated as "risky."

A biographical inventory about financial "lifestyle" might include information about such matters as:

(1) ratio of low-risk to high-risk investment holdings,

(2) extent of leveraged investments in real estate,

(3) ratio of personal debt to personal assets,

(4) number of voluntary job changes relative to number of years of work experience (this is particularly important if the client terminated one job before securing new employment),

(5) ratio of life insurance to annual salary,

(6) extent of recreational gambling,

(7) tendency to write "floating" checks,

(8) frequency of buying stocks short or long,

(9) tendency to use conventional methods (e.g., bank loans) versus unconventional methods (e.g., use of credit card borrowing privileges) for obtaining start-up money for business ventures, etc.

The advantage of this category of test is that all the questions are "real world" and personal to the client himself. The major weakness is that the client may not be able to provide accurate information.

IV. SELF-REPORTS OF ATTITUDES TOWARD RISK—Self-ratings of attitudes toward risk can range from one or two very global questions to questionnaires consisting of many items.

Global questions are frequently of this type:

"Are you a risk-taker or are you a risk-avoider?"

The individual is required to select one of these two options (risk-taker, or risk-avoider) or is asked to rate himself on a scale with opposite points labeled risk-taker and risk-avoider.

More elaborate questionnaires include a series of items that are designed to identify conditions under which people will take greater or lesser risks. Questions tapping the same issue in slightly different language may be used to reduce the possibility that the specific phrasing of any one question influenced the client to answer it in a specific way. The answers from a series of questions are then added together to arrive at a "sum score." Asking a series of questions rather than just one question tends to reduce the measurement error. Therefore, a score derived from the summation of a set of similar questions generally produces more accurate information than the answer to any one question within that set. Other things being equal, the more items that are used to measure a psychological characteristic, the more precise and reliable the result.

The advantage of this method is that it is very easy to administer and appears to give a very realistic and personal appraisal. Its disadvantage is that often people tend to consider and rate themselves as greater risk-takers than they are in reality.

HOW CLIENTS MAKE DECISIONS INVOLVING UNCERTAIN OUTCOMES

Various models have been constructed to explain how a "rational" client would make a decision regarding an uncertainty. The basic assumption underlying these models is that a person tries to make a choice that appears to have the greatest value ("utility"). For instance, offered two choices a rational person should select the choice that has the greatest monetary (utility) value.

How does this hypothetical rational client calculate the utility of a given choice (gamble)? According to the so called "utility theory," only simple multiplication and subtraction skills are needed once the client is given the appropriate probability of success.

To compute the net utility of a gamble is a three step process:

Step 1:	To compute the value of a win:	
	A. State the Probability of Win	_____
	B. State the Monetary Reward	$_____
	C. Multiply A X B for Utility	$_____
Step 2:	To compute the value of a loss:	
	A. State the Probability of a Loss on the Gamble	_____
	B. State the Amount of the Potential Loss	$_____
	C. Multiply A X B for Utility	$_____
Step 3:	To compute the overall utility of the gamble:	
	A. State the Utility of a Win (STEP 1 C)	$_____
	B. State the Utility of a Loss (Step 2 C)	$_____
	C. Subtract B from A	$_____

At this stage, faced with a choice, the investor should compare the utility of one gamble with the utility of the second. If a decision were made on this basis (alone), the client would choose (put his money on) the gamble with the highest positive utility.

An example may be helpful: Suppose you were offered two bets (choices). Which of these two should you choose (based solely on the utility theory)?

Bet 1: A 25% chance (probability) of winning $1,000 and a 75% chance of losing $50.
Bet 2: An 80% chance of winning $3,000 and a 20% chance of losing $200.

Which bet, before you do the math, looks (feels) better?

The net utility of Bet 1 is:

WIN:	.25 (probability)	X	$1,000 (reward)	= $250.00	(utility)
Loss:	.75 (probability)	X	50 (loss)	= $ 37.50	(utility)
Net:				$212.50	

The net utility of Bet 2 is:

WIN:	.80 (probability)	X	$3,000 (reward)	= $2,400	(utility)
Loss:	.20 (probability)	X	200 (loss)	= $ 40	(utility)
Net:				$2,360	

Measuring risk in this manner, it is clear that Wager 2 has a far higher overall utility ($2,360) than Wager 1 ($212.50) so the rational investor should take Wager 2.

Utility-based predictions of behavior are often incorrect, however, for a number of reasons. First, in many financial planning decisions, neither the planner nor the client knows what the true probability is. Second, most clients don't understand the (relatively simple) mathematics underlying utility theory. Third, many clients don't behave as they "should"; in other words, their thinking becomes clouded by certain distortions which are discussed below.

Despite these drawbacks, utility theory can be used by the financial planner to help peg a client's risk tolerance. For instance, suppose you offered a client a bet on the toss of a coin. The probability of either heads or tails on any given flip is 50 percent. A coin is just as likely to land "heads" as it is "tails." Here's the bet:

Bet 1: "Heads" or "tails" you win $1,000.
Bet 2: "Heads" you win $2,000. "Tails you win $0.

Which bet would you take? Which bet do you think most of your clients would take? Before you do the math, which bet do you feel has the greater utility?

After you've done the math, you find:

Bet 1:	1.0 (probability)	X	$1,000 (reward)	=	$1,000 (utility)
Bet 2:	.50 (probability)	X	$2,000 (reward)	=	$1,000 (utility)

A risk-averse client will probably select the "sure thing" offered by Bet 1.

A risk-seeking client will probably select the "Long-Shot Big Killing" offered by Bet 2.

A risk-neutral (risk-indifferent) client would just as readily select Bet 2 as Bet 1.

FRAMING THE ISSUE

Presentation format will significantly influence the choice a client makes. The "framing" of the issue (the way questions are asked and the sequence in which they occur), especially with respect to probabilities, can significantly affect the results of a risk-taking propensity test. In an article in the Fall 1987 issue of the Journal of Certified Financial Planners, the following fictitious lottery is discussed:

How would you decide if given the choice between:

Choice 1: A certain win of $30, or

Choice 2: An 80% chance of winning $45 (if you lose you win $0).

What percentage of people do you think will select the certain win versus the 20 percent chance of losing all?

About 78 percent go for the sure win and only 22 percent take choice 2. How does that compare with (a) what you personally would have decided and (b) the percentage of your own clients who you think would have selected each choice?

Studies have shown that most people lean toward the "risk-averse" end of the spectrum when faced with a choice between a sure gain and an uncertain outcome, even if the mathematical value of the uncertain outcome is much higher. (This "utility of the sure thing" principle was discussed above). It also may show that most people don't know how to compute the higher value outcome. How would you decide if given the choice between:

Choice 1: A 25% chance of winning $30 (if you lose you win $0), or

Choice 2: A 20% chance of winning $45 (if you lose you win $0).

In one study, 42 percent selected the first choice and 58 percent selected the second choice. How does that compare (a) with your choice and (b) with the percentage of your clients who you think would have selected each choice?

In this set of choices neither option is a sure gain. When faced with a decision in which neither choice is a sure gain, more people will pick the higher value. (However, the split between choice 1 and choice 2 is rather close considering that choice 2 is a better value.)

What happens when both choices involve the possibility of a loss instead of a gain? For example, suppose the two choices are:

(1) a certain loss of $3,000, or

(2) an 80 percent chance of losing $4,000 and a 20 percent chance of losing nothing.

It has been found that under these circumstances most people will take choice (2), despite its riskier nature. Apparently, it is more important to most clients to avoid loss than to avoid risk. (Note: the utility value of Choice 1 is a $3000 loss, whereas for Choice 2 the utility value is a loss of $3200.)

One conclusion a planner should derive from this and other studies is that multiple ways of framing a question should be used to assess a client's risk-taking propensities.

Perhaps a more important point to be derived is that the way real life choices are framed by a planner to the client will drastically affect the decision the client will make. Knowing how clients tend to react to choices should change the way you state them.

For example, your client purchased a mutual fund from you one month ago and paid $10 a share. The fund is now selling for $8 a share. When he asks you what to do, you tell him he must decide to (a) realize the loss or (b) continue to hold. Given that statement, most clients will choose to hold the fund and hope to attain an expected gain in the future or just to break even. They are, of course, unwittingly assuming more risk since the per share price is equally likely to go up or down. But most people, once they have committed time, money, and effort into a particular course of action tend to continue to support it even if they believe the expected return may be unfavorable. They are reluctant to cut their losses.

One reason investors may be reluctant to accept and realize losses is that they believe the very act of doing so will prove that their first judgment was wrong. Would the client react differently if you suggested that "a transfer of assets" might help "reduce the impact of past losses?" Framing the issue properly and helping a client to remove the mental obstacles to proper decision making is an essential part of the professionalism of financial planning.

ILLUSTRATIVE MAJOR FINDINGS ABOUT RISK

Listed below are some other major findings about risk, including personal attributes and conditions that appear to influence one's risk tolerance in various contexts. This research information has come from various kinds of situations and has been collected through a wide range of measurement techniques.

Respected authorities disagree as to whether risk tolerance constitutes a general, durable personality attribute or whether it is nonstatic, multifaceted, and essentially situation-specific. Therefore, one should exercise caution in applying these findings to risk tolerance with regard to investments, especially when making judgments about individual clients. However, this research information can be quite valuable in alerting financial planners to personal attributes and circumstances that may contribute to the subjective aspects of their clients' risk propensities. These findings may be divided into three broad categories: (1) Characteristics of risk-tolerant and risk-averse persons; (2) Mental processing of risk information; and (3) Other psychological influences on behavior in risky situations.

I. Characteristics of Risk-Tolerant and Risk-Averse Persons

1. In general, females tend to be more risk-aversive than males in financial matters as well as other spheres of life.

2. Risk-aversiveness in investment (as well as in general) contexts seems to increase with age.

3. Other things being equal, the first-born child in a family is more likely to be risk-aversive than younger siblings.

4. Unmarried individuals are more prone to take risks than married individuals.

5. In the generations who are nearing or at retirement, those who work(ed) in the "public sector" (e.g. for government agencies or in school systems) are frequently more risk-aversive than people of the same generation who are (were) employed in the private sector. With younger people, this generalization is less likely to be true.

6. Other things being equal, people who work on commissions are typically more risk-tolerant than those who work on a straight salary.

7. Risk-aversiveness appears to decrease with increasing wealth and/or income. Compared to other upper income persons, millionaires have a disproportionate number of risk-takers in their ranks. (Does this mean more millionaires have become risk-takers or did they become millionaires because they are risk-takers?)

8. Individuals who are successful in their work tend to take more risks.

9. Business executives tend to be more risk-tolerant with business investments than with investments of their own personal funds.

10. Risk-taking is valued in our society. People tend to admire those who make a more risky choice in a given situation than they themselves have made.

11. A personality type called the "thrill seeker" or the "sensation seeker" has been identified by some psychologists. These individuals seem to engage in certain activities for the thrill of the risk itself. Questions have been raised about the extent to which these people may also seek risks when making investment decisions. Financial planners can identify the thrill seeker by the following characteristics:

    a. more likely to be male than female,

    b. outgoing (extroverted),

    c. spontaneous (impulsive),

    d. reaches decisions very quickly,

    e. seeks new experiences (e.g., volunteers for scientific experiments),

    f. particularly strong sex drive (likely to have multiple partners),

    g. takes part in risky sports (mountain climbing, sky diving, scuba diving),

    h. intensely dislikes "boring" people (is likely to associate with "unusual" people),

    i. likes to gamble (particularly blackjack),

    j. enjoys spicy, sour, and crunchy foods,

    k. more likely to use "recreational drugs," and experiment with a wide variety of drugs rather than just one.

    The percentage of "thrill seekers" using investing as a means of experiencing excitement is not known. The number may be relatively small where sizable sums of money relative to the person's income and assets are involved. Nevertheless, a financial planner who encounters this type of person must be extremely cautious and particularly careful to document due diligence. This type of person is likely to make brash decisions without consideration for the consequences. If the investment fails, such a person may pursue litigation against the planner if for no other reason than the thrill of the experience (especially if he has never sued anyone before).

12. Are there certain people who are consistently risk-tolerant or risk-aversive across a wide range of activities, including investment decisions? It was indicated earlier that psychologists disagree on this matter. But there is some suggestion that certain people are more consistent than others.

    The first type are the "thrill-seekers" discussed above. They are more likely to be consistently high in risk-taking in multiple contexts.

    "Defensive-Anxious" individuals are another category of personality that tends to be consistent. But this type of person can be either consistently a risk-avoider or a consistent risk-taker. To this type of individual, satisfaction or dissatisfaction with a particular decision may not depend so much on the financial outcome of the transaction as on whether he feels the choice was consistent with an overall risk strategy. Again, financial planners must take extra care to perform and document due diligence in connection with this type of client. Consistency in either risk-taking or risk-avoidance in all aspects of a client's life should be a "red flag" to the planner.

13. There are individual differences in people's attitudes toward risk that go beyond their demographic characteristics. Thus, two people with approximately the same wealth and circumstances can differ substantially in their tolerance for risk.

II. Mental Processing of Risk Information

1. All investors, no matter where they fall on the risk-tolerant—risk-indifferent—risk-adverse continuum, generally desire to realize a return on the investments they make. However, these three types of investors may differ significantly as one moves from relatively "safe" investments to relatively "risky" investments. Findings have shown that:

   Risk-Tolerant investors will settle for a disproportionately *smaller* increase in expected returns with each increase in the risk they are willing to assume.

   Risk-indifferent investors require only a *proportional* increase in expected return with each increase in the risk they assume.

   Risk-Aversive investors demand a disproportionately *larger* expected return with each increase in the risk they will undertake.

This pattern of a demand for a disproportionately higher return by more risk-aversive clients can be illustrated by the graph in Figure 16.4.

2. People frequently are not aware of their true tolerance for risk.

3. As compared with risk-takers, risk-avoiders tend to want more information, need to be more in control, and should therefore be given more attention by the financial planner before as well as after making decisions. Because of their need for control, this type of person will probably prefer direct ownership over an indirect form such as a limited partnership.

4. In general, people tend to be risk-averse. In a Fortune Magazine article (Investor's Guide, 1988, page 63) the author reports on a pair of questions used by psychologists who asked subjects to choose between different pairs of risks and rewards. In one test the subjects were asked,

   "If faced with the prospect of two possible gains, which one would you choose?"

   (1) a 100% chance to win $3,000, or

   (2) an 80% chance to win $4,000.

   Most people choose the guaranteed $3,000. But the second choice, according to probability theory, has a higher value. (Multiply the chance of winning, 80 percent by the amount that could be won, $4,000, to arrive at $3,200). In the long run, therefore, an investor would be better off if the second choice had been taken.

Figure 16.4

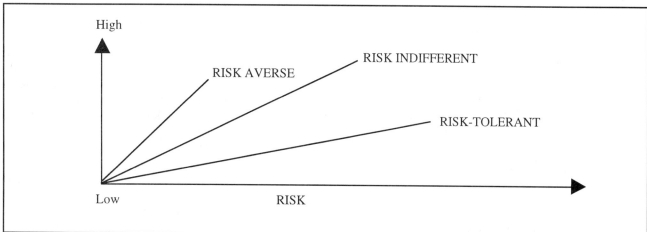

Why then, do most people pick the first (lower value) choice? Because most investors give greater preference to certainty and tend to avoid risk whenever and to whatever extent possible. Some have called this the "sure thing" principle.

5. Typically a person labels himself as more of a risk-taker than he really is as revealed by his actions in betting game simulations and in real-life activities.

6. The way questions are asked (how they are presented, and in what sequence they occur) can greatly influence the manner in which people describe their attitudes about risk. This is the "framing concept" discussed previously.

7. A loss of a certain amount—e.g., $1,000—causes more dissatisfaction than a gain of a comparable amount produces satisfaction. This can be illustrated in another question from the Fortune Magazine article mentioned above.

Fear of loss is a concept little understood by most planners. Would you take this bet?

(1) Heads you win $1,500

(2) Tails you lose $1,000.

Note that although the potential payoff is 1.5 times the possible loss, most clients will refuse to take that bet. The point is that loss aversion is a surprisingly powerful emotion that in many cases may keep clients from taking good investment risks. This may, in fact, explain why certain stocks are substantially undervalued in the marketplace (and also why contrarians who carefully purchase "out of favor" stocks can reap such high rewards).

Why do most investors steer clear of troubled companies when the prices of those companies drop into what is clearly the "bargain basement" level? Again, the answer is probably the terror of potential loss (perhaps as much for the loss of face and loss of personal esteem as for the financial consequences) in the case of those who have low "social risk" tolerances.

8. People greatly undervalue the reduction in the probability of a hazard relative to its complete elimination. In other words, most investors would place more value on eliminating the possibility of loss (100 percent sure of not suffering a loss) than on reducing the odds of loss in return for a potential gain.

9. A "sure thing" is overweighted in comparison with events of moderate or high probability.

10. Decisions reached by group consensus are typically more extreme and usually more risky in nature than decisions made individually by most members of the same group. Psychologists call this the "Risky Shift" phenomenon. This may tell the financial planner something about family decision-making dynamics.

11. Risk tolerance is greater if the outcome of the decision will occur later rather than sooner. That is, the tendency to take risks increases if the consequences of the decision are delayed.

12. There is a tendency to believe, in retrospect, that past events were more predictable than they really were. This is particularly true when the client suffers a loss. ("I should have known" or "My planner should have known.")

13. Predictions about an individual's risk tolerance for a given financial matter can better be based on his risk tolerance for other financial matters rather than on his risk tolerance for life events more generally.

14. People tend to overestimate the likelihood of improbable events occurring, exaggerate remote possibilities, underestimate the likelihood of very probable events occurring, and really don't understand probability in general.

For instance, consider another question from the Fortune Magazine interview cited above:

Choose one:

(1) a 2 percent chance to win $3,000

(2) a 1 percent chance to win $6,000

Which would you take? Most people would take the second choice, a 2 to 1 favorite. Yet the utilities are not two to one. The value of both choices are exactly the same! The monetary value for both choices is $60. (.02 times $3,000 is the same as .01 time $6,000). Why aren't investors rational thinkers? Why do they abandon, in this case, simple mathematics? The reason appears to be, the interviewed psychologists tell us, that "the less likely the long-term payoff, the more our mental calculations break down and overestimate its probability. That, they say, is why people go on buying lottery tickets." (Could it be that "wishful thinking" is more powerful than logic?)

This "Long Shot Big Kill" syndrome, of course, will transfer into market decisions. Investors will tend to both over and undervalue stocks. For example, investors, upon hearing news that a drug company is about to release an exciting new breakthrough, will then pay prices for the stock that are absurd. They aren't betting that the new drug will be successful; rather, they're betting on the remote possibility that it will be a blockbuster and will not encounter competition.

III. Other Psychological Influences on Risk Behavior

1. There is a concept known as "Fear of Regret." It may also be called the "Hollywood Push-Pull" Principle. According to this theory, most investors will push away from an "ugly investment," one such as an already depressed company. But the same investors will pull toward a "pretty investment," one which they feel will help them be admired if they purchase it. They feel that if you purchased the type of investment which isn't currently in favor and it drops in price, others will tend to think that the investment (and perhaps the investor) was a loser all along. But if they purchased a "star" stock, such as IBM, that is generally held in great esteem, and if that drops in price, others would consider it (and the investor) blameless since the drop could be considered an unpredictable "Act of God."

    Some investors (and also investment managers?) may avoid "better bet" stocks of the less admired companies and settle for mediocre performance from investments with "Hollywood Star" reputations mainly to avoid the fear of regret.

    Once the client has purchased the stock, the fear of regret can metamorphose into a "Pride-Shame" relationship. According to this concept, an investor will tend to overvalue stocks he owns (he has a certain pride and also defensiveness with respect to that stock) and undervalue stocks which he doesn't own (stocks the investor perceives are not admired by others and therefore that he would be ashamed to own). This helps to explain why investors gravitate toward stocks making new highs rather than to those making new lows. (Are professional stock analysts prey to the desire to have their names linked with "Hollywood Stars" and therefore tend to tout them?)

    Planners considering the impact of the "Fear of Regret," "Hollywood Push-Pull," and the "Pride-Shame" theories should consider the self-fulfilling prophesy potential. Because so many investors tend to follow these principles, the price recovery of a sound but out of favor company or industry may be slow.

2. "Heuristics," the sometimes necessary mental shortcuts we take when processing information, can result in costly errors of judgment for investors. A common example of a heuristic is the tendency clients have to conclude that two things are the same if they have some similar characteristic. For this reason, they often trust a financial planner merely because he "dresses for success" or looks like someone else who the client knows is honest. Clients tend to conclude that if a money manager (or an investment) has done well recently, that good recent performance means that the money manager is talented (or that the stock is sound and likely to continue to climb in value and pay dividends in the future). The same principle works against out of favor companies or industries. A mental shortcut (laziness?) that tells us the oil industry is down and out and therefore will stay that way forever fails to recognize that no trends are forever.

3. "Golden Blinders" is another related disease that infects many investors; they tend to forget distant lessons and exaggerate what is recent and easily recallable. The bloodbath that fixed-income recipients took during the late '70s and early '80s because of double digit inflation has long been forgotten or dismissed but this morning's dire headlines are stamped in big bold letters indelibly in our minds. Investors lose perspective and tend to overemphasize the impact of current events.

4. "Contagious Enthusiasm" is often the flimsy evidence of value that triggers "buy" or "sell" orders. Making a rational decision requires that the source of an investor's information be both accurate and objective. Yet studies show that many investors (including a shocking number of institutional professional investors) base buying and selling decisions on such sources as investment letters, word of mouth recommendations, or "what's hot on the street." A shockingly small percentage of investors actually study a company's financial reports and read the security analyst's data.

WHERE CAN I FIND OUT MORE?

Listed below are some sources where you can find more information about risk tolerance measures, research findings, theory, and opinions about risk tolerance. When reading these sources, you may want to keep in mind the cautions noted above about the extent to which such literature is relevant to risk-taking in the financial arena as opposed to other facets of life.

1. N. Kogan and M. A. Wallachs' (1964; Holt, Rinehart and Winston) book, *Risk Taking*, contains seminal information about the field and, more importantly, includes (in the Appendix) copies of various measures that have been used to measure risk in research projects.

2. Another reference is *Taking Risks: The Management of Uncertainty* by K. R. MacCrimmon, D. A. Wehrung, and W. T. Stanbury (1986; The Free Press). This book contains a "portfolio" of risk measures and discusses the relationships between variables addressed by those measures.

3. Louis Harris and Associates, Inc. conducted a survey in 1984 for The Insurance Information Institute (Study No. 837008) entitled: "Public Attitudes Toward Risk" that provides valuable insights on the subject.

4. K. Haddad and A. WongBoren's paper, "Proper Framing: Asking the Right Questions," (*Journal of the Institute of Certified Financial Planners*, Fall, 1987, pages 195-200) discusses how the way one asks questions about risk attitudes can influence the answers clients provide.

5. Few commercially published measures of risk tolerance exist today. However, it is anticipated that more tests may become available in the future. There are two organizations that produce indices and critiques of commercially published tests—Buros Mental Measurements Institute, and Test Corporation of America. The financial planner wishing to keep abreast of developments in this area should consult the publications of these organizations, which are available in many libraries:

    A. *Tests: A Comprehensive Reference for Assessments in Psychology, Education, and Business* (edited by D. J. Keyser and R. C. Sweetland; Test Corp. of America) contains brief descriptions of tests, costs, scoring procedures, and publishers.

    B. *Tests in Print* (Buros Institute of Mental Measurements) contains information about tests similar to the above.

    C. The above two references are simply listings of available tests. Both organizations also publish works in which tests are critiqued by experts on measurement. These two publications are: *Test Critiques* (Test Corp. of America), and *The Mental Measurements Yearbook* (Buros).

6. MDRV Standards for Educational and Psychological Testing (1985; AERA/APA/NCME Joint Committee Washington, D.C., American Psychological Association) is the major reference to be consulted when judging tests in terms of their reliability, validity and other psychometric standards.

QUESTIONS AND ANSWERS

Question — Why can't I just ask my clients if they are "risk-tolerant" or "risk-aversive"? It seems as though doing more is a time consuming expensive overkill!

Answer — There are several reasons why a financial planner will not obtain accurate feedback merely by asking the client whether he is or is not "risk-tolerant":

First, it is very difficult to know whether your interpretation of "risk-tolerant" is the same as your client's meaning of the term; thus, he may have some difficulty in understanding your question.

Second, from a measurement perspective, answers to global questions of this sort are notoriously unreliable, even under the best of circumstances. In other words, your clients may not be able to give accurate answers even if they do fully understand your question.

Third, clients may not even be aware of their feelings, concerns and hopes relevant to their investments. Clients can differ markedly in the way they think of "risk" in an investment context, with some dwelling on how much they could lose and others focusing on how much they might gain. They may or may not have adequate perspectives about their views in the context of other investors.

Question — Do clients totally disregard objective ratings of investment products when making investment decisions?

Answer — No, clients do take such objective information into account in formulating their risk-return expectations. But there are other, quite subjective, influences on clients' risk tolerance. Even classifying a client in terms of wealth, age, gender and other pertinent variables may not adequately take into account how that particular client, at that time, feels about risks.

Question — Are the psychological questions necessarily better than the questions typically asked or the "gut feelings" received by financial planners?

Answer — Not necessarily better. However, this information about your clients can supplement the investment product and investment history information that is commonly obtained by financial planners and should help your clients to better understand themselves.

Question — What is the "best" way to measure a client's risk tolerance?

Answer — At present, there is no single instrument that has been widely acknowledged as being the "best" instrument. The above descriptions of influences on risk-taking propensities can serve as a check list of items that you may want to explore in discussions with your client.[1]

Question — How can I, as a financial planner working with clients, use this information about risk tolerance?

Answer — This chapter summarizes observations about risk tolerance, including situational and personal influences on one's risk propensity. These observations reflect group patterns involving a variety of life events, some of which are related to investment decisions. In using this information, the financial adviser should:

(a) consider the broader context of information described above when obtaining and using the client's comments about how risk-tolerant he is,

(b) be aware that personal characteristics and circumstances may combine to alter predicted results, and

(c) recognize that these observations should be used with care when drawing conclusions about an individual client's risk tolerance for investments. The information, thus, can indicate circumstances and personal attributes that may influence a client's risk tolerance.

1. Dr. Snelbecker has developed an instrument to measure risk tolerance and risk-aversion that will be useful for financial planners. If you would like to offer suggestions on the development of this instrument or would like further information about it, contact: Dr. Glenn E. Snelbecker, C/O M*A*T*C*H, 8905 Patton Rd. Wyndmoor, PA. 19118.

Chapter 17

ASSET ALLOCATION AND PERSONAL PORTFOLIO MANAGEMENT

Successful investors apply fundamental investment and portfolio management principles in a manner that is consistent with their investment goals and objectives and within the constraints of their personal investment profile. Easier said than done!

A person's investment goals and objectives drive the process, but without the application of sound investment principles, the chances of success are limited. The following sections discuss the fundamentals of investing and personal portfolio management, the role and importance of strategic asset allocation, the personal financial life cycle, the risks of tactical asset allocation or market timing, and the role of mutual funds in asset allocation planning.

WHAT ARE THE FUNDAMENTAL INVESTMENT AND PORTFOLIO MANAGEMENT PRINCIPLES?

In the 1950s, Harry Markowitz published his seminal book *Portfolio Selection.* The essential conclusion of Markowitz's theory was that portfolios or risky stocks could be put together in such a way that the portfolio as a whole could actually be less risky than any one of the individual stocks in it. Assuming that people prefer higher expected returns and less dispersion or likelihood of deviations from the expected return, Markowitz showed that investors can choose from among all possible portfolios a set that is *efficient* in the sense that for any given level of desired return they can find the portfolio with the least dispersion or variance about its expected return. How does this work? The mathematical development is rather complex, but it depends essentially on two basic concepts: *covariance* or *correlation* and *diversification*.

COVARIANCE/CORRELATION — THE CONCEPT

What is covariance? As the term suggests, covariance means varying together. Covariance is a measure of the degree to which two variables move in a systematic or predictable way, either positively or negatively. Correlation is a normalized measure of covariance that ranges from 1 when two

variables are perfectly and positively covariable to -1 when they are perfectly but negatively covariable.

Perfect Positive or Negative Covariance or Correlation

Let us look at what could be considered variables that are perfectly covariable or perfectly correlated. For a given policy type and age at issue an insurance agent knows what first year commission to expect for whatever premium amount is paid. The premium and the commission are perfectly dependent — the higher the premium, the larger the commission; the lower the premium, the smaller the commission. Therefore the premium and the commission are perfectly and positively covariable and the correlation between them is 1.

Another example of dependence, and thus covariability, is perfect negative covariance or correlation. That is, if one variable is larger, the second is smaller; if one is positive, the other is negative. For example, in a perfect bond market the interest rate and the price of a bond would be perfectly and negatively covariable. Interest rates and prices are related; the price must adjust to equate the bond's yield with the market rate of interest. For any randomly selected market rate of interest there exists a bond price that will equate the yield on a bond having a fixed coupon with the market rate of interest. As the market interest rate goes up, the price of the bond must go down. The correlation is -1.

What does this have to do with Markowitz's portfolio theory? Consider the following very simplistic but informative example. Suppose an individual has an opportunity to purchase shares in two businesses. The first is a suntan lotion manufacturer. The second is a manufacturer of umbrellas. Each of these businesses is affected by the weather. Assume that if the summer season is rainy, the umbrella manufacturer will earn a return of 25 percent, and that if it is sunny, the umbrella manufacturer will lose 10 percent. In contrast, the suntan lotion manufacturer will earn a return of 25 percent if the summer season is sunny and will lose 10 percent if the summer season is rainy. If, on the average, one-half of the seasons are sunny and one-half are rainy, an investor who has purchased stock in the umbrella manufacturer would find that half of the time he earns a 25 percent return and the other half

Figure 17.1

Investment	100% in Umbrella Company	100% in Suntan Lotion Company
If Sunny	-10.0%	25.0%
If Rainy	25.0%	-10.0%
Expected Return	7.5%	7.5%

Investment	50% in Umbrella Company	Plus	50% in Suntan Lotion Company	Certain Return
If Sunny	-10% x 50%	+	25% x 50%	7.5%
If Rainy	25% x 50%	+	-10% x 50%	7.5%
Expected Return	7.5%		7.5%	7.5%

of the time he loses 10 percent of his investment. On the average he would earn a return of 7.5 percent. (This is called the expected return, meaning the return the investor expects after averaging all possible outcomes.)

In a similar manner, an investor who has purchased stock in the suntan lotion company will also get an average return of 7.5 percent, but the incidence of the gains and losses will be reversed. Investing in only one business or the other would be fairly risky because there could be several sunny or rainy seasons in a row.

Suppose, however, that an investor invests equal amounts in each company. Regardless of whether the sun shines or the rain falls, he will earn 25 percent on half his investment and -10 percent on the other half. Therefore, the net return will be 7.5 percent in either case. This investor eliminates all his risk and still gets the same expected return of 7.5 percent by splitting his investment equally between the two companies rather than putting all of his money in either one or the other. Obviously the "portfolio" combination of equal shares in each company is the best possible combination since it minimizes the risk (variability of possible outcomes) for the given level of expected return. Figure 17.1 demonstrates these results.

This example of Markowitz's portfolio theory demonstrates that investors should choose the combination of securities that minimizes the risk of the entire portfolio for a specified expected return. Any one security may have great variability of outcomes by itself, but when combined with the other securities in a portfolio, the important factor is the covariance or correlation.

Independence — The Opposite of Perfect Covariability or Correlation

Two variables are independent if they exhibit no covariance; that is, if the correlation is 0. For example, each roll of a fair die is independent of any other roll. The outcome of a flip of a coin is unaffected by any previous flips.

Covariance or Correlation and Independence Combined

Unfortunately, the real world offers very few opportunities for perfect covariability or complete independence. Most "real-world" variables are neither completely dependent (perfectly covariable) nor completely independent. For instance, the weight and height of humans have positive covariance or are positively correlated. The taller an individual is, the more likely it is that his or her weight is greater. However, knowing an individual's height or weight alone does not allow one to know or predict the other factor with certainty, although one could probably make a better guess than if one knew nothing about the individual. Other independent factors, such as bone structure, muscle tone, fat content, gender, and so forth, affect the relationship between height and weight.

Most real-world securities have some common factor or factors that influence them mutually and many other factors that affect each independently. For example, many common economic factors will influence the earnings of Ford and General Motors in similar ways. However, each company's earnings will also be influenced by many independent factors that will have no effect whatsoever on the other company — for example, the company president's health or a fire in a warehouse. Consequently, one would expect the earnings of Ford and GM to have very positive covariability, but not perfect covariability. One would expect the correlation to be greater than zero but less than 1.

The real world has instances of negative covariability as well. Higher oil and gas prices may mean greater earnings for Exxon but lower earnings for Consolidated Trucking. Obviously both Exxon and Consolidated are influenced by many factors in addition to the price of gasoline, but many of those factors will be independent events unrelated to most other events affecting either firm.

DIVERSIFICATION

Why Is It Important to Distinguish Those Factors That Covary From Those That Do Not?

The risk resulting from the independent factors, the factors that do not covary, can be eliminated by *diversification*. The principle of diversification is probably intuitively understood by almost everyone and yet it is difficult to explain without technical jargon and mathematical analysis. In simple terms, diversification is the process of combining securities in such a way that the variability of the independent factors tends to be canceled out, leaving only the covariability between the securities' returns. For example, when a single dart is thrown at a target, chances are not good that the dart will hit the bull's-eye. However, if more and more darts are thrown, those darts hitting above the bull's-eye will tend to equal in number those below, and those to the right will tend to equal those to the left, so that, on average, the errors cancel. Therefore the larger the "portfolio" of throws, the more likely the average throw is a bull's-eye.

A similar process describes the diversification of a portfolio of securities. As more and more securities are added to the portfolio, the random and independent factors that cause one security to perform poorly are likely to be offset by other independent factors that cause another security to perform above average. These independent factors, like the scattering of darts, tend to offset one another. The variability of the portfolio will depend less and less on the independent factors and more and more on the covariances or correlation between the securities as the number of securities in the portfolio increases.

How Many Securities Must the Average Investor Hold to Gain the Advantages of Diversification?

Most individuals are surprised when they discover how few securities they need to virtually eliminate the diversifiable

risk (the independent variability) from their portfolio. By the time the 20th equity security is added, about 90 percent of all the independent variability is eliminated. In general, even fewer securities are required to eliminate most of the diversifiable risk in a portfolio of fixed-income securities.

Diversification cannot eliminate all risk or variability from a portfolio of securities. There will always be some common or covariable factors that affect all securities. However, about 50 to 70 percent of a stock's variability is attributable to factors that can be diversified away. This proportion varies by industry or market sector and by asset class, but is generally at least half. The relatively few securities that are required to eliminate so much risk (variability) at no loss of expected return indicates the power and importance of this principle. A well diversified portfolio will always be preferred to a less-diversified portfolio with the same expected return because the variability of outcomes will be reduced with no loss in expected returns.

What Is Systematic (Market) and Unsystematic (Diversifiable) Risk?

Other researchers soon realized that Markowitz's principles would have significant implications if applied to asset pricing in the marketplace. If investors *do* seek to minimize risk for any given level of expected returns, as Markowitz suggested, then prices in the stock market should tend to reflect these risk-reducing activities. These researchers suggested that each security should be valued on the basis of its covariability with the market as a whole. On the basis of Markowitz's principles, the only risk (or variability) the investor could not diversify away was that part directly related to the overall market variability. That is, even if an investor diversified as completely as possible by buying some shares of all securities in the market, he or she could not eliminate all risk or variability since the market as a whole is variable. The part of a security's total risk or variability that relates to the market as a whole is called its *systematic* or *market* risk. The remaining risk that results from factors exclusive to the company itself, such as a new product or a warehouse fire, is called its *unsystematic, diversifiable,* or *residual risk.*

This type of risk can be explained by extending the dart and target analogy used above to describe the principle of diversification. Suppose that there is a wind that will blow either from the left or the right across the path of the darts, but you won't know how hard or in which direction it has been blowing until you've thrown all the darts. The wind is analogous to the systematic or market risk of a portfolio. The wind will tend to move the whole shot-grouping of the darts either to the left or right of the bull's eye. This is similar to the effect of general market or economic conditions on portfolio returns.

If general market conditions are good, returns on many of the securities within the portfolio will be better than average; if bad, many security returns will be lower than average.

The dart and target with wind analogy has its deficiencies, however. Not all asset classes are affected by market conditions in the same way or to the same degree. And there is more than one "market" factor that affects the returns on securities. For example, stocks tend to be more sensitive to business cycle conditions than bonds, but bonds are generally more affected by inflation and interest rate changes. And while U.S. stocks and bonds may be depressed, foreign stocks and bonds may be doing quite well. It is in this area of portfolio management that the principles of asset allocation apply.

WHAT IS ASSET ALLOCATION?

Asset allocation, in its generic use, is simply the diversification among different asset classes to take advantage of less than perfect correlations among these classes and thereby to reduce the overall risk of an investment portfolio (variability or returns in various economic environments) without reducing the total expected return. In particular, asset allocation is the process of selecting investment proportions for the traditional portfolio asset classes such as stocks, bonds, and money market instruments together with less traditional asset classes such as real estate, precious metals and commodities, and foreign stocks and bonds. The objective is to even out performance over varying economic cycles. Losses suffered by those asset classes or market segments that decline in value can be offset by gains in other asset classes or market segments that increase in value throughout any economic cycle. Since investment returns from different asset classes tend to have low correlations, investing "across the board" in many asset classes reduces risk without a commensurate reduction in return.

The concept of diversification has traditionally referred to the reduction of risk attributable to spreading investment dollars among a number of securities within a given asset class. For example, most mutual finds invest in basically one asset class, such as common stocks or bonds, and provide investors with the benefit of a substantial reduction of risk (with presumably the same expected return) relative to the risk investors would bear if they invested directly in only a few securities within the class. Asset allocation simply expands this concept to diversification *among* the asset classes. As such, the asset allocation decision is just one part of the overall personal portfolio management process. But, as is explained further below, empirical evidence shows that it is by far the most important part of this process.

This concept can be explained using the dart and target analogy once again. However, this time assume you have several types of darts, each with different size feathers. The darts with larger feathers are more affected by any possible wind than those with smaller feathers, but, perhaps in the absence of wind, the darts with larger feathers are more accurate. If you use only darts with larger feathers and there is little wind, you will score higher than if you use only darts with smaller feathers. However, if there is a large wind, using the darts with small feathers would be better. Since you do not know how the wind will blow, you can minimize the variance of your score if you use some of each. If you also had a set of darts with feathers that spiralled the opposite way from those of other sets of darts, which would cause them to curve into, rather than with, the wind, you could reduce the variance of your score even further by including them within your portfolio of dart throws. This is equivalent to securities, asset classes, or market segments that are negatively correlated.

In everyday use, the term "asset allocation" is not quite so singularly defined as may have been suggested above. The term is frequently used to mean slightly different things to different people or in different contexts. Essentially 3 basic and one hybrid investment models or philosophies are associated with the concept of asset allocation. These models may be described as follows:

- **Strategic Asset Allocation**: is essentially a passive management philosophy that focuses on long-range policy decisions (i.e., the normal asset mix) where no attempt is made to outguess or time the market. The selection of asset classes to include in the portfolio and the proportion of the portfolio to be invested in each class is based on the investor's long-term goals and objectives and remains fixed until the investor's goals and objectives change.

- **Dynamic Asset Allocation**: is also essentially a passive management philosophy that makes no attempt to beat or time the market but that does employ predetermined or automatic defensive asset-shifting strategies to limit downside risk. For example, portfolio weights among asset classes may be changed as dictated by portfolio insurance techniques or other program trading strategies, such as by using limit orders or hedging with put options or financial or stock index futures.

- **Tactical (or Active) Asset Allocation**: is an active management philosophy that attempts to beat the market using market timing or sector or group rotation techniques (that is, periodically shifting the investment weights among the different market segments or asset classes). Decisions may rest either on predictions of fundamental economic factors such as future interest rates, money supply and inflation rates, and leading economic indicators of the business cycle or on technical indicators such as charts, trendlines, volume and trading patterns, and measures of investor sentiment.

- **Dynamic Tactical Asset Allocation**: is a hybrid management philosophy that attempts to beat the market using market timing or sector rotation techniques while retaining some of the attributes of portfolio insurance or other program trading techniques.

All tactical or active asset allocation schemes are somewhat at odds with the basic premise of asset allocation — reduction of risk by covering all the bases. Such an "all-weather" investment philosophy helps to assure adequate returns in any investment environment. However, what is called tactical allocation encompasses a wide range of active management procedures, usually based on probability weighted economic scenarios or projections. The more conservative plans may limit portfolio adjustments to a narrow band around the fixed-mix portfolio weights of the underlying strategic allocation policy. At the other extreme is outright market timing techniques which may involve large or complete shifts in and out of various asset classes or market segments.

HOW IMPORTANT IS THE STRATEGIC ASSET ALLOCATION POLICY?

Asset allocation policy, not individual security selection or market timing, is the MAJOR determinant of total portfolio performance.

A study reported in the *Financial Analysts Journal* examined the relative importance of strategic asset allocation, tactical asset allocation or market timing, and security selection in determining the performance of the portfolios of 91 large U.S. company pension plans over the 10-year period from 1974 through 1983.[1] The authors compared the performance of the pension portfolios to that of similar but "passive" portfolios with fixed asset allocation proportions equal to the average asset allocation proportions of the pension funds over the 10-year period. The study concluded that 93.6 percent of the variation in performance between the actual portfolios and the "passive" portfolios was due to asset allocation decisions. This means that only 6.4 percent of the variation was attributable to the fund managers' differing abilities to time the markets and to select individual securities within the asset classes or markets. In other words, the selection of the asset classes in which to invest and the assignment of portfolio weights to each of those classes was almost 15

times more important in explaining differences in portfolio performance than the market timing and security selection decisions combined.

This conclusion has been reconfirmed in another context that may be more relevant to individual investors. Mark Hulbert, the author of the *Hulbert Financial Digest*, applied similar methodology in a study of the portfolio recommendations of eleven different investment newsletters from January 1988 through December 1991.[2] Figure 17.2 shows the results of this study.

His study found that, on average, about 71 percent of the actual performance of the investment newsletters was explained by strategic asset allocation decisions. Of the almost 29 percent (28.94%) of performance that was not explained by the asset allocation decisions, about 18 percent was explained by market timing and, implicitly, 11 percent by security selection. He argued that the reason the market timing and security selection components explained as much of the performance as they did relative to the original study was that his study covered only four years, not ten.

Furthermore, in seven out of the eleven cases, the actual contribution of the market timing and security selection policies to overall portfolio performance was negative. In this majority of cases, an investor following an investment newsletter's recommendations would have been better off just adhering to its average asset allocation portfolio weighting scheme and ignoring both its specific security recommendations and its market timing recommendations regarding changes in portfolio weights or shifts in asset categories.

The conclusion: **the most important element in the successful management of your personal portfolio is the strategic asset allocation policy.**

WHAT ARE THE PRINCIPAL ASSET CLASSES TO CONSIDER IN AN ASSET ALLOCATION STRATEGY?

The primary asset allocation classes include

(a) Domestic fixed income assets (government and corporate)

    (1) cash equivalents and short debt

    (2) intermediate and long debt

    (3) life insurance cash values

Figure 17.2

	JANUARY 1988 THROUGH DECEMBER 1991				
	Returns (%)			Percentage of Market Timing Return Not Explained by Asset Allocation	Percentage of Return Not Explained by Asset Allocation
Newsletters	**(A) Asset Allocation**	**(B) Market Timing**	**(C) Actual**		
Donoghue's Moneyletter ("Venture-some" Portfolio)	62.87	58.42	59.60	7.08	5.20
FXC Report	61.19	59.12	73.90	3.38	20.77
Fund Exchange					
a. Conservative Balanced	48.07	34.06	31.20	29.14	35.09
b. Aggressive Balanced	50.48	35.62	36.10	29.44	28.49
Garside Forecast					
a. Aggressive	34.57	44.41	n/a	28.46	n/a
b. Total Return	22.02	25.48	n/a	15.71	n/a
Growth Fund Guide	43.90	32.39	26.60	26.22	39.41
Investech Mutual Fund Advisor	42.72	45.23	51.00	5.88	19.38
Kinsman's Telephone Growth & Income Service	51.89	40.98	25.10	21.03	51.63
Outlook	71.77	59.28	43.30	17.40	39.67
Peter Dag's Investment Letter	40.46	46.30	48.90	14.43	20.86
Average of Newsletters				18.02	28.94

Index Return (%)

Stocks 91.82	Bond 53.32	Gold -27.41	Cash 30.70

* The stock portion of these portfolios earned the rate of return of the Wilshire 5000 value-weighted total-return index, the bond portion, Shearson Lehman Hutton's total-return all-maturities government bond index; the gold portion, London's P.M. Fixing price; and cash, the 90-day Treasury bill rate.

(b) International fixed income assets (government and corporate)

    (1) cash equivalents and short debt

    (2) intermediate and long debt

(c) Equity assets

    (1) domestic stocks

    (2) foreign stocks

(d) Natural resources

    (1) marketable energy and extractive

    (2) private energy LPs

(e) Real Estate

    (1) residential

    (2) investment

    (3) farm

(f) Tangibles

    (1) precious metals

    (2) collectibles

    (3) commodities

Each of these asset classes has subclasses. For example, among the equities are small capitalization stocks, large

Figure 17.3

	Total Return (%)		
Year	Treasury Bills	S&P 500	All-Weather Portfolio
INVESTMENT RETURNS OF A SIMULATED ALL-WEATHER PORTFOLIO 1968-1987			
1968	5.2	11.1	15.4
1969	6.6	-8.5	-2.6
1970	6.5	4.0	0.6
1971	4.4	14.3	14.5
1972	3.8	19.0	15.8
1973	6.9	-14.7	0.0
1974	8.0	-26.5	-1.3
1975	5.8	37.2	22.8
1976	5.1	23.8	15.3
1977	5.1	-7.2	11.1
1978	7.2	6.6	16.3
1979	10.4	18.4	18.6
1980	11.2	32.4	23.5
1981	14.7	-4.9	1.4
1982	10.5	21.4	16.1
1983	8.8	22.5	14.7
1984	9.9	6.3	3.4
1985	7.7	32.2	31.4
1986	6.2	18.5	19.7
1987	5.2	4.7	6.4
1968-1987 average annual compound	7.4	9.2	11.8
Standard deviation	2.70	16.77	9.45

stocks, income stocks, and growth stocks as well as distinct market sectors, each with their own unique and less than perfect cross correlations. Similarly, among the fixed income classes are investment grade and junk bonds, municipals, and collateralized security obligations. The broadest diversification and benefit from asset allocation can be obtained by including as many of these asset classes as is feasible.

HOW IS THE OPTIMAL ASSET MIX DETERMINED?

The naive approach is to invest in each asset class in proportion to its weight in the "world" portfolio. From a theoretical perspective, this would provide the greatest possible diversification.

The benefit of diversifying across a broad range of asset classes is demonstrated in Figure 17.3, which shows the performance of an asset allocation mix roughly in proportion to estimated world wealth (excluding real estate) — the all-weather portfolio 1968-1987. The performance was compared to an investment in the S&P 500 or Treasury Bills.

The "all weather" portfolio used mutual fund categories with allocation weights as follows:

(1) small-capitalization stock funds	15%
(2) large-capitalization stock funds	15%
(3) international equity funds	15%
(4) international bond funds	10%
(5) domestic bond funds	20%
(6) gold funds	10%
(7) money market funds	15%

Figure 17.4

CORRELATION MATRIX OF INVESTMENT CATEGORIES (BASED ON ANNUAL RETURNS FROM 1973-1989)

	S&P 500	NASDAQ Composite	London Index	Tokyo Index	EAFE Index	Long-Term Corporate Bonds	Long-Term Gov't Bonds	1-Month Treasury Bills	Gold	Single-Family Homes	Inflation (CPI)
S&P 500	1.00										
NASDAQ Composite	0.90	1.00									
London Index	0.63	0.57	1.00								
Tokyo Index	0.52	0.41	0.31	1.00							
EAFE Index	0.56	0.52	0.44	0.69	1.00						
Long-Term Corporate Bonds	0.54	0.38	0.33	0.33	0.28	1.00					
Long-Term Gov't Bonds	0.40	0.25	0.11	0.28	0.23	0.93	1.00				
1-Month Treasury Bills	(0.02)	0.02	(0.11)	0.08	(0.39)	(0.09)	(0.02)	1.00			
Gold	(0.37)	(0.24)	(0.48)	(0.55)	(0.30)	(0.43)	(0.25)	(0.05)	1.00		
Single-Family Homes	(0.25)	0.01	0.04	(0.46)	(0.29)	(0.56)	(0.55)	0.15	0.51	1.00	
Inflation (CPI)	(0.33)	(0.14)	(0.23)	(0.59)	(0.52)	(0.72)	(0.61)	0.37	0.59	0.82	1.00

The all-weather portfolio outperformed the S&P 500 by 2.6 percent while reducing risk as measured by standard deviation to less than three fifths that of the S&P 500. It also had only two years of negative returns, as compared to 5 for the S&P 500, and the greatest loss was only 2.6 percent, ten times less than the S&P 500's greatest loss of 26.5 percent.

To create "efficient portfolios," that is, portfolios with the lowest risk or variability of return for a given level of expected return, one must know cross-correlations (covariances) among the asset classes within the portfolio. If an investor wishes to create portfolios with anything other than naive asset allocation based as closely as possible on world market weights (naive is not used here in a pejorative sense, but rather to indicate the absence of any formalized asset allocation scheme), then asset allocation weights should be determined using the tools of modern portfolio theory. There are now a number of investment allocation software programs available for use with personal computers (with prices ranging from several hundred to several thousand dollars) which, as part of the service, provide the necessary cross-correlations and risk and return characteristics for the various asset classes.

Figure 17.4 shows the relationships (correlations) among a wide range of asset classes that is fairly representative of a world portfolio. The less than perfect correlations, and even negative correlations among some asset classes make it clear that broad diversification can reduce risk. The relationships in the table suggest that most people should allocate part of their portfolio to large and small domestic stocks, international common stocks, fixed-income securities, and real estate assets. The S&P 500 index is highly but not perfectly correlated with OTC stocks. The foreign stock indexes are correlated, but not perfectly, with our domestic equity markets, so their inclusion should reduce risk without reducing return. Homes, gold, and T-bills are positively correlated with inflation and negatively correlated with most equities. Their inclusion should enhance overall performance.

However, trying to diversify across all asset classes in the world is, in practice, impractical and unnecessary. First, nobody really knows the relative value of all asset classes in the world portfolio. Second, and perhaps more importantly, it takes no account of the investors' personal investment goals and objectives and his or her personal investment profile.

Each investor has his or her own unique investment characteristics: risk tolerance, tax status, liquidity needs, investment planning horizon, and income/growth preferences. In addition, all investors are subject to constraints: the size of their portfolio, their investable cash flow, the portion of their wealth tied up in relatively inflexible investments such as a family business and their homes. In many cases, a large part of one's wealth is tied up in retirement plans where the investment options may be limited. Even a person's job is a factor, since salaries and bonuses often depend in part upon the performance of the company, which may be highly correlated with a given market segment. Finally, people's investment characteristics and objectives tend to vary throughout their life.

Figure 17.5 presents broad guidelines as to the asset classes to emphasize based on an investor's broad objectives.

LIFE CYCLE PERIODS

An individual typically moves through 5 financial stages throughout his or her life, which are characterized by various issues and objectives that are distinct to each stage. As you review the following characteristics and goals of these various life cycle stages, try to determine which stage best describes your or your client's own situation.

Early career: age 25 or under-35

- Often newly married and have young children

- Establishment of employment patterns for one or both spouses

- Accumulation of income for home purchase

- Creation of college education funding for children

- Accumulation for starting one's own business

- Little consideration for retirement planning, particularly in early years of this period

Career development: age 35-50

- Enhancement of career, upward career mobility, or rapid growth in income from profession or business

- Accumulation and expenditure of funds for children's college education

- Integration of employee benefits with investment strategy

- Employee benefit coordination between spouses

- Retirement income planning (financial independence)

- Purchase of vacation home, travel

Figure 17.5

	Explanation	Range	Security Groups With These Characteristics
		THE PERSONAL INVESTMENT PROFILE	
Risk Tolerance	How much of a loss can you stomach over a one-year period without abandoning your investment plan?	Loss: 0% to 5% loss Moderate: 6% to 15% loss High: 16% to 25% loss	Low: Money market funds, CD Moderate: Intermediate and long-term bonds, conservative high dividend paying stocks High: Growth Stocks
Return Needs	What form of portfolio return do you need to emphasize: income, growth or both?	Income: Steady source of annual income Growth/Income: Some steady annual income, but some growth is also needed Growth: Growth to assure real (after inflation) increase in portfolio value	Income: Bonds Growth/Income: Dividend-paying stocks Growth: Growth stocks
Time Horizon	How soon do you need to take the money out of your investment portfolio?	Short: 1 to 5 years Long: Over 5 years	Short: Money market funds, CDs, short-term bonds; intermediate-term bonds (less than 5 years) Long: Growth stocks, aggressive growth stocks
Tax Exposure	Based on your annual income, at what tax bracket will additional income from portfolio earnings and gains be taxed?	Lower: Annual income is such that marginal tax bracket is among lower rates Higher: Annual income is such that marginal tax bracket is among higher rates	Higher tax exposures securities (stressed by lower tax-exposure investors): Fixed income securities, high dividend paying stocks Lower tax exposure securities (stressed by high-tax exposure investor): Municipal bonds, non-dividend-paying growth stocks

- Beginning of general wealth building beyond basic objectives

- Geographic relocation

Peak accumulation: age 50-62 (approximately)

- In general, peak of career with possible lessening of work-related activities

- Period of maximum ability to accumulate wealth for all purposes. These are the years for maximum wealth accumulation in excess of needs for specific objectives

- Basically a continuation of

  - retirement income planning

  - coordination of benefits from employment with investment strategy — also, integration for retirement planning

  - vacation home, travel

Figure 17.6

INVESTMENT ALLOCATION PERCENTAGES			
	Investment Categories		
Life Cycle Stage	**(1)** **low risk,** **secure** **income-oriented**	**(2)** **medium** **risk** **growth type**	**(3)** **high** **risk** **speculative**
early career	40 down to 10	60 up to 80	0 up to 20
development	40 down to 30	50 up to 70	0 up to 20
peak accumulation	50 down to 30	40 up to 60	0 up to 15
preretirement	80 down to 40	20 up to 40	0 up to 10
retirement	80 down to 60	10 up to 40	0 up to 10

- Beginnings of some reduced investment risk as portfolio begins to emphasize income production for retirement (particularly near the end of this period)

- Concerns of minimizing both income and taxes

Preretirement years: 3-5 years prior to planned retirement age

- Winding down of career and income potential

- Restructuring of portfolio to reduce risk and enhance income

- Further tax planning

- Integration of plan distribution options with income needs and tax consequences

Retirement

- Hoped-for enjoyable life style

- Adequacy of retirement income

- Preservation of purchasing power

- New job (paid or volunteer)

INVESTMENT ALLOCATION GUIDELINES

Figure 17.6 provides guidelines for determining appropriate asset allocation percentages to suit your or your client's personal needs. A range of acceptable investment percentages is presented for each life cycle stage and are allocated to three broad investment categories: (1) low risk, secure, and income-oriented investments; (2) medium risk, growth-type investments; and (3) high risk, speculative investments. Although there is certainly some overlap between the investment categories, broadly stated, each category includes the following types of investments. Category (1) includes savings accounts, T-bills, money-market funds, government bonds, high-grade corporate bonds, participation certificates, and similar types of investments. Category (2) includes municipal bonds, convertible bonds, lower-grade corporate bonds, preferred stocks, high-quality growth stocks, and similar investments. Category (3) includes more-speculative growth stocks, most real estate investments, REITs, options, commodities and futures contracts, and similar types of investments. In addition, mutual funds are available that fit within each of these general classes of investments.

Which investment percentage is chosen within each class should now depend on an assessment of risk tolerance and the investment horizon. For example, if your client is 55 years old, considers himself in the peak accumulation stage of his financial life cycle, plans to take early retirement at age 62, and considers himself relatively risk averse, he should probably invest up to 50 percent of his portfolio in class (1), up to 50 percent in class (2), and close to 0 percent in class (3). In contrast, if he is more risk tolerant and plans to continue working past age 65, he should probably invest closer to only 30 percent class (1), between 50 and 60 percent in class (2), and perhaps up to 15 percent in class (3).

HOW IMPORTANT IS THE INVESTMENT PLANNING HORIZON IN THE ASSET ALLOCATION DECISION?

The investment planning horizon is extremely important in the asset allocation decision. Figure 17.7 shows risk/return

Figure 17.7

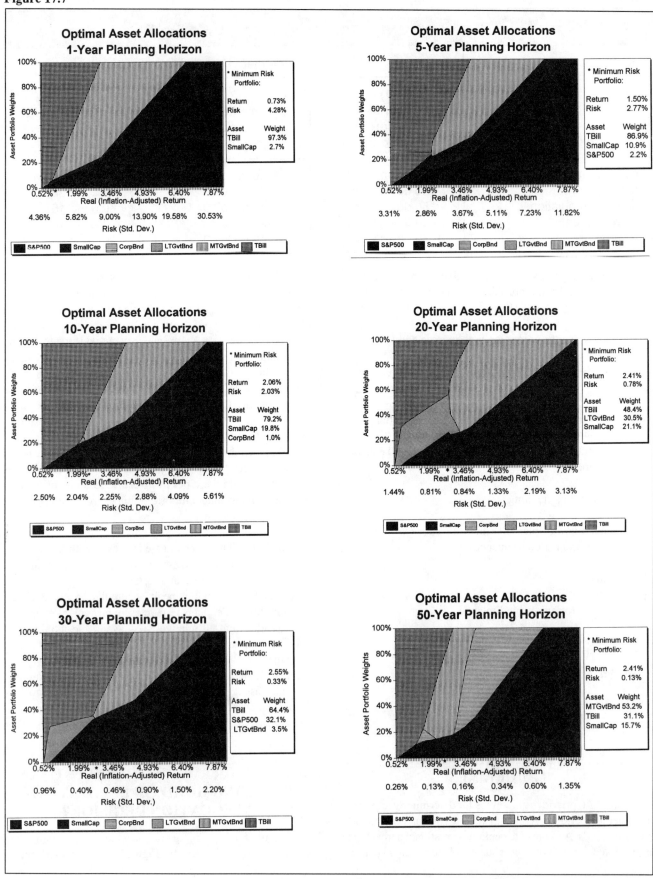

Figure 17.8

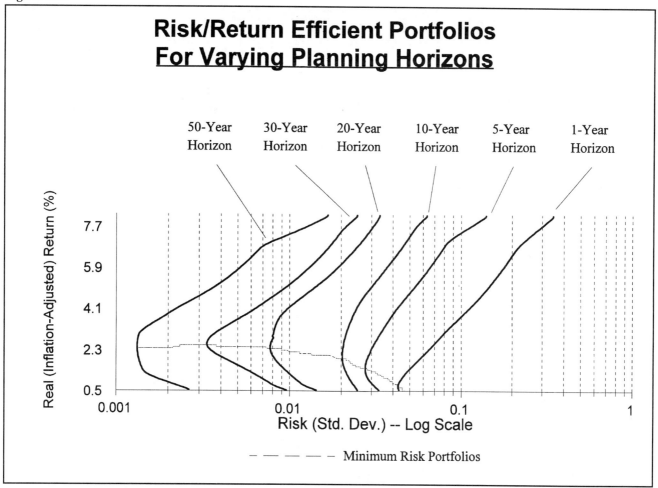

Risk/Return Efficient Portfolios
For Varying Planning Horizons

efficient portfolios composed of 6 asset categories: S&P 500 stocks, small stocks, corporate bonds, long-term government bonds, medium-term (5-year) government bonds, and T-bills for investment planning horizons ranging from 1 to 50 years based on inflation-adjusted returns. These portfolios are "efficient" in the sense that the asset allocations among the asset classes provide the lowest risk (standard deviation) for the given rate of return based on the historical correlations (1926 through 1990) between the various asset classes. Clearly, the efficient "frontier" moves significantly toward lower risk for the same level of return as the investment planning horizon increases.

Figure 17.8 shows the asset allocation weights corresponding to each planning horizon. Among the most salient observations is the fact that in no case is an investment in T-bills alone optimal, even though T-bills have the lowest risk as measured by standard deviation. Even in the 1-year case, a very risk-averse person would be better off investing some small portion of his or her portfolio in what are typically considered high-risk small capitalization stocks than in T-

bills alone. As the horizon is increased to 5 years, the optimal minimum risk portfolio includes over 13 percent equities.

Another interesting result is that long-term bonds, either government or corporate, rarely enter the asset allocation scheme above the minimum risk portfolio. However, medium-term government bonds are a major component of the optimal allocation scheme for intermediate risk/return portfolios for all planning horizons.

Finally, for 5-, 10-, and 20-year horizons, the proportion of the portfolio allocated to S&P stocks declines while that of small capitalization stocks increases. But for even longer horizons, the weight of S&P 500 stocks increases once again.

Although these analyses are somewhat limited in that they do not include many other important asset classes, especially international stocks and bonds, they are instructive. As the investment horizon increases, risk decreases with respect to return in optimal portfolios. But the optimal portfolios' asset allocation weights change as well with the planning horizon.

Figure 17.9

MONTHLY STOCK RETURNS (1926 THROUGH 1987)				
	Average Return (%)	Variation* (%)	% of Positive Months	% of Months Accounting for 62-Year Cumulative Returns	% of Months Accounting for 62-Year Return Above Treasuries
S&P 500	0.79	5.90	61	6.7	3.5
Small Stocks	0.95	8.89	60	4.0	2.3

* Measures the range around the average return in which two-thirds of the actual returns fell.

CAN TACTICAL ASSET ALLOCATION OR MARKET TIMING ENHANCE PORTFOLIO RETURNS?

This question is constantly debated. However, the overwhelming evidence is that even professional market timers cannot consistently outperform the market. Market timing is a zero-sum game whereas investing in the market as a whole is a positive-sum game. What does this mean?

Economists describe many economic and financial phenomena in terms of games. A positive-sum game is one in which you can have more winners than losers. The market is positive-sum game since the economy is growing; in theory, every investor could come out ahead. However, market timing is a zero-sum (or negative-sum, if you consider transactions costs) game since a market timer can gain only at the expense of another market timer. Why?

If everyone invested in the market portfolio (however defined), nobody could gain at anyone else's expense. And, since it is the market portfolio, every asset must be held by someone. Now suppose only half the people hold the market while the rest try to time it, moving in and out of cash and the market. Clearly, the people who hold the market cannot lose out to those who time the market; they will get the market return regardless of what the timers do. Since everyone's returns must sum up to the market return, if one timer "beats" the market, his gain must come at the expense of some other market timer taking an opposite position who "lost" to the market. It can't be any other way.

The argument is sometimes made that timing reduces risk, since one is invested in cash or T-bills a portion of the time and in the market the rest of the time. Since T-bills are less risky than stocks, the argument goes, the overall risk is lower.

The fallacy here is in failing to account for the risk of missing the big gains in the market. Most of the gains in the market are made during relatively short periods surrounded by long periods of relative stagnation. Figure 17.9 shows monthly stock returns from 1926 through 1987 on S&P 500 and small stocks. *All* of the return to S&P 500 stocks occurred in just 6.7 percent of the months; for small stocks, just 4 percent of the months account for all of the return over this period. Only 3.5 percent and 2.3 percent, respectively, of the months accounted for all of the return in excess of T-bills. In other words, if you were invested in the market 96.5 percent of the time, but you were out for the months of greatest gain, you would have done no better than investing in T-bills.

A similar study of the bull market from 1982 to 1987 gave similar results, based on days, rather than months in the market. This study showed that if you missed just the 40 biggest days, or just 3 percent of the 1,276 trading days of this bull market, you would have missed 83.7 percent of the market's 26.3 percent annual compounded return over the period. See Figure 17.10.

Clearly, the risk of *not* being in the market when it makes its run is very significant, and conveniently overlooked when the market timers try to sell their concept. Best advice: invest for the long term and be in the market consistently. No market timer can claim to be accurate over 80 percent of the time, so timing will inevitably lead to cases where the big market runs are missed.

WHAT IS THE ROLE OF MUTUAL FUNDS IN ASSET ALLOCATION?

With the growth in world markets and many more asset classes available to diversify and reduce risk, mutual funds

Figure 17.10

COST OF NOT BEING IN THE MARKET		
Period if Investment	**S&P 500 Annualized Return (%)**	**% of Return Missed**
Entire 1,276 Trading Days	26.3	0.0
Less the 10 Biggest Gains Days	18.3	30.4
Less the 20 Biggest Gain Days	13.1	50.2
Less the 30 Biggest Gain Days	8.5	67.7
Less the 40 Biggest Gain Days	4.3	83.7
University of Michigan Study: *Bull Market of 1982-1987* (1,276 trading days ending August 25, 1987)		

provide the easiest way for investors to do their own asset allocation by providing them with well diversified portfolios representing most of the various asset classes. (See chapter 34 for more information on mutual funds.)

A relatively recent study shows that by diversifying among mutual fund categories, the higher risks of some of the better performing mutual fund categories can be reduced without significantly reducing the associated returns.[3] To better illustrate the relationship between risk and return for mutual fund categories, Figure 17.11 presents the average annual returns and risk of mutual fund categories for the 10-year period 1978-1987. The data clearly indicates that the higher the return, the higher the risk.

An asset allocation approach to mutual funds is contingent on the funds' reaction to one another relative to return performance. Figure 17.12 details these relationships. The categories that exhibit little or no correlation would benefit most from diversification since the low returns in one category can be balanced by the higher returns in another.

Figure 17.13 presents the results of the study. Samples of possible mutual fund portfolio combinations with their expected risk and return levels are shown. Several findings are significant:

(1) Although international stock funds, when viewed alone, are riskier than small-capitalization stock funds, because of their negative correlation with money market funds, they may be combined with money market funds to achieve lower portfolio risk than combinations of small-stock funds and money market funds.

(2) Only 3 or 4 mutual fund categories out of the 6 categories included in the study are generally necessary to form a particular efficient portfolio.

(3) A portfolio of 4 mutual fund categories can achieve 78% less risk than the risk of the average mutual fund category taken alone (portfolio 9).

(4) A combination of international stock, small-company stock, and growth stock mutual funds can achieve 18% less risk than international funds taken alone while sacrificing only 1% in total return (portfolio 2).

(5) The same combination of international, small-stock, and growth stock funds can achieve 13% less risk than small-stock funds taken alone and with 2 percent higher returns (portfolio 2).

(6) A combination of international stock, growth stock, and money market mutual funds can achieve 35% less risk while providing a similar return to small-stock funds taken alone (portfolio 4).

(7) A different combination of international stock, growth stock, and money market mutual funds can achieve 29% less risk while providing a similar return to growth stocks taken alone (portfolio 5).

(8) A combination of international stock, domestic corporate bond, and money market mutual funds (the lowest-risk portfolio) can achieve 85% less risk while providing a similar return to Treasury bond funds taken alone (portfolio 10).

(9) The same combination of international stock, domestic corporate bond, and money market mutual funds can achieve 77% less risk while providing more than 1% greater total return than corporate bond funds taken alone (portfolio 10).

(10) The same combination of international stock, domestic corporate bond, and money market mutual funds

Figure 17.11

AVERAGE ANNUAL RETURNS AND RISK OF MUTUAL FUND CATEGORIES (1978-1987)		
Category	Average Annual Return	Volatility*
International Stock Funds	20.3%	19.2%
Small-Company Stock Funds	17.0	18.2
Growth Stock Funds	16.2	14.1
Corporate Bond Funds	9.7	10.5
Treasury Bond Funds	10.7	16.4
Money Market Funds	9.9	3.4

*As measured by standard deviation. The figure represents the amount by which returns varied around the average; the greater the future, the greater the volatility and therefore the greater the risk.

can achieve 29% less risk while providing 1% greater total return than money market mutual fund taken alone (portfolio 10).

The results of this study provide significant evidence that following an asset allocation approach when making mutual fund investments can help an investor to realize the benefits of substantial returns but with lower risk.

When selecting mutual funds to implement an asset allocation strategy, two considerations are critical:

(1) whether or not a given fund truly reflects the desired characteristics of that fund category, and

(2) the degree of management discretion in the asset composition of the fund.

Read the prospectus to assure yourself that the fund invests (exclusively, if possible) in the securities required for the desired asset class. Compare the performance of the fund over the past 5 to 10 years with the average performance of the fund class. Performance should not differ substantially.

Select mutual funds in which management discretion in the asset composition of the fund is minimal. Although mutual fund managers who perform market timing decisions and move assets into and out of the specified asset class based on their assessment of economic and market conditions may provide a valuable service when an investor is looking to the fund as his or her sole investment, such management discre-

tion is counterproductive when the fund is part of an asset allocation scheme. The success of an asset allocation strategy depends on the investments within each asset category of the portfolio performing in various economic circumstances as the underlying assets within that category do in the economy at large. If the fund managers vary their asset weights in various economic environments (for instance, in the case of a growth stock fund by shifting out of stocks into cash equivalents when they expect the market to decline) the actual portfolio weights in the various asset categories of the asset allocator's portfolio will not reflect those he or she has selected.

For example, assume a simple asset allocation investment scheme of 50% in growth stock mutual funds and 50% in money market mutual funds. If the mutual fund manager shifts from the normal position of 90% equities and 10% cash equivalents (most stock funds hold a percentage of their assets in cash equivalents to facilitate redemptions without having to liquidate stock positions) to 10% stocks and 90% cash, the asset allocator who thinks he or she has about a 50/50 mix between growth stocks and money market mutual funds will in reality have about a 95/5 money market to growth stock portfolio.

Real estate, precious metals, natural resources and energy, and commodities were not included in the study. Even further risk reduction may be possible without loss of potential returns by including real estate investment trusts, gold and silver stocks or funds, natural resource and energy sector funds, and commodity funds or futures contracts in the portfolio weighting scheme.

FOOTNOTES REFERENCES

Asset Allocation and Personal Portfolio Management

1. "Determinants of Portfolio Performance," Gary Brinson, Randolph Hood, and Gilbert Beebower, *Financial Analysts Journal* (July-August 1986).

2. "The Relative Importance of Asset Allocation Decisions," Mark Hulbert, *AAII Journal* (June 1992).

3. "The Benefits of Diversifying Among Mutual Fund Categories," Jeff Madura and John M. Cheney, *AAII Journal*, Vol. XI, No. 1 (January 1989), pp. 8-10.

Figure 17.12

CORRELATIONS AMONG MUTUAL FUND CATEGORIES (1978-1987)						
Category	International Stock Funds	Small Company Stock Funds	Growth Stock Funds	Corporate Bond Funds	Treasury Bond Funds	Money Market Funds
International Stock Funds	1.00	-	-	-	-	-
Small-Company Stock Funds	0.30	1.00	-	-	-	-
Growth Stock Funds	0.38	0.96	1.00	-	-	-
Corporate Bond Funds	-0.07	0.14	0.14	1.00	-	-
Treasury Bond Funds	0.07	0.11	0.15	0.97	1.00	-
Money Market Funds	-0.56	0.12	0.02	0.02	-0.10	1.00

* Indicate how one category behaves versus another. A 1.00 indicates perfect correlation: The returns in one category rise and fall at the same time and to the same degree as the returns in the other.

Figure 17.13

EXAMPLES OF DIVERSIFIED MUTUAL FUND PORTFOLIOS				Percentage Allocated Mutual Fund Category				
	Portfolio	Return (%)	Volatility* (%)	International (%)	Small-Company (%)	Growth Stock (%)	Corporate Bond (%)	Treasury Bond (%)
Max. Return, Max. Risk	1	20.3	19.2	100.0	0.0	0.0	0.0	0.0
	2	19.3	15.8	68.4	29.2	2.4	0.0	0.0
	3	18.2	13.7	53.9	0.0	42.3	0.0	0.0
	4	17.1	11.8	47.8	0.0	35.7	0.0	0.0
	5	16.1	9.9	41.7	0.0	29.1	0.0	0.0
	6	15.0	8.1	35.6	0.0	22.4	0.0	0.0
	7	14.0	6.2	29.5	0.0	15.8	0.0	0.0
	8	12.9	4.5	23.4	0.0	9.2	0.0	0.0
	9	11.8	3.0	17.4	0.0	2.5	3.3	0.0
Min. Return, Min. Risk	10	10.9	2.4	10.1	0.0	0.0	6.4	0.0

* As measured by standard deviation. The figure represents the amount by which returns varied around the average; the greater the figure, the greater the volatility and therefore the greater the risk.

Chapter 18

ANNUITIES

WHAT IS IT?

Annuities are the only investment vehicles that can guarantee investors that they will not outlive their income, and they do this in a tax-favored manner. In addition, annuities are available with a host of differing features to meet a wide variety of investor needs.

Technically, annuities are contracts providing for the systematic liquidation of principal and interest in the form of a series of payments over time. The annuity may be paid for a fixed period such as 5, 10, or 30 years, or for the life (or lives) of the annuitant (or annuitants). The investor makes a single large cash payment or a series of periodic payments to the insurance company which invests the money. In return, the company agrees to pay an annuitant (or annuitants) a specified amount (the annuity) periodically.

If the annuity is a life annuity, the company promises that payouts will continue for as long as the annuitant (or annuitants) lives; the income stream can never be outlived. If the annuity is a fixed period annuity (also called a term-certain annuity), the company promises to pay stipulated amounts for a fixed or guaranteed period of time independent of the survival of the annuitant. The living proceeds received from a life insurance contract are also considered annuities if they consist of payments of both principal and interest.

There are many different types of annuities available. Consequently, annuities can be classified in a number of ways including according to: (1) How premiums are paid; (2) What residual values, if any, are paid upon the death of the annuitant; (3) When benefit payments begin; (4) How many lives are covered; (5) What investment options are available to the owner of the annuity contract; and (6) How benefits are calculated. Figure 18.1 illustrates how annuities are classified.

1. *Premium Paying Method*: Single premium annuities are often the ideal vehicles for people who have come into large cash sums. A single premium annuity will convert such amounts, for example, from an inheritance, from the sale of a business or a large piece of real estate, or from a qualified pension or profit-sharing plan lump-sum distribution, into a lifetime or certain fixed period stream of payments.

Fixed premium annuities are favored by investors who do not have large cash sums to invest but who desire a regular investment program with a "forced saving" feature. Typically, fixed annual (semiannual, quarterly, monthly or even weekly) premium payments continue until the desired annuity starting date (the date when payouts begin). Since the periodic premiums are fixed, the total accumulation and, therefore, the ultimate annuity payout is very predictable.

Flexible-premium annuities allow the contract owner to invest (make premium contributions) at any time and in any amount desired. The insurance company usually requires certain minimum annual contributions within the first few years, but after this initial period generally no restrictions or requirements apply with regard to the timing or amount of further contributions.

2. *Disposition of Proceeds*: A life annuity with no refund feature continues annuity payouts only as long as one or more annuitants survive. Payments are assured for the life or lives of the annuitant or annuitants, but once the annuitant(s) dies, annuity payments cease, even if the total paid out of the annuity is less than the amount invested in the contract.

Insurance companies also offer annuity contracts with minimum payback guarantees, since many investors are reluctant to forfeit a portion of their investment in the event of the premature death of the annuitant. These guarantees take two forms.

Refund annuities promise to pay the difference between the amount invested in the contract (generally the total of the premiums paid) and the annuity payments actually paid out before the death of the annuitant. This refund takes the form either of lump-sum cash payments or of installment payouts. Period certain annuities promise to make payments for a stipulated period, such as 5, 10, or 20 years, or for the annuitant's life, whichever is longer.

The payout period may also be short term, that is, for a specified period generally shorter than the expected life (or lives) of the annuitant(s). Term-certain annuities operate similarly to the amortization of a loan. Payments

Figure 18.1

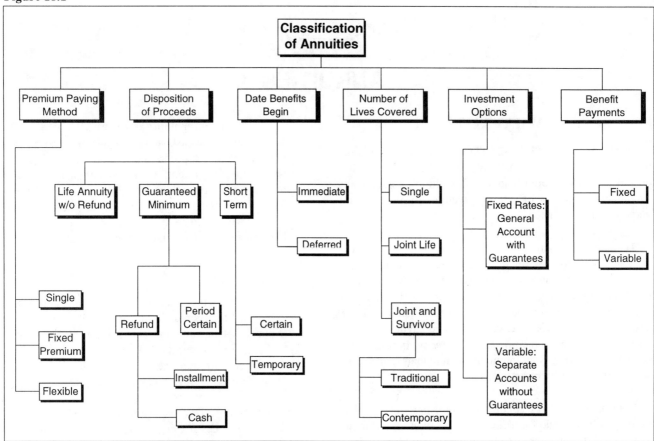

continue for a specified term only, regardless of when the annuitant dies. A temporary annuity is a variation on the period certain annuity concept. However, rather than paying a specified amount for the longer of the annuitant's life or the specified term, a temporary annuity continues payments only for the shorter of the annuitant's life or the specified term.

3. *Date Benefits Begin*: An immediate annuity begins annuity payments within one year after all premiums are contributed. Immediate annuities are commonly used when a person wishes to convert a large lump-sum amount, such as a lump-sum distribution from a qualified pension or profit-sharing plan, into an immediate income stream. As the name suggests, payments from deferred annuities are delayed or deferred for a period of time after the premiums or contributions have been completed. Deferred annuities are frequently used when a person has cash to invest before retirement and wishes to postpone the beginning of the annuity payments until retirement or later.

4. *Number of Lives Covered*: The annuity payout period may depend on one, two, or, less common, more lives. A single life annuity (with no refund feature) makes pay-

ments until the single covered life dies. In the case of annuities based on two or more lives, payouts may continue until the last annuitant dies or only until the first annuitant dies. Annuities whose payments continue until the last death of the covered lives are called joint and last survivor annuities, or just joint and survivor annuities. Those annuities whose payments cease upon the first death are called joint life annuities.

A joint and survivor annuity may pay one amount while both annuitants are alive and another amount after the first death. The surviving annuitant may receive some specified percentage (called the survivor benefit ratio) of the amount payable before the first death. Survivor benefit ratios typically range from 50 percent to 100 percent, with 50, 66, 75, and 100 percent being the most common. For example, a joint and 75 percent survivor annuity paying a $50,000 annual joint benefit would pay $37,500 per year to the survivor after the first death.

The benefit payable to the survivor may also depend on which annuitant dies first. The traditional joint and survivor annuity has a principal annuitant and a secondary annuitant or beneficiary. The survivor benefit ratio applies only to the benefit payable to the surviving secondary annuitant after the principal annuitant's death. If the principal annuitant outlives the secondary annuitant, the benefit payments are not reduced. In recent years an alternative form of the joint and survivor annuity has become popular. This contemporary joint and survivor annuity pays the reduced benefit to the survivor regardless of which annuitant dies first. For a given total investment, insurance companies can afford to pay relatively higher joint and survivor benefits on these annuities than on traditional joint and survivor annuities.

5. *Investment Options*: Fixed rate annuities are similar to universal life policies in that amounts credited to cash values are based on the insurer's current declared rate, subject to a minimum guarantee of about 4 percent to 4.5 percent. Rates paid on new money (current contributions) may be guaranteed for one to five years. The currently declared rate depends on the performance of the insurer's general investment portfolio or general account, which is largely invested in fixed income investments such as bonds and mortgages. Although interest credits to the annuity depend on market rates on these types of fixed-income investments, the cash value itself is not market valued. Similar to a savings account, once interest is credited, the cash value will not decline if the market value of the underlying assets in the insurer's general account declines. The insurer bears the market risk.

Analogously, variable annuities are similar to variable insurance policies. The annuity owner may choose to invest contributions and cash values in a broad spectrum of investment options or separate accounts, which are similar to mutual funds. The investment options usually include diversified stock, bond, and money market funds and frequently include specialized stock funds, foreign stock and bond funds, real estate equity and mortgage funds, and even asset allocation funds (a type of balanced fund where the insurer's investment manager allocates investments among the other funds). In contrast with fixed rate annuities, cash values depend on the market value of the underlying assets in the selected separate accounts. Variable annuity owners bear the market risk of investment and forego minimum interest rate guarantees. However, they have the flexibility to choose their investment portfolio and the potential to earn far greater total returns than they would earn on fixed rate annuities.

6. *Benefit Payments*: Fixed benefit annuities guarantee a minimum annuity benefit payment per dollar of accumulated value, similar to settlement options under life insurance policies. Variable benefit annuities make no guarantees. Annuity benefit payments depend on the market value of the assets in the separate accounts.

WHEN IS THE USE OF THIS TOOL INDICATED?

Since there is such a fundamental difference in the risk and return characteristics of fixed and variable annuities, each type is more or less suitable for various purposes. However, some form of annuity would be indicated in the following circumstances.

1. When a tax deferred accumulation of interest is desired. The interest earned inside an annuity owned by an individual grows income tax free and is not taxed until it is withdrawn.

2. When liquidity is desired. Owners may usually withdraw cash, within limits, before the annuity starting date.

3. When an investment with immediate and high collateral value is wanted.

4. When the a person wants a retirement income that can never be outlived. .

5. When the person would like to avoid probate and pass a large sum of money by contract to an heir to reduce the possibility of a will contest.

6. When an investor wants to be free of the responsibility of investing and managing assets.

7. As a replacement for or an alternative to an IRA. With less opportunity for pre-tax contributions to IRAs, many clients are seeking opportunities of making regular after-tax contributions to an investment vehicle. The annuity may be a good choice because the contribution can be much more than the IRA limitations.

8. When a retired individual wants a monthly income equal to or higher than other conservative investments and is willing to have principal liquidated.

9. Fixed annuities, in particular, would be indicated: (1) when safety of principal is a paramount consideration. This is particularly important for retirement planning; (2) when an investor wants a guarantee that a given level of interest will be credited to his investment for a long period of time; and (3) when a conservative complement to other investment vehicles is desired.

10. Variable annuities, in particular, would be indicated: (1) when an investor wants more control over his or her investment and is willing to bear the risk associated with his or her investment selections; and (2) when a person is looking for potentially increasing retirement income.

ADVANTAGES

1. Protects and builds a person's cash reserve. The insurer guarantees principal, interest, and the promise (if purchased) that the annuity can never be outlived. This makes the annuity particularly attractive to those who have retired and desire or require fixed monthly income and lifetime guarantees.

2. A client can "time" the receipt of income and shift it into lower bracket years. This ability to decide when to be taxed allows the annuitant to compound the advantage of deferral.

3. The guarantees of safety, interest rates, and lifelong income give the purchaser peace of mind and psychological security.

4. Because the interest on an annuity is tax-deferred, an annuity paying the same rate of interest (after expenses) as a taxable investment will result in a higher effective yield.

DISADVANTAGES

1. Receipt of a lump sum at retirement could result in a significant tax burden since income averaging is not available.

2. A long term cash flow stream of a fixed amount may not keep pace with inflation.

3. A 10 percent penalty tax is generally imposed on withdrawals of accumulated interest prior to age 59½ or disability.

4. With a few limited exceptions, if an annuity contract is held by a corporation or other entity that is not a natural person, the contract is not treated as an annuity contract for federal income tax purposes. This means that income on the contract for any taxable year is treated as current taxable ordinary income to the owner of the contract regardless of whether or not withdrawals are made.

5. If the client is forced to liquidate the investment in the early years of an annuity, management and maintenance fees and sales costs could prove expensive. Total management fees and mortality charges can run from one to two percent of the value of the contract. There may be a "back end" surrender charge if the contract is terminated within the first few years to compensate the insurer for the sales charges which are not typically levied "up front."

TAX IMPLICATIONS

1. A client's investment in an annuity is returned in equal tax-free amounts during the payment period. Any additional amount received is taxed at ordinary income rates. This means part of each payment is considered return of capital and is therefore nontaxable and part of each payment is considered return on capital (income) and is therefore taxable at ordinary rates.

The formula for determining the nontaxable portion of each year's payment is:

$$\frac{\text{INVESTMENT IN CONTRACT}}{\text{EXPECTED RETURN}}$$

This is called the "exclusion ratio." It is expressed as a percentage and applied to each annuity payment to find the portion of the payment that is excludable from gross income. For instance, assume a 70-year-old purchases an annuity. He pays (the investment in the contract is) $12,000 for the annuity. Assume his expected return is $19,200.

The exclusion ratio is $12,000/$19,200, 62.5 percent. If the monthly payment he receives is $100, the portion that can be excluded from gross income is $62.50 (62.5% of $100). The $37.50 balance of each $100 monthly payment is ordinary income.

The full amount of each annuity payment received would be tax free if the investment in the contract exceeds the expected return.

The excludable portion of any annuity payment may not exceed the unrecovered investment in the contract (unless the annuity started before January 1, 1987). The "unrecovered investment in the contract" is the policyowner's premium cost (reduced by any dividends received in cash or used to reduce premiums and by the aggregate amount received under the contract on or after the annuity starting date to the extent it was excludable from income). This rule limits the total amount the policyowner can exclude from income to the total amount of his contribution. Once an annuitant actually lives longer than his or her actuarial life expectancy, 100 percent of each payment will be taxable.

Some annuities provide a refund if the annuitant dies before recovering his entire cost, or provide a "period-certain" guarantee (payments will be made for a specified period regardless of how long the annuitant lives). The value of the refund or period-certain guarantee must be ascertained by government tables and subtracted from the investment in the contract.

The "expected return" is the total amount that the annuitant (or annuitants) should receive given the payments specified multiplied by the life expectancy according to the government's tables. For instance, assume that under the applicable table a 70-year-old has a life expectancy of 16 years. If he (or she, since the life expectancy tables are unisex) receives $100 a month, the expected return would be $19,200 ($1,200 a year x 16 years).

2. When an annuitant dies before receiving the full amount guaranteed under a refund or period certain life annuity, the beneficiary receiving the balance of the guaranteed amount will have no taxable income (unless the amount received by the beneficiary plus the amount that had been received tax free by the annuitant exceeds the investment in the contract).

   If the refund or commuted (present) value of the remaining installments is applied by the beneficiary to purchase a new annuity, payments received will be taxed under the annuity rules to the beneficiary. The refund amount will be considered the beneficiary's investment in the new contract and a new exclusion ratio must be determined.

3. If the annuitant was receiving payments under a joint and survivor annuity, the survivor excludes from income the same percentage of each payment that was excludable by the first annuitant. An income tax deduction may be available to the survivor annuitant to the extent inclusion of the annuity in the estate of the first to die generated an estate tax. A similar deduction may be available if the annuity generated a generation skipping transfer tax.

4. When an annuitant makes a partial withdrawal from the contract and takes a reduced annuity for the same term, a portion of the amount withdrawn will be subject to income tax.

5. When an annuitant makes a partial withdrawal from the contract (allocable to an investment in the contract made after August 13, 1982) and chooses to take the same payments for a different term, to the extent the cash surrender value of the contract exceeds the investment in the contract, gain will be realized in the form of a taxable withdrawal of interest.

6. The purchaser of a variable annuity (see Questions and Answers below) is not taxed on income during the accumulation period. No tax will be payable until the earlier of (a) the surrender of the contract or (b) the time payments under the annuity begin (the "annuity starting date"). To obtain annuity treatment, however, the underlying investments of the segregated asset account must be "adequately diversified" according to IRS regulations.

Payments made as an annuity under a variable annuity are not subject to the same exclusion ratio as is a regular fixed annuity. This is because it is impossible to determine the expected return. Instead, the following formula is used:

$$\frac{\text{INVESTMENT IN CONTRACT}}{\text{NUMBER OF YEARS OF EXPECTED RETURN}}$$

If there is a period certain or refund guarantee, the investment in the contract is adjusted accordingly. If payments are made for a fixed number of years without regard to life expectancy, the divisor is that fixed number of years. If payments are made for a single life, use IRS Table V. If payments are to be made on a joint and survivor basis, use Table VI.

The exclusion ratio no longer applies once an annuitant reaches his life expectancy. So if a person's actual life exceeds his actuarial expectancy as anticipated when benefits began, the total amount that can be excluded is limited to the total amount of his investment. For instance, assume a 65-year-old paid $40,000 for his life annuity. Since his life expectancy is 20 years, his yearly exclusion is $2,000 ($40,000 ÷ 20). The $2,000 continues to be excludable until the annuitant has recovered the $40,000.

If payments drop below the excludable amount ($2,000 in this example) in any given year, the annuitant can elect to redetermine the excludable amount in the next tax year in which he receives an annuity payment. The loss in exclusions is divided by the number of years remaining (in the case of a fixed period annuity). In the case of a life annuity the loss is divided by the annuitant's life expectancy computed as of the first day of the first period for which an amount is received as an annuity.

For instance, assume a 65-year-old taxpayer purchased an annuity for $20,000. The contract provides variable monthly payments for life. Since his life expectancy is 20 years (Table V), he may exclude $1,000 of each annuity payment from income ($20,000 ÷ 20). Assume on his 70th birthday he receives only $200, $800 less than his excludable amount. At age 70 his life expectancy is 16 years. He may elect to add $50 ($800 ÷ 16) to his $1,000 exclusion, a total of $1,050 which he may exclude that year and in subsequent years.

7. If an annuitant dies before payments received equal cost, a loss deduction can be taken for the amount of the unrecovered investment, provided the annuity starting date was after July 1, 1986. This same result applies where one person purchases an annuity on the life of another who dies prematurely. So if a wife purchases a single premium nonrefundable annuity on the life of her husband, and the husband dies before all costs have been recovered, a loss deduction will be allowed.

   The deduction for the unrecovered investment in the contract is an itemized deduction, but not a miscellaneous deduction. Therefore, it is not subject to the 2 percent floor.

8. Amounts payable under a deferred annuity contract at the death of an annuitant (prior to the contract's maturity) will be taxed as ordinary income to the beneficiary. The excess of (a) the death benefit (plus aggregate dividends and other amounts that were received tax free) over (b) total gross premiums is taxable.

   Beneficiaries can elect to delay reporting of the gain in the year of the annuitant's death if the beneficiary applies the death benefit under a life income or installment option within 60 days of the annuitant's death. The beneficiary will then report income according to an exclusion ratio. The beneficiary's investment in the contract will be the same as the annuitant's investment in the contract. The expected return is based on the income the beneficiary will receive and the beneficiary's life expectancy.

9. The owner of an annuity often takes dividends, makes cash withdrawals, or takes other amounts out of the annuity contract before the date the annuity is to start (the "annuity starting date"). Such amounts are taxable as income to the extent that the policy cash value exceeds the investment in the contract. (Different rules apply to contracts purchased on or before August 13, 1982).

   The so called "interest first" (amounts received are treated first as interest income and further amounts are considered a recovery of cost) rule was imposed to discourage the use of annuity contracts as short term investment vehicles. Under this rule, a loan is considered a cash withdrawal.

   Likewise, to the extent the contract is used as collateral for a loan, amounts borrowed will be taxable (to the extent the amount received equals or is less than any gain inherent in the contract). If the amount received exceeds the built-in gain, the excess of what was borrowed over potential gain is considered a tax free return of the contract owner's investment. With respect to contracts entered into after October 21, 1988, amounts borrowed increase investment in the contract to the extent they are includable in income under these rules.

   In applying the interest first rule, all contracts entered into after October 21, 1988 and issued by the same company to the same policyholder during any calendar year are treated as one contract.

10. "Premature" distributions (those made before certain dates listed below) are subject, not only to the normal tax on ordinary income, but also to a penalty tax of 10 percent.

   The penalty for premature distributions will not apply to any of the following:

      (A) payments part of a series of substantially equal periodic payments made for the life (or life expectancy) of the taxpayer or the joint lives (or joint life expectancies) of the taxpayer and his beneficiary (unless the series of payments is modified under certain circumstances);

      (B) payments made on or after the time the contract owner becomes age 59½;

      (C) payments made on account of the contract owner's disability;

      (D) payments made from qualified retirement plans and IRAs (but these are subject to other similar premature distribution requirements);

      (E) payments made to a beneficiary (or annuitant's estate) on or after the death of an annuitant;

      (F) distributions under an immediate annuity contract;

      (G) an annuity contract purchased on the termination of certain qualified employer retirement plans and held until the employee separates from service;

      (H) payments allocable to investment in the contract before August 14, 1982.

11. If an annuity owner dies before the starting date of the annuity payments, the cash value of the contract must either be distributed within 5 years of death or used within one year of death to provide a life annuity or installment payments payable over a period not longer than the beneficiary's life expectancy. However, if the surviving spouse is the beneficiary; the distribution requirements

are applied by treating the spouse as the owner of the annuity contract.

The 10 percent premature distribution penalty tax does not apply to required after-death distributions.

If the annuity contract is transferred by gift, the tax deferral on the inside build-up that was allowed to the original contract owner is terminated. The donor of the gift is treated as having received non-annuity income in an amount equal to the excess of the cash surrender value of the contract at the time of the transfer over the investment in the contract at that time.

12. Tax free build-up within the contract is allowed only to "natural persons." If an annuity contract is held by a person who is not a natural person, then the annuity contract is not treated as an annuity and the income on the contract is treated as ordinary income received or accrued by the owner during that taxable year.

Corporations are not "natural persons." Neither is the typical trust although a trust acting as the agent for a natural person would itself be considered a natural person. But if an employer is the agent for its employees, the contract will be considered as if owned by the employer. The employer will therefore be taxed on the inside build-up. This means annuities are no longer appropriate tax advantaged investments for nonqualified deferred compensation agreements. Exceptions from the "natural persons" rules allow tax free build up of the following:

(A) annuities received by the executor of a decedent at the decedent's death,

(B) annuities held by a qualified retirement plan or IRA,

(C) annuities considered "qualifying funding assets" (used to provide funding for structured settlements and by property or casualty insurance companies to fund periodic payments for damages),

(D) annuities purchased by an employer on termination of a qualified plan and held until all amounts under the plan are distributed to the employee or his beneficiary,

(E) annuities which are "immediate," i.e., those which have a starting date no more than one year from the date the annuity was purchased and provide for a series of substantially equal periodic payments to be made at least annually over the annuity period.

ALTERNATIVES

1. Municipal bond funds are an attractive option for retirement savings. The income they produce is exempt from federal and in many cases state income tax (although the sale of the bonds will be taxable and some municipal bonds may be subject to the AMT (alternative minimum tax)).

   If a municipal bond fund's average yield is 6 percent, the equivalent taxable yield is almost 8.7 percent if the investor in the 31 percent personal tax bracket. Money can be withdrawn from a municipal bond fund at any time without IRS penalty. A drawback of municipal bond funds as compared with annuities is the lack of a guaranteed return.

2. Single Premium Life Insurance (SPLI) offers many of the same advantages of annuities and others as well.

   Generally, no income tax or penalties are payable until or unless the policy is surrendered. Single premium life insurance policies issued after June 21, 1988 are modified endowment contracts (MECs). Distributions from MECs are taxed under essentially the same rules as annuity contracts. This means that any policy distributions, including loans, will be taxed at the time received to the extent that the cash value of the contract immediately before the payment exceeds the investment in the contract. Additionally, a 10 percent penalty tax may apply to certain distributions. In effect, the MEC rules remove the tax-free borrowing possibilities previously associated with the SPLI policy.

   A client should not be directed to a product — any product — merely for its tax advantages since these are at the mercy of Congress. Certainly, if a client doesn't need life insurance, the costs and restrictions make single premium life insurance less attractive since there is a cost for the death benefit which, in turn, leaves less capital available for investment.

3. Mutual funds offer another alternative. During the accumulation period, variable annuities offer investment options which are essentially the same as mutual funds. Mutual funds do not enjoy the tax-deferred accumulation associated with variable annuities. However, tax on the capital appreciation of the assets in a mutual fund is deferred until the gains are realized. In addition, the realized gains are taxed as either long-term or short-term capital gains, depending on the holding period. In contrast, all gains and income on the assets in separate accounts are taxed at ordinary income tax rates when

paid. Also, mutual funds receive a step-up in basis at death in the hands of the heir. There is no step-up in basis in annuity values in the hands of the beneficiary when the annuity contract owner dies.

WHERE AND HOW TO GET IT

Almost all life insurance companies and many stock brokerage firms offer annuities to their customers. In addition, some banks now offer annuities.

Variable annuities are considered securities under the federal securities laws. Consequently, they may be offered only by agents who are licensed and who have passed specific securities examinations. In addition, prospective buyers must be given a prospectus which describes the product and its features and the company offering the product, explains and details expense charges, contract options, investment options, and related information.

WHAT FEES OR OTHER ACQUISITION COSTS ARE INVOLVED?

There are five fees or charges which are often incurred in annuities (particularly in variable annuities). These include:

1. investment management fees which run from a low of about 0.25 percent to a high of about 1 percent

2. administration expense and mortality risk charges which range from a low of about 0.5 percent to a high of about 1.3 percent

3. annual maintenance charges which typically range from none to $100

4. charges per fund exchange which generally range from none to $10, but most funds will permit a limited number of charge-free exchanges per year

5. maximum surrender charges which range from 5 percent of premium decreasing to 0 percent over 9 years to 8 percent of premium decreasing to 0 percent over 8 years.

HOW DO I SELECT THE BEST OF ITS TYPE?

1. Compare, on a spreadsheet, the costs and features of selected annuities. Consider all of the five costs discussed

above as well as how much can be withdrawn from the contract each year without fee.

2. Compare the total outlay with the total annual annuity payment in the case of fixed annuities.

3. In an analysis of variable annuities, compare the average 12 month total return for variable annuity funds in general (Lipper Analytical Services, Inc. computes this) with the return of the annuities in question.

4. Compare the relative financial strength of the companies through services such as A.M. Best. Insist on a high credit rating.

WHERE CAN I FIND OUT MORE ABOUT IT?

Information on annuities can be obtained in newspapers (especially the *Wall Street Journal*'s quarterly report on mutual funds and variable annuities) and in three major statistical sources: (a) A.M. Best Co., (b) Lipper Analytical Services Inc., and (c) Barron's.

QUESTIONS AND ANSWERS

Question — What happens to the money paid to the insurance company when the annuitant dies?

Answer — A "pure life annuity" is one in which the continuation of payments by the insurer is contingent upon the continuing existence of one or more lives. The consideration (premium) paid for the annuity is fully earned by the insurer immediately upon the death of the annuitant. This is why annuities payable for the life or lives of one or more annuitants frequently include a minimum payment guarantee. In other words, many annuities include both life and fixed period or refund elements so that if death occurs prematurely, the annuitant and the annuitant's survivors will recover a total of at least a minimum amount. Therefore, each annuity payment where a minimum guarantee has been purchased is composed of (a) return of principal, (b) interest or earnings on invested funds, and (c) a survivorship element.

If an annuitant dies before having recovered the full amount guaranteed under a refund or period certain life annuity, the balance of the guaranteed amount is not taxable income to the refund beneficiary - until the total amount received tax free by the annuitant plus the total amount received tax free by the beneficiary equals the investment in the contract. From that point on, all additional amounts received are ordinary income.

Question — What is the difference between a "fixed" annuity and a "variable" annuity?

Answer — Although annuities have many other distinguishing features, the two major types of annuities being sold today are the fixed annuity and the variable annuity. About 90 percent of all outstanding annuity contracts fall into the fixed rate category, but variable annuities are becoming increasingly popular. The investment account in a fixed rate contract operates much like the cash value account of a universal life policy. The annuity investment earns a fixed rate which is guaranteed for the first one to five years of the contract. After that time, the rate depends on the investment success of the insurer's general portfolio (subject to a guaranteed floor, typically about 4 percent).

In many fixed rate contracts, if the contract return falls below that minimum rate, there is often a "bailout rate." Once the return falls below the bailout rate (often 1 percent below the guaranteed minimum rate), the contract owner can terminate the contract without cost. The fixed rate contract gives the contract owner no choice or say in the underlying investments.

Variable rate annuities are popular because, in return for the assumption of greater risk, the contract owner may obtain both greater investment flexibility and a higher return. The contract owner can select from among a number of separate accounts that are similar to mutual fund investments. The investment options typically include diversified stock, bond, and money market funds. Most insurer's also now offer a broad array of alternative funds such as specialized stock funds (sector funds, small-capitalization stock funds, index funds), foreign stock and bond funds, junk bond funds, real estate equity and mortgage funds, GNMA-type funds, and asset-allocation funds (where the company's investment manager selects portfolio weights allocating investments among the other funds).

Question — What is the difference between a joint annuity and a joint and last survivor annuity?

Answer — A joint life annuity is a contract that provides a specified amount of income for two or more persons named in the contract. Income ends upon the first death. A joint and last survivor contract is much more popular because payments continue until the last death among the covered lives. Obviously, this form of annuity is more expensive than other forms since, on average, it will pay

income for a longer time. This increased cost is reflected in a lower income than would be paid under a single life annuity at either of the two ages.

Clients can purchase the joint and survivor annuity on either a pure life basis (ending at the later death) or with a certain number of payments guaranteed. Most insurers offer a form of joint and survivor annuity that pays the full amount while both annuitants are alive and then two thirds or one half that income when the first annuitant dies. This is called a "joint and two thirds" or "joint and one half annuity."

Question — How does the variable annuity work?

Answer — The variable annuity was the product of a search for a tool which would provide a guaranteed lifetime income that could never be outlived that also provided a relatively stable purchasing power in times of inflation. The variable annuity is based on equity type investments and works like this:

Premiums are paid to the insurance company during the "accumulation period." That money is placed into one or more separate accounts. The funds in these accounts are invested separately from the other assets of the insurer. Each year, some money is taken out of the contract owner's premium for expenses. The balance is applied to purchase "units of credit" in the separate accounts.

The number of credits purchased depends on the current valuation of a unit in terms of dollars. For instance, if each unit was valued at $10 a unit based on current investment results, a $100 level premium (after expenses) would purchase 10 units. If the value of a unit dropped because of investment experience, the premium would purchase more units. If the value of a unit increased, the same premium would buy fewer units. This unit purchasing continues until the "maturity" of the contract.

At the maturity of the contract, the insurer credits the contract owner's total units to a retirement fund. A given number of accumulation units will purchase so many retirement income units (based on actuarial principals and upon the current value of each unit). Note that the variable annuity does not promise to pay a fixed number of dollars each month but rather a fixed number of annuity units. In other words, the dollar amount of each payment depends on the dollar value of an annuity unit when the payment is made. The dollar value of an annuity unit is in turn based on the investment results of the special account. For instance, assume an annuitant was entitled to a payment based on 10 annuity units each month. If the dollar value of an annuity unit varied from $12.10 to $12.50 to $12.80, the annuitant would be paid $121, $125, and $128.

Question — What are the risks being assumed by the contract owner under a variable annuity?

Answer — Under a variable annuity, the insurer assumes only the risk of fluctuations due to mortality and expenses (guaranteeing that the annuitant will not outlive his or her income and that expense fluctuations will be absorbed). This means the contract owner is assuming the investment risk. If the special account is invested poorly or in the wrong investments, the annuitant will receive fewer dollars of income than would have been paid under a conventional fixed-dollar annuity.

Question — Although the investment options in variable annuities are similar to mutual funds, mutual funds are taxed differently than annuities and annuities charge higher fees and loads to cover various guarantees within the annuity contract. How can one determine if and when a variable annuity is a better investment than a mutual fund?

Answer — Conceptually, variable annuities are simply mutual funds wrapped in an instrument that permits tax on all income, whether ordinary or capital gain, to be deferred until monies are distributed. If annuitized, distributions are taxed under the rules of Internal Revenue Code Section 72, which essentially prorates the recovery of basis over the distribution period. An investor must pay a price for this tax advantage, however.

First, the amount of each annuity payment in excess of the amount of basis recovery is taxed at ordinary income tax rates, regardless of whether that amount is attributable to ordinary investment income (i.e., interest or dividends) or capital appreciation. That is, investors whose marginal ordinary income tax rate exceeds the applicable capital gains rate will forfeit the favorable lower tax treatment on the portion of their payments that is attributable to previously unrecognized capital gains.

Second, variable annuities incur a mortality charge that averages about 1.25 percent in addition to the usual fund expenses which average from about 0.6 percent to one percent on equity funds depending on the type of fund.

Third, most variable annuities impose surrender charges if money is withdrawn within the first five to nine years. The charge typically declines to zero by one

percent per year. As a general rule, variable annuities are less attractive than mutual funds if there is any possibility the contract will be surrendered within the first 5 to 7 years. The period of tax deferral will generally be insufficient to overcome the additional fees and surrender charges.

Fourth, potentially more problematic is the 10-percent early-withdrawal penalty on distributions from annuities before age 59½. Distributions that are not part of series of substantially equal periodic payments for the life or life expectancy of the annuitant or the lives or joint life expectancy of the annuitant and a second life or beneficiary are in most cases subject to a 10-percent penalty tax in addition to the ordinary income tax.

Keep in mind, equity mutual funds do not enjoy the same degree of tax deferral as variable annuities, but they are, nonetheless, tax-favored investments. Although the tax on ordinary dividend and interest income earned by a fund is paid by the shareholders in the year the income is earned, the tax on capital gains is deferred until the gains are recognized, either through buy and sell transactions within the mutual fund portfolio or when the investor sells his shares in the fund.

Therefore, when trying to decide whether variable annuities or mutual funds will provide the greater overall return, the results depend on certain critical assumptions regarding the size of the differential in fees and loads, the rate of return, the ordinary and capital gains tax rates, the length of accumulation period, and whether annuity distributions will be subject to a 10 percent penalty. In addition, the relative merit depends on how the variable annuity will be liquidated. Variable annuities are relatively more attractive if proceeds will be annuitized rather than taken in a lump-sum.

For any combination of assumptions regarding the fee differential, tax rates, and rates of return and distribution options there is a "break even holding period" after which an investor can withdraw the accumulated value in a variable annuity, pay the regular income tax and, if applicable, the 10 percent penalty, and be left with as much as he would accumulate in a taxable mutual fund.

Figure 18.2 compares the effective after-tax rates of return of a variable annuity with a no-load mutual fund over various accumulation periods and a range of assumed before-tax and before-expense rates of return. Additional assumptions include that:

- Both the mutual fund and variable annuity are invested in common stocks;

- There are no front-end loads on either the mutual fund or the variable annuity;

- The variable annuity has surrender charges that grade to zero after year seven;

- The investor's marginal tax rate for current taxable (ordinary) income is 35 percent and for deferred gains is 20 percent (applicable state and local taxes are ignored);

- Regarding the mutual fund, 40 percent of the total returns are attributable to dividends and 60 percent to capital gains;

- The investor will be age 59½ or older at the end of the investor's variable annuity holding period (i.e., withdrawals from the variable annuity will not be subject to the 10-percent early-withdrawal penalty);

- All of the earnings from the variable annuity will be deferred until distributions are made;

- Total annual expense charges for administration and management of the mutual fund are one percent;

- Total annual expense charges for the variable annuity are two percent (one percent, comparable to the administrative and management charges for the mutual fund, plus a one percent annual mortality charge); and

- The average annual turnover rate (for the calculation of taxes on gains recognized when the fund buys and sells securities) for the mutual fund is 20 percent (i.e., the average holding period for securities within the mutual fund is five years).

Figure 18.2 shows the effective after-tax and after-expense rate of return for the investment in the mutual fund and the variable annuity for the various accumulation periods and the various assumed before-tax and before-expense rates of return. The values are computed by assuming that both the mutual fund and the variable annuity are liquidated at the end of the specified accumulation period and that all taxes on the tax-deferred gains and tax-deferred income, respectively, are paid at that time. The vehicle with the largest effective return is the better performing investment; that is, it is the one that would provide the investor with the greatest after-tax balance at the end of the accumulation period.

Figure 18.2 shows that even if the total before-tax and before-expense average annual compound rate of return on investment is as great as 12 percent, the variable

annuity becomes the better accumulation vehicle only if the accumulation period approaches 20 years. That is, under the assumptions listed above, if an investor is planning to accumulate funds for a period shorter than about 20 years, the mutual fund would be the better accumulation vehicle.

The period of years until the variable annuity becomes the better accumulation vehicle is even longer for lower assumed total rates of return. For instance, the average annual compound rate of return on the S&P 500 index since 1926 has been just slightly over 10 percent. Using this rate of return as a general guideline for a broadly diversified portfolio of stocks, an investor would have to wait almost 27 years before the variable annuity would provide the greater after-tax accumulation. If the rate of return is expected to be eight percent or less, even 40 years is not a sufficient accumulation period for the variable annuity to outperform the mutual fund after taxes and expenses.

In most cases, investors who accumulate substantial sums for retirement, either inside or outside of an annuity, do not take a lump-sum distribution, which would then trigger the immediate recognition and taxation of all deferred income or accumulated gains. Instead, they make periodic withdrawals (annuity-type payments) which enables them to continue to enjoy the benefits of tax deferral on the remaining balance over the distribution years. This continuation of tax deferral increases the relative benefit of the variable annuity as compared to the mutual fund.

Assuming a distribution period of 20 years, Figure 18.3 shows the effective annual compound after-tax and after-expense rates of return for the entire accumulation and distribution period and the number of years in the accumulation period (the crossover year) until the variable annuity would outperform (provide greater annual after-tax distributions than) the mutual fund. These crossover years were calculated using the same assumptions as listed above plus the following assumptions with regard to the taxation of distributions during the 20-year distribution period:

- Distributions from the annuity are assumed to be level and taxed under the rules of Code section 72. Under these rules, basis is recovered in a pro rata fashion over the distribution period. For example, if the basis is $100,000 and the distribution period is 20 years, 1/20 of the basis, or $5,000 of each annual payment is treated as a nontaxable recovery of basis. The remaining portion of each annual payment is taxable as ordinary income. Given the assumptions of a level 35

Figure 18.2

EFFECTIVE AFTERTAX RATE OF RETURN **Mutual Fund v. Variable Annuity**							
Lump-Sum Distribution at End of Accumulation Period							
Accum Period		**Total Before-Tax and Before-Expense Rate of Return**					
		12%	**11%**	**10%**	**9%**	**8%**	**7%**
5	MF	7.82	7.09	6.37	5.65	4.93	4.22
	VA	6.91	6.19	5.47	4.76	4.05	3.36
	Dif	0.91	0.90	0.90	0.89	0.88	0.86
10	MF	7.94	7.20	6.46	5.72	4.99	4.26
	VA	7.37	6.57	5.78	5.00	4.24	3.49
	Dif	0.57	0.63	0.68	0.72	0.75	0.77
15	MF	8.00	7.25	6.50	5.75	5.01	4.28
	VA	7.50	6.89	6.05	5.21	4.40	3.61
	Dif	0.50	0.36	0.45	0.54	0.61	0.67
19	MF	8.03	7.27	6.52	5.77	5.03	4.29
	VA	8.01	7.12	6.23	5.37	4.52	3.70
	Dif	0.02	0.15	0.29	0.40	0.51	0.59
20	MF	8.04	7.28	6.52	5.77	5.03	4.29
	VA	8.07	7.17	6.28	5.40	4.55	3.72
	Dif	-0.03	0.11	0.24	0.37	0.48	0.57
22	MF	8.05	7.29	6.53	5.78	5.04	4.30
	VA	8.18	7.26	6.36	5.47	4.60	3.76
	Dif	-0.13	0.03	0.17	0.31	0.44	0.54
23	MF	8.05	7.29	6.53	5.78	5.04	4.30
	VA	8.23	7.31	6.40	5.51	4.63	3.78
	Dif	-0.18	-0.02	0.13	0.27	0.41	0.52
26	MF	8.06	7.30	6.54	5.79	5.04	4.30
	VA	8.38	7.44	6.51	5.60	4.71	3.84
	Dif	-0.32	-0.14	0.03	0.19	0.33	0.46
27	MF	8.07	7.30	6.54	5.79	5.04	4.30
	VA	8.42	7.48	6.55	5.63	4.73	3.85
	Dif	-0.35	-0.18	-0.01	0.16	0.31	0.45
33	MF	8.08	7.32	6.56	5.80	5.05	4.31
	VA	8.65	7.69	6.73	5.79	4.87	3.96
	Dif	-0.57	-0.37	-0.17	0.01	0.18	0.35
34	MF	8.08	7.32	6.56	5.80	5.05	4.31
	VA	8.68	7.72	6.76	5.82	4.89	3.98
	Dif	-0.60	-0.40	-0.20	-0.02	0.16	0.33
40	MF	8.09	7.33	6.56	5.81	5.06	4.31
	VA	8.85	7.88	6.91	5.95	5.00	4.07
	Dif	-0.76	-0.55	-0.35	-0.14	0.06	0.24
Crossover Yr.		**19.4**	**22.5**	**26.9**	**33.3**	**43.6**	**62.2**

Figure 18.3

Total ROR	Effective Aftertax ROR		Crossover Year
	MF	VA	
12%	8.0920%	8.0920%	13.8
11%	7.3265%	7.3265%	16.5
10%	6.5683%	6.5683%	20.4
9%	5.8156%	5.8156%	26.4
8%	5.0670%	5.0670%	36.3
7%	4.3235%	4.3235%	54.5

Mutual Fund Versus Variable Annuity
20-Year Annuitization

percent tax rate on ordinary income and level annual distributions, the after-tax payments from the annuity will also be level each year over the distribution period;

- The amount withdrawn in any given year from the mutual fund is the amount necessary to provide equal after-tax annual distributions over the 20-year distribution period. It is assumed that the after-tax dividend income each year is the first money withdrawn. If, in a given year, the after-tax dividend income is less than the desired after-tax distribution, shares in the mutual fund must be sold to make up the difference. It is assumed that gain is recognized and taxed on the sale of such shares in the same proportion as the ratio of the total accumulated gains within the portfolio to the total value of the portfolio. For example, if the total value of the portfolio is $100,000 and the built-in gain is $40,000, a sale of $5,000 worth of securities would result in the recognition and taxation of $2,000 of gains. The remaining $3,000 would be tax-free recovery of basis.

The variable annuity becomes relatively more advantageous when the continuing benefits of tax deferral over an extended payout period are also included in the analysis. However, even if funds are to be liquidated over a 20-year period, the variable annuity becomes the better alternative (under the listed assumptions) only if the accumulation period is still quite long.

For example, assume an investor expects to invest at a total before-tax and before-expense rate of return of about 10 percent (matching the long-term compound annual rate of return on the S&P 500 index). The investor can expect the variable annuity to outperform a mutual fund only if the investor plans to accumulate money in the variable annuity for about 20.4 years before beginning distributions over a 20-year payout period. Stated another way, an investor

who plans to retire at age 65, for instance, would gain by making contributions to a variable annuity before age 45. However, any further investments made after age 44 would be better invested in the mutual fund outside the variable annuity. The after-tax payments associated with a systematic liquidation of the mutual fund for a twenty year period starting at age 65 for contributions after age 44 would be greater than for comparable contributions to the variable annuity.

Question — What is an FPDA?

Answer — An FPDA is a flexible premium deferred annuity. As the last two words indicate, the contract provides for the accumulation of funds to be applied at some future time designated by the contract owner to provide an income for the annuitant. Premiums can be paid as frequently or infrequently as the owner desires. They can be paid monthly, annually, or one or more years can be skipped since there is no specified contribution amount or required payment frequency. Most insurers do set a minimum payment level for administrative purposes. (This runs from $25 to 50 in most companies).

Most FPDA contracts have no front end load. Annual loads vary but many are under $50 a year. Some companies charge loads based on a percentage of each contribution, as a percentage of the annuity fund balance, or as a percentage of both. The insurer does charge a "back end" load (a surrender charge) when a cash withdrawal in a year exceeds a stipulated percentage of the fund balance. This load will typically reduce year by year to 0 by the 7th or 8th contract year.

Insurers guarantee minimum interest rates (typically 4 to 4.5 percent) but actually pay much higher rates. The actual rate will depend on the earnings rate of the insurer. Current rates are subject to rapid change as interest rates trend upward or downward. Focus should be placed on the net (after loading) return earned when comparing annuities.

Question — What is an SPDA?

Answer — An SPDA is a single premium deferred annuity. It provides, as its name implies, a promise that an annuity will begin at some time in the future in return for a single premium. A minimum stated rate of interest is guaranteed but most insurers pay competitive market rates (the actual rate paid is a function of (a) the current investment earnings of the insurer and (b) how competitive the insurer is determined to be. The rate is subject to change by the insurer.

The SPDA, like the FPDA, is back end loaded. No front end charges are imposed. Surrender charges are graded and partial withdrawals are often allowed without charge. Bailout provisions allow the contract owner to withdraw all funds without the imposition of a surrender charge if the interest rate actually credited falls below the "bailout rate" (typically set at the inception of the contract as 1 to 3 percent below the rate being credited at that time). Keep in mind that on any withdrawal there may be both an ordinary income tax and a penalty tax.

Question — What is a "temporary life annuity"?

Answer — A temporary life annuity is one which provides for fixed payments until the annuitant dies or if earlier the end of a specified number of years. To compute the annuity exclusion ratio, expected return is found by multiplying one year's annuity payments by a multiple from the appropriate IRS annuity table.

Chapter 19

CERTIFICATES OF DEPOSIT

WHAT IS IT?

A certificate of deposit is a debt instrument issued by a commercial bank, savings and loan, or other thrift institution (herein collectively referred to as "bank") in exchange for a deposit made by an investor. "CDs" are usually issued in minimum amounts of $10,000, but often are available in smaller denominations. The term of these certificates can range from three months up to five years. Interest rates on these certificates are frequently tied to the rate paid on 6-month U.S. Treasury bills.

WHEN IS THE USE OF THIS TOOL INDICATED?

1. When the investor requires absolute safety of principal.

2. When immediate access or availability of the funds is desired. (However, the premature redemption of a CD will generally result in the imposition of some type of penalty—for example, the forfeiture of a portion of interest earned to date.)

3. When an individual desires an investment with a relatively limited, but highly flexible time horizon.

ADVANTAGES

1. CDs are generally insured by various agencies of the federal government up to a maximum of $100,000 per account. Individuals who wish to invest more than this amount in their own name should open accounts with different banks to maximize the government insurance protection on their funds.

2. Almost all banks will redeem their certificates prior to maturity on demand. However, there are penalties for early withdrawal of funds from a certificate. First, there may be a withdrawal penalty. For example, an investor who wishes to redeem a 6-month certificate after only three months may be charged the equivalent of one month's interest as a penalty. A second penalty is a reduction in the rate of interest earned on the certificate to the level of passbook rates. (This assumes that CD rates are higher than passbook rates.)

3. As opposed to bonds and common stocks, which are typically longer term investments, CDs may be purchased with maturities that match investors' short-term needs. In addition to formal certificates of deposit, some institutions may offer certificate-like accounts with maturities as short as seven days. The interest paid on these accounts will normally be very similar to that paid on longer term certificates. The availability of these accounts is particularly advantageous for investors who need a safe, liquid, and reasonably profitable "parking place" for cash while considering other investments.

Investors may purchase a portfolio of certificates with differing maturities or simply roll over short-term CDs on an ongoing basis. For example, an investor with $100,000 could purchase four $25,000 CDs, one maturing at the end of each of the next four years. Alternatively, the entire $100,000 could be invested in a single 6-month certificate that would mature and automatically be reinvested (rolled over) in another 6-month certificate.

DISADVANTAGES

1. The rate of return on CDs is lower than rates typically available on higher risk alternatives. For example, CDs typically pay a rate of interest several points below that paid on long-term government bonds. An even greater spread would be available from an investment in corporate bonds.

2. A substantial penalty is charged if the investor redeems the certificate prior to maturity. This penalty can significantly reduce the overall rate of return on the investment.

TAX IMPLICATIONS

1. All of the income from certificates of deposit is fully taxable and subject to ordinary income tax rates.

2. Unlike other investments which are subject to price changes, CDs will be redeemed at maturity for their original investment value. This, together with the fact that there is no market for CDs, means that there can be neither capital gain nor loss with this type of investment. For example, Suzanne Carnes recently invested $50,000

in 6-month certificates of deposit. At maturity, the bank will pay her $50,000 for the certificates. Thus, there is no capital gain or loss.

3. Penalties paid by investors who redeem CDs prior to the maturity date are deductible for federal income tax purposes. For instance, in the example above, if Suzanne Carnes redeemed her CDs two months before they were to have matured, the penalty paid to the bank (actually deducted from the interest and/or principal she otherwise would have received) is deductible.

   You must report on your tax return the gross amount of interest paid or credited to your account during the year without subtracting the penalty. You then deduct the penalty in calculating adjusted gross income (i.e., regardless of whether deductions are itemized). You may deduct the entire penalty even if it exceeds your interest income. Both the gross interest and the penalty amount will be reported to the taxpayer on Form 1099-INT by the financial institution issuing the certificate.

4. The foregone interest in the event of a premature redemption is not deductible. For instance, in the example above, Suzanne Carnes did not earn as much interest as she would have had she kept the certificate until its maturity date. The tax law does not allow a deduction for the loss of interest that might have been earned.

ALTERNATIVES

1. Money market mutual funds typically offer higher rates of return than passbook accounts. These funds also commonly offer check writing features which provide a high degree of liquidity. However, in making a comparison to CDs, the investor should consider that banks offer deposit insurance guarantees up to $100,000.

2. Direct purchase of treasury bills is another investment similar to certificates of deposit. The timing of maturities, safety of principal, and amount of required investment are comparable to investing in bank CDs. Most individuals find it easier to deal with their local banks than to purchase treasury bills through the Federal Reserve system. Furthermore, some banks offer a slightly higher return on CDs than that available from treasury bills.

3. Many banks offer short-term "money market deposit accounts" (MMDA) that are similar in many ways to CDs. These accounts pay competitive rates tied to fluctuations in short-term interest rates. The rate paid normally changes on a weekly basis with interest credited quarterly.

WHERE AND HOW DO I GET IT?

Certificates of deposit are offered by virtually all commercial banks, savings and loans, mutual savings banks, and similar financial institutions.

The investor simply walks into the bank, deposits his or her funds, and receives a certificate in exchange. An investor already dealing with a bank may call the institution, obtain rate quotations, and decide on the maturity date of the certificate and the amount to be purchased. The customer's account will be charged, the CD will be issued and held in safekeeping by the bank, and the need to actually visit the bank has been avoided.

The most popular maturity of these certificates is six months, but maturities can extend for as long as five years. These certificates should be kept in a safe deposit box or other secure location.

Typically, the investor will be notified two to three weeks prior to the maturity of the certificate. If no action is taken, the CD will simply be "rolled over" into another certificate with a similar maturity, but at the bank's current rate of interest. The investor also has the option of redeeming the certificate for cash or making an additional investment.

It is usually recommended that individuals with large amounts to invest in CDs purchase multiple certificates rather than one large certificate. This would make it possible to redeem part of the investment without disturbing the other certificates or paying the premature withdrawal penalty on the entire amount. For example, an investor with $100,000 should purchase ten certificates of $10,000 each rather than one certificate for $100,000.

Diversification of the CDs by bank and geographic location also enhances safety of principal as well as convenience. For additional protection of principal and interest against loss due to troubled savings and loan institutions, it may be desirable to spread investments among several institutions in more than one state. Individuals who live or work a significant part of the time in states other than their legal domicile might consider purchasing and storing CDs in more than one state.

WHAT FEES OR OTHER ACQUISITION COSTS ARE INVOLVED?

There are normally no specific fees or other acquisition costs associated with the purchase of CDs. However, it is important to note that a premature redemption fee is assessed by most banks, and that a lower interest rate may be paid for the period of the investment.

HOW DO I SELECT THE BEST OF ITS TYPE?

1. The investor should compare the interest rates offered by several institutions on CDs for a given maturity. Higher rates are often available from banks and thrift institutions in other parts of the country. For this reason, investors, particularly those with larger amounts to invest, should shop around for the most attractive rates. Information on interest rates offered by out of state institutions may be found in *Barron's*, *The Wall Street Journal*, *The New York Times*, *The Investor's Daily*, and other major financial newspapers.

WHERE CAN I FIND OUT MORE ABOUT IT?

1. The leading source of information on investments in certificates of deposit would be the various financial institutions themselves. All of these sources provide information on rates offered, length of maturity, and any early withdrawal penalties.

2. Financial newspapers and magazines such as *The Wall Street Journal*, *New York Times*, *Barron's*, *Forbes*, and *Investor's Daily* provide information on CDs offered by major financial institutions throughout the country. Local newspapers will also carry ads from regional banks and thrift institutions.

QUESTIONS AND ANSWERS

Question — Are all CDs insured by the federal government?

Answer — No, not all CDs are insured by the federal government and there is a limit to the amount of insurance on those that are covered. Some institutions are insured by state organizations rather than the federal government.

These state insurance arrangements are not as secure as federal insurance. This was evidenced by the failure of certain S&Ls during the mid-80s. It is recommended that investors place their funds with those institutions that do have federal deposit insurance. Also, amounts in excess of $100,000 per account are not covered. This indicates the need to diversify an ultra large investment among a number of different accounts or institutions. For instance, Lara Leimberg wishes to invest a million dollar gift she has recently received from her father. She should consider the purchase of certificates using not only her own name, but also the names of her husband and children (jointly with her own, or separately) so that no one certificate exceeds the federal insurance limit of $100,000. (Note that there may be gift tax implications where certificates are purchased in the names of other individuals.) Another alternative would be for Lara to purchase ten individual certificates in her own name from ten different banks.

Question — Can a CD be used as collateral for a loan?

Answer — Yes. An investor can pledge a CD as security for a loan from the issuing institution or another lender. Banking law (Regulation Q) requires that a bank lending money to customers who use their own CDs as collateral must charge at least one percent over the rate of interest being paid on the CD. This does not apply, however, when an investor is borrowing money from a bank other than the one that issued the CD.

Question — When does the purchaser of a CD receive his interest income?

Answer — Interest is normally calculated daily and paid when the certificate matures. Interest may be withdrawn at that time. Otherwise, it often will be automatically reinvested along with the principal of the certificate. For longer term certificates, those with maturities up to five years, interest may be withdrawn on a quarterly basis.

Chapter 20

COLLECTIBLES

WHAT IS IT?

An investment quality collectible is any item of property which meets the following three criteria:

(1) Rarity

(2) Popularity

(3) Ready marketability

The specific value of a particular collectible will depend on its history, aesthetic qualities, condition, composition, and the number of similar items in existence.

Examples of popular investment quality collectibles include rare coins, art, stamps, gems, oriental rugs, antiques, and certain wines.

WHEN IS THE USE OF THIS TOOL INDICATED?

1. When the investor has little or no need for immediate income and desires long-term capital appreciation.

2. When the investor has a particular knowledge of factors affecting the value of a specific type of collectible. For instance, an artist or art historian may have a unique insight into the quality, rarity, and marketability of middle eastern or oriental art. This sophistication gives such an individual a significant advantage in buying and selling such items.

3. When an investor has unusual access to the sources of supply and demand for a particular type of collectible. For example, an investor with political or social connections in a country famed for its oriental rugs might be told of a collection coming to market or be given favored status in bargaining for a particular item.

4. When an investor wishes to combine the potential for capital appreciation with the psychological pleasure of owning a collectible. For instance, a stamp collector can derive many hours of personal satisfaction from his "hobby" at the same time that it provides a source of financial security. A comic book collector can be entertained, amused, and possibly even rewarded.

5. When an individual is looking for an investment with relative capital stability. Many investors, because of their personal attachment to the items collected, are reluctant to sell. Because collectibles are not controlled by individuals who must sell continually, many items are not freely circulated which adds to their value. The likelihood of a panic sell-off is minimal because collectible investors really wish to own the objects they have collected.

ADVANTAGES

1. Collectibles have the potential for long-term capital growth.

2. Above average returns can be realized by investors with specialized knowledge or information.

3. Collectibles are fun!

4. Collectibles have proven to be a relatively stable form of investment with steady appreciation.

DISADVANTAGES

1. Collectibles generally provide no current income for the investor.

2. Most individuals are not expert enough in a particular area to judge the specific quality of the item they are purchasing. Therefore, they are dependent upon the dealer and any appraiser they may employ. An independent appraisal will add to the cost of purchasing the item.

3. Collectibles are subject to swings in popularity. Fads come and go, and even if the number of collectors increases, the price of a particular item may fall or may not appreciate as rapidly as expected.

4. The absence of an organized market puts both buyers and sellers at a disadvantage; neither is likely to have adequate knowledge of supply, demand, or what is a "fair" price for a particular item.

5. Investors must take the risk that an item will be damaged, stolen, or destroyed. For example, the pages of a rare book may be torn, wine may turn to vinegar, or a fine old

toy bank may rust. Safekeeping, storage, and insurance costs will reduce the overall rate of return on these types of investments.

6. The value of a particular collectible may drop precipitously if a supply previously unknown to the market is discovered.

7. More than in any other area of investment, the potential for fraud and forgery must be considered. Although few experts will be fooled, and copying may be difficult, there is a risk that cannot be discounted. (Investors should insist that sellers verify or guarantee the authenticity of a particular item.)

TAX IMPLICATIONS

1. With the exception of dealers, an individual who invests in collectibles is typically purchasing a capital asset. Therefore, any gain realized on the sale of such an item will be subject to long-term capital gain treatment, assuming that it is held for the requisite period of time. The long-term capital gain on a collectible is taxed at a maximum rate of 28 percent (see "Capital gain" in the Glossary and the discussion of capital gains and losses in Chapter 8, "Income Tax Concepts"). Likewise, any loss will be treated as either long-term or short-term capital loss. Most collectibles are held for at least one to two years, and therefore will usually result in either a long-term gain or a long-term loss.

2. Since there is no fixed maturity date on collectible investments, the individual can control the timing of any gain or loss. Obviously this makes it advantageous to delay any sale of an investment until a year when the investor's income is low, deductions are high, or a year in which tax brackets have dropped.

3. The increase in value of collectibles occurs on a tax-deferred basis year after year. The investor pays no tax until he chooses to sell.

ALTERNATIVES

1. The investor may switch from one area of collectibles to another as his personal tastes and interests change. For example, a stamp collector may turn to rare coins. A collector of ancient Japanese woodcuts may decide to acquire rare and historically valuable photographs.

2. Gold, silver, platinum, and other precious metals share some of the same characteristics as collectibles. These include their tangible nature, and emphasis on capital appreciation.

WHERE AND HOW DO I GET IT?

Specialty stores typically offer the finest investment grade collectibles. Such stores will usually concentrate in a particular area of collectibles such as antique furniture or clocks. The investor can expect to pay a premium in doing business with such establishments due to their relatively high overhead.

Auctions are another important source of fine collectibles. They provide the investor with useful pricing information, an opportunity to meet other investor-collectors, and they add to the psychological pleasure of buying, selling, and owning collectibles.

Collector "conventions" are gathering places for large groups of buyers and sellers. They offer many of the same opportunities as auctions, but in a somewhat less formal setting.

Local newspapers are a source of information on estate sales. The pressure to pay taxes and other estate settlement expenses—or to dispose of unwanted assets—often makes valuable items available at favorable prices.

Many general interest newspapers carry advertisements for collectibles. Collectors' magazines such as *The Antique Trader* are directed at collectors in general. A third source of market information is the very specific and narrowly focused periodicals; for example, there are magazines directed exclusively at antique gun collectors.

Flea markets are an important source of collectibles for the modest investor. These carnival-like gatherings provide an opportunity to view a large array of items on sale at what are often bargain prices. The investor has an opportunity to negotiate the price, or just plain haggle, with the seller.

Fellow collectors may provide one of the most important sources of information as well as supply and demand for collectibles. Many develop expert knowledge in a particular field and may maintain personal contact with a large number of individuals who share similar interests.

WHAT FEES OR OTHER ACQUISITION COSTS ARE INVOLVED?

Typically, there are no commissions or fees associated with the purchase of collectibles. One important exception would be the formal auction where a percentage of the bid price is added and paid to the auction house by both the buyer and seller of the item.

As with all tangible investments, shipping, storage, and insurance costs must be factored into the investment equation. Appraisal costs may also add significantly to the purchase price of an item.

HOW DO I SELECT THE BEST OF ITS TYPE?

1. There are authoritative (but not always totally accurate) price guides in the collectibles marketplace. These serve as useful tools for investors, but fall far short of being as indicative of value as are the transactions of buyers and sellers on an organized exchange.

2. Wealthy investors may wish to hire authorities and experts in a particular area of collectibles. For instance, an individual could employ an appraiser or art consultant to locate and negotiate the price for a specific painting.

3. Dealers in collectibles can provide access to information as well as share their expertise with valued customers.

4. As much as in any other investment, if not more so, the purchase of collectibles requires knowledge on the part of the investor. Specifically, this means knowledge of the particular characteristics which make the investment valuable. This insight can be obtained through courses given through colleges and adult continuing education programs. There are also programs available through museums and galleries. These educational experiences enhance the collector's psychological enjoyment as well as increase the potential for investment gain.

WHERE CAN I FIND OUT MORE ABOUT IT?

1. There are many reference books for the collector available in libraries and local bookstores. Such references include *The Encyclopedia of Collectibles*, *The Concise Encyclopedia of Antiques*, *Investments You Can Live With and Enjoy*, and *A Guide to the Grading of U. S. Coins*.

2. Periodicals are available for almost every type of collectible. Examples include *Antique Monthly*, *Antique Toy World*, and *Antique Trader*. Potential investors may want to browse through several of these magazines in their particular areas of interest before making an investment.

3. Clubs, museums, and auction houses often publish newsletters, articles, and catalogs of interest to the collector-investor.

QUESTIONS AND ANSWERS

Question — How do you determine a fair price for a painting?

Answer — A number of factors must be considered before purchasing a painting (or any other art) for investment purposes. These include: (1) the identity of the artist (an artist whose works are traded in the international art market will bring a higher price than one who is not so well known), (2) the time in the life of the artist when the particular work was done (certain styles adopted either early or late in an artist's life may be more sought after and therefore bring larger sums than others), (3) the quality of the art (a top quality work will bring a higher price than work by the same artist that is executed in a less professional manner), (4) the condition of the art (scratches, chips, other damages, overcleaning and overpainting may all adversely affect the value of the art), (5) the subject (ugly scenes are less in demand than pleasant ones and certain subjects have a higher popularity than others), (6) the size (very small works of art may be worth more—or less—than larger versions, and the size must be suitable for use or display), (7) exhibitions (if the work was ever exhibited in a prominent museum or gallery, its quality is presumed to be higher and it is considered more authentic and prestigious), (8) the pedigree (if the past ownership can be traced, the authenticity and quality of the art work are easier to establish), (9) whether there is a genuine signature (the signature of a recognized artist enhances the value), (10) the artist's price history (the various prices the artist has received in the past are indicators of current value), and (11) the identity of the seller (many large and reputable auction galleries will guarantee the authenticity and pedigree of the art).

Question — What should the collector-investor look for when purchasing stamps?

Answer — The first factor in stamp investing is scarcity. The condition of the stamp or stamps is the second major characteristic which should be examined. The shading of the color and the design "centering" are also key factors in determining value. If a stamp is canceled lightly or is unused it will be more valuable. (A "mint" stamp is one which is both unused and in perfect condition while an "unused" stamp is one which has never been used for postage, but is not in perfect condition.) A stamp which is interesting, easily understood, and physically attractive will have stronger appeal, and therefore greater value. Another factor is the country of origin of the stamp. Stamps of countries with a stable government and sound currency which also have wealthy stamp collectors are likely to be more valuable than stamps from countries which do not. A stamp is likely to increase in value at a greater rate if its "topic" is of considerable interest. For instance, a stamp depicting the first moonwalk will have greater value—other things being equal—than a similar stamp carrying the picture of Colonel Arthur Young.

Question — What are the factors that affect the price of a rare coin?

Answer — The four major factors that affect the price of a rare coin are: (1) quality (the condition of the coin), (2) the supply available, (3) the historical significance, and (4) its attractiveness and physical appeal.

Question — Why do so few people become investors in collectibles if the potential for high return is so great?

Answer — It is a good rule of thumb when it comes to collectibles (and perhaps also to investments in gems) to invest in only what can be enjoyed without sacrificing measured income or liquidity needs. There are many reasons for this position:

(1) collectibles, precious metals, and gems are costly to own, store, or insure yet produce no income to help purchase or carry those costs,

(2) the acquisition costs, markup, and commissions are high relative to alternatives,

(3) market value fluctuations are common and often significant,

(4) price changes are often due to both unpredictable and uncontrollable forces, and

(5) perhaps most importantly, it is difficult to find reputable, trustworthy, experienced, and knowledgeable advisers whose income is related to results.

Assets such as gold, diamonds, or platinum are often called "hard assets" and are often purchased as a defensive measure against political instability and inflation.

Chapter 21

COMMODITIES

WHAT IS IT?

A commodity purchase represents ownership of a definite physical item such as sugar, wheat, corn, lumber, or pork bellies. Other commodities include orange juice, cotton, cocoa, coffee, and eggs. The purchaser is buying—not a paper ownership right—but the actual item itself. The units of purchase are measured by given weights, sizes, or shapes. For example, a wheat contract may be described as "No. 2, soft red winter wheat" and each contract represents a 5,000 bushel purchase.

Most investors purchasing commodities buy a contract to either make or accept a delivery of a specified commodity on a given future date, thus the term, "futures contract." If the contract runs to its termination, the investor must complete the contract by either making a delivery of the commodity or paying cash in acceptance of the commodity.

WHEN IS THE USE OF THIS TOOL INDICATED?

1. When the investor is willing to take very high risks. Although the potential rewards of commodities trading are extremely high (it is possible for an investor to double his money in only a few days), over 70% of commodities speculators will lose money, and aggregate losses are typically five to six times greater than gains. If a commodities contract is allowed to expire (for example, because the price of soybeans plummets from $13 to $5, and the investor's contract allows him to purchase soybeans at $10 per bushel), the investor has no equity, his entire position is eliminated, and the value of his contract is zero.

2. When the investor is able to risk at least $10,000 of capital. This amount is the suggested minimum necessary to allow reasonable diversification of positions, and to respond to "margin calls." *Margin* is an amount of money deposited by both buyers and sellers of futures contracts to ensure performance of the terms of the contract. A brokerage firm may "call" for additional margin to bring the funds in a customer's account up to the required level.

3. When the investor desires a very high degree of leverage in his investments. This leverage comes from the low margin requirements on commodities investments. Compared to margins of fifty percent when investing in common stocks, margins on commodity investments are extremely low. An investor can finance ninety to ninety-five percent of the value of the contract at the time of purchase. (The actual cash required will vary according to the commodity and the standards of the broker handling the transaction.) The margin for commodities is considered a security deposit. Therefore, unlike margins for securities which are interest bearing, the investor pays no interest on the unpaid balance in a commodities contract.

4. When the investor has the emotional stability to accept frequent and possibly significant losses. Clearly, commodities trading is not for the fainthearted.

5. When the producer of a particular commodity would like to "hedge" one risk by taking an offsetting one. For example, assume a farmer plants winter wheat. He has calculated that he must receive a price of $ X.XX per bushel to break even. Yet, he has no assurance of what the price will be when he is ready to bring the wheat to market. To assure himself of at least a minimum price he enters into a futures contract guaranteeing a price of $ Y.YY per bushel upon delivery of the wheat.

If the cash market price is below the price guaranteed in the futures contract the farmer will exercise the contract, deliver the wheat, and obtain his expected profit. Conversely, if the cash price is above the contract price, the farmer will likely sell his wheat in the cash market, buy back his futures contract, and presumably increase his profit.

In essence, the commodities exchange serves the function of finding someone to complete the opposite side of the contract. That someone is the investor (speculator). This individual assumes the risk because he feels he can profit from price movements on wheat before the delivery date of the contract. For example, the speculator may feel that wheat prices will rise sharply in the next few months, and that there will be a corresponding increase in the value of his contract. That is because the contract gives him the right to buy wheat at a fixed price below the expected market price.

ADVANTAGES

1. A speculator in commodities has the potential of making enormous profits in a relatively short period of time. Assume corn is selling at $2.90 per bushel and an investor purchases one 5,000 bushel contract. Instead of putting up $14,500, he is allowed to deposit only $1,000. If the price of corn rises to $3.19 (a price change of only ten percent), he will have made a profit of $1,450 ($0.29 x 5,000 bushels), less commissions. But, if we compare his profit of $1,450 to his outlay of $1,000, the percentage return is 145% (lowered slightly by commissions).

2. For a given investment budget, the extremely low margin requirements for commodities permits more diversification than would be possible in the stock and bond markets.

3. Producers of various commodities can transfer the risk of price changes to speculators, and lock in a particular price when they bring their commodity to market.

DISADVANTAGES

1. An investor's position can be completely wiped out by a relatively small change in the price of the commodity. This is due to the very low margin requirements of the contract, and the inherent volatility of the commodity markets. In the example above, the investor purchased a 5,000 bushel contract for corn selling at $2.90 per bushel. Instead of putting up $14,500 ($2.90 x 5,000), his broker allows him to deposit only $1,000. If the price of corn were to drop by twenty cents per bushel, the value of the contract would have declined by $1,000 and his margin would have been eliminated. This would result in a call from his broker for additional margin in order to maintain his position.

   It is very likely that an investor who puts up small amounts of margin will often have that margin eliminated. Unless the investor is willing to put up additional margin, his position will be closed out and the contract terminated. This may occur a number of times before the investor will be able to discern and follow a trend in the market.

2. Unlike other securities markets, positions in commodities are "marked to the market" on a daily basis. This means that at the close of trading each day, the clearinghouse for the exchange calculates the gains and losses on all open positions and transfers those gains or losses into or out of all margin accounts. Profits may be removed by investors, but losses are deducted immediately from the investor's account. If the remaining margin declines below the level of the required maintenance margin, a "margin call" will be issued asking that additional funds be added to the account to bring it back to the minimum margin level. Should the investor fail to do so, his position will be "closed" by the firm handling his account. In other words, the brokerage firm will terminate the investor's interest in the contract. It does this by either buying or selling an offsetting contract.

3. Each commodity has a daily price limit, and once that limit is reached trading stops for the day. For example, the maximum daily price movement for soybeans, one of the most active commodity markets, is twenty cents per bushel. This represents a value of $1,000 per contract on a 5,000 bushel contract. The purpose of this limit is to protect the commodity markets from severe price fluctuations which could result from news of crop damage, weather reports, and other natural or market occurrences. This restriction on trading can cause the investor to be "locked in" to a position when the market is unavailable to buy or sell the commodity.

   For instance, Marty Satinsky owns a futures contract for wheat. A newly issued crop report indicates a tremendous surplus which causes a panic in the market. Prices fall sharply, and before Marty can act, the drop in price has reached the maximum daily limit. That causes all trading in wheat to stop and Marty is forced to hold his contract until trading resumes. By that time it may be even more difficult to close out his position.

TAX IMPLICATIONS

1. Net gains on all speculative commodity futures contracts are taxed at a maximum effective rate of 27.84%. This is due to the fact that net gains on all speculative transactions are treated as though they are forty percent short-term capital gains and sixty percent long-term capital gains. Applying the 1998 maximum tax rate of 39.6% and a 20% capital gains rate results in a 27.84% overall rate ((39.6% x 40%) + (20% x 60%)). The usual holding period rule for determining whether a gain or loss is short-term or long-term is ignored.

2. All "open" positions (those which have not been closed out, exercised, or expired) at the end of the tax year are treated as if they had been closed on the last day of the year. In other words, any gain or loss inherent in a futures contract at the end of the year, or at any time during the year, must be reported annually, even if the investor has not actually realized those gains or losses. Therefore, if a contract has not been terminated or transferred before the

end of the tax year, it is artificially treated as though the investor had sold it for its fair market value on the last business day of the year. Profits or losses from these open positions are combined with those positions that were actually closed during the rest of the year.

3. Net futures trading losses may be applied against the investor's other capital gains. If a net loss on futures transactions still exists, these may be carried back three years. If any loss still remains it may be carried forward into succeeding years.

ALTERNATIVES

1. Rather than buying commodities directly, an investor may purchase shares in a mutual fund that specializes in these investments. This alternative is especially attractive for the individual who does not have the expertise or time necessary to watch his investments on a day-to-day basis. Such attention is absolutely essential in the commodities area due to the rapid price movements and low margin positions. Commodity funds offer professional management and the constant attention demanded by this volatile market.

2. A "commodity pool" is an alternative to mutual funds, but has many of the same characteristics. For instance, in order to participate in a diversified portfolio of commodity futures with professional management, individuals will purchase units in the pool. Their money is combined and invested in a number of active commodities. In many cases the pool will be closed out when fifty percent of the original capital is lost. These are normally structured as limited partnerships requiring a minimum investment of $5,000 or more. In addition to a minimum investment these pools typically require that investors have a minimum income and wealth position.

WHERE AND HOW DO I GET IT?

Investors may trade contracts on commodities through their brokerage firms in much the same way as they buy and sell securities. A separate margin account is required and settlement on this account will be made on a daily basis as described above.

An investor may also take part in a so-called "managed account" program with a particular commodities broker or trading firm. Under this arrangement the commodities broker has the discretionary power to trade for the investor's account. An added characteristic of these managed accounts is that the broker may participate in the profits earned on the account in addition to any commissions that may be generated by the trading activity.

Investors may also invest in commodities through mutual funds which may be purchased through a broker, or in the case of some funds, directly from the fund itself. Minimum investments generally range from $1,000 up to $10,000. An advantage of these funds is that they enable individuals to participate in a portfolio of commodity contracts which provides a degree of diversification that the small investor may not be able to achieve.

WHAT FEES OR OTHER ACQUISITION COSTS ARE INVOLVED?

A commission or service charge is applied to a commodities trade in much the same fashion as the buying or selling of stocks and bonds.

HOW DO I SELECT THE BEST OF ITS TYPE?

1. Investors should concentrate their attention on a few commodities rather than spread their investment over a large number of different contracts. More time and effort will be needed to follow commodity positions than similar investments in stocks and bonds, and the average investor will generally be less knowledgeable about commodity markets.

2. Select markets which are active and which have a large "open interest." This is the number of contracts in a commodity that have not been closed out, exercised, or allowed to expire. The level of open interest is reported daily in newspaper commodity pages. Conversely, beginning investors should avoid "thin" markets which are especially prone to volatile price swings because of the relatively low number of contracts and the small number of active traders. Some of the more active commodities are soybeans, wheat, cocoa, and copper.

3. Inexperienced traders should begin with a conservative position of one or two contracts that mature in a distant month. This will require a relatively small investment and give the investor time to study the market and get better acquainted with its characteristics before making greater commitments. Also, buying contracts in distant months will reduce the amount of trading and the amount of commissions charged.

4. It is generally a good idea to put in a "stop-loss order" five percent below the market price when buying a commod-

ity, and five percent above the market for a short sale. This approach will limit the investor's losses while allowing for continued gains if the market moves in the anticipated direction.

5. Never put up additional margin to maintain a contract. If you are asked to do so it means that the market is moving against you and will likely continue to do so. It is better to liquidate your position and take a small loss rather than continue to increase your investment and risk a major loss of capital.

6. This is an area where an experienced broker can be invaluable. Investors should look for a firm with a strong background in commodities, and deal with a broker who is a specialist in the field. It is not likely that a broker whose area of expertise is stocks and bonds will also be knowledgeable in the area of commodities. Diversified investors may want to maintain a separate brokerage account for their commodities trading activity.

WHERE CAN I FIND OUT MORE ABOUT IT?

1. Daily price quotations on various commodities can be found in *The Wall Street Journal* and other major financial newspapers.

2. Most of the major brokerage firms have departments that specialize in trading commodities. They can be a source of reports and charts on the various commodity contracts.

3. Serious traders may wish to subscribe to the monthly *Commodities Magazine* published by Norwood Securities, Inc., Chicago, Illinois.

4. The Chicago Board of Trade publishes a reference book entitled, *Commodity Trading Manual.*

QUESTIONS AND ANSWERS

Question — Why are the margins on commodity contracts so low in comparison with those on stocks and bonds?

Answer — The margin on a commodity contract is a security deposit to ensure performance on the contract. It is not a down payment on the commodity itself or a payment of equity as in the case of stocks and bonds. A similar concept applies in the field of real estate where a security deposit is typically paid to the seller of a house by the buyer to ensure that final payment will be made at the time of closing.

Question — Is commodities trading regulated?

Answer — Yes, the Commodity Futures Trading Commission (CFTC), an agency of the federal government, regulates the trading of all domestically traded commodities. The CFTC sets price fluctuation limits, prohibits excessive market positions, oversees the handling of investors' funds by brokers, and allows trading only on designated exchanges.

Question — Where can an investor obtain information on the commodities themselves?

Answer — A commodities investor must be concerned with a number of fundamentals and their relationship to each other. These include: (1) the amount produced, (2) surplus from prior years, (3) the amount which must be saved, and is therefore not available for current use, and (4) the amount that is currently needed.

The United States Department of Agriculture (USDA) makes public announcements of most of this information. Until the public release, this information is a closely guarded secret.

Other factors which will directly or indirectly affect the price of various commodities are the weather, crop and animal blights and diseases, political influences, technological changes, and the expectations of farmers and other commodity producers.

Chapter 22

COMMON STOCKS

WHAT IS IT?

Common stock represents an ownership interest in a corporation. Each shareholder is entitled to a proportionate share of the control, profits, and assets of the corporation. Stockholders exercise control through voting rights and receive a share of corporate profits through dividends. In the event the corporation is sold or liquidated, owners of common stock will share the net proceeds.

WHEN IS THE USE OF THIS TOOL INDICATED?

1. When an investor is willing to accept the risk of fluctuating share prices in return for potential capital growth and increasing dividend income.

2. When the investor is concerned that the purchasing power of fixed income securities may not keep pace with inflation.

ADVANTAGES

1. Over the long run, common stocks have provided an average annual rate of return almost twice that of fixed income investments. Returns on stocks have averaged 9% to 10% over the past fifty years while fixed income securities such as corporate bonds and government securities have averaged only 4%. From 1990 through 1997, the Standard & Poor's 500 Stock Index averaged a compound annual return of about 16%.

2. Common stocks are highly marketable. This means that they can quickly and easily be converted to cash if necessary. This liquidity itself enhances their value.

3. The huge number of common stocks available makes it possible for investors to select securities that are compatible with their own particular investment requirements and risk-taking preferences. For example, public utility stocks have traditionally been selected by investors with a preference for security and stable income while growth stocks may be more attractive to those who are willing to accept greater risk and do not need current income.

4. Unlike many real estate investments, common stocks do not require a high degree of personal management. Typically, a stock portfolio does not require day-to-day management as may be necessary in more active types of investments.

DISADVANTAGES

1. The market price of stocks can fluctuate widely over time. Day-to-day changes in share prices are inevitable and beyond the investor's control. This volatility may be unsettling to conservative investors for whom preservation of capital is a high priority.

2. The prices of individual securities may be adversely affected by factors unrelated to the financial condition of the business itself. These may include political events, changes in tax laws or interest rates, and general economic conditions.

3. It is possible that an investor could lose all or a significant portion of his investment. For instance, if an individual were forced to sell shares during a depressed market the result may be a permanent loss of capital.

4. Payment of dividends on common stock is not guaranteed. Although many corporations have traditionally paid regular dividends, declaration of a dividend, as well as the specific amount, is at the discretion of the corporation's board of directors. Thus, dividends may vary with changes in the general financial condition of a company. This would be a potential problem for investors who desire a regular income.

TAX IMPLICATIONS

1. Dividends on common stock are taxed as ordinary income.

2. Capital gains are taxable at various rates depending on the holding period of the investment. Short-term gains (12 months or less) are taxable at ordinary income rates up to a maximum of 39.6%. Long-term gains (more than 12 months) are taxable at only a 10% rate for investors in the 15% bracket, and 20% for investors in all other brackets.

3. Losses on the sale of common stock will be short-term or long-term depending on how long the stock was held (see "Capital gain" in the Glossary for the necessary holding period). Capital losses are deductible dollar for dollar against short-term capital gain, long-term capital gain, and finally, to a limited degree, against ordinary income. Assume Dick Goldman had a capital "paper loss" of $8,000 and an actual realized short-term gain of $5,000 in the same year. If he sold the depressed shares and recognized the $8,000 loss, $5,000 of the loss would be used to wipe out the entire short-term gain. This would leave a $3,000 loss that could be used to reduce his ordinary income. (The maximum amount of ordinary income that may be offset in one tax year is $3,000; any excess capital loss may be carried over to the succeeding tax year.)

4. Year-to-year appreciation in share prices is not taxable unless and until the investor realizes the gain by selling the stock or otherwise disposing of it in a taxable transaction. This makes it possible to defer the gain until a tax year in which the investor is in a lower tax bracket. For example, Bob Norton might deliberately delay the sale of highly appreciated stock until after retirement when he will be in a lower tax bracket.

It may be possible to avoid taxation on the gain entirely. If an investor holds appreciated stock until his death, the gain is never taxed. This is because the "basis" of the stock is "stepped-up" to its fair market value for federal estate tax purposes. For example, if Bob Norton had purchased the stock for $30 per share and it was worth $130 per share at the time of his death, the new basis of the stock in his executor's hands would be stepped up to

$130. If the executor sold the stock the next day for $130 there would be no gain. This is because the "amount realized" ($130) minus the adjusted basis ($130) is zero and, therefore, there is no taxable gain.

ALTERNATIVES

1. Certain types of real estate investments offer similar features in regard to capital gain potential, deferral of taxation, and the opportunity for increasing income over time.

2. Convertible bonds (see Chapter 23) are often thought of as an alternative to more direct investments in common stock. Interest income will generally be greater than the dividends paid on common shares of equal value. The conversion feature offers the potential for bondholders to share in the future appreciation of common stock.

3. Securities options ("puts" and "calls") give the investor the right to sell, in the case of puts, or buy, in the case of calls, a certain number of shares of stock at a fixed price for a limited period of time. Options provide the opportunity for substantial leverage based on a relatively small capital outlay. (See Questions and Answers below.)

WHERE AND HOW DO I GET IT?

Common stocks are typically purchased through a stock brokerage firm. Once your account is established by providing certain personal and financial information, brokers will transact orders for the purchase or sale of shares. These orders

Figure 22.1 — Example of a client confirmation

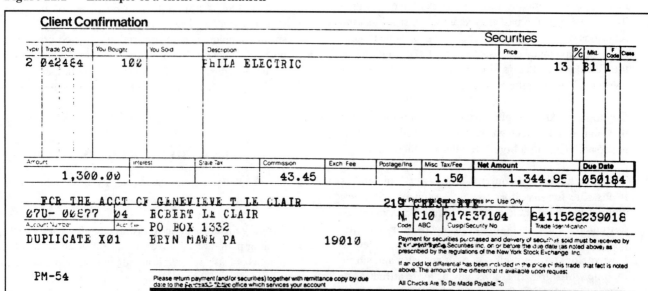

may be submitted in person but are commonly transacted over the telephone.

It is also possible to buy and sell securities directly through many banks, mutual funds, and other financial institutions. Although these institutions may not provide the full range of services offered by the typical brokerage firm, they generally charge substantially lower commissions to buy and sell shares.

Recently, investors have been able to buy and sell securities using personal computers and the Internet. Such electronic trading, often through discount brokerage firms, is growing rapidly. One factor contributing to this growth is the very low cost of such transactions. Fees paid on these trades can be as low as $8, which is a small fraction of the regular brokerage commission charge.

Once stock has been bought or sold the investor is notified by mail in the form of a written confirmation. The confirmation will show the date of the transaction, the name of the company involved, the number of shares, the transaction price per share, the total value of the transaction, and the commissions or fees charged. A typical confirmation is shown in Figure 22.1.

The ownership of stock is evidenced by certificates. An example of a stock certificate is shown in Figure 22.2.

Investors can have their broker send them the actual stock certificates or they can ask the broker to hold them for safekeeping. This relieves the investor of the expense and trouble of providing security for the shares and makes it easier and faster to sell the shares at a later date.

When shares are held by the broker on behalf of the investor, they are registered in the name of the broker. This is commonly referred to as holding shares in "street name." As long as shares are held in street name any dividends paid on the stock are remitted to the brokerage firm which will pay them to the investor or retain them in the investor's account.

Many investors prefer to own common stocks indirectly through mutual funds. These funds provide a number of advantages such as: (1) diversification, (2) professional management, (3) automatic reinvestment of dividends, and (4) ease of record keeping. (See Chapter 34 for a more detailed discussion of mutual funds.)

WHAT FEES OR OTHER ACQUISITION COSTS ARE INVOLVED?

When common stocks are purchased directly from a broker or a bank there is a sales charge commonly called a brokerage commission or fee. The amount of the fee will be dependent upon the amount invested and the number of shares purchased.

Commission charges will vary widely and investors should compare the rates charged by various sources when buying or selling shares. However, transaction costs are not the only factor to consider in buying or selling shares of stock. The information, advice and other services that are provided by a firm may easily justify a higher commission rate.

HOW DO I SELECT THE BEST OF ITS TYPE?

1. Professional security analysts rate common stocks according to their (1) overall quality, (2) security, and (3) growth potential. The process involves an analysis of various factors such as product and industry position, corporate resources, and financial policy. Among the rating services which can be found in your local library are Standard & Poor's, Moody's, and the Value Line Investment Survey. Their rankings of stocks should not be considered as a forecast of future market price performance. Instead, the rating assigned should basically be considered an appraisal of past performance of earnings and dividends.

   The rankings do not take into account the current price of a stock, which is a critical factor in making a particular purchase or sale. A highly rated stock may be overpriced while a stock with a low rating may be attractively priced and a good buy. Ratings by professional services should be only one of the factors an investor would look at in making stock investment decisions.

   Conservative investors usually avoid those stocks rated "B" or lower by Standard & Poor's or Moody's or those with a Value Line ranking lower than "3."

2. Extensive information and investment advisory services are offered by most brokerage firms. They can provide recommendations on specific industries or individual companies in the form of research reports by their own analysts. Brokerage firms also make available information which they in turn purchase from one or more professional research firms.

3. A wealth of information can be obtained at no cost by writing to the headquarters of a company and requesting a copy of its "annual report." This report contains information on the company's activities, its financial condition, products or services, general outlook, management personnel, dividend payments, and future prospects. A more detailed version of this report, known as a "10-K report,"

Figure 22.2 — Example of a stock certificate

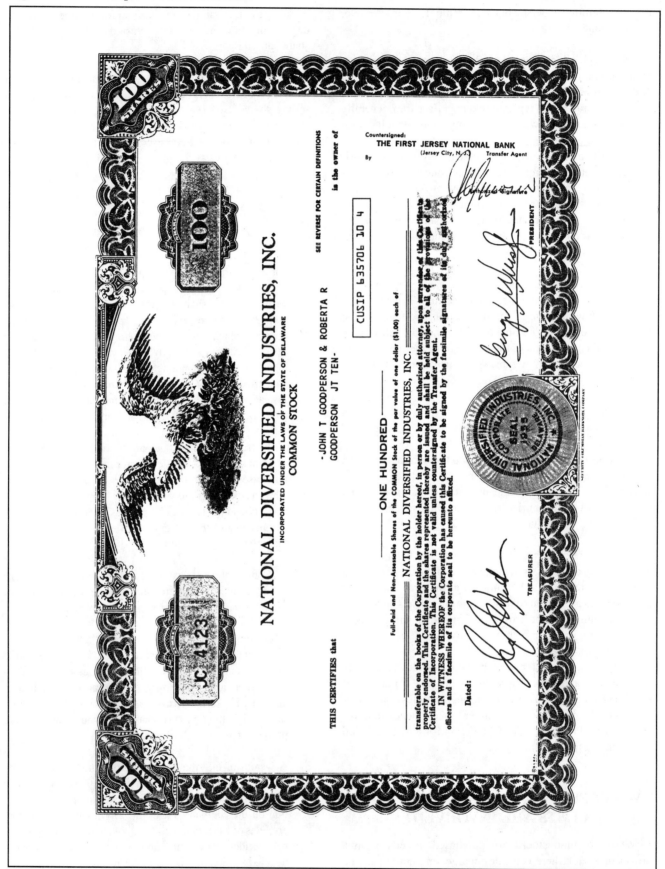

can also be obtained by writing to the company or to the Securities and Exchange Commission, Washington, D.C.

4. Investors seeking current income should examine the dividend payment record of the stock in question. The services listed above will indicate the current dividend being paid on the stock, if any, and the amounts paid in prior years. Brokerage firms can provide lists of companies that have paid dividends consistently for many years and those firms that have increased their dividends regularly. The Value Line Investment Survey ranks stocks according to their current dividend yield percentage. This ranking would enable an investor to quickly select those stocks providing the highest level of dividend income per dollar of investment.

WHERE CAN I FIND OUT MORE ABOUT IT?

1. As noted above, your local library can provide a wealth of information on common stocks. In addition to receiving rating services such as Standard & Poor's or Moody's, many libraries will have a variety of books on investment, security analysis, portfolio management, and related topics. Periodicals such as *Business Week*, *Forbes*, and *Fortune* regularly carry reports on various industries and individual companies. Larger libraries may have collections of annual reports received from individual companies, particularly those with headquarters located in the immediate area.

2. *The Wall Street Journal*, *The New York Times*, and most major newspapers will carry daily listings of the trading activity on the larger stock and bond exchanges.

3. Research reports and other information on specific issues and current market conditions can be obtained by calling major brokerage firms and the trust departments of many banks.

4. A great deal of investment information is now available on the Internet using a personal computer. Most larger companies and many smaller ones provide their annual reports, press releases, and other useful information electronically. Additional information is available from the Securities and Exchange Commission though its Electronic Data Gathering, Analysis, and Retrieval (EDGAR) website (www.sec.gov/edgarhp.htm).

QUESTIONS AND ANSWERS

Question — Of what value is a stock's "price/earnings ratio" in deciding whether or not it is a good buy?

Answer — The "P/E ratio" is simply the stock's current market price divided by the company's most recent twelve months earnings. The ratio can be compared with that of other similar companies to determine the relative value of various companies' earnings. An investor interested in a particular company could also compare the current P/E ratio with the historic high and low ratio for the same company. Many investors prefer to purchase a stock when its P/E ratio is at or near its historic low point in anticipation that the rate will increase in the future. Conservative stocks tend to have price/earnings ratios of six to ten while more speculative issues can have ratios of twenty or thirty times earnings.

For example, a stock selling at $50 per share, with earnings of $4 per share, has a P/E ratio of 12.5 (50 ÷ 4).

Question — Why do some companies "split" their common stock?

Answer — The main reason for stock splits is to lower the stock's price per share. For example, if a stock were selling for $75 per share before a 3:1 split, after the split each shareholder would have three times the number of shares held previously but the price per share would now be $25. Many companies desire to maintain a relatively low stock price, between $20 and $50 per share, so that small investors can buy one hundred share lots. The purchase of one hundred shares of a stock is often called a "round lot."

Question — What is a "stock dividend?"

Answer — A stock dividend is a dividend paid in additional shares of stock rather than cash. Since all common stockholders receive their proportionate share of the dividend the total value of all the common stock of the company is unchanged, while at the same time, the value of each share is proportionately reduced.

Question — Will I receive dividends if I purchase a call option on a particular stock?

Answer — No, option holders are not entitled to receive dividends during the option period since they do not actually own the stock. Only the actual owner of the stock is able to receive dividends.

Question — When would it be desirable to buy a call option on a stock rather than the stock itself?

Answer — Investors utilize this tool because with a minimal outlay of funds they have the potential for greater capital gains than if they purchased the shares directly. For example, ABC Company's common shares are currently selling for $50 per share. An investment of $5,000 will purchase 100 shares of stock. If the stock doubles in price to $100 per share the investor will have a gain of 100% on his investment. At the same time an option to buy 100 shares of ABC Company may cost $500. If the stock price were to double, the value of an option could triple or quadruple and the investor would have a return of 300% or 400%. (For a more complete explanation, see Chapter 38, Put and Call Stock Options.)

Question — What is a stock "right"?

Answer — When a corporation wants to sell additional stock, the issuance of such stock must be approved by the board of directors and there must be enough "authorized and unissued" stock available. "Rights" (often called "subscription rights") are sometimes offered to existing shareholders, enabling them to purchase any new shares before the public at large.

This subscription right gives the stockholder the privilege of purchasing stock at a stipulated price for a limited period of time. The subscription price is set below the current market price as an inducement to encourage the purchase of additional shares.

Subscription rights typically expire in a few weeks. They have no theoretical value if the market price of the common stock falls below the subscription price of the new shares.

Corporations will specify (a) the record date, (b) the subscription price, and (c) the expiration date of the stock rights when the common stock offering is announced. One right is usually issued for each outstanding share of stock to stockholders listed in the corporate records on the stated record date.

The following equation shows how to calculate the value of a right:

$$X = \frac{MP - SP}{N}$$

where

X = estimated value of a right

MP = market price per share

SP = subscription price to buy one share

N = number of rights needed to buy one new share

For example, if the market price of a stock is $15 per share, the subscription price to buy one share of the same stock is $10, and five "rights" were needed to buy one the share, the estimated value of one "right" would be $1.

Question — What is "selling short" and how does it work?

Answer — Selling short is a technique used by both aggressive and conservative investors. The aggressive investor who feels the price of the stock will fall can earn money by selling short. In the past, the conservative investor used short selling to defer the tax on gains. Short selling means that you sell shares you "borrow" from a broker with the hope that the stock will decline in price in the near future.

Short selling works like this:

(a) the client calls the broker and says, "Sell X number of shares of Y stock short."

(b) The broker tells the client that the stock is currently selling for $U dollars per share. In a short sale the client must buy on an "uptick." That means he can buy only if the last sale was at a price higher than the sale preceding it. The client can specify a target price for the sale (this is called a "limit" order) or the client can specify that the stock is to be sold "at market" or on the next uptick.

(c) Assume the stock "ticks up" to the sell price and the broker sells X shares from its inventory. (If the firm doesn't have enough of the stock in its inventory, it will borrow the stock and charge the client a small premium.) The client will be charged the standard commission for selling the stock.

(d) The purchaser of the stock pays the broker and in return receives the stock certificates.

(e) The client must put up 50 percent of the value of the borrowed stock in cash (or 100% of the value of the borrowed stock in securities) since this is a credit transaction. The money or securities are placed in the client's margin account. Interest is typically not charged on the transaction since the broker has the proceeds from the short sale as well as the initial margin.

(f) If the stock drops in value, the client "closes out" the short sale. He tells his broker to buy the same number of shares he previously sold and specifies that the purchase is to cover the short sale. The brokerage firm returns that number of shares to its inventory. The client has a profit (or loss) equal to the difference between the sale price and the purchase price. But note that the percentage return is much greater than it appears because the client never invested the full amount; he put up only the 50 percent margin amount. His gain is further reduced (or his loss is increased) by the two brokerage commissions.

Selling short is highly risky because, if the stock goes up instead of down, the client will have to buy back the stock at its higher price. The leverage that increases the client's gain if he is right increases his loss if he is wrong. If the stock increases rapidly in value, the stock brokerage firm will issue the client a "maintenance call." This is a notice from the firm that the client must put more money into his margin account. This call will typically be issued when the margin account balance (the sum of what the client put into the account plus the proceeds from the short sale) falls below 130 percent of the current market value of the stock. The broker will automatically close out the client's position if the additional call money is not added to the account. (Most experts advise that it's better to take the loss than to put up more margin and lose more money).

Selling short should be considered only if (a) the market is a bear market, and (b) the client has researched the particular stock and the state of its industry group thoroughly and (c) the client has checked the volume of short sales of that stock (if many others have also shorted the stock, when they begin to buy the stock to cover their positions, it may drive the price of the stock back up) and (d) the client has considered the tax implications. (All gains from short sales will be taxed at ordinary rates regardless of when the short sale is covered.)

Selling short could have been used as a tax as well as an investment strategy in the past. It enabled the deferral of gain on the sale of a stock by selling short the exact number of shares you owned. This is called, "selling short against the box" (because the client's shares are kept in his safe deposit box). After TRA '97 the tax treatment of this strategy has been revised by requiring investors to recognize gain upon entering into a *constructive sale* of an *appreciated financial position*. An *appreciated financial position* is generally any position with respect to any stock, debt instrument, or partnership interest if there would be gain were such position sold, assigned, or otherwise terminated at its fair market value. A *constructive sale* is deemed to have been made if the taxpayer (or related person) enters into certain transactions including (i) a short sale of the same or substantially identical property, (ii) an offsetting notional principal contract with respect to the same or substantially identical property, or (iii) a futures or forward contract to deliver the same or substantially identical property.

Question — How can an investor evaluate new issues of stock?

Answer — New issues should be evaluated very much the same as seasoned stocks, very carefully and according to a standard procedure. That procedure should include studying the prospectus. Specifically, look for positive answers to:

(a) What does the firm do?

(b) What is its major product?

(c) Who are the firm's major competitors? Look for businesses with a unique product that can't be quickly or easily copied by major competitors.

(d) How long has the firm been in business and has it survived major economic downturns?

(e) How stable and experienced is the management of the company and what exceptional talent or experience does it possess?

(f) What is the size of the company's profit and what is the trend?

(g) How large is the company?

(h) What is the source of the company's revenues and how dependent is it on any one source?

(i) What is unique about the company—not only from the positive side but also from the negative side (what unusual down side risks or liabilities does it have)?

(j) Has the firm been audited by a national accounting firm and, if so, has the firm qualified its endorsement?

(k) What is the expected dividend per share for the issue? (Find price/earnings ratio by dividing net earnings for the latest 12 month period by the number of shares the company intends to issue.) Divide the expected offering price by the company's past earnings per share to estimate a price/earnings for the new issue. Most new growth oriented companies have P/E ratios higher than the average S&P.

(l) What are brokers and statistical studies saying about the stock? Independent services that can be found in public libraries or that can be purchased directly include: (i) *The Value Line New Issues Service*, (ii) *Standard and Poor's Emerging and Special Situations*, (iii) *Going Public: The IPO Reporter*, and (iv) *New Issues*.

Chapter 23

CONVERTIBLE SECURITIES

WHAT IS IT?

Typically, convertibles are bonds or preferred stocks that may be converted at a specified conversion price (per share) or conversion ratio (number of shares) into the common stock of the firm issuing the securities. However, there are many other variations. They allow a holder to exchange, trade in, or convert the security being held into another type of security. Convertible securities are hedge-type instruments that allow investors to enjoy much of the upside potential of a riskier investment while bearing the smaller downside risk more commonly associated with investments offering less upside potential.

WHEN IS THE USE OF THIS TOOL INDICATED?

1. When the investor would like to combine an element of certainty (through a fixed interest or dividend rate and a known payment schedule) with the opportunity for significant capital gains.

2. When the investor needs current cash flow that provides a higher rate of return than available from the dividends on common stock.

3. When the investor at the same time is willing to accept a somewhat lower rate of return than might be available on bonds and preferred stocks that do not have the conversion feature.

ADVANTAGES

1. Such issues provide the investor with a relatively high degree of security for both principal and income. The general credit of the issuing corporation stands behind payments to convertible bond holders. Preferred stockholders are protected by the cumulative nature of most preferred dividends. This means that if the issuing corporation fails to pay the stated dividend on the cumulative preferred shares, the dividend accumulates and must be paid at some future time. Until preferred dividends are fully paid no payment of dividends can be made to common stockholders.

2. Convertible securities offer the potential for capital growth through ownership of the common stock. Convertible securities provide two opportunities for this appreciation. The first is through conversion and actual ownership of the common stock of a corporation. The second is through the appreciation in the market value of the convertible bond or preferred stock that occurs as a result of an increase in the price of the common stock. If the underlying stock price rises above the value of the convertible as a fixed income security, the convertible's price will move in almost direct relation to the price of the common.

   For example, a bond convertible into 50 shares of common stock which sells for about $1,000 as a fixed income security, will sell for at least $1,500 if the common stock increases in value from $20 per share to $30 per share.

3. The basic form of a convertible bond or preferred stock offers some protection in the event that common stock prices decline. If the price of the company's common stock falls below the convertible's value as a fixed income security, the investor would still have a bond or preferred stock with a price determined by its intrinsic worth as a bond or preferred stock. This concept is often referred to as providing a "floor" under the price of the convertible security.

4. A company's convertible securities, whether bonds or preferred stock, typically pay a higher rate of return in the form of interest or dividends than is available from its common shares. (Many companies that issue convertible securities pay no current dividends on their common stocks.)

5. The investor controls the form of investment and the timing of the conversion. (Note, however, that in some cases a corporation may effectively force conversion by exercising the call feature common to almost all convertible securities.)

6. The change in the nature of the investment can be effected quickly and with little or no cost to the investor. The investor merely sends the convertible security to the issuer and requests the change. Typically there are no fees or charges associated with this transaction.

DISADVANTAGES

1. Until the conversion has been made the investor is relatively unprotected from the effects of inflation. This is due to the fixed nature of interest payments on convertible bonds and the fixed dividend rate on convertible preferred stocks.

2. The yields provided by convertible securities often are significantly below the yields of alternative investments. Since convertibles provide both upside potential and downside protection, investors must pay a premium for these securities. For example, it would not be unusual for convertible bonds to pay yields one to two percentage points below the rate paid on comparable bonds without a conversion feature.

3. If the price of the underlying common stock does increase substantially, the value of the convertible will never increase as much as the value of the underlying common, because of the premium paid for the convertible. Consequently, investors who buy convertibles will generally receive lower cash yields than they would have gotten from nonconvertible securities and less appreciation than they would have gotten from outright purchase of the underlying stock. However, they also generally receive higher cash yields than they would have received from the underlying stock and higher appreciation than they would have received from the nonconvertible securities.

4. Convertible bonds, like regular bonds, typically are callable by the issuing corporation at a price slightly above their par value. Companies can use this feature to force conversion if the price of the bond has appreciated to a point well above the call price. For example, a bond convertible into fifty shares of common stock will sell for at least $1,500 if the stock is trading at $30 per share. The same bond may have a call price of only $1,080. If the issuer were to call the bond, investors would be forced to convert their bonds into common stock or face the loss of $420 per bond.

   If the price of the underlying stock increases quickly, conversion may be forced earlier than the investor planned. In that case, the investor will not have recovered the premium paid to purchase the convertible, making the return less than if the underlying common stock had been purchased outright.

5. Convertible bonds are subject to many of the disadvantages of regular corporate bonds, often referred to as "straight bonds" (see Chapter 24). Likewise, convertible preferred stocks have some of the same weaknesses as other preferred stocks (see Chapter 36).

6. Many convertible issues tend to be of relatively small size when compared with regular bond and stock issues. With relatively few convertible bonds or preferred shares outstanding, trading is less active and may result in a lack of liquidity when buying or selling a particular issue.

7. Convertible bonds are generally subordinated to all other debt issued by the firm. Therefore, default risk is higher than for other nonconvertible debt.

8. Because of the complex nature of convertibles as hybrid securities, a more involved and detailed selection process is necessary. The multiplicity of factors that must be considered includes the financial condition of the issuing company, the trend of current interest rates, and estimates of future stock prices.

TAX IMPLICATIONS

1. Income received from a convertible bond or preferred stock is subject to ordinary income tax rates.

2. Appreciation is not taxable until the investor sells the bond, preferred stock, or the common shares received on conversion. (However, original issue discount on a convertible bond may be includable as it accrues.)

3. Conversion itself is not a taxable event. A deferral of taxation is allowed because the investor takes as his cost basis the price paid for the original investment. If the conversion feature is not detachable, there is no allocation of basis to the two components of the security. That basis is carried over to the common shares acquired in the exchange. For instance, Nancy Manzi purchased a convertible bond for $800. She later converted the bond into 40 shares of the issuing company's common stock. Nancy's cost basis for those 40 shares of common stock is $800, a carryover of her original investment. This results in a cost basis for the common stock of $20 per share ($800 ÷ 40 shares).

4. Profits or losses on the sale of a convertible bond or preferred stock, or on the maturity of a convertible bond, are treated as capital gains or losses. (Market discount and original issue discount realized on sale or maturity of a bond may have to be treated as interest. See Chapter 8, "Income Tax Concepts.") Long-term capital gains are generally taxable at a maximum rate of 20%. Capital losses may be used to offset only capital gains and up to $3,000 of ordinary income per year. (See "Capital gain" in the Glossary and the discussion of capital gains and losses in Chapter 8.)

ALTERNATIVES

1. Convertible bonds with a premium put. These bonds are convertibles with additional downside protection. They are generally issued at their face value and include a put option that allows the investor to redeem the bonds for cash at a premium relative to the bonds' face value at a future date. Because of their added safety, they typically pay even lower interest than nonconvertibles, all else being equal. These convertibles are especially attractive when investors wish to protect themselves from potential bond price declines if interest rates rise.

2. Mutual funds specializing in convertible securities.

3. Bonds issued with equity warrants. These bonds are essentially just convertible bonds with a detachable conversion feature. If the warrant is detachable, generally the bond and warrant will be treated for tax purposes as separate instruments. Also, sale of the bond and exercise of the warrant will typically be a taxable transaction.

4. Investors considering convertibles could also "package" their own form of convertible by combining stock purchase warrants or call options with straight bonds.

A "stock purchase warrant" is an option to buy stock at a stated price for a given period of time. Warrants pay no income but do allow the investor to determine the timing of his purchase and offer the opportunity for appreciation. Warrants also provide leverage in that the exercise price of the warrant is generally fixed in the same manner as the conversion price of a convertible bond or convertible preferred stock.

For example, the illustration in Figure 23.1 assumes a warrant selling for $5 which enables the holder to purchase the common stock of a company at a price of $52 per share. If the current price of the company's stock is $46 per share, there is no reason to exercise the warrants and obtain the stock; it would be cheaper to simply purchase the shares directly rather than use the warrants and pay a price of $52 per share. However, if the price of the stock were to go up to $69, a gain of 50 percent, the value of the warrants would increase to at least $17 ($69 - $52), or an increase of 240%.

The package of a stock purchase warrant and a straight bond satisfies the investor's twin objectives of capital gain potential (through the warrant) and current income (through the straight bond). The major advantages of this strategy are the leverage and capital gains potential of the warrants coupled with the one to two percentage points of additional return provided by straight bonds.

Because listed calls are short-term in nature, the investor who combines straight bonds with listed call options would have to roll over the call position continuously and the premiums paid for the calls will vary over time and will not necessarily match the income given up by investing in the convertible. Furthermore, the exercise of the artificially created conversion feature (sale of bonds and exercise of call) will generally be a taxable event.

Figure 23.1

COMPUTING WARRANT VALUE, PREMIUM, AND LEVERAGE		
	TO COMPUTE VALUE:	
INPUT:	MARKET PRICE OF STOCK	$46.00
INPUT:	SUBSCRIPTION PRICE OF STOCK	$52.00
INPUT:	NUMBER OF SHARES PER WARRANT	1
	THEORETICAL WARRANT VALUE	$ 0.00
	TO COMPUTE PREMIUM:	
INPUT:	MARKET PRICE OF WARRANT	$ 5.00
	PREMIUM	$ 5.00
	PERCENT PREMIUM	0.000
	TO COMPUTE POTENTIAL LEVERAGE:	
INPUT:	PROJECTED MARKET PRICE OF COMMON	$69.00
	PROJECTED VALUE OF WARRANT	$17.00
	GAIN IN MARKET VALUE	240.00%

Reprinted with permission from *Financial Planning* TOOLKIT, Leimberg & LeClair, Inc.

WHERE AND HOW DO I GET IT?

Convertible bonds may be purchased directly by calling a full-service brokerage firm and placing an order. They may also be purchased through discount brokerage firms or through the discount brokerage services offered by many banks and thrift institutions.

In addition to a direct purchase, convertible bonds may also be acquired indirectly by investing in one of several mutual funds that specialize in convertibles. These funds offer the benefits of diversification and professional management which can be particularly advantageous to the small investor. A mutual fund also eliminates the need for the investor to analyze various bonds and to select the most attractive at any given time.

WHAT FEES OR OTHER ACQUISITION COSTS ARE INVOLVED?

Brokerage fees on the purchase of convertible bonds will be very similar to those paid in buying regular bonds. You can expect to pay from $5 to $20 per bond depending on the total value of the transaction, the number of bonds purchased, and whether or not a discount broker is used. Some firms will charge a minimum fee of $30 regardless of the number of bonds being bought or sold.

HOW DO I SELECT THE BEST OF ITS TYPE?

Evaluating the purchase of a convertible bond is more complicated than buying either bonds or stocks separately. Buyers are purchasing a combination of features that may look like a bond today but be converted into common stock tomorrow. The following suggestions may be helpful in selecting convertible issues:

(1) Look for a record of increasing earnings for at least the past five years and assets well in excess of the face value of the bonds.

(2) For a new issue, the investment banking firm that underwrites the issue and offers it to the public should be a member of a major stock exchange.

(3) Investors may prefer convertibles that are offered by companies in growth industries. Eventually, buyers will want to convert their bonds into stock or sell the bonds at an appreciated value. Companies that are experiencing growth in earnings per share are likely to have their stock price increase as well. This gain in value will be reflected in a higher price for the firm's convertible bonds.

(4) The conversion price of the bond should be within 15% of the current price of the company's common stock. For example, assume ABC Company has an issue of convertible bonds with a conversion price of $40 per share. These bonds would meet this guideline if the common stock of ABC Company were selling for at least $35 per share. If the conversion price of the bond is more than 15% above the current stock price, then the stock must appreciate a great deal in value before it becomes attractive to convert the bond. The closer the conversion value to the current price of the stock, the more attractive the convertible bond.

(5) The interest paid on the convertible bond should be within two percentage points of the rate paid on similar quality, nonconvertible bonds. If nonconvertible issues are yielding 10%, then an attractive convertible bond should be paying no less than 8%. Investors should not sacrifice too much in terms of current income in exchange for the speculative feature of converting to common stock in the future.

WHERE CAN I FIND OUT MORE ABOUT IT?

1. *Standard & Poor's Bond Guide, Moody's Investors Service*, and other statistical rating agencies provide information on convertible as well as regular bonds. These services should be available at most local libraries.

2. Several services specialize in providing investors with information on convertible bonds. The best of these are:

   Value Line Convertible Survey
   Arnold Bernhard & Company, Inc.
   711 Third Avenue
   New York, NY 10017

   RHM Convertible Survey
   417 Northern Boulevard
   Great Neck, NY 11201

3. Most brokerage firms offer some coverage of convertible issues through various publications and can supply basic information on companies that have convertible bonds outstanding.

4. While most convertible bonds are traded on the over-the-counter market, some of the larger issues of better known companies are listed on the New York Stock Exchange. The *Wall Street Journal*, *The New York Times*, and many other metropolitan newspapers will carry daily listings of their trading activity.

QUESTIONS AND ANSWERS

Question — Are convertible bonds rated in the same way as bonds that are not convertible?

Answer — Yes. Rating agencies such as Standard & Poor's evaluate convertible issues and assign quality ratings in much the same manner as regular bonds. However, since most convertible issues are somewhat speculative, their ratings tend to be relatively low. There are very few convertible bonds with ratings of AAA, AA, or even A. Most convertibles have a rating in the B or even C range.

Question — Should a convertible bond always be exchanged for common stock when the stock price goes above the conversion price of the bond?

Answer — There may be several good reasons for continuing to hold the bond rather than converting into common stock. First, an investor may prefer the bond form of investment rather than common stock. Bonds are generally more secure and provide income based on regularly scheduled interest payments. A company's common shares are likely to be more speculative and dividends, if any are being paid, are not guaranteed. Second, the current yield available on a company's convertible bonds is likely to be higher than the dividend yield on the same company's common stock. Some issuers pay no current dividends on their common stock while providing relatively attractive yields on their convertible bonds. Finally, since the convertible bonds generally will appreciate in value along with the common stock, the capital gain potential is also available to bond holders.

Question — What is "Exchangeable Debt"?

Answer — Exchangeable debt combines a long-term bond issue with an option (sometimes detachable) to exchange the bonds not for common stock of the issuing company but rather for common stock in a third company, which is typically held by the company issuing the bonds. For investors, exchangeable debt serves essentially the same function as regular convertible bonds—reasonable and predictable cash flow and upside appreciation potential with downside loss protection.

As with regular bonds, investors generally receive less interest than they would on nonconvertible bonds and, consequently, risk that the overall yield on the exchangeable bond will be lower than they could get on other types of debt.

Exchangeable debt may be less risky than regular convertible bonds because default risk on convertible bonds generally increases when the underlying firm's stock price falls. Since the firm issuing the exchangeable bond is different from the firm issuing the stock, there would generally be little relation between the stock price and the default risk on the exchangeable bond.

The exchange of the debt for the common stock is generally a taxable event, which is not the case with most conversions of regular convertible bonds into the underlying stock of the same company. If the option is detachable, basis should be allocated between the debt instrument and the option to buy the stock. Otherwise, the entire basis should be allocated to the debt.

Question — What are "Flip Flop Notes"?

Answer — They are debt instruments that allow investors to convert to and from two (and sometimes more) types of securities. Typically, they will allow investors to convert a long-term variable rate bond into a short-term or intermediate-term fixed-rate bond and back again, if desired.

These notes allow investors to invest long-term and to receive variable rate interest only slightly lower than on nonconvertible long-term variable rate debt, while retaining the flexibility of switching to short-term (and less price-volatile) debt when funds may be needed for some potential expenditure on relatively short notice. For example, this type of instrument might be suitable for the portfolios of older investors since they would be converted to their short-term form at death, leaving them much less subject to interest-rate risk and price fluctuations while the estate is being settled.

In whatever form the notes are held, they have the same risk characteristics as regular bonds of the same type and quality. The principle risk is that the value of the conversion feature does not warrant the lower interest rate typically paid on these bonds because of their conversion features. Also, there may be some uncertainty regarding maturity dates and interest rates on flip flop notes.

Investors who convert from a floating-rate bond to a fixed-rate bond may have to treat the conversion as a taxable event.

Question — What are LYONs?

Answer — LYONs (Liquid Yield Option Notes) are zero-coupon notes convertible into a fixed number of shares of common stock of the issuer. They are discussed in Chapter 50.

Chapter 24

CORPORATE BONDS

WHAT IS IT?

A bond is the legal evidence of a long-term loan made by the bondholder to the corporation which issued the bond. Typically the loan must be repaid as of a specified date, referred to as the "maturity date." Until the bonds are redeemed (paid off by the corporation), interest at a stated rate is paid, generally every six months, by the corporation to the bondholder. The interest rate paid on the bonds is usually fixed when the bonds are issued and does not change during the life of the bond.

WHEN IS THE USE OF THIS TOOL INDICATED?

1. When a primary concern of the investor is safety of principal.

2. When a relatively high current return on investment is desired.

3. When a secure and consistent flow of income is necessary. ("Zero coupon" corporate bonds, which pay no current interest, may be suitable for investors who do not need additional income; see Chapter 50.)

4. When an investor anticipates holding the investment for a minimum of three to five years.

5. When an investor's cash flow and capital needs can be planned to coincide with scheduled bond interest payments and maturities.

ADVANTAGES

1. Income and principal are relatively safe. Semiannual interest payments and eventual repayment of the principal on an unsecured corporate bond (a "debenture") are guaranteed by the general credit of the issuing corporation. Obviously, the security of both interest and principal are in direct proportion to the financial strength of the issuer. Income and principal payments on a secured bond are backed by specified collateral, such as real property owned by the corporation, as well as by the earning power and other assets of the firm.

Payment of both interest and principal to bondholders takes precedence over payment of dividends on either preferred or common stock. In the event of corporate insolvency or bankruptcy, holders of secured bonds generally will receive better treatment than either unsecured creditors, general creditors, or stockholders.

2. Bonds normally pay interest income on a regular basis. Once issued, the amount and timing of bond payments cannot be changed by the issuing corporation regardless of its financial condition (unless it files a petition under the bankruptcy code). Unlike the payment of dividends on stocks, which is made at the discretion of the board of directors, interest payments on bonds are a nondiscretionary legal obligation. Because of this fixed commitment it is possible for an investor, through careful selection of individual issues, to be assured of a regular income. For example, by selecting six bonds, each with a different semiannual payment date, an investor can receive an interest check every month.

3. Gain on the sale of a bond held for more than one year is eligible for long-term capital gains treatment. (See "capital gain" in the Glossary for the appropriate holding period.) Likewise, if the bond is held to maturity, and the maturity value (par value) exceeds the price paid for a bond purchased on the market, the difference would be treated as a long-term capital gain. For example, if an investor had purchased an AT&T bond in 1998 at a price of $900, and the bond matures in 2008 at its par value of $1,000, the difference of $100 would be treated as a long-term capital gain.

The Tax Reform Act of 1984 changed the treatment of market discount on bonds issued after July 18, 1984 or purchased after April 30, 1993. When such a bond is purchased at a price less than the original issue price, the difference between the purchase price and the original issue price must be treated as interest income rather than capital gain. That income can be recognized on an annual basis, when the bond is sold, or when it matures. The law also provides for certain limits on the deductibility of interest expense incurred to purchase or carry market discount bonds.

In addition, if the original issue price of the bond is less than the maturity value, the excess of the maturity value over the original issue price must be included as interest income (original issue discount) as it accrues over the life of the bond.

4. Compared to many other investments, corporate bonds provide a high current rate of return on capital. Historically, the current yield on corporate bonds has ranged from 2% to 8% higher than the dividend yield on common stocks. In early 1998, the current yield on long-term AA bonds was approximately 6.5% while the dividend yield on the Standard & Poor's 500 Stock Average was 1.6%, and many public utility stocks paid dividends yielding about 7%.

DISADVANTAGES

1. While the interest payments on bonds are fixed in amount and almost certain to be paid, their purchasing power may be eroded by inflation. The longer the period of time to maturity the more likely that the purchasing power of each fixed dollar payment will decline.

For example, assume that an inflation rate of 3% annually exists and that you purchase a bond paying $80 each year. Your "inflation-adjusted" interest income would be equivalent to $69.01 after five years and only $59.53 after ten years. Looked at another way, your income after five years would have to be $92.74 and after ten years $107.51, to keep pace with a 3% annual inflation rate.

2. Interest payments are fixed when the bonds are issued. The dollar amount of these payments will not change even if the financial condition of the company or the economy improves. Since bondholders are creditors and not owners of the corporation, they do not share in the growth or prosperity of the company. This means that the fixed interest on bonds may be unattractive when compared with potentially increasing payments available from alternative investments. For example, dividends from common stocks and rental income from real estate investments can increase substantially over time.

3. Inflation will also reduce the purchasing power of a bondholder's principal. The longer the period of time the bondholder has to wait for repayment of principal, the more significant that effect may be. Assume that you purchase a bond for $1,000 and that the bond will mature in ten years. At a 3% rate of inflation, the $1,000 repayment you will receive in ten years would be equivalent to only $744.09 in current dollars.

4. Bond prices fluctuate with changes in current market interest rates. If interest rates paid on newly issued bonds

increase, older bonds paying lower rates of interest will be less attractive to investors. In order to sell older bonds having lower interest rates, their price must be reduced. The effect of this decline in price is to make old bonds competitive with new ones in terms of their "yield to maturity." (Yield to maturity is the average annualized rate of return that an investor will earn if a bond is held until it matures.)

For example, if market interest rates increase from 8% to 10%, a 20-year bond paying 8% will fall in price from $1,000 to $828. Why? Because, by purchasing new bonds investors can now earn 10% on every $1,000 they invest rather than 8%. Therefore, the price of the 8% bond must be lowered until it produces a yield to maturity equivalent to the yield on the new 10% bond.

Of course, the reverse is also true. If market interest rates fall, the price of previously issued bonds will rise. In this situation bondholders will demand a higher price for their bonds since they are more attractive than new issues with lower interest rates.

5. If the overall financial condition of the issuing corporation deteriorates, the resale price of their bonds is likely to fall. A decline in the financial strength of the corporation would be reflected in a lower credit standing for the firm and, therefore, a lower quality rating for the bond issue. The lower quality rating results in a perception of increased risk and diminished worth in the minds of investors. In return for this increased risk potential buyers will demand a higher rate of return. Since interest payments cannot be increased, the only way to satisfy a potential buyer's demand for a higher rate of return is for the seller to lower the price. An improvement in the issuer's financial condition and credit rating will typically result in higher bond prices.

6. An investor's ability to sell his bonds at a given time may be adversely affected by any one or more of the following factors:

(a) The smaller the size of the issue, the less likely the bonds are to be actively traded.

(b) The issue may be owned in large blocks by only a few large institutions, such as banks and pension funds, resulting in low levels of trading activity and a relatively restricted market.

(c) If the quality rating of the issuer has declined since the bond was purchased, there may be fewer interested buyers. This, of course, makes a sale more difficult.

7. Today, most corporate bonds are issued as general credit obligations ("debentures"). Although such bonds provide a greater degree of security for investors than an equity (stock) investment, they still involve a greater degree of risk than a "secured" debt obligation, such as a mortgage. Bonds backed by real assets of the corporation provide an investor with the specific security of the mortgaged property.

Corporate bonds also are often issued in the form of "subordinated debentures" which generally have security preference over only the equity of the issuing company. Such debentures are subordinated in security to all other creditors, including general creditors. Because of the higher risk associated with subordinated debentures, they usually will pay a higher interest rate than general credit obligations, and often are issued with warrants for the purchase of common stock of the issuing company, or are convertible into such stock.

TAX IMPLICATIONS

1. Interest income paid on a regular basis is generally taxable when received at ordinary income rates.

2. Profits or losses on the sale or maturity of corporate bonds are treated as capital gains or losses (see "capital gain" in the Glossary and the discussion of capital gains and losses in Chapter 8, "Income Tax Concepts").

Long-term capital gains are generally taxable at a maximum rate of 20%. Capital losses may be used to offset only capital gains and up to $3,000 of ordinary income per year. Unused losses may be carried forward by individuals and applied against future income.

3. If a bond is sold at a loss and then repurchased, the investor may be subject to the "wash sale" rules.

4. Bonds held at death in the sole name of the investor will be subject to both federal estate tax and state death tax. Fifty percent of bonds owned jointly between spouses will be includable in the gross estate of a decedent but will generate no federal estate tax upon the death of the first spouse because of the unlimited marital deduction.

5. Bonds issued with "original issue discount," such as "zero coupon bonds," yield taxable income to the bondholders with respect to the discount over the life of the bond. This occurs even though the discount "income" will not be received until the bond matures. (Original issue discount is discussed in detail in the question and answer section of this chapter.)

6. Special rules apply where bonds are purchased at a "market discount" (that is, a price below the original issue price and the maturity or face value). Generally, the amount of market discount need not be recognized as income until the bond is sold or matures. However, there is a limit on the deductibility of interest expense on debt incurred to purchase or carry market discount bonds. Such interest expense can be deducted to the extent there is interest income on the bond (including original issue discount) which is includable in income. Beyond that amount, interest expense may be deducted only to the extent it is more than the market discount allocable to the days the bond was held in the year. The amount of interest expense not currently deductible may be deducted in the year the investor disposes of the bond. (The interest disallowance rules do not apply if the investor elects to recognize a prescribed portion of the market discount as income each year until the bond matures.)

ALTERNATIVES

1. Municipal bonds generating a comparable or higher after-tax yield.

2. Single-premium deferred annuities providing a fixed annual payment.

3. Certain preferred stocks with a fixed dividend.

4. Intermediate or long-term securities of the federal government or federal agencies that provide a comparable or slightly lower after-tax yield.

5. Investors who do not need current income may want to consider "zero coupon" bonds (which pay no interest until maturity), but offer a comparable overall yield.

WHERE AND HOW DO I GET IT?

Corporate bonds can be purchased directly by calling any brokerage firm as well as many banks and other financial institutions. Bond prices are established through dealers on the basis of supply and demand. Most bonds are traded on the "over-the-counter" (OTC) market rather than on an organized stock exchange. However, many of the most active and largest bond issues are traded on the New York Stock Exchange (NYSE).

Information on new bond issues will generally appear in the form of "tombstone ads" in the business section of major newspapers. The example shown in Figure 24.2 at the end of this chapter indicates the issuer of the bond as well as the size of the issue, its maturity date, and interest rate. Also shown are the "underwriters," the brokerage firms who originally purchased the bonds from the issuing corporation. The bonds are available from other brokerage firms, but there is a big advantage in purchasing them from one of the original underwriters: there is no commission payable on the purchase.

In periods of changing interest rates, bonds will frequently trade at a "premium" (sell above par value) or at a "discount" (sell below par value).

The prices of bonds are also influenced by their maturity date. The period of time to maturity can range from a few days to more than thirty years. Price volatility is directly related to the length of time to maturity. Long-term bonds tend to fluctuate more in price than short-term bonds.

The majority of bonds are held by institutional investors who tend to trade in "round lots": large blocks of securities amounting to $100,000 or more. Individual investors typically make smaller purchases referred to as "odd lots."

The selection of a particular broker or bond dealer can affect the price you pay for the bond for the following reasons:

(1) The commission or fees charged by different brokers can vary considerably, as noted below.

(2) Some brokers may be willing to sell bonds at a lower price in order to reduce their inventory of a particular issue.

Some investors prefer to achieve safety of principal and income through the diversification available from a mutual fund of corporate bonds. These bond funds are managed portfolios holding a large variety of corporate bonds of different maturities and issuers.

There are two common ways of purchasing a corporate bond fund: directly from the fund itself ("no-load") or through a brokerage firm ("load").

A no-load fund is generally advertised in the newspaper, carries out its transaction by mail, and charges no sales commission on the purchase of its shares.

A load fund is typically distributed through brokerage firms and the purchaser is charged a sales fee in addition to the value of the fund's shares. The price of a bond fund's shares will be determined by changes in the value of bonds in the fund's portfolio.

WHAT FEES OR OTHER ACQUISITION COSTS ARE INVOLVED?

The investor will pay no commission on the purchase of a new issue. The corporation selling the bonds or the underwriter absorbs the sales costs. In all other cases buyers and sellers can expect to pay a brokerage fee ranging from $2.50 to $20.00 per bond. Some brokers will charge a minimum fee of $30 regardless of the number of bonds being bought or sold.

HOW DO I SELECT THE BEST OF ITS TYPE?

1. Investors interested in buying corporate bonds should consider the following:

   (a) The quality rating of the bond as assigned by a professional appraisal service such as Standard & Poor's Bond Guide or Moody's Investors Service. These run from "AAA" (highest rating) to "D" (default), though conservative investors probably should not consider bonds rated lower than BBB. This rating is a current assessment of the credit worthiness of the issuer and is based on information furnished by the company or obtained by the rating service. The ratings take into consideration the nature and provisions of the obligation, likelihood of default, and protection afforded the holder in the case of bankruptcy.

   (b) Current yield - the rate of return based on the current market price of the bond. This is obtained by dividing the annual interest amount by the current purchase price of the bond.

   (c) Yield to Maturity - the rate of return on a bond held to its maturity date and redeemed by the issuer at its par value. Yield to maturity includes any gain (or loss) if the bond was purchased below (or above) its par value.

2. A maturity date should be consistent with the investor's projected cash flow or capital needs objectives. An investor seeking to provide college education funds in ten years might select an issue with a similar maturity date. (Such an investor should consider whether purchasing the bonds under the "Uniform Gifts to Minors Act" (UGMA) or a "2503(c) trust" would shift income taxation to the child's relatively lower bracket. See the discussions of the "kiddie tax" in Chapter 8, "Income Tax Concepts" and in Chapter 4, "Education Funding.")

3. It may be desirable to coordinate maturities with potential shifts in tax brackets. In other words, an investor should

select maturities which delay the gain until he or she will be in a lower tax bracket or can utilize offsetting deductions.

4. Preference should be given to the larger issues of strong, well-managed corporations. The bonds of such firms are likely to be actively traded. This increased marketability will make the bonds easier and less costly to sell in a short time.

5. Bonds with shorter maturity dates will generally have a greater price stability than longer term bonds with the same quality rating (although the tradeoff may be a lower yield).

WHERE CAN I FIND OUT MORE ABOUT IT?

1. Standard & Poor's Bond Guide, Moody's Investors Service, and other statistical rating agency reports are available at most libraries. Such services provide information on the issuers of bonds as well as price and yield information on the bonds themselves. Their ratings are based on past performance, present financial condition, and potential strength of the company. The rating represents a judgment as to the degree of protection for both interest and principal payments to bondholders.

2. *The New York Times, The Wall Street Journal,* and many other newspapers quote bond prices daily.

3. Additional information on specific issues and current market conditions can be obtained by calling major brokerage firms or banks.

QUESTIONS AND ANSWERS

Question — Why do corporations issue bonds?

Answer — A bond is a debt obligation of a corporation. The corporation issues a certificate that states the terms of the issue including the specified rate of interest. Corporations use bonds to raise funds for capital improvements or expansion. The interest paid by a corporation is tax deductible by the corporation as a business expense.

Question — What is an "indenture"?

Answer — An indenture is the legal document that authorizes a corporate bond issue. It contains the terms and features of the issue such as the amount of bonds, the rate of interest, the maturity date, and interest payment dates.

The indenture will also provide a description of the company and its business, a listing of the major corporate officers, and the intended use of the funds to be raised through the bond issue.

Question — What is the most important factor in determining the price of a bond?

Answer — The level of interest rates and the direction in which they are moving (up or down) are the key factors in determining bond prices. Bond values go up when interest rates go down and prices fall when rates increase. Typically, long-term bonds (10 years or more to maturity) will fluctuate much more in price as rates change than will short-term issues (1-3 years).

Question — Why do the prices of long-term bonds fluctuate more than those of notes or short-term issues?

Answer — The reason is that a change in interest rates that extends over only a few months will require a smaller price change than the same interest rate change when projected far into the future. For instance, if interest rates decrease by one percent, a $1,000 short-term issue may drop in value by only $10. However, a bond with twenty years to maturity may lose as much as $100 in its price because investors recognize the compounding effect of the interest rate change.

Question — What is the difference between a corporate "bond" and a corporate "note"?

Answer — This distinction is more a matter of terminology than anything else. A debt security that is issued with a maturity date of more than 7-10 years generally is referred to as a bond. If the debt has an original maturity date less than 7-10 years into the future, it is frequently called a note.

Question — What is an "original issue discount" bond?

Answer — When bonds are originally sold by a corporation at a price below their eventual maturity value they are said to have original issue discount (OID). For example, if a 20-year bond with a maturity value of $1,000 is issued for only $950, the $50 difference between the maturity value and the issue price is original issue discount. (The extreme example of an OID bond is a "zero coupon" bond. A zero coupon bond pays no periodic interest. The purchaser's total return is the price appreciation.)

For federal income tax purposes, original issue discount on bonds issued after May 27, 1969 is taxable to the bondholder over the life of the bond even though no cash is received until the bond is sold or matures. With respect to OID bonds issued after July 1, 1982, the amount of OID income which is taxable each year is computed based on the bond's yield to maturity. Annual compounding is used if the bond was issued before January 1, 1985 and semiannual compounding if issued on or after January 1, 1985. Consequently, the amount of OID income will be lowest in the first year of the bond, but will increase each year as the prior year's OID income is added to the value of the bond for interest computation purposes.

For example, assume that on January 1, 1984 a corporation issued a 20-year, zero coupon bond priced at $760 which will be redeemed for $10,000 at maturity. The yield to maturity for anyone who purchases the bond for $760 will be 13.75%. In the first year of the bond, the OID income, taxable to the bondholder as ordinary interest income, would be $104.50 (13.75% x $760). In the second year, the $104.50 of income recognized in the prior year would be added to the original purchase price of $760, resulting in an $864.50 value for computing income at a 13.75% rate. The second year taxable income would be $118.87 (13.75% x $864.50).

For OID bonds issued on or before July 1, 1982, the annual amount of the OID income is computed by dividing the total amount of the discount by the period from issuance until maturity. Thus, in our example, the annual OID income for the twenty year period of the bond would be $460 ($10,000 - $760 = $9,240, divided by twenty years). As this example illustrates, the newer OID rules provide an advantage for investors over the older rules since the total OID income is recognized at a slower rate. However, it should be remembered that even under the newer rules, OID still results in taxable income without the receipt of any cash to pay the resulting tax. For this reason, OID bonds (especially zero coupon bonds) are most often purchased by tax-exempt entities such as pension trusts.

Question — What is a "mortgage bond"?

Answer — A mortgage bond is a corporate debt security backed by a claim against property such as land or buildings owned by the corporation. In the event of default on payments of principal or interest, the bondholders can claim the assets, sell them, and use the proceeds to pay their claims.

Question — What is a "debenture"?

Answer — A debenture bond is a corporate obligation that is not secured by any property. Its only backing is the

general credit of the corporation. Some investors prefer the additional security of a claim on corporate assets and will not purchase a debenture issue unless it offers a somewhat higher yield than a mortgage bond.

Question — What is the difference between "bearer bonds" and "registered bonds"?

Answer — At one time most bonds were issued in "bearer" form. That meant the bonds were negotiable by the person holding them. Interest coupons were attached to these bonds. Interest, payable twice a year, was claimed by removing the coupons from the bonds and presenting them to a paying agent. (This is where the phrase "clipping coupons" came from.)

Although there still are some bearer bonds outstanding, long-term corporate debt must be in the form of "registered bonds" in order to avoid certain adverse tax treatment. Registration is designed to assure the basic security of the bond. A bond may be registered as to principal to protect the owner from loss. This means the name and address of the bondholder are recorded with the issuing company. A registered bond is transferred in the same way as common stock is exchanged. Interest is paid to bondholders by mail and, because the names of the owners are recorded, they will automatically receive notices of redemption. The major advantage of registration is that if the bonds are lost, stolen, or destroyed, the owner is protected against loss.

Question — What is meant by "nominal yield" and how is it different from the actual yield on a bond?

Answer — Nominal yield (also called "coupon yield" or "stated yield") is the interest rate stated on the bond. For example, the bond may indicate that it will pay 8%. The percentage is multiplied by the par value of the bond to arrive at the actual dollar amount of interest to be paid. Since almost all bonds have a par value of $1,000, an 8% nominal yield represents $80 (8% x $1,000) in actual cash received by the bondholder.

The actual yield earned by an investor is based on the purchase price rather than the par value of the bond. If the bond is purchased below par value, at $800, for example, the actual rate of return will be higher than the nominal yield. Conversely, if the bond is purchased at a premium (above par) the actual yield will be lower than the nominal yield.

The printout from the *Financial Planning TOOLKIT* shown in Figure 24.1 shows yield calculations for a

Figure 24.1

+--+
| **COMPREHENSIVE BOND CALCULATOR** |
+--+

INPUT: FACE VALUE OF BOND $1,000.00
INPUT: ORIGINAL PURCHASE PRICE .... $ 890.00
INPUT: CURRENT MARKET PRICE .... $ 980.00
INPUT: COUPON INTEREST RATE 0.0875
INPUT: YEARS TO MATURITY 7

BOND CALCULATIONS:
          ANNUAL INTEREST PAID .... $ 87.50
          GAIN (OR LOSS) .... $ 90.00
          ORIGINAL ACCRETION (OR AMORTIZATION) .... $ 110.00
          CURRENT YIELD 0.089
          APPROXIMATE YIELD TO MATURITY 0.091

Reprinted with permission from *Financial Planning* TOOLKIT, Leimberg and LeClair, Inc.

bond paying a coupon rate of 8.75% and selling for $980. Since the bond is selling at a slight discount, the current yield is 8.9% ($87.50/$980) and the yield to maturity is 9.1%.

Question — What is an "income bond" and how does it differ from other bonds?

Answer — An income bond pays interest only if the corporation earns enough money to make such payments. If the firm does not have sufficient earnings to pay the bondholders, then payment on those obligations is deferred until income is adequate to do so. The corporation is not placed in default and can continue to operate as if it had made the required payments. Income bonds are riskier than standard bonds (where interest payments must be made) and generally offer a higher rate of return in order to attract investors.

Question — Are there any bonds for which the interest rates are not fixed and which pay interest based on changing market rates?

Answer — Yes, there are "floating rate" bonds (also called "adjustable rate bonds") on which the rate of interest will vary with changes in a specified market index such as the yield on Treasury bills or Treasury bonds. For example, a floating-rate bond may adjust its rate every six months and pay one percent more than the rate on 5-year Treasury notes. Floating rate bonds provide greater stability of principal since their price tends to return to near par whenever the rate is reset.

Figure 24.2 — Example of a "tombstone" ad.

This announcement is neither an offer to sell nor a solicitation of an offer to buy these securities. The offer is made only by the Prospectus Supplement and the related Prospectus.

New Issues/August 2, 1985

$200,000,000

Phibro-Salomon Inc

$100,000,000

10.70% Notes Due 1992

Price 100% and accrued interest from August 1, 1985

$100,000,000
$11\frac{5}{8}$% Debentures Due 2015

Price 99.375% and accrued interest from August 1, 1985

Copies of the Prospectus Supplement and the related Prospectus may be obtained in any State in which this announcement is circulated only from such of the undersigned as may legally offer these securities in such State.

Salomon Brothers Inc.

Lazard Freres & Co.

Merrill Lynch Capital Markets

Prudential-Bache
Securities

Shearson Lehman Brothers Inc.

The First Boston Corporation   Goldman, Sachs & Co.   Morgan Stanley & Co.
Incorporated

ABD Securities   Banque Nationale de Paris   Bear, Stearns & Co.   Deutsche Bank Capital
Corporation

Dillon, Read & Co. Inc.   Donaldson, Lufkin & Jenrette   E.F. Hutton & Company Inc.   Kidder, Peabody & Co.
Securities Corporation   Incorporated

Nomura Securities International, Inc.   Paine Webber   L.F. Rothschild, Unterberg, Towbin
Incorporated

Smith Barney, Harris Upham & Co.   Swiss Bank Corporation International   UBS Securities Inc.
Incorporated   Securities Inc.

S.G. Warburg & Co. Ltd.   Wertheim & Co., Inc.   Darn Witter Reynolds Inc.

Chapter 25

FINANCIAL FUTURES

WHAT IS IT?

Financial futures are standardized contracts calling for future delivery of a product (such as Treasury bonds, Treasury Bills, GNMA bonds, or foreign currencies). The price at which delivery will be made is determined at the present time. In other words, the transaction takes place at the present time, but delivery is scheduled for some future date.

For example, an investor may deal through the Chicago Board of Trade on June 15 to purchase a futures contract in GNMA certificates for actual delivery on November 26. The price and the number of contracts to be traded are set at the time of purchase or sale (June 15) and not at the time of delivery (November 26).

Most investors in the financial futures market do not plan to take delivery of the item purchased (or make delivery in the case of a sale). Less than three percent of contracts traded are settled by the buyer's receiving and the seller's making delivery of the actual instrument on which the contract is based. The real purpose of the transaction is to transfer the risk (and potential reward) of price fluctuations from hedgers to speculators, and not to take actual possession of the asset.

Most investors "close out" their sale or purchase positions by entering into an offsetting transaction instead of taking or making delivery. This is accomplished by simply reversing their original position. For example, if an investor buys a futures contract on Treasury bills, he can close out the position by selling the identical contract prior to expiration.

WHEN IS THE USE OF THIS TOOL INDICATED?

1. When an investor desires to speculate on price movements in financial instruments (such as bonds and mortgages) caused by changes in market conditions, interest rates, or foreign currency values. Such individuals can take large risks (and hope for similarly large returns) by purchasing financial futures contracts without actually owning the underlying securities or currencies.

2. When an investor is exposed to the risk of significant price changes in financial instruments, such as bonds or mortgages, because of the nature of its business. These

are generally institutional investors such as banks, savings banks, savings and loans, insurance companies, and pension funds. They typically hold large portfolios of mortgages and long-term securities which can fluctuate significantly in price as market conditions change. Such investors can "hedge" their positions through the sale of financial futures, and thereby reduce the capital risk of their portfolios.

3. When an individual or corporation is involved with substantial foreign currency transactions, as would be the case in international trade. The financial success of these multinational business transactions can be greatly affected by changes in the relative value of the currencies involved. For example, changes in the relationship of the dollar to the British pound or Japanese yen will either add to or subtract from the actual profit or loss on transactions in British wool or Japanese automobiles.

ADVANTAGES

1. The terms of futures contracts are standardized by the various exchanges where they are traded. The coupon rate, maturity, issuer, and other terms are the same for each contract of a particular type. For example, a contract for Treasury bills will state the value of the underlying bills (typically one million dollars), the maturity date of the contract, and the exchange where it is traded, the International Monetary Mart. These terms are identical for all similar contracts, and they remain fixed for the life of the contract. The only item that varies is the price of the contract making for ease of quotation and trading.

2. Financial futures offer investors a high degree of "leverage" on their investments because of the low margin requirements involved. For example, the initial margin for the Chicago Board of Trade contract on $100,000 of Treasury bonds is only $2,000. This leverage offers speculators the opportunity for large returns on the relatively small investment they have to make. Low margins also make it possible for institutions to hedge their portfolios at a reasonable cost.

3. The financial futures market is highly liquid. On any given day billions of dollars of futures contracts will be traded on the various organized exchanges. New posi-

tions can be created and old ones closed out with little difficulty, and at relatively low cost in terms of commissions and fees.

4. All futures contracts are "guaranteed" by the clearinghouse which processes the transactions. In actuality the clearinghouse becomes the other side of every trade — the buyer from every seller and the seller to every buyer. This arrangement improves market performance by eliminating concern over the credit worthiness of the opposing parties, assuring delivery of the underlying securities, and adding to flexibility in closing out positions.

DISADVANTAGES

1. Financial futures are an extremely volatile investment area where substantial price changes can take place in a very short period of time. Investors must have both the financial and emotional capacity to operate in this area where gains and losses are settled on a daily basis.

2. Since all accounts are settled on a daily basis investors are subject to frequent margin calls, and must be prepared to invest additional funds or risk having their futures position closed out by the brokerage firm.

3. Trading strategies in financial futures tend to be complex arrangements compared to many other kinds of investments such as the simple purchase of a stock or a bond. This is due to the fact that a futures transaction generally accompanies some other investment rather than being carried out in isolation. For example, an investor in GNMA bonds may "hedge" that investment with a GNMA futures contract. Keeping track of these multi-part investments requires much more time and energy than most other investments.

TAX IMPLICATIONS

1. Financial futures generally are considered to be so-called "executory contracts," contracts which require performance at some future date. Gains and losses on regulated futures contracts are capital gains and losses regardless of the nature of the underlying property.

2. Any gain or loss required to be reported by an investor on a futures contract is treated as if forty percent of the gain or loss is short-term and sixty percent is long-term gain or loss. *Net capital gains* (i.e., the excess of long-term capital gains over short-term capital losses) are generally taxable at a maximum rate of 20%.

3. Under the "mark-to-market" tax rules, gains and losses on futures contracts owned by an investor at the end of the tax year, or at any time during the year, must be reported annually, even if such gains or losses have not been realized by the investor. A contract which is still in existence at the end of the year is, therefore, treated as if it were sold for its fair market value on the last business day of that year.

ALTERNATIVES

1. Put and call stock options frequently can be used to accomplish some of the same purposes as financial futures. Investors with large portfolios of common stocks can use options to hedge their stock positions while increasing the income from those portfolios. Similarly, speculators can purchase calls (puts) in anticipation of an increase (decrease) in stock prices, and invest a relatively small sum compared with the cost of actually buying (or selling) the underlying stock.

2. Stock purchase warrants also offer some of the same advantages in terms of leverage and relatively low investment that make financial futures attractive. Warrants are particularly attractive to speculators who hope to profit from a much larger percentage increase in the value of a warrant if the underlying stock increases in value.

3. Another alternative method of participating in futures is through a managed financial futures account, which is similar in concept to a common stock mutual fund. It is the only method of participation in which the investors do not have their own individual trading accounts. Instead, investor's money is combined with that of other pool participants and, in effect, traded as a single account. Gains or losses are shared in proportion to each participant's investment in the pool. The advantages of this arrangement are that it offers potentially greater diversification of risks, participant's losses are generally limited to their investment in the pool (because most pools are formed as limited partnerships), and the individual participants are not generally subject to margin calls. The disadvantages include the risk of bad management and the additional management fees and organizational or administrative expenses that may reduce the amount available for investment in futures contracts.

WHERE AND HOW DO I GET IT?

Financial futures are traded on several organized exchanges, most of which are located in either Chicago or New York.

These include the Chicago Board of Trade (CBT), the Chicago Board Options Exchange (CBOE), the American Stock Exchange (ASE), and the New York Futures Exchange.

Buying or selling financial futures is quite similar in many ways to buying or selling stocks or bonds. Transactions must be carried out through a "margin account" with a brokerage firm which sends orders to the trading floors of the various futures exchanges. Orders are executed on the exchange floor, and the results of the trade are reported back to the brokerage firm, and in turn to the customer.

To execute a transaction an investor can call his broker and state, "Buy a Treasury Note Futures contract for my account at 79." This represents a contract for $100,000 face value of U.S. Treasury Notes. The price paid by the investor is 79, or $79,000. However, only a relatively small margin position ($2,000) will typically have to be deposited by the investor. A written record of the transaction will be sent to the buyer confirming the transaction. This is the only evidence of the purchase that the investor will receive. This is due to the fact that the futures transaction involves a contract to buy or sell rather than an actual security.

Once the trade has been made the position of the buyer or seller remains "open" until one of two events occurs. One possibility is that the buyer will accept delivery of the underlying instruments (T-bills, GNMAs, etc.) on the settlement date. The seller of the contract is obligated to make delivery to the buyer. As noted above, less than three percent of futures contracts are settled in this fashion.

Much more common will be a "closing out" of the buyer's or seller's position by executing another trade which is the opposite of the first transaction. The buyer sells or the seller buys, and the original positions are offset and eliminated. Continuing our example of the buyer of a Treasury Note contract, he may decide to close out his position when the price of the contract reaches 81, or $81,000. At that point he would sell the identical contract and recognize a profit of $2,000, the difference between the purchase price of $79,000 and the sale price of $81,000. (This example does not include commission costs and is intended for illustration purposes only.)

WHAT FEES OR OTHER ACQUISITION COSTS ARE INVOLVED?

Commissions on the purchase or sale of a financial futures contract are similar to those paid on other security transactions. Brokerage firms typically charge a percentage of the value of the transaction with a minimum commission of $25 or $30. Brokerage charges are relatively high on single unit

trades, and most active investors will trade in multiples of five or ten contracts at a time.

HOW DO I SELECT THE BEST OF ITS TYPE?

1. An accurate forecast of interest rates is an essential part of an effective financial futures strategy. Estimating the direction of interest rate changes and the amount of change is critical to establishing profitable contract positions. For example, buyers of financial futures contracts will generally benefit if interest rates fall. When this happens the value of securities such as T-bills and GNMA certificates will increase, and so will the value of contracts to take delivery on these issues in the future. Sellers of futures contracts will tend to lose money under these circumstances.

   Conversely, when interest rates rise, buyers of futures contracts will see the value of their contracts decline while sellers will benefit from the fall in value of the underlying securities.

2. Individuals and institutions seeking to hedge their portfolios should determine the appropriate maturity structure of those portfolios in selecting the best financial futures contract. The portfolio hedged by the futures contract should be of approximately the same maturity as the securities underlying the futures contract. For example, an investor with a long-term bond portfolio would hedge that portfolio by using a futures contract on Treasury bonds rather than one based on short-term Treasury Bills.

3. The period of time to settlement of the futures contract should be considered before any purchase or sale is made. The longer the term of the contract the more risk is generally involved for sellers and the more advantage for buyers. These conditions are reflected in price of the contracts along with the volatility of the underlying securities.

WHERE CAN I FIND OUT MORE ABOUT IT?

1. Major brokerage firms can usually provide brochures on the financial futures market as well as an analysis of current market conditions that may or may not make financial futures attractive for investment purposes.

2. Each of the futures exchanges publishes a number of booklets that explain the nature of futures trading, the contracts that are available, and various strategies for

investors. For example, you may contact the Chicago Board of Trade at:

> Chicago Board of Trade
> Marketing Dept.
> LaSalle at Jackson
> Chicago, IL 60604
> (312) 435-3558

3. Larger brokerage firms generally will have specialists who concentrate on financial futures and may even manage discretionary accounts for their clients. Such firms often publish their own reports and recommendations.

QUESTIONS AND ANSWERS

Question — What is the meaning of the term "hedge"?

Answer — Hedging an investment refers to balancing the risk of a position in the current or cash market with an offsetting position in the futures market. For example, an investor who owns (is long) long-term debt and is concerned that interest rates may rise (and bond prices fall), may sell (go short) financial futures to hedge that risk. If bond prices decline, the profits from the short position in futures will offset, or at least partially offset, the losses on the long-term debt position.

Question — What is the usual length of time of a futures contract?

Answer — While it is possible to enter into a futures contract that covers two or three years, the vast majority of activity takes place in contracts that require settlement (mature) within twelve months. Therefore, investors who maintain permanent portfolios may enter into a series of contracts, "rolling over" or entering into new contracts when the old ones are settled or closed out.

Question — What does the phrase "marked to market" mean in regard to trading futures contracts?

Answer — Marked to market means that brokerage accounts trading financial futures, like all commodity trading accounts, are settled at the end of each day based on the closing prices of those futures contracts. Any paper gains or losses are recognized immediately and posted to the investor's account rather than when a security is bought or sold. This procedure coupled with the small margin required on such accounts may subject the investor to daily margin calls if futures prices move against them.

Question — What are "Index Futures"?

Answer — Index futures are contracts to purchase a given index of stocks at a prespecified price at some specified time in the future — the delivery date. The concept is to use a futures contract as a substitute for the dollar amount of stock that otherwise would have been purchased. The purchasers pay 10 percent of the specified price at the time they purchase the contracts and pay the remainder at the time the contract expires. Since they will owe 90 percent of the price when the contract comes due, this is a leveraged, and speculative, position. If the index rises by the delivery date, the holders will receive an index whose value is higher than the price they have agreed to pay. Conversely, if the market drops, they will receive an index whose value is below their purchase price. Figure 25.1 lists index futures contracts.

Question — Is there a way investors can reduce the leveraged and speculative nature of index futures?

Answer — Investors can "unleverage" (or reduce the leverage of) the index contract and, consequently, reduce their speculative nature by buying a futures contract and simultaneously investing in Treasury bills an amount equal to (or in some proportion of) the entire amount that will be due when the contract expires.

This strategy is economically equivalent to buying the index of stocks outright except the investor

(a) gets the T-bill interest rate rather than the dividends on the stocks (T-bill interest would typically be greater than the dividend income), and

(b) pays any premium that the futures contract has over the actual index (there is a premium typically).

Arbitragers keep the premium very close to the difference between T-bill interest and dividends.

There are three advantages to this approach over outright purchase of the stocks in the index:

(a) The bid/ask spread, which is a significant part of the transactions costs, is narrower. For blue chip stocks the typical round-trip spread is about 1 percent, versus 0.1 percent for a futures contract. Assuming that futures contracts will have to be traded 3 times as often because they expire, the spread differential is still 0.3 percent to 1 percent.

(b) The average commission costs are lower. For an equivalent portfolio of stocks with a discount broker

Figure 25.1

Index Futures Contracts	Market	Underlying Index
S&P 500 Index	Chicago Mercantile Exchange	The index is based on the market-weighted stock prices of 500 large-capitalization companies. The market value of the 500 firms is equal to about 80 percent of the value of all stocks listed on the New York Stock Exchange.
S&P MIDCAP	Chicago Mercantile Exchange	This index represents the "middle" of the market. Like the S&P 500, the S&P MidCap 400 is market weighted, but it tracks the market performance of medium capitalization stocks instead of large-cap firms.
S&P 500/BARRA GROWTH & VALUE Indices	Chicago Mercantile Exchange	Each S&P 500 stock is assigned to either the *Growth* or *Value* Index so that the two indices "add up" to the S&P 500. The indices are rebalanced twice a year based on a variety of factors so that each represents about 50 percent of the S&P 500 capitalization. Companies in the Growth Index have generally higher market capitalizations than those in the Value Index, so there are many more companies in the Value Index.
NASDAQ 100 Index	Chicago Mercantile Exchange	The NASDAQ 100 Index comprises 100 of the largest domestic, non-financial common stocks listed on the NASDAQ Stock Market. It is a market-weighted index that has about a 94-percent correlation to the NASDAQ Composite Index.
Russell 2000	Chicago Mercantile Exchange	The Russell 2000 Index, based on 2,000 stocks, is the most widely recognized market-weighted small-capitalization U.S. benchmark.
MAJOR MARKET Index	Chicago Mercantile Exchange	The Major Market Index (MMI) was developed by the American Stock Exchange and is designed to measure the performance of the blue-chip sector of the U.S. stock market. It is a price-weighted rather than market-weighted index based on 20 large-capitalization, well known U.S. companies.
NIKKEI 225 Stock Average	Chicago Mercantile Exchange	The Nikkei 225 Stock Average is Japan's most widely followed and most frequently quoted equity index. Like the MMI, the Nikkei is price weighted and comprises the 225 top-tiered (the "bluest" chip) Japanese companies listed in the First Section of the Tokyo Stock
IPC	Chicago Mercantile Exchange	The Indice de Precios y Cortizaciones (IPC) is the principal stock index of the Bolsa Mexicana de Valores (BMV), Mexico's stock exchange. It is a broad-based, market-weighted index consisting of 35 stocks traded at the BMV selected from different economic sectors of the Mexican economy to ensure complete market coverage.
GSCI	Chicago Mercantile Exchange	The Goldman Sachs Commodity Index represents every major commodity group: energy, livestock, grains and oil seeds, food and fiber and metals. The GSCI comprises 22 liquid, exchange-traded physical commodity futures contracts. It is production weighted, similar to a market-weighted stock index.
KC Value Line Index	Kansas City Board of Trade	The close to 1,700 stocks followed by Value Line Investment Services.
KC Mini Value Line Index	Kansas City Board of Trade	The Mini is like the Value Line in all respects but the size of the investment. A Mini contract is one-fifth the size of a Value Line contract.
Eurotop 100 Index	New York Mercantile Exchange	The Optiebeurs N.V. (European Options Exchange, also known as the EOE) Eurotop 100 Index is designed to measure the collective performance of the European equities market, as reflected by the major stock exchanges of the United Kingdom, France, Germany, Italy, Switzerland, the Netherlands, Spain, Sweden, and Belgium.
PSE Technology 100 Index	Pacific Stock Exchange	The PSE Technology 100 is a price-weighted, broad-based index comprised of 100 listed and over-the-counter stocks from 15 different industries (including computer hardware and software development, semiconductors, networking, communications, and data storage and processing). The PSE is the tech sector equivalent of the Dow Jones industrial Average used to gauge the performance of the technology sector of the U.S. equity market.
Wilshire Small Cap Index	Pacific Stock Exchange	The Wilshire Small Cap Index™ measures the performance of the small capitalization sector of the United State equity market. It is a market-weighted index comprised of 250 stock and is designed to be a trading instrument for institutional and individual investors. Component issues were chosen on the basis of market capitalization, liquidity, and industry group representation. The Small Cap Index originates from the Wilshire Next 1750 Index, a benchmark for institutional investors in the small cap sector.
Morgan Stanley Emerging Growth Index	Pacific Stock Exchange	Developed in partnership by the Pacific Exchange and Morgan Stanley, EGI is a broad-based, capitalization-weighted average of 50 rapidly growing new companies. It is the first index designed specifically for investors who want to participate in the movement of the emerging growth market.
NYSE Composite Index	New York Futures Exchanges	The NYSE Composite Index is a market-weighted measure of the changes in the aggregate market value of all NYSE common stocks, adjusted to eliminate the effects of capitalization changes, new listings and delistings.

the commission is about 13 times greater than the commission on a futures contract.

(c) The speed and ease of trading the futures contracts and T-bills is an advantage over the stock portfolio.

The market risks are essentially the same as investing in the stocks of the underlying index.

Premiums on index futures will increase in busy up or down markets, so there is some risk that the premium as well as the basic index will change. However, this difference should be neutral over the long-term.

For contracts traded on domestic exchanges, gain or loss is capital in nature and is deemed to be 60 percent long term and 40 percent short term regardless of actual holding period. The contracts are marked to market at year end, so that all unrealized gains and losses are recognized at year end. Taking or making delivery under the contract is a taxable event. The timing and characterization of gains or losses may be affected if the futures contracts are part of a straddle.

One alternative to index futures is the purchase of the stocks in the index outright or through an index mutual fund. The unleveraged index futures contract technique requires the investor to put up an amount equal to the striking price (price for the index) at the time the contract is purchased. For instance, an S&P 500 futures contract covers about $160,000 of stock. An investor can acquire shares in Vanguard's First Index Trust (based on the S&P 500 portfolio) with an initial purchase of only $2,500.

Any of the exchanges making markets in index futures have informational brochures on index futures. Most brokerage firms have similar information.

Chapter 26

GOLD AND OTHER PRECIOUS METALS

WHAT IS IT?

Gold, silver, and platinum are the most common of the precious metal investments. They are valued primarily because of their scarcity, and to a lesser extent, because of their utility for scientific and industrial purposes.

WHEN IS THE USE OF THIS TOOL INDICATED?

1. When the investor anticipates instability in traditional capital markets. Historically, when stock and bond markets have fallen, the price of gold and other precious metals has tended to increase.

2. When the worldwide political outlook is one of uncertainty and fear, precious metals tend to be viewed as a more stable and secure investment.

3. When the investor anticipates that the purchasing power of the dollar will be eroded by high rates of inflation.

4. When the value of the investor's dollars is declining because of international currency fluctuations. For example, as the value of the U.S. dollar declines, the price of gold and other precious metals generally increases.

5. When the investor desires to diversify a portfolio which already contains significant amounts of stocks, bonds, and real estate.

ADVANTAGES

1. Gold and the other precious metals offer a potentially high return (gold increased from $200 an ounce in 1979 to more than $850 per ounce in 1980).

2. Since precious metals are tangible, or physically possessable assets, they provide a degree of psychological security matched by few other investments.

3. Precious metals can be purchased in relatively small quantities and in a variety of forms. For instance, an investor can purchase gold by the bar or purchase an ounce or even less at a time by buying a coin such as the Canadian Maple Leaf. Such coins are available in amounts as low as one-half or one-quarter ounce.

4. Since all of the precious metals have some utility for scientific and industrial purposes, there is an underlying demand for them as a commodity in addition to their speculative or investment value. Silver, for example, is used extensively for both jewelry and photographic purposes.

5. Historically, precious metals held over a very long period have proven to be a relatively safe and stable form of investment. Many investors have purchased gold, for example, as a long-term hedge against inflation.

DISADVANTAGES

1. Precious metals are a highly speculative form of investment. For example, the price of gold is determined more by international political and psychological factors than by normal economic factors of supply and demand.

2. Historically, the prices of precious metals have been highly volatile and the investor is subject to a high risk of significant loss of capital. Panic buying of gold could quickly reverse itself. For instance, the price of gold dropped from $375 an ounce in December of 1996 to $295 an ounce in December of 1997.

3. Precious metals have frequently been controlled by various governments. For instance, the United States government hoarded gold in its vaults for many years and forbade U.S. citizens from owning and selling gold privately for investment or speculation until 1975.

4. Direct investments in precious metals typically yield no current income. This makes gold relatively "expensive" when alternative investments are yielding high rates of return in the form of dividends or interest. (But metal's prices do not always follow a logical or consistent pattern. For instance, when interest rates were hitting 21% gold was also skyrocketing to its high of $880 per ounce.)

5. Precious metal investments involve storage costs either directly or indirectly. These costs may amount to more than a dollar per ounce on an annual basis. There may also be shipping and insurance charges.

6. Sales tax may be payable.

7. There may be assay costs involved in the purchase.

TAX IMPLICATIONS

1. Taxable gain is realized and must be recognized (reported) to the extent an investor receives more upon disposition than he paid. Therefore, to the extent that the selling price exceeds the investor's tax basis he must realize a gain.

2. No gain is reportable until the investment is disposed of in a taxable transaction. Therefore, the appreciation on a precious metals investment will remain untaxed until the asset is sold. This can be particularly advantageous to high tax bracket investors.

3. A loss from a precious metals transaction is allowable to the extent an investor paid more for the asset than he received from the sale. To the extent that the investor's basis exceeds his selling price, he has a deductible loss.

4. Gain or loss on a precious metals transaction is a capital gain or capital loss assuming the metal is held as an investment rather than by a dealer for trading purposes. The length of time the metal was held prior to disposition will determine whether the gain or loss will be long-term or short-term.

5. No gain or loss must be reported if one precious metal is exchanged solely for another. This favorable rule applies only if the metal received is of the same nature and same character as the metal given up in the exchange. Therefore, if an investor exchanges gold coins for gold bullion, or trades gold bullion for certificates of gold, no gain or loss is recognized on the transaction. Likewise, if bullion-type coins of one country are exchanged for bullion-type coins of another country, no taxable income or loss would be generated.

   Note that the tax-free exchange rules are strictly construed. A gain or loss would be triggered by the exchange of a "numismatic" coin for a "bullion" type coin. (A numismatic coin such as the twenty dollar U.S. gold piece is valued for its rarity and condition; its metal content is only one of many factors contributing to its value. Conversely, a bullion coin such as the Canadian Maple Leaf is valued solely for its metal content and the type of metal, purity, and weight are the primary value determinants.)

   An exchange of any two different types of metals will trigger the recognition of gain or loss. For instance, gain or loss would be triggered by the exchange of a silver bullion type coin for a gold bullion type coin.

6. The exchange of a precious metal for property other than a similar type of precious metal will result in a reportable gain or loss.

7. Coins acquired in a taxable transaction must be valued for tax purposes at their fair market value rather than at their face value. For instance, a Fifty Peso Mexican coin with a gold content of 1.2057 ounces may be worth a lot more than fifty pesos.

ALTERNATIVES

1. From the standpoint of form of an investment, alternatives to precious metals would include speculative real estate (raw land), collectibles, diamonds and other gemstones, and art.

2. From a risk-return standpoint, alternatives would include speculative stocks, "junk bonds," securities options, commodity futures, limited partnerships, and other capital gain oriented investments.

WHERE AND HOW DO I GET IT?

There are a number of ways of investing, depending on the type of metal. Gold or silver can be purchased as (1) coins of the bullion type, such as the U.S. Gold Eagle, the Canadian Maple Leaf, or the Mexican Peso; or (2) bars (ingots of one or more ounces); or (3) certificates. Certificates certify that a specific warehouse is holding a given amount of that metal for the investor.

There are dealers such as Deak-Perera who specialize in precious metals. Investors can establish accounts and obtain a firm, binding quote over the telephone. Payment must be made by cashier's check or wired funds typically postmarked by noon of the day after purchase.

Many investors prefer to purchase gold in the form of small wafers called ingots. Ingots are sold in standard weights which range from as little as one gram (0.0322 oz.) to as much as four hundred troy ounces. The typical investor will purchase ingots in one ounce quantities.

Gold should be purchased only from a recognized dealer. Its fineness (the maximum is 0.999) should be stamped on the ingot. Investors should not purchase a bar with a lesser fineness. The ingot should be stamped with the name of a recognized refiner and should be accompanied by an assay certificate. This assures the purchaser of its purity and authenticity, and will typically save the cost of another assay when sold.

Investors who wish to buy small quantities of gold should consider coins. They are easy to purchase, store, and resell.

The most popular bullion type coins have included the South African Kruggerand and the Canadian Maple Leaf and have a fine-gold content of exactly one troy ounce. These coins generally have no numismatic value. This means that the value of an investor's holding can be figured by multiplying the price of gold for immediate delivery (the so-called "spot" or cash price) by the number of ounces held.

A number of banks act as an agent for their customers who choose to purchase precious metals. As an accommodation, the bank will "bulk" the orders of a number of smaller investors together. For instance, Citibank has generally accepted a minimum investment of $1,000 from a number of its customers. It then goes to the New York Commodities Exchange and purchases gold in four hundred ounce bars of 0.995 fineness or better and silver in five thousand ounce bars of 0.999 fineness or better. This is the equivalent of buying wholesale since there is no markup. Citibank's customers have thus received the advantage of both a bulk purchase buy and the best price available on the New York Comex.

WHAT FEES OR OTHER ACQUISITION COSTS ARE INVOLVED?

Gold, as well as silver and platinum, is purchased at the market value plus a premium. That premium generally ranges from 2% to 3% and covers both the dealer's profit as well as the cost of fabricating the metal. Premiums decline with the quantity of the metal purchased and may be less than 2% for a one hundred ounce bar.

An investor who desires to take physical possession of a precious metal must pay insurance and shipping costs in addition to possible sales taxes. A representative shipping and insurance charge for six ounces of gold is $18.

Many investors prefer not to accept the risk as well as the expense involved in taking physical possession of a precious metal. Rather than accept delivery, such investors may utilize the certificate programs offered by a number of large dealers, banks, and brokerage firms. The investor will receive a certificate stating that he owns a specified number of troy ounces in an independent bank depository. This bank may be located in Delaware or in Switzerland. The investor can sell his holding at any time or take delivery of the bullion.

The obvious advantage of storage certificate programs is the savings in delivery costs. But, the investor also may save sales taxes and fabrication charges by using an independent bank depository. The minimum investment required for these certificate programs is $1,000. Deak-Perera has allowed additional investments of amounts as small as one hundred dollars. A typical commission is 3% on orders up to $1,000; 2.5% to $10,000, and 2% to $50,000. Annual storage charges are 0.5% of the value of the investor's holdings and a 1% commission is paid upon the sale of the metal.

HOW DO I SELECT THE BEST OF ITS TYPE?

1. In making a selection among the various types of precious metals an investor should consider the following factors:

    (a) The price of one metal compared with another. For instance, if silver were trading at $8 per ounce and gold were trading at $340 per ounce, and if other factors were equal, the small investor might opt for an investment in silver because it is more "affordable."

    (b) The position of the price relative to recent highs and lows of the metal. An optimistic investor might choose platinum at $370 per ounce if its recent high was $1,040 per ounce over gold selling at $400 per ounce with an expected high of $600 per ounce.

    (c) The potential downside risk. One metal may be used for many more scientific and industrial purposes than another and, therefore, may have a higher "floor" than the other.

    (d) Other value determinants such as sensitivity to political changes and supply and demand influences. For instance, an individual anticipating a major gold mining strike might prefer to invest in gold rather than silver or platinum.

2. Compare the premium charge imposed by a number of dealers. Premiums can vary significantly from one dealer to another.

3. Deal only with reputable dealers who are willing to ship within forty-eight hours of payment if delivery is requested and who are willing to exchange gold for cash.

4. When storing gold, deal only with a firm which has been in business for a minimum of five years, and is periodically audited by an independent CPA. Gold should be stored in a segregated account and not be subjected to either the claims of the dealer's creditors or the custodian's creditors. If an investor's bullion is mingled with that of other registered holders, his holdings should be clearly identified and available for delivery after the payment of any appropriate charges.

WHERE CAN I FIND OUT MORE ABOUT IT?

1. Newspapers such as *The Wall Street Journal*, *The New York Times*, and *Barron's* carry the daily price "fixings" for gold and the other precious metals as well as stories and reports on market activity.

2. *American Metal Market*, printed by Fairchild Publications of New York, is also a respected source of information for metals investors.

3. *Financial Times*, an English publication, offers an international perspective, which can be important due to the global nature of these markets.

4. Statistics on precious metals production and use can be found in *Mineral Commodities Summaries* published by the U.S. Bureau of Mines and in an annual review of markets published by Handy and Harman. The multinational mining concern of Consolidated Goldfields Limited publishes an annual review of the statistics on gold.

5. Major brokerage firms and commodity trading houses also publish reports on metal markets and related investments.

QUESTIONS AND ANSWERS

Question — How are gold prices established?

Answer — The price of gold and other precious metals is determined by prevailing market forces of supply and demand. This takes place at four major exchanges: in Zurich, London, New York, and Hong Kong. The price is "fixed" at various times in each of these locations by selected gold specialists and bank officials representing individual investors and commodity traders throughout the world. Reports of these prices are published daily in major newspapers and broadcast by television and radio stations.

Question — Should an individual invest directly in gold mining stocks?

Answer — At certain times, gold shares have been among the most profitable equity investments from the standpoint of return. Gold stocks typically follow the price of gold, but at times may be even more volatile than the price of the metal itself. Investing in gold stocks may be more convenient than buying gold directly. The purchaser can also avoid the cost of shipping, insurance, and storage.

An investor should distinguish between the purchase of shares of gold mining companies in North America and those in South Africa. First, the size and quality of the mines is much higher in South Africa than in the United States. For instance, one South African mine alone produces more gold than the total U.S. production. Second, profits earned by South African mining companies are paid out more rapidly than those of U.S. concerns. Third, these advantages may be offset by the potential risk associated with the political and social unrest of South Africa. These threaten to disrupt production and may even endanger the investor's capital.

Question — Are there any mutual funds which invest in gold or other precious metals?

Answer — Yes, there are a variety of funds which concentrate their investments in the stocks of gold mining and other precious metals companies. Such investments provide the opportunity for relative safety through diversification of mine locations, accessibility of ore deposits, and remaining years of life. They also offer investment management expertise not available to the typical small investor.

Question — How does silver compare with gold as a precious metals investment?

Answer — Silver has always been considered a less valuable commodity than gold. Its price has swung even more widely than gold in recent years and is influenced by many of the same market factors that determine the price of gold—inflation, interest rates, and political tensions. However, silver has a value independent of its rarity. It is used in large quantities in film manufacturing and in the production of electronic products, and is therefore stockpiled for its use in national defense. Silver is also used in the production of coins, jewelry, and works of art. The world actually consumes more silver than it produces each year. This deficit is made up by recycling many of these same coins, jewelry, and artwork.

Question — How does an investor buy silver?

Answer — Like gold, silver can be purchased through brokers in many forms. These forms include silver bars or ingots, bags of silver coins, silver forward contracts, silver futures contracts, silver options, and silver shares. Silver bars are purchased and sold in weights of one thousand ounces. Purchasers must pay a premium of 5% to 8% over the "spot" price of the metal in addition to sales taxes in many states, if the bullion is actually delivered. There also may be assay and warehousing expenses. For these reasons, many owners choose to store silver bullion in warehouses and accept warehouse receipts as evidence of ownership.

Purchasers can obtain bags of silver coins. These coins are standard U.S. issue and are ninety percent pure silver. Each bag has a weight of about sixty-five pounds and the price of a bag is determined by daily spot quotations for silver. They are popular among speculators as an investment even though they are difficult to move and store.

Forward contracts are arrangements for future delivery of the actual metal made on the London Metal Exchange. Silver futures are contracts for future delivery on the Comex and Chicago Board of Trade that serve primarily as a device for hedging or speculation rather than for trading in physical silver. Silver options consist of put and call contracts which give the holder the right to sell or buy a certain amount of silver at a stated price for a given period of time.

Investors can also purchase the stock of silver producers on organized exchanges or the over-the-counter market. The prices of these companies' shares will typically follow the rise and fall of silver metal prices.

Question — What are some of the major factors an investor should consider before purchasing platinum?

Answer — Platinum is the rarest of the major precious metals, with world production less than one-fifth the amount of gold produced. South Africa is one of only two major sources of the metal, the other being the Soviet Union. The metal has commercial uses as well as being valued as a precious metal. Also, there is only a small unmined stock of platinum as compared with relatively large inventories of gold and silver. As a result, prices tend to respond quickly to changing market conditions. The same disadvantages present in the purchase of gold and silver, such as assay charges, shipping, storage, and insurance costs are present in owning platinum. The price of platinum has tended to parallel the price of gold. It is affected by many of the same political, social and psychological forces that influence the price of gold, and also reacts to factors stemming from its industrial uses.

Chapter 27

ROTH IRAS

WHAT IS IT?

A Roth IRA is an individual retirement plan that is designated at the time of establishment of the plan as a Roth IRA.[1] The basic idea of this new breed of IRA is that contributions are nondeductible and "qualified distributions" are tax free. In addition to tax free qualified distributions, the Roth IRA offers other benefits, including (1) no minimum required distributions during the lifetime of the owner, (2) no maximum age limitation for making contributions, and even (3) a tax-favored rule for "nonqualified" distributions.

As described in Code section 408A(a), "a Roth IRA shall be treated for purposes of this title in the same manner as an individual retirement plan," except as provided elsewhere in Section 408A. This means that all the rules applicable to regular or "traditional" IRAs apply also to Roth IRAs, except where the Code has a specifically different rule.

WHEN IS THE USE OF THIS TOOL INDICATED?

1. When an investor desires to shelter investment income from income taxation.

2. When long-term accumulation and deferral of distributions is an important objective.

3. When a person over age 70½ has earned income and wishes to invest up to $2,000 per year tax free.

4. When a person anticipates higher future tax rates and wants to convert currently tax-deferred traditional IRAs (or, in a two-step rollover process from qualified plans to traditional IRAs and then to Roth IRAs) into tax-free investments by rolling money into a Roth IRA and paying the tax currently.

ADVANTAGES

1. Eligible individuals may contribute up to $2,000 after tax to a Roth IRA per year and avoid all income tax on the future investment income, provided certain requirements are met.

2. There is no age restriction on the creation of Roth IRAs or on contributions to Roth IRAs after age 70½.

3. Distributions from a Roth IRA are not required until the IRA-owner dies and then they may be spread over the life expectancy of the designated beneficiary under the minimum required distribution rules.

4. A surviving spouse who is named as a beneficiary may roll the Roth IRA of his deceased spouse over to his own accounts, or treat it as his own, name new designated beneficiaries, and continue deferring distributions until after his death.

5. Under the distribution ordering rules, even nonqualified distributions are first treated as a nontaxable return of regular contributions. Consequently, the owner may withdraw up to the total amount of his regular annual contributions at any time, even before age 59½, without any tax or penalty.

6. Qualified distributions of any amount are entirely tax free. (Qualified and nonqualified distributions are defined below.)

7. A taxpayer may roll amounts out of a traditional IRA and into a Roth IRA before age 59½. He must pay regular income tax on the rollover amount, but no penalty tax. After a five-year period, he may then withdraw up to the entire rollover amount, even before age 59½, without the imposition of the 10-percent early withdrawal penalty (to the extent such distribution does not exceed the aggregate amount of contributions).

DISADVANTAGES

1. Annual contributions (not counting rollover contributions) to Roth IRAs may not exceed $2,000 (less all other annual deductible or nondeductible contributions, if any, to traditional IRAs).

2. Contributions are nondeductible.

3. The $2,000 contribution limit is phased out ratably for single taxpayers with AGI between $95,000 and $110,000,

for married taxpayers filing jointly with AGI between $150,000 and $160,000, and for married taxpayers filing separately with AGI between $0 and $10,000.

4. A 10-percent penalty may be imposed on a portion of distributions made within the first five years of the taxable year of the first annual contribution to a Roth IRA or within five years of a distribution attributable to a rollover contribution.

5. In order to be eligible to roll over amounts from a traditional IRA to a Roth IRA, a taxpayer must have AGI below $100,000 and not be a married taxpayer filing separately.

6. There is some tax risk and tax uncertainty with regard to Roth IRAs. If the recently repealed 15-percent excise tax on excess retirement distributions and accumulations from qualified plans and IRAs is any indication of the type of tax legislation that could be enacted in the future, taxpayers who use Roth IRAs should beware. They certainly bear some non-negligible risk that future tax legislation will impose some type of tax on Roth IRA accumulations or distributions, despite the current promise of future tax-free distributions. Also, it is unclear at this time whether Roth IRA earnings may be considered preference income for alternative minimum tax purposes or whether Roth IRA earnings may be counted in the modified adjusted gross income calculation when computing the taxability of Social Security.

TAX IMPLICATIONS

Contributions

1. *Nondeductible contributions.* Contributions to a Roth IRA are nondeductible.[2]

2. *Contribution limits.* Contributions cannot exceed, on an annual basis, the excess of the maximum contribution permitted (i.e., the lesser of $2,000 or 100% of compensation includable in gross income) over the aggregate amounts contributed to all other IRAs.[3] Therefore, the maximum contribution to all Roth IRAs is the lesser of $2,000 or earned income, reduced by any deductible or nondeductible contributions to any traditional IRAs. Also, up to $2,000 may be contributed to the spousal Roth IRA (less any deductible or nondeductible amounts contributed to traditional IRAs) of a nonworking spouse.

3. *No contribution age limit.* In contrast with traditional IRAs, a person may make contributions to a Roth IRA even after reaching the age of 70½.[4]

4. *Year of contribution.* Similar to traditional IRAs, contributions are deemed to be made on the last day of the preceding taxable year if they are made by the due date for the filing of the income tax return in respect of the preceding taxable year (without regard to extensions).[5]

5. *Phase-out of contributions.* The maximum contribution amount to a Roth IRA is phased out in a pro-rata fashion for individual filers with AGI between $95,000 and $110,000 and for joint filers with AGI between $150,000 and $160,000. The phase-out range of AGI for married taxpayers filing separate returns is $0 to $10,000.[6] However, a husband and wife who file separate returns but live apart at all times during the taxable year are not treated as married for this purpose,[7] in which case, each of them could make contributions based on the $95,000 to $110,000 phase-out range.

For these purposes, AGI is determined with regard to Social Security inclusion and passive loss limitations, but without regard to the exclusions for education savings bonds, adoption expenses, foreign housing or earned income.[8] Also, in computing the AGI limit, no amount required to be included in income as a result of a rollover from a non-Roth IRA to a Roth IRA is included in AGI.

6. *Qualified rollover contributions.* In general, rollover contributions from an IRA other than a Roth IRA to a Roth IRA are permitted if the contributions are "qualified rollover contributions" and the taxpayer has AGI of $100,000 or less and is not a married taxpayer filing separately.[9] Such contributions are not counted against the maximum annual contribution limit.[10]

A qualified rollover contribution means a rollover contribution or plan-to-plan transfer to a Roth IRA from another such account, or a rollover contribution, plan-to-plan transfer, or conversion from a traditional IRA, but only if such rollover contribution, plan-to-plan transfer, or conversion meets the rollover requirements applicable to IRAs generally.[11]

7. *Taxation of qualified rollover contributions.* In the case of any distribution from an individual retirement plan (other than a Roth IRA) which is contributed to a Roth IRA in a qualified rollover contribution, the taxpayer must include in gross income and pay income tax on any amount which would be includable were it not part of a qualified rollover contribution.[12] For example, if the taxpayer rolls $100,000 from a traditional IRA to a Roth IRA and $10,000 of the rollover contribution is attributable to nondeductible contributions to the traditional IRA, $90,000 must be included in gross income. For these purposes a conversion (including an IRA-to-IRA

transfer) is treated as though a distribution had been made.[13]

8. *Special 4-year ratable inclusion rule for 1998 conversions and rollovers.* If a qualified rollover distribution or conversion is made before January 1, 1999, the conversion is included in income ratably over a four-taxable-year period beginning in 1998, unless the taxpayer elects otherwise. This election could be changed, but not after the (extended) due date of the tax return.[14]

If a taxpayer who elected to include 1998 conversion income ratably over the 1998 through 2001 tax years dies during this period, the amount of conversion income not previously reported will be included in the decedent's final tax return. However, if the spouse is the beneficiary of the Roth IRA, the spouse can elect to continue to report the conversion income on the same schedule as the decedent would have. This election cannot be made or rescinded after the due date of the spouse's tax return for the year of the decedent's death.[15] Special rules apply to amounts withdrawn during this 4-year period. (See Tax Implications — Distributions.)

9. *No early withdrawal penalty tax on rollover contributions.* Although subject to income tax, distributions from a traditional IRA which are subsequently rolled over into a Roth IRA are not subject to the 10-percent additional penalty tax even if the taxpayer is not yet 59½ years of age.[16] However, a subsequent distribution from the Roth IRA may be subject to the 10-percent early withdrawal penalty if it occurs within five taxable years of the taxable year of the rollover and before the taxpayer reaches age 59½ and it is deemed (under the ordering rules described below) to be attributable to the taxable portion of the rollover or earnings.

10. *AGI limitation.* Qualified rollovers or conversions from a traditional IRA to a Roth IRA may be made only by taxpayers (1) with $100,000 or less of AGI and (2) who are not married taxpayers filing separately.[17] The $100,000 AGI limit is computed, for this Code section only, without including the income that results from the conversion or rollover. For example, a taxpayer has total AGI of $105,000 before consideration of an active participation rental loss of $6,000. In the absence of any income resulting from the conversion, his AGI would be $99,000. If this taxpayer is permitted to convert his traditional IRA to a Roth IRA, he will recognize $75,000 of income upon the distribution from the traditional IRA. However, now if he includes this $75,000 of income in his regular computation of AGI, he loses the $6,000 rental loss under the AGI phase-out rule for rental losses. For purposes of the $100,000 AGI limitation only, the amount includable

in income due to the rollover amount is disregarded. The AGI for conversion purposes is still $99,000 ($105,000 - $6,000 rental loss), even though the rental loss will not be permitted on his actual tax return when the conversion amount is included in income.

11. *AGI limitation beginning after 2004.* For tax years beginning after 2004, for conversion eligibility purposes only, AGI is computed without including any amount otherwise included in gross income by reason of required minimum distributions from traditional IRAs. Before 2005, some taxpayers over age 70½ may be prevented from converting traditional IRAs to Roth IRAs simply because the required distributions from their traditional IRAs push their AGI over the $100,000 limit. This problem is eliminated for tax years beginning after 2004.[18]

12. *Married taxpayers filing separate returns.* Married taxpayers filing separate returns are not permitted to roll over or convert traditional IRAs to Roth IRAs.[19]

13. *One-rollover-in-12-month-rule.* For purposes of the one-rollover-in-a-12-month-period rule for IRAs, any qualified rollover contribution from an individual retirement plan (other than a Roth IRA) to a Roth IRA is disregarded.[20]

Distributions

1. *Aggregation rule.* Similar to traditional IRAs, all Roth IRAs must be aggregated and treated as one Roth IRA when determining the tax consequences of distributions from any one Roth IRA.[21] This rule makes it unnecessary to segregate Roth IRAs into those that receive only annual contributions and those that receive conversion amounts from traditional IRAs.

2. *Qualified distributions.* Qualified distributions from Roth IRAs are not includable in income; that is, they are entirely tax free.[22] Qualified distributions are distributions (1) that occur after the completion of a five-taxable-year nonexclusion period *and* (2) which are:

- made on or after the date on which the individual reaches age 59½,[23]

- made to a beneficiary on or after the death of the individual,[24]

- attributable to the individual's being disabled,[25] or

- for a "qualified special purpose" distribution (i.e., first-time homebuyer expenses up to $10,000).[26]

For regular annual Roth IRA contributions, the Roth IRA nonexclusion period is defined as the five-taxable-year period beginning with the first taxable year for which a taxpayer made a contribution of any kind to any Roth IRA.

There is a no longer a separate five-year nonexclusion period starting with the tax year of the conversion for each rollover contribution from a traditional IRA to a Roth IRA, as a result of changes by the IRS Restructuring and Reform Act of 1998. As a result, a subsequent rollover will not start the running of a new five-year period. However, the 10-percent penalty tax may apply to distributions attributable to taxable conversion amounts within five taxable years of the conversion or rollover. (See item # 6 below.)

3. Ordering rules for nonqualified distributions. Income taxation and the application of the 10-percent early withdrawal penalty on distributions that are not qualified distributions is determined by the application of a set of ordering rules. The ordering rules encompass two concepts: (1) segregation and separate tracking of Roth IRA assets according to three basic source categories: contributory assets, conversion assets, and total earnings and (2) a first-in-first-out (FIFO) rule.

Contributory assets represent the total amount of assets contributed as regular Roth IRA contributions to all Roth IRAs of the taxpayer up to the time of the distribution (less amounts recovered as a result of prior distributions).

Conversion assets represent the total amount of assets rolled over or converted from traditional IRAs to Roth IRAs up to the time of the distribution (less amounts recovered as a result of prior distributions). Conversion assets are further subcategorized into the taxable and nontaxable (attributable to nondeductible contributions to traditional IRAs) portions of the rollover or conversion assets.

Total earnings are the aggregate earnings that have accumulated within all Roth IRAs by the time of the distribution. The total earnings may be computed by subtracting the total of all undistributed contributory amounts and the total of all undistributed conversion amounts from the total value of all Roth IRAs.

Once the Roth IRA assets have been categorized by source, the ordering rules specify the order in which each asset source is recovered when distributions occur. The FIFO rule simply says that distribution amounts attribut-able to a category are recovered from the assets in that category on a first-in-first-out basis.

The ordering rules require the Roth IRA owner to treat any amounts distributed as coming from the following sources in the order listed:

1. contributory assets, until all contributory assets are recovered, then

2. conversion assets, chronologically by tax year of conversion, and within each tax year's conversions, by taking taxable conversion assets first, followed by nontaxable conversion assets, until all conversion assets are recovered, and finally

3. total earnings.

Example 1: In 2003, Lou Anne rolls $20,000 from a traditional IRA to a Roth IRA. Of this amount, $2,500 is treated as recovery of nondeductible contributions she had made over the years. She must include $17,500 in her gross income on her tax return for 2003 ($20,000 less $2,500 nontaxable recovery of her nondeductible contributions). In 2004, Lou Anne converts the remainder of her traditional IRA balances, $30,000, to a Roth IRA. The portion of the conversion treated as nondeductible contributions is $3,500. She must report $26,500 of gross income on her tax return in the year 2004.

By the year 2005, she has made $8,000 of annual contributions to her Roth IRAs. In the year 2005, her Roth IRAs have a balance of $70,000 and she withdraws $60,000. The ordering rules would treat the distribution as coming from the following sources in the following order:

$8,000	from regular annual Roth IRA contributions
$17,500	from taxable conversion assets in the 2003 rollover
$2,500	from nontaxable conversion assets in the 2003 rollover
$26,500	from taxable conversion assets in the 2004 rollover
$3,500	from nontaxable conversion assets in the 2004 rollover
$2,000	from total earnings
$60,000	Total distribution

The tax and penalty consequences of this distribution are described below.

Roth IRAs

4. *Income taxation of nonqualified distributions.* The income tax consequences of a nonqualified distribution depend on the source or category of asset received. The portion of any distribution categorized as coming from earnings is taxable and the portions categorized as coming from regular Roth IRA contributions and conversion assets are recovered income-tax free. However, a special income acceleration rule applies to taxpayers who converted assets from traditional IRAs to Roth IRAs in 1998, elected to pro-rate the income over a 4-year period, and withdraw amounts attributable to such a conversion within the 4-year period.

5. *Income acceleration rule.* Taxpayers who converted traditional IRAs to Roth IRAs in 1998, elected to pro-rate the income on the conversion amount over the 4-year period from 1998 through 2001, and who then take withdrawals from a Roth IRA within the 4-year period must accelerate the reporting and taxation of the conversion income.[27] The rule requires the taxpayer to increase the amount required to be included in income under the ratable taxation rule by any distributions of 1998 taxable conversion amounts distributed from Roth IRAs between 1998 and 2000. However, the amount includable is limited and cannot exceed the remaining taxable amount of the conversion.

Example 2: A taxpayer converted $95,000 of a traditional IRA to a Roth IRA in 1998. Of this amount, $15,000 is treated as nontaxable recovery of nondeductible contributions; $80,000 is taxable conversion amount. If the taxpayer elected to pro-rate the recognition and taxation of income under the 4-year rule, he would include $20,000 of the taxable conversion amount per year in his gross income in the years 1998 through 2001. Assume the taxpayer has made no other contributions to Roth IRAs and that he makes a $13,000 withdrawal from the Roth IRA in the year 2000. He would already have reported $40,000 of the taxable conversion amount on his tax returns in the years 1998 and 1999. In 2000, he must report in his gross income that year's pro-rata share of the taxable conversion amount, $20,000, plus the $13,000 he withdraws from the Roth IRA that year, a total of $33,000. In the year 2001, he will report the remaining $7,000 of the original taxable conversion amount.

Assume, contrary to the assumption above, that the taxpayer has made $5,000 of regular annual contributions to the Roth IRA. In this case, under the ordering rules the first $5,000 of the $13,000 distribution would be categorized as a recovery of his contributions and only $8,000 would be categorized as coming from his taxable conversion amount. Therefore, he would report $28,000 in gross income in the year 2000 and the remaining $12,000 of his original taxable conversion amount in gross income in the year 2001.

6. *Section 72(t) 10-percent early withdrawal penalty tax on nonqualified distributions.* The 10-percent penalty tax for withdrawals before age 59½ applies to the portions of any nonqualified distributions that are attributable to taxable conversion amounts within five taxable years of the conversion or earnings, unless the distribution qualifies under one of the exceptions to the 10-percent penalty tax.[28] The exceptions to the 10-percent penalty tax for distributions from IRAs include distributions

- paid to the beneficiary after the death of the death of the owner,[29]

- made on account of the disability of the owner,[30]

- that are part of a series of substantially equal periodic payments over the life or life expectancy of the owner or the joint life or joint life expectancies of the owner and the beneficiary,[31]

- to the extent used to pay certain unreimbursed medical expenses in excess of 7.5% of AGI during the year,[32]

- to the extent used to pay the health insurance premiums of an unemployed owner (within limits),[33]

- to pay certain qualifying higher education expenses,[34] or

- to pay certain qualified first-time homebuyer acquisition costs up to $10,000.[35]

7. *Tax and penalty summary table.* The tax and penalty rules described above for distributions from Roth IRAs are summarized in the following table by the source of the distribution as described by the ordering rules, by the reason for the distribution, and by whether the distribution occurs before or after the 5-year nonexclusion period.

Example 1 (continued): Assume that Lou Anne's $60,000 withdrawal from her Roth IRA in the year 2005 occurs before she reaches age 59½ and that she does not qualify under one of the exceptions to the Section 72(t) 10-percent penalty tax. The tax and penalty consequences of her distribution would be as follows:

Figure 27.1

Roth IRA Tax and Penalty Summary Table

Source of Distribution Under Ordering Rules

Reason for Distribution	Contribution Assets				Taxable Conversion Asset				Nontaxable Conversion Asset				Earnings			
	Before 5-yr. Period[1]		After 5-yr. Period[1]		Before 5-yr. Period[2]		After 5-yr. Period[2]		Before 5-yr. Period[2]		After 5-yr. Period[2]		Before 5-yr. Period[1]		After 5-yr. Period[1]	
	Tax	Penalty	Tax	Penalty	Tax	Penalty	Tax	Penalty	Tax	Penalty	Tax	Penalty	Tax	Penalty	Tax	Penalty
After age 59½	No	No	No	No	No†	No	No	No	No	No	No	No	Yes	No	No	No
Before age 59½ no penalty exception	No	No	No	No	No†	Yes	No	No	No	No	No	No	Yes	Yes	Yes	Yes
Before age 59½ with penalty exception:																
Death	No	No	No	No	No†	No	No	No	No	No	No	No	Yes	No	No	No
Disability	No	No	No	No	No†	No	No	No	No	No	No	No	Yes	No	No	No
First-time homebuyer	No	No	No	No	No†	No	No	No	No	No	No	No	Yes	No	No	No
Substantially equal periodic pmts.	No	No	No	No	No†	No	No	No	No	No	No	No	Yes	No	Yes	No
Medical expenses	No	No	No	No	No†	No	No	No	No	No	No	No	Yes	No	Yes	No
Insurance prems. by unemployed	No	No	No	No	No†	No	No	No	No	No	No	No	Yes	No	Yes	No
Higher ed. expenses	No	No	No	No	No†	No	No	No	No	No	No	No	Yes	No	Yes	No

[1] The 5-year period beginning with the first taxable year for which a contribution is made to any Roth IRA.

[2] The 5-year period beginning with the taxable year in which the regular IRA to which the conversion assets are attributable was converted to a Roth IRA.

† For conversions in 1998 in which the conversion income is pro-rated over 4 years, the conversion income scheduled for inclusion in later years may be accelerated, reported, and taxed in the year of the distribution.

$8,000	from regular annual Roth IRA contributions (no tax, no penalty)
$17,500	from taxable conversion assets in the 2003 rollover (no tax, penalty)
$2,500	from nontaxable conversion assets in the 2003 rollover (no tax, no penalty)
$26,500	from taxable conversion assets from the 2004 rollover (no tax, penalty)
$3,500	from nontaxable conversion assets from the 2004 rollover (no tax, no penalty)
$2,000	from total earnings (tax, penalty)
$60,000	Total distribution

8. *Application of the required minimum distribution rules.* The mandatory distribution rules applicable to the owner of a traditional IRA after reaching age 70½ and prior to death do not apply to the owner of a Roth IRA.[36] Thus, distributions do not have to begin by April 1 of the year following the year in which the owner reaches age 70½. In fact, no distributions need to be made during the lifetime of the owner.

If the Roth IRA passes to the spouse, the surviving spouse may treat the Roth IRA as his own (by rollover or otherwise) and thereby defer the application of the lifetime mandatory distribution rules until he dies. If the successor to the Roth IRA is not a designated beneficiary or a surviving spouse, the balance of the Roth IRA must be distributed over a five-year period beginning with date of death.[37] However, if the owner has named a designated beneficiary, the balance of the Roth IRA must be distributed, beginning within one year of the death of the owner, over the lifetime or a period not in excess of the life expectancy (without recalculation) of the designated beneficiary.[38]

Also, the minimum distribution incidental death benefit (MDIB) requirements do not apply to a Roth IRA.[39] This essentially only clarifies that no distribution is required under the MDIB rules while no distribution is required under the regular minimum distribution rules.

9. *Nondeductible contributions to traditional IRAs still available.* The law still permits taxpayers to make nondeductible contributions to traditional IRAs. Thus, an individual who cannot (or does not) make contributions to a deductible IRA or a Roth IRA may make nondeductible contributions to a traditional IRA. In no case can contributions (not counting rollover contributions or conversions) to all an individual's traditional IRAs and Roth IRAs for a taxable year exceed $2,000 in the aggregate.

ALTERNATIVES

1. *Tax-free municipal bonds.* There is no $2,000 limit on the amount one may invest in tax-free municipals (or municipal bond funds). However, the return on tax-free bonds is considerably lower than on taxable bonds or, generally, on equities. Therefore, one could generate much greater tax-free returns by investing in taxable bonds or equities within a Roth IRA rather than in a tax-free municipal bond.

2. *Nondeductible contributions to traditional IRAs.* The maximum annual nondeductible contribution to either a traditional IRA or a Roth IRA is $2,000. A person should never make a nondeductible contribution to a traditional IRA if he has the opportunity to make a similar nondeductible contribution to a Roth IRA. In either case, the contribution is nondeductible, but earnings in the Roth IRA are potentially tax free; earnings in the traditional IRA are only tax deferred.

3. *Annuities.* The amount invested each year may exceed $2,000. Similar to nondeductible contributions to traditional IRAs, annuities permit investors to defer tax on their investment income until the money is distributed. However, annuities are taxed in most respects like traditional nondeductible IRAs. Therefore, a person should never make a nondeductible contribution to an annuity if they can make the same nondeductible contribution to a Roth IRA; in the Roth IRA, the earnings are potentially tax free rather than just tax deferred.

4. *Deductible contributions to traditional IRAs.* Sometimes making deductible contributions to a traditional IRA where the investment earnings are tax deferred will be better than making nondeductible contributions to a Roth IRA where investment earnings are potentially tax free. The result depends on a number of factors that are addressed in the question and answer section at the end of this chapter.

WHERE AND HOW DO I GET IT?

Almost all banks, savings and loans, mutual savings banks, insurance companies, mutual funds, and brokerage houses offer IRA services. Your Roth IRA may be in the form of a savings account or savings certificates, an annuity contract, shares in a mutual fund, or an account at a brokerage house.

WHAT FEES OR OTHER ACQUISITION COSTS ARE INVOLVED?

Many institutions do not charge any fee for establishing an IRA account. In many cases there may be a nominal annual fee ranging from $10 to $20. However, there may be normal commissions or other charges involved in buying certain investment products in the account. For example, a "load" mutual fund may not charge anything to open an IRA, but would charge its normal, or sometimes a reduced, sales commission to buy shares of the fund. On the other hand, some firms will reduce or eliminate certain sales charges altogether in order to attract an investor with an IRA account.

HOW DO I SELECT THE BEST OF ITS TYPE?

Federal laws regulate the structure of Roth IRAs making all of these accounts similar in their basic design. All accounts are subject to the same contribution limits and federal income tax treatment. The only significant differences in IRA plans are in the investments chosen by an individual for his specific accounts. Some people may elect to use a savings account or certificate. Others will purchase mutual fund shares or a plan offered by an insurance company. The long run performance of these plans may vary, but the differences will be due to the different investment vehicles selected rather than the basic structure of the IRA.

WHERE CAN I FIND OUT MORE ABOUT IT?

Most banks, savings and loan companies, insurance companies, mutual funds, and brokerage houses have brochures describing their IRA plans, including Roth IRAs. These will indicate the types of investments available as well as any charges that may be applied to such accounts.

The Internal Revenue Service offers taxpayers information on IRAs through a special booklet (Publication 590) entitled, Individual Retirement Arrangements (IRAs). This booklet is available from local offices of the IRS or by writing to: Internal Revenue Service, Washington, DC 20224.

QUESTIONS AND ANSWERS

Question — Assuming a person qualifies for either type of contribution, will he be better off making a $2,000 tax-deductible contribution to a traditional IRA or a $2,000 nondeductible contribution to a Roth IRA?

Answer — The answer depends on a number of factors, including (1) how and when he anticipates taking distributions, (2) tax rates, and (3) investment opportunities. However, some relatively simple concepts may help to clarify the decision. The first concept is this: If a taxpayer's tax rate will be the same at the time he anticipates taking distributions from the IRAs as when he makes the contribution, the after-tax amount he would accumulate with a $2,000 before-tax contribution to a traditional IRA will exactly equal the after-tax amount he would accumulate by investing the equivalent after-tax amount in the Roth IRA.

A simple example demonstrates the point. Assume a taxpayer is in the 28 percent tax bracket and is considering a $2,000 deductible (before tax) contribution to his traditional IRA. If he does not make the $2,000 deductible contribution, he will have, after tax, just $1,440 [$2,000 x (1-0.28)] available to invest in the Roth IRA. Assume, for illustration, an investment rate of return of 10 percent and an accumulation period of 10 years.

The $2,000 invested in the traditional IRA will accumulate to $5,187.48 in 10 years before tax ($2,000 x $(1.10)^{10}$ = $2,000 x 2.59374 = $5,187.48). At a 28-percent tax rate the after-tax amount he would accumulate assuming he withdraws the money in 10 years (and assuming no 10-percent penalty) is $3,734.99 [$5,187.48 x (1-0.28)]. The $1,440 invested in the Roth IRA will also accumulate to $3,734.99 at a 10-percent tax-free rate of return ($1,440 x $(1.10)^{10}$ = $1,440 x 2.59374). It makes no difference what accumulation period or rate of return one assumes, if the tax rate remains the same, the after-tax balances will also be the same. Under this scenario, if the taxpayer's tax rate at the time of distribution is greater than the tax rate at the time of the contribution, the after-tax accumulation with the Roth IRA will be greater than the after-tax accumulation with the traditional IRA, and vice-versa.

If that were all there were to it, the decision might be relatively simple. However, the analysis so far ignores a second very important concept. The Roth IRA permits a taxpayer to convert what would otherwise be taxable investments into tax-free Roth IRA investments. The taxpayer may contribute up to $2,000 to the Roth IRA, not just the after-tax equivalent of the $2,000 before tax contribution to the traditional IRA.

Continuing the example, the taxpayer may contribute $2,000 to the Roth IRA, not just $1,440. As shown above, if the tax rate remains the same, the $1,440 contribution to the Roth IRA and the $2,000 contribution to the traditional IRA will give the taxpayer the same after-tax accumulation. But the Roth IRA permits the taxpayer to contribute an additional $560. In order to do so, he would either have to liquidate some other investment to raise the additional $560 for his Roth IRA contribution or forego putting $560 of available cash into some other taxable investment (or, he could possibly borrow the money). In any event, the taxpayer is converting $560 from a taxable to a tax-free investment. Assuming the investment opportunities are the same both inside and outside of the Roth IRA, the taxpayer will always be better off investing the $560 inside the Roth IRA, where the returns are tax free, rather than outside, where they are subject to tax. Therefore, the taxpayer may be better off investing in the Roth IRA rather than in the traditional IRA even if the tax rate is expected to be lower when the money is ultimately withdrawn than when it was contributed.

For illustration, assume the taxpayer is investing both inside and outside of the IRAs in an S&P Index mutual fund that is expected to earn 10 percent before tax. The taxpayer generates the additional $560 contribution for the Roth IRA by simply investing the $560 in the S&P fund inside the Roth IRA rather than outside of the Roth IRA. All else remains the same. Therefore, we can compute how much better off he will be by investing in the Roth IRA rather than in the traditional IRA by simply comparing the future value of the $560 as a taxable investment and as a tax-free investment. The after-tax value of the $560 invested inside the Roth IRA at a 10-percent tax-free rate for 10 years is $1,452.50 [$560 x $(1.10)^{10}$ = $560 x 2.59374 = $1,452.50].

Outside the Roth IRA, the mutual fund will be subject to current taxation on the ordinary income portion and capital gains tax on the capital appreciation element, when the gain is recognized. Historically, about 70 percent of the return on the S&P 500 has been attributable to capital appreciation and about 30 percent attributable to ordinary dividend income. Assuming very little of the capital appreciation is recognized in the intervening term as a result of portfolio transactions, the fund will grow at a rate of about 9.16 percent after paying the 28 percent ordinary income tax rate on the ordinary dividend income component of return [10% - 7% = 3% ordinary income; 3% x (1-0.28) = 2.16% after ordinary income tax; 7% + 2.16% = 9.16%]. The $560 accumulating at a 9.16% percent rate in the S&P Index fund outside the Roth IRA will grow to $1,345.31 [$560 x $(1.0916)^{10}$ = $560 x 2.4023444 = $1,345.31] in 10 years. At that time, the accumulated and as yet untaxed capital gains will be about $600.13. Assuming the tax rate on recognized long-term gains is 20 percent, the tax on the gains when the balance is withdrawn at the end of the 10-year accumulation period would be $120.03. Therefore, the after-tax value of the investment outside the Roth IRA would be about $1,225.28 ($1,345.31 - $120.03). This amount is about $227.22, or 15.6 percent, less than the taxpayer would accumulate inside the Roth IRA. In other

words, even if the ordinary income tax rate remains the same, by investing $2,000 in the Roth IRA rather than in the traditional IRA, the taxpayer can expect to be better off by $227.22 after-tax over this 10-year period because he is able to invest an additional $560 inside of, rather than outside of, the tax-free Roth IRA. The advantage would be greater for longer deferral periods.

Even if the taxpayer expects his tax rate to fall to a lower level by the time he anticipates taking money form his IRAs, he may still be better off by investing $2,000 after tax in the Roth IRA rather than $2,000 before tax in the traditional IRA.

Assume in this case that all else remains the same except that the taxpayer's tax rate on ordinary income falls just before the money is withdrawn in ten years. The tax rate could fall to as low as about 23.6 percent before the taxpayer would be worse off investing in the Roth IRA. Looking out 20 years, rather than just 10 years, the taxpayer's tax rate on ordinary income could fall to as low as about 21 percent before the taxpayer would be worse off investing in the Roth IRA rather than the traditional IRA.

A third consideration that enhances the attractiveness of the Roth IRA is the fact that distributions may be forced out of the traditional IRA after the owner reaches age 70½ because of required minimum distributions, even if the taxpayer doesn't need or want to take distributions. No distributions are required from the Roth IRA until after the owner's death. These forced traditional IRA distributions are subject to tax and the after-tax proceeds will no longer grow tax-deferred. Even if the after-tax value of the forced distributions were greater than the corresponding tax-free amount that otherwise would have accumulated in the Roth IRA at the time of the distribution, the amount accumulated with tax-free growth in the Roth IRA would, at some later point, exceed the traditional IRA's after-tax distribution amount reinvested in a taxable instrument.

For example, assume the $2,000 contribution described above is forced out of the traditional IRA after the 10-year accumulation period, but the taxpayer's ordinary income tax rate falls to 20 percent. The before-tax balance in either IRA, as shown above, would be $5,187.48. If he invested in the traditional IRA, the extra $560 he would have had invested outside his IRA, as shown above, would have grown to $1,345.31 with accumulated but as yet untaxed capital gains of $600.13. The after-tax distribution from the traditional IRA would be $4,149.98 [$5,187.48 x (1-0.20)]. So his total after-tax balance from his traditional IRA and his outside fund would be

$5,495.29, with an accumulated but as yet untaxed capital gain of $600.13. If his capital gains tax rate were now only 15 percent and he recognized the gain, he could pay the $90.02 capital gains tax and still have $5,405.27 after all taxes. This amount is $217.79 more than he would have accumulated in the Roth IRA. However, had he invested in the Roth IRA he would not have to take the money out at this time and he would continue to enjoy tax-free earnings.

So how much longer would the $5,187.48 in the Roth IRA have to continue to be invested at 10 percent tax free to end up with more money after tax than he would have by investing the after-tax proceeds from the traditional IRA in the taxable investment? That depends upon rates of returns and tax rates. However, assuming the tax rate on ordinary income is at 20 percent and the capital gains tax rate is at 15 percent, it will take only about 4.2 years for the Roth IRA to overcome the deficit.

The $5,495.29 from the after-tax proceeds of the traditional IRA plus the side fund balance would grow at a 9.4 percent (before-capital-gains tax) rate to $8,019.53 in 4.2 years assuming all other characteristics of the investment remain the same except the ordinary income tax rate on dividend income, which is now 20 percent. The accumulated gains at the end of the 4.2 year period would be about $1,879.75. At a 15-percent capital gains tax rate, the tax would be $281.94, leaving $7,737.57 after all taxes are paid. In 4.2 years, the Roth IRA would grow to $7,741.15. So in this case, even if tax rates are expected to fall to a level where the traditional IRA would outperform the Roth IRA on an after-tax basis for a given period, the Roth IRA may be superior if it permits the taxpayer to defer distributions from the Roth IRA for just over 4 years or more after they would otherwise have to be distributed from the traditional IRA.

Question — Can a taxpayer who is past her required beginning date and whose required distributions for the year from her traditional IRAs push her over the $100,000 AGI limit still convert a traditional IRA to a Roth IRA?

Answer — The first possibility is that the realization of the deemed income that arises from conversion may "count" as fulfilling her minimum distribution requirement for the year. The point of the minimum distribution rules is to require the participant to pay some tax on the IRA. By converting, the owner actually pays tax on all of it, not just an the amount required to be distributed. Will that suffice?

Unfortunately, no. The purpose of the minimum distribution rules is not just to pay some tax, but also, to take amounts out of the tax-favored vehicle. Otherwise, using the logic here, a taxpayer could take just the distribution amount required each year, pay tax on it, and roll it over to a Roth IRA. The taxpayer ends up paying the same tax she would have anyway, but now she will ultimately convert all of the traditional IRA balance into a Roth IRA and enjoy tax-free compounding on the Roth IRA's investment return.

A second possibility might be to convert to the Roth IRA first and then take the distribution from the Roth IRA. Unfortunately, this won't work either because minimum required distributions may not be rolled over to another IRA, including, it seems, a Roth IRA.[40]

Could this problem be avoided by converting most of the traditional IRA balance to the Roth IRA and leaving only the required minimum distribution amount in the traditional IRA? The owner would then take only so much of the required distribution from the original IRA so that she is still left with an AGI that is less than $100,000. The taxpayer would fail to meet the required minimum distribution for the year and incur a 50-percent penalty tax on the underpayment, but that might be worth it to be able to convert all the rest of the original IRA to the Roth IRA. Unfortunately, it appears even this will not work, since the regulations state that "the first dollars distributed are deemed to be part of the minimum required distribution until the minimum required distribution has been entirely distributed."[41] The Roth IRA may not accept ANY rollover from the traditional IRA until the entire required minimum for the year has been distributed.

Therefore, if a taxpayer's required minimum distribution pushes AGI above the $100,000 limit, it appears there is no way, in that year, to convert the traditional IRA to a Roth IRA.

The only alternative if one wants to roll at least some of the traditional IRA over to a Roth IRA may be to accelerate or increase IRA withdrawals above the required minimum in the current year so as to reduce the IRA balance and, consequently, the required distribution in the subsequent year. By manipulating the recognition of other income in the subsequent year to reduce AGI to the minimum extent possible and careful planning to minimize the "excess" distribution taken from the traditional IRA in the current year, a taxpayer may be able to reduce the required minimum in a subsequent year to a level where his AGI falls under the $100,000 limit. The taxpayer can then convert the remaining traditional IRA balance to a Roth IRA.

Roth IRAs

For taxpayers who can wait, there is relief from this problem after 2004. Effective in tax years beginning after 2004, for qualification under the $100,000 AGI limitation only, amounts required to be distributed under the minimum distribution rules do not count in the AGI computation. The effect of this change will be to allow more taxpayers, at age 70½ and above, to rollover from a traditional IRA to a Roth IRA. This will enlarge the group of taxpayers who can enjoy the benefits of the Roth IRA.

Question — Are amounts rolled over or converted from a traditional IRA to a Roth IRA subject to a 10-percent penalty tax if the owner is less than 59½ years of age at the time of the rollover?

Answer — Although a conversion is not subject to the 10-percent early withdrawal penalty when the conversion occurs, it may be subject to the penalty if withdrawals from the Roth IRA occur within five years of the conversion and the reason for the withdrawal does not qualify as one of the exceptions to the Section 72(t) 10-percent penalty tax.

If a portion of the distribution is categorized as a taxable conversion asset under the ordering rules and the distribution occurs within five taxable years of the taxable year of the conversion, the portion of the distribution attributable to amounts that were includable in income due to the conversion is subject to the 10-percent penalty tax. If the distribution occurs after the five-year period, the penalty tax does not apply.

Question — Can a taxpayer roll the proceeds from a qualified plan into a Roth IRA?

Answer — The proceeds of a qualified plan cannot be rolled over to a Roth IRA... directly. However, nothing precludes a participant from rolling a qualified plan to a traditional IRA and thereafter rolling ("converting") the traditional IRA into a Roth IRA.[42]

Question — Who benefits from a traditional IRA to Roth IRA conversion?

Answer — Roth IRAs have their greatest attraction to those people who do not need to withdraw any funds from their IRAs during life, especially those individuals who expect to live well beyond the average life expectancy due to their sex, genetic heritage and/or health. A traditional IRA participant approaching age 70½ is required to take distributions which will substantially diminish if not eliminate the account over a long life span.

Converting to a Roth IRA just before death should be considered when benefits will otherwise have to be paid out just after death since such conversion may permit the longer post-death deferral of distributions.

For estate planning purposes, if an IRA must be used to fund the credit shelter trust, part of the advantage of escaping estate taxes is mitigated by the necessity of the trust to pay income taxes out of its principal; in many cases the tax rate on such taxable income will be higher for the trust than for any of the beneficiaries. While this can be corrected by a withdrawal from the IRA of a sufficient amount (grossed-up by the income tax), this requires the loss of continued deferral inside the IRA. With the Roth IRA conversion, the income taxes are removed from the estate but the deferral of taxes continues and the credit shelter pays no income taxes on the receipt of distributions from the Roth IRA.

Question — Can the owner of a Roth IRA change his designated beneficiary after reaching the age of 70½?

Answer — The Roth IRA participant enjoys the advantage of being able to change his "designated beneficiary" after age 70½, and have that change be effective for determining minimum required distributions after his death. The new designated beneficiary's life expectancy at the date of the owner's death will be used for determining the amount of the required distributions.

In addition, an owner who at his required beginning date (age 70½) with respect to a traditional IRA named the "wrong" (or no) beneficiary, or who regrets his choice of a method of determining life expectancy under the minimum distribution rules, can get a fresh start by converting to a Roth IRA, and naming the "right" beneficiary.

A participant who named his spouse as the designated beneficiary of his traditional IRA at his required beginning date, but whose spouse might die before him (thus causing loss of the potential for spousal rollover and eventual long-term payout over the life expectancies of younger generation beneficiaries), can convert to a Roth IRA so that the long-term post-death payout will be available regardless of which spouse dies first.

For example, Jack, age 75, named his spouse Jill as the designated beneficiary of his $500,000 traditional IRA as of his required beginning date. Jill predeceased him, Jack is precluded from naming a new beneficiary and changing his required minimum distribution. He will be required to take his required minimum distribution based on the elections he made at his required beginning date, presumably over both his and his deceased spouse's remaining life expectancy (depending upon his election with respect to recalculation of life expectancies). When Jack dies, the IRA must be distributed over a period depending on the original choices. In general, this would require distributions be paid either over the joint life expectancies of Jack and Jill (if life expectancies were not being recalculated) or by the end of the year following his death (if both life expectancies were being recalculated).

However, assume the same facts except that the IRA is a Roth IRA rather than a traditional IRA. After Jill's death, Jack can name a new designated beneficiary, say, a son, for tax purposes. Therefore, he could then name the son as the designated beneficiary, but still have no required distribution during his lifetime. At his death his son will then be able to take the Roth IRA out over his single life expectancy. This allows for substantially more deferral when compared to the previous example where the wife was named as the designated beneficiary of a traditional IRA.

Also, with a traditional IRA, a nonspouse's life expectancy is determined once, when the owner reaches his required beginning date. Thus, when the owner dies, the designated beneficiary receives benefits over that designated beneficiary's life expectancy computed at the designated beneficiary's age as of the owner's required beginning date, reduced by the number of years between the required beginning date and date of owner's death. In contrast, because there is no required beginning date in a Roth IRA, the benefits are paid after the owner's death over the beneficiary's life expectancy as determined on the date of the owner's death. The life expectancy payout period will always be longer in the second case. For example, assume the nonspouse designated beneficiary is age 40 at the IRA owner's required beginning date. The single life expectancy factor for a person age 40 is 42.5 years. If the IRA owner dies 20 years later (and has elected to recalculate his life expectancy), the IRA balance must be distributed over the 22.5 years of the designated beneficiary's life expectancy remaining from the original 42.5 years. In contrast, if the IRA is a Roth IRA, the life expectancy factor is determined for the designated beneficiary's age at the time of the IRA owner's death; in this case, age 60. The life expectancy factor for a 60-year-old person is 24.2 years, or about ten-percent longer than with the traditional IRA. Thus, this actuarial difference reflecting the longer life expectancy represents a hidden advantage of a Roth IRA.

FOOTNOTE REFERENCES

ROTH IRAs

1. IRC Secs. 408A(b), 7701(a)(37).
2. IRC Sec. 408A(c)(1).
3. IRC Sec. 408A(c)(2).
4. IRC Sec. 408A(c)(4).
5. IRC Sec. 408A(c)(7).
6. IRC Secs. 408A(c)(3)(A), 408(c)(3)(C).
7. IRC Secs. 408A(c)(3)(D), 219(g)(4).
8. IRC Sec. 408A(C)(3)(C)(i). See IRC Sec. 219(g)(3)(A).
9. IRC Secs. 408A(c)(6)(A), 408A(e).
10. IRC Sec. 408A(c)(6)(B).
11. Prop. Reg. §1.408A-4, A-1.
12. IRC Sec. 408A(d)(3)(A)(i).
13. IRC Sec. 408A(d)(3)(C).
14. IRC Sec. 408A(d)(3)(A)(iii).
15. IRC Sec. 408A(d)(3)(E)(ii).
16. IRC Sec. 408A(d)(3)(A)(ii).
17. IRC Sec. 408A(c)(3)(B).
18. IRC Sec. 408A(c)(3)(C)(i), as added by IRSRRA '98 Sec. 7004(a).
19. IRC Sec. 408A(c)(3)(B)(ii).
20. IRC Sec. 408A(e).
21. IRC Sec. 408A(d)(4)(A) referencing Section 408(d)(2).
22. IRC Sec. 408A(d)(1).
23. IRC Sec. 408A(d)(2)(A)(i).
24. IRC Sec. 408A(d)(2)(A)(ii).
25. IRC Sec. 408A(d)(2)(A)(iii).
26. IRC Secs. 408A(d)(2)(A)(iv), 408A(d)(5). See IRC Sec. 72(t)(2)(F).
27. IRC Sec. 408A(d)(3)(E)(i).
28. IRC Sec. 408A(d)(3)(F).
29. IRC Sec. 72(t)(2)(A)(ii).
30. IRC Sec. 72(t)(2)(A)(iii).
31. IRC Sec. 72(t)(2)(A)(iv).
32. IRC Sec. 72(t)(2)(B).
33. IRC Sec. 72(t)(2)(D).
34. IRC Sec. 72(t)(2)(E).
35. IRC Sec. 72(t)(2)(F).
36. IRC Sec. 408A(c)(5)(A).
37. IRC Sec. 401(a)(9)(B)(ii).
38. IRC Sec. 401(a)(9)(B)(iii).
39. IRC Sec. 408A(c)(5)(B).
40. IRC Sec. 408(d)(3)(E).
41. Reg. §1.402(c)(2), A-7.
42. Prop. Reg. §1.408A-4, A-5.

Chapter 28

INDIVIDUAL RETIREMENT ACCOUNTS: TRADITIONAL

WHAT IS IT?

Traditional individual retirement accounts (IRAs) include any one of three vehicles accorded the same basic tax treatment:

- An individual retirement account is a trust or custodial account established by an individual with a bank or similarly qualified firm which acts as a trustee or custodian of investments contributed by the individual or purchased with funds contributed by the individual.[1]

- An individual retirement annuity is an annuity contract (or, rarely, an endowment contract) issued by an insurance company into which an individual pays premiums instead of contributions.[2]

- A group individual retirement account is a plan sponsored by an employer or labor union. With the advent of simplified employee pensions (SEPs) and SIMPLE IRAs, group IRAs are now rarely used.[3]

Traditional IRAs provide certain tax benefits to encourage retirement savings. Depending upon an individual's status as an active participant in an employer-sponsored qualified retirement plan and the level of his adjusted gross income, generally an individual may make some combination of deductible and nondeductible contributions of up to $2,000 per year to an IRA. Earnings on the amounts in the account accumulate tax-deferred.

There are number of special terms used to describe certain types of traditional IRAs. A "spousal IRA" is a traditional IRA established for a nonworking spouse or for a spouse with limited gross income.[4] Up to $2,000 may be contributed per year to a deductible spousal IRA. While the combined total maximum contribution for both spouses is $4,000, the deduction for each spouse is computed separately.

The spousal IRA rules apply to any individual (1) who files a joint return for the tax year and (2) whose total compensation (if any) includable in gross income is less than the compensation includable in the gross income of the spouse. However, the aggregate contributions for both spouses cannot exceed the greater of the combined compensation of both spouses or $4,000, subject to certain limitations on AGI.

The term "conduit IRA" or "rollover IRA" refers to a traditional IRA that has been set up to receive a (lump-sum) distribution from a qualified pension or profit sharing plan or a Section 403(b) tax deferred annuity plan (TDA), with the intent, if the amounts are never commingled with other IRA funds, to preserve the right to roll the monies back into a qualified plan or TDA similar to that from which the funds originally were paid. The objective is to preserve certain tax-preferred options available only from qualified plans.[5]

The IRAs associated with employer-sponsored Simplified Employee Pensions (SEPs) and SIMPLE IRAs are essentially traditional IRAs, with certain special rules in each case. The only real distinction between a SEP-IRA and a traditional IRA is the annual contribution limit. For contribution limit purposes, the SEP-IRA is treated like a qualified profit sharing plan. In a SEP-IRA, the employer may contribute up to *the lesser of* 15 percent of compensation or $30,000 (the Section 415 limits), subject to the limit on covered compensation (under Section 401(a)(17)), which is $160,000 as indexed in 1998. Effectively, this means the employer may contribute a maximum of $24,000 to the account of an employee earning $160,000 or more (in 1998). Essentially all the other rules applicable to traditional IRAs apply to SEP-IRAs. (See Chapter 44, SEPs.)

The IRAs associated with SIMPLE plans are subject to most of the same rules as traditional IRAs, except for the annual contribution limits and certain differences or limitations on withdrawals and penalties within the first two years. The maximum annual contribution to a SIMPLE IRA is $12,000, composed of a maximum of $6,000 of employee elective deferrals and $6,000 of employer matching contributions. The employer match cannot exceed 3 percent of compensation, so an employee must earn $200,000 or more to get the maximum $12,000 contribution. In contrast with SEP-IRAs, an employee is not permitted to use the SIMPLE IRA to receive up to $2,000 of contributions under the traditional IRA rules while the SIMPLE plan is in existence and the employee is not separated from service. Once the employee separates from service, the SIMPLE IRA is treated as a traditional IRA. During the first two years of its existence, any taxable distribution from a SIMPLE IRA that does not meet one of the exceptions to the 10 percent pre-59½ early distribution penalty, is subject, not to a 10 percent penalty but rather, to a 25 percent penalty. After the two-year period, early distributions from SIMPLE IRAs are treated like early distributions from traditional IRAs. (See Chapter 45, SIMPLE Plans.)

The Taxpayer Relief Act of 1997 (TRA '97) introduced a new type of IRA called the Roth IRA. A Roth IRA is a type of nondeductible IRA where qualifying distributions are free from federal income tax. In addition to the tax-free status of distributions, these IRAs have a number of unique features that are distinctly different from traditional IRAs. Although many of the rules that apply to traditional IRAs also apply to Roth IRAs, the substantial differences warrant a separate discussion. (See Chapter 27, Roth IRAs.) One important consideration with respect to traditional IRAs is the linkage in the contribution limits. A taxpayer may contribute no more than $2,000 in total to his traditional IRAs and Roth IRAs in any given year. Therefore, if a person contributes, say $1,500, to a Roth IRA, the maximum contribution permitted to a traditional IRA for that taxpayer is $500.

TRA '97 also introduced another tax-favored accumulation vehicle called an Education IRA to help taxpayers fund college educations. Despite its name and some similarity in tax treatment, an Education IRA is not really an IRA. Education IRAs are discussed elsewhere. (See Chapter 4, Education Funding.)

WHEN IS THE USE OF THIS TOOL INDICATED?

1. When there is a desire to shelter current earned income from taxation.

2. When it is desirable to defer taxes on investment income.

3. When long-term accumulation, especially for retirement purposes, is an important objective.

4. When an investor anticipates holding the investments in the IRA for a minimum of five to seven years.

ADVANTAGES

1. Eligible individuals may generally contribute up to $2,000 to a traditional IRA per year and deduct this amount from their current taxable income.

2. Investment earnings within the IRA are entirely tax deferred.

3. Distributions from an IRA are not required until the IRA-owner reaches age 70½ and then may be spread over the life or life expectancy of the IRA-owner or the joint lives

or life expectancies of the IRA-owner and a designated beneficiary under the minimum required distribution rules.

4. An IRA may serve as a temporary tax-deferred repository for lump-sum distributions from qualified plans and Section 403(b) TDAs. These amounts may be rolled back into a plan similar to the distributing plan at a later date if so desired so long as certain requirements are met.

DISADVANTAGES

1. Although funds may be withdrawn from an IRA at any time, if the need arises, the imposition of the traditional income tax as well as the 10 percent penalty tax associated with distributions before age 59½ makes that choice very costly. However, in the case of tax-deductible contributions, the immediate tax deduction together with tax deferral on earnings will often provide a sufficiently greater accumulation after a period of years relative to what could be accumulated outside the IRA. As a result, it is possible that the investor will accumulate more after tax even if the withdrawal is subject to the 10 percent penalty. In addition, certain distributions before age 59½ are exempt from the 10 percent penalty. (These exceptions are described in the "Tax Implications" section below.)

2. Traditional IRAs may not be established and further contributions to an established traditional IRA are not permitted once a person reaches age 70½, even if he still has earned income.

3. Distributions from traditional IRAs must commence when the IRA-owner reaches age 70½ under the minimum distribution rules, even if the IRA-owner has no need for the funds. Failure to take the required minimum distributions subjects the underpayments to an excise tax of 50 percent.

TAX IMPLICATIONS

Contributions

1. *Amount of contributions.* An IRA cannot accept more than $2,000 or 100% of compensation includable in the taxpayer's gross income for any taxable year (not including rollover amounts).[6] In certain circumstances a married individual may make IRA contributions of more than $2,000 per taxable year. The contributions must be made to a combination of the married individual's own IRA and

the nonworking spouse's IRA, because neither IRA is permitted to receive more than $2,000 in contributions per taxable year (excluding rollover contributions).

2. *Contributions prohibited to "inherited IRAs."* The term "inherited IRA" describes an IRA after the death of its owner. No deduction is allowed for any amount contributed to an inherited IRA.[7] Nondeductible contributions are prohibited also. However, the prohibition does not apply to a beneficiary who is the surviving spouse of the IRA owner if the surviving spouse elects to treat the IRA as his own for all purposes including deductible contributions.

3. *Deductible amount.* An IRA owner may never deduct more than the lesser of $2,000 or compensation includable in gross income for the taxable year.[8] This amount may be further limited if the IRA owner is an "active participant" in an employer-sponsored retirement plan.

4. *Active participation.* An individual (or his spouse) who is an active participant in one of certain types of retirement plans will be unable to make a deductible contribution to an IRA unless his income is below an applicable dollar amount.[9] If it is, a full or partial deduction may be available, depending upon the individual's income level. Active participant status and the deductibility of IRA contributions is determined separately for each spouse of a married couple except for married couples whose AGI exceeds $150,000, as explained below.

An active participant is a person who actively participates in a pension, profit-sharing, stock bonus, Section 403(a), Section 403(b) account or contract, a SEP, SIMPLE plan, or certain governmental plans, such as civil service. A person is not considered an active participant simply because he has earned income subject to FICA tax ("participating" in Social Security) or because he participates in a (nonqualified) Section 457 plan. It is not necessary that a participant's rights in any of these plans be fully vested in order for the participation to be considered active.[10]

A participant is an active participant in a defined benefit plan if, for any portion of the plan year ending with or within the individual's taxable (calendar) year, he is not excluded from the plan's eligibility provisions. Note, even an employee who accrues no benefit because he has not met the required minimum hours is nonetheless an active participant for the year, because such provisions only affect the accrual of a benefit, not the eligibility to participate.[11]

If all accruals for participants under a defined benefit plan have ceased, a person will cease to be an active participant in such frozen plan in those taxable years following the taxable year in which the plan was frozen.

This exception does not apply if the benefit may vary with future compensation. For example, a final average salary plan, though frozen, is still adjusted for what the final average salary turns out to be. Note that this can likewise affect non-key employees in a top-heavy frozen plan.

For example, Jack is a calendar year individual who is not excluded by reason of the provisions of a defined benefit plan with a plan year ending November 30. Jack separates from service on December 2 and accrues no benefit. However, since Jack was not excluded on December 1, he is considered an active participant for the following calendar year within which ends the plan's November 30 plan year.

Generally, a participant in a defined contribution plan is an active participant if, with respect to a plan year ending with or within the individual's taxable year, employer contributions or forfeitures are allocated to the individual's account.[12] Employment is not required by the employer; many plans, however, provide that an employee must be employed on the final day of the plan year in order to receive any allocation. So active participation may, for a separated employee, depend not only on the plan provisions, but also on whether any forfeitures of account balances took place during the plan year.

If an individual elects not to participate in the plan, that person is not an active participant, but this election can endanger the plan from qualifying under the coverage requirements.

If a top-heavy plan is required to make a contribution on behalf of a non-key employee, that person, whether employed or not, will be treated as an active participant.

Even if contributions are not made, but are required to be, the participant can be held an active participant for the "constructive" allocation.

If an employee makes an elective deferral[13] or even a nondeductible contribution to the plan,[14] he will be considered an active participant.

For timing purposes, if no amount of forfeitures has been allocated by the end of the plan year and contributions are purely discretionary and have not been made by the end of the plan year, the participant will not be considered active for that plan year; however, if the employer makes a contribution that is allocated after the plan year, the person will be considered active for the taxable year of the individual in which the contribution is made.

For example, suppose Jack is a participant in a profit-sharing plan with purely discretionary contributions and a plan year ending October 31. As of October 31, no contributions had been made and no forfeitures were made. The employer makes a contribution on January 14 of the following year for the previous October 31 plan year. Jack is not considered an active participant for the previous calendar year, but is considered an active participant in the calendar year in which the January 14 contribution is made, even if the employer makes no other contribution in that calendar year for the plan year ending October 31 of that year and no forfeitures are allocated to Jack's account.

Suppose, instead, the employer makes the contribution on December 14, rather than on the following January 14. Now Jack is an active participant in the plan for the previous calendar year when the contribution is made.

5. *Deductible IRA phaseout formula.* The deductibility of contributions to traditional IRAs for active participants is phased out in a pro-rata fashion over the applicable phaseout range of AGI. For example, if the applicable phaseout range of AGI is $50,000 to $60,000, a taxpayer with AGI of $54,000 who actively participates in a qualified plan would be permitted to contribute $2,000 to an IRA, but would be permitted to deduct only $1,200 of that $2,000 contribution. The remaining $800 (4/10 of $2,000) would be a nondeductible contribution.

6. *AGI phaseout ranges.* The phaseout range depends upon filing status and the year in which the contribution is made. The Tax Reform Act of 1997 created the following phaseout ranges:

Taxable years beginning in:	Joint Returns Phase-out range	Single Taxpayers Phase-out range
1998	$50,000 - $60,000	$30,000 - $40,000
1999	$51,000 - $61,000	$31,000 - $41,000
2000	$52,000 - $62,000	$32,000 - $42,000
2001	$53,000 - $63,000	$33,000 - $43,000
2002	$54,000 - $64,000	$34,000 - $44,000
2003	$60,000 - $70,000	$40,000 - $50,000
2004	$65,000 - $75,000	$45,000 - $55,000
2005	$70,000 - $80,000	$50,000 - $60,000
2006	$75,000 - $85,000	$50,000 - $60,000
2007 and thereafter	$80,000 - $100,000	$50,000 - $60,000

The maximum deductible IRA contribution for an individual who is not an active participant, but whose spouse is, is phased out for taxpayers with AGI between $150,000 and $160,000. If an individual is an active participant and his spouse is not, the deduction for contributions to the individual's own IRA may be limited by the phaseout rules; however, such an individual's contribution to the spousal IRA is deductible subject only to the phaseout starting at $150,000 of AGI for individuals who are not active participants but whose spouses are active participants.

7. *Floor amount and rounding rules.* There is a $200 floor on the deductible amount, unless adjusted gross income is equal to or greater than the amount at which the deductible limit has been reduced to zero.[15] Therefore an individual always can deduct $200 (assuming at least $200 in compensation) as long as the individual's adjusted gross income is below the top of the applicable phaseout range.

The amount of the dollar reduction from $2,000 (or to each $2,000 contribution in a spousal IRA situation) will be rounded to the next lowest $10 increment.[16]

For example, S is unmarried and has adjusted gross income of $34,015 when the applicable phaseout range is $32,000 to $42,000. The formula would reduce her $2,000 maximum deductible dollar limit for IRA contributions by $403 ($2,015/$10,000), which would result in a limit of $1,597. The reduction is rounded down to $400, yielding a maximum dollar limit of $1,600 in deductible contributions.

8. *Nondeductible contributions.* An active participant may generally make IRA contributions of $2,000 each year, but some or all of the contributions may not qualify for a deduction. The contributions can be withdrawn as excess contributions or can be left in the IRA as designated nondeductible contributions. In an IRA, nondeductible contributions generate tax-deferred earnings.

An individual may make the maximum deductible contributions (if any) and then make nondeductible contributions until the total of both types of contributions equals the limit of $2,000 (or 100 percent of compensation includable in income if less).[17]

For example, H is an unmarried active participant in his employer's Section 401(a) qualified plan. Assuming his adjusted gross income is $38,000 (and he had more than $2,000 of compensation) when the applicable phaseout range is $33,000 to $43,000, he may make no more than $1,000 in deductible IRA contributions. He is allowed to make up to $1,000 in nondeductible IRA contributions.

In a second case, B is an unmarried active participant in her employer's qualified plan whose AGI exceeds the applicable phaseout range. She may not make any deductible IRA contributions for the year. However, she may make up to $2,000 in nondeductible IRA contributions for the year.

In a third case, G and M are married and file jointly. Each has earned income in excess of $2,000. G is an active participant in his employer's qualified plan but M is not. Their combined adjusted gross income is $65,000 and the applicable phaseout range is $60,000 to $70,000. G can make up to $1,000 in deductible IRA contributions and up to $1,000 in nondeductible IRA contributions. M can make a fully deductible $2,000 IRA contribution to her account since she is not an active participant in a qualified plan (and their combined income is not in the $150,000 to $160,000 phaseout range for a married couple where one spouse is an active participant).

9. *Federal payroll taxes.* Amounts paid by an employer to an employee that are contributed by the employee to an IRA or that are paid directly into the employee's IRA by the employer are considered taxable income and are subject to Social Security (FICA) and unemployment (FUTA) taxes. However, employer contributions to an IRA that is part of a SEP arrangement are not taxable and are not included in wages for FICA or FUTA purposes unless the contributions are made pursuant to a salary reduction election.

Contributions to the IRA of a self-employed individual are neither excludable nor deductible in figuring compensation subject to self-employment taxes.

10. *Excise tax on excess contributions.* An excise tax of six percent per year on the amount of an excess contribution is imposed for the taxable year in which it is made and for each subsequent year at the end of which the excess contribution remains in the IRA. An excess contribution is an IRA contribution that (1) is made in excess of the maximum contribution available, (2) does not meet the rollover requirements, or (3) is made by a person ineligible to make the contribution.[18]

For example, P establishes an IRA by transferring to his IRA trustee certificates of stock worth $1,800. Unless the stock had been distributed to him from a qualified plan and thereby qualified as a rollover contribution to the IRA, the contribution is an excess contribution because

IRA contributions other than rollover contributions must be in cash.

In a second example, M has $1,500 in compensation during the year and establishes an IRA by contributing $2,000 in cash. Unless the $2,000 had been distributed to him from a qualified plan or other retirement plan and thereby qualified as a rollover contribution to the IRA, $500 of the $2,000 contribution is an excess contribution.

In a third example, M is age 75. He establishes an IRA and makes a contribution of $2,000. Unless the $2,000 had been distributed to him from a qualified plan no more than 60 days prior to the contribution, such that the contribution was a rollover contribution to the IRA, M has made a $2,000 excess contribution because he had attained age 70½ by the end of the year.

The Code authorizes two corrective techniques to reverse excess contributions. If a person who makes an excess contribution fails to use one of these authorized techniques, the excess is subject to the six percent excise tax each year, and withdrawal of the amount of the excess contribution would be taxable just as would any other IRA distribution (other than the return of nondeductible contributions), including a 10 percent early distribution tax if otherwise applicable.

The first technique the taxpayer may employ is to carry forward the amount of the excess contribution by treating it as an additional IRA contribution in later taxable years (up to the appropriate annual limit).[19] Carry forward treatment generally occurs automatically (for purposes of computing the six percent excise tax) if the taxpayer does not actually contribute the maximum deductible amount to his IRA for a taxable year in which excess contributions remain in the IRA. Over time, the entire excess may be "absorbed." However, each year any remaining excess is still subject to the six percent excise tax. The carry forward technique eliminates the need to break investments, such as a long-term certificate of deposit, and avoids the tax that would apply to a distribution.

The second technique is to simply withdraw the excess contribution in its entirety. An actual withdrawal is generally better for large excess contributions, but the amounts withdrawn are subject to income tax and may also be subject to the 10 percent early distribution penalty.

11. *Rollover contributions.* Contributions of qualified rollover distributions from a qualified plan, Section 403(b) TDA, or another IRA to a (conduit) IRA are not subject to tax,

provided certain requirements are met. However, only the taxable portion of a distribution from a qualified plan may be rolled over. Any nontaxable portion attributable to the participant's basis in the plan may not be rolled over, but there is no tax since the amount represents a recovery of the taxpayer's basis. Any amount that is rolled over must be deposited in the rollover IRA within 60 days of receipt of the distribution. The entire amount of the distribution need not be rolled over, but the portion that is not rolled over is subject to tax and possibly the 10 percent early distribution penalty if received before age 59½.

Distributions

1. *General federal income tax rules on distributions.* Except in the case of a rollover, an actual distribution generally is taxed as ordinary income in the taxable year in which the distribution is received.[20]

2. *Recovery of basis.* If nondeductible contributions have been made to the IRAs, a portion of the distribution is a tax-free return of those contributions. The nondeductible contributions give the IRA owner a tax basis in the IRA, which is an investment in the contract for purposes of applying the Section 72 rules regarding distributions. In computing what portion of a distribution is a tax-free return of nondeductible contributions, all distributions during the taxable year are added together and treated as one distribution.[21] Similarly, all nondeductible contributions that have been made to any IRAs he owns as of the close of the year must be aggregated.[22]

The amount of a nontaxable return of nondeductible contributions is generally the portion of the taxable year's distributions that bears the same ratio to the total amount of the taxable year's distributions as the amount of nondeductible contributions held in all IRAs as of the end of the calendar year in which the taxable year begins bears to the total balance of all IRAs as of the end of that calendar year.[23]

The amount of a calendar year's distributions must be added to the calendar year-end balance in order to compute the denominator of the fraction.[24] In effect the calculation of the portion attributable to nondeductible contributions is made at the beginning of each calendar year before any distributions. Distributions that are nontaxable because they are a return of excess contributions are not added back, however.

For example, V has made $8,000 of deductible and $6,000 of nondeductible contributions to her only IRA over a period of prior years. On March 1 of 1998, she withdraws $1,000. On May 1, she withdraws another $1,000. On July 1 she withdraws another $1,000. On September 1 she withdraws another $1,000. On November 1 she withdraws another $1,000, for a total of $5,000 withdrawn during the year. At the end of the current year, her IRA balance is $12,500. The portion of the $5,000 in total distributions that is treated as a nontaxable return of her nondeductible contributions is $1,714.29, calculated as follows:

$$\frac{\$6,000}{\$12,500 + \$5,000} \quad x \quad \$5,000 \quad = \quad \$1,714.29$$

She pays tax for the 1998 year on only $3,285.71 ($5,000 less $1,714.29).

The amount of nondeductible contributions considered to be distributed must be subtracted from the total amount of nondeductible contributions, in order for the formula to work properly in later years.

For example, returning to the facts of V's IRA, above, assume further that V makes no further withdrawals until June 30, 1999, when she withdraws $3,000. She makes no additional contributions. Her IRA balance on December 31, 1999 is $10,875. In applying the formula, she must reduce her total nondeductible contributions by the portion of the prior distribution that was a return of nondeductible contributions ($1,714.29). The total nondeductible contributions accordingly are lowered from $6,000 to $4,285.71. The portion of the 1999 distribution that is nontaxable is calculated as follows:

$$\frac{\$4,285.71}{\$10,875 + \$3,000} \quad x \quad \$3,000 \quad = \quad \$926.64$$

The $926.64 of the $3,000 distribution is a tax-free return of basis. The remainder, $2,073.36, is taxable income to V.

It is not possible for an IRA owner to designate a distribution as being from nondeductible contributions only, even if the IRA owner attempts to characterize his nondeductible contributions as being kept in a separate IRA and takes withdrawals only from that IRA. Nor is it possible to roll over only the taxable portion of an IRA distribution. In rolling over amounts from one IRA to another, the IRA owner must roll over amounts attributable to nondeductible contributions as well as deductible contributions.[25]

Also, the amount of any outstanding rollover must be added to the fraction's denominator.[26] An outstanding rollover is an amount that (1) is distributed from the IRA within 60 days of the end of the taxable year (generally between November 2 and December 31), (2) is not rolled over into another IRA by the end of the taxable year, and (3) is ultimately rolled over (in the following taxable year) to another IRA (i.e., by the end of the 60-day period).[27] Therefore, the complete formula for the portion of a distribution that is a nontaxable return of nondeductible contributions is the following:

$$\frac{\text{Total Nondeductible Contributions}}{\text{Total IRA Balances} + \text{Distributions} + \text{Outstanding Rollovers}} \times \text{Distributions} = \text{Nontaxable Portion}$$

For example, J has two IRAs, IRA-1 and IRA-2. He has made a total of $6,000 in nondeductible contributions between the two of them. There have been no distributions from either IRA. On December 11 he withdraws $7,000 from IRA-1 and on October 10 he withdraws $300 from IRA-2. As of December 31 neither distribution had been rolled over into another IRA. The balances in the IRAs on December 31 are the following:

IRA-1	$3,000
IRA-2	$20,000
Total	$23,000

On the following January 30, J rolls $7,000 into another IRA. The $300 that was distributed from IRA-2 is not rolled over, however. To calculate the portion of the $300 that is a tax-free return of nondeductible contributions, the "outstanding rollover" of $7,000 as of December 31 is added to the denominator. The nontaxable portion is:

$$\frac{\$6,000}{\$23,000 + \$300 + \$7,000} \times \$300 = \$59.41 \text{ nontaxable}$$

The remaining $240.59 is taxable and, assuming J is less than 59½ years old, subject to the 10 percent penalty tax on premature distributions.

The IRA owner is responsible for keeping track of his nondeductible contributions and calculating the taxable amount of any distribution that is not rolled over.

3. *Ten percent early distribution penalty tax.* An IRA owner who receives a distribution from the IRA before age 59½[28] is liable for an additional tax equal to 10 percent of the taxable amount of the distribution.[29]

The 10 percent additional tax does not apply to the extent a distribution is a nontaxable return of nondeductible contributions or is rolled over into another IRA or a qualified plan.

For example, S maintains an IRA into which he has made only deductible contributions. A family emergency arises while S is age 33 and he withdraws $1,000 from the IRA to pay the sudden expenses. S must include the $1,000 withdrawal in his taxable income for the year pursuant to the usual IRA distribution tax rules. In addition, he must pay an additional 10 percent penalty tax of $100 due to the early distribution.

Assume instead, some of S's contributions to the IRA had been designated as nondeductible contributions and that S includes only $600 in income for the year (assuming $400 is a return of nondeductible contributions). In this case he has to pay an additional penalty tax of only $60 (10 percent of the $600 taxable amount).

4. *List of exceptions to the 10 percent penalty tax.* There are no hardship exceptions to the 10 percent additional tax, but certain other exceptions apply. A distribution before the IRA owner has attained age 59½ is not subject to the 10 percent additional tax if the distribution meets one of several exceptions. The exceptions to the 10 percent additional tax for distributions from IRAs include distributions

- paid to the beneficiary after the death of the owner,[30]

- made on account of the disability of the owner,[31]

- that are part of a series of substantially equal periodic payments over the life or life expectancy of the owner or the joint life or joint life expectancies of the owner and the beneficiary,[32]

- to the extent used to pay certain medical expenses during the year,[33]

- to the extent used to pay the health insurance premiums of an unemployed owner (within limits),[34]

- to pay certain qualifying higher education expenses,[35]

- to pay certain qualified first-time homebuyer acquisition costs,[36]

- that are rolled over, on a tax-deferred basis, into another qualified plan or IRA,

- made on account of a levy under Section 6331 on an IRA, for tax years beginning after 1999.[37]

5. *Application of exceptions to 10 percent penalty tax.* For purposes of the disability exception to the 10 percent additional tax, an individual is considered disabled if he cannot participate in any substantial gainful activity because of a medically determinable physical or mental condition which can be expected to result in death or to be of long-continued and indefinite duration.

A distribution to a beneficiary or to the estate of the IRA owner after the death of the IRA owner is not subject to the 10 percent additional tax even though the IRA owner had not attained age 59½ by the time of the distribution.

Distributions made to an owner from an IRA are not subject to the 10 percent penalty to the extent such distributions are used to pay medical expenses during the taxable year and do not exceed the amount allowable as a deduction (on schedule A) for medical expenses in excess of 7.5 percent of AGI (Code section 213), determined without regard to whether the employee/owner itemizes deductions for such taxable year.

Distributions from IRAs to unemployed individuals that are used to pay health insurance premiums are not subject to the 10 percent penalty (1) if such individual has received unemployment compensation for 12 consecutive weeks under any Federal or State unemployment compensation law, (2) if such distributions are made during any taxable year during which such unemployment compensation is paid or the succeeding taxable year, and (3) to the extent such distributions do not exceed the amount paid during the taxable year for insurance described in Code section 213(d)(1)(D) with respect to the individual and the individual's spouse and dependents. This exemption continues to apply to distributions until the individual has been re-employed for 60 days. In the case of self-employed individuals, the exemption applies in the same manner as to common law employees if, under the Federal or State law, the individual would have qualified to receive unemployment compensation but for the fact that the individual was self-employed.

The Taxpayer Relief Act of 1997 added an additional exception to the early withdrawal tax for IRAs with respect to a qualified first-time homebuyer distribution, subject to a $10,000 life-time cap. A qualified first-time homebuyer distribution means (1) any payment or distribution received by an individual, (2) to the extent such payment or distribution is used by the individual before the close of the 120th day after the day on which such payment or distribution is received, (3) to pay qualified acquisition costs, (4) with respect to a principal residence of a first-time homebuyer, and (5) the first-time homebuyer

is such individual, the spouse of such individual, or any child, grandchild, or ancestor of such individual or the individual's spouse.[38]

The qualified acquisition costs are the costs of acquiring, constructing, or reconstructing a residence, including any usual or reasonable settlement, financing, or other closing costs.[39]

An individual is a first-time homebuyer if such individual (and if married, such individual's spouse) had no present ownership interest in a principal residence during the two-year period ending on the date of acquisition of the principal residence.[40]

The Taxpayer Relief Act of 1997 added another exception to the 10 percent additional tax for distributions from an IRA to pay for qualified higher education expenses to the extent such distributions (other than those already excluded from the penalty) do not exceed the qualified higher education expenses of the taxpayer for the taxable year.[41] For these purposes, qualified higher education expenses are those qualified higher education expenses for education furnished to (1) the taxpayer, (2) the taxpayer's spouse, or (3) any child[42] or grandchild of the taxpayer or the taxpayer's spouse, at an eligible educational institution.[43]

The term qualified higher education expenses means tuition, fees, books, supplies, and equipment as well as reasonable costs for room and board, up to a maximum of the minimum amount that the school allocates for room and board per student for a particular academic period.[44]

The amount of qualified higher education expenses for any taxable year is reduced by the amount of scholarships or fellowship grants excludable from gross income under Section 117, any other tax-free educational benefits received by the student during the taxable year (such as employer-provided educational assistance excludable under Section 127), and any payment (other than a gift, bequest, devise, or inheritance within the meaning of Section 102(a)) which is excludable under any United States law. Additionally, qualified higher education expenses are reduced by any amount excludable from gross income relating to the redemption of a qualified U.S. Savings Bond and certain scholarships and veterans benefits.[45]

The IRS Restructuring and Reform Act of 1998 added yet another exception to the 10-percent penalty tax for early withdrawals. For tax years beginning after 1999, distributions which are made on account of an IRS levy on an IRA under Section 6331 will not be subject to the

10% penalty for distributions made prior to the individual attaining age 59½. It has been indicated that this exception will apply only if the IRA itself has been levied; the exception will not apply if the amount is withdrawn to pay taxes in the absence of a levy, or in order to release a levy on other interests.[46]

6. *Distributions under the "substantially equal periodic payments" exception to the 10 percent penalty tax.* The exception for a distribution that is part of a series of substantially equal periodic payments made not less frequently than annually over the life (or life expectancy) of the IRA owner or the joint lives (or joint life and last survivor expectancy) of the IRA owner and the IRA owner's designated beneficiary offers important planning opportunities and some potential pitfalls.

If the IRA owner changes the method of distribution (other than because of death or disability) before age 59½, or if after he reaches age 59½, within five years of the date of the first payment, to a method that no longer qualifies for this exception, the 10 percent additional tax is imposed on all distributions received before age 59½. This tax is payable in the first taxable year in which the modification is made, and equals the tax that would have been imposed had the exception never applied. Interest is also due on the recaptured tax.[47]

For example, T begins receiving payments at age 53 in 1994 under a distribution method that provides for substantially equal payments over her life expectancy. At age 57 in 1998, she elected to withdraw the balance of her IRA in a single sum. She is liable for a 10 percent additional tax on the amount of the lump sum and on the total of the amounts she has received since 1994, as well as interest due on the recaptured tax.

Note that substantially equal periodic payments to an IRA owner under age 59½ generally must be received for at least five years.[48] The IRA owner not only is prohibited from changing the method of distribution before age 59½ to a method that no longer qualifies for the exception for substantially equal periodic payments, he generally must wait at least five years to do so, even if he attains age 59½ before the end of the five-year period.[49] If the IRA owner does not, the exception from the 10 percent additional tax is canceled to the extent amounts were received before attaining age 59½. Interest is also due on the recaptured tax.

For example, L begins receiving distributions in substantially equal payments at age 57 in 1994. Four years later at age 61 she decides to alter the distribution method and she withdraws the balance in a single sum. She is liable for the 10 percent additional tax in 1998 on the total of the distributions she received before she turned age 59½, as well as interest on that tax. She is not liable for the 10 percent additional tax on amounts received after age 59½.

The prohibition against changing the method of distribution within five years does not apply if the reason the method of distribution is changed is the death or disability of the IRA owner.[50]

Suppose that in the previous example, the reason L needs to withdraw the balance four years later at age 61 is that she has become disabled since the time she started to receive her distributions. The 10 percent additional tax is not due, even for amounts received before she attained age 59½.

If the 10 percent additional tax must be recaptured due to a change in method of distribution before 59½ or within five years of the start of payments, the IRA owner also is liable for interest on the additional tax. Interest is computed over a "deferral period," which is the period beginning with the taxable year in which the distributions would have been taxable but for the substantially equal payments exception and ending with the taxable year in which the change in method of distribution occurs.[51]

The IRS has recognized three approaches or methods to the application of this exception:[52]

- Life expectancy method: annual distribution of the required minimum distribution amount (as calculated under the Section 401(a)(9) and Section 408(a)(6) rules), based on either the life expectancy of the IRA owner or the joint life and last survivor expectancy of the IRA owner and a designated beneficiary;[53]

- Amortization method: amortization of the IRA's account balance over a number of years equal to the life expectancy of the IRA owner or joint life and last survivor expectancy of the IRA owner and a designated beneficiary, at an interest rate that does not exceed a reasonable interest rate on the date payments commence; or

- Annuity method: division of the IRA's account balance by an annuity factor derived using a reasonable mortality table and an interest rate which does not exceed a reasonable interest rate on the date payments commence.

For example, S is a 50 year-old woman who has no designated beneficiary. ("Designated beneficiary" is a defined term under the required minimum distribution rules. A beneficiary other than an individual, with an exception for a trust under certain circumstances, cannot qualify as a designated beneficiary.) S's beneficiary is the University of Pennsylvania Wharton School. S wishes to begin receiving substantially equal payments from her IRA, which has a balance of $100,000.

Under the first exception, she would use one of the formulas available for meeting the required minimum distribution rules. For example, she might choose the formula that allows for recalculation of life expectancy, meaning that in the first year her minimum distribution would be $100,000 divided by her projected life expectancy of 33.1 years[54] or $3,021.15; in the second year, the minimum distribution would be the first year's account balance divided by 32.2 years, or, assuming the balance is now $105,000, the distribution would be $3,360.87.

Second, she could satisfy the substantially equal periodic payments exception by amortizing the IRA. Under this method she would amortize the $100,000 account balance using a reasonable interest rate over her life expectancy of 33.1 years at the time distributions commence. Assuming a rate of eight percent is reasonable, S would receive $8,679 annually.

Finally, under the third method, S can divide the account balance by an annuity factor derived from a reasonable mortality table and a reasonable rate of interest. Assuming an interest rate of eight percent, the annuity factor from the UP-1984 Mortality Table is 11.109. This factor would yield an annual distribution of $9,002 ($100,000/11.109 = $9,002).

One of the practical problems with relying on the minimum distribution method is the fact that the IRA owner must receive the exact amount determined under that method, and no more. Even though the method is based upon the required "minimum" distribution amount that would be required if those rules applied to the IRA owner currently (they do not apply until approximately age 70½), the portion of a taxable year's distributions in excess of that amount would be subject to the 10 percent additional tax.

According to the IRS, the exception for distributions that are part of a series of substantially equal periodic payments applies to each IRA owned by the taxpayer, rather than the aggregate of all IRAs.[55] An IRA owner who desires the flexibility in the future to increase the amounts being withdrawn annually has this planning opportunity: divide an existing IRA into several IRAs, and begin to take the substantially equal periodic distri-

butions from only one of the IRAs. Thereafter, if additional funds are needed on an annual basis, one or more of the other IRAs can begin making substantially equal periodic distributions as well.

The reasonable interest rate factor used in the amortization or the annuity factor methods is flexible and may offer some planning opportunities. One may use an interest rate that is lower than the highest reasonable rate and by doing so, the amount of the periodic distributions decreases.

Among the rates authorized by the IRS are:

- Interest rate provided in PBGC Regs. Section 2619.41, et seq., for valuing annuities.[56]

- Federal long-term monthly rate in effect on the date of the initial distribution.[57]

- Average of the adjusted federal long-term rates used for purposes of Section 382 for the prior 12 months.[58]

- Eight percent.[59]

What life expectancy may be used?

- Life expectancy may be based on the participant's age alone or on the participant's and his designated beneficiary's ages to derive the joint and survivor life expectancy of the participant and designated beneficiary.

- The unisex Tables V or VI.[60]

- The UP-1984 Mortality Table.

- No particular life expectancy authority has been indicated in the case of the annuity method.

Although there is no statutory, regulatory, case, or private letter ruling authority for doing so, one may also reasonably assume that the mortality factors and implicit life expectancies associated with Table 80CNSMT are also reasonable. Table 80CNSMT is the mortality table underlying the annuity factors in the IRS's ALPHA volume of the actuarial tables for valuing life estates, remainders, and annuities for gift and estate tax purposes. Since the Table 80CNSMT factors are used to value gifts of partial interests in trust, and taxpayers may elect to retain one interest, for example, a life estate, and to give away the rest, the remainder interest, or vice-versa, the factors are close to actuarially neutral to prevent "actuarial arbitrage." Actuarial arbitrage would occur if the tables either overestimated or underestimated life expectancies and taxpayers were able to retain the more favorable side of the partial interest to undervalue the gift or estate tax value of the transferred interest. The term actuarial neutral means that the mortality factors are loaded neither towards longevity (as are annuity tables) nor towards premature death (as are life insurance tables).

The life expectancies associated with Table 80CNSMT are approximately 20 percent shorter than those associated with Table V of the Section 72 regulations. For instance, at age 65 the life expectancy value from Table V is 20 years, from Table 80CNSMT, 16.5 years. Consequently, for a given balance in an IRA account, the annual amount one could withdraw without penalty would be greater if one uses the values from Table 80CNSMT, rather than the values from Table V (for a single life) or Table VI (for joint lives), to determine payments under the substantially equal periodic payments exception.

The life expectancy method will generally result in the lowest allowable payments, but required payments will increase each year as mortality and the accrued account balance increase. The amortization and annuity methods will provide a level annual payment schedule (unless an interest rate index is used and the amortization amount is recomputed each year). Allowable payments will be larger if a higher interest rate or lower life expectancy is used to compute the required payments, and vice versa.

For planning purposes, the IRA owner's ability to roll any portion of one IRA over to another IRA and the rule that the substantially equal periodic payments may be computed separately from each account means that one has virtually unlimited flexibility to arrange exactly the desired periodic payout.

For example, your client, age 52, has $350,000 in an IRA and wishes to withdraw $20,000 a year from his IRA under the substantially equal periodic payments exception to the 10 percent penalty tax. Using the IRS-preferred single-life expectancy Table V from the Section 72 regulations, his life expectancy is 31.3 years. Also using the IRS's safe harbor interest rate of eight percent (from Notice 89-25), one can determine the principal sum necessary under the amortization method to derive annual payments of $20,000. In other words, given a payment amount of $20,000, an interest rate of eight percent, and a number of years such as 31.3, one can find the corresponding present value (principal amount). The answer is $227,521.03. All your client has to do is roll $227,521.03 out of his current IRA into a new IRA and

then take his desired $20,000 annual payments from the new account. If some other set of assumptions regarding the interest rate and life expectancy are deemed to be more suitable assumptions, then one can simply compute the required principal amount using those assumptions and roll that amount out of the current IRA into a new IRA. In other words, the assumptions one uses are almost irrelevant since one can always back into the required principal amount and then create a new rollover IRA with that principal amount in the account.

Keep in mind, the payouts depend in no way upon the actual investment performance of the funds in the IRA; once the method of determining the substantially equal payments and the corresponding interest rate and life expectancy assumptions are made, they remain constant, regardless of the actual performance of the funds in the IRA. Therefore, from your client's perspective it makes no difference that he has split his IRA funds into two accounts assuming he continues to invest each account in the manner he would have anyway if he had not split his current account into two accounts.

7. *Required distributions.* An IRA owner generally must begin to receive distributions by April 1st of the year following the year in which he attains age 70½.[61] In addition, the amounts received at that time must meet the minimum distribution rules. Underpayments are subject to a 50 percent excise tax in addition to the traditional income tax.

8. *Withholding rules.* Distributions of the entire amount of an IRA generally are subject to withholding at a flat rate of 10 percent.[62] Periodic (annuity-type) distributions generally are subject to withholding at the rate which applies to wages paid to an employee.[63] Distributions from an individual retirement account that are payable upon demand are not treated as periodic distributions even if the recipient has scheduled installment payments over a period of years.

The recipient may elect out of withholding for any reason and must be notified at certain intervals of the right to make or revoke such an election.[64] Interest and dividend payments on investments of an IRA are not subject to backup withholding.

9. *No 5-year or 10-year lump-sum tax averaging.* Lump-sum distributions from IRAs, even from conduit IRAs that contain only amounts (and the earnings thereon) that were rolled over from a qualified plan and which might otherwise have qualified for the lump-sum tax averaging election, do not qualify for the lump-sum tax averaging election.

10. *Rollovers to Roth IRAs.* Individuals with less than $100,000 of AGI may roll their traditional IRAs over into a Roth IRA. The amount rolled over is subject to federal income tax (but not the 10 percent penalty) just as if the amount were distributed from the traditional IRA and not rolled over (with a special 4-year income spreading provision for 1998 rollovers, unless the taxpayer elects otherwise). Note that the rollover is not included in income for the purposes of the $100,000 limitation on AGI. The amount rolled into the Roth IRA now accumulates entirely tax free. There is no federal income tax on qualified distributions from the Roth IRA. (See Chapter 27, Roth IRAs, for a further discussion of the Roth IRA rules and the traditional IRA to Roth IRA rollover provisions.)

ALTERNATIVES

1. Self-employed individuals may make contributions to so-called Keogh plans which are the self-employed person's qualified retirement plan. Keogh plans can be even more attractive than deductible IRAs because the annual limit for certain defined contribution-type plans can be as high as 20 percent of the individual's before-contribution self-employment income up to a maximum of $30,000 (as indexed for inflation in 1998). (See Chapter 29 for details on Keogh plans.) Permitted contributions might be even higher for a defined benefit Keogh plan if adopted by an older individual. Similarly, a somewhat less expensive and less difficult to administer plan for self-employed individuals is a Simplified Employee Pension (SEP). An individual may contribute, effectively, up to just over 13 percent of their before-contribution self-employment income up to a maximum of $24,000 (as indexed for inflation and limited by the covered compensation limit of $160,000 in 1998). One further inexpensive and simple alternative is to adopt a SIMPLE IRA. Total contributions (in 1998) to a SIMPLE IRA may be as high as $12,000 for individuals with self-employment income exceeding $200,000.

2. Employees whose employers sponsor various thrift, savings, or cash or deferred arrangements (Section 401(k) plans) may elect to contribute up to 15 percent of their compensation up to a maximum of $10,000 (as indexed in 1998). Similar to deductible IRAs, the amounts contributed are generally not subject to federal income tax and investment earnings in the plan are tax deferred.

3. Individuals may contribute up to $2,000 to a Roth IRA, subject to certain limitations on adjusted gross income. Although the contributions are not tax deductible, the investment earnings within the Roth IRA are potentially tax free.

WHERE AND HOW DO I GET IT?

An individual retirement account must have a written governing instrument which contains certain statutory language and provisions, and the IRA must be operated according to its terms.[65] Generally, either of two IRS-issued forms may be used to establish an individual retirement account. Form 5305 establishes a trust, under which an individual deposits funds or assets with a trustee. Form 5305-A establishes a custodial agreement, under which an individual deposits funds or assets with a custodian.

An individual may also establish an account using an approved prototype IRA agreement. An individual who uses an IRS-approved prototype IRA has all the rights and privileges of an individual who uses either of the IRS-issued forms. For practical purposes, every financial institution that offers IRA accounts has their prototype IRAs approved by the IRS. The trustee of an IRA must be a bank, or must be a company that demonstrates to the IRS that it is capable of administering an IRA under criteria prescribed by the IRS.[66] An individual cannot qualify as a trustee or custodian of an IRA.[67]

Almost all banks, savings and loans, mutual savings banks, insurance companies, mutual funds, and brokerage houses offer IRA services. Your IRA may be in the form of a savings account or savings certificates, an annuity contract, shares in a mutual fund, or an account at a brokerage house.

WHAT FEES OR OTHER ACQUISITION COSTS ARE INVOLVED?

Many institutions do not charge any fee for establishing an IRA account. In many cases there may be a nominal annual fee ranging from $10 to $20. However, there may be normal commissions or other charges involved in buying certain investment products in the account. For example, a "load" mutual fund may not charge anything to open an IRA, but would charge its normal, or sometimes a reduced, sales commission to buy shares of the fund. On the other hand, some firms will reduce or eliminate certain sales charges altogether in order to attract an investor with an IRA account.

HOW DO I SELECT THE BEST OF ITS TYPE?

Federal laws regulate the structure of IRAs, making all of these accounts similar in their basic design. All accounts are subject to the same contribution limits and federal income tax treatment. The only significant differences in IRA plans are in the investments chosen by individuals for their specific accounts. Some people may elect to use a savings account or certificate. Others will purchase mutual fund shares or a plan offered by an insurance company. The long run performance of these plans may vary, but the differences will be due to the different investment vehicles selected rather than the basic structure of the IRA.

WHERE CAN I FIND OUT MORE ABOUT IT?

Most banks, savings and loan companies, insurance companies, mutual funds, and brokerage houses have brochures describing their IRA plans. These will indicate the types of investments available as well as any charges that may be applied to such accounts.

The Internal Revenue Service offers taxpayers information on IRAs through a special booklet (Publication 590) entitled, *Individual Retirement Arrangements (IRAs)*. This booklet is available from local offices of the IRS or by writing to: Internal Revenue Service, Washington, DC 20224.

QUESTIONS AND ANSWERS

Question — Are there any circumstances where I could lose or forfeit amounts I have contributed to a traditional IRA?

Answer — An IRA must be fully vested at all times.[68] The Code permits no conditions or forfeiture provisions which would cause the IRA owner to lose the value of some or all of the assets of the IRA. The IRA must be fully vested even if contributions have been made by an employer for the benefit of the employee-IRA-owner rather than by the employee-IRA-owner himself.

Question — How much may I contribute to a traditional IRA?

Answer — Contributions are limited to 100 percent of compensation up to $2,000 per taxable year for any individual.[69] The IRS apparently never has disqualified an IRA for accepting more than $2,000 in a given year. However, various adverse tax consequences and potential penalties arise from such a contribution. Keep in mind, the $2,000 limit includes contributions to Roth IRAs as well so that total contribution to all IRAs cannot exceed $2,000. A taxpayer with compensation of $4,000 or more, may also contribute up to $2,000 to a nonworking spouse's IRA, but in no event can the total contributed for any single person's benefit exceed $2,000.

Question — What kind of income is eligible to be contributed to an IRA?

Answer — The income must be produced from personal services which would include wages, salaries, professional fees, sales commissions, tips, and bonuses. Unearned income such as dividends, interest, or rent cannot be used in determining the amount of your IRA contribution.

Question — Are IRA contributions locked into any one particular investment?

Answer — No. First, you may select more than one organization which sponsors IRA programs, as long as the total of all investments made each year are within your personal contribution limit. For example, you could place part of your contribution in a savings account and the remainder in a stock mutual fund. Second, you may transfer directly from one sponsoring organization to another an unlimited number of times per year, if you so desire. Additionally, you may withdraw the funds and roll them over into the same or a new IRA account. However, the reinvestment must take place within 60 days, and you are generally allowed to make a rollover from any one plan only once every 12 months.

Question — Are there any restrictions on the investments I may include in my IRA?

Answer — Generally, the IRA-owner may include any of the normal forms of investment, such as stocks, bonds, and mutual funds, or property held for the production of income, such as real estate or leased equipment, in an IRA. However, certain types of investments are prohibited or limited.

No part of the account may be invested in "life insurance contracts."[70] In fact, IRA provisions prohibit the owner from using IRA funds to purchase any kind of insurance whatsoever. The only slight exception to this rule is the "insurance" element of an annuity, which is considered incidental and permissible. The insurance element of an annuity arises in those annuities that guarantee the owner that if the balance in the annuity account in the event of death before the payout period begins is less than the sum of the premiums paid, the death benefit will be equal to the sum of premiums paid.

IRAs may not own "collectibles." An IRA that purchases a collectible is treated as having distributed the cost of the collectible to the IRA owner, in effect removing the tax advantages of IRAs for such investments.[71]

The cost of the collectible deemed distributed to the IRA owner is its fair market value at the time of acquisition.[72] Any such deemed distribution is subject to the 10 percent additional tax on distributions to the IRA owner before age 59½.[73] The owner obtains a basis in the IRA equal to this amount but is not otherwise taxed on any appreciation until the collectible is actually distributed. The rules do not require divestiture or distribution of the collectible itself. In fact, distribution of the collectible could present additional tax problems. Although the acquisition of the collectible creates a nontaxable basis in the IRA equal to its acquisition value, distribution of the collectible will not generally be treated entirely as a nontaxable recovery of basis. The basis allocation rules will apply to the distribution and basis will be recovered on the value of the distribution in the ratio of the total basis in all IRAs held by the taxpayer to the total value of all IRA accounts.

The only exception to the above-described tax treatment for collectibles is provided by statute for (1) gold or silver coins minted by the United States ("American Eagle" bullion coins) acquired after December 31, 1986, (2) coins issued under the laws of any state if those coins are acquired by an IRA after November 10, 1988, or (3) certain platinum coins and certain gold, silver, platinum or palladium bullion.[74]

Also, although not specifically prohibited, any investment in a trade or business regularly carried on by the IRA that is not substantially related to the exercise by the IRA of its tax-exempt purpose will generate what is called unrelated business taxable income. The implications of this are discussed below.

Question — What if I am rolling a distribution from a qualified plan that includes life insurance contracts into an IRA?

Answer — The restriction on life insurance in IRAs can cause a problem when the individual is rolling over assets from a qualified plan, which can hold life insurance within certain limits defined by the incidental benefit rule. The plan participant-IRA owner has several options. If he wants to roll as much money as possible over to the IRA, he may ask the qualified plan administrator to surrender the policy(ies) and distribute the cash values along with the remaining account balance. Alternatively, especially if he wishes to keep the life insurance in force, he may request that the plan administrator sell the policy(ies) to him. This last option is generally preferred to simply distributing the policies since (1) in either case the insured continues the life insurance coverage, (2) the amount that is distributed from the qualified plan and that may be rolled over includes the value of the policy(ies), and (3) the participant-IRA-owner avoids both the income tax

and the potential 10 percent early withdrawal penalty tax on the monetary value of the distributed policies.

Question — When will income earned in an IRA be taxed as unrelated business taxable income?

Answer — Earnings in an IRA are generally exempt from tax, but certain investments cause taxable income, called "unrelated business taxable income" (UBTI).[75] UBTI is income from a trade or business regularly carried on by the IRA that is not substantially related to the exercise by the IRA of its tax-exempt purpose.[76] Many types of income are exempt from the UBTI provisions. Statutory "modifications" exclude the following types of income: (1) dividends, (2) interest, (3) annuities, (4) royalties, (5) most rents from real property and (6) gains from the sale, exchange or other disposition of property other than inventory or property held for sale in the ordinary course of a trade or business.[77]

The most common source of UBTI in an IRA arises from "unrelated debt-financed income."[78] Interest, rents and the other general exemptions lose their status as not UBTI to the extent they are generated by properties, such as real estate, acquired or improved through the use of debt.[79] An IRA subject to unrelated business income tax must make quarterly estimated tax payments, just as corporations do.[80] Taxes are payable on the unrelated business taxable income when the return is filed, at the rates applicable to estates and trusts.[81]

Question — Are there any types of transactions that are prohibited in IRA accounts?

Answer — The IRA owner and the IRA's beneficiaries, IRA trustees, custodians and issuers acting as fiduciaries, as well as employers or employee organizations (usually labor unions) sponsoring group IRAs are all considered disqualified persons for purposes of the prohibited transactions rules. The following types of transactions are prohibited:[82]

- Sale or exchange, or leasing, of any property between a plan and a disqualified person;

- Lending of money or other extension of credit between a plan and a disqualified person;

- Furnishing of goods, services or facilities between a plan and a disqualified person;

- Transfer to, or use by or for the benefit of, a disqualified person, of any assets or income of a plan;

- A "self-dealing" act by a fiduciary whereby the fiduciary deals with the assets or income of a plan in the fiduciary's own interest or for the fiduciary's own account; and

- The receipt of consideration (i.e., a kickback) by a fiduciary for the fiduciary's own account from any party dealing with a plan in connection with a transaction involving the assets or income of the plan.

Examples of prohibited transactions include the borrowing of money from an individual retirement account by its owner, the sale of property by the IRA owner to the IRA, or the IRA owner's receipt of unreasonable compensation for managing the IRA's investments. In addition, a self-directed IRA owner who directs the lending of funds in the IRA to a business he owns is considered to be engaging in a prohibited transaction.

If the owner of an individual retirement account (or, after the IRA owner's death, a beneficiary entitled to a distribution) engages in a prohibited transaction with the account, the account ceases to qualify as an IRA. The account's earnings cease to be tax-exempt as of the first day of the taxable year in which the prohibited transaction occurs and a constructive distribution of the fair market value of the account as of the first day of that year occurs.[83] The usual excise tax on disqualified persons does not apply to the owner or beneficiary, however.[84]

The pledge of an individual retirement account as security for a loan is not treated as a prohibited transaction, but rather as a constructive distribution which is taxed in the same manner as a regular distribution.[85] The owner would then treat the amount of the constructive loan as additional nontaxable basis in the IRA.

Loophole: the short-term loan. An IRA owner may withdraw funds from an IRA and then contribute those funds to another IRA or even the original IRA, if the transaction is completed within 60 days of distribution and if the transaction otherwise qualifies as a rollover.[86] Although, in effect, the transaction is a 60-day interest-free loan, the IRS has not yet treated such transactions as loans. IRS has ruled that the return of part of a distribution from an IRA back to that IRA within 60 days of the distribution qualifies as an IRA-to-IRA rollover.[87] Great caution is advised in using this technique since failure to "repay" the loan by rolling the distribution back into an IRA within 60 days will subject the distribution to income tax and, possibly, the 10 percent early withdrawal penalty.

Question — What restrictions or limitations apply to IRA contributions other than the $2,000 annual contribution limit?

Answer — Except for rollover contributions, all contributions to an IRA must be made in cash.[88] No deduction is allowed for contributions of property other than cash. If a traditional IRA owner is age 70½ or over at the end of the taxable year for which a contribution is made, no contribution, deductible or otherwise, is permitted.[89]

A contribution is considered made for a particular taxable year if it is contributed (1) during that taxable year, or (2) after the taxable year has ended but is made "on account of" that year and is made before the due date (not including extensions) for filing the IRA owner's tax return for that year.[90] A contribution is timely if it is mailed and postmarked by the due date for the taxpayer's return, even though the IRA trustee does not receive the contribution for crediting to the IRA until after the due date.

Question — What are the reporting and disclosure requirements for IRA owners?

Answer — An IRA owner reports the deductible contributions to such accounts on the individual income tax return.

Any nondeductible contributions for a taxable year are reported using Form 8606, which is filed along with the taxpayer's Form 1040. The form must be filed even if the taxpayer's income is less than the minimum amount required to file a return and he is not required to file an income tax return. Keeping accurate records of nondeductible contributions to an IRA is extremely important since the burden of proof in establishing how much of a given distribution from a taxpayer's IRA is a nontaxable recovery of nondeductible contributions lies with the taxpayer.

Form 5329 must be filed by an individual who:

- owes taxes on excess contributions to an IRA,

- receives a distribution subject to the 10 percent additional tax on early distributions, or

- fails to receive a required minimum distribution from an IRA after age 70½.

Form 5329 must be filed even if the taxpayer is not required to file Form 1040 because his income was less than the amount where one is required to file. It is filed with the IRS at the time and place he would file Form 1040.

An IRA owner is required to attach Copy B of Form 1099-R to his Form 1040 if a distribution was received from an IRA and federal income taxes were withheld from the distribution.

FOOTNOTE REFERENCES

Individual Retirement Accounts - Traditional

1. IRC Sec. 408(a).
2. IRC Sec. 408(b).
3. IRC Sec. 408(c).
4. IRC Sec. 219(c).
5. The 5-year tax averaging election for qualifying lump-sum distributions from qualified plans is scheduled to expire for distributions after December 31, 1999. However, under a grandfathering provision, taxpayers who were born before January 1, 1936 (age 64 or older in the year 2000) may still elect to use the old 10-year lump-sum averaging provisions for qualifying lumps-sum distributions. Similarly, although the election to treat the amount of a lump-sum distribution attributable to participation in a qualified plan before January 1, 1974 as separately taxable capital gain has expired, taxpayers born before January 1, 1936 are grandfathered and may still elect to make the election to treat the amount attributable to participation before January 1, 1974 as capital gains taxable at a flat rate of 20 percent. Generally, taxpayers may elect to use the lump-sum averaging election and/or the capital gains election only once in a lifetime, although taxpayers born before January 1, 1936 who elected to use the lump-sum averaging or the capital gains treatment before 1986 are still entitled to elect to use these provisions once more in their lifetimes.
6. IRC Sec. 408(o)(2).
7. IRC Sec. 219(d)(4).
8. IRC Sec. 219(b)(1).
9. IRC Sec. 219(g)(1).
10. IRC Sec. 219(g)(5).
11. Notice 87-16, 1987-1 CB 446.
12. Note that an allocation of plan earnings is not sufficient to trigger active participation status.
13. Conversely, Let. Rul. 8929019 held a person who declined to make any contribution to a plan's Section 401(k) arrangement (with no resulting employer contribution) was not an active participant for such year.
14. Let. Rul. 8805066.
15. IRC Sec. 219(g)(2)(B).
16. IRC Sec. 219(g)(2)(C).
17. IRC Sec. 408(o)(2)(B).
18. IRC Secs. 4973(a), 4973(b).
19. IRC Sec. 219(f)(6).
20. IRC Secs. 408(d)(1), 72.
21. IRC Sec. 408(d)(2)(B).
22. IRC Sec. 408(d)(2)(C).
23. IRC Sec. 72(b).
24. IRC Sec. 408(d)(2) (flush language).
25. Notice 87-16, 1987-1 CB 446, Q&A D-2, D-3, D-4.
26. Notice 87-16, 1987-1 CB 446, Q&A D-6.
27. IRC Sec. 408(d)(3)(A).
28. Code section 72(t)(2)(A)(i) exempts all distributions after the IRA owner reaches this age.
29. IRC Sec. 72(t)(1).
30. IRC Sec. 72(t)(2)(A)(ii).
31. IRC Sec. 72(t)(2)(A)(iii).
32. IRC Sec. 72(t)(2)(A)(iv).
33. IRC Sec. 72(t)(2)(B).
34. IRC Sec. 72(t)(2)(D).
35. IRC Sec. 72(t)(2)(E).
36. IRC Sec. 72(t)(2)(F).
37. IRC Sec. 72(t)(2)(A)(vii), as added by IRSRRA '98 Sec. 3436(a).
38. IRC Sec. 72(t)(8).
39. IRC Sec. 72(t)(8)(C).
40. IRC Sec. 72(t)(8)(D)(i). A longer period is provided in the event the individual had owned a principal residence outside the United States or was a member of the Armed Forces.
41. IRC Sec. 72(t)(2)(E).
42. Under Code section 151(c)(3), a child includes a son, daughter, stepson, or step daughter, and under Section 152, an adopted child and, in certain circumstances, a foster child are also considered a child.
43. IRC Sec. 72(t)(7)(A).
44. IRC Sec. 529(e)(3).
45. IRC Sec. 72(t)(2)(B).
46. IRC Sec. 72(t)(2)(A)(vii), as added by IRSRRA '98 Sec. 3436(a).
47. IRC Sec. 72(t)(4)(A)(ii).
48. IRC Sec. 72(t)(4)(A)(ii)(I).
49. IRC Sec. 72(t)(4)(A)(ii)(II).
50. IRC Sec. 72(t)(4)(A)(ii).
51. IRC Sec. 72(t)(4)(B).
52. Notice 89-25, 1989-1 CB 662, A-12. See also Let. Rul. 9312035 (method of determining annual periodic payments from IRA at end of current year by amortizing sum of stock and cash transferred to IRA over a number of years equal to the current year single life expectancy of account owner, assuming an eight percent interest rate of return, results in substantially equal periodic payments); PLR 9416036 (monthly distributions from IRA over taxpayer's projected life expectancy constitute a series of substantially equal periodic payments and are not subject to Section 72(t)(1) tax).
53. See Chapter 6, How to Evaluate Life Insurance Products.
54. This life expectancy is derived from tables published in Reg. §1.72-9, Table V.
55. Let. Rul. 9050030.
56. Let. Rul. 8911069.
57. Let. Rul. 8911070.
58. Let. Rul. 8911071.
59. Notice 89-25, 1989-1 CB 662.
60. Reg. §1.72-9. This is probably the safest choice for all alternatives.
61. IRC Sec. 408(a)(6); see IRC Sec. 401(a)(9).
62. IRC Sec. 3405(b)(1).

63. IRC Sec. 3405(a)(1).

64. IRC Secs. 3405(a)(2), 3405(a)(3), 3405(b)(2), 3405(e)(B)(i).

65. IRC Sec. 408(a); Reg. §1.408-2(b).

66. IRC Sec. 408(a)(2); Reg. §1.408-2(b)(2).

67. Consequently, a disadvantage to rolling over a distribution from a tax-qualified retirement plan to an IRA is the loss of the ability of an individual to serve as trustee with respect to the assets.

68. IRC Sec. 408(a)(4).

69. IRC Sec. 219(b)(1).

70. IRC Sec. 408(a)(3); Reg. §1.408-2(b)(3).

71. Code section 408(m)(2) defines a collectible as any work of art, rug or antique, metal (except as provided below with respect to certain coins), gem, stamp, coin, alcoholic beverage (e.g., vintage wines), musical instrument, historical object (such as a document or clothes), or other item of tangible personal property that the IRS determines is a collectible.

72. IRC Sec. 408(m)(1).

73. IRC Sec. 72(t).

74. IRC Secs. 408(m)(3)(A), 408(m)(3)(B).

75. IRC Sec. 511.

76. IRC Sec. 513.

77. IRC Sec. 512.

78. IRC Sec. 514.

79. There are limited exceptions to this in the case of certain real estate financings. IRC Sec. 514(c)(9).

80. IRC Sec. 6655.

81. IRC Sec. 511(b)(1).

82. IRC Sec. 4975(c).

83. IRC Sec. 408(e)(2).

84. IRC Sec. 4975(c)(3).

85. IRC Sec. 408(e)(4); Reg. §1.408-1(c)(4).

86. IRC Sec. 408(d)(3)(A)(i).

87. Let. Rul. 8502044.

88. IRC Sec. 219(e)(1).

89. IRC Sec. 219(d)(1).

90. IRC Sec. 219(f)(3).

Chapter 29

KEOGH PLANS

WHAT IS IT?

A Keogh plan, sometimes referred to as an H.R. 10 plan, is a special investment program available to self-employed individuals. The purpose of the program is to enable self-employed persons to accumulate a private retirement fund that will supplement their pension and Social Security benefits.

WHEN IS THE USE OF THIS TOOL INDICATED?

1. When a self-employed person has a need to shelter some of his current earnings from federal income tax.

2. When an employee has self-employment income from sources other than his employer and wishes to invest this secondary income and defer taxes on it.

3. When it is desirable to defer taxes on investment income.

4. When long-term capital accumulation, particularly for retirement purposes, is an important objective.

5. When a self-employed investor anticipates holding the investments in a Keogh plan arrangement for at least five or six years.

ADVANTAGES

1. Keogh contributions are deducted from gross income and the tax is deferred until funds are withdrawn from the plan at a later date.

2. Income generated by the investments in a Keogh plan is also free of income taxes until it is withdrawn from the plan. This reinvestment of income and build-up of tax deferred earnings is one of the main features that make Keogh plans attractive for self-employed individuals.

   For example, the following table shows the results of investing $7,500 annually in a Keogh plan where the rate of return is eight percent, compounded daily.

Number of Years	Total Contribution	Tax Deferred Interest	Total Value
5	$ 37,500	$ 10,645	$ 48,145
10	75,000	45,365	120,365
15	112,500	116,201	228,701
20	150,000	241,213	391,213
25	187,500	447,490	634,990

As can be seen, the tax-deferred earnings portion of the program will eventually exceed the amount of personal annual contributions. This is a strong incentive to start early and continue to make the largest possible contribution to such a plan. (Unrelated business income of a plan trust is subject to tax: for example, investment in a limited partnership.)

3. The limits on Keogh plan contributions are more liberal than those applied to the Individual Retirement Account (IRA). IRAs have an annual contribution limit of $2,000 (a couple may contribute up to $2,000 each, for a total of $4,000) as compared with the maximum possible contribution of $30,000 permitted under a Keogh plan. (See "Tax Implications" below regarding the computation of the maximum *deductible* Keogh plan contribution.) Thus, a self-employed person may contribute considerably more to a Keogh plan than to an IRA. Keogh plans offer an opportunity to accumulate much larger sums during one's working years and to provide really significant benefits after retirement. In addition, the contributions to traditional IRAs may not be deductible, or may be limited, depending upon participation in employer-provided retirement plans and income levels (see Chapter 28).

4. An investor may also be eligible to participate in a Keogh plan, even as an employee, if the owner of the business for which he works establishes such a plan. Employees of the business must be included as participants in the plan on a nondiscriminatory basis. The percentage of net income, not net earnings, contributed to a defined contribution plan on behalf of employees generally may not be less than that contributed on behalf of owners. However, the employer has the right to select the period of employment that is required for eligibility of the owner-employee and any employees. Such a period of eligibility cannot be longer than 24 months.

5. Rather than specifying a limit on the amount that is contributed each year, a "defined benefit" plan lets the contribution be tailored to obtain a specific level of income upon retirement. In effect, you decide how much income you want from your plan and for how long you expect to receive it.

The defined benefit plan often allows a self-employed individual to make larger contributions to his plan than are allowed by a defined contribution Keogh plan. He is permitted to make whatever contributions are necessary to fund his own life annuity upon retirement.

The maximum annual retirement benefit allowed cannot exceed the lesser of (a) 100% of the average of his high three years of preretirement self-employment earnings or (b) $90,000, indexed for inflation ($130,000 in 1998). Depending on his present age, current income, and desired benefits, a self-employed individual may be able to put more than $30,000 into a defined benefit Keogh plan and reduce his taxable income by the same amount.

DISADVANTAGES

1. In-service distributions (distributions from the employer's plan while still employed) are generally prohibited from qualified pension plans (whether the pension is a defined benefit or defined contribution plan), including Keogh plans. In general, distributions from qualified pension plans are permitted only after separation from service. Distributions may be permitted from qualified *profit-sharing* plans, including Keogh profit sharing plans, for contributions held at least two years within the plan.

2. Taxable amounts withdrawn from a Keogh Plan prior to the participant's becoming age 59½ are subject to a 10-percent excise tax unless the withdrawal qualifies under one of the exceptions to the penalty tax. This tax is intended to discourage early withdrawals and insure that funds are available for retirement. The exceptions to the 10-percent additional tax for distributions from qualified plans and IRAs include distributions:

    • paid to the beneficiary after the death of the owner,[1]

    • made on account of the disability of the owner,[2]

    • that are part of a series of substantially equal periodic payments over the life or life expectancy of the owner or the joint life or joint life expectancies of the owner and the beneficiary,[3]

    • made to an employee following separation from service after age 55 (this exception does not apply to IRAs),[4]

    • that are dividends paid on stock of a corporation held in an ESOP (this exception does not apply to IRAs),[5]

    • to the extent used to pay certain medical expenses during the year,[6]

    • made to alternate payees under a qualified domestic relations order (QDROs) (this exception does not apply to IRAs),[7]

    • to the extent used to pay the health insurance premiums of an unemployed owner (within limits),[8]

    • to pay certain qualifying higher education expenses,[9]

    • to pay certain qualified first-time homebuyer acquisition costs (this exception applies to IRAs only),[10]

    • that are transfers of assets from a terminated defined benefit plan to a Section 401(k) plan maintained by the same employer (this exception does not apply to IRAs),[11]

    • that are rolled over, on a tax-deferred basis, into another qualified plan or IRA,

    • that constitute employer contributions and trust income that are treated as having been applied to the purchase of life insurance protection for a plan participant, even though these amounts are includable in the participant's gross income (this exception does not apply to IRAs),[12]

The following are additional exceptions to the 10-percent additional tax but do not apply to IRAs:

    • distributions of elective deferrals and employee contributions that exceed the annual limitations imposed under Section 415,

    • corrective distributions of excess aggregate contributions, which are employer matching contributions, employee after-tax contributions, and certain other contributions that exceed the amounts allowed for the plan year under the average contribution percentage (ACP) test described in Section 401(m),

    • that are corrective distributions of excess contributions, which are the amounts of elective deferrals made by highly compensated participants under a Section 401(k) plan that exceed the limits prescribed for the plan year by the average deferral percentage (ADP) test described in Section 401(k), and

• that are corrective distributions of excess elective deferrals, which are elective deferrals make by an individual in excess of the applicable dollar limit established under Section 402(g) for the taxable year.

For example, assume that Tom Brinker, a partner, has a Keogh profit-sharing plan and wishes to make a withdrawal of $10,000. The withdrawal does not meet one of the exceptions listed above. Since he is not yet 59½, Tom is subject to the excise tax in addition to his regular tax which normally is in the 28% bracket. Assuming that Tom has no cost basis in the plan (e.g., after-tax contributions), the entire amount will be includable in income; thus, the total tax due on the withdrawal will be $2,800 in ordinary income taxes plus the excise tax of $1,000 (10% x $10,000). After taxes, Tom's ten thousand dollar withdrawal will result in $6,200 of spendable income.

Despite these tax considerations, contributions to a Keogh plan can be advantageous even if withdrawals are subject to the 10% penalty. The benefit of the initial deduction from gross income plus the tax free build-up can offset the additional tax if funds remain in the account for a minimum of five or six years. The specific period of time will depend on the investor's tax bracket and the rate of return earned on the investments in the plan.

3. In the case of a SIMPLE IRA (see Chapter 45), the 10% early withdrawal penalty described above is increased to 25% during the first two years of participation; subject to the exceptions described above.

4. Withdrawals from Keogh plans are generally *required* by April 1 of the calendar year after the year in which the individual reaches age 70½; however, in the case of a nonowner-employee or an owner of less than a 5% interest in the employer, distributions may be delayed until April 1 of the calendar year after the calendar year in which he retires, if that is later than the year in which he becomes age 70½. The minimum amount generally is calculated on the basis of remaining life expectancy. Thus, Keogh plans are not intended as a means of avoiding income taxes and passing capital on to succeeding generations tax free.

5. Most self-employed investors may not borrow funds from their Keogh plans although it is generally possible in limited circumstances for regular employees.

TAX IMPLICATIONS

1. An investor is eligible to create a Keogh retirement plan if he is self-employed either as a sole proprietor or as a partner. Even if he is employed elsewhere, he may make Keogh contributions on the basis of his self-employment income earned in the trade or business for which the plan is established. Such income must be earned from personal services and cannot include "unearned income" from such sources as dividends, interest, etc.

2. The amount that may be contributed to a Keogh plan depends on the type of plan that is adopted. Code section 415(c) limits annual additions for defined contribution plan accounts to the lesser of (i) $30,000 (in 1998 as indexed), or (ii) 25% of compensation; however, the employer's deduction under Section 404(c)(3)(A) for contributions to a profit sharing plan is limited to 15% of the compensation paid or accrued to participating employees. (See item 3, below, regarding the special computation of the deductible percentage for self-employed individuals). A self-employed person wishing to take a deduction for $30,000 (or, if less, 25% of compensation) to a defined contribution Keogh plan may wish to adopt a money purchase pension plan.

3. The maximum deductible contribution rate (15% for profit sharing plans) is, in effect, reduced for a Keogh plan, because in the case of a self-employed person "earned income" is used in place of "compensation" and earned income is defined as the self-employed individual's net income from the business after all deductions, *including the deduction for Keogh plan contributions*, have been taken. IRS Publication 560 explains the complex steps necessary to arrive at the "net" contribution rate for a self-employed person. Consequently, if the desired plan contribution rate is 15%, the net rate (after taking into account the self-employment tax and the planned Keogh contribution amount) for a self-employed person will be 13.0435%. For a desired plan contribution rate of 25%, the net rate will be 20%. See IRS Publication 560 for details and contribution rate tables.

Example 1: Bill Barnard is self-employed as a builder of sailboats. His net earnings derived solely from his business (after deducting one-half of his self-employment tax) equal $200,000; however, the maximum compensation amount he may take into account (as indexed for 1998) is $160,000. Bill's Keogh plan is a money purchase pension; thus, his maximum deductible contribution is *the lesser of* $30,000 or 25% of his net earnings *after* the Keogh contribution is deducted. The 25% computation is made as follows: ($160,000 ÷ 1.25) x .25 = $32,000; thus, the maximum deductible contribution Bill can make is $30,000.

Example 2: Joe Johnson is self-employed as a management consultant. His net earnings derived solely from his business (after deducting one-half of his self-employment tax) equal $160,000. Joe makes contributions to a profit-sharing Keogh plan; thus, his maximum deductible contribution is 15% of his net earnings *after* the Keogh contribution is deducted (or 13.0435%, as described above). The computation of his deductible contribution is made as follows: ($160,000 ÷ 1.15) x .15 = $20,869.60; thus, the maximum deductible contribution Joe can make is 13.0435%, or $20,869.60.

4. A 10% penalty may be imposed if a self-employed person contributes more than he can deduct in a year.

5. Keogh benefits may be paid out in a lump sum or in substantially equal amounts on at least an annual basis. The payout period must be less than or equal to the owner's life expectancy or the joint and survivor life expectancy of the owner of the plan and his designated beneficiary. The appropriate life expectancy period is determined as of the date payments begin to be made from the plan, and may be recomputed annually.

6. Withdrawals from a Keogh plan prior to age 59½ or disability are generally subject to a 10% premature withdrawal tax (see the exceptions listed above, under "Disadvantages") similar to that which applies to IRAs. In addition, if the participant has no cost basis in the plan, the full amount that is withdrawn is considered ordinary income for income tax purposes. Therefore, a dollar withdrawn from a Keogh plan prior to age 59½ may be subject to two taxes and thus will not actually provide a dollar of disposable income.

Rather than make unnecessary withdrawals from a Keogh plan it may be wiser to borrow for short-term needs.

ALTERNATIVES

1. Traditional IRAs enable an individual, whether self-employed or not, to invest up to $2,000 of earned income and, subject to certain limitations (See Chapter 28 on Individual Retirement Accounts), to deduct his investment from annual taxable income. The amount of the contribution to an IRA is not based on a percentage of earned income as is the Keogh contribution. Therefore, if the amount of self-employment income is relatively small, a person may be permitted to make a larger

contribution to an IRA than to a Keogh plan. However, if the individual's adjusted gross income is below certain limits (see Chapter 39), he may be able to make fully deductible contributions to both the Keogh plan and the traditional IRA.

2. Simplified employee pensions (SEPs) are low-cost and easy-to-administer plans that permit contributions essentially equal to those permitted for Keogh profit-sharing plans. (See Chapter 44).

3. SIMPLE IRAs are also relatively easy-to-administer plans that permit salary-reduction contributions similar to Section 401(k) plans, but at lower maximum levels. (See Chapter 45).

WHERE AND HOW DO I GET IT?

Like IRAs, Keogh plans may be created through a broad range of financial institutions. These include banks, thrift institutions, insurance companies, and mutual funds. Each of these is anxious to increase its retirement plan business, especially in the form of Keogh plans. Such plans generally involve stable, long-term investments that require only a modest degree of customer servicing. Alternatively, a self-employed person may want to have an individually designed plan prepared for him by an attorney or through a pension consultant.

WHAT FEES OR OTHER ACQUISITION COSTS ARE INVOLVED?

The vast majority of plans involve little or no cost to the investor. Most banks, thrift institutions, mutual funds, and insurance companies will establish a Keogh plan at no charge. Some plans, especially those involving mutual funds, may have an annual maintenance fee of $5 to $10 per year. Also, more complicated plans that require the use of an attorney or a pension consultant will result in fees paid for such services.

HOW DO I SELECT THE BEST OF ITS TYPE?

A self-employed person may have a defined contribution or defined benefit pension plan, a target plan, or a profit sharing plan. Different assets can be used in the account— stocks, bonds, mutual funds, or annuities. The contribution limits and federal income tax treatment are generally the same as for corporate plans. Which investments are the "best" will depend on the financial circumstances and personal risk attitudes of each person who establishes such a plan.

Keogh Plans

WHERE CAN I FIND OUT MORE ABOUT IT?

1. Keogh plan arrangements are widely advertised, particularly at the end of the calendar year and near the federal income tax filing deadline. You should not have any difficulty in obtaining information from banks, brokerage firms, savings and loans, savings banks, mutual funds, and insurance companies as to the types of plans that they offer.

2. A special booklet, *Self-Employed Retirement Plans* (Publication 560), is available from the Internal Revenue Service and provides information on these plans and how they are treated for income tax purposes. This booklet is available from local offices of the Internal Revenue Service, or by writing to: Internal Revenue Service, Washington, DC 20224.

QUESTIONS AND ANSWERS

Question — Who can establish a Keogh retirement plan?

Answer — Any sole proprietor or partnership, whether or not the business has employees: for example; doctors, lawyers, accountants, writers, etc. Generally, employees of the business must be included as participants in the plan on the same general basis as the key employees.

Question — How much can I contribute to a Keogh plan?

Answer — Employers may contribute to a defined contribution plan 25% of earned income or $30,000, whichever is less, in each taxable year. Earned income is computed after deducting the Keogh contribution and the Keogh contribution must be determined after computing the self-employment tax and taking a deduction of one-half of the tax. (See item 3 under "Tax Implications" above.) If the plan is a defined benefit plan, the employer may contribute the amount actuarially necessary to fund an annual benefit not in excess of $90,000 as indexed for inflation ($130,000 in 1998) or 100% of the average of the participant's high three years of net self-employment earnings, whichever is less.

Question — When can Keogh plan benefits be paid?

Answer — Distributions to a participant can begin upon termination of employment, but generally not earlier than age 59½. For 5% owners, distributions must commence no later than April 1 of the calendar year following the year they reach age 70½. For nonowner-employees or less than 5% owners, distributions must commence by April 1 of the year following the year in which they retire, if later than April 1 of the year following the year in which they reach age 70½.

Question — Can I collect benefits if I become disabled?

Answer — In the event that any participant in the plan becomes so disabled as to render him or her unable to engage in any substantial gainful activity, all contributed amounts plus earnings may be paid immediately without being subject to a premature distribution penalty.

Question — What happens to my plan if I die?

Answer—In the event that any participant dies, all contributed amounts plus earnings may be immediately paid to the participant's designated beneficiary or estate.

Question — May I set up a Keogh plan in addition to an Individual Retirement Account?

Answer — Yes. If you are eligible to set up a Keogh plan you may also create an IRA as well. Remember, though, that the general limit on all IRA contributions is $2,000 (a couple may contribute up to $2,000 each, for a total of $4,000) and that above certain income limits, IRA contributions will not be tax deductible (see Chapter 28).

FOOTNOTE REFERENCES

Keogh Plans

1. IRC Section 72(t)(2)(A)(ii). A distribution to a beneficiary or to the estate of the IRA owner after the death of the IRA owner is not subject to the 10-percent additional tax even though the IRA owner had not attained age 59½ by the time of the distribution.
2. IRC Section 72(t)(2)(A)(iii). For purposes of the disability exception to the 10-percent additional tax, an individual is considered disabled if he cannot perform any substantial gainful activity because of a medically determinable physical or mental condition which can be expected to result in death or to be of long-continued and indefinite duration.
3. IRC Section 72(t)(2)(A)(iv).
4. IRC Section 72(t)(2)(A)(v).
5. IRC Section 72(t)(2)(A)(vi).
6. IRC Section 72(t)(2)(B). Distributions made to an employee from a qualified plan or to an owner from an IRA are not subject to the 10-percent penalty to the extent such distributions are used to pay medical expenses during the taxable year and do not exceed the amount allowable as a deduction (on Schedule A) for medical expenses in excess of 7.5 percent of AGI (see IRC Sec. 213), determined without regard to whether the employee/owner itemizes deductions for such taxable year.
7. IRC Section 72(t)(2)(C).

8. IRC Section 72(t)(2)(D). Distributions from qualified plans or IRAs to unemployed individuals that are used to pay health insurance premiums are not subject to the 10 percent penalty (1) if such individual has received unemployment compensation for 12 consecutive weeks under any Federal or State unemployment compensation law, (2) if such distributions are made during any taxable year during which such unemployment compensation is paid or the succeeding taxable year, and (3) to the extent such distributions do not exceed the amount paid during the taxable year for insurance described in Code section 213(d)(1)(D) with respect to the individual and the individual's spouse and dependents. This exemption continues to apply to distributions until the individual has been re-employed for 60 days. In the case of self-employed individuals, the exemption applies in the same manner as to common law employees if, under the Federal or State law, the individual would have qualified to receive unemployment compensation but for the fact that the individual was self-employed.

9. IRC Section 72(t)(2)(E). The Taxpayer Relief Act of 1997 added an additional exception to the 10-percent additional tax for distributions from an IRA to the extent such distributions (other than those already excluded from the penalty) do not exceed the qualified higher education expenses of the taxpayer for the taxable year. For these purposes, qualified higher education expenses are those qualified higher education expenses for education furnished to (i) the taxpayer, (ii) the taxpayer's spouse, or (iii) any child, at an eligible educational institution. IRC Secs. 72(t)(2)(E), 72(t)(7)(A), 529(e)(3). Under Code section 151(c)(3), a child includes a son, daughter, stepson, or step daughter, and under Section 152, an adopted child (and, in certain circumstances, a foster child) is also considered a child or grandchild of the taxpayer or the taxpayer's spouse. Qualified higher education expenses are reduced by any amounts excludable from gross income relating to the redemp-

tion of a qualified U.S. Savings Bond and by certain scholarships and veterans benefits. IRC Sec. 72(t)(7)(B). The amount of qualified higher education expenses for any taxable year is reduced by the amount of scholarships or fellowship grants excludable from gross income under Section 117, any other tax-free educational benefits received by the student during the taxable year (such as employer-provided educational assistance excludable under Section 127), and any payment (other than a gift, bequest, devise, or inheritance within the meaning of Code section 102(a)) which is excludable under any United States law.

10. IRC Section 72(t)(2)(F). The Taxpayer Relief Act of 1997 added an additional exception to the early withdrawal tax, for IRAs only, with respect to a qualified first-time homebuyer distribution, subject to a $10,000 lifetime cap. See IRC Sec. 72(t)(8)(B). A qualified first-time homebuyer distribution means any payment or distribution received by an individual to the extent such payment or distribution is used by the individual before the close of the 120th day after the day on which such payment or distribution is received to pay qualified acquisition costs with respect to a principal residence of a first-time homebuyer who is the individual, the spouse of such individual, or any child, grandchild, or ancestor of such individual or of the individual's spouse. IRC Sec. 72(t)(8)(A). The qualified acquisition costs are the costs of acquiring, constructing, or reconstructing a residence, including any usual or reasonable settlement, financing, or other closing costs. IRC Sec. 72(t)(8)(C). An individual is a first-time homebuyer if the individual (and if married, the individual's spouse) had no present ownership interest in a principal residence during the two-year period ending on the date of acquisition of the principal residence. IRC Sec. 72(t)(8)(D)(i).

11. Let. Rul. 8531078.

12. Notice 89-25, 1989-1 CB 662, A-11.

Chapter 30

LIFE INSURANCE

WHAT IS IT?

Life insurance is a contract that promises to pay a specified amount of money to a designated beneficiary when the insured person dies. The contract is between the insurance company and the policyowner who pays premiums in exchange for the promised death benefits. Frequently the policyowner is the person insured, but the policy can be owned by someone other than the insured.

The insurance company charges a premium for the contract which is combined with other premium payments on other contracts and with earnings on the investment of these premium payments to provide adequate funds to pay death benefits when they come due and cover insurance company expenses and profits. Consequently, the death benefit is significantly larger than the premium(s) paid for the individual policy.

There are different types of life insurance policies and they can be classified in different ways. One method of classification is by the number of lives insured. Most policies cover only one life, but policies are available that cover two or more lives. Such policies may pay a death benefit at the first death only, or may be payable at the second or last death of the insureds.

More commonly, life insurance policies are classified as

(1) term,

(2) whole life,

(3) universal life,

(4) interest sensitive or current assumption whole life, or

(5) variable life.

Each of these types of life insurance is discussed in detail in the Question and Answer portion of this chapter.

WHEN IS THE USE OF THIS TOOL INDICATED?

1.   When a client wants to provide income for dependent family members until they become self supporting after the head of the household dies.

2.   When a client wants to liquidate consumer or business debts or mortgages, or to create a fund that would enable his family to do so at his death.

3.   When a client wants to provide large amounts of cash at death for college expenses or other capital needs.

4.   When cash is needed to pay estate and inheritance taxes.

5.   When a client wants to provide funds for the continuation of a business through a "buy-sell" agreement. Business continuation "buy-sell" uses include funding the purchase of ownership interests following the death of an owner in a proprietorship, partnership, or closely held corporation with life insurance coverage on the life of each owner.

6.   When a business seeks economic indemnification for the loss of a key individual. This is known as "key person" life insurance. Insurance owned by and payable to the business is purchased on the lives of employees or owners whose deaths could result in serious financial loss to the firm.

7.   When an employer seeks to recruit, retain, or retire one or more key employees through a salary continuation plan and finance its obligations under that plan to the dependents of a deceased owner or key employee.

8.   When a client is seeking an inexpensive and effective way to transfer capital to children, grandchildren or others without the erosion often caused by probate costs, inheritance taxes, income taxes, federal estate taxes, transfer fees, or the generation-skipping transfer tax.

9.   When a client wants to provide greatly enhanced charitable gifts. Although there are many ways life insurance is used in charitable gift planning, the two most common involve the use of policies owned by the charity and the naming of the charity as beneficiary of new or existing policies.

ADVANTAGES

1.   Life insurance provides a guarantee of large amounts of cash payable immediately at the death of the insured. The amount of the death benefit payable is significantly greater than the premiums paid for the policy.

2. Life insurance proceeds are not part of the probate estate. Only when the estate is named as the beneficiary of the policy are the proceeds subject to probate (or if the proceeds are paid for the estate's benefit). Therefore, the proceeds can be paid to the beneficiary without delay caused by administration of the estate.

3. There will be no public record of the death benefit amount or to whom it is payable.

4. Life insurance policies offer some protection against creditors of both the policyowner and of the beneficiary. The amount of protection varies from state to state.

5. Life insurance cash values provide instant availability of cash through policy loans. The interest rate for policy loans is known in advance and may be lower than the rate on loans from other sources.

6. The death benefit proceeds from a life insurance policy are generally not subject to federal income taxes.

7. The increases in the cash value of a life insurance policy enjoy favorable federal income tax treatment. Interest earned on policy cash values is not taxable unless or until the policy is surrendered for cash.

8. Life insurance proceeds are often exempt from state inheritance taxes.

DISADVANTAGES

1. Life insurance is often not available to persons in extremely poor health. However, individuals in moderately poor health can generally obtain insurance if they are willing to pay higher premiums.

2. Life insurance is a complex product which is hard to evaluate and compare. The time required to gather policy information, decipher it, and compare it with other policies discourages purchasers from engaging in comparison shopping.

3. The cost of coverage reduces the amount of funds available for current consumption or investment.

TAX IMPLICATIONS

1. In general there is no deduction permitted for premium payments on life insurance policies. The notable exception is the premium payment on group term life insurance provided by an employer to employees.

2. Dividends received by the policyowner are generally not subject to federal income taxation. Dividends will not be taxable income unless the aggregate of dividends paid (and other amounts withdrawn) exceeds the aggregate of premiums paid by the policyowner.

3. The cash value increases in a life insurance policy resulting from investment income are not taxable income as long as the policy remains in force. The cash value build-up in a life insurance policy enjoys deferral from taxation while the policy remains in force and exemption from income tax if the policy terminates in a death claim. However, if the policy is surrendered for cash, the gain on the policy is subject to federal income taxation. The gain on a surrendered policy is the amount by which the net cash value payable and policy loan forgiveness exceeds the owner's basis in the policy.

Basis in the policy equals the premiums paid less policyowner dividends and less any other amounts previously withdrawn. For example, a policy on which $35,000 has been paid in premiums and $7,000 has been received in dividends would have a basis of $28,000 ($35,000 - $7,000). If that policy were surrendered for $10,000 in cash and a policy loan of $50,000 canceled (as if a total of $60,000 was received at the time of surrender), there would be a taxable gain of $32,000 ($60,000 - 28,000).

4. The deductibility of interest paid on policy loans is limited:

(1) Interest on loans to purchase single premium policies is not deductible;

(2) Interest on loans to purchase periodic premium policies may be deductible if certain exceptions are met;

(3) Interest paid on policy loans on a policy covering a "key person" is deductible to the extent that the indebtedness does not exceed $50,000.

In any event, the availability of a deduction that is not disallowed under the rules above depends also upon how the interest is classified. "Personal" interest is generally not deductible. In general, if policy loans are used to pay premiums on the policy or for any other personal purpose, the interest is not deductible.

Interest paid on policy loans used for investment purposes is subject to a different set of deductibility limits. In general, the interest on loan proceeds, including proceeds of life insurance policy loans, used to finance investments is deductible each year only to the extent it does not exceed the taxable investment income from all investments. If interest expense exceeds investment income in one year, the excess may be carried forward and deducted in future years when there is adequate investment income.

The rules concerning the different types of interest are explained in Chapter 8, "Income Tax Concepts."

5. The death benefits payable under a life insurance policy are generally free from federal income taxation. Proceeds from corporate owned life insurance policies can increase "adjusted current earnings," a portion of which may be taxed under the corporate "alternative minimum tax" (AMT). In a worst case scenario, this tax amounts to roughly 15 percent of the total policy proceeds paid to a corporate beneficiary. The AMT is basically a tax that takes into consideration items that receive preferential treatment under the regular income tax rules. The AMT is applicable only if there are large amounts of such preferentially treated items relative to the regular corporate income. Consequently, it is possible that the AMT will not apply if the death benefit proceeds are paid in a year when there are few preference items. Additionally, after 1997 corporations meeting the definition of a "small corporation" are exempt from the AMT. A small corporation is generally one which has average annual gross receipts for the previous three years which do not exceed $5,000,000.

6. Life insurance policies which have been transferred by one policyowner to another may be subject to the transfer for value rule. Under this rule, the death proceeds of a policy transferred for a valuable consideration are taxed as income to the extent the death proceeds are greater than the purchase price plus premiums and certain interest amounts relating to policy indebtedness paid by the transferee.

In other words, if an existing life insurance policy or an interest in an existing policy is transferred for any type of valuable consideration in money or money's worth, all or a significant portion of the death benefit proceeds may lose income tax free status. However, policies can be transferred safely to:

(a) the insured,

(b) a partner of the insured,

(c) a partnership in which the insured is a partner, or

(d) a corporation in which the insured is a shareholder or officer,

without subjecting the proceeds to income tax, even if the transfer is for a valuable consideration.

7. The proceeds of a life insurance policy will be included in the estate of the insured for federal estate tax purposes if the insured held any "incident of ownership" at any time during the three years prior to death or the proceeds from the policy were payable to or for the benefit of the estate of the insured. Incidents of ownership include such things as the right to (a) change the beneficiary, (b) take out a policy loan, or (c) surrender the policy for cash.

8. Distributions such as cash withdrawals or policy loans from a life insurance policy classified as a modified endowment contract may be taxed differently than if the policy is not so classified. If a policy falls into this category by failing the seven pay test, distributions from the policy will be taxed less favorably than if the seven pay test is met.

A policy fails the seven pay test if the cumulative amount paid at any time during the first seven years of the contract exceeds the net level premiums that would have been paid during the first seven years if the contract provided for paid-up future benefits. If a material change in the policy's benefits occurs, a new seven year period for testing must begin.

Distributions, including policy loans, from modified endowment contracts are taxed as income at the time received to the extent that the cash value of the contract immediately before the payment exceeds the investment in the contract. In effect, this means that policy distributions are taxed as income first and recovery of basis second, much as distributions from annuity contracts are taxed. Additionally, a penalty tax of 10 percent applies to distribution amounts included in income unless the taxpayer has become disabled, or reached age 59½ or the distribution is part of a series of substantially equal payments made over the taxpayer's life.

For the purpose of determining the amount includable in gross income, all modified endowment contracts issued by the same company to the same policyholder during any calendar year are treated as one modified endowment contract.

With some exceptions, life insurance policies issued on or before June 21, 1988, are grandfathered and not required to comply with the seven pay test.

ALTERNATIVES

There are no good alternatives to life insurance for providing tax-free cash upon death. If an individual is uninsurable and, therefore, cannot obtain life insurance the best alternatives are accumulation funds and tax-deferred investments.

WHEN AND HOW DO I GET IT?

There are nearly 1,500 life insurance companies actively marketing coverage in the United States. In addition to commercial insurance companies, coverage is also available through fraternal organizations, some savings banks, professional associations, membership organizations, and employer group benefit packages. Policies can be purchased through many financial planners or agents representing a licensed insurance company.

For persons having difficulty finding coverage because of health problems, there are agents who specialize in what is called the "substandard" market. They know which insurance companies are likely to write coverage for people with specific problems. Life insurance coverage can be obtained for people who cannot obtain it in any other way through "credit life insurance." This is a form of "group insurance" associated with loans for the purchase of automobiles, furniture, and even homes. This coverage is extremely expensive because it is priced to cover all ages and health conditions for the same premium, but it is available to anyone who qualifies for the loan.

WHAT FEES OR OTHER ACQUISITION COSTS ARE INVOLVED?

Life insurance is generally sold on a specified price basis. Life insurance companies are free to set their premiums according to their own marketing strategies. All but a few states have statutes prohibiting any form of "rebating" (sharing the commission with the purchaser) by the agent. The premium set by the insurance company includes a "loading" (a specified part of each premium payment) to cover such things as commission payments to agents, premium taxes payable to the state government, operating expenses of the insurance company, such as rent or mortgage payments and salaries, and any other applicable expenses.

There are some life insurance companies that sell "no load" life insurance policies. These policies do not provide a commission to the selling agent. However, these companies tend to charge a premium that is as high as companies charge who do pay commissions to agents. Evidently they have other marketing costs which make up for the reduction in costs from commission savings.

The bulk of an insurance company's expenses for a policy are incurred when the policy is issued. It may take an insurance company five to nine years or even longer to recover all of its front-end costs. The state premium tax applicable to all life insurance premium payments is an ongoing expense. The average level of this tax is about 2½ percent of each premium payment.

With most cash value policies, the aggregate of commissions payable to the selling agent is approximately equal to the first year premium on the policy. About half of it is payable in the year of sale and the other half will be paid on a renewal basis over a period of three to nine years. On single premium policies (where the entire cost for the policy is paid at once rather than over time) the commission payable usually ranges between two to eight percent of the premium. A lower commission is usually paid on term insurance than on cash-value policies.

HOW DO I SELECT THE BEST OF ITS TYPE?

Policy selection should be broken down into two components. In the first stage the planner should find the appropriate type or combination of types of policies suitable for the client. The second stage of policy selection should focus on the selection of the specific policy (i.e., the exact product the client should purchase).

Appropriate Types of Policies

There is no such thing as the "best" type of policy for a particular client since there may be many policies that will be appropriate and competitively priced. But the policies that the planner should consider should meet certain criteria. Factors to consider include:

(a) duration of the need,

(b) the preferences of the client as to living benefits,

(c) the amount of premiums the client can afford and the client's cash-flow abilities and timing preferences, and

(d) the type and amount of risk he or she is willing to assume in return for potential enhanced cash value, dividend, and death benefits.

Some generally accepted rule-of-thumb guidelines in policy selection are:

(a) For durations of 10 years or less, term insurance is usually appropriate;

(b) For durations between 10 and 15 years both term insurance and cash value coverage should be evaluated;

(c) For durations in excess of 15 years cash value forms of coverage are usually more cost effective than term;

(d) Clients who prefer maximum premium flexibility and death benefit flexibility will want to consider universal life and variable universal life;

(e) Clients preferring to direct the investments behind the policy and who are willing to assume the investment risk will want to consider variable life insurance or universal variable life;

(f) Clients desiring a maximum of guarantees and a minimum of risk assumption will prefer the more traditional contracts such as whole life and term.

Individual preferences relative to "pre-funding" (paying higher payments at the beginning in order to avoid payment increases in later years) or "pay-as-you-go" (paying the lowest possible price initially subject to substantial increases with age) will influence the premium paying pattern appropriate for the client. Clients willing and able to pre-fund totally may consider single premium policies, while those who are willing to pre-fund only partially generally prefer level premium payments for a specified period. Clients not willing to pre-fund life insurance will purchase term insurance and pay increasing premiums at each renewal of the term coverage. Pre-funding of life insurance results in increased policy cash values. The tax deferred earnings on those cash values help defray or eliminate future premium payments.

Specific Policies

Selecting a specific policy involves a combination of factors which include:

(a) an evaluation of the insurance company's financial soundness, and

(b) a comparison of policy guarantees and projections (benefit promises).

The company should have an "A++ or A+ " rating from the A.M. Best Company preferably for the last 5 or 10 consecutive years. The company should also have a reputation for prompt and courteous service in handling policy changes and claims. The agent should have a minimum of 5 years experience and be well versed in both insurance knowledge and tax knowledge at the federal and state levels.

It is important to give close attention to the full name and city of domicile for insurance companies since many of them have very similar names. The ratings given by the A.M. Best Company fall into the following classifications for over-all performance and ability to meet obligations:

A++, A+ (Superior)

A, A- (Excellent)

B++, B+ (Very Good)

B, B- (Good)

C++, C+ (Fair)

C, C- (Marginal)

Insurers are also ranked by financial size as follows:

Category	Adjusted Surplus (in $ millions)		
FSC I	Up	to	1
FSC II	1	to	2
FSC III	2	to	5
FSC IV	5	to	10
FSC V	10	to	25
FSC VI	25	to	50
FSC VII	50	to	100
FSC VIII	100	to	250
FSC IX	250	to	500
FSC X	500	to	750
FSC XI	750	to	1,000
FSC XII	1,000	to	1,250
FSC XIII	1,250	to	1,500
FSC XIV	1,500	to	2,000
FSC XV	2,000	or	more

Ratings sometimes are accompanied by modifiers which indicate further considerations are necessary. These modifiers are all lower case letters of the alphabet, some of which include:

"e" — parent rating (based on the rating of the parent who owns at least 50 percent of the subsidiary)

"p" — pooled rating (based on all operations of companies under common management which pool 100% of their business that is not reinsured)

"r" — reinsured rating (rating is that of the company reinsuring 100% of the company's coverage)

While A.M. Best may be the most recognized, other rating services do exist and may provide helpful information. For more detailed information on HOW DO I SELECT THE BEST OF ITS TYPE? see Chapter 6, "How To Evaluate Life Insurance Products."

WHERE CAN I FIND OUT MORE ABOUT IT?

1. Leimberg, Stephan R., et al., *The Tools & Techniques of Life Insurance Planning*, 1st ed. Cincinnati, Ohio: The National Underwriter Company, 1993.

2. *Tax Facts 1*, Cincinnati, Ohio; The National Underwriter Company, (revised annually)

3. Kenneth Black, Jr., and Harold Skipper, Jr., *Life Insurance*, Englewood Cliffs, New Jersey; Prentice Hall Incorporated

4. Joseph M. Belth, *Life Insurance: A Consumers Handbook*, (available from Indiana University Press, Bloomington, Indiana)

5. *Best's Reports*, Oldwick, New Jersey; The A.M. Best Company (available in some libraries)

6. *Journal of the American Society of CLU & ChFC* (American Society of CLU & ChFC, Bryn Mawr, Pennsylvania)

QUESTIONS AND ANSWERS

Question—What is Term Insurance?

Answer—Term life insurance is insurance for a specified period of time such as 1 year, 5 years, 10 years, or to a specified age such as age 65. At the end of the specified period the contract expires. Continuing coverage can be obtained by renewing the term insurance policy for another successive period and paying the new, higher premium applicable for the new attained age of the insured. For 1 year term insurance (also called "YRT"—yearly renewable term—or "ART"—annually renewable term), the premium would increase every year if the contract is renewed for a new 1-year period of coverage. Some companies impose an upper age limit (such as age 70) on the renewability of term insurance. Because of the relatively short durations of coverage, these policies do not typically develop cash surrender values or have any policy loan availability.

Most term insurance policies can be converted to whole life or other cash value forms of life insurance that do not limit the upper age of renewability or coverage. Therefore, planners should compare not only term insurance rates but also the rates and quality of the whole life policies into which the term insurance may be converted. There is usually an upper age limit (such as age 65) on the privilege of conversion. A conversion privilege allows the insured to exchange the type of coverage without undergoing a physical examination or otherwise showing evidence of good health. Sometimes there is a separate premium charged for the convertibility and the renewability features of term life insurance contracts. Other policies automatically include these provisions without charging a separate premium for them. There are also term insurance policies which do not include convertibility and renewability privileges. These coverages can neither be converted to another form of coverage nor can they be renewed once they expire. Planners should utilize these policies only in very special circumstances.

Question—What is Whole Life Insurance?

Answer—Whole life insurance is the traditional policy with level premium payments designed to remain in force over the entire lifetime of the insured individual. Premium payments in the early policy years are deliberately higher than would be required to cover the probability of death alone. This excess charge in early years makes it possible for the insurer to build up a "reserve." These reserves will be needed—together with interest earned on them and continuing premiums—to pay the necessary premiums in years when the insured is older and more likely to die. In other words, the reserve established in early years makes it possible to keep the premium level in later years when the premium might otherwise become prohibitively high.

As a result of the reserves, the whole life contract builds up internal "cash values" (amounts that can be borrowed from the insurer or obtained by surrendering the policy and releasing the insurer from any liability while the insured is still alive). Cash values enable life insurance companies to make policy loans available to the policyowner a few days after the policyowner requests them. The amount available for such loans is usually 90 percent or more of the existing cash value in the policy. The interest rate charged will be set forth in the life insurance contract as either a specific flat rate, such as 8 percent, or a fluctuating rate with limitations imposed by a specified index, such as Moody's average yield on seasoned corporate bonds.

Although the premium payable on whole life policies is usually level for the lifetime of the insured, it can be based on a shorter premium-paying period such as 10 years, 20 years, or to some specified age such as 65. These policies are known as "limited pay" or "limited-payment whole life policies" (the premium is payable with level premium payments for a given period only). The ultimate limited-payment policy is the "single premium whole life policy" which is discussed in more detail below.

The premium paying period influences the cash value buildup in the policy. The shorter the time to build up a reserve adequate for future years, the greater the necessary premium payment amount and the higher the early reserve amounts. A single premium policy starts off with a relatively high cash value which continues to grow with policy duration and will eventually equal the "face amount" (contractually promised death benefit) of the policy if the insured lives to age 95.

The level premium whole life policy, on the other hand, starts with a very low cash value that gradually builds up to the face amount of the contract. For any type of cash value life insurance policy, the cash value will build up more rapidly during the premium paying period than it does after the end of the premium paying period. Ultimately, if the insured lives long enough, the cash values will build up to the same amount, regardless of how premiums are paid. Cash value buildup is fastest for a single premium whole life policy and slowest for a "continuous-pay" (level premium over life) policy.

As mentioned above, cash values are merely the residual effect of level premium payments used to pay for a long-term contract that has increasing costs with increasing duration of that contract. In essence, the cash values represent some pre-funding of the future death benefit obligation. Each insurance company is free to adopt its own approach to the degree of advanced funding it incorporates into the policy design. There are statutory limitations on both minimum and maximum cash values relative to a given death benefit. However, there is a wide latitude of acceptable values within the upper and lower limits. In general, companies charging a higher premium for the same level of death benefit will provide higher levels of cash value in their policies than those for policies with lower premiums and the same death benefit.

Whole life policies are designed to provide a lifetime of protection. The death benefit will be payable whenever the insured dies and may be payable before death since the full death benefit is typically payable at age 95 (although many policies are "paid up" at much earlier ages).

Question—What is Universal Life?

Answer—Universal life insurance is a variation of whole life insurance. Universal life differs from traditional whole life in several major ways. First, policyholders have a great deal of flexibility as to the premiums they pay. Second, policyholders may, within limits, change the death benefit levels of the policies. In addition, universal life contracts provide separate disclosure about expenses, mortality charges, and interest rates and allow policyholders access to cash values either through policy loans or through direct withdrawals. Similar to traditional whole life policies, standard universal life policies provide interest, mortality, and expense guarantees.

The first year of premium is the only required premium under a universal life policy. After the first policy year the policyowner is free to make whatever level premium payments he or she desires, if any, as long as there is enough cash value to keep the policy in force. Policyowners may contribute extra premiums at any time as long as they do not result in high enough aggregate premiums or cash value to violate the definition of life insurance set forth in Internal Revenue Code section 7702.

Alternatively, policyowners may reduce the level of premium payments or even skip premium payments as long as there is a sufficient cash value to cover the mortality charge. The level of premium payments made into the policy will determine whether it develops high or low cash values over any particular duration. Policyowners who choose to make low premium payments are treating the policy as if it were term insurance while policyowners who choose to make high premium payments are treating it as cash-value life insurance.

Universal life policyowners have access to the cash value amounts through policy loans or partial withdrawals. Partial withdrawals are not policy loans and therefore do not involve any borrowing or interest charges. Partial cash withdrawals do not have to be repaid and are not deducted from the death benefit of the policy when the death proceeds are paid, as are policy loans. However, they do reduce the cash value which is part of the death benefit of type B universal life policies.

Policyowners may choose between two different death benefit designs for these policies. One design, typically called design A, has a level death benefit until the insured reaches a relatively advanced age. The other death benefit design, typically called design B, provides the policy cash value *plus* a fixed level amount of protection as the death benefit. This second design results in an increasing death benefit at successive durations of coverage which are tied directly to the cash value increases.

Under either design the amount at risk is the difference between the face amount of the coverage and the cash value in the policy. The insurance company deducts a mortality charge from the cash value every month. That mortality charge is based on the amount at risk and the mortality rate for the attained age of the insured.

Universal life policies specify a maximum mortality rate that can be charged at each attained age. However, the mortality rate actually charged is a discretionary amount and is set by the insurance company management based upon the company's mortality experience. Policyowners actually bear some of the mortality risk in that the rates actually charged could be increased all the way to the guaranteed maximum. Of course, policyowners of traditional participating whole life policies similarly bear some mortality risk since the dividends they receive will similarly reflect the company's mortality experience.

Universal life insurance expenses incurred by the insurance company are treated in many different ways depending upon the individual insurance company policy design. Policies from some companies explicitly identify a front-end expense loading that will be deducted out of each and every premium payment. Other life insurers do not provide for any explicit disclosure of insurer overhead expenses. Instead they rely on surrender charges (a form of back-end expense) and on the spread between the portfolio earnings and the lower rate of interest credited to the cash value accounts to cover overhead expenses.

The cash value of any universal life policy is explicitly increased by premium payments and monthly interest earnings and decreased by a mortality charge each month. The insurance company must provide the policyowner with a summary of the cash value account transactions at least on an annual basis. This requirement is expensive because it mandates individualized computer processing for each policy.

Like traditional whole life policies, universal life insurance policies guarantee a minimum interest rate (often 4 percent) on the cash value of the policy. However, the interest rate actually credited to the cash value is a discretionary decision of the insurance company management that is made at least annually and is generally higher than the guaranteed rate. Many companies tie their current rate to some well-known index of interest rates, such as the average rate on U.S. government bonds with 5 years to maturity, so that prospective buyers have a standard for comparison. However, much life insurance marketing focuses only on the current interest rate applicable to cash values. This can be misleading if no attention is paid to the level of mortality charges and other expense loadings. Also universal life policy illustrations may sometimes be misleading because they have been based on interest rates in excess of what can realistically be expected over the full duration of the policy.

The interest rate credited to the cash value typically will be affected by outstanding policy loans. A lower interest rate is credited to a portion of the cash value equal in amount to the outstanding policy loan. This lower interest may be, for example, two percent lower than the current rate being paid on the non-borrowed portion of the cash value. In some cases, the minimum guaranteed interest rate specified in the policy is the rate credited to the "borrowed" portion of the cash value. The obvious purpose of the differential is to discourage policy loans when investment returns are significantly higher than policy loan interest rates.

Universal life policies are applicable in any situation where whole life policies are appropriate. The extreme flexibility of these policies makes them adaptable to the changes in economic circumstances during an individual's life cycle. A single policy can be reconfigured to suit changing needs. Generally, new evidence of insurability is required only in those cases where a significant increase in the amount at risk for the insurance company is involved. (Typically, this occurs when the death benefit amount is substantially increased).

Question—What is Interest Sensitive Whole Life?

Answer—Interest sensitive or current assumption whole life policies are variations on the whole life insurance contract. All whole life policies promise a certain minimum interest rate on cash value accumulations and use that rate to determine the premium. With traditional whole life policies the premium and cash value schedule are fixed. If the insurance company earns a rate of return that is higher than that assumed, the policyholder may receive dividends that, in effect, reduce the fixed premium. However, the nominal premium remains the same and cash values continue to build as presented in the contract.

Interest sensitive policies rely on a higher assumed interest rate and typically do not have a fixed required premium or fixed cash value schedule. However, these policies do guarantee that the premium payments necessary to keep the policy in force will never exceed the amount guaranteed at issue. Required future premium payments may be less than the guaranteed maximum if investment experience warrants such a reduction. The investment earnings in excess of the minimum interest guarantee under these policies, called "excess investment return," gives rise to an "accumulation fund." The "accumulation fund" supplements the "scheduled cash value" (which is based on the minimum interest guarantee). The policyholder's aggregate cash value is equal to the "scheduled cash value" plus the "accumulation fund."

Rather than pay dividends, these policies make premium adjustments or cash value adjustments. If the investment performance is better than assumed when computing the required premium, the policyholder may either pay a lower premium or continue to pay the premiums at the initial value and accumulate greater cash values. These policies generally subject the cash value to a surrender charge in the event of early policy termination.

Question—What is Variable Life?

Answer—Variable life is more like traditional whole life insurance than universal life since it has fixed premiums and a minimum guaranteed death benefit. The difference is that the investment risk and return is shifted to the policyowner. Much like selecting among mutual funds, the policyowner is able to direct the funds backing the policy into one or more of a group of segregated investment accounts made available by the life insurance company. The number and types of accounts available differs from one company to another and may be as few as three or as many as nine. Typically, the policyowner is able to allocate assets among at least a stock fund, a bond fund, and a money market fund. Because the policyowner picks the portfolio of investments in which the cash value of the policy is invested there is no minimum cash value guarantee.

When the performance on the portfolio of funds chosen by the policyowner is good, both the cash value and the death benefit of a variable life policy increase proportionately. However, when the portfolio performance is below expectations, the death benefit may drop, but never below the original amount of coverage when the policy was issued. The principal advantage to policyowners is that they capture the benefit from good portfolio performance. However, the major drawback is that they also must bear investment losses. By transferring the investment risk and potential investment returns to the policyowners the insurance company greatly reduces the incentive for policyowners to withdraw funds from the policy as they would with traditional whole life policies when opportunities elsewhere are better.

Variable life policies are particularly suitable for policyowners who desire to choose how the portfolio backing the life insurance policy will be invested and are willing to assume the investment risk that goes with that responsibility. If invested in equities, for instance, which have outperformed inflation over the long term, these policies may provide a protection against loss of purchasing power. However, for shorter periods in particular, the policyowner must bear some risk that the portfolio performance may not correspond to increases in the level of inflation in the economy. Consequently, these policies may not be appropriate for persons who become anxious

over short term fluctuations in stock and bond prices. Since most companies offer a short-term money market account option, policyowners generally may select a conservative investment strategy. However, even this strategy is riskier than traditional whole life policies since money market rates, theoretically and actually, can fall below minimum guaranteed rates on traditional policies.

Question—What is Variable Universal Life?

Answer—Variable universal life insurance, which is a variation on the whole life policy, is a hybrid of universal life and variable life insurance. It provides policyowners with the ability to adjust premiums and to reconfigure the death benefit level. Both investment risk and mortality risk are shifted to the policyowner under this contract. As in the variable life contract the policyowner gets to choose the investment medium under this contract and there are no guarantees as to cash value levels or growth. Most of these policies give the policyowner the option of deciding whether favorable investment results will increase the death benefit level or will be directed only to cash value growth.

Question—What is Joint Life?

Answer—Joint life insurance is a whole life policy which insures two or more lives rather than just one. There are two basic types: first death and second (or last) death joint life. With a first death policy, the policy pays the face amount and terminates after the first death with no benefits remaining for the surviving insured. Because the policy provides only one death benefit it is a less expensive way of providing insurance than purchasing separate policies on each life. This policy is often used for business buy-sell agreements and for estate taxes when the husband and wife intend to pay some estate taxes after the first death.

The second death variation of joint life also covers more than one life and pays only one death benefit. It is known as survivorship whole life because the death benefit is paid upon the last death of two or more insureds. Since the death proceeds are paid only once and only after *all* insureds have died, the premium burden for such a policy is significantly lower than that for two or more separate policies. This type policy has increased in popularity as a result of the unlimited marital deduction which permits married couples with large estates to defer estate tax liabilities until the second death.

Question—What are dividends?

Answer—Certain policies are called, "participating" because their policyowners participate to some extent in the favorable experience of the insurance company. (Policies in which the policyowners do not share in such experience are called "nonparticipating" or "nonpar.") Dividends payable on participating whole life policies are considered a return of premium. Therefore they are not taxable income until the aggregate of all dividends and other amounts actually received exceeds the entire value of all premiums paid. The dividends payable on some life insurance policies exceed the premium payment after the policy has been in force for several years. Policyowner dividends effectively decrease the final cost of coverage for the policy.

Dividends are influenced by three factors, (a) the mortality experience of the insurance company, (b) the "loading" (overhead costs) experienced by the insurance company, and (c) the investment return on the insurance company portfolio. The more careful and conservative the underwriting and the fewer deaths in relation to those anticipated, the higher the dividends, assuming that the other two factors remain equal. The lower the business expenses compared to those anticipated when the premium rates were constructed, the higher the dividends. Finally, the higher the investment return over that anticipated, the greater the dividends. Dividends tend to increase with increasing policy duration and provide an incentive for the policyowner to retain the policy (which in turn helps the insurance company recover its costs over a longer period of time and therefore reduce its loading costs).

Question—Since my state has a life insurance guarantee fund, should I be concerned about the rating of the insurance company?

Answer—Many states have established special funds called "life insurance guarantee funds." These are intended to pay policy benefits in case of an insurance company failure. However, these funds are designed to rescue policyowners and beneficiaries of a weak or troubled company by assessing other insurance companies. Competitive forces in recent years have whittled away at the safety margin of many companies and there is a greater danger that the financial guarantee mechanism may prove inadequate in the face of multiple life insurance company failures. Even if the guarantee mechanism does provide protection, it is a slow and inefficient bureaucracy that could delay settlement for years. The best way to avoid such problems is to deal with an insurance company that is financially sound and likely to remain so throughout the desired period of coverage.

Question—Is "single premium whole life" a good investment?

Answer—Single premium whole life is a fully pre-funded life insurance policy. Purchasing this type of policy entails paying mortality charges which may or may not be explicitly identified. Most of these policies have an initial cash value equal to the full single premium payment. This cash value grows year by year. This cash value buildup escapes income taxation if the policy terminates in a death claim. In any case, it enjoys tax deferral until the policy is terminated either by death or surrender prior to a death claim.

These policies can provide a respectable return to policyowners even after mortality charges and other expenses. However, single premium whole life policies are subject to significant surrender charges in the early years of the contract. These surrender charges can drastically reduce the investment performance if the policy is surrendered for cash while they are applicable. These policies are not strictly an investment and should not be purchased for that purpose alone.

There are limits to the favorable taxation of policy distributions from policies which do not meet certain requirements. (See number 8 under "Tax Implications"). No deduction is allowed for policy loan interest on single premium whole life policies.

Question—Is there a difference between a single premium whole life policy and a universal life policy paid for by a single premium payment?

Answer—Yes. There is a guarantee that the single premium whole life policy is adequately funded and no further premium payments will be required. Under a universal life policy, the single premium payment will be adequate only if the interest assumptions and mortality assumptions turn out to be in line with future actual experience under the policy. There is a risk that investment performance has been over-estimated and mortality expenses have been underestimated. If this is true, the premium paid will eventually be inadequate. Under these circumstances, the policyowner could maintain the policy benefits by paying additional premiums. Otherwise, the benefits (face value of coverage) must be reduced to keep the policy in line with the premium actually paid.

Question—Why do insurance premiums vary?

Answer—There are three main cost elements to life insurance policies: (1) mortality charges, (2) insurer expenses, and (3) investment performance. Each insurance company has varying degrees of efficiency associated with each of these factors.

Contrary to popular belief, there are many different mortality tables applicable to insurance products. Insurance companies tend to charge mortality rates based on the experience of their own policies. Standardized mortality tables such as the "1980 CSO (Commissioners Standard Ordinary) Mortality Table" are used for reserve purposes (i.e., for the insurer to create a reserve under the policy large enough to meet potential future claims) but are rarely used in setting the premium for the policy. Part of the variation in premiums from company to company is explained by differences in mortality rates used. An even larger portion of the variation is explained by differences in investment return.

Insurance company expenses vary significantly from one company to another. Part of that difference is a function of the amount of services provided to policyowners. Some variation in expenses is due to the differing efficiencies of the insurance company and its procedures.

One of the most important factors explaining variation in life insurance premiums is the investment return. Relatively small changes in the rate of investment return can result in sizable changes in the premium that must be charged. The decrease in life insurance policy premiums over the past decade is mainly the result of increased investment earnings for life insurance companies.

Question—What is the difference between a "limited payment" policy and a "vanishing premium" policy?

Answer—A limited payment policy guarantees that a specified number of fixed premium payments will be sufficient to fully pay for the life insurance policy. This guarantee is not present in vanishing premium policies. Vanishing premium policies have fixed premiums but utilize policy dividends to pay anticipated premiums after the policy has been in force the prescribed period of time. If the dividends are as large as or larger than expected, the policyowner will not have to pay premiums beyond the specified policy duration. However, there is the possibility that dividend experience will fall short of expectations. Consequently, the policyowner may have to make additional premium payments to supplement the dividends and cover the entire premium due.

With some life insurance companies the dividend expectation is very conservative and it is highly unlikely that future dividends will not be adequate to cover premium payments. On the other hand, there are some insurance companies using such aggressive estimates of future dividends that it is unlikely future dividends will live up to these expectations. Policyowners with these companies may be both surprised and perturbed in the future to find that their vanishing premium has suddenly reappeared. Planners should review past dividend records and compare the actual experience with the company's original projections to obtain some idea of how conservative or aggressive the company has been with respect to its dividend projections.

Question—What is the purpose of a delay clause in the beneficiary designation?

Answer—Sometimes both the insured and the beneficiary die within a short time. If the beneficiary survives the insured for a very short period of time, the proceeds of the policy will be payable to the beneficiary and flow through the beneficiary's estate when the beneficiary dies. A delay clause makes payment of the death proceeds contingent upon the beneficiary surviving a stated period of time, such as 90 days after the insured dies. If the beneficiary does not survive the specified period of time, the proceeds are payable to a contingent beneficiary specified in the beneficiary designation. Hence, the death benefits completely bypass the primary beneficiary's estate, avoiding unnecessary taxes and other estate expenses. If the delay clause exceeds 180 days, the policy proceeds will not qualify for the federal estate tax marital deduction.

Chapter 31

MONEY MARKET FUNDS

WHAT IS IT?

A money market fund is a mutual fund that invests solely in short-term debt instruments. The term "money market" is applied to high quality, short-term debt instruments that mature within one year. These debt instruments include:

U. S. TREASURY BILLS — short-term certificates issued by the federal government which typically mature in three months to one year.

CERTIFICATES OF DEPOSIT (CDs) — short-term obligations of major banks that generally mature within 180 days (see Chapter 19). These may include certificates of foreign banks as well as domestic institutions. Although the risk associated with foreign CDs is somewhat higher, they pay a slightly greater rate of return. Most funds will tend to diversify their portfolios by holding both foreign and domestic issues.

COMMERCIAL PAPER — short-term debt of major industrial corporations which matures in sixty days to one year.

WHEN IS THE USE OF THIS TOOL INDICATED?

1. When an investor desires a high degree of "liquidity," the ability to convert an investment into cash quickly and with little or no cost. This is an ideal vehicle for those investors who find themselves with large amounts of idle cash.

2. When there is a need or desire for a high degree of safety of principal. Security is provided by the combination of short maturities and the high quality of the issuers of money market securities.

3. When an investor desires a higher rate of return than is available from a passbook type account yet desires more flexibility than would be found in longer term investments.

ADVANTAGES

1. An investment in a money market fund can be converted easily and conveniently into cash. Most funds offer shareholders personalized check writing services as well

as the ability to wire transfer money from the fund to the investor's bank account.

2. Due to the financial strength of the issuers of the underlying assets held by money market funds they provide a secure investment; the investor knows that there will be little or no fluctuation in the market value of the investment and the return of capital is virtually assured.

3. The rate of return offered by money market funds is highly sensitive to changes in short-term interest rates. This means that if rates increase, the return provided by the fund will quickly follow. This is because the holdings of the average fund will "turn over" (i.e., will mature and be reinvested) within twenty to forty days.

4. Most money market funds do not impose a sales charge on purchases of the fund or a redemption fee when shares are sold. (However, there are management fees of approximately 0.5% to 0.7% of the fund which are applied annually and administrative charges which are typically $10 per account each year.)

DISADVANTAGES

1. Normally, these funds do not pay as high a rate of return as longer term investments such as bonds. In fact, six-month CDs may yield a higher rate of return.

2. All of the income generated by a money market investment will be taxed as ordinary income. The investor has no control over the timing of income received and must report all income currently.

3. Investments in money market funds are not insured or guaranteed by any federal agency. Unlike banks which have federally mandated reserve requirements, money market funds are relatively unregulated.

TAX IMPLICATIONS

1. Dividends received by investors in these funds are fully and currently taxable. These "dividends" actually are considered to be interest payments for tax purposes.

2. There are a few funds which specialize in short-term, tax-exempt investments. The payments received by investors from these funds would retain this tax-free status and are therefore federal income tax free, subject to the effects of the alternative minimum tax (see Chapter 8, "Income Tax Concepts").

3. Because money market funds are mutual funds, they are exempt from the requirement that certain pass-through entities report to shareholders, as income, their shares of expenses of the fund which would be miscellaneous itemized deductions if incurred by the shareholder individually.

ALTERNATIVES

1. Commercial banks, savings and loans, and mutual savings banks, now offer "money market deposit accounts." The interest rate paid on these accounts is normally competitive with the rates on six-month CDs, Treasury bills, and that paid by money market mutual funds. Money market deposit accounts are convenient because they can be obtained at the same location where the investor banks and is known. These accounts are also insured up to a limit of $100,000 by various agencies of the federal government.

2. The direct purchase of Treasury bills, CDs, commercial paper, or other similar instruments. However, such an approach may not provide the diversification or professional management available from a money market fund.

WHERE AND HOW DO I GET IT?

1. Almost all major brokerage firms make money market funds available to their customers. Customers are encouraged to leave on deposit in such funds the proceeds of any security sales or any dividends or interest received in the account.

2. Many brokerage firms also offer special accounts which provide a comprehensive package of investment services to customers. A money market account is typically included in the system in order to keep excess cash balances fully invested at all times.

3. Virtually all mutual fund organizations include a money market fund among their offerings. This enables a mutual fund investor to move assets within a "family of funds" conveniently, quickly, and with minimal cost.

Money market mutual funds are purchased from the fund sponsor itself either in person or by phone or mail. Direct mail and newspaper ads will provide the address and phone number of organizations offering money market funds.

WHAT FEES OR OTHER ACQUISITION COSTS ARE INVOLVED?

Generally there is no sales charge associated with the purchase of a money market fund. Even those mutual fund organizations which typically charge a "load" fee will not do so in the case of a money market fund. Brokerage firms also do not charge a sale or redemption fee when funds are added to or removed from a money market account.

As noted above, however, there is a management fee based on the total value of the assets owned by the fund.

This fee, which averages 0.5% to 0.7% of the value of the fund, is deducted from the assets of the fund and is not paid directly by the shareholders. In addition, most funds will deduct an annual account fee of about $10.

HOW DO I SELECT THE BEST OF ITS TYPE?

1. Compare the yields offered by various funds. These returns are generally stated in terms of the average yield paid by the fund during the past seven days or during the past thirty days. If the funds are comparable in other respects, choose the fund that offers the highest yield.

2. Select funds with short average maturities. Assuming stable interest rates, if two funds each have the same yield, investors should favor the one that has the shorter average maturity of its holdings. For example, assume Fidelity Cash Reserves and Rowe Price Prime Reserve Fund are both yielding 2.75%. If the average maturity of the Fidelity portfolio is 30 days and that of the Rowe Price fund is 40 days, investors may prefer the Fidelity fund because of its shorter maturity.

3. There are rating services that evaluate the quality of securities in a money market fund's portfolio. Investors who have substantial amounts invested in these funds may wish to obtain these ratings as a means of comparing the safety of individual funds.

WHERE CAN I FIND OUT MORE ABOUT IT?

1. The financial sections of *The Wall Street Journal*, *The New York Times*, and other major newspapers publish a

weekly listing of money market funds. These reports typically show the average maturity of assets held by each fund and its most recent yield.

2. Many of the reports and statistics published on money market funds are produced by the Donoghue organization, a pioneer in the analysis of money market funds. Investors wishing to obtain information on their publications should write to:

    Donoghue's Money Fund Report
    P.O. Box 540
    Holliston, MA 01746

3. Investors interested in obtaining more information on money market mutual funds can also write or call:

    Investment Company Institute
    1401 H Street, N.W.
    Washington, D.C. 20005
    (202) 326-5800

QUESTIONS AND ANSWERS

Question — How do money market funds compare with the money market deposit accounts offered by banks, savings and loans, and mutual savings banks?

Answer — The yields available from these two investments generally will be very similar. Banks and thrift institu-

tions will offer rates on their accounts that will compete with those provided by money market funds. Occasionally, one or the other may offer a higher return, but these differences are likely to average out over time. The most important difference between the two investments is that the accounts offered by banks and thrift institutions are insured by various agencies of the federal government. Investors are protected against loss on these accounts up to a maximum of $100,000. Investments in money market funds are not insured by any government agency, though they are generally considered safe due to the high quality of their assets.

Question — How is it possible to ascertain the best CD rates?

Answer — Several newsletters publish a list of the highest yields available nationwide. Local newspapers often publish in their business sections similar listings for savings institutions. There are several nationwide services that will help an investor shop for the highest rates. These services compare yields at banks across the country and can often open an account for the investor over the phone.

Question — How can an investor obtain a list of the highest yields on money market funds?

Answer — There are services which can be obtained at libraries or purchased directly which show the current rates, safety ratings, and minimum investments in various taxable and tax free funds.

Chapter 32

MORTGAGE-BACKED SECURITIES

WHAT IS IT?

Mortgage-backed securities are debt-type securities which are typically secured by a "pool" of residential mortgages. A trustee is assigned to hold the titles of all mortgages in the pool and to see that all mortgages and properties are in acceptable form and that payments are properly made.

Three of the best known sources of these instruments are the Government National Mortgage Association (GNMA), the Federal National Mortgage Association (FNMA), and the Federal Home Loan Mortgage Corporation (FHLMC). GNMA is a wholly owned U.S. government corporation within the Department of Housing and Urban Development. FNMA is a government-sponsored corporation owned entirely by private stockholders, though it is regulated by Housing and Urban Development. FHLMC was created by Congress and is owned by the twelve Federal Home Loan Banks.

The securities they issue are appropriately nicknamed, "Ginnie Maes," "Fannie Maes," and "Freddie Macs." State and local government agencies, as well as institutions in the private sector, such as the Bank of America, also issue various types of mortgage-backed securities. These privately issued securities are known collectively as "Connie Macs."

WHEN IS THE USE OF THIS TOOL INDICATED?

1. When an investor desires a relatively secure type of investment that in most cases is guaranteed by the U.S. Treasury or a federal agency. Private issues are generally offered by large money center banks which also offer a high degree of security. Another factor contributing to the safety of these issues is the broad geographical distribution of the underlying mortgages. Many mortgage-backed securities obtain their underlying mortgages from throughout the country and therefore are not overly influenced by economic conditions in any one state or region.

2. When the investor desires a relatively high rate of return. The competitive yield on instruments such as GNMAs is generally higher than other long-term government securities.

3. When the investor requires a high level of cash flow. These instruments typically provide monthly payments which consist of both interest and the return of some portion of the loan principal. Payments to investors in the pass-through type of instrument may vary somewhat from month to month because some mortgages within the pool may be paid off before maturity and others may be partially prepaid.

4. When the investor desires a high level of liquidity. There is a very active secondary market for these issues since they are bought and sold through investment bankers and their price and yield quotations are easily found in the financial sections of most major newspapers.

5. When the investor seeks to diversify his portfolio beyond the holding of stocks and corporate bonds. Mortgage-backed securities are essentially an investment in real estate and therefore provide an alternative to money market funds and other income-oriented corporate securities.

ADVANTAGES

1. Mortgage-backed bonds are virtually risk free in terms of return of principal and certainty of income.

2. Because interest rates on residential mortgages are usually higher than short-term money market rates or even long-term corporate bond rates, these issues provide one of the highest rates of return available from debt instruments. GNMAs, for example, offer the highest yield of any actively traded, federally guaranteed security. They have tended to yield 15 percent to 20 percent more than the yield on intermediate Treasury bonds. They have also outperformed AAA-rated corporate bonds over the period from 1985-1995 by about five percent.

3. Holders of mortgage-backed securities are usually guaranteed a monthly payment of interest and principal whether or not these sums have actually been collected by the issuer. (In the case of "straight pass-through" certificates, GNMA guarantees only the proper performance of the mortgage servicing and the payment of only that interest and principal actually collected. In the case of "modified

pass-through" certificates, GNMA guarantees the timely payment of principal and interest, whether or not collected by the originating association.)

4. Payments are generally made by the fifteenth day of the calendar month following the month in which collections on mortgages are made. Monthly principal payments to investors may actually increase at times because homeowners may voluntarily pay off their mortgage loans (for example, when they sell their homes) or accelerate payments of principal (for instance, to reduce the term of their mortgage and the overall amount of interest paid on the loan.)

5. There is a well developed secondary market for mortgage-backed securities, especially for those issued by federal agencies. In the private sector, the larger the issuer, the more active the market for mortgage-backed securities of that issuer. This means that investors will have little or no difficulty in selling their securities if the need arises.

However, the selling price of an issue is not guaranteed and is subject to change as the level of mortgage interest rates changes. For example, if mortgage rates rise, the price of previously issued securities tends to decline because more attractive rates are available in the marketplace. Likewise, if rates fall, the price of existing issues will tend to increase.

6. Early repayments of mortgage loans may be subject to prepayment penalties. This operates to the advantage of the investor since these amounts are passed through and added to his monthly income.

DISADVANTAGES

1. Like other interest sensitive assets, the price of mortgage-backed securities will tend to fall when market interest rates rise. This potential for capital depreciation could seriously affect the investor who is forced to sell his investment before it matures.

2. Mortgage-backed securities are subject to two types of inflation risk: (1) the risk that the purchasing power of their income will be eroded over time, and (2) the risk that the purchasing power of capital received at maturity will have diminished. This second risk is minimized to a degree by the very nature of the instrument itself; the investor constantly recovers principal which is available for reinvestment or current consumption.

3. A direct investment in mortgage-backed securities is difficult for many investors because a high minimum investment is required. For instance, a GNMA certificate has a principal value of $25,000 at its inception. (The actual amount an investor pays may be less than $25,000 if the pool of mortgages has been in existence for some time and some of the original principal has been repaid.) However, this disadvantage may be overcome by investing in mutual funds which specialize in mortgage-backed securities. These funds are discussed in more detail below.

4. Mortgage-backed securities carry the risk that the underlying mortgages will be paid off more quickly than anticipated, and thus the holder will receive the stated interest for a shorter time period than desired.

Mortgages are prepaid for a variety of reasons as homeowners relocate and refinance. The prepayment experiences on mortgage-backed securities vary depending on the underlying mortgages, and there is no way of accurately predicting an individual security's life. However, the general level of interest rates will affect prepayments, because refinancing becomes more or less economically advantageous. A new 30-year 9 percent mortgage would have an average life of 21 years based on the scheduled amortization included in the monthly payments. When a large group of these mortgages are aggregated, however, about 10 percent of these mortgages on average are pre-paid when interest rates and housing conditions remain constant. If you assume an annual prepayment rate of 10 percent, a mortgage pool's average life is reduced to about 8 years. This average life could be shorter, though, if market interest rates decline substantially below the existing mortgage rates, leading more homeowners to refinance.

Figure 32.1 shows the cash flow patterns for three mortgage securities in which the underlying mortgages are prepaid at annual rates of 5 percent, 15 percent, and 25 percent. The mortgage securities with prepayments running at about 15 percent provide annual cash flows (both interest and principal) of 20 percent to 25 percent of one's initial investment in the first few years, with declining rates of cash flow as the years pass. In contrast, the mortgage security that is experiencing 5 percent in prepayments has a much steadier cash flow. The security experiencing 25 percent prepayments has even higher cash flows in the initial years. As the figure illustrates, owning a portfolio of mortgage securities is like owning a substantial portion of bonds with a relatively short maturity, a moderate portion of bonds with an intermediate maturity, and a small portion of bonds with a long

Figure 32.1

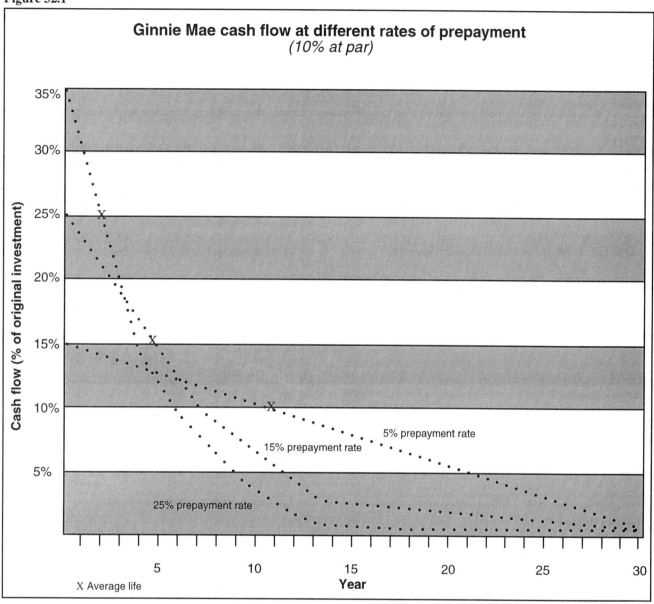

Ginnie Mae cash flow at different rates of prepayment
(10% at par)

maturity. This helps explain why mortgage securities generally experience less dramatic interest-rate-related price changes than most 10-year or longer-maturity bonds.

5. Since the periodic payments from mortgage-backed securities include both interest and a return of principal, mortgage-backed bondholders face greater reinvestment risk than regular bondholders. The periodic payments must be reinvested, and if interest rates have fallen, that money will be reinvested at lower rates, thus lowering future total return. Also, prepayments generally accelerate when it is least desirable from the mortgage-backed security holder's point of view. If market interest rates

decline substantially below the existing mortgage rates, more homeowners are likely to refinance, forcing the mortgage-backed security holder to reinvest the payments at lower yields. Conversely, prepayments are generally delayed when it is most desired, under conditions of higher interest rates.

Investors who purchase mortgage-backed securities at a premium in the secondary market are at especially high risk from early prepayment. Rapid payoffs will reduce their realized yield. This occurs because investors are unlikely to fully amortize (recover) the premium before the bonds are repaid.

TAX IMPLICATIONS

1. The interest income from mortgage-backed securities is reportable as ordinary income in the year received. (Each investor will receive from the issuer a monthly statement indicating what part of the distribution represents (a) scheduled amortization of principal, (b) interest, and (c) unscheduled collection of principal.)

2. The portion of each monthly payment which represents the return of principal is a nontaxable repayment of the original investment. However, principal payments in some cases may represent a discount on the purchase of the mortgages in the past or, if the bond is acquired in the secondary market, a market discount, and to this extent must be included as ordinary income. The investor must therefore report as ordinary income his ratable share of any discount income realized on the purchase of each of the mortgages in the pool under the "original issue discount" and "market discount" rules. These rules are discussed in more detail in Chapter 24, "Corporate Bonds."

3. Prepayment penalties, assumption fees, and late payment charges passed through to the investor are ordinary income reportable in the year received.

4. Gains on the sale of these issues are typically capital gains. But, if an investor purchased a new issue at a discount (called "original issue discount") the remaining unrecognized portion of the discount will be taxed as ordinary income. Similarly, any remaining unrecognized market discount will be taxed as ordinary income.

5. Amounts withheld from the investor by the issuer of the certificate to pay servicing, custodian, and guarantee fees are expenses incurred for the production of income and as such are deductible as miscellaneous itemized deductions. However, these miscellaneous items must be combined with certain miscellaneous items from other sources, and the total is deductible only to the extent it exceeds two percent of the investor's adjusted gross income.

ALTERNATIVES

1. Many large mutual fund organizations sponsor funds which specialize in mortgage-backed securities. They invest shareholders' funds in a diversified portfolio of securities issued by GNMA, FNMA, the Federal Home Loan Mortgage Corporation, and private issuers such as the Bank of America. These funds are particularly attractive to small investors who may not be able to invest $25,000 directly in mortgage-backed securities. They also offer automatic monthly reinvestment of interest,

principal, or both for investors who do not need additional income. In some cases mutual funds employ financial futures and put and call options to hedge against changes in interest rates that affect the rate of prepayments. This provides investors with some additional protection against the prepayment risk and reinvestment risk inherent in direct ownership of mortgage-backed securities.

2. Real Estate Investment Trusts (REITs) offer some of the same features as mortgage-backed securities even though they are quite different in form. Investors in REITs purchase common shares in the REIT rather than bonds. These funds are then invested by the investment trust in a diversified portfolio of real estate such as apartment buildings, shopping centers, office complexes, and real estate mortgages. In order to qualify as a real estate investment trust under the Internal Revenue Code, ninety-five percent of the entity's income must be obtained from rents, dividends, interest, and gains from the sale of securities and real estate properties. REITs are discussed in Chapter 41.

3. Collateralized mortgage obligations and REMIC bonds are quite similar in many respects to pass-through participation certificates and other mortgage-backed-bonds. These are discussed in Chapter 42.

WHERE AND HOW DO I GET IT?

An investor can call a brokerage firm and purchase mortgage-backed securities in much the same fashion as stocks and bonds. Also, these issues may be purchased through those banks and thrift institutions which offer their customers investment services.

WHAT FEES OR OTHER ACQUISITION COSTS ARE INVOLVED?

Investors can expect to pay a modest commission or service charge to the brokerage firm or bank handling the transaction. This fee is typically $15 to $25 for each thousand dollars invested, and the fee may be included in the total cost of the securities purchased rather than shown separately as a commission or service charge.

HOW DO I SELECT THE BEST OF ITS TYPE?

At first glance it may appear that all mortgage-backed securities are similar. Yet there are a number of distinctions an

Figure 32.2

Types of Mortgage-Backed Securities				
	Ginnie Mae	Freddie Mac PC	Freddie Mac GMC	FNMA CMBS	Mortgage-Backed Bond
Payment Stream	Monthly; guaranteed 15-day delay. Periodic prepayments.	Monthly; guaranteed 44-day delay. Periodic prepayments	Semi-annually; annual principal payments.	Monthly; guaranteed 25-day delay. Periodic prepayments.	Semi-annually; principal at maturity or sale.
Underlying Asset	FHA/VA mortgages	Conventional mortgages	Conventional mortgages	Conventional mortgages	General assets
Guarantee	Full faith and credit of U.S. Treasury	Freddie Mac net worth; private mortgage insurance on mortgages with LTV over 80	Freddie Mac net worth; private mortgage insurance on mortgages with LTV over 80	Freddie Mac net worth;private mortgage insurance on mortgages with LTV over 80	Overcollateralized by 150-200% with mortgage portfolio
Liquidity/ Secondary Market	Active market due to high volume of issue, risk-free status	Active market due to high volume of issue, low-risk status	Less active due to high volume of issue, lower issue volume	Unknown at this time	Same as Institution PC
First Issued	1970	1971	1971	1981	1975
Rating/Risk Equivalent	Government security; no rating required	Considered nearly equivalent to a government security; no rating	Same as Freddie Mac PC	Same as Freddie Mac PC	AAA due to continuous maintenance of overcollateralized position

investor should consider in the selection process. These include:

(1) The identity of the issuer. A U.S. government guarantee assures the investor of the highest degree of safety of principal. A guarantee by a private mortgage issuer, such as the Bank of America, may be safe and yet an investor should not have quite the same level of confidence that payments of principal and interest will be made.

(2) The age of the mortgages in the pool. The payments received from older mortgages are made up of larger amounts of mortgage principal and smaller amounts of interest. This is because the early payments made on a mortgage are almost all interest and only a small amount is used to reduce the outstanding principal of the loan. Principal amounts in excess of basis will be taxed as capital gains while interest will be taxed as ordinary income.

(3) The nature of the underlying mortgages included in the pool. Safety of principal and certainty of income

payments depend upon (a) the quality of the mortgages, (b) the number and size of the mortgages, (c) the distribution of mortgage maturities, and (d) geographic distribution of mortgages. These factors will affect the amount of monthly cash flow and the breakdown between principal and interest as well as the regularity, predictability, and certainty of payment.

(4) The guarantees on the security and the mortgages. There are four types of guarantees that are given by issuers in order to enhance their credit worthiness. These include (a) guarantees on interest payments, (b) guarantees on principal payments, (c) mortgage guarantee insurance, and (d) hazard insurance (covering such risks as earthquakes and floods). Because not all of these guarantees will apply to every issue, the investor should select the issues which provide those guarantees which are most important.

(5) The risk-return tradeoff. The securities which provide the lowest level of risk and which offer the most prompt payment (GNMAs) trade at a lower yield than other mortgage-backed securities. Conversely, vari-

ous private issues trade at much higher yields because of their somewhat higher risk. A compromise is the Freddie Mac issue which provides a level of security and guarantee of timely payment only slightly lower than a GNMA but which may trade at a yield ranging from fifteen to forty basis points higher.

The table in Figure 32.2 illustrates the various factors that should be considered by an investor with respect to each of the major types of mortgage-backed securities.

WHERE CAN I FIND OUT MORE ABOUT IT?

1. Listings of mortgage-backed securities issued by GNMA and FNMA are carried daily in the *Wall Street Journal* and other major newspapers. These listings show the securities available, current prices, and the yield on each issue.

2. The larger brokerage houses and mortgage-banking firms publish a variety of booklets on mortgage-backed securities. Two of the best sources of information are First Boston Corporation and Salomon Brothers, both located in New York City. An excellent guide to mortgage-backed securities and other U. S. government issues is the *Handbook of Securities of the United States Government and Federal Agencies* published by First Boston Corporation.

QUESTIONS AND ANSWERS

Question — What are the two major types of mortgage-backed securities?

Answer — The two general types of mortgage-backed securities are: (1) "pass-through" certificates, and (2) mortgage-backed bonds. In the pass-through arrangement, investors actually own a share of the pooled mortgages. The stream of income generated by payments of principal and interest on mortgage loans is passed through to the investor. Mortgage-backed bonds are general obligations of issuing institutions and do not constitute a sale of assets as is the case with the pass-through arrangement. This debt is collateralized by a pool of mortgages that is held by a trustee representing the bondholders. Payments of principal and interest on mortgage-backed bonds are made out of the institution's overall asset earnings generated primarily through mortgage loans.

Question — How does a pass-through certificate work?

Answer — There are several variations of pass-through certificates. A straight pass-through pays principal and inter-

est as they are collected from the mortgage pool. If payments on the underlying mortgages are delayed, payments to holders of pass-through investors are similarly delayed. A partially modified pass-through guarantees that monthly principal and interest payments will be made to a certain extent, even if not collected from the mortgage pool. For example, the issuer might guarantee payments up to 5 percent of the original or current principal amount of the certificate. A modified pass-through guarantees payment of the scheduled monthly principal and interest payments, irrespective of the amounts that are collected from the mortgage pool.

Question — What types of mortgage-backed bonds are there?

Answer — There are essentially four types of mortgage-backed bonds;

(1) "pay-through bonds,"

(2) "straight bonds,"

(3) collateralized mortgage obligations, and

(4) REMIC bonds.

Pay-throughs (also called "cash-flow" bonds) are designed so that the required amortization from the pool of mortgages will at all times be at least equal to the payments of both interest, at the coupon rate, and scheduled principal on the bonds. Additional payments of principal are made to bondholders when there are prepayments on the mortgage pool. The life of the bonds, therefore, is determined by the life of the mortgage pool. Although these instruments are treated differently than pass-throughs from the issuer's standpoint (since they are considered the debt of the issuer rather than a sale of claims on the underlying mortgage pool), they are functionally equivalent to pass-throughs from the investor's perspective. (Some pay-throughs are not fully amortizing; some may have balloon payments due at maturity.)

Straight mortgage-backed bonds are similar to conventional corporate bonds, except that they are secured by a mortgage pool rather than the general assets of a regular corporation. They feature scheduled interest payments on a monthly, quarterly, semi-annual, or annual basis. Principal is typically not scheduled to be repaid until the bonds mature, although interim principal repayments are not uncommon. The issuer is often required to maintain a specified amount of mortgages in the mortgage pool. If a mortgage is prepaid or foreclosed, the issuer usually must substitute similar mortgages into the pool. Many straight mortgage-backed bonds are callable at the discretion of the issuer, similar to most conventional corporate bonds. In many cases these issues have a sinking fund feature that requires the issuer to deposit principal received on the underlying mortgages in an escrow account and to call (buy back) a specified portion of the outstanding bonds at specified intervals or when the sinking fund reaches certain levels. The bonds are generally called by random lot. In other words, some bondholders, determined at random, are periodically required to redeem their bonds before the maturity date.

Collateralized mortgage obligations (CMOs) and *REMIC bonds* (regular interests in Real Estate Mortgage Investment Conduits) are more complicated hybrid securities combining features of pass-through certificates and conventional corporate bonds. These bond issues typically have several classes of interests (technically called "tranches") with differing rights to interest and principal from the underlying mortgage pool. They are designed to give investors the benefit of the high yields characteristic of other mortgage-backed securities without the same degree of uncertainty as to when principal will be repaid. Because of their importance as well as their unique and complex features, CMOs and REMICs are discussed in Chapter 42 and will not be discussed further in the remainder of this chapter.

Question — What is the minimum investment in a GNMA or FNMA certificate?

Answer — Initially these certificates have a principal value of $25,000. The amount actually paid may be less depending on whether the certificate is being sold at a lower amount due to amortization of principal, which may have occurred after the establishment of the particular pool. In such cases, the certificates may be purchased for substantially less since the original mortgage pool is actually lower in value. Increments above the $25,000 initial minimum are $5,000 for GNMA issues. There are no similar restrictions above the $25,000 minimum on FNMA issues.

Question — What if one or more of the mortgages in a pool goes into default?

Answer — In most cases, the issuer of the mortgage-backed security, such as GNMA or FNMA, must continue to pay the full amount of principal and interest payments even though a mortgage may be in default. As a matter of fact, the security holder will not be aware of any defaults and is not affected by them.

Question — What is the average maturity of a mortgage-backed security?

Answer — Most of the residential mortgages which make up the pools behind these issues are thirty year mortgages. However, homeowners may pay off their mortgages in advance (which typically occurs when a home is sold), make partial prepayments which reduce the average life of the pool, or go into default. Taking all of these factors together, the average life of most mortgage-backed securities tends to be about 81/2 years in length. However, older pools with lower interest rate mortgages are not likely to be paid off as quickly and will have a longer average life. Mortgage pools of VA and FHA mortgages tend to have longer average lives than other mortgage pools. Mortgage-backed bonds are typically issued with maturities ranging from 5 to 12 years.

Question — Can the yield on these issues be compared to those available on corporate bonds?

Answer — Yes, but there are some important differences. Mortgage-backed securities lack a definite maturity date and their average life can only be estimated. This uncertainty can have a major impact on the actual rate of return earned on such an investment. Also, most corporate bonds pay interest semiannually, while the interest on GNMAs and FNMAs is paid monthly. This means that interest on mortgage-backed securities can be compounded monthly rather than just twice each year. Over the course of six monthly payments the effective rate of return earned on the mortgage-backed bond will be higher than one paying interest semiannually even though the stated rate on each issue is the same.

Question — How is the yield on a mortgage-backed security determined?

Answer — The yield an investor will actually receive on mortgage-backed securities depends critically on the rate of prepayments on the underlying mortgages. Both the yield quotation and the projected maturity depend on the specific prepayment assumption. Realized prepayment depends on the demographic, financial, and contractual nature of the underlying mortgage assets as well as on the structure and guarantees of the mortgage-backed security issue itself.

Question — How is the quoted yield on mortgage-backed securities determined?

Answer — The quoted yield on a mortgage-backed security is the internal rate of return (IRR) of all cash inflows (the interest and principal payments) and cash outflows (the price paid for the security). Simply stated, the IRR can be viewed as follows: If the investor placed the purchase price of the security in an interest-bearing savings ac-

Figure 32.3

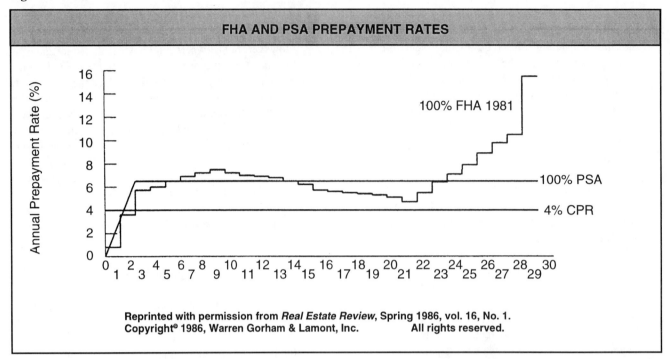

FHA AND PSA PREPAYMENT RATES

count paying interest equal to the IRR, he could withdraw cash from the account exactly matching the projected cash flows from the security with no balance left over. The quoted yield (IRR) depends critically on when prepayments of principal are assumed to occur. Yields have been quoted in different ways by different dealers, making comparisons based on quoted yields extremely difficult, and often irrelevant.

Question — What prepayment assumptions are used to determine quoted yields?

Answer — The weighted average life (WAL) is commonly used in the secondary mortgage market as a measure of the effective maturity of a mortgage pool. The WAL will be longer if the assumed prepayments are slower but shorter if the assumed prepayments occur faster. A number of conventional specifications of assumed prepayment rates have been used.

The first and simplest specification is to assume the "standard mortgage yield." This specification assumes there are no prepayments whatsoever until year 12 on 30-year mortgages, when all the mortgages in the pool are assumed to prepay entirely. Of course, in reality some prepayments are inevitable before year 12. Therefore, a quoted yield based on this "standard" prepayments assumption seriously understates the potential yield on a security trading at a deep discount. It overstates the potential yield on one selling at a premium.

A second prepayment specification bases assumed prepayments on FHA experience. The FHA compiles historical data on the actual incidence of prepayment on the mortgage loans it insures. The quoted yield is determined by assuming some ratio of FHA experience. For example, if prepayments are expected to be slower than historical FHA experience, a ratio of 75% of the FHA experience might be used. The benefit of this method is that it uses historically validated assumptions, including in particular the tendency to have higher prepayments in the first few years of the mortgage pool than in later years. The problem with this method is that it incorporates information on a variety of market conditions and mortgages that may not reflect the attributes of the underlying mortgage pool. Figure 32.3 shows the annual FHA prepayment rates based on 1981 experience.

A third prepayment specification is the constant prepayment rate (CPR). This specification assumes that the percentage of the principal balance that is prepaid during a given year is a constant, such as 6 percent. Because of its simplicity, the CPR method has often been used to determine quoted yields. Figure 32.3 shows the annual prepayment rates based on a 4 percent constant assumed rate.

Finally, many quoted yields are now based on the standard prepayment experience offered by the Public Securities Association (PSA), an industry trade group. The PSA's goal is to bring some standardization to the marketplace. Essentially, the PSA standard is a combination of the PSA experience method and the CPR method. The first 30 months of the PSA standard calls for a steadily rising prepayment rate. After that, the rate is assumed constant at 6 percent. Figure 32.3 shows the assumed annual prepayments using the PSA standard method. Similar to the FHA method, the prepayments may be expected to be faster or slower than normal. For example, 150 percent of the PSA standard would project prepayment rates that are half again as great as under normal conditions.

Question — How are the yields an investor will actually realize related to the quoted yield and the rate at which prepayments occur?

Answer — The yield an investor actually realizes may vary significantly from the quoted yield if the actual rate of prepayments of principal differs from the assumed rate of prepayments that was used to calculate the quoted yield.

Investors who buy mortgage-backed securities at a premium (when the coupon rate paid on the security exceeds the current market rate of return for comparable securities) will realize yields that are less than the quoted yields if actual prepayments are faster than assumed when computing the quoted yield. This general principle can be demonstrated with a simple example. A regular bond maturing in 2 years with a face value of $1,000 and paying an annual coupon of $100 is priced at $1,017.59— a $17.59 premium over the face value. The quoted yield (IRR), assuming the bond is not called (prepaid) before the end of the second year, is therefore 9 percent. In other words, bonds of similar quality selling at their face values of $1,000 carry coupon rates of 9 percent. However, if the bond is called (prepaid) for $1,000 after the first year, the actual yield is 8.1 percent. (The $100 coupon less the $17.59 loss in value on the bond divided by the original investment of $1,017.59 equals 8.1 percent.) Consequently, the realized yield when principal is prepaid after year 1 (rather than after year 2 as assumed when computing the quoted yield) is less than the quoted yield of 9 percent. Although assumed and actual principal repayment schedules for mortgage-backed securities are more involved than in this simple example, the same general relationship between quoted and realized yields holds.

Conversely, realized yields on mortgage-backed securities purchased for premiums will be higher than quoted yields if actual prepayments are slower than assumed. This relationship can be demonstrated by simply reversing the example described above. An investor who purchases the bond for $1,017.59 and anticipates that it will be called (prepaid) after one year for $1,000

expects a yield (quoted yield) of 8.1 percent. If the bond is not called as expected after one year, the actual realized yield will be 9 percent.

Similarly, investors who buy mortgage-backed securities at a discount (when the promised interest rate is less than current market rates for comparable securities) will realize yields that are greater than the quoted yields if actual prepayments are faster than assumed prepayments. For example, an investor who buys a $1,000 face-value bond with an 8 percent annual coupon and a 2 year maturity for $982.41 (a $17.59 discount) has an expected yield to maturity (quoted yield) of 9 percent. If the $1,000 face value of the bond is prepaid at the end of the first year, the realized yield is 9.93 percent. (The $80 coupon plus the $17.59 appreciation on the bond divided by the $982.41 purchase price equals 9.93 percent.) Therefore, when actual prepayments of principal are faster than assumed, the realized yield on debt instruments purchased at a discount is greater than the quoted yield based on the assumed prepayments. Conversely, realized yields will be lower than quoted yields if actual prepayments are slower than assumed prepayments.

Investors who buy mortgage-backed securities at par (when the promised interest rate is equal to current market rates for comparable securities) will realize yields equal to the quoted yield, regardless of when prepayments occur.

In addition, regardless of whether investors purchase their securities at a premium, a discount, or par, the timing of prepayments will also significantly affect their potential total return including reinvestment. Specifically, if actual prepayments are faster than assumed, reinvestment return will be lower than expected if interest rates have fallen. If interest rates have risen, reinvestment return will increase. Conversely, if actual prepayments are slower than assumed, reinvestment return will be either higher or lower than expected depending on whether interest rates have risen or fallen, respectively.

The greater the difference between the assumed prepayments and the actual prepayments, the greater the difference will be between the quoted and realized yield. Consequently, to compare potential investments in mortgage-backed securities and to determine a realistic estimate of the potential yield, investors must understand the types of prepayment assumptions that are used to compute quoted yields.

Question — Are there any tax free issues of mortgage-backed securities?

Answer — Yes, a small number of tax-exempt issues are available through the municipal bond departments of investment banking and brokerage firms. These securities are designed to raise funds for low income housing construction and subsidized low interest mortgage loans. They are generally issued by state and local housing authorities.

Question — Are there marketable securities backed by other types of loan agreements?

Answer — Yes, in recent years investment bankers have been extremely creative and have come up with new marketable securities backed by every kind of loan agreement imaginable. Securities have been issued that are backed by auto loans, computer leases, and even credit-card charge accounts.

Some lesser-known loan-backed securities come close to the record that Ginnie Mae 30-year, home-mortgage securities have experienced for high yields and safety. Specifically, the Student Loan Marketing Association (Sallie Mae) is a government-chartered corporation that creates a market in federally-guaranteed student loans. It buys the loans from lending institutions and finances those purchases by issuing bonds to the public. Unlike mortgage pass-throughs, which are set up so that both interest and principal payments are "passed through" to investors each month, these bonds, called Sallie Maes, are in the form of conventional bonds. They pay interest semiannually, have set maturity dates, and return all principal when they mature. Although the bonds don't carry an explicit government guarantee, they are virtually risk-free because the underlying student loans are federally guaranteed. Sallie Maes, which are issued in minimum denominations of $10,000, yield about 0.25 percent more than Treasury bonds of comparable maturities.

Few investors realize that the same agency that issues Ginnie Maes also issues pass-through securities backed by mobile-home loans. These high-yielding, government-guaranteed securities have shorter maturities than conventional Ginnie Maes and tend to have less prepayment risk. That's a plus for investors seeking high-yield securities that sell at a premium. The securities are sold in four maturities: 12-years, 15-years, 18-years, and 20-years.

Question — Are Ginnie Maes subject to state taxation?

Answer — Federal statues provide that all Treasury bonds, Treasury notes, and other obligations of the federal government are not subject to state income taxation; however, Ginnie Maes are not direct obligations of the federal government. They are issued by private financial institutions, and the timely payment of interest and principal is guaranteed by the Government National Mortgage Association. Even though Ginnie Maes are backed by the full faith and credit of the federal government, the securities are *not* direct federal government obligations. Therefore, Ginnie Maes are subject to state income and personal property taxes as well as local taxation. The United States Supreme Court made this determination in June, 1987. *Rockford Life Insurance Company v. Illinois Department of Revenue*, 107 S.Ct. 2312 (1987). This decision also extends to other privately issued securities guaranteed by the federal government.

Chapter 33

MUNICIPAL BONDS

WHAT IS IT?

A municipal bond, also known as a tax-exempt bond, is a debt instrument issued by a state, county, city, or other governmental agency. Like corporate bonds, these issues typically pay a fixed rate of interest. Interest from these bonds is exempt from federal income tax and may also be exempt from state, county, and local taxes as well. (It should be noted that some municipal bonds may be issued in taxable form.)

WHEN IS THE USE OF THIS TOOL INDICATED?

1. When the investor's tax bracket (including any state and local taxes) is high enough that the lower yield of a tax-exempt instrument results in a higher after-tax rate of return than would be produced by a comparable taxable investment. (See below.)

2. When a steady and consistent flow of income is desired.

3. When a secure and relatively conservative investment is indicated.

4. When an investor anticipates holding the investment for a minimum of 3 to 5 years.

ADVANTAGES

1. Income from these bonds is exempt from federal income tax. Compared to an alternative investment producing taxable income, municipal bonds may provide a higher after-tax return. For example, a tax-exempt yield of 7.92% is equivalent to a 11% taxable yield assuming the investor is in a 28% tax bracket. Of course, the higher an investor's tax bracket, the greater the advantage of tax-exempt income.

If the investor were in a lower bracket, the utility of the tax-free bond would be reduced. For instance, if the investor described above were in a 15% rather than a 28% bracket, a tax-exempt yield of 7.92% would be equivalent to only a 9.32% taxable return.

To compare tax-free with taxable yields, use the following formula:

$$\frac{\text{Tax Free Return}}{(100\% - \text{Tax Rate})} \times 100\% = \text{Taxable Equivalent Yield}$$

For example, if a tax-exempt bond yields 10% and the investor is in a 28% tax bracket, the taxable equivalent yield is:

$$\frac{10\%}{100\% - 28\%} \times 100\% = 13.89\%$$

The chart "After-Tax Equivalents of Tax-Exempt Yields" in Appendix G shows the relationship between taxable and tax-free income for individuals in various tax brackets.

2. Income from municipal bonds may also be exempt from state, county, and city income taxes. Generally, the income is exempt from taxation only within the state where the bond was issued. The chart in Figure 33.1 shows the tax status of municipal bond income in the various states.

3. Principal and income are relatively safe. This is because a "general obligation" municipal bond is a debt obligation which has a strong claim on tax revenues. Payment on most tax-exempt municipals has priority over many other government obligations. However, some bonds, known as "revenue bonds," must be paid from specific revenues rather than from general taxes. Examples would be bonds issued for the construction of toll roads or sewage treatment plants. Such bonds are considered riskier than general obligation bonds and pay a higher yield.

DISADVANTAGES

1. As with any fixed-income investment, municipal bonds provide minimal protection against inflation. For example, the fixed income may not keep pace with an increasing cost of living. Similarly, the bond principal, at maturity or sale, may not provide the purchasing power that would have been available through an alternative investment.

2. Bond prices may fluctuate with changes in market interest rates. When interest rates rise, bond values typically decline (of course, if interest rates drop, bond prices generally rise).

3. There may be a limited market for municipal bonds, particularly those issued in small amounts which are not traded actively. The result is that an investor who wants to sell an issue quickly may have to accept a lower price. (This may be advantageous to buyers.)

4. Tax-free bonds can seldom be purchased directly for less than $5,000.

5. The primary advantage of these bonds diminishes as tax rates are lowered. To a taxpayer in a 31% bracket, a 7% tax-free return is equal to a 10.14% return from a taxable investment. If the same taxpayer were in a 28% bracket, a 7% tax-free return would be equal to a 9.72% return from a taxable investment.

TAX IMPLICATIONS

1. The exemption of interest income from federal income and often state and local taxation has been explained above. Note that in calculating the relative advantage of a tax-exempt bond the tax rate applicable after all allowable deductions and adjustments should be used, rather than the rate shown for gross income.

2. Capital gains (or losses) realized on the sale of these bonds are subject to normal capital gain (or loss) treatment. (See "capital gain" in the Glossary and the discussion of capital gains and losses in Chapter 8, "Income Tax Concepts"). Special rules apply to the very few municipal bonds having original issue discount.

3. Although municipal bonds are loosely called "tax-exempt," gifts of these bonds are generally subject to federal (and in many cases state) gift taxation. A bequest of municipals is subject to the federal estate tax as well as applicable state death taxes.

4. The interest earned on most "private activity" municipal bonds issued after August 7, 1986 is a tax preference for purposes of the alternative minimum tax. (See the discussion of the alternative minimum tax in Chapter 8, "Income Tax Concepts.") So-called "private activity" municipal bonds are tax-exempt bonds used for nongovernmental purposes, such as "industrial development" bonds or other bonds the proceeds of which are used in the trade or business of persons other than state or local governments. Bonds used, for example, for student loans, quali-

fied mortgages and veterans' mortgages, and qualified waste disposal facilities are private activity bonds.

ALTERNATIVES

1. Taxable bonds generating a comparable or higher after-tax yield.

2. Single premium deferred annuities providing a fixed annual payment.

3. Certain preferred stock with a fixed dividend.

WHERE AND HOW DO I GET IT?

Municipal bonds can be purchased by calling a brokerage firm, contacting a bank (in some cases the bank will take an order over the phone), savings and loan, or savings bank.

Each dealer in bonds establishes a price based on cost and demand. Larger dealers set prices based on the amount for which similar lots of the same bonds can be sold or acquired. The point is that there is no national auction as there is for stocks.

When comparing bonds be sure to check the yield to maturity of each bond. For example, a 10-year, 10% bond selling at par ($1,000) will provide the same current yield as a 12% bond selling at $1,124 which also matures in 10 years. Both will yield 10% if held to maturity.

An investor will profit from purchasing bonds in registered form although most older municipals (those issued prior to January 1, 1983) are in "bearer" form. Why? Registered bonds often can be purchased at bargain yields because large buyers don't want the delay and expense of registration.

Frequently, municipals are offered in serial form. This means that specific amounts mature regularly over the life of the issue. Coupons attached to bearer bonds state the date when interest comes due, generally on a semiannual basis. The coupons are detached from the bond and presented to either a paying agent or a commercial bank for payment.

Most investors will purchase small blocks of bonds. These purchases ($25,000 or less) are called "odd lots." Larger investors, such as banks, like the convenience of large blocks of $100,000 or more. A tradeoff occurs which favors—for a change—the small investor. The small investor will often be able to buy 10 bonds of $10,000 each for a lower price than a bank would pay for a $100,000 bond. The difference could amount to as much as $10 per $1,000 bond.

Figure 33.1 — State Individual Income Tax of Municipal Bond Interest

State	Resident State Interest	Nonresident State Interest
Alabama	Exempt	Taxable
Alaska	No Income Tax	No Income Tax
Arizona	Exempt	Taxable
Arkansas	Exempt	Taxable
California	Exempt	Taxable
Colorado	Exempt (exceptions)	Taxable
Connecticut	Exempt	Taxable
Delaware	Exempt	Taxable
D.C.	Exempt	Exempt[1]
Florida	No Income Tax	No Income Tax
Georgia	Exempt	Taxable
Hawaii	Exempt	Taxable
Idaho	Exempt	Taxable
Illinois	Taxable (limited exceptions)	Taxable
Indiana	Exempt	Exempt[2]
Iowa	Taxable (limited exceptions)	Taxable
Kansas	Some taxable[3]	Taxable
Kentucky	Exempt	Taxable
Louisiana	Exempt	Taxable
Maine	Exempt	Taxable
Maryland	Exempt	Taxable
Massachusetts	Exempt	Taxable
Michigan	Exempt	Taxable
Minnesota	Exempt	Taxable
Mississippi	Exempt	Taxable
Missouri	Exempt	Taxable
Montana	Exempt	Taxable
Nebraska	Exempt	Taxable
Nevada	No Income Tax	No Income Tax
New Hampshire	Exempt	Taxable
New Jersey	Exempt	Taxable
New Mexico	Exempt	Taxable
New York	Exempt	Taxable
North Carolina	Exempt	Taxable
North Dakota	Exempt	Taxable
Ohio	Exempt	Taxable
Oklahoma	Some taxable[3]	Taxable
Oregon	Exempt	Taxable
Pennsylvania	Exempt	Taxable
Rhode Island	Exempt	Taxable
South Carolina	Exempt	Taxable
South Dakota	No Income Tax	No Income Tax
Tennessee	Exempt	Taxable
Texas	No Income Tax	No Income Tax
Utah	Exempt	Exempt
Vermont	Exempt	Taxable
Virginia	Exempt	Taxable
Washington	No Income Tax	No Income Tax
West Virginia	Exempt	Taxable
Wisconsin	Taxable	Taxable
Wyoming	No Income Tax	No Income Tax

[1] taxable if purchased after 1991
[2] taxable only for gross income tax purposes
[3] specified issues exempt

Rather than purchase bonds on their own, some investors prefer the greater diversification available through municipal bond unit trusts while others utilize municipal bond mutual funds. A "unit trust" is a fixed portfolio; the underlying bonds don't change and are not "managed"; that is, there is no continual buying and selling. Small investors find this approach appealing because of (1) the increased safety through diversification, (2) professional selection, (3) security (the unit trust safeguards the securities themselves), and (4) convenience (interest and principal are collected by the unit trust and paid out on a regular basis or automatically reinvested).

Therefore, unit trusts are best for long-term holdings when a certain fixed income is desired. As the unit trust's holdings mature (or as the bonds are paid off through sinking funds), fund holders are paid on a pro rata basis. Unit trusts are "self liquidating," which means that when assets drop below approximately twenty percent of the original investment, the fund ends and unit holders receive their share of the current price of the portfolio.

A municipal bond mutual fund is similar to a unit trust except that its underlying portfolio is "managed"; there is a regular sale and purchase of bonds to take advantage of changing market conditions. Shares of a municipal bond mutual fund are bought and sold on the open market. The prices fluctuate with the changing worth of the underlying securities. If an investor expects to sell in a relatively short period of time (within three years) a managed tax-exempt fund is a better choice than a unit trust.

WHAT FEES OR OTHER ACQUISITION COSTS ARE INVOLVED?

When a municipal bond is purchased directly from a broker or a bank there is a sales charge or brokerage commission. These fees will vary depending on the amount invested and the number of bonds purchased. Some institutions charge fees based on the number of bonds while others calculate fees on the total dollars invested. These costs range from five to ten dollars per bond.

If municipal bonds are purchased through a unit trust, a "load" (sales charge) of 3.5% to 5.0% is typically added to the value of the purchase. For example, an investor may pay $40 per unit (units are generally valued at $1,000). This means less money is at work and penalizes an investor who liquidates holdings quickly.

Purchasers of municipal bond mutual funds may pay a sales charge (a "load" fund) or may select a fund with no sales charge (a "no-load" fund). Both of these types of funds charge

an annual management fee which will usually range from 0.5% to 1.0% of net asset value. This annual management fee is deducted from the assets of the fund itself and is not paid directly by individual investors.

HOW DO I SELECT THE BEST OF ITS TYPE?

1. Investors contemplating a direct purchase of municipal bonds should compare:

    (a) The quality rating of each bond. Bond ratings can be found in your local library through services such as Standard & Poor's, Moody's and Fitch's; ratings of AAA or A+ indicate the highest quality bonds while those rated CCC or lower are quite speculative. An "A" rated bond will be safer and yield only slightly less than a lower quality issue.

    (b) Current yield (coupon amount divided by investor's cost); for example, a bond paying $90 per year in interest and that costs $850 will have a current yield of 10.6%.

    (c) Yield to maturity (coupon return plus gain or minus loss at maturity); for example, the bond described above, maturing in five years, will have a yield to maturity of 13.2% when the gain of $150 is included with the current yield. (See Chapter 24 for a more detailed explanation of the yield to maturity calculation.

2. Purchasing a bond issued in the investor's state of residence may result in a higher after-tax yield. If the investor lives in Pennsylvania, for example, which has an income tax, the income from Pennsylvania Turnpike Bonds would be exempt. The income would be exempt from both federal and state (and sometimes city) income taxes.

3. Select a maturity date of ten years or less. For two bonds with the same quality rating, the bond with the shorter maturity date will typically have greater price stability (though perhaps a lower yield as well).

4. Schedule maturities according to projected cash flow or capital needs. An investor planning to retire in ten years should select a discount bond maturing in a decade.

5. Search for a large issue of general obligation bonds of state governments and revenue bonds of large, well-known authorities. These bonds are more marketable and will be easier and less costly to sell quickly.

WHERE CAN I FIND OUT MORE ABOUT IT?

1. Your local library should have Moody's Municipal Bond Guide, Standard & Poor's Bond Guide, or Fitch's rating service. These are services which list large numbers of bonds and give quality rating, coupon rate, current yield, and yield to maturity.

2. Major brokerage firms and banks can provide information on specific issues and current market conditions.

QUESTIONS AND ANSWERS

Question — What is the difference between a general obligation bond (a "GO") and a "revenue" bond?

Answer — A general obligation bond is backed by the "full faith and credit" of the issuing entity. These bonds are generally considered safer than revenue bonds and therefore have a lower rate of return.

A revenue bond is issued for a particular project (for example, Florida Pollution Control bonds). The interest and principal of these bonds are paid out of the income only of the particular enterprise and may be less secure than general obligation bonds. For that reason they generally sell at lower prices to yield a higher return.

Question — Can a tax-exempt bond be purchased in "bearer" form?

Answer — Since December 31, 1982, long-term obligations (maturing in more than one year) of state and local governments must be in registered form. This means that the right to principal and interest is transferable only through an entry on the books of the obligation's issuer or holder. The book entry system requires that any person or his agent holding an obligation in a "street name" account or for safekeeping must make it possible to identify the beneficial owner by creating ownership records.

Most bonds issued prior to January 1, 1983 are fully negotiable, meaning that title passes with possession. They are obviously prime targets for theft or misappropriation and should be kept in a safe deposit box or with a broker.

Question — Is a municipal bond an appropriate investment for a pension plan?

Answer — Qualified retirement plans such as a pension or profit sharing plan have many advantages. Among these is the fact that income earned by plan assets is free of all current income taxes. Therefore, bonds providing additional exemption are unnecessary and should not be held in such portfolios.

Question — What is the advantage of a "serial" maturity?

Answer — Serial maturity means that a portion of the bond issue comes due each year until the final redemption. This regular payment schedule makes it easier for the borrower to handle its cash flow obligations. This serial feature is also beneficial to the investor who can purchase bonds that will be redeemed as cash flow is needed. For example, bonds from a single issue may be purchased to mature in the same year or years that college tuition comes due or retirement income is needed.

Question — Can you buy a tax-exempt bond on margin?

Answer — Technically, you can borrow up to 80% of the current market price of a municipal bond. But, the interest you pay to buy such bonds, or previously purchased tax-exempt securities, will not be deductible for federal income tax purposes because the income produced by the bonds is nontaxable.

Question — Is there any given time during the year when it is better to buy tax-exempt bonds?

Answer — Late in the tax year many investors are trying to set up tax losses that can be used against earned income. They may swap (exchange) bonds to realize capital losses. This activity temporarily may "flood" the market and lower prices. The end result may be a higher yield for the individual who buys at the end of the year.

Question — Is there such a thing as a short-term, tax-exempt bond?

Answer — It is possible to purchase municipal obligations with a maturity of less than 270 days. An investor in a high tax bracket who would like to put funds to work for a short period of time will find this an excellent way to invest.

There are also short-term, tax-exempt bond funds, in essence a type of money market fund. The cash received from the sale of shares is invested in municipals with an average maturity of about 180 days. Chances of a capital loss are slight because of the frequent maturities, although the tradeoff for this safety is a yield slightly lower than those of regular funds.

Question — What are the advantages of tax-exempt bond funds?

Answer — There are six major advantages of tax-exempt bond funds:

(1) Ease of investing — most bond funds allow an investor to begin with as little as $1,000 and then add contributions as low as $100.

(2) Diversification — fund managers purchase different types of bonds, select issuers in widespread geographic location, and pick bonds with varied maturities.

(3) Automatic reinvestment — interest and capital gains are immediately and automatically reinvested. This maximizes the potential of compound interest.

(4) Ability to exchange funds — a single fund management group may offer many different types of funds. An investor could exchange shares in a tax-exempt fund for shares of a stock fund or a taxable bond fund paying higher returns.

(5) Convenience — funds provide safekeeping of securities and may be selected on the basis of whether they pay interest monthly, quarterly, or semiannually.

(6) Tax reports and records — detailed reports are provided to investors covering the purchase and sale of shares making it easy to determine any capital gain or loss for tax purposes.

Chapter 34

MUTUAL FUNDS

WHAT IS IT?

A mutual fund is a company (or a trust) that sells shares of its own stock and utilizes the proceeds to make other investments. These investments may include the stocks of publicly traded companies, corporate or municipal bonds, real estate, or short-term money market instruments. The investor, by purchasing shares in a mutual fund, obtains a number of benefits that would otherwise be unavailable.

WHEN IS THE USE OF THIS TOOL INDICATED?

1. When an investor has limited capital to work with and cannot afford to purchase a broad enough range of assets to achieve adequate diversification.

2. When the investor is unwilling or unable to select, manage or keep records on a large number of securities.

3. When the investor wants to be able to sell shares or increase his holdings at any time.

ADVANTAGES

1. Mutual funds can provide a high degree of security of both principal and income through diversification of investments. Few individuals could afford to buy as many different types of stocks or other investments as the typical mutual fund. This spreading of risk makes it unlikely that poor performance by any one asset will result in financial disaster.

2. The purchase of shares in a mutual fund frees the investor from having to make a number of difficult decisions, and from other related responsibilities. These include: (1) analyzing securities, (2) timing purchases and sales, (3) reinvesting of income, (4) safekeeping of securities, and (5) detailed record keeping.

3. Most mutual funds "maintain a market" in their own shares. Such funds are referred to as "open end" investment companies. This means that the mutual fund company has obligated itself to buy back its shares from investors. An investor can require the fund to redeem its

shares at any time. This requirement provides the purchaser of fund shares with a high degree of liquidity.

A small category of funds, referred to as "closed end" funds, do not buy and sell their own shares. Instead, their shares are traded on the open market much like the shares of other companies. Some of these funds are listed on the organized stock exchanges but most are traded on the over-the-counter market. (Although closed-end funds technically are not mutual funds, the shareholders of a fund which qualifies and makes the necessary election to be taxed as a regulated investment company will be taxed like mutual fund shareholders.)

4. Mutual fund organizations have promoted the concept of a "family of funds." A company will sponsor a number of funds with different investment objectives and underlying assets. The investor can choose to switch assets back and forth from one fund to another. The advantage is that the investor can quickly, conveniently (and without any additional sales charges) move assets into one or more funds which better meet his investment needs or desires.

DISADVANTAGES

1. Purchasing shares from many mutual funds involves payment of a sales charge, commonly called a "load." This charge covers the cost of marketing the fund through brokerage firms and certain other fees. Sales charges can be as high as 8.5% of the original investment; however, the growing number of no-load funds has forced the load down to an average of about 4.75% for bond funds and 5.75% for stock funds. (There are many "no-load" funds which market their products directly to the public by mail and through newspaper advertising. These funds do not charge a sales fee.)

2. Diversification, which is typically considered an advantage, can work against an investor because it reduces the potential for very large gains. Even if the fund should happen to "pick a winner" it will not have much of an impact on the performance of the fund as a whole. This is because any one investment is only a small portion of the fund's total assets. (Most funds are limited to having no more than five percent of their assets invested in any one company.)

3. Annual management fees and administrative charges can reduce the overall return on the investment. Management fees can range from 0.5% to 3% or more of the value of the investment. Administrative charges are imposed in addition to management fees and frequently cost from $5 to $10 annually per account.

4. While professional management relieves the investor of certain obligations and responsibilities, it also eliminates his personal involvement in the management of the fund. As a practical matter the purchaser of a mutual fund cannot control the selection of specific assets or the timing of purchases and sales. Unlike the investor who buys stock directly, and who can select the best time to sell and recognize a gain or loss, the mutual fund shareholder has no choice. He cannot control the amount of any capital gain distribution or when it must be reported. Capital gain distributions are paid annually and must be reported each year to the IRS.

TAX IMPLICATIONS

1. Ordinary income distributions from mutual funds are taxed to individual shareholders at ordinary tax rates. (See the question and answer section at the end of this chapter for a description of tax strategies to consider when acquiring shares and when disposing of shares.)

2. Capital gain distributions are generally treated as long-term capital gain, and are taxable in the year in which the distribution is declared. (See the discussion of capital gains and losses in Chapter 8, "Income Tax Concepts.")

3. The income paid from municipal bond funds is not subject to federal income tax, but is normally taxed at the state level. Capital gains, however, are fully taxable.

4. Every time a switch is made within a family of funds, shares of one fund are technically sold and shares of another fund are purchased. These sales are taxable events and result in a gain or loss immediately reportable by the investor. Of course, if the funds are purchased through an IRA, Keogh, or qualified corporate pension or profit sharing plan, tax is deferred until an actual or constructive distribution occurs.

5. The sale or other disposition of less than all of an investor's shares (or of shares acquired on various dates at various prices) can cause difficulty in determining the basis of the shares sold. Several methods are available for establishing the basis of shares and, thus, for determining the amount of taxable gain. These are explained in the question and answer section at the end of this chapter.

6. Some funds are set up as limited partnerships in order to allow investors an exemption from state and local taxes on interest from U.S. government securities; however, this exemption does not apply in all states.

ALTERNATIVES

1. A variable annuity has many of the characteristics and features of a mutual fund. Typically, these include ownership of a large portfolio of securities and management by professional investment advisers. (See the question and answer section at the end of this chapter for more information on variable annuities.)

2. Real estate investment trusts (REITs) are similar to mutual funds in many respects but differ mainly in the nature of their underlying assets. REITs generally have the majority of their assets invested in shopping centers, apartment buildings, office buildings and other large-scale real estate ventures. Some investors have a preference for real estate as opposed to securities, for investment purposes. REITs are discussed fully in Chapter 41.

WHERE AND HOW DO I GET IT?

Most load funds are sold through brokerage firms which receive part of the load charge as a fee for selling shares in the fund. Many brokerage firms are affiliated with particular fund groups or have their own set of mutual funds that they market to their clients. These funds will generally include a money market fund (see Chapter 31), one or more common stock funds, bond funds, and a fund which specializes in tax-exempt securities. Orders to buy and sell fund shares are treated like any other transaction and require that the investor have an account with the brokerage firm. Investors will receive confirming receipts of any trades, and activity will be shown on the monthly statement received from their broker.

Investors should realize that brokers naturally are biased toward selling their own funds rather than those of other mutual fund organizations. Also, brokers typically will not sell shares in no-load funds for which they receive no commissions. Investors should be careful to review the recommendations of brokers to see that they are conforming with the investor's particular needs and desires.

As noted, no-load mutual funds are rarely sold through brokerage firms. These funds are bought and sold directly through the funds themselves. No-load funds are widely advertised in the newspapers and most carry on an active campaign of direct mail advertising and solicitation. Investors interested in a specific fund or a particular group of funds will normally write or call the fund (many have toll-free "800" phone numbers) for additional information or the forms needed to open an account.

Once an account has been established with a no-load mutual fund organization it is relatively easy to purchase additional shares, to switch investments from one fund in the group to another, or to sell shares. Most of these transactions can be done on the telephone or by mail. After a transaction is made the fund will send a confirming receipt to the investor within a few days.

WHAT FEES OR OTHER ACQUISITION COSTS ARE INVOLVED?

The sales charge for purchasing a load fund can range from 3% to 8.5% of the net asset value of the fund. Net asset value is the total value of the fund's assets, minus any liabilities, divided by the number of shares of the fund outstanding. For example, let's assume that Consolidated Fund, a hypothetical mutual fund, charges an 8.5% load to purchase its shares. If the fund's shares had a net asset value of $10.00 per share, the sales charge would be $0.85, and the purchase price of a share for investors would be $10.85.

The load fee for mutual funds may be as high as 8.5%. However, quite a few funds charge less than this amount and are referred to as "low-load" funds. Investors should be cautious in purchasing these funds since many also charge a redemption fee that may be as high as 5% of the value of any shares sold. This fee is assessed whenever the investor sells shares of the fund and would be subtracted from the amount the investor would be paid. This redemption fee may be waived if the investor sells shares of the fund but reinvests the money in another fund of the same group. The load plus the 12b-1 fee plus the redemption charges cannot exceed 8.5%.

The costs for buying and selling shares of so-called "closed-end" funds are similar to those of buying and selling any shares of stock. The transaction cost will be determined by the number of shares traded and the total value of the transaction. Typically this cost will be 2% to 3% of the total value of the shares purchased or sold.

As their names implies, no-load funds do not charge a fee for the purchase or sale of their shares. These funds may be identified in newspaper listings of mutual funds by the indication of "N.L." in the column of offering prices. These funds may be purchased or sold at their indicated net asset value with no additional sales charges. However, investors should be aware that while these funds do not charge a sales fee, they do assess administrative charges and management fees and may charge 12b-1 fees to cover the costs of marketing and adver-

tising, typically on an annual basis. These fees can range from 0.5% to 1.25%. Further, service charges of 0.5% to 3% of the investment may be charged when shares are purchased or dividends reinvested. Back-end redemption fees beginning at 5% or 6% and declining to zero if the shares are held for 5-8 years may also be imposed.

HOW DO I SELECT THE BEST OF ITS TYPE?

Today there are more than 6,000 different mutual funds available to investors. These funds have a wide variety of investment objectives and vary considerably in terms of size, fees, management performance, and services offered to investors. Selecting the right fund for a particular investment situation may not be easy and should be given a great deal of thought. Described below are some of the important factors to consider in making such a decision:

(1) The selection process should begin with an evaluation of the fund's investment objective. This information can be found in the fund's "prospectus" which can be obtained from a brokerage firm or from the fund itself. In addition to describing the fund's investment objectives, the prospectus will indicate its current investments and provide some data on its historical performance. While there are a great many mutual funds, their objectives can be grouped into a few common categories:

GROWTH FUNDS — more aggressive than common stock funds, these funds concentrate on long-term capital gains and high future income; generally invest in more speculative issues that provide little or no current income; most of their investments are in common stocks, and possibly a few convertible bonds. The most aggressive funds with above-average growth potential, high portfolio turnover, high leverage, and high risk are called performance or "go-go" funds.

INCOME FUNDS — specialize in securities that pay higher-than-average current rates of return from either dividends or interest by investing in securities not generally favored by the investment community; frequently invest a high percentage of their assets in bonds rather than common stocks.

BALANCED FUNDS — these are the most conservative of the funds investing in common stock; have as their primary objective the preservation of capital and moderate growth of income and principal; secondary consideration is capital gains; generally diversify their investments among both stocks and bonds; during bear markets typically offer the best investor protection.

TAX-EXEMPT FUNDS — operate principally to provide investors with high after-tax returns on their investments; generally limit their investments to municipal securities or other types of issues that offer tax-sheltered income.

INDEX FUNDS — grew out of the "efficient markets" theory that, on the average, it is impossible to consistently outperform the market; accordingly, try to match the performance of some market index by creating a portfolio patterned after the index. The objective is to reduce the cost of poor security analysis and portfolio turnover, and allow the investor to decide, on his own, the degree of leverage desired and how to time the market. (See the question and answer section at the end of this chapter for more information on index funds.)

SECTOR FUNDS — restrict investments to a particular sector of the market, such as energy, electronics, chemicals, or health care; these funds tend to be more volatile than a more diversified portfolio. (See the question and answer section at the end of this chapter for more information on sector funds.)

DIVERSIFIED COMMON STOCK FUNDS — concentrate principally on long-term capital growth, with current income being a secondary consideration; a majority of the assets are invested in good quality common stocks with the balance in cash or short-term government notes. These funds follow a more conservative approach.

SPECIALTY FUNDS — seek to achieve their objectives by concentrating their investments in a single industry, in a group of related industries, in industry within a specific geographic region, or even in non-security assets such as real estate investment trusts that purchase real property or loans secured by real property.

HEDGE FUNDS — use the most aggressive techniques, including high leverage, short sales, and the purchase of put and call options to achieve maximum growth of capital; for the most speculative investor.

MONEY MARKET FUNDS — typically no-load funds that invest exclusively in money market instruments such as T-bills, CDs, and corporate commercial paper, providing current income and relative safety of principal; offer competitive services such as check-writing privileges and free conversion privileges to other types of funds managed by the same investment group.

COMMODITY FUNDS — designed to bring the small investor into the commodities market; organized as limited partnerships, these funds offer inflation-hedge in an inflationary environment and an opportunity for large gains, but with a high degree of risk.

BOND FUNDS — possess several advantages over direct bond investing, provided expenses are kept low; offer a variety of portfolio types, and proven track records; allows an investor to indirectly participate in the bond market without acquiring the expertise necessary to invest in the market directly. (See the question and answer section at the end of this chapter for more information on bond funds.)

FOREIGN STOCK AND BOND FUNDS — open-end and closed-end funds that invest in foreign stocks and bonds; some invest exclusively in the securities of one nation while others invest more broadly in foreign regions, or in all foreign markets; during 1980's these funds performed better than U.S. stocks by 4% on average.

ASSET ALLOCATION FUNDS — in essence, these funds offer one-stop shopping for a complete investment portfolio and offer a substitute for the investor's own allocation of investment dollars among several different traditional funds. These funds offer diversification not only within asset classes but among asset classes, and they may include nontraditional asset classes such as commodities and real estate. (See the question and answer section at the end of this chapter for more information on asset allocation funds.)

(2) Another important selection factor is the fund's historical performance. Relatively few funds have outperformed the market as a whole over long periods of time, but some have consistently done better than others. Each fund's prospectus will give some indication of its rate of return during the last five or ten years. Most funds will show what a typical investment would have returned in the form of dividends and capital gains. Various investment sources (see below) will also provide comparative information on large numbers of mutual funds. Investors should use this information to select those funds which have regularly been above average in their investment performance.

In analyzing the performance of mutual funds it is important to note that many funds perform quite differently in bull markets as compared to bear markets. Growth funds, especially those that concentrate in speculative issues, tend to do well when economic conditions are good and the general trend of the stock market is up. However, these same funds have been relatively poor performers when market conditions are weak and the economy is in a decline. In contrast, income funds and some balanced funds tend to do better than growth funds when the market is weak. Few funds have been able to turn in better than average performance under all market conditions. Given this situation, investors should be prepared to move from one fund to another as market conditions change.

(3) Investors should concentrate on those funds with low sales charges, management fees, and expense ratios. As noted above, funds differ considerably as to the cost of purchasing their shares. This should not be the only consideration, but high sales charges can sharply reduce an investor's overall rate of return on investment. Similarly, funds that charge high portfolio management fees have to provide better than average returns to compensate for those charges. Funds also have normal business expenses and these charges, referred to as a fund's "expense ratio," should be a factor in selecting a particular mutual fund for investment. A well-managed fund will typically have an expense ratio of no more than 0.6% to 0.75% of its assets.

(4) The range of services offered by the fund is another important consideration in making a selection. Most funds will provide for automatic reinvestment of dividends into additional shares of the fund. Another common feature is automatic payout of a specified amount on a monthly, quarterly, or annual basis. This feature is especially important to older investors who may be using the fund to provide retirement income. In addition, many offer convenient methods for purchasing shares at the day's net asset value, either by telephone or by wire transfer.

(5) It is desirable that a fund be a part of a "family of funds" that provide the investor with flexibility in terms of diversification and the opportunity to alter his investment objective. As noted above, few funds have done well under all market conditions, and the investor should be prepared to transfer investments when market conditions change. Also, it is not unusual for one person to have a variety of investment needs, and the opportunity to make investments in a number of funds within the same management group is attractive.

(6) A sample worksheet for evaluating mutual funds is included in Figure 34.1. It is designed to allow an investor to systematically evaluate data to arrive at an investment decision. A fund's prospectus can supply most of the required information.

(a) The first section, beyond requesting basic information, requires the investor to focus on his investment objectives as they relate to risk, return, and portfolio diversification.

(b) The second section examines a fund's performance for five years, both on its own and relative to an index and the average for its investment category. The Treasury bill rate is a reference point for examining riskless return. Returns should include any reinvestments of capital gains and income distributions.

Comparison of a fund's performance to an index is an indication of the performance of the fund's management. An index is unmanaged (no management fees or expenses). Fund performance greater than the index indicates that the fund manager is doing a good job, and essentially, worth his fees.

Comparison of a fund's performance to the average for its category is an indication of how well a fund is performing relative to its counterparts with the same investment objectives and fees. If a fund performs worse than the average, it should not be considered for a portfolio, typically.

(c) The next section examines risk. The first differentiation required concerns diversified vs. non-diversified funds. This is important because non-diversified funds are more risky than diversified funds due to their unlikeliness to follow the market and to exhibit more variation in return.

The worst annual performance in the past five years is an indication of how much risk an investor can withstand without ruining long-term investment plans. Although overall performance is more important, if this poor performance signifies more risk than you can tolerate, this figure is significant.

The stock and bond funds sections focus on the risk involved with each. For example, sector funds and small stocks are riskier than equity funds and large stocks. The risk associated with bonds focuses on the creditworthiness of the issuer and the maturity of the bond. The federal government is more creditworthy and, hence, less risky than a corporate issuer. Likewise, bonds with longer average maturity dates are

Figure 34.1

MUTUAL FUND WORKSHEET

Fund
Name _____

Address _____

Telephone _____

Minimum Initial Investment $ _____

Minimum Subsequent Investment $ _____

Telephone Exchange? ____Yes____With money market fund?
                ____No

Investment Objective

____ Aggressive Growth Stock
____ Growth Stock
____ Growth and Income Stock
____ Balanced, Stock and Bond
____ Bond
____ Tax-Exempt Bond
____ International Stock
____ International Bond
____ Other:_____

Performance

	Total Annual Return for Most Recent 5 Years (%)				
	1	2	3	4	5
Fund	___	___	___	___	___
Index*	___	___	___	___	___
Average for Category	___	___	___	___	___
Fund Return Less Index*	___	___	___	___	___
Fund Return Less Category Average	___	___	___	___	___
Treasury Bill Rate	___	___	___	___	___

*Stock index for stock funds; bond index for bond funds
Consistency of Performance:
In how many years did the fund outperform the average for its category?_____

Portfolio Manager:_____ No. of years in position:_____

Risk

____Diversified   ____Non-Diversified   Worst annual performance over last 5 years:_____%

Stock Funds:

____Yes
____No
Industry:_____

Investments:
____Large Stocks
____Small Stocks

Bond Funds:

Investments:
____Governments
____High-Quality Corporates
____Low-Quality Corporates
____High-Quality Municipals
____Low-Quality Municipals
____Mortgages

Average Maturity:
____Short-term (less than three years)
____Intermediate-term (three to 10 years)
____Long-term (over 10 years)

Figure 34.1 continued

MUTUAL FUND WORKSHEET

Expenses

12b-1 annual charge: _____%	Greater than 0.50% _____ Yes
Annual expense ratio: _____%	_____ No

_____ No-Load	Greater than:
	    1.1% for bond funds?
	    1.4% for stock funds? _____ Yes
	    _____ No

Load: Front-End _____% Bank-End or Redemption _____%	Disappears after 6 months? _____ Yes _____ No

Taxes

Distribution dates: Income _____

                              Capital gains _____

Net Investment Income as a percentage of average net asset value: _____%

Portfolio turnover rate: _____%	Greater than 50% _____ Yes _____ No

Tax-exempt interest: _____ Federal   _____ State   _____ Local

Account Status: IRA, Keogh, Simplified employee Pension, or 403(b)   _____ Yes
                                                                                                 _____ No

more risky as interest rates fluctuate than bonds with shorter average maturity dates.

(d) The mutual fund expense section focuses on the expenses and fees associated with the fund's operation. Annual fees charged for the administration of the fund, management fees, and sales fees can grow to substantial amounts that reduce the overall return of the fund. Although it is unwise to judge a fund solely by its cost structure, excessive expenses are a very important factor in evaluating a mutual fund's attractiveness.

(e) The final section examines taxes to avoid paying them unnecessarily. To approximate required taxes, the ratio of net investment income to average net asset value of the fund is useful. This calculation estimates interest or dividend yield, essentially. The higher the yield, the greater the tax potential. Also useful is the portfolio turnover rate. This measure indicates how often the fund buys or sells securities during the year.

The greater the number of transactions, the greater the potential for capital gains and subsequent distributions which are taxable. A benchmark portfolio turnover figure of 50% or less is usually desirable.

WHERE CAN I FIND OUT MORE ABOUT IT?

1. An excellent source of information on mutual funds is Weisenberger's *Investment Companies*, a reference book on mutual funds that is available from most libraries. This manual provides information on the investment objectives of several hundred mutual funds as well as a record of their past investment performance. It also includes the address of the fund where investors may write for additional information.

2. *Forbes* magazine publishes an annual survey of mutual funds in one of its August issues. This survey is unique in

evaluating the performance of funds in both up and down markets. Investors can quickly see how well a fund has done under various conditions and match that performance to their own assessment of current market circumstances.

3. Most brokerage houses will be happy to provide information on the mutual funds which they offer to their customers. They are also required by law to provide a current prospectus on the fund before they solicit an investor to buy shares in the fund.

4. The funds themselves are good sources of investment information. In addition to a prospectus, funds publish quarterly reports which indicate their performance during the period and the investments currently in their portfolio. They may also make available information in the form of booklets which describe the various funds available, the objective of each fund in the group, and how those funds can be used to meet investors' needs.

5. Investment Company Institute
    1401 H Street, N.W.
    Washington, DC 20005
    (202) 326-5800

6. *Dow Jones-Irwin No-Load Mutual Funds*, William G. Droms and Peter D. Heerwagen, Dow Jones-Irwin, Homewood, IL. 60430.

7. *Barron's*: Dow Jones and Company, 200 Burnett Road, Chicopee, Mass. 01020; Weekly; Separate listing of selected funds and listing of prices by exchange.

8. *The Wall Street Journal*: Dow Jones and Company, 200 Liberty Street, New York, NY 10281; Daily, Monday issue has a separate listing of selected funds and listing of prices by exchange.

9. *Moody's Bank and Finance Manual*: Moody's Investors Service, 99 Church Street, New York, NY 10007; Annual; Financial details and summaries of selected funds.

10. *The Value Line Investment Service*: Arnold Bernhard & Company, 711 Third Avenue, New York, NY 10017; Closed-end fund industry summary and evaluation of selected funds.

QUESTIONS AND ANSWERS

Question — What is a "family of funds"?

Answer — Most sponsors of mutual funds offer a number of funds with different investment objectives. For instance,

a typical fund organization would offer a growth stock fund, an income fund, a tax-free municipal bond fund, and a money market fund. A few of the larger sponsors may offer specialty funds such as an international stock fund, or a fund that concentrates in a particular area such as high-tech industries, defense issues, or precious metals such as gold and silver. Although each fund is a separate entity, the sponsor allows investors to transfer funds from one fund to another without charge. Each transfer is a taxable event unless it is done in an IRA, Keogh, or qualified retirement plan.

Dealing with a sponsor who offers a family of funds is advantageous because it allows the investor to satisfy changing investment needs without incurring repeated sales charges when moving from one organization to another.

Question — How do I compare one mutual fund with another?

Answer — Some of the factors that apply to the selection of mutual funds are:

(1) fund objective,

(2) performance record,

(3) sales charges (if any),

(4) advisory fees,

(5) management fees,

(6) special services.

Fund objectives should match the investor's personal goals. Each fund states its objectives in its advertising and provides a more detailed explanation in its prospectus.

An investor should review a fund's performance record over a period of at least five years. This information can be found in most local libraries. Some of the more common sources are Weisenberger's *Investment Companies, Forbes* magazine, and publications from the Investment Company Institute and the No-Load Mutual Fund Association.

"Load" and "no-load" are terms used to indicate whether or not a fund levies a direct sales charge. Such charges can range from 3% to 8.5% of the initial investment. It would appear that investors would always be better off by purchasing no-load funds. This is not necessarily the case; the overall performance record of a good load fund can far offset the absence of a sales charge in a mediocre no-load fund.

While all funds charge an advisory fee, these vary considerably from fund to fund. Investors should search for those funds with good performance records and relatively low advisory fees. These fees are reported in the fund's prospectus or annual report.

All funds charge a management fee in addition to any sales charges and investment advisory fees. These fees are typically five to ten dollars per account per year.

Investors should select funds from those organizations which provide a wide range of special services to fund holders. These services include: (a) ability to transfer from one fund to another; (b) automatic reinvestment of dividends; (c) automatic payments from the fund (typically requires a minimum investment of $10,000); (d) service and information provided with respect to Keogh and IRA accounts; (e) toll-free "hot line" for information and service. (Some funds offer direct computer access to accounts through an investor's touch-tone telephone. The investor can obtain 24-hour account information and even make transactions by phone.)

Question — What is a beta coefficient and how can it be used to measure how well a mutual fund will do in a bull market?

Answer — A beta coefficient measures the fund's relative volatility against a well known market index such as the Standard & Poor's index of 500 common stocks. The index selected would be assigned a beta of 1. If the fund tends to rise (or fall) twice as high (or low) as the selected index, then the fund would be given a beta of 2.

A fund which rose or fell only half as much as the selected index would be given a beta coefficient of .5. The beta of a fund will change according to the time period over which it is analyzed. High volatility does not assure that the fund will skyrocket in an up market. But in general, funds with the highest betas tend to go up further and faster in up markets than those with a lower beta.

Question — How can an investor determine the number of additional shares that have been purchased when a distribution is reinvested in additional shares of the fund?

Answer — Divide the amount of the distribution by the fund's NAV (net asset value) on the date of the distribution. For example, suppose the shares in a mutual fund have a NAV of $8.17. The fund pays a capital gains distribution of $0.30 per share and a dividend of $0.38 a share. You would divide $0.68 (.30 + .38) by $8.17. That equals .083231 additional shares.

Question — What are "Sector Funds"?

Answer — Sector funds are mutual funds that restrict their investments to a particular sector of the market. For example, a health care sector fund would confine its investments to those industries related to this segment of the market: drug companies, hospital management firms, medical suppliers, and biotech concerns. The portfolio would consist of promising growth stocks from these particular industries. Among the more popular sector funds are those that concentrate their investments in energy; financial services; gold; leisure and entertainment; natural resources; electronics; chemicals; computers and peripherals; telecommunications; utilities; and health care.

The underlying investment objective of a sector fund is generally growth. The idea behind the sector fund concept is that the really attractive returns come from small segments of the market. Rather than diversifying widely across the market, the philosophy is to put your money where the action is. These funds should be considered only by aggressive investors who are willing to take on the added risks that often accompany these funds. Since sector funds are, by design, not well diversified, investors face greater price volatility than with more broadly diversified portfolios.

Some investors use sector funds to implement a market timing investment strategy. Because various sectors of the economy tend to "peak" and "trough" at different times within the business cycle, market timers shift from one sector fund to another as they anticipate the economy moving from one phase of the business cycle to another. This is an extremely risky technique, since (1) investors may miss-time the business cycle and shift their portfolios at incorrect times and (2) any given sector fund may not behave in the same manner as the entire sector in each business cycle. Research does not suggest that many, if any, investors have been able to consistently predict changes in the business cycle. If anyone can predict the way various industries will perform, he should be able to predict the entire market. There is more to be gained from knowing when to shift from stocks to Treasury bills than there is from knowing when to shift from health care to leisure and entertainment.

If the fund's managers do not select appropriate stocks for the fund, it may not truly reflect the performance of the sector it is supposed to mimic.

Question — What are dual-purpose funds?

Answer — Dual-purpose funds are closed-end investment companies established on or before June 12, 1989, that offered two types of shares to investors: (1) income shares that received all income from the fund's investments, and (2) capital shares that received all capital gains. Mutual funds that registered with the SEC after June 12, 1989, are not permitted to distribute different types of income disproportionately between classes of stock. As a result, only a few funds registered prior to that date still exist.

Question — What are variable annuities and how do they compare as an alternative to mutual funds?

Answer — A variable annuity allows the holder of an annuity contract, usually issued by an insurance company, to invest in a family of mutual funds with the purpose of accumulating savings, usually for retirement. The balance accumulated is then disbursed as a series of payments or a lump-sum payment upon retirement or other planned event. The amount available for distribution is contingent on the performance of the mutual funds selected.

As an alternative to mutual funds, variable annuities offer the advantages of tax-deferral for any dividends or capital gains earned until the income is withdrawn, and a waiver on taxes normally required for fund transfers between mutual funds. Further, investment advisory fees are, in essence, "tax-deductible" because they are not added back to taxable income. Generally, variable annuities also guarantee that a beneficiary will never receive less than the sum of the contributions if the annuity holder dies before the annuity starting date.

On the other hand, money in variable annuities is tied up for long periods of time; a disadvantage if the investment strategy is not long-term in focus. Variable annuities are also illiquid because the IRS imposes a 10% penalty tax on premature distributions (generally before age 59½ — see Chapter 18) and insurance companies also impose surrender charges. Expenses, too, are high; usually 2% of total assets versus a 1% charge for mutual funds. Finally, declining back-end surrender charges are frequently imposed over a seven-year period whereas no-load mutual funds carry no such levy. Load mutual funds, however, impose a sales charge up to 8.5% that is paid up-front and does not decline if no withdrawals are made during the first few years.

Overall, variable annuities perform similarly to mutual funds. Specifically, though, variable annuities exhibit lower levels of stock market and total risk than the market as a whole.

On the whole, variable annuities present better investment opportunities when:

(1) the investor's tax rate is higher during the accumulation phase and lower during the payout phase,

(2) the accumulation period is longer,

(3) the rate of return is higher,

(4) the annual expense differential is smaller, and/or

(5) payments will be taken from the annuity contract in the form of one of the annuity options rather than as a lump sum.

Figure 34.2

COMPARISON OF VARIABLE ANNUITY VERSUS MUTUAL FUND					
	No-Load Mutual Fund After-Tax Value		Variable Annuity After-Tax Value		
End of	Total	Total Retirement Payouts Over 20 Years	Total	Lump-sum Surrender	Total Retirement Payout Over 20 Years
5 Years	$33,361	$57,880	$36,733	$32,744	$57,880
10 Years	44,518	77,240	53,973	44,122	81,060
15 Years	59,407	103,080	79,304	60,841	115,120
20 Years	79,276	137,560	116,324	85,406	165,160

Also, a variable annuity is more likely the better investment if you are comparing it to a load mutual fund rather than a no-load mutual fund.

Figure 34.2 compares the after-tax accumulation of a variable annuity with a no-load fund over various accumulation periods assuming a $25,000 initial investment, 9 percent pretax rate of return (after investment management expenses), a 1 percent annual charge in excess of the annual mutual fund expenses, a 34 percent combined federal and state income tax rate, annuity payment/withdrawals that commence after age 59½ (no 10 percent penalty), and no surrender charges on the annuity after year 5.

The comparison shows that the variable annuity breaks even with the mutual fund in 5 years and outperforms the mutual fund for every holding period beyond 5 years. The annuity builds to over $116,000, versus the $79,000 you would get from the mutual fund, if you invest for 20 years before taking a lump-sum withdrawal. The advantage is even greater if you take distributions from the annuity over 20 years. In this case you would receive a total of over $165,000 after tax, which is about 20 percent more than if you systematically withdrew funds from the mutual fund during the 20 year retirement period. If your tax bracket were to drop to 25 percent after retirement from 34 percent before retirement, your retirement payout would increase to over $184,000.

The annuity break-even period is quite sensitive to changes in some assumptions. For example, if the assumed rate of return is lower, 6 percent for instance, the break-even accumulation period for a lump-sum withdrawal is about 3 times longer, just under 15 years. If the annuity is withdrawn over 20 years rather than as a lump sum, the break-even accumulation period is about 9 years.

It should be noted that variable annuities are taxable as ordinary income, while mutual funds may be taxable at capital gains or ordinary income rates.

Question — Is it better strategy to invest in bonds directly or through a mutual fund?

Answer — With a diversified portfolio, an investor can reap the benefits provided by both bonds and funds. However, bond mutual funds possess several advantages over direct bond investing, provided expenses are maintained at low levels. In addition to diversification and professional management, mutual funds offer a variety of portfolio types, and proven track records. Furthermore, as an individual investor it is more difficult and costly to deal directly in the bond markets due to their professional orientation. Therefore, by investing in bond mutual funds

an individual can realize transaction cost economies by allowing the professionals to make the investments. Bond mutual funds offer greater liquidity, too, because an investor can take money out of a no-load fund without incurring transaction costs or unfavorable prices. Selling bonds before their maturity date carries penalties. Finally, direct bond investors rarely realize a bond's promised yield because rates of return are highly unpredictable. Bond mutual fund investors have a greater chance of realizing returns due to their ability to reinvest any distributions as they are received and by having their interest compounded.

Overall, bonds, whether invested directly or through mutual funds, generally realize lower total returns than stocks. Therefore, it is necessary to maintain low costs in order to offset this disadvantage.

Question — What are index funds?

Answer — Index funds are mutual funds that try to match the performance of some market index by creating a portfolio in the same manner that is used to create the index. For example, the Vanguard Index Trust, which was the first publicly offered index fund, seeks to provide investment results that correspond to the price and yield performance of publicly traded stocks as represented by the Standard & Poor's 500 composite stock price index. The S&P 500 index is a value-weighted index (that is, the weighting of stocks in the index are in proportion to their value in the market relative to all the stocks in the index) which studies indicate is one of the best measures of overall market performance.

Index funds are useful when the investor wants to minimize underperformance. If you believe, as many studies indicate and general factors suggest, that it is nearly impossible to consistently outperform the market on a risk-adjusted basis, index funds provide a means to closely match the market, or given segments of the market, at low cost with broad diversification and convenience. On average, about 75 percent of the common stock mutual funds classified as either growth or aggressive growth fail to beat the market in any given year. In addition, for investors who wish to make their own market timing decisions, index funds, together with money market funds, provide convenient, inexpensive, and flexible vehicles for moving money in and out of the market.

Index funds offer several advantages that include:

(1) Diversification.

(2) Low initial investment requirements.

(3) Lower transaction costs. On average, the typical common stock fund incurs about a 4 percent transactions cost on a round-trip trade. The average common stock fund turns over about 80 percent of its portfolio each year. Therefore, even if the performance of a fund matches the market, annual average returns would be reduced by about 3.2 percent relative to the market. The portfolio turnover rate for the Vanguard Index Trust has averaged about 20 percent per year (since it trades only when necessary to keep the fund in line with the S&P index). Consequently, the Vanguard Index Trust has averaged 4 times lower transaction costs than the average common stock mutual fund.

(4) Lower management fees and expenses. These fees have averaged about 1.2 percent per year for the average common stock mutual fund. Index funds that passively match a specified index charge no, or a very low, management fee. Consequently, fees and expenses for index funds are many times lower than for the average common stock mutual fund. For example, the expense ratio for the Vanguard Index Trust has averaged about 0.33 percent during the last five years or about 4 times less than the average stock fund.

(5) More consistent performance. On average, any common stock mutual fund that "beats" the market one year has about a 50-50 chance of underperforming the market in the subsequent year. Index funds tend to closely match the specified index year after year.

Index funds also possess several disadvantages. Investors bear essentially the same market risk as the underlying index. Also, some of the new entries into the index fund market are actually managed actively rather than passively (most notably, the Gateway Option Income Fund). Therefore, their performance can deviate substantially from the ideal. When selecting an index fund, read the prospectus carefully to determine the degree of latitude the management has in the active management of the fund.

Several tax related issues are relevant when considering index funds. The principal tax consideration is that index funds, like all other mutual funds, must declare and pay both regular and capital dividends at least once annually. Investors do not have the same degree of latitude in the timing of sales of specified securities within the funds as they would if they held the underlying portfolio directly. Consequently, they may have to recognize gains when they would otherwise choose not to do so. However, investors may choose when to buy and sell shares in the funds and gains will be treated as long-term if they have held the shares for the required period, even if some of the underlying stocks in the portfolio have not been held for the long-term holding period.

Index funds can be effectively incorporated into a mutual fund portfolio by utilizing a core portfolio approach. This approach splits a stock portfolio into two portions: (1) a passively managed portion and (2) an actively managed portion. The passive portion focuses on index funds and should account for at least fifty percent of the total stock portfolio. It should track a broad-based index like the Standard & Poor's 500. The active portion focuses on specialty funds or a particular market segment not covered by the index fund, or that offers the potential for undiscovered market value. Although the active management of some of the new entries is classified as a disadvantage of index funds, active management in this instance works to the advantage of the investor.

Question — What accounts for the differences in returns among mutual fund rankings?

Answer — Although mutual fund rankings take into account both return and risk, this question focuses on the variations in returns reported by various organizations providing mutual fund rankings. A number of factors are responsible. They include:

(1) The time period covered: Not all mutual fund ranking services use the same time period for their calculations, due to publication deadlines. Some use a calendar year while others use only certain quarters of the year. Trying to compare time periods that are not exactly the same will distort data as extraordinary or unusual events occurring during those time periods take effect. A related problem occurs when some ranking sources provide returns for bull and bear markets while others do not. The definition of a bear or bull market is intuitive and varies with the individual. In addition, not all funds were in existence during all the bear and bull markets to-date.

(2) Return figure composition: Total returns consist of capital gains plus income minus the operating expenses of the fund, brokerage costs, and commissions. Fund load charges and redemption fees are not normally included, although this is where the problem arises. Some sources include these load charges which distort the short-term performance of the fund.

(3) Reinvestment of fund distributions: Although almost all sources include the reinvestment of distributions of the fund, not all report these reinvestments at the same time period. Some report reinvested distributions at the end of the month during which the reinvestment

occurred. Others report reinvestment distributions on the exact day of reinvestment which may not be the end of the month. If the fund prices differ when reinvestments are made, the returns will subsequently differ.

(4) How the return performance is reported: Three reporting formats are common. Reporting by dollar returns, annualized returns, or unannualized returns. Each will report a different return since the calculations for each differ and since different time periods are used for the calculations.

Question — What tax strategies should be considered when acquiring mutual fund shares?

Answer — Several strategies are useful. They include:

(1) Time purchases wisely. For the investor, the purchase of mutual fund shares carries the extra burden of the fund's untaxed dividends and capital gains to-date. When distributions are received, the shareholder is taxed on those previously accumulated dividends and gains.

By timing purchases wisely, the investor can reduce his tax liability. Purchasing shares on or soon after the ex-distribution date (the date a shareholder is no longer entitled to the distribution) relieves the investor of this added tax because there is no taxable income to report. This factor is very important if very large capital gains are expected because they carry a large tax burden.

(2) Take advantage of tax deferrals. Taxes on unrealized gains on stocks are deferred until the shares are sold. Because these gains are compounded on a pre-tax basis, tax deferral on the gains results in a lower effective tax rate. The longer the deferral, the lower the tax rate.

Likewise, a stock mutual fund investor obtains the same advantages for as long as the fund holds the appreciated shares. Therefore, the lower the portfolio turnover rate, the better the opportunity for tax deferral.

(3) It is best to try to time the disposition of fund shares so that short-term capital gains can be used to offset long-term capital losses, rather than being treated as ordinary income. A fund's turnover rate is a good indicator of potential short-term gains. A high turnover may mean a greater potential for short-term gains, while a low turnover would indicate a lower proportion of short-term gains.

(4) Maximize mutual fund capital loss carryovers. Because capital losses are not passed on to shareholders, but are offset against capital gains, an investor could use carryover losses to reduce capital gains and subsequent taxes.

Question — What tax strategies should be considered when disposing of mutual fund shares?

Answer — The cost method used when calculating gains and/or losses on partial share purchases and redemptions affects taxable income. Four methods can be used:

(1) Average cost method. An investor whose mutual fund shares are held by a custodian can use this method. The choice of the single-category or double-category method is up to the investor and affects the classification (long-term or short-term) and amounts of taxable gain. The double-category method gives taxpayers greater control over the amount of gains or losses recognized.

(2) Specific Identification Method. This is a more flexible method that allows shareholders to choose the specific portions of shares sold in a partial redemption. Identification of shares sold is required.

(3) FIFO method. This method states that when a sale is made, the shares sold are those purchased earliest. If the price per share has risen since acquisition, then use of this method results in the largest overall gains.

(4) LIFO method. This method assumes the most recently purchased shares are sold. If prices have gone up, gains are reduced.

Investors should choose wisely the cost method used in order to reduce their tax liability.

Question — What are asset allocation funds?

Answer — In recent years, a number of mutual funds referred to as asset allocation funds have been created to offer diversification into asset categories not traditionally offered by conventional mutual funds. Specifically, these funds invest in traditional asset categories of domestic stocks, bonds, and money market instruments; but they also invest in the nontraditional asset categories of foreign stocks and bonds, real estate securities, precious metals securities, commodities, and natural resources. Although mutual funds that invest in one of these nontraditional asset categories have proliferated in recent years, balanced mutual funds, which invest in some mix of common stocks, fixed-income securities (such as bonds and preferred stocks), and money market instruments, were generally the only types of funds that offered a limited kind of asset allocation.

The asset allocation funds attempt to use the imperfect correlations between the nontraditional asset classes and the traditional asset classes to provide either higher returns for a given level of risk or lower risk for a given level of return relative to traditional mutual funds.

However, the term "asset allocation" is used by asset allocation mutual funds in both its strategic and tactical sense. In other words, some asset allocation funds employ strategic asset allocation to broadly diversify with relatively fixed-mix asset proportions invested in traditional as well as nontraditional asset classes. Other asset allocation funds employ tactical asset allocation to time the market and to shift investments among both the traditional and nontraditional asset classes depending on their manager's forecast of economic and market trends.

These asset allocation funds differ from one another in a number of important ways:

(1) By the asset classes that are included or permitted within the portfolio.

• Some funds permit investments in virtually all asset classes.

• Others restrict investments to a subset of all asset classes and, by doing so, may better be described as hybrids between traditional balanced mutual funds and genuine asset allocation funds.

• However, for practical reasons of cost and efficiency, even the asset allocation funds that have virtually no restrictions on the asset classes in which they may invest usually restrict their investment to a subset of all the major asset classes. It is possible to create efficient portfolios (that give the highest potential returns for a given level of risk) while limiting investments to a subset of all asset categories.

(2) By investment strategy and philosophy.

• Some asset allocation funds employ strict strategic asset allocation by applying a fixed-mix asset allocation scheme to their asset categories. In other words, the proportion of the portfolio invested in each asset class remains fixed in all economic and market environments.

• Some asset allocation funds employ unrestricted tactical asset allocation and set no minimum limit on

the amount that must be invested in any one asset class. Fund managers are given the flexibility of investing virtually all or none of the fund's assets in any asset class depending on their assessment of the current economic and market environments.

• Most asset allocation funds set a restricted high/low range on the amount that must be invested in any given asset class. Managers are given limited discretion to shift funds among asset classes when, in their judgment, current economic and market conditions so warrant.

• Some asset allocation funds employ dynamic hedging or portfolio insurance strategies, or permit the use of put and call options, short selling, or stock index futures trading to limit downside risk.

When selecting an asset allocation fund, determine whether a fixed-mix strategic asset allocation strategy or a variable-mix tactical asset allocation best fits your own personal investment philosophy and select from those funds which match your philosophy. Review the fund's prospectus for the following information:

(1) The permitted asset classes (more is generally better).

(2) The asset classes in which the fund has actually invested. Although some funds may permit investments in a broad range of asset classes, they may, in fact, not invest in many or most of those categories. Some of the funds are virtually nothing more than glorified balanced funds with their investments predominantly in U.S. stocks and bonds.

(3) The limits or restrictions on the portfolio weights in each asset category. If you want tactical asset allocation and market timing, more flexible and broad limits may be better. However, if you wish to assure at least some diversification among nontraditional asset classes, look for more restricted ranges or limits on the required investment in each asset class.

(4) Minimum initial and subsequent investments. Some funds have very low or minimal initial required investments and permit additional investment of nominal sums. Others require quite sizable initial and subsequent investments.

(5) Expense ratios. Look at the history (which in many cases may be quite limited) of the fund's expense ratio as a percent of assets being managed. The expense ratio is an indicator of efficiency of management. However, expect expense ratios for asset allocation

funds to be higher on average than for traditional mutual funds. Diversification into more asset classes and into nontraditional asset categories will entail some additional expense.

(6) The use of dynamic hedging techniques or portfolio insurance strategies. The prospectus should explain whether the fund will employ strategies to limit downside performance through various hedging or portfolio insurance techniques. These techniques may be beneficial for investors with a relatively short-term planning horizon. However, for investors with a longer-term planning horizon, the cost of such techniques will generally outweigh the benefits.

Chapter 35

OIL AND GAS

WHAT IS IT?

Exploration for and production of oil and natural gas involves a high degree of risk, large amounts of capital, a great deal of technical expertise, and offers in return, incredible rewards.

The combined efforts and capital of many groups of individuals in the form of corporations (including S corporations), trusts, general and limited partnerships, and joint ventures are necessary to achieve profitable exploration and production.

There are four basic types of oil and gas investments:

(1) exploratory drilling (the search for oil or gas in new areas),

(2) development (the search for oil or gas near previous successful wells),

(3) income (investment in the production of oil or gas reserves already located and drilled), and

(4) diversified (a combination of the first three).

WHEN IS THE USE OF THE TOOL INDICATED?

1. When the investor is in a high income tax bracket and in need of tax shelter.

2. When the investor is psychologically willing and able to take relatively high risks in return for possible large rewards.

3. When the investor desires a completely passive role and does not wish to be actively involved in the operation of the investment.

ADVANTAGES

1. There are a number of major tax advantages associated with an investment in oil and/or gas. These result in both high front-end deductions (often exceeding sixty percent of the initial investment) and a continuing deferral of tax. These tax advantages include:

(a) A deduction is allowed for the depletion of the oil or gas reserves in the ground. There are two types of depletion and an investor must generally use the method that generates the largest deduction. "Percentage depletion" allows for a deduction of a specified percentage of the gross income derived from the property (after reduction for any rents or royalties the investor must pay with respect to that property). The alternative to percentage depletion is "cost depletion" which essentially bases the deduction on proration of the investor's basis in the property between the number of oil or gas units sold during the year and the number of estimated units remaining. Stated as a formula, cost depletion for the tax year is computed as follows:

$$\frac{\text{Investor's Basis}}{\text{Barrels of oil (1,000's of cubic feet of gas) remaining}} \quad X \quad \begin{array}{c} \text{Barrels (cubic feet)} \\ \text{sold during the} \\ \text{taxable year} \end{array}$$

The percentage depletion allowance can be a major tax advantage since it generally will permit a deduction greater than the amount computed on a cost depletion basis and the investor may continue to use it even when the right to use cost depletion has been exhausted. There is an overall annual limitation to the percentage depletion allowance. The annual deduction is limited to 100% of the taxable income (calculated before the depletion deduction) derived from the property.

(b) Intangible Drilling Costs (IDC) incurred in exploratory and development programs (as well as any small amount of IDC associated with an income program) are deductible.

(c) Investors may elect to take an "enhanced oil recovery credit" in lieu of deductions for depreciable property and IDCs equal to 15% of the investor's qualified enhanced oil recovery costs for certain projects begun after December 31, 1990 (the credit is phased out as the price of crude oil exceeds a certain level). The credit is a component of the general business credit; thus, it is subject to the general limitations and carryback and carryforward rules of the general business credit itself.

(d) The interest expenses on funds borrowed to finance the investment are deductible, subject to limitations discussed in Chapter 8, "Income Tax Concepts."

(e) Losses are currently tax deductible, subject to the "passive activity" limitations discussed in Chapter 8, "Income Tax Concepts."

(f) The investor has the potential to receive long term capital gain treatment upon the sale of his or her interest.

(g) If an investor has purchased an interest in the form of a limited partnership unit, within certain limitations, participants (the general and limited partners) can agree to divide up income, deductions, and credits in a manner disproportionate to their ownership interests.

2. The investment required is relatively small when compared with the potential profit. A successful exploratory well could easily produce a return of $10 for every $1 of capital invested. Even development wells have the potential for returning profits that double the taxpayer's investment in a short period of time.

3. Since most investors becoming involved in an oil and gas venture do so as limited partners, their liability is limited to the extent of (a) their capital contributions to the partnership, (b) any contributions investors contractually agree to make in the future, and (c) any partnership debts the investors agree to guaranty in order to leverage their tax benefits.

DISADVANTAGES

1. An investor in oil and gas assumes an extremely high degree of risk if the investment is in exploratory drilling. An investor may lose 100% of capital since only one out of ten "wildcat" wells is successful. However, by participating in only developmental or income drilling, the degree of risk can be reduced. But even with productive wells, success is not guaranteed. Many wells never produce reserves of sufficient quantity to enable a recovery of drilling costs. For these reasons, many advisors recommend that an investor split the total investment among two or three different types of drilling programs.

The chance of drilling a "dry hole" is not the only risk assumed by the investor. Since most investors do not live near enough to the drilling site to constantly inspect operations or monitor costs, the risk of mismanagement and/or fraud is high.

2. The tax advantages of investments in oil and gas are offset by two disadvantages:

(a) the possibility of paying the alternative minimum tax because of preference items, and

(b) the "at risk" and "passive loss" rules.

Two tax advantages of investments in oil and gas, the deduction for IDC on productive wells and the percentage depletion allowance, are considered preference items for certain producers and royalty holders and may result in the required payment of the alternative minimum tax. Only a portion of the intangible drilling cost is considered a preference item. This preference amount is computed using a very complex formula. The amount by which percentage depletion on a property exceeds its tax basis is also a preference. Investors subject to this rule may therefore recover the basis of the property through depletion allowances, but then subject all subsequent percentage depletion to the alternative minimum tax. (For tax years beginning after 1992, these preference rules apply only to integrated oil companies rather than to "independent producers." Because most oil and gas investments qualify as independent producers, the alternative minimum tax should affect fewer investors.)

The current deductibility of "losses" generated by the exploration and exploitation of oil and gas reserves is limited to the amount that the investor stands to lose in the economic sense. This amount that the investor has "at risk" consists of his actual (cash or property) investment in the property plus the amount of partnership debt incurred that the investor may personally be called upon to repay. In other words, a person is at risk to the extent he is not protected against the loss of the money or other property actually contributed or that he may be called upon to contribute.

To the extent the investor may not deduct the loss in the current tax year, the excess may be carried over indefinitely. The excess loss may be deducted in a subsequent year, when the investor has a sufficient amount "at risk" to absorb it.

In addition, investments in oil and gas are subject to the "passive activity" loss limitations (except so-called "working interests" in oil and gas properties).

3. The "time line" of the investment varies, but is often long term (3 to 5 years).

4. The value of an investor's interest can quickly drop due to the volatility of energy prices coupled with increased conservation and reduced consumption.

TAX IMPLICATIONS

The implications of oil and gas as a tax shelter investment have already been described above. Specifically, the investor may hope to achieve three results:

(1) a deduction for intangible drilling costs,

(2) a deduction for percentage depletion, and

(3) a credit for enhanced oil recovery costs.

The investor's tax benefits may be reduced by:

(1) the impact of the alternative minimum tax,

(2) the limitations on the depletion deduction, and

(3) the "at risk" and "passive loss" rules.

ALTERNATIVES

1. "Exotic" tax shelters such as leasing "masters" (plates or recordings) for stamps, recordings, and lithographs as well as movie deals and cattle feeding programs, are all very high risk with possible high return.

2. On the basis of potential tax shelter, certain rental real estate investments would be appropriate for upper-middle to high income investors who are able to take significant risks. (In general, rental real estate is less risky than oil and gas).

WHERE AND HOW DO I GET IT?

Few investors buy a direct interest in oil or gas drilling operations. Those that do acquire a fractional, undivided working interest in a co-owned oil or gas property. Such investors participate in every item of income and expense attributable to the operation in accordance with his fractional ownership interest. Each co-owner signs an operating agreement that names one of the co-owners as the "operator" of each property. The co-ownership arrangement is often considered a partnership for tax purposes and co-owners are taxed

as partners. (There are provisions allowing co-owners to "opt-out" of partnership taxation. If they are willing to take their share of production "in kind" and meet certain other requirements, co-owners can be treated under the tax law as individual owners.)

The advantage of co-ownership over the more popular limited partnership method of investing in oil and gas is that a co-owner's interest is more transferable and has a greater collateral value than a partnership interest. A co-owner may also make his own elections with regard to various tax matters and is not restricted by elections made by the partnership.

The major disadvantage of co-ownership is liability. When compared with the limited partner, the co-owner bears a significantly broader level of risk. Co-ownership involves an investment of more than merely a greater amount of funds than a limited partnership investment; a co-owner must be willing to invest a considerable amount of personal time and effort. Another disadvantage is that co-owners cannot allocate costs with the same flexibility as limited partners, who can make "special" allocations of deductions and credits among themselves.

Most investors prefer the limited partnership as the vehicle for participating in an oil and gas venture. They generally perceive the advantages of limited liability as outweighing the disadvantages of not participating in the operating decisions.

Revenues and costs are shared by partners according to an agreement appropriately termed the "sharing arrangement." Usually, capital costs are allocated to the general partners and tax deductible expenditures are allocated to the limited partners. There are many types of sharing agreements. Most fall into one of the following four categories:

(1) Functional allocation of costs (also known as tangible-intangible allocation). The general partner participates in revenues from the beginning of the venture. The percentage of that participation is decided by agreement among the partners and is often higher than 35%.

This arrangement is very popular because it maximizes the tax deductions of the limited partners. (Limited partners pay costs that are deductible when incurred, while the general partner pays costs that must be capitalized.) The disadvantage of the functional allocation is that limited partners bear both the full cost of drilling unproductive wells and the majority of the cost of drilling productive wells.

(2) Promoted interest. In this type of sharing agreement the general partner arranges to participate in revenues

in excess of his participation in costs. In more simple language, this means that the general partner pays for (say) 8% of costs for a 22% participation in revenues. The 14% difference is the "promoted interest."

(3) Carried interest. Here, limited partners "carry" the general partner with respect to costs. The general partner participates in revenues from the beginning of the venture while paying a relatively minimal share of costs. For example, the general partner may receive more than 10% of the operation's revenues while paying perhaps only 1% or 2% of its costs. The general partner's income interest will typically increase a few more percentage points once the limited partners have recovered their investment from their share of production.

(4) Reversionary interest. The general partner in this method of sharing receives only a small percentage of the revenues and pays only a small portion of the costs until the limited partners have recouped their investment from revenues. At that point the general partner's interest becomes significant. For example, the general partner may begin with a minimal participation in both costs and revenues of only 1%. But after the pay out to the limited partners of their costs, the general partner may share costs and revenues at a level of 20% or greater.

WHAT FEES OR OTHER ACQUISITION COSTS ARE INVOLVED?

There are numerous fees a typical investor in an oil and gas syndication can expect to pay. These include:

(1) sales commissions,

(2) management fees (sometimes given exotic names such as "drilling overseeing fees"),

(3) broker-dealer fees,

(4) loan origination fees and points,

(5) guarantee fees (generally paid to the general partner for such commitments as providing a guaranteed minimum cash flow from the investment), and

(6) other "syndication" fees paid to promoters or syndicators.

These fees will generally range from 13% to 20% of the equity invested in the partnership by the limited partners.

HOW DO I SELECT THE BEST OF ITS TYPE?

As is the case with any other tax shelter, oil and gas sharing arrangements should be measured by the investment standards of risk and cost versus economic reward. Six helpful guidelines in analyzing alternatives are:

(1) Compare the "track records" of the sponsors. Give top rating to a sponsor with established programs (one that has been in business at least seven or eight years) and a history of consistently returning the investors' capital. A lower rating should be given to a program that has been in operation for four to six years and in which the limited partners have received a return of at least 20% of their original investment. Programs that have been in operation for less than four years should typically be considered only by investors with an ultra high risk taking propensity.

(2) Determine the sponsor's success ratio. Compare wells completed and producing to wells drilled. Be careful to look not only at the ratio of success but also the location of the drilling. In certain areas of the country (Pennsylvania, West Virginia, and Ohio) the success ratio should be relatively high. A percentage of 80% to 90% should be expected. In other parts of the country (such as Oklahoma and Alaska), a lower ratio can be expected. A 15% to 20% ratio is considered successful. Of course, it is not only the percentage of completed and producing wells to wells drilled that is important; the amount of oil lifted from the ground and the cost of doing so, measured on a "per well" basis, are equally as important.

(3) Use "time value of money" measurements in the analysis process. In comparing sponsors' histories, check to see how quickly investors' money was returned as well as the amount of each payment. The more quickly the sponsor was able to return investors' money, the better. Also, the financial advisor should consider not only alternative drilling programs, but also alternative investments, other than oil and gas.

(4) Ascertain the location of the wells to be drilled. The reliability of past history is directly proportionate to the location of the wells to be drilled. The sponsor that has been successful in one state or region may now be seeking funds for exploration in an entirely different type of geological formation.

(5) Measure one sponsor's financial participation against another's. Give top grade to the sponsor with the greatest identity of interest with the limited partners.

Identity of interest is reflected in a greater commitment of money and a larger share of the cost. Check to see if the sponsor is compensated merely for each well drilled. Higher scores should go to those sponsors who are in the business of finding oil or gas rather than to those who are in the business of just drilling wells.

Many sponsors will contribute land they already own to the oil or gas partnership. Higher marks should go to sponsors who place that acreage into the venture at their cost. The sponsor should not have the right to pick and choose which acreage will be drilled for its own account. Give low grades to general partners who reserve the right to be selective in the choice of which land they will drill and which land the limited partners' money will be sunk into. An examination should be made of each sponsor's prospectus or offering memorandum for a section describing these and other possible conflicts of interest.

(6) Compare the cost/return ratios. The cost of finding and selling oil and gas entails more than merely finding it and pumping it from the ground. For example, once the oil is removed, it must be transported through pipeline hookups and held in storage facilities until it can be shipped. The investor should compare the cost information provided in the offering materials of the alternative sponsors.

WHERE CAN I FIND OUT MORE ABOUT IT?

1. Lewis D. Solomon, *Taxation of Investments*, (Clifton, NJ, Prentice Hall Law & Business, 1987).

2. *Tax Facts on Investments (Tax Facts 2)* (Cincinnati, The National Underwriter Company).

QUESTIONS AND ANSWERS

Question — What is the difference between a "wildcat," a "step out," and a "deeper test" exploratory program?

Answer — Exploratory programs are organized to drill in areas with no known production. Pure wildcat programs are those that drill in completely unproven territory.

Step out programs involve drilling in unproven areas that are near producing fields. The step out is really an extension of the proven field and serves to test its boundaries.

Deeper test are those programs that extend the limits of a known field in terms of depth rather than surface boundary.

Question — Why are assessments often levied against the investors in oil and gas programs?

Answer — Additional capital is often required of investors to provide funds for drilling costs. An assessment provision in an oil or gas program requires that limited partners must put up more money if called upon to do so by the general partner. Investors who fail to make additional contributions are typically subject to certain penalties that can significantly reduce the viability of the investment. Obviously, the presence or absence of an assessment provision (more likely to be present in development programs) must be considered in the comparison of various ventures and in the overall decision of whether to invest in oil and gas at all.

Question — What items are involved in "intangible drilling and development costs?"

Answer — Intangible drilling costs include labor, fuel, repair, hauling, supply, and other expenditures incurred in

(1) ground clearing,

(2) road making,

(3) surveying and geological work needed to prepare a site for drilling, and

(4) construction of physical structures such as derricks, tanks, and pipelines.

Expenditures to acquire tangible property that has a salvage value are not considered intangible drilling costs. Therefore, the costs incurred to obtain the following items would not be considered intangible drilling costs (although depreciation deductions may be available):

(1) drilling tools,

(2) pipes,

(3) casings,

(4) tubings,

(5) tanks, and

(6) other machinery or materials used in the construction of the wells or on the well sites.

Question — What is the tax treatment of an intangible drilling cost?

Answer — An investor with an interest in oil or gas property has two choices with respect to intangible drilling and development costs: He can (1) capitalize the intangible drilling costs, or (2) deduct it currently in the taxable year the expense is paid or incurred.

In actuality, the election to capitalize or expense intangible drilling costs is made by the general partner. This is another reason that a potential investor should examine the prospectus because the general partner's intent as to this election is stated there. Where the investment is marketed as a tax shelter, the general partner will typically elect to expense the intangible drilling expenses.

Each limited partner can recover his share of capital expenditures on his personal income tax return through depletion or depreciation if the limited partnership elects to capitalize intangible drilling and development costs. On the other hand, if the partnership elects to expense intangible drilling costs, each partner has two choices as to how to treat his allocated share of intangible drilling costs: (1) take a current deduction for the allocable share, or (2) elect to amortize such costs ratably over a 60-month period.

Question — What is a "swap deal?"

Answer — A swap deal is an innovation designed to make oil or gas tax shelter investments more marketable. A newly organized public corporation exchanges shares of its stock for the oil and gas interests of the partnership's investors. Procedurally, after the exchange, the limited partnership is terminated and the individual investors own stock in the new corporation. If properly structured, the swap should be tax free to both the investors and the corporation. Because the investor now owns stock in a publicly traded company, the liquidity of his investment is significantly improved.

Perhaps even more appealing than the increased liquidity, the investor now owns stock which if sold at a profit may give rise to long term capital gain. The transaction has eliminated the exposure of recapture of IDC and depreciation previously deducted individually by the investor. It therefore successfully converts what would

have been ordinary income upon the disposition of the investment into capital gain.

A successful swap deal requires that both parties come to terms as to the value of the investor's oil or gas interest. Its major drawback is that the value of the investor's new interest (the stock) now fluctuates according to the vagaries of the stock market. The future price of the stock may be much more or much less than the value of an investor's share of the underlying oil or gas reserves held by the partnership prior to the exchange.

Question — What is the difference between a "royalty" interest and a "working" interest?

Answer — A land owner owns both the right to the surface of the land and the minerals beneath its surface. It is possible to sever these two rights and sell or lease one without the other. Therefore the owner of the land can retain the surface rights and sell or lease the rights to the minerals under the land.

The owner of the mineral rights in turn can lease or assign either a royalty interest or a working interest. The owner of the mineral rights may grant an operator the right to exploit that interest in return for a fraction of the total production. For instance, an operator who believes a farmer's pasture land may have high oil or gas potential will bargain with the farmer for the right to drill and extract any oil or gas. In return for a lease allowing the operator to drill and extract any oil or gas found, the farmer will be given (technically he reserves) a royalty interest. The exact percentage depends on the operator's expectations as well as the farmer's bargaining abilities. The fraction may be as small as 1/8 or as large as 1/4 of production revenue.

An operator who acquires the right to exploit the minerals under the land has generally acquired a working (operating) interest in the mineral rights. This involves not only the benefits but also the burdens (the operating costs) of extracting the oil or gas.

Few owners of a working mineral interest have the capital to undertake the large and risky task of exploiting the minerals under the land. Therefore, the working owner may assign most of his rights and all of his obligations under the lease to another party. That other party is often a syndicated limited partnership.

Chapter 36

PREFERRED STOCK

WHAT IS IT?

A preferred stock is a hybrid security that combines some of the features of both bonds and common stocks. Most preferred stocks do not carry voting rights under normal circumstances. Preferred stocks, as their name implies, have a preferred position with respect to the earnings of a corporation. Dividends on preferred stocks must be paid before any dividends can be paid to holders of common shares. Owners of preferred stock have precedence over common stockholders with respect to the assets of the corporation in the event of a sale or liquidation of the company.

WHEN IS THE USE OF THIS TOOL INDICATED?

1. When the investor is primarily interested in safety of principal.

2. When a current rate of return on investment at a rate higher than that available from the same company's common stock is desired.

3. When a fixed amount and steady flow of income is needed. Most preferred stocks pay a fixed dollar amount of dividend, or a dividend based on a stated percentage of the preferred stock's par value. For example, Wheeling Pittsburgh Steel Company has a 6% preferred stock issue outstanding with a par value of $100 per share. The stock pays a quarterly dividend of $1.50 ($100 x 6% ÷ 4) per share in January, April, July and October.

4. When the purchaser of the stock is a corporation. Generally, a corporation is entitled to deduct 70 percent of the dividends it receives from other domestic corporations from its taxable income. Therefore, only 30 percent of the dividends received by a corporation are subject to federal income tax.

    If a corporation owned 500 shares of the Wheeling Pittsburgh Steel preferred described above it would receive $3,000 (500 x $6) annually in dividends. The receiving corporation would have to declare 30 percent of those dividends, or $900 (30% x $3,000) as income. The remaining $2,100 would be excluded from federal income taxes.

    Current law allows accumulations of up to $250,000 ($150,000 for most professional corporations) even if the corporation is used to avoid personal income tax by allowing preferred dividends to accumulate at favorable corporate rates.

5. When there is no particular date on which the investor must have his capital returned. Unlike bonds, preferred stocks have no specified maturity date. In order to regain their capital investors must sell their preferred shares. Preferred stocks give investors more control over the timing of their recovery of capital than is true of bonds.

ADVANTAGES

1. Income from preferred shares is relatively certain, especially when compared to dividends on common stock. Typically, dividends on preferred shares are paid on a quarterly basis. While preferred dividends are not a fixed, legal obligation (in the sense that interest on bonds must be paid to avoid default), they must be paid before any common shareholders can receive dividends. Although preferred stockholders typically cannot vote and demand payment of dividends, pressure from common shareholders who want dividend payments will make preferred dividend payments more likely.

    Perhaps even more important than pressure by common shareholders is the generally "cumulative" nature of preferred dividend payments. This means that any preferred dividends that are "passed" (not paid quarterly as anticipated) must be accumulated by the corporation and eventually paid before any dividends can be paid to common stockholders. For example, if Wheeling Pittsburgh Steel skipped payment of a quarterly dividend of $1.50 per share for one year, it would have to make up the arrearage of $6.00 before resuming payment of common stock dividends.

2. The investor's capital is relatively secure. This is because (after bondholders and other creditors) preferred shareholders take precedence over common stockholders in the event of a corporate sale or liquidation. If XYZ Corp. were to be liquidated, for example, any assets remaining after creditors had been paid would be first allocated to

preferred shareholders in proportion to the value of their interests. (In some cases, a corporation may have more than one preferred stock issue outstanding. Each of these issues would be assigned an order of priority in terms of sale or liquidation.)

3. The prices of preferred stocks tend to be more stable than those of common stocks. Common stock prices are affected most directly by changes in corporate earnings, which can be highly erratic. Preferred stock prices are more likely to reflect changes in interest rates, which are relatively less volatile than changes in the earnings of a corporation. This is especially true for high quality preferreds issued by financially sound companies.

However, when interest rates do decline, the prices of preferred shares tend to increase. Obviously, the opposite result occurs when interest rates rise; the price of preferred stocks will typically decline since investors can obtain higher rates on new issues of preferred stock or newly issued bonds.

4. Some preferred stocks are "convertible." This means that they may be exchanged at a predetermined rate for common stock of the same corporation at the discretion of the preferred stockholder. This will be advantageous when the price of common shares is increasing due to the fixed rate of exchange. Therefore, the preferred stock investor will be able to participate in the equity growth in a manner similar to common stockholders while retaining the relative security afforded the preferred shareholders.

DISADVANTAGES

1. The purchasing power of future fixed preferred stock dividends may be eroded by inflation. The longer the holding period of the investment the more likely that the purchasing power of each fixed dollar payment will decline. For instance, assume inflation takes place at a three percent annual rate. A preferred dividend of $10.00 per year will have the purchasing power equivalent of only $7.37 ten years later.

2. Dividend payments on preferred stock will not increase even if the financial condition of the company or the economy improves. Preferred shareholders do not participate in the growth and prosperity of their company in the same way as do common stockholders.

Some preferred stocks are "participating" issues. This means that preferred stockholders may be entitled to payments above the normal level of dividends in certain situations. This would occur once common stockholders had received dividends of a specified amount.

For example, the terms of the preferred stock issue may provide that once common shareholders have received dividends amounting to $5.00 per share, both common and preferred stockholders will share equally in any further dividend payments.

3. Preferred stocks do not provide much opportunity for capital growth. The fixed nature of the dividend payments and the lack of voting rights limit the market's enthusiasm for these issues. (As noted above, however, the convertibility feature of certain preferreds may offset this disadvantage and provide the opportunity for significant capital appreciation.)

TAX IMPLICATIONS

1. Dividends received on preferred stocks are generally taxable at ordinary income rates.

2. Profits on the sale of preferred shares are long-term or short-term capital gains depending on how long the stock has been held by an investor. (See "Capital gain" in the Glossary for an explanation of the holding periods.) *Net capital gains* (i.e., the excess of long-term capital gains over short-term capital losses) are generally taxable at a maximum rate of 20 percent.

3. Losses on the sale of preferred stock are subject to capital loss rules. Certain limits are imposed on the utility of capital losses in offsetting ordinary income. Unused capital losses may be carried forward by individuals and applied against future income.

4. If a share of preferred stock is sold at a loss and then repurchased within a given time period, the investor will be subject to the so-called "wash sale" rules discussed in Chapter 8, "Income Tax Concepts."

5. Dividends received on preferred stocks of domestic corporations are subject to the "dividends received" deduction if the dividends are received by a corporate investor. Up to 30 percent of the dividend will be subject to corporate tax rates.

6. Preferred stocks held at death in the sole name of the investor will be subject to both federal and state death taxes. Fifty percent of preferred stocks held jointly between spouses will be includable in the gross estate of the first joint owner to die but will generate no federal estate tax because of the unlimited marital deduction.

ALTERNATIVES

1. Government, municipal, or corporate bonds generally will provide many of the same characteristics of high quality preferred stocks. Investors should consider bonds that generate a comparable or higher after-tax yield.

2. An investor considering convertible preferred stocks may wish to explore convertible bonds of the same or similar companies.

3. Single-premium deferred annuities providing a fixed annual payment. (Until the annuity payout period begins, this alternative may not be suitable. In addition, unless the annuity has a guaranteed payout or a joint and survivor provision, the value of the annuity, unlike preferred stock, will terminate at the owner's death and provide no benefit to heirs.)

WHERE AND HOW DO I GET IT?

Preferred stocks may be purchased directly through a brokerage firm much like common stock, bonds, or other investments. They may also be purchased through banks which offer brokerage services and through discount brokerage houses.

Quite a few preferred stocks are listed on the organized stock exchanges such as the New York or American stock exchanges. Their listings are shown immediately below the listings for the same company's common stock. However, the majority of preferred issues are unlisted and trade on the over-the-counter market.

The trading in preferred stocks is dominated by corporations and other institutional investors. This is due to the dividends received deduction, discussed above, and tends to work against individual investors. Also, the market for preferred stocks is not as active as the market for common shares and trading volume is relatively low.

Individuals may also invest in preferred stocks indirectly through the purchase of shares in a mutual fund. Income funds, which emphasize a high rate of current return on investment, frequently purchase large blocks of preferred stock. The mutual fund approach offers the added attractions of diversification and professional management in addition to high yield and relative price stability.

WHAT FEES OR OTHER ACQUISITION COSTS ARE INVOLVED?

When preferred stocks are purchased through a broker, a regular sales commission is added to the price of the preferred shares. Typically, this brokerage commission will be two to three percent of the value of the shares purchased. Banks and discount brokers may charge a flat fee of $10 to $40 for buying shares or a fee based on the number of shares purchased regardless of price. For example, one discount brokerage house advertises that it will charge a fee of $0.10 per share no matter what the price of the stock, with a $30 minimum charge.

If shares are purchased indirectly through a mutual fund, the fund's regular sales fee will apply in the case of a "load" fund. If a "no-load" fund is used there will be no sales charge added to the purchase price of the shares. Both types of funds will normally charge a management fee and an account maintenance fee in addition to any sales fees.

HOW DO I SELECT THE BEST OF ITS TYPE?

1. Since preferred stockholders are mainly interested in security and a high yield, the financial condition of the issuer is of primary concern. Investors should evaluate the soundness of the company or rely on the published ratings of firms such as Standard & Poor's or Moody's Investors Services. The following factors will be important in evaluating the company's financial condition:

    (a) The company's earnings record, particularly the growth of earnings or at least a pattern of stable earnings during the past ten years.

    (b) Earnings available to pay preferred dividends should be several times the amount actually required. Preferred stockholders do not have first claim on a company's earnings. Earnings are first used to pay any interest due to bondholders. Then, preferred dividends are paid before any payments are made to common stockholders. The company should have enough earnings to pay interest and dividends even if earnings should decline for a year or two.

    This concept of a "margin of safety" is important due to the limitations placed on the dividends from preferred issues. One prominent investment text states preferreds should be selected "on a recession or depression basis." Since preferred dividends will not be increased no matter how prosperous the firm may be, the investor must be more concerned with the payment of those dividends under the worst of circumstances.

    (c) Since preferred dividends are paid from cash, investors should review the liquidity of the company before they invest. An attractive company will have a substantial cash position as well as large amounts of short-term assets.

(d) The preferred stock issue should be relatively small compared with the other capital of the firm. This means that the amount of preferred dividends will be a small obligation compared with bond interest or even common dividends. This relatively small size generally adds to the overall security of the issue.

2. Investors should compare the dividend yield available from a preferred stock with other issues of apparent similar quality. If one issue offers a rate of return substantially higher than other similar issues, it may be an indication of excessive risk and the stock should be avoided.

3. Depending on their own risk preferences, investors may want to compare the yields available from bonds as an alternative to a preferred stock. Bonds do provide a greater degree of security than preferreds because the interest payments on bonds must be made in order for the firm to avoid bankruptcy. Preferred dividends can be passed, or deferred, even if they are cumulative. This may be difficult for some investors, particularly those who are dependent on a regular flow of investment income.

WHERE CAN I FIND OUT MORE ABOUT IT?

1. Publications from Standard & Poor's and Moody's Investors Services are available at most local libraries. These will provide information on the issuing companies as well as the historical record of any preferred stocks.

2. Major brokerage firms can usually provide information on specific issues as well as current market conditions that may or may not make preferreds attractive for investment.

3. An investor interested in an issue of a particular company can write to the president or treasurer of the firm and request an annual report. This financial statement will provide details on the issue itself as well as the overall financial condition of the company.

QUESTIONS AND ANSWERS

Question — What does it mean when a preferred stock is "cumulative"?

Answer — The cumulative feature is common among preferred stocks. It means that any preferred dividends that are not paid as scheduled must be accumulated by the company and paid at some future date. No specific date is stated, but if any preferred dividends have not been paid the company is normally prohibited from paying any dividends to common stockholders. This feature puts management under pressure to maintain preferred dividends and provides greater security for preferred stockholders.

Question — When would a "convertible" preferred stock be a desirable investment?

Answer — A convertible preferred would be attractive when the price of the company's common stock is expected to go up. The price of the preferred will increase along with the common, but not necessarily in direct proportion. Rather than convert their stock, preferred shareholders may continue to hold it, particularly if the preferred dividend yield is higher than that on the common stock.

Question — Does preferred stock have voting rights?

Answer — Generally not. In exchange for their preferred status in regard to dividends and liquidation, preferred shareholders give up voting control of the corporation to common stockholders. However, if preferred dividends are in arrears, preferred stockholders may be given the same voting rights as common stockholders.

Question — Are preferred dividends taxable if the company has no earnings but continues to pay dividends?

Answer — If a company has no earnings, then any "dividends" paid to stockholders, whether common or preferred, are really a return of capital and are not taxable as income to the shareholder. Under these circumstances dividends are not considered taxable income, but shareholders must reduce the cost basis of their stock to reflect the pay out of capital. This will result in a larger amount of taxable capital gain when the stock is eventually sold.

Chapter 37

PUBLICLY TRADED (MASTER) LIMITED PARTNERSHIPS

WHAT IS IT?

A publicly traded limited partnership (PTP), including what has frequently been called a "master limited partnership," (MLP) is a limited partnership whose units are traded on an organized exchange, in the over-the-counter market, or in a well-established secondary market created by investment bankers or other institutions or persons. A PTP allows unit holders to trade their units in a manner similar to common stock in a corporation. As such, PTPs provide the tax attributes of a partnership with the liquidity and convenience of a stock. The PTP form provides a mechanism for distributing cash flow to investors without double taxation (corporate tax and individual tax) because partnerships are not generally taxable entities.

The Revenue Act of 1987 contains provisions to tax certain PTPs as corporations. Many existing PTPs became subject to the corporate tax rules as of December 31, 1997. Others are exempt from the rules altogether. Also, certain PTPs may elect out of the corporate tax rules. These exceptions are discussed in more detail below under "Tax Implications."

WHEN IS THE USE OF THIS TOOL INDICATED?

Most PTPs may be viewed as hybrid securities which combine the income attributes of yield-oriented investments with the equity appreciation (or fluctuation) potential of common stock. Investors looking for investments with these characteristics can find PTPs operating in the following industries:

(1) real estate ownership,

(2) hotels and motels,

(3) fast food franchises,

(4) oil and gas,

(5) natural gas pipelines,

(6) timber,

(7) agriculture,

(8) cable television,

(9) mortgage banking,

(10) home building,

(11) real estate and land development,

(12) nursing and retirement homes,

(13) equipment leasing, and others.

Most PTPs have been formed to operate mature businesses having relatively low risk and high distributable cash flow. They have typically been structured to appeal to the retail individual investor looking for liquidity and a high current cash-on-cash yield. An ideal candidate for the PTP form of business is a firm that has substantial cash flow not required for reinvestment which could be distributed to investors.

PTPs are formed for several reasons using several different methods including "roll-ups," "original acquisitions," "roll-outs," and "liquidations." PTPs originated in the oil and gas industry and were formed by "rolling up" several existing untraded partnerships into a PTP by means of an exchange offer. Roll-ups are now used in a variety of industries. In a roll-up transaction, limited partners in existing private partnerships are offered the opportunity to exchange their interests for interests in the PTP. This accomplishes several goals:

(1) relatively small, limited-asset-base partnerships are combined to form a pool of assets that is substantially larger (and therefore often stronger) in terms of value of assets and diversity of assets (adding safety);

(2) investors accepting the exchange offer receive a liquid security with a determinable market value and loan value in exchange for their illiquid and unmarginable holdings;

(3) Because of its broader base of pooled assets, the PTP may realize operating efficiencies and have greater access to financing at lower costs; and

(4) the PTP may have a greater capacity for growth because of its enhanced ability to finance its operations and to make acquisitions.

The success of the roll-up PTPs led to the use of PTPs in other cases. Original acquisition PTPs are formed as PTPs from the start. They invest in properties similar to those in which normal untraded limited partnerships seeking income tend to invest. But original acquisition PTPs, unlike normal untraded limited partnerships, provide immediate liquidity to unit holders. The PTP issues units to the public for cash which is used to purchase assets, often from the sponsor, who is also the PTP general partner. In some cases these PTPs are organized as "blind pools" to buy unidentified assets of a certain type — for instance, apartment complexes or producing oil and gas properties.

"Roll-out" PTPs are formed when corporate-owned assets are transferred to a newly formed PTP in exchange for units. These units are then sold to the public. Roll-out PTPs are created principally to serve the interests of the corporation that rolls the assets out of its corporate structure. For example, a roll out may help the corporation avoid a takeover bid or it may be a less costly method of raising capital than issuing stock or using retained earnings. The roll-out PTP is similar to taking a subsidiary public. This technique serves several purposes including:

(1) cash flow and/or losses can be transferred to a separate entity, which may result in a more efficient market valuation for these assets than when the assets are included with other assets inside the corporation;

(2) for companies valued on the basis of cash flow, the PTP structure ensures that valuation methodology will still be valid and appropriate when the PTP operation begins incurring a tax liability; and

(3) when the operations begin generating taxable income, all or a portion of the cash flow may still be distributable without a double (corporate and individual) taxation (but see "Tax Implications").

Finally, many PTPs have been formed when a corporation was completely liquidated. Prior to the Tax Reform Act of 1986, generally no gain would be recognized (subject to certain exceptions for recapture of depreciation and other expenses) when the corporation issued PTP units in a complete liquidation. However, with the repeal of this favorable tax treatment under the Tax Reform Act of 1986, very few, if any, new PTPs will be formed with this result as an objective.

ADVANTAGES

1. Liquidity. The principal advantage of PTPs is liquidity. Unit holders can trade their units in a ready market at short notice and at well established market values. In contrast, although interests in larger untraded partnerships may often be traded, the market is a "thin" agency market, not an auction market where bid and ask prices are constantly quoted. As a result, if an untraded partnership unit must be sold in the early years the price is usually at a substantial discount to original cost.

2. Limited Liability. Similar to investments in untraded limited partnership interests and common stock investments, PTP investors generally can lose no more than they have paid for their units plus their share of any undistributed income. They are typically protected from claims against the partnership.

3. High Current Yield. To support secondary markets, current yields are usually a lot higher for PTPs than for untraded partnerships. The businesses that are most attractive for PTP purposes are generally those that have a high cash flow which is not required for reinvestment in the business. Non traded partnerships often have other objectives of principal importance such as some potential for tax shelter or an emphasis on capital appreciation rather than income.

In some cases, PTPs artificially support yields through the use of zero-coupon financing, subordinated or deferred general partnership interests, additional purchase of limited partner units by the general partner with the proceeds paid to existing LP units, or borrowing to pay cash distributions, especially in the early years. This acceleration of benefits may improve overall performance, but not without a potential downside. Cash distributions may fall after the support period. In addition, most support techniques dilute ownership or increase debt, potentially reducing the long-term investment value of the units. If earnings on the PTPs assets do not grow as anticipated to make up for the advanced funding of distributions, the market value of the PTP units could fall substantially.

4. Investment Flexibility. The general partner of a PTP is generally able to sell and repurchase assets, enabling active portfolio management and changes in the portfolio's diversification and/or asset mix over time. PTPs are more like actively managed investment companies than traditional non traded partnerships. A PTP is similar to a "sector" mutual fund that invests in one particular industry or sector of the economy. Non traded partnerships are

generally more like unit trusts because they do not generally reinvest asset sale proceeds.

5. Avoidance of Corporate Tax. PTPs that qualify under the "passive-type income" test, described below, are not taxed as corporations. Also, certain PTPs may elect out of corporate taxation in exchange for paying a small rate of tax on the PTPs gross income. Consequently, investors enjoy most of the benefits of the corporate form of ownership, in particular, limited liability and liquidity, without the adverse double taxation on income.

DISADVANTAGES

1. Basis of Valuation and Price Volatility. The return from an untraded partnership must ultimately reflect the performance of the underlying assets. But the return on a PTP may not. Because PTPs are valued principally on the basis of their cash flow, the return on a PTP will reflect changes in interest rates, possibly the performance of the stock market, and only partly the performance of the underlying assets. PTP units tend to sell on the basis of current yield and not on asset value. Similar to common stock, but in contrast to untraded LP units, the PTP's market price may not reflect the liquidation value of the underlying assets. Consequently, the prices of PTP units will generally fluctuate with more volatility than the underlying assets in the PTP's portfolios.

2. Uncertain Front-end Costs. Front-end costs on untraded limited partnerships are spelled out in the offering circular. Although investments in PTPs also involve the equivalent of front-end costs, the costs are not easily identified.

3. Timing Risk. Most untraded limited partnerships have limited lives of from 6 to 12 years and are typically purchased with the intent to hold the units until the partnership is liquidated. In contrast, most PTPs have longer lives ranging from 30 to 40 years or longer. Consequently, PTP investors must decide when is the "right time" to sell.

4. Interest Rate Risk. Because PTPs generally emphasize cash flow, they tend to be valued on the basis of their yield. Consequently, the values of PTP units, similar to other yield-oriented investments such as preferred stocks and bonds, will tend to fluctuate inversely with changes in interest rates.

5. Tax Risk. Tax risks are significantly greater for PTPs than for untraded limited partnerships. Also, the application of partnership tax rules to PTPs is much more complicated than to untraded limited partnerships. The tax implications for PTPs are discussed in more detail below.

TAX IMPLICATIONS

1. Taxation as Corporations. The Revenue Act of 1987 contains provisions to tax "traded" partnerships — PTPs — as corporations rather than as partnerships, with *certain important exceptions*. Generally, partnerships are not taxable entities; all income and loss and other tax attributes, such as credits and intangible drilling costs, flow through to the partners according to the partnership agreement. Therefore, tax is determined at the partner level and is paid only once. A PTP that is taxed as a corporation will have to pay tax on income at the entity level and unit holders will again have to pay tax on a personal level when cash is distributed, similar to when a corporation earns income and then pays dividends on its stock.

The tax difference between a partnership (single direct tax to partners) and a corporate (tax at both the corporate and personal levels) characterization can be significant. Assuming, for example, a 34% corporate tax rate and a 28% investor tax rate, the effective tax rate on income can be as high as 52.5% if the partnership is taxed as a corporation. (For instance, the tax on $100 of income taxed at the corporate rate of 34% is $34, leaving only $66 left to distribute to investors. If the $66 that is distributed to investors is taxed at a 28% rate, the tax on the distribution is $18.48 (.28 x $66). The total tax paid on the $100 of income is therefore $52.48 ($34 + $18.48), for an effective tax rate of 52.5%.) In contrast, income from a partnership that is not taxed as a corporation is taxed only at the investor's tax rate of 28%.

A publicly traded partnership for the purpose of these corporate tax provisions is defined as any partnership traded on an "established securities market" (such as the New York or American Stock Exchanges or the over-the-counter market) or "readily tradable" on a secondary market. "Readily tradable" means price quotes can be regularly obtained from persons or institutions "making a market" in the units. A person or institution that "makes a market" in a security generally keeps an inventory of securities and offers to buy and sell the securities at quoted bid and ask prices which change up or down as the volume of trading and values fluctuate. If an investor has the opportunity to sell units with the speed characteristic of a market maker, even if there is no readily identifiable market maker, the partnership will be treated as publicly traded.

However, trading on computerized systems or other "informal" secondary markets, such as NAPEX (National Partnership Exchange), will not generally cause a partnership to be considered publicly traded. Also, if general partners or partnerships occasionally repurchase, or offer to repurchase, units or assist in identifying and bringing together buyers and sellers, the partnership will not generally be considered publicly traded. In contrast, a regular and ongoing redemption program would generally be considered a secondary market which would cause the partnership to be considered publicly traded.

The exemption from the corporate tax provisions hinges on the characterization of the partnership's income. If a partnership generates income, 90% or more of which is "passive-type" income, it retains its flow-through character and is exempt from the corporate tax provisions. "Passive-type" income includes income derived from:

(a) interest;

(b) dividends;

(c) real property rents;

(d) gains from the disposition of real property;

(e) exploration, development, mining, production, processing, refining, transportation, or marketing of minerals and natural resources;

(f) disposition of a capital asset; or

(g) commodities and their related futures, forward contracts and options.

Many (but not all) real estate PTPs and virtually all oil and gas/natural resource PTPs and certain pipeline and hydrocarbon transporting partnerships are exempt from the corporate tax provisions. Because not all interest and rent is passive-type, not all real estate or mortgage-loan PTPs will escape corporate taxation. The types of real estate PTPs that are likely to escape the corporate tax provisions are those investing in shopping centers, income properties, and home building. Restaurant and hotel or motel PTPs are likely to be taxed as corporations.

A PTP that was "grandfathered" from being taxed as a corporation until December 31, 1997 may continue to be exempt from corporate taxation after 1997 if the partnership makes an election and consents to pay a 3.5 percent tax on the gross income from the PTP's active trades and businesses.

An existing PTP will lose its exemption if, during the exemption period, it adds a substantial new line of business. A substantial new line of business is one that is not closely related to a preexisting line of partnership business. However, the new activity will not be considered substantial if the partnership does not derive more than 15% of gross income from the new line and does not devote more than 15% of the value of partnership assets to the business. The new line of business also will not be considered substantial to the extent it generates passive-type income. However, existing PTPs may expand their current lines of business and issue new units without triggering corporate taxation.

2. Net passive income from a PTP is classified as investment income. Before the Revenue Act of 1987, PTPs were a popular way to generate passive-activity income to offset losses from other passive activities. Under the prior rules, most limited partnership interests were automatically treated as passive activities subject to the passive-activity loss rules enacted under the Tax Reform Act of 1986. Income from PTPs, other than actual portfolio-type income (such as interest, dividends, and the like) was passive-activity income that could be used to offset passive-activity losses from an investor's other passive activities. Now, income from PTPs can no longer be used to offset losses from other passive-activity investments or PTPs.

Furthermore, passive losses from PTPs retain their passive-activity character and, consequently, cannot be used to offset an investor's other earned or portfolio income. Losses are suspended and may be used only to offset income in later years from the same PTP. When a PTP is sold, any unused losses first offset gains from the sale, then passive income from other partnership investments, and finally any remaining losses offset any other income or gains.

3. PTP income is UBTI (Unrelated Business Taxable Income) when received by tax-exempt organizations. This provision of the Revenue Act of 1987 acts to close the institutional equity market to PTPs. Tax-exempt organizations, such as hospitals, schools, and charitable organizations must recognize and pay tax on income from PTP units acquired after December 17, 1987.

4. Tax Complexity. To trade effectively, PTP units must be fungible — that is, one unit must be treated for tax and economic purposes just like any other unit in the PTP. This introduces a number of complications into the tax accounting and tracing necessary whenever units are traded.

Many PTPs do not make Code section 754 elections. Because of this, each purchaser of units may have, as his or her share of the basis of PTP properties, a basis different than the price paid for the units. The reason PTPs do make the election is because thousands of units may be traded in any given year and the administrative burdens can become exorbitant, even with the aid of computers. Also, because units will be traded at different prices and on different dates, difficulties will arise in assigning the various purchase prices and holding periods through the PTP to the tax basis of the underlying assets. Certain assumptions would need to be made to make the election workable. These assumptions may not conform with the "letter" of the law and consequently could result in adverse IRS rulings.

ALTERNATIVES

1. Real Estate Investment Trusts (REITs). REITs are mutual fund-like investment vehicles that invest in real estate and/or real estate mortgages. There is no tax at the entity (REIT) level, so the double taxation of the corporate form is avoided, similar to PTPs. REITs must distribute most of their income and shareholders are taxed on the income when it is distributed, just as with dividends on common stock. If the REIT has taxable losses, the losses do not flow through to investors as they would with most PTPs. In addition, REITs have restrictions on the type of property in which they may invest and on how actively the portfolio of assets may be managed which do not apply to PTPs. REITs are covered more fully in Chapter 41.

2. Sector Funds. Sector funds are mutual funds that invest in the common stocks of firms in specific sectors or segments of the market. (See Chapter 34.) Similarly, PTPs generally invest in the assets or businesses of one sector of the market. Similar to PTPs (that are not subject to the corporate tax provisions), sector funds are not subject to tax at the entity (Fund) level and, consequently, there is no double taxation of income. The funds are required to distribute virtually all of their income and capital gains which are then subject to tax at the shareholder level. In contrast, PTPs may, but usually do not, retain income to purchase additional assets and to fund further growth. However, they often do use the proceeds from sales of assets to acquire additional assets rather than to distribute income to investors. Income and gains from sector funds and net passive income from a PTP are treated as investment income for tax purposes. Any sector fund tax losses do not flow through to investors as they do with PTPs. However, a net passive loss from a PTP cannot be aggregated with other passive losses of the investor.

3. Untraded Limited Partnerships. Many untraded limited partnerships are available that have investment characteristics similar to PTPs. (See the Question and Answer section below for a comparison of the investment characteristics of untraded limited partnerships and PTPs.) Although selling interests in untraded limited partnerships is difficult and may result in loss, the market is not entirely illiquid. NAPEX (the National Partnership Exchange, based in Tampa, Florida) is a computer network of bid/ask prices for large, but irregularly traded, limited partnerships. NAPEX also publishes the quarterly *Trade Price Reporter* which lists prices for recent exchanges of limited partnership interests.

WHERE AND HOW DO I GET IT?

Many of the PTPs available are traded on organized exchanges or on the over-the-counter market and can be acquired from brokers and investment bankers in the same manner as common stocks. Other partnership units that will now be treated as "publicly traded," although not traded on an exchange, are generally available from the promoter/sponsor of the partnership.

WHAT FEES OR OTHER ACQUISITION COSTS ARE INVOLVED?

For units traded on organized exchanges, the acquisition fees are similar in amount to commissions for common stock purchases of comparable dollar outlays. However, units are usually priced in thousands of dollars, rather than in tens or hundreds of dollars, as is common for stocks. Consequently, the necessary minimum outlay is generally higher than the minimum required for a common stock purchase. However, because common stocks are generally purchased in "round lots" (multiples of 100 shares), for most investors the amount expended for stocks or for PTP units will be comparable in amount.

For units traded on the over-the-counter market or with a "market maker," the cost is essentially equal to the difference between the bid and ask price quotes. The bid-ask spread will generally vary over time and will depend on both the number of units outstanding and the volume of trading. The bid-ask spread will tend to be larger when the number of units outstanding is larger and when the trading volume is higher.

HOW DO I SELECT THE BEST OF ITS TYPE?

Several factors combine to make the selection of PTPs a difficult process. First, partnerships typically have more involved tax possibilities, basis allocation rules, and accounting methods than stocks. Second, information is not reported in the same manner and in the same depth for partnerships as it is for most stocks. Third, institutional investors and brokerage firms have tended not to follow the PTP market as closely as the market for stocks and so less institutional research has been available for these investments. Fourth, the PTP market is relatively new — the first PTP having been offered in 1981 — and so there is very little history on which to base evaluations and make performance comparisons.

To a great extent, investors must rely on a PTP's management and the due diligence of the firm that brought the PTP public. As for management, look for a track record in partnership management beyond 5 years. In particular, be sure the management is experienced in the particular business in which the PTP is engaged. Check to see whether any of the other properties the management has purchased or partnerships they have managed are in financial trouble.

Because yield is the most important factor when valuing most PTPs, compare the promised yield with that of bonds. Keep in mind that yields are sometimes initially artificially supported above the earnings from the business with the anticipation that earnings growth in later years will provide the funds necessary to "repay" for the earlier support. Supporting yields may increase the overall investment performance but it does involve downside risks. Most support techniques dilute ownership or increase debt, which may reduce the long-term return from the investment. In addition, especially if the yield support technique involves the use of borrowing, unit values may become more sensitive to changes in interest rates and overall price volatility may increase. Finally, because the level of distributions may drop off significantly after the period of support, yield supports may affect the investor's ability to sell the PTP units without suffering a capital loss. This would generally be avoided only if the investor holds the units until the annual earnings grow back to the initial support level.

The risk involved with support techniques will generally decline when the initial spread between the PTP earnings and the advertised yield is small. Clearly, the larger the initial gap, the more earnings must grow during the support period to avoid a decline in the market value of the PTP.

The Stanger Organization (see references below) publishes the Stanger MLP Index which measures the performance of MLPs (PTPs) and periodically ranks the individual performance of all of the PTPs in the market.

WHERE CAN I FIND OUT MORE ABOUT IT?

1. *The Stanger Report: A Guide To Partnership Investing* (published by Robert A. Stanger & Co., LP, P.O. Box 7490, 1129 Broad Street, Shrewsbury, N.J. 07702) is a monthly newsletter with articles and data on PTPs and other partnerships.

2. *The Stanger Register* (published by Robert A. Stanger & Co., LP) is a monthly magazine with articles on the investment environment, investment product ideas, financial planning ideas, and departments on mutual funds and partnership listings and rankings.

3. *Investment Limited Partnerships Law Report* (published by Clark Boardman Callaghan, 375 Hudson Street, New York, NY 10014) is a monthly newsletter typically addressing in considerable detail each month one particular topic concerning the legal and tax aspects of limited partnership investments.

4. *Investment Limited Partnerships Handbook* (published by Clark Boardman Callaghan) is an annual compendium of up-to-date, authoritative information on all aspects of limited partnership investments.

5. The *Wall Street Journal, Barrons, Forbes, Financial Planning* and various other financial news journals and magazines and various tax and accounting journals provide occasional articles on PTPs and other partnership investments.

QUESTIONS AND ANSWERS

Question — What types of businesses do PTPs invest in?

Answer — PTPs tend to invest in businesses that have high cash yields that can be distributed to investors. Largely, this includes oil and gas exploration and production, oil and gas distribution and processing, real estate operating businesses (fast food and restaurants, motels and hotels, principally), real estate income properties or mortgage loans, other natural resources, and services, media, and the like.

Question — How do PTP units compare with common stock?

Answer — Units of PTPs that are now taxed as corporations are virtually identical to common stocks from the investor's perspective. Units of the PTPs that are exempt from the corporate tax provisions will combine features of both common stock and limited partnership investments. Fig-

Figure 37.1

COMPARISON OF PTP UNITS AND COMMON STOCK	
Common Stock	**PTP Units**
	Personal Liability
None.	No personal liability for limited partners, except to the extent that return of capital contributions are wrongfully made or are necessary to meet obligations to creditors. General liability for partnership debts is imposed only on those limited partners who are, in effect, silent general partners.
	Organizational Life
Infinite life.	Has finite life but can be structured to have infinite life. However, majority approval of unit holders is required to continue with a new general partner if and when the general partner withdraws, dies, or is declared bankrupt. The general partner may be a corporation. Must be reformed if over 50% of units are traded in one year.
	Voting Rights
Each shares entitles its owner to cast one vote in the election of directors and any other matter in which voting is permitted or required.	The general partner has total management responsibility; there is no board of directors. Limited partners have limited voting rights on matters relating to the partnership.
	Cash Distributions
Each share entitles its owners to common stock dividends from funds legally available for that purpose as declared by the board. No cash distributions are specified in the corporate charter.	Each unit entitles its holder to distributions from available partnership cash flow legally available for that purpose as designated by the general partner. Intended cash distributions may be stated in the partnership agreement.
	Liquidation Rights
Each share entitles its owner to receive a prorated share of any assets available for holders of common stock on liquidation of the corporation.	Each unit entitles its owner to receive a prorated share of any assets available for holders of units on liquidation of the partnership.
	Liquidity
Liquid markets for publicly traded shares on organized exchanges and over-the-counter.	Liquid markets for publicly traded units on organized exchanges and over-the-counter.

Figure 37.1 (continued)

COMPARISON OF PTP UNITS AND COMMON STOCK	
Common Stock	**PTP Units**

Ability to Attract Funds

Established record of acquiring large levels of funding in financial markets attributed to divisibility of ownership into transferable shares, liability, liquid market for shares, and infinite life.	Expected to establish a record of acquiring large levels of funding based on attributes of divisibility of ownership into transferable units, limited liability, liquid market for units, and infinite life.

Reporting Requirements

Subject to the requirements of the Exchange Act of 1934 must file quarterly and annual reports. Must report net taxable income and dividends paid to shareholders.	Subject to the requirements of the Exchange Act of 1934 must file quarterly and annual reports. Must allocate income or losses among the partners, report on form K-1 to the partners their shares of income or loss in total and by state, allocate each partner's gain on the sale of partnership interests as to ordinary income or capital gain. If a Section 754 election is made, the MLP must prepare individualized computations for each transferee partner. Must report to partners any adjustments proposed by auditors.

Restrictions on Ownership

Citizens of some foreign countries are restricted from owning stock in firms in certain industries.	Citizens of some foreign countries are restricted from being partners in certain industries under U.S. or state statutes. Oil and gas leases are one example.

Taxation

Taxable entity with respect to income after allowable deductions and credits. Shareholders are not taxed with respect to company income, but are taxed on dividends from the company after allowable exclusions. Capital gain or loss based on the difference between shareholder's cost per share and amount realized per share is recognized on the sale of shares.	Not a taxable entity (unless taxed as corporation). Each unit holder includes his/her share of the income, deductions, and credits attributable to the partnership operations in computing his/her taxable income, without regard to the cash distributed to him/her. Cash distributions themselves are not taxable to the extent they do not exceed the unit holder's basis. Gain or loss based on the difference between unit holder's basis and the amount realized is recognized on the sale of units. Losses on unit sales are capital losses; gains may be a combination of ordinary income and capital gain.

Figure 37.2

COMPARISON OF INVESTMENT CHARACTERISTICS: PTPS VERSUS UNTRADED PARTNERSHIPS		
Characteristics	**PTPs**	**Untraded Partnerships**
Liquidity	Marketable	Limited marketability
Current Yield	Higher, often artificially	Lower
Offering Costs	8%-10%, true costs hard to judge	12%-30%
Asset Acquisition	By Appraisal	Actual transaction
Investment Risk/Growth	Similar to Untraded Partnerships	Similar to PTPs
Stock Market/Interest Rate Risk	Significant	Limited
Price Discount From Asset Value	Depends on interest rates	Large initially, but narrows to zero
Marginable	Yes	No
Tax Risks	Significant	Some, but more limited than PTPs
Portfolio Management	Can change assets	More like a unit trust
Diversification	Generally limited	Varies
Investment Decisions	Continuous	Once, on purchase

Reprinted with permission from *The Stanger Register*, September 1987.

ure 37.1 shows a comparison of the features of PTP units with common stock.

Question — How do units of PTPs that are not subject to the corporate tax provisions compare with interests in untraded partnerships?

Answer — The principal and most significant difference between PTP units and interests in untraded limited partnerships is the liquidity of the investment. However, they differ in other ways as well. Figure 37.2 shows a comparison of the investment characteristics of PTP units and untraded partnership interests.

Question — How does a real estate PTP compare with a real estate investment trust (REIT)?

Answer — First, a PTP, unless taxed as a corporation, is a "complete" pass-through entity that passes through income and losses and other tax attributes, such as credits and depreciation, to investors. Tax is determined and paid entirely at the investor's level and at the investor's rate. REITs are "net" pass-through entities — that is, items of income and loss, credits and depreciation are determined at the entity level. Although the REIT will pay no tax at the entity level if it meets the cash distribution requirements, distributions are still treated as dividends and taxed as such to investors. If the REIT realizes a taxable loss, the loss cannot be passed through to investors, except to the extent that it may be reflected in share price values when a shareholder sells his or her shares. Note, however, that while income from a REIT and net passive income from a PTP is treated as investment income, a net passive loss from a PTP retains its passive character and such a loss cannot be aggregated with other passive losses of the investor. Also, the $25,000 rental real estate exemption under the passive loss rules is available with respect to a publicly traded partnership only with respect to the rehabilitation and low-income housing credits.

Second, PTPs have operating and management benefits over REITs because REITs are restricted to passively, rather than actively, managing properties in the portfolio.

Finally, REITs have restrictions on the types of properties in which they can invest that do not apply to real estate PTPs.

For further discussion of REITs, see Chapter 41.

Chapter 38

PUT AND CALL STOCK OPTIONS

WHAT IS IT?

A call option is a contract which gives the holder the right to purchase a specified number of shares of common stock at a fixed price for a stated period of time. For example, an investor who anticipated an increase in the price of AT&T stock could purchase a call option for 100 shares instead of the stock itself. The call option could have a term of up to nine months and would have a fixed exercise price. At any time during the period of the contract the holder could exercise his option and purchase 100 shares of the stock at the stated price regardless of how high the actual price of AT&T had risen.

A put option is a contract which gives the holder the right to sell a specified number of shares of common stock at a set price for a given period of time. For example, if an individual owned 100 shares of AT&T and expected the price of the stock to decline, he could purchase a put option giving him the right to sell his shares at a stated price any time during the term of the option contract regardless of the actual market price of AT&T stock.

Most investors typically think of either buying or selling the stock itself. But, since both puts and calls are property, these may be bought or sold independently of the underlying stock. Investors may buy or sell either of these contracts depending upon their own investment strategies. For instance, Charlee Leimberg expects AT&T to increase in value and therefore buys a call that gives her the right to purchase the stock at a fixed price, say $65, for the next six months. Assume that the current market price of AT&T is $62 per share. The cost of her call option might be $2 per share, or $200 for the contract.

If the market price of AT&T stock were to jump to $70 per share, the value of her call would also increase. The minimum value of the contract would be $500 (the difference between the market price of $70 and her exercise price of $65 times the 100 shares of the contract). The value of her contract could actually be higher than $500 if the contract still had a significant amount of time until the expiration date. That is because investors might anticipate further appreciation in the value of the stock which in turn would be reflected in the price of the call option.

Charlee's sister, Lara, might have an entirely different opinion about the price of AT&T stock. If she expects the price to decline, she may decide to sell a call on 100 shares of the stock. This means that Lara would be on the "other side" of her sister's transaction; she would receive $200 in return for agreeing to sell 100 shares of the stock at a price of $65 per share any time during the next six months. If the price of AT&T remains below $65 per share, Charlee will let her option to buy the stock expire, and the right which she never used will have cost her $200.

Lara will have a profit of $200 from the transaction and will not have to deliver the stock.

Put options work in the opposite fashion from a call. An investor would buy a put if he expected a stock's price to decline. The put would give him the right to sell at a fixed price higher than the actual market price of the stock. If John Mullen expects AT&T to decline from its current price of $62 per share, he could purchase a put option that would give him the right to sell the stock at a price of $60. If the share price were to fall to $58, he could exercise his option and receive $60 per share instead of the lower market price.

The seller of a put contract expects the market price of the stock to remain stable or to increase. John's associate, Mike Dunleavy, feels that the price of AT&T will not go below $60 per share and offers to sell a put at that price for $1 per share. If he is correct, then the option will not be exercised, he will not have to purchase the stock, and he will have a profit of $100. If the stock's price does decline, the option will be exercised, and Mike will have to purchase the stock for $60 per share even though the actual market price may be significantly less. His "loss" will be offset by the $100 premium he received for writing the contract.

WHEN IS THE USE OF
THIS TOOL INDICATED?

1. When investors wish to speculate on a movement in the stock market—either up or down—without actually buying or selling stocks themselves.

2. When an investor wishes to create a leveraged situation in his investment portfolio. In this case the leverage comes about due to the fixed price at which either a put or a call contract is exercised. This price, also referred to as the "striking price," does not change during the life of the

contract regardless of the movements in the price of the underlying stock.

For example, assume a stock is currently selling for $60 per share. A call option is available on that same stock and has an exercise price of $55 per share. The option alone will sell for at least $5 per share and possibly more. If the price of the underlying stock were to double to $120 per share, the investor who merely purchased the stock would have a gain of 100%. If the stock did increase to $120 per share, the value of the option would increase to at least $65 per share ($120 minus the exercise price of $55). This is an increase of 1300%, a 1200% advantage over the purchase of the stock.

3. When an investor has limited funds but still wishes to speculate with some of his investments. Puts and calls are generally traded at small fractions of the price of their underlying stocks. For example, if General Motors stock were selling at $70 per share, a call option to purchase 100 GM shares at an exercise price of $70 might trade for $200 to $300.

4. When an investor wishes to generate additional income from a stock portfolio by selling call options on shares in his portfolio to speculators. The seller or "writer" of these options receives a fee or "premium" for taking part in the contract. For instance, Lara Leimberg, in the example above, received $200 for selling a call contract.

5. When an investor desires to "hedge" a stock or his entire portfolio against unexpected moves in the price of the stock. John Mullen, in the example above, was protecting himself against a substantial decline in the value of his AT&T shares by buying a put contract guaranteeing him a right to sell his stock at a minimum price of $60 per share.

ADVANTAGES

1. The fixed exercise price of these option contracts creates a *leverage* factor which may be advantageous to the investor. For example, if a common stock were to double in value, a 100% increase, the value of a call option on the same stock might increase as much as 500% or more.

2. Option trading requires a relatively small investment on the part of the investor.

3. Income earned from the sale of either put or call contracts is paid to the investor immediately no matter what the term of the contract may be.

DISADVANTAGES

1. Leverage operates in both directions and a decline (rise) in the price of a stock will typically result in a much larger percentage loss for the buyer of a call (put) option. For example, if stock purchased at $60 per share were to drop to $30, the result is a 50% decline in market value. If an investor purchased an option to buy the stock at $55 per share when the market price was $60 per share, the call would have been worth at least $5 per share. But, when the stock drops to $30 per share, the value of the option will become almost nil.

2. Both puts and calls have a relatively short life span—not more than nine months. Therefore, they are sometimes referred to as "wasting assets" which will be of no value after a particular point in time, the expiration date.

3. Call options, though they enable the holder to purchase shares of common stock, have neither voting rights nor are they entitled to receive any dividends declared and paid during the term of the option. Even though the life of an option is relatively short, no more than nine months, this lack of income can be an important disadvantage.

TAX IMPLICATIONS

1. Options generally are classified as capital assets for tax purposes, though they are subject to some special rules because of their unique nature. See the discussion of capital gains and losses in Chapter 8, "Income Tax Concepts."

2. Investors who buy call options will have a capital gain or loss if the option is sold in a "closing" transaction. Gain or loss is calculated by taking the sale price of the option minus the purchase price (including any brokerage fees included in either transaction). Because exchange-traded call options are issued for a term of only nine months, any capital gain or loss will be short-term.

3. No gain or loss is realized upon the exercise of a call option. A capital gain or loss is realized only when the stock acquired through exercise of the call is sold. The cost of the call is added to the purchase price of the stock in computing the gain or loss for tax purposes. The holding period is measured from the day after the call option is exercised, not from the date the call was purchased.

4. Investors who write calls and then close out their positions by repurchasing them will recognize any capital gain upon the closing. However, since dispositions in-

volving options are subject to the wash sale rule, loss on the sale of a call option within 30 days before or after the date of purchase of substantially identical stocks or securities may not be recognized. Instead, such a loss will generally increase the basis of the replacement stock or securities. If the option expires unexercised, the investor will realize a short-term capital gain.

5. An investor who writes a call option that is exercised will realize a capital gain or loss upon exercise. The premium the investor received for writing the call is added to the selling price of the stock in calculating the amount of capital gain or loss.

6. Investors who purchase put options and sell them will recognize any capital gain on the sale at the time of closing. However, since dispositions involving options are subject to the wash sale rule, loss on the sale of a put option within 30 days before or after the date of purchase of substantially identical stocks or securities may not be recognized. Instead, such a loss will generally increase the basis of the replacement stock or securities. A capital loss will result if the put option expires without being exercised.

7. Exercising a put option constitutes a sale of the stock. The cost of the put is subtracted from the selling price of the stock in computing capital gain or loss for tax purposes. The date of exercise of the put option is treated as the sale date of the stock.

8. Investors who write puts and repurchase their put obligations will realize a short-term capital gain or loss on the closing. If the option expires unexercised, the investor will realize a short-term capital gain.

9. When a put option is exercised the writer is required to purchase the stock put to him. However, this is not treated as a taxable event for the writer of the put contract. Instead, the put writer deducts the premium received for writing the put from the purchase price of the stock. The holding period for the stock is measured from the date of exercise of the put.

ALTERNATIVES

1. Stock purchase warrants have many of the same features as call options. They enable the owner of the warrant to purchase a certain number of shares of stock at a fixed price for a given period of time. The original term of the warrant is generally much longer than a put or call option, frequently lasting for several years. However, warrants are offered by corporations and are frequently issued in connection with the sale of other securities such as bonds or preferred stock. Some warrants are listed on the organized securities exchanges, but the majority are traded in the over-the-counter market. The fixed exercise price of warrants creates the same type of leverage provided by options.

2. Stock "rights" are another form of option that enable existing shareholders to purchase new stock being issued by a corporation. Generally one right is issued for each share of stock an investor owns, and the rights entitle the stockholder to purchase additional shares at a stated price. Rights have an extremely short life span and generally must be exercised within a month or so of the new stock offering.

WHERE AND HOW DO I GET IT?

Put and call stock options are traded on several organized exchanges, most of which are related to stock exchanges. The first exchange to be organized especially for trading of options was the Chicago Board Options Exchange (CBOE) which began operating in April, 1973. The CBOE was an extension of the Chicago Board of Trade which had a long history of trading options on agricultural commodities. Since 1973, trading in puts and calls has extended to the American Stock Exchange (ASE), the Pacific Coast Stock Exchange, the Philadelphia Stock Exchange, and the New York Stock Exchange (NYSE). Today these options may be traded on more than 1,500 different underlying stocks.

Buying or selling puts and calls is very similar to buying or selling the underlying stocks. However, option trades must be made through a "margin account" which allows a customer to buy securities with money borrowed from a broker. Transactions are made through brokerage firms which relay the orders they receive to the trading floors of the options exchanges. Orders are carried out by the exchange and the results of the trade are reported back to the brokerage firm, which in turn notifies its customer.

To execute a transaction an investor can merely call his broker and state, "Please purchase five AT&T April-60 call option contracts for my account." A written record of the trade automatically will be sent to the buyer or seller of the option contract confirming the transaction. This is the only evidence of the purchase or sale that the investor will receive. This is due to the fact that the option is a contract to buy or sell rather than an actual security.

Once a trade has been made the position of the buyer or seller remains "open" until one of three events occurs. The first possibility is that the option may expire without being exercised. Expiration of an option series will "close out" all positions open at that time. This is the result frequently desired by sellers of call options who hope to keep the premium they received and to keep their shares of stock as well.

A second possible outcome is that the option will be exercised and that the underlying shares of stock will have to be transferred. For example, if a call option is exercised, the seller will have to deliver shares of stock at the exercise price to be paid by the buyer of the call.

A third possibility is that the buyer or seller of the option will wish to close out his original position. This is done simply by entering an order opposite to the first order. For instance, assume Greg Murphy had purchased a put option allowing him to sell GM stock at a price of $70 per share. Greg now wishes to close out his position and may do so by *selling* the exact same option contract. The two option contracts offset each other and, at that point, Greg has neither an option to buy or sell. He may have had a profit or loss on his original position. The amount of the gain or loss will depend upon the change in price of the initial option contract from the date of purchase or sale until the position is closed.

For example, Greg may have paid $5 per share, or $500 for the original put option. If the contract were selling for $300 when he closed out his position, he would have a loss of $200 on the transaction.

WHAT FEES OR OTHER ACQUISITION COSTS ARE INVOLVED?

Commissions on the purchase or sale of option contracts are similar to those paid on other security transactions. Brokerage firms typically charge a percentage of the value of the transaction with a minimum commission of $25 or $30. For example, a single contract trade amounting to $250 may involve a commission of $25. Ten contracts amounting to $2,500 may result in a commission of $150.

HOW DO I SELECT THE BEST OF ITS TYPE?

1. Since investors can either buy or sell either puts or calls there are a great many different option strategies available at any given time. Perhaps the first decision that must be made is an estimate of whether the stock market as a whole, or any one stock, is likely to advance or decline. If the market is moving upward, investors are more likely to want to buy calls or sell put options. If the market or a stock is weak, then a strategy of buying puts or selling calls may be in order.

2. The volatility of the underlying stock has a lot to do with the movement of both put and call options. The more active a particular issue, the more likely the option will have a wide swing in price. Speculators should look for stocks that experience fairly rapid movements, either up or down, over a relatively short period of time. More conservative investors may want to concentrate on options where the underlying stock is relatively stable in price.

3. The period of time to expiration of the option should be considered before any purchase or sale is made. The longer the term of the option the more likely the price of the stock to change significantly, and the greater the volatility of the option. Again, investors who wish to speculate will prefer longer term options, while conservative investors will prefer shorter maturities.

4. The dividends paid on the underlying stock have a significant impact on the value of an option. Option holders do not receive any dividends, which are paid only to holders of actual stock. Therefore, options on high dividend-paying stocks will tend to be less valuable than those on issues with low dividends or none at all.

WHERE CAN I FIND OUT MORE ABOUT IT?

1. Each of the option exchanges publishes a variety of booklets dealing with the mechanics of option trading and various strategies for investors. These booklets generally are also available through most brokerage firms.

2. Larger brokerage firms have specialists who concentrate on options and may even manage option funds for their clients. Such firms frequently publish their own reports and recommendations.

3. Several of the major investment advisory services include information on options in their publications. Both Standard & Poor's and Value Line collect data on puts and calls though they do not make recommendations or assign a quality rating as they do with stocks and bonds.

QUESTIONS AND ANSWERS

Question — How long does an option contract last?

Answer — Option contracts can have maturities up to several months. However, most trading activity takes place on those options that will expire within the next two or three months. New options are introduced by the various exchanges as old options expire.

Question — Are options available for all stocks?

Answer — No, options are available on a relatively limited number of stocks. The five options exchanges trade puts and calls on about 1,500 issues, but this is a small percentage of the thousands of listed stocks and the many thousands more that are traded on the over-the-counter market. Options are generally available on those issues that are widely held or that are very actively traded. The exchanges review their lists on a regular basis and add new issues from time to time.

Question — Do I have to own a particular stock before I can trade its options?

Answer — No, you may trade options—both puts and calls—without actual ownership of the underlying stock. This is referred to as "trading naked" or "uncovered" as opposed to owning the stock and being "covered." The additional risk in naked trading is the possible need to buy the stock for delivery if the option is exercised. This can be particularly expensive since double commissions are involved as well as the cost of purchasing the underlying stock.

Question — If I acquire stock by exercising a call option, what is the actual cost basis of my shares?

Answer — The cost basis of the stock for tax purposes will be the exercise price paid for the shares plus the premium paid for the call option. For example, if an investor paid $500 for a call on 100 shares of stock, and later exercised the option at a price of $50 per share, the cost basis of the stock would be $55 per share.

Question — If I buy an option and let it expire without being exercised, is my loss on the transaction a capital loss?

Answer — Yes, if the option expires, it is treated as if it were sold on the expiration date. The premium that was paid to acquire the option is treated as a short-term capital loss.

Question — How is the premium income received by option writers taxed?

Answer — First, there is no tax due at the time the option is written and the premium is paid to the seller. For tax purposes, the premium is considered to be deferred until the transaction is completed, even though the writer actually receives the funds immediately. If the option expires without being exercised, the premium is recognized as a short-term capital gain and is included in the writer's income for the tax year in which the option expired. If the option is exercised, the writer adds the premium to the striking price to calculate the total amount received. This amount is compared with the writer's cost basis to determine whether a taxable gain or loss has been realized. Any gain or loss that results from a "closing purchase" is considered short-term capital gain or loss.

Chapter 39

QUALIFIED PENSION AND PROFIT SHARING PLANS

An employer's qualified pension and profit sharing plans are perhaps the major sources of retirement savings for employees. These plans are designed to meet employer as well as employee objectives. Generally, employees do not have direct control over the specific features of the plan. However, employees who own or control a business may be in a position to dictate the design features of their company's qualified plan. So for these employees, the plan's design is an important part of their personal tax and financial planning. Keogh (HR-10) plans, discussed in Chapter 29, are qualified plans used by unincorporated self-employed individuals.

The design, administration, and installation of qualified pension and profit sharing plans is a very complex subject, and the details are beyond the scope of this book. However, because of the great importance of these plans for financial and retirement planning, every financial planner should have a basic understanding of how these plans are structured and what they can do.

WHAT IS A QUALIFIED PLAN?

A qualified pension or profit sharing plan is a plan by which part of the compensation an employee would otherwise receive currently is deferred (both actually and for tax purposes) and deposited into a trust fund, or insurance or annuity contract, for the benefit of the employee. Benefits from the fund are paid when the employee retires or terminates employment. Qualified pension and profit sharing plans are, therefore, plans of deferred compensation. A qualified plan receives tax benefits that are not available for a "nonqualified" deferred compensation plan (a plan that does not meet the Code requirements for qualified plans described below).

These tax benefits are:

(1) Amounts paid into a qualified plan to finance future retirement benefits are deductible by the employer in the year for which they are made.

(2) The employee is not taxed when the employer makes contributions to the plan fund, even if the employee is fully vested in the retirement benefit.

(3) The tax on salary put into the plan is deferred to the time when benefits are received by the employee or

the employee's beneficiary. Some lump-sum benefits are eligible for a special 5-year averaging tax computation (see Chapter 14) if they are received before January 1, 2000.

(4) The plan fund is tax exempt; therefore, earnings accumulate tax free to the plan itself and are not taxed to the employee or the employee's beneficiary until benefits are paid. This significantly increases the effective investment return.

Deferral of tax on both plan contributions and plan earnings is a very valuable tax benefit. This feature permits plan funds to build up much faster than comparable savings outside the plan in most cases.

Types of Qualified Plans

Qualified plans are either defined contribution or defined benefit plans. As the names imply, the type depends on whether the plan specifies an employer contribution rate on the one hand, or guarantees a specified benefit level on the other.

DEFINED CONTRIBUTION PLANS

In a defined contribution plan, the employer establishes and maintains an individual account for each plan participant. When the participant becomes eligible to receive benefit payments—usually at retirement or termination of employment—the benefit is based on the total amount in the participant's account. The account balance includes employer contributions, employee contributions in some cases, and earnings on the account over all the years of deferral.

The employer does not guarantee the amount of the benefit a participant will ultimately receive in a defined contribution plan. Instead, the employer generally must make contributions under a formula specified in the plan. There are three principal types of defined contribution plan formulas:

(1) The *money-purchase pension plan.* Under a money-purchase plan, the employer must contribute each year to each participant's account a percentage of the participant's compensation. This percentage is usually about 10 percent, although percentages up to 25

Figure 39.1 Comparison of Money-Purchase Plans and Target Plans

Employee Age	Annual Compensation	Annual Contribution		Accumulation at Age 65 (5½%)	
		Money-Purchase (14%)	Target	Money-Purchase	Target
30	$30,000	$4,200	$1,655	$444,214	$175,000
40	30,000	4,200	3,243	226,657	175,000
50	30,000	4,200	7,402	99,292	175,000

are possible. The money-purchase plan is probably the simplest of all types of plans and is one of the most common.

(2) The *target-benefit pension plan.* A target plan is similar to a money-purchase plan in that the employer must make annual contributions to each participant's account under a formula based on compensation. In a target plan, however, the participant's age at plan entry is also taken into account in determining the contribution percentage. This is done on an actuarial basis so that older entrants can build up retirement accounts faster. The objective—the target—is to provide approximately the same benefit level (as a percentage of compensation) for each participant at retirement. The employer does not guarantee this level, however, and the employee bears the risk as well as reaping any benefit of varying investment results.

The money-purchase and target plans are best illustrated by looking at a simple comparison of contribution levels and plan accumulations for a hypothetical employer having three employees with the same annual compensation but varying ages at plan entry. This comparison is made in Figure 43.1.

(3) The *profit sharing plan.* A profit sharing plan is a defined contribution plan under which the employer determines the amount of the contribution each year, rather than having a contribution obligation based on each employee's compensation. In a profit sharing plan, the employer can decide not to contribute to the plan at all in certain cases. Typically, plan contributions are based on the employer's profits in some manner. If a contribution is made, the total amount must be allocated to each participant's account using a nondiscriminatory formula. Such formulas are usually based on compensation, but age and/or service can be taken into account.

For example, suppose an employer contributes $10,000 to a profit sharing plan and the plan allocates this contribution to employees on the basis of compen-

sation—that is, each employee receives a fraction of the employer contribution equal to the ratio of his compensation to the total payroll. Then, for three employees with compensation as indicated, the employer allocation would be as follows:

Employee	Annual Compensation	Share of $10,000 Employer Contribution
A	$20,000	$2,000
B	30,000	3,000
C	50,000	5,000

Profit sharing plans often feature employee contributions, typically with an employer match. For example, the plan could provide that employees may contribute up to X percent of their compensation to the plan, with the employer contributing 50¢ for every $1 of employee contribution. This type of plan is referred to as a *thrift* or *savings* plan.

Another variation on the profit sharing plan design is the *Section 401(k)* plan (i.e., a *cash or deferred arrangement* or CODA). Under this type of plan, employees can make tax deferred contributions by electing salary reductions, which are limited to $7,000 annually per employee. (This amount is indexed for inflation each year—$10,000 in 1998.) Employers often match employee salary reductions in order to encourage employee participation in these plans.

DEFINED BENEFIT PLANS

Defined benefit plans provide a specific amount of benefit to the employee at normal retirement age. There are many different types of formulas for determining this benefit. These formulas are typically based on the employee's earnings averaged over a number of years of service. The formula also can be based on the employee's service—the "unit-credit" approach. For example:

(1) A flat percentage defined benefit formula might provide a retirement benefit equal to 50 percent of the employee's average earnings prior to retirement. Under this formula, a participant whose average earnings

were $100,000 prior to retirement would receive an annual pension of $50,000.

(2) A unit credit defined benefit formula might provide 1.5 percent of earnings for each of the employee's years of service, with the total percentage applied to the employee's earnings averaged over a specified period. Under this formula, a participant with average annual compensation of $100,000 who retired after 30 years of service would receive an annual pension of $45,000.

In these formulas, earnings can be averaged over the employee's entire career (a "career-average" formula) or over a number of years—usually 3 to 5 immediately prior to retirement (a "final-average" formula).

Employers must fund defined benefit plans with periodic deposits determined actuarially so that the plan fund will be sufficient to pay the promised benefit as each participant retires. (Contributions to most defined benefit plans must be made on at least a quarterly basis.) The objective is to accumulate a fund at the employee's retirement age that is sufficient to "buy an annuity" equal to the retirement benefit. For example, suppose the actuary estimates that an annuity of $50,000 per year beginning at age 65 is equivalent to a lump sum of $475,000 at age 65. For a participant aged 45 at plan entry, the employer has 20 years to fund this benefit. The actuary will use various methods and assumptions to determine how much must be deposited quarterly. In this case, a "level funding" (equal annual payment) method with a 6 percent interest assumption would require the employer to deposit $3,158 quarterly for 20 years. This shows how investment return works for the benefit of the employer; the 80 deposits of $3,158 total only $252,640, but at age 65 the fund will actually total $475,000 at 6 percent investment return.

Actuarial methods and assumptions are chosen to provide the desired pattern for spreading the plan's cost over the years it is in effect. The actuarial method and assumptions often have to be adjusted over the years to make sure the fund is adequate. It is even possible for a defined benefit plan to become overfunded, in which case employer contributions must be reduced or eliminated for a period of time. To back up the employer's funding obligation and safeguard employees, defined benefit plans are insured by the federal Pension Benefit Guaranty Corporation (PBGC) up to specified limits.

Because of the actuarial computations required and the PBGC involvement, defined benefit plans are more complicated and expensive to administer and explain to employees than are defined contribution plans.

The actuarial funding for defined benefit plans means that, for a given benefit level, the annual funding amount is greater for employees who are older at entry into the plan, since the time to fund their benefits is less. This makes defined benefit plans attractive to professional and closely held business owners; they tend to adopt retirement plans for their businesses when they are relatively older than their regular employees. A large percentage of the total cost for a defined benefit plan in this situation funds these key employees' benefits.

ADVANTAGES OF DEFINED CONTRIBUTION PLANS

1. The participant can benefit from good investment results.

2. Plans are relatively simple and inexpensive to adopt and administer.

3. Employer funding of profit sharing plans is flexible.

4. Plans featuring employee contributions or 401(k) salary reductions allow participants some control over the level of their retirement savings.

DISADVANTAGES OF DEFINED CONTRIBUTION PLANS

1. Neither the employer nor the PBGC guarantees benefit levels; participants bear the risk of poor investment results.

2. Benefits may be inadequate for participants who enter the plan at later ages.

3. For a highly-compensated employee, the $30,000/25 percent of compensation annual additions limit (discussed below) may restrict plan contributions more than the corresponding defined benefit plan limit.

4. For profit sharing plans, annual employer deductions are limited to 15 percent of the payroll of covered employees.

ADVANTAGES OF DEFINED BENEFIT PLANS

1. Retirement benefits at adequate levels can be provided for all employees regardless of age at plan entry.

2. Benefit levels are guaranteed both by the employer and, within limits, by the PBGC.

3. For an older highly-compensated employee, defined benefit plans tend to allow the maximum amount of tax-deferred retirement savings.

DISADVANTAGES OF DEFINED BENEFIT PLANS

1. Actuarial services and PBGC requirements result in higher installation and administration costs.

2. The plans are complex to design and to explain to employees.

3. Employees who leave before retirement may receive relatively little benefit.

4. The employer has a recurring funding obligation regardless of whether, in a given year, it has made a profit or incurred a loss.

QUALIFIED PLAN REQUIREMENTS

In order to obtain the tax advantages of qualified plans, complex Internal Revenue Code and IRS regulatory requirements must be met. The following will summarize these requirements as briefly as possible. These rules have many exceptions and qualifications that will not be covered in detail.

Eligibility and Coverage

A qualified plan must cover a broad group of employees, not just key employees and business owners. Two types of rules must be satisfied: the "age and service" ("waiting period") requirements and the "overall coverage" requirement.

Minimum waiting period and age requirements are often used in plans to avoid burdening the plan with employees who terminate after short periods of service. However, the plan cannot require more than one year of service for eligibility, and cannot exclude, on the basis of age, any employee who has attained the age of at least 21. As an alternative, the plan waiting period can be up to 2 years if the plan provides immediate 100 percent vesting upon entry. No plan can impose a maximum age for entry. For eligibility purposes, a year of service generally means a 12-month period during which the employee has at least 1,000 hours of service.

The overall coverage of a qualified plan must satisfy at least one of the following coverage tests of the Code:

(1) the plan must cover at least 70 percent of employees who are not highly compensated (the "percentage test"), or

(2) the plan must cover a percentage of non-highly compensated employees that is at least 70 percent of the percentage of highly compensated employees covered (the "ratio test"), or

(3) the plan must meet the "average benefit test." Under the average benefit test, the plan must benefit a nondiscriminatory classification of employees, and the average benefit, as a percentage of compensation, for non-highly compensated employees must be at least 70 percent of that for highly compensated employees.

(Regulations combine the percentage and ratio tests into one test.)

In addition, a defined benefit plan must cover the lesser of 50 employees or 40 percent of all employees (a "minimum participation" test).

"Highly compensated employee" is defined under the Internal Revenue Code as an employee who (i) owns more than 5 percent of the business, or (ii) earned more than $80,000 in the preceding year *and*, if the employer elects to follow the "top paid group" rule, was in the top paid group. (See IRC Sec. 414(q)). The "top paid group" is defined as the top 20% of employees, ranked by compensation. The limit of $80,000 (in 1998) is indexed annually for inflation.

Certain employees are not counted in applying the above three coverage tests, which means that they can effectively be excluded from the plan. For example, if the employees are included in a collective bargaining unit, they can be excluded if there was good faith bargaining on retirement benefits.

When the coverage rules are applied, all related employers must be treated as a single employer. Thus, an employer generally cannot break up its business into a number of corporations or other separate units to avoid covering rank-and-file employees. However, if the employer actually has bona fide separate lines of business, it is possible to apply the coverage test and, within limits, the minimum participation test separately to employees in each line of business.

Nondiscrimination in Benefits and Contributions

Qualified plans may not discriminate in favor of highly compensated employees either in terms of benefits or in terms of employer contributions to the plan. However, some nondiscriminatory formulas will provide a higher benefit for highly compensated employees. Contributions or benefits can be based on compensation or years of service, for example. Also, qualified plan benefit or contribution formulas can be "integrated" with Social Security. In an integrated plan, greater contributions or benefits may be provided for higher paid employees earning compensation above certain levels. This is

The Tools and Techniques of Financial Planning

generally permitted because Social Security provides a higher retirement income, relatively speaking, for lower paid employees (i.e., a higher percentage of income for lower paid employees is replaced by Social Security). A special nondiscrimination test is applied to employee contributions and employer matching contributions.

Vesting

If a qualified plan provides for employee contributions, the portion of the benefit or account balance attributable to employee contributions must at all times be 100 percent vested (nonforfeitable). The portion attributable to employer contributions must be vested under a specified vesting schedule that is at least as favorable as one of two alternative minimum standards:

(1) 5-year vesting. A plan's vesting schedule satisfies this minimum requirement if an employee with at least 5 years of service is 100 percent vested. No vesting at all is required before 5 years of service.

(2) 3-year to 7-year vesting. The plan must provide vesting that is at least as fast as the following schedule:

Years of Service	Vested Percentage
3	20%
4	40
5	60
6	80
7 or more	100

Funding Requirements

Employer and employee contributions to a qualified plan must be deposited into an irrevocable trust fund or insurance or annuity contract that is for the "exclusive benefit" of plan participants and their beneficiaries. This means that plan funds are not available for the employer's use.

The minimum funding standards of federal law provide a mathematical calculation of the minimum amount that must be contributed to a qualified pension plan. *Pension* plans, whether defined benefit or defined contribution, must meet these minimum funding standards or be subject to a penalty. The minimum amount must be paid in (at least) quarterly deposits to avoid a further penalty.

Profit sharing plans are not subject to the minimum funding standards as such, but contributions must be "substantial and recurring" or the IRS can deem the plan to be terminated. Substantial and recurring is not clearly defined in the law so that there is always some risk in repeatedly omitting contributions.

There are strict limits on the extent to which an employer can exercise control over the plan fund. The plan trustee can be a corporation or an individual, even a company president or shareholder, but plan trustees are subject to stringent federal fiduciary rules requiring them to manage the fund solely in the interest of plan participants and beneficiaries. Loans to employees are permitted within limits, but the employer is penalized for borrowing from the plan.

Limitation on Benefits and Contributions

To prevent a qualified plan from being used primarily as a tax shelter for highly compensated employees, there is a limitation on plan benefits or employer contributions.

Defined benefit limits. Under a defined benefit plan, the benefit at age 65 or the social security retirement age, if later, cannot exceed the lesser of

(1) 100 percent of the participant's compensation averaged over the 3 years of highest compensation, or

(2) $90,000.

The $90,000 limit is adjusted under a cost-of-living indexing formula. For 1998, the dollar limit $130,000. The dollar limit is also adjusted actuarially for retirement ages earlier or later than the Social Security retirement age.

Defined Contribution Limits. For a defined contribution plan, the "annual addition" (employer contributions, employee salary reductions, employee contributions, and plan forfeitures reallocated from other participants' accounts) to each participant's account is limited. This annual addition cannot exceed the lesser of

(1) 25% of the participant's annual compensation, or

(2) $30,000 (in 1998, as indexed).

The $30,000 limit is subject to indexing for inflation in increments of $5,000; thus, it will increase only when the sum of the inflation adjustments equals or exceeds $5,000.

In limitation years beginning before January 1, 2000, if there is both a defined benefit and a defined contribution plan covering the same employee, the defined benefit and defined contribution limits are adjusted under a combined formula. This formula is repealed for limitation years beginning after December 31, 1999.

The $150,000 Compensation Limit. Finally, a further limitation on plan benefits or contributions is that only the first

$150,000 (as indexed for inflation—$160,000 in 1998) of each employee's annual compensation can be taken into account in the plan's benefit or contribution formula. For example, if an employee earns $300,000 in 1998 and the employer has a 10 percent money-purchase plan, the maximum contribution for that employee is $16,000 (10% of $160,000).

Payout Restrictions

The restrictions, tax treatment, and penalties relating to plan benefit payments are extremely important in financial planning for individuals and are covered in detail in Chapter 14. To summarize, there is a 10 percent penalty on withdrawal of funds from any qualified plan before separation from service at age 55, or before age 59½, death, or disability, with certain exceptions. Also, payments cannot be delayed unduly; generally, benefit payments must begin by April 1 of the later of (i) the year after the participant attains age 70½, or (ii) the year the participant retires (unless he is a 5% owner, in which case distributions must begin by April 1 of the year after he reaches age 70½). The payment must be made (at least) in specified minimum annual amounts.

The Code provides a participant's spouse with specified rights to the participant's retirement benefits. Payments from a pension plan must automatically be in the form of a qualified joint and survivor annuity, meaning an annuity for the joint lives of the participant and his spouse with an annuity of at least 50 percent of this amount to the surviving spouse. Furthermore, if a vested participant dies before retirement, the surviving spouse has the right to a survivor annuity from the plan. Survivorship benefits in the form of joint and survivor annuities and survivor annuities are not required in the case of a profit sharing plan if the plan provides that the participant's spouse is the beneficiary of the participant's entire vested account balance in the event of the participant's death.

Top-Heavy Requirements

Plans for closely held businesses often predominantly benefit the business owners. A "top-heavy" plan is one that provides more than 60 percent of its aggregate accrued benefits or account balances to key employees. If a plan is top-heavy for a given year, it must provide more rapid vesting than generally required. The plan can either provide 100 percent vesting after 2 years of service, or 6-year graded vesting as follows:

Years of Service	Vested Percentage
2	20%
3	40
4	60
5	80
6 or more	100

In addition, a top-heavy plan must provide minimum benefits or contributions for non-key employees. For defined benefit plans the benefit for each non-key employee must be at least 2 percent of compensation multiplied by the employee's years of service, up to 20 percent. The average compensation used for this formula is based on the highest 5 years of compensation. For a defined contribution plan, employer contributions during a top-heavy year must be at least 3 percent of compensation.

In limitation years beginning before January 1, 2000, even more stringent rules may apply if the plan is deemed to be "super top-heavy"—that is, if it provides more than 90 percent of its accrued benefits or account balances for key employees.

FINANCIAL PLANNING CHECKLIST FOR QUALIFIED PLAN PARTICIPANTS

A client's qualified plan benefits are a critical part of his or her financial picture; this is particularly true for middle and upper-middle income employees. The financial planner should help to maximize these benefits for the client. Some steps include:

(1) Obtain and review the Summary Plan Description (SPD) for plans in which the client currently participates and also plans in which he participated in the past. Employers are legally obligated to furnish an SPD. The SPD will usually explain the benefits from the plan adequately, but if not, employers must allow access to other plan documents for review and copying. In addition, employers must furnish on request (at least annually) a Personal Benefit Statement that provides the exact dollar value of the participant's current and projected benefit.

(2) Determine whether current and projected benefits provide adequate retirement savings and, if not, what supplemental action is necessary. Consider the effect on plan benefits if the client plans to change employers in the future.

(3) If the plan provides for employee contributions or salary reductions, determine if these should be increased or decreased.

(4) If the client is nearing retirement, consider what benefit payment options are available and which would be best. Planning for retirement plan distributions is discussed in Chapter 14.

(5) If the client is a key or controlling employee of the business consider what improvements might be made in the plan for his benefit.

Chapter 40

REAL ESTATE AS AN INVESTMENT

WHAT IS IT?

Real estate is land, and the buildings and improvements on land as well as the natural assets, such as minerals, under the land. Because of the obvious limited supply of land, especially in "desirable" locations, real estate has long been viewed as an attractive investment alternative.

Real estate can be classified into four major categories:

(1) land,

(2) residential,

(3) commercial, and

(4) industrial.

"Land" can be subdivided into five categories: (a) unimproved, (b) farm land, (c) recreational, (d) ranches, and (e) subdivided lots.

"Residential" can be subdivided into three categories: (a) single family dwellings, (b) multiple family dwellings (such as apartments and condominiums), and (c) hotels and motels (transient dwellings).

"Commercial" can be subdivided into five categories: (a) residential rental, (b) office buildings, (c) retail stores, (d) shopping centers, and (e) specialty buildings (such as banks, movie theaters, stadiums, and bowling alleys).

"Industrial" can be subdivided into four categories: (a) factories, (b) warehouses, (c) industrial parks, and (d) utility facilities (such as power plants).

An investor should select the type of real estate that will best meet the specific objectives of the investment plan. For example, unimproved land can provide substantial, long term appreciation, but cannot be looked to for a significant current flow of income.

WHEN IS THE USE OF THIS TOOL INDICATED?

1. When an investor desires an investment with tax shelter potential.

2. When a long term hedge against inflation is needed.

3. When a relatively constant cash flow is required.

4. When an investor is looking for long term appreciation.

5. When the investor would like a tangible investment. Many investors — for psychological reasons — are more comfortable with an asset that they can see, touch, and physically possess.

6. When the investor wants to make maximum use of leverage. Lenders are willing to advance large sums of money on the security of real estate for long periods of time at relatively low interest because real estate is not only tangible and stationary, but is also reasonably stable in value.

ADVANTAGES

1. Real estate has numerous different tax related advantages. (Those tax advantages relating more specifically to real estate are discussed below. Those tax advantages of a more general nature are covered in greater depth in Chapter 8, "Income Tax Concepts.") Real estate's tax advantages include:

(a) Expenditures which are considered ordinary and necessary in the production or collection of income or in the preservation of its value as an investment are deductible.

(b) The costs of supplies, labor, and other components necessary to keep the property in good repair can be deducted.

(c) Real estate property taxes are deductible.

(d) A tenant leasing business property may deduct reasonable rental costs.

(e) Interest on the unpaid balance of the mortgage is deductible (subject to limitations imposed by the tax law).

(f) The full cost of buildings and real estate improvements (i.e., cost *excluding* land) is depreciable.

(g) Gain on the sale of real estate can be reported over more than one taxable year. This may allow the investor to defer the payment of tax until cash proceeds from an "installment sale" of the property are received (although interest payments may be due on certain deferred tax liabilities).

(h) Losses incurred on the sale of real estate are deductible (subject to limitations discussed below).

(i) One parcel of real estate can be exchanged for another without the immediate recognition of taxable income. Tax on appreciation can be postponed an indefinite number of times (and for an indefinite period of time) if each trade meets the strict requirements of the tax free exchange rule of the Internal Revenue Code (Code section 1031).

(j) Upon the "involuntary conversion" of real estate (such as through fire or condemnation), the investor does not have to pay any tax upon the receipt of cash from insurance or condemnation award, so long as the cash is reinvested in "qualified property" (essentially property of similar use) having equal or greater value.

(k) Liquidity (cash) can be obtained from real estate, including any appreciation, without paying taxes, through a mortgage on the property. (Of course, upon sale of the property, the investor is taxed upon the entire appreciation.)

(l) The cost of rehabilitating certain buildings or structures may qualify for a special investment tax credit.

However, real estate is also subject to special "passive activity" tax rules that may limit the ability to use real estate losses to offset income from other sources. The "passive activity" rules are discussed in Chapter 8, "Income Tax Concepts."

2. Real estate is tangible. As mentioned above, many investors prefer an asset that can be seen, touched, fenced in, and built upon. It feels more "real" than intangible investments, such as life insurance or common stocks, which do not exist in a physical sense.

3. Real estate has historically proven itself as an excellent hedge against inflation. Real estate tends to increase in value while prices are rising and the value of the dollar is declining.

4. Each parcel of real estate is unique. Because no two parcels can share the same location, no two can be exactly alike. The "monopoly" each real estate owner has on each individual location is itself of value.

5. Because of its great value as security for a loan, real estate enables an investor to obtain maximum potential leverage.

DISADVANTAGES

1. Real estate is almost always relatively illiquid. Because there is no organized market on the national or local level for real estate comparable to the stock or commodity exchanges, real estate is difficult to convert to cash quickly.

Other reasons that real estate is not as liquid as other investments include: (a) the usual difficulty in finding a "willing buyer" at the desired selling price (because the property must suit the buyer with respect to a multiplicity of factors, including location, financing, timing, potential income, etc.), (b) the length of time involved in the "closing" process (typically 2 to 6 months), and (c) the need for the purchaser to obtain financing in most cases.

2. Some degree of management is necessary with all real estate investments. For example, a properly managed real estate investment requires that someone maintain the physical premises, collect rents, and pay bills. If the investor does not possess the requisite expertise (or have the time or inclination to obtain or exercise that expertise), a professional manager must be hired. This makes many small real estate investments impractical.

3. Typically the investment in real estate is large in amount and will require the commitment of investable funds for a long period of time. Compared to stocks, which can be purchased for as low as pennies per share and can be sold within a matter of hours, real estate requires many thousands of dollars (not all of which need be put up by the investor, but can be leveraged) which may remain "locked in" for many years.

4. Costs related to the purchase or sale of real estate reduce its value as an investment that can produce a short term gain. Such costs, which include transfer taxes, title insurance, appraisals, financing fees and "points," title recording and notary fees, and sales commissions, may run as high as 10% to 15% of the cost of the real estate itself.

5. Real estate, by definition, cannot be moved. This immobility can become a distinct disadvantage when the inves-

tor moves to a new location and can no longer properly manage the investment personally.

6. Once land has been improved with a building, that "improvement" is often difficult and expensive to modify or remove. For instance, a building designed as a warehouse can be converted to an apartment house to meet a shift in market demand, but only at great expense and considerable trouble. This disadvantage is often referred to as "fixity" of investment.

7. It is often difficult or impossible to assess the economic risks and projected return on a real estate investment with exactness. This is because unpredictables (such as changes in consumer demand, levels of maintenance and repair expenses, changes in tax laws) are involved in the analysis.

8. Because the investment return on real estate is significantly affected by the available tax benefits, such investments are most susceptible to the risk of challenge by the IRS.

TAX IMPLICATIONS

1. All the ordinary and necessary expenses paid or incurred by a real estate investor during the taxable year in carrying on a trade or business are deductible. Deductible expenses include costs incurred in the production or the collection of investment income. Expenditures for the management, conservation, or maintenance of real estate property held either to produce income or for appreciation are also deductible.

Typical deductible expenses that a real estate investor might incur include utilities such as electric and gas, rental commissions, trash removal, and insurance.

2. Routine repair and maintenance expenses — those that do not appreciably add to the value of the property or significantly add to its life span but merely keep it in efficient running order — are deductible in the year the outlay is incurred.

The cost of improvements must be "capitalized." This means that the cost of an item that increases the longevity or the value or alters the use for which the property is suitable cannot be deducted currently. However, such expenditures can be added to the investor's basis in the property. They are then recovered through depreciation deductions.

3. Amounts paid for real property taxes (subject to a limitation for certain taxes incurred during construc-

tion) are deductible when paid. An investor is allowed to deduct real estate taxes paid in the year property is acquired. However, those taxes must be allocated on a day-by-day basis between the buyer and the seller according to the number of days each owns the property.

Certain "taxes" are in fact improvement assessments that add to the value of the property and therefore must be capitalized rather than currently deducted. Examples of such "taxes" include assessments for sidewalks and sewers. The cost of these items is deductible over a period of years according to a cost recovery schedule provided in the Internal Revenue Code.

Construction period taxes must be capitalized and then amortized as part of the basis of the constructed property. Such taxes may therefore only be depreciated over the life of the property (generally 27½ years for residential real estate and 39 years for other real estate).

4. Rental expenses for the use of business property are deductible currently. This deduction by the lessee of property enables the owner/investor of the property to charge a higher rental, thus increasing the value of the property.

5. Interest paid to finance the purchase of investment real estate may be deductible currently. Certain special rules, however, must be considered by the investor. These rules may limit the deductibility of

   (a) construction period interest,

   (b) "investment interest,"

   (c) prepaid interest,

   (d) "points," and

   (e) "passive losses."

Construction period interest must be capitalized and added to the basis of the property being constructed. For example, if an investor incurred $10,000 of interest expense during a one year construction period, the entire amount could not be currently deducted. Instead, the investor could depreciate the interest as part of the cost of the constructed property.

Financing through debt is almost universal in real estate investment. This makes it critical that the advisor and the client be aware that there are limitations on the deduction of interest expense.

The applicable "passive activity" rules as they relate to interest expense are discussed in Chapter 8, "Income Tax Concepts."

Real estate investments are subject to the "at risk" rules which may limit the deductibility of losses from real estate which is leveraged. The "at risk" rules are discussed in Chapter 8, "Income Tax Concepts."

6. Land is not depreciable. But improvements upon the land are eligible for depreciation deductions. In fact, in most cases the "tax losses" generated by depreciation deductions are the most important part of the tax shelter afforded by real estate. However, such "tax losses" are subject to the "passive activity" rules.

The key to the tax shelter value of real estate lies in the fact that depreciation is a "non-cash" charge against income. Depreciation creates an artificial loss enabling an investor to recover the cost of the asset over a specified period of time. In many cases this tax benefit precedes any actual cost (resulting from reduction in the value of the property due to wear and tear or obsolescence). In addition, by financing (i.e., using leverage), the investor may depreciate the full cost of the building and improvements even though

(a) most of the costs have been borrowed from the mortgagee,

(b) the investor may have no personal liability on the mortgage debt, and

(c) the actual cash outlay to repay the debt may not be paid for many years.

7. Tax on the gain upon the sale of real estate can be deferred. Subject to certain limitations, the "installment sale rules" of Code section 453 permit an investor to delay reporting any gain or paying any tax until money is received. For example, an individual in a high tax bracket this year could agree to sell the property before year end but defer receipt of any sales proceeds until next year. In fact, installment sales rules are so flexible that a seller does not have to accept any cash proceeds for five, or ten, or even fifteen years. The law does not set a limit as to how long the parties can agree to extend the payment period. As long as at least one payment will be received by the seller after the close of the taxable year in which the disposition occurs, installment sales treatment is available.

Installment sales are often used as a vehicle for financing the sale, rather than (or in addition to) third party financing, such as from a bank. However, just as a bank requires the payment of interest for the use of the unpaid balance of the loan, tax law "expects" that the parties will provide for interest on the loan inherent in an installment sale. Tax law cannot dictate the stated interest rate agreed to by the parties or even that there be interest actually charged. But, if an interest obligation is not stated in the installment sale agreement, or if the stated rate is insufficient under the law, Code section 483 will treat a portion of the sales price as built-in interest.

This imputation of interest on the unpaid balance of the sales proceeds has the effect of reducing the potential capital gain on the sale of the property, and increasing the ordinary income to the seller.

For instance, Alex Benjamin sells a parcel of unimproved land to Sara Gail for $500,000. He paid $100,000 for the land five years ago. Alex agrees to accept $200,000 in cash at closing, with the balance in installments of $100,000 each on January 1 of each of the next three years.

It appears the sales price is $500,000. But when interest is imputed on the $300,000 unpaid balance, it becomes obvious that if part of that $300,000 is treated as interest, then the real sales price must be significantly less than $500,000. In this example, if the Service were to impute a 10% interest rate on the $300,000 unpaid balance, the effect would be to treat approximately $51,314 of the total installment payment as interest (taxable to the seller and deductible by the buyer) and only $248,686 of the installment payments as principal. For tax purposes, the total sales price would be only $448,686 ($200,000 received at settlement plus the $248,686 principal payments on the installments). The adjusted capital gain would be $348,686 ($448,686 adjusted sales proceeds less $100,000 basis).

The benefits of installment sales of real estate may be limited if the seller pledged the installment receivable as security for a loan. This limitation, as well as other restrictions on the use of the installment method, are discussed in Chapter 8, "Income Tax Concepts."

In addition, the purchaser of real estate that is financed by seller-provided installment sale debt, will be subject to the "at risk" rules, which may limit the deductibility of certain loss. (See the discussion of the "at risk" rules in Chapter 8, "Income Tax Concepts.")

8. Losses on the sale of real estate held for investment or used in a trade or business are generally deductible in the year incurred. Such losses are measured by the excess of

(a) the investor's adjusted basis (generally cost less accumulated depreciation) in the property over (b) the proceeds from the sale of the property.

Losses incurred upon the sale of personal use realty, such as an individual's residence, are not deductible (even if the owner expected the property to appreciate).

The tax treatment for losses incurred on the sale of real property held purely for investment (such as unimproved land) will be different from the treatment of losses from the sale of real property used in a "trade or business" (such as a manufacturing plant).

Real estate held purely for investment is treated as a capital asset. If all capital losses exceed all capital gains, they offset ordinary income dollar-for-dollar up to a maximum of $3,000 per year. Any unused losses may be carried forward.

Real property used in a trade or business is not a capital asset. Such property, if held for the long-term holding period before being sold, is called "Section 1231 Property." A loss from the sale of real estate that is Section 1231 property is totaled with all other losses and gains from the sale of Section 1231 property recognized during the year. If the net of all Section 1231 gains and losses is a gain, the net gain will be treated as a capital gain. If the net of all Section 1231 gains and losses is a loss, the total loss will be treated as an ordinary loss.

9. It is possible, under certain circumstances, for an investor to trade (exchange) properties with another party and postpone all or a portion of the gain that would normally have to be recognized on a sale. This postponement or partial avoidance of taxation is known as a "like-kind" exchange. (Although this is sometimes referred to as a "tax-free" exchange because no tax is payable at the time of the transaction, it is more proper to refer to it as a "tax deferred" exchange; the tax on the exchange is usually paid when the property received in the transaction is subsequently sold.)

10. Tax deferral may also be available upon what is known as an "involuntary conversion." Involuntary conversion is the destruction of property by fire or other casualty. It may also be caused by the condemnation of property by a governmental body utilizing its right to take private property and convert it to the use of the public.

When the investor receives payment through insurance or governmental compensation for property involuntarily converted, tax law treats that money as if it were the proceeds from a sale. Fortunately, any gain realized

on that "sale" can usually be deferred if the investor reinvests the full proceeds in similar ("like kind") property within three years from the end of the year in which the proceeds are received. If less than the entire proceeds are reinvested, only a proportionate amount of the gain can be deferred.

11. An investor can convert part of the appreciated value of property into cash without either selling it or otherwise triggering a tax on any gain. This can be accomplished by using the property as security for a loan. However, there may be limitations on the deductibility of the loan interest.

12. The cost of constructing or rehabilitating certain buildings or structures may qualify for a special investment tax credit. The properties eligible for this credit include (a) qualified low income housing, (b) certified historic structures, and (c) buildings that were first placed in service before 1936.

ALTERNATIVES

Few investments are comparable to real estate because of its unique characteristics, location, potential for significant tax shelter benefits and relatively constant cash flow, and psychological comfort. Other investments, such as stocks, do provide a long term hedge against inflation, the possibility of substantial appreciation, and the potential to maximize the use of leverage. However, no other investments possess all these characteristics to the extent of real estate.

WHERE AND HOW DO I GET IT?

An individual will typically purchase real estate in his own name directly from the seller or through a real estate broker or agent. However, most real estate acquired for tax shelter investment purposes is acquired by purchasing an interest in a partnership or other investment entity.

Real estate may be held by an investor in any of the following forms:

(a) outright ownership,

(b) general partnership or joint venture,

(c) limited partnership,

(d) corporate ("C" corporation),

(e) S corporation, or

(f) real estate investment trust (REIT).

Real Estate as an Investment

Each of these forms of ownership has advantages and disadvantages with respect to the liability incurred, management efforts required, income tax implications, transferability, and continuity of the entity upon the death of the investor.

Outright ownership of real estate does not protect the individual investor from full personal liability relating to the ownership and operation of the property. For example, an investor can be held financially accountable for negligent acts resulting in injury to a visitor on the property. Debts incurred with respect to the investment typically require the personal guarantees of the outright owner and therefore subject all his other assets to the claims of creditors.

An outright owner has full management responsibility. Agents can be hired, however, to assume such tasks as maintenance, rental collection, and paying the bills.

All the tax benefits and costs of outright ownership are personal to the investor. The investor's individual tax return will reflect the taxable income and deductible expenses of the property.

An outright owner can convey the title to all or a portion of the property at any time without restriction.

The death of an individual owner results in the termination of the individual ownership form. The property will then pass through the investor's estate to his heirs or by operation of law to his joint owners.

A general partnership is one in which two or more individuals join together for investment purposes. Usually, a general partner is jointly and severally liable for all the debts and any obligations incurred by the partnership.

If a partner cannot pay his part of the obligations of a partnership, the remaining partners are liable to the total extent of their financial resources. Suppose Howard and Jonathan form a partnership and each invested $30,000 in cash which is used to buy real estate. A visitor slips on the doorstep and successfully sues the partnership for $80,000. Howard has no assets other than his investment in the partnership. Jonathan has other investments totalling $500,000. Assuming there is no insurance, the injured party would first take over the partnership property (worth $60,000) and then look to Jonathan for the remaining $20,000.

Although all the general partners may be held responsible by law for the management of the property, usually only one or a few partners are actively involved in operations. Subject to specific exceptions included in the partnership agreement, each general partner has the authority to bind the partnership (and therefore the other partners) to any contracts or commitments.

Partnerships are not taxed as separate entities. Income, deductions, and credits flow through to the partners according to their proportionate ownership. Each partner reports his or her share of partnership income, deductions, and credits as if each owned that percentage of the property individually. A partner's share of partnership losses is deductible only to the extent of his basis (investment) in the partnership.

A partner's rights to transfer his or her interest in the property is limited by the terms of the partnership agreement. Such agreements generally preclude the sale or gift of an individual's partnership interest without approval of the other partners or without first offering that interest to the other partners.

The death of an individual partner may cause the termination of the partnership unless the terms of the partnership agreement provide otherwise. In most cases the partnership agreement provides for the purchase of the deceased partner's interest by the remaining partners.

A limited partnership permits certain partners (so-called "limited partners") the benefit of limited liability. (Such partnerships must have at least one general partner with full liability). For this reason, limited partnerships are quite popular as a means of owning real estate. In fact, most tax shelter real estate investments are syndicated in this form.

Many limited partnership investments are heavily leveraged. Where the limited partners are not "at risk" to pay a proportionate amount of the debt in the event the partnership activities cannot generate enough cash to pay off the loans, the limited partners may not be able to fully deduct partnership losses. These "at risk" rules are discussed in Chapter 8, "Income Tax Concepts."

Limited partners are passive investors and cannot actively participate in daily management without risking full personal liability. (Limited partners may participate in general policy decisions concerning the long term goals of the venture.) Management authority in a limited partnership is vested solely in the general partner.

As in the case of a general partnership, income, deductions, and credits of a limited partnership flow through to the partners according to their proportionate ownership. Each partner, whether general or limited, reports his or her share of partnership income, deductions, and credits as if each owned that percentage of the property individually. A limited partner's share of partnership losses is deductible only to the extent of his basis (investment) in the partnership.

A limited partner's rights to transfer his or her interest in the property is limited by the terms of the partnership agreement. Limited partnership agreements are generally more restrictive than general partnership agreements in precluding the transferability of an individual's partnership interest.

The death of an individual limited partner generally will not cause the termination of the partnership. In most cases the partnership agreement provides for the deceased partner's heirs to succeed to his interest. However, the death of the sole general partner who is an individual may cause the dissolution of the partnership, unless the partnership agreement provides for a successor general partner. This is one reason why many general partners are corporations.

A major benefit of investing in corporate form is the limited liability it provides. (This applies whether the corporation is being taxed as a regular ("C") corporation or has elected to be taxed as an "S" corporation.) Specifically, the investor is not personally liable for negligent acts of the corporation and its employees and officers. Unless the investor has been personally negligent (outside his role as a corporate employee), full liability stops with the corporation.

Limited liability also applies to corporate borrowing; technically, a creditor can look only to the corporation for payment of a debt and may not reach through to the assets of the individual shareholders. But, as a matter of practice, many lenders will not make loans to closely-held corporations unless the individual shareholders personally cosign or guarantee payment of the debt. Once a shareholder does sign as an individual, the lender can look to that person for payment if the corporation defaults on its obligations.

Centralized management is another feature of the corporate form. The responsibility to manage and authority to run a corporation rests with the board of directors elected by the shareholders. These directors, who typically in closely-held corporations are the controlling shareholders, select officers to handle the day-to-day operations. (Often these officers are also shareholders and members of the board of directors. But it is also common for shareholders to be purely passive investors who do not participate in any way in the operation or management of the company.)

Continuity of life is another feature of the corporate form. A corporation does not terminate at the death of one or more of its owners. Legally, the corporation has an indefinite life. This continuity enhances the corporation's ability to raise large amounts of capital for long term investment.

Finally, enhanced transferability of interests is another feature of the corporate form. A shareholder in a regular corporation (unless restricted by corporate bylaws or a shareholders' agreement) can transfer any number of shares to any party at any time. A shareholder in an S corporation has similar freedom of transferability. However, the transfer of shares to certain restricted parties (see below) will terminate S corporation status.

A regular ("C") corporation is treated for tax purposes as a tax entity entirely separate from its owners. A C corporation must file its own tax return and its income is subject to a special corporate income tax rate schedule. Because the corporation is considered a separate tax entity, once it earns and pays tax on the income, the net remaining after taxes belongs to the corporation itself, and not its shareholders. Those net corporate earnings can generally be distributed to the shareholders only as a dividend, which is then taxable to them upon receipt.

Note that corporate earnings paid to shareholders will typically be taxed twice, once to the corporation and then again to the shareholders when paid out to them. This means that the real estate investor operating in corporate form suffers two disadvantages; first, the earnings of the investment are taxed twice, and second, if the corporation operates at a loss, that loss can be utilized only by the corporate entity and cannot be passed through to the investor.

An S corporation is treated essentially the same as a C corporation except for taxation. (S corporations are also subject to certain shareholder limitations designed to insure that income is still taxed at the shareholder level — the corporation may not have more than 75 shareholders, all of whom are individuals or certain trusts, none of whom are nonresident aliens, and with not more than one class of stock.) An S corporation in many respects is taxed similarly to a partnership. Although it provides the corporate benefits of limited liability, centralized management, continuity of life, and free transferability of interests, its profits, losses, deductions, and credits are passed through the entity to the tax returns of the individual shareholders. Essentially, the corporation pays no federal income tax. The shareholders are taxed on the net income of the S corporation, whether or not it is distributed to them.

The obvious advantage of an S corporation to investors is this ability to enjoy the benefits of partnership-like flow-through taxation. The total of the deductions for interest, depreciation, and other expenses of operating and maintaining the investment property is netted against the corporation's operating income. A shareholder's share of losses is deductible only to the extent of the shareholder's (a) basis in the stock, plus (b) the amount of any loans which may have been made by the shareholder to the corporation. Any losses disallowed in a given year as a result of this limitation can be carried forward to future years.

A real estate investment trust (REIT) is a vehicle specifically designed to facilitate large scale public participation in real estate investments. In many respects, a REIT operates similarly to a mutual fund. Having many investors (called the beneficiaries or shareholders), each contributing relatively small amounts of capital, enables the management of the REIT to make diversified and large scale investments on their behalf.

To qualify as a REIT for federal income tax purposes, the trust must generally meet the following requirements:

(a) Five or fewer persons may not own more than 50% of the trust. (This requirement is designed to assure public ownership.)

(b) At least 75% of the REIT's assets must consist of real estate, government securities, or cash.

(c) At least 100 "shareholders" must own an interest in the REIT.

(d) An owner's interest in a REIT must be fully transferable. (This requirement is designed to help maintain a market for the shares.)

(e) At least one trustee must be responsible for the REIT's management.

(f) Certain restrictions on the source of the REIT's income must be met. (These limitations are designed to insure that the nature of the REIT's income is passive.)

(g) At least 95% of the annual taxable income of the REIT must be distributed to the beneficiaries.

Because the REIT essentially operates and will be taxed as a regular ("C") corporation (even though it is called a "trust"), its owners are entitled to many of the benefits of corporate ownership. One of the most important of these is limited liability.

REIT law requires that one or more trustees accept management responsibility. Therefore, a REIT is similar to a corporation in the sense that it provides centralized management.

If the REIT distributes at least 95% of its taxable income, beneficiaries are taxed in a manner similar to that of mutual fund shareholders: all distributions are considered ordinary income dividends and are includible when received by the beneficiaries unless the distribution consists of capital gain income and is designated as such by the REIT. The REIT is entitled to a deduction for these distributions. This eliminates the double taxation that would occur if the REIT were treated precisely the same as a regular corporation for tax purposes.

Similar to a regular corporation, a REIT has an indefinite life. The death of an individual beneficiary does not affect the continuity of the REIT. REITs are more fully discussed in Chapter 41.

The most common form of tax shelter oriented real estate investment ownership is a limited partnership. Interests in such a partnership are generally sold by real estate syndicators.

A syndicated partnership consists of two types of owners, the syndicator-promoters (sometimes referred to as developers) and the investors. A promoter will typically acquire a property (sometimes the promoter will merely obtain an option to buy the property) and then attempt to sell it to a group of investors. In addition to fees, the promoter will retain an ownership interest as a portion of the compensation for its efforts. Alternatively, promoters may form an investment group, raise cash, and then seek to obtain suitable property on behalf of the investors.

An interest in a syndication can be obtained through a representative of a registered broker-dealer. An offering brochure (usually called an "offering memorandum") is provided to potential investors and describes the objectives, benefits, and risks of the venture.

WHAT FEES OR OTHER ACQUISITION COSTS ARE INVOLVED?

An investor purchasing real estate on his own can expect to pay a number of acquisition costs. These include brokers's commissions, legal fees, title examination and registration fees, title insurance, and state and/or local transfer taxes.

The costs of investing in a syndicated real estate venture will be higher than an investment where the owner finds, develops, and manages the property because these responsibilities are assumed by the developer/promoter. An investor can expect to pay more when investing through a public offering than a "private placement" (one which is not required to meet certain state and/or federal securities commission disclosure standards). This is because a private placement does not involve all the costs associated with full SEC registration.

Total fees and commissions in a typical public syndication will range from 16% to 26% of the amount invested. In the case of a private offering, total costs generally range from 13% to 25%. Obviously, the actual total costs will vary considerably with each investment. It is therefore critical that the investor thoroughly review the offering materials and factor the estimated costs into any investment analysis.

HOW DO I SELECT THE BEST OF ITS TYPE?

Because of the unique nature of real estate, "best" is a relative term — at best. An investor should study each of the following major criteria:

(1) Location of the property. (This is the most important single factor and will determine present and future market demand.)

(2) Soundness of construction and appropriateness of design for intended use. (Maintenance costs will be higher with poor construction and rental income may be lower than anticipated if the project is not suited for its intended use.)

(3) Cost of capital. (The interest rate that must be paid on the purchase debt will significantly affect the ultimate profitability of the venture.)

(4) Financing fee. (Requiring payment of "points" has become a prevalent practice. These are paid to the lender on both the construction financing and the permanent mortgage. Each point is 1% of the borrowed amount.)

(5) The cost of operating and maintaining the property. (A review of the track record of the promoter/manager in similar projects is particularly helpful.)

(6) Organization and offering expenses.

(7) Sales commissions.

(8) Construction costs. (Check to see if the general partner's fee will be reduced if costs of construction are higher than projected.)

(9) Fees paid to the general partner for managing the partnership and the underlying investment property.

(10) Projected cash flow and tax results from operations.

WHERE CAN I FIND OUT MORE ABOUT IT?

1. *Tax Facts On Investments (Tax Facts 2)* (Cincinnati, The National Underwriter Company).

2. Gary Barr, *J.K. Lasser's Real Estate Investment Guide* (New York, J.K. Lasser Institute, 1989).

3. David F. Windish, *Tax-Advantaged Investments* (New York, New York Institute of Finance, 1989).

4. Jack Crestol and Herman M. Schneider, *Tax Planning For Investors* (Chicago, Commerce Clearing House, 1991).

The real estate industry offers many educational programs and courses. Some of these include:

(a) The National Marketing Institute of the National Association of Realtors.

(b) The CCIM (Certified Commercial Investment Member) designation for those interested in commercial and investment property.

(c) MAI (Member of the Appraisal Institute) for advisors interested in real estate appraising.

(d) FLI (Farm and Land Institute) for those interested in farm and ranch brokerage.

(e) GRI (Graduate of a Real Estate Institute).

(f) CRB (Certified Residential Broker).

Related courses and certificate programs are also available by calling state and local realtor associations. Many universities and graduate schools also include real estate in their higher education programs.

QUESTIONS AND ANSWERS

Question — What deductions, if any, are available to an investor who purchases unimproved real estate?

Answer — Land is purchased for its future development potential. This investment is suitable mainly for upper income investors who are able to bear the risk of a long term investment while realizing no immediate return.

Tax deductions are available only for interest, real estate taxes, and maintenance expenses. Alternatively, an investor may have the option of capitalizing certain expenditures, foregoing current deductions, and using the increased basis to reduce the gain at sale.

When unimproved land is sold, it is subject to capital gains treatment if the owner is not considered a "dealer."

An individual's gain will be taxed as ordinary income if the property was held "primarily for sale to customers in the ordinary course of trade or business." This "dealer" treatment may apply once the individual has bought and sold a number of parcels of land and then subdivided that land or participated actively in its sale.

In making the distinction between an investor and a dealer, courts focus on the following factors:

(a) The purpose and use for which the investor purchased and held the property.

(b) The length of time between the acquisition and disposition of the property.

(c) The number and frequency of sales.

(d) The degree of active participation of the investor (or his agents).

(e) The developments and improvements made by the investor to place the property on the market.

(f) The manner in which the individual advertises in newspapers and telephone directories, and the presence or absence of (1) a business office to sell the property, and (2) memberships in professional realty associations.

(g) The percentage of income derived from sales of developed and promoted real estate in comparison to the investor's other income.

It is possible for an individual to be considered an investor with respect to some properties while treated as a dealer with respect to others.

Question — Why might an investor exchange rather than sell a real estate investment?

Answer — The tax benefits of exchanging rather than selling real estate have been discussed above in the "tax implications" section: All or a portion of the tax that otherwise would be paid currently on the gain from the sale of property may be postponed. But there are several non-tax reasons for exchanging rather than selling real estate. One reason is that it may not be possible for the potential buyer to obtain adequate financing. A second reason is that the investor may want to acquire land in another location from a person who does not want to recognize a gain on the sale of that property.

Question — What are some of the sources for financing the purchase of real estate?

Answer — Approximately 60% to 70% of the value (as much as 80% for multiple family residential property) of investment real estate to be acquired can be borrowed from various financial institutions. The conventional financing sources include savings and loan associations, commercial banks, mortgage banking companies, and most life insurance companies.

Less conventional sources of real estate financing include mortgage brokers, private lenders, pension funds, REITs, and seller financing ("purchase money" financing).

Question — What are some of the techniques for financing the purchase of real estate?

Answer — Historically, most real estate purchases have been financed by use of long term (15 to 30 year) fixed rate mortgages. For example, an investor could finance 80% of the cost of purchasing a $1,000,000 building by obtaining a 30 year bank loan of $800,000, bearing a fixed rate of interest on the unpaid balance. However, because of uncertainties in interest rates and the effects of inflation, other techniques of structuring the financing of real estate have become more popular. These techniques include

(1) adjustable rate mortgages (ARMs) — The applicable interest rate payable is adjusted periodically (usually annually) as the "money market" dictates.

(2) Equity participation loans — The lender agrees to a fixed or only moderately adjustable interest rate on the condition that upon the sale of the property he will share in the gain realized.

(3) Lease with purchase option — Typically, a third party purchases the property and leases it to the user. The user is given an option to purchase the property at the end of the lease period. The option price is either predetermined or established by the fair market value at the date of the sale. This technique is employed when the user does not have either the immediate ability to purchase the property from the seller or a high enough tax bracket to utilize the tax benefits of ownership.

Question — What marginal tax bracket must an investor be in before real estate makes sense as a tax shelter?

Answer — There is no special breakpoint formula or number at which a real estate (or any other investment) does or does not make sense. The psychological as well as financial character of the investor must be matched to the attributes of the investment.

There is a formula that can be used to help answer the ultimate question with regard to the numbers involved: Will the "bottom line" of this investment increase the client's wealth more than any alternative investment?

The following formula will help regardless of the marginal tax bracket of the investor:

(1) State total cash invested .... $_____
(2) Subtract total tax savings ...... $_____

     After Tax Cost .... $_____

(3) State cash anticipated
     upon disposition .... $_____
(4) Subtract total tax due .... $_____

     After Tax Return .... $_____

(5) Subtract After Tax Return
     from After Tax Cost

     NET GAIN (LOSS) .... $_____

Will the end result of a particular real estate investment increase wealth significantly more than any appropriate alternative? Let's try an example:

Assume

(1) State total cash invested $100,000
(2) Subtract total tax savings .... $ 18,000

     After Tax Cost .... $ 82,000

(3) State cash anticipated
     upon disposition $250,000
(4) Subtract total tax due .... $ 50,000

     After Tax Return $200,000

(5) Subtract After Tax Return
     from After Tax Cost

     NET GAIN (LOSS) $118,000

It is important for the financial planner to recognize that this type of analysis is over simplified. It does not take into account such factors as (1) the time value of money (see Chapters 12 and 13), (2) the investor's personal cash flow needs, (3) the investor's liquidity needs, (4) the investor's personal investment preferences and risk taking propensity.

Chapter 41

REITS (REAL ESTATE INVESTMENT TRUSTS)

WHAT IS IT?

A Real Estate Investment Trust (REIT) is essentially a publicly-traded closed-end investment company that invests in a managed, diversified portfolio of real estate or real estate mortgages and construction loans rather than in financial securities such as stocks and bonds. Although REITs are corporations or trusts, they are not subject to tax at the corporate level if they distribute at least 95% of their net annual earnings to shareholders and meet certain other requirements (discussed below). Investors must pay the tax on the REIT's earnings as the earnings are distributed. Therefore, REITs allow investors to share, with limited liability, the financial and tax benefits of real estate while avoiding the double taxation inherent in corporate ownership.

Investors have three types of REITs to choose from:

(1) Equity REITs acquire ownership interests in commercial, industrial, or residential properties. Income is primarily received from the rentals of these properties.

(2) Mortgage REITs invest in real estate indirectly by lending funds for construction and/or permanent mortgages. In some cases mortgage REITs invest in mortgage-backed securities such as Ginnie Maes or other mortgage-backed obligations.

(3) Hybrid REITs combine the features of both equity and mortgage REITs.

WHEN IS THE USE OF THIS TOOL INDICATED?

1. When an investor has limited capital and cannot afford to purchase real estate properties or mortgages directly.

2. When an investor wants the added safety a broadly diversified portfolio of real estate investments or mortgages provides.

3. When an investor does not have the skill or inclination to manage his own real estate investments.

4. When an investor desires a long-term hedge against inflation, equity REITs are indicated.

5. When an investor desires an investment that provides potentially growing cash flows and the possibility for long-term capital appreciation, equity REITs are indicated.

6. When an investor desires high current income, mortgage REITs are indicated.

7. When an investor desires an investment combining the features of equity REITs and mortgage REITs, hybrid REITs are indicated.

ADVANTAGES

1. Limited liability. REIT shareholders are treated like common stockholders in a regular corporation. Their liability is limited to the amount of their investment.

2. No corporate-level tax. If the REIT distributes 95% of its income to shareholders (and meets certain other requirements described under "Tax Implications" below), there is no corporate-level tax. Therefore, REIT shareholders enjoy limited liability while avoiding the double tax of corporate ownership.

3. Pooling of resources. REITs pool individual investors' funds to acquire real estate interests and provide the investors with access to real estate investment opportunities not normally available to small investors through direct investment in real estate.

4. Knowledgeable professionals. REITs use the services of knowledgeable professionals who provide expert management and have a proven track record. Management compensation represents only a small portion of the overall expenses of these trusts. Thus, the major portion of the REITs' profits flows directly to the investors.

5. Record keeping. The REIT keeps detailed records of transactions, income and loss, distributions, and expenses, and reports regularly to investors, sparing them record keeping responsibility and inconvenience.

6. Small denominations. Most REITs sell for less than $50 a share and, as with other stock investments, there is no minimum number of shares an investor must buy. How-

ever, because of the transactions costs involved, it is generally best to purchase shares in multiples of 100.

7. Ability to leverage investments. Many REITs use both short-term and long-term debt to finance their asset purchases. If the returns on the REIT's investments exceed the interest paid on the debt, the investor's returns are enhanced. However, the use of debt increases the investor's risk because actual returns may not be adequate to pay the interest on the debt.

8. Utility as collateral. An investor's shares in a REIT may also be used as collateral for loans from the investor's bank or broker, subject to limits set by the Federal Reserve.

9. Liquidity. REITs are easily marketable and are traded widely on the various exchanges. In contrast, direct investments in real estate are generally extremely illiquid. In addition, if an investor sells a direct investment in real estate, he must typically sell the entire asset. The REIT investor may sell as few shares as the situation requires and continue holding the balance.

10. Discounts from book value. REITs have generally sold at discounts ranging from 5% to 20% of their book values. In other words, the price paid for a share has typically been less than an investor would have to pay to buy a pro-rata share of the assets in the REIT portfolio directly. This discount in effect creates positive leverage for the investor. For example, assume a mortgage REIT is selling at a 10% discount from book value and the mortgages are yielding 10% inside the REIT. Since the REIT investor is in essence acquiring interests in the mortgage pool at 90 cents on the dollar, his pro-rata share of interest is ten cents for every 90 cents invested. This translates into a yield of 11.1%.

11. High dividend payouts. This is based on the requirement that REITs distribute 95% of their income.

12. Automatic dividend reinvestment. Most REITs allow investors to automatically reinvest dividends (similar to the reinvestment option allowed by mutual funds).

13. Diversification in real estate portfolio. REITs can provide investors with a high degree of risk reduction through diversification because the investment policy of many trusts requires them to spread their investments over wide geographical regions as well as among various property types.

14. Inflation hedge. Real estate has historically proven itself as an excellent hedge against inflation. Equity REITs should provide the same inflation-hedging potential as direct real estate investments. In contrast, mortgage REITs, because they invest in mortgages and other loans where interest rates and principal balances are fixed, will tend to be poor inflation hedges. However, mortgage REITs that invest in variable-rate mortgages and loans will provide some inflation-hedging potential because interest rates will tend to move in concert with inflation.

15. Diversification beyond stocks and bonds. By including real estate investments in their portfolios, investors can reduce their risks and enhance their expected returns beyond what they would enjoy with either a portfolio containing only stocks and bonds or only real estate. In some years when stocks and bonds perform poorly, real estate performs well; in other years, the opposite is often true. Consequently, the returns on a portfolio that includes stocks, bonds, and real estate will tend to fluctuate less severely than returns on portfolios containing only one of these asset categories.

DISADVANTAGES

1. Loss of control. Professional management makes the investment easier for the investor, but it also reduces the investor's control and flexibility in the management of the investment. With direct investments the investor can choose to buy and sell specific assets when it is advantageous for tax or other reasons to do so. With an investment in a REIT, assets are bought and sold at the discretion of the REIT management. Since 95% of the income from both rents or interest and gains on sales of assets must be distributed to investors, the timing of such transactions may be disadvantageous to the investor.

2. Lower potential returns. Although diversification reduces risk, it also reduces the potential for substantial gains. An investor who can afford to invest directly in real estate and who is knowledgeable enough to manage his own real estate portfolio can expect to do better than he could with REIT investments.

3. Management fees and administrative charges. Although management fees are small relative to the overall amount of money involved, typically 0.5% to 1.5% of the value of the investment, they are still an additional expense that an investor may not incur if he manages his own investments. However, these fees are at least in part offset by economies of scale that reduce other transaction costs, such as legal fees and loan origination charges, that would typically be higher for an individual investor.

4. No flow-through of tax benefits. Only tax-sheltered income can be passed through to the investor; losses cannot

be passed through. In contrast, losses may be passed through to investors with direct investments in real estate or with interests in limited partnerships (other than those taxed as corporations).

5. Discounts from book values. As described earlier in the discussion of advantages, REIT shares have generally sold at a discount from their book values. Purchase at a discount enhances an investor's yield, but since these discounts vary over time an investor is faced with the additional risk that share values may decline. If the discount increases after investors have acquired shares in a REIT, they may suffer a capital loss when they sell their shares.

6. Considerable risk. REIT share prices can be just as volatile as stock prices. The amount and sources of risk vary considerably depending on (a) the type of REIT, (b) the management philosophy, and (c) its actual asset/liability makeup. (See "How Do I Select the Best of Its Type?" below for a further discussion of risk.)

7. Poor inflation hedge. Mortgage REITs, which have investment characteristics similar to bonds, are not likely to be good inflation hedges. If inflation rises and causes interest rates to rise, the value of the underlying mortgages and loans will typically fall. Consequently, in inflationary times, share values in mortgage REITs are likely to decline. However, mortgage REITs that invest in variable-rate mortgages and loans will provide some inflation-hedging potential because interest rates will tend to move in concert with inflation.

TAX IMPLICATIONS

1. REITs will not be subject to federal income tax if they satisfy several Internal Revenue Code provisions that require

   (a) that distribution of 95% of net annual earnings be made to shareholders;

   (b) that at least 75% of gross income be derived from real estate—usually rents, mortgage interest, and gains for selling real estate;

   (c) that at least 75% of the REIT's portfolio be invested in real estate, loans secured by real property or mortgages on real estate, shares in other REITs, cash or cash items, or government securities;

   (d) that there be at least 100 shareholders and that no more than half the outstanding shares may be owned by five

   or fewer individuals at any time during the second half of each taxable year; and

   (e) the REIT to be managed by one or more trustees or directors.

2. Although REITs invest in real estate (which is generally subject to the passive activity rules), distributions are treated as investment income, like dividends on stock, and not as passive activity income. (See Chapter 8, "Income Tax Concepts," for a discussion of the passive activity rules.)

3. Shareholders pay taxes on distributions (dividends paid) from the REIT's earnings. Unlike a real estate limited partnership that is not taxed as a corporation, REITs cannot offer flow-through tax benefits, but some trustees pass on cash flow in excess of income as a nontaxable return of capital. Consequently, distributions may include portions that are treated as ordinary income, capital gains or losses, and return of capital.

   Distributed income is taxed as ordinary income to shareholders. Capital gains and losses on the sale of assets in the REIT's portfolio retain their character and are taxed as gains or losses by the investors when distributed. For tax purposes, depreciation, which is a noncash expense, is subtracted from net operating income to derive the REIT's taxable income. Therefore, cash distributions may exceed net income. Distributions in excess of net income are treated as a nontaxable return of capital. Shareholders must reduce the basis in their shares by any such excess distributions.

4. Gains or losses realized when investors sell their shares in a REIT are treated as capital gains or losses. The cost basis for determining gain or loss on sale is the original cost of the shares less cash distributions received in excess of the REIT's net income.

5. REITs are exempt from the requirement that certain pass-through entities report to shareholders, as income, their shares of expenses of the fund which would be miscellaneous itemized deductions if incurred by the shareholders individually.

ALTERNATIVES

1. Direct investments in real estate. Equity REITs allow investors to enjoy many of the benefits of direct investments in real estate; however, by investing through a REIT, investors give up many of the potential advantages of direct real estate investments. One of the major distinc-

tions is that distributions are treated as investment income and not passive activity income as they would be if the real estate were held directly. Also, taxable losses on REIT properties do not flow through to shareholders as they would if the properties were held directly. Consequently, REIT shareholders cannot use taxable losses (income) on REIT properties to offset taxable income (losses) from other real estate investments or other passive activities.

2. Real estate limited partnership interests (RELPs). Many real estate limited partnerships offer investors a pooled real estate investment similar to an equity REIT. However, similar to direct real estate investments, real estate limited partnerships (other than those taxed as corporations) have the flow-through characteristic that is lacking in a REIT.

3. Mutual Funds. Mutual funds that invest in mortgages or mortgage-backed securities offer an investment opportunity that is very similar to a mortgage REIT. One important distinction is the potential leveraging. Most mutual funds that invest in real estate mortgages or mortgage-backed securities limit the amount of borrowing the fund may employ to leverage its investments. Although the amount of borrowing allowed varies from one mortgage REIT to another, many mortgage REITs employ substantial borrowing to finance their asset acquisitions. This feature has both pros and cons, since such leverage can either enhance or depress returns to investors, depending on whether the returns generated by the assets acquired with the debt exceed the interest that must be paid on the debt. Other advantages associated with real estate mutual funds include a high level of diversification, professional management, and ease of ownership.

4. Mortgage-backed securities. Mortgage-backed pass-through certificates, mortgage-backed bonds, CMOs and REMIC bonds are all investments in pools of mortgages that are similar to mortgage REITs.

Except for pass-through certificates such as Ginnie Maes, mortgage-backed securities are typically treated as debt for tax purposes whereas shares in mortgage REITs are treated like common stock. From the investor's perspective, in many cases this may be a distinction without a difference. However, certain items are treated differently for tax purposes at the investor level such as original issue discounts and market discounts on the underlying mortgages and the timing of recognition of principal repayments. In these respects mortgage REITs are much less complicated investments for investors.

Also, most mortgage-backed securities are backed by a fixed pool of mortgages; the pool is liquidated as the mortgages are repaid. Most mortgage REITs have indeterminate lives. They continue to acquire additional mortgages as the older mortgages in the pool are paid off. However, some REITs, called "finite-life REITs," or "FREITs," liquidate their holdings by a given date and distribute the proceeds to investors. FREITs are also unincorporated trusts, while REITs are incorporated.

Some mortgage REITs invest in mortgage-backed securities. Investors who buy shares in these REITs are essentially buying a pool of mortgages and are getting the ultimate in diversification.

5. Residual interests in REMICs. Although residual interests in REMICs have generally been privately placed and are not available to the general public, if the market for these instruments grows as anticipated, residual interests will become publicly traded. Such interests will have characteristics very similar to hybrid REITs, that is, cash flow and appreciation potential similar to a combined investment in equity and mortgage REITs.

WHERE AND HOW DO I GET IT?

Many REITs are listed on the national and regional exchanges. Others are traded in the over-the-counter market. Like common stocks, shares can be acquired from stock brokerage firms, discount brokers, and through many banks and other financial institutions.

WHAT FEES OR OTHER ACQUISITION COSTS ARE INVOLVED?

A commission is commonly charged when shares are purchased or sold. The fee will depend on (1) the amount invested, (2) the number of shares purchased, (3) whether purchased through a full-service broker or a discount broker, and (4) the market in which the shares are traded.

Like common stocks, REIT shares trade in round lots of 100 shares, with odd-lot transactions (less than 100 shares) involving higher commissions. Regular full-service commissions typically range from two to three percent of the dollar value of the shares purchased or sold. Discount brokerage fees range from about 15% to 70% of the regular full-service rate. In either case, there is typically a minimum fee of about $30.

The fee paid to acquire shares that are traded over-the-counter is essentially the "bid-ask spread." Market makers in the OTC market maintain a bid price at which they will purchase shares and an ask price at which they will sell shares. The bid price is always lower than the ask price. The difference, or "spread," is the broker's profit for making a market in the shares. The size of the spread depends on how many shares are outstanding and the volume of trading in the shares. The spread is smaller for very actively traded shares with a large number of shares outstanding.

HOW DO I SELECT THE BEST OF ITS TYPE?

There are over 300 REITs available to investors. These REITs have a wide variety of investment objectives and vary considerably in terms of (1) size, (2) fees, (3) management performance, (4) investment philosophy, (5) capital structure, and (6) asset characteristics. The selection process for REITs is at least as involved as that for stocks or mutual funds, since REITs share many of the characteristics of each. Investors should consider many factors when making their selections. When selecting a REIT:

(1) Ascertain the type of REIT which best meets the investor's objectives with regard to income versus growth and tolerance for risk. Equity REITs generally provide moderate income and opportunities for growing cash flows and capital appreciation. Mortgage REITs generally provide higher income, but less opportunity for growth. Hybrid REITs provide a combination of both types of REITs. As a group, equity REITs are considered riskier than mortgage REITs, but in individual cases the opposite is often the case. Risk factors are discussed below.

(2) Determine whether the management's investment philosophy is consistent with the investor's. The prospectus which accompanies an initial offering always includes a section describing the proposed activities of the trust. Read that section to see if the fund's objective and methods are consistent with the client's. Investors who buy REIT shares in the market after the original offering should obtain a copy of the original prospectus from their broker, if possible. They should also look at the annual reports for the most recent several years to confirm that the REIT management is maintaining a consistent investment philosophy. Among the items that should be considered are

(a) the types of assets that the REIT will invest in,

(b) whether leverage will be employed and, if so, whether there are limits on the amount of debt it can employ,

(c) whether the trust will provide broad diversification or concentrate its investments in a particular type of real property such as motels, health care facilities, or apartments,

(d) whether the trust will diversify geographically,

(e) whether the trust will limit the placement of assets in any one project, and

(f) whether the trust will emphasize income or capital appreciation when selecting its investments.

Each of these items warrants further discussion:

(a) The type of assets the REIT acquires is critical in determining the risk and return characteristics of the REIT and the relative emphasis on income versus capital growth. For example, mortgage REITs that provide construction and development loans will be significantly riskier, and potentially much more profitable, than REITs that invest in government-insured mortgage-backed securities. However, since the default experience on construction and development loans is much higher than on other types of mortgage financing, cash flows from REITs that invest in these loans may fluctuate year to year much more than from REITs that invest in more secure mortgages.

Investors seeking stable income should avoid REITs that direct their investments to construction and development loans. In contrast, these types of REITs are recommended for investors who are looking for high yields and are less concerned with yearly fluctuations.

Some equity REITs focus on new construction and recently completed new properties that have not yet been fully rented up. Others invest only in "proven" properties that have a well-established rental history. The REITs that focus on new properties typically provide low cash flows from rents, but considerable growth potential and substantial capital gains when properties are sold. REITs that invest in proven properties generally provide higher and more predictable cash flows from rents, but less potential for growth and only moderate capital gains when properties are sold. Investors should seek out those REITs whose investment focus will provide the income and growth characteristics they desire.

(b) Leverage can increase investor's returns, but only with a corresponding increase in risk and greater fluctuations in annual returns. In the early 1970s, many REITs had dismal performances, in large part because they were over-leveraged and managed their debt poorly. Since then, in general, REITs have been more conservative in the use of debt to finance their asset acquisitions. However, many REITs still employ debt to leverage their investments. Investors should look at what limits, if any, are placed on the use of leverage. In general, only the most aggressive and risk tolerant investors should consider REITs that use debt extensively.

(c) Some REITs restrict their investments to specific segments of the market, such as health care facilities or motels or residential construction loans. The advantage of such segmentation is that the managers typically know the chosen market segment better than other market segments and can use their expertise to select the better opportunities within that market segment.

The disadvantage is that the REIT is less well diversified and therefore is exposed to additional economic risk. For example, if a REIT specializes in motels, a general downturn in travel and tourism or overbuilding may adversely affect its returns. However, at the same time, demand for health care facilities, or new office space may be booming.

REITs that invest across many market segments will be less affected by economic and business factors that are detrimental to any one segment of the market. Unless an investor feels that one particular market segment offers exceptional opportunities, he will often be better off selecting a REIT that invests in many market segments.

(d) Some REITs also limit their diversification by investing within one geographical region. The advantage of regional specialization is that managers are closer to their market. Successful real estate investing requires a great deal of hands-on management and local knowledge. REITs that invest within a region they know well are less likely to make poor investments. Consequently, many of the smaller REITs are limited in their geographical scope. However, such regional specialization exposes the REIT to the same kind of risk as market segmentation. One geographical region may be suffering adverse business conditions while other regions are booming. Investors who invest in REITs that are geographically diversified reduce their exposure to this kind of risk.

(e) One last aspect of diversification should not be ignored. REITs may limit the proportion of their total assets that may be invested in one project. Clearly, if a major portion of a REIT's total investment is in one or two projects, the REIT essentially lives or dies by those projects. Unless an investor holds considerable assets elsewhere and therefore provides his own diversification, he should generally look for REITs that limit the proportion of their total investment that may be placed in any given project.

(f) To a great extent, the type of assets the REIT acquires will dictate its policy regarding income and capital appreciation. Clearly, mortgage REITs will typically emphasize income, while equity REITs will typically seek at least some capital appreciation. However, how the management directs the portfolio and, in particular, its policy regarding when it sells properties will affect cash flows and growth potential.

Those equity REITs that pursue essentially a "buy-and-hold" philosophy will often provide relatively stable, but growing, cash flows. As the values of the properties in the REIT's portfolio increase, the REIT's share value should also appreciate. Equity REITs that specialize in new construction will often hold properties until they are rented to capacity, and then sell, presumably for substantial gains. Since 95% of the REIT's net income, including gains on sales, must be distributed, investors have to recognize and pay taxes on the gains to the extent cash is distributed. Consequently, such REITs may earn substantial gains on their properties; but the net effect to investors is higher and more volatile cash flows and less potential appreciation in their share value. Therefore, the management's philosophy and policy regarding how they direct their portfolio will greatly affect the degree to which returns are realized as cash flows or as appreciation in share value.

(3) Evaluate the historical performance of those REITs that match the investor's investment objectives and philosophy. Unfortunately, there is no standardized means to compare REITs. Unlike the stock market where performance can be compared with a broad and long-term measure of the market, such as the S&P 500 index, no such commonly accepted measure exists for REITs.

(a) The single most important factor in selecting a REIT is the quality of management. Some of the personal data about management personnel can be found in *Who's Who in Business, Who's Who in America,* or *Dun's Reference Book of Corporate Managements.* Investors should also try to evaluate the management's experience by looking at the performance of previous real estate ventures managed by the team. Success in the past does not guarantee success in the future, but a history of poor performance does suggest less than average prospects for future success.

(b) The critical factors that reflect on the quality of management and the potential performance of a REIT are the (1) dividend payout record, (2) expense ratios, (3) vacancy rates, (4) length of time the REIT management has been in business, (5) the quality or value of the properties in which the REIT invests, and (6) the percentage of ownership held by the managers of the company.

Historical information regarding earnings, dividends, assets, liabilities, expense ratios and the like can be obtained for many REITs from reports issued by investment advisory services such as Value Line, Moody's, and Standard & Poor's. Additional information is presented in the REITs' annual reports. REITs are also rated by the advisory services. Conservative investors should generally avoid REITs that are rated "B" or lower by Moody's or Standard & Poor's, as well as those with a Value Line rating lower than "3."

(4) Project future performance. This, of course, is the most difficult step in the selection process. Growth will depend on the future income from the REIT's holdings. Income will depend on the rent and, sometimes, the sales level of the REIT's properties. Some reliance may be placed on professional appraisals of the REIT's properties to estimate future income growth and appreciation potential. But appraisals do not always reflect the same standards and may be derived using different assumptions regarding rent multipliers or capitalization rates (which are techniques used to value the projected rental stream from a property). In addition, vacancy rates, poor regional economic growth, and overbuilding in the geographic region or the particular market segment favored by the REIT can all affect REIT income. High levels of debt may also cause shareholder dividends to be low.

Given the complexity of selecting the "best" REIT of its type, investors should consider buying shares in several REITs that have the basic investment characteristics and investment philosophy the investor is seeking. By diversifying among several REIT holdings, rather than buying just one, investors can expect about average performance. But they also minimize downside exposure.

WHERE CAN I FIND OUT MORE ABOUT IT?

1. Two books published annually by the National Association of Real Estate Investment Trusts, 1101 17th Street N.W., Washington D.C., are a good place to start finding out more about REITs: *REIT Fact Book* and *The State and Course of the Real Estate Investment Trust Industry*. The *Fact Book* can be acquired for a nominal fee of $1.00 and the *State and Course* book for $16.95.

2. In addition, the investment advisories listed below provide information not only about industries and companies but also about the outlook for the national economy. The investment advisory services cost several hundred dollars per year, but they, along with the books from the National Association of Real Estate Investment Trusts, are available for use in most libraries.

   a. *Value Line Investment Surveys*, 5 East 44th Street, New York, NY;

   b. *Realty Stock Review*, a twice-monthly newsletter which tracks the performance of 100 REITs ($264/year; Audit Investments, 136 Summit Avenue, Montvale, NJ 07645);

   c. *Moody's Handbook of Common Stock*, Moody's Investment Services, 99 Church Street, New York, NY;

   d. *Stock Guide*, Standard & Poor's Corporation, 345 Hudson Street, New York, NY.

3. *The Wall Street Journal, The New York Times*, and most major newspapers will carry daily listings of the trading activity and prices for REITs listed on the major exchanges.

4. Articles on REITs appear periodically in various financial magazines and journals such as *Barron's, Forbes, Fortune, The Wall Street Journal, Money Magazine*, and *Changing Times*.

5. Research reports and other information on specific REITs and current market conditions can be obtained by calling major brokerage firms—especially those firms that make a market in various REIT issues.

QUESTIONS AND ANSWERS

Question—How have REITs performed historically?

Answer—Figure 41.1 shows annual total returns (dividends and gains (losses) in share value) for the various types of

REITS (Real Estate Investment Trusts)

Figure 41.1

Real Estate Investment Trusts Annual Total Return (%), 1972 - 1997				
Year	All	Equity	Mortgage	Hybrid
1972	11.19	8.01	12.17	11.41
1973	(27.22)	(15.52)	(36.26)	(23.37)
1974	(42.23)	(21.40)	(45.32)	(52.22)
1975	36.34	19.30	40.79	49.92
1976	48.97	47.59	51.71	48.19
1977	19.08	22.42	17.82	17.44
1978	(1.64)	10.34	(9.97)	(7.29)
1979	30.53	35.86	16.56	33.81
1980	28.02	24.37	16.80	42.46
1981	8.58	6.00	7.07	12.23
1982	31.64	21.60	48.64	29.56
1983	25.47	30.64	16.90	29.90
1984	14.82	20.93	7.26	17.25
1985	5.92	19.10	(5.20)	4.32
1986	19.18	19.16	19.21	18.75
1987	(10.67)	(3.64)	(15.67)	(17.58)
1988	11.36	13.49	7.30	6.60
1989	(1.81)	8.84	(15.90)	(12.14)
1990	(17.35)	(15.35)	(18.37)	(28.21)
1991	35.68	35.70	31.83	39.16
1992	12.18	14.59	1.92	16.59
1993	18.55	19.65	14.55	21.18
1994	0.81	3.17	(24.30)	4.00
1995	18.31	15.27	63.42	22.99
1996	35.75	35.27	50.86	29.35
1997	18.86	20.26	3.82	10.75
Source: National Association of Real Estate Investment Trusts (www.nareit.com)				

REITs from 1972 through 1997. In the early to mid-1970s REITs performed poorly, along with the general stock market. Economic conditions were partly responsible, but many of the trusts themselves were shaky. The period from 1987 through 1990 was also one of relatively weak returns.

REITs have enjoyed renewed popularity over the past few years due to a strong real estate market, falling interest rates, and a vibrant commercial rental market. Figure 41.2 compares the annualized total returns on equity REITs to those of the S&P 500 stock market index (figures shown are for periods ending December 31, 1996).

Question—Are REITs sensitive to the stock market?

Answer—No, REITs do not normally react substantially to changes in the stock market. REITs are more sensitive to interest rate fluctuations. Generally, the behavior of REITs is opposite that of the behavior of interest rates; as interest rates rise, REITs decline, and as interest rates fall, the cash flow of REITs increases. In this instance, they provide a better source of current income than bonds.

Question—How can diversification be achieved with REITs?

Answer—REIT portfolio diversification is possible in several ways.

(1) Diversification through the real estate portfolio. This is accomplished in two ways. Investments can be made in a variety of property sectors, such as hospitals.

Figure 41.2

Annualuzed Total Returns Equity REITs versus S&P 500 Stock Index					
Investment	1 year	3 year	5 year	10 year	20 year
Equity REITs	35.27%	17.17%	17.14%	11.67%	16.13%
S&P 500	22.96%	19.63%	15.18%	15.27%	14.55%
Source: National Association of Real Estate Investment Trusts (www.nareit.com)					

hotels, or office buildings, rather than in one specific sector. Second, investments can be spread over a wide geographical area that may include foreign countries.

(2) Diversification beyond stocks and bonds. By investing in real estate in addition to stocks and bonds, an investor can enjoy greater returns with less risk. The balance created between the three investment options reduces the fluctuations of returns and risks associated with investments in just one of the assets.

Question — How do REITs and RELPs differ?

Answer—Real Estate Limited Partnerships (RELPs) offer an alternative to REITs; however, they do differ in operational structure, tax treatment, and liquidity.

(1) Operational structure. A REIT is managed by a board of directors that is accountable to shareholders. A RELP is managed by an autonomous general partner.

(2) Tax treatment. REITs are categorized as portfolio investments; therefore, dividends and capital gains and losses are taxed in the same way as any other stock. RELPs, on the other hand, are "passive activity" investments. Accordingly, different tax laws apply regarding gains and losses.

(3) Liquidity. REITs are very liquid due to their active trading on most stock exchanges. RELPs, with the exception of a small group of publicly traded partnerships, are generally illiquid.

Chapter 42

REAL ESTATE MORTGAGE INVESTMENT CONDUITS (REMICs)

WHAT IS IT?

A Real Estate Mortgage Investment Conduit (REMIC) is a limited-life, self-liquidating entity that invests exclusively in real estate mortgages or in securities backed by real estate mortgages.

REMICs may issue two types of securities: "regular interests" and "residual interests." The REMIC may issue multiple classes of regular interests (REMIC bonds) but only one class of residual interests. REMIC bonds are treated for tax purposes as debt securities. Investors who hold REMIC bonds receive a specified cash flow from the underlying pool of mortgages. In this respect REMIC bonds are very similar to collateralized mortgage obligations. They essentially are a hybrid security combining features of conventional bonds and mortgaged-backed participation certificates (PCs) such as Ginnie Mae pass-through certificates. Residual interests are treated for tax purposes much like interests in a partnership or grantor trust. As such, they are roughly comparable to the equity interest in the REMIC entity. Residual interest holders take into account all of the REMIC's net income that is not taken into account by the REMIC bondholders.

A REMIC is typically exempt from federal income tax. In other words, it is a flow-through entity, similar to a partnership; thus, it acts as a conduit and holders of REMIC securities must report any taxable income from the underlying mortgages. A REMIC terminates when its mortgages are repaid.

Eventually, REMICs are intended to be the exclusive means for issuing multiple-class real estate mortgage-backed securities. This means they will eventually replace all collateralized mortgage obligations. In addition, they may become the favored vehicle for issuing securities similar to mortgage-backed participation certificates such as Ginnie Maes.

WHEN IS THE USE OF THIS TOOL INDICATED?

1. When an investor is interested in an income-producing investment with risk and return characteristics similar to conventional bonds, regular interests in REMICs would be indicated.

2. When an investor desires a potentially high-yielding investment with risk and return characteristics similar to common stocks or partnership interests, residual interests will be indicated. Most residual interests have been privately placed and are not generally available to the investing public. However, if the REMIC market grows as anticipated, residual interests will become available to the general public.

3. When an investor wants the added safety provided by pooling a number of mortgages into one investment.

4. When an investor desires a relatively high rate of return on a debt-type instrument. The holders of REMIC bonds should receive a competitive yield on mortgage-backed securities that is generally higher than on other bond-type investments of similar quality and maturity.

5. When an investor wants to diversify beyond the holding of stocks and traditional corporate and government bonds. By investing in REMICs, an investor is expanding his portfolio into real estate and capturing the additional protection such diversity provides.

6. When an investor wants liquidity. Because of their specialized nature, REMIC bonds may not enjoy the same breadth of market as conventional bonds. However, the growth of this market is expected to be significant. It is anticipated that secondary markets will develop for REMIC bonds that are similar to those that currently exist for Ginnie Maes, Fannie Maes, and other mortgage-backed participation certificates. In many cases, the issuers guarantee to maintain a secondary market in these securities. Also, some REMICs are structured to permit REMIC bondholders to redeem their holdings at par value before maturity, subject to limits and other restrictions.

7. When an investor wants a relatively secure type of investment. Regular interests are treated like debt and will have risk characteristics similar to comparably rated traditional bonds. Some REMICs offer both a senior and a subordinated class of interests. Investors who desire low risk may acquire the senior class, which receives all payments of interest and principal before the subordi-

nated class. Investors who are willing to subordinate their interests to the senior class of security holders can expect to receive higher returns for bearing the slightly higher risk.

8. When an investor wants more predictability regarding prepayments of principal than is available with other mortgage-backed securities such as Ginnie Mae pass-through certificates. Since REMICs may issue multiple classes of regular interests, many are structured to offer a short-term class that matures in 3 to 5 years, intermediate-term class(es) that mature(s) in 5 to 15 years, and long-term class(es) that mature(s) in 15 to 30 years. Consequently, investors can invest in classes that match their investment horizons and avoid a great deal of the uncertainty regarding when principal will be repaid.

ADVANTAGES

1. Taxation of REMIC interests is established by statute without regard to their form, provided such interests qualify as regular or residual REMIC interests. Consequently, although regular interests may be issued as stock, bonds, or interests in trusts, they will always be treated as debt (bonds) for tax purposes.

2. Regular interests in many REMICs are virtually risk free in terms of return of principal and certainty of income. The quality of the mortgages in the pool determines the quality of the issue. Many REMICs invest in mortgages guaranteed by the Government National Mortgage Association, the Federal National Mortgage Association, or the Federal Home Loan Mortgage Corporation. In addition, many REMICs have received triple A ratings from one or more of the bond rating companies (Moody's, Standard and Poor's, or Fitch's). However, the use of REMICs to pool both residential and nonresidential mortgages that are not guaranteed by government agencies is expected to grow considerably. In these cases, the risk will depend on (a) the reputation of the issuing agency, (b) the quality of the mortgages in the pool, and (c) the existence and nature of the private insurance, if any, behind the mortgages.

3. REMICs offer investors a way to minimize the "prepayment risk" inherent in a mortgage pool. Prepayment risk arises because the mortgages in the underlying pool may be paid off earlier than anticipated. When prepayments exceed expectations, investors may be forced to reinvest the proceeds at lower current interest rates. When prepayments are slower than expected, investors may lose the opportunity to reinvest at higher current rates. Investors in regular mortgage-backed securities such as Ginnie

Mae pass-through certificates share the prepayment risk in proportion to their ownership of the pool. Since prepayments tend to increase when interest rates fall (because people are more likely to refinance their mortgages), prepayments force investors to reinvest more of their capital when yields on reinvestment opportunities are less.

REMICs can issue different classes of REMIC bonds with different maturity dates, different interest rates, etc., enabling them to appeal to investors with different purposes—for example, safety, yield, long-term or short-term investments. Certain investors have claim to predetermined principal repayment cash flows. As a result, the prepayment risk is not shared equally; rather it is borne sequentially by specific subgroups of the overall investors in the mortgage pool. Consequently, REMICs offer some protection against prepayments to investors who acquire the later maturing classes.

4. REMICs combine the predictable cash flow of bonds with the relatively high yields of mortgage securities. Interest rates on mortgages are typically higher than short-term money market rates or even long-term corporate bond rates. Each class of REMIC bonds will usually yield more than bonds of comparable maturity. Also, since each successive class of securities receives principal repayments only after the prior class has been fully repaid, the cash flow is more predictable than for traditional mortgage-backed participation certificates and more closely resembles the cash flows for traditional bonds. For example, assume a REMIC creates a Class A security paying 8% and a Class B security paying 10%. Holders in Class A must be paid in full before principal may be paid on the Class B securities. A third class might be paid an even higher rate, but only after the Class A and B holders are paid.

5. By segregating the cash flows to create issues with different maturities, investors who have little desire to hold thirty-year mortgages in their portfolios can still participate in the high yields associated with mortgage-secured investments by purchasing one of the shorter-term issues.

6. As the number of these issues grows, the secondary market will also grow. For larger issuers, secondary markets have arisen to provide liquidity if investors need to sell their securities. In some cases, issuers promise to maintain a secondary market or to provide limited redemptions at par value before maturity.

7. The price volatility of REMIC bonds tends to be less than for bonds of similar quality and maturity. Bond prices

generally fall when interest rates increase and rise when interest rates decrease. The longer the term of the bond, the more sensitive the bond price is to a given change in interest rates. The prices of REMIC bonds move in the same general manner, but the velocity of the move is dampened by changes in the rate of prepayments. Prepayments on mortgages tend to accelerate when interest rates decline and homeowners find it advantageous to refinance. As prepayments increase, the average maturity of a given class of regular interests decreases. Consequently, the price of the regular interests will not tend to rise as much as the price of bonds with a similar maturity before the interest rate increase. Prepayments may also slow down somewhat when interest rates increase, since there are fewer refinancings. However, the slowdown in prepayments caused by increases in interest rates is rather limited because mortgagors must still make their required mortgage payments of both principal and interest. In other words, they cannot extend the maturity of their mortgages when interest rates increase. Since some principal is usually repaid on REMIC bonds before the ultimate maturity, even when interest rates rise, the price of REMIC bonds will tend to fall less than the price of bonds of similar maturity when interest rates rise.

8. Although many REMICs have been issued with minimum purchase requirements of $10,000 or more, the minimum purchase requirement is still less than the $25,000 minimum for Ginnie Maes. Most REMICs issue regular interests with smaller denominations that will attract smaller investors. In most cases, REMIC bonds are issued in $1,000 units, similar to conventional corporate bonds.

9. REMICs allow a great deal of flexibility in the forms of the securities it may issue. REMICs may soon offer such features as coupon-stripping, adjustable and variable rates and other innovative forms of securities.

10. REMIC bonds with variable interest rates may provide some inflation-hedging protection since interest rates typically move in concert with inflation.

11. REMICs provide a number of advantages to the issuers, which ultimately will permit a more efficient (less costly) method for packaging and selling multiclass securities and, therefore, provide better returns and features for investors. First, there will no longer be the need (as in the case of CMOs) to follow both debt format and substance. Second, there will be no need for excess equity capital to build in at least a minimum investment risk for the residual holders. Consequently, more capital will be used to acquire high-yielding mortgages rather than to fund excess reserve accounts paying low money-market rates.

Third, the risk that the REMIC may be taxed as a corporation, rather than a flow-through entity, is eliminated if the REMIC rules are followed. Fourth, REMIC regular and residual interests are qualifying assets for thrift institutions and REITs. Residual interests may also be acquired by pension plans without the income being taxed as unrelated business taxable income (with some restrictions). This will broaden both the original issue and secondary markets for these securities. Fifth, residual interests are freely transferable, which means more institutions are likely to create REMICs and further expand the market.

DISADVANTAGES

1. As with other interest-sensitive investments, the price of regular interests in REMICs will tend to fall when market interest rates rise. Investors who must sell their interests before maturity may have to sell them at a loss.

2. The actual yield an investor will realize on a REMIC bond is uncertain, mainly because of the unpredictability of prepayments on the underlying mortgage pool. (See "How Do I Select The Best of Its Type" for an explanation of quoted and realized yields.)

3. Secondary markets are expected to grow significantly as the number of REMIC offerings increases. However, because of their specialized nature, secondary markets for REMIC bonds may never be as well developed as for conventional bonds. For example, except for very large issues with standard features, REMIC bonds will not typically be listed on organized security exchanges. Consequently, investors who must sell their securities before maturity may have to sell at a sizable discount. The size of the discount will depend on the size of the issue, the reputation of the issuer, and the quality of the mortgages backing the security. In some cases, the underwriters and other investment banking firms and financial institutions have promised to maintain secondary markets in the securities. Also, some mortgage-backed securities have been issued with put or redemption features that allow investors to redeem the bonds before maturity at face value, subject to limits and restrictions. Some REMIC issues may include similar features.

4. REMIC bonds with fixed interest rates, similar to fixed-rate bonds and other mortgage-backed debt-type securities, are subject to two types of inflation risk: (1) the risk that the purchasing power of income will be eroded over time, and (2) the risk that the purchasing power of capital received at maturity will have diminished. The second risk is somewhat less than with conventional bonds

because principal is recovered over a period of years and can be reinvested or consumed. It is somewhat higher for the later-maturing classes of REMIC bonds than with pass-through certificates because principal recovery is delayed on these securities until the early-maturing classes have been completely repaid.

5. Similar to many conventional corporate bond issues, many REMIC bonds are callable at the discretion of the issuer. Others are issued with a sinking fund feature which requires that a specified number of securities be redeemed at specified dates. The bonds that are redeemed are typically determined by random lot. Consequently, like conventional callable corporate bonds, REMIC bonds may be redeemed before the holder would otherwise choose to redeem them.

TAX IMPLICATIONS

1. There is a great deal of flexibility in the form of entity that may be used for a REMIC. A trust, partnership, corporation, association, or merely a segregated pool of mortgages is suitable. Once the entity elects REMIC status at startup, the initial form of the issuing entity is ignored and the entity is taxed under the special REMIC rules. REMICs are taxed as pass-through entities, that is, there is no entity-level tax. Except for certain prohibited transactions, REMIC taxable income or loss flows through to the holders of residual interests on a pro-rata basis.

2. REGULAR INTERESTS

   (a) A regular interest is treated as debt, regardless of its form.

   (b) REMIC bonds have two unique features for tax purposes. First, holders of REMIC bonds must use the accrual method to report income on their bonds, even if they are cash-basis taxpayers for other purposes. Second, a special rule requires that a part of the gain on sale or exchange of a REMIC bond be taxed as ordinary income.

      On a sale or exchange, the owner of a REMIC bond recognizes gain if the amount received exceeds the adjusted basis of the bond (or loss if the amount received is less than its adjusted basis). The adjusted basis will generally equal the investor's cost, increased by any original issue discount or market discount that has been included in income, and reduced by (1) any previous principal payments received and (2) premium amortization. The gain or loss, adjusted by any unrecognized market discount

and the part of the gain subject to the special rule cited above, will be taxed as a capital gain or loss. The portion of gain attributable to market discount is taxed as ordinary income.

The portion of gain on the sale or exchange of a REMIC bond that is treated as ordinary income under the special rule is an amount equal to the excess of (1) the amount that would have been includable on the bond if its yield were 110% of the applicable Federal rate (AFR) in effect when the holder's holding period began, over (2) the amount actually included by the holder in gross income during the time the bond was held.

For example, assume a REMIC bond paying 8% interest per year is acquired for $1,000. The AFR at the time of acquisition is 9%. In three years the bond is sold for $1,100. The gain, assuming no payments of principal have been received, is $100. The amount of interest actually included in income is $240. The amount that would have been includable in income if the yield were 110% of the 9% AFR is $297 (9.9% times $1,000 times 3). Therefore, $57 ($297-$240) of the $100 gain on sale is treated as ordinary income and the remaining $43 is treated as long-term capital gain.

   (c) Each investor is required to report as ordinary income the interest paid or accrued on the indebtedness, and the "original issue discount" or "market discount," if applicable. The amount that must be reported as ordinary income is decreased by "premium amortization," if applicable.

      Original issue discounts (OIDs), market discounts, and premiums arise when there is a difference between the acquisition price of a debt instrument and the total principal amounts that will be repaid on the security until it matures. If a debt instrument is acquired for a price that is greater than the total principal payments that will be repaid on the security, the difference is called a premium. A premium typically arises when the coupon rate on a debt instrument is greater than the market rate of interest for comparable debt securities. For example, a regular $1,000 face-value bond with a 10% coupon rate and 25 years to maturity would sell for, perhaps, $1,100, or a $100 premium, if the market rate of interest on comparable bonds is 9%. Conversely, if the purchase price in the after-original issue (secondary) market of a debt instrument (originally issued at par) is less than the total principal payments, the difference is called a market discount. Market discount typically occurs when market interest rates rise above the coupon rate on the debt instrument.

Real Estate Mortgage Investment Conduits (REMICs)

Figure 42.1

year	cash interest	Straight-line			Constant-rate		
		accrued discount	taxable interest	accum'd discount	accrued discount	taxable interest	accum'd discount
1	$50.00	$41.67	$91.67	$41.67	$37.50	$87.50	$37.50
2	50.00	41.67	91.67	83.34	41.25	91.25	78.75
3	50.00	41.66	91.66	125.00	46.25	96.25	125.00

An original issue discount is essentially the same as a market discount, except that it arises when a debt instrument is acquired from the original issuer, rather than in the secondary market. Despite the similarity, OIDs and market discounts are accounted for separately because they are treated differently for tax purposes.

OIDs in REMICs may arise in two ways: (1) the mortgages in the pool are acquired with an OID (which is not typically the case), or (2) the class of regular interests is structured so that the issue price is less than the redemption price (which is more common). If OID arises in the second way and the term of such indebtedness is in excess of one year, OID must be reported as ordinary income by each investor as it accrues, in accordance with a constant-rate method that takes compounding into account and in advance of the cash attributable to such income.

A special rule exists for calculating OID on debt instruments that have a maturity that is initially fixed but may accelerate based on prepayments. In general, OID on such indebtedness is calculated and included in the holder's income by (1) accruing the discount using the original yield to maturity for the instrument assuming that a certain level of prepayments will occur, (2) increasing the amount of income recognized as more frequent prepayments occur, and (3) decreasing the amount of accrued income (but never below zero) if there is a reduction in prepayments.

If OID arises because the mortgages in the pool are acquired with an OID, the residual interest holders, not the regular interest holders, must report the OID. In these cases the residual interest holders will typically have reportable income in excess of the cash income on the mortgages and in excess of the deductible interest payments on the regular interests. (The original issue discount rules are discussed in more detail in Chapter 24, "Corporate Bonds.")

Market discount may also arise in two ways: (1) mortgages in the pool are acquired at a market discount from the total of the principal payments that will be paid on the mortgages, or (2) the investor acquires the REMIC bond for a price that is less than the unpaid principal balance on the bond. In the second case, investors have an option as to when the market discount will be taxed and at what rate it will accrue. Market discount will accrue either (1) at a constant rate, or (2) in proportion to original issue discount accrual, if there is such discount, or ratably in proportion to stated interest on regular interests.

These two market discount accrual methods can best be understood by example. Assume a 5-percent coupon bond ($50 per year in interest) that matures in 3 years for $1,000 is selling for $875, a $125 discount. The market rate of interest is 10%. Using the straight-line method the investor would accrue one-third of the discount, or $41.67, each year. Adding this together with the $50 coupon amount, the investor would report and be taxed on $91.67 ($50 plus $41.67) of interest each year. Using the constant-rate method the investor would report interest at the rate of 10% each year based on the outstanding principal balance on the bond. The principal balance in the first year is $875. Therefore the taxable interest is $87.50. Of this amount, $37.50 ($87.50 taxable interest minus $50 cash interest) is attributable to recovery of the discount. Because the investor receives no cash for the discount until the bond matures, it is added to the outstanding principal balance. In the second year the outstanding principal balance is $912.50 ($875 original price plus $37.50 accrued discount). Therefore, the investor must report $91.25 as taxable interest. The amount of the discount accrued in the second year is $41.25 ($91.25 taxable interest minus $50 cash interest) which is added to $912.50 to determine the $953.75 principal balance outstanding in the third year. At the end of the third year when the $1,000 face value of the bond is repaid, the investor reports $96.25 of taxable interest ($50 cash interest plus the remaining $46.25 of unrecovered discount).

In summary, the two methods provide the cash flows and taxable interest each year shown in Figure 42.1.

Since the amount of market discount that accrues before the maturity of the debt instrument is always less with the constant-rate method than with the straight-line method, investors are always better off for tax purposes if they elect to use the constant-rate method to compute accrued market discount.

Investors may choose not only the method for computing the accrued market discount, but also may decide when they will recognize the accrued market discount for tax purposes. Unless the investor elects otherwise, the accrued market discount will generally be recognized upon receipt of payments treated as principal payments. Alternatively, investors may elect to recognize market discount currently as it accrues, but before principal payments are actually received. In most cases, investors are better off deferring recognition of market discounts until principal payments are received.

If mortgages in the pool are acquired at a market discount, once again, the residual interest holders, not the regular interest holders, will take the discount into income and pay any taxes that might be due. The residual holders have the same elections available for timing of recognition of market discounts as the regular interest holders do for their market discounts.

If the unpaid principal balance on a debt instrument is less than the investor's cost, the excess purchase price is deemed to be premium. Premium may be amortized and deducted by the investor over the life of the debt instrument using the constant-rate method.

(d) Principal payments received are considered nontaxable return of capital to the extent of the investor's basis in the security, except to the extent of any market discount. (Payments of principal in excess of basis would typically arise only in circumstances where the investor contributed property, instead of cash, to acquire the securities and the investor's basis in the contributed property was less than the fair market value.)

3. RESIDUAL INTERESTS.

(a) Residual interest holders must compute their taxable income from the REMIC on an accrual basis even if they are cash-basis taxpayers for other purposes. In essence, they are taxed as if they owned a pro-rata partnership interest in the REMIC's taxable income. REMIC taxable income generally means

the REMIC's gross income, including

(i) interest,

(ii) original issue discount income,

(iii) accrued market discount income on the qualified mortgages owned by the REMIC, and

(iv) income on reinvestment of cash flows and reserve assets,

minus deductions, including

(i) interest and original issue discount expense on the REMIC bonds,

(ii) premium amortization,

(iii) servicing fees on qualified mortgages, and

(iv) bond administration expenses.

(b) Taxable losses are limited to the residual holder's adjusted basis. (In other words, residual interest holders cannot take losses in excess of their investment in the interest.) However, losses may be carried over indefinitely and used to offset future income generated by the same REMIC.

(c) An individual investor will be allowed to deduct certain expenses, including expenses for the production of income such as mortgage servicing fees and possibly administrative expenses of REMICs, only to the extent that his miscellaneous deductions in the aggregate exceed 2 percent of the investor's adjusted gross income.

(d) As a result of the multiclass structure of the regular interests, a REMIC's taxable income may include what is called "phantom income." Phantom or noncash income arises as a result of timing differences between the recognition of accrued income on the underlying mortgages and the corresponding interest deductions for payments on the regular interests. It results in part from the fact that the interest deductions accrue at a rate that increases over time as the typically lower-yielding classes of REMIC bonds are retired, whereas the interest income on the underlying mortgages accrues at a constant rate. This phantom income in the early years will generally be recovered by offsetting "phantom losses" in the later years (when cash income exceeds taxable income).

(e) Residual holders are also subject to a complicated set of rules that limit the deductions that may be passed through the REMIC to reduce their taxable income from the REMIC. In general, these rules provide that a residual holder's taxable income shall in no event be less than what is called the excess inclusion. Excess inclusion arises because of the phantom income problem described above.

(f) In addition to reporting the taxable income of the REMIC, residual holders will have taxable income to the extent cash distributions from the REMIC exceed their basis in their residual interests. Basis is equal to the amount of money paid for the interest increased by the amount of taxable income reported by the holder and decreased by the amount of loss reported by the holder. Cash distributions paid to the holder reduce the basis.

(g) Gains or losses on the sale or exchange of residual interests or liquidation of the REMIC generally will be treated as capital gains or losses. However, certain losses on dispositions of residual interests will be disallowed or deferred if the seller of the interest, during a six-month period before or after the disposition, acquires any residual interest in any REMIC that is economically comparable to the residual interest that was sold.

ALTERNATIVES

1. Many large mutual fund families offer funds that invest in mortgage-backed securities such as PCs (participation certificates) issued by GNMA, FNMA, FHLMC, and private issuers, and CMOs. Minimum required investments are usually less than $2,500, which is considerably less than the $25,000 required for direct investment in participation certificates and less than the minimum investment required for many REMIC bonds. They also allow investors automatically to reinvest interest, principal, or both, if desired. These mutual funds hold a broadly diversified portfolio of mortgage-backed securities with various maturities and yields. Therefore,

(a) the yield uncertainty is typically less than with direct investments in PCs, CMOs, or REMIC bonds, and

(b) the price volatility generally will be less than with these instruments if the average maturity of the fund's portfolio is less than the maturity of these instruments.

However, mutual fund investors are not able to get the prepayment protection available to REMIC bond investors who acquire classes of REMIC bonds that do not repay principal until classes with shorter maturities are fully repaid.

2. Ginnie Maes, Fannie Maes, Freddie Macs and other PCs offered by private institutions possess many of the features of REMIC bonds, but without the flexibility to match maturity to the desired holding period and without the prepayment protection of the longer-maturity REMIC bonds. (Chapter 32, "Mortgage-Backed Securities," discusses the characteristics of PCs in more detail.)

3. Real Estate Investment Trusts (REITs) offer some of the same features as REMICs. In fact, some REITs may be organized as REMICs. (Chapter 41, "REITs (Real Estate Investment Trusts)," discusses the features of this investment vehicle.)

4. Expect to see mutual funds offering REMIC funds before long. These funds will provide investors with double diversification by pooling REMIC interests which themselves hold a pool of mortgages.

5. Collateralized mortgage obligations (CMOs) are mortgage-backed securities with features very similar to REMIC bonds.

WHERE AND HOW DO I GET IT?

Interests in REMICs can be acquired from a brokerage firm in much the same fashion as stocks and bonds. Some issues are offered by thrift institutions and banks that offer investment services.

WHAT FEES OR OTHER ACQUISITION COSTS ARE INVOLVED?

The fees or acquisition costs depend on how the investor acquires the security. Investors will pay no commission on new issues. The issuer or underwriter absorbs the initial sales costs. If the security is acquired in the secondary after-issue market, an investor can expect to pay a fee ranging from $2.50 to $20.00 per unit, depending on how many units are acquired. In most cases, the fee will not be less than $30.00.

HOW DO I SELECT THE BEST OF ITS TYPE?

REMICs are complex vehicles. To select the best of its type an investor must evaluate both the underlying mortgages backing the security and the characteristics of the security itself. Some of the distinctions an investor should consider when evaluating a REMIC include:

(1) The identity of the issuer of the underlying mortgages. Mortgages guaranteed or backed by a U.S. Government Agency provide the highest degree of safety of principal. Those insured by private institutions, though still quite secure, are somewhat less safe than government-backed mortgages.

(2) The types of guarantees on the underlying mortgages. Guarantees may assure that both interest and principal are paid in a timely manner or they may simply guarantee that interest is paid in a timely manner and that principal is ultimately paid (perhaps up to a year after it is due). Some issues include hazard insurance as well (covering such risks as earthquakes and floods).

(3) The risk-return tradeoff. The safest mortgages with the most prompt payoff are those guaranteed by GNMA. They trade at a lower yield than other types of mortgages. Mortgages insured by private institutions trade at higher yields because of the slightly higher risk of default or delay in payment of principal. Mortgages insured by FNMA or FHLMC represent a middle ground with yields slightly higher than on GNMAs and lower than on privately insured mortgages.

(4) The quoted yield and the assumed prepayment rate on the underlying mortgages. The return actually realized by an investor may differ substantially from the quoted yield if actual prepayments on the underlying mortgages differ substantially from the assumptions used to compute the quoted yield. (See the Question and Answer section for a discussion of how the yield is computed.)

(5) The characteristics of the mortgage pool that serves as collateral for the REMICs. FHA and VA mortgages tend to prepay more slowly than conventional loans because they are often assumable and are not due on sale. Also, conventional mortgages tend to have higher original principal balances (because of the ceiling on the amount the FHA and VA will guarantee) which means they also imply higher-income homeowners who have a greater tendency to trade up or to relocate.

(6) The similarity in the coupon rates and maturity dates of the mortgages in the pool. Some REMICs are issued from pools of mortgages that all have the same coupon rate, others may have mortgages having coupons spanning a range of rates. A pool of mortgages with a weighted average coupon rate of 10 percent where individual mortgages within the pool have coupon rates ranging from 8 to 12 percent is likely to have a different prepayment rate than a pool where all the mortgages in the pool have a coupon rate of 10 percent. Similarly, pools with varying final maturity dates on individual mortgages are likely to have a different prepayment pattern than pools where all the mortgages have the same final maturity date, even though the weighted average life is the same in both pools.

(7) The pool size and diversification. A large, geographically diversified pool of mortgages is more likely to experience "average" prepayment experience than a smaller and less geographically diversified pool. However, it may be easier to estimate actual prepayment experience for a smaller, geographically isolated pool of mortgages.

(8) The relative size and number of classes of REMIC bonds in the issue. A particular class has protection from prepayments as long as a faster-paying class exists. If the first few classes are small relative to the size of the overall issue, they could be paid off quickly if the actual prepayment rate is higher than expected.

(9) The return on collection accounts and reserve funds. Payments of interest and principal on the underlying mortgages may not correspond with the timing of payments to REMIC bond holders. Consequently, the issuer must place cash flows from the underlying mortgages in a collection account invested in high-grade money-market instruments until the funds are paid to REMIC bond holders. In some cases, the REMIC has reserve funds that serve as additional collateral for the regular interests. The bond rating agencies require that the issuer assume a conservative below-market reinvestment rate (3 to 5 percent) on these short-term investments. That assumption is built into the quoted yield. Some issuers use the excess earned on these funds over the assumed rate to pay off principal on the earliest maturing classes. This shortens the effective maturity of the REMIC bonds and raises the realized yield over the quoted yield. Other issuers pay the excess cash flow to the residual interest holders. The size of the collection and reserve funds, the rate assumed earned on these funds, and whether or not the issuer uses the excess earned on these funds to pay off the REMIC bonds all affect the quoted yield

and the potential yield investors can expect on the REMIC bonds.

(10) The existence of a secondary market in the securities or the presence of a put or redemption feature for the REMIC bond holder. Liquidity varies considerably among REMIC offerings. In some cases, issuers, together with the underwriting syndicate of investment bankers, agree to make a secondary market in the securities to make the offering more attractive to potential investors. Also, some issues have a put (sell back) feature that allows bondholders to redeem their bonds before maturity, subject to certain limits and restrictions. This additional liquidity comes at a price. Typically, REMICs with such features will yield less than those without them.

WHERE CAN I FIND OUT MORE ABOUT IT?

Investment bankers and brokerage firms that have underwritten these offerings have brochures available that describe the basic operation of these types of securities. Since REMICs are complex instruments and each offering has its own characteristics, the only thorough description of any given REMIC is the initial offering prospectus, which can be acquired from brokers who participate in the offering. Also, brokerage firms making a secondary market in these securities should be able to provide bid and ask price quotes and yield information.

For a broad discussion of REMICs consider the following articles:

(1) Robert A. Rudnick and Joseph R. Parise, "Real Estate Mortgage Investment Conduits: An Introduction," *The Journal Of Taxation Of Investments* (Summer 1987), pp. 238-257

(2) Michael Hirchfeld and Thomas A. Humphreys, "Tax Reform Brings New Certainty to Mortgage-Backed Securities," *The Journal Of Taxation* (May 1987), pp. 280-286

(3) Arnold C. Johnson, "Real Estate Mortgage Investment Conduits—A Flexible New Tax Structure for Issuers and Investors," *Tax Notes* (March 2, 1987), pp. 911-918

(4) Charles M. Levitin, "REMICs: Removing Tax Obstacles to More Efficient Trading of Mortgage-backed Securities," *Real Estate Review* (Summer 1987), pp. 26-34

For a discussion of all types of loan-backed securities, including mortgage-backed securities and securities backed by nonmortgage loans, consider

(5) Christine Pavel, "Securitization," *Economic Perspectives*, Federal Reserve Bank of Chicago, Vol. 10, No. 5 (July/August 1986), pp. 16-31.

QUESTIONS AND ANSWERS

Question — How is the yield on a REMIC bond determined?

Answer — To determine the actual yield on a REMIC bond an investor must analyze and assess two key factors: (1) the probability of realizing the quoted yield and (2) the probability of realizing the expected maturity. Both the yield quotation and the projected maturity depend on the specific prepayment assumption. Realized prepayment depends on the demographic, financial, and contractual nature of the underlying mortgage assets as well as on the structure of the REMIC issue itself.

(1) The quoted yield on a REMIC bond is the internal rate of return (IRR) of all cash inflows (the interest and principal payments) and cash outflows (the price paid for the security). Simply stated, the IRR can be viewed as follows: If the investor placed the purchase price of the REMIC bond in an interest bearing savings account paying interest equal to the IRR, he could withdraw cash from the account exactly matching the projected cash flows from the security with no balance left over. The quoted yield (IRR) depends critically on when prepayments of principal are assumed to occur. The problem is that yields have been quoted in different ways by different dealers, making comparisons based on quoted yields all but impossible.

(2) The yield actually realized by an investor may vary significantly from the quoted yield depending on when prepayments of principal actually occur as compared with the assumed prepayments that were used to calculate the quoted yields.

Investors who buy REMIC bonds at a premium (when the interest rate promised exceeds current market rates of return for comparable securities) will realize yields that are less than the quoted yields if actual prepayments are faster than assumed prepayments. Conversely, realized yields will be higher than quoted yields if actual prepayments are slower than assumed prepayments.

Figure 42.2

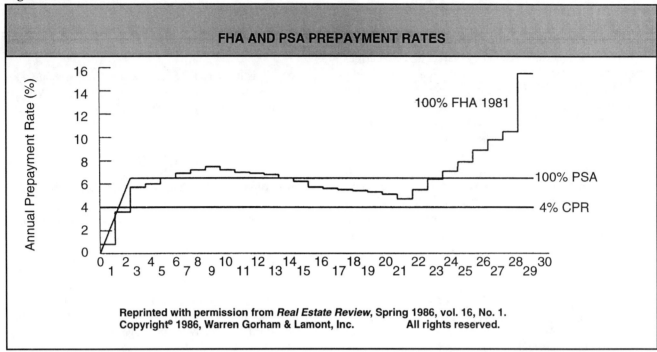

FHA AND PSA PREPAYMENT RATES

Investors who buy REMIC bonds at a discount (when the interest rate promised is less than current market rates for comparable securities) will realize yields that are less than the quoted yields if actual prepayments are slower than assumed prepayments. Realized yields will be greater than quoted yields if actual prepayments are faster than assumed prepayments.

Investors who buy REMIC bonds at par (when the interest rate promised is equal to current market rates for comparable securities) will realize yields equal to the quoted yield, regardless of when prepayments occur.

In addition, regardless of whether investors purchase their interests at a premium, at a discount, or at par, the timing of actual prepayments will significantly affect their potential total return including reinvestment. Specifically, if actual prepayments are faster than assumed and interest rates have fallen, reinvestment return will be lower than expected. If interest rates have risen, reinvestment return will increase. Conversely, if actual prepayments are slower than assumed, reinvestment return will be either higher or lower than expected depending on whether interest rates have risen or fallen, respectively.

(3) The quoted yield will not accurately reflect an investor's potential realized yield unless actual prepayments

equal assumed prepayments. The difference between the quoted and realized yield will be greater, the greater the difference between assumed and actual prepayments. Consequently, to compare potential investments in mortgage-backed securities and to determine a realistic estimate of the potential yield, investors must understand the types of prepayment assumptions that are used to compute quoted yields.

The weighted average life (WAL) is commonly used in the secondary mortgage market as a measure of the effective maturity of a mortgage pool. The slower the assumed payments the longer the WAL. The shorter the WAL the faster the assumed prepayments. A number of conventional specifications of assumed prepayment rates have been used.

The first and simplest specification is to assume the "standard mortgage yield." This specification assumes there are no prepayments whatsoever until year 12 on 30-year mortgages, when all the mortgages in the pool are assumed to prepay entirely. Of course, some prepayments are inevitable before year 12. Therefore, a quoted yield based on this "standard" prepayment assumption seriously understates the potential yield on a security trading at a deep discount and overstates the potential yield on one selling at a premium.

A second prepayment specification bases assumed prepayments on FHA experience. The FHA compiles historical data on the actual incidence of prepayment on the mortgage loans it insures. The quoted yield is determined by assuming some ratio of FHA experience. For example, if prepayments are expected to be slower than historical FHA experience, a ratio of 75% of the FHA experience might be used. The benefit of this method is that it uses historically validated assumptions, including in particular the tendency to have higher prepayments in the first few years of the mortgage pool than in later years. The problem with this method is that it incorporates information on a variety of market conditions and mortgages that may not reflect the attributes of the underlying mortgage pool. Figure 42.2 shows the annual FHA prepayment rates based on 1981 experience.

A third prepayment specification is the constant prepayment rate (CPR). This specification assumes that the percentage of the principal balance that is prepaid during a given year is a constant, such as 6 percent. Because of its simplicity, the CPR method has often been used to determine quoted yields. Figure 42.2 shows the annual prepayment rates based on a 4% constant assumed rate.

Finally, many quoted yields are now based on the standard prepayment experience offered by the Public Securities Association (PSA), an industry trade group. The PSA's goal is to bring some standardization to the marketplace. Essentially, the PSA standard is a combination of the FHA experience method and the CPR method. The first 30 months of the PSA standard calls for a steadily rising prepayment rate. After that, the rate is assumed constant at 6 percent. Figure 42.2 shows the assumed annual prepayments using the PSA standard method. Similar to the FHA method, the quoted yield may be computed using some ratio of the PSA standard if prepayments are expected to be faster or slower than the normal. For example, 150% of the PSA standard would project prepayment rates that are half again as great as under normal conditions.

Question — How do REMICs operate to reduce the prepayment risk inherent in other mortgage-backed securities such as pass-through participation certificates?

Answer— One problem investors have with mortgage-backed participation certificates (PCs) such as Ginnie Maes is that their maturity is uncertain due to the unpredictability of prepayments. PCs on a given mortgage pool are all identical, have a single stated maturity, and pass through a pro-rata share of all cash flows to all participants in the mortgage pool. REMIC bonds are debt instruments, not pass-through securities. Instead of having a single stated maturity, they bear maturities that are staggered or "fast-pay, slow-pay." In other words, some classes of interests (technically called tranches) receive all the principal that is repaid on the underlying mortgages before others. Within each tranche, cash flow is distributed in a pro-rata fashion. By packaging a mortgage pool in such a way, investors have the opportunity to acquire securities with short-term, intermediate-term, or long-term characteristics even though the mortgages backing the securities may have 25-year or 30-year maturities.

Figure 42.3 shows how a REMIC backed by a pool of 30-year mortgages and with 3 tranches of securities would operate. Panel A of Figure 42.3 shows the cash flows of a typical PC based on a pool of 30-year mortgages assuming a 6% annual prepayment rate. The height of the bars indicates the relative magnitude of the anticipated cash flows each year. The dark section of each bar represents the principal repayment portion of each cash flow and the remaining portion represents interest. The weighted average life (WAL) is 11.57 years. If prepayments materialized as assumed, a PC holder would receive decreasing payments of both interest and principal over the life of the certificate.

Panel B shows the cash-flow pattern of the class A securities which receive all scheduled and unscheduled principal payments on the pool until that class is entirely paid off. The WAL of the class A securities is just over 3 years. The class B securities (panel C) are paid interest only until the class A securities are paid off and then all principal payments are allocated to the class B securities. The WAL of the class B securities is about 10½ years. Finally, the class C securities (Panel D) are paid interest only until the class B securities are paid off and then all principal payments are allocated to class C securities until the mortgage pool is liquidated. The WAL of the class C securities is about 21 years.

Question — May issuers of REMICs offer a redemption feature?

Answer — Yes, issuers may offer a redemption feature to make the offering more attractive to investors and enhance marketability. These securities include a "put" (sell back right) that allows holders to redeem their securities at par value before maturity, subject to limits. In this manner investors are even better able to pick their desired maturity. This put option is usually combined with a "call" (buy back) provision and a "sinking fund" provision that allows the issuer to redeem some or all of the securities before maturity. In these circumstances the

Figure 42.3

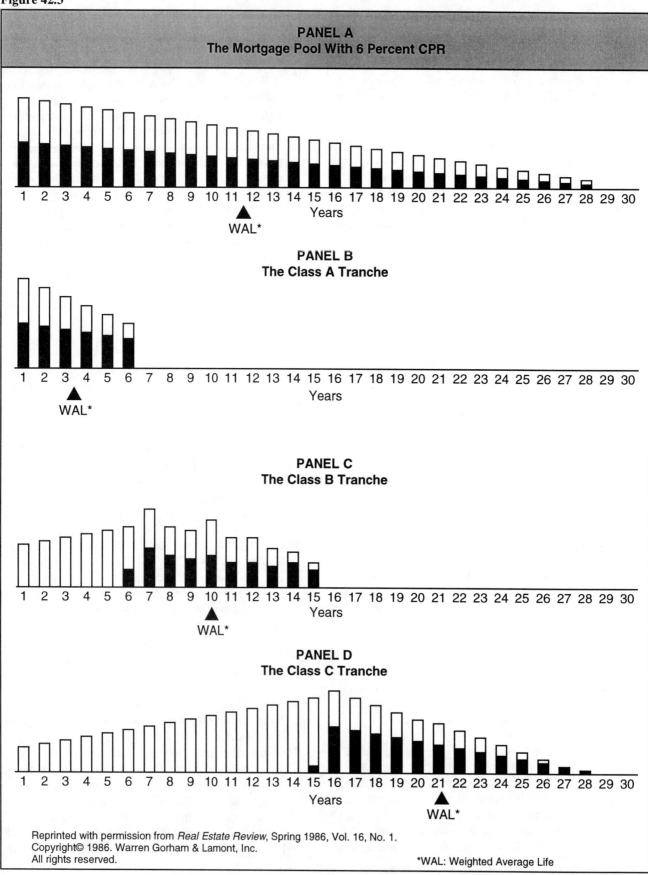

PANEL A
The Mortgage Pool With 6 Percent CPR

Years

WAL*

PANEL B
The Class A Tranche

Years

WAL*

PANEL C
The Class B Tranche

Years

WAL*

PANEL D
The Class C Tranche

Years

WAL*

redemption fund is equal to the amount that has built up in the sinking fund. Security holders who wish to redeem their bonds may do so to the extent funds are available in the redemption fund. If desired redemptions exceed the amount in the redemption fund, redemptions are usually allowed on a first-come, first-served basis within a specified priority schedule. For instance, priority may be given first to deceased bondholders for up to $100,000 each; second to all other holders for up to $10,000 each; third to any remaining bonds for deceased bond holders; and finally to any other redemption requests in the order received.

Typically, if desired redemptions do not exceed the amount in the redemption fund on specified dates, the issuer will call (redeem) additional bonds, determined by random lot, until the redemption fund is depleted.

Question — Can one class of REMIC bonds be subordinated to another class?

Answer — Yes. An interest in a REMIC will still be a regular interest even if the payments of principal are subordinated to other regular interests.

Issuers may use this arrangement to make the senior class more attractive to investors. If cash flows are insufficient to pay principal and interest on all securities, the senior class will be paid first.

Question — What is a "full accrual bond" (also called a "Z-class bond")?

Answer — REMIC issues may include an accrual bond, typically designated class Z. The Z class bond is effectively a zero-coupon bond. The interest that is earned by the Z-class bond is not paid to the Z-class bond holder. Instead it is used to pay down principal on the earlier maturing tranches, effectively shortening their maturities. The compounded accrued interest that it has earned is added to the outstanding principal balance. Once all earlier maturing tranches are paid off, all interest and principal from the underlying mortgage pool is paid to the Z-class bond holders. Often, when all other tranches have been paid off, the issuer will liquidate the remaining mortgages in the pool and pay off the Z-class bond holders in one lump sum. The Z-class bonds are especially suitable for pension funds which do not have to pay tax on the accruing interest. For unsheltered investors, the accrued but unpaid interest is taxable as it accrues.

Consequently, such investors would have to pay tax on the interest that accrues even though they are not currently receiving any cash flow from the investment.

Question — May REMICs issue REMIC bonds with variable interest rates?

Answer — Yes. Variable rate interests may be issued where the interest paid is based on a weighted average of the interest rates on the qualifying mortgages held by the REMIC or where it is based on some other index, independent of the rates on the underlying mortgages. However, if the variable rate is not based on a weighted average of the underlying mortgages, the variable rate REMIC bonds must qualify as "variable rate debt instruments" under regulations dealing with original issue discount. These regulations insure that the variable rates are not constructed in such a fashion so as to avoid the original issue discount rules.

Question — A regular interest in a REMIC is clearly a type of bond, where the owner looks to interest and principal payments in return for his or her investment. But what do residual interest holders receive for their investment?

Answer — A residual interest is defined very broadly and simply (but not very descriptively) as any interest that is not a regular interest. Generally, residual interests are meant to be rights to payments that are contingent on the speed of prepayments. For example, a right to receive part of the income from a mortgage that represents what is called "excess servicing" may be a residual interest because that income is contingent on the prepayment rate of the underlying mortgage pool. For instance, assume a bank originates a loan with a 10% coupon rate. Later it decides to sell the loan when the market rate of interest is 9%. The 10% loan may be difficult to sell because investors are reluctant to pay a premium when they risk that the loan will be prepaid before the premium is amortized. The bank therefore sells the loan at a lower price to yield 9% so that the buyers do not have to risk losing the premium if the mortgage is prepaid. The bank then retains the excess one percent. This retained interest above the market rate is called excess servicing. Also, REMIC residual interests may receive the earnings on qualified reserve funds that are set aside to pay for unexpected expenses or as additional collateral in the case of defaults and on cash flows that are reinvested until needed to pay the amounts guaranteed to holders of regular interests.

Chapter 43

RETIREMENT PLAN ROLLOVERS

WHAT IS IT?

Tax free "rollovers" of distributions from qualified plans, IRAs and SEPs, and Section 403(b) tax-deferred annuity plans are specifically allowed by the Internal Revenue Code. A rollover means a distribution of money or property from a retirement plan can be transferred or "rolled over" to a special type of traditional IRA — the traditional rollover IRA. Alternatively, in some cases the distribution can be rolled over to another plan of the same type — for example, from a qualified plan of one employer to another employer's qualified plan.

The rollover is an important financial planning technique for this reason: If the rollover is made within 60 days of receipt of the distribution and follows statutory rules, the tax on the distribution is deferred. In other words, the receipt of the distribution is not a taxable event to the participant so long as the rollover is properly completed.

WHEN IS THE USE OF THIS TOOL INDICATED?

1. When a retirement plan participant receives a large plan distribution upon retirement or termination of employment and wants to defer taxes (and avoid early distribution penalties, if any) on part or all of the distribution.

2. When a participant in a qualified retirement plan or a 403(b) annuity plan receives a large distribution upon the termination of the qualified retirement or 403(b) annuity plan, has no current need for the income, and wishes to defer taxes on it.

3. When a participant in a qualified plan, 403(b) annuity plan, or IRA would like to continue to defer taxes on the money in the plan, but wants to change the form of the investment or gain greater control over it.

ADVANTAGES

1. A rollover converts an otherwise taxable distribution from a retirement plan into a nontaxable event (assuming the rollover is made within the 60 day period and the distribution is an "eligible rollover distribution").

2. When plan money is rolled over into an IRA, the rollover IRA can give the plan participant greater investment discretion than was possible under the original qualified retirement plan or 403(b) annuity.

3. Distributions from a rollover IRA can often be structured to provide greater flexibility in planning than was possible under the original qualified plan or 403(b) annuity plan. Payouts from a rollover IRA can be structured to match the circumstances and meet the needs of a participant.

4. A rollover can be used as a means of terminating a Keogh or other qualified plan that is dormant and no longer useful to a self-employed person. If the Keogh plan is simply terminated and "frozen," ERISA annual reporting requirements such as filing Form 5500 continue to apply. However, if the terminated Keogh plan proceeds are rolled over into an IRA, the ERISA reporting requirements no longer apply.

5. The IRA rollover can be used as a means of avoiding the early distribution penalty for distributions from qualified plans. For example, if a plan participant under age 59½ receives a lump-sum plan termination distribution, it is generally subject to penalty tax. But if the same distribution is rolled over, distributions from the rollover IRA can be structured to avoid the penalty.

6. If a plan participant leaves his or her job and goes to work for another employer, a rollover IRA can be used as a "conduit" to receive a distribution from the first plan. Then the distribution can later be transferred from the rollover IRA into a second qualified plan if it permits such transfers. It is also possible to roll over the distribution from the first plan directly to the second plan.

DISADVANTAGES

1. If part or all of a lump-sum distribution from a qualified plan is rolled over to an IRA, any available 5-year (or 10-year, where applicable) averaging tax computation for these lump-sum distributions is lost, unless the rollover amount is kept segregated and later rolled over into another qualified plan. Special averaging cannot be used for a subsequent lump-sum distribution from the rollover

IRA. The special 5-year averaging provisions were repealed for distributions after December 31, 1999. However, persons born before January 1, 1936 may continue to elect after December 31, 1999 to use 10-year averaging and to treat amounts attributable to participation in a plan before January 1, 1974 as separately taxable capital gains taxed at a rate of 20 percent. Also, if only part of the qualified plan distribution is rolled over to an IRA, any otherwise-available 5-year (or 10-year) averaging tax computation becomes unavailable for the part of the distribution that is *not* rolled over.

Thus, for a lump-sum distribution from a qualified plan, the advantages of 5-year (or 10-year) averaging must be weighed against the advantages of tax deferral that a rollover can make possible. It is not always easy to quantify these benefits because many assumptions must be made about the future rates of investment earnings, future tax rates, and the time at which withdrawals will be made from the rollover IRA.

2. Since a participant's spouse has spousal rights under federal law in the participant's qualified plan benefit, the spouse must consent in writing to any plan distribution which would qualify for rollover. These rights can have a considerable dollar value to the spouse. So only a "fully informed" consent is likely to be recognized legally. In many cases, it will not be in the spouse's interest to consent to such a distribution and, thereby, to the termination of any spousal rights.

3. Statutory requirements such as the 60-day limit must be strictly adhered to. Any deviation from Code requirements will result in a complete loss of the tax deferral of the rollover and possibly in the imposition of a penalty tax if the excess contribution to the IRA is not withdrawn in a timely manner.

4. Distributions from a rollover IRA are subject to all of the same limitations and rules applicable to traditional IRAs in general. The distribution rules for traditional IRAs are in some ways more restrictive than the rules for qualified plans. Specifically, distributions from IRAs must commence under the minimum distributions rules by April 1 of the year following the calendar year in which the owner reaches age 70½. For anyone other than a 5% or more owner, distributions from qualified plans must commence by the *later* of April 1 of the year following the calendar year in which the participant (1) reaches the age of 70½, or (2) retires.

5. Rollovers are not available for all qualified plan or Section 403(b) tax deferred annuity distributions (see the discussion under "Tax Implications").

6. Amounts from a qualified plan that constitute the participant's nontaxable basis may not be rolled over to a conduit IRA. Only the taxable portion of a distribution from a qualified plan (i.e., the amount defined as an "eligible rollover distribution") may be rolled over to an IRA. What this means is that the participant will no longer earn tax-deferred income on that portion of the distribution which represents his or her basis in the plan. A participant may acquire nontaxable basis in a qualified plan in a number of ways. For instance, basis will include such things as any nondeductible voluntary contributions made to the plan (when such contributions were permitted), any, P.S. 58 costs associated with the "pure-death-costs" element of life insurance owned by the plan on the life of the participant, and any loan balances from the plan that were treated as deemed distributions (generally for failure to repay the loan on a timely basis, even though the loan still had to be repaid).

7. Since IRAs may not own life insurance, any life insurance owned by a qualified plan on the life of a participant may not be rolled over to a conduit IRA. There are several possible remedies to this problem. The plan administrator may surrender the policy and distribute the cash value along with the rest of the plan balance. In this case the entire amount may be rolled over to the IRA. However, since life insurance that may have been acquired by the plan when the participant was much younger is usually a valuable asset, it would often be better if the policy could remain in force. The plan administrator may distribute the policy along with the cash balance. In this case, the value of the policy (its "interpolated terminal reserve," which is essentially its cash value plus any unearned premiums) will be taxable to the participant and may be subject to the 10-percent penalty tax if received before age 59½. Alternatively, the participant may negotiate to purchase the policy from the plan, if he has the necessary resources to do so. In this case, he preserves the policy while also preserving the maximum amount for rollover to the IRA.

8. Qualified plans often include provisions to permit loans from the plan. IRAs may not permit loans. Therefore, rolling qualified plan balances to an IRA may restrict a person's access to funds through loans when needed for relatively short-term purposes. The only alternative is to withdraw funds which will be subject to tax and possibly the early distribution penalty.

TAX IMPLICATIONS

1. In general, any part of the taxable portion of a distribution received from a qualified retirement plan or a tax sheltered annuity, other than a required minimum distribu-

tion, can be rolled over to a traditional IRA without incurring income tax. Under certain circumstances a distribution from a qualified plan may be rolled over to another qualified plan and a distribution from a tax sheltered annuity may be rolled over to another tax sheltered annuity. However, no tax-free rollover is permitted if the distribution is part of a series of substantially equal payments made over the life expectancy of the plan participant or the joint life expectancies of the participant and his or her beneficiary or over a period of ten or more years.

Further, any qualified retirement plan or tax sheltered annuity must allow its participants to elect to have any distribution that is eligible for rollover treatment handled by means of a direct rollover. If this method is not elected, but rather the funds are distributed to the individual participant, a mandatory income tax withholding rate of 20% will apply. The participant cannot elect out of withholding from such a distribution. This mandatory 20 percent withholding rate applies even if the participant receiving the distribution rolls the funds over within 60 days.

2. The distribution from the qualified plan must be transferred to the IRA not later than the 60th day after the distribution. Failure to meet this requirement subjects the distribution to income taxes; however, in the case of distributions received before January 1, 2000, the participant may be eligible to elect special 5-year averaging to cushion the blow if the distribution meets certain requirements. Furthermore, persons born before January 1, 1936 may elect to use 10-year averaging for certain distributions, regardless of when they are made.

3. Distributions from the rollover IRA are not eligible for any otherwise-available 5-year (or 10-year) averaging tax treatment.

4. Distributions from the rollover IRA are subject to the same rules and limitations as all traditional IRA distributions, discussed in Chapter 28. To summarize, distributions must: (a) begin no later than April 1 of the year after the participant attains age 70½, and (b) be made in minimum amounts based on a life or joint life annuity payout. Distributions from rollover IRAs are generally fully taxable as ordinary income; however, if a participant in a qualified retirement plan has a basis in the plan, (e.g., if nondeductible employee contributions were made) those amounts will be excludable from income. Distributions prior to age 59½ are subject to the 10 percent early withdrawal penalty, with the exceptions explained in Chapter 28.

5. Loans from a rollover IRA, like loans from any other IRA, are not permitted.

6. If a participant dies before withdrawing all of the rollover IRA account, the death benefit is includable in the deceased participant's estate for federal estate tax purposes. If payable to the participant's surviving spouse in a qualifying manner, the marital deduction will defer estate taxes.

7. An IRA can be used as a conduit to hold qualified plan funds for transfer from one qualified plan to another when an employee changes employers. The initial transfer from the qualified plan to the IRA is tax free if the amount is transferred within 60 days. If the IRA contains no assets other than those attributable to the distribution from the qualified plan, then the amount in the IRA may subsequently be transferred tax free to another qualified plan, if the plan allows such transfers. An existing IRA should not be used for conduit rollovers; a new one should be established. Note that unless the transfer from the first qualified retirement plan to the rollover IRA is accomplished by means of a direct rollover, a mandatory income tax withholding rate of 20% will apply.

An IRA can also be used as a conduit between two Section 403(b) annuity plans. However, conduit rollovers are not permitted between a qualified plan and a Section 403(b) annuity plan.

As an alternative to a conduit IRA, an eligible rollover distribution can be rolled over directly to another qualified plan covering the employee, without using an IRA. However, the second qualified plan must be in existence and must permit such rollovers.

ALTERNATIVES

1. In cases where the rollover IRA is an alternative to leaving the money in the existing qualified plan, it may be better — or no worse — to leave the money in the plan if the participant is satisfied with the qualified plan's investment performance and the payout options available under that plan meet the participant's needs.

2. Results similar to a rollover IRA can be achieved if the qualified plan distributes an annuity contract to a participant in lieu of a cash distribution. The annuity contract does not have to meet the requirements of an IRA, but the tax implications and distribution restrictions are generally similar.

3. If a participant's objective is to absorb an existing Keogh or other qualified pension or profit-sharing plan account to avoid continuing administrative requirements, there is an alternative to the rollover IRA. Simply make a direct rollover by transferring all the assets directly from the trustee of the old Keogh plan to the trustee of the new transferee plan. This can be advantageous because a distribution from the plan may then be eligible for special averaging (if such treatment is otherwise available; see Chapter 39). However, there are potential tax traps in this type of transaction and it should be done only under the guidance of an experienced tax adviser.

WHERE AND HOW DO I GET IT?

Rollover IRAs are administered on much the same basis as traditional IRAs and therefore are available from many banks, thrift institutions, insurance companies, and mutual funds. Since a rollover IRA typically involves much more money that the usual $2,000 annual contribution IRA, many of these organizations are eagerly looking for this type of business and it should be easy to obtain information about rollover IRAs from them.

WHAT FEES OR OTHER ACQUISITION COSTS ARE INVOLVED?

As with other traditional IRAs, rollover IRAs involve minimal cost. Many banks, insurance companies, and other providers will establish the rollover IRA with no initial charge, and may charge only a small annual maintenance fee, such as $10 per year, to maintain the account. Where substantial amounts are involved, as is often the case, the participant should have the advice of a tax professional before going ahead with the transaction, to make sure that all the requirements for a rollover IRA are satisfied.

HOW DO I SELECT THE BEST OF ITS TYPE?

The choice of the best provider of a rollover IRA is similar to the choice for any other IRA as discussed in Chapter 28, except that since more money is typically involved, the investigation should be correspondingly thorough. Investment performance, investment flexibility, and reliability of service are important.

WHERE CAN I FIND OUT MORE ABOUT IT?

1. The technical requirements for rollover IRAs are explained in IRS publication 590. This booklet is available from local offices of the Internal Revenue Services or by writing to: Internal Revenue Service, Washington, D.C. 20224.

2. Providers of rollover IRAs such as banks, thrift institutions, insurance companies, and mutual funds, are generally willing to provide information on their services and investment products for rollover IRAs without charge. The same providers who advertise traditional IRAs, Roth IRAs and Keogh plans usually provide rollover IRAs as well.

QUESTIONS AND ANSWERS

Question — Can I take out just part of the money in my qualified plan or 403(b) annuity plan and roll it over to an IRA tax free?

Answer —Yes. Generally, an "eligible rollover distribution," which is defined as any distribution made to an employee of any portion of the balance to his or her credit, can be rolled over to an IRA. Thus, it is possible for an employee to roll over something less than the full amount to his or her credit in the plan to a rollover IRA.

Question — Suppose the original plan participant dies and leaves a plan benefit to a beneficiary. Can the beneficiary avoid current income tax on this death benefit by rolling it over into an IRA?

Answer — Only a participant's spouse can roll over a death benefit distribution to an IRA, and the rollover must be made within 60 days of receipt. Alternatively, the spouse can elect to treat an inherited IRA as the spouse's own IRA, with much the same results as a rollover. Beneficiaries other than a surviving spouse of the participant are not eligible for these provisions.

Question — Is there a $2,000 annual limit or other limit on rollover IRAs?

Answer — There is no dollar limit on the amount of a distribution that can be rolled over from a qualified plan or 403(b) plan to an IRA.

Question — Can my existing traditional IRA be used for receiving rollovers from my qualified plan?

Answer — Yes, an existing IRA can be used to receive rollovers from qualified plans; however, it is generally advisable to set up a separate account. The use of the IRA as a conduit for later rollovers to another qualified plan requires a separate rollover IRA. This is because no amount in the IRA used as a conduit can be attributable to any source other than an eligible rollover distribution from a qualified plan.

Question — If I receive a distribution of property such as company stock from my qualified plan, can I sell the property and roll over the cash proceeds to an IRA?

Answer — The Code requires that either the same property received from the qualified plan or the proceeds of a bona fide sale of the property must be rolled over to the IRA. The IRS has ruled that it is not permissible to keep the property received and then roll the equivalent cash over to an IRA.

Question — If I have a rollover IRA, can I continue contributing to a traditional or Roth IRA?

Answer — The existence of a rollover IRA does not affect your continuing eligibility for annual IRA contributions. Traditional IRA contributions may be deductible if you are not an active participant in a regular qualified plan, a 403(b) annuity plan, or a simplified employee pension. If either you or your spouse is an active participant in an employer-provided retirement plan, you may still deduct all or a portion of your IRA contributions if you fall below the adjusted gross income limits, as discussed in Chapter 28.

Question — If an employee has made after tax (nondeductible) contributions to a qualified plan, a portion of the plan distribution is nontaxable, reflecting the prior after tax contributions. Can the entire amount of such a distribution be rolled over to an IRA?

Answer — No, only the taxable portion of a distribution may be rolled over to an IRA. The amount that reflects after tax contributions is nontaxable and is not eligible for rollover.

Question — May I roll my qualified plan balances into a Roth IRA?

Answer — Effectively, yes, but it must be done indirectly. There is no provision permitting a participant to roll qualified plan balances into a Roth IRA. However, an eligible rollover distribution from a qualified plan may be rolled over to a traditional IRA, and then the traditional IRA may be rolled over or converted to a Roth IRA if the IRA owner meets all of the qualifying criteria. (See Chapter 27 on Roth IRAs for a discussion of the traditional IRA to Roth IRA rollover rules.)

Chapter 44

SIMPLIFIED EMPLOYEE PENSION (SEP)

WHAT IS IT?

A simplified employee pension (SEP) is a relatively easily administered, compliance simple, and low-cost IRA-based, small business retirement plan that is similar to a qualified profit-sharing plan. Essentially, a SEP is simply a nondiscriminatory plan maintained by a small employer who makes contributions to IRAs maintained by employees. In contrast with ordinary IRAs, where each individual's annual contributions are limited to $2,000, the employer may contribute up to *the lesser of* 15 percent of compensation or $30,000 (the Section 415 limits), subject to the limit on covered compensation (under Section 401(a)(17)), which is $160,000 as indexed in 1998. Effectively, this means the employer may contribute a maximum of $24,000 to the account of an employee earning $160,000 or more (in 1998).

Similar to profit-sharing plans, the employer has great flexibility in the selection of the contribution rate for employees each year as long as the rate is uniform and nondiscriminatory for all eligible employees. SEPs may be integrated with Social Security and, if the plan was adopted before January 1, 1997, may include elective employee salary reduction provisions (SARSEPs). SEPs adopted after December 31, 1996 may not include salary reduction provisions.

WHEN IS IT INDICATED?

1. When a small employer is looking for a "no-frills" profit-sharing or defined contribution type plan that is easier to adopt and administer than a qualified plan. The simplest method of implementing a SEP is to adopt the IRS model plan using Form 5305-SEP. In such a case, the reporting and disclosure requirements are simplified, and the employer is not required to file the annual 5500 series report form. However, if this model plan form is used, the plan may not be integrated with Social Security, the employer may not maintain any other qualified plans, and the employer must not have *ever* maintained a defined benefit plan. In addition, the plan is automatically assumed to be top heavy, thus requiring certain minimum contributions for all nonhighly compensated employees.

2. Employers looking for a relatively easily administered "add-on" profit-sharing type plan to compliment their already established qualified defined benefit or defined contribution type plan or who wish to implement a plan that is integrated with Social Security may install a prototype plan with the desired features. In theory, the employer will have to bear the added expense of a custom design; however, in practice, many banks, mutual fund families, brokerage houses, and other financial institutions have an assortment of IRS approved SEP prototype plans that include the most commonly desired features excluded from the IRS model plan. Such a plan can be installed at minimal cost, and may include Social Security integration or the provisions necessary to coordinate benefits with another employer-sponsored qualified plans.

3. SEPs are **NOT** indicated when the employer wishes to install a salary reduction plan since SEPs adopted after December 31, 1996 are not permitted to include salary reduction provisions. Employers wishing to use a salary reduction feature without being subject to the compliance requirements of a qualified plan may wish to consider a SIMPLE IRA plan (see Chapter 45).

ADVANTAGES

1. The adoption procedures and administrative and compliance requirements are generally much less complex and less expensive for SEPs than for qualified plans.

2. Since the employer makes contributions to employee-owned IRAs and all contributions are 100 percent vested in the employees, the SEP accounts are entirely portable.

3. Similar to profit-sharing plans, the employer has great flexibility in the amount and timing of contributions to the plan and may even skip contributions in any given year if desired.

4. Individual employees are responsible for directing the investments in their accounts, which permits the employees to benefit from superior investment results.

5. The employer does not have the same fiduciary duty to participants with respect to investment advice and counsel as with a qualified profit-sharing or Section 401(k) plan. It is generally not legally necessary to monitor the investment performance of an IRA trustee for compliance with an ERISA standard of prudence in the selection of investments. Instead, each employee takes on this responsibility in selecting the investments used for his or her IRA.

DISADVANTAGES

1. As with any type of profit-sharing plan, employees have no assurance they will accumulate adequate retirement benefits. Employers are not required to make regular or significant annual contributions. This problem is especially acute for older employees who have only a limited number of years to accumulate their retirement nest egg.

2. Employees bear all of the investment risk. Even if the employer makes regular and sizable annual contributions, the account balance at retirement may be inadequate if the investment results are poor.

3. Similar to qualified profit-sharing plans, the maximum annual contribution is constrained by the contribution limits of Section 415 and the covered compensation limit of Section 401(a)(17). These limits mean, respectively, (I) that annual contributions may not exceed the lesser of (a) 15 percent of compensation or (b) $30,000 and (II) the maximum amount of compensation that may be taken into account is (in 1998, as indexed) $160,000. For highly-compensated employees, the maximum contribution (in 1998) is $24,000 (15% x $160,000), In contrast, the maximum contribution in a defined contribution plan (in 1998) is $30,000, since the Section 415 percentage limit is 25 percent of compensation (subject still to the covered compensation limit).

4. Unlike qualified plans, SEPs, as IRA-based account plans, may not permit employee loans. Therefore, employees who need money for their children's educations, to buy a home, or for any other financial difficulty, may not borrow money from the plan. Since they do own the IRAs and the amounts are completely vested, employees may withdraw money from their accounts at their discretion, but most withdrawals are subject to both ordinary income tax and the 10-percent early withdrawal penalty if withdrawn before age 59½.

5. Distributions from SEP-IRA accounts must commence under the minimum distribution rules by age 70½, even if an employee is still working. In contrast, for rank-and-file employees distributions from qualified plans do not have to begin under the minimum distribution rules until after retirement, even if they remain employed after age 70½.

TAXATION

1. An employer may deduct contributions of up to 15% to a SEP (effectively $24,000 in 1998 because of the $160,000 covered compensation limit) if the contributions meet the various requirements applicable to SEPs. The major SEP requirements are:

- A SEP must cover all employees: (1) who are at least 21 years of age, (2) who have worked for the employer, full or part time, during three of the last five calendar years, and (3) whose compensation for the calendar year was at least $400 (in 1998, as indexed for inflation).

  For this purpose, employees of affiliated employers must be covered. Affiliated employers include (1) other corporations in a controlled group of corporations with the sponsoring employer, (2) all trades or businesses, whether or not incorporated, that are under common control with the sponsoring employer, and (3) all organizations that are members of an affiliated service group with the sponsoring employer.

- The plan must not discriminate in favor of highly-compensated employees, which means that SEP formulas must usually provide allocations as a uniform percentage of total compensation of each employee. IRS rulings have permitted allocations based upon a flat amount for each employee, since such an allocation formula essentially discriminates against, rather than for, highly-compensated employees. Plans that are integrated with Social Security under the integration rules applicable to qualified defined contribution plans are deemed not to discriminate in favor of highly-compensated employees.

- A SEP may exclude employees who are (1) members of a collective bargaining unit if retirement benefits have been the subject of good-faith bargaining or (2) nonresident aliens with no U.S. earned income.

2. Employer contributions (and employee salary reductions in the grandfathered SARSEP plans) are not included in the employee's taxable income for federal income tax purposes. However, salary reductions, but not direct employer contributions, are subject to Social Security (FICA) and federal unemployment (FUTA) taxes.

3. If an employer maintains a SEP and also maintains a regular qualified plan, SEP contributions reduce the amounts that can be deducted for contributions to the regular qualified plan.

4. Distributions to employees are treated as distributions from a traditional IRA. All of the normal rules for traditional IRA distributions apply to SEP-IRAs, including the rollover rules, the pre-59½ withdrawals penalty provisions and exceptions, and the minimum distribution

rules. The 5-year and 10-year lump-sum averaging provisions (see Chapter 39 on qualified plans) are not available to SEP participants.

ALTERNATIVES

1. Qualified defined contribution and/or profit sharing plan. These plans offer greater flexibility and options for the employer but also impose greater administrative, fiduciary, compliance and reporting duties and generally greater costs on the employer.

2. Section 401(k) cash or deferred arrangement. These are salary reduction profit-sharing type plans that, depending on the contribution formula, can be funded almost entirely through salary reductions, rather than employer contributions. Similar to other qualified plans, the administrative, fiduciary, compliance, and reporting duties apply to 401(k) plans; thus, the operational costs generally are greater for these plans than for SEPs.

3. SIMPLE IRA or SIMPLE 401(k) Plan. SIMPLE IRAs were enacted as a replacement for salary reduction SEPs (SARSEPs) as the relatively easily and inexpensively installed and administered salary reduction plan option for small employers. However, both types of SIMPLE plans offer the employer much less flexibility with respect to employer contributions than with a regular SEP or salary reduction SEP plan. SIMPLE 401(k) plans maintain many of the compliance requirements of a traditional 401(k) plan, but offer a design-based funding formula that eliminates ADP/ACP testing.

WHERE CAN I FIND OUT MORE?

IRS Publication 334, Tax Guide for Business, and Publication 535, Business Expense Deductions, are published annually and are available free from the IRS.

QUESTIONS AND ANSWERS

Question — Must the employer be a corporation to adopt a SEP plan?

Answer — No. Partners and sole proprietors and other employees of nonincorporated business ventures may be covered under a SEP plan. In the case of partners and sole proprietors, earned income is used in place of compensation in computing SEP contributions.

Question — Under the rules for traditional IRAs, no contributions are deductible after age 70½. Does this mean that an employer may not make contributions to SEP-IRAs on behalf of employees who are over age 70½?

Answer — No. Employers may make contributions on behalf of employees over age 70½, even though the contributions are to IRA accounts. Note, however, that in contrast with regular qualified pension or profit sharing plans, distributions for all employees must commence at age 70½ under the minimum distribution rules for traditional IRAs, even if the individual is still employed.

Question — What happens if an employer contributes too much to the account of an employee?

Answer — If the actual contributions to the SEPs of the employees exceed the amounts the employees should have received under the allocation formula, some employees may be penalized according to procedures set forth in IRS regulations.[1] The smallest percentage of compensation actually contributed to the SEP of an employee is used as a baseline; that percentage is applied to the other employees to determine the "excess" allocations made to their SEPs. The excess allocations do not disqualify their SEPs; instead those allocations are treated as excess IRA contributions.[2] As excess contributions, they will be subject to a 6-percent excise tax annually until corrected.

Although the excess allocations are not deductible as SEP contributions, they will be considered payment of compensation by the employer to the employees and usually will be deductible as business expenses or expenses of producing income, subject to the requirements that the compensation be ordinary and necessary and be reasonable in amount. Finally, the excess allocations will not be considered SEP contributions for purposes of the usual exemption from FICA and FUTA (social security and federal unemployment) taxes, resulting in increased taxes on the employer and employees.

Question — How is a SEP plan integrated with Social Security?

Answer — A SEP arrangement is permitted to provide some disparity in contributions based on Social Security integration, under the same rules that apply to defined contribution Section 401(a) qualified plans.[3] Therefore, a SEP arrangement may provide employees whose compensation is above the Social Security taxable wage base with a contribution that has a higher excess percentage of their compensation than the base percentage provided for employees earning less than the taxable wage base. The difference can be as much as 5.7 percent.[4]

For example, In 1998 a SEP arrangement provides for contributions of 10 percent of compensation up to $68,400 (the 1998 Social Security wage base) and 15.7 percent of compensation in excess of $68,400. There are three eligible employees, A, B and C, who have compensation for the 1998 plan year in the following amounts and receive the indicated allocations:

	A	B	C
Compensation	$100,000.00	$25,000.00	$15,000.00
Allocation amount	$11,801.20	$2,500.00	$1,500.00
Effective contribution rate	11.80%	10.00%	10.00%

The arrangement is properly integrated even though A (who is a highly compensated employee) receives a total allocation under the plan that is a higher percentage than that provided for B or C.

Question — Can an employee participating in a SEP also make deductible contributions to his own IRA?

Answer — Active participation in a SEP is treated like active participation in a qualified plan for purposes of deducting IRA contributions. Employees are considered active participants in a SEP plan in any year in which salary reductions or employer contributions are allocated to their SEP-IRA accounts. Participants whose income is below the "active participation" phaseout range can make fully deductible contributions of up to $2,000 to their own IRAs. Participants whose adjusted gross income falls within the phaseout range are permitted to make a $2,000

contribution to their IRAs, but the deduction is reduced in pro-rata fashion. For instance, if the phaseout range is $50,000 to $60,000 and a participant's adjusted gross income is $54,000, $800 of the $2,000 IRA contribution would be nondeductible and the remaining $1,200 would be deductible. The phaseout ranges for single and married taxpayers change each year until the year 2007 as shown in the following table:[5]

Taxable Years Beginning in:	Joint Returns Phase-out Range	Single Taxpayers Phase-out Range
1998	$50,000 —$60,000	$30,000 — $40,000
1999	$51,000 — $61,000	$31,000 — $41,000
2000	$52,000 — $62,000	$32,000 — $42,000
2001	$53,000 — $63,000	$33,000 — $43,000
2002	$54,000 — $64,000	$34,000 — $44,000
2003	$60,000 — $70,000	$40,000 — $50,000
2004	$65,000 — $75,000	$45,000 — $55,000
2005	$70,000 — $80,000	$50,000 — $60,000
2006	$75,000 — $85,000	$50,000 — $60,000
2007 and thereafter	$80,000 — $100,000	$50,000 — $60,000

FOOTNOTE REFERENCES

Simplified Employee Pension (SEP)

1. Prop. Regs. §1.408-7(f).
2. See the explanation in Chapter 28, Individual Retirement Accounts, regarding excess contributions to an IRA.
3. IRC Section 408(k)(3)(D).
4. See IRC Section 401(l).
5. See Chapter 28 on Individual Retirement Accounts for a more complete explanation of the phaseout rules and the deductibility of IRA contributions.

Chapter 45

SIMPLE PLAN

WHAT IS IT?

The "SIMPLE" in SIMPLE plans stands for Savings Incentive Match PLan for Employees. Small businesses may adopt these new types of employer-sponsored cash or deferred arrangement (CODA) elective salary reduction retirement plans effective for years beginning after December 31, 1996.[1]

Employees may choose whether to have the employer make payments as contributions under the SIMPLE plan or to receive these payments directly in cash. An employer that chooses to establish a SIMPLE plan must make either matching contributions or nonelective contributions on behalf of all eligible employees.

There are two types of SIMPLE plans: SIMPLE IRAs and SIMPLE 401(k)s. SIMPLE IRAs were essentially designed to replace salary reduction simplified employee pensions, or SARSEPS, while retaining the basic design and administrative convenience associated with these plans. The salary reduction provisions for SEPs were repealed for SEPs; thus, no new SARSEPS may be adopted after December 31, 1996. Employers who wish to implement easily administered plans with no salary reduction or elective deferral features may still adopt "plain vanilla" SEPs (without a salary reduction feature).

SIMPLE 401(k)s are Section 401(k) salary reduction plans with features similar to those for SIMPLE IRAs. The design-based formula for SIMPLE 401(k) plans makes nondiscrimination testing of such plans unnecessary.

In general application, the availability, plan design and contribution rules are very similar for the two types of SIMPLE plans. However, there are a number of distinctions explained throughout this chapter that should be considered in the planning process.

WHEN IS IT INDICATED?

1. When a small employer (i.e., one with 100 or fewer employees earning less than $5,000 annually[2]) is looking for a simplified retirement plan that is relatively inexpensive to implement, permits employee elective deferrals similar to Section 401(k) plans, and is easy to adopt and administer.

2. When an employer employs many part-time workers earning less than $5,000. Both types of SIMPLE plans may exclude employees who are expected to earn less than $5,000 and have not earned at least $5,000 in any two preceding years. In contrast, the earnings threshold for SEPs is $400 (in 1998) and for traditional Section 401(k) plans it is the first dollar of income. By excluding such employees, the employer reduces required contributions and, perhaps more importantly, the administrative hassle and expense of many small accounts that may be largely forfeited anyway under the deferred vesting schedule of a regular qualified plan.

3. When the elective deferral rates by nonhighly compensated employees in a regular Section 401(k) cash or deferred arrangement or salary reduction SEP are so low that, under the ADP and ACP tests and top-heavy rules, the ability of the key employees to contribute is severely limited. Since both types of SIMPLE plans contain contribution requirements designed to insure nondiscrimination, key employee salary reduction contributions do not depend in any way on nonhighly compensated employee participation rates.

ADVANTAGES

1. Similar to other defined contribution and salary reduction plans, participants can direct their own investments within the SIMPLE IRA plan or select from range of offerings within the SIMPLE 401(k) plan and benefit from good investment results.

2. SIMPLE plans give participants some control over the level of their retirement savings.

3. SIMPLE plans are relatively inexpensive and easy to adopt and administer.

4. A SIMPLE IRA established using a model plan provided by the IRS (i.e., Form 5304-SIMPLE or Form 5305-SIMPLE) is not subject to the nondiscrimination rules generally applicable to qualified plans (including the top-heavy rules[3]) and simplified reporting requirements apply.[4] SIMPLE 401(k) plans automatically meet the top heavy requirements and the ADP and ACP tests, and are subject to simplified rules for the annual summary plan

description, annual account statement, and notice of rights to each employee.

5. In contrast with Section 401(k) plans and other qualified plans, and similar to traditional IRAs, there is no limitation on in-service distributions from SIMPLE IRAs; however, early distributions (before age 59½) may be subject to either a 25 percent (in the first two years of participation) or a 10 percent early distribution penalty tax. Distributions from SIMPLE 401(k) plans are subject to the same restrictions on distributions that apply to regular Section 401(k) plans.

6. The elective contribution to a SIMPLE IRA is a dollar amount rather than a percentage of compensation, so participants in a SIMPLE IRA plan can elect to contribute as much as 100 percent of compensation up to the $6,000 SIMPLE IRA limit, even if they only earn $6,000 of wages (grossed up by employment tax). In contrast, elective contributions to SIMPLE 401(k) plans must comply with the Section 415 limitations. Therefore, SIMPLE 401(k) plan participants must not be permitted to elect to contribute a percentage of compensation that, when added to the employer's matching contribution, exceeds 25 percent of compensation.

7. From the employer's perspective, the higher ($5,000) compensation-eligibility threshold for both SIMPLE IRAs and SIMPLE 401(k)s (as contrasted with the relatively small threshold for a SEP ($400 in 1998) and the zero threshold applicable to a Section 401(k) arrangement) is advantageous since it eliminates the administrative and contribution requirements for very low income employees.

DISADVANTAGES

1. Investment results are not guaranteed; participants bear the risk of poor investment results.

2. The elective salary reduction contribution limit ($6,000 in 1998) is less generous for SIMPLEs than the elective deferral limits for Section 401(k) plans, SARSEPs, or Section 403(b) plans ($10,000 in 1998).

3. As with traditional IRAs, a participant has no access to SIMPLE IRA funds through borrowing. Section 401(k) plans (including SIMPLE 401(k) plans) may include hardship provisions as part of the plan design.

4. The early-access problem is further exacerbated by a 25-percent early distribution penalty which is imposed during the first two years of participation in a SIMPLE IRA.

This restriction does not apply to employees whose distributions qualify under one of the exceptions to the 10-percent early-withdrawal penalty.[5] Both traditional and SIMPLE 401(k) plans may generally permit distributions only in the case of hardship (if the plan so provides), or in the case of the participant's death, disability, or separation from service. Taxable pre-59½ distributions from SIMPLE 401(k) plans, including hardship withdrawals, which do not qualify under one of the exceptions to the penalty provisions are apparently subject to the 10-percent penalty, not the 25-percent penalty, even if received within two years of beginning participation in the SIMPLE 401(k) plan.

5. Generally, an employer who sponsors any other qualified pension or profit sharing plan or SEP is ineligible to adopt a SIMPLE IRA. In the case of a SIMPLE 401(k) plan, the employer may maintain another plan provided it does not cover any of the same employees who are covered under the SIMPLE 401(k) plan.

TAX IMPLICATIONS

1. The employer may deduct contributions (both employee salary reduction amounts and employer matching contributions) to a SIMPLE plan if certain Code requirements are met. The principal SIMPLE plan requirements are:[6]

- the employer must have 100 or fewer employees (only employees with at least $5,000 in compensation for the preceding year are counted) on any day in the year.

- contributions may be made to an IRA established for each employee (in the case of a SIMPLE IRA) or to the employee's 401(k) account (if the plan is a SIMPLE 401(k) plan). (See the questions and answers below for a comparison of SIMPLE 401(k) plans with traditional 401(k) plans.)

- employees who earned at least $5,000 from the employer in any 2 preceding years, and are reasonably expected to earn at least $5,000 in the current year, can contribute (through salary reductions) up to $6,000 (as indexed for 1998) annually.

- the employer is required to make a contribution equal to either;

    (a) a dollar for dollar matching contribution up to 3 percent of the employee's compensation (in the case of a SIMPLE IRA *only*, the employer can elect a lower percentage, not less than 1 percent, in no more than 2 out of the 5 years ending with the current year),[7] or

(b) a nonelective contribution of 2 percent of compensation for all eligible employees earning at least $5,000 (whether or not they elect salary reductions).[8]

- employees must be 100 vested in all contributions (whether they are salary deferral, matching, or nonelective contributions) to SIMPLE IRAs and SIMPLE 401(k) plans at all times.[9] No deferred vesting schedules are available; however, the limitations on distributions that apply to traditional 401(k) plans apply to SIMPLE 401(k) plans.

2. Contributions to a SIMPLE IRA or SIMPLE 401(k) plan are generally deductible by the employer, and are not subject to the 15% deduction limit.[10] The employee may make a salary deferral contribution to the SIMPLE IRA subject to the $6,000 limitation.[11] For matching contributions, the employer is allowed a deduction for a year only if the contributions are made by the due date (including extensions) for the employer's tax return.[12] Contributions to a SIMPLE IRA or SIMPLE 401(k) plan are excludable from the employee's income.[13] Earnings within SIMPLE IRAs and SIMPLE 401(k)s, like traditional IRAs, are tax-deferred.

3. Distributions from SIMPLE IRAs and SIMPLE 401(k) plans are generally taxed under the rules applicable to traditional IRAs and traditional 401(k) plans, respectively (with the exception of the higher early distribution penalty, described below).[14] Thus, they are includable in income when withdrawn. Distributions from SIMPLE IRAs are reported on Form 1099-R.

4. Participants may roll over proceeds from one SIMPLE IRA to another SIMPLE IRA tax free.[15] A SIMPLE IRA can be rolled over to a regular IRA or transferred in a direct trustee-to-trustee transfer from the SIMPLE IRA to another regular IRA on a tax-free basis only after a two-year period has expired since the individual first participated in the SIMPLE IRA plan.[16] A distribution from a SIMPLE 401(k) may be rolled over to a regular IRA if it is an eligible rollover distribution under the rules applicable to qualified plans.

No rollover or trustee-to-trustee transfer is permitted from a SIMPLE IRA to a traditional IRA during the first two years of an employee's participation in the SIMPLE IRA.[17] In fact, such a distribution will generally be subject to income taxation and, potentially, a *25-percent* early-withdrawal penalty tax. The contribution to the traditional IRA will also be treated as an excess contribution which will be subject to the 6-percent excise tax each year until it is corrected.[18]

5. Early withdrawals (before age 59½) from a SIMPLE IRA are generally subject to the 10-percent early withdrawal tax applicable to regular IRAs unless the distribution qualifies for one of the exceptions from the penalty[19]; *however*, withdrawals of contributions during the two-year period beginning on the date the employee first participated in the SIMPLE IRA plan are subject to a 25-percent early withdrawal penalty tax (rather than 10 percent).[20] If one of the exceptions to the application of the 10-percent tax applies, the exception also applies to distributions otherwise subject to the 25-percent penalty tax.

To the extent an employee is no longer participating in a SIMPLE IRA plan (e.g., the employee has terminated employment) and two years have expired since the employee first participated in the SIMPLE IRA plan, the employee's SIMPLE IRA is treated as a traditional IRA.[21]

6. Rollovers from SIMPLE 401(k)s to other qualified plans or to traditional IRAs are governed by the rules applicable to traditional Section 401(k) plans and qualified plan rollovers generally.

7. Distributions from SIMPLE 401(k) plans are subject to the same restrictions as those from traditional Section 401(k) plans. Thus, for example, in-service withdrawals other than hardship distributions are generally prohibited.[22] Withdrawals are permitted after separation from service but they may be subject to the 10-percent early-withdrawal penalty tax.

8. Employer matching or nonelective contributions to a SIMPLE IRA plan are not treated as wages for employment tax purposes.[23] Employee elective salary reduction contributions are treated as wages and are subject to employment taxes.

ALTERNATIVES

1. A traditional Section 401(k) plan. These plans permit greater flexibility in employer matching contribution formulas and the use of deferred vesting schedules, but they entail considerably greater expense and administrative and compliance burdens than SIMPLE IRA plans. SIMPLE 401(k) plans are subject to many of the same administrative and filing requirements as traditional 401(k) plans, but are exempt from ADP/ACP testing, since they are required to use a nondiscriminatory design-based contribution formula.

2. A Simplified Employee Pension (SEP). SEPs are IRA-based employer-sponsored defined contribution/profit-sharing type retirement plans for small businesses. Like SIMPLE IRAs, they offer simplified administration and convenience at relatively low cost to the employer. SEPs adopted before January 1, 1997 were permitted to include provisions for employee elective deferrals, similar to Section 401(k) plans, but these provisions are unavailable for SEPs adopted after 1996. Therefore, SEPs now serve primarily as a small business alternative to a defined contribution pension plan or profit-sharing plan.

WHERE AND HOW DO I GET IT

Most banks, mutual fund companies, insurance companies, brokerage houses, and other financial institutions have pro-forma SIMPLE IRA plans that are available virtually "off the shelf." The IRS has published two model SIMPLE IRA plans that may be adopted by simply following the instructions included with them (Form 5304-SIMPLE and Form 5305-SIMPLE). Many institutions also have prototype SIMPLE 401(k) plans that can be easily implemented. Employers who wish to amend existing Section 401(k) plans to conform to the SIMPLE provisions (and who are prepared to make the contributions required of a SIMPLE 401(k) plan sponsor) should consult with their pension administrators or legal counsel and follow the guidelines of Revenue Procedure 97-9, 1997-1 CB 624.

QUESTIONS AND ANSWERS

Question — Can an unincorporated business adopt a SIMPLE IRA or SIMPLE 401(k) plan covering partners or a sole proprietor?

Answer — Yes. Partners and proprietors can be covered under the SIMPLE IRA or SIMPLE 401(k) of an unincorporated employer, as well as regular employees; however, for a partner or proprietor, "earned income" is used in place of compensation in computing SIMPLE contributions.

Question — Can an employee who is over age 70½ participate in a SIMPLE IRA or SIMPLE 401(k) plan?

Answer — Although an individual cannot make contributions to his or her own IRA after attaining age 70½, employers can make contributions to SIMPLE IRAs (including both matching contributions and salary reductions) and SIMPLE 401(k) plans for employees who are over age 70½. In fact, the age discrimination law, if applicable, would generally require such contributions to be made.

Question — Can an employee participating in a SIMPLE IRA also make deductible contributions to his or her own IRA?

Answer — For individual IRA purposes, a SIMPLE IRA participant is treated the same as a participant in a regular qualified plan. That is, if the individual is an "active participant" in the plan, individual IRA contributions can be made and deducted, but the $2,000/$4,000 deduction limit is reduced for individuals with adjusted gross income (AGI) of more than $25,000 or married couples with AGI of more than $40,000. If the individual is not an active participant in the plan, the full IRA deduction is available. These rules are discussed in greater detail in Chapter 28.

An employee covered under a SIMPLE IRA or SIMPLE 401(k) plan would be considered an active participant in any year in which salary reductions or employer contributions were allocated to his or her account. However, in a year in which no allocation was made to the individual's account, the individual would have a full individual IRA deduction available (up to the $2,000/$4,000 limit). The higher SIMPLE plan limit is not available for individual IRA contributions, only for employer contributions or salary reductions under a SIMPLE IRA plan.

Question — How do the rules for SIMPLE 401(k) plans compare with the rules for traditional Section 401(k) plans?

Answer — The table on page 473 summarizes and compares the key features and rules for SIMPLE 401(k)s and traditional Section 401(k) plans.

FOOTNOTES

SIMPLE Plan

1. IRC Section 408(p)(1).
2. See IRC Sections 408(p)(2)(D), 401(k)(11)(C).
3. IRC Section 416(g)(4)(G).
4. IRC Section 408(l)(2).
5. See Chapters 28 (regarding traditional IRAs) and 39 (regarding qualified plans) for an explanation of the exceptions to the 10-percent penalty for pre-59½ distributions.
6. See IRC Section 408(p) with respect to SIMPLE IRAs; see IRC Section 401(k)(11) with respect to SIMPLE 401(k) plans.
7. IRC Section 408(p)(2)(A)(iii). The compensation limit under Code section 401(a)(17) is not applicable for purposes of the matching contribution; thus, the 3% match could reach the maximum of $6,000 for an employee with compensation of $200,000 in a year. See Notice 98-4, 1998-2 IRB 25.

Figure 45.1

Comparison Traditional Section 401(k) Plan versus SIMPLE Section 401(k) Plan (1998 Values*)		
	Traditional Section 401(k) Plan	**SIMPLE Section 401(k) Plan**
Elective Deferral Limit	About 15% of compensation up to a limit of $10,000	About 15% of compensation up to a limit of $6,000
Maximum Total Potential Contributions	$24,000	$10,800
Employers Eligible	All	100 or fewer employees
Employer Contribution	Not required	2% flat or 3% matching for all employees with at least $5,000 of annual compensation (2-out-of-5-year rule permits employer match as low as 1 percent in only 2 out of each 5 years)
Vesting of Employer Contributions	Regular qualified plan deferred vesting schedules permitted	All benefits attributable to contributions are nonforfeitable at all times
Other Retirement Plans	Yes	Only if none of the same employees are covered under both plans
ADP/ACP/Top-heavy Testing	Yes	No
Reporting and Disclosure	Full: 5500, Summary Plan Description	Simplified annual summary plan description; annual account statement and notice of rights to each employee
Fiduciary Liability	Full liability ERISA 404(c)	Employer liable only during 1st year of contributions if no affirmative election by employee

*The 415 and 401(a)(17) limitations as well as the $6,000 SIMPLE limitation are indexed for inflation so dollar values are subject to change in future years.

8. IRC Section 408(p)(2)(B). "Compensation" for purposes of the 2% nonelective contribution is subject to the limits of Code section 401(a)(17); thus, the maximum that could be contributed in nonelective contributions for an employee would be $3,200 (i.e., 2% of $160,000 (as indexed for 1998)). See IRC Section 408(p)(2)(B)(ii); Notice 97-58, 1997-45 IRB 7.
9. IRC Sections 408(p)(3), 401(k)(11)(A)(iii).
10. IRC Sections 404(m)(2)(A), 404(a)(3)(i)(II).
11. See IRC Section 219(b)(4).
12. IRC Section 404(m)(2)(B).
13. IRC Section 402(k).

14. IRC Section 402(h)(3).
15. IRC Section 408(d)(3)(G)(i).
16. IRC Section 408(d)(3)(G); Notice 98-4, 1998-2 IRB 25.
17. Notice 98-4, 1998-2 IRB 25, A-2.
18. IRC Section 4973(a).
19. IRC Section 72(t)(6).
20. IRC Section 72(t)(6).
21. IRC Section 408(d)(3)(G)(ii). See IRC Section 72(t)(6).
22. IRC Section 401(k)(2)(B)(I)(IV); Reg. §1.401(k)-1(d)(1).
23. IRC Sections 3121(a)(5)(H), 3306(b)(5)(H), 3401(a)(12)(D). See also Section 209(a)(4)(J) of the Social Security Act.

Chapter 46

STRIPPED BONDS

WHAT IS IT?

Stripped bonds are artificially "manufactured" zero-coupon bonds. These zero-coupon bonds are "manufactured" when investment bankers buy blocks of coupon-paying bonds (typically long-term government treasuries) and separate them into two components: (1) the coupons (which have been "stripped" from the bond) and (2) the principal (the "stripped" bond). Each component is sold separately. The principal is sold at enough of a discount to provide a competitive market yield to maturity.

WHEN IS THE USE OF THIS TOOL INDICATED?

1. Investors are assured of reinvestment at the yield to maturity (unless the bond is called or sold before maturity).

2. Because of the certainty of the reinvestment rate, investors can better predict and plan for specific accumulated values at the maturity date.

3. Taxable strips are very suitable conservative investments for retirement plans.

4. Tax-exempt strips are an excellent vehicle for children under age 14 who are subject to their parents' tax rate on unearned income.

ADVANTAGES AND DISADVANTAGES

1. Prices of strips are more sensitive to interest rate changes than prices of coupon-paying bonds of the same quality and maturity.

2. Many stripped bonds are callable at the discretion of the issuer. If a strip is called before maturity — which is more likely to occur when interest rates have fallen — the investor will generally not be able to reinvest the proceeds at the yield to maturity he enjoyed on the strip.

   However, some strips are issued with call protection to assure investors that the bond will not be called for a specified period, or not at all.

TAX IMPLICATIONS

1. Unless the bond is a tax-exempt municipal issue, interest is subject to tax as it accrues even though no cash is paid until the bond matures or is called.

2. If the underlying securities are federal government issues, there is some question as to whether the interest is exempt from state taxation. If the interest is U.S. government interest, the interest is exempt from state tax. If the interest is from the investment banker who "manufactures" the strip, the interest would be subject to state taxation.

ALTERNATIVES

1. Stripped Federal Government Securities have many different names, depending on the investment banker that "manufactures" the stripped bond, including

   (a) CATs — Certificates of Accrual on Treasury Certificates

   (b) COUGRs — Certificates of Government Receipts

   (c) STAGs — Sterling Transferable Accruing Government Securities

   (d) STRIPs — Separate Trading of Registered Interest and Principal of Securities

   (e) TIGRs — Treasury Investment Growth Certificates

   (f) ZEBRAs — Zero-Coupon Eurosterling Bearer or Registered Accruing Certificates

2. Stripped tax-free municipal bonds have one very important advantage over original issue zero-coupon municipals (which have been available for years) — most of the tax-free strips are not callable while virtually all of the zero-coupon municipals are callable. Consequently, investors who buy tax-free strips get much more certainty about the holding period and their reinvestment yield.

   In addition, some of the new tax-free strips are guaranteed by "pre-refunding." They are backed by U.S.

Treasury bonds that have been purchased to guarantee payment if the municipality goes bankrupt or is slow in paying when the bond matures.

3. Another way to purchase zero-coupon instruments is through a target-maturity mutual fund. These open-end no-load mutual funds, which typically require $1,000 as a minimum investment, specify a particular termination date. They invest in STRIPS and coupon-paying Treasury bonds that match the specified termination date. They pay little or no interest during the life of the fund, and pay out a lump sum at the fund's termination date. For example, in 1998, the Benham Target Maturity Funds have termination dates ranging from 2000 to 2025 in five-year increments. The imputed interest, similar to actual zero-coupon bonds, is taxable each year and is reported on the 1099-DIV form. The fund managers argue that since they are bulk purchasers of STRIPS, they can get better prices and pass the savings on to shareholders in the form of higher yields. On the other hand, the management and operating expenses of these funds range from about 0.7% to 1% of the fund value annually which, given current yields (in 1998) that have ranged from about 5% to 6%, is a substantial drain on return.

Chapter 47

TAX SHELTERS — GENERAL CONCEPTS

(TAX ORIENTED INVESTMENTS)

WHAT IS IT?

A tax shelter is an investment vehicle that attempts to use favorable federal income tax rules to maximize the resulting economic return. The most important word in this definition is "investment." Tax shelters should be used to increase the return on the funds invested and not merely to reduce current income taxes. If the investment has little or no chance of providing a reasonable economic return without the tax benefits, it is unlikely the tax benefits alone will make the investment a sound alternative.

Many tax and investment advisors no longer use the term "tax shelter," and prefer to emphasize the economic aspects of the investment. Consequently, terms such as "tax oriented investment" and "tax benefit investment" have become widely used.

HOW DOES IT WORK?

Historically, tax shelters have worked because of three basic principles:

(1) deferral,

(2) leveraging, and

(3) conversion.

However, as will be discussed in this chapter, because tax shelters were a primary target of the Tax Reform Act of 1986, the ability to utilize these principles has been significantly reduced.

Deferral is the ability to delay the imposition of tax. This deferral is accomplished by taking advantage of the tax deductions allowed with respect to certain investments. These deductions are used to offset income from other sources that would otherwise be currently taxable. For example, if in 1998 Phyllis Friedman, a single taxpayer, earned a salary of $180,000 and reported a taxable income of $160,000, the resulting tax would be $46,058. However, if Phyllis purchased a $275,000 residential real estate investment for that year and took a depreciation deduction of $10,000, she could reduce her

taxable income by $10,000 to $150,000. This would reduce her tax liability for the year to $42,458, a difference of $3,600.

Deferral serves merely to delay the imposition of the tax; it does not eliminate it. In most cases, the tax must eventually be paid. Phyllis will have to pay the deferred tax when she sells the real estate. The depreciation deductions she claims over the years reduce her "basis" (cost) in the property. Her gain on the sale is computed on the difference between the amount she "realizes" on the sale (the proceeds) and her "adjusted basis" (original cost adjusted downward for the total depreciation she has claimed).

Sales proceeds		$275,000
Original cost	$275,000	
Total depreciation	$100,000	
Adjusted basis		$175,000
Gain on sale		$100,000

The total depreciation of $100,000 offset otherwise taxable income in earlier years. However, Phyllis had to reduce her basis in the property by the same amount, $100,000. Therefore, in the year of sale, when her investment in the real estate ended, so did the *deferral*. The gain on the sale is increased by the amount of the deductions she had taken.

So what then are the benefits of the *deferral*? If Phyllis has to increase her gain on the sale by $100,000, the same amount she used to reduce her income in the past, it appears there is no advantage to deferral. However, Phyllis has the use of the tax dollars each year as a result of the deductions. In effect, the government makes her an interest free loan for the period of the deferral.

Furthermore, if Phyllis sells the property in a year in which she is in a lower tax bracket than in the year the deferral deductions were claimed, she may realize an additional advantage. This advantage results from the tax rate differential.

A third advantage to *deferral* is the possibility of a "step up" in basis of the investment property at the death of the client. As a result, the deferred tax never has to be paid.

The Tax Reform Act of 1986 reduced the benefits of *deferral* by limiting the kind of income a tax shelter loss can offset. Since 1987, most tax shelter losses are treated as "passive activity" losses and can only be used to offset "passive activity" income. Therefore, Phyllis might not be able to utilize the full tax shelter loss generated by her real estate investment to offset her salary income. (The "passive activity" rules are discussed in more detail in Chapter 8, "Income Tax Concepts.")

Leveraging (as explained in greater detail in Chapter 10) is the use of borrowed funds in order to increase the size of a tax shelter investment. By increasing the size of the investment, a person may also increase the related tax benefits. For example, if in 1998 Phyllis could borrow an additional $275,000, she could double the size of the real estate investment and the related tax benefits. A $20,000 deduction (instead of a $10,000 deduction) would reduce her 1998 taxable income from $150,000 to $140,000. This could drop her tax an additional $3,600, from $42,458 to $38,858.

There are economic costs associated with *leveraging*; namely the costs of borrowing money. In evaluating the economic return from a leveraged tax shelter investment, the interest expense must be considered. However, interest expenses associated with the purchase of "passive activity" investments, such as most tax shelter investments, are treated as "passive activity" expenses and are only deductible against "passive activity" income. To the extent the interest expense can be deducted, the cost of *leveraging* can be reduced.

Conversion is the third characteristic of a tax shelter investment. Conversion is the ability to change what would otherwise be ordinary income into long-term capital gain, and historically has perhaps been the most beneficial feature of tax shelters.

WHEN IS THE USE OF THIS TECHNIQUE INDICATED?

1. When the investor is in a high marginal income tax bracket. (The decision as to whether the tax bracket is high enough to yield the desired tax benefits from the investment must be made by both the investor and the investment sponsor.)

2. When the investor has adequate cash flow and/or capital to support his or her current standard of living regardless of the outcome of the investment. (Although this should be a major factor in any investment decision, it is particularly important with respect to a tax shelter.)

3. When the investor has sufficient psychological stability to accept the inherent risks of the investment. (These

types of investments entail not only economic risk, but also the risk of IRS challenge to the tax advantage aspects as well as the possibility of changes in the tax law.)

4. When the investor, with the aid of his advisors, is sophisticated enough to analyze the specific tax shelter under consideration and form a considered judgment as to the appropriateness of that particular investment and its effect on his overall financial plan.

ADVANTAGES

1. Deferral of the payment of taxes that would otherwise be currently due.

2. Permanent reduction of tax.

3. Creation of income taxable at favorable rates.

DISADVANTAGES

1. The risk that the tax advantage aspects of the investment will be challenged by the IRS.

2. The risk that the tax law upon which the tax advantages are based may be adversely changed. This is, in fact, what occurred with the Tax Reform Act of 1986.

3. The interplay of the basic economic considerations with the tax aspects of the investment complicates the evaluation of the risks and rewards.

4. The investor's potential for gain may be reduced by the costs of promoting and syndicating the investment.

HOW IS IT IMPLEMENTED?

The implementation of a tax shelter depends upon what type of shelter it is. The major types of shelters are discussed and implementation procedures are covered in detail in the chapters on Real Estate and Oil and Gas investments.

WHERE CAN I FIND OUT MORE ABOUT IT?

1. *Tax Facts on Investments (Tax Facts 2)* (Cincinnati, The National Underwriter Company).

2. Jack Crestol and Herman Schneider, *Tax Planning for Investors* (Chicago, Commerce Clearing House, 1991).

3. *The Financial Services Professional's Guide to the Tax Reform Act of 1986* (Bryn Mawr, Pa., The American College, 1986).

4. David F. Windish, *Tax Advantaged Investments* (New York, New York Institute of Finance, 1989).

QUESTIONS AND ANSWERS

Question — What is the difference between a "public" and a "private" offering of a tax shelter investment?

Answer — An offering is a solicitation for investors to become involved in the purchase of an interest in a tax shelter investment. Most shelter investments are offered by reputable brokerage houses or other sales organizations.

A public offering is one that is registered with the Securities and Exchange Commission (SEC) for *inter*state sale or with a state agency for *intra*state sale. A public offering must be accompanied by a prospectus or offering circular that explains in detail the objectives and risks of the proposed investments.

A private offering is a solicitation that is not registered with any federal or state securities agency. Private offerings must be limited to a specified number of highly sophisticated investors who satisfy certain requirements as to both income and net worth. A private placement memorandum that describes the proposed investment and furnishes information sufficient for an individual to make an informed investment decision must accompany the offering.

Investors should typically avoid the purchase of investments — sold as tax shelters — that do not satisfy the requirements of either a public or private offering. However, because a tax shelter can be broadly defined as any investment that has tax advantages as a significant factor, "do-it-yourself" tax oriented investments, such as a con-

dominium unit purchased for investment, should be considered.

Question — How can an investor learn about the promoter of a tax shelter?

Answer — The first place an investor should look is the prospectus, in the case of a public offering, or the private placement memorandum, in the case of a private offering. Then the investor should check with sources dealt with in the past in the brokerage, banking, and investment advisory communities. Personal references of investors who have previously dealt with the promoter are particularly helpful.

Question — What tax aspects of a shelter investment are most often questioned by the IRS?

Answer — The primary question the IRS will generally ask about a tax oriented investment is whether the investment was entered into for a profit or purely to obtain the tax benefits. If the investment does not provide the investors with a reasonable possibility of earning a profit, the IRS will have a strong basis for disallowing deductions for such expenses as depreciation. The IRS would be able to disallow those expenses as not ordinary and necessary business expenses.

In addition the IRS will also look closely at such specific tax aspects of an investment as:

(1) the depreciable life of an asset (e.g., is it real estate or personal property eligible for faster depreciation deductions),

(2) the deductibility of interest expense,

(3) the reasonableness of certain fees and expenses related to the promotion and syndication of the investment, and

(4) when certain items of income are taxable and certain expenses are deductible.

Chapter 48

U.S. GOVERNMENT SECURITIES

WHAT IS IT?

U.S. government securities are issues of the United States Treasury and various government agencies used to finance the activities of the federal government. Government securities include direct issues of the Treasury such as bills, notes, and bonds, as well as bonds of governmental agencies such as the Government National Mortgage Association (GNMA) and the Federal Land Bank.

A Treasury bill is a short-term debt security with a maturity of either thirteen, twenty-six, or fifty-two weeks. It is purchased in minimum amounts of $1,000. These bills are issued on a "discount basis" (sold at less than their par or face value) and redeemed at face value without interest on their maturity date.

A Treasury note is a medium-term debt security, paying interest semiannually. Notes have a fixed maturity date greater than one year and can extend for up to ten years from the date of issue. The minimum face value denomination for a Treasury note is $1,000.

A Treasury bond is a long-term debt security which, like Treasury notes, also pays interest on a semiannual basis. Bonds have a fixed maturity of ten years up to a maximum of thirty years. The minimum denomination for a Treasury bond is $1,000, and interest is paid semiannually.

WHEN IS THE USE OF THIS TOOL INDICATED?

1. When the individual desires a high quality investment that has little or no risk of default. The U.S. Government has never defaulted on even one of its obligations in more than two hundred years.

   To only a slightly lesser degree, the securities of U.S. government agencies such as the World Bank, the Postal Service, and the Federal Home Loan Bank offer low risk and high quality.

2. When an investor needs certainty of income. Because the Treasury can simply print money or raise taxes to pay interest on its obligations, an investor can be sure that payments will be timely made in the amounts promised.

3. When an investor seeks an investment with unquestioned utility as collateral. Due to the low risk of loss of capital and certainty of income, U.S. government securities are readily accepted by lenders as security for loans.

4. When an investor desires a security with the highest degree of marketability. Government securities are traded daily in very large volume by thousands of individuals and institutions. This insures a ready market and the availability of information on prices and returns.

5. When the investor is either unable or unwilling to accept the uncertainty and risk inherent in equity, tax sheltered, and corporate fixed-income investments.

ADVANTAGES

1. U.S. government securities are virtually free of the risk of default.

2. The income from government securities is assured.

3. Government securities are readily accepted by virtually every financial institution as collateral for loans.

4. The securities of the federal government and its agencies are easily and quickly converted to cash.

5. Government issues provide a high degree of security and comfort for risk conscious investors.

6. Because of the variety of government issues, purchases can be tailored to meet the investor's goals and objectives.

7. The interest earned on Treasury securities is not subject to state and local taxation. This can be of considerable advantage to an investor in a high tax bracket.

DISADVANTAGES

1. U.S. government securities provide a rate of return that is generally lower than other fixed-income securities.

2. Long-term government issues, like any long-term, fixed-income investment, are subject to a high degree of interest-rate risk. Therefore, the prices of U.S. government and agency bonds fluctuate substantially with changes in interest rates.

3. As is the case with all fixed-income investments, the purchasing power of the fixed amount of dollars paid by these issues will be eroded over time by the effects of inflation. This problem can be particularly acute if the instruments are long term.

TAX IMPLICATIONS

1. All interest from T-bills, notes, and bonds is subject to federal income tax. This income is taxable at ordinary income rates.

2. Interest from U.S. government securities is entirely exempt from all state and local taxes.

3. Interest from a Treasury bill is not reportable until the year that the T-bill matures. Therefore, if an investor purchased a 13-week T-bill in November 1997 and the bill matured in February 1998, the interest earned on this bill will be declared on his 1998 federal income tax return.

4. If an investor sells a T-bill on the open market prior to its maturity, he must report as ordinary income the difference between the price he paid and the selling price. If the bill is sold for more than he paid, the gain will be ordinary income. If the bill is sold for less than he paid, the loss is treated as a capital loss.

5. A Treasury note or bond may be subject to capital gains treatment. If a note or bond is sold before maturity on the open market, gain or loss is treated as capital gain or capital loss. (If the gain includes original issue discount or market discount, it may be necessary to treat part of the gain as ordinary income.)

ALTERNATIVES

1. Short-term certificates of deposit issued by banks and savings institutions are comparable to Treasury bills. The interest rate paid on CDs is usually the same as or slightly higher than the current T-bill rate. Many institutions will pay up to a quarter point premium over the bill rate in order to attract investors away from government securities.

2. Longer term certificates of deposit, also issued by banks, savings and loans, and mutual savings banks, are competitive with Treasury notes and bonds and the securities of other government agencies.

3. High quality corporate bonds (for example, Standard & Poor's ratings of AA or AAA) should be considered as an alternative to long-term government securities such as notes and bonds. Corporate issues involve greater risk but also provide considerably higher rates of return.

WHERE AND HOW DO I GET IT?

T-bills are offered according to a regular schedule. Thirteen and twenty-six week bills (3 and 6 month maturities) are offered every week by the Treasury. Every Tuesday the offering is announced publicly in major newspapers such as *The Wall Street Journal* or *The New York Times*. The following Monday the bills are auctioned. Fifty-two week (one year maturity) T-bills are issued every four weeks. Every fourth Friday the offering is publicly announced and the bills are auctioned the following Thursday. You can find out the date of the next scheduled offering of notes and bonds by phoning the nearest Federal Reserve Bank or branch.

Federal government securities can be purchased: (1) directly from the United States Treasury through a Federal Reserve bank (on issue) or (2) from a commercial bank or (3) through a brokerage firm.

An investor who wants to purchase a new issue directly from the U.S. Treasury submits a standardized form known as a "tender" either by mail or in person at the appropriate Federal Reserve bank or one of its branches. (The investor should send a certified personal or cashier's check drawn on a bank in the same federal reserve district.)

Most individual investors prefer the convenience of purchasing U.S. government securities from their local bank or brokerage firm. They merely call their banker or broker and indicate the amount they desire to invest and the particular security they desire to purchase. The bank will then send the security to the investor while a broker may offer to hold the security in the customer's account.

WHAT FEES OR OTHER ACQUISITION COSTS ARE INVOLVED?

When an investor purchases a security directly from the United States Treasury, there are no charges or commissions.

Making a purchase through a bank or broker will typically be more expensive. Banks may charge a commission as well as a premium on purchases under $100,000. Since these charges may vary considerably, it is wise for an investor to compare the fees and premiums charged by a number of banks and brokers.

Aside from commissions, an investor's cost in purchasing government securities from a bank or broker will be different from the cost of a direct purchase from the federal government. First, the bank or broker will either purchase the securities on the open market or will sell the investor issues from their inventory. This means the investor must pay the "asked" market price (which may be higher or lower) than the price at which the note or bond was originally issued.

Another consideration is the amount of interest accrued on the note or bond since the last interest payment date. The investor is entitled only to the interest beginning with the date of his purchase. Therefore he must pay the seller of the security the amount of interest accrued since the last payment date, in addition to the price of the note or bond itself. Of course, on the next payment date the investor will receive the full amount of interest for the period.

HOW DO I SELECT THE BEST OF ITS TYPE?

Unlike most other investments, all government securities with similar maturities have the same risk and reward characteristics. Therefore, selecting the "best of its type" will depend on the investor's goals and objectives. Planners should focus on the investor's needs for liquidity, income, and tax deferral in selecting among T-bills, notes, and bonds.

For example, Anne Lewis desires to have a high degree of liquidity since she feels interest rates are likely to increase sharply in the months ahead. Clearly, she should not purchase long-term notes or bonds since they will decline in value as rates increase. Anne should concentrate any investments in short-term issues such as T-bills which mature relatively quickly and which will enable her to reinvest at the higher interest rate.

WHERE CAN I FIND OUT MORE ABOUT IT?

1. Financial publications such as *The Wall Street Journal*, and *Barron's* regularly quote prices for bills, notes, and bonds issued by the federal government.

2. Banks and brokerage firms will also provide investors with information on available issues and current prices.

3. Investors may also write or call the Treasury itself for information concerning the purchase of government securities on issue. Inquiries should be addressed to: Bureau of the Public Debt, Department W, Washington, DC 20226.

4. A useful book on government issues is *Buying and Selling Treasury Securities* published by Dow Jones-Irwin, Homewood, Illinois, 60430.

Figure 48.1

RATE OF RETURN ON A U.S. TREASURY BILL			
INPUT: Enter face value of Treasury Bill			$10,000
INPUT: Enter current price of Treasury Bill			$ 9,800
Enter date information:			
	Year	Month	Day
INPUT: Maturity	98	12	15
INPUT: Current	98	9	15
Number of Days to Maturity			91
Annualized rate of return			0.082

Reprinted with permission from *Financial Planning* TOOLKIT, Leimberg & LeClair, Inc.

5. Information on government securities transactions may also be obtained through electronic data networks such as *Dow Jones News/Retrieval Service*.

QUESTIONS AND ANSWERS

Question — How is interest paid on U.S. Treasury bills?

Answer — Treasury bills do not pay interest in the same way as other securities. Bills are sold on a discount basis which means they are offered at a price below their face value or redemption value. The difference between the offering price and the maturity value represents the interest earned by investors. For example, a Treasury bill may be offered at a price of $9,800 with the face value of $10,000 to be paid in thirteen weeks, or 91 days. This represents a rate of return to the investor of 8.2%, as shown in Figure 48.1.

Question — What is the difference between a Treasury "note" and a "bond"?

Answer — The difference is in the length of time until maturity. Notes generally mature in one to ten years. Bonds, on the other hand, typically have maturities of ten to thirty years.

Question — Are there any mutual funds which specialize in Treasury securities?

Answer — Yes, a mutual fund may restrict its portfolio to issues of the U.S. government. Although these funds are not insured, they are fully invested in Treasury securities which gives them a high degree of security. Such mutual funds provide the same services as money market funds and investors can make automatic withdrawals and redemptions by telephone, check, or wire.

Treasury mutual funds should be compared with money market funds which may invest in T-bills and other government securities but also place funds in many other short-term obligations such as bank certificates of deposit. Investors will typically receive higher yields from money market funds since their underlying assets are securities bearing higher risks than comparable Treasury securities.

Question — What is the "Treasury Direct" system the Treasury uses to issue bills, notes, and bonds?

Answer — In July of 1986, the U.S. Treasury Department changed the way it issues bills, notes, and bonds as well as the way it handles investor accounts. The familiar engraved certificates were replaced with a book-entry securities system which operates alongside the commercial system already in place.

Investors under the system, called "Treasury Direct," receive a statement of account instead of engraved certificates. Statements provide a record of the investor's entire portfolio of Treasury securities (much like the system that has been in place for years with T-bills). All holdings (unless maintained under different registration options or with different payment instructions) are held under a single master account for simplified record keeping and flexibility. The account statement is similar to the statements issued by securities dealers to purchasers of stocks and bonds.

Treasury Direct provides more security to clients because it eliminates the possibility of certificates being lost or stolen. Clients also receive simplified and more accurate records, a broad choice of registration options, direct deposit of Treasury payments, and an automatic reinvestment option.

Investors can obtain information and conduct transactions on their accounts at Federal Reserve Banks or the U.S. Treasury. There are 37 locations which have been designated as Treasury Direct servicing centers at which investors can purchase Treasury bills, notes, or bonds, transfer securities from one account to another, or request detailed information on their accounts.

Question — How can a lost U.S. Savings Bond be replaced?

Answer — Write to the Bureau of Public Debt, Department of the Treasury, P.O. Box 1328, Parkersburg, WV 26102. Request form PD-1048. The form will request information about:

(a) the name the bond was registered in,

(b) the issue date,

(c) the address given at time of issue,

(d) current address, and

(e) serial numbers.

Chapter 49

WORLD WIDE INVESTING: ADRs, INTERNATIONAL AND GLOBAL FUNDS, SINGLE COUNTRY FUNDS

Studies indicate that investors can increase overall returns and reduce overall risk (as measured by volatility) by including foreign investments in their portfolios. (See Figure 49.1 for reference and display of returns by components of a world market portfolio.)

A recent study by Goldman Sachs International (London) indicated that the U.S. stock market was ranked seventh out of 17 countries and areas surveyed. During the period from 1986 through 1994, the world average for equity performance was 11.5% (in terms of U.S. dollars) while the comparable U.S. figure was 9.4%. Returns were quite a bit higher in specific countries such as Japan (18.7%), Spain (17.8%), and Sweden (17.6%). It seems safe to assume that investors who limit themselves only to the U.S. market earn rates of return lower than those in many other countries.

Another study by Reilly and Wright also demonstrated similar results for investors in bonds. The performance of the U.S. bond market was fourth out of six countries; fifth when exchange rates were factored in.

Overall, investors can generally improve their investment returns by adding foreign stocks and bonds to their portfolios. Many foreign securities offer investors higher risk-adjusted returns than domestic securities. In addition, the low positive or negative correlation between foreign and U.S. securities makes them useful for building a diversified portfolio.

Unfortunately, the benefits of direct international diversification are offset in part by political and exchange-rate risk, as well as by institutional barriers to trading. However, investors interested in international investing have several options open to them including ADRs (American Depositary Receipts), international and global funds, single-country closed-end funds and PFICs (Passive Foreign Investment Companies.)

AMERICAN DEPOSITARY RECEIPTS

What Is It?

ADRs are simply receipts issued by a U.S. bank on foreign securities that were purchased by the bank through a foreign correspondent bank and held in trust for the benefit of the ADR holder.

ADRs are priced in U.S. dollars and are typically listed on the over-the-counter market. Some ADRs are listed on the New York or American Stock Exchanges. Therefore, investors can buy or sell ADRs in the same way they trade American stocks. Dividends on the stocks underlying an ADR are received by the depository bank, which turns over the proceeds, net of foreign withholding taxes and in U.S. dollars, to the ADR holder. The depository bank acts something like a U.S.-based international mutual fund, performing all the functions that individuals investing directly in foreign securities may not be able to perform, but it provides investors with the ability to purchase whole and selected foreign shares, rather than pro-rata shares of a portfolio of foreign securities.

When Is The Use Of This Tool Indicated?

ADRs allow investors to buy foreign stocks and diversify internationally without the difficulties and restrictions of direct foreign investments.

In addition, ADRs internalize the costs of foreign currency exchange for U.S. dollars with every dividend or interest payment, and they eliminate the costs of buying and selling securities in a foreign currency.

Advantages And Disadvantages

1. It is possible that political or economic turmoil could cause the country of a foreign security to restrict capital flows. Therefore, receipt of interest, dividends, and, perhaps, principal could be delayed or, in the extreme, forfeited altogether.

2. Currency differences can have a major effect on ADR performance. An investor could actually lose money on the stock and end up making money because of currency fluctuations, or vice-versa.

Figure 49.1

WORLD MARKET PORTFOLIO: TOTAL ANNUAL RETURNS 1960-1984					
	Compound return	Standard deviation*		Compound return	Standard deviation*
Equities			Cash equivalents		
United States			United States		
NYSE	8.71%	16.30%	U.S. Treasury bills	6.25%	3.10%
Amex	7.28	23.49	Commercial paper	7.03	3.20
OTC	11.47	22.42	U.S. cash total	6.49	3.22
United States total	8.81	16.89			
Foreign			Foreign	6.00	7.10
Europe	7.83	15.58			
Asia	15.14	30.74	Cash total	6.38	2.92
Other	8.14	20.88			
Foreign total	9.84	16.07	U.S. real estate		
			Business	8.49	4.16
Equities total	9.08	15.28	Residential	8.86	3.77
			Farms	11.86	7.88
Bonds					
United States			Real estate total	9.44	3.45
Corporate					
Intermediate-term	6.37	7.15	Metals		
Long-term	5.03	11.26	Gold	9.08	29.87
Corporate total**	5.35	9.63	Silver	9.14	75.34
Government					
Treasury notes	6.32	5.27	Metals total	9.11	29.69
Treasury bonds	4.70	9.70			
U.S. agencies	6.88	6.15	U.S. market portfolio	8.63	5.06
Government total	5.91	6.43			
United States total	5.70	7.16	Foreign market portfolio	7.76	8.48
Foreign			World Market Portfolio		
Corporate domestic	8.35	7.26	Excluding metals	8.34	5.24
Government domestic	5.79	7.41	Including metals	8.39	5.80
Cross border	7.51	5.76			
Foreign total	6.80	6.88	U.S. inflation rate	5.24	3.60
Bonds total	6.36	5.56			

* The standard deviation indicates that two-thirds of the returns varied around the average by plus or minus the amount indicated. The average used is the arithmetic mean, not the compound return presented in our table. The differences, however, are only slight.

** Including preferred stock.

Source: Roger G. Ibbotson, Lawrence B. Siegel, and Kathryn S. Love, *"World Wealth: U.S. and Foreign Market Values and Returns,"* The Journal of Portfolio Management, Fall 1985.

Reprinted by permission of *American Association of Individual Investors Journal.*

3. Information on foreign securities is less available generally and less reliable than what Americans have come to expect for domestic securities.

Tax Implications

1. Foreign taxes are generally withheld before interest and dividends are passed through to the ADR holder. U.S. treaties can result in partial reclamation of withholdings in some countries.

2. Foreign taxes paid can be offset to some extent against federal income taxes.

3. There is often no capital gain tax imposed by foreign governments, though such gains are taxed by the U.S. government.

4. Special rules apply to 10 percent or more ownership of a foreign corporation.

Where Can I Find Out More About It?

1. *Morgan Stanley Capital International Perspective*, Morgan Stanley, 1251 Avenue of the Americas, New York, NY; a publication with reams of information about the stocks of over 2,100 companies located worldwide—primarily for institutional investors; price $5,000 annually; can be viewed at Morgan Stanley offices in major cities around the country.

2. ADR prices are listed in *The Wall Street Journal* and other newspapers as well as in electronic databases.

3. *Dessaurer's Journal*, P.O. Box 1718, Orleans, Mass. 02653.

4. *Worldwide Investment Notes*, 7730 Carondelet Avenue, St. Louis, MO 63105.

INTERNATIONAL AND GLOBAL FUNDS

What Is It?

These funds are investment companies that invest in foreign stocks and bonds and ADRs. There are both open-end and closed-end funds available. International funds typically invest only in non-U.S. securities. Global funds invest in foreign and domestic securities.

When Is The Use Of This Tool Indicated?

1. When an investor wants international investments with the diversification, pooling, economies of scale, professional management, and flexibility of an investment company.

2. When it is important to increase total return on your portfolio while reducing overall risk relative to a portfolio containing only domestic securities.

Advantages And Disadvantages

1. Because investing in foreign securities requires currency exchanges, share values will be affected not only by the underlying economic performance of the securities in the portfolio, but also by exchange rates.

2. Although individual foreign markets may tend to be more volatile than the U.S. market, when foreign investments are included within a person's total portfolio (many advisers recommend up to 25 percent of one's portfolio should be invested in foreign securities) overall volatility of the portfolio will generally diminish.

Tax Implications

International and global funds are taxed in the same manner as domestic mutual funds and closed-end investment companies. See Chapter 34.

Where Can I Find Out More About It?

1. *Wiesenberger Investment Companies Service*, Warren, Gorham, & Lamont, Inc., 210 South Street, Boston, Mass. 02111

2. *Dow Jones-Irwin No-Load Mutual Funds*, William G. Droms and Peter D. Heerwagen, Dow Jones-Irwin, Homewood, Ill. 60430

SINGLE-COUNTRY CLOSED-END FUNDS

What Is It?

Single-country closed-end funds are investment companies that invest exclusively in the stocks and/or bonds of one country. There are over 30 such funds available to American investors. Almost all trade on the New York Stock Exchange; only two trade on the American Stock Exchange.

When Is The Use Of This Tool Indicated?

1. Similar to international or global funds, single-country closed end funds give American investors the opportunity easily to include foreign investments in their portfolios and, by doing so, to increase their portfolios' return while reducing their overall risk.

2. Investors get the benefit of professional management and diversification within the selected market as is typical with any mutual fund or closed-end fund investment.

3. Most single-country funds have capital appreciation as a primary objective with income, at best, a secondary consideration. Most foreign stocks pay lower dividend yields than their American counterparts. Also, given the possibility of some double-taxation (both in the foreign country and in the U.S.) and the potential currency exchange problems, income is often avoided.

4. Single-country funds are to international investing what sector funds are to domestic investing. Market timers attempt to select the country that "is on the move" and then switch when economic indicators suggest another country will perform better. This is, however, a high-risk strategy, since picking the "hottest" countries, like picking the "hottest" sectors, is difficult. A few timing mistakes can more than offset the gains from successful switches.

5. Most of the single-country funds are closed-end funds because many of the securities in these markets are thinly traded. By sticking to the closed-end format, portfolio managers do not need to worry about dumping stocks, perhaps at substantial discounts, to meet redemptions by shareholders. The managers would find it difficult to buy or sell securities in thin markets if they had large inflows or outflows of cash coming at unpredictable times. Consequently, the closed-end format protects investors from the excessive swings in share values that could arise with the open-end format.

Advantages And Disadvantages

1. Investors must depend on the portfolio manager to select appropriate investments and decide when to buy and sell those investments. Management may elect to sell securities when it is not timely for a given investor for tax or other reasons.

2. Similar to any other foreign investment, the performance of the fund depends not only on the economic performance of the securities in the fund, but also on currency exchange rates. It is possible for the securities in the fund to show gains in their own market, but to show losses for American investors after adjusting for currency fluctuations.

3. Similar to domestic closed-end funds, single-country closed-end funds generally trade at a price that is different from their net asset values (the market value of the portfolio if acquired outside the fund). Most of these funds sell at a discount from net asset value and the discount often changes. A fund's net asset value and current market price do not necessarily move in the same direction. Consequently, investors may sustain a loss when selling their shares, not because the market value of the shares in the portfolio has fallen, but simply because the discount has increased. Of course, investors may also benefit if the discount decreases.

4. Although the fund may be broadly diversified within its selected market, each foreign market itself is subject to wide variability compared with the overall international market.

5. Single-country funds are more volatile than other closed-end funds. Therefore, it is important to invest conservatively with a long-term approach. The timing of a purchase also becomes a more important consideration.

Tax Implications

Shares in closed-end funds are taxed like regular shares of common stock.

Alternatives

1. ADRs, international or global mutual funds, and passive foreign investment companies.

2. Investing in multinational corporations listed on the U.S. stock exchanges.

QUESTIONS AND ANSWERS

Question — What are emerging markets and the potential risks involved in investing in them?

Answer — Although definitions vary, emerging markets are generally identified as those established markets like Hong Kong and New Zealand that are typically involved in foreign stock funds. Such markets may also include various immature markets like Chile, Turkey, and Argentina. More and more of these markets will begin to "emerge" now as markets witness the potential for industrialization, and are no longer bound by Communism.

Investors are monitoring these markets for growth potential among these underdeveloped countries and for individual companies within those countries.

The potential risks associated with emerging markets are high. One such risk is currency risk. Changes in the value of the dollar compared to foreign currency can affect a fund's performance. The politics and the underlying economies of foreign countries also increases the risks involved. In addition, many of these countries are unable to handle the increased trading volume and the related responsibilities. For example, registration of stock certificates occasionally takes months to complete. In other cases, stock certificates have been lost or forged.

These risks have been identified as those most problematic to-date. Unfortunately, it is difficult to predict the impact these risks will have in the future, or the emergence of any other substantial risks. This can be attributed to the fact that these markets do not have substantial, long-term performance data available to analyze.

Question — What are the advantages and disadvantages associated with direct investments in international assets?

Answer — Due to the expected lowering of brokerage and transaction costs associated with cross border trades, mutual fund investors' desire to achieve more precise geographic asset distributions, and a belief that mutual funds do not offer returns commensurate with calculated risk levels, some individuals are considering direct investments in international assets. It is important to consider both the benefits and risks involved before acting.

A benefit of direct international investing is risk diversification. By adding international investments to a U.S.-based portfolio, overall risk is lowered. The risk of an entire portfolio is generally lower than the risk of a sole investment because the risks are spread over a greater area. This is conditioned on the fact, though, that the correlation among the investments is low. Another advantage is an investor's ability to pick and choose those assets that best satisfy the geographic distribution desired for his portfolio.

The disadvantages are related to costs and expertise. Directly purchasing foreign investments is very costly. The investor must bear the costs of both domestic and foreign brokerage commissions, as well as those related to the international clearing process. Furthermore, information costs are high because it is more difficult to obtain and analyze data about the investments offered by foreign companies due to differences in culture and accounting standards. In addition, a number of countries consider it legal and customary practice to use insider information in evaluating investments. Investors should be aware of such unconventional sources.

Individuals possessing the knowledge and expertise to evaluate the cryptic information can overcome the risks and reap the benefits of greater returns and diversification.

Chapter 50

ZERO-COUPON BONDS

WHAT IS IT?

Zero-coupon bonds are sold at a deep original issue discount from their face value. Investors receive the face value at maturity rather than periodic interest payments. Corporations and government entities issue zero-coupon bonds. Some zero-coupon bonds issued by state and municipal governments are tax-exempt. For example, a zero-coupon bond issued at $500 and maturing in 10 years at $1,000 provides a yield of 7.18%

WHEN IS THE USE OF THIS TOOL INDICATED?

1. With zero-coupon bonds, investors know their yield to maturity exactly since they do not have to worry about reinvesting cash flows at, perhaps, lower rates of interest than they are receiving on the bond. If the bond is held to maturity and does not default, the return is guaranteed. Consequently, zero-coupon bonds are especially appropriate when investors wish to "lock in" a rate of return and be assured of a specified accumulation at a given future date (the maturity date).

2. Taxable zeros are very attractive conservative investments for retirement plans. The tax shelter of the retirement plan allows the unpaid but otherwise taxable accruing interest to be tax deferred.

3. Tax-exempt zeros are suitable conservative investments for high-tax-bracket investors who wish to accumulate wealth, have little need for cash flow, and who do not desire to worry about reinvestment of cash flows. They are also attractive investments for gifts to children under age 14 who, under the "kiddie tax" rules, are subject to tax on their unearned income at their parents' tax rates.

4. Zero-coupon securities frequently are used to meet specific financial or investment goals, especially when the date of a future need is known well in advance. For example, Eva and Brad Rogers know their son, Zachary, will be entering his first year of college in 12 years. They can purchase zeros maturing in 12 years and know that a specific amount of money will be available for tuition. They may even wish to purchase additional zero-coupon bonds maturing in 13, 14, and 15 years to provide funds for the typical four year college funding period.

ADVANTAGES AND DISADVANTAGES

1. Although investors are assured that they will receive a reinvestment rate equal to the yield to maturity if they hold the bond to maturity, they derive this certainty by foregoing the opportunity to reinvest at higher rates if market interest rates rise.

2. Prices of zero-coupon bonds are more sensitive to changes in interest rates than coupon bonds of comparable term and quality. Consequently, if an investor has to sell a zero-coupon bond before maturity, there is no assurance that he will realize the anticipated yield.

3. Many zero-coupon bonds are callable at the discretion of the issuer. If a zero-coupon bond is called before maturity — which is more likely to occur when interest rates have fallen — the investor will generally not be able to reinvest the proceeds at the yield to maturity he enjoyed on the zero-coupon bond.

TAX IMPLICATIONS

The investor must generally include accruing interest in income — unless it is a tax-exempt issue — even though no cash is received until the bond matures, is sold, or is called.

ALTERNATIVES

Deep-discount, low-coupon (market discount) bonds. Investors may acquire low-coupon bonds at substantial discounts from their face values, depending on the coupon rate and the remaining time to maturity. Investors are assured that the portion of the interest that is cash-deferred until the bond matures will be effectively reinvested at the original yield to maturity, similar to zero-coupon bonds. (See chapter 24 for an explanation of the tax treatment of market discount bonds.)

QUESTIONS AND ANSWERS

Question — What are LYONs (Liquid Yield Option Notes)?

Answer — LYONs are zero-coupon convertible notes. Corporations issue zero-coupon bonds that are convertible into

The Tools and Techniques of Financial Planning

a fixed number of shares of common stock of the issuer. Investors who choose to convert forfeit all accrued interest on the bonds.

These bonds are generally less valued as convertibles than as zero-coupon bonds because it becomes more expensive to convert as time passes (since the investor must forego accrued interest).

Question — What are "Bunny Bonds"?

Answer — A bunny bond is a bond in which investors reinvest the income into bonds with the same terms and conditions as on the original bond (thus, the term "bunny" bond because they multiply like bunnies). This reinvestment feature makes bunny bonds very similar to zero-coupon bonds.

These bonds eliminate the reinvestment problem characteristic of all income-producing assets, namely, the uncertainty of the rate of return at which the income can be reinvested. These bonds are especially well suited for retirement funds and other tax-sheltered vehicles or for tax-exempt entities, since investors must include interest in taxable income even though they receive no cash until the bonds mature.

The principal risk is that interest rates will rise and the investor will be "locked" into reinvesting at the lower specified rate. Because of the automatic reinvestment feature, the price of these bonds is more sensitive to interest rate changes than the price of a conventional bond of similar quality and maturity. The price will tend to fall more than conventional bonds of comparable quality and maturity when interest rates rise. On the other hand, if interest rates fall, the investor reinvests at the higher rate and the price of the bond will rise more than conventional bonds of similar quality and term to maturity.

Bunny bonds can be compared to bonds issued with detachable or nondetachable warrants. A warrant is like a long-term call option that allows the investor to acquire more bonds of the same issue or a new issue at a specified price and yield.

Appendix A

COMPOUND INTEREST TABLE
(Future Value of a Lump Sum)

(The use of this table is explained in Chapter 12)

YEARS	3.0%	3.5%	4.0%	4.5%	5.0%	5.5%
1	1.0300	1.0350	1.0400	1.0450	1.0500	1.0550
2	1.0609	1.0712	1.0816	1.0920	1.1025	1.1130
3	1.0927	1.1087	1.1249	1.1412	1.1576	1.1742
4	1.1255	1.1475	1.1699	1.1925	1.2155	1.2388
5	1.1593	1.1877	1.2167	1.2462	1.2763	1.3070
6	1.1941	1.2293	1.2653	1.3023	1.3401	1.3788
7	1.2299	1.2723	1.3159	1.3609	1.4071	1.4547
8	1.2668	1.3168	1.3686	1.4221	1.4775	1.5347
9	1.3048	1.3629	1.4233	1.4861	1.5513	1.6191
10	1.3439	1.4106	1.4802	1.5530	1.6289	1.7081
11	1.3842	1.4600	1.5395	1.6229	1.7103	1.8021
12	1.4258	1.5111	1.6010	1.6959	1.7959	1.9012
13	1.4685	1.5640	1.6651	1.7722	1.8856	2.0058
14	1.5126	1.6187	1.7317	1.8519	1.9799	2.1161
15	1.5580	1.6753	1.8009	1.9353	2.0789	2.2325
16	1.6047	1.7340	1.8730	2.0224	2.1829	2.3553
17	1.6528	1.7947	1.9479	2.1134	2.2920	2.4848
18	1.7024	1.8575	2.0258	2.2085	2.4066	2.6215
19	1.7535	1.9225	2.1068	2.3079	2.5270	2.7656
20	1.8061	1.9898	2.1911	2.4117	2.6533	2.9178
21	1.8603	2.0594	2.2788	2.5202	2.7860	3.0782
22	1.9161	2.1315	2.3699	2.6337	2.9253	3.2475
23	1.9736	2.2061	2.4647	2.7522	3.0715	3.4262
24	2.0328	2.2833	2.5633	2.8760	3.2251	3.6146
25	2.0938	2.3632	2.6658	3.0054	3.3864	3.8134
26	2.1566	2.4460	2.7725	3.1407	3.5557	4.0231
27	2.2213	2.5316	2.8834	3.2820	3.7335	4.2444
28	2.2879	2.6202	2.9987	3.4297	3.9201	4.4778
29	2.3566	2.7119	3.1187	3.5840	4.1161	4.7241
30	2.4273	2.8068	3.2434	3.7453	4.3219	4.9840
31	2.5001	2.9050	3.3731	3.9139	4.5380	5.2581
32	2.5751	3.0067	3.5081	4.0900	4.7649	5.5473
33	2.6523	3.1119	3.6484	4.2740	5.0032	5.8524
34	2.7319	3.2209	3.7943	4.4664	5.2533	6.1742
35	2.8139	3.3336	3.9461	4.6673	5.5160	6.5138
36	2.8983	3.4503	4.1039	4.8774	5.7918	6.8721
37	2.9852	3.5710	4.2681	5.0969	6.0814	7.2501
38	3.0748	3.6960	4.4388	5.3262	6.3855	7.6488
39	3.1670	3.8254	4.6164	5.5659	6.7048	8.0695
40	3.2620	3.9593	4.8010	5.8164	7.0400	8.5133
41	3.3599	4.0978	4.9931	6.0781	7.3920	8.9815
42	3.4607	4.2413	5.1928	6.3516	7.7616	9.4755
43	3.5645	4.3897	5.4005	6.6374	8.1497	9.9967
44	3.6715	4.5433	5.6165	6.9361	8.5572	10.5465
45	3.7816	4.7024	5.8412	7.2482	8.9850	11.1266
46	3.8950	4.8669	6.0748	7.5744	9.4343	11.7385
47	4.0119	5.0373	6.3178	7.9153	9.9060	12.3841
48	4.1323	5.2136	6.5705	8.2715	10.4013	13.0653
49	4.2562	5.3961	6.8333	8.6437	10.9213	13.7838
50	4.3839	5.5849	7.1067	9.0326	11.4674	14.5420

COMPOUND INTEREST TABLE (continued)
(Future Value of a Lump Sum)

YEARS	6.0%	6.5%	7.0%	7.5%	8.0%	8.5%
1	1.0600	1.0650	1.0700	1.0750	1.0800	1.0850
2	1.1236	1.1342	1.1449	1.1556	1.1664	1.1772
3	1.1910	1.2079	1.2250	1.2423	1.2597	1.2773
4	1.2625	1.2865	1.3108	1.3355	1.3605	1.3859
5	1.3382	1.3701	1.4026	1.4356	1.4693	1.5037
6	1.4185	1.4591	1.5007	1.5433	1.5869	1.6315
7	1.5036	1.5540	1.6058	1.6590	1.7138	1.7701
8	1.5938	1.6550	1.7182	1.7835	1.8509	1.9206
9	1.6895	1.7626	1.8385	1.9172	1.9990	2.0839
10	1.7908	1.8771	1.9672	2.0610	2.1589	2.2610
11	1.8983	1.9992	2.1049	2.2156	2.3316	2.4532
12	2.0122	2.1291	2.2522	2.3818	2.5182	2.6617
13	2.1329	2.2675	2.4098	2.5604	2.7196	2.8879
14	2.2609	2.4149	2.5785	2.7524	2.9372	3.1334
15	2.3966	2.5718	2.7590	2.9589	3.1722	3.3997
16	2.5404	2.7390	2.9522	3.1808	3.4259	3.6887
17	2.6928	2.9170	3.1588	3.4194	3.7000	4.0023
18	2.8543	3.1067	3.3799	3.6758	3.9960	4.3425
19	3.0256	3.3086	3.6165	3.9515	4.3157	4.7116
20	3.2071	3.5236	3.8697	4.2479	4.6610	5.1120
21	3.3996	3.7527	4.1406	4.5664	5.0338	5.5466
22	3.6035	3.9966	4.4304	4.9089	5.4365	6.0180
23	3.8197	4.2564	4.7405	5.2771	5.8715	6.5296
24	4.0489	4.5331	5.0724	5.6729	6.3412	7.0846
25	4.2919	4.8277	5.4274	6.0983	6.8485	7.6868
26	4.5494	5.1415	5.8074	6.5557	7.3964	8.3401
27	4.8223	5.4757	6.2139	7.0474	7.9881	9.0490
28	5.1117	5.8316	6.6488	7.5759	8.6271	9.8182
29	5.4184	6.2107	7.1143	8.1441	9.3173	10.6528
30	5.7435	6.6144	7.6123	8.7550	10.0627	11.5583
31	6.0881	7.0443	8.1451	9.4116	10.8677	12.5407
32	6.4534	7.5022	8.7153	10.1174	11.7371	13.6067
33	6.8406	7.9898	9.3253	10.8763	12.6760	14.7632
34	7.2510	8.5092	9.9781	11.6920	13.6901	16.0181
35	7.6861	9.0623	10.6766	12.5689	14.7853	17.3796
36	8.1473	9.6513	11.4239	13.5115	15.9682	18.8569
37	8.6361	10.2786	12.2236	14.5249	17.2456	20.4598
38	9.1543	10.9467	13.0793	15.6143	18.6253	22.1988
39	9.7035	11.6583	13.9948	16.7853	20.1153	24.0857
40	10.2857	12.4161	14.9745	18.0442	21.7245	26.1330
41	10.9029	13.2231	16.0227	19.3976	23.4625	28.3543
42	11.5570	14.0826	17.1443	20.8524	25.3395	30.7644
43	12.2505	14.9980	18.3444	22.4163	27.3666	33.3794
44	12.9855	15.9729	19.6285	24.0975	29.5560	36.2167
45	13.7646	17.0111	21.0025	25.9048	31.9204	39.2951
46	14.5905	18.1168	22.4726	27.8477	34.4741	42.6352
47	15.4659	19.2944	24.0457	29.9363	37.2320	46.2592
48	16.3939	20.5485	25.7289	32.1815	40.2106	50.1912
49	17.3775	21.8842	27.5299	34.5951	43.4274	54.4574
50	18.4202	23.3067	29.4570	37.1898	46.9016	59.0863

COMPOUND INTEREST TABLE (continued)
(Future Value of a Lump Sum)

YEARS	9.0%	9.5%	10.0%	10.5%	11.0%	11.5%
1	1.0900	1.0950	1.1000	1.1050	1.1100	1.1150
2	1.1881	1.1990	1.2100	1.2210	1.2321	1.2432
3	1.2950	1.3129	1.3310	1.3492	1.3676	1.3862
4	1.4116	1.4377	1.4641	1.4909	1.5181	1.5456
5	1.5386	1.5742	1.6105	1.6474	1.6851	1.7234
6	1.6771	1.7238	1.7716	1.8204	1.8704	1.9215
7	1.8280	1.8876	1.9487	2.0116	2.0762	2.1425
8	1.9926	2.0669	2.1436	2.2228	2.3045	2.3889
9	2.1719	2.2632	2.3579	2.4562	2.5580	2.6636
10	2.3674	2.4782	2.5937	2.7141	2.8394	2.9699
11	2.5804	2.7137	2.8531	2.9991	3.1518	3.3115
12	2.8127	2.9715	3.1384	3.3140	3.4985	3.6923
13	3.0658	3.2537	3.4523	3.6619	3.8833	4.1169
14	3.3417	3.5629	3.7975	4.0464	4.3104	4.5904
15	3.6425	3.9013	4.1772	4.4713	4.7846	5.1183
16	3.9703	4.2719	4.5950	4.9408	5.3109	5.7069
17	4.3276	4.6778	5.0545	5.4596	5.8951	6.3632
18	4.7171	5.1222	5.5599	6.0328	6.5436	7.0949
19	5.1417	5.6088	6.1159	6.6663	7.2633	7.9108
20	5.6044	6.1416	6.7275	7.3662	8.0623	8.8206
21	6.1088	6.7251	7.4003	8.1397	8.9492	9.8350
22	6.6586	7.3639	8.1403	8.9944	9.9336	10.9660
23	7.2579	8.0635	8.9543	9.9388	11.0263	12.2271
24	7.9111	8.8296	9.8497	10.9823	12.2392	13.6332
25	8.6231	9.6684	10.8347	12.1355	13.5855	15.2010
26	9.3992	10.5869	11.9182	13.4097	15.0799	16.9491
27	10.2451	11.5926	13.1100	14.8177	16.7386	18.8982
28	11.1671	12.6939	14.4210	16.3736	18.5799	21.0715
29	12.1722	13.8998	15.8631	18.0928	20.6237	23.4948
30	13.2677	15.2203	17.4494	19.9926	22.8923	26.1967
31	14.4618	16.6662	19.1943	22.0918	25.4104	29.2093
32	15.7633	18.2495	21.1138	24.4114	28.2056	32.5684
33	17.1820	19.9832	23.2252	26.9746	31.3082	36.3137
34	18.7284	21.8816	25.5477	29.8069	34.7521	40.4898
35	20.4140	23.9604	28.1024	32.9367	38.5749	45.1461
36	22.2512	26.2366	30.9127	36.3950	42.8181	50.3379
37	24.2538	28.7291	34.0040	40.2165	47.5281	56.1268
38	26.4367	31.4584	37.4043	44.4392	52.7562	62.5814
39	28.8160	34.4469	41.1448	49.1053	58.5593	69.7782
40	31.4094	37.7194	45.2593	54.2614	65.0009	77.8027
41	34.2363	41.3027	49.7852	59.9589	72.1510	86.7500
42	37.3175	45.2265	54.7637	66.2545	80.0876	96.7263
43	40.6761	49.5230	60.2401	73.2113	88.8972	107.8498
44	44.3370	54.2277	66.2641	80.8984	98.6759	120.2525
45	48.3273	59.3793	72.8905	89.3928	109.5302	134.0816
46	52.6767	65.0204	80.1795	98.7790	121.5786	149.5009
47	57.4177	71.1973	88.1975	109.1508	134.9522	166.6936
48	62.5852	77.9611	97.0172	120.6117	149.7969	185.8633
49	68.2179	85.3674	106.7190	133.2759	166.2746	207.2376
50	74.3575	93.4773	117.3909	147.2698	184.5648	231.0699

COMPOUND INTEREST TABLE (continued)
(Future Value of a Lump Sum)

YEARS	12.0%	12.5%	13.0%	13.5%	14.0%	14.5%
1	1.1200	1.1250	1.1300	1.1350	1.1400	1.1450
2	1.2544	1.2656	1.2769	1.2882	1.2996	1.3110
3	1.4049	1.4238	1.4429	1.4621	1.4815	1.5011
4	1.5735	1.6018	1.6305	1.6595	1.6890	1.7188
5	1.7623	1.8020	1.8424	1.8836	1.9254	1.9680
6	1.9738	2.0273	2.0820	2.1378	2.1950	2.2534
7	2.2107	2.2807	2.3526	2.4264	2.5023	2.5801
8	2.4760	2.5658	2.6584	2.7540	2.8526	2.9542
9	2.7731	2.8865	3.0040	3.1258	3.2519	3.3826
10	3.1058	3.2473	3.3946	3.5478	3.7072	3.8731
11	3.4785	3.6532	3.8359	4.0267	4.2262	4.4347
12	3.8960	4.1099	4.3345	4.5704	4.8179	5.0777
13	4.3635	4.6236	4.8980	5.1874	5.4924	5.8140
14	4.8871	5.2016	5.5348	5.8877	6.2613	6.6570
15	5.4736	5.8518	6.2543	6.6825	7.1379	7.6222
16	6.1304	6.5833	7.0673	7.5846	8.1372	8.7275
17	6.8660	7.4062	7.9861	8.6085	9.2765	9.9929
18	7.6900	8.3319	9.0243	9.7707	10.5752	11.4419
19	8.6128	9.3734	10.1974	11.0897	12.0557	13.1010
20	9.6463	10.5451	11.5231	12.5869	13.7435	15.0006
21	10.8038	11.8632	13.0211	14.2861	15.6676	17.1757
22	12.1003	13.3461	14.7138	16.2147	17.8610	19.6662
23	13.5523	15.0144	16.6266	18.4037	20.3616	22.5178
24	15.1786	16.8912	18.7881	20.8882	23.2122	25.7829
25	17.0001	19.0026	21.2305	23.7081	26.4619	29.5214
26	19.0401	21.3779	23.9905	26.9087	30.1666	33.8020
27	21.3249	24.0502	27.1093	30.5414	34.3899	38.7033
28	23.8839	27.0564	30.6335	34.6644	39.2045	44.3153
29	26.7499	30.4385	34.6158	39.3441	44.6931	50.7410
30	29.9599	34.2433	39.1159	44.6556	50.9502	58.0985
31	33.5551	38.5237	44.2010	50.6841	58.0832	66.5227
32	37.5817	43.3392	49.9471	57.5265	66.2148	76.1685
33	42.0915	48.7566	56.4402	65.2925	75.4849	87.2130
34	47.1425	54.8512	63.7774	74.1070	86.0528	99.8588
35	52.7996	61.7075	72.0685	84.1115	98.1002	114.3384
36	59.1356	69.4210	81.4374	95.4665	111.8342	130.9174
37	66.2318	78.0986	92.0243	108.3545	127.4910	149.9005
38	74.1797	87.8609	103.9874	122.9824	145.3397	171.6360
39	83.0812	98.8436	117.5058	139.5850	165.6873	196.5232
40	93.0510	111.1990	132.7815	158.4289	188.8835	225.0191
41	104.2171	125.0989	150.0431	179.8169	215.3272	257.6469
42	116.7231	140.7362	169.5487	204.0921	245.4730	295.0057
43	130.7299	158.3283	191.5901	231.6446	279.8392	337.7815
44	146.4175	178.1193	216.4968	262.9166	319.0167	386.7598
45	163.9876	200.3842	244.6414	298.4103	363.6791	442.8400
46	183.6661	225.4322	276.4447	338.6957	414.5942	507.0518
47	205.7060	253.6113	312.3825	384.4197	472.6373	580.5743
48	230.3907	285.3127	352.9923	436.3163	538.8066	664.7576
49	258.0376	320.9768	398.8813	495.2190	614.2395	761.1474
50	289.0022	361.0989	450.7358	562.0736	700.2330	871.5138

COMPOUND INTEREST TABLE (continued)
(Future Value of a Lump Sum)

YEARS	15.0%	16.0%	17.0%	18.0%	19.0%	20.0%
1	1.1500	1.1600	1.1700	1.1800	1.1900	1.2000
2	1.3225	1.3456	1.3689	1.3924	1.4161	1.4400
3	1.5209	1.5609	1.6016	1.6430	1.6852	1.7280
4	1.7490	1.8106	1.8739	1.9388	2.0053	2.0736
5	2.0114	2.1003	2.1924	2.2878	2.3864	2.4883
6	2.3131	2.4364	2.5652	2.6996	2.8398	2.9860
7	2.6600	2.8262	3.0012	3.1855	3.3793	3.5832
8	3.0590	3.2784	3.5115	3.7589	4.0214	4.2998
9	3.5179	3.8030	4.1084	4.4355	4.7854	5.1598
10	4.0456	4.4114	4.8068	5.2338	5.6947	6.1917
11	4.6524	5.1173	5.6240	6.1759	6.7767	7.4301
12	5.3503	5.9360	6.5801	7.2876	8.0642	8.9161
13	6.1528	6.8858	7.6987	8.5994	9.5964	10.6993
14	7.0757	7.9875	9.0075	10.1472	11.4198	12.8392
15	8.1371	9.2655	10.5387	11.9737	13.5895	15.4070
16	9.3576	10.7480	12.3303	14.1290	16.1715	18.4884
17	10.7613	12.4677	14.4265	16.6722	19.2441	22.1861
18	12.3755	14.4625	16.8790	19.6733	22.9005	26.6233
19	14.2318	16.7765	19.7484	23.2144	27.2516	31.9480
20	16.3665	19.4608	23.1056	27.3930	32.4294	38.3376
21	18.8215	22.5745	27.0336	32.3238	38.5910	46.0051
22	21.6447	26.1864	31.6293	38.1421	45.9233	55.2061
23	24.8915	30.3762	37.0062	45.0076	54.6487	66.2474
24	28.6252	35.2364	43.2973	53.1090	65.0320	79.4969
25	32.9190	40.8742	50.6578	62.6686	77.3881	95.3962
26	37.8568	47.4141	59.2697	73.9490	92.0918	114.4755
27	43.5353	55.0004	69.3455	87.2598	109.5892	137.3706
28	50.0656	63.8004	81.1342	102.9666	130.4112	164.8447
29	57.5755	74.0085	94.9271	121.5006	155.1893	197.8136
30	66.2118	85.8499	111.0647	143.3707	184.6753	237.3763
31	76.1435	99.5858	129.9456	169.1774	219.7636	284.8516
32	87.5651	115.5196	152.0364	199.6293	261.5187	341.8219
33	100.6998	134.0027	177.8826	235.5626	311.2072	410.1863
34	115.8048	155.4431	208.1226	277.9639	370.3366	492.2236
35	133.1755	180.3141	243.5035	327.9974	440.7006	590.6683
36	153.1519	209.1643	284.8991	387.0369	524.4337	708.8019
37	176.1247	242.6306	333.3319	456.7035	624.0761	850.5623
38	202.5434	281.4515	389.9984	538.9102	742.6505	1020.6748
39	232.9249	326.4837	456.2981	635.9140	883.7541	1224.8098
40	267.8636	378.7211	533.8687	750.3785	1051.6674	1469.7717
41	308.0431	439.3165	624.6264	885.4467	1251.4842	1763.7261
42	354.2496	509.6071	730.8129	1044.8271	1489.2662	2116.4713
43	407.3871	591.1443	855.0511	1232.8960	1772.2268	2539.7655
44	468.4951	685.7273	1000.4098	1454.8172	2108.9499	3047.7187
45	538.7694	795.4437	1170.4795	1716.6843	2509.6504	3657.2624
46	619.5848	922.7147	1369.4610	2025.6875	2986.4839	4388.7149
47	712.5225	1070.3491	1602.2694	2390.3113	3553.9159	5266.4579
48	819.4009	1241.6049	1874.6552	2820.5674	4229.1599	6319.7495
49	942.3111	1440.2617	2193.3466	3328.2695	5032.7003	7583.6994
50	1083.6577	1670.7035	2566.2155	3927.3581	5988.9133	9100.4393

Appendix B

PRESENT VALUE TABLE
(Present Value of a Future Lump Sum)

(The use of this table is explained in Chapter 12)

YEARS	3.0%	3.5%	4.0%	4.5%	5.0%	5.5%	6.0%
1	0.9709	0.9662	0.9615	0.9569	0.9524	0.9479	0.9434
2	0.9426	0.9335	0.9246	0.9157	0.9070	0.8985	0.8900
3	0.9151	0.9019	0.8890	0.8763	0.8638	0.8516	0.8396
4	0.8885	0.8714	0.8548	0.8386	0.8227	0.8072	0.7921
5	0.8626	0.8420	0.8219	0.8025	0.7835	0.7651	0.7473
6	0.8375	0.8135	0.7903	0.7679	0.7462	0.7252	0.7050
7	0.8131	0.7860	0.7599	0.7348	0.7107	0.6874	0.6651
8	0.7894	0.7594	0.7307	0.7032	0.6768	0.6516	0.6274
9	0.7664	0.7337	0.7026	0.6729	0.6446	0.6176	0.5919
10	0.7441	0.7089	0.6756	0.6439	0.6139	0.5854	0.5584
11	0.7224	0.6849	0.6496	0.6162	0.5847	0.5549	0.5268
12	0.7014	0.6618	0.6246	0.5897	0.5568	0.5260	0.4970
13	0.6810	0.6394	0.6006	0.5643	0.5303	0.4986	0.4688
14	0.6611	0.6178	0.5775	0.5400	0.5051	0.4726	0.4423
15	0.6419	0.5969	0.5553	0.5167	0.4810	0.4479	0.4173
16	0.6232	0.5767	0.5339	0.4945	0.4581	0.4246	0.3936
17	0.6050	0.5572	0.5134	0.4732	0.4363	0.4024	0.3714
18	0.5874	0.5384	0.4936	0.4528	0.4155	0.3815	0.3503
19	0.5703	0.5202	0.4746	0.4333	0.3957	0.3616	0.3305
20	0.5537	0.5026	0.4564	0.4146	0.3769	0.3427	0.3118
21	0.5375	0.4856	0.4388	0.3968	0.3589	0.3249	0.2942
22	0.5219	0.4692	0.4220	0.3797	0.3418	0.3079	0.2775
23	0.5067	0.4533	0.4057	0.3634	0.3256	0.2919	0.2618
24	0.4919	0.4380	0.3901	0.3477	0.3101	0.2767	0.2470
25	0.4776	0.4231	0.3751	0.3327	0.2953	0.2622	0.2330
26	0.4637	0.4088	0.3607	0.3184	0.2812	0.2486	0.2198
27	0.4502	0.3950	0.3468	0.3047	0.2678	0.2356	0.2074
28	0.4371	0.3817	0.3335	0.2916	0.2551	0.2233	0.1956
29	0.4243	0.3687	0.3207	0.2790	0.2429	0.2117	0.1846
30	0.4120	0.3563	0.3083	0.2670	0.2314	0.2006	0.1741
31	0.4000	0.3442	0.2965	0.2555	0.2204	0.1902	0.1643
32	0.3883	0.3326	0.2851	0.2445	0.2099	0.1803	0.1550
33	0.3770	0.3213	0.2741	0.2340	0.1999	0.1709	0.1462
34	0.3660	0.3105	0.2636	0.2239	0.1904	0.1620	0.1379
35	0.3554	0.3000	0.2534	0.2143	0.1813	0.1535	0.1301
36	0.3450	0.2898	0.2437	0.2050	0.1727	0.1455	0.1227
37	0.3350	0.2800	0.2343	0.1962	0.1644	0.1379	0.1158
38	0.3252	0.2706	0.2253	0.1878	0.1566	0.1307	0.1092
39	0.3158	0.2614	0.2166	0.1797	0.1491	0.1239	0.1031
40	0.3066	0.2526	0.2083	0.1719	0.1420	0.1175	0.0972
41	0.2976	0.2440	0.2003	0.1645	0.1353	0.1113	0.0917
42	0.2890	0.2358	0.1926	0.1574	0.1288	0.1055	0.0865
43	0.2805	0.2278	0.1852	0.1507	0.1227	0.1000	0.0816
44	0.2724	0.2201	0.1780	0.1442	0.1169	0.0948	0.0770
45	0.2644	0.2127	0.1712	0.1380	0.1113	0.0899	0.0727
46	0.2567	0.2055	0.1646	0.1320	0.1060	0.0852	0.0685
47	0.2493	0.1985	0.1583	0.1263	0.1009	0.0807	0.0647
48	0.2420	0.1918	0.1522	0.1209	0.0961	0.0765	0.0610
49	0.2350	0.1853	0.1463	0.1157	0.0916	0.0725	0.0575
50	0.2281	0.1791	0.1407	0.1107	0.0872	0.0688	0.0543

The Tools and Techniques of Financial Planning

PRESENT VALUE TABLE (continued)
(Present Value of a Future Lump Sum)

YEARS	6.5%	7.0%	7.5%	8.0%	8.5%	9.0%	9.5%
1	0.9390	0.9346	0.9302	0.9259	0.9217	0.9174	0.9132
2	0.8817	0.8734	0.8653	0.8573	0.8495	0.8417	0.8340
3	0.8278	0.8163	0.8050	0.7938	0.7829	0.7722	0.7617
4	0.7773	0.7629	0.7488	0.7350	0.7216	0.7084	0.6956
5	0.7299	0.7130	0.6966	0.6806	0.6650	0.6499	0.6352
6	0.6853	0.6663	0.6480	0.6302	0.6129	0.5963	0.5801
7	0.6435	0.6227	0.6028	0.5835	0.5649	0.5470	0.5298
8	0.6042	0.5820	0.5607	0.5403	0.5207	0.5019	0.4838
9	0.5674	0.5439	0.5216	0.5002	0.4799	0.4604	0.4418
10	0.5327	0.5083	0.4852	0.4632	0.4423	0.4224	0.4035
11	0.5002	0.4751	0.4513	0.4289	0.4076	0.3875	0.3685
12	0.4697	0.4440	0.4199	0.3971	0.3757	0.3555	0.3365
13	0.4410	0.4150	0.3906	0.3677	0.3463	0.3262	0.3073
14	0.4141	0.3878	0.3633	0.3405	0.3191	0.2992	0.2807
15	0.3888	0.3624	0.3380	0.3152	0.2941	0.2745	0.2563
16	0.3651	0.3387	0.3144	0.2919	0.2711	0.2519	0.2341
17	0.3428	0.3166	0.2925	0.2703	0.2499	0.2311	0.2138
18	0.3219	0.2959	0.2720	0.2502	0.2303	0.2120	0.1952
19	0.3022	0.2765	0.2531	0.2317	0.2122	0.1945	0.1783
20	0.2838	0.2584	0.2354	0.2145	0.1956	0.1784	0.1628
21	0.2665	0.2415	0.2190	0.1987	0.1803	0.1637	0.1487
22	0.2502	0.2257	0.2037	0.1839	0.1662	0.1502	0.1358
23	0.2349	0.2109	0.1895	0.1703	0.1531	0.1378	0.1240
24	0.2206	0.1971	0.1763	0.1577	0.1412	0.1264	0.1133
25	0.2071	0.1842	0.1640	0.1460	0.1301	0.1160	0.1034
26	0.1945	0.1722	0.1525	0.1352	0.1199	0.1064	0.0945
27	0.1826	0.1609	0.1419	0.1252	0.1105	0.0976	0.0863
28	0.1715	0.1504	0.1320	0.1159	0.1019	0.0895	0.0788
29	0.1610	0.1406	0.1228	0.1073	0.0939	0.0822	0.0719
30	0.1512	0.1314	0.1142	0.0994	0.0865	0.0754	0.0657
31	0.1420	0.1228	0.1063	0.0920	0.0797	0.0691	0.0600
32	0.1333	0.1147	0.0988	0.0852	0.0735	0.0634	0.0548
33	0.1252	0.1072	0.0919	0.0789	0.0677	0.0582	0.0500
34	0.1175	0.1002	0.0855	0.0730	0.0624	0.0534	0.0457
35	0.1103	0.0937	0.0796	0.0676	0.0575	0.0490	0.0417
36	0.1036	0.0875	0.0740	0.0626	0.0530	0.0449	0.0381
37	0.0973	0.0818	0.0688	0.0580	0.0489	0.0412	0.0348
38	0.0914	0.0765	0.0640	0.0537	0.0450	0.0378	0.0318
39	0.0858	0.0715	0.0596	0.0497	0.0415	0.0347	0.0290
40	0.0805	0.0668	0.0554	0.0460	0.0383	0.0318	0.0265
41	0.0756	0.0624	0.0516	0.0426	0.0353	0.0292	0.0242
42	0.0710	0.0583	0.0480	0.0395	0.0325	0.0268	0.0221
43	0.0667	0.0545	0.0446	0.0365	0.0300	0.0246	0.0202
44	0.0626	0.0509	0.0415	0.0338	0.0276	0.0226	0.0184
45	0.0588	0.0476	0.0386	0.0313	0.0254	0.0207	0.0168
46	0.0552	0.0445	0.0359	0.0290	0.0235	0.0190	0.0154
47	0.0518	0.0416	0.0334	0.0269	0.0216	0.0174	0.0140
48	0.0487	0.0389	0.0311	0.0249	0.0199	0.0160	0.0128
49	0.0457	0.0363	0.0289	0.0230	0.0184	0.0147	0.0117
50	0.0429	0.0339	0.0269	0.0213	0.0169	0.0134	0.0107

PRESENT VALUE TABLE (continued)
(Present Value of a Future Lump Sum)

YEARS	10.0%	10.5%	11.0%	11.5%	12.0%	12.5%	13.0%
1	0.9091	0.9050	0.9009	0.8969	0.8929	0.8889	0.8850
2	0.8264	0.8190	0.8116	0.8044	0.7972	0.7901	0.7831
3	0.7513	0.7412	0.7312	0.7214	0.7118	0.7023	0.6931
4	0.6830	0.6707	0.6587	0.6470	0.6355	0.6243	0.6133
5	0.6209	0.6070	0.5935	0.5803	0.5674	0.5549	0.5428
6	0.5645	0.5493	0.5346	0.5204	0.5066	0.4933	0.4803
7	0.5132	0.4971	0.4817	0.4667	0.4523	0.4385	0.4251
8	0.4665	0.4499	0.4339	0.4186	0.4039	0.3897	0.3762
9	0.4241	0.4071	0.3909	0.3754	0.3606	0.3464	0.3329
10	0.3855	0.3684	0.3522	0.3367	0.3220	0.3079	0.2946
11	0.3505	0.3334	0.3173	0.3020	0.2875	0.2737	0.2607
12	0.3186	0.3018	0.2858	0.2708	0.2567	0.2433	0.2307
13	0.2897	0.2731	0.2575	0.2429	0.2292	0.2163	0.2042
14	0.2633	0.2471	0.2320	0.2178	0.2046	0.1922	0.1807
15	0.2394	0.2236	0.2090	0.1954	0.1827	0.1709	0.1599
16	0.2176	0.2024	0.1883	0.1752	0.1631	0.1519	0.1415
17	0.1978	0.1832	0.1696	0.1572	0.1456	0.1350	0.1252
18	0.1799	0.1658	0.1528	0.1409	0.1300	0.1200	0.1108
19	0.1635	0.1500	0.1377	0.1264	0.1161	0.1067	0.0981
20	0.1486	0.1358	0.1240	0.1134	0.1037	0.0948	0.0868
21	0.1351	0.1229	0.1117	0.1017	0.0926	0.0843	0.0768
22	0.1228	0.1112	0.1007	0.0912	0.0826	0.0749	0.0680
23	0.1117	0.1006	0.0907	0.0818	0.0738	0.0666	0.0601
24	0.1015	0.0911	0.0817	0.0734	0.0659	0.0592	0.0532
25	0.0923	0.0824	0.0736	0.0658	0.0588	0.0526	0.0471
26	0.0839	0.0746	0.0663	0.0590	0.0525	0.0468	0.0417
27	0.0763	0.0675	0.0597	0.0529	0.0469	0.0416	0.0369
28	0.0693	0.0611	0.0538	0.0475	0.0419	0.0370	0.0326
29	0.0630	0.0553	0.0485	0.0426	0.0374	0.0329	0.0289
30	0.0573	0.0500	0.0437	0.0382	0.0334	0.0292	0.0256
31	0.0521	0.0453	0.0394	0.0342	0.0298	0.0260	0.0226
32	0.0474	0.0410	0.0355	0.0307	0.0266	0.0231	0.0200
33	0.0431	0.0371	0.0319	0.0275	0.0238	0.0205	0.0177
34	0.0391	0.0335	0.0288	0.0247	0.0212	0.0182	0.0157
35	0.0356	0.0304	0.0259	0.0222	0.0189	0.0162	0.0139
36	0.0323	0.0275	0.0234	0.0199	0.0169	0.0144	0.0123
37	0.0294	0.0249	0.0210	0.0178	0.0151	0.0128	0.0109
38	0.0267	0.0225	0.0190	0.0160	0.0135	0.0114	0.0096
39	0.0243	0.0204	0.0171	0.0143	0.0120	0.0101	0.0085
40	0.0221	0.0184	0.0154	0.0129	0.0107	0.0090	0.0075
41	0.0201	0.0167	0.0139	0.0115	0.0096	0.0080	0.0067
42	0.0183	0.0151	0.0125	0.0103	0.0086	0.0071	0.0059
43	0.0166	0.0137	0.0112	0.0093	0.0076	0.0063	0.0052
44	0.0151	0.0124	0.0101	0.0083	0.0068	0.0056	0.0046
45	0.0137	0.0112	0.0091	0.0075	0.0061	0.0050	0.0041
46	0.0125	0.0101	0.0082	0.0067	0.0054	0.0044	0.0036
47	0.0113	0.0092	0.0074	0.0060	0.0049	0.0039	0.0032
48	0.0103	0.0083	0.0067	0.0054	0.0043	0.0035	0.0028
49	0.0094	0.0075	0.0060	0.0048	0.0039	0.0031	0.0025
50	0.0085	0.0068	0.0054	0.0043	0.0035	0.0028	0.0022

PRESENT VALUE TABLE (continued)
(Present Value of a Future Lump Sum)

YEARS	14.0%	15.0%	16.0%	17.0%	18.0%	19.0%	20.0%
1	0.8772	0.8696	0.8621	0.8547	0.8475	0.8403	0.8333
2	0.7695	0.7561	0.7432	0.7305	0.7182	0.7062	0.6944
3	0.6750	0.6575	0.6407	0.6244	0.6086	0.5934	0.5787
4	0.5921	0.5718	0.5523	0.5337	0.5158	0.4987	0.4823
5	0.5194	0.4972	0.4761	0.4561	0.4371	0.4190	0.4019
6	0.4556	0.4323	0.4104	0.3898	0.3704	0.3521	0.3349
7	0.3996	0.3759	0.3538	0.3332	0.3139	0.2959	0.2791
8	0.3506	0.3269	0.3050	0.2848	0.2660	0.2487	0.2326
9	0.3075	0.2843	0.2630	0.2434	0.2255	0.2090	0.1938
10	0.2697	0.2472	0.2267	0.2080	0.1911	0.1756	0.1615
11	0.2366	0.2149	0.1954	0.1778	0.1619	0.1476	0.1346
12	0.2076	0.1869	0.1685	0.1520	0.1372	0.1240	0.1122
13	0.1821	0.1625	0.1452	0.1299	0.1163	0.1042	0.0935
14	0.1597	0.1413	0.1252	0.1110	0.0985	0.0876	0.0779
15	0.1401	0.1229	0.1079	0.0949	0.0835	0.0736	0.0649
16	0.1229	0.1069	0.0930	0.0811	0.0708	0.0618	0.0541
17	0.1078	0.0929	0.0802	0.0693	0.0600	0.0520	0.0451
18	0.0946	0.0808	0.0691	0.0592	0.0508	0.0437	0.0376
19	0.0829	0.0703	0.0596	0.0506	0.0431	0.0367	0.0313
20	0.0728	0.0611	0.0514	0.0433	0.0365	0.0308	0.0261
21	0.0638	0.0531	0.0443	0.0370	0.0309	0.0259	0.0217
22	0.0560	0.0462	0.0382	0.0316	0.0262	0.0218	0.0181
23	0.0491	0.0402	0.0329	0.0270	0.0222	0.0183	0.0151
24	0.0431	0.0349	0.0284	0.0231	0.0188	0.0154	0.0126
25	0.0378	0.0304	0.0245	0.0197	0.0160	0.0129	0.0105
26	0.0331	0.0264	0.0211	0.0169	0.0135	0.0109	0.0087
27	0.0291	0.0230	0.0182	0.0144	0.0115	0.0091	0.0073
28	0.0255	0.0200	0.0157	0.0123	0.0097	0.0077	0.0061
29	0.0224	0.0174	0.0135	0.0105	0.0082	0.0064	0.0051
30	0.0196	0.0151	0.0116	0.0090	0.0070	0.0054	0.0042
31	0.0172	0.0131	0.0100	0.0077	0.0059	0.0046	0.0035
32	0.0151	0.0114	0.0087	0.0066	0.0050	0.0038	0.0029
33	0.0132	0.0099	0.0075	0.0056	0.0042	0.0032	0.0024
34	0.0116	0.0086	0.0064	0.0048	0.0036	0.0027	0.0020
35	0.0102	0.0075	0.0055	0.0041	0.0030	0.0023	0.0017
36	0.0089	0.0065	0.0048	0.0035	0.0026	0.0019	0.0014
37	0.0078	0.0057	0.0041	0.0030	0.0022	0.0016	0.0012
38	0.0069	0.0049	0.0036	0.0026	0.0019	0.0013	0.0010
39	0.0060	0.0043	0.0031	0.0022	0.0016	0.0011	0.0008
40	0.0053	0.0037	0.0026	0.0019	0.0013	0.0010	0.0007
41	0.0046	0.0032	0.0023	0.0016	0.0011	0.0008	0.0006
42	0.0041	0.0028	0.0020	0.0014	0.0010	0.0007	0.0005
43	0.0036	0.0025	0.0017	0.0012	0.0008	0.0006	0.0004
44	0.0031	0.0021	0.0015	0.0010	0.0007	0.0005	0.0003
45	0.0027	0.0019	0.0013	0.0009	0.0006	0.0004	0.0003
46	0.0024	0.0016	0.0011	0.0007	0.0005	0.0003	0.0002
47	0.0021	0.0014	0.0009	0.0006	0.0004	0.0003	0.0002
48	0.0019	0.0012	0.0008	0.0005	0.0004	0.0002	0.0002
49	0.0016	0.0011	0.0007	0.0005	0.0003	0.0002	0.0001
50	0.0014	0.0009	0.0006	0.0004	0.0003	0.0002	0.0001

Appendix C

COMPOUND ANNUAL ANNUITY, IN ADVANCE
(Future Value of Annuity Due)

(The use of this table is explained in Chapter 12)

YEARS	3.0%	3.5%	4.0%	4.5%	5.0%	5.5%
1	1.0300	1.0350	1.0400	1.0450	1.0500	1.0550
2	2.0909	2.1062	2.1216	2.1370	2.1525	2.1680
3	3.1836	3.2149	3.2465	3.2782	3.3101	3.3423
4	4.3091	4.3625	4.4163	4.4707	4.5256	4.5811
5	5.4684	5.5502	5.6330	5.7169	5.8019	5.8881
6	6.6625	6.7794	6.8983	7.0192	7.1420	7.2669
7	7.8923	8.0517	8.2142	8.3800	8.5491	8.7216
8	9.1591	9.3685	9.5828	9.8021	10.0266	10.2563
9	10.4639	10.7314	11.0061	11.2882	11.5779	11.8754
10	11.8078	12.1420	12.4864	12.8412	13.2068	13.5835
11	13.1920	13.6020	14.0258	14.4640	14.9171	15.3856
12	14.6178	15.1130	15.6268	16.1599	16.7130	17.2868
13	16.0863	16.6770	17.2919	17.9321	18.5986	19.2926
14	17.5989	18.2957	19.0236	19.7841	20.5786	21.4087
15	19.1569	19.9710	20.8245	21.7193	22.6575	23.6411
16	20.7616	21.7050	22.6975	23.7417	24.8404	25.9964
17	22.4144	23.4997	24.6454	25.8551	27.1324	28.4812
18	24.1169	25.3572	26.6712	28.0636	29.5390	31.1027
19	25.8704	27.2797	28.7781	30.3714	32.0660	33.8683
20	27.6765	29.2695	30.9692	32.7831	34.7193	36.7861
21	29.5368	31.3289	33.2480	35.3034	37.5052	39.8643
22	31.4529	33.4604	35.6179	37.9370	40.4305	43.1118
23	33.4265	35.6665	38.0826	40.6892	43.5020	46.5380
24	35.4593	37.9499	40.6459	43.5652	46.7271	50.1526
25	37.5530	40.3131	43.3117	46.5706	50.1135	53.9660
26	39.7096	42.7591	46.0842	49.7113	53.6691	57.9891
27	41.9309	45.2906	48.9676	52.9933	57.4026	62.2335
28	44.2188	47.9108	51.9663	56.4230	61.3227	66.7114
29	46.5754	50.6227	55.0849	60.0071	65.4388	71.4355
30	49.0027	53.4295	58.3283	63.7524	69.7608	76.4194
31	51.5028	56.3345	61.7015	67.6662	74.2988	81.6775
32	54.0778	59.3412	65.2095	71.7562	79.0638	87.2248
33	56.7302	62.4532	68.8579	76.0303	84.0670	93.0771
34	59.4621	65.6740	72.6522	80.4966	89.3203	99.2514
35	62.2759	69.0076	76.5983	85.1640	94.8363	105.7652
36	65.1742	72.4579	80.7022	90.0413	100.6281	112.6373
37	68.1594	76.0289	84.9703	95.1382	106.7095	119.8873
38	71.2342	79.7249	89.4091	100.4644	113.0950	127.5361
39	74.4013	83.5503	94.0255	106.0303	119.7998	135.6056
40	77.6633	87.5095	98.8265	111.8467	126.8398	144.1189
41	81.0232	91.6074	103.8196	117.9248	134.2318	153.1005
42	84.4839	95.8486	109.0124	124.2764	141.9933	162.5760
43	88.0484	100.2383	114.4129	130.9138	150.1430	172.5727
44	91.7199	104.7817	120.0294	137.8500	158.7002	183.1192
45	95.5015	109.4840	125.8706	145.0982	167.6852	194.2457
46	99.3965	114.3510	131.9454	152.6726	177.1194	205.9842
47	103.4084	119.3883	138.2632	160.5879	187.0254	218.3684
48	107.5406	124.6018	144.8337	168.8594	197.4267	231.4336
49	111.7969	129.9979	151.6671	177.5030	208.3480	245.2175
50	116.1808	135.5828	158.7738	186.5357	219.8154	259.7594

COMPOUND ANNUAL ANNUITY, IN ADVANCE (continued)
(Future Value of Annuity Due)

YEARS	6.0%	6.5%	7.0%	7.5%	8.0%	8.5%
1	1.0600	1.0650	1.0700	1.0750	1.0800	1.0850
2	2.1836	2.1992	2.2149	2.2306	2.2464	2.2622
3	3.3746	3.4072	3.4399	3.4729	3.5061	3.5395
4	4.6371	4.6936	4.7507	4.8084	4.8666	4.9254
5	5.9753	6.0637	6.1533	6.2440	6.3359	6.4290
6	7.3938	7.5229	7.6540	7.7873	7.9228	8.0605
7	8.8975	9.0769	9.2598	9.4464	9.6366	9.8306
8	10.4913	10.7319	10.9780	11.2298	11.4876	11.7512
9	12.1808	12.4944	12.8164	13.1471	13.4866	13.8351
10	13.9716	14.3716	14.7836	15.2081	15.6455	16.0961
11	15.8699	16.3707	16.8885	17.4237	17.9771	18.5492
12	17.8821	18.4998	19.1406	19.8055	20.4953	21.2109
13	20.0151	20.7673	21.5505	22.3659	23.2149	24.0989
14	22.2760	23.1822	24.1290	25.1184	26.1521	27.2323
15	24.6725	25.7540	26.8881	28.0772	29.3243	30.6320
16	27.2129	28.4930	29.8402	31.2580	32.7502	34.3207
17	29.9057	31.4101	32.9990	34.6774	36.4502	38.3230
18	32.7600	34.5167	36.3790	38.3532	40.4463	42.6655
19	35.7856	37.8253	39.9955	42.3047	44.7620	47.3770
20	38.9927	41.3490	43.8652	46.5525	49.4229	52.4891
21	42.3923	45.1016	48.0057	51.1190	54.4568	58.0356
22	45.9958	49.0982	52.4361	56.0279	59.8933	64.0537
23	49.8156	53.3546	57.1767	61.3050	65.7648	70.5832
24	53.8645	57.8877	62.2490	66.9779	72.1059	77.6678
25	58.1564	62.7154	67.6765	73.0762	78.9544	85.3546
26	62.7058	67.8569	73.4838	79.6319	86.3508	93.6947
27	67.5281	73.3326	79.6977	86.6793	94.3388	102.7437
28	72.6398	79.1642	86.3465	94.2553	102.9659	112.5620
29	78.0582	85.3749	93.4608	102.3994	112.2832	123.2147
30	83.8017	91.9892	101.0730	111.1544	122.3459	134.7730
31	89.8898	99.0335	109.2182	120.5659	133.2135	147.3137
32	96.3432	106.5357	117.9334	130.6834	144.9506	160.9203
33	103.1838	114.5255	127.2588	141.5596	157.6267	175.6836
34	110.4348	123.0347	137.2369	153.2516	171.3168	191.7017
35	118.1209	132.0969	147.9135	165.8205	186.1021	209.0813
36	126.2681	141.7482	159.3374	179.3320	202.0703	227.9382
37	134.9042	152.0269	171.5610	193.8569	219.3159	248.3980
38	144.0585	162.9736	184.6403	209.4712	237.9412	270.5968
39	153.7620	174.6319	198.6351	226.2565	258.0565	294.6825
40	164.0477	187.0480	213.6096	244.3008	279.7810	320.8156
41	174.9505	200.2711	229.6322	263.6983	303.2435	349.1699
42	186.5076	214.3537	246.7765	284.5507	328.5830	379.9343
43	198.7580	229.3517	265.1209	306.9670	355.9496	413.3137
44	211.7435	245.3246	284.7493	331.0645	385.5056	449.5304
45	225.5081	262.3357	305.7518	356.9694	417.4260	488.8255
46	240.0986	280.4525	328.2244	384.8171	451.9001	531.4607
47	255.5645	299.7469	352.2701	414.7534	489.1321	577.7198
48	271.9584	320.2954	377.9990	446.9349	529.3427	627.9110
49	289.3359	342.1796	405.5289	481.5300	572.7701	682.3684
50	307.7560	365.4863	434.9860	518.7197	619.6717	741.4548

COMPOUND ANNUAL ANNUITY, IN ADVANCE (continued)
(Future Value of Annuity Due)

YEARS	9.0%	9.5%	10.0%	10.5%	11.0%	11.5%
1	1.0900	1.0950	1.1000	1.1050	1.1100	1.1150
2	2.2781	2.2940	2.3100	2.3260	2.3421	2.3582
3	3.5731	3.6070	3.6410	3.6753	3.7097	3.7444
4	4.9847	5.0446	5.1051	5.1662	5.2278	5.2900
5	6.5233	6.6189	6.7156	6.8136	6.9129	7.0134
6	8.2004	8.3426	8.4872	8.6340	8.7833	8.9349
7	10.0285	10.2302	10.4359	10.6456	10.8594	11.0774
8	12.0210	12.2971	12.5795	12.8684	13.1640	13.4663
9	14.1929	14.5603	14.9374	15.3246	15.7220	16.1300
10	16.5603	17.0385	17.5312	18.0387	18.5614	19.0999
11	19.1407	19.7522	20.3843	21.0377	21.7132	22.4114
12	21.9534	22.7236	23.5227	24.3517	25.2116	26.1037
13	25.0192	25.9774	26.9750	28.0136	29.0949	30.2207
14	28.3609	29.5402	30.7725	32.0600	33.4054	34.8110
15	32.0034	33.4416	34.9497	36.5313	38.1899	39.9293
16	35.9737	37.7135	39.5447	41.4721	43.5008	45.6362
17	40.3013	42.3913	44.5992	46.9317	49.3959	51.9993
18	45.0185	47.5135	50.1591	52.9645	55.9395	59.0942
19	50.1601	53.1222	56.2750	59.6308	63.2028	67.0051
20	55.7645	59.2638	63.0025	66.9970	71.2651	75.8257
21	61.8733	65.9889	70.4028	75.1367	80.2143	85.6606
22	68.5319	73.3529	78.5430	84.1311	90.1479	96.6266
23	75.7898	81.4164	87.4973	94.0698	101.1741	108.8536
24	83.7009	90.2459	97.3471	105.0522	113.4133	122.4868
25	92.3240	99.9143	108.1818	117.1877	126.9988	137.6878
26	101.7231	110.5012	120.0999	130.5974	142.0786	154.6369
27	111.9682	122.0938	133.2099	145.4151	158.8173	173.5351
28	123.1354	134.7877	147.6309	161.7887	177.3972	194.6067
29	135.3075	148.6875	163.4940	179.8815	198.0209	218.1015
30	148.5752	163.9078	180.9434	199.8740	220.9132	244.2981
31	163.0370	180.5741	200.1378	221.9658	246.3236	273.5074
32	178.8003	198.8236	221.2516	246.3772	274.5292	306.0758
33	195.9824	218.8068	244.4767	273.3518	305.8374	342.3895
34	214.7108	240.6885	270.0244	303.1588	340.5896	382.8793
35	235.1247	264.6489	298.1268	336.0954	379.1644	428.0254
36	257.3760	290.8855	329.0395	372.4905	421.9825	478.3633
37	281.6298	319.6146	363.0434	412.7070	469.5106	534.4901
38	308.0665	351.0730	400.4478	457.1462	522.2667	597.0714
39	336.8825	385.5200	441.5926	506.2515	580.8261	666.8496
40	368.2919	423.2394	486.8518	560.5129	645.8269	744.6524
41	402.5282	464.5421	536.6370	620.4718	717.9779	831.4024
42	439.8457	509.7686	591.4007	686.7263	798.0655	928.1287
43	480.5218	559.2916	651.6408	759.9376	886.9626	1035.9785
44	524.8588	613.5193	717.9049	840.8360	985.6385	1156.2310
45	573.1861	672.8987	790.7954	930.2288	1095.1688	1290.3125
46	625.8628	737.9191	870.9749	1029.0079	1216.7473	1439.8135
47	683.2805	809.1164	959.1724	1138.1587	1351.6996	1606.5070
48	745.8657	887.0774	1056.1896	1258.7703	1501.4965	1792.3704
49	814.0837	972.4448	1162.9086	1392.0462	1667.7711	1999.6079
50	888.4412	1065.9220	1280.2995	1539.3161	1852.3359	2230.6779

COMPOUND ANNUAL ANNUITY, IN ADVANCE (continued)
(Future Value of Annuity Due)

YEARS	12.0%	12.5%	13.0%	13.5%	14.0%	14.5%
1	1.1200	1.1250	1.1300	1.1350	1.1400	1.1450
2	2.3744	2.3906	2.4069	2.4232	2.4396	2.4560
3	3.7793	3.8145	3.8498	3.8854	3.9211	3.9571
4	5.3528	5.4163	5.4803	5.5449	5.6101	5.6759
5	7.1152	7.2183	7.3227	7.4284	7.5355	7.6439
6	9.0890	9.2456	9.4047	9.5663	9.7305	9.8973
7	11.2997	11.5263	11.7573	11.9927	12.2328	12.4774
8	13.7757	14.0921	14.4157	14.7468	15.0853	15.4317
9	16.5487	16.9786	17.4197	17.8726	18.3373	18.8142
10	19.6546	20.2259	20.8143	21.4204	22.0445	22.6873
11	23.1331	23.8791	24.6502	25.4471	26.2707	27.1220
12	27.0291	27.9890	28.9847	30.0175	31.0887	32.1997
13	31.3926	32.6126	33.8827	35.2048	36.5811	38.0136
14	36.2797	37.8142	39.4175	41.0925	42.8424	44.6706
15	41.7533	43.6660	45.6717	47.7750	49.9804	52.2928
16	47.8837	50.2493	52.7391	55.3596	58.1176	61.0203
17	54.7497	57.6554	60.7251	63.9681	67.3941	71.0132
18	62.4397	65.9873	69.7494	73.7388	77.9692	82.4551
19	71.0524	75.3608	79.9468	84.8286	90.0249	95.5561
20	80.6987	85.9058	91.4699	97.4154	103.7684	110.5568
21	91.5026	97.7691	104.4910	111.7015	119.4360	127.7325
22	103.6029	111.1152	119.2048	127.9162	137.2970	147.3987
23	117.1552	126.1296	135.8315	146.3199	157.6586	169.9165
24	132.3339	143.0208	154.6195	167.2081	180.8708	195.6994
25	149.3339	162.0234	175.8501	190.9162	207.3327	225.2208
26	168.3740	183.4013	199.8406	217.8249	237.4993	259.0228
27	189.6989	207.4515	226.9499	248.3662	271.8892	297.7261
28	213.5827	234.5079	257.5834	283.0306	311.0937	342.0414
29	240.3327	264.9464	292.1992	322.3748	355.7869	392.7824
30	270.2926	299.1897	331.3151	367.0304	406.7370	450.8809
31	303.8477	337.7135	375.5160	417.7145	464.8202	517.4036
32	341.4294	381.0526	425.4631	475.2409	531.0350	593.5721
33	383.5210	429.8092	481.9033	540.5335	606.5199	680.7851
34	430.6635	484.6604	545.6808	614.6405	692.5727	780.6439
35	483.4631	546.3679	617.7493	698.7520	790.6729	894.9823
36	542.5987	615.7889	699.1867	794.2185	902.5071	1025.8997
37	608.8305	693.8875	791.2109	902.5730	1029.9981	1175.8002
38	683.0101	781.7485	895.1983	1025.5553	1175.3378	1347.4362
39	766.0914	880.5920	1012.7041	1165.1403	1341.0251	1543.9594
40	859.1423	991.7910	1145.4856	1323.5693	1529.9086	1768.9785
41	963.3594	1116.8899	1295.5288	1503.3861	1745.2358	2026.6254
42	1080.0825	1257.6262	1465.0775	1707.4783	1990.7089	2321.6311
43	1210.8124	1415.9544	1656.6676	1939.1228	2270.5481	2659.4126
44	1357.2299	1594.0737	1873.1643	2202.0394	2589.5648	3046.1724
45	1521.2175	1794.4579	2117.8057	2500.4498	2953.2439	3489.0124
46	1704.8836	2019.8902	2394.2504	2839.1455	3367.8381	3996.0642
47	1910.5896	2273.5015	2706.6330	3223.5652	3840.4754	4576.6385
48	2140.9804	2558.8141	3059.6252	3659.8815	4379.2820	5241.3960
49	2399.0180	2879.7909	3458.5065	4155.1005	4993.5215	6002.5434
50	2688.0202	3240.8898	3909.2423	4717.1741	5693.7545	6874.0572

COMPOUND ANNUAL ANNUITY, IN ADVANCE (continued)
(Future Value of Annuity Due)

YEARS	15.0%	16.0%	17.0%	18.0%	19.0%	20.0%
1	1.1500	1.1600	1.1700	1.1800	1.1900	1.2000
2	2.4725	2.5056	2.5389	2.5724	2.6061	2.6400
3	3.9934	4.0665	4.1405	4.2154	4.2913	4.3680
4	5.7424	5.8771	6.0144	6.1542	6.2966	6.4416
5	7.7537	7.9775	8.2068	8.4420	8.6830	8.9299
6	10.0668	10.4139	10.7720	11.1415	11.5227	11.9159
7	12.7268	13.2401	13.7733	14.3270	14.9020	15.4991
8	15.7858	16.5185	17.2847	18.0859	18.9234	19.7989
9	19.3037	20.3215	21.3931	22.5213	23.7089	24.9587
10	23.3493	24.7329	26.1999	27.7551	29.4035	31.1504
11	28.0017	29.8502	31.8239	33.9311	36.1802	38.5805
12	33.3519	35.7862	38.4040	41.2187	44.2445	47.4966
13	39.5047	42.6720	46.1027	49.8180	53.8409	58.1959
14	46.5804	50.6595	55.1101	59.9653	65.2607	71.0351
15	54.7175	59.9250	65.6488	71.9390	78.8502	86.4421
16	64.0751	70.6730	77.9792	86.0680	95.0217	104.9306
17	74.8364	83.1407	92.4056	102.7403	114.2659	127.1167
18	87.2118	97.6032	109.2846	122.4135	137.1664	153.7400
19	101.4436	114.3797	129.0329	145.6280	164.4180	185.6880
20	117.8101	133.8405	152.1385	173.0210	196.8474	224.0256
21	136.6316	156.4150	179.1721	205.3448	235.4384	270.0307
22	158.2764	182.6014	210.8013	243.4869	281.3618	325.2369
23	183.1679	212.9776	247.8076	288.4945	336.0105	391.4843
24	211.7930	248.2140	291.1049	341.6035	401.0425	470.9811
25	244.7120	289.0883	341.7627	404.2722	478.4305	566.3773
26	282.5688	336.5024	401.0323	478.2212	570.5223	680.8528
27	326.1041	391.5027	470.3779	565.4810	680.1116	818.2234
28	376.1697	455.3032	551.5121	668.4475	810.5228	983.0680
29	433.7452	529.3117	646.4391	789.9481	965.7121	1180.8816
30	499.9570	615.1616	757.5038	933.3188	1150.3874	1418.2580
31	576.1005	714.7474	887.4494	1102.4962	1370.1510	1703.1096
32	663.6656	830.2670	1039.4858	1302.1255	1631.6697	2044.9315
33	764.3655	964.2697	1217.3684	1537.6881	1942.8770	2455.1178
34	880.1703	1119.7129	1425.4911	1815.6519	2313.2136	2947.3414
35	1013.3458	1300.0269	1668.9946	2143.6493	2753.9142	3538.0096
36	1166.4977	1509.1912	1953.8937	2530.6862	3278.3478	4246.8116
37	1342.6224	1751.8218	2287.2256	2987.3897	3902.4239	5097.3739
38	1545.1657	2033.2733	2677.2239	3526.2999	4645.0745	6118.0487
39	1778.0906	2359.7570	3133.5220	4162.2139	5528.8286	7342.8585
40	2045.9542	2738.4781	3667.3907	4912.5924	6580.4960	8812.6302
41	2353.9974	3177.7946	4292.0172	5798.0391	7831.9803	10576.3562
42	2708.2470	3687.4017	5022.8301	6842.8661	9321.2465	12692.8275
43	3115.6340	4278.5460	5877.8812	8075.7621	11093.4733	15232.5931
44	3584.1292	4964.2733	6878.2911	9530.5793	13202.4232	18280.3117
45	4122.8985	5759.7170	8048.7705	11247.2637	15712.0736	21937.5741
46	4742.4834	6682.4318	9418.2315	13272.9512	18698.5575	26326.2890
47	5455.0059	7752.7808	11020.5009	15663.2625	22252.4734	31592.7469
48	6274.4068	8994.3857	12895.1561	18483.8299	26481.6333	37912.4963
49	7216.7179	10434.6474	15088.5027	21812.0994	31514.3336	45496.1957
50	8300.3756	12105.3509	17654.7181	25739.4575	37503.2469	54596.6350

Appendix D

COMPOUND ANNUAL ANNUITY, IN ARREARS
(Future Value of an Ordinary Annuity)

(The use of this table is explained in Chapter 12)

YEARS	3.0%	3.5%	4.0%	4.5%	5.0%	5.5%
1	1.0000	1.0000	1.0000	1.0000	1.0000	1.0000
2	2.0300	2.0350	2.0400	2.0450	2.0500	2.0550
3	3.0909	3.1062	3.1216	3.1370	3.1525	3.1680
4	4.1836	4.2149	4.2465	4.2782	4.3101	4.3423
5	5.3091	5.3625	5.4163	5.4707	5.5256	5.5811
6	6.4684	6.5502	6.6330	6.7169	6.8019	6.8881
7	7.6625	7.7794	7.8983	8.0192	8.1420	8.2669
8	8.8923	9.0517	9.2142	9.3800	9.5491	9.7216
9	10.1591	10.3685	10.5828	10.8021	11.0266	11.2563
10	11.4639	11.7314	12.0061	12.2882	12.5779	12.8754
11	12.8078	13.1420	13.4864	13.8412	14.2068	14.5835
12	14.1920	14.6020	15.0258	15.4640	15.9171	16.3856
13	15.6178	16.1130	16.6268	17.1599	17.7130	18.2868
14	17.0863	17.6770	18.2919	18.9321	19.5986	20.2926
15	18.5989	19.2957	20.0236	20.7841	21.5786	22.4087
16	20.1569	20.9710	21.8245	22.7193	23.6575	24.6411
17	21.7616	22.7050	23.6975	24.7417	25.8404	26.9964
18	23.4144	24.4997	25.6454	26.8551	28.1324	29.4812
19	25.1169	26.3572	27.6712	29.0636	30.5390	32.1027
20	26.8704	28.2797	29.7781	31.3714	33.0660	34.8683
21	28.6765	30.2695	31.9692	33.7831	35.7193	37.7861
22	30.5368	32.3289	34.2480	36.3034	38.5052	40.8643
23	32.4529	34.4604	36.6179	38.9370	41.4305	44.1118
24	34.4265	36.6665	39.0826	41.6892	44.5020	47.5380
25	36.4593	38.9499	41.6459	44.5652	47.7271	51.1526
26	38.5530	41.3131	44.3117	47.5706	51.1135	54.9660
27	40.7096	43.7591	47.0842	50.7113	54.6691	58.9891
28	42.9309	46.2906	49.9676	53.9933	58.4026	63.2335
29	45.2188	48.9108	52.9663	57.4230	62.3227	67.7114
30	47.5754	51.6227	56.0849	61.0071	66.4388	72.4355
31	50.0027	54.4295	59.3283	64.7524	70.7608	77.4194
32	52.5028	57.3345	62.7015	68.6662	75.2988	82.6775
33	55.0778	60.3412	66.2095	72.7562	80.0638	88.2248
34	57.7302	63.4532	69.8579	77.0303	85.0670	94.0771
35	60.4621	66.6740	73.6522	81.4966	90.3203	100.2514
36	63.2759	70.0076	77.5983	86.1640	95.8363	106.7652
37	66.1742	73.4579	81.7022	91.0413	101.6281	113.6373
38	69.1594	77.0289	85.9703	96.1382	107.7095	120.8873
39	72.2342	80.7249	90.4091	101.4644	114.0950	128.5361
40	75.4013	84.5503	95.0255	107.0303	120.7998	136.6056
41	78.6633	88.5095	99.8265	112.8467	127.8398	145.1189
42	82.0232	92.6074	104.8196	118.9248	135.2318	154.1005
43	85.4839	96.8486	110.0124	125.2764	142.9933	163.5760
44	89.0484	101.2383	115.4129	131.9138	151.1430	173.5727
45	92.7199	105.7817	121.0294	138.8500	159.7002	184.1192
46	96.5015	110.4840	126.8706	146.0982	168.6852	195.2457
47	100.3965	115.3510	132.9454	153.6726	178.1194	206.9842
48	104.4084	120.3883	139.2632	161.5879	188.0254	219.3684
49	108.5406	125.6018	145.8337	169.8594	198.4267	232.4336
50	112.7969	130.9979	152.6671	178.5030	209.3480	246.2175

COMPOUND ANNUAL ANNUITY, IN ARREARS (continued)
(Future Value of an Ordinary Annuity)

YEARS	6.0%	6.5%	7.0%	7.5%	8.0%	8.5%
1	1.0000	1.0000	1.0000	1.0000	1.0000	1.0000
2	2.0600	2.0650	2.0700	2.0750	2.0800	2.0850
3	3.1836	3.1992	3.2149	3.2306	3.2464	3.2622
4	4.3746	4.4072	4.4399	4.4729	4.5061	4.5395
5	5.6371	5.6936	5.7507	5.8084	5.8666	5.9254
6	6.9753	7.0637	7.1533	7.2440	7.3359	7.4290
7	8.3938	8.5229	8.6540	8.7873	8.9228	9.0605
8	9.8975	10.0769	10.2598	10.4464	10.6366	10.8306
9	11.4913	11.7319	11.9780	12.2298	12.4876	12.7512
10	13.1808	13.4944	13.8164	14.1471	14.4866	14.8351
11	14.9716	15.3716	15.7836	16.2081	16.6455	17.0961
12	16.8699	17.3707	17.8885	18.4237	18.9771	19.5492
13	18.8821	19.4998	20.1406	20.8055	21.4953	22.2109
14	21.0151	21.7673	22.5505	23.3659	24.2149	25.0989
15	23.2760	24.1822	25.1290	26.1184	27.1521	28.2323
16	25.6725	26.7540	27.8881	29.0772	30.3243	31.6320
17	28.2129	29.4930	30.8402	32.2580	33.7502	35.3207
18	30.9057	32.4101	33.9990	35.6774	37.4502	39.3230
19	33.7600	35.5167	37.3790	39.3532	41.4463	43.6655
20	36.7856	38.8253	40.9955	43.3047	45.7620	48.3770
21	39.9927	42.3490	44.8652	47.5525	50.4229	53.4891
22	43.3923	46.1016	49.0057	52.1190	55.4568	59.0356
23	46.9958	50.0982	53.4361	57.0279	60.8933	65.0537
24	50.8156	54.3546	58.1767	62.3050	66.7648	71.5832
25	54.8645	58.8877	63.2490	67.9779	73.1059	78.6678
26	59.1564	63.7154	68.6765	74.0762	79.9544	86.3546
27	63.7058	68.8569	74.4838	80.6319	87.3508	94.6947
28	68.5281	74.3326	80.6977	87.6793	95.3388	103.7437
29	73.6398	80.1642	87.3465	95.2553	103.9659	113.5620
30	79.0582	86.3749	94.4608	103.3994	113.2832	124.2147
31	84.8017	92.9892	102.0730	112.1544	123.3459	135.7730
32	90.8898	100.0335	110.2182	121.5659	134.2135	148.3137
33	97.3432	107.5357	118.9334	131.6834	145.9506	161.9203
34	104.1838	115.5255	128.2588	142.5596	158.6267	176.6836
35	111.4348	124.0347	138.2369	154.2516	172.3168	192.7017
36	119.1209	133.0969	148.9135	166.8205	187.1021	210.0813
37	127.2681	142.7482	160.3374	180.3320	203.0703	228.9382
38	135.9042	153.0269	172.5610	194.8569	220.3159	249.3980
39	145.0585	163.9736	185.6403	210.4712	238.9412	271.5968
40	154.7620	175.6319	199.6351	227.2565	259.0565	295.6825
41	165.0477	188.0480	214.6096	245.3008	280.7810	321.8156
42	175.9505	201.2711	230.6322	264.6983	304.2435	350.1699
43	187.5076	215.3537	247.7765	285.5507	329.5830	380.9343
44	199.7580	230.3517	266.1209	307.9670	356.9496	414.3137
45	212.7435	246.3246	285.7493	332.0645	386.5056	450.5304
46	226.5081	263.3357	306.7518	357.9694	418.4260	489.8255
47	241.0986	281.4525	329.2244	385.8171	452.9001	532.4607
48	256.5645	300.7469	353.2701	415.7534	490.1321	578.7198
49	272.9584	321.2954	378.9990	447.9349	530.3427	628.9110
50	290.3359	343.1796	406.5289	482.5300	573.7701	683.3684

COMPOUND ANNUAL ANNUITY, IN ARREARS (continued)
(Future Value of an Ordinary Annuity)

YEARS	9.0%	9.5%	10.0%	10.5%	11.0%	11.5%
1	1.0000	1.0000	1.0000	1.0000	1.0000	1.0000
2	2.0900	2.0950	2.1000	2.1050	2.1100	2.1150
3	3.2781	3.2940	3.3100	3.3260	3.3421	3.3582
4	4.5731	4.6070	4.6410	4.6753	4.7097	4.7444
5	5.9847	6.0446	6.1051	6.1662	6.2278	6.2900
6	7.5233	7.6189	7.7156	7.8136	7.9129	8.0134
7	9.2004	9.3426	9.4872	9.6340	9.7833	9.9349
8	11.0285	11.2302	11.4359	11.6456	11.8594	12.0774
9	13.0210	13.2971	13.5795	13.8684	14.1640	14.4663
10	15.1929	15.5603	15.9374	16.3246	16.7220	17.1300
11	17.5603	18.0385	18.5312	19.0387	19.5614	20.0999
12	20.1407	20.7522	21.3843	22.0377	22.7132	23.4114
13	22.9534	23.7236	24.5227	25.3517	26.2116	27.1037
14	26.0192	26.9774	27.9750	29.0136	30.0949	31.2207
15	29.3609	30.5402	31.7725	33.0600	34.4054	35.8110
16	33.0034	34.4416	35.9497	37.5313	39.1899	40.9293
17	36.9737	38.7135	40.5447	42.4721	44.5008	46.6362
18	41.3013	43.3913	45.5992	47.9317	50.3959	52.9993
19	46.0185	48.5135	51.1591	53.9645	56.9395	60.0942
20	51.1601	54.1222	57.2750	60.6308	64.2028	68.0051
21	56.7645	60.2638	64.0025	67.9970	72.2651	76.8257
22	62.8733	66.9889	71.4028	76.1367	81.2143	86.6606
23	69.5319	74.3529	79.5430	85.1311	91.1479	97.6266
24	76.7898	82.4164	88.4973	95.0698	102.1741	109.8536
25	84.7009	91.2459	98.3471	106.0522	114.4133	123.4868
26	93.3240	100.9143	109.1818	118.1877	127.9988	138.6878
27	102.7231	111.5012	121.0999	131.5974	143.0786	155.6369
28	112.9682	123.0938	134.2099	146.4151	159.8173	174.5351
29	124.1354	135.7877	148.6309	162.7887	178.3972	195.6067
30	136.3075	149.6875	164.4940	180.8815	199.0209	219.1015
31	149.5752	164.9078	181.9434	200.8740	221.9132	245.2981
32	164.0370	181.5741	201.1378	222.9658	247.3236	274.5074
33	179.8003	199.8236	222.2516	247.3772	275.5292	307.0758
34	196.9824	219.8068	245.4767	274.3518	306.8374	343.3895
35	215.7108	241.6885	271.0244	304.1588	341.5896	383.8793
36	236.1247	265.6489	299.1268	337.0954	380.1644	429.0254
37	258.3760	291.8855	330.0395	373.4905	422.9825	479.3633
38	282.6298	320.6146	364.0434	413.7070	470.5106	535.4901
39	309.0665	352.0730	401.4478	458.1462	523.2667	598.0714
40	337.8825	386.5200	442.5926	507.2515	581.8261	667.8496
41	369.2919	424.2394	487.8518	561.5129	646.8269	745.6524
42	403.5282	465.5421	537.6370	621.4718	718.9779	832.4024
43	440.8457	510.7686	592.4007	687.7263	799.0655	929.1287
44	481.5218	560.2916	652.6408	760.9376	887.9626	1036.9785
45	525.8588	614.5193	718.9049	841.8360	986.6385	1157.2310
46	574.1861	673.8987	791.7954	931.2288	1096.1688	1291.3125
47	626.8628	738.9191	871.9749	1030.0079	1217.7473	1440.8135
48	684.2805	810.1164	960.1724	1139.1587	1352.6996	1607.5070
49	746.8657	888.0774	1057.1896	1259.7703	1502.4965	1793.3704
50	815.0837	973.4448	1163.9086	1393.0462	1668.7711	2000.6079

COMPOUND ANNUAL ANNUITY, IN ARREARS (continued)
(Future Value of an Ordinary Annuity)

YEARS	12.0%	12.5%	13.0%	13.5%	14.0%	14.5%
1	1.0000	1.0000	1.0000	1.0000	1.0000	1.0000
2	2.1200	2.1250	2.1300	2.1350	2.1400	2.1450
3	3.3744	3.3906	3.4069	3.4232	3.4396	3.4560
4	4.7793	4.8145	4.8498	4.8854	4.9211	4.9571
5	6.3528	6.4163	6.4803	6.5449	6.6101	6.6759
6	8.1152	8.2183	8.3227	8.4284	8.5355	8.6439
7	10.0890	10.2456	10.4047	10.5663	10.7305	10.8973
8	12.2997	12.5263	12.7573	12.9927	13.2328	13.4774
9	14.7757	15.0921	15.4157	15.7468	16.0853	16.4317
10	17.5487	17.9786	18.4197	18.8726	19.3373	19.8142
11	20.6546	21.2259	21.8143	22.4204	23.0445	23.6873
12	24.1331	24.8791	25.6502	26.4471	27.2707	28.1220
13	28.0291	28.9890	29.9847	31.0175	32.0887	33.1997
14	32.3926	33.6126	34.8827	36.2048	37.5811	39.0136
15	37.2797	38.8142	40.4175	42.0925	43.8424	45.6706
16	42.7533	44.6660	46.6717	48.7750	50.9804	53.2928
17	48.8837	51.2493	53.7391	56.3596	59.1176	62.0203
18	55.7497	58.6554	61.7251	64.9681	68.3941	72.0132
19	63.4397	66.9873	70.7494	74.7388	78.9692	83.4551
20	72.0524	76.3608	80.9468	85.8286	91.0249	96.5561
21	81.6987	86.9058	92.4699	98.4154	104.7684	111.5568
22	92.5026	98.7691	105.4910	112.7015	120.4360	128.7325
23	104.6029	112.1152	120.2048	128.9162	138.2970	148.3987
24	118.1552	127.1296	136.8315	147.3199	158.6586	170.9165
25	133.3339	144.0208	155.6195	168.2081	181.8708	196.6994
26	150.3339	163.0234	176.8501	191.9162	208.3327	226.2208
27	169.3740	184.4013	200.8406	218.8249	238.4993	260.0228
28	190.6989	208.4515	227.9499	249.3662	272.8892	298.7261
29	214.5827	235.5079	258.5834	284.0306	312.0937	343.0414
30	241.3327	265.9464	293.1992	323.3748	356.7869	393.7824
31	271.2926	300.1897	332.3151	368.0304	407.7370	451.8809
32	304.8477	338.7135	376.5160	418.7145	465.8202	518.4036
33	342.4294	382.0526	426.4631	476.2409	532.0350	594.5721
34	384.5210	430.8092	482.9033	541.5335	607.5199	681.7851
35	431.6635	485.6604	546.6808	615.6405	693.5727	781.6439
36	484.4631	547.3679	618.7493	699.7520	791.6729	895.9823
37	543.5987	616.7889	700.1867	795.2185	903.5071	1026.8997
38	609.8305	694.8875	792.2109	903.5730	1030.9981	1176.8002
39	684.0101	782.7485	896.1983	1026.5553	1176.3378	1348.4362
40	767.0914	881.5920	1013.7041	1166.1403	1342.0251	1544.9594
41	860.1423	992.7910	1146.4856	1324.5693	1530.9086	1769.9785
42	964.3594	1117.8899	1296.5288	1504.3861	1746.2358	2027.6254
43	1081.0825	1258.6262	1466.0775	1708.4783	1991.7089	2322.6311
44	1211.8124	1416.9544	1657.6676	1940.1228	2271.5481	2660.4126
45	1358.2299	1595.0737	1874.1643	2203.0394	2590.5648	3047.1724
46	1522.2175	1795.4579	2118.8057	2501.4498	2954.2439	3490.0124
47	1705.8836	2020.8902	2395.2504	2840.1455	3368.8381	3997.0642
48	1911.5896	2274.5015	2707.6330	3224.5652	3841.4754	4577.6385
49	2141.9804	2559.8141	3060.6252	3660.8815	4380.2820	5242.3960
50	2400.0180	2880.7909	3459.5065	4156.1005	4994.5215	6003.5434

COMPOUND ANNUAL ANNUITY, IN ARREARS (continued)
(Future Value of an Ordinary Annuity)

YEARS	15.0%	16.0%	17.0%	18.0%	19.0%	20.0%
1	1.0000	1.0000	1.0000	1.0000	1.0000	1.0000
2	2.1500	2.1600	2.1700	2.1800	2.1900	2.2000
3	3.4725	3.5056	3.5389	3.5724	3.6061	3.6400
4	4.9934	5.0665	5.1405	5.2154	5.2913	5.3680
5	6.7424	6.8771	7.0144	7.1542	7.2966	7.4416
6	8.7537	8.9775	9.2068	9.4420	9.6830	9.9299
7	11.0668	11.4139	11.7720	12.1415	12.5227	12.9159
8	13.7268	14.2401	14.7733	15.3270	15.9020	16.4991
9	16.7858	17.5185	18.2847	19.0859	19.9234	20.7989
10	20.3037	21.3215	22.3931	23.5213	24.7089	25.9587
11	24.3493	25.7329	27.1999	28.7551	30.4035	32.1504
12	29.0017	30.8502	32.8239	34.9311	37.1802	39.5805
13	34.3519	36.7862	39.4040	42.2187	45.2445	48.4966
14	40.5047	43.6720	47.1027	50.8180	54.8409	59.1959
15	47.5804	51.6595	56.1101	60.9653	66.2607	72.0351
16	55.7175	60.9250	66.6488	72.9390	79.8502	87.4421
17	65.0751	71.6730	78.9792	87.0680	96.0217	105.9306
18	75.8364	84.1407	93.4056	103.7403	115.2659	128.1167
19	88.2118	98.6032	110.2846	123.4135	138.1664	154.7400
20	102.4436	115.3797	130.0329	146.6280	165.4180	186.6880
21	118.8101	134.8405	153.1385	174.0210	197.8474	225.0256
22	137.6316	157.4150	180.1721	206.3448	236.4384	271.0307
23	159.2764	183.6014	211.8013	244.4869	282.3618	326.2369
24	184.1679	213.9776	248.8076	289.4945	337.0105	392.4843
25	212.7930	249.2140	292.1049	342.6035	402.0425	471.9811
26	245.7120	290.0883	342.7627	405.2722	479.4305	567.3773
27	283.5688	337.5024	402.0323	479.2212	571.5223	681.8528
28	327.1041	392.5027	471.3779	566.4810	681.1116	819.2234
29	377.1697	456.3032	552.5121	669.4475	811.5228	984.0680
30	434.7452	530.3117	647.4391	790.9481	966.7121	1181.8816
31	500.9570	616.1616	758.5038	934.3188	1151.3874	1419.2580
32	577.1005	715.7474	888.4494	1103.4962	1371.1510	1704.1096
33	664.6656	831.2670	1040.4858	1303.1255	1632.6697	2045.9315
34	765.3655	965.2697	1218.3684	1538.6881	1943.8770	2456.1178
35	881.1703	1120.7129	1426.4911	1816.6519	2314.2136	2948.3414
36	1014.3458	1301.0269	1669.9946	2144.6493	2754.9142	3539.0096
37	1167.4977	1510.1912	1954.8937	2531.6862	3279.3478	4247.8116
38	1343.6224	1752.8218	2288.2256	2988.3897	3903.4239	5098.3739
39	1546.1657	2034.2733	2678.2239	3527.2999	4646.0745	6119.0487
40	1779.0906	2360.7570	3134.5220	4163.2139	5529.8286	7343.8585
41	2046.9542	2739.4781	3668.3907	4913.5924	6581.4960	8813.6302
42	2354.9974	3178.7946	4293.0172	5799.0391	7832.9803	10577.3562
43	2709.2470	3688.4017	5023.8301	6843.8661	9322.2465	12693.8275
44	3116.6340	4279.5460	5878.8812	8076.7621	11094.4733	15233.5931
45	3585.1292	4965.2733	6879.2911	9531.5793	13203.4232	18281.3117
46	4123.8985	5760.7170	8049.7705	11248.2637	15713.0736	21938.5741
47	4743.4834	6683.4318	9419.2315	13273.9512	18699.5575	26327.2890
48	5456.0059	7753.7808	11021.5009	15664.2625	22253.4734	31593.7469
49	6275.4068	8995.3857	12896.1561	18484.8299	26482.6333	37913.4963
50	7217.7179	10435.6474	15089.5027	21813.0994	31515.3336	45497.1957

Appendix E

COMPOUND DISCOUNT TABLE
(Present Value of an Ordinary Annuity)
(The use of this table is explained in Chapter 12)

YEARS	3.0%	3.5%	4.0%	4.5%	5.0%	5.5%	6.0%
1	0.9709	0.9662	0.9615	0.9569	0.9524	0.9479	0.9434
2	1.9135	1.8997	1.8861	1.8727	1.8594	1.8463	1.8334
3	2.8286	2.8016	2.7751	2.7490	2.7232	2.6979	2.6730
4	3.7171	3.6731	3.6299	3.5875	3.5460	3.5051	3.4651
5	4.5797	4.5151	4.4518	4.3900	4.3295	4.2703	4.2124
6	5.4172	5.3286	5.2421	5.1579	5.0757	4.9955	4.9173
7	6.2303	6.1145	6.0021	5.8927	5.7864	5.6830	5.5824
8	7.0197	6.8740	6.7327	6.5959	6.4632	6.3346	6.2098
9	7.7861	7.6077	7.4353	7.2688	7.1078	6.9522	6.8017
10	8.5302	8.3166	8.1109	7.9127	7.7217	7.5376	7.3601
11	9.2526	9.0016	8.7605	8.5289	8.3064	8.0925	7.8869
12	9.9540	9.6633	9.3851	9.1186	8.8633	8.6185	8.3838
13	10.6350	10.3027	9.9856	9.6829	9.3936	9.1171	8.8527
14	11.2961	10.9205	10.5631	10.2228	9.8986	9.5896	9.2950
15	11.9379	11.5174	11.1184	10.7395	10.3797	10.0376	9.7122
16	12.5611	12.0941	11.6523	11.2340	10.8378	10.4622	10.1059
17	13.1661	12.6513	12.1657	11.7072	11.2741	10.8646	10.4773
18	13.7535	13.1897	12.6593	12.1600	11.6896	11.2461	10.8276
19	14.3238	13.7098	13.1339	12.5933	12.0853	11.6077	11.1581
20	14.8775	14.2124	13.5903	13.0079	12.4622	11.9504	11.4699
21	15.4150	14.6980	14.0292	13.4047	12.8212	12.2752	11.7641
22	15.9369	15.1671	14.4511	13.7844	13.1630	12.5832	12.0416
23	16.4436	15.6204	14.8568	14.1478	13.4886	12.8750	12.3034
24	16.9355	16.0584	15.2470	14.4955	13.7986	13.1517	12.5504
25	17.4131	16.4815	15.6221	14.8282	14.0939	13.4139	12.7834
26	17.8768	16.8904	15.9828	15.1466	14.3752	13.6625	13.0032
27	18.3270	17.2854	16.3296	15.4513	14.6430	13.8981	13.2105
28	18.7641	17.6670	16.6631	15.7429	14.8981	14.1214	13.4062
29	19.1885	18.0358	16.9837	16.0219	15.1411	14.3331	13.5907
30	19.6004	18.3920	17.2920	16.2889	15.3725	14.5337	13.7648
31	20.0004	18.7363	17.5885	16.5444	15.5928	14.7239	13.9291
32	20.3888	19.0689	17.8736	16.7889	15.8027	14.9042	14.0840
33	20.7658	19.3902	18.1476	17.0229	16.0025	15.0751	14.2302
34	21.1318	19.7007	18.4112	17.2468	16.1929	15.2370	14.3681
35	21.4872	20.0007	18.6646	17.4610	16.3742	15.3906	14.4982
36	21.8323	20.2905	18.9083	17.6660	16.5469	15.5361	14.6210
37	22.1672	20.5705	19.1426	17.8622	16.7113	15.6740	14.7368
38	22.4925	20.8411	19.3679	18.0500	16.8679	15.8047	14.8460
39	22.8082	21.1025	19.5845	18.2297	17.0170	15.9287	14.9491
40	23.1148	21.3551	19.7928	18.4016	17.1591	16.0461	15.0463
41	23.4124	21.5991	19.9931	18.5661	17.2944	16.1575	15.1380
42	23.7014	21.8349	20.1856	18.7235	17.4232	16.2630	15.2245
43	23.9819	22.0627	20.3708	18.8742	17.5459	16.3630	15.3062
44	24.2543	22.2828	20.5488	19.0184	17.6628	16.4578	15.3832
45	24.5187	22.4955	20.7200	19.1563	17.7741	16.5477	15.4558
46	24.7754	22.7009	20.8847	19.2884	17.8801	16.6329	15.5244
47	25.0247	22.8994	21.0429	19.4147	17.9810	16.7137	15.5890
48	25.2667	23.0912	21.1951	19.5356	18.0772	16.7902	15.6500
49	25.5017	23.2766	21.3415	19.6513	18.1687	16.8628	15.7076
50	25.7298	23.4556	21.4822	19.7620	18.2559	16.9315	15.7619

The Tools and Techniques of Financial Planning

COMPOUND DISCOUNT TABLE (continued)
(Present Value of an Ordinary Annuity)

YEARS	6.5%	7.0%	7.5%	8.0%	8.5%	9.0%	9.5%
1	0.9390	0.9346	0.9302	0.9259	0.9217	0.9174	0.9132
2	1.8206	1.8080	1.7956	1.7833	1.7711	1.7591	1.7473
3	2.6485	2.6243	2.6005	2.5771	2.5540	2.5313	2.5089
4	3.4258	3.3872	3.3493	3.3121	3.2756	3.2397	3.2045
5	4.1557	4.1002	4.0459	3.9927	3.9406	3.8897	3.8397
6	4.8410	4.7665	4.6938	4.6229	4.5536	4.4859	4.4198
7	5.4845	5.3893	5.2966	5.2064	5.1185	5.0330	4.9496
8	6.0888	5.9713	5.8573	5.7466	5.6392	5.5348	5.4334
9	6.6561	6.5152	6.3789	6.2469	6.1191	5.9952	5.8753
10	7.1888	7.0236	6.8641	6.7101	6.5613	6.4177	6.2788
11	7.6890	7.4987	7.3154	7.1390	6.9690	6.8052	6.6473
12	8.1587	7.9427	7.7353	7.5361	7.3447	7.1607	6.9838
13	8.5997	8.3577	8.1258	7.9038	7.6910	7.4869	7.2912
14	9.0138	8.7455	8.4892	8.2442	8.0101	7.7862	7.5719
15	9.4027	9.1079	8.8271	8.5595	8.3042	8.0607	7.8282
16	9.7678	9.4466	9.1415	8.8514	8.5753	8.3126	8.0623
17	10.1106	9.7632	9.4340	9.1216	8.8252	8.5436	8.2760
18	10.4325	10.0591	9.7060	9.3719	9.0555	8.7556	8.4713
19	10.7347	10.3356	9.9591	9.6036	9.2677	8.9501	8.6496
20	11.0185	10.5940	10.1945	9.8181	9.4633	9.1285	8.8124
21	11.2850	10.8355	10.4135	10.0168	9.6436	9.2922	8.9611
22	11.5352	11.0612	10.6172	10.2007	9.8098	9.4424	9.0969
23	11.7701	11.2722	10.8067	10.3711	9.9629	9.5802	9.2209
24	11.9907	11.4693	10.9830	10.5288	10.1041	9.7066	9.3341
25	12.1979	11.6536	11.1469	10.6748	10.2342	9.8226	9.4376
26	12.3924	11.8258	11.2995	10.8100	10.3541	9.9290	9.5320
27	12.5750	11.9867	11.4414	10.9352	10.4646	10.0266	9.6183
28	12.7465	12.1371	11.5734	11.0511	10.5665	10.1161	9.6971
29	12.9075	12.2777	11.6962	11.1584	10.6603	10.1983	9.7690
30	13.0587	12.4090	11.8104	11.2578	10.7468	10.2737	9.8347
31	13.2006	12.5318	11.9166	11.3498	10.8266	10.3428	9.8947
32	13.3339	12.6466	12.0155	11.4350	10.9001	10.4062	9.9495
33	13.4591	12.7538	12.1074	11.5139	10.9678	10.4644	9.9996
34	13.5766	12.8540	12.1929	11.5869	11.0302	10.5178	10.0453
35	13.6870	12.9477	12.2725	11.6546	11.0878	10.5668	10.0870
36	13.7906	13.0352	12.3465	11.7172	11.1408	10.6118	10.1251
37	13.8879	13.1170	12.4154	11.7752	11.1897	10.6530	10.1599
38	13.9792	13.1935	12.4794	11.8289	11.2347	10.6908	10.1917
39	14.0650	13.2649	12.5390	11.8786	11.2763	10.7255	10.2207
40	14.1455	13.3317	12.5944	11.9246	11.3145	10.7574	10.2472
41	14.2212	13.3941	12.6460	11.9672	11.3498	10.7866	10.2715
42	14.2922	13.4524	12.6939	12.0067	11.3823	10.8134	10.2936
43	14.3588	13.5070	12.7385	12.0432	11.4123	10.8379	10.3138
44	14.4214	13.5579	12.7800	12.0771	11.4399	10.8605	10.3322
45	14.4802	13.6055	12.8186	12.1084	11.4653	10.8812	10.3490
46	14.5354	13.6500	12.8545	12.1374	11.4888	10.9002	10.3644
47	14.5873	13.6916	12.8879	12.1643	11.5104	10.9176	10.3785
48	14.6359	13.7305	12.9190	12.1891	11.5303	10.9336	10.3913
49	14.6816	13.7668	12.9479	12.2122	11.5487	10.9482	10.4030
50	14.7245	13.8007	12.9748	12.2335	11.5656	10.9617	10.4137

COMPOUND DISCOUNT TABLE (continued)
(Present Value of an Ordinary Annuity)

YEARS	10.0%	10.5%	11.0%	11.5%	12.0%	12.5%	13.0%
1	0.9091	0.9050	0.9009	0.8969	0.8929	0.8889	0.8850
2	1.7355	1.7240	1.7125	1.7012	1.6901	1.6790	1.6681
3	2.4869	2.4651	2.4437	2.4226	2.4018	2.3813	2.3612
4	3.1699	3.1359	3.1024	3.0696	3.0373	3.0056	2.9745
5	3.7908	3.7429	3.6959	3.6499	3.6048	3.5606	3.5172
6	4.3553	4.2922	4.2305	4.1703	4.1114	4.0538	3.9975
7	4.8684	4.7893	4.7122	4.6370	4.5638	4.4923	4.4226
8	5.3349	5.2392	5.1461	5.0556	4.9676	4.8820	4.7988
9	5.7590	5.6463	5.5370	5.4311	5.3282	5.2285	5.1317
10	6.1446	6.0148	5.8892	5.7678	5.6502	5.5364	5.4262
11	6.4951	6.3482	6.2065	6.0697	5.9377	5.8102	5.6869
12	6.8137	6.6500	6.4924	6.3406	6.1944	6.0535	5.9176
13	7.1034	6.9230	6.7499	6.5835	6.4235	6.2698	6.1218
14	7.3667	7.1702	6.9819	6.8013	6.6282	6.4620	6.3025
15	7.6061	7.3938	7.1909	6.9967	6.8109	6.6329	6.4624
16	7.8237	7.5962	7.3792	7.1719	6.9740	6.7848	6.6039
17	8.0216	7.7794	7.5488	7.3291	7.1196	6.9198	6.7291
18	8.2014	7.9451	7.7016	7.4700	7.2497	7.0398	6.8399
19	8.3649	8.0952	7.8393	7.5964	7.3658	7.1465	6.9380
20	8.5136	8.2309	7.9633	7.7098	7.4694	7.2414	7.0248
21	8.6487	8.3538	8.0751	7.8115	7.5620	7.3256	7.1016
22	8.7715	8.4649	8.1757	7.9027	7.6446	7.4006	7.1695
23	8.8832	8.5656	8.2664	7.9845	7.7184	7.4672	7.2297
24	8.9847	8.6566	8.3481	8.0578	7.7843	7.5264	7.2829
25	9.0770	8.7390	8.4217	8.1236	7.8431	7.5790	7.3300
26	9.1609	8.8136	8.4881	8.1826	7.8957	7.6258	7.3717
27	9.2372	8.8811	8.5478	8.2355	7.9426	7.6674	7.4086
28	9.3066	8.9422	8.6016	8.2830	7.9844	7.7043	7.4412
29	9.3696	8.9974	8.6501	8.3255	8.0218	7.7372	7.4701
30	9.4269	9.0474	8.6938	8.3637	8.0552	7.7664	7.4957
31	9.4790	9.0927	8.7331	8.3980	8.0850	7.7923	7.5183
32	9.5264	9.1337	8.7686	8.4287	8.1116	7.8154	7.5383
33	9.5694	9.1707	8.8005	8.4562	8.1354	7.8359	7.5560
34	9.6086	9.2043	8.8293	8.4809	8.1566	7.8542	7.5717
35	9.6442	9.2347	8.8552	8.5030	8.1755	7.8704	7.5856
36	9.6765	9.2621	8.8786	8.5229	8.1924	7.8848	7.5979
37	9.7059	9.2870	8.8996	8.5407	8.2075	7.8976	7.6087
38	9.7327	9.3095	8.9186	8.5567	8.2210	7.9089	7.6183
39	9.7570	9.3299	8.9357	8.5710	8.2330	7.9191	7.6268
40	9.7791	9.3483	8.9511	8.5839	8.2438	7.9281	7.6344
41	9.7991	9.3650	8.9649	8.5954	8.2534	7.9361	7.6410
42	9.8174	9.3801	8.9774	8.6058	8.2619	7.9432	7.6469
43	9.8340	9.3937	8.9886	8.6150	8.2696	7.9495	7.6522
44	9.8491	9.4061	8.9988	8.6233	8.2764	7.9551	7.6568
45	9.8628	9.4173	9.0079	8.6308	8.2825	7.9601	7.6609
46	9.8753	9.4274	9.0161	8.6375	8.2880	7.9645	7.6645
47	9.8866	9.4366	9.0235	8.6435	8.2928	7.9685	7.6677
48	9.8969	9.4448	9.0302	8.6489	8.2972	7.9720	7.6705
49	9.9063	9.4524	9.0362	8.6537	8.3010	7.9751	7.6730
50	9.9148	9.4591	9.0417	8.6580	8.3045	7.9778	7.6752

COMPOUND DISCOUNT TABLE (continued)
(Present Value of an Ordinary Annuity)

YEARS	14.0%	15.0%	16.0%	17.0%	18.0%	19.0%	20.0%
1	0.8772	0.8696	0.8621	0.8547	0.8475	0.8403	0.8333
2	1.6467	1.6257	1.6052	1.5852	1.5656	1.5465	1.5278
3	2.3216	2.2832	2.2459	2.2096	2.1743	2.1399	2.1065
4	2.9137	2.8550	2.7982	2.7432	2.6901	2.6386	2.5887
5	3.4331	3.3522	3.2743	3.1993	3.1272	3.0576	2.9906
6	3.8887	3.7845	3.6847	3.5892	3.4976	3.4098	3.3255
7	4.2883	4.1604	4.0386	3.9224	3.8115	3.7057	3.6046
8	4.6389	4.4873	4.3436	4.2072	4.0776	3.9544	3.8372
9	4.9464	4.7716	4.6065	4.4506	4.3030	4.1633	4.0310
10	5.2161	5.0188	4.8332	4.6586	4.4941	4.3389	4.1925
11	5.4527	5.2337	5.0286	4.8364	4.6560	4.4865	4.3271
12	5.6603	5.4206	5.1971	4.9884	4.7932	4.6105	4.4392
13	5.8424	5.5831	5.3423	5.1183	4.9095	4.7147	4.5327
14	6.0021	5.7245	5.4675	5.2293	5.0081	4.8023	4.6106
15	6.1422	5.8474	5.5755	5.3242	5.0916	4.8759	4.6755
16	6.2651	5.9542	5.6685	5.4053	5.1624	4.9377	4.7296
17	6.3729	6.0472	5.7487	5.4746	5.2223	4.9897	4.7746
18	6.4674	6.1280	5.8178	5.5339	5.2732	5.0333	4.8122
19	6.5504	6.1982	5.8775	5.5845	5.3162	5.0700	4.8435
20	6.6231	6.2593	5.9288	5.6278	5.3527	5.1009	4.8696
21	6.6870	6.3125	5.9731	5.6648	5.3837	5.1268	4.8913
22	6.7429	6.3587	6.0113	5.6964	5.4099	5.1486	4.9094
23	6.7921	6.3988	6.0442	5.7234	5.4321	5.1668	4.9245
24	6.8351	6.4338	6.0726	5.7465	5.4509	5.1822	4.9371
25	6.8729	6.4641	6.0971	5.7662	5.4669	5.1951	4.9476
26	6.9061	6.4906	6.1182	5.7831	5.4804	5.2060	4.9563
27	6.9352	6.5135	6.1364	5.7975	5.4919	5.2151	4.9636
28	6.9607	6.5335	6.1520	5.8099	5.5016	5.2228	4.9697
29	6.9830	6.5509	6.1656	5.8204	5.5098	5.2292	4.9747
30	7.0027	6.5660	6.1772	5.8294	5.5168	5.2347	4.9789
31	7.0199	6.5791	6.1872	5.8371	5.5227	5.2392	4.9824
32	7.0350	6.5905	6.1959	5.8437	5.5277	5.2430	4.9854
33	7.0482	6.6005	6.2034	5.8493	5.5320	5.2462	4.9878
34	7.0599	6.6091	6.2098	5.8541	5.5356	5.2489	4.9898
35	7.0700	6.6166	6.2153	5.8582	5.5386	5.2512	4.9915
36	7.0790	6.6231	6.2201	5.8617	5.5412	5.2531	4.9929
37	7.0868	6.6288	6.2242	5.8647	5.5434	5.2547	4.9941
38	7.0937	6.6338	6.2278	5.8673	5.5452	5.2561	4.9951
39	7.0997	6.6380	6.2309	5.8695	5.5468	5.2572	4.9959
40	7.1050	6.6418	6.2335	5.8713	5.5482	5.2582	4.9966
41	7.1097	6.6450	6.2358	5.8729	5.5493	5.2590	4.9972
42	7.1138	6.6478	6.2377	5.8743	5.5502	5.2596	4.9976
43	7.1173	6.6503	6.2394	5.8755	5.5510	5.2602	4.9980
44	7.1205	6.6524	6.2409	5.8765	5.5517	5.2607	4.9984
45	7.1232	6.6543	6.2421	5.8773	5.5523	5.2611	4.9986
46	7.1256	6.6559	6.2432	5.8781	5.5528	5.2614	4.9989
47	7.1277	6.6573	6.2442	5.8787	5.5532	5.2617	4.9991
48	7.1296	6.6585	6.2450	5.8792	5.5536	5.2619	4.9992
49	7.1312	6.6596	6.2457	5.8797	5.5539	5.2621	4.9993
50	7.1327	6.6605	6.2463	5.8801	5.5541	5.2623	4.9995

Appendix F

PRESENT VALUE OF AN ANNUITY DUE

(This table is used in the same way as Appendix E,
but for payments made at the beginning of a period)

YEARS	3.0%	3.5%	4.0%	4.5%	5.0%	5.5%	6.0%
1	1.0000	1.0000	1.0000	1.0000	1.0000	1.0000	1.0000
2	1.9709	1.9662	1.9615	1.9569	1.9524	1.9479	1.9434
3	2.9135	2.8997	2.8861	2.8727	2.8594	2.8463	2.8334
4	3.8286	3.8016	3.7751	3.7490	3.7232	3.6979	3.6730
5	4.7171	4.6731	4.6299	4.5875	4.5459	4.5052	4.4651
6	5.5797	5.5151	5.4518	5.3900	5.3295	5.2703	5.2124
7	6.4172	6.3286	6.2421	6.1579	6.0757	5.9955	5.9173
8	7.2303	7.1145	7.0021	6.8927	6.7864	6.6830	6.5824
9	8.0197	7.8740	7.7327	7.5959	7.4632	7.3346	7.2098
10	8.7861	8.6077	8.4353	8.2688	8.1078	7.9522	7.8017
11	9.5302	9.3166	9.1109	8.9127	8.7217	8.5376	8.3601
12	10.2526	10.0016	9.7605	9.5289	9.3064	9.0925	8.8869
13	10.9540	10.6633	10.3851	10.1186	9.8633	9.6185	9.3838
14	11.6350	11.3027	10.9856	10.6829	10.3936	10.1171	9.8527
15	12.2961	11.9205	11.5631	11.2228	10.8986	10.5896	10.2950
16	12.9379	12.5174	12.1184	11.7395	11.3797	11.0376	10.7122
17	13.5611	13.0941	12.6523	12.2340	11.8378	11.4622	11.1059
18	14.1661	13.6513	13.1657	12.7072	12.2741	11.8646	11.4773
19	14.7535	14.1897	13.6593	13.1600	12.6896	12.2461	11.8276
20	15.3238	14.7098	14.1339	13.5933	13.0853	12.6077	12.1581
21	15.8775	15.2124	14.5903	14.0079	13.4622	12.9504	12.4699
22	16.4150	15.6980	15.0292	14.4047	13.8212	13.2752	12.7641
23	16.9369	16.1671	15.4511	14.7844	14.1630	13.5832	13.0416
24	17.4436	16.6204	15.8568	15.1478	14.4886	13.8750	13.3034
25	17.9355	17.0584	16.2470	15.4955	14.7986	14.1517	13.5504
26	18.4131	17.4815	16.6221	15.8282	15.0939	14.4139	13.7834
27	18.8768	17.8904	16.9828	16.1466	15.3752	14.6625	14.0032
28	19.3270	18.2854	17.3296	16.4513	15.6430	14.8981	14.2105
29	19.7641	18.6670	17.6631	16.7429	15.8981	15.1214	14.4062
30	20.1885	19.0358	17.9837	17.0219	16.1411	15.3331	14.5907
31	20.6004	19.3920	18.2920	17.2889	16.3724	15.5337	14.7648
32	21.0004	19.7363	18.5885	17.5444	16.5928	15.7239	14.9291
33	21.3888	20.0689	18.8735	17.7889	16.8027	15.9042	15.0840
34	21.7658	20.3902	19.1476	18.0229	17.0025	16.0751	15.2302
35	22.1318	20.7007	19.4112	18.2468	17.1929	16.2370	15.3681
36	22.4872	21.0007	19.6646	18.4610	17.3742	16.3906	15.4982
37	22.8323	21.2905	19.9083	18.6660	17.5469	16.5361	15.6210
38	23.1672	21.5705	20.1426	18.8622	17.7113	16.6740	15.7368
39	23.4925	21.8411	20.3679	19.0500	17.8679	16.8047	15.8460
40	23.8082	22.1025	20.5845	19.2297	18.0170	16.9287	15.9491
41	24.1148	22.3551	20.7928	19.4016	18.1591	17.0461	16.0463
42	24.4124	22.5991	20.9931	19.5661	18.2944	17.1575	16.1380
43	24.7014	22.8349	21.1856	19.7235	18.4232	17.2630	16.2245
44	24.9819	23.0627	21.3708	19.8742	18.5459	17.3630	16.3062
45	25.2543	23.2828	21.5488	20.0184	18.6628	17.4578	16.3832
46	25.5187	23.4954	21.7200	20.1563	18.7741	17.5477	16.4558
47	25.7754	23.7009	21.8847	20.2884	18.8801	17.6329	16.5244
48	26.0247	23.8994	22.0429	20.4147	18.9810	17.7137	16.5890
49	26.2667	24.0912	22.1951	20.5356	19.0772	17.7902	16.6500
50	26.5017	24.2766	22.3415	20.6513	19.1687	17.8628	16.7076

The Tools and Techniques of Financial Planning

PRESENT VALUE OF AN ANNUITY DUE (continued)

YEARS	6.5%	7.0%	7.5%	8.0%	8.5%	9.0%	9.5%
1	1.0000	1.0000	1.0000	1.0000	1.0000	1.0000	1.0000
2	1.9390	1.9346	1.9302	1.9259	1.9217	1.9174	1.9132
3	2.8206	2.8080	2.7956	2.7833	2.7711	2.7591	2.7473
4	3.6485	3.6243	3.6005	3.5771	3.5540	3.5313	3.5089
5	4.4258	4.3872	4.3493	4.3121	4.2756	4.2397	4.2045
6	5.1557	5.1002	5.0459	4.9927	4.9406	4.8897	4.8397
7	5.8410	5.7665	5.6938	5.6229	5.5536	5.4859	5.4198
8	6.4845	6.3893	6.2966	6.2064	6.1185	6.0330	5.9496
9	7.0888	6.9713	6.8573	6.7466	6.6392	6.5348	6.4334
10	7.6561	7.5152	7.3789	7.2469	7.1191	6.9952	6.8753
11	8.1888	8.0236	7.8641	7.7101	7.5613	7.4177	7.2788
12	8.6890	8.4987	8.3154	8.1390	7.9690	7.8052	7.6473
13	9.1587	8.9427	8.7353	8.5361	8.3447	8.1607	7.9838
14	9.5997	9.3577	9.1258	8.9038	8.6910	8.4869	8.2912
15	10.0138	9.7455	9.4892	9.2442	9.0101	8.7861	8.5719
16	10.4027	10.1079	9.8271	9.5595	9.3042	9.0607	8.8282
17	10.7678	10.4466	10.1415	9.8514	9.5753	9.3126	9.0623
18	11.1106	10.7632	10.4340	10.1216	9.8252	9.5436	9.2760
19	11.4325	11.0591	10.7060	10.3719	10.0555	9.7556	9.4713
20	11.7347	11.3356	10.9591	10.6036	10.2677	9.9501	9.6496
21	12.0185	11.5940	11.1945	10.8181	10.4633	10.1285	9.8124
22	12.2850	11.8355	11.4135	11.0168	10.6436	10.2922	9.9611
23	12.5352	12.0612	11.6172	11.2007	10.8098	10.4424	10.0969
24	12.7701	12.2722	11.8067	11.3711	10.9629	10.5802	10.2209
25	12.9907	12.4693	11.9830	11.5288	11.1041	10.7066	10.3341
26	13.1979	12.6536	12.1469	11.6748	11.2342	10.8226	10.4376
27	13.3924	12.8258	12.2995	11.8100	11.3541	10.9290	10.5320
28	13.5750	12.9867	12.4414	11.9352	11.4646	11.0266	10.6183
29	13.7465	13.1371	12.5734	12.0511	11.5665	11.1161	10.6971
30	13.9075	13.2777	12.6962	12.1584	11.6603	11.1983	10.7690
31	14.0587	13.4090	12.8104	12.2578	11.7468	11.2737	10.8347
32	14.2006	13.5318	12.9166	12.3498	11.8266	11.3428	10.8947
33	14.3339	13.6466	13.0155	12.4350	11.9001	11.4062	10.9495
34	14.4591	13.7538	13.1074	12.5139	11.9678	11.4644	10.9996
35	14.5766	13.8540	13.1929	12.5869	12.0302	11.5178	11.0453
36	14.6870	13.9477	13.2725	12.6546	12.0878	11.5668	11.0870
37	14.7906	14.0352	13.3465	12.7172	12.1408	11.6118	11.1251
38	14.8879	14.1170	13.4154	12.7752	12.1897	11.6530	11.1599
39	14.9792	14.1935	13.4794	12.8289	12.2347	11.6908	11.1917
40	15.0650	14.2649	13.5390	12.8786	12.2763	11.7255	11.2207
41	15.1455	14.3317	13.5944	12.9246	12.3145	11.7574	11.2472
42	15.2212	14.3941	13.6460	12.9672	12.3498	11.7866	11.2715
43	15.2922	14.4524	13.6939	13.0067	12.3823	11.8134	11.2936
44	15.3588	14.5070	13.7385	13.0432	12.4123	11.8380	11.3138
45	15.4214	14.5579	13.7800	13.0771	12.4399	11.8605	11.3322
46	15.4802	14.6055	13.8186	13.1084	12.4653	11.8812	11.3490
47	15.5354	14.6500	13.8545	13.1374	12.4888	11.9002	11.3644
48	15.5873	14.6916	13.8879	13.1643	12.5104	11.9176	11.3785
49	15.6359	14.7305	13.9190	13.1891	12.5303	11.9336	11.3913
50	15.6816	14.7668	13.9479	13.2122	12.5487	11.9482	11.4030

PRESENT VALUE OF AN ANNUITY DUE (continued)

YEARS	10.0%	10.5%	11.0%	11.5%	12.0%	12.5%	13.0%
1	1.0000	1.0000	1.0000	1.0000	1.0000	1.0000	1.0000
2	1.9091	1.9050	1.9009	1.8969	1.8929	1.8889	1.8850
3	2.7355	2.7240	2.7125	2.7012	2.6901	2.6790	2.6681
4	3.4869	3.4651	3.4437	3.4226	3.4018	3.3813	3.3612
5	4.1699	4.1359	4.1024	4.0696	4.0373	4.0056	3.9745
6	4.7908	4.7429	4.6959	4.6499	4.6048	4.5606	4.5172
7	5.3553	5.2922	5.2305	5.1703	5.1114	5.0538	4.9976
8	5.8684	5.7893	5.7122	5.6370	5.5638	5.4923	5.4226
9	6.3349	6.2392	6.1461	6.0556	5.9676	5.8820	5.7988
10	6.7590	6.6463	6.5370	6.4311	6.3282	6.2285	6.1317
11	7.1446	7.0148	6.8892	6.7678	6.6502	6.5364	6.4262
12	7.4951	7.3482	7.2065	7.0697	6.9377	6.8102	6.6869
13	7.8137	7.6500	7.4924	7.3406	7.1944	7.0535	6.9176
14	8.1034	7.9230	7.7499	7.5835	7.4235	7.2698	7.1218
15	8.3667	8.1702	7.9819	7.8013	7.6282	7.4620	7.3025
16	8.6061	8.3938	8.1909	7.9967	7.8109	7.6329	7.4624
17	8.8237	8.5962	8.3792	8.1719	7.9740	7.7848	7.6039
18	9.0216	8.7794	8.5488	8.3291	8.1196	7.9198	7.7291
19	9.2014	8.9451	8.7016	8.4700	8.2497	8.0398	7.8399
20	9.3649	9.0952	8.8393	8.5964	8.3658	8.1465	7.9380
21	9.5136	9.2309	8.9633	8.7098	8.4694	8.2414	8.0248
22	9.6487	9.3538	9.0751	8.8115	8.5620	8.3256	8.1016
23	9.7715	9.4649	9.1757	8.9027	8.6446	8.4006	8.1695
24	9.8832	9.5656	9.2664	8.9845	8.7184	8.4672	8.2297
25	9.9847	9.6566	9.3481	9.0578	8.7843	8.5264	8.2829
26	10.0770	9.7390	9.4217	9.1236	8.8431	8.5790	8.3300
27	10.1609	9.8136	9.4881	9.1826	8.8957	8.6258	8.3717
28	10.2372	9.8811	9.5478	9.2355	8.9426	8.6674	8.4086
29	10.3066	9.9422	9.6016	9.2830	8.9844	8.7043	8.4412
30	10.3696	9.9974	9.6501	9.3255	9.0218	8.7372	8.4701
31	10.4269	10.0474	9.6938	9.3637	9.0552	8.7664	8.4957
32	10.4790	10.0927	9.7331	9.3980	9.0850	8.7923	8.5183
33	10.5264	10.1337	9.7686	9.4287	9.1116	8.8154	8.5383
34	10.5694	10.1707	9.8005	9.4562	9.1354	8.8359	8.5560
35	10.6086	10.2043	9.8293	9.4809	9.1566	8.8542	8.5717
36	10.6442	10.2347	9.8552	9.5030	9.1755	8.8704	8.5856
37	10.6765	10.2621	9.8786	9.5229	9.1924	8.8848	8.5979
38	10.7059	10.2870	9.8996	9.5407	9.2075	8.8976	8.6087
39	10.7327	10.3095	9.9186	9.5567	9.2210	8.9089	8.6183
40	10.7570	10.3299	9.9357	9.5710	9.2330	8.9191	8.6268
41	10.7791	10.3483	9.9511	9.5839	9.2438	8.9281	8.6344
42	10.7991	10.3650	9.9649	9.5954	9.2534	8.9361	8.6410
43	10.8174	10.3801	9.9774	9.6058	9.2619	8.9432	8.6469
44	10.8340	10.3937	9.9886	9.6150	9.2696	8.9495	8.6522
45	10.8491	10.4061	9.9988	9.6233	9.2764	8.9551	8.6568
46	10.8628	10.4173	10.0079	9.6308	9.2825	8.9601	8.6609
47	10.8753	10.4274	10.0161	9.6375	9.2880	8.9645	8.6645
48	10.8866	10.4366	10.0235	9.6435	9.2928	8.9685	8.6677
49	10.8969	10.4448	10.0302	9.6489	9.2972	8.9720	8.6705
50	10.9063	10.4524	10.0362	9.6537	9.3010	8.9751	8.6730

Appendix F

PRESENT VALUE OF AN ANNUITY DUE (continued)

YEARS	14.0%	15.0%	16.0%	17.0%	18.0%	19.0%	20.0%
1	1.0000	1.0000	1.0000	1.0000	1.0000	1.0000	1.0000
2	1.8772	1.8696	1.8621	1.8547	1.8475	1.8403	1.8333
3	2.6467	2.6257	2.6052	2.5852	2.5656	2.5465	2.5278
4	3.3216	3.2832	3.2459	3.2096	3.1743	3.1399	3.1065
5	3.9137	3.8550	3.7982	3.7432	3.6901	3.6386	3.5887
6	4.4331	4.3522	4.2743	4.1993	4.1272	4.0576	3.9906
7	4.8887	4.7845	4.6847	4.5892	4.4976	4.4098	4.3255
8	5.2883	5.1604	5.0386	4.9224	4.8115	4.7057	4.6046
9	5.6389	5.4873	5.3436	5.2072	5.0776	4.9544	4.8372
10	5.9464	5.7716	5.6065	5.4506	5.3030	5.1633	5.0310
11	6.2161	6.0188	5.8332	5.6586	5.4941	5.3389	5.1925
12	6.4527	6.2337	6.0286	5.8364	5.6560	5.4865	5.3271
13	6.6603	6.4206	6.1971	5.9884	5.7932	5.6105	5.4392
14	6.8424	6.5831	6.3423	6.1183	5.9095	5.7147	5.5327
15	7.0021	6.7245	6.4675	6.2293	6.0081	5.8023	5.6106
16	7.1422	6.8474	6.5755	6.3242	6.0916	5.8759	5.6755
17	7.2651	6.9542	6.6685	6.4053	6.1624	5.9377	5.7296
18	7.3729	7.0472	6.7487	6.4746	6.2223	5.9897	5.7746
19	7.4674	7.1280	6.8178	6.5339	6.2732	6.0333	5.8122
20	7.5504	7.1982	6.8775	6.5845	6.3162	6.0700	5.8435
21	7.6231	7.2593	6.9288	6.6278	6.3527	6.1009	5.8696
22	7.6870	7.3125	6.9731	6.6648	6.3837	6.1268	5.8913
23	7.7429	7.3587	7.0113	6.6964	6.4099	6.1486	5.9094
24	7.7921	7.3988	7.0442	6.7234	6.4321	6.1668	5.9245
25	7.8351	7.4338	7.0726	6.7465	6.4509	6.1822	5.9371
26	7.8729	7.4641	7.0971	6.7662	6.4669	6.1951	5.9476
27	7.9061	7.4906	7.1182	6.7831	6.4804	6.2060	5.9563
28	7.9352	7.5135	7.1364	6.7975	6.4919	6.2151	5.9636
29	7.9607	7.5335	7.1520	6.8099	6.5016	6.2228	5.9697
30	7.9830	7.5509	7.1656	6.8204	6.5098	6.2292	5.9747
31	8.0027	7.5660	7.1772	6.8294	6.5168	6.2347	5.9789
32	8.0199	7.5791	7.1872	6.8371	6.5227	6.2392	5.9824
33	8.0350	7.5905	7.1959	6.8437	6.5277	6.2430	5.9854
34	8.0482	7.6005	7.2034	6.8493	6.5320	6.2462	5.9878
35	8.0599	7.6091	7.2098	6.8541	6.5356	6.2489	5.9898
36	8.0700	7.6166	7.2153	6.8582	6.5386	6.2512	5.9915
37	8.0790	7.6231	7.2201	6.8617	6.5412	6.2531	5.9929
38	8.0868	7.6288	7.2242	6.8647	6.5434	6.2547	5.9941
39	8.0937	7.6338	7.2278	6.8673	6.5452	6.2561	5.9951
40	8.0997	7.6380	7.2309	6.8695	6.5468	6.2572	5.9959
41	8.1050	7.6418	7.2335	6.8713	6.5482	6.2582	5.9966
42	8.1097	7.6450	7.2358	6.8729	6.5493	6.2590	5.9972
43	8.1138	7.6478	7.2377	6.8743	6.5502	6.2596	5.9976
44	8.1173	7.6503	7.2394	6.8755	6.5510	6.2602	5.9980
45	8.1205	7.6524	7.2409	6.8765	6.5517	6.2607	5.9984
46	8.1232	7.6543	7.2421	6.8773	6.5523	6.2611	5.9986
47	8.1256	7.6559	7.2432	6.8781	6.5528	6.2614	5.9989
48	8.1277	7.6573	7.2442	6.8787	6.5532	6.2617	5.9991
49	8.1296	7.6585	7.2450	6.8792	6.5536	6.2619	5.9992
50	8.1312	7.6596	7.2457	6.8797	6.5539	6.2621	5.9993

The Tools and Techniques of Financial Planning

Appendix G

TAX EXEMPT EQUIVALENTS

TAX EXEMPT YIELDS	15%	16%	17%	18%	19%	20%	21%	22%	23%
3.00	3.53	3.57	3.61	3.66	3.70	3.75	3.80	3.85	3.90
3.25	3.82	3.87	3.92	3.96	4.01	4.06	4.11	4.17	4.22
3.50	4.12	4.17	4.22	4.27	4.32	4.38	4.43	4.49	4.55
3.75	4.41	4.46	4.52	4.57	4.63	4.69	4.75	4.81	4.87
4.00	4.71	4.76	4.82	4.88	4.94	5.00	5.06	5.13	5.19
4.25	5.00	5.06	5.12	5.18	5.25	5.31	5.38	5.45	5.52
4.50	5.29	5.36	5.42	5.49	5.56	5.63	5.70	5.77	5.84
4.75	5.59	5.65	5.72	5.79	5.86	5.94	6.01	6.09	6.17
5.00	5.88	5.95	6.02	6.10	6.17	6.25	6.33	6.41	6.49
5.25	6.18	6.25	6.33	6.40	6.48	6.56	6.65	6.73	6.82
5.50	6.47	6.55	6.63	6.71	6.79	6.88	6.96	7.05	7.14
5.75	6.76	6.85	6.93	7.01	7.10	7.19	7.28	7.37	7.47
6.00	7.06	7.14	7.23	7.32	7.41	7.50	7.59	7.69	7.79
6.25	7.35	7.44	7.53	7.62	7.72	7.81	7.91	8.01	8.12
6.50	7.65	7.74	7.83	7.93	8.02	8.13	8.23	8.33	8.44
6.75	7.94	8.04	8.13	8.23	8.33	8.44	8.54	8.65	8.77
7.00	8.24	8.33	8.43	8.54	8.64	8.75	8.86	8.97	9.09
7.25	8.53	8.63	8.73	8.84	8.95	9.06	9.18	9.29	9.42
7.50	8.82	8.93	9.04	9.15	9.26	9.38	9.49	9.62	9.74
7.75	9.12	9.23	9.34	9.45	9.57	9.69	9.81	9.94	10.06
8.00	9.41	9.52	9.64	9.76	9.88	10.00	10.13	10.26	10.39
8.25	9.71	9.82	9.94	10.06	10.19	10.31	10.44	10.58	10.71
8.50	10.00	10.12	10.24	10.37	10.49	10.63	10.76	10.90	11.04
8.75	10.29	10.42	10.54	10.67	10.80	10.94	11.08	11.22	11.36
9.00	10.59	10.71	10.84	10.98	11.11	11.25	11.39	11.54	11.69
9.25	10.88	11.01	11.14	11.28	11.42	11.56	11.71	11.86	12.01
9.50	11.18	11.31	11.45	11.59	11.73	11.88	12.03	12.18	12.34
9.75	11.47	11.61	11.75	11.89	12.04	12.19	12.34	12.50	12.66
10.00	11.76	11.90	12.05	12.20	12.35	12.50	12.66	12.82	12.99
10.25	12.06	12.20	12.35	12.50	12.65	12.81	12.97	13.14	13.31
10.50	12.35	12.50	12.65	12.80	12.96	13.13	13.29	13.46	13.64
10.75	12.65	12.80	12.95	13.11	13.27	13.44	13.61	13.78	13.96
11.00	12.94	13.10	13.25	13.41	13.58	13.75	13.92	14.10	14.29
11.25	13.24	13.39	13.55	13.72	13.89	14.06	14.24	14.42	14.61
11.50	13.53	13.69	13.86	14.02	14.20	14.38	14.56	14.74	14.94
11.75	13.82	13.99	14.16	14.33	14.51	14.69	14.87	15.06	15.26
12.00	14.12	14.29	14.46	14.63	14.81	15.00	15.19	15.38	15.58
12.25	14.41	14.58	14.76	14.94	15.12	15.31	15.51	15.71	15.91
12.50	14.71	14.88	15.06	15.24	15.43	15.63	15.82	16.03	16.23
12.75	15.00	15.18	15.36	15.55	15.74	15.94	16.14	16.35	16.56
13.00	15.29	15.48	15.66	15.85	16.05	16.25	16.46	16.67	16.88
13.25	15.59	15.77	15.96	16.16	16.36	16.56	16.77	16.99	17.21
13.50	15.88	16.07	16.27	16.46	16.67	16.88	17.09	17.31	17.53
13.75	16.18	16.37	16.57	16.77	16.98	17.19	17.41	17.63	17.86
14.00	16.47	16.67	16.87	17.07	17.28	17.50	17.72	17.95	18.18
14.25	16.76	16.96	17.17	17.38	17.59	17.81	18.04	18.27	18.51
14.50	17.06	17.26	17.47	17.68	17.90	18.13	18.35	18.59	18.83
14.75	17.35	17.56	17.77	17.99	18.21	18.44	18.67	18.91	19.16
15.00	17.65	17.86	18.07	18.29	18.52	18.75	18.99	19.23	19.48

TAX EXEMPT EQUIVALENTS (continued)

TAX EXEMPT YIELDS	24%	25%	26%	27%	28%	29%	30%	31%	32%
3.00	3.95	4.00	4.05	4.11	4.17	4.23	4.29	4.35	4.41
3.25	4.28	4.33	4.39	4.45	4.51	4.58	4.64	4.71	4.78
3.50	4.61	4.67	4.73	4.79	4.86	4.93	5.00	5.07	5.15
3.75	4.93	5.00	5.07	5.14	5.21	5.28	5.36	5.43	5.51
4.00	5.26	5.33	5.41	5.48	5.56	5.63	5.71	5.80	5.88
4.25	5.59	5.67	5.74	5.82	5.90	5.99	6.07	6.16	6.25
4.50	5.92	6.00	6.08	6.16	6.25	6.34	6.43	6.52	6.62
4.75	6.25	6.33	6.42	6.51	6.60	6.69	6.79	6.88	6.99
5.00	6.58	6.67	6.76	6.85	6.94	7.04	7.14	7.25	7.35
5.25	6.91	7.00	7.09	7.19	7.29	7.39	7.50	7.61	7.72
5.50	7.24	7.33	7.43	7.53	7.64	7.75	7.86	7.97	8.09
5.75	7.57	7.67	7.77	7.88	7.99	8.10	8.21	8.33	8.46
6.00	7.89	8.00	8.11	8.22	8.33	8.45	8.57	8.70	8.82
6.25	8.22	8.33	8.45	8.56	8.68	8.80	8.93	9.06	9.19
6.50	8.55	8.67	8.78	8.90	9.03	9.15	9.29	9.42	9.56
6.75	8.88	9.00	9.12	9.25	9.38	9.51	9.64	9.78	9.93
7.00	9.21	9.33	9.46	9.59	9.72	9.86	10.00	10.14	10.29
7.25	9.54	9.67	9.80	9.93	10.07	10.21	10.36	10.51	10.66
7.50	9.87	10.00	10.14	10.27	10.42	10.56	10.71	10.87	11.03
7.75	10.20	10.33	10.47	10.62	10.76	10.92	11.07	11.23	11.40
8.00	10.53	10.67	10.81	10.96	11.11	11.27	11.43	11.59	11.76
8.25	10.86	11.00	11.15	11.30	11.46	11.62	11.79	11.96	12.13
8.50	11.18	11.33	11.49	11.64	11.81	11.97	12.14	12.32	12.50
8.75	11.51	11.67	11.82	11.99	12.15	12.32	12.50	12.68	12.87
9.00	11.84	12.00	12.16	12.33	12.50	12.68	12.86	13.04	13.24
9.25	12.17	12.33	12.50	12.67	12.85	13.03	13.21	13.41	13.60
9.50	12.50	12.67	12.84	13.01	13.19	13.38	13.57	13.77	13.97
9.75	12.83	13.00	13.18	13.36	13.54	13.73	13.93	14.13	14.34
10.00	13.16	13.33	13.51	13.70	13.89	14.08	14.29	14.49	14.71
10.25	13.49	13.67	13.85	14.04	14.24	14.44	14.64	14.86	15.07
10.50	13.82	14.00	14.19	14.38	14.58	14.79	15.00	15.22	15.44
10.75	14.14	14.33	14.53	14.73	14.93	15.14	15.36	15.58	15.81
11.00	14.47	14.67	14.86	15.07	15.28	15.49	15.71	15.94	16.18
11.25	14.80	15.00	15.20	15.41	15.63	15.85	16.07	16.30	16.54
11.50	15.13	15.33	15.54	15.75	15.97	16.20	16.43	16.67	16.91
11.75	15.46	15.67	15.88	16.10	16.32	16.55	16.79	17.03	17.28
12.00	15.79	16.00	16.22	16.44	16.67	16.90	17.14	17.39	17.65
12.25	16.12	16.33	16.55	16.78	17.01	17.25	17.50	17.75	18.01
12.50	16.45	16.67	16.89	17.12	17.36	17.61	17.86	18.12	18.38
12.75	16.78	17.00	17.23	17.47	17.71	17.96	18.21	18.48	18.75
13.00	17.11	17.33	17.57	17.81	18.06	18.31	18.57	18.84	19.12
13.25	17.43	17.67	17.91	18.15	18.40	18.66	18.93	19.20	19.49
13.50	17.76	18.00	18.24	18.49	18.75	19.01	19.29	19.57	19.85
13.75	18.09	18.33	18.58	18.84	19.10	19.37	19.64	19.93	20.22
14.00	18.42	18.67	18.92	19.18	19.44	19.72	20.00	20.29	20.59
14.25	18.75	19.00	19.26	19.52	19.79	20.07	20.36	20.65	20.96
14.50	19.08	19.33	19.59	19.86	20.14	20.42	20.71	21.01	21.32
14.75	19.41	19.67	19.93	20.21	20.49	20.77	21.07	21.38	21.69
15.00	19.74	20.00	20.27	20.55	20.83	21.13	21.43	21.74	22.06

TAX EXEMPT EQUIVALENTS (continued)

TAX EXEMPT YIELDS	33%	34%	35%	36%	37%	38%	39%	40%	41%
3.00	4.48	4.55	4.62	4.69	4.76	4.84	4.92	5.00	5.08
3.25	4.85	4.92	5.00	5.08	5.16	5.24	5.33	5.42	5.51
3.50	5.22	5.30	5.38	5.47	5.56	5.65	5.74	5.83	5.93
3.75	5.60	5.68	5.77	5.86	5.95	6.05	6.15	6.25	6.36
4.00	5.97	6.06	6.15	6.25	6.35	6.45	6.56	6.67	6.78
4.25	6.34	6.44	6.54	6.64	6.75	6.85	6.97	7.08	7.20
4.50	6.72	6.82	6.92	7.03	7.14	7.26	7.38	7.50	7.63
4.75	7.09	7.20	7.31	7.42	7.54	7.66	7.79	7.92	8.05
5.00	7.46	7.58	7.69	7.81	7.94	8.06	8.20	8.33	8.47
5.25	7.84	7.95	8.08	8.20	8.33	8.47	8.61	8.75	8.90
5.50	8.21	8.33	8.46	8.59	8.73	8.87	9.02	9.17	9.32
5.75	8.58	8.71	8.85	8.98	9.13	9.27	9.43	9.58	9.75
6.00	8.96	9.09	9.23	9.38	9.52	9.68	9.84	10.00	10.17
6.25	9.33	9.47	9.62	9.77	9.92	10.08	10.25	10.42	10.59
6.50	9.70	9.85	10.00	10.16	10.32	10.48	10.66	10.83	11.02
6.75	10.07	10.23	10.38	10.55	10.71	10.89	11.07	11.25	11.44
7.00	10.45	10.61	10.77	10.94	11.11	11.29	11.48	11.67	11.86
7.25	10.82	10.98	11.15	11.33	11.51	11.69	11.89	12.08	12.29
7.50	11.19	11.36	11.54	11.72	11.90	12.10	12.30	12.50	12.71
7.75	11.57	11.74	11.92	12.11	12.30	12.50	12.70	12.92	13.14
8.00	11.94	12.12	12.31	12.50	12.70	12.90	13.11	13.33	13.56
8.25	12.31	12.50	12.69	12.89	13.10	13.31	13.52	13.75	13.98
8.50	12.69	12.88	13.08	13.28	13.49	13.71	13.93	14.17	14.41
8.75	13.06	13.26	13.46	13.67	13.89	14.11	14.34	14.58	14.83
9.00	13.43	13.64	13.85	14.06	14.29	14.52	14.75	15.00	15.25
9.25	13.81	14.02	14.23	14.45	14.68	14.92	15.16	15.42	15.68
9.50	14.18	14.39	14.62	14.84	15.08	15.32	15.57	15.83	16.10
9.75	14.55	14.77	15.00	15.23	15.48	15.73	15.98	16.25	16.53
10.00	14.93	15.15	15.38	15.63	15.87	16.13	16.39	16.67	16.95
10.25	15.30	15.53	15.77	16.02	16.27	16.53	16.80	17.08	17.37
10.50	15.67	15.91	16.15	16.41	16.67	16.94	17.21	17.50	17.80
10.75	16.04	16.29	16.54	16.80	17.06	17.34	17.62	17.92	18.22
11.00	16.42	16.67	16.92	17.19	17.46	17.74	18.03	18.33	18.64
11.25	16.79	17.05	17.31	17.58	17.86	18.15	18.44	18.75	19.07
11.50	17.16	17.42	17.69	17.97	18.25	18.55	18.85	19.17	19.49
11.75	17.54	17.80	18.08	18.36	18.65	18.95	19.26	19.58	19.92
12.00	17.91	18.18	18.46	18.75	19.05	19.35	19.67	20.00	20.34
12.25	18.28	18.56	18.85	19.14	19.44	19.76	20.08	20.42	20.76
12.50	18.66	18.94	19.23	19.53	19.84	20.16	20.49	20.83	21.19
12.75	19.03	19.32	19.62	19.92	20.24	20.56	20.90	21.25	21.61
13.00	19.40	19.70	20.00	20.31	20.63	20.97	21.31	21.67	22.03
13.25	19.78	20.08	20.38	20.70	21.03	21.37	21.72	22.08	22.46
13.50	20.15	20.45	20.77	21.09	21.43	21.77	22.13	22.50	22.88
13.75	20.52	20.83	21.15	21.48	21.83	22.18	22.54	22.92	23.31
14.00	20.90	21.21	21.54	21.88	22.22	22.58	22.95	23.33	23.73
14.25	21.27	21.59	21.92	22.27	22.62	22.98	23.36	23.75	24.15
14.50	21.64	21.97	22.31	22.66	23.02	23.39	23.77	24.17	24.58
14.75	22.01	22.35	22.69	23.05	23.41	23.79	24.18	24.58	25.00
15.00	22.39	22.73	23.08	23.44	23.81	24.19	24.59	25.00	25.42

The Tools and Techniques of Financial Planning

TAX EXEMPT EQUIVALENTS (continued)

TAX EXEMPT YIELDS	42%	43%	44%	45%	46%	47%	48%	49%	50%
3.00	5.17	5.26	5.36	5.45	5.56	5.66	5.77	5.88	6.00
3.25	5.60	5.70	5.80	5.91	6.02	6.13	6.25	6.37	6.50
3.50	6.03	6.14	6.25	6.36	6.48	6.60	6.73	6.86	7.00
3.75	6.47	6.58	6.70	6.82	6.94	7.08	7.21	7.35	7.50
4.00	6.90	7.02	7.14	7.27	7.41	7.55	7.69	7.84	8.00
4.25	7.33	7.46	7.59	7.73	7.87	8.02	8.17	8.33	8.50
4.50	7.76	7.89	8.04	8.18	8.33	8.49	8.65	8.82	9.00
4.75	8.19	8.33	8.48	8.64	8.80	8.96	9.13	9.31	9.50
5.00	8.62	8.77	8.93	9.09	9.26	9.43	9.62	9.80	10.00
5.25	9.05	9.21	9.38	9.55	9.72	9.91	10.10	10.29	10.50
5.50	9.48	9.65	9.82	10.00	10.19	10.38	10.58	10.78	11.00
5.75	9.91	10.09	10.27	10.45	10.65	10.85	11.06	11.27	11.50
6.00	10.34	10.53	10.71	10.91	11.11	11.32	11.54	11.76	12.00
6.25	10.78	10.96	11.16	11.36	11.57	11.79	12.02	12.25	12.50
6.50	11.21	11.40	11.61	11.82	12.04	12.26	12.50	12.75	13.00
6.75	11.64	11.84	12.05	12.27	12.50	12.74	12.98	13.24	13.50
7.00	12.07	12.28	12.50	12.73	12.96	13.21	13.46	13.73	14.00
7.25	12.50	12.72	12.95	13.18	13.43	13.68	13.94	14.22	14.50
7.50	12.93	13.16	13.39	13.64	13.89	14.15	14.42	14.71	15.00
7.75	13.36	13.60	13.84	14.09	14.35	14.62	14.90	15.20	15.50
8.00	13.79	14.04	14.29	14.55	14.81	15.09	15.38	15.69	16.00
8.25	14.22	14.47	14.73	15.00	15.28	15.57	15.87	16.18	16.50
8.50	14.66	14.91	15.18	15.45	15.74	16.04	16.35	16.67	17.00
8.75	15.09	15.35	15.63	15.91	16.20	16.51	16.83	17.16	17.50
9.00	15.52	15.79	16.07	16.36	16.67	16.98	17.31	17.65	18.00
9.25	15.95	16.23	16.52	16.82	17.13	17.45	17.79	18.14	18.50
9.50	16.38	16.67	16.96	17.27	17.59	17.92	18.27	18.63	19.00
9.75	16.81	17.11	17.41	17.73	18.06	18.40	18.75	19.12	19.50
10.00	17.24	17.54	17.86	18.18	18.52	18.87	19.23	19.61	20.00
10.25	17.67	17.98	18.30	18.64	18.98	19.34	19.71	20.10	20.50
10.50	18.10	18.42	18.75	19.09	19.44	19.81	20.19	20.59	21.00
10.75	18.53	18.86	19.20	19.55	19.91	20.28	20.67	21.08	21.50
11.00	18.97	19.30	19.64	20.00	20.37	20.75	21.15	21.57	22.00
11.25	19.40	19.74	20.09	20.45	20.83	21.23	21.63	22.06	22.50
11.50	19.83	20.18	20.54	20.91	21.30	21.70	22.12	22.55	23.00
11.75	20.26	20.61	20.98	21.36	21.76	22.17	22.60	23.04	23.50
12.00	20.69	21.05	21.43	21.82	22.22	22.64	23.08	23.53	24.00
12.25	21.12	21.49	21.88	22.27	22.69	23.11	23.56	24.02	24.50
12.50	21.55	21.93	22.32	22.73	23.15	23.58	24.04	24.51	25.00
12.75	21.98	22.37	22.77	23.18	23.61	24.06	24.52	25.00	25.50
13.00	22.41	22.81	23.21	23.64	24.07	24.53	25.00	25.49	26.00
13.25	22.84	23.25	23.66	24.09	24.54	25.00	25.48	25.98	26.50
13.50	23.28	23.68	24.11	24.55	25.00	25.47	25.96	26.47	27.00
13.75	23.71	24.12	24.55	25.00	25.46	25.94	26.44	26.96	27.50
14.00	24.14	24.56	25.00	25.45	25.93	26.42	26.92	27.45	28.00
14.25	24.57	25.00	25.45	25.91	26.39	26.89	27.40	27.94	28.50
14.50	25.00	25.44	25.89	26.36	26.85	27.36	27.88	28.43	29.00
14.75	25.43	25.88	26.34	26.82	27.31	27.83	28.37	28.92	29.50
15.00	25.86	26.32	26.79	27.27	27.78	28.30	28.85	29.41	30.00

Appendix H

INVESTMENT CHARACTERISTICS MATRIX AND INVESTMENT PRIORITY VALUATOR

All investment alternatives ("tools") possess certain important functional characteristics. These characteristics include:

(1) Liquidity

(2) Tax Advantages

(3) Current Income

(4) Security (Safety)

(5) Substantial Appreciation Potential

(6) Moderate Appreciation (Inflation Hedge).

The degree to which any investment will perform these functions may vary dramatically. For example, an investment such as a money market fund may provide a great degree of liquidity, but has no potential for substantial appreciation. On the other hand, an individual retirement plan may have outstanding tax advantages, but provides no current income to investors until withdrawals are made upon retirement.

This appendix provides the financial planner with two useful devices for comparing and analyzing the performance of investment alternatives:

(1) The *Investment Characteristics Matrix* provides a basic appraisal of how well the investment tools discussed in this volume might be expected to perform each of the six functional characteristics listed above.

(2) The *Investment Priority Valuator* uses the Investment Characteristic Matrix to provide the financial planner with a simple method of incorporating the investor's individual goals and priorities into the comparative analysis process.

The *Investment Characteristics Matrix* provides a rating for each of the six functional characteristics for each investment alternative. The highest rating given is a five (5). The lowest possible rating is a one (1).

Liquidity is an extremely important characteristic. A higher rating is given to an investment which can be readily converted to cash-in-hand without any loss in value. If the immediate sale of the investment is difficult and will result in a sacrifice in cash proceeds, a lower rating is warranted.

For example, money market funds and certificates of deposit, especially short term certificates, are considered highly liquid. Publicly traded stocks and bonds are easily converted to cash, but the value at the time of sale may not be worth what the investor had hoped for. Real estate will generally receive a low liquidity rating because of the difficulty in obtaining the full value of real property in a "forced sale" situation.

The more an investment utilizes certain benefits available in the tax law to enhance the investor's return, the higher the rating it receives in the *tax advantage* category. Individual retirement accounts, Keogh plans, and municipal bonds are obviously rated the highest. Common stocks, for example, receive a moderate rating because of the potential for capital gain treatment (net long-term capital gains are taxed at a maximum rate of 28%). Money market funds and certificates of deposit, which have no tax advantages, receive the lowest rating.

Higher ratings for *current income* are given to those investments which provide both the highest amount and greatest certainty of providing regular cash flow to investors (without regard to tax benefits). Annuities, corporate bonds and mortgage backed securities receive the highest rank in this category. Collectibles, commodities, and unimproved real estate, for instance, receive the lowest rating. These investments provide the investor with no income on a regular, recurring basis.

The risk of loss of capital invested is the primary criterion in evaluating the security or safety of an investment. Generally, investments which are guaranteed or otherwise secured by the federal government are considered the most secure. U.S. Government securities (such as Treasury notes and bonds) and FDIC-insured certificates of deposit are in this category. Highly rated (AAA) municipal bonds are considered relatively safe. The more speculative investments, such as commodities and financial futures, usually receive low ratings for security.

An investment which is more likely to have a rapid or extreme increase in market value is considered to have *substantial appreciation potential*. Investments which receive high ratings in this category tend to be more speculative and therefore less secure. These include collectibles, commodities, gold and other precious metals, and exploratory oil and gas investments.

Certificates of deposit, corporate bonds, municipal bonds, and other fixed income assets are examples of investments with little or no potential for appreciation. These "fixed dollar" investments will in fact lose value in periods of high inflation, even though the face value will remain secure.

An investment is considered to provide *moderate appreciation* (and therefore a hedge against inflation) if it is likely that the value of the investment will increase (at least moderately) during a period of inflation, but will not reduce substantially during a deflationary period. An investment receiving a high rating in this category tends to hold its value because of such factors as limited supply (e.g., real estate), variable income potential (e.g., variable IRAs and mutual funds), and general ability to fluctuate with market conditions (e.g., growth oriented common stocks). Fixed income investments, such as certificates of deposit, and corporate and municipal bonds, which do not react positively to inflationary conditions, receive lower ratings.

The *Investment Priority Valuator* enables the financial planner to make a comparative analysis of alternative investments based upon the investor's own valuation of the importance of each of the six functional criteria of the Investment Characteristics Matrix. Each characteristic of each alternative investment is given two ratings: (1) Importance, and (2) Performance.

Importance is the personal value given by the investor to each of the functional criteria. The values for Importance can range from one (1), for a characteristic of little importance to the investor, to five (5) for a criterion of utmost importance to the investor.

The *Performance* value is the rating ascribed in the Investment Characteristics Matrix to each functional criterion for each investment type. (Alternatively, the financial planner and investor can modify these ratings based on information more appropriate to the investor's individual circumstances.)

The following steps should be followed in using the Investment Priority Valuator:

(1) For each characteristic, insert the investor's Importance rating under the "Importance" column for all of the investments. (The same Importance rating for a particular characteristic should be used for all of the investment alternatives.)

(2) For each investment, insert the Performance ratings (from the Investment Characteristics Matrix or as otherwise determined) under the "Performance" column for each characteristic.

(3) Multiply the Importance rating by the Performance rating for each characteristic of each investment and insert the result in the appropriate space under the "Value" columns.

(4) Add the computed values for each characteristic of each investment. For each investment, insert the total amount in the "Total Value" column.

(5) Compare the "Total Value" computed for each alternative investment. The investments with the highest total values are most likely to fulfill the investor's investment goals.

The final exhibit of this appendix provides an example of a completed Investment Priority Valuator, using the Performance ratings from the Investment Characteristics Matrix and the following Importance ratings of the investor:

Liquidity = 4

Tax Advantage = 4

Current Income = 3

Security = 5

Substantial Appreciation Potential = 2

Moderate Appreciation (Inflation Hedge) = 5

Based on these priorities, the investments receiving the highest ratings are Real Estate Investment Trusts (REITs)—equity (80), common stocks (77), convertible securities (75), annuities (75), individual retirement accounts—variable (73), Keogh plans—variable (73), mutual funds (73), real estate—commercial (73), real estate—apartments (73), Real Estate Investment Trusts (REITs)—hybrid (73) and municipal bonds (72).

The investments receiving the lowest ratings (and therefore are least appropriate based on the investor's goals) are commodities (47), individual retirement accounts—fixed (59), Keogh plans—fixed (59), life insurance—variable (60), Real Estate Mortgage Investment Conduits (REMICs)—regular interests (60), and financial futures (60).

INVESTMENT CHARACTERISTICS MATRIX

	Liquidity	Tax Advantage
Annuities	2	4
Certificates of Deposit	5	1
Collectibles	2	3
Commodities	1	3
Common Stocks	4	3
Convertible Securities	4	3
Corporate Bonds	4	2
FInancial Futures	4	2
Gold & Other Precious Metals	3	3
Individual Retirement Accounts — Fixed	1	5
Individual Retirement Accounts — Variable	1	5
Keogh (HR-10) Plans — Fixed	1	5
Keogh (HR-10) Plans — Variable	1	5
Life Insurance — Whole Life	2	4
Life Insurance — Interest Sensitive Whole Life	2	4
Life Insurance — Universal	2	4
Life Insurance — Variable	2	4
Money Market Funds	5	1
Mortgage Backed Securities	4	3
Municipal Bonds	4	5
Mutual Funds (Balanced Fund)	4	3
Oil & Gas (Balanced Program)	1	4
Preferred Stock	4	3
Puts & Calls	4	3
Real Estate — Apartments	2	4
Real Estate — Commercial	2	4
Real Estate — Unimproved Land	2	2
Real Estate Investment Trusts (REITs) — Equity	4	3
Real Estate Investment Trusts (REITs) — Mortgage	4	3
Real Estate Investment Trusts (REITs) — Hybrid	4	3
Real Estate Mortgage Investment Conduits (REMICs) — Regular Interest	4	2
Real Estate Mortgage Investment Conduits (REMICs) — Residual Interest	3	2
U.S. Government Securities	4	2

Appendix H

INVESTMENT CHARACTERISTICS MATRIX

Current Income	Security (Safety)	Substantial Appreciation Potential	Moderate Appreciation (Inflation Hedge)
4	4	2	3
3	5	1	1
1	2	4	4
1	1	4	3
2	3	4	4
3	3	4	3
4	4	1	1
1	1	4	4
1	3	4	4
1	5	1	1
1	4	3	4
1	5	1	1
1	4	3	4
1	4	2	2
1	3	3	4
1	4	3	3
1	2	4	3
3	5	1	1
4	4	1	1
3	4	1	1
3	3	3	3
3	2	4	3
3	3	2	2
1	2	4	3
2	3	4	4
2	3	4	4
1	3	4	4
3	3	4	4
3	3	2	2
3	3	3	3
3	4	1	1
3	3	3	3
3	5	1	1

INVESTMENT PRIORITY VALUATOR

	Liquidity			Tax Advantage		
	Impor-tance x	Perfor-mance	= Value	Impor-tance x	Perfor-mance	= Value
Annuities	4	2	8	4	4	16
Certificates of Deposit	4	5	20	4	1	4
Collectibles	4	2	8	4	3	12
Commodities	4	1	4	4	3	12
Common Stocks	4	4	16	4	3	12
Convertible Securities	4	4	16	4	3	12
Corporate Bonds	4	4	16	4	2	8
Financial Futures	4	4	16	4	2	8
Gold & Other Precious Metals	4	3	12	4	3	12
Individ. Retirement Accounts — Fixed	4	1	4	4	5	20
Individual Retirement Accounts — Variable	4	1	4	4	5	20
Keogh (HR-10) Plans — Fixed	4	1	4	4	5	20
Keogh (HR-10) Plans — Variable	4	1	4	4	5	20
Life Insurance — Whole Life	4	2	8	4	4	16
Life Insurance — Int. Sens. W. L.	4	2	8	4	4	16
Life Insurance — Universal	4	2	8	4	4	16
Life Insurance — Variable	4	2	8	4	4	16
Money Market Funds	4	5	20	4	1	4
Mortgaged Backed Securities	4	4	16	4	3	12
Municipal Bonds	4	4	16	4	5	20
Mutual Funds (Balanced Fund)	4	4	16	4	3	12
Oil & Gas (Balanced Program)	4	1	4	4	4	16
Preferred Stock	4	4	16	4	3	12
Puts & Calls	4	4	16	4	3	12
Real Estate — Apartments	4	2	8	4	4	16
Real Estate — Commercial	4	2	8	4	4	16
Real Estate — Unimproved Land	4	2	8	4	2	8
Real Estate Investment Trusts (REITs) — Equity	4	4	16	4	3	12
Real Estate Investment Trusts (REITs) — Mortgage	4	4	16	4	3	12
Real Estate Investment Trusts (REITs) — Hybrid	4	4	16	4	3	12
Real Estate Mortgage Investment Conduits (REMICs) — Regular Interest	4	4	16	4	2	8
Real Estate Mortgage Investment Conduits (REMICs) — Residual Interest	4	3	12	4	2	8
U.S. Government Securities	4	4	16	4	2	8

Appendix H

INVESTMENT PRIORITY VALUATOR

Current Income			Security (Safety)			Substantial Appreciation Potential			Moderate Appreciation (Inflation Hedge)			Total Value
Impor-tance x	Perfor-mance =	Value	Impor-tance x	Perfor-mance =	Value	Impor-tance x	Perfor-mance =	Value	Impor-tance x	Perfor-mance =	Value	Total Value
3	4	12	5	4	20	2	2	4	5	3	15	75
3	3	9	5	5	25	2	1	2	5	1	5	65
3	1	3	5	2	10	2	4	8	5	4	20	61
3	1	3	5	1	5	2	4	8	5	3	15	47
3	2	6	5	3	15	2	4	8	5	4	20	77
3	3	9	5	3	15	2	4	8	5	3	15	75
3	4	12	5	4	20	2	1	2	5	1	5	63
3	1	3	5	1	5	2	4	8	5	4	20	60
3	1	3	5	3	15	2	4	8	5	4	20	70
3	1	3	5	5	25	2	1	2	5	1	5	59
3	1	3	5	4	20	2	3	6	5	4	20	73
3	1	3	5	5	25	2	1	2	5	1	5	59
3	1	3	5	4	20	2	3	6	5	4	20	73
3	1	3	5	4	20	2	2	4	5	2	10	61
3	1	3	5	3	15	2	3	6	5	4	20	68
3	1	3	5	4	20	2	3	6	5	3	15	68
3	1	3	5	2	10	2	4	8	5	3	15	60
3	3	9	5	5	25	2	1	2	5	1	5	65
3	4	12	5	4	20	2	1	2	5	1	5	67
3	3	9	5	4	20	2	1	2	5	1	5	72
3	3	9	5	3	15	2	3	6	5	3	15	73
3	3	9	5	2	10	2	4	8	5	3	15	62
3	3	9	5	3	15	2	2	4	5	2	10	66
3	1	3	5	2	10	2	4	8	5	3	15	64
3	2	6	5	3	15	2	4	8	5	4	20	73
3	2	6	5	3	15	2	4	8	5	4	20	73
3	1	3	5	3	15	2	4	8	5	4	20	62
3	3	9	5	3	15	2	4	8	5	4	20	80
3	3	9	5	3	15	2	2	4	5	2	10	66
3	3	9	5	3	15	2	3	6	5	3	15	73
3	3	9	5	4	20	2	1	2	5	1	5	60
3	3	9	5	3	15	2	3	6	5	3	15	65
3	3	9	5	5	25	2	1	2	5	1	5	65

INVESTMENT PRIORITY VALUATOR

	Liquidity			Tax Advantage		
	Impor-tance	x Perfor-mance	= Value	Impor-tance	x Perfor-mance	= Value
Annuities						
Certificates of Deposit						
Collectibles						
Commodities						
Common Stocks						
Convertible Securities						
Corporate Bonds						
Financial Futures						
Gold & Other Precious Metals						
Individ. Retirement Accounts — Fixed						
Individual Retirement Accounts — Variable						
Keogh (HR-10) Plans — Fixed						
Keogh (HR-10) Plans — Variable						
Life Insurance — Whole Life						
Life Insurance — Int. Sens. W. L.						
Life Insurance — Universal						
Life Insurance — Variable						
Money Market Funds						
Mortgaged Backed Securities						
Municipal Bonds						
Mutual Funds (Balanced Fund)						
Oil & Gas (Balanced Program)						
Preferred Stock						
Puts & Calls						
Real Estate — Apartments						
Real Estate — Commercial						
Real Estate — Unimproved Land						
Real Estate Investment Trusts (REITs) — Equity						
Real Estate Investment Trusts (REITs) — Mortgage						
Real Estate Investment Trusts (REITs) — Hybrid						
Real Estate Mortgage Investment Conduits (REMICs) — Regular Interest						
Real Estate Mortgage Investment Conduits (REMICs) — Residual Interest						
U.S. Government Securities						

Appendix H

INVESTMENT PRIORITY VALUATOR

Current Income			Security (Safety)			Substantial Appreciation Potential			Moderate Appreciation (Inflation Hedge)			
Impor- tance	Perfor- x mance	= Value	Impor- tance	Perfor- x mance	= Value	Impor- tance	Perfor- x mance	= Value	Impor- tance	Perfor- x mance	= Value	Total Value

Appendix I

INCOME TAX RATE TABLES

Individuals, Estates and Trusts

(Tax Years Beginning in 1998)

Col. 1 Taxable Income $	Separate Return Tax on Col. 1 $	Separate Return Rate on Excess %	Joint Return Tax on Col. 1 $	Joint Return Rate on Excess %	Single Return Tax on Col. 1 $	Single Return Rate on Excess %	Head of Household Tax on Col. 1 $	Head of Household Rate on Excess %	Trusts and Estates Tax on Col. 1 $	Trusts and Estates Rate on Excess %
0	0	15	0	15	0	15	0	15	0	15
1,700	255	15	255	15	255	15	255	15	255	28
4,000	600	15	600	15	600	15	600	15	899	31
6,100	915	15	915	15	915	15	915	15	1,550	36
8,350	1,253	15	1,253	15	1,253	15	1,253	15	2,360	39.6
21,175	3,176	28	3,176	15	3,176	15	3,176	15	7,439	39.6
25,350	4,345	28	3,803	15	3,803	28	3,803	15	9,092	39.6
33,950	6,753	28	5,093	15	6,211	28	5,093	28	12,498	39.6
42,350	9,105	28	6,353	28	8,563	28	7,445	28	15,824	39.6
51,150	11,569	31	8,817	28	11,027	28	9,909	28	19,309	39.6
61,400	14,747	31	11,687	28	13,897	31	12,779	28	23,368	39.6
77,975	19,885	36	16,328	28	19,035	31	17,420	28	29,932	39.6
87,700	23,386	36	19,051	28	22,050	31	20,143	31	33,783	39.6
102,300	28,642	36	23,139	31	26,576	31	24,669	31	39,564	39.6
128,100	37,930	36	31,137	31	34,574	36	32,667	31	49,781	39.6
139,225	41,935	39.6	34,586	31	38,579	36	36,116	31	54,187	39.6
142,000	43,034	39.6	35,446	31	39,578	36	36,976	36	55,285	39.6
155,950	48,558	39.6	39,770	36	44,600	36	41,998	36	60,810	39.6
278,450	97,068	39.6	83,870	39.6	88,700	39.6	86,098	39.6	109,320	39.6

Corporations†

(Tax Years Beginning in 1998)

Col. 1 Taxable Income	Tax on Col. 1	Rate on Excess
-0-	-0-	15%
$ 50,000	7,500	25%
$ 75,000	13,750	34%
$ 100,000	22,250	39% *
$ 335,000	113,900	34%
$10,000,000	3,400,000	35%
$15,000,000	5,150,000	38% **
$18,333,333	——	35%

† Personal Service Corporations are taxed at a flat rate of 35%.

* A 5% surtax is imposed on income above $100,000 until the benefit of the 15 and 25% tax rates has been canceled. Thus, taxable income from $100,001 to $335,000 is taxed at the rate of 39%.

** Corporations with taxable income over $15,000,000 are subject to an additional tax of the lesser of 3% of the excess over $15,000,000 or $100,000. Thus, taxable income exceeding $18,333,333 is taxed at 35%. See Ann. 93-133, 1993-32 IRB 12.

MILLION DOLLAR GOAL GUIDE
20 Years
To reach $1,000,000

I have now	I need	My money has to earn	or	If the money I have now earns 5%, it will be worth	Shortfall	Return needed to meet goal if $10,000 invested annually	or	If the annual investment earns 5%, I need to invest each year
$ 20,000	$980,000	21.48%		$ 53,066	$946,934	13.28%		$27,274
40,000	960,000	17.46%		106,132	893,868	12.82%		25,746
60,000	940,000	15.10%		159,198	840,802	12.33%		24,217
80,000	920,000	13.46%		212,264	787,736	11.81%		22,689
100,000	900,000	12.20%		265,330	734,670	11.25%		21,160
120,000	880,000	11.18%		318,396	681,604	10.64%		19,632
140,000	860,000	10.33%		371,462	628,538	9.98%		18,103
160,000	840,000	9.60%		424,528	575,472	9.26%		16,575
180,000	820,000	8.95%		477,594	522,406	8.46%		15,047
200,000	800,000	8.38%		530,660	469,340	7.57%		13,518
220,000	780,000	7.86%		583,725	416,275	6.56%		11,990
240,000	760,000	7.40%		636,791	363,209	5.39%		10,461
260,000	740,000	6.97%		689,857	310,143	4.01%		8,933
280,000	720,000	6.57%		742,923	257,077	2.33%		7,404
300,000	700,000	6.20%		795,989	204,011	.19%		5,876
320,000	680,000	5.86%		849,055	150,945	**		4,348
340,000	660,000	5.54%		902,121	97,879	**		2,819
360,000	640,000	5.24%		955,187	44,813	**		1,291
380,000	620,000	4.96%		1,008,253	(8,253)	**		**
400,000	600,000	4.69%		1,061,319	(61,319)	**		**
420,000	580,000	4.43%		1,114,385	(114,385)	**		**
440,000	560,000	4.19%		1,167,451	(167,451)	**		**
460,000	540,000	3.96%		1,220,517	(220,517)	**		**
480,000	520,000	3.74%		1,273,583	(273,583)	**		**
500,000	500,000	3.53%		1,326,649	(326,649)	**		**

*Figures courtesy of Financial Planning Toolkit.

Appendix K

EXAMPLE OF A LETTER OF INSTRUCTIONS

To my dear wife,

Thanks for a wonderful life together. I pray that you've still got many more wonderful years ahead with our children and friends. The sooner you start enjoying them the better. This letter is an expression of my love. I hope it will help get you off to a smooth start. Keep in mind these thoughts are simply guidelines.

<u>What to do first</u>: Records you'll need immediately are in our safe deposit box at The Bryn Mawr Trust Company.

Here's what needs to be done first:

- Call our estate lawyer, Morey Rosenbloom, CPA, our accountant, Marty Satinsky, CLU, and Johnny Thorne or Bill Thornton, our financial planner. Their addresses, and numbers are listed on the attached sheets. Arrange to meet them soon as possible after the funeral.

- You'll need some ready cash for immediate expenses. There's a list of our checking and savings accounts, along with a money-market fund. I've made sure there's enough in your personal checking account. There's also a list of investments held in your name that can be quickly sold, if necessary. But that shouldn't be necessary because of the policy you own on my life.

- Our current financial statement is attached. It will tell you what my estate includes, and which long-term bills are still outstanding.

- I've stored some of our less important documents and past year's tax returns in the home safe. The key is in my top center desk drawer. You'll find originals of my will and trust (our lawyer has duplicates), life insurance policies, birth and marriage certificates, armed-services discharge papers, and pension-plan papers in the bank safe deposit box. Securities are held by our broker, Sam Wasserman, and his phone number is listed on the attached sheet.

- Johnny Thorne or Bill Thornton will help you submit claims for my life insurance as soon as possible, and apply for other death benefits you're entitled to such as: Social Security, veterans' benefits, and my company pension-plan.

- Pay the usual household bills, such as the phone, heating, and electricity bills, If you have any doubts about whether to pay a bill, ask our lawyer, Morey Rosenbloom.

<u>My funeral</u>: I wish to be cremated and have my ashes scattered at sea. Keep the ceremony simple and modest — just family and close friends. Serve champagne and lots of shrimp. On second thought, serve lots of champagne, too. Play '40s swing. Maybe you won't feel up to that, but you get the idea that I don't want solemnity. I had a good life. Should you want to have a simple memorial service, fine. I'd prefer donations to the American Cancer Society instead of flowers. Speaking of donations, be sure to look in my wallet for my instructions on organ donations.

<u>My practice</u>: I've made arrangements so that you won't have to shop around for a buyer for my practice. My partner and I have a "buy-sell agreement." It pays the family of the first of us to die a fair price for his share of the practice. Since we're incorporated, the agreement is in the form of a stock-redemption plan. The corporation has purchased and paid the premiums on $150,000 of life insurance for each of us. The corporation is the beneficiary. If I die first,

the corporation will get the money and will pay you this total amount. You, in turn, are obligated to accept this amount as full payment for my share of the practice. This plan frees you from having to concern yourself with patients, accounts receivable, records, the office lease, and almost everything else involved in shutting down a practice.

One thing you must do, though, is notify the state board of medical examiners and the Drug Enforcement Agency of my death. As executor of my estate, you must comply with all regulations concerning narcotics. Check the exact regulations with my partner and our lawyer.

Our wills and trust: Remember what our goals were when we devised this plan: I wanted to make sure you were financially secure for life. We wanted to make sure the estate was divided upon your death, according to our wishes. We also wanted to make sure the children inherited the maximum amount possible, while protecting the estate from unnecessary taxes, charges, and fees.

Whatever you are left outright is federal estate-tax-free under present law. You'll receive all but about $625,000. The exact amount depends on what goes into the bypass trust we've set up for the children, with you as trustee. The trust will receive the maximum allowed free of estate taxes. (In 1998, that maximum is $625,000.) You will receive the income from this trust until your death. Then the principal will pass to the children, but without the tax consequences that would result if the money were in your estate.

Advisers and counsel: Fortunately, over the years we've managed to find a few trusted people upon whom you can rely for advice and help on taxes, legal advice, investments, and the like. I recommend using our CPA, Marty Satinsky, and/or Johnny Thorne or Bill Thornton, our financial planner whenever problems arise in managing your assets. Again, your own good judgment is what you should ultimately rely on. Whatever you do, however, don't give anyone discretionary power over the assets; nothing should be withdrawn from your accounts without your informed consent and signature.

Remaining obligations: As you can see in the attached financial statement, we have only a few outstanding obligations. I suggest paying these off from the life insurance proceeds. The home mortgage has about 10 years to go, and it's up to you whether or not you want to stay in the house.

I hope this letter helps you. If you have any questions about financial arrangements, please don't hesitate to ask the advisers I've listed.

My warmest love and thanks to you again.

GLOSSARY

ACCELERATION CLAUSE. The clause in a note, bond, or mortgage giving the creditor (mortgagee) the right to demand, upon default of the debtor (mortgagor), the immediate payment of the unpaid balance of the loan or mortgage.

ACCRUED INTEREST. Interest accrued on a bond or other debt obligation since the last interest payment was made. The buyer of a bond pays the market price plus accrued interest. Exceptions include bonds that are in default and income bonds.

AMORTIZE. To pay off a debt by periodic payments set aside for the purpose, or to allocate the cost of an asset over its life.

ANNUAL EXCLUSION. A federal gift tax exclusion of $10,000 (indexed after 1998) allowed the donor each year for each donee, provided the gift is one of present interest (that is, the donee must be given an immediate right to possession or enjoyment of the property interest).

ANNUAL REPORT. The formal financial statement issued yearly by a corporation.

ANNUITY. A series of payments of a fixed amount for a specified number of years.

ASKED PRICE. The price at which securities are offered to potential buyers; or the price sellers offer to take.

ASSESSED VALUE. Value assigned to property by a public body for property tax purposes.

ASSIGNMENT. The act of transferring any interest in property to another party. The one who transfers the right is the "assignor;" the receiver of the right is "assignee."

BALANCE SHEET. A statement of the financial position of a business entity at a given time, disclosing the assets, liabilities, and invested capital.

BALLOON PAYMENT. The balance due on a debt instrument at maturity that is in excess of a regular principal payment.

BANKRUPTCY. The condition of a business or individual which has been declared insolvent (unable to pay debts) by a court proceeding and whose financial matters are being administered by the court through a receiver or trustee.

BEAR. Someone who believes that the stock market will decline. See Bull.

BEAR MARKET. A declining market. See Bull Market.

BEARER BOND. A bond which does not have the owner's name registered on the books of the issuing company and which is payable to the holder. See Coupon Bond, Registered Bond.

BENEFICIARY. The recipient of funds, property, or other benefits from an insurance policy, will, or other settlement. The individual or entity entitled to the beneficial interest of a trust.

BID PRICE. The price buyers offer to pay for securities; the price at which sellers may dispose of them.

BIG BOARD. A popular term for the New York Stock Exchange.

BLUE CHIP. A company known nationally for the quality and wide acceptance of its products or services, and for its ability to earn income and pay dividends.

BLUE LIST. The trade offering sheets of bond dealers, which list dealers' offerings of municipal bonds for sale all over the country.

BOND. An IOU or promissory note of a corporation or governmental body, usually issued in multiples of $1,000 or $5,000, although $100 and $500 denominations are not unknown. A bond is evidence of a debt on which the issuer usually promises to pay the bondholders a specified amount of interest for a specified length of time, and to repay the loan on the expiration date.

BOOK VALUE. The net amount at which an asset appears on the books of a company.

Glossary

BROKER. An agent who handles the public's orders to buy and sell securities, commodities, or other property. For this service a commission is charged.

BULL. A person who believes that the stock market will rise. See Bear.

BULL MARKET. An advancing market. See Bear Market.

CALL. The process of redeeming a bond or preferred stock issue before its normal maturity. Sometimes used to refer to a "call option."

CALL OPTION. An option to buy (or "call") shares of stock at a specified price for a set period of time.

CAPITAL GAIN or CAPITAL LOSS. Profit or loss from the sale of a capital asset. A capital gain is either short-term or long-term. Capital gain is short-term if the asset was held for 1 year or less; the gain is long-term if the asset was held for more than 1 year. This more-than-1-year period necessary to qualify a capital gain as long-term is often referred to as the "long-term capital gain holding period." *Net* long-term capital gain (i.e., the excess of long-term capital gains over short-term capital losses) is taxed at special 10% and 20 % tax rates. (See Chapter 8, "Income Tax Concepts.")

CAPITAL STOCK. All shares representing ownership of a business, including preferred and common. See Common Stock, Preferred stock.

CAPITALIZATION. The total amount of all the securities issued by a corporation.

CASH FLOW. The amount of cash generated over time from an investment, usually after any tax effects.

CERTIFICATE. The actual piece of paper which is evidence of ownership of stock in a corporation, or of other intangible property.

CHARITABLE DEDUCTION. A deduction allowed for a reportable gift to a charitable organization.

CLOSING. The conclusion or consummation of a real estate transaction where all documents are signed and a deed or land contract, etc., is transferred.

COMMERCIAL PAPER. Unsecured, short-term promissory notes of large firms, usually issued in denominations of $1 million or more.

COMMON STOCK. Securities which represent an ownership interest in a corporation.

CONGLOMERATE. A corporation that has diversified its operations usually by acquiring enterprises in widely varied industries.

CONVERTIBLE. A bond, debenture, or preferred share which may be exchanged by the owner for common stock or another security, usually of the same company, in accordance with the terms of the issue.

CORPORATION. A legal unit organized under state laws which has a continuous life span independent from its ownership. In the event of dissolution, its owners are not responsible for its debt (beyond the amount of their original investment). Corporations can raise capital by issuing securities.

COUPON. Evidence of interest due on a bond, usually every six months. With a bearer bond, the coupon is detached from the bond and presented for payment of interest to the issuer's agent or the bondholder's bank. In the case of a registered bond, the issuing corporation will mail a check for the semiannual interest to the owner of record on each interest payment date.

COUPON BOND. A bond with interest coupons attached. The coupons are removed ("clipped") as they come due and are presented by the holder for payment of interest. See Bearer Bond, Registered Bond.

COUPON RATE. The stated rate of interest on a bond.

COVERED OPTION. An option on stock is covered if the individual who, on exercise of the option, would be required to sell the stock owns the subject stock. Thus, a call option is covered if the writer of the call owns the subject stock; a put is covered if the purchaser of the put option (who by exercising the put elects to sell his stock) owns the subject stock.

CUMULATIVE PREFERRED. A preferred stock having a provision that if one or more dividends are omitted, the omitted dividends must be paid in full before dividends may be paid on the company's common stock.

CURRENT YIELD. The percent relation of the annual interest received to the current price of a bond, or other debt obligation.

DEALER. A person or firm acting as a principal in buying and selling securities.

The Tools and Techniques of Financial Planning

DEBENTURE. A promissory note backed by the general credit of a company and usually not secured by a mortgage or lien on any specific property. See Bond.

DEBT SERVICE. The amount of cash needed to cover periodic mortgage payments or bond interest, including interest and principal.

DEFAULT. Failure to pay principal or interest promptly when due.

DISCOUNT. The amount by which a preferred stock or bond may sell below its par value. Also used as a verb to mean "takes into account," as "the price of the stock has discounted the expected dividend cut." See Premium.

DIVIDEND. A payment made from earnings to the stockholders of a corporation. It is authorized by the board of directors and paid among the shares outstanding. In the case of common shares, payment is made on a pro rata basis; however, preferred shares may be entitled to a specific dividend rate which is different from that paid common shareholders.

DIVIDEND YIELD. The ratio of the current dividend to the current price of a share of stock.

DOLLAR COST AVERAGING. A system of buying securities at regular intervals with a fixed dollar amount of capital.

DOMICILE. A location legally regarded as the main place of residence of an individual or business entity.

DONEE. The recipient of a gift. The term also is used to refer to the recipient of a power of appointment.

DONOR. The person who makes a gift. The term also refers to the person who grants a power of appointment to another.

EARNINGS PER SHARE. The earnings available to common stockholders divided by the number of common shares outstanding.

ESTATE. An interest in real property. All assets owned by an individual.

ESTATE TAX. A tax imposed upon the right of a person to transfer property at death. This type of tax is imposed not only by the federal government, but also by a number of states.

EXPIRATION DATE. The last day on which an option (call or put) can be exercised.

EXTRA. The short form of "extra dividend." A dividend in the form of stock or cash in addition to the regular or usual dividend a company has been paying.

FIDUCIARY. A person occupying a position of trust, (e.g., an executor, administrator, or trustee).

FLOATING-RATE BOND. A bond on which the interest rate is adjusted, usually every six months, for the subsequent six months, according to a formula based on the then prevailing interest rates. The prime rate, federal funds rate, commercial paper rate, and Treasury bill rates are frequently used indices.

GENERAL OBLIGATION BOND. A municipal bond backed by the general taxing power of its issuer.

GIFT. Property or property rights or interest gratuitously passed on or transferred for less than an adequate and full consideration in money or money's worth to another, whether the transfer is in trust or otherwise, direct or indirect.

GOVERNMENT BONDS. Obligations of the U.S. Government, regarded as the highest grade issues in existence.

GROWTH STOCK. Stock of a company with a record of rapid growth in earnings.

INCOME STATEMENT. A statement that summarizes the revenues and expenses of a business for a specified period of time.

INDENTURE. A written agreement under which bonds and debentures are issued, setting forth maturity date, interest rate, and other terms.

IN-THE-MONEY. Description of a *call* option when the stock price is above the striking price of the call. Description of a *put* option when the stock price is below the striking price of the put.

INTERVIVOS TRUST. A trust created during the settlor's lifetime. It becomes operative during one's lifetime as opposed to a trust under a will, which does not become operative until the settlor dies.

INTEREST. Payments a borrower pays a lender for the use of money. A corporation pays interest on its bonds to its bondholders. See Bond.

INVESTMENT. The use of money for the purpose of making more money in order to gain income, increase capital, or both.

INVESTMENT COMPANY. See Mutual Fund.

JOINT TENANCY. The holding of property by two or more persons in such a manner that, upon the death of one, the survivor or survivors take the entire property.

LESSEE. The party to whom a lease is granted.

LESSOR. The party who grants a lease.

LEVERAGE. The use of funds borrowed at a fixed rate in an attempt to reinvest them at a higher rate. Borrowing against the established equity. The term is also used with investments which offer enhanced return without increased investment, such as options and warrants, even without borrowing.

LIEN. A claim against property that has been pledged or mortgaged to secure the performance of an obligation. A bond may be secured by a lien against specific property owned by the company issuing the bonds.

LIMIT ORDER. An order to purchase or sell securities at a set price determined by the customer.

LISTED STOCK. The stock of a company that is traded on an organized securities exchange.

LIQUID ASSETS. Cash or assets that can readily be converted into cash without a serious loss of capital.

LOAD. The portion of the offering price of shares of a mutual fund which covers sales commissions and all other costs of distribution. The load is usually incurred only on purchase and not when shares are sold (redeemed).

MARGIN. The buying of stocks or bonds on credit, known as "buying on margin."

MARKETABILITY. The ease or difficulty with which a security or other asset can be sold in the secondary market.

MARKET ORDER. An order by a customer to buy or sell securities at the best obtainable price.

MARKET PRICE. In the case of a security, market price is usually considered the last reported price at which a stock or bond has been sold.

MATURITY. The date on which a loan, bond, or debenture comes due and is to be paid off.

MODIFIED ENDOWMENT CONTRACT (MEC). A life insurance policy which has failed the seven pay test of Code section 7702A. Distributions (including loans) from a MEC are taxed less favorably than distributions from a life insurance policy which has met the requirements of the seven pay test.

MONEY MARKET. Financial markets in which funds are borrowed or lent for short periods, typically less than one year.

MONEY MARKET FUND. A type of mutual fund which invests in short-term government securities, commercial paper, and repurchase agreements.

MORTGAGE. A pledge of designated property as security for a loan.

MORTGAGE BOND. A bond backed by a lien on a specific property.

MORTGAGEE. One who lends funds on the security of specific property (mortgage).

MORTGAGOR. The borrower who uses specific property as collateral for a loan.

MUNICIPAL BOND. A bond issued by a state or a political subdivision, such as a county, city, town, or village. The interest paid on many municipal bonds is exempt from federal income taxes and state and local income taxes within the state of issue.

MUTUAL FUND. An investment company that uses the proceeds from the sale of its shares in order to invest in the securities of other companies.

NET ASSET VALUE. A term used in connection with mutual funds, meaning net asset value per share—the total market value of all securities owned by the fund minus liabilities, divided by the number of fund shares outstanding.

NEW ISSUE. Securities offered to the public for the first time.

NO-LOAD FUND. A mutual fund on which no sales commission is paid.

ODD LOT. An amount of a security less than the established "round lot." See Round Lot.

OVER THE COUNTER. Unlisted securities; those not traded on a major exchange.

PAR VALUE. The nominal or face value of a stock or bond.

PARTNERSHIP. An association of two or more individuals to carry on a business for profit. The life span of the partnership is directly linked to that of the owners. Technically, if a partner dies, the partnership has ended. A partnership can only raise money based on personal credit available to the owners.

PAY OUT RATIO. The percentage of earnings paid out in the form of dividends.

PORTFOLIO. Securities held by an individual or institution. A portfolio may consist of bonds, stocks, or other securities of various types of institutions.

PREFERRED STOCK. A class of stock with a claim on the company's earnings before payment may be made on the common stock and usually entitled to priority over common stock if the company liquidates.

PREMIUM. The amount by which a bond or preferred stock may sell above its par value.

PRICE-EARNINGS RATIO. The price of a share of stock divided by earnings per share for a 12-month period. For example, a stock selling for $20 with earnings per share of $2 is said to be selling for a price-earnings ratio of 10 to 1.

PRIMARY MARKET. The market for new issues of stocks or bonds.

PRINCIPAL. The property comprising the estate or fund that has been set aside in trust, or from which income is expected to accrue (corpus).

PROPRIETORSHIP. A type of business owned by one person. It can raise money based only on the owner's personal credit.

PROSPECTUS. A document issued for the purpose of describing a new security issue.

PROXY. Written authorization given by a shareholder to someone else to represent him and vote his shares at a stockholders' meeting.

PUT. An option to sell a particular security at a specified price within a designated period of time.

RATING. A formal opinion by an outside professional service on the credit reputation of an issuer and the investment quality of its securities.

REAL ESTATE INVESTMENT TRUST (REIT). An organization similar to a mutual fund in which investors pool funds that are invested in real estate or used to make construction or mortgage loans.

REFUNDING. The redemption of a bond issue by the sale of a new bond issue, usually at terms more favorable to the issuer.

REGISTERED BOND. A bond which is registered on the books of the issuing company in the name of the owner. It can be transferred only when endorsed by the registered owner. See Bearer Bond, Coupon Bond.

REIT. See Real Estate Investment Trust.

REVENUE BOND. A municipal bond backed by revenues produced from a particular project, such as a turnpike. See General Obligation Bond.

REVOCABLE TRUST. A trust that can be changed or terminated during the grantor's lifetime and the property recovered.

ROUND LOT. A unit of trading or multiple thereof. On the NYSE the unit of trading is generally 100 shares in stocks and $10,000 par value in the case of bonds.

SECONDARY MARKET. Where existing issues are bought and sold. It may be either an over-the-counter market or through an organized exchange.

SERIAL BOND. A part of an issue which matures in relatively small amounts at periodic stated intervals. See Term Bond.

SETTLEMENT DATE. The date on which money and securities are exchanged.

SHORT-TERM TRUST. Also known as Clifford Trust. An irrevocable trust running for a period of *more than* 10 years (10 years and one day is sufficient) or the life of the beneficiary, whichever is shorter, in which the income is payable to a person other than the grantor, and established under the provisions of the Internal Revenue Code. The income is taxable to the income beneficiary and not to the grantor. In the case of any short-term trust created after March 1, 1986, the income is taxed to the grantor, not to the trust beneficiary.

SINKING FUND. Money set aside by the issuer to be used to retire a bond issue.

SPECIALIST. A member of a stock exchange whose function is to maintain an orderly market in certain stocks. Each specialist is responsible for specific issues and must make a market in those issues.

SPREAD. The difference between what a dealer pays for a security and the price at which he offers to sell it.

STANDARD DEDUCTION. The amount set forth in the Internal Revenue Code which may be deducted (along with personal exemptions) by a taxpayer who does *not* itemize.

STOCK DIVIDEND. A dividend paid in shares of stock rather than cash.

STOCK EXCHANGE. A central market place where securities are traded.

STRIKING PRICE. The price at which an option can be exercised.

SYNDICATE. A group of investment bankers and/or banks who underwrite a bond or stock issue and offer it for public sale.

SYSTEMATIC WITHDRAWAL. An arrangement where a mutual fund automatically liquidates sufficient shares to pay an investor a predetermined amount of money at regular intervals.

TAX CREDIT. A direct reduction of income tax liability based on items such as investments, political contributions, child care, energy conservation, and foreign taxes.

TAX SHELTER. A tax-favored investment, generally in the form of a partnership or joint venture.

TAXABLE YEAR. A 12-month period, usually the calendar year in the case of individuals, which is used in the calculation of taxable income.

TERM BOND. Part of a bond issue which has a single maturity. See Serial Bond.

TRANSFER AGENT. A professional agency, typically a bank, employed by a corporation to handle the issuance and transfer of securities, payment of dividends, and maintenance of books of the corporation.

UNDERWRITER. The investment banker (or bankers) who buy the entire issue of securities from the issuer and then sell the securities to individual and institutional investors.

VARIABLE ANNUITY. An annuity contract under which the annuity holder has the ability to allocate the annuity premiums among several available investment choices. The annuity holder, not the company issuing the contract, assumes the investment risk associated with the investment decisions.

WARRANT. A right or option to buy a stated number of shares of stock at a specified price over a given period of time. It is usually of longer duration than a call option.

WARRANTY DEED. A deed by which a grantor conveys and guarantees good title to real property; the safest form of deed for the buyer.

YIELD. Also known as return. The dividends or interest paid by a company expressed as a percentage of the current price. A stock with a current market value of $25 per share paying dividends at a rate of $2.50 is said to return 10% ($2.50 ^ $25.00).

YIELD TO MATURITY. The average annualized rate of return that an investor will receive if a bond is held until its maturity date. It differs from "yield" or "current yield" in that it takes into consideration the increase to par of a bond bought at a discount and the decrease to par of a bond bought at a premium.

ZERO COUPON BOND. A bond that pays no interest during the life of the bond and which is normally issued at a substantial discount from par. The face amount of the bond, when it is paid at maturity, includes the payment of interest.

INDEX

A

Accumulation 24
Adjusted Rate of Return (ARR) 181, 187
ADR, *See* American Depository Receipts
ADV, *See* Form ADV
Alternative Minimum Tax (AMT) 145
American College 18
American Depository Receipts (ADR) 485
American Society of CLU & ChFC 18
Annuities
    generally 247
    immediate (due) 253
    joint and survivor 191, 255
    life 247
    period certain 191, 251
    single premium deferred 260
    taxation 250
    variable 255
Antiques, *See* Collectibles
Appointment of Fiduciaries Clause 125
Art, *See* Collectibles
Asset Allocation 229
At Risk Rules 130

B

Balance Sheet, Personal 163, 165
Basis 129
Bearer Bonds 292, 373
Belth Yearly Rate of Return 112
Beta Coefficient 383
Bills, *See* Treasury Bills
Bond Maturity Premium 200
Bonds
    bunny 492
    convertible 281, 282, 284, 285
    corporate 287, 482
    foreign 485
    government, U. S. 481, 483
    mortgage backed 359
    municipal 369, 475
    returns, historical 199, 200
    stripped 475
    zero coupon 74, 289, 291, 491-492
Brochure Rule 154

Budgeting 27
Bunny Bonds 492
Business Energy Tax Credits 132

C

Calls, *See* Put and Call Options
Canadian Maple Leaf, *See* Precious Metals
Capital Gains (Losses) 134
Carryover basis 131
Cash Flow Statement, Personal 163, 166-167, 171-172
Cash on Cash Comparison 181, 188
Cash Value 348
Certificates of Deposit 261, 357, 482
Clifford Trusts 64
CMOs, *See* Collateralized Mortgage Obligations
Codicil 81
Coins, *See* Collectibles
Collateralized Mortgage Obligations (CMO) 365, 451
Collectibles 265
College for Financial Planning 18
College Funding, *See* Education Funding
Commodities 269
Commodity Pool, *See* Commodities
Common Stock
    generally 273
    options 274, 277, 411
    returns, historical 199, 200
Comparison, Tools for
    Comparing Investments .... Appendix H
Compound Interest 174
Compound Interest
    (Future Value) Tables .... Appendices A, C, D
Connie Macs 359, 451
Constructive Receipt 143
Conversion price 281
Convertible Securities 281-285
Corporate Bonds 287-294
Cumulative Dividends 400

D

Death Taxes, State 99
Debenture 292
Deductible Investment Expenses 138

Deep Discount Bond 491
Defined-Benefit Plan
    distributions 191, 422, 459
    generally 418-419
Defined-Contribution Plan
    distributions 192, 422, 459
    generally 417-418
Diversification 5
Dividends
    cash 273
    stock 277

E

ECU, *See* European Currency Unit
Education Funding
    expenses 37
    financial aid 47, 55, 61
    funding sources 47
        financial aid (scholarships & loans) 47, 55, 61
        pay-as-you-go 47
        planned accumulation 43, 62, 65
        prepayment programs 65
        working student 60
    generally 37
    income shifting 63
    tax considerations 63
    worksheet 44
Energy Credits 132
Equity Risk Premium 201
Estate Administration 83
Estate Planning
    definition 77
    objectives 24, 77
    problems 78
    process 79
Estate Tax 91
Example of letter of instructions .... Appendix K
Exchangeable Debt 285
Exordium clause 119

F

Family of Funds 382
Fannie Maes 359, 451
Federal Estate Tax 91
Federal Home Loan Mortgage Assoc. 359
Federal National Mortgage Assoc. 359
Financial Futures 295-300
Financial Objectives 23

Financial Planning
    definition 1, 21
    education 17
    objectives 23
    principles 4
    process 3, 21
    report 15
FHLMC, *See* Federal Home Loan Mortgage Corp.
Financial Statements, Personal 163-172
Flip Flop Notes 285
Floating Rate Bonds 293
FNMA, *See* Federal National Mortgage Assoc.
Foreign Investments 485-489
Form ADV 156, 157
Freddie Macs 359, 451
Funding Requirements 419
Future Value 174, 176
Future Value Tables .... Appendices A, C, D

G

Gas, *See* Oil and Gas
Gems, *See* Collectibles
Generation Skipping Transfer Tax 99
Gifts 88
Ginnie Maes, *See* Govt. Natl. Mortgage Assoc.
Global Funds 485, 487
Glossary 543
GNMA, *See* Government National Mortgage Assoc.
Gold, *See* Precious Metals
Government National Mortgage Assoc. 359, 451, 481
Government Securities 475, 481

H

Hedging 269
Highly Compensated Employees 420
HR-10 Plans, *See* Keogh Plans

I

IAFP 19
IBCFP 18
ICFP 18
Income Shifting 63
Income Statement 163
Income Tax Rate Tables .... Appendix I

Index

Income Taxes
    children 148
    generally 129
    rates 147
Indenture 291
Index Funds 378
Index Futures 298
Individual Retirement Accounts
  Roth
    contributions 308
    conversion from traditional IRA 316, 317
    generally 307
    qualified distributions 309
    tax and penalty summary table 312
    tax implications 308
  Traditional
    contributions 319, 320-324, 331, 333
    distributions 324-330
    generally 319-320
    rollovers 319, 323, 332
    SIMPLE IRAs 319
    spousal IRAs 319
Installment Sales 132
Intangible Drilling Costs 391
Interest-Adjusted Net Cost Index 108
Interest-Sensitive Whole Life 350
Internal Rate of Return (IRR) 181, 184
International Funds 485, 487
International Investments 485-489
Intestacy 82
Investment Adviser, *See* Registered Investment Adviser
Investment Advisers Act of 1940 151
Investment Company, *See* Mutual Funds
Investment Company Institute (ICI) 382
Investment Counsel 155
IRAs, *See* Individual Retirement Accounts

J

Jewelry, *See* Collectibles
Joint Life Insurance 351
Joint Ownership 84

K

Keogh Plans 321-324
Kiddie Tax 148

L

Letter of instructions .... 82, Appendix K
Leverage 159-162, 478

Life Insurance
    company comparisons 116
    coverage, amount 103
    generally 343
    policy comparisons 105
    policy illustrations 104
    rating information 116, 347
    right product 101, 346
Limited Partnerships
    publicly traded 401
    untraded 405, 409
Linton Yield 111
Liquid Yield Option Notes (LYONs) 285
Load Fee 377, 382
Lump-Sum Distributions 194
LYONs 285, 491-492

M

Margin Requirements 269
Market Discount Rules 289
Master Limited Partnership (MLP) 401
Medical Payments, *See* Personal Automobile Policy
Million Dollar Accumulation Guide .... Appendix J
MLP, *See* Master Limited Partnership
Money Market Deposit Accounts 356-357
Money Market Funds 355
Money-Purchase Pension Plan 417-418
Mortgage-Backed Securities 359, 438, 451
Mortgage Pool 359
Municipal Bonds 369
Mutual Funds
    balanced funds 377
    dual-purpose funds 384
    expenses 377
    generally 375
    global funds 485, 487
    growth funds 377
    income funds 377
    index funds 378
    international funds 485, 487
    load fees 377, 382
    sector funds 383, 405
    single country funds 485, 487-488
    tax-exempt funds 378

N

Net Present Value 181, 182-184
No-Load Fund 377, 382
Nonqualified Deferred Compensation 417
Notes, *See* Government Securities

Index

O

Oil and Gas 391
Open Interest 271
Options, *See* Put and Call Options
Oriental Rugs, *See* Collectibles
Original Issue Discount (OID) 289, 291

P

Pay-through Certificates 364
Passive activity 137, 424
Pay-Back Period 181, 188
Percentage Depletion 391
Performance Measurement 25
Personal Financial Statements 163-172
Platinum, *See* Precious Metals
Precious Metals 301-305
Preferred Stock
    cumulative 400
    generally 397
Prepayment Risk 360
Present Value 175, 177, 181, 182-184
Present Value Tables .... Appendices B, E, F
Price-earnings ratio 277
Probate 80, 81, 83
Profit-Sharing Plans 418
Publicly Traded Partnerships 401
Put and Call Options 274, 411

Q

Qualified Plans 417-422

R

Rare Coins, *See* Collectibles
Rate of Return 173-180, 181-190
Real Estate 423-433, 435
Real Estate Investment
    Trust (REIT) 362, 405, 427, 430, 435-443, 451
Real Estate Mortgage Investment
    Conduit 362, 365, 438, 445-457
Rehabilitation Tax Credits 132
REIT, *See* Real Estate Investment Trust
REMIC, *See* Real Estate Mortgage Investment Conduit
Registered Bonds 292
Registered Investment Adviser (RIA)
    definition 151, 153
    exclusions 151
    exemptions 151, 152

Registered Investment Adviser (RIA) (Cont'd)
    financial planners 152-154
    legal requirements, generally 151
    withdrawal 157
Residuary Clause 123
Retirement Plan Distributions 191-197, 459
Retirement Planning 24
Returns, Historical 199, 200
Reversionary Interest 394
RIA, *See* Registered Investment Adviser
Rights 278
Risk 199, 215
Risk Premiums 200
Risk Tolerance 215-227
Riskless Interest Rate 200
Rollovers 459
Roth IRAs, *See* Individual Retirement Accounts

S

Savings 23
Savings Bonds, Replacement of Lost 484
SEC, *See* Security and Exchange Commission
Sector Funds, *See* Mutual Funds
Security and Exchange Commission 151
Selling Short, *See* Short Sale
Serial Maturity 373
Short Sale 278
Silver, *See* Precious Metals
Simple Plan
    generally 469
    simple 401(k) 469
    simple IRA 469
Single Country Closed End Funds 485, 487-488
Single Premium Deferred Annuity 260
Single Premium Whole Life Insurance 352
Small Stock Premium 201
Stamps, *See* Collectibles
Standard of Living 23
State Death Taxes 99
Stock
    common
        generally 273
        options 274, 277, 411
        returns, historical 199, 200
    preferred 397
Stock Dividend 277
Stock Right 278, 413
Stock Split 277
Stock Warrants 413
Striking Price 411
Stripped Bonds 475

The Tools and Techniques of Financial Planning

Index

T

Target-Benefit Pension Plan 418
Taxable Equivalent Yields .... Appendix G
Tax Basis 129
Tax-Exempt Equivalent Yields .... Appendix G
Tax-Free Bonds, *See* Municipal Bonds
Tax Preference Items 145
Tax Shelters 477
Term Insurance 343, 348
Thrift Plans 418
Time Value of Money 173, 181
Top-Heavy Plans 422
Treasury Bills
    generally 481
    returns, historical 199, 200
Treasury Bonds 481, 484
Treasury Direct System 484
Treasury Notes 481, 484
Trusts 85

U

UGMA, *See* Uniform Gifts to Minors Act
Uniform Gifts to Minors Act 68
Universal Life Insurance 349
Untraded Limited Partnerships 405, 409
U. S. Government Securities 481

V

Variable Life Insurance 351
Variable Universal Life Insurance 351
Vesting 421

W

Warrants 413
Whole Life Insurance 343, 348
Wills
    appointment clause 125
    bequest clauses 122, 123
    codicil 181
    contesting 81
    debts clause 120
    devise clause 123
    exordium clause 119
    generally 80, 119
    powers clause 124
    review, how to 119
    residuary clause 123
    revocation 81
    safeguarding 82
    tax clause 121
Wines, *See* Collectibles

Y

Yield
    coupon 292
    current 290
    nominal 292
    to maturity 288, 290

Z

Zero Coupon Bond 74, 289, 291, 491-492